ASSEMBLY LANGUAGE PROGRAMMING

Third Edition

ASSEMBLY LANGUAGE PROGRAMMING

For the IBM System 370 and Compatible Computers

Michael D. Kudlick

University of San Francisco

wcb
Wm. C. Brown Publishers
Dubuque, Iowa

Book Team

Editor *Earl McPeek*
Developmental Editor *Nova A. Maack*
Designer *K. Wayne Harms*
Visuals Processor *Joseph P. O'Connell*

wcb group

Chairman of the Board *Wm. C. Brown*
President and Chief Executive Officer *Mark C. Falb*

wcb

Wm. C. Brown Publishers, College Division

President *G. Franklin Lewis*
Vice President, Editor-in-Chief *George Wm. Bergquist*
Vice President, Director of Production *Beverly Kolz*
National Sales Manager *Bob McLaughlin*
Director of Marketing *Thomas E. Doran*
Marketing Information Systems Manager *Craig S. Marty*
Marketing Manager *Matt Shaughnessy*
Executive Editor *Edward G. Jaffe*
Manager of Visuals and Design *Faye M. Schilling*
Manager of Design *Marilyn A. Phelps*
Production Editorial Manager *Julie A. Kennedy*

Cover art by ArtNET

Library of Congress Catalog Card Number: 87–071181

ISBN 0–697–06255–4

Printed in the United States of America by Wm. C. Brown Publishers
2460 Kerper Boulevard, Dubuque, IA 52001

10 9 8 7 6 5 4 3 2 1

To Elaine

Contents

PART

I
Fundamental Concepts

PART

II
Fundamental Techniques

P A R T

III

Noninteger Arithmetic

P A R T

VI

The Assembler

List of Figures

Preface

In writing this textbook I have attempted to provide a thorough tutorial discussion of the topics that comprise problem-mode assembly language programming for the IBM System 370 and compatible computers. Since the publication of the first edition of this book, other IBM computer systems in addition to the older IBM 360 now use essentially the same nonprivileged instructions as the IBM 370 does: in particular, writing problem-mode assembly language programs for the IBM 30xx and 4300 systems is hardly different from doing so for the IBM 370. Other manufacturers have also used a similar instruction set for some of their computer systems.

Thus, although throughout this book references are made to the 360 and 370, that should not preclude the book's applicability to compatible systems except perhaps in the area of I/O programming. This applicability includes such fundamentals as base-displacement addressing, binary integer arithmetic, byte and bit manipulations, subroutines, and floating-point and decimal arithmetic. Only I/O programming, dependent as it is on macros and on the computer's operating system, may differ significantly from one system to another. In this book we have limited our I/O programming discussions to the OS/VS and DOS/VS operating systems for the IBM 370.

Students using this text are expected to have completed one course in programming, on the order of an introductory Fortran course. Elementary concepts such as defining constants, reserving memory space, controlling loops, and processing arrays are explained with reference to allied concepts in Fortran; concepts with no immediate analogy in high-level languages (e.g., base-displacement addressing) are explained without assuming prior knowledge of these concepts by the students.

I have attempted to reinforce students' understanding of the various topics through numerous examples, explanations, and programming solutions to problems. In addition, the student is frequently reminded of the important distinctions between assembly-time and run-time events, and of the interactions that take place among the assembler, loader, operating system, user's program, and central processing unit (CPU). The Summary, Review, and Exercises appearing at the end of each chapter and the sample problems (with complete programming solutions) that appear at the end of several of the chapters will, it is hoped, enhance the text's usefulness for students.

NEW TO THIS EDITION

In this third edition, all the features of the well-received earlier editions have been retained, and several additions have been made at the suggestion of reviewers and students. The additions are:

1. Separation of the former Chapter 9, Subroutines, into two chapters: Chapter 9, Internal Subroutines, and Chapter 10, External Subroutines, with the former Chapter 10 now moved to Chapter 23
2. A section in the new chapter on internal subroutines illustrating how to use them to write a program following top-down design principles
3. A section in the new chapter on external subroutines illustrating how recursive procedures are written in assembly language
4. Review sections and review questions at the end of each chapter
5. Marginal notes on almost every page to assist students in their studies
6. Appendixes on debugging tips, on reading the assembler listing, and on converting integers between their EBCDIC and binary representations via macros

TEXT ORGANIZATION

With the exception of the introductory chapters, the text's six parts may be covered in a number of different ways, depending on the topics the instructor wishes to emphasize.

There are perhaps three different approaches to the teaching of assembly language. They are not necessarily mutually exclusive, but given the constraints of time in a single semester, one of the approaches will probably dominate the other two. The first approach concentrates on the manner in which arithmetic processes are carried out. For this, Chapters 1–5 and 11–13 form the heart of the course. The second approach concentrates on the manner in which nonarithmetic processes are carried out. For this, Chapters 1–4, 7 and 8, and 18–22 are emphasized. The third approach uses assembly language as a means of introducing more systems-oriented topics. For this, Chapters 1–10, 14–17, and 23 are most helpful. The amount of emphasis given to any one chapter, regardless of the approach used, depends on the instructor as well as the capabilities of the students.

The three chapters in Part I include (1) the essentials of binary and hexadecimal integer arithmetic, (2) assembly language statement formats and their use in a simple program that reads and writes arbitrary text data, and (3) the seven types of instruction formats and the purpose and methods of using base-displacement addressing.

In Part II, most of the elementary operations are discussed and illustrated. Chapter 4 introduces loop control and integer I/O techniques and shows how to obtain snaps of selected memory contents at run time. Chapter 5 covers binary integer arithmetic, including an explanation of two's complement arithmetic. Chapter 6 describes the techniques of defining run-time and assembly-time constants, of reserving memory space, and of assuring desired boundary alignments. Chapter 7 discusses byte manipulations, including the handling of variable-length strings; Chapter 8 covers bit manipulations; Chapter 9 discusses how to write and use internal subroutines, expecially when following top-down design principles; and Chapter 10 discusses the linkage conventions and other topics related to external subroutines, and also illustrates how recursive subroutines are written in assembly language.

The three chapters of Part III deal with noninteger arithmetic. Chapter 11 briefly presents the rationale for decimal and floating-point hardware, Chapter 12 describes the use of the decimal arithmetic instruction set and data formats, and Chapter 13 describes the floating-point instruction set and data formats. In Chapter 12, special emphasis is given to the problem of retaining sufficient accuracy through shifting, in the 360 as well as the 370, and to the problem of converting to and from EBCDIC format. In Chapter 13, the emphasis is on the advantages and limitations of floating-point arithmetic, its similarities to and differences from fixed-point arithmetic, and the problem of converting to and from internal floating-point format.

Part IV, on the use of directives, begins with a discussion of the elementary directives in Chapter 14, discusses control sections and related directives in Chapter 15, introduces the concept of conditional assemblies in Chapter 16, and demonstrates the usefulness and power of macros in Chapter 17. A somewhat more extensive coverage of macros than is usually found in introductory texts is provided in Chapter 17, in order to motivate advanced students to explore their capabilities.

The discussion of I/O programming in Part V is, as far as I have been able to determine, more thorough than that found in any other introductory text on assembly language. Chapter 18 is primarily a description of the space and time constraints of using disks that are similar to the IBM 3330 system. Chapter 19 presents a comprehensive overview of the software facilities available for sequential and indexed sequential files through I/O macros. Chapter 20 illustrates how to create and maintain sequential files via QSAM, and Chapter 21 does the same for indexed sequential files via QISAM and BISAM. Chapter 22 contains corresponding information for VSAM files.

Part VI consists of a single chapter that explains the need for, and methods used by, a two-pass assembler. It includes a complete description of an object module. It also includes an introduction to the techniques of searching and sorting tables, and of handling one-way lists such as the assembler's cross-reference list.

Information summarizing the mnemonic instructions and directives, condition code settings, causes of run-time errors, and the EBCDIC and ASCII code schemes can be found in Appendixes A–F. Appendix G describes the content of an assembler listing, and Appendix H describes two macros—one converts a signed or unsigned EBCDIC integer to its full-word binary representation, and the other converts a full-word binary integer to its EBCDIC representation with leading zeroes suppressed. Appendix I gives references to related books and IBM manuals.

Throughout the text, the approach taken in presenting the material is to illustrate all concepts and techniques with examples. These range in scope from simple demonstrations of the effects of individual instructions and directives to complete programs showing how instructions and directives are used in concert to produce desired results. I believe that one of the most effective methods of learning how to *write* assembly language programs is to *read* programs written by others. For this reason, a number of programs are included in the text.

Though I have attempted to cover many details and concepts, inevitably some have been omitted or passed over lightly. Therefore students are encouraged to seek additional information from reference manuals. In addition to compensating for those details that have not been adequately covered, this should have the beneficial effect of exposing students to the importance of using manuals at an early stage of the learning experience.

Students can purchase a solutions manual that contains answers to all review questions and all odd-number exercises. For teachers, supplementary materials to accompany this text are available from the publisher in the form of an Instructor's Manual.

ACKNOWLEDGMENTS

The previous editions of this book would not have been so well received were it not for the patience, encouragement, and wisdom of my editor, Robert Stern. The present edition has similarly benefited from the editorial assistance of Nova Maack (developmental editor), Mary Monner (production editor), and Nikki Herbst (copy editor). I consider myself extremely fortunate to have had such superb editors.

Many other persons have provided various suggestions that have helped me. My colleague George Ledin suggested the need for the approach I have used in this text. My former students Bruce Barton and Warren Chave contributed a number of constructive criticisms and Mr. Barton provided invaluable assistance in the formulation of the VSAM chapter. It is also a pleasure once again to thank the prepublication reviewers of the first edition: their diligence and insights were exceptionally beneficial to me. Thus to Ken Danhoff of Southern Illinois University, John Forsythe of Michigan State University, Clinton Foulk of Ohio State University, Alfred Newhouse of the University of Houston, Udo Pooch of Texas A & M, and Alfred Weaver of the University of Virginia, I extend my sincerest appreciation for all the time, energy, and care they gave in reviewing my manuscripts. I am similarly indebted to Charles Downey of the University of Nebraska and Mondest C. Richards of Madison Area Technical College for providing very thoughtful and useful suggestions for incorporation into the second edition. To Alan Canton and Louis Hatton I extend my gratitude for valuable explanations of basic DOS concepts.

I would also like to thank the reviewers of the third edition: John Atkins of West Virginia University, Tom Parkinson of Oakland Community College, Richard Detmer of Northwest Missouri State, Dennis Heckman of Portland Community College, Richard Davis of Tulsa Junior College, Ron McCarty of Behrend College, and Peter Gingo of the University of Akron.

I am particularly indebted to Prof. Richard Detmer of Northwest Missouri State University for writing the pseudocode descriptions of about twenty-five algorithms. These descriptions have replaced the flow diagrams that were in previous editions, and they definitely improve the pedagogical aspects of the text.

From all these persons and from daily contact with students using the text I have learned a great deal. Obviously, however, no blame is to be placed on any of these persons for inadequacies that appear in these pages.

Program testing was done on one of the University of San Francisco's computer systems, a Univac Series 90 Model 90/60E. I owe many thanks to the former Director of USF's Computer Center, Michael Kelly, for his gracious and knowledgeable assistance, and to the continued support of the Center's staff. I also wish to thank my former secretary, Sarah Flowers, whose superb typing, editing, and organizational skills made preparation of the first edition much simpler than it otherwise would have been.

I

Fundamental Concepts

1

Computer System Concepts

The computer systems that we will be concerned with in this textbook, primarily the IBM 360 and 370 systems, consist of two broad categories of components: hardware and software. The term **hardware** refers to a computer system's electronic, electromagnetic, and electromechanical components: in short, its physical equipment. **Software** consists of the computer programs, procedures, rules, and documentation used in the operation of a computer system.

Program

Broadly speaking, a program is a plan that specifies actions that may be taken and the conditions under which they are to be taken. We will use the terms **program** and **computer program** interchangeably to mean a sequence of actions and conditions written in such a way that they may either be processed directly by the hardware or be translated into a form that may be processed directly by the hardware. A program that can be processed directly by the hardware is known as a **machine language** program. A program that can be translated into machine language is said to be written in a computer **programming language.**

Source Module

IBM 360 and 370 Assembly Language is a computer programming language. An assembly language program consists of statements that are processed by a program known as the *assembler*. The statements are collectively called the **source code,** or **source module.** A significant portion of an assembly language program consists of statements that represent the detailed operations—known as **instructions**—that the hardware is capable of executing. Whereas programming languages such as Fortran and Cobol do not closely reflect the structure of a computer's hardware, assembly language does. For this reason, programming in assembly language is qualitatively different from programming in almost any other language.

1.1 ASSEMBLY LANGUAGE PROGRAMMING

When the assembler processes a source module, it produces two things: an object module and a listing. The **object module** contains the numeric instructions and data formats that constitute the machine language representation of the source module statements. Thus one function of the assembler is to translate source module statements into machine language. The listing produced by the assembler is

Figure 1.1 Sample listing produced by an assembler.

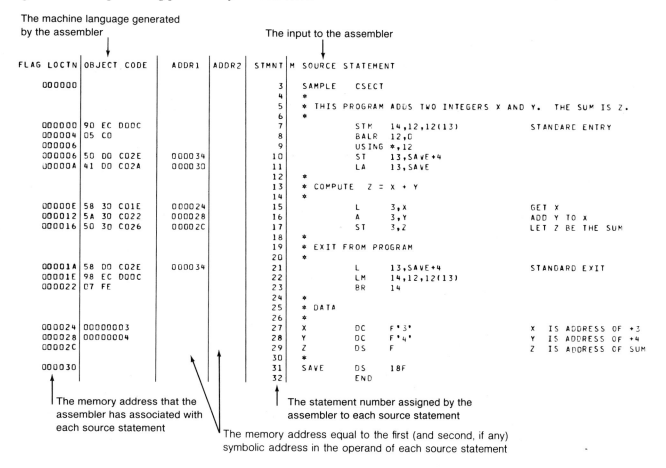

The machine language generated by the assembler

The input to the assembler

```
FLAG LOCTN OBJECT CODE    ADDR1   ADDR2  STMNT M SOURCE STATEMENT

     000000                               3     SAMPLE    CSECT
                                          4     *
                                          5     * THIS PROGRAM ADDS TWO INTEGERS X AND Y.  THE SUM IS Z.
                                          6     *
     000000 90 EC D00C                    7               STM    14,12,12(13)          STANDARD ENTRY
     000004 05 C0                         8               BALR   12,0
     000006                               9               USING  *,12
     000006 50 D0 C02E       000034       10              ST     13,SAVE+4
     00000A 41 D0 C02A       000030       11              LA     13,SAVE
                                          12    *
                                          13    * COMPUTE  Z = X + Y
                                          14    *
     00000E 58 30 C01E       000024       15              L      3,X                   GET X
     000012 5A 30 C022       000028       16              A      3,Y                   ADD Y TO X
     000016 50 30 C026       00002C       17              ST     3,Z                   LET Z BE THE SUM
                                          18    *
                                          19    * EXIT FROM PROGRAM
                                          20    *
     00001A 58 D0 C02E       000034       21              L      13,SAVE+4             STANDARD EXIT
     00001E 98 EC D00C                    22              LM     14,12,12(13)
     000022 07 FE                         23              BR     14
                                          24    *
                                          25    * DATA
                                          26    *
     000024 00000003                      27    X         DC     F'3'                  X  IS ADDRESS OF +3
     000028 00000004                      28    Y         DC     F'4'                  Y  IS ADDRESS OF +4
     00002C                               29    Z         DS     F                     Z  IS ADDRESS OF SUM
                                          30    *
     000030                               31    SAVE      DS     18F
                                          32              END
```

The memory address that the assembler has associated with each source statement

The statement number assigned by the assembler to each source statement

The memory address equal to the first (and second, if any) symbolic address in the operand of each source statement

a printed record of the source module statements together with the information contained in the object module. A portion of such a listing is shown in Figure 1.1. Not shown in Figure 1.1, but also included in such listings, is information that is useful for analyzing program errors.

When submitting a source module to a computer system for processing, an assembly language programmer does not communicate directly with the hardware. Rather, the source module is literally the input data processed by the assembler. As is illustrated in Figure 1.2, another program, the *loader,* processes the object module one step further in order to prepare it for execution by the hardware. This entails copying, or *loading,* the machine language version of the program into the main memory of the computer system.

It is useful at this point to emphasize that when a programmer's source module is being processed by the assembler, it is the assembler program that is being executed by the hardware, not the programmer's. The period of time during which this happens is known as **assembly time.** Similarly, when an object module is being processed by the loader, it is the loader program that is being executed, not the programmer's. This is known as **load time.** The programmer's program can be executed only after the loader program has been executed. The period of time during which the programmer's program is being executed by the hardware is known as **run time;** while being executed, the program is said to be *running* in the computer.

Because some of the statements in a source module are specifically intended for use during assembly time and/or load time, and not during run time, the distinctions between assembly time, load time, and run time are of critical importance to the understanding of assembly language programming. An example of a statement used only at assembly time is the USING directive shown in Figure 1.1.

Assembly Time

Load Time

Run Time

Figure 1.2   Relationship of assembler and loader.

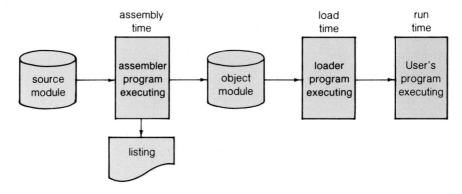

In general, a source module statement may be a comment or may specify an instruction or a directive. Comment statements are identified by an asterisk in the first position of the statement; instructions and directives are specified by an operation code in one of the statement's fields. For example, the three statements

```
L      3,X
A      3,Y
ST     3,Z
```

in Figure 1.1 specify the three instructions Load, Add, and Store, respectively; the statement

END

specifies a directive that identifies the statement as being the last one in the source module. The distinction between an instruction and a directive is that an **instruction** is a symbolic representation of a single machine language operation that will be executed by the hardware at run time, while a **directive** is a request to the assembler to perform some function other than translating instructions into machine language. Therefore, in your study of IBM 360 and 370 Assembly Language, it is important to learn the various capabilities provided by instructions and directives and how to specify them.

1.2   THE OPERATING SYSTEM

In addition to interacting with the assembler and loader programs, an assembly language programmer needs to become familiar with certain capabilities of the computer system's master control program. In the IBM 360 and 370, the master control program is more commonly known as the operating system. This program manages the operation of the computer in such a way as to make it practicable for a number of users to efficiently utilize the computer's facilities without interfering with one another.

In many IBM 360 and 370 computers, the operating system is known as OS; in others it is DOS. OS is essentially more complex and more versatile than DOS, having been designed for systems that cater to a larger variety of user needs than DOS. In this text, we will use the term **operating system** to refer to both OS and DOS; however, we will delineate any differences that exist between OS and DOS Assembly Language. Except for these differences, which are primarily in the manner in which input and output operations are specified, programs written in IBM 360 or 370 Assembly Language use the same instructions and directives whether they are written for OS or DOS. However, since there are different versions of each of these operating systems, it is important to note that this text is oriented to the OS/VS and DOS/VS versions.

Figure 1.3   Typical output processes.

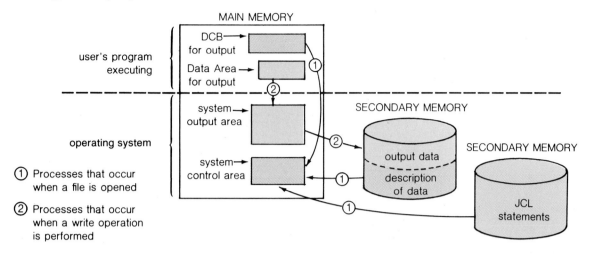

① Processes that occur when a file is opened

② Processes that occur when a write operation is performed

There are two mechanisms for communicating with the operating system: (1) by means of job control language (JCL) statements and (2) by means of instructions. The principal functions of JCL statements are to identify the user and the user's accounting parameters, to initiate and terminate jobs, and to describe files and request certain activities related to files. In this context, a **job** is a unit of work such as assembling, loading, and running a program that is to be performed by the computer system; a **file** is a set of related data that is treated as a unit and is identified by name. Probably the most important function of instructions that communicate with the operating system is to request that data be read from files and written to files at run time. The process of reading data is known as **input,** that of writing data as **output.**

Figure 1.3 indicates in a general way the processes that occur in order for output to take place. Every file to be processed by a program must be named on a JCL statement, and certain characteristics of that file must be described either by JCL statements or by data control (DCB or DTF) directives. The file must be "opened" at run time prior to its use and may then be written to in accordance with the specifications given when it was opened. When a file is opened, the operating system collects the specifications of the file into a control area and allocates space for the anticipated output operations. When a write operation is performed, data is transferred from the user program area to the system output buffer and from there it is transferred to the file by the operating system. A similar process takes place for input operations.

In a computer system in which many users can have access to the same facilities, each user's programs and data must be protected from being inadvertently or intentionally interfered with by other users' programs. Part of the function of the operating system is to provide that protection, and for this reason it controls all input and output operations. But in order to ensure that no user program can bypass that control function, another degree of protection is provided by the hardware. When a user's program is being run, the hardware, or more precisely, the central processing unit (see next section), is in what is known as **problem mode;** this means that only those instructions that cannot be used to affect the system's integrity are allowed to be executed. When the operating system is being run, the central processing unit is said to be in **supervisor mode,** in which all the instructions of the computer can be executed. Since input and output instructions are among those that can be used to affect system integrity, they can only be executed in supervisor mode and are therefore known as **privileged** instructions.

In the IBM 360 and 370 systems, there are some 180 executable instructions, of which about thirty are privileged. In the 3033 extension feature of the 370, there are also a dozen or so semiprivileged instructions used in the dual-address-space facility. These privileged and semiprivileged instructions will not be discussed in this text. Instead, attention will be focused on the 150 or so nonprivileged instructions and on the approximately fifty directives that can be used in IBM 360 and 370 Assembly Language.

Figure 1.4   Relationship of hardware components.

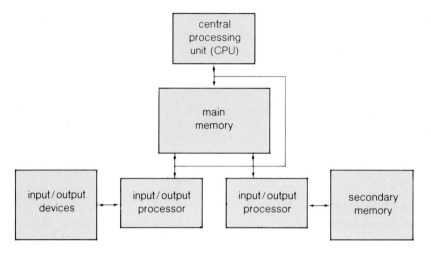

1.3   HARDWARE

Assembly language programmers are forced, by the nature of the language, to become familiar with some aspects of a computer system's hardware. Chief among these are the machine language instructions and data formats, the methods of addressing information in main memory, and the manner in which arithmetic is accomplished. In this section, the functions of the principal hardware components are summarized, and some fundamental characteristics of two of these components, main memory and the central processing unit, are discussed.

The hardware can be represented in a general way by the diagram in Figure 1.4. **Main memory** contains the operating system and any other program that is being executed by the hardware. In addition, it contains data and control information required by the operating system and the programs that are being executed. The **central processing unit** (CPU) contains the electronics required to interpret and execute machine language instructions, to control the transfer of data and programs into and out of main memory, and to detect various errors as they arise. The **input/output processors,** called data channels in IBM systems, contain the electronics required to transmit data between main memory and input/output devices, and between main memory and secondary memory. **Secondary,** or **auxiliary, memory** serves as storage space for data and for programs when they are not being executed. Secondary memory commonly consists of magnetic tapes, disks, and drums. **Input devices** generate signals required for the transmission of data into main memory from sources external to the computer system; common devices include card readers, terminals, and optical and magnetic ink character readers. **Output devices** receive signals transmitted from main memory for use outside the computer system; common devices include printers, terminals, card punches, and plotters.

Bits and Bytes   Main memory consists of a large number of elements whose purpose is to store programs and data in such a way that the instructions can be executed, and the data operated on, by the CPU. The fundamental unit of information in main memory is the binary digit, or **bit,** which may be either a 0 or a 1. *All data and programs are represented as sequences of bits.* In most computers some fixed number of bits is stored, accessed, and processed as a single unit of information. The term **byte** is used to denote a small number of consecutive bits, and the term **word** is generally used to denote a somewhat larger number of consecutive bits. In a unit of information consisting of k consecutive bits, the bits are usually numbered from 0 to $k-1$, starting at the high-order bit position:

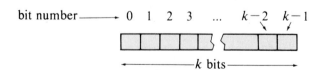

As shown, the high-order bit position is usually depicted as the left-most bit. It should be noted that with k bits, one can represent exactly 2^k different sequences of bits. For example, if $k = 2$, the four sequences are 00, 01, 10, and 11.

Memory Location

In the IBM 360 and 370 systems, a byte consists of 8 bits, and a word of 32 bits. Two other frequently used units are a half word, consisting of 16 bits (2 bytes), and a double word, consisting of 64 bits (8 bytes). A word is often called a *full word*, to distinguish it from half and double words. Each byte in main memory is said to occupy a location, or physical position, in memory, and each location is identified by a numeric name called its **address.** The set of all addresses in a main memory *Memory Address* that contains N byte locations is the set of nonnegative integers $0,1,2,...,N-1$, as represented by this diagram:

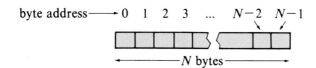

In a one megabyte (*mega* means million) memory, there are approximately one million byte locations— $N = 2^{20} = 1,048,576$.

Each byte in the main memory of IBM 360 and 370 systems is characterized by two quantities: *Memory Contents* its address and the sequence of 8 bits contained in the byte. The latter are often called the **contents** of the byte. Similarly, one speaks of the contents of a word, of a half word, and of a double word. The address of these larger units is the address of their most significant byte, usually depicted in diagrams as the left-most byte. It should be noted, however, that in some computer systems individual bytes may not be addressable. In those systems, a word is usually the smallest addressable unit of information.

The CPU executes instructions that it obtains from main memory and, in doing so, frequently *Machine Language Instruction Format* processes data that it also obtains from main memory. As has already been mentioned, the instructions and data are represented in machine language. This is a numeric language, the format and content of which usually differ considerably from one manufacturer's computer system to another's. The differences among various machine languages account for the differences among various assembly languages, since the format of the instructions and data represented in an assembly language is closely tied to that of machine language. Despite these differences, however, the general form of a machine language instruction can be depicted as follows:

opcode	operand

The sequence of bits in the opcode field identifies the particular instruction to be executed by the CPU, for example, add, compare, go-to. The bits in the operand field usually represent either the address of the data to be operated on by the instruction, or the data itself. In many instructions, two items of data are represented in the operand field, and in some instructions three are represented. These are known as two-operand or three-operand instructions, respectively. In go-to type instructions, the operand specifies the address of the next instruction to be executed.

Most CPU's execute only one instruction at a time. At any instant, the address of the next *The PC* instruction to be executed is contained in a hardware element known as the **program location counter (PC).** In the IBM 360 and 370 systems, the PC is part of the program status word (PSW), which records various information about the instantaneous state of a running program. The address in the PC is initially set by the operating system to refer to the first instruction in a program. But once program execution is under way, the address in the PC is controlled by the CPU as follows: When an instruction is obtained from memory, the CPU anticipates that the next instruction will be obtained from the next sequential location in memory. Therefore, it increments the address in the PC to refer to that location and then executes the instruction that was just fetched from memory.

When the executed instruction is anything other than a go-to type of instruction, the CPU uses the incremented PC address to fetch the next instruction upon completion of the current one. When the executed instruction is a go-to type of instruction, the address specified in that instruction's operand replaces the address in the PC, thereby changing the location of the next instruction from that which was anticipated by the CPU. In this way, the PC always contains the address of the next instruction that is to be fetched and executed by the CPU. Thus, through the mechanism of the PC, program execution proceeds from one instruction to the next in the same logical sequence as that given in the source module.

Use of Registers   In addition to fetching instructions and data directly from main memory, the CPU and main memory often are interfaced to one another through registers. **Registers** are special memory elements designed to provide faster access to data than is possible through main memory. Therefore, the use of registers contributes substantially to the speed with which a program can be executed. For this reason, most of the computations and comparisons performed by instructions use registers as well as main memory. But, because registers are more expensive than are main memory elements, there are far fewer registers than main memory locations in a computer system. (Compared to main memory, the higher cost of registers is due not only to their greater speed but also to their greater complexity. Registers are specifically designed to be used by the CPU for various arithmetic and logical operations, whereas main memory isn't.) One task of any program, therefore, is to copy data into and out of registers on an as-needed basis. Instructions specifically designed for this purpose are usually known as load and store instructions, respectively. In the three instructions of Figure 1.1 mentioned earlier,

```
L     3,X
A     3,Y
ST    3,Z
```

the first instruction is a load instruction, the only purpose of which is to copy an integer into a register (Register 3 in this example) so that the addition specified by the second instruction can be performed in that register. The third instruction is a store instruction, the purpose of which is to copy the sum from the register into main memory, so that the register can then be used for other purposes. In Fortran, an assignment statement would look like this:

```
Z = X + Y
```

In assembly language, it is necessary to specify the detailed sequence of instructions needed to carry out the process.

1.4   REPRESENTATION OF DATA IN MEMORY

In a computer's memory, all data are represented as one or more sequences of bits. The bit sequences that are used generally depend on how the data are to be processed by the CPU.

Arithmetic vs. Nonarithmetic Processing   One of the main processing distinctions is between arithmetic and nonarithmetic processes. Clearly, data that are to be used for arithmetic processes must be represented in such a way that the rules of arithmetic can be consistently and correctly applied to the data. Similarly, data used for nonarithmetic processes must be represented so that these processes can be carried out in a consistent manner. Usually the two sets of requirements are not compatible. Invariably, in a computer's memory, *a different representation is used for numbers that participate in arithmetic processes than is used for numbers that participate in nonarithmetic processes.* An example of a number used in an arithmetic process is the mathematical constant $\pi = 3.14159....$ An example of a number used in a nonarithmetic process is a telephone number, such as 555–1346.

Yet, all data that are transmitted between a computer's main memory and external input or output devices, such as card readers, printers, and terminals, are almost invariably transmitted in a form known as *character data*. This form is well suited for many nonarithmetic processes but is not well suited for arithmetic processes.

A **character** is any letter, digit, punctuation mark, or other symbol that can be represented on a punched card or typed on a keyboard. In the form of data representation known as character data, each character is represented as a sequence of bits in a code that uniquely identifies that character. Thus for purposes of data transmission, a number may be thought of as a sequence of one or more characters, each of which is represented in a unique code that is suitable for data transmission but not for arithmetic processes.

There are presently two main sets of character codes in widespread use. One is known as the American National Standard Code for Information Interchange (ASCII, usually pronounced *ask-ee*); the other is the Extended Binary-Coded Decimal Interchange Code (EBCDIC, pronounced *ebb-sid-ik*). EBCDIC is used in IBM devices and computer systems, as well as other computer systems; ASCII is used in terminals and computer systems not manufactured by IBM. *The two sets of codes are not the same.* EBCDIC is an 8-bit code, giving 256 possible character representations. ASCII is a 7-bit code, giving 128 possible character representations. For example, the digit "1" is represented as 0110001 in 7-bit ASCII but as 11110001 in 8-bit EBCDIC. The reader can ascertain other differences as well as similarities between the two schemes from the tables given in Appendix F.

In this text we will be concerned almost solely with the EBCDIC representations of characters. But whichever representation is used, one of the immediate problems the programmer has to face is that of translating input data from its character representation to the representation required in computer memory when the data is to be used in arithmetic processes. The programmer will also be faced with the reverse translation problem, to transmit arithmetic results from the computer's memory to an external device such as a printer or terminal. It must be emphasized that when a number is transmitted between memory and an external device, it is transmitted as character data—a sequence of digits, and possibly a plus or minus sign, punctuation marks, and/or a decimal point—each of which is represented in character form. This form is not used for the arithmetic processes of addition, subtraction, multiplication, and division in a computer system and is not even used to algebraically compare two numbers.

We will face these problems of translation in stages. First, we will consider only arithmetic processes involving integers. This discussion begins in the next section and continues, in various forms, through the first ten chapters. The representation and processing of numbers that are not integers will be dealt with in Chapters 11, 12, and 13.

1.5 BINARY AND HEXADECIMAL INTEGERS

In the binary number system, only two digits are used in the representation of numbers: 0 and 1. With only two digits, the rules of arithmetic are especially simple and require much simpler electronics than if the decimal system were used.

From a programming standpoint, the methods used to represent binary integers and to compute arithmetic functions of them in computer systems must be thoroughly understood for two reasons: (1) calculations involving addresses are of critical importance in assembly language programming, and almost all such calculations are based on the binary system, and (2) the range of integers that can be represented in computer systems is not infinite and attempts to generate an integer whose value is outside the allowable range usually produce erroneous results.

In this section, we will show how to express an integer in the binary and hexadecimal number systems and how to convert an integer from its decimal system representation to either the binary or hexadecimal system. These operations are necessary for an understanding of the material to be covered in subsequent chapters.

Positional Notation

In a decimal integer such as 423, the position of each digit determines the value of the integer. Thus, the value of 423 is computed as

$$4 \times 10^2 + 2 \times 10^1 + 3 \times 10^0$$

In general, for a decimal integer consisting of k digits

$$d_0 d_1 d_2 ... d_{k-2} d_{k-1}$$

where d_n denotes any decimal digit (and below, b_n any binary digit, and h_n any hexadecimal digit), the value of the integer is computed as

$$d_0 \times 10^{k-1} + d_1 \times 10^{k-2} + d_2 \times 10^{k-3} + ... + d_{k-2} \times 10^1 + d_{k-1} \times 10^0$$

The representation $d_0 d_1 d_2 ... d_{k-2} d_{k-1}$ is said to use **positional notation** for the base 10.

Analogous to decimal integers, any nonnegative binary integer is a sequence of the binary digits 0 and 1 arranged in such an order that the position of each bit implies its value in the integer. For example, the positional value of each bit in the binary integer 10101 is computed as follows:

$$
\begin{array}{llll}
1 & 0 & 1 & 0 & 1 \\
\end{array}
$$

$$
\begin{aligned}
1 \times 2^0 &= 1 \\
0 \times 2^1 &= 0 \\
1 \times 2^2 &= 4 \\
0 \times 2^3 &= 0 \\
1 \times 2^4 &= 16
\end{aligned}
$$

The value of the binary integer 10101 is the sum of the positional values (represented here in the decimal system) of each bit:

$$
\begin{array}{ccccc}
1 & 0 & 1 & 0 & 1 \\
\end{array}
$$

$$
16 + 0 + 4 + 0 + 1 = 21
$$

In general, for a k-bit binary integer

$$
b_0 b_1 b_2 ... b_{k-2} b_{k-1}
$$

the value of the integer is computed as

$$
b_0 \times 2^{k-1} + b_1 \times 2^{k-2} + b_2 \times 2^{k-3} + ... + b_{k-2} \times 2^1 + b_{k-1} \times 2^0
$$

Binary numbers are therefore known as base 2 numbers. To avoid misinterpretation, they are often written with a subscript 2, as in 10101_2.

In the hexadecimal (base 16) system, there are sixteen digits, represented by the symbols 0,1,2,3,4,5,6,7,8,9,A,B,C,D,E, and F. The first ten symbols have their usual meaning; the remaining six—*A* through *F*—represent the values ten through fifteen when used as hexadecimal digits. In a hexadecimal integer, the value implied by each digit's position is a multiple of a power of sixteen, not of two as in binary or of ten as in decimal integers. For example, the positional values of the digits in the hexadecimal integer A423 is computed as follows:

$$
\begin{array}{cccc}
A & 4 & 2 & 3
\end{array}
$$

$$
\begin{aligned}
3 \times 16^0 &= 3 & (16^0 &= 1) \\
2 \times 16^1 &= 32 & (16^1 &= 16) \\
4 \times 16^2 &= 1024 & (16^2 &= 256) \\
10 \times 16^3 &= 40960 & (16^3 &= 4096)
\end{aligned}
$$

The value of A423 is therefore $40960 + 1024 + 32 + 3 = 42019$ in decimal notation.

In general, for a k-digit hexadecimal integer

$$
h_0 h_1 h_2 ... h_{k-2} h_{k-1}
$$

the value of the integer is computed as

$$
h_0 \times 16^{k-1} + h_1 \times 16^{k-2} + h_2 \times 16^{k-3} + ... + h_{k-2} \times 16^1 + h_{k-1} \times 16^0
$$

Hexadecimal integers are often written with a subscript 16, and sometimes with a subscript x, as in $800_{16} = 800_x$.

It will prove worthwhile to gain complete familiarity with the representations of the first sixteen binary and hexadecimal integers shown in Figure 1.5 since both the binary and hexadecimal forms will be used extensively in subsequent chapters. This use will include addition and subtraction of two binary integers, addition and subtraction of two hexadecimal integers, and conversion from binary to hexadecimal and vice versa.

Figure 1.5   Representations of integers.

name	decimal	binary	hexadecimal
zero	0	0000	0
one	1	0001	1
two	2	0010	2
three	3	0011	3
four	4	0100	4
five	5	0101	5
six	6	0110	6
seven	7	0111	7
eight	8	1000	8
nine	9	1001	9
ten	10	1010	A
eleven	11	1011	B
twelve	12	1100	C
thirteen	13	1101	D
fourteen	14	1110	E
fifteen	15	1111	F
sixteen	16	10000	10

Addition and Subtraction in Base 2

Addition of two binary integers is a simple matter, since there are only four rules to learn: $0 + 0 = 0$, $0 + 1 = 1$, $1 + 0 = 1$, and $1 + 1 = 10$ (two, in binary). In the last rule, a carry of 1 is generated and must be added to the next higher-order digit sum, an operation that is analogous to the handling of carries in decimal addition. You should be able to verify that the following sums are correct:

$$
\begin{array}{r} 10110 \\ + 1100 \\ \hline 100010 \end{array}
\qquad
\begin{array}{r} 10110 \\ + 11 \\ \hline 11001 \end{array}
\qquad
\begin{array}{r} 11111 \\ + 1 \\ \hline 100000 \end{array}
\qquad
\begin{array}{r} 11001 \\ + 11001 \\ \hline 110010 \end{array}
$$

Subtraction of two binary integers is also straightforward, since the only situation in which a borrow operation can arise is that of subtracting 1 from 0. As with decimal integers, subtraction of two binary integers is best done by subtracting the smaller from the larger integer. The following examples illustrate how subtraction is accomplished when the result is positive:

$$
\begin{array}{r} 10110 \\ - 101 \\ \hline 10001 \end{array}
\qquad
\begin{array}{r} 10110 \\ - 1010 \\ \hline 1100 \end{array}
\qquad
\begin{array}{r} 10000 \\ - 1 \\ \hline 1111 \end{array}
\qquad
\begin{array}{r} 10010 \\ - 1101 \\ \hline 101 \end{array}
$$

Addition and Subtraction in Base 16

Addition and subtraction of two hexadecimal integers require some practice; it is an essential skill because it is used in address computations. In *addition* of two hexadecimal digits, the sum is a single digit if its value is less than sixteen; otherwise a carry of 1 is generated. In *subtraction,* a borrow of 10_x (sixteen, in hexadecimal) is necessary when the first digit is smaller than the second. The following examples illustrate these concepts. Note that all the integers here are in hexadecimal notation.

$$
\begin{array}{r} 4 \\ + 6 \\ \hline A \end{array}
\quad
\begin{array}{r} 4 \\ + A \\ \hline E \end{array}
\quad
\begin{array}{r} A \\ + 6 \\ \hline 10 \end{array}
\quad
\begin{array}{r} B \\ - 6 \\ \hline 5 \end{array}
\quad
\begin{array}{r} 10 \\ - 8 \\ \hline 8 \end{array}
\quad
\begin{array}{r} 18 \\ - 9 \\ \hline F \end{array}
\quad
\begin{array}{r} DE \\ + C8 \\ \hline 1A6 \end{array}
\quad
\begin{array}{r} DE \\ - C8 \\ \hline 16 \end{array}
\quad
\begin{array}{r} 40C \\ - E \\ \hline 3FE \end{array}
\quad
\begin{array}{r} FFF \\ + 1 \\ \hline 1000 \end{array}
$$

Conversion of Positive Integers from One Base to Another

The method for converting a positive integer from its representation in one base (the old base) to its representation in another (the new) depends on which number system the computations are performed in. When converting *from* decimal to another base, it is convenient to do the calculations in the decimal system, which, in this case, is the old base. When converting *to* decimal from another base, it is still convenient to calculate in the decimal system, which, in this case, is the new base. As we shall now see, calculating in the old base requires division; calculating in the new base requires multiplication.

Suppose that an integer J is represented in the decimal system as

$$d_0 d_1 d_2 ... d_{k-2} d_{k-1}$$

and that we wish to determine its binary representation

$$b_0 b_1 b_2 ... b_{m-2} b_{m-1}$$

The value of J can be computed in the decimal system (the old base) by either of these equations:

$$J = d_0 \times 10^{k-1} + d_1 \times 10^{k-2} + ... + d_{k-2} \times 10^1 + d_{k-1} \times 10^0 \qquad (1.1)$$

$$J = b_0 \times 2^{m-1} + b_1 \times 2^{m-2} + ... + b_{m-2} \times 2^1 + b_{m-1} \times 2^0 \qquad (1.2)$$

(Note that m is usually not equal to k.)

Conversion from Base 10 to Base 2

Since the d_j digits are known but the b_j are not, we know the value of J as given by Equation 1.1 and we can use this value to determine the b_j from Equation 1.2 by successive iterations, as follows.

We first divide by 2, producing an integer quotient and an integer remainder. Let the quotient be Q_1; the remainder is just b_{m-1}, i.e., the low-order digit in the binary representation of J.

$$\frac{J}{2} = b_0 \times 2^{m-2} + b_1 \times 2^{m-3} + ... + b_{m-2} \times 2^0 + \frac{b_{m-1}}{2} = Q_1 + \frac{b_{m-1}}{2}$$

We now obtain the next digit, b_{m-2}, by dividing Q_1 by 2.

$$\frac{Q_1}{2} = b_0 \times 2^{m-3} + b_1 \times 2^{m-4} + ... + b_{m-3} \times 2^0 + \frac{b_{m-2}}{2} = Q_2 + \frac{b_{m-2}}{2}$$

The process continues by dividing each successive integer quotient, Q_j, by 2 and collecting the integer remainders. When a quotient of 0 is obtained, the remainder will be the most significant digit b_0.

To illustrate, let $J = 18$ in decimal notation. Then

$$\begin{aligned}
J/2 &= 9 + 0/2, & \text{so } Q_1 &= 9 \text{ and } b_{m-1} = 0 \\
Q_1/2 &= 4 + 1/2, & \text{so } Q_2 &= 4 \text{ and } b_{m-2} = 1 \\
Q_2/2 &= 2 + 0/2, & \text{so } Q_3 &= 2 \text{ and } b_{m-3} = 0 \\
Q_3/2 &= 1 + 0/2, & \text{so } Q_4 &= 1 \text{ and } b_{m-4} = 0 \\
Q_4/2 &= 0 + 1/2, & \text{so } Q_5 &= 0 \text{ and } b_{m-5} = 1 = b_0
\end{aligned}$$

Thus the binary representation of 18_{10} is 10010_2.

It is perhaps simplest to perform the above operations as follows:

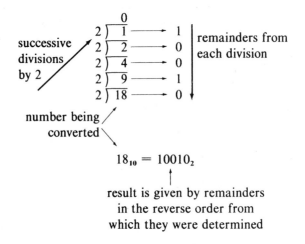

result is given by remainders
in the reverse order from
which they were determined

The process just described is not limited to conversions from decimal to binary. It can be used to convert from any base, P, to any other base, R, provided that *the calculations are performed in the base P system*. Equations 1.1 and 1.2 must be replaced by their equivalent representations in the base P system. If we assume that the known base P representation is $p_0p_1p_2...p_{k-1}$ and that the desired base R representation is $r_0r_1r_2...r_{m-1}$, then the appropriate equations are

$$J = p_0 \times P^{k-1} + p_1 \times P^{k-2} + ... + p_{k-2} \times P^1 + p_{k-1} \times P^0 \tag{1.3}$$

$$J = r_0 \times R^{m-1} + r_1 \times R^{m-2} + ... + r_{m-2} \times R^1 + r_{m-1} \times R^0 \tag{1.4}$$

To begin the iteration procedure, divide Equation 1.4 by R, obtaining an integer quotient, Q_1, and an integer remainder, r_{m-1}. Then divide Q_1 by R to obtain Q_2 and r_{m-2}, and so forth. The calculations must be done in the base P system and are terminated when a zero quotient is obtained.

The reader can verify that if $P = 10$ (ten) and $R = 16$, then the conversion of the decimal integer $J = 18$ to the hexadecimal system proceeds as follows:

Conversion from Base 10 to Base 16

$$J/16 = 1 + 2/16, \quad \text{so } Q_1 = 1 \text{ and } r_{m-1} = 2$$

$$Q_1/16 = 0 + 1/16, \quad \text{so } Q_2 = 0 \text{ and } r_{m-2} = 1 = r_0$$

Thus the hexadecimal representation of 18_{10} is 12_{16}.

These methods are useful when converting by hand from the decimal system to any other system. But when converting from some other base to base 10, it makes sense to do the conversions in the new base (10). This is the method that we used when converting 10101_2 to 21_{10}, and $A423_{16}$ to 42019_{10}. In general we simply represent the value of the known integer in the new base, and calculate that value in the new base. Thus if the old base is P and the new base is R, and if the known integer J is represented in the base P system as $p_0p_1p_2...p_{k-1}$, then we represent each digit, p_j, as an integer in the base R system and calculate this expression:

$$\bar{p}_0 \times P^{k-1} + \bar{p}_1 \times P^{k-2} + ... + \bar{p}_{k-2} \times P^1 + \bar{p}_{k-2} \times P^0$$

Here, $\bar{p}_j$ is the representative of p_j in the base R system. For example, with J represented as $A423_{16}$, then $P = 16$, $p_0 = A$, $p_1 = 4$, $p_2 = 2$, and $p_3 = 3$. If $R = 10$ (ten), then $\bar{p}_0 = 10$, $\bar{p}_1 = 4$, $\bar{p}_2 = 2$, and $\bar{p}_3 = 3$ so that in the base 10 system, the hexadecimal integer $A423_{16}$ is represented as

Conversion from Base 16 to Base 10

$$10 \times 16^3 + 4 \times 16^2 + 2 \times 16^1 + 3 \times 16^0 = 42019_{10}$$

A useful method of performing this type of calculation is to group terms as follows:

$$[(10 \times 16 + 4) \times 16 + 2] \times 16 + 3 = 42019_{10}$$

Conversions between Binary and Hexadecimal Integers

Conversions between the hexadecimal and binary representations will frequently be required throughout this text. The binary system is simply too cumbersome to work with easily, and the hexadecimal system provides a useful and convenient substitute. Because the base 16 and base 2 systems are related by the equation $16 = 2^4$, *conversions between the two systems do not require use of the general procedures described earlier*. Instead, the following two rules are almost always used:

1. To convert from hexadecimal to binary, replace each hexadecimal digit with its equivalent four-bit binary representation.

2. To convert from binary to hexadecimal, replace every four consecutive binary digits by their equivalent hexadecimal digit, starting from the right-hand digit and adding zeroes on the left, if necessary.

The following examples demonstrate these rules. The reader should verify that the results obtained are equivalent to those that would be obtained using the general procedures described earlier. Note that spaces are used after each set of four binary digits to facilitate reading; they have no other purpose.

binary:	0001	0010		
hexadecimal:	1	2		
binary:	0100	0000		
hexadecimal:	4	0		
binary:	1110	0010	0100	1010
hexadecimal:	E	2	4	A
binary:	1111	1101	1011	
hexadecimal:	F	D	B	

Thus, $10010_2 = 12_x$, $1000000_2 = 40_x$, $1110001001001010_2 = E24A_x$, and $111111011011_2 = FDB_x$.

One further example should serve to indicate why the substitution rules are valid. Consider this binary integer: 10101010011011. Applying the rules, we mark off groups of four binary bits from right to left, starting at the low-order bit, appending binary zeroes at the left, high-order end so that the last group also contains 4 bits: 0010 1010 1001 1011. Now we replace each group of 4 bits with its equivalent hexadecimal representation:

0010	1010	1001	1011
2	A	9	B

Notice that the value of the binary integer representation can be calculated as follows:

$$1 \times 2^{13} + 1 \times 2^{11} + 1 \times 2^9 + 1 \times 2^7 + 1 \times 2^4 + 1 \times 2^3 + 1 \times 2^1 + 1 \times 2^0$$

The value of the hexadecimal integer representation can similarly be calculated:

$$2 \times 16^3 + 10 \times 16^2 + 9 \times 16^1 + 11 \times 16^0$$

But since $16 = 2^4$, and since

$$10 = 2^3 + 2^1$$
$$9 = 2^3 + 2^0$$
$$11 = 2^3 + 2^1 + 2^0$$

then the hexadecimal calculation is equivalent to the expression

$$2 \times (2^4)^3 + (2^3 + 2^1) \times (2^4)^2 + (2^3 + 2^0) \times (2^4)^1 + (2^3 + 2^1 + 2^0) \times (2^4)^0$$

and this reduces precisely to the expression given for the binary calculation.

1.6 SUMMARY

Computer systems consist of two broad classes of components, hardware and software. Some aspects of the structure of the hardware, particularly the main memory and the instructions that are executable by the CPU, are reflected in assembly language, thereby making the language qualitatively different from almost all other programming languages. Among the concepts an assembly language programmer must be familiar with are the ways in which data are represented in memory for arithmetic and nonarithmetic processes; the organization of memory into bytes, words, and other units of information, each of which is accessed by means of its address; and the use of registers as an interface between the central processing unit and main memory. Important, too, are the distinctions between assembly time, load time, and run time, and the role of the operating system in input and output operations.

The terminology used in conjunction with assembly language programming reflects its relationship to the hardware. One speaks of bits, bytes, words, addresses, registers, and so forth, because these entities have fundamental uses in assembly language. Definitions will be given whenever new terms are introduced, but you may also want to refer to the following dictionaries:

American National Dictionary for Information Processing. American National Standards Committee X3; Technical Report # X3/TR-1-77. Published by the Computer and Business Equipment Manufacturers Association, Washington, DC.

Data Processing Glossary. IBM Publication #GC20-1699. Obtainable from the IBM Data Processing Division, White Plains, NY.

Standard Dictionary of Computers and Information Processing. Martin H. Weik. Published by Hayden Book Co., Inc., Rochelle Park, NJ.

Dictionary of Computers, Data Processing, and Telecommunications. Jerry M. Rosenberg. Published by John Wiley & Sons, Inc., New York, NY.

1.7 REVIEW

Programs   A program is a plan that specifies actions that may be taken by a computer, together with the conditions (including the data) under which the actions are to be taken. Computer programs are always written in a precise language that can be either processed directly by the computer's hardware or translated into a form that can be processed by the hardware.

Machine Language   In a computer, the hardware component known as the central processing unit interprets (i.e., executes, or carries out the plan that is specified by) programs coded in machine language, whose instructions and data are entirely numeric.

Assembly Language   Assembly language consists of mnemonic instructions and directives. The mnemonic instructions represent a computer's machine language instructions; the mnemonic directives have many different purposes, one of them being to represent a computer's machine language data. Therefore, when writing an assembly language program you are writing a program that is a symbolic form of machine language.

Operating Systems   An operating system is the master control program for a computer. It manages and controls the programs that are executed by the hardware. In the IBM 360 and 370 systems, there are two principal families of operating systems: OS and DOS. Except for the manner in which input and output operations are specified, there are very few differences between OS and DOS Assembly Language.

Privileged Instructions   Operating systems and related programs utilize privileged instructions to control and safeguard the integrity of the programs and data stored in the computer. User programs, such as the ones that you and I write, are not permitted to use privileged instructions. Consequently, this textbook only discusses the *non*privileged instructions of the IBM 360 and 370 computer systems.

Memory Locations   The main memory of a modern-day computer may contain millions of individually identifiable cells, or locations, in which data or instructions are stored and used. Each location is identified by its unique numeric name; this name is known as the location's address. In the IBM 360 and 370 systems, the smallest addressable location is a byte, consisting of eight consecutive bits. Larger addressable units are a half word (two bytes), full word (four bytes), and double word (eight bytes).

Registers   Registers are special high-speed memory elements that serve as interfaces between the CPU and main memory. By design, many assembly language instructions must specify and use registers in order to accomplish their tasks. The hardware is designed that way to achieve greater efficiency and speed.

Data   The way that data is represented in a computer depends on how it is going to be used. Data used for numeric processes are represented differently from data used for nonnumeric processes. Data that is transmitted between main memory and an input/output device such as a terminal or printer is always represented in character format.

EBCDIC   The coding scheme used for character format in the IBM 360 and 370 systems is known as EBCDIC. In it, each character is represented by a unique pattern of eight bits. One of the tasks of an assembly language program is to convert numeric data between its main memory representation and its character format in order to perform input and output operations.

Binary and Hexadecimal Number Systems   All numbers used in a computer for arithmetic processing are represented in the binary (base 2) number system, i.e., using just two digits: 0 and 1. Since it is tedious for humans to work with binary numbers, we will almost always use hexadecimal (base 16) numbers, because they are easily derived from and converted into binary numbers. The hexadecimal system uses sixteen digits, each of which represents one four-digit binary number from zero to fifteen (see Fig. 1.5).

1.8   REVIEW QUESTIONS

1. In what important way are assembly time, load time, and run time different?
2. What is the most important distinction between an assembly language instruction and an assembly language directive?
3. What are the two important characteristics of each main memory location?
4. How many bits are contained in a byte? How many bytes are contained in a half word? A full word? A double word? How many words are contained in a 16-megabyte memory?
5. Why is it necessary to convert numeric data to or from the EBCDIC code scheme in order to perform input/output operations?
6. In what important way (or ways) does main memory differ from secondary memory?
7. In converting between binary and hexadecimal numbers, how many bits are represented by each hex digit? What role do leading zeroes play when converting integers between the two number systems?

1.9   EXERCISES

1. The use of instructions and directives in IBM 360 and 370 Assembly Language has its counterpart in the use of executable and nonexecutable statements in high-level languages like Fortran and Cobol. Describe the fundamental distinction between executable and nonexecutable statements. In what way is this distinction related to the concepts of assembly time and run time as defined in Chapter 1?

2. The distinction between the address of a memory location and the contents of that location exists in high-level languages as well as in assembly language. Explain this distinction in either the Fortran assignment statement Z = X + Y or the corresponding Cobol assignment statement COMPUTE Z = X + Y.

3. Suppose that the title of a programming course is COMPUTER SCIENCE 102. Using the 8-bit EBCDIC codes given in Appendix F, write the EBCDIC character representation of the course name.

4. Assume that the 7-bit ASCII codes given in Appendix F are extended to 8 bits by appending a high-order bit of "1" to each code, so that, for example, the 7-bit code for the letter *A* (namely, 1000001) is extended to the 8-bit code 11000001. By extending each 7-bit ASCII code in this manner, write the 8-bit ASCII character representation of COMPUTER SCIENCE 102.

5. Assume that the 7-bit ASCII codes are extended to 8 bits by appending a high-order bit, which makes the number of 1's in each extended 8-bit code an even number. Using this scheme, for example, the 7-bit code for the letter B (1000010) becomes 01000010 while the 7-bit code for the letter C (1000011) becomes 11000011. The bit that is so appended is known as the parity bit. By extending each 7-bit ASCII code in this manner, write the 8-bit ASCII character representation of COMPUTER SCIENCE 102.

6. What is the EBCDIC character representation of each of the decimal integers given below? What is the binary number system representation of each of these decimal integers? What is the hexadecimal representation?

a.	0	**e.**	32	**i.**	31
b.	10	**f.**	64	**j.**	63
c.	49	**g.**	128	**k.**	4095
d.	102	**h.**	256	**l.**	255

7. State a rule that will allow you to determine whether an arbitrarily chosen binary integer is odd or even, without having to do any calculations. State a similar rule that will allow you to determine, without calculation, whether a given binary integer is exactly divisible by 4, by 8, and in general by 2^k for any positive integer k.

8. What is the hexadecimal representation of each of the following binary integers?

a. 0100 0000 **d.** 1110 1011 1100 1101
b. 1111 1111 **e.** 0010 0100 0110 1000
c. 0101 1010 **f.** 0011 1110 0000

9. What is the binary representation of each of the following hexadecimal integers? If each of these two-digit hexadecimal numbers is interpreted as the 8-bit EBCDIC code for a character, what character does it represent?

a.	4E	**e.**	5D	**i.**	F9
b.	60	**f.**	40	**j.**	C3
c.	4B	**g.**	7D	**k.**	83
d.	5C	**h.**	6B	**l.**	7A

10. Perform the indicated additions and subtractions using the rules of hexadecimal arithmetic:

a.	88C	**b.**	EC0	**c.**	6A	**d.**	CB	**e.**	DE4
	+ 2A		− FF		+A6		−BC		+ 21C

11. In the base 8 number system (known as the octal system), there are only eight digits: 0,1,2,3,4,5,6,7. The value of an octal number such as 345_8 is computed in the decimal system as

$$3 \times 8^2 + 4 \times 8^1 + 5 \times 8^0 = 229_{10}$$

  a. Determine the octal system representations of the decimal integers 8 through 16.
  b. State a method of converting integers from the binary system to the octal system, and vice versa, that is analogous to the method of converting between the binary and hexadecimal systems. Prove that the method is equivalent to the general iterative procedures of Section 1.5.
  c. In some computer systems it is more useful to represent binary integers in the octal system than in the hexadecimal system. Under what conditions might this be done?

2

Fundamentals of the IBM 360 and 370 Assembly Language

In this chapter we describe the general format of assembly language statements for the IBM 360 and 370 computer systems, indicate how statements should be organized in a source module, and illustrate how input and output operations are written.

2.1 STATEMENT FORMATS

Each statement in a source module must be written in accordance with well-defined rules. The rules depend on the type and purpose of the statement, but the general format of all statements falls into one of two categories: (1) the format used for comment statements and (2) the format used for instructions and directives. In both cases, the general format is designed to accommodate the constraints imposed by an eighty-column input line.

The eighty characters are divided into four fields for the comment statement format, and six fields for the format of instructions and directives. Although the length and position of some fields may be varied, as will be seen, they are usually defined as shown in Figure 2.1. The statements shown in Figure 2.2 illustrate the use of these formats.

Comment Statement Format

The first position of a comment statement must contain an asterisk (*). Comment statements may appear anywhere in a source module, and there may be any number of them. They are printed on the listing along with the other statements of the source module and therefore are used to provide a description of the purpose and techniques of the statements following the comments.

Positions 2 through 71 may contain any text desired by the programmer. The continuation field (position 72) is normally blank. If not blank, the continuation field indicates that the comment's text is continued on the subsequent line of the source module, in the manner described in the next section for instructions and directives. The identification field (positions 73 through 80) is also used in the same manner as that for instructions and directives.

Figure 2.1   Statement formats.

comment statement format:

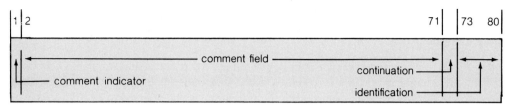

format for instructions and directives:

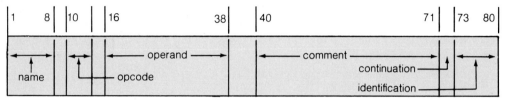

Figure 2.2   Assembly language statement examples.

name	opcode	operand	comment	continuation	identification
*		EVERY STATEMENT WITH AN ASTERISK IN THE FIRST POSITION			ALP00010
*		IS A COMMENT STATEMENT.			ALP00020
*					ALP00030
*	THE OPERAND AND COMMENT FIELDS OF AN	INSTRUCTION OR DIRECTIVE			ALP00040
*	MAY BE CONTINUED ONTO THE FOLLOWING	LINE BY PUTTING A NONBLANK			ALP00050
*	CHARACTER IN	POSITION 72, AS FOLLOWS:			ALP00060
*					ALP00070
LINE	DCB	DSORG=PS,MACRF=(PM),DDNAME=SYSPRINT,RECFM=FB,LRECL=132,		-	ALP00080
		BLKSIZE=4092			ALP00090
*					ALP00100
*	NORMALLY CONTINUATION IS NOT REQUIRED, AS IN THESE STATEMENTS:				ALP00110
*					ALP00120
OUTER	L	4,=F'5'	SET LINE COUNT TO 5		ALP00130
*READ ONE CARD	AND PRINT IT				ALP00140
INNER	GET	CARD,INAREA	READ CARD INTO 'INAREA'		ALP00150
	MVC	OUTAREA(80),INAREA	COPY DATA TO 'OUTAREA'		ALP00160
	PUT	LINE,OUTAREA	WRITE CARD IMAGE ON PRINTER		ALP00170
	BCT	4,INNER	REPEAT READ/WRITE LOOP 5 TIMES		ALP00180
*PRINT BLANK LINE					ALP00190
	MVC	OUTAREA(132),=132C' '	COPY 132 BLANKS TO 'OUTAREA'		ALP00200
	PUT	LINE,OUTAREA	WRITE BLANK LINE ON PRINTER		ALP00210
	B	OUTER	REPEAT ENTIRE READ/WRITE PROCESS		ALP00220

Format for Instructions and Directives

The two principal requirements in instructions and directives are these: (1) The first position must not contain an asterisk. It must either be blank or be the first character of the name-field symbol (see below). (2) The opcode field must contain a string of from one to five characters that is a valid assembly language instruction or directive.

In addition, the information in each of the six fields is constrained by the requirements outlined in the following paragraphs.

Name Field.   When the first character of the name field is not blank, the name field must consist of from one to eight characters followed by a blank. A name-field entry is called a **symbol,** and its purpose is to identify the statement so that the statement can be referred to by that symbol elsewhere in the source module.

Except as discussed in Chapters 16 and 17, the first character of a symbol must be a letter and the remaining characters, if any, must be letters or digits. No other characters are permitted. It should be noted that in the IBM 360 and 370 Assembly Language, the word **letter** is used to denote any of the twenty-six alphabetic characters A through Z and the three characters $ (dollar sign), # (number sign), and @ (at sign).

Valid Symbols   The following are examples of valid symbols:

```
Q
A101
LOOP
FOUND
REP12A
#1
CONTINUE
@HERE
$###2
```

Invalid Symbols   For the reasons stated, the following are examples of invalid symbols:

3
101A } first character not a letter

F(1)   parentheses
LOOP 1   blank   not among
LOOP.1   period   the allowable
LOOP-1   hyphen   characters

ENCOUNTER   too many characters: maximum is 8

Opcode Field.   As mentioned earlier, the opcode field must contain a valid assembly language code of from one to five alphabetic characters that identifies one of the instructions or directives that exist in the language. An alphabetical summary of valid operation codes is given in Appendixes A, B, and E. The last character of the operation code must be followed by a blank.

Operand Field.   The format of the operand field depends on whether the opcode field designates an instruction or a directive, and it also depends on which instruction or directive is specified. But despite the fact that there are differences among operand formats, they all share two characteristics. First, unless the operand is blank, as it may be in some directives, it always consists of one or more subfields written without intervening blanks. Every two adjacent subfields are separated by a comma, and a blank must immediately follow the last character of the last operand subfield. And second, blanks cannot be used indiscriminately within an operand. Use of a blank must follow prescribed rules that apply only to special cases such as text strings that are enclosed within apostrophes.

A few examples illustrating some of the varieties possible in operand fields were given in Figure 2.2.

Comment Field. The comment field may contain any information. The information in the comment field supplements the information specified in comment statements. It is usually a brief description of the purpose of the statement. Care must be taken, however, not to extend the comment field information into the continuation field. Examples of valid comment field entries were given in Figure 2.2.

Continuation Field. The operand and comment fields of a statement may in some cases contain more information than can fit on a single line of source code. In these cases the statement may be extended over two or more lines by means of the continuation field. If the continuation field contains any nonblank character, then the following line will be assumed to be a continuation of the line whose continuation field is nonblank.

When continuing a statement in this manner, each continuation line must begin in position 16, called the **continuing position.** In Figure 2.2 the statement shown below consists of two lines, the second being a continuation of the first because of the nonblank character in position 72.

```
           position 16                                                      position 72
              |                                                                |
LINE   DCB DSORG=PS,MACRF=(PM),DDNAME=SYSPRINT,RECFM=FB,LRECL=132, -ALP00080
           BLKSIZE=4092
```

Identification Field. The identification field may consist of any combination of letters, digits, and blank spaces. When the field is not all blank, its purpose is twofold: (1) to identify the source module in which the statement appears and (2) to record the sequential position of the statement within the source module.

The identification field contents are always printed on the listing, but otherwise they are ignored by the assembler unless the ISEQ directive has been used to initiate sequence checking of statements. If an ISEQ directive has initiated sequence checking in the manner described in Chapter 14, the assembler compares the identification field contents of each line with the same field of the preceding line. With the exception that blank fields are ignored, the two fields must be in increasing sequence; otherwise a warning message is printed on the listing. An out-of-sequence condition does not affect the assembly of the source module in any other way.

2.2 STATEMENT FORMAT VARIATIONS

The field positions for the statement format defined in the preceding section are said to be in the **standard fixed format** of the IBM 360 and 370 Assembly Language. Position 1 of the standard fixed format is called the *beginning* position of a statement, position 71 is called the *ending* position, and position 16 is called the *continuing* position.

As previously stated, the beginning position is used for two purposes: (1) to distinguish a comment statement from statements containing instructions or directives and (2) as the first position of the name field. If the beginning position contains an asterisk, the statement is a comment statement. If the beginning position does not contain an asterisk, the statement is either an instruction or a directive. Any character other than an asterisk or a blank in the beginning position of a statement is assumed to be the first character of a name-field symbol.

Other characteristics of standard fixed format include the following:

1. Any field that is omitted must be blank.
2. All nonblank fields must be left-justified within the field boundaries and be filled with trailing blanks.
3. Positions 9, 15, and 39 must be blank.
4. Information in the operand and/or comment fields of one line of a statement may be continued on the following line, provided that the continuation field contains a nonblank character. The information that is continued must begin in the continuing position.

Figure 2.3   Use of standard fixed and standard free formats.

name	opcode	operand	comment	continuation	identification
*	PROGRAM	LOGIC AND STRUCTURE CAN BE DEPICTED USING FREE FORMAT			ALP01010
*	IN OPC	ODE, OPERAND, AND COMMENT FIELDS OF INSTRUCTIONS AND			ALP01020
*	DIRECT	IVES AS IN THE FOLLOWING STATEMENTS:			ALP01030
*					ALP01040
OUTER	L	4,=F'5'	SET LINE COUNT TO 5		ALP01050
*					ALP01060
* INNER	LOOP	READS 5 CARDS ONE AT A TIME	AND PRINTS EACH ONE		ALP01070
*					ALP01080
INNER		GET CARD,INAREA	READ CARD INTO 'INAREA'		ALP01090
		MVC OUTAREA(80),INAREA	COPY DATA TO 'OUTAREA'		ALP01100
		PUT LINE,OUTAREA	WRITE CARD DATA ON PRINTER		ALP01110
		BCT 4,INNER	REPEAT READ/WRITE LOOP		ALP01120
*					ALP01130
* OUTER	LOOP	PRINTS ONE BLANK LINE AFTER EVERY FIFTH DATA LINE			ALP01140
*					ALP01150
		MVC OUTAREA(132),=132C' '	COPY 132 BLANKS TO 'OUTAREA		ALP01160
		PUT LINE,OUTAREA	WRITE BLANK LINE ON PRINTER		ALP01170
		B OUTER	REPEAT ENTIRE READ/WRITE PROCESS		ALP01180

Fixed vs. Free Format

These standard fixed format constraints may be overridden in one of two ways. One way is that the positions used for beginning, ending, and continuing a line may be redefined. This is done by means of the ICTL directive, which will not be discussed further until Chapter 14. The second method utilizes the fact that in the IBM 360 and 370 Assembly Language, the opcode, operand, and comment fields need not begin in positions 10, 16, and 40, respectively; the information in any of these fields needs only to be separated by one or more blanks from the information in the immediately preceding field. This capability is called **free format.**

Free format can be used anywhere in a source module. It permits longer operands than can fit in the fixed positions 16 through 38; alternatively, it permits comments to be started before position 40. Another advantage is that it permits one to indent the opcode and operand fields and thereby emphasize the structure of the logic more clearly than if indentation were not employed. Figure 2.3 illustrates this for some of the statements that were given in Figure 2.2. It should be noted, however, that whichever is used, standard fixed format or standard free format, the positions of the continuation and identification fields remain fixed in positions 72 and 73–80, respectively; and the beginning, ending, and continuing positions remain fixed in positions 1, 71, and 16, respectively.

2.3   SOURCE MODULE REQUIREMENTS

In this section the conventional requirements for writing source modules in IBM 360 and 370 Assembly Language are described. The requirements may vary somewhat among different computer installations, but those given here will probably be sufficient in most operating environments. Most of the statements provide an interface to the operating system and other programs at run time, as will be explained in Chapter 10. Two—the BALR instruction and the USING directive—have fundamental roles related to addressing within a program (see Chap. 3).

There are two different sets of requirements: one for OS systems and one for DOS systems.

Requirement 1. Except for comment statements, which may be placed anywhere in a source module, the first statements of a source module should be these:

In OS

name field	opcode	operand
modname	CSECT	
↑	STM	14,12,12(13)
this symbol	BALR	12,0
used as name	USING	*,12
of the source	ST	13,SAVE+4
module	LA	13,SAVE

In DOS

name field	opcode	operand
modname	CSECT	
	BALR	12,0
	USING	*,12
	LA	13,SAVE

Requirement 2. The last executable statements of a source module should be these:

In OS

name field	opcode	operand
exitname	L	13,SAVE+4
↑	LM	14,12,12(13)
any valid	BR	14
symbol		

In DOS

name field	opcode	operand
exitname	EOJ	

Requirement 3. The last statements of a source module should be these:

In OS

name field	opcode	operand
SAVE	DS	18F
↑	END	
this symbol		
must be SAVE		

In DOS

name field	opcode	operand
SAVE	DS	9D
	END	

Executable vs. Nonexecutable Statements

Some of the statements given in Requirements 1–3 are directives and some are instructions. Instructions are known as **executable statements** because they are translated into machine language by the assembler and executed at run time by the hardware. Some directives, like EOJ in Requirement 2 for DOS, are also executable because they cause the assembler to generate instructions. All other directives, including the CSECT, USING, and END directives previously mentioned, are called **nonexecutable statements.**

Object Module Size

All executable statements, and those nonexecutable statements that define constants and data areas, are assembled into an object module that, as was indicated in Chapter 1, is in a form that can be loaded into main memory and executed at run time. However, if the three requirements are followed and the object module size is greater than 4096 bytes, it may not run properly. Techniques for dealing with this situation will be described in Chapter 9. None of the examples and exercises in the first eight chapters require object modules larger than 4096 bytes.

In this section the minimum IBM 360 and 370 Assembly Language requirements for reading and writing data in EBCDIC character format are summarized. This will provide for input from the input data stream and output to the printer. Methods of conversion to and from binary integer format will be described in Chapter 4; other aspects of input/output operations will be more fully described in Chapters 18 through 22.

OPEN
CLOSE
DCB/DTF
GET
PUT
DS
DC

Each file that is read or written from an assembly language program must be opened before any input or output operations are executed and closed after all such operations have been executed. Opening a file is achieved by the OPEN macro, and closing by the CLOSE macro. In addition, each file to be used must be described by a data control block (DCB) macro in OS systems and by a define-the-file (DTF) macro in DOS systems. To read data from the input data stream, we use the GET macro; to write it onto the printer, the PUT macro. The OPEN, CLOSE, GET, and PUT macros are directives that cause the assembler to generate the instructions needed to request that the corresponding operations be performed by the operating system. The areas of memory to be used for the input and output data must be reserved by the define storage (DS) and define constant (DC) directives.

The OS program in Figure 2.4a and the DOS one in Figure 2.4b indicate how the I/O macro operations are to be used. The only difference between the programs are the I/O macros and the three sets of required statements given in the preceding section. All other differences between OS and DOS Assembly Language are exceedingly minor, and will be discussed in subsequent chapters.

A brief explanation of the I/O macros is given below for both OS and DOS systems. For our purposes, these macros will be sufficient for all the programs we will discuss until the chapters in Part Five.

Nevertheless, before using the DCB's or DTF's, you should determine whether the values of the parameters given below are correct for your computer. After making any necessary changes to these parameters, you should submit the program for assembly and execution on your computer system. In typing the statements, take care to ensure that the information in the name field, opcode field, and operand field is exactly as shown in the figures.

OS I/O Macros

In OS Assembly Language, there must be a DCB macro associated with each file that is used in a program. The DCB macro informs the operating system how you intend to use the file. The macro must be placed in the data area of your program and must have a name-field symbol. Whenever you open, close, read, or write to the file, you must refer to the DCB name-field symbol, indicated below as "symbol1." For our purposes, we will use the following forms of the DCB macro:

input file
```
symbol1    DCB   DSORG=PS,MACRF=(GM),DDNAME=SYSIN,EODAD=symbol2,        X
                 RECFM=FB,LRECL=80,BLKSIZE=4080
```

printer file
```
symbol1    DCB   DSORG=PS,MACRF=(PM),DDNAME=SYSPRINT,                   X
                 RECFM=FBA,LRECL=133,BLKSIZE=3990
```

NOTE: The "X" (or any other nonblank character) in column 72 of the first line in a macro says that the operand is continued on the next line.

For the *input file,* the DSORG=PS parameter says that we are reading a sequential file. MACRF=(GM) indicates we will use the GET macro. DDNAME=SYSIN names the job control language (JCL) statement that identifies the standard system input file (SYSIN). The field "symbol2" in the EODAD= parameter of the input file's DCB is the name-field symbol of the statement to which control will be transferred when there are no more data to be read, i.e., when end-of-file is detected. In Figure 2.4a, that symbol is FINISH. RECFM=FB says that the records are all of the

Figure 2.4a Sample assembly language program for OS.

```
DEMO    CSECT
*
* THIS PROGRAM READS RECORDS FROM THE INPUT DATA STREAM
*  AND PRINTS THEM, SINGLE-SPACED, ON THE SYSTEM PRINTER.
*
        STM    14,12,12(13)            STANDARD ENTRY TO PROGRAM
        BALR   12,0
        USING  *,12
        ST     13,SAVE+4
        LA     13,SAVE
*
* OPEN INPUT DATA FILE AND STANDARD PRINTER FILE
*
        OPEN   (INDCB,(INPUT))         OPEN INPUT DATA STREAM FILE
        OPEN   (OUTDCB,(OUTPUT))       OPEN PRINTER OUTPUT FILE
*
* READ AND PRINT EACH RECORD
*
IOLOOP  MVC    INAREA,=80C' '          BLANK OUT 'INAREA'
        GET    INDCB,INAREA            READ DATA INTO 'INAREA'
        MVI    OUTCARR,C' '            SET SINGLE-SPACE CONTROL CHAR
        MVC    OUTLINE(80),INAREA      COPY DATA TO OUTPUT LINE AREA
        PUT    OUTDCB,OUTAREA          WRITE DATA FROM 'OUTAREA'
        B      IOLOOP                  CONTINUE UNTIL END-OF-FILE
*
* WHEN INPUT END-OF-FILE IS DETECTED, CONTROL IS TRANSFERRED HERE
*
FINISH  CLOSE  (INDCB)                 CLOSE INPUT FILE
        CLOSE  (OUTDCB)                CLOSE OUTPUT FILE
EXIT    L      13,SAVE+4               STANDARD EXIT FROM PROGRAM
        LM     14,12,12(13)
        BR     14
*
* DATA CONTROL BLOCKS FOR INPUT AND OUTPUT FILES
*
INDCB   DCB    DSORG=PS,MACRF=(PM),DDNAME=SYSIN,EODAD=FINISH       X
               RECFM=FB,LRECL=80,BLKSIZE=4080
OUTDCB  DCB    DSORG=PS,MACRF=(GM),DDNAME=SYSPRINT,                X
               RECFM=FBA,LRECL=133,BLKSIZE=3990
*
* AREAS RESERVED FOR INPUT RECORD AND PRINTER LINE
*
INAREA  DS     CL80              80 BYTES FOR AN INPUT RECORD
*
OUTAREA DS     0CL133            133 BYTES FOR A PRINTER LINE ...
OUTCARR DC     CL1' '              1 BYTE FOR CARRIAGE CONTROL CHAR
OUTLINE DC     CL132' '            132 BYTES FOR DATA TO BE PRINTED
*
* REQUIRED STATEMENTS
SAVE    DS     18F
        END
```

same fixed length and are stored on the disk in larger units called "data blocks." LRECL=80 shows that the length of each record is 80 bytes; BLKSIZE=4080 indicates that there are up to 51 (=4080/80) records in each data block.

For the *printer file*, DSORG=PS indicates that we are writing to a sequential file. MACRF=(PM) says we will use the PUT macro. DDNAME=SYSPRINT names the JCL statement that identifies the system's printer output file. RECFM=FBA says that the records are of fixed length and are stored in fixed-length data blocks, and that an ANSI carriage control character will be used for printer line-spacing. LRECL=133 states that the output area is 133 bytes long.

Figure 2.4b   Sample assembly language program for DOS.

```
DEMO    CSECT
*
* THIS PROGRAM READS RECORDS FROM THE INPUT DATA STREAM
*   AND PRINTS THEM, SINGLE-SPACED, ON THE SYSTEM PRINTER.
*
        BALR  12,0                  STANDARD ENTRY TO PROGRAM
        USING *,12
        LA    13,SAVE
*
* OPEN INPUT DATA FILE AND STANDARD PRINTER FILE
*
        OPEN  INDTF                 OPEN INPUT DATA STREAM FILE
        OPEN  OUTDTF                OPEN PRINTER OUTPUT FILE
*
* READ AND PRINT EACH RECORD
*
IOLOOP  MVC   INAREA,=80C' '        BLANK OUT 'INAREA'
        GET   INDTF,INAREA          READ DATA INTO 'INAREA'
        MVI   OUTCARR,C' '          SET SINGLE-SPACE CONTROL CHAR
        MVC   OUTLINE,INAREA        COPY DATA TO OUTPUT LINE AREA
        PUT   OUTDTF,OUTAREA        WRITE DATA FROM 'OUTAREA'
        B     IOLOOP                CONTINUE UNTIL END-OF-FILE
*
* WHEN INPUT END-OF-FILE IS DETECTED, CONTROL IS TRANSFERRED HERE
*
FINISH  CLOSE INDTF                 CLOSE INPUT FILE
        CLOSE OUTDTF                CLOSE OUTPUT FILE
EXIT    EOJ                         STANDARD EXIT FROM PROGRAM
*
* DTF'S FOR INPUT AND OUTPUT FILES
*
INDTF   DTFCD DEVADDR=SYSIPT,IOAREA1=INBUF,WORKA=YES,           X
              EOFADDR=FINISH,BLKSIZE=80
OUTDTF  DTFPR DEVADDR=SYSLST,IOAREA1=OUTBUF,WORKA=YES,          X
              CTLCHR=ASA,BLKSIZE=133
*
* AREAS RESERVED FOR INPUT RECORD AND PRINTER LINE
*
INAREA  DS    CL80           80 BYTES FOR INPUT "WORKA"
INBUF   DS    CL80           80 BYTES FOR INPUT "IOAREA1"
*
OUTAREA DS    0CL133         133 BYTES FOR PRINTER "WORKA" ...
OUTCARR DC    CL1' '           1 BYTE FOR CARRIAGE CONTROL CHAR
OUTLINE DC    CL132' '         132 BYTES FOR DATA TO BE PRINTED
OUTBUF  DS    CL133          133 BYTES FOR PRINTER "IOAREA1"
*
* REQUIRED STATEMENTS
SAVE    DS    9D
        END
```

BLKSIZE=3990 shows that there are up to 30 (=3990/133) records in each data block. The first byte of each record must be the ANSI control character, as discussed below; the remaining 132 bytes contain the characters to be printed.

As can be seen in Figure 2.4a, the OPEN macro specifies two things: the name of the corresponding DCB macro, and how the file is to be used, in that order.

```
        OPEN   (INDCB,(INPUT))      OPEN INPUT DATA STREAM FILE
        OPEN   (OUTDCB,(OUTPUT))    OPEN PRINTER OUTPUT FILE
```

The GET and PUT macros also specify two items: the name of the DCB macro, and the name of the I/O area for the data, in that order.

```
        GET     INDCB,INAREA              READ DATA INTO 'INAREA'

        :::

        PUT     OUTDCB,OUTAREA            WRITE DATA FROM 'OUTAREA'
```

The CLOSE macro simply specifies the name of the corresponding DCB macro:

```
FINISH  CLOSE   (INDCB)                   CLOSE INPUT FILE
        CLOSE   (OUTDCB)                  CLOSE OUTPUT FILE
```

DOS I/O Macros

In DOS Assembly Language, there must be a DTF macro associated with each file that is used in a program. The DTF macro informs the operating system how you intend to use the file. The macro must be placed in the data area of your program, and it must have a name-field symbol. Whenever you open, close, read, or write to the file, you must refer to the DTF name-field symbol, indicated below as "symbol1." For our purposes, we will use the following forms of the DTF macro:

input file
```
symbol1  DTFCD   DEVADDR=SYSIPT,IOAREA1=symbol2,WORKA=YES,        X
                 EOFADDR=symbol3,BLKSIZE=80
```

printer file
```
symbol1  DTFPR   DEVADDR=SYSLST,IOAREA1=symbol2,WORKA=YES,        X
                 CTLCHR=ASA,BLKSIZE=133
```

> **NOTE:** The "X" (or any other nonblank character) in column 72 of the first line in a macro says that the operand is continued on the next line.

For the *input file,* the DEVADDR=SYSIPT parameter says that we are reading from the standard system input device. The "symbol2" in the IOAREA1= parameter identifies the area into which each input record will be read. WORKA=YES indicates that after the input data has been read, it will be available to your program in the "work area" whose name is specified in the GET macro. The "symbol3" in the EOFADDR= parameter of the input file's DTF is the name-field symbol of the statement to which control will be transferred when there are no more data to be read, i.e., when end-of-file is detected. In Figure 2.4b, that symbol is FINISH. BLKSIZE=80 gives the length of IOAREA1; it is 80 when, as assumed here, the standard input record is a card. The length of the work area must also be 80 bytes.

For the *printer file,* DEVADDR=SYSLST says that we are writing to the standard listing device. The "symbol2" in the IOAREA1= parameter identifies the area from which each output record will be written. WORKA=YES indicates that the output line will be created in the work area whose name is specified in the PUT macro. CTLCHR=ASA says that an ANSI carriage-control character will be used for printer line-spacing. The first byte of each record must be the ANSI control character, as discussed below; the remaining 132 bytes contain the characters to be printed. BLKSIZE=133 gives the length of IOAREA1, and also of the work area. Note that printer lines are 132 bytes long rather than 133; the value of BLKSIZE is 133 to provide space for a printer carriage-control character.

As can be seen from Figure 2.4b, each OPEN macro specifies the name of the corresponding DTF macro:

```
        OPEN    INDTF                     OPEN INPUT DATA STREAM FILE
        OPEN    OUTDTF                    OPEN PRINTER OUTPUT FILE
```

The GET and PUT macros specify two items: the name of the DTF macro, and the name of the work area for the data, in that order.

```
GET     INDTF,INAREA          READ DATA INTO 'INAREA'

:::

PUT     OUTDTF,OUTAREA        WRITE DATA FROM 'OUTAREA'
```

The CLOSE macro simply specifies the name of the corresponding DCB macro:

```
FINISH  CLOSE   INDTF                 CLOSE INPUT FILE
        CLOSE   OUTDTF                CLOSE OUTPUT FILE
```

ANSI Carriage-Control Characters

The American National Standards Institute (ANSI) has established that certain printer line- and page-spacing operations be triggered by "carriage-control" characters. These characters are in the standard character set of the computer, but when they are in the first position of the print line they are not printed; instead, they cause the printer to adjust the paper position before printing the line.

The ANSI carriage-control characters and their functions are these:

ANSI	character	function	action
C' '	(blank)	single spacing:	print on the next available line
C'0'	(zero)	double spacing:	leave one blank line before printing
C'−'	(minus)	triple spacing:	leave two blank lines before printing
C'1'	(one)	skip to new page:	print on first line of next page
C'+'	(plus)	suppress spacing:	print without advancing the paper

In Figures 2.4a and 2.4b, the only carriage-control character that is used is the blank, for single spacing. A somewhat more elaborate program, involving single spacing, double spacing, and skipping to a new page, is given in Chapter 20, Figure 20.4.

> **NOTE:** In OS's DCB macro, the "A" in the RECFM=FBA parameter causes the operating system to put the printer carriage under software control. If you do not wish to use printer carriage-control characters, then replace the second line of the printer file DCB with this line:
>
> ```
> RECFM=FB,LRECL=132,BLKSIZE=4092
> ```
>
> In DOS's DTFPR macro, the CTLCHR=ASA parameter causes the operating system to put the printer carriage under software control. If you do not wish to use printer carriage-control characters, then replace the second line of the printer file DTFPR with this line:
>
> ```
> BLKSIZE=132
> ```

2.5   ASSEMBLY LISTINGS

As mentioned in Chapter 1, the assembler produces a listing of your program that shows the machine language together with your source language statements and indicates what (if any) errors have been detected during the assembly process. The appearance of the listing can be enhanced by using the following simple assembly language directives:

```
EJECT—Starts a new page on the listing
TITLE—Puts a title line at the beginning of each page
SPACE—Inserts one or more blank lines on a page
PRINT NOGEN,NODATA—Limits the amount of detail printed
```

It is easy to use these directives. Since their use can make the listing much more readable, you are advised to learn how to use them now by reading Sections 14.1 through 14.4 and by inserting the directives at appropriate places in the program of Figures 2.4a and 2.4b.

The listing also includes an index of the name-field symbols defined in the source module. This index, known as the **cross-reference** list (XREF), is very useful when debugging and modifying programs. It identifies the statement in which each symbol is defined and the statements in which each is used—i.e., where it appears in an operand field. The cross-reference list also gives the *value* of each symbol and the *length* of the instruction or data field that the symbol is associated with. If your installation's assembler does not always produce a cross-reference list, it is possible to request one with a JCL statement: // OPTION XREF in DOS, and // EXEC ASMFC,PARM=XREF(FULL) in OS. (Details are in the *OS/VS-VM/370 Assembler Programmer's Guide,* IBM Publication GC33–4021 or –4024.)

2.6   SUMMARY

The format of an assembly language statement is designed to accommodate the constraints of an eighty-column line but can be varied somewhat within those constraints. In the standard format, the first character position is used to distinguish between comment statements and all other statements; an asterisk (∗) is used to denote a comment. The purpose of any statement that is not a comment is determined by the opcode field, which must contain a valid abbreviation of from one to five characters for an instruction or directive. The purpose of each instruction or directive is further defined by the information in its operand field. All instructions and directives may optionally include free-form comments following the operand. All statements may optionally include identification that can be used for checking the sequence of the statements. Statements whose operand or comments fields are too long to be contained on one line may be continued on the following line through appropriate use of the continuation field.

Certain instructions and directives are, by convention, required in every source module. These were described in Section 2.3. They provide an interface to the operating system and other programs at run time and have important roles related to addressing.

To read data from the input data stream and print information on the printer, several things are required: certain attributes of the data must be described by a DCB or DTF macro and corresponding job control language statements; the input data stream must be opened before any data can be read at run time, and the printer must be opened before any data can be printed at run time; reading and printing are performed, respectively, by the GET and PUT macros; and the two files must be closed at completion of processing. In addition, an area must be reserved for the input data as well as the output data. All data read or written are in EBCDIC character form. The program in Figures 2.4a and 2.4b will serve as a model for all input and output operations required until Chapter 18.

The differences between OS and DOS Assembly Language are almost solely confined to statements that are used for input and output and to the required statements mentioned in Section 2.3. There are no differences in statement formats, and the other differences that do exist are quite minor ones, which do not affect any of the examples or programs that are given later in this text. Those minor differences will simply be pointed out at the appropriate places in the text.

2.7   REVIEW

Statement Formats   For instructions and directives, the format provides for up to six fields: the name, opcode, operand, comment, continuation, and identification fields. For comment statements, there are only three fields: the comment-indicator field, the comment field, and the identification field. The formats are the same in OS and DOS systems.

Standard Format   In standard format, the name field begins in column 1, the optional continuation field is in column 72, and the optional identification field begins in column 73. For instructions and directives, information in each of the other fields must be preceded by at least one blank.

Name-Field Symbols   Symbols must be from 1 to 8 characters in length, beginning with a letter and containing only letters and digits. Letters are defined to include not only the alphabet, but also three special characters: dollar sign ($), number sign (#), and at sign (@).

Required Statements   Assembly language source modules written for the IBM 360 and 370 systems should begin with a CSECT directive whose name field contains the program's name, and should end with an END directive. (The precise nature and purpose of the other required statements will be discussed in subsequent chapters.)

Executable Statements   Any statement whose opcode causes the assembler to generate one or more machine language instructions is known as an executable statement, because machine language instructions may be executed by the CPU at run time. All other statements, including most directives and all comment statements, are nonexecutable.

Input/Output (I/O) Macros   The format and operand parameters used in I/O macros depend in significant ways on whether one is using an OS system or a DOS system. But in both systems, the OPEN, GET, PUT, and CLOSE macros are executable statements, whereas OS's DCB and DOS's DTF macros are nonexecutable statements.

Assembly Listings   Readability of the program listings produced by the assembler can be enhanced by use of the EJECT, TITLE, SPACE, and PRINT directives. Each of these directives can appear anywhere, and any number of times, in a source module. EJECT starts a new listing page; TITLE starts a new page and puts a heading at the top of each page; SPACE inserts one or more blank lines in the listing; and PRINT can be used to suppress unwanted details.

2.8   REVIEW QUESTIONS

1. Given that there is provision for comments via comment statements, of what use is the comment field in statements containing instructions or directives?
2. What is the purpose of the continuation field in an assembly language statement? Of the identification field? Which (if either) of these two fields are required?
3. What positions (columns) are used for the beginning of each of the six fields in standard fixed format?
4. Can the same symbol be used in the name field of two or more different statements within a source module? Why or why not?
5. Can the name field of an instruction or directive statement be blank? Why or why not?
6. Can the opcode field of an instruction or directive statement be blank? Why or why not?
7. When end-of-file is detected while attempting to read from an input file, the program can be directed to transfer to some other instruction. How is the location of that instruction specified in assembly language? (Hint: See Fig. 2.4a or 2.4b.)
8. In what way or ways does your computer installation suggest that you specify the parameters in a DCB (or DTF) macro? How does that differ from the specifications that will be used throughout this textbook?
9. What job control language (JCL) statements, if any, are required at your computer installation in order that your program can read from the input data stream and write to the printer?
10. What assembly language directives can you use to improve the readability of a program listing? Where in a source module would you put each of those directives?

2.9   EXERCISES

1. Determine what job control language (JCL) statements are required to assemble a source module at your computer installation, and use those statements to assemble the source module given in Figure 2.4a or 2.4b.

2. In conjunction with Exercise 1, determine what JCL statements are required to execute the object code produced by the assembler, and use those statements to run the program whose source module is given in Figure 2.4a or 2.4b. (**Note:** You will have to prepare some input data records. There may be any number of them, and they may contain any information whatsoever because the program does not examine or manipulate any of the data; it only reads and prints it. It is recommended that you prepare at least ten data records, in order to demonstrate the printer line-spacing provided by the program.)

3. If you have reasonably inexpensive and frequent access to the computer, you may want to deliberately create some error situations to see how the assembler responds. Several conditions that will cause assembly-time errors follow; i.e., errors that the assembler will detect and note on the listing. Make the changes specified below to the source module of Figure 2.4a or 2.4b and assemble the changed module using the JCL statements determined in Exercise 1. The error messages that will be printed on the listing are explained in IBM Publication GC33-4021, *OS/VS-VM/370 Assembler Programmer's Guide*.

   a. Delete and do not replace the following statements:

   ```
   INDCB        DCB        DSORG=PS,...
                END
   ```

   b. Insert the following statements anywhere in the module:

name field	opcode	operand
EXIT	B	FINISH
ERROR	BT	4,INNER
	LM	14,12
	MVC	OUTAREA,132C'
	L	3,X
12345	ST	13,SAVE+4

4. What assembly-time error would occur if the name field of the CSECT directive of Figures 2.4a and 2.4b began in column 2 instead of column 1?

5. Based on your understanding of the assembly language statement formats, deliberately generate some source module errors, incorporate them into the source module of Figure 2.4a or 2.4b, and submit the module for assembly to see how the assembler responds. The errors should include mistakes in the name, opcode, operand, comment, and continuation fields. Is there any way to generate an invalid comment statement? Is there any way that a comment statement can cause an error in another statement or statements?

6. What assembly-time error would occur if the operand fields of the OPEN macros in Figures 2.4a and 2.4b were omitted?

7. Some types of programming errors are not detected by the assembler. Instead of causing assembly-time errors, they cause run-time errors. For example, such errors can cause execution of your program to be abnormally terminated, a situation known as an "abend." These types of errors are called *logic* errors. To see how the operating system responds to a run-time error, assemble and run the program of Figure 2.4a or 2.4b with the following statement deleted from the source module:

   ```
   BALR  12,0
   ```

   The reason that omission of this statement causes a run-time error will be explained in Chapter 3.

8. There are a few directives that enable a programmer to gain some control over the appearance of the listing. Chief among these are the TITLE, EJECT, SPACE, and PRINT directives described in Chapter 14. Read Sections 14.1 through 14.4 now, and experiment with use of these directives. Note particularly the effect of inserting the following directive immediately after line 1 of the source module in Figure 2.4a or 2.4b:

opcode	operand
PRINT	NOGEN

9. Without submitting a job for assembly, determine which of the following statements would, if inserted in the source module of Figure 2.4a or 2.4b following the CSECT directive, cause an assembly-time error. Explain the reason for each error.

name field	opcode	operand
A#1	STM	14,12,12(13)
	BALR	
	USNIG	*,12
	ST	13,SAVE+$
	OPEN	(INAREA,(INPUT))
	GET	CARD,OUTAREA

CHAPTER

3

Instructions and Addresses

Every machine language instruction contains two types of information: (1) a numeric opcode that identifies the purpose of the instruction and (2) an operand that identifies the information required for execution of the instruction.

Every assembly language instruction is a symbolic representation of a machine language instruction. The opcode and operand fields of an assembly language instruction correspond one for one to those of a machine language instruction. At assembly time, the assembler translates each symbolic assembly language instruction into its numeric machine language representation. At run time, the translated instructions are executed by the central processing unit.

In this chapter we describe the formats of assembly language and machine language instructions and show how addresses are represented and processed at assembly time and at run time in the 360 and 370 computer systems. You may wish to review the processes of converting integers from decimal to binary and hexadecimal, especially the correspondences between the first sixteen integers, that were given in Figure 1.5.

See Summaries in Figures 3.4 and 3.6

3.1   ADDRESSES

Each byte in memory is referred to by its address. A **memory address** is an unsigned integer in the range 0 through $2^n - 1$, where 2^n is the total number of bytes available in memory, i.e., the memory's capacity. The first byte in memory has address 0, the second address 1, the third 2, and so forth. Memory addresses are almost invariably written in hexadecimal notation, as in this diagram.

Main Memory Addresses

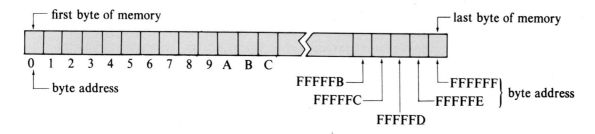

Figure 3.1   Schematic representation of memory.

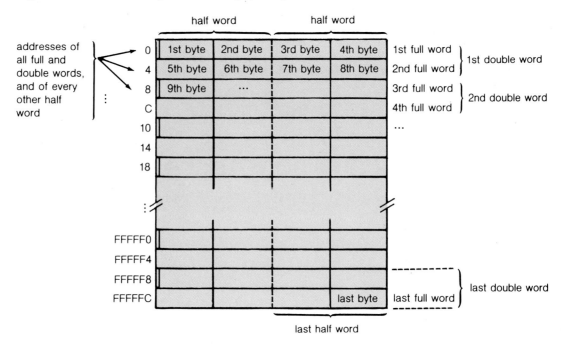

All addresses are shown in hexadecimal notation. In this notation, the low-order digit of a double-word address is either 0 or 8; that of a full-word address is 0, 4, 8, or C. Half-word addresses are even numbers ending in 0,2,4,6,8,A,C, or E.

The address of the last byte in this diagram is $2^{24}-1$, the largest allowable memory address in most IBM 360 and 370 computer systems. As a binary number, $2^{24}-1$ is represented with 24 bits, all of which are 1's; therefore as a hexadecimal number it is represented with six digits, FFFFFF. In more familiar terms, $2^{24} = 16,777,216$—what is commonly known as a 16-megabyte memory.

The linear diagram on the previous page is not an especially useful way to represent memory, because bytes are very often grouped into units called full words, half words, and double words. A **full word** is any four consecutive bytes in which the address of the first byte is a number exactly divisible by four: 0, 4, 8, C, 10, 14, 18, 1C,.... In a **half word,** the address of the first byte is exactly divisible by two; in a **double word,** by eight. The first byte of a full word is said to be at the full-word *Boundaries* **boundary.** Half-word and double-word boundaries are at the beginning byte of each half and double word, respectively. Thus an alternative and more frequently used representation of memory is that shown in Figure 3.1. The concept of boundaries is important because all machine language instructions must be aligned on a half-word boundary, and some data should be aligned on half-, full-, or double-word boundaries.

As mentioned in Chapter 1, the execution of an instruction may require that data be in a reg-*Register* ister. There are 16 general-purpose registers in the IBM 360 and 370 systems, and each is referred *Addresses* to by an address that is an unsigned integer in the range from 0 through 15_{10} (Fig. 3.2). Each register contains 32 bits (4 bytes), but neither the bits nor the bytes of a register are individually addressable. For purposes of discussion, the 32 bits in a register are numbered from 0 to 31. In diagrams, bit 0 is always shown at the left, bit 31 at the right. The left-most bits are the most significant, or high-order, bits of a register; the right-most bits are the least significant, or low-order, bits. The 32-bit quantity in a register is often called the *contents* of that register.

The information required for the execution of an instruction may be in a memory location, or it may be in a register. In either case, the address of that memory location or register is designated in the operand of the instruction. A register address is always represented by 4 bits in an instruction's operand. This is sufficient for all sixteen register addresses. But although a memory address may require up to 24 bits for its representation as a binary integer, only 16 bits are allocated for it in a machine language instruction. This is apparently insufficient, but the following fundamentally important scheme permits the 16 bits to refer to any one of the $2^{24}-1$ memory addresses.

Figure 3.2   Schematic diagram of the 16 general registers.

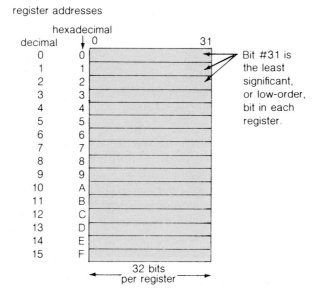

The 16 bits that are used to represent a memory address do not represent a single integer; they represent two integers, each with a different purpose. One of the integers is 4 bits long and designates the address of a register known as the **base register.** The other integer is 12 bits long and represents an adjustment factor known as the **displacement.** This 16-bit representation of a memory address is known as the *base-displacement form* of that address. It will frequently be depicted like this:

Base- Displacement Addresses

B	D

where   B = base register address (4 bits)
         D = displacement (12 bits)

At run time, the base-displacement form of an address is translated by the central processing unit (CPU) into a 24-bit memory address. The memory address (M) is computed by the CPU from this formula:

$$M = \left\{ \begin{array}{l} \text{contents of} \\ \text{base register} \end{array} \right\} + \{\text{displacement}\}$$

Note that it is not the address of the base register that is added to the displacement, rather it is the *contents* of the register, more precisely, bits 8 through 31 of the register designated by that address, that is added. The quantity so added is known as the **base address** for memory address M. Both the base address and the displacement are always considered to be nonnegative integers, so that the resulting memory address is always a nonnegative integer, as it must be. M is known as the **effective address** generated from the base-displacement address. Thus, another way to write the previous equation is this:

Base Address vs. Effective Address

$$M = \{\text{base address}\} + \{\text{displacement}\}$$
$$= \text{effective address}$$

There are two main reasons for the use of the base-displacement form rather than the full 24-bit memory address in an instruction. One is that it conserves space in the instruction. In other words, if space for a 24-bit address were available in each instruction, then most of the time this space would be only partly used, since most of the instructions in a program do not normally refer to addresses whose values require 24 bits. Most programs are simply not that big. If leading zeroes are disregarded, then the memory addresses used in most programs can be specified in fewer than 24 bits. The base-displacement form allows 16 bits to be used to refer to large addresses when they are needed but does not waste the space when it is not needed.

Note that although memory addresses are always 24-bit integers in many models of the IBM 370 and compatible computers, there are some models—namely those that use the so-called "extended architecture" (XA)—in which memory addresses are 31-bit integers. The number of bits in an address determines the maximum size of main memory and is a property of the design of the computer. With 24-bit addresses, up to $2^{24} = 16,777,216$ memory locations (i.e., 16 megabytes) can be individually accessed by a program. With 31-bit addresses, up to $2^{31} = 2,147,483,648$ locations (2 gigabytes) can be individually accessed by a program.

In this text we will only be concerned with 24-bit addresses, not only because most problem-mode programs don't need to access more than 16 megabytes of memory, but also because the base-displacement format—4 bits for the base register's address, and 16 bits for the displacement—is the same whether or not the extended architecture is used.

The other reason for the use of the base-displacement form is that when a program is loaded into memory by the loader program, it is almost never assigned a starting address of 000000. Instead, it is assigned whatever address is available, depending on what memory locations are being used by other programs. Thus, a program that, when assembled, is assigned memory addresses from 000000 through 000500_{16}, may, when loaded, be assigned addresses from 005000 through 005500_{16}. This is *Relocation* known as **program relocation.** When a relocated program is executed at run time, its instructions must refer to the addresses assigned by the loader, not to the addresses assigned by the assembler. All the assembler-assigned main memory addresses must be incremented by a constant factor, known as the relocation factor (005000_{16} in the example cited). The relocation factor can be a different number each time a program is loaded. But, since the base-displacement form of address is used in the operands of instructions, a program can be relocated simply by adding the relocation factor to the base address. Neither the B nor the D components of a base-displacement address need to be changed. This greatly facilitates the process of program relocation.

In addition to the advantages just mentioned, there are two important constraints associated *Displacement* with the use of the base-displacement form of address. First, the base address must be large enough *Size* so that the corresponding displacement is not larger than FFF_{16}. If the displacement were larger than FFF_{16}, the displacement would not fit in the 12-bit displacement field. Second, the register chosen for use as the base register should ordinarily not be Register 0 since the IBM 360 and 370 hardware *Register 0 as Base* are designed to disregard the contents of Register 0 if that register is designated as the base register. *Register* If, however, Register 0 is the base register, then the base address is always assumed to be 000000.

3.2 INSTRUCTIONS

Each machine language instruction consists of a certain number of bytes. The number of bytes comprising an instruction is known as the instruction's *length*. In many computer systems, the length of all instructions is the same. In some computers, the length of an instruction depends on the type of instruction it is. We speak of a **variable-length** instruction set in the latter case and a **fixed-length** *Fixed- and* instruction set in the former. The IBM systems 360 and 370 have a variable-length instruction set; *Variable-Length* some of its instructions occupy two consecutive bytes, some occupy four, and some occupy six. *Instructions*

The use of a variable-length instruction set, though apparently more complex than use of a fixed-length set, has one significant advantage: the number of bytes required for any instruction is just sufficient to provide only the information required in that instruction. This results in an overall saving of memory space in a program. In fixed-length sets, the length used for *all* instructions is the length needed by the instructions that contain the most information. This can result in unusable, hence wasted, memory space.

The address of an instruction is always the address of its first byte. Any two consecutive instructions in memory occupy consecutive locations. Thus, if we add the length of an instruction to its address, we obtain the address of the instruction immediately following it in memory.

One question that naturally arises is, How is the address of an instruction assigned? The answer is that it is assigned by the assembler at assembly time. The assembler maintains a counter, called the **memory location counter (MLC),** whose initial value is 0. When assembling an instruction, the assembler assigns it an address whose value equals the value of the memory location counter. Before the next instruction is assembled, the assembler increases the memory location counter by an amount equal to the length of the instruction that was just assembled.

Memory Location Counter

$$\left\{ \begin{array}{c} \text{memory} \\ \text{location} \\ \text{counter} \end{array} \right\} = \left\{ \begin{array}{c} \text{address} \\ \text{assigned} \\ \text{to an} \\ \text{instruction} \end{array} \right\} = \left\{ \begin{array}{c} \text{address} \\ \text{assigned to} \\ \text{preceding} \\ \text{instruction} \end{array} \right\} + \left\{ \begin{array}{c} \text{length of} \\ \text{preceding} \\ \text{instruction} \end{array} \right\}$$

The value of the memory location counter maintained by the assembler at assembly time is thus comparable to the value of the program location counter (PC) maintained by the CPU at run time.

When a machine language instruction refers to another instruction, as in a go-to type of instruction (known as a *branch* instruction), the address of the instruction to which the branch is to be made is specified in base-displacement form in the branch (B) instruction itself. In assembly language, the programmer need not specify the base-displacement form of an address. Instead, he or she can specify an address symbolically, by using the symbol defined in a statement's name field. The assembler translates that symbol into its appropriate base-displacement form when assembling an instruction. For example, in the sequence

```
LOOP      ---      ----
          ---      ----
B         LOOP
```

the assembler translates the symbol LOOP specified in the operand of the B instruction into the base-displacement representation of the address of the instruction named LOOP. At the time that the instruction named LOOP was assembled, the assembler assigned a value to LOOP equal to the address assigned to that instruction. That address was just the value of the memory location counter.

$$\left\{ \begin{array}{c} \text{address assigned} \\ \text{to a symbol} \end{array} \right\} = \left\{ \begin{array}{c} \text{memory} \\ \text{location} \\ \text{counter} \end{array} \right\} = \left\{ \begin{array}{c} \text{address assigned to} \\ \text{instruction identified} \\ \text{by that symbol} \end{array} \right\}$$

The assembler maintains a list of all symbols defined in an assembly language program, together with the address values it has assigned to them. This list is known as the assembler's *symbol table.* Whenever the assembler processes a statement that contains a symbol in its name field, that symbol is entered into the symbol table, along with the value assigned to it. (Duplicate names, that is, the same name on two different statements, are not allowed; they are flagged as multiply defined symbols.) When the assembler assembles a statement that contains a symbol in its operand field, it uses the value recorded for that symbol in its symbol table. The manner in which these processes are carried out will be discussed in Chapter 23. For present purposes, the important thing to note is that in assembly language the programmer need not specify the numeric address of an instruction or data; he or she need only specify a symbolic address, i.e., the symbol whose value is equal to the numeric address.

Further discussion of assembly language statement formats is deferred until Section 3.4. The following section is a description of the machine language instruction formats upon which all assembly language instructions are based.

3.3 MACHINE LANGUAGE FORMATS

You will recall that machine language instructions on the IBM 360 and 370 are of variable length; some are 2 bytes long, some 4, and some 6. The length of an instruction, together with the type of information contained in the operand field of the instruction, constitute the instruction's *format.*

Figure 3.3   Machine language instruction formats.

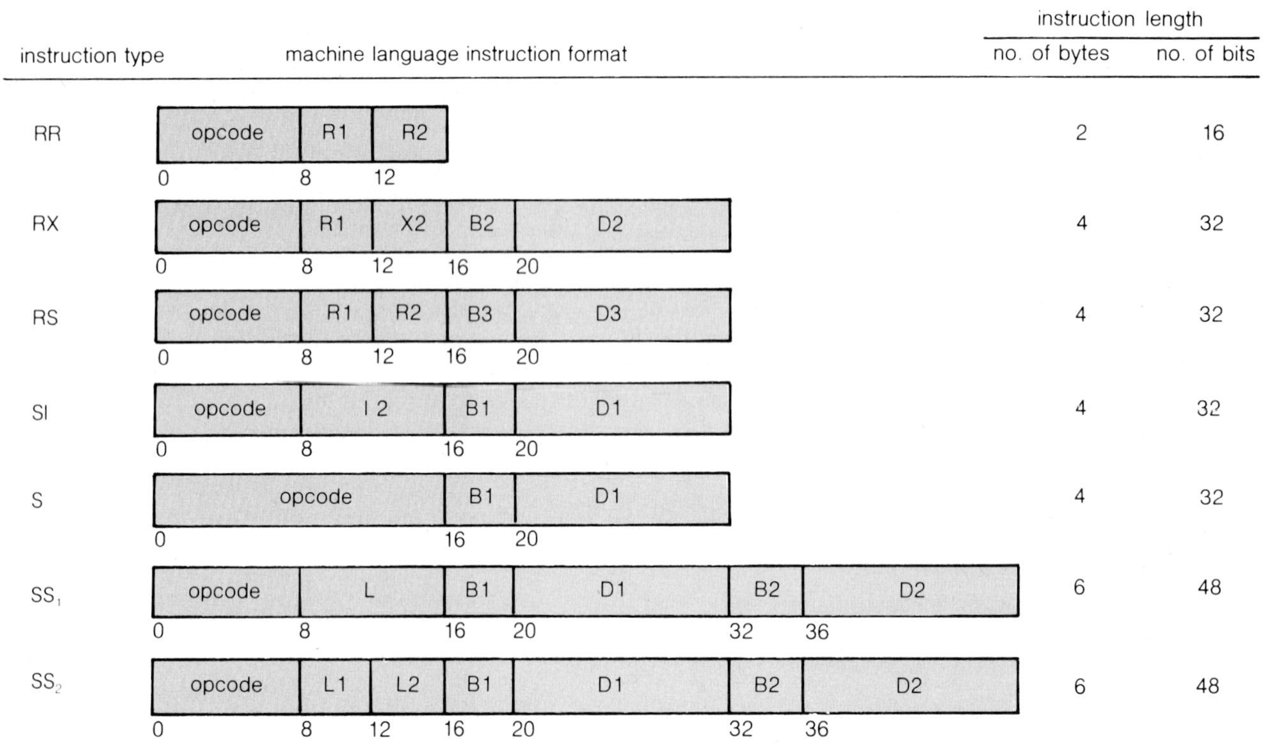

instruction type	machine language instruction format	instruction length	
		no. of bytes	no. of bits

RR	opcode R1 R2 (0, 8, 12)	2	16
RX	opcode R1 X2 B2 D2 (0, 8, 12, 16, 20)	4	32
RS	opcode R1 R2 B3 D3 (0, 8, 12, 16, 20)	4	32
SI	opcode I2 B1 D1 (0, 8, 16, 20)	4	32
S	opcode B1 D1 (0, 16, 20)	4	32
SS₁	opcode L B1 D1 B2 D2 (0, 8, 16, 20, 32, 36)	6	48
SS₂	opcode L1 L2 B1 D1 B2 D2 (0, 8, 12, 16, 20, 32, 36)	6	48

Note: For the RS format, the IBM reference manuals use R3 where we have used R2, and use B2 and D2 where we have used B3 and D3.

There are seven different instruction formats. These are known as the RR, RX, RS, SI, S, SS₁, and SS₂ formats. All seven are available on the 370, and all but the S format are available on the 360. Although the SS₁ and SS₂ formats are often referred to simply as *the* SS format, we will maintain the distinction between SS₁ and SS₂ since it is useful.

Machine Language Instruction Format

Each machine language instruction has one and only one format. For all instructions of a given format, the information required in the instruction is represented in the manner dictated by that format. The seven formats are illustrated in Figure 3.3. They all have the following general structure:

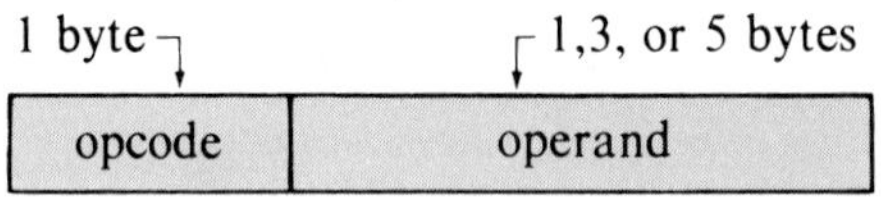

Each operand field contains either a register address, data, or a displacement. A displacement, denoted by D1, D2, or D3, is always immediately preceded by its associated base-register address, denoted by B1, B2, or B3. Together, the two constitute the base-displacement form of memory address that was previously discussed.

For the RS instruction format, we have departed from the notation convention used in IBM reference manuals. This departure allows us to refer to the second operand of assembly language RS instructions as R2, and to the third field in those instructions as D3(B3). For the other formats, the notation of Figure 3.3 is consistent with that used in IBM reference manuals.

The following three examples illustrate the manner in which all but one of the fields occurring in a machine language instruction are specified at run time. The exception is the X2 field, which will be discussed separately. Note the following points in the examples:

1. The opcode field contains the 8-bit numeric code that identifies the instruction. A list of these codes is given in Appendix A.
2. The fields designated as R1 and R2 contain register addresses, 4 bits each. Data to be operated on by the instruction are obtained at run time from the designated registers.
3. The fields designated as D1, D2, and D3, 12 bits each, are paired with the corresponding B1, B2, and B3 fields, 4 bits each. Each pair is the base-displacement form of a memory address.
4. The field designated as I2 contains an 8-bit constant that is used as data in the execution of the instruction.
5. The field designated as L contains an 8-bit unsigned integer that represents the number of bytes to be operated on. The contents of the L field is one less than the actual number of bytes that it represents.

Example 1.   Add two integers (RR format)

The RR-type instruction for adding two integers has the opcode $1A_{16}$. Using Figure 3.3, we find that the machine language format for RR-type instructions is as follows:

If we choose Register 3 for R1 and Register 4 for R2, then the machine language instruction is this:

When executed at run time, this instruction adds the integer contained in the register whose address is 4 to the integer contained in the register whose address is 3. The result will be in Register 3.

Example 2.   Compare 2 bytes (SI format)

The SI-type instruction for comparing two bytes has the opcode 95_{16}. From Figure 3.3, we find that the machine language format for SI-type instructions is as follows:

opcode	I2	B1	D1

Let us assume that the base-displacement form for a memory address in this instruction specifies Register 12 with a displacement of 32_{10}, so that the B1 field is C, and the D1 field is 020_{16}. Then, to compare the byte at that memory address with the 1-byte constant, 40_{16}, the machine language instruction is as follows:

9 5	4 0	C	0 2 0

Note that the 1-byte constant, 40_{16}, is contained in the I2 field of the instruction. Since these data are specified in the instruction and are available to the CPU at the same time that it obtains the instruction, they are known as **immediate** data.

Example 3.   Compare five bytes (SS$_1$ format)

The **SS$_1$**-type instruction for comparing bytes at one memory location with those at another has the opcode D5$_{16}$. From Figure 3.3, we find that the machine language format for SS$_1$-type instructions is as follows:

opcode	L	B1	D1	B2	D2

In an SS$_1$-compare instruction, one or more bytes beginning at the memory address whose base-displacement form is given in the B1, D1 fields are compared to the same number of bytes at the memory location whose base-displacement address is given in the B2,D2 fields. The number of bytes to be compared is specified in the L field of the instruction. When the contents of that field is 0, one byte is compared; when it is 1, two bytes are compared; and so forth. Since L is an 8-bit field, the maximum number of bytes that can be compared is 256.

Let us assume that the base-displacement address specified in the B1,D1 fields designates Register 12 with a displacement of 64$_{10}$, and that the base-displacement address specified in the B2,D2 fields designates Register 12 with a displacement of 200$_{10}$. To compare 5 bytes, the contents of the L field must be 4, so that under the assumptions just cited the machine language instruction is as follows:

D5	04	C	040	C	0C8

In SS$_2$-type instructions (not illustrated here), the fields designated as L1 and L2 serve the same purpose as the L field of an SS$_1$ instruction. They are byte counts. L1 is the number of bytes to be used starting at the memory address designated by B1,D1; L2, the number of bytes starting at B2,D2. L1 and L2 are 4-bit fields whose contents are in the range 0 through 15, representing counts of 1 through 16 bytes.

Indexed (RX) Instructions

The only field not yet mentioned is X2 in the RX format. The register designated by the X2 field is known as the **index register.** RX-type instructions are said to be *indexed* instructions. This type of instruction permits an additional factor to be used in the computation of an effective address at run time. This factor, known simply as the *index,* provides the principal means by which subscripting of arrays (as in Fortran DO-loops) is accomplished in assembly language.

The CPU uses the X2 field at run time as follows: If the X2 field designates Register 0, then no indexing is performed; if the X2 field designates any register other than Register 0, then indexing is performed. The effective address is then computed by this formula:

$$\begin{Bmatrix} \text{effective} \\ \text{address} \end{Bmatrix} = \begin{Bmatrix} \text{base} \\ \text{address} \end{Bmatrix} + \{\text{displacement}\} + \{\text{index}\}$$

The index consists of bits 8 through 31 of the register designated by the X2 field and is considered to be an unsigned nonnegative binary integer, as are the other factors in this formula.

Important Details

The examples discussed illustrate three important aspects of machine language instructions: (1) The position of the hex digits in an instruction, as well as the value of each digit, is crucial to a correct execution at run time. (2) There is no indication in an instruction that it *is* an instruction. In Example 3, the twelve hex digits D504C040C0C8 that constitute the instruction are indistinguishable from the same twelve digits that might be used to represent data. A similar statement could be made for any instruction. (3) Except for the I2 field in the SI-type instruction of Example 2, the data that an instruction operates on are not contained in the instruction. Instead, either they are contained in a register whose address is given in the instruction, or they are contained in a memory location whose address is represented in base-displacement form in the instruction.

The position and value of each hex digit in an instruction are determined by the assembler when it translates an assembly language instruction into machine language. The translated instruction is often referred to as the *object code*. At run time, the CPU assumes that the object code is correct. If it is not, it is executed anyway, with the likelihood that the results will not be as intended by the programmer. Therefore considerable care must be taken when writing instructions in assembly language. Moreover, when an instruction is executed, the data to be operated on must already exist in the designated registers and memory locations. If this is not the case, the instruction will be executed anyway, and the results will very likely not be what was wanted. Failure to specify an instruction correctly and failure to ensure the correct placement of data are two common causes of run-time errors and invalid results.

We will see in the next section that there is a one-to-one correspondence between the fields required in a machine language instruction and those that are represented in an assembly language instruction. We will show how the operand format of each assembly language instruction is defined by the type of machine language instruction into which it is translated. Though often written symbolically rather than numerically, each operand format essentially mimics the format of the corresponding machine language instruction. For that reason, it is extremely useful, if not absolutely necessary, that you become familiar with the seven machine language formats shown in Figure 3.3.

3.4 ASSEMBLY LANGUAGE FORMATS

An assembly language instruction must specify the same information as that contained in the machine language instruction that it represents. Some of the fields in a machine language instruction must be explicitly represented in the assembly language instruction, while others can either be explicitly represented or implied.

The fields that must be explicitly represented are the opcode field, the R1 and R2 register address fields, and the I2 immediate data field. The fields that can be implied or explicit are the base-displacement fields, B1,D1, B2,D2, and B3,D3, and the length fields, L, L1, and L2.

The opcode is represented symbolically by a mnemonic abbreviation consisting of from one to five alphabetic characters. The mnemonic abbreviation usually serves as a reminder of the name and purpose of the instruction. For example, B is the abbreviation for the Branch instruction. The mnemonic abbreviations that are available in the IBM 360 and 370 Assembly Language are summarized in Appendix A.

An assembly language instruction's *type* is defined to be the same as that of the machine language instruction that it represents. Thus, there are seven types of assembly language instructions: RR, RX, RS, SI, S, SS$_1$, and SS$_2$. As in machine language instructions, the opcode appearing in an assembly language instruction determines that instruction's type. The opcode also determines the instruction's operand format, although there may be more than one permissible format for a given type of instruction. The number of permissible formats is determined by the number of possible combinations of explicit and implicit fields in the operand. These are summarized in Figure 3.4.

Explicit Formats

With one exception, the notation used in Figure 3.4 for explicit formats is the same as that used in machine language instructions. The exception is that in assembly language the length field designators L, L1, and L2 represent the exact number of bytes that are to be operated on, whereas in machine language these designators represent one less than the exact number of bytes. The assembler calculates the correct length for the machine language instruction at assembly time, so that the programmer can almost always ignore the difference of 1 when writing instructions. As examples of the use of explicit formats, the instructions illustrated in the preceding section are repeated (see Examples 1 through 3). These are followed by a discussion of the RX format. For the RX explicit format, there are three possibilities: X2 or B2 or both. Examples 4 through 5b use assumed values for the various fields.

In Example 4, each field in the assembly language operand is assembled into the corresponding field in the machine language operand. In Example 5a the omission of the X2 field is indicated by the comma immediately following the left parenthesis: 4(,11). When X2 is omitted in this fashion, the assembler assigns it a value of 0. In Example 5b, it is B2 that is omitted; this is indicated by the absence of a comma following the X2 field: 4(11). However, at run time the X2 and B2 fields are processed in exactly the same way in the calculation of the effective address. Consequently, *the two assembly language forms, D2(,B2) and D2(X2), have the same effect at run time.* The second form will often be used when omitting either X2 or B2.

Figure 3.4 Instruction format summary.

type	machine language instruction formats	assembly language operand formats	notes
RR	op | R1 | R2 (0, 8, 12)	explicit: R1,R2	
RX	op | R1 | X2 | B2 | D2 (0, 8, 12, 16, 20, 31)	explicit: R1,D2(X2,B2) R1,D2(,B2) R1,D2(X2) R1,D2 implicit: R1,S2(X2) R1,S2	1
RS	op | R1 | R2 | B3 | D3 (0, 8, 12, 16, 20, 31)	explicit: R1,R2,D3(B3) implicit: R1,R2,S3	2
SI	op | I2 | B1 | D1 (0, 8, 16, 20, 31)	explicit: D1(B1),I2 implicit: S1,I2	3
S	op | B1 | D1 (0, 16, 20, 31)	explicit: D1(B1) implicit: S1	
SS₁	op | L | B1 | D1 | B2 | D2 (0, 8, 16, 20, 32, 36, 47)	explicit: D1(L,B1),D2(B2) implicit: S1,S2 mixed: D1(L,B1),S2 S1(L),D2(B2) S1(L),S2 S1,D2(B2)	4,5
SS₂	op | L1 | L2 | B1 | D1 | B2 | D2 (0, 8, 12, 16, 20, 32, 36, 47)	explicit: D1(L1,B1),D2(L2,B2) implicit: S1,S2 mixed: D1(L1,B1),S2(L2) D1(L1,B1),S2 S1(L1),S2(L2) S1(L1),S2 S1,S2(L2) S1(L1),D2(L2,B2) S1,D2(L2,B2)	5,6

Notes:

1. RX: When the index field X2 is omitted, it is assumed to be 0. An X2 field of 0 means no indexing.

2. RS: IBM manuals give R1,R3,D2(B2) where we have given R1,R2,D3(B3).

3. SI: The I2 field is one byte, used as immediate data.

4. SS₁: In machine language, the length field L is represented by a number that is one less than that used in assembly language.

5. SS₁, SS₂: Any of the length fields can be omitted in assembly language when a symbolic address is used. If so omitted, the assembler uses the length attribute of the corresponding symbol.

6. SS₂: In machine language the length fields L1 and L2 are represented by numbers that are one less than those used in the corresponding assembly language fields.

Example 1.   Add two integers (RR format)

machine language

op \| R1 \| R2

1A \| 3 \| 4

assembly language

op   R1,R2

AR   3,4

Example 2.   Compare 2 bytes (SI format)

machine language

op	I2	B1	D1

9 5	4 0	C	0 2 0

assembly language

op   D1(B1),I2

CLI   32(12),X'40'

Note that in assembly language, numbers are assumed to be in decimal notation unless otherwise indicated. X'...'denotes a hexadecimal number within the two delimiting apostrophes.

Example 3.   Compare 5 bytes (SS₁ format)

machine language

op	L	B1	D1	B2	D2

D 5	0 4	C	0 4 0	C	0 C 8

assembly language

op   D1(L,B1),D2(B2)

CLC   64(5,12),200(12)

Example 4.   Add two integers (RX format, X2 and B2 specified)

machine language

op	R1	X2	B2	D2

5 A	3	A	B	0 0 4

assembly language

op   R1,D2(X2,B2)

A   3,4(10,11)

Example 5a.   Add two integers (RX format, X2 omitted)

machine language

op	R1	X2	B2	D2

5 A	3	0	B	0 0 4

assembly language

op   R1,D2(,B2)

A   3,4(,11)

Example 5b.   Add two integers (RX format, B2 omitted)

machine language

op	R1	X2	B2	D2

5 A	3	B	0	0 0 4

assembly language

op   R1,D2(X2)

A   3,4(11)

There is one other important rule. When the B1, B2, or B3 field is specified in an explicit format, the corresponding D1, D2, or D3 field must not represent a memory address. Instead, it must represent a constant in the range 0 through 4095_{10}.

Implicit Formats

In the notation of Figure 3.4, S1, S2, and S3 are used to indicate an address that is written in implicit form rather than in explicit base-displacement form. Use of implicit formats has a decided advantage over use of explicit formats: they are simpler to use, less error prone, and greatly facilitate the writing and modifying of source statements. Consequently, implicit formats are used frequently in assembly language programming.

The simplest implicit form of address consists of a statement name-field symbol. For example, this Add instruction,

$$\text{A} \qquad \text{3,Z}$$

Implicit Base-Displacement Address

corresponds to the following implicit form for an RX-type instruction given in Figure 3.4:

$$\text{op} \qquad \text{R1,S2}$$

In the Add instruction, the symbol Z is assumed to have been defined in the name field of some statement in the source module in which the Add occurs. The value of Z is an address, namely the address that the assembler assigned to the statement in which Z was the name-field symbol. When assembling the machine language instruction corresponding to A 3,Z, the assembler generates the required base-displacement form of the address that is represented by Z. *The programmer must not specify the displacement or the base register when using an implicit form of address.*

The instructions shown in Figure 3.5 illustrate a few of the other implicit forms of address. The phrase "symbolic address is Z" used in the explanation column of Figure 3.5 means "the memory address that is equal to the value of the symbol Z." In each of the instructions, the implicit form of address is given by a statement-name symbol. In the last example of Figure 3.5, the implicit format

$$\text{op} \qquad \text{S1,S2}$$

Implicit Length

indicates that the length field L is implied, as in the instruction

$$\text{CLC} \qquad \text{X,Z}$$

The value of the implied length is assumed by the assembler to be the number of bytes represented by the symbol X. This is known as the **length-attribute** of X and will be discussed further in Chapter 6.

In all the examples of Figure 3.5, the assembler must generate the correct base-displacement form of a symbolic address. Thus, for the RX-type Add instruction

$$\text{A} \qquad \text{3,Z}$$

the assembler must generate a base register address for the B2 field and a displacement for the D2 field of the assembled machine language instruction. The machine language opcode for this Add instruction is 5A, so from Figure 3.4 we see that the assembled instruction will have the following form:

5 A	3	0	?	?
op	R1	X2	B2	D2

The contents of the B2 and D2 fields must be such that the formula

$$\left\{ \begin{array}{l} \text{memory address} \\ \text{represented by Z} \end{array} \right\} = \left\{ \begin{array}{l} \text{base} \\ \text{address} \end{array} \right\} + \left\{ \begin{array}{l} \text{implied} \\ \text{displacement} \end{array} \right\}$$

is satisfied. The base address in this formula is the contents of the base register that is implied by symbolic address Z. That register must be designated by the contents of the B2 field in the machine language instruction. The implied displacement must be calculated by the assembler and represented in the D2 field of the instruction.

Figure 3.5 Examples of implicit formats.

type	implicit format	instruction		explanation
RX	R1,S2	A	3,Z	Add the integer whose symbolic address is Z to the contents of Register 3.
RX	R1,S2(X2)	A	3,Z(5)	Add to Register 3 the integer whose address is the sum of the index in Register 5 and the symbolic address Z.
SI	S1,I2	CLI	Z,X'40'	Compare the byte whose symbolic address is Z to the one-byte constant X'40', given as immediate data.
SS₁	S1(L),S2	CLC	X(5),Z	Compare the five bytes at the location whose symbolic address is X to the five bytes whose symbolic address is Z.
SS₁	S1,S2	CLC	X,Z	Compare the n bytes at the location whose symbolic address is X to the n bytes whose symbolic address is Z. Note: The value of n is implied and is the length attribute of X.

The question is, What should the B2 and D2 fields be, and what is the value of the base address, in order that this formula be satisfied? The assembler can determine the memory address represented by Z—the left-hand side of the formula—by means of its symbol table, but how can it determine the quantities in the right-hand side of the equation? It appears that we have one equation and three unknowns: the base address, the implied base register designated by the B2 field, and the implied displacement in the D2 field. To resolve this situation, the following method must be used.

The programmer is required to specify the base address and the address of the implied base register by means of a USING directive. *The USING directive must occur before any statement in the source module that contains an operand for which an implied displacement must be calculated.* Its format is

opcode	operand
USING	A,R

where A represents the base address and R represents the implied base register.

Given this information, the assembler can resolve the situation described. The implied displacement from the formula given on the previous page can be written as follows:

$$\left\{\begin{array}{l}\text{implied}\\\text{displacement}\end{array}\right\} = \left\{\begin{array}{l}\text{memory address}\\\text{represented by Z}\end{array}\right\} - \{\text{base address}\}$$

In general, whenever an implicit form of address is specified in the operand of an assembly language instruction, the assembler uses the base address and the implied base register that are specified in the USING directive and computes the required implied displacement from the following formula:

Implied Displacement Calculated at Assembly Time

$$\left\{\begin{array}{l}\text{implied}\\\text{displacement}\end{array}\right\} = \left\{\begin{array}{l}\text{memory}\\\text{address}\end{array}\right\} - \left\{\begin{array}{l}\text{base}\\\text{address}\end{array}\right\}$$

To return to our Add instruction,

$$\text{A} \quad \text{3,Z}$$

we are now entitled to assume that the memory address represented by Z is a known value, that the address of the implied base register is known, and that the base address is known. "Known," of course, means "known to the assembler." Suppose, then, that the addresses just mentioned are as follows:

$$\text{memory address Z} = 80A_{16}$$

$$\text{implied base register} = C_{16}$$

$$\text{base address} = 6_{16}$$

The implied displacement can then be calculated from the previously mentioned formula:

$$\text{implied displacement} = 80A - 6$$
$$= 804$$

The assembled instruction therefore becomes the following:

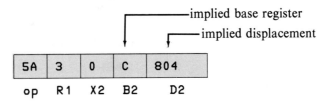

The only constraint placed on the determination of the implied displacement is that the displacement must be a nonnegative integer in the range from 000 through FFF_{16} (0 through 4095_{10}). For this reason, it is always advisable to write programs that do not exceed 4096 bytes in length when assembled.

3.5 THE BALR-USING SEQUENCE

In the preceding section, we showed that in order to use the implicit form of address, the programmer must specify the base address and the implied base register in a USING directive, of the form

$$\text{USING} \quad A,R$$

where A represents the base address and R represents the implied base register. Given that information, the assembler is able to calculate the implied displacement and generate the required base-displacement form of the address.

But what will happen at run time? At run time the computation of the effective address in RX, RS, SI, S, SS_1, and SS_2 instructions uses the base address that is in the base register:

Effective Address Calculated by CPU at Run Time

$$\left\{\begin{array}{c}\text{effective}\\\text{address}\end{array}\right\} = \left\{\begin{array}{c}\text{base address}\\\text{in designated}\\\text{base register}\end{array}\right\} + \{\text{displacement}\}$$

Consequently, *there must be an instruction in the program that puts the base address into the implied base register at run time.* The instruction that is used for this purpose is the BALR instruction, an RR-type instruction. As shown in Figure 3.4, the format of the BALR instruction is as follows:

opcode	operand
BALR	R1,R2

For the present purposes, we will use it with R1 = 12 and R2 = 0:

$$\text{BALR} \quad 12,0$$

In this form, the BALR instruction, *when executed at run time,* places the address of the instruction that immediately follows the BALR into Register 12. Since the BALR's length is 2 bytes, the address placed into Register 12 is 2 plus the address of the BALR instruction itself. For example, if the address of the BALR 12,0 instruction is 0004, the address placed into Register 12 is 0006.

If in the USING directive we let R = 12 and A = {2 plus the address of the BALR instruction}, then the effective addresses computed for the RX, RS, SI, S, SS_1, and SS_2 instructions at run time will be identical with the effective addresses designated in those instructions at assembly time.

To specify the desired value of A and R in the USING directive, the programmer writes the BALR and USING statements in the following manner and in the following sequence:

$$\text{BALR} \quad 12,0$$
$$\text{USING} \quad *,12$$

The asterisk symbol (∗), when used in this manner, represents the value of the memory location counter that is maintained by the assembler. As stated in Section 3.2, this value is equal to the address assigned to the preceding instruction, plus the length of that instruction. In other words, *it is the same as the address that the BALR instruction will place into Register 12 at run time.*

Register 12= Implied Base Register

Throughout this book, Register 12 will be used as the implied base register. This is the standard base register convention in the IBM 360 and 370 systems. The reason for choosing Register 12 rather than any other register is this: Registers 1, 13, 14, and 15, which are used in the standard subroutine linkage convention (as will be described in Chapter 10), ordinarily should not be used for any other purpose; Register 0 cannot be used, since its contents are disregarded by the IBM 360 and 370 hardware when it is used as a base register. By choosing Register 12, we have ten consecutive registers free for other use in the program.

Finally, it should be noted that no implicit forms of address may be used in the operands of statements that occur before the USING directive. If these forms were used, the assembler could not calculate the implied displacement and would not know what register to use as the implied base register in those operands.

As an illustration of these concepts, consider the sequence of statements that are required at the beginning of each assembly language program:

```
NAME       CSECT
           STM       14,12,12(13)
           BALR      12,0
           USING     *,12
           ST        13,SAVE+4
           LA        13,SAVE
```

The assembler initializes the memory location counter to 0 and then processes the statements one by one. The results can be depicted as shown below. Note that there is no opcode corresponding to a directive, only to an instruction.

assembly language statement		memory location counter	opcode	type	number of bytes	assembled object code	
NAME CSECT		0000	none	directive	0	none	
STM	14,12,12(13)	0000	STM = 90	RS	4	90ECD00C	(explicit)
BALR	12,0	0004	BALR = 05	RR	2	05C0	
USING	*,12	0006	none	directive	0	none	
ST	13,SAVE+4	0006	ST = 50	RX	4	50D0C---	(implicit)
LA	13,SAVE	000A	LA = 41	RX	4	41D0C---	(implicit)

The following observations summarize the results just depicted. First, before assembling a statement, the memory location counter is increased by the number of object code bytes (if any) required by the preceding statement. Then, the current value of the memory location counter is assigned to the name-field symbol (if any) appearing in a statement, and to the symbol used to represent the memory location counter, namely the asterisk (∗). Next, each instruction is translated into its appropriate machine language format, using the numeric equivalent of the mnemonic opcode. Operand fields given in explicit base-displacement form can be immediately translated, as in the STM instruction; but operands given implicitly, as in the ST instruction, cannot be translated until three things are known: the base address, the implied base register, and the value of the symbolic address. Fourth, the USING ∗,12 directive informs the assembler that the base address is 0006 and that the base register is Register 12. And finally, to translate the ST instruction, the assembler must calculate the implied displacement from the formula given earlier,

$$\left\{ \begin{array}{c} \text{implied} \\ \text{displacement} \end{array} \right\} = \left\{ \begin{array}{c} \text{memory address} \\ \text{represented} \\ \text{symbolically by} \\ \text{SAVE+4} \end{array} \right\} - \left\{ \begin{array}{c} \text{base address} \\ \text{in implied} \\ \text{base register} \end{array} \right\}$$

The base address is 0006, and the implied base register B2 is 12; but the memory address represented symbolically by SAVE+4 cannot be determined until the statement in which SAVE is the name-field symbol is processed. This statement is not shown on the previous page, but to complete the example let us assume that when it is processed the value assigned to SAVE is 500_{16}. Then the implied displacement will be

$$4FE = (500 + 4) - 0006$$

and the object code corresponding to the ST 13,SAVE+4 instruction will be as follows:

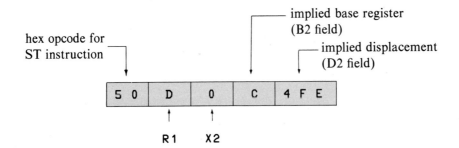

3.6   MNEMONIC OPCODES

The entire set of nonprivileged assembly language instructions is summarized in Figure 3.6. We will describe in later chapters how to use these instructions. Through repeated usage they will become familiar to you; therefore, it is not necessary to begin learning them now.

Ultimately you will have to learn each instruction's mnemonic opcode and type (RR, RX, etc.). Together, the opcode and type dictate not only what operation is to be performed but also what kind of data is being operated on (binary, decimal, etc.) and whether the data are in memory or in registers.

The letters used in the opcodes are designed to help you remember each opcode and its purpose, as in *A* for Add and *B* for Branch. For this reason the opcodes are said to be **mnemonic,** from the Greek words meaning mindful and remember. For some instructions the type is easy to remember once the opcode is learned; for example, in most RR-type instructions the opcode ends in the letter *R*. For the others, however, learning the type will require frequent recourse to tables such as Figure 3.6. A very useful set of these and other data is provided in IBM's pocket-sized *System/370 Reference Summary,* Publication GX20–1850, known as the "yellow booklet."

3.7   SUMMARY

Perhaps more than any other single fact, what makes assembly language qualitatively different from just about every other programming language is that *there is a one-to-one correspondence between the opcode and operand fields of a machine language instruction and those of an assembly language instruction.* Therefore, since in the IBM 360 and 370 systems there are seven different machine language instruction formats—RR, RX, RS, SI, S, SS$_1$, and SS$_2$—there are seven correspondingly different assembly language instruction formats.

Although in machine language all fields in an instruction contain binary numbers, in assembly language the fields are usually written symbolically or with decimal numbers. The assembler translates the field representations into the binary formats required for execution at run time.

In each of the seven machine language formats, the opcode field occupies the first 8 bits. This means that there can be up to 256 ($=2^8$) different opcodes. As can be seen from the opcodes listed in Appendix A, there are in fact only about 150 nonprivileged opcodes. Some of the remaining 100 or so opcodes are privileged or semiprivileged instructions that will not be discussed in this text; the others are not associated with hardware operations, i.e., they are invalid. In IBM 360 and 370 Assembly Language, the valid opcodes are represented mnemonically by codes of from one to five letters. In this text, their study will be undertaken in accordance with the functional categories depicted in Figure 3.6.

The operand field of a machine language instruction specifies the data on which the instruction is to operate. The specification can take one of four forms:

1. The data itself (only in SI-type instructions)
2. The numeric address of a register containing the data
3. The numeric address of a memory location containing the data, the address being given in base-displacement form
4. The number of bytes (length) of the data at a memory location (given only in SS_1- and SS_2-type instructions)

These fields must also be specified in assembly language, though this is often done symbolically rather than numerically, and implicitly rather than explicitly. The correspondences between the operand fields of a machine language instruction and those of an assembly language instruction were given in Figure 3.4. The choice of which operand format to use depends on the instruction's type. The functional summary of mnemonic opcodes in Figure 3.6 and the alphabetical summary in Appendix A state each instruction's type. Without knowledge of an instruction's type or knowledge of how the operand must be specified for that type of instruction, a programmer cannot write an assembly language instruction correctly.

The use of base-displacement addressing in the IBM 360 and 370 systems requires that there be statements in each assembly language source module that specify the implied base register and base address to the assembler and that cause the base address to be loaded into the implied base register at run time. The convention adopted for use in the IBM 360 and 370 systems is that Register 12 be used for the implied base register. In this book we will adhere to this convention by employing the following two statements in the order given:

```
BALR        12,0
USING       *,12
```

The first of these satisfies the run-time requirement; the second satisfies the assembly time requirement. In satisfying the convention in this way, we are restricted to creating object modules whose size does not exceed 4096 bytes. In Chapters 9 and 10 we will see how to circumvent this restriction. We will also see that Registers 1, 13, 14, and 15 have conventionally recognized purposes in calling subroutines. Because of these conventions and because the same registers are used by all input/output macros, programmers should avoid using these registers except in conjunction with subroutines and system macros. Registers 2 through 11 have no restrictions associated with their use.

3.8 REVIEW

Memory Addresses   A memory address is an unsigned integer that identifies the location of a byte, half word, full word, or double word. No address can exceed the total number of bytes available in main memory (i.e., the memory's capacity). Double-word addresses are exactly divisible by 8, full-word addresses by 4, and half-word addresses by 2.

Boundaries   The first byte of a half word, full word, and double word in memory is known as a half-word boundary, full-word boundary, and double-word boundary, respectively. By design of the hardware in both the IBM 360 and 370, each machine language instruction must always be located at a half-word boundary. The IBM 360's design (but not the 370's) also dictates that most numeric data be located at a half-word, full-word, or double-word boundary.

Registers   The sixteen general-purpose registers have numeric addresses in the range 0 through 15. Each register contains exactly 32 bits. The content of a register depends on the use to which it is put. For data used in numeric calculations, the high-order bit (bit# 0) is used for a number's algebraic sign.

Base Register   The content of a base register is a memory address known as the "base address." It is used by the CPU to calculate an effective address at run time. Any of the general-purpose registers except Register 0 can be used as a base register.

Figure 3.6   Mnemonic opcode summary.

instruction category	general description	see section	RR	RX	RS	SI	S	SS₁	SS₂
			mnemonic opcodes by instruction type						
Branching and loop control	Unconditional branch	3.2;8.4	BR	B		(none)			
	Branch and link to subroutine	3.5; 9.2;10.3	BALR BASR	BAL BAS					
	Conditional branch, depending on index	4.6			BXH BXLE				
	Conditional branch, depending on count	4.5	BCTR	BCT					
	Conditional branch, depending on condition code	5.4;5.5 7.4; 8.4; 12.4; 13.5	BCR BER BNER BLR BNLR BHR BNHR BZR BNZR BMR BNMR BPR BNPR BOR BNOR	BC BE BNE BL BNL BH BNH BZ BNZ BM BNM BP BNP BO BNO					
Binary integer operations	Add	5.3	AR ALR	A AH AL		(none)			
	Subtract	5.3	SR SLR	S SH SL					
	Multiply	5.3	MR	M MH					
	Divide	5.3	DR	D					
	Shift, with sign preserved	5.3;8.1			SRA SRDA SLA SLDA				
	Compare	5.5	CR	C CH					
	Test	5.4	LTR						
	Sign	5.6	LCR LNR LPR						
	Copy into register	5.2	LR	L LH	LM				
	Copy into memory	5.2		ST STH	STM				
	Convert decimal to binary	4.4;12.8		CVB					
	Convert binary to decimal	4.3;12.8		CVD					

			RR	RX	RS	SI	S	SS₁	SS₂
Decimal operations	Add	12.3		(none)					AP ZAP
	Subtract	12.3							SP
	Multiply	12.3							MP
	Divide	12.3							DP
	Shift	12.6							MVO
	Shift and round	12.5							SRP
	Compare	12.4							CP
	Copy	12.6						MVN MVZ	
	Convert zoned to packed	4.4;12.8							PACK
	Convert packed to zoned	4.3;12.8							UNPK
	Convert packed to EBCDIC	12.9						ED EDMK	

Figure 3.6   continued

mnemonic opcodes by instruction type

instruction category	general description	see section	RR			RX			RS	SI	S	SS₁	SS₂
			short	long	ext'd	short	long	ext'd					
Floating-point operations	Add	13.7	AER AUR	ADR AWR	AXR	AE AU	AD AW		(none)				
	Subtract	13.7	SER SUR	SDR SWR	SXR	SE SU	SD SW						
	Multiply	13.7	MER	MDR	MXDR MXR	ME	MD	MXD					
	Divide	13.7	DER	DDR		DE	DD						
	Halve	13.7	HER	HDR									
	Round	13.7			LRER LRDR								
	Compare	13.5	CER	CDR		CE	CD						
	Test	13.5	LTER	LTDR									
	Sign	13.6	LCER LNER LPER	LCDR LNDR LPDR									
	Copy into register	13.4	LER	LDR		LE	LD						
	Copy into memory	13.4				STE	STD						

instruction category	general description	see section	RR	RX	RS	SI	S	SS₁	SS₂
Byte manipulations	Compare	7.3; 7.8	CLR CLCL	CL	CLM	CLI		CLC	
	Copy	7.2; 7.8	MVCL	IC STC	ICM STCM	MVI		MVC MVCIN	
	Translate	7.9						TR	
	Translate and test	7.9						TRT	
Bit manipulations	And	8.2	NR	N		NI		NC	
	Or	8.2	OR	O		OI		OC	
	Exclusive Or	8.2	XR	X		XI		XC	
	Test	8.3				TM	TS		
	Shift	8.1			SRL SRDL SLL SLDL				
Miscellaneous	Load address	4.5		LA					
	Execute	7.7		EX					
	Set program mask	11.4	SPM						
	No-op	6.5; 8.4	NOPR	NOP					
	Supervisor call	19.4	SVC						
	Monitor call	---					MC		
	Store clock	---					STCK		
	Compare and swap	---			CS CDS				

Base-Displacement Address   The operand of an instruction in the IBM 360 and 370 systems specifies a memory location by a pair of numbers known as a "base-displacement" address. One component of this pair is the 4-bit address of a base register; the other component is a 12-bit displacement.

Effective Address   The base-displacement address in an instruction's operand is used by the CPU at run time to calculate the actual memory address designated by the operand. The address so calculated is known as the "effective address." The calculation is straightforward:

either   {effective address} = {base address} + {displacement}
  or   {effective address} = {base address} + {displacement} + {index}, for RX only.

Implied Base Register   The base register used by the CPU when an assembly language operand address is written in implicit form is known as the implied base register. By convention, it is Register 12.

BALR-USING   The USING directive specifies the address of the implied base register together with the base address that the assembler should use when creating a base-displacement address at assembly time. The BALR instruction specifies the same implied base register and base address as the USING directive does, so that at run time the CPU can calculate the effective address.

Instruction Formats   The number of bytes in a machine language instruction depends on what type of instruction it is. One byte contains the opcode. From 1 to 5 bytes contain the operand fields. See Figure 3.3.

Assembly Language Instructions   The assembler translates each mnemonic instruction code into a machine language opcode. Correspondingly, each operand field of an assembly language instruction is translated into a machine language operand field. See Figure 3.4.

Explicit Operand Format   When an assembly language instruction's operand field is in base-displacement form, it is said to be in explicit format.

Implicit Operand Format   When an assembly language instruction's operand field contains a symbolic address, it is said to be in implicit format because the machine language base-displacement form is implied rather than explicitly stated.

Register Usage Convention   Use of Registers 2 thru 11 is, in general, unrestricted. The other registers should not normally be used except as follows: Register 12 is reserved for the implied base register; and Registers 0, 1, 13, 14, and 15 are reserved for use in subroutine linkage.

3.9   REVIEW QUESTIONS

1. Why is the concept of address boundaries important?
2. What are the two components of a base-displacement address, and what is the purpose of each component?
3. What are the smallest and largest possible values of a displacement? Are negative displacements permitted?
4. What is the "memory location counter"? How does the assembler determine its value?
5. The RX and SI types of instructions each have one characteristic that is unique to that type. What is that characteristic for RX-type instructions? For SI-type?
6. RR-type instructions are the only kind that are two bytes long. What else distinguishes RR-type instructions from all the other types?
7. As shown in Figure 3.4, there are two implicit operand formats for RX-type instructions: R1,S2(X2) and R1,S2. What does the X2 field represent? What value is assigned to the X2 field when it is omitted from an operand?
8. What is the purpose of the USING directive? Why must it occur before any source module statement that contains an operand field in implicit format?
9. In the BALR-USING sequence, what is the purpose of the BALR instruction?
10. By convention, what register is used for the implied base register? What registers have no conventions associated with their usage?

1. What is the difference in meaning between the phrase "the contents of a memory location" and the phrase "the address of a memory location"?

2. In the following assembly language ADD instruction, what is the purpose of the name-field symbol LOOP?

name field	opcode	operand
LOOP	A	3,X

In this instruction, what meaning does the assembler attach to the number 3 in the operand?

3. Why is there no implicit form of operand in an assembly language RR-type instruction?

4. Analogous to the meanings of the symbols X, Y, and Z in the assembly language sequence

```
L      3,X
A      3,Y
ST     3,Z
```

what meanings should be attached to the variables X, Y, and Z in the Fortran assignment statement

```
Z = X + Y
```

5. The following questions pertain to the BALR-USING sequence:

```
BALR     12,0
USING    *,12
```

   a. What would be the effect at assembly time if the BALR instruction were omitted from this sequence?
   b. What would be the effect at assembly time if the USING directive were omitted from this sequence?
   c. Why must the BALR instruction precede the USING directive as shown? Why couldn't the sequence be written in the reverse order, as

```
USING    *,12
BALR     12,0
```

and still achieve exactly the same purpose as the given sequence?

6. What is fundamentally incorrect about the following revision to the six statements required at the beginning of each OS source module, and why is it incorrect?

```
BOMB     CSECT
         STM     14,12,12(13)
         ST      13,SAVE+4
         LA      13,SAVE
         BALR    12,0
         USING   *,12
```

7. Assume that Register 12 has been designated as the implied base register by the BALR-USING sequence:

```
BALR     12,0
USING    *,12
```

Assume also that the address placed in Register 12 by the BALR 12,0 instruction is 000006. What implied displacements would be required to represent each of the following effective addresses in base-displacement form:

```
00012C
00FF2A
000006
00008E
001005
```

8. In an expression such as SAVE+4, which is used in the instruction

```
ST        13,SAVE+4
```

the assembler determines the value of the symbol SAVE, adds 4 to that value, and generates the base-displacement address for the sum. Suppose that the value of SAVE is 000F4C, and suppose that Register 12 has been designated as the implied base register with base address 00001E. What is the base-displacement address corresponding to each of the operands in the following instructions:

a.	L	5,4(1)		d.	ST	6,SAVE(4)
b.	ST	5,SAVE		e.	L	11,SAVE+4(8)
c.	L	6,SAVE+4		f.	ST	11,SAVE-4

9. What base address always results from use of the convention that the first six statements in an OS source module be:

```
PROG      CSECT
          STM       14,12,12(13)
          BALR      12,0
          USING     *,12
          ST        13,SAVE+4
          LA        13,SAVE
```

Given this convention and resulting base address, what is the largest possible value of the symbol SAVE in a source module? What is the base-displacement form of address corresponding to that value of SAVE? In what way does this limit the size of an object module?

10. Suppose that, at load time, the loader program places the object module into main memory beginning at address 02000_{16}. Assuming that the source module statements were written in accordance with the conventions stated in Exercise 9, what would be the memory addresses of the first four instructions in the program at run time? What would be the base address at run time? If the value of the symbol SAVE was 000248 at assembly time, what effective address would be represented at run time by the B2,D2 field of the assembled ST 13,SAVE+4 instruction?

11. Suppose that the contents of Registers 4, 5, and 6 are 000000, 000004, and 000008, respectively. Suppose also that the value of the symbol X is 00020A. What effective addresses would be represented by the second operand field of each of the following RX-type ADD instructions?

```
A   8,X(4)
A   8,X(5)
A   8,X(6)
```

12. In some computer systems, the concept of base-displacement addresses is not employed. Instead, the memory address field of each instruction contains a single binary integer, which itself *is* the desired effective address. If in such a system the memory address field is 16 bits in length, what is the largest effective address that can be represented in an instruction? If in such a system the assembler assigns addresses beginning at 0000 and the loader places an object module into main memory beginning at address 0800, what would be required before that object module could be run?

13. From the summary given in Figure 3.6 together with the names and properties of the instructions given in Appendix A, we can determine a few general characteristics of the mnemonic opcodes and the instructions they represent. For example, the opcodes of almost all RR-type instructions end in the letter R to remind us of their type; almost all operations on binary integers are either RR or RX instructions; and there is no single instruction that can be used to calculate a square root, or perform exponentiation, or compute more complicated mathematical functions. Missing from the summaries are any instructions that perform input or output, since, as was mentioned in Chapter 1, these are all privileged instructions. What other patterns and general characteristics can you determine from these summaries?

II

Fundamental Techniques

4

Elementary Operations:
Loops and Integer I/O

The manner in which registers are used for the computation of an effective address at run time was discussed in Chapter 3. In this chapter, we will demonstrate some of the other uses of registers: for integer computations, array variable subscripts, and loop control.

The chapter begins with an explanation of how to add two integers. Next, methods of defining integer constants and of reserving memory space for integers are described. In Section 4.3 the instructions required to translate the binary representation of nonnegative integers into a character representation that can be used for printed output are summarized. Section 4.4 covers the reverse translation process, from character input to binary integer. Handling of negative integers is illustrated in the end-of-chapter exercises.

The important question of how loops may be initialized and controlled in assembly language is introduced in Sections 4.5 and 4.6. To demonstrate the use of loop-control techniques, we will show how to add two integer arrays. This also introduces the notions of subscripts and of memory allocation for one-dimensional arrays.

The chapter concludes with a brief discussion of some assembly language programming considerations.

4.1   ADDITION OF TWO BINARY INTEGERS

To add two binary integers in the IBM 360 and 370, *the arithmetic must be done in a register*. For example, to add the binary integers that are located at symbolic addresses X and Y, the programmer must decide which of the 16 registers to use, copy one of the integers into that register, and add the other integer to it. Using Register 3, the following two instructions will compute the sum of the two integers:

```
L          3,X
A          3,Y
```

The Load instruction L 3,X copies the integer that is at symbolic address X into Register 3. In doing so, it replaces whatever was previously in Register 3 but does not alter or erase the integer at X. The Add instruction A 3,Y adds the integer that is at symbolic address Y to the contents of Register 3. The sum replaces the integer that had been loaded into Register 3 by the previous instruction, but the number being added—the integer at symbolic address Y—is not changed.

Now, if we want to use Register 3 for any other purpose, we must first copy the sum out of that register because it may be replaced or altered by a subsequent instruction using that register. Therefore, the usual sequence for adding two binary integers is

```
L          3,X
A          3,Y
ST         3,Z
```

The Store instruction ST 3,Z copies the sum into the memory location whose symbolic address is Z. In doing so, it replaces whatever was previously at that location but does not alter or erase the contents of Register 3. Once the sum is copied into a memory location, Register 3 can be used for other purposes.

In using the implicit form of address in each of the previous three RX-type instructions, namely

```
opcode      R1,S2
```

we have tacitly assumed that a base address and implied base register have been established in the program containing the instructions. This assumption is necessary in order to avoid having to use the explicit base-displacement form of address. The assumption also has one other consequence: In choosing a register for our computation, we were free to choose any register *except* the implied base register. Had we chosen the implied base register, Register 12, then a load instruction such as

```
L     12,X
```

would have replaced the base address with the integer that is at symbolic address X. The computation of the effective address in the execution of subsequent instructions would therefore probably have produced incorrect results. Consequently, in this text Register 12 will be used only as the implied base register. Similar considerations will cause us to avoid using Registers 0, 1, 13, 14, and 15 for computations.

Use Registers 2 through 11

4.2 BINARY INTEGER CONSTANTS AND MEMORY ALLOCATION

The example in the preceding section gives rise to two questions: How is integer data specified in an assembly language program, and how can memory space be reserved for results of calculations?

There are two methods for specifying binary integer constants. One is to define the constants by means of a directive designed for that purpose. The other is to specify the constants in the instructions that are to use them. The directive that is used to define an integer constant is the **Define Constant (DC) directive,** written in its simplest form as

The DC Directive for Full-Word Binary Integer Constants

name field	opcode	operand
{ any symbol, or blank }	DC	F'x'

In the operand, the letter *x* denotes a signed or unsigned decimal integer. The assembler converts that integer to its binary representation, and the symbol in the name field becomes the symbolic address of that integer. For example, if these statements were in an assembly language program

```
X     DC     F'40'
Y     DC     F'-10'
```

then the Load and Add instructions of the previous section

```
L        3,X
A        3,Y
```

would compute the sum of $+40$ and -10, i.e., $+30$.

Alternatively, the constants could be specified in the operand of the Load and/or Add instruction as

```
L        3,=F'40'
A        3,=F'-10'
```

*"Literals" for
Full-Word Binary
Integer Constants*

In this case, there need be no corresponding DC directive. The assembler generates the binary representation of the constant so specified, and assigns an address to it. The notation $=F'x'$ where x denotes a signed or unsigned decimal integer is known as a **literal constant.** Other types of literal constants, and other forms of the DC directive, will be discussed in Chapter 6.

To reserve memory space for the result of a calculation, we use the **Define Storage (DS) directive.** In its simplest form, it is written

name field	opcode	operand
{ any symbol, or blank }	DS	F

In the operand, the letter F denotes that one full word is to be reserved. The symbol in the name field becomes the symbolic address of that word. To continue the example, we can now write these statements in an assembly language program:

```
          L        3,X
          A        3,Y
          ST       3,Z
                   .
                   .
                   .
X         DC       F'40'
Y         DC       F'-10'
Z         DS       F
```

*Do Not Intermix
Data with
Instructions*

The three dots indicate that there are other statements in the program between the ST instruction and the DC directive. Since the CPU cannot distinguish an instruction from data, do not intermix instructions with DC or DS directives. If there were no instructions following the ST that would ultimately terminate the program's execution at run time, then the CPU would, as it proceeded from one instruction to the next, attempt to execute data as though they were instructions! At best, the result would be undesirable; most likely, the program would be terminated due to an invalid instruction.

It is possible to use the DS directive to reserve more than one memory location, as would be needed for an array. We will see how to do this shortly. Other forms of the DS directive will be described in Chapter 6.

4.3 PRINTING NONNEGATIVE INTEGERS

You will recall that the representation of integer data in memory is different from that used by most input and output devices. Integer data used for arithmetic purposes are represented in the binary number system, whereas all data transmitted between memory and most input and output devices are in character format. In the IBM 360 and 370 systems, the EBCDIC character format is used. This consists of a unique 8-bit code for each letter, digit, punctuation mark, and other symbol that can be typed at a keyboard, displayed at a terminal, or printed by a printer.

In producing a line of printed output, the hardware literally copies each line, character by character, from main memory to the printer device. This means that each line must be set up in memory in exactly the form in which it is to be transmitted to the printer. Therefore, *to print an integer that is represented in binary form in memory, it must first be converted to its character form.*

There is no single instruction in the IBM 360 or 370 systems that converts a binary integer to its representation as a decimal integer in character form. Instead, a sequence of instructions must be used. In this section, we present the instructions that are required to convert nonnegative integers to a form suitable for printing and discuss the manner in which the DC and DS directives can be used to allocate memory areas for the characters that are to be printed. A similar but slightly more complex procedure is used to convert negative integers; this will be discussed in Exercise 11 at the end of the chapter.

The conversion procedures to be discussed are the same whether you are using assembly language in OS or in DOS. The difference between the two systems is not in the conversion process but in the output process; namely, the use of OPEN, PUT, CLOSE, and DCB or DTF macros. Since this was already discussed in Section 2.4, we will confine our examples to OS output procedures.

Allocating a Memory Area

It is characteristic of virtually all printers that each printed line consists of a fixed number of print positions (the same number for each line), that each printed character—including blanks—may only be printed in a print position, and that no two characters may be printed in the same position of a given line. For the high-speed printers to which we restrict our attention, the number of print positions per line is usually 132.

Therefore, to allocate a memory area sufficient to accommodate any printed line, 132 bytes of memory must be reserved for the entire line. Some of these bytes must be allocated for the integers that are to be printed, others for any text that is also to be printed, and the remainder for blanks that fill out the line. Each such allocation will designate the print positions that are to be used.

To achieve the desired allocations, we will use the following four forms of the DC and DS directives:

1. To define the beginning and length of a printed line:

```
either:   LINE    DS    0CL132    Used when carriage control omitted.
    or:   LINE    DS    0CL133    Used when carriage control included.
```

2. To reserve space for an integer that consists of *n* characters, including one position for the sign:

```
symbol    DS    CLn     n is an unsigned decimal integer, and
                        symbol is any valid name-field symbol.
```

3. To define text that is to be printed on the line:

```
          DC    C'...'    The three dots represent any text
                          characters other than an apostrophe (')
                          or an ampersand (&).
```

4. To assign *m* blanks to unused print positions:

```
          DC    CLm' '    m, an unsigned decimal integer, is the
                          number of consecutive blanks to be
                          printed; the apostrophes enclose a single
                          blank.
```

As an example of the use of these directives, suppose we wanted to print the following line in order to see the result of the addition processes described earlier.

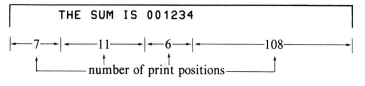

Then the directives to be used are those shown here:

```
LINE    DS    0CL133            DEFINE BEGINNING AND LENGTH OF LINE
        DC    CL1' '            CARRIAGE CONTROL FOR SINGLE SPACING
        DC    CL7' '            DEFINE 7 CONSECUTIVE BLANKS
        DC    C'THE SUM IS '    DEFINE TEXT THAT IS TO BE PRINTED
SUM     DS    CL6               RESERVE 6 POSITIONS FOR THE INTEGER
        DC    CL108' '          DEFINE 108 CONSECUTIVE BLANKS
```

Except for the printing of leading zeroes, the following Fortran format statement will provide the same print position definitions:

$$\text{FORMAT (' ', 7X, 'THE SUM IS ', I6, 108X)}$$

In Cobol, a working storage definition for this print line might be

```
01  LINE.

    02    FILLER    PICTURE X(1)      VALUE SPACE.
    02    FILLER    PICTURE X(7)      VALUE SPACES.
    02    FILLER    PICTURE X(11)     VALUE 'THE SUM IS '.
    02    SUM       PICTURE 9(6).
    02    FILLER    PICTURE X(108)    VALUE SPACES.
```

It should be noted that in assembly language, as in Fortran and Cobol, the print positions are designated relative to the beginning of the line, by the sequence in which the information is specified, and by the number of positions reserved for each item.

Conversion from Binary to Character Representation

Conversion of an integer from its representation in the binary number system to its representation as a sequence of decimal digits in character form is not a trivial process. For example, the binary integer representation of 12_{10} is

$$0000 \quad 0000 \quad 0000 \quad 0000 \quad 0000 \quad 0000 \quad 0000 \quad 1100$$

whereas its representation as the two digits 1 and 2 in character form is

$$\underbrace{1111 \quad 0001}_{1} \qquad \underbrace{1111 \quad 0010}_{2}$$

In the IBM 360 and 370 systems, there are instructions that enable the conversion to be done in two steps: (1) the binary integer is converted to its representation as a binary-coded decimal number by means of the Convert to Decimal (CVD) instruction, and (2) the binary-coded decimal representation is converted to its EBCDIC character representation by means of the Unpack (UNPK) instruction. This two-step process works for negative as well as nonnegative integers, but the manner in which the sign is handled is not entirely satisfactory in either case. Whether the binary integer being converted is negative or nonnegative, its sign is encoded into the low-order digit of the EBCDIC representation by the UNPK instruction.

For example, the binary representation of $+12_{10}$ would be converted not to the two characters *1* and *2,* but to the characters *1* and *B;* the representation of -12_{10} would be converted to the characters *1* and *K.* The *B* represents the 2 encoded as $+2$, the *K* the 2 encoded as -2. In general, low-order digits (1,2,3,...,9) are encoded, respectively, as A,B,C,...,I for positive numbers and as J,K,L,...,R for negative numbers. A low-order zero digit is encoded as a left-brace "{" if the number is zero or positive, and as a right-brace "}" if it is negative. Since it is awkward to read numbers with their low-order digits encoded, instructions that supplement the CVD and UNPK instructions are used to decode the sign's representation.

There are a number of ways to resolve the sign problem. Some general solutions will be discussed in Exercise 11 at the end of this chapter, and in Chapter 12, Sections 12.8 and 12.9. The representation known as binary-coded decimal, or packed decimal, will also be discussed at length in Chapter 12. For present purposes, we will restrict our attention to the simplest case, that in which the numbers to be converted are either positive or zero. In this case, the conversion can be accomplished in four instructions, provided we impose the following conditions: *all nonnegative integers will be printed as ten-digit numbers, without punctuating commas, and with leading zeroes printed as zeroes. The sign will not be printed.*

For example, the number +12 would be printed as 0000000012, the number 123,456,789 would be printed as 0123456789, and the number 0 would be printed as 0000000000.

The sequence of four instructions required to convert a binary integer to the form just described is shown below and in Figure 4.1. As can be seen from the figure, these instructions must be supplemented with three directives: one that defines the binary integer that is to be converted, one that allocates the 10-byte memory area required for the character form of the number, and one that reserves an area for the intermediate binary-coded decimal representation created by the CVD instruction.

There are a lot of details to learn, but it is not necessary at this point to know how the conversion instructions work. For now you only need to know how to write the required instructions and directives. A more detailed explanation will be given in Chapter 12.

The four conversion instructions are:

```
L       5,Z         COPY THE BINARY INTEGER INTO A REGISTER
CVD     5,BCD       CONVERT IT TO BINARY-CODED DECIMAL FORM
UNPK    SUM,BCD     CONVERT THAT TO CHARACTER FORM
OI      SUM+9,X'F0' ELIMINATE THE SIGN CODE IN LOW-ORDER DIGIT
```

General Procedure

It should be emphasized that these four instructions will convert *any* 32-bit nonnegative binary integer to the character form described provided that these procedures are followed:

1. The address of the binary integer must be specified in the second operand of the Load (L) instruction.
2. The address of the ten-byte memory area that is allocated for the character representation of the number must be specified in the first operand of the UNPK instruction.
3. The address of the *low-order byte* of the ten-byte character area must be specified in the first operand of the OI instruction.
4. The address of the area reserved for the intermediate binary-coded decimal representation must be specified in the second operand of both the CVD and the UNPK instructions.

Note that any register may be used by the L and CVD instructions, but the same register must be used by both instructions. Note also that in reserving an area for the intermediate binary-coded decimal representation, we have used a DS directive whose operand contains the single letter *D*. This reserves eight bytes on a double-word boundary, an alignment required in the IBM 360 but optional in the IBM 370.

4.4 READING NONNEGATIVE INTEGER INPUT DATA

As discussed, conversion from binary integer to character form is not a trivial process. Neither is the reverse conversion trivial. The reverse conversion is done as a two-step process in the IBM 360 and 370 systems. The PACK instruction converts from character form to binary-coded decimal, and the Convert to Binary (CVB) converts from binary-coded decimal to 32-bit binary integer form. The PACK-CVB sequence, the counterpart of the CVD-UNPK sequence used for printing, suffers the same limitation in its handling of the sign. Whereas negative as well as nonnegative integers may be converted, the PACK instruction assumes that the sign is encoded in the low-order digit of the character representation, using the same sign-encoding scheme that is used by the UNPK instruction.

Converting from Character to Binary

At this stage, we will avoid these sign considerations as much as possible. Therefore, in this section we present the instructions and supplementary DC and DS directives that can be used to convert nonnegative integers from character form to 32-bit binary integer form. One method of handling negative integers will be described in Exercise 12 at the end of this chapter. We impose the conditions that *the character form of the decimal integer occupies exactly ten positions, right-justified with either leading zeroes or leading blanks. Its sign is omitted; it is assumed to be nonnegative.*

Figure 4.1   Program to print the sum of two binary integers.

```
PRINTEX  CSECT
*
*   THIS PROGRAM WILL COMPUTE THE SUM OF TWO BINARY INTEGERS,
*    CONVERT THE SUM TO A 10-BYTE CHARACTER FORM SUITABLE FOR
*    PRINTING, AND PRINT THE RESULT.
*
*   THE CONVERSION PROCESS USED IS VALID ONLY FOR NONNEGATIVE
*    INTEGERS: I.E., THE SUM IN THIS PROCESS IS PRINTED AS A
*    10-DIGIT NUMBER WITHOUT PUNCTUATING COMMAS, WITH LEADING
*    ZEROES PRINTED AS ZEROES, AND WITH THE SIGN NOT PRINTED.
*
*   THE INTEGERS USED TO COMPUTE THE SUM ARE DEFINED WITHIN THE
*    PROGRAM: THEY ARE NOT READ AS INPUT DATA.
         STM     14,12,12(13)     STANDARD ENTRY
         BALR    12,0
         USING   *,12
         ST      13,SAVE+4
         LA      13,SAVE
*
         OPEN    (PRINTER,(OUTPUT))   OPEN THE PRINTER OUTPUT FILE
* ADD
         L       3,X              COMPUTE THE SUM OF THE INTEGERS GIVEN
         A       3,Y              AT SYMBOLIC ADDRESSES X & Y, AND
         ST      3,Z              STORE THE SUM AT SYMBOLIC ADDRESS Z.
* CONVERT
         L       5,Z              COPY THE SUM INTO REGISTER 5
         CVD     5,BCD            CONVERT IT TO BINARY-CODED DECIMAL FORM
         UNPK    SUM,BCD          CONVERT THAT TO CHARACTER (EBCDIC) FORM
         OI      SUM+9,X'F0'      ELIMINATE SIGN CODE IN LO-ORDER DIGIT.
* PRINT
         PUT     PRINTER,LINE     WRITE THE SUM, TOGETHER WITH TEXT, ONTO
* EXIT                            THE PRINTER.
         CLOSE   (PRINTER)
         L       13,SAVE+4        STANDARD EXIT
         LM      14,12,12(13)
         BR      14
*
* INTEGER CONSTANTS, AND AREA RESERVED FOR THEIR SUM
X        DC      F'437'           BINARY REPRESENTATION OF DECIMAL +437
Y        DC      F'562'           BINARY REPRESENTATION OF DECIMAL +562
Z        DS      F                BINARY SUM, TO BE CONVERTED TO EBCDIC
* AREA RESERVED FOR INTERMEDIATE BINARY-CODED DECIMAL REPRESENTATION
BCD      DS      D                8 BYTES RESERVED ON DOUBLE-WORD BOUNDARY
* AREA RESERVED FOR 132-BYTE PRINT LINE
LINE     DS      0CL132           BEGINNING AND LENGTH OF LINE
         DC      CL7' '              COLS  1 - 7    BLANK
         DC      C'THE SUM IS '           8 - 18   EXPLANATORY TEXT
SUM      DS      CL10                    19 - 28   10-BYTE SUM
         DC      CL104' '                29 - 132  BLANK
*
*   DATA CONTROL BLOCK FOR OUTPUT TO PRINTER
PRINTER  DCB     DSORG=PS,MACRF=(PM),DDNAME=SYSPRINT,RECFM=FB,          X
               LRECL=132,BLKSIZE=4092
* REQUIRED STATEMENTS:
SAVE     DS      18F
         END
```

For example, either of these are acceptable forms for the decimal integer $+12_{10}$, the symbol ⌣ denoting one blank:

$$⌣⌣⌣⌣⌣⌣⌣⌣12 \quad\quad \text{or} \quad\quad 0000000012$$

but the following two forms are not acceptable under the given conditions:

$$⌣⌣⌣⌣⌣⌣⌣+12 \quad\quad\quad +0000000012$$

The instructions and directives used in the conversion procedures when reading integers are the same whether you use OS or DOS Assembly Language. It is only the input procedure—OPEN, GET, CLOSE, and DCB or DTF macros—that differs between OS and DOS. Since this was discussed in Section 2.4, we will restrict our examples to OS input procedures.

Allocating a Memory Area

In reading a line of input data, the hardware literally copies each line, character by character, from the input device into main memory. This means that an area of memory equal to the length of the line must be reserved for the data transmission.

Each character in an input line occupies a unique position, analogous to a character in a print line position. In other words, each position in a line contains exactly one character, which may of course be a blank. Assuming that the maximum line length is 80 positions, as it would be on most terminals, we therefore reserve 80 bytes of memory for the entire line. We allocate some of these bytes for the integers in each line, others for additional data that may be included in a line, and the remainder for blanks. We use the same forms of the DC and DS directives that were used for printer output.

For example, if given this input line format

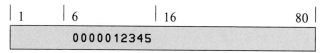

then the directives required to allocate the memory area for the data can be written as shown below.

```
CARD    DS      0CL80       DEFINE BEGINNING AND LENGTH OF CARD
        DS      CL5' '      RESERVE 5 BYTES FOR UNUSED POSITIONS
INT     DS      CL10        10 BYTES FOR CHARACTER FORM OF INTEGER
        DS      CL65' '     65 BYTE POSITIONS FOR REMAINDER OF CARD
```

Conversion from Character Form to 32-Bit Binary Integer Form

Under the conditions imposed at the beginning of this section—namely that the character form of a decimal integer consist of exactly ten bytes, that the integer be nonnegative, that the sign not be represented, and that either leading zeroes or leading blanks may be used to the left of the most significant digit—only three instructions are required for the conversion to 32-bit binary integer form. These are:

```
        PACK    BCD,INT     CONVERT FROM CHAR. TO BINARY-CODED DECIMAL
        CVB     5,BCD       CONVERT THAT TO 32-BIT BINARY IN REGISTER 5
        ST      5,X         STORE THE BINARY FORM AT SYMBOLIC ADDRESS X
```

General Procedure

The symbolic address INT was defined by the DS directive given above, and is repeated here for convenience:

```
INT     DS      CL10        RESERVE 10 BYTES FOR THE CHARACTER FORM
```

The symbolic address BCD must be defined, as when performing the reverse conversion for output, as follows:

```
BCD     DS      D           RESERVE 8 BYTES ON A DOUBLE-WORD BOUNDARY
```

And the symbolic address X must be defined by a DS directive of the following form:

```
X       DS      F         RESERVE ONE FULL WORD FOR A BINARY INTEGER
```

It should be noted that these three instructions can be used to convert *any* decimal integer represented in character form under the previously mentioned conditions. The requirements are:

1. The address of the 10-byte memory area that is allocated for the input character representation of the number must be specified in the second operand of the PACK instruction.
2. The address of the area reserved for the intermediate binary-coded decimal representation of the number must be specified in the first operand of the PACK instruction and in the second operand of the CVB instruction.
3. The address of the area reserved for the binary integer must be specified in the second operand of the ST instruction.

Note that any register may be used by the CVB and ST instructions, but the same register must be used by both instructions.

A program that will read a line containing two nonnegative integers, compute their sum, and write the sum on the printer is given in Figure 4.2. Note that only one GET macro is used; it reads the entire contents of the line. As in Chapter 2, the data is assumed to be in the input data stream.

4.5 ADDITION OF INTEGER ARRAYS: THE BCT AND LA INSTRUCTIONS

Suppose there are two sets of integers, $\{X\}$ and $\{Y\}$, whose components are indicated by subscripts

$$X_1, X_2, X_3,...,X_n$$
$$Y_1, Y_2, Y_3,...,Y_n$$

In Fortran, we could add each corresponding pair of integers to produce a third set, $\{Z\}$, by means of a DO-loop such as

```
        DO   10   J = 1,N
        Z(J) = X(J) + Y(J)
   10   CONTINUE
```

In Fortran, the variable *J* can serve both as the loop-control variable and as the subscript. In assembly language, we frequently use separate variables for loop control and subscripts. Both subscripting and loop control are accomplished by means of registers: loop control is accomplished by counting the number of iterations using a counter in a register, and subscripting is accomplished by using an index register in RX-type instructions.

Loop Control

The simplest way to control the number of iterations in a loop is to determine how many iterations are desired, and either count up (by 1's) to that number or count down (again by 1's) to zero. These methods work even though the number of iterations may depend on the data, as it does in the Fortran DO-loop.

Counting Down by 1's Via BCT

In the IBM 360 and 370, there is one instruction especially suited to controlling the number of loop iterations by the method of "counting down by 1's." That is the Branch on Count (BCT) instruction. It is an RX-type instruction, for which we will use the implicit format

opcode	operand
BCT	R1,S2

When a BCT instruction is executed, two things take place *in this order:*

1. First, a $+1$ is algebraically subtracted from the register designated by the first operand, R1, and the result is placed into that register.

2. Then the result obtained is tested to see if it is zero. If it is not zero, a branch is made to the address designated by the second operand. But if the result is zero, no branch is made; instead, execution proceeds at the instruction that immediately follows the BCT.

For example, suppose that the location whose symbolic address is N contains the binary integer +5. Then, in the sequence

```
          L       4,N
LOOP      ---     ---
          ---     ---
          ---     ---
          BCT     4,LOOP
          ---     ---
```

the four instructions beginning with the statement named LOOP will be repeated five times. The first time the instruction at LOOP is executed, Register 4 will contain +5. Then the BCT instruction will reduce that value to +4, and branch back to the instruction at LOOP. The second time the BCT instruction is executed, it will reduce the value in Register 4 from +4 to +3, and again branch back to LOOP. The third time the value will be reduced from +3 to +2, the fourth time from +2 to +1, and the fifth time from +1 to 0. At this point the BCT instruction will no longer branch; instead, the instruction following the BCT will be executed.

Similarly, if we suppose that the location whose symbolic address is N contains any positive binary integer, then in the previous illustration the four instructions will be repeated *n* times, where *n* denotes the value of the integer at address N. Thus, *n* serves as the loop-control variable, or *counter,* for the loop.

To illustrate how the Fortran DO-loop given earlier can be implemented in assembly language, we must introduce two further concepts: (1) the manner in which an array is stored in memory and (2) the manner in which its individual components can be accessed using index registers.

Address of an Array Component

The components of an array are stored in consecutive memory locations, as depicted in Figure 4.3. Since we are concerned only with binary integers at this time, each component occupies one full word, which we assume is located at a full-word boundary. Thus the address of any component in the array can be determined once the address of the first component is known. If the first component's address is Z, then the second component's is Z+4, the third one is at Z+8, and so forth. In general, the address of Z_J for J = 1,2,... is given by the formula

$$\left\{ \begin{array}{c} \text{address} \\ \text{of } Z_J \end{array} \right\} \;=\; \left\{ \begin{array}{c} \text{address} \\ \text{of } Z_1 \end{array} \right\} \;+\; \{4*(J-1)\}$$

Thus, if the index $4*(J-1)$ is in an index register, say Register 5, then the following three instructions will compute the sum $Z_J = X_J + Y_J$:

```
          L       3,X(5)
          A       3,Y(5)
          ST      3,Z(5)
```

In this sequence, we are using the indexed implicit format for RX-type instructions

```
          opcode      R1,S2(X2)
```

At run time, the effective address computed for each of these three instructions is

instruction		effective address	
L	3,X(5)	address of X +	index in Register 5
A	3,Y(5)	address of Y +	index in Register 5
ST	3,Z(5)	address of Z +	index in Register 5

Use of Index Register

Figure 4.2   Program to read two integers and print their sum.

```
RDPRT     CSECT
*
*   THIS PROGRAM READS TWO NONNEGATIVE INTEGERS FROM A DATA CARD
*    THAT IS IN THE INPUT DATA STREAM, COMPUTES THEIR SUM, AND
*    PRINTS THE RESULT IN A SINGLE LINE ON THE PRINTER.
*
*   THE INPUT DATA IS ASSUMED TO BE REPRESENTED AS 10-BYTE UNSIGNED
*    DECIMAL INTEGERS, WITH EITHER LEADING ZEROES OR LEADING BLANKS.
*
*   THE SUM IS PRINTED AS A 10-BYTE UNSIGNED DECIMAL INTEGER, WITH
*    LEADING ZEROES PRINTED AS ZEROES.
*
          STM    14,12,12(13)    STANDARD ENTRY
          BALR   12,0
          USING  *,12
          ST     13,SAVE+4
          LA     13,SAVE
*
*   OPEN   INPUT AND OUTPUT FILES
          OPEN   (TRANS,(INPUT))      CARDS FROM INPUT DATA STREAM
          OPEN   (PRINTER,(OUTPUT))   PRINTER IS SYSOUT
*
*   READ ONE DATA CARD
          GET    TRANS,CARD           INPUT AREA IS 'CARD'
*
*   CONVERT EACH NUMBER TO 32-BIT BINARY
          PACK   BCD,INT1             FIRST INTEGER IS AT 'INT1'
          CVB    5,BCD                ITS 32-BIT BINARY INTEGER FORM IS
          ST     5,X                   STORED AT 'X'.
          PACK   BCD,INT2             SECOND INTEGER IS AT 'INT2'.
          CVB    5,BCD                ITS 32-BIT BINARY INTEGER FORM IS
          ST     5,Y                   STORED AT 'Y'.
*
*   COMPUTE THE SUM, AND STORE BINARY INTEGER RESULT AT 'Z'.
          L      3,X                  COMPUTE THE SUM OF THE INTEGERS GIVEN
          A      3,Y                  AT SYMBOLIC ADDRESSES X & Y, AND
          ST     3,Z                  STORE THE SUM AT SYMBOLIC ADDRESS Z.
*
*   CONVERT THE SUM TO UNSIGNED 10-BYTE CHAR. FORM WITH LEADING ZEROES.
          L      5,Z                  PUT THE SUM IN A REGISTER
          CVD    5,BCD                CONVERT IT TO BINARY-CODED DEC.
          UNPK   SUM,BCD              CONVERT THAT TO CHAR (EBCDIC)
          OI     SUM+9,X'F0'          ELIMINATE SIGN CODE
*
*   PRINT THE RESULT
          PUT    PRINTER,LINE
*
*   EXIT FROM PROGRAM
EOJ       CLOSE  (PRINTER)            CLOSE ALL FILES
          CLOSE  (TRANS)
          L      13,SAVE+4            STANDARD EXIT
          LM     14,12,12(13)
          BR     14
*
*   AREAS RESERVED FOR TWO BINARY INTEGERS AND THEIR SUM
X         DS     F         BINARY REPRESENTATION OF INTEGER AT 'INT1'
Y         DS     F         BINARY REPRESENTATION OF INTEGER AT 'INT2'
Z         DS     F         SUM OF 'X' AND 'Y' INTEGERS
*
*   AREA RESERVED FOR INTERMEDIATE BINARY-CODED DECIMAL REPRESENTATION
BCD       DS     D         SAME AREA USED FOR ALL CONVERSIONS
```

Figure 4.2 **continued**

```
*
*  AREA RESERVED FOR 80-BYTE INPUT CARD
CARD     DS       0CL80         BEGINNING AND LENGTH OF AREA
         DS       CL5           COLS  1 -  5 UNUSED
INT1     DS       CL10                 6 - 15 FIRST 10-BYTE DECIMAL INTEGER
         DS       CL5                 16 - 20 UNUSED
INT2     DS       CL10                21 - 30 SECOND 10-BYTE DECIMAL INTEGER
         DS       CL50                31 - 80 UNUSED
*
*  AREA RESERVED FOR 132-BYTE PRINT LINE
LINE     DS       0CL132              BEGINNING AND LENGTH OF LINE
         DC       CL7' '        COLS  1 -  7 BLANK
         DC       C'THE SUM IS '       8 - 18 EXPLANATORY TEXT
SUM      DS       CL10                19 - 28 10-BYTE SUM
         DC       CL104' '            29 - 132 BLANK
*
*  DATA CONTROL BLOCKS FOR INPUT AND OUTPUT FILES
*
TRANS    DCB      DSORG=PS,MACRF=(GM),DDNAME=SYSIN,EODAD=EOJ,RECFM=FB,       X
                  LRECL=80,BLKSIZE=4080
PRINTER  DCB      DSORG=PS,MACRF=(PM),DDNAME=SYSPRINT,RECFM=FB,              X
                  LRECL=132,BLKSIZE=4092
*
*  REQUIRED STATEMENTS
*
SAVE     DS       18F
         END
```

As shown in Figure 4.3, the address of X is identical to that of X_1, and similarly for Y and Z. Thus, using the assumption that the index in Register 5 is $4*(J-1)$, it follows that the effective address computed when the L 3,X(5) instruction is executed is the address of X_J; the effective address computed when the A 3,Y(5) instruction is executed is the address of Y_J; and the effective address computed when the ST 3,Z(5) instruction is executed is the address of Z_J. In other words, when Register 5 contains $4*(J-1)$, the three instructions compute the sum $Z_J = X_J + Y_J$.

To compute each of the sums Z_J for $J = 1,2,...,N$, we use a loop containing the three instructions, repeat the loop N times, and on each repetition ensure that the appropriate index $4*(J-1)$, namely $0,4,8,...,4*(N-1)$, is in Register 5. To ensure that Register 5 contains the appropriate index during each repetition of the loop, we use the Load Address (LA) instruction. We could also use an add instruction to increase the contents of an index register by $+4$ or by any other number. But the use of LA has become fairly common for this type of operation because the constant to be added is generally a small positive number and can be specified in the displacement field. LA is an RX-type instruction that places the effective address specified in its second operand into the register designated in its first operand.

The LA Instruction

typical forms	examples	main purpose
LA R1,S2	LA 5,W	initialize a register with a (implicit) memory address
LA R1,D2	LA 5,4	initialize a register with the explicit displacement
LA R1,D2(X2)	LA 5,4(5)	increase a register's index or counter by adding the explicit displacement to it
LA R1,D2(X2,B2)	LA 5,4(5,6)	increase a register's index or counter by adding two numbers to it: the explicit displacement and the number in the explicit base register

Figure 4.3   Placement of arrays in memory.

The elements of each array are 32-bit integers. Consequently, each occupies one full word. Consecutive integers in each array are stored in consecutive full words. The size of each array is assumed to be 12 full words ($N= 12$), for purposes of illustration.

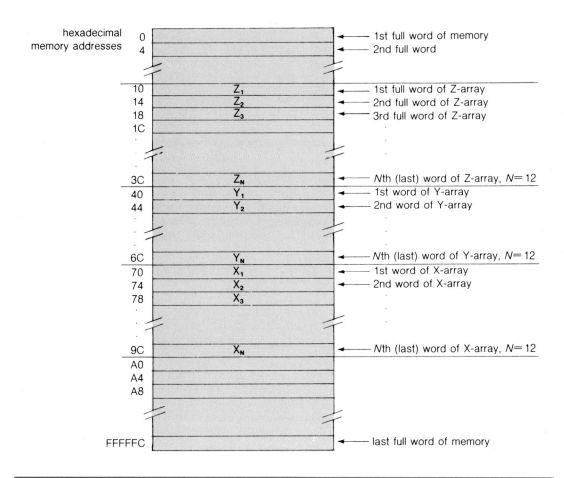

When an LA instruction is executed, the effective address replaces the quantity that was in the R1 register. However, the effective address is computed using the quantities that existed in the base and index registers just *before* the instruction is executed. Therefore the R1 field may designate the same register as either or both of the X2 and B2 fields without affecting the manner in which the effective address is computed.

These descriptions of the LA's execution can be summarized by the formula

$$\begin{Bmatrix} \text{contents of} \\ \text{the register} \\ \text{designated by} \\ \text{the R1 field} \end{Bmatrix} = \begin{Bmatrix} \text{effective} \\ \text{address} \\ \text{represented by} \\ \text{S2 or B2,D2} \end{Bmatrix} + \begin{Bmatrix} \text{contents of} \\ \text{the register} \\ \text{designated by} \\ \text{the X2 field} \end{Bmatrix} = \begin{Bmatrix} \text{base} \\ \text{address} \end{Bmatrix} + \{\text{displacement}\} + \{\text{index}\}$$

Note that the sum indicated by the right-hand side of this formula is just the second-operand address that is computed by the CPU when executing any RX-type instruction, as was explained in Chapter 3. That is why the instruction's name is "Load *Address*." As in all such address computations, it is only bits 8 through 31 of the designated registers that participate in the addition; the result is a 24-bit nonnegative address. Therefore, bits 0 through 7 of the R1 register are set to 0's. For similar

Register 0   reasons, the value assumed for the index is zero if the X2 field designates Register 0, and the value assumed for the base address is zero if the B2 field designates Register 0.

Figure 4.4 Adding two arrays. (See Figure 4.3.)

```
* STATEMENTS TO ADD TWO SETS OF INTEGERS, X(J) + Y(J) = Z(J)
*
* INITIALIZATION OF LOOP CONTROL VARIABLE AND SUBSCRIPT
          L     4,N              1: REG 4 GETS LOOP CONTROL COUNTER
          L     5,=F'0'          2: REG 5 GETS INITIAL INDEX, 0
*
* COMPUTATION WITHIN LOOP
LOOP      L     3,X(5)           3: REG 3 GETS X(J)
          A     3,Y(5)           4: Y(J) ADDED TO X(J)
          ST    3,Z(5)           5: RESULT STORED IN Z(J)
*
* LOOP CONTROL MECHANISM
          LA    5,4(5)           6: ADD 4 TO INDEX
          BCT   4,LOOP           7: REPEAT TILL NO MORE TO DO
          .
          .
          .
* DIRECTIVES TO RESERVE MEMORY AREAS FOR THE ARRAYS
Z         DS    12F              12 WORDS FOR Z ARRAY
Y         DS    12F              12 WORDS FOR Y ARRAY
X         DS    12F              12 WORDS FOR X ARRAY
N         DC    F'12'            NUMBER OF COMPONENTS IN EACH ARRAY
```

As illustrations of these concepts, suppose that the following conditions existed at run time just prior to the execution of each of the LA instructions shown below:

$$\text{contents of Register 5} = 00000550_{16}$$
$$\text{contents of Register 6} = 00000040_{16}$$
$$\text{symbolic address W} = 00000400_{16}$$

Then, after execution of each of these instructions, the contents of the registers would be as indicated here in hexadecimal:

		before execution		after execution	
		Reg 5	Reg 6	Reg 5	Reg 6
LA	5,W	00000550	00000040	00000400	00000040
LA	5,4	00000550	00000040	00000004	00000040
LA	5,4(5)	00000550	00000040	00000554	00000040
LA	5,4(5,6)	00000550	00000040	00000594	00000040

Note that LA 5,4(5) adds $+4$ to the contents of Register 5. Note also that LA 5,4 is equivalent to LA 5,4(0,0); if a register address is omitted in the base or index field of an explicit operand the assembler assumes that the omitted address is zero. Thus the effective address in R1,D2 format is simply equal to the displacement, since at run time the CPU always ignores the contents of Register 0 when it is used as an index register or base register. The LA instruction can therefore be used in R1,D2 format to load a nonnegative integer constant (in the previous case, $+4$) into a register. But note that since a displacement cannot be negative or greater than 4095_{10}, the instruction LA 5,-4 is invalid, as is LA 5,8000.

Negative Displacements Are Invalid

Given these descriptions of the BCT and LA instructions, the sequence of assembly language instructions that can be used to compute the sums $Z_J = X_J + Y_J$ for $J = 1,2,...,N$ is shown in Figure 4.4. Since we want the index to be the successive values $0,4,8,...,4*(N-1)$, it is initialized to 0 and incremented by 4. And since we want the sums to be computed in a loop that is repeated N times, the loop-control counter is initialized to the number of components in the arrays and reduced by $+1$ after each repetition of the loop.

The first three repetitions of the loop are described in Figure 4.5, assuming that the number of components in the arrays is 12 and that the addresses assigned to the arrays are as shown in Figure 4.3. Subsequent repetitions would be executed in similar fashion.

Figure 4.5   Partial trace for statements of Figure 4.4 (N = 12).

			Reg 5	effective address	Reg 4
Initialization steps					
L	4,N	Put loop-control counter into Reg 4	--		12
L	5,=F'0'	Put initial value of index into Reg 5	0		12
First time through the loop					
LOOP L	3,X(5)	Copy X_1 from memory into Reg 3	0	70 = X_1's addr	12
A	3,Y(5)	Compute $X_1 + Y_1$ in Reg 3	0	40 = Y_1's addr	12
ST	3,Z(5)	Copy sum from Reg 3 to Z_1 in memory	0	10 = Z_1's addr	12
LA	5,4(5)	Increase index in Reg 5 by 4	4		12
BCT	4,LOOP	Decr loop count by 1, and go to LOOP	4		11
Second time through the loop					
LOOP L	3,X(5)	Copy X_2 from memory into Reg 3	4	74 = X_2's addr	11
A	3,Y(5)	Compute $X_2 + Y_2$ in Reg 3	4	44 = Y_2's addr	11
ST	3,Z(5)	Copy sum from Reg 3 to Z_2 in memory	4	14 = Z_2's addr	11
LA	5,4(5)	Increase index in Reg 5 by 4	8		11
BCT	4,LOOP	Decr loop count by 1, and go to LOOP	8		10
Third time through the loop					
LOOP L	3,X(5)	Copy X_3 from memory into Reg 3	8	78 = X_3's addr	10
A	3,Y(5)	Compute $X_3 + Y_3$ in Reg 3	8	48 = Y_3's addr	10
ST	3,Z(5)	Copy sum from Reg 3 to Z_3 in memory	8	18 = Z_3's addr	10
LA	5,4(5)	Increase index in Reg 5 by 4	12		10
BCT	4,LOOP	Decr loop count by 1, and go to LOOP	12		9

loop-control counter in Reg 4 = the number of times the loop is still to be repeated

effective memory address = address used to access the *J*th elements of X, Y, and Z

index in Reg 5 is used in the role of a subscript

(see fig. 4.3)

It should be noted that the machine language instructions corresponding to the instructions in Figure 4.5 do not change during the execution of the loop at run time. It is the effective addresses that change, due to the changes in the index. Since an instruction's execution is dependent on the value of the effective address, it will access different memory locations for different effective addresses. But since the instructions themselves are not changed, the same loop could be used many times during execution of a program, provided that the loop-control counter and the index are initialized each time the loop is used.

Finally, note that the DS directives in Figure 4.4 reserve memory for the array data but that no data is specified. It is assumed that some other portion of the program read the data, converted it to binary form, and stored it in the arrays.

4.6   FURTHER ASPECTS OF LOOP CONTROL: THE BXH AND BXLE INSTRUCTIONS

Either the *B*ranch on Inde*x H*igh (BXH) or the *B*ranch on Inde*x L*ess Than or *E*qual (BXLE) instruction can be used to cause three things to happen during each iteration of a loop: (1) incrementing or decrementing the index, (2) counting the number of iterations of the loop, and (3) testing to see whether the loop should be repeated. BXH is usually used when an index, and hence an effective address, is to be *decreased* during each repetition of a loop; BXLE, when an effective address is to be *increased* during each iteration. But each is general enough to be used in either situation, and both are very useful in manipulating arrays. Neither instruction will be used in the examples given in this textbook, since their functions can readily be accomplished by the methods already illustrated, and they are not as simple to use as are the methods already cited. The following brief descriptions therefore serve merely as an illustration of the capabilities of these two instructions.

When either the BXH or BXLE instruction is executed, the index is incremented by a factor that is specified by one of the operands of the instruction. The factor can be either positive or negative. After the index is incremented, it is compared to some limit, which is also specified by one of the operands in the instruction. The BXH instruction branches if the new index is higher than the limit; the BXLE instruction branches if the new index is less than or equal to the limit. Like the increment, the limit may be a positive or negative number. The address to which the BXH and BXLE instructions branch is specified in an operand field of the instruction.

Thus, there are four factors that must be specified by the operand fields of a BXH or BXLE instruction: the index, the increment, the limit, and the branch address. The first three of these must be in registers whose addresses are designated in the operand fields. The branch address must be specified in the operand. This is done in the following manner. Both BXH and BXLE are RS-type instructions, which may be written in one of two forms

	opcode	operand
explicit form:	BXH	R1,R2,D3(B3)
	BXLE	R1,R2,D3(B3)
implicit form:	BXH	R1,R2,S3
	BXLE	R1,R2,S3

The three operand fields have the same meanings in both instructions: R1 designates the register that contains the *index*; R2 designates the register that contains the *increment*; and S3 and D3(B3) specify the *branch address*. The *limit* (the number to which the index is compared after it has been incremented) *must be in an odd-numbered register* whose address depends on the R2 field. If the R2 field designates an odd-numbered register, then the limit is in that register; in this case, the limit and the increment are one and the same. If the R2 field designates an even-numbered register, then the limit is in the odd-numbered register whose address is one more than that designated by the R2 field. For example, if R2 designates Register 3, then both the increment and the limit are in Register 3; but if R2 designates Register 4, then the increment is in Register 4 and the limit is in Register 5.

Since three of the four quantities required for execution of the BXH and BXLE instructions must be in registers, it should be clear that before the loop iterations are begun, the index, increment, and limit must be placed into the registers. As an example, consider the following sequence of statements that could be used to compute the sums $Z_J = X_J + Y_J$ discussed earlier.

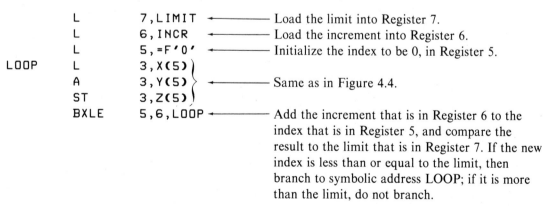

```
          L     7,LIMIT  ←————— Load the limit into Register 7.
          L     6,INCR   ←————— Load the increment into Register 6.
          L     5,=F'0'  ←————— Initialize the index to be 0, in Register 5.
LOOP      L     3,X(5)  ⎫
          A     3,Y(5)  ⎬ ←————— Same as in Figure 4.4.
          ST    3,Z(5)  ⎭
          BXLE  5,6,LOOP ←————— Add the increment that is in Register 6 to the
                                index that is in Register 5, and compare the
                                result to the limit that is in Register 7. If the new
                                index is less than or equal to the limit, then
                                branch to symbolic address LOOP; if it is more
                                than the limit, do not branch.
```

In this sequence, it is assumed that the location whose symbolic address is INCR contains the constant 4, corresponding to the increment of 4 in the instruction LA 5,4(5) given in Figure 4.4. It is also assumed that the location whose symbolic address is LIMIT contains the limit factor $4*(N-1)$, where N is the number of components in each of the arrays. Note that under these conditions, the above sequence accomplishes the same purpose as the sequence given in Figure 4.4.

4.7 SOME PROGRAMMING CONSIDERATIONS

The computer programs that we shall be considering in this text have the overall structure depicted by the diagram

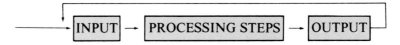

The meaning of this diagram is that each program obtains data from its input operations, processes those data to produce some output results, and then repeats the procedure. This iterative procedure is repeated until either there are no more data to be obtained or until a processing step determines that no more processing is required.

In assembly language, the programmer must specify not only the processing steps but must also define all constants that are to be used at run time as well as reserve memory areas for all input and output data. In addition, the programmer must describe all the files that are to be used for input and output and indicate what is to be done when there are no more input data. It is good practice to separate all statements that constitute instructions and associated comments for input, processing, and output from those that constitute data, data areas, file descriptions, and comments associated with these.

Getting Started

Given what may seem to be a bewilderingly complex set of instructions and directives, the beginning assembly language programmer may well ask some fundamental questions at this point. For example, how does one decide what the processing steps should be for the solution to a given problem? Having decided the steps, in what order should they be carried out, and what should be the interrelationships among them? How are they to be coded in assembly language? How can the processing steps be expressed so that they are relatively easy to modify when it is necessary to accommodate new or previously unforeseen requirements?

There is no surefire formula for deciding what processing steps are needed to arrive at a programming solution to a problem or how best to represent them in assembly language. But there are certain ways of approaching a problem that may prove more fruitful than others. One way to think about technical problems in general, and a methodology for thinking about solving them, is described in G. Polya's book, *How to Solve It* (Princeton University Press, 1973). A collection of papers and a bibliography relevant to programming in particular is contained in *Tutorial on Software Design Techniques,* edited by Peter Freeman and Anthony Wasserman (IEEE Computer Society, 1976). Perhaps of overriding importance in following the guidelines given in these books is the following set of principles:

1. *You must understand the problem for which a programming solution is desired.* This means not only understanding the technical aspects of the problem but also the manner in which the solution is to be used so that the results can be presented in a useful manner. To do this you must know what results are expected, what input data will be provided, and what tools are available for solving the problem, e.g., formulas, existing solution procedures for all or part of the problem, and the capabilities and limitations of the programming language to be used.
2. *Before beginning to devise a programming solution to a problem, you must know how to solve the problem without a computer system.* This does not necessarily mean solving it, but it means knowing *how* to solve it if there were sufficient time to do so.

You should not try to write a program until you have decided upon the program's overall design and its detailed design. The design should begin with the details of the desired output and the required input. Once those details have been decided upon, the next step is to determine an overall design for the solution: the names, inputs and outputs, and purposes of the principal components of the solution. After the overall design has been completed, each component of the solution should be designed in detail so that its actions are fairly well understood. Only after the overall and detailed designs have been done with a reasonable degree of completeness should the program statements be coded.

For many years, flow diagrams (also known as flowcharts) were used to depict a program's design. More recently, use of pseudocode—a structured, English-like rendition of the principal programming steps in a solution—has been found to be a better design tool than flow diagrams. Pseudocode not only mimics the statements in a high-level programming language, it also mimics the structure and intended readability of the programming solution, and it is easy to change when the design changes. So, whereas earlier editions of this textbook used flow diagrams to depict the logic of a solution, the current edition uses pseudocode for the same purpose. When pseudocode doesn't appear in the text explicitly, you may find it useful to write your own pseudocode version of the text's programming solutions in order to better understand the logic used in those solutions.

The more programs you write, the better your understanding will be of the capabilities and limitations of assembly language. It is also helpful to study programs written by other persons. For these reasons, a number of programs are included in the text, and a number of programming problems are included in the exercises at the end of the chapter.

Detecting Errors

Errors in the logic of a procedure, as well as errors in the use of instructions and data constants, are often not detected until a program is run. However, many errors can be anticipated and corrected before running a program, by thinking through a programming solution instruction by instruction, mentally mimicking the way the CPU processes the instructions at run time. For this task, it is useful to have some systematic way of recording the expected actions of the CPU. One such method was illustrated in Figure 4.5; similar techniques will be discussed in subsequent chapters. It is also extremely useful to design data that will test as many as possible of the different types of conditions that a program is expected to encounter at run time. Since it is not feasible to test every possible data condition that may arise, you should attempt to reduce the complexity of the solution's logic and thereby reduce the likelihood that there will be errors in logic. One means of achieving this is to reduce the number of interconnections among processing steps, by making each step have just one point at which it is entered and one from which it is exited. This is one of the cardinal rules of writing well-structured programs. In practice, this principle leads to the use of subroutines and macros and to a sharp reduction in the number of unconditional branches that might otherwise be used.

Despite all precautions, you may still find yourself with run-time programming errors that need to be unraveled and corrected. For this task the *memory dump* is an indispensable aid. The memory dump is a printing of the contents of a program's memory and registers and related information at the time an error occurred. Instructions on how to read memory dumps may be found in a number of sources, among them Rindfleisch's *Debugging System 360/370 Programs Using OS and VS Storage Dumps* (Prentice-Hall, 1976) and the IBM *Debugging Guide* manual (GC24–5093). For MVS users, Robert Binder's *Application Debugging* (Prentice-Hall, 1985) is very useful. An explanation of the numeric code that is printed on a memory dump to identify the immediate cause of a run-time error may be found in the IBM *System Messages* manual (GC38–1001). A summary of the run-time error conditions that are detectable by the CPU and that will generally cause program termination is given in Appendix D.

In addition to a memory dump, it is often useful when debugging an assembly language program to print selected portions of memory while a program is running and before an error occurs. This type of memory print is known as a snapshot, or *snap,* and is obtained in OS by the SNAP macro and in DOS by the PDUMP macro. The idea is to insert a SNAP or PDUMP macro into the source module at places where you would like to have the contents of the registers and/or selected memory locations printed at run time.

Memory Snapshots

SNAP. The following summary shows the essential aspects of using SNAP and will prove satisfactory for most debugging needs. Figure 4.6 shows how to interpret the information that is printed by the SNAP macro. A complete discussion of the SNAP macro may be found in the IBM *Supervisor Services and Macro Instructions* manual (GC24–5103).

1. Before the first SNAP is executed, we must open the SNAP data set by using the OPEN macro

```
OPEN   (snapdcb,(OUTPUT))
```

where "snapdcb" is the name of the associated DCB macro described on the next page.

Figure 4.6 Example of use of SNAP macro.

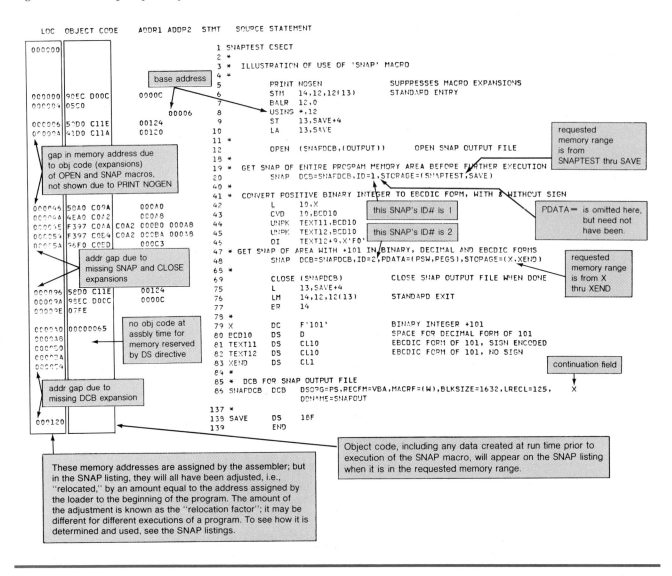

2. Wherever we wish a snap of registers and memory locations, the following macro should be inserted:

name field	opcode	operand
{any symbol,} or blank	SNAP	DCB=snapdcb,ID=k,PDATA=(PSW,REGS),STORAGE=(s1,s2)

where

ID=k ($0 \leq k \leq 127$) will be used to identify the snap on the snap listing

PDATA=(PSW,REGS) will cause printing of the PSW and all register contents

STORAGE=(s1,s2) will cause printing of memory contents between the symbolic addresses s1 and s2 inclusive

It should be noted that the three parameters, ID=, PDATA=, and STORAGE=, may be given in any order, and any of them may be omitted. The DCB= parameter may not be omitted. The example in Figure 4.7 shows one use of SNAP with PDATA omitted and one with it included.

Figure 4.6 *continued*

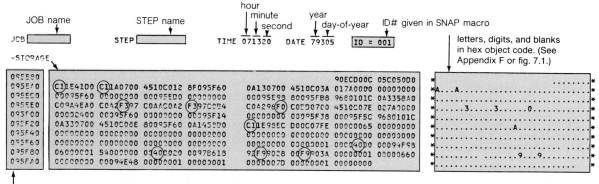

SNAP listing addresses are always real memory addresses that are exactly divisible by 32_{10} (20_{16}), and are equal to or just preceding the beginning of the desired memory range.

The addresses shown are the addresses of the first byte (first two hex digits) of the corresponding line. Addresses of other bytes on a line must be determined by hex counting and hex addition.

For example, the address of the full word 90ECD00C on the first line is 095E98 = 095E80 + 18, since the hex 90 in that word is in the twenty-fourth byte relative to the first byte of that line. *In this way it is determined that the loader has assigned real memory address 095E98 to the beginning of this program.* This number, 095E98, is the "relocation factor."

All addresses assigned by the assembler must be adjusted by the relocation factor to determine the corresponding real memory addresses. For example, SAVE = 000120 + 095E98 = 095FB8 in real memory.

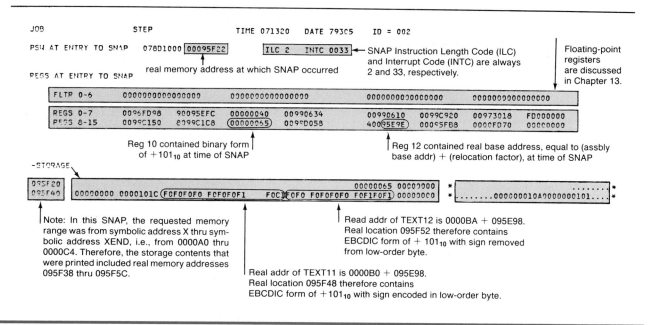

Note: In this SNAP, the requested memory range was from symbolic address X thru symbolic address XEND, i.e., from 0000A0 thru 0000C4. Therefore, the storage contents that were printed included real memory addresses 095F38 thru 095F5C.

Real addr of TEXT11 is 0000B0 + 095E98. Real location 095F48 therefore contains EBCDIC form of + 101_{10} with sign encoded in low-order byte.

Read addr of TEXT12 is 0000BA + 095E98. Real location 095F52 therefore contains EBCDIC form of + 101_{10} with sign removed from low-order byte.

Reg 10 contained binary form of + 101_{10} at time of SNAP

Reg 12 contained real base address, equal to (assbly base addr) + (relocation factor), at time of SNAP

---

3. As part of the program termination procedure, we should close the SNAP output file by using the CLOSE macro:

```
CLOSE   (snapdcb)
```

4. Among the constants and data areas, we must include the DCB macro that describes the SNAP output file, as follows[1]:

```
snapdcb DCB DSORG=PS,RECFM=VBA,MACRF=(W),BLKSIZE=1632,LRECL=125,  X
            DDNAME=snapdd
```

1. Before using the SNAP macro, you should verify that the LRECL= and BLKSIZE= values given in the DCB macro are the same as those required at the computer installation being used.

The name-field symbol 'snapdcb' must be the same as that used in the OPEN, SNAP, and CLOSE macros shown previously. The DDNAME= parameter must identify the following JCL statement in the execution step:

```
//snapdd    DD    SYSOUT=A
```

NOTE: When executing the OPEN, CLOSE, or SNAP macros, Register 13 must contain the address of the SAVE area. Execution of any of these macros may alter the contents of Registers 0, 1, 14, and 15, but all other register contents will remain intact. The use of PRINT NOGEN, as shown in Figure 4.6, suppresses printing of the source and object code that is produced by the assembler when it processes the macros. This makes the assembly listing easier to read and less lengthy than if PRINT NOGEN were not used (see Chap. 14).

PDUMP.   In DOS, run-time snapshots of memory and register contents are obtained via the PDUMP macro, which may be written in any of four ways:

opcode	operand
PDUMP	s1,s2
PDUMP	(r1),(r2)
PDUMP	(r1),s2
PDUMP	s1,(r2)

In each case, the first operand designates the starting memory address for the snapshot, and the second one designates the ending address. The ending address should not be less than the starting address.

When a parenthesized operand field (r1) or (r2) is used, the corresponding memory address is in a register. The address of that register is what is enclosed in the parentheses. When parentheses are not used, then we just specify a symbolic address s1 or s2, as illustrated below. In all four cases, the contents of all registers are always printed.

For example, the purpose of the SNAP macro shown in Figure 4.6 can be achieved by either of these two forms of PDUMP:

```
(1)        PDUMP        SNAPTEST,SAVE

(2)      ⎧ LA           5,SAVE
         ⎩ PDUMP        SNAPTEST,(5)
```

The PDUMP output is always placed on the SYSLST printer file. No JCL, DTF, or other I/O statements are required unless SYSLST is a disk file. If it *is* a disk file, then a SYSLST DTF is required, and an OPEN macro must immediately follow each execution of PDUMP. For further details, see IBM publication #GC33–5373, *DOS/VS Supervisor and I/O Macros*.

4.8   SUMMARY

The instruction we will use to count the number of iterations of a loop in the IBM 360 and 370 systems is Branch on Count (BCT). Each time the BCT is executed, it subtracts +1 from the counter, and if the resulting new count is not zero, the BCT will branch to the effective address specified in its second operand. If the new counter is zero, the BCT will not branch.

Subscripting can be achieved through index registers because of the manner in which an index register participates in the formation of an effective address at run time. To simplify the process, a systematic scheme is used to store each array's data in memory, as is illustrated in Figure 4.3 for one-dimensional integer arrays. The instruction we will use to increment the index is the Load Address (LA) instruction. Together, the LA and BCT instructions will be the heart of the loop-control mechanisms used in this text.

An alternative method of controlling the number of loop iterations and achieving the effect of subscripting involves use of either the Branch on Index High (BXH) or Branch on Index Less Than or Equal (BXLE) instructions. These instructions combine the iteration-counting and index-incrementing operations into a single operation. Consequently, their use requires slightly different loop initialization steps than does the LA-BCT pair.

The character representation of integers is always used when they are printed, displayed at terminals, or read from cards or terminals. Since this representation cannot be used for arithmetic processes—there being no instructions to do so—integer input must be converted to binary, and integer output must be converted from binary. Two sets of instructions simplify the conversion processes considerably: PACK and CVB for converting from character to binary integer representation, and CVD and UNPK for converting from binary integer to character representation. Since neither pair's handling of the sign is entirely satisfactory, additional instructions are used to compensate.

In this chapter we have shown how to convert positive integers from character to binary format (and vice versa) under certain simple conditions. A procedure for converting negative as well as positive integers from character to binary format is given in Exercise 12 at the end of this chapter, and a more general procedure is given at the end of Section 12.8. Similarly, a procedure that converts integers from binary to character format is given in Exercise 11, and others are given at the end of Section 12.9.

4.9   REVIEW

Register Usage   In binary integer arithmetic, at least one of the two integers being operated on must be in a register. The result is also in a register. Although in principle any of the registers may be used, Registers 2 thru 11 are the ones that are normally used since they are the only ones not reserved for other purposes.

Load and Store   The "Load" (L) instruction copies an integer from memory into a register. "Store" (ST) copies it from a register into memory.

"Literal" Constants   A literal constant may be specified in the second operand field of a Load instruction and any binary arithmetic instruction (add, subtract, multiply, divide). For a binary integer, specify the literal constant as follows: =F'...' The dots indicate a signed or unsigned decimal integer.

The DC Directive   DC defines (i.e., specifies) a constant for use by your program at run time.

For a full-word binary integer, use DC this way: X DC F'...' where X is the symbolic address of the constant, and the dots indicate a signed or unsigned decimal integer. The assembler converts the decimal integer to its full-word binary representation.

For a character constant consisting of n consecutive blanks, use DC this way: X DC CLn' ' where X is the symbolic address of the constant, and n is a decimal integer.

For a character constant consisting of an arbitrary sequence of characters, use DC this way: X DC C'...' The dots indicate the characters you want.

The DS Directive   DS defines (i.e., reserves) a memory area for use by your program at run time.

For full-word binary integer data, use DS this way: X DS nF   As before, X is the symbolic address of the area; n specifies the maximum number of full-word binary integers that you may store in the area at run time.

For character data, use DS this way: X DS CLn   Here, n specifies the number of characters that you may store in the area at run time.

Printer Output Lines   An output line on most high-speed printers contains a maximum of 132 character positions. One character is printed in each position. Each space counts as one character. Numbers must be printed as a sequence of digits, each digit being in EBCDIC format.

Printer Output Areas   A memory area must be reserved for a printer output line. The area can be reused for each line that is printed. Character constants (including blanks) can be defined within the area. The area should begin with a DS directive that defines the name and length of the line, as in this example: LINE DS 0CL132

> **NOTE:**   In Figure 4.2, the DS and DC directives in the area reserved for the 132-byte printer line near the end of the program covers all 132 print positions. In general, the number of print positions covered by DC's and DS's in a print-line area must equal the value of n specified in the DS 0CLn directive that defines the beginning and length of the area.

Integer Output   Binary integers must be converted to EBCDIC format in order to be printed. This sequence of instructions will convert a positive integer whose symbolic address is Z into its 10-character unsigned EBCDIC representation at symbolic address SUM:

```
        L       5,Z
        CVD     5,BCD
        UNPK    SUM,BCD
        OI      SUM+9,X'F0'
```

Integer Input   Integers must be converted from EBCDIC to binary format in order to be operated on by the binary integer instructions. This sequence will convert an unsigned positive integer whose symbolic address is INT into its full-word binary integer representation at symbolic address X:

```
        PACK    BCD,INT
        CVB     5,BCD
        ST      5,X
```

Integer Arrays   The components of a one-dimensional full-word binary integer array are stored in consecutive memory locations. Subscripting is done via index registers. The value of the index for the Jth component is $4*(J-1)$.

Loop Control   Loops are most easily controlled via a combination of the LA and BCT instructions. LA adds a nonnegative increment to the index. BCT subtracts $+1$ from the loop-control counter each time it is executed, and exits from the loop when the count reaches zero.

Snapshots   For debugging, the OS "SNAP" and DOS "PDUMP" macros will print the contents of a memory area exactly as it existed when the macro was executed at run time. The starting and ending addresses of the area must be specified in the operand of the SNAP and PDUMP macros.

4.10   REVIEW QUESTIONS

1. What is the purpose of the L (Load) instruction? The ST (Store) instruction?
2. How would you specify $+36$ as a full-word binary integer constant in a DC directive? As a literal?
3. What three instructions are required to add the integers -78 and $+32$, with the result stored as a full-word binary integer at symbolic address Z?
4. In each of the following situations, what DC or DS directive will correctly allocate the indicated area?

    a. a 10-byte character area
    b. an area containing 50 consecutive blanks
    c. an area containing these words: TIME OF DAY

5. Why is it necessary to reserve an area for a printer output line? What directives will correctly reserve an area for a line containing four consecutive 10-byte nonnegative integers in character format, with 3 blanks between the first and second, second and third, and third and fourth integers?
6. What instructions and/or directives are needed to correctly convert a full-word nonnegative binary integer stored at symbolic address A to its 10-byte character representation at symbolic address B?
7. What instructions and/or directives are needed to correctly convert a 10-byte nonnegative integer stored in character format at symbolic address A to its full-word binary representation at symbolic address B?
8. In Figure 4.2, what is the purpose of the DC CL104' ' directive that appears at the end of the 132-byte print-line area defined near the end of the program? Would there be an assembly-time error or a run-time error if that statement were omitted from the program? Why or why not?
9. When controlling the number of loop iterations with a BCT instruction, the loop-control counter must be initialized to some number N. What fact determines the value of N?

10. When using RX-type instructions such as Load (L), Add (A), and Store (ST) in a loop to process the components of a one-dimensional binary integer array, use of an index register enables each component of the array to be accessed by the same three instructions. What value should the index register normally be initialized to, and by what amount should its contents be increased each time through the loop?

11. Recall that the Load Address (LA) instruction loads the sum of three quantities that it obtains via its second operand field: the displacement, the contents of the index register, and the contents of the base register. What will be the contents of Register 7 after the following three consecutive LA instructions are executed at run time in the sequence given here:

```
LA   7,4
LA   7,4(7)
LA   7,4(7)
```

12. Suppose that X is the symbolic address of a full-word binary integer. Then what is the fundamental difference between these Load (L) and Load Address (LA) instructions:

```
L    7,X
LA   7,X
```

Problem Statement

Write a program that will read input data containing class enrollments in the format described below and print all the input data followed by a line giving the total enrollment in all classes.

The input data format is this:

> columns 1–6: course i.d.
> 10–50: course name
> 55–64: number of students enrolled

Solution Procedure

The procedure (Figs. 4.7a–4.7b) requires that for each input data record that is read, the number of enrolled students be converted to binary integer format and added to a cumulative tally. After having read and printed all input data and having accumulated all the enrollments in the tally, the tally must be converted to its EBCDIC representation and printed.

Note that the tally cannot be printed until the end-of-data portion of the program is entered. This is done when the operating system, in responding to the input GET macro, detects that there are no more data. It then transfers control not to the instruction following the GET macro but to the instruction whose symbolic address is specified by the EODAD= parameter in the input DCB macro. It is at that point that the tally is converted to EBCDIC and printed.

Figure 4.7a   Pseudocode for sample problem solution in Figure 4.7b.

```
PROGRAM:

    open input and output files;
    total_enrollment := 0;
    print heading line;

    REPEAT WHILE there is more data to read

      read one input record;
      convert enrollment from EBCDIC to binary;
      add class_enrollment to total_enrollment;
      print the input record;

    END WHILE;

    print one blank line;
    convert total_enrollment from binary to EBCDIC;
    print total_enrollment;
    close all files;

    EXIT PROGRAM.
```

Figure 4.7b   Solution to sample problem.

```
FLAG LOCTN OBJECT CODE     ADDR1 ADDR2 STMNT M SOURCE STATEMENT

     000000                              3  SPCH4     CSECT
                                         4  *
                                         5  * SPCH4 READS INPUT DATA CARDS CONTAINING CLASS ENROLLMENTS
                                         6  *  IN THE FORMAT DESCRIBED BELOW, AND PRINTS EACH INPUT DATA
                                         7  *  CARD, THE LAST CARD BEING FOLLOWED BY A PRINTED LINE GIVING
                                         8  *  THE TOTAL ENROLLMENT IN ALL CLASSES.
                                         9  *
                                        10  * INPUT DATA IS IN TEXT (EBCDIC CHARACTER) FORM, AS FOLLOWS
                                        11  *     COLS   1-6    COURSE I.D.
                                        12  *           10-50   COURSE NAME
                                        13  *           55-64   NUMBER OF STUDENTS ENROLLED
                                        14  *     OTHER COLUMNS ARE UNUSED.
                                        15  *
     000000 90 EC D00C                  16            STM   14,12,12(13)          STANDARD ENTRY
     000004 05 C0                       17            BALR  12,0
     000006                             18            USING *,12
     000006 50 D0 C3FE      000404      19            ST    13,SAVE+4
     00000A 41 D0 C3FA      000400      20            LA    13,SAVE
                                        21  *
                                        22  * INITIALIZE TOTAL ENROLLMENT
                                        23  *
     00000E 58 60 C442      000448      24            L     6,=F'0'
     000012 50 60 C0D6      0000DC      25            ST    6,ENROLLED
                                        26  *
                                        27  * OPEN INPUT AND OUTPUT FILES
                                        28  *
     000016                             29            OPEN  (SYSIN,(INPUT))       INPUT IS 'SYSIN' DATA STREAM
     000022                             35            OPEN  (SYSPRNT,(OUTPUT))    OUTPUT IS 'SYSOUT' PRINTER

                                        41  * DOS  *******
                                        42  *          OPEN  SYSIN
                                        43  *          OPEN  SYSPRNT
                                        44  ***************

                                        45  *
                                        46  * PRINT HEADING LINE FOR START OF OUTPUT
                                        47  *
     00002E                             48            PUT   SYSPRNT,HEADING
                                        53  *
                                        54  * MAIN PROCESSING LOOP ...
                                        55  *        READS ONE INPUT CARD
                                        56  *        CONVERTS COURSE ENROLLMENT TO BINARY INTEGER
                                        57  *        ADDS COURSE ENROLLMENT TO TOTAL ENROLLMENT
                                        58  *        PRINTS THE CARD
                                        59  *        WHEN END-OF-DATA OCCURS, CONTROL TRANSFERS TO 'EOD'
                                        60  *
     00003C                             61  LOOP      GET   SYSIN,INAREA          GET INPUT CARD INTO INPUT AREA
                                        66  *
     00004A F2 79 C0CAC110 000000 000116 67           PACK  BCD,DATA             CONVERT INPUT DATA TO DECIMAL
     000050 4F 60 C0CA      000000      68            CVB   6,BCD                CONVERT DECIMAL TO BINARY
     000054 50 60 C0D2      0000D8      69            ST    6,BINARY             AND SAVE IT IN MEMORY
                                        70  *
     000058 58 60 C0D6      0000DC      71            L     6,ENROLLED           GET TOTAL ENROLLMENT
     00005C 5A 60 C0D2      0000D8      72            A     6,BINARY             ADD COURSE ENROLLMENT TO TOTAL
     000060 50 60 C0D6      0000DC      73            ST    6,ENROLLED           AND RETURN NEW TOTAL TO MEMORY
                                        74  *
     000064 D2 4F C134C0DA 00013A 0000E0 75           MVC   OUTLINE,INAREA       COPY INPUT DATA TO OUTPUT AREA
     00006A                             76            PUT   SYSPRNT,OUTAREA       PUT OUTPUT LINE ONTO PRINTER FILE
     000078 47 F0 C036      00003C      81            B     LOOP                 BRANCH BACK TO GET NEXT CARD
                                        82  *
                                        83  * WHEN END-OF-DATA IS SENSED BY 'GET', CONTROL IS TRANSFERRED HERE
                                        84  *
     00007C                             85  EOD       PUT   SYSPRNT,BLANKS        PRINT ONE BLANK LINE
                                        90  *
     00008A 58 60 C0D6      0000DC      91            L     6,ENROLLED           GET TOTAL ENROLLMENT
     00008E 4E 60 C0CA      0000D0      92            CVD   6,BCD                CONVERT TOTAL TO DECIMAL
     000092 F3 97 C272C0CA 000278 000000 93           UNPK  TOTAL,BCD            AND THEN TO EBCDIC (TEXT)
     000098 96 F0 C27B      000281      94            OI    TOTAL+9,X'F0'        REMOVE SIGN CODE
                                        95  *
     00009C                             96            PUT   SYSPRNT,TOTALS       PRINT TOTAL LINE
                                       101  *
                                       102  * TERMINATION OF PROGRAM
                                       103  *
     0000AA                            104            CLOSE (SYSIN)
     0000B6                            110            CLOSE (SYSPRNT)
     0000C2 58 D0 C3FE      000404     116            L     13,SAVE+4            STANDARD EXIT
     0000C6 98 EC D00C                 117            LM    14,12,12(13)
     0000CA 07 FE                      118            BR    14

                                       119  * DOS  *******
                                       120  *          CLOSE SYSIN
                                       121  *          CLOSE SYSPRNT
                                       122  *          EOJ
                                       123  ***************

                                       124  *
                                       125  *
                                       126  * DATA AREAS AND CONSTANTS
                                       127  *
```

Figure 4.7b continued

```
FLAG LOCTN OBJECT CODE    ADDR1  ADDR2  STMNT M SOURCE STATEMENT

     000000                                128   BCD      DS      D                                    DECIMAL COURSE ENROLLMENT
     0000D8                                129   BINARY   DS      F                                    BINARY COURSE ENROLLMENT
     0000DC                                130   ENROLLED DS      F                                    BINARY TOTAL ENROLLMENT
                                           131   *
                                           132   * INPUT CARD AREA
                                           133   *
     0000E0                                134   INAREA   DS      0CL80                                DEFINITION OF INPUT AREA ...
     0000E0                                135   ID       DS      CL6                                  COLS 1-6   COURSE I.D.
     0000E6                                136            DS      CL3                                       7-9   UNUSED
     0000E9                                137   NAME     DS      CL41                                    10-50   COURSE NAME
     000112                                138            DS      CL4                                     51-54   UNUSED
     000116                                139   DATA     DS      CL10                                    55-64   ENROLLMENT
     000120                                140            DS      CL16                                    65-80   UNUSED
                                           141   *
                                           142   * OUTPUT LINE AREA
                                           143   *
     000130                                144   OUTAREA  DS      0CL132                               DEFINITION OF OUTPUT AREA
     000130 4040404040404040               145            DC      CL10' '                              COLS 1-10   BLANKS
     00013A                                146   OUTLINE  DS      CL80                                    11-90   SPACE FOR INPUT CARD
     00018A 4040404040404040               147            DC      CL42' '                                 91-132  BLANKS
                                           148   *
                                           149   * BLANK LINE FOR OUTPUT
                                           150   *
     0001B4                                151   BLANKS   DS      0CL132                               DEFINITION OF BLANK LINE ...
     0001B4 4040404040404040               152            DC      CL132' '                             COLS 1-132   BLANKS
                                           153   *
                                           154   * LINE FOR TOTALS
                                           155   *
     000238                                156   TOTALS   DS      0CL132                               DEFINITION OF TOTAL LINE ...
     000238 4040404040404040               157            DC      CL54' '                              COLS 1-54   BLANKS
     00026E E3D6E3C1D340407E               158            DC      CL10'TOTAL   ='                          55-64   TOTAL  =  (FOR INFO)
     000278                                159   TOTAL    DS      CL10                                    65-74   TOTAL ENROLLMENT
     000282 4040404040404040               160            DC      CL58' '                                 75-132 BLANKS
                                           161   *
                                           162   * HEADING LINE
                                           163   *
     0002BC                                164   HEADING  DS      0CL132                               DEFINITION OF HEADING LINE ...
     0002BC 4040404040404040               165            DC      CL10' '                              COLS 1-10   BLANKS
     0002C6 40C94BC44B40                   166            DC      CL6' I.D.'                              11-16   I.D. HEADING
     0002CC 404040                         167            DC      CL3' '                                  17-19   BLANKS
     0002CF 40C3D6E4D9E2C540               168            DC      CL41' COURSE NAME'                       20-60   COURSE NAME HEADING
     0002F8 404040                         169            DC      CL4' '                                  61-64   BLANKS
     0002FC C5D5D9D6D3D3D4C5               170            DC      CL10'ENROLLMENT'                         65-74   ENROLLMENT HEADING
     000306 4040404040404040               171            DC      CL58' '                                 75-132 BLANKS
                                           172   *
                                           173   *
                                           174   * DCB'S FOR INPUT AND OUTPUT FILES
                                           175   *
     000340                                176   SYSIN    DCB     DSORG=PS,MACRF=(GM),DDNAME=SYSIN,EODAD=EOD,              X
                                           177                    RECFM=FB,LRECL=80,BLKSIZE=4080
                                           229   *
     0003A0                                230   SYSPRNT  DCB     DSORG=PS,MACRF=(PM),DDNAME=SYSPRINT,                     X
                                           231                    RECFM=FB,LRECL=132,BLKSIZE=4092

                                           283   * DOS  *******
                                           284   *SYSIN   DTFCD DEVADDR=SYSIPT,WORKA=YES,IOAREA1=INBUF,EOFADDR=EOD,       X
                                           285                  DEVICE=2540
                                           286   *SYSPRNT DTFPR DEVADDR=SYSLST,WORKA=YES,IOAREA1=OUTBUF,BLKSIZE=132,      X
                                           287   *              DEVICE=1403
                                           288   *
                                           289   *INBUF   DS      CL80
                                           290   *OUTBUF  DC      CL132' '
                                           291   ***************

                                           292   *
                                           293   * SAVE AREA
                                           294   *
     000400                                295   SAVE     DS      18F

                                           296   * DOS  *******
                                           297   *SAVE    DS      9D
                                           298   ***************

                                           299   * LITERALS
     000448 00000000                       301                    =F'0'
                                           302            END
```

Figure 4.7b   *continued*

```
                              CROSS-REFERENCE


         SYMBOL    LEN   VALUE  DEFN    REFERENCES


         BCD       00008 000000 00128   00067  00068  00092  00093
         BINARY    00004 0000D8 00129   00069  00072
         BLANKS    00084 0001B4 00151   00087
         DATA      0000A 000116 00139   00067
         ENROLLED  00004 0000DC 00130   00025  00071  00073  00091
         EOD       00004 00007C 00086   00198
         HEADING   00084 0002BC 00164   00050
         ID        00006 0000E0 00135
         INAREA    00050 0000E0 00134   00063  00075
         LOOP      00004 00003C 00062   00081
         NAME      00029 0000E9 00137
         OUTAREA   00084 000130 00144   00078
         OUTLINE   00050 00013A 00146   00075
         SAVE      00004 000400 00295   00019  00020  00116
         SPCH4     00001 000000 00003
         SYSIN     00004 000340 00177   00033  00062  00108
         SYSPRNT   00004 0003A0 00231   00039  00049  00077  00086  00097  00114
         TOTAL     0000A 000278 00159   00093  00094
         TOTALS    00084 000238 00156   00098
```

1. What is the main advantage gained by storing the elements of an array in consecutive locations in memory?

2. Suppose that in Figure 4.4, Statement 6,

```
LA   5,4(5)
```

is replaced by this statement:

```
LA   5,8(5)
```

What would be the effect on the computations at run time?

3. Assume that for the statements shown in Figure 4.4, the following conditions are true:

$$\begin{aligned}
&\text{base address} = 00006\\
&\text{base register} = 12\\
&\text{symbolic address LOOP} = 500_x\\
&\text{symbolic address N} = 800_x
\end{aligned}$$

Using the values of the symbolic addresses for X, Y, and Z given in Figure 4.3, what is the machine language representation of the instructions given in Figure 4.4?

4. Show how to change the program segment of Figure 4.4 so that instead of computing $Z_j = X_j + Y_j$ for $J = 1,2,...,N$, it computes $Z_j = X_j + 8$.

5. Show how to change the program segment of Figure 4.4 so that instead of computing $Z_j = X_j + Y_j$ for $J = 1,2,...,N$, it computes $Z_j = X_j + Y_j$ for $J = 2,4,...,N$ (assume that N is an even number).

6. Show how to change the program segment of Figure 4.4 so that instead of computing $Z_j = X_j + Y_j$ for $J = 1,2,...,N$, it computes $Z_j = X_j + Y_j$ for $J = N, N-1, N-2,...,1$. Do this using the same register for both the loop-control variable and the array index.

7. Suppose there are fifty input records, each with a positive integer in columns 1–10 (right-justified). Write an assembly language program that will read the fifty integers into an array and then print them in the reverse order from that in which they were read.

8. Use the same input data as in Exercise 7. Write an assembly language program that will print them two per line as follows: the first and twenty-sixth integers on the first line, the second and twenty-seventh on the second line, and so on up to the twenty-fifth and fiftieth on the last line.

9. Write an assembly language program that will print the positive integers $+1, +2,..., +9, +10$ and the negative integers $-1, -2,..., -10$. The integers should be converted to character form by just three instructions similar to these:

```
L      5,Z
CVD    5,BCD
UNPK   SUM,BCD
```

The OI instruction given in Section 4.3 has been omitted so that you can observe the effect of the UNPK instruction on the low-order digit of positive and negative integers. Note that, as in Section 4.3, the symbolic address SUM is the address of the integer in its character form, ready for printing; and the symbolic address Z is the address of the integer in its 32-bit binary form.

10. Repeat Exercise 9, except that the conversions from binary integer to character form should be done by these four instructions for both the positive and the negative integers:

```
        L       5,Z
        CVD     5,BCD
        UNPK    SUM,BCD
        OI      SUM+9,X'F0'
```

The purpose of including the OI instruction for negative as well as positive integers is to demonstrate its effect: it eliminates the code used for the sign in the low-order digit position. From the table of EBCDIC characters given in Appendix F, we can see what is happening: the code used to represent a $+1$ is changed from 1100 0001 (the letter A) to 1111 0001 (the digit 1); the code used to represent a -1 is changed from 1101 0001 (the letter J) to 1111 0001; and similarly for the other codes. The OI instruction performs the Boolean "or" function and is described in Section 8.2.

11. The following eight instructions can be used to convert a 32-bit binary integer to its representation as a decimal integer in EBCDIC character form. The sign is represented by a blank if the integer is positive or zero and by a dash (the familiar minus sign) if the integer is negative. Ten bytes are used for the character representation: the left-most byte is used for the sign, and the remaining 9 bytes for the digits. Zeroes are not suppressed. The notation is the same as that given in Section 4.3.

```
* CONVERT FROM BINARY TO EBCDIC
          L      5,Z          COPY AN INTEGER INTO REGISTER 5.
          CVD    5,BCD        CONVERT TO BINARY-CODED DECIMAL.
          UNPK   SUM,BCD      CONVERT THAT TO EBCDIC (10 BYTES).
          MVI    SUM,X'40'    ASSUME IT'S NONNEG, AND PUT BLANK
          LTR    5,5          (X'40') IN 1ST POSITION. THEN TEST:
          BNM    NONNEG       IF NONNEGATIVE, LEAVE SIGN BLANK.
          MVI    SUM,X'60'    IF NEGATIVE, PUT DASH (X'60') IN.
NONNEG    OI     SUM+9,X'F0'  ELIMINATE SIGN IN LO-ORDER DIGIT.
```

Repeat Exercise 9, using these eight instructions to convert each integer. The LTR and BNM instructions are discussed in Section 5.4; they enable the sign of the integer to be determined. The MVI instruction is discussed in Chapter 7, Section 7.2; it copies 1 byte from its immediate data field into the byte whose address is given in its first operand.

12. The following six instructions can be used to convert a decimal integer from its 10-byte EBCDIC representation to its 32-bit binary integer representation. If the decimal integer is positive or zero, its sign must be represented by a blank in the left-most character position. If the integer is negative, its sign must be represented by a dash (the minus sign) in the left-most character position. Leading zeroes may be present or suppressed. The notation is the same as that given in Section 4.4.

```
* CONVERT FROM EBCDIC TO BINARY
          PACK   BCD,INT      CONVERT EBCDIC TO BINARY-CODED DECIMAL.
          CVB    5,BCD        CONVERT THAT TO 32-BIT BINARY INTEGER.
          CLI    INT,X'60'    SEE IF LEFT-MOST BYTE WAS A DASH (X'60').
          BNE    NODASH       IF NOT, ACCEPT SIGN AS CONVERTED.
          LNR    5,5          IF SO, FORCE INTEGER TO BE NEGATIVE.
NODASH    ST     5,X          STORE 32-BIT INTEGER.
```

Write an assembly language program that will read exactly five input records, each containing an integer in columns 1–10 in the format described. Use the above six instructions to convert them to 32-bit binary representation, and compute their sum. Print the sum after converting it to EBCDIC with the instructions from Exercise 11.

> **NOTE:** See Appendix G for an alternative method of converting signed and unsigned integers between the EBCDIC character representation and full-word binary integer representation. With the alternative method, you will only need one statement for each conversion. The macro definitions given in Appendix G must be either in your source module or in a "macro library" accessible to the assembler.

5

Integer Arithmetic

The term **integer arithmetic** includes several types of instructions that operate on full-word and half-word binary numbers: copying data into and out of a register; addition, subtraction, multiplication, and division of two binary integers; changing sign, and generating the absolute value of a binary integer; testing for a positive, negative, or zero numeric result; and comparing two binary integers algebraically. The reason for emphasizing the word **binary** is that there are two other types of numeric data: packed-decimal numbers and floating-point numbers. Each of these requires its own set of arithmetic instructions, different from those required for binary integers. Packed-decimal arithmetic will be discussed in Chapter 12, floating-point arithmetic in Chapter 13.

See Summary in Figure 5.12

There are two general characteristics of the binary integer arithmetic instructions:

1. Almost all the instructions operate on two integers. One of the integers must be in a register, and the other must be either in a register or in memory, depending on the instruction. The instructions that require that both integers being operated on be in registers are recognizable by their opcodes, which end in the letter *R:* AR, SR, MR, DR, CR.

General Characteristics

2. On the IBM 360, almost all the instructions require that the data that are in memory be aligned on full-word boundaries when being operated on. Those that don't require full-word alignment require half-word alignment. The latter are all recognizable by their opcodes, which end in the letter *H:* LH, STH, AH, SH, MH, CH. On the IBM 370, neither full-word nor half-word alignment is necessary; byte alignment is all that is required. However, the 370's performance may be degraded if the data are not aligned the way they must be on the 360.

Section 5.1 discusses the method used to represent binary integers in the IBM 360 and 370 systems. This is followed by several sections that describe the various instructions that operate on integers and two sections (5.7 and 5.8) of examples that illustrate how these instructions can be used in programs. It should be noted that although we are restricting our discussions to integers, the instructions described in this chapter can be used to process numbers other than integers, i.e., mixed numbers. To do so, the mixed numbers must be represented as integers, with an implied but fixed position of the decimal point. For this reason, the more general term used for the instructions described in this chapter is **fixed-point arithmetic.** A brief summary of the methods of using binary integers to represent mixed numbers is given in Chapter 11.

5.1 TWO'S COMPLEMENT ARITHMETIC

Representation of Binary Integers

Using the notation of Chapter 1, we will let b_n represent the nth bit in a binary integer, so that each integer can be represented as $b_0b_1b_2...b_{k-1}$, where b_0 is used to designate the sign bit: $b_0 = 0$ for positive integers and $b_0 = 1$ for negative integers. The number of bits, k, determines the maximum value that a binary integer may have in a computer: $(2^{k-1} - 1)$. In the IBM 360 and 370 systems, k may be either 32 or 16; the former are full-word integers, the latter are half-word integers. Without loss of generality we will write $b_0b_1b_2...b_{k-1}$ for the binary representation of an integer and understand that k is the same for all integers being discussed.

Two main methods are used for the representation of integers in computer systems. One is known as the sign-magnitude form, the other as the two's complement form. The two's complement form, which has certain advantages over the sign-magnitude form, is used in the IBM 360 and 370 systems.

In the sign-magnitude form, bits b_1 through b_{k-1} represent the absolute value, or magnitude, of the integer, and bit b_0 represents the sign. To illustrate, we take $k = 4$ for simplicity; then 2^4 integers can be represented as follows:

Sign-Magnitude Form

decimal	binary	decimal	binary
+0	0000	−0	1000
+1	0001	−1	1001
+2	0010	−2	1010
+3	0011	−3	1011
+4	0100	−4	1100
+5	0101	−5	1101
+6	0110	−6	1110
+7	0111	−7	1111

The value of each integer $b_0b_1b_2b_3$ can be computed as

$$(1 - 2b_0) \times \{b_1 \times 2^2 + b_2 \times 2^1 + b_3 \times 2^0\}$$

For example, $1101_2 = (1 - 2 \times 1) \times \{1 \times 2^2 + 0 \times 2^1 + 1 \times 2^0\} = -1 \times \{4 + 1\} = -5_{10}$.

To perform arithmetic on two integers that are in sign-magnitude form, we must process the sign bit in a separate manner from the magnitude bits. In *addition,* we must determine whether the signs of the two integers are the same or different and proceed according to the rules of algebra. In *subtraction,* we change the sign of the second factor, and then proceed as in addition. In both addition and subtraction, the result may be too large to be represented in k bits. This is known as **overflow** and causes an erroneous result. For example, with $k = 4$

Overflow

decimal	binary	
4	0100	no overflow:
+ (−5)	+ 1101	the smaller magnitude is subtracted
−1	1001	from the larger when the signs are not the same
−4	1100	
+ (−5)	+ 1101	
−9	1001	overflow:
		the carry out of the high-order digit
		is lost, and the result is in error

Of course, a larger value than $k = 4$ is usually used, but overflow always occurs when an attempt is made to generate a result whose magnitude exceeds $(2^{k-1} - 1)$, whatever value is used for k. However, the disadvantages of using sign-magnitude form do not lie in the problem of overflow. The main disadvantages are the need to process the sign bit separately and the need to determine which of the two factors in additions and subtractions is larger when their signs are different. Another, but lesser, disadvantage is that the number 0 is represented in two forms, $+0$ and -0. *The use of the two's complement form eliminates all these problems except that of overflow.* The overflow problem is inherent in all methods that use a fixed number of bits to represent an integer.

In two's complement form, the leading bit is still used for the sign, but it participates in arithmetic operations as though it represented the value $-b_0 \times 2^{k-1}$. The remaining bits represent the magnitude of nonnegative integers, as is done in the sign-magnitude form. But the negative form of an integer is obtained by reversing the value of each bit and adding $+1$ to the result. The process of bit reversal—0 becomes 1, and 1 becomes 0—is known as **complementing the bit.** The maximum positive value that can be represented is $2^{k-1} - 1$; the minimum negative value is -2^{k-1}. The number zero is always represented with its sign bit $b_0 = 0$.

Two's Complement Sign Bit

For example, with $k = 4$, the largest positive integer is $2^3 - 1 = 7$, and the smallest negative integer is $-2^3 = -8$. The integers 0 through 7 are represented as in sign-magnitude format:

decimal	binary
0	0000
$+1$	0001
$+2$	0010
$+3$	0011
$+4$	0100
$+5$	0101
$+6$	0110
$+7$	0111

Four-Bit Two's Complement for Nonnegative Integers

The representations of the negative integers -1 through -7 are obtained by complementing the positive binary integers, and adding $+1$ as shown here:

integer	0001	0010	0011	...	0110	0111
complement	1110	1101	1100	...	1001	1000
$+1$	$+$ 0001	$+$ 0001	$+$ 0001	...	$+$ 0001	$+$ 0001
result:	1111	$+$ 1110	1101	...	1010	1001

The remaining 4-bit representation, 1000, is -8, since the sign bit in general must represent the value $-b_0 \times 2^{k-1}$. The negative integers, therefore, are represented as

decimal	binary
-1	1111
-2	1110
-3	1101
-4	1100
-5	1011
-6	1010
-7	1001
-8	1000

Four-Bit Two's Complement for Negative Integers

The value of each positive or negative (or zero) integer $b_0 b_1 b_2 b_3$ can be computed as

$$-b_0 \times 2^3 + b_1 \times 2^2 + b_2 \times 2^1 + b_3 \times 2^0$$

For example, $1011_2 = -1 \times 2^3 + 0 \times 2^2 + 1 \times 2^1 + 1 \times 2^0 = -8 + 2 + 1 = -5_{10}$.

It should be noted that the negative of a negative integer is represented properly by the above method, except that $+8$, i.e., $-(-8)$, cannot be represented in 4 bits.

For integers represented by k bits, $b_0 b_1 b_2 ... b_{k-1}$, the methods illustrated above are essentially the same. The value of a k-bit integer is computed as

$$J = -b_0 \times 2^{k-1} + b_1 \times 2^{k-2} + ... + b_{k-2} \times 2^1 + b_{k-1} \times 2^0$$

Figure 5.1 *Two's complement integers in IBM 360 and 370 systems.*

	full-word integers		half-word integers
-2^{31}:	1000 0000 0000 0000 0000 0000 0000 0000		
$-2^{31} + 1$:	1000 0000 0000 0000 0000 0000 0000 0001		
$-2^{31} + 2$:	1000 0000 0000 0000 0000 0000 0000 0010	-2^{15}:	1000 0000 0000 0000
	... ...	$-2^{15} + 1$:	1000 0000 0000 0001
-2:	1111 1111 1111 1111 1111 1111 1111 1110		...
-1:	1111 1111 1111 1111 1111 1111 1111 1111	-1:	1111 1111 1111 1111
0:	0000 0000 0000 0000 0000 0000 0000 0000	0:	0000 0000 0000 0000
$+1$:	0000 0000 0000 0000 0000 0000 0000 0001	$+1$:	0000 0000 0000 0001
$+2$:	0000 0000 0000 0000 0000 0000 0000 0010		...
	... ...	$2^{15} - 2$:	0111 1111 1111 1110
$2^{31} - 2$:	0111 1111 1111 1111 1111 1111 1111 1110	$2^{15} - 1$:	0111 1111 1111 1111
$2^{31} - 1$:	0111 1111 1111 1111 1111 1111 1111 1111		

When the integer is positive, then $b_0 = 0$, and this reduces to the familiar expression for evaluating positive integers. When the integer is negative in two's complement form, the previous expression for J also gives its value, for $-J$ is then positive, and

$$-J = +b_0 \times 2^{k-1} - b_1 \times 2^{k-2} - ... - b_{k-2} \times 2^1 - b_{k-1} \times 2^0$$

But by writing $-J = (2^{k-1} - J) - 2^{k-1}$, and noting that

$$2^{k-1} = 1 + 2^{k-2} + 2^{k-3} + ... + 2^1 + 2^0$$

the expression for $-J$ can be rewritten as

$$-J = 1 + \{-(1-b_0) \times 2^{k-1} + (1-b_1) \times 2^{k-2} + ... + (1-b_{k-1}) \times 2^0\}$$

The value within braces $\{...\}$ is the value of the bit-for-bit complement of the representation we started with, $b_0 b_1 b_2 ... b_{k-1}$. Consequently, the expression for $-J$ represents the algorithm previously given for computing the two's complement, and the expression for J is therefore valid for evaluating both positive and negative k-bit integers represented in two's complement form.

The name *two's complement* is due to the fact that the negative of a k-bit integer $b_0 b_1 b_2 ... b_{k-1}$ is the representation obtained by subtracting the $(k+1)$-bit integer $0 b_0 b_1 b_2 ... b_{k-1}$ from 2^k, as can be readily verified. For this reason, the name *two's complement* is also often used to designate the representation of a negative integer.

In the IBM 360 and 370 systems, the range of numbers that can be represented as full-word integers ($k = 32$) is from -2^{31} through $2^{31} - 1$; that for half-word integers ($k = 16$) is from -2^{15} through $2^{15} - 1$. This is illustrated in Figure 5.1.

Clearly, all the integers that can be represented in a half word can also be represented in a full word. Moreover, *a half-word representation is converted to the full-word representation of the same integer by copying its sign into each of the 16 high-order bits of the full word, and copying the low-order bits of the half word, one by one, into the corresponding low-order bits of the full word.* For example:

Half Word to Full Word

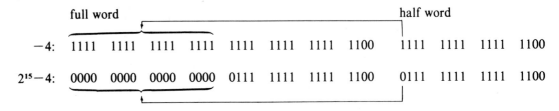

Fundamental Techniques

The reason that the sign bit must be copied, or **propagated,** in this manner is that the additional bits must contribute a net value of zero to the value of the integer, while the new high-order bit must become the sign bit. In general, to change from an m-bit representation $b_0b_1b_2...b_{m-1}$ to an equivalent k-bit representation with $k > m$, the new form is

$$\underbrace{b_0b_0b_0...b_0b_0b_1b_2...b_{m-1}}$$
$$\uparrow\!\;\;\;\;\;\; k-m \text{ bits}$$

The value of the new representation may be computed as $J = K + L$, where L is the value of the low-order m bits

$$L = b_0 \times 2^{m-1} + b_1 \times 2^{m-2} + ... + b_{m-1} \times 2^0$$

and K is the value of the $k-m$ high-order bits

$$K = b_0 \times \{-2^{k-1} + 2^{k-2} + ... + 2^{m+1} + 2^m\}$$

The value contributed by the term in braces $\{...\}$ is -2^m, so that

$$J = K + L = -b_0 \times (2^m - 2^{m-1}) + b_1 \times 2^{m-2} + ... + b_{m-1} \times 2^0$$
$$= -b_0 \times 2^{m-1} + b_1 \times 2^{m-2} + ... + b_{m-1} \times 2^0$$

Since this is just the value of the original m-bit integer $b_0b_1b_2...b_{m-1}$, the propagation of the sign bit has not altered that value.

Integer Arithmetic

When integers are represented in two's complement form, the operations of addition, subtraction, multiplication, and division are much simpler than when sign-magnitude form is used. All bits participate in the arithmetic. The sign bit contributes a value of $-b_0 \times 2^{k-1}$, and the remaining bits contribute values $b_j \times 2^{k-j-1}$ for $j = 1,2,...,k-1$. Except when overflow occurs, the sign of the result is algebraically correct. We will illustrate how arithmetic is performed with $k = 4$, since the methods carry over without change for larger values of k.

Addition and Subtraction

When adding or subtracting two 4-bit integers, the result must be a 4-bit integer. If the value of the result exceeds $2^3 - 1$ or is less than -2^3, it cannot be represented in 4 bits. This situation is known as **overflow,** and the 4-bit representation of the result is incorrect. As examples of the addition and subtraction processes, we have

$+6$	0110	-6	1010	$+5$	0101	-5	1011
$+ (+1)$	0001	$+ (-1)$	1111	$+ (+6)$	0110	$+ (-6)$	1010
	0111		1 1001		0 1011		1 0100
	no overflow		no overflow		overflow		overflow

Note that in all cases the sum is computed as though these were unsigned 4-bit integers, and the carries into and out of the sign bit position are examined to determine whether there is overflow. The rule for determining overflow is this: *if the carry into the sign bit from position b_1 is different from the carry out of the sign bit position, then there is overflow.* Otherwise, there is no overflow. When two negative numbers cause overflow, the resulting representation is positive; when two positive numbers cause overflow, the result is negative. Addition of two numbers with opposite signs cannot cause overflow.

That the carry rule detects overflow situations correctly depends in part on the fact that the sum of two binary digits can at most produce a carry of 1. This can occur only when both digits are 1's, or when at least one of them is 1 and a carry from the previous digit is added to their sum: $1 + 0 + \text{(carry)} = 10$, $1 + 1 + \text{(carry)} = 11$. The rule also depends on two other properties of binary integers that are represented in two's complement form: (1) If P is positive, then its high-order numeric bit b_1 is a 1 if and only if $P \geq \frac{1}{2}(2^{k-1} - 1)$; (2) if N is negative, then its high-order numeric bit b_1 is a 1 if and only if $N \geq -\frac{1}{2}(2^{k-1})$.

Using these properties, the correctness of the carry rule can be demonstrated by considering the three cases cited below.

Case 1. Adding two positive integers, P_1 and P_2

Since the sign bits in both integers are both 0's, there can be no carry out of b_0. Moreover, there is a carry out of b_1 if and only if $P_1 + P_2 > (2^{k-1} - 1)$.

Case 2. Adding two negative integers, N_1 and N_2

Since the sign bits in both integers are both 1's, there will always be a carry out of b_0. Moreover, there is a carry out of b_1 if and only if $N_1 + N_2 \geq -(2^{k-1})$.

Case 3. Adding a positive integer, P, and a negative integer, N

Since the sum must always be correctly representable in k-bit two's complement form, the sign of the sum must be the same as the sign of whichever integer is larger in magnitude. But since the sign bit of P is a 0 and that of N is a 1, the sign of the sum will be negative if there is no carry out of b_1 (and thus no carry out of the sign bit) and positive if there is a carry out of b_1 (and thus also a carry out of the sign bit).

Multiplication

In multiplication of two integers, the product may contain more significant bits than either of the two factors. The largest possible product of two k-bit integers is $(-2^{k-1}) \times (-2^{k-1}) = 2^{2k-2}$, which requires $2k - 1$ bits. To allow for this, most computers generate a $2k$-bit product when multiplying k-bit integers. In doing so, each of the two factors is considered to be extended on the left with as many copies of the sign bit as are needed to generate the $2k$-bit product. As demonstrated earlier, this does not change the value of either factor. Since there can be no overflow when a $2k$-bit product is generated, the correct representation for the product is assured.

For $k = 4$, we illustrate the above concepts with the following examples:

$$
\begin{array}{rl}
+6 & 0110 \\
\times\,(+2) & \underline{0010} \\
& 0000\ 1100 \\
& \underbrace{} \\
& +12
\end{array}
\qquad
\begin{array}{rl}
+6 & 0110 \\
\times\,(-2) & \underline{1110} \\
& 1111\ 0100 \\
& \underbrace{} \\
& -12
\end{array}
\qquad
\begin{array}{rl}
-3 & 1101 \\
\times\,(+6) & \underline{0110} \\
& 1110\ 1110 \\
& \underbrace{} \\
& -18
\end{array}
\qquad
\begin{array}{rl}
-3 & 1101 \\
\times\,(-6) & \underline{1010} \\
& 0001\ 0010 \\
& \underbrace{} \\
& +18
\end{array}
$$

To verify that these are the correct 8-bit representations of the products, we can carry out the multiplications by hand rather easily, since the multiplication table is simply $1 \times 1 = 1$, $1 \times 0 = 0 \times 1 = 0 \times 0 = 0$. But since the sign bit b_0 participates in k-bit arithmetic operations as though it represented the value $-b_0 \times 2^{k-1}$, then with $k = 4$ the sign bit represents the value -2^3, i.e., -8. To account for this in 4-bit hand calculations, we must propagate the sign bit four positions to the left before doing the calculations. For example:

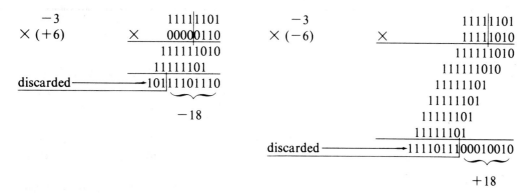

$$\begin{array}{r} -3 \\ \times\,(+6) \end{array} \qquad \begin{array}{r} 1111|1101 \\ \times \quad 00000110 \\ \hline 11111010 \\ 11111101 \\ \hline \end{array}$$

discarded ————→ 101|11101110

−18

$$\begin{array}{r} -3 \\ \times\,(-6) \end{array} \qquad \begin{array}{r} 1111|1101 \\ \times \quad 1111|1010 \\ \hline 11111010 \\ 111111010 \\ 11111101 \\ 11111101 \\ 11111101 \\ 11111101 \\ \hline \end{array}$$

discarded ————→ 1111011|00010010

+18

It should be noted that even though a $2k$-bit product is generated, there might be only k or fewer significant bits in the product. There are, of course, not many situations in which this can occur when $k = 4$, but, for larger k, products will often be developed containing fewer than k significant bits. This means that the product can still be represented in the same fixed number of bits used for other integers, a decided advantage when programming. If $k = 8$, then all products in the range from -128 through $+127$ can be represented in 8 bits; if $k = 16$, the range is $-32,768$ through $+32,767$; and if $k = 32$, the range is $-2,147,483,648$ through $2,147,483,647$, i.e., -2^{31} through $2^{31} - 1$.

In the IBM 360 and 370, we can multiply two 32-bit integers and obtain a 64-bit product, using either of two instructions designed for this purpose. There is also an instruction for multiplying two 16-bit integers to produce a 32-bit product, but one of the factors must first be extended to 32 bits. We shall see how this is done when the multiply instructions are discussed later in this chapter.

Division

Turning to division, we note that the result of dividing two integers K and L can be written as

$$\frac{K}{L} = Q + \frac{R}{L}$$

where the quotient, Q, and the remainder, R, are both integers. For example, in decimal arithmetic

$$\frac{7}{4} = 1 + \frac{3}{4}$$

and the same division problem could be represented in 4-bit notation as

$$\begin{array}{r} 0001 \longleftarrow \text{ integer quotient } Q \\ 0100\overline{)\ 0111} \\ 0100 \\ \hline 0011 \longleftarrow \text{ integer remainder } R \end{array}$$

However, in two's complement arithmetic division of two k-bit integers, we cannot in general develop a k-bit quotient and a k-bit remainder. What is required is that the dividend, K, be represented by $2k$ bits. The following examples illustrate this for $K = -7$, $L = 4$, and $k = 4$.

$$\begin{array}{r} 0001 \longleftarrow Q \neq -1 \\ 0100\overline{)\ 1001} \\ 0100 \\ \hline 0101 \longleftarrow R \neq -3 \end{array}$$

only k bits are retained after each intermediate calculation

$$\begin{array}{r} 1111 \longleftarrow Q = -1 \\ 0100\overline{)\ 11111001} \\ 0100 \\ \hline 10110 \\ 0100 \\ \hline 00100 \\ 0100 \\ \hline 00001 \\ 0100 \\ \hline 1101 \longleftarrow R = -3 \end{array}$$

The quotient is represented in 4 bits (in general, in k bits) with its proper algebraic sign. The remainder is also a k-bit integer; its sign is the same as that of the dividend. It should be noted that it is possible to generate a quotient that is too large to be represented in k bits. This will occur if the original k-bit dividend is -2^{k-1} and the divisor is -1; in this situation the quotient $+2^{k-1}$ could not be represented in k bits. It could also occur in other situations, since the dividend that is used in the division process is $2k$ bits, while the divisor is only k bits.

In the IBM 360 and 370 systems, we can divide a 64-bit dividend by a 32-bit divisor, using either of two instructions designed for this purpose. These instructions will be described later in this chapter.

5.2 COPYING DATA TO AND FROM A REGISTER

Since almost all the instructions considered in this chapter require that the data be in a register in order to be operated on, it is necessary to use instructions that copy data into a register prior to performing the desired arithmetic operations and to use instructions that copy the results from the register into memory after the operations are completed.

To copy data into a register, we use a *LOAD* instruction. To copy data out of a register, we use a *STORE* instruction.

The LOAD instructions are

opcode	meaning	type
L	copy a full word from memory into a register	RX
LH	copy a half word from memory into a register	RX
LM	copy from 1 to 16 consecutive full words from consecutive memory locations into consecutively numbered registers	RS
LR	copy a full word from one register into another	RR

Since the half-word LOAD instruction (LH) copies a half word (2 bytes) from memory into a full-word area—a register—its effect is slightly different from the other LOAD instructions. The same applies to the half-word STORE instruction (STH). The differences will be illustrated in Examples 3a, 3b, and 4.

The STORE instructions are

opcode	meaning	type
ST	copy a full word from a register into memory	RX
STH	copy a half word from a register into memory	RX
STM	copy from 1 to 16 full words from consecutively numbered registers into consecutive memory locations	RS

From these two lists, it can be seen that, with one exception, the LOAD and STORE instructions are paired. The exception is LR, for which a counterpart STORE instruction would be meaningless. The pairings are

$$\left.\begin{array}{l} \text{L} \\ \text{ST} \end{array}\right\} \text{ copy a full word}$$

$$\left.\begin{array}{l} \text{LH} \\ \text{STH} \end{array}\right\} \text{ copy a half word}$$

$$\left.\begin{array}{l} \text{LM} \\ \text{STM} \end{array}\right\} \text{ copy from 1 to 16 consecutive full words}$$

In each LOAD and STORE instruction, the operand field that designates where the data are copied *from* is called the **source operand.** The field that designates where the data are copied *to* is called the **destination operand.** Data from the source always replace the data that existed at the destination. But the source data itself is not changed when one of these instructions is executed.

In summary, three instructions copy data from memory to a register, three corresponding instructions copy data from a register to memory, and one instruction copies data from register to register. This is illustrated in the following table and in Examples 1 through 7.

instruction	operand	source field	destination field
L	R1,D2(X2,B2)	D2(X2,B2)	R1
LH	R1,D2(X2,B2)	D2(X2,B2)	R1
LM	R1,R2,D3(B3)	D3(B3)	R1 thru R2
ST	R1,D2(X2,B2)	R1	D2(X2,B2)
STH	R1,D2(X2,B2)	R1	D2(X2,B2)
STM	R1,R2,D3(B3)	R1 thru R2	D3(B3)
LR	R1,R2	R2	R1

In the examples, the data that exist at the source and destination are shown in hexadecimal notation with values that are assumed to exist *before* the instruction is executed, and with the values that would exist *after* the instruction is executed. The examples are not related to one another, except that the address represented by the symbol A is assumed to be 1000 (in hex) in each example.

Example 1.

				Register 3		memory address 1000
L	3,A	{	before execution:	0246	0357	0001 0010
			after execution:	0001	0010	0001 0010

Example 2.

				Register 4		memory address 1000
ST	4,A	{	before execution:	0123	0456	0ABC 0DEF
			after execution:	0123	0456	0123 0456

Example 3a.

Load Positive Half Word

				Register 5		memory address 1000
LH	5,A	{	before execution:	0159	0260	4321
			after execution:	0000	4321	4321

Note that although only a half word is loaded into Register 5, the entire content of that register is replaced. The half word is loaded into the right-hand half of the register—the so-called *low-order* half of the register—and the left-hand half of the register is replaced by all zeroes. (However, see the next example.)

Example 3b.

Load Negative Half Word

				Register 5		memory address 1000
LH	5,A	{	before execution:	0159	0260	9876
			after execution:	FFFF	9876	9876

As in Example 3a, a half word is loaded into the low-order (right-hand) half of Register 5, but the left-hand half is replaced by all F's (not zeroes as in Example 3a). The rule for the left-hand portion of the register, whenever the LH is used, is: The sign bit of the half word that is loaded is *copied into each bit* of the left-hand portion of the register. This is called propagating the sign bit to the left.

In the hexadecimal number 4321 = 0100 0011 0010 0001, the sign bit is 0, so 4321 is extended to the full-word integer 00004321.

In the hexadecimal number 9876 = 1001 1000 0111 0110, the sign bit is 1, so 9876 is extended to the full-word integer FFFF9876.

This rule for the LH instruction guarantees that a half-word integer's sign and value will be the same in a 32-bit representation as it is in a 16-bit representation.

Example 4.

Store Half Word

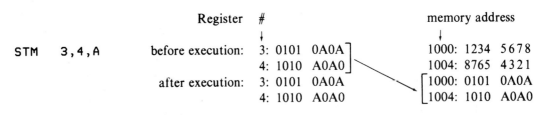

		Register 6	memory address 1000
STH 6,A	before execution:	0123 0246	0ABC
	after execution:	0123 0246	0246

Note that only the low-order 16-bits are copied from a register by the STH instruction.

Example 5.

Load Three Consecutive Full Words

		Register #	memory address
LM 2,4,A	before execution:	2: 0000 1 2 3 4	1000: 0001 ABCD
		3: 0000 3 4 5 6	1004: 0002 BCDE
		4: 0000 5 6 7 8	1008: 0003 CDEF
	after execution:	2: 0001 ABCD	1000: 0001 ABCD
		3: 0002 BCDE	1004: 0002 BCDE
		4: 0003 CDEF	1008: 0003 CDEF

In the LM instruction, the destination is registers R1 thru R2 inclusive. Here, R1 = 2, and R2 = 4.

Example 6.

		Register #	memory address
STM 3,4,A	before execution:	3: 0101 0A0A	1000: 1234 5678
		4: 1010 A0A0	1004: 8765 4321
	after execution:	3: 0101 0A0A	1000: 0101 0A0A
		4: 1010 A0A0	1004: 1010 A0A0

Example 7.

		Reg 3	Reg 4
LR 3,4	before execution:	ABCD EF00	1234 5678
	after execution:	1 2 3 4 5678	1234 5678

Recall that in all LOAD instructions, the source is the second operand; the destination is the first operand. Thus, in this example, the number in Register 4 is copied into Register 3.

The instructions for these four operations all operate on two binary integers; therefore they all require two operand fields. The number that is addressed by the second operand field is combined with the number addressed by the first field. **The result replaces the number addressed by the first field.**

In the descriptions that follow, we will use this notation:

V_1 = the number whose address is specified by the *first* operand field of the instruction
V_2 = the number whose address is specified by the *second* operand field of the instruction

Addition

There are five binary integer addition instructions: A, AL, AR, ALR, and AH.

opcode	meaning	type
A	ADD	RX
AL	ADD LOGICAL	RX
	Both A and AL add the full word V_2 to the full word V_1. V_2 is in memory, V_1 in a register. The result replaces V_1. The distinction between A and AL is discussed below.	
AR	ADD REGISTERS	RR
ALR	ADD LOGICAL REGISTERS	RR
	Both AR and ALR add the full word V_2 to the full word V_1. V_1 and V_2 are in registers. The result replaces V_1. The distinction between AR and ALR is discussed below.	
AH	ADD HALF WORD	RX
	Adds half word V_2 to full word V_1. V_2 is in memory, V_1 in a register. The result, a full word, replaces V_1.	

The result of an A, AR, and AH instruction is a 32-bit integer. If there is no overflow, i.e., if the sum is within the range from -2^{31} though $2^{31}-1$, the sum is correctly represented as a positive, negative, or zero quantity. However, if an overflow occurs during an addition, the 32-bit result cannot and does not represent the true sum. Remember that in two's complement addition, overflow occurs if the carry out of the sign bit position is different from the carry out of the high-order numeric bit position.

When an overflow occurs during an A, AR, or AH instruction, execution of the program may be interrupted by the hardware, and the program may be terminated by the operating system. The only way to prevent such a hardware interruption is by means of the program mask, a capability of the IBM 360 and 370 systems that will be discussed further in Chapter 11.

In the AL and ALR instructions, the quantities V_1, V_2, and $V_1 + V_2$ are treated as *unsigned* 32-bit integers. Thus bit b_0 of each quantity is not a sign bit; instead, it is the high-order numeric bit, with positional value $b_0 \times 2^{32}$. When an overflow occurs during an AL or ALR instruction, execution of the program is not interrupted by the hardware. Instead, execution proceeds with the next instruction in the program.

A hardware indicator known as the **condition code** records the nature of the result of all five add instructions. The meaning of the condition code that is recorded depends on which add instruction was executed, as shown in the following table:

	condition code and its meaning			
instruction	0	1	2	3
A,AR,AH	result was zero	result was negative	result was positive	overflow occurred
AL,ALR	result was zero with no carry out of the sign bit position	result was not zero with no carry out of the sign bit position	result was zero with a carry out of the sign bit position	result was not zero with a carry out of the sign bit position

Since there are only a few problems in which AL or ALR is used, they will not be considered further in this text.

In Examples 1 through 4 and in the rest of this chapter, we will often specify the second operand as a **literal constant,** recognizable by an equal sign (=). For example:

$$= F'10' \text{ specifies a full-word integer, } +10 \text{ (} 0000000A \text{ in hex)}$$
$$= H'8' \text{ specifies a half-word integer, } +8 \text{ (} 0008 \text{ in hex)}$$

Similarly, $=F'-10'$ and $=H'-8'$ specify full- and half-word negative integers. Note that in this notation, the integer is written in the decimal system; the assembler translates this to its binary representation.

Example 1.   64 + 10 = 74

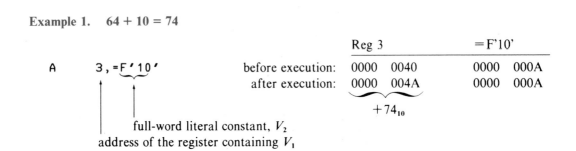

Example 2.   4096 + (−1) = 4095

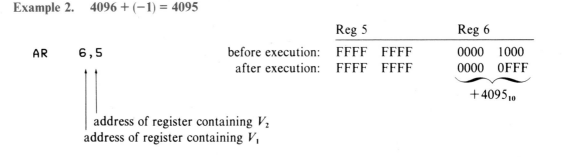

Example 3.   80 + 8 = 88

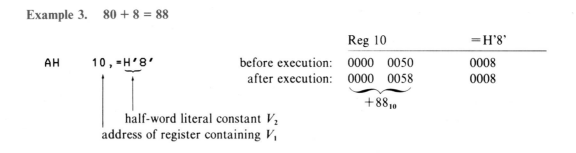

Example 4.   80 + (−8) = 72

		Reg 10	= H'−8'
AH	10,=H'-8'		
	before execution:	0000 0050	FFF8
	after execution:	0000 0048	FFF8

When the AH instruction is executed, the half-word integer V_2 is extended to 32 bits just prior to the addition, without changing the representation of V_2 in memory. As discussed earlier, the extension of a half-word integer to a 32-bit integer is done by propagating the sign bit into the 16 high-order bits, so that, for example, 0008 becomes 00000008 and FFF8 becomes FFFFFFF8.

Subtraction

There are five binary integer subtraction instructions: S, SL, SR, SLR, and SH.

opcode	meaning	type
S	SUBTRACT	RX
SL	SUBTRACT LOGICAL	RX
	Both S and SL subtract the full word V_2 from the full word V_1. V_2 is in memory, V_1 in a register. The result replaces V_1. The distinction between S and SL is discussed below.	
SR	SUBTRACT REGISTERS	RR
SLR	SUBTRACT LOGICAL REGISTERS	RR
	Both SR and SLR subtract the full word V_2 from the full word V_1. V_1 and V_2 are in registers. The result replaces V_1. The distinction between SR and SLR is discussed below.	
SH	SUBTRACT HALF WORD	RX
	Subtracts half word V_2 from full word V_1. V_2 is in memory, V_1 in a register. The result, a full word, replaces V_1.	

In the S, SR, and SH instructions, the quantities V_1, V_2, and $V_1 - V_2$ are signed integers, and two's complement arithmetic is performed. If overflow occurs, execution may be interrupted and the program terminated. In the SL and SLR instructions, V_1, V_2, and $V_1 - V_2$ are treated as *un*signed integers: bit b_0 is the high-order numeric bit, with positional value $b_0 \times 2^{32}$, and overflow does not cause program interruption.

The condition code is set for each subtract instruction as indicated in the following table.

	condition code and its meaning			
instruction	0*	1	2	3
S, SR, SH	result was zero	result was negative	result was positive	overflow occurred
SL, SLR	---	result was not zero with no carry out of the sign bit position	result was zero with a carry out of the sign bit position	result was not zero with a carry out of the sign bit position

*Condition code 0 is never set during an SL or SLR instruction due to the manner in which subtraction is performed by the hardware.

Compared to the S, SR, and SH instructions, there are not many problems for which SL and SLR are used. Consequently, the two logical subtracts will not be considered further in this text.

Example 1.   64 − 10 = 54

			Reg 3		= F'10'	
S	3,=F'10'	before execution:	0000	0040	0000	000A
		after execution:	0000	0036	0000	000A

Example 2.   4096 − (−1) = 4097

			Reg 5		Reg 6	
SR	6,5	before execution:	FFFF	FFFF	0000	1000
		after execution:	FFFF	FFFF	0000	1001

Example 3.　$8 - 80 = -72$

		Reg 10	= H'80'
SH　　10,=H'80'	before execution:	0000　0008	0050
	after execution:	FFFF　FFB8	0050

In half-word subtraction, as in half-word addition, the second factor, V_2, is extended to 32 bits by propagating its sign bit into the 16 high-order bits. The CPU does this without affecting the representation of V_2 in memory.

Multiplication

There are three binary integer multiply instructions: M, MR, and MH. The M and MR instructions work similarly to one another, while the MH works somewhat differently.

In the M and MR instructions, V_1 must always be in an odd-numbered register. The product is a 64-bit signed integer that occupies two consecutive registers. These two registers are called an **even-odd register pair,** because the first of them is an even-numbered register and the second is the next consecutively addressed register. The following diagram shows the relationship of the registers that contain V_1 and its product with V_2.

V_1 Is Multiplicand

V_2 Is Multiplier

$V_1 \times V_2$ Is Product

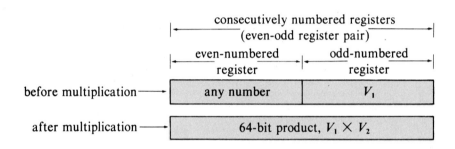

opcode	meaning	type
M	MULTIPLY Multiply V_1 by V_2. V_2 is a full word in memory. V_1 is a full word in an *odd*-numbered register. Result is a 64-bit double word, replacing the contents of the even-odd register pair that contained V_1.	RX
MR	MULTIPLY REGISTERS Multiply V_1 by V_2. V_2 is a full word in a register. V_1 is a full word in an *odd*-numbered register. Result is a 64-bit double word, replacing the contents of the even-odd register pair that contained V_1.	RR

In both the M and the MR instructions, the first operand must specify the address of the even-numbered register of the even-odd pair containing V_1. Examples 1 and 2 illustrate this.

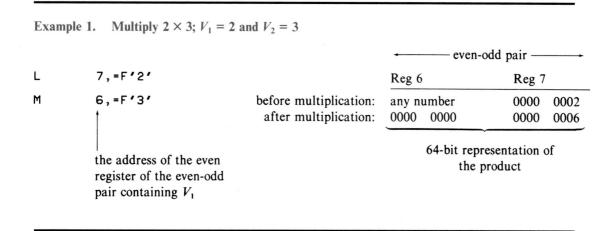

Example 1. Multiply 2×3; $V_1 = 2$ and $V_2 = 3$

			even-odd pair	
			Reg 6	Reg 7
L	7,=F'2'			
M	6,=F'3'	before multiplication:	any number	0000 0002
		after multiplication:	0000 0000	0000 0006

the address of the even
register of the even-odd
pair containing V_1

64-bit representation of
the product

Example 2. Multiply $65,536 \times 65,536$ (i.e., $2^{16} \times 2^{16}$)

			even-odd pair	
			Reg 6	Reg 7
L	7,=F'65536'	before multiplication:	any number	0001 0000
MR	6,7	after multiplication:	0000 0001	0000 0000

64-bit product

the address of V_2 is Reg 7

the address of the even
register of the even-odd
pair containing V_1 is Reg 6

Note that $V_1 = V_2$ and both are in the same register, yet the two register addresses in the MR instruction are different. This example illustrates one method of multiplying a number by itself.

In Example 1, all the significant bits of the product, together with its sign, can be contained in the low-order 32 bits, that is, in the odd-numbered register. The high-order 32 bits are all nonsignificant; they do not contribute to the value of the product. In Example 2, the high-order 32 bits contain some significant bits. This is because the value of the product $2^{16} \times 2^{16} = 2^{32}$ is greater than $2^{31} - 1$ and so cannot be contained within 31 bits. *This is not considered an overflow;* the program is not interrupted. It is the responsibility of the programmer to know whether a product might exceed $2^{31} - 1$ (or less than -2^{31}); if it will, there must be appropriate provisions in the program to ensure that the high-order significant bits are not lost. Alternatively, the programmer may want to use floating-point numbers, since the maximum allowable floating-point number is 2^{252} (approximately 10^{75}), rather than $2^{31} - 1$. Floating-point numbers are discussed in Chapter 13.

Overflow Cannot Occur in Multiplications

Because the MH instruction does not require that an even-odd register pair be used, it is simpler to use than the M or MR instructions. *Any* register can be used for V_1, and the address of V_1 specifies the register that contains it. However, because the product generated by MH is always a 32-bit number—31 bits for numeric value, 1 bit for sign—MH should not be used if the product could exceed $2^{31} - 1$ or be less than -2^{31}. If the product's value lies outside the range of a 32-bit number, the most significant bits are lost *and there is no overflow*. The MH instruction is summarized by the following description and examples.

opcode	meaning	type
MH	MULTIPLY HALF WORD	RX
	Multiply V_1 by V_2. V_2 is a half word in memory. V_1 is a full word in any register. Result replaces V_1.	

Example 3.   Multiply 2 × 5, for a half word, 5

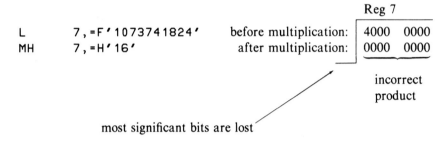

			Reg 7	
L	7,=F'2'	before multiplication:	0000	0002
MH	7,=H'5'	after multiplication:	0000	000A

correct 32-bit product

the address of V_1 is
the register containing it

Example 4.   Multiply $2^{30} \times 2^4$, for a half word, 2^4

			Reg 7	
L	7,=F'1073741824'	before multiplication:	4000	0000
MH	7,=H'16'	after multiplication:	0000	0000

incorrect
product

most significant bits are lost

Division

There are two binary integer division instructions, D and DR. (Note that there is no half-word division instruction.)

opcode	meaning	type
D	DIVIDE Divide V_1 by V_2. V_2 is a full word in memory. V_1 is a double word in an even-odd register pair. Result replaces V_1 (see below).	RX
DR	DIVIDE REGISTERS Divide V_1 by V_2. V_2 is a full word in a register. V_1 is a double word in an even-odd register pair. Result replaces V_1.	RR

V_1 Is Dividend

V_2 Is Divisor

In the D and DR instructions, V_1 is a 64-bit integer and must always be in an even-odd register pair. Its position is specified by the even register of the pair.

Q Is Integer Quotient

The result of an integer division consists of two signed integers: an integer quotient, Q, and an integer remainder, R, defined as

$$\frac{V_1}{V_2} = Q + \frac{R}{V_2}$$

R Is Integer Remainder

The sign of the quotient is determined by the rules of algebra. The sign of the remainder is the same as that of the dividend, V_1, except when $R = 0$ and $V_1 < 0$. (The sign bit of a zero remainder is always 0, as is that of a zero quotient.) For example, if $V_1 = 150$ and $V_2 = 40$, then $Q = 3$ and $R = 30$. If $V_1 = -150$ and $V_2 = 40$, then $Q = -3$ and $R = -30$. If $V_1 = -120$ and $V_2 = 40$, then $Q = -3$ and $R = 0$. The quotient Q replaces the low-order half of V_1 (i.e., Q replaces the contents of the odd-numbered register), and the remainder, R, replaces the high-order half of V_1. The following diagram illustrates this:

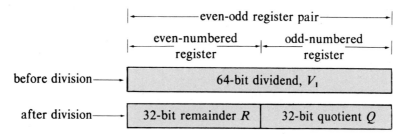

These concepts are illustrated in Examples 1 and 2.

Example 1. Divide 7 by 2; $V_1 = 7$, $V_2 = 2$

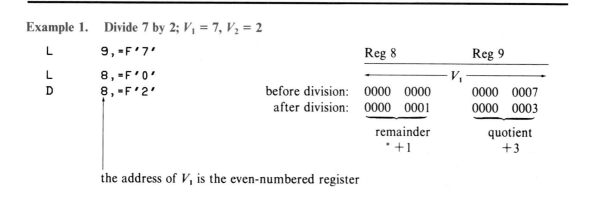

```
L     9,=F'7'
L     8,=F'0'
D     8,=F'2'
```

	Reg 8		Reg 9	
		V_1		
before division:	0000	0000	0000	0007
after division:	0000	0001	0000	0003
	remainder		quotient	
	$+1$		$+3$	

the address of V_1 is the even-numbered register

Example 2. Divide 150 by -40; $V_1 = +150$, $V_2 = -40$

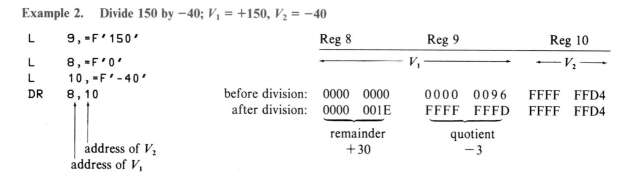

```
L     9,=F'150'
L     8,=F'0'
L     10,=F'-40'
DR    8,10
```

	Reg 8		Reg 9		Reg 10	
		V_1			V_2	
before division:	0000	0000	0000	0096	FFFF	FFD4
after division:	0000	001E	FFFF	FFFD	FFFF	FFD4
	remainder		quotient			
	$+30$		-3			

address of V_2
address of V_1

In both examples, the dividend, V_1, was a positive number. Changing it from a full-word 32-bit integer to a double-word 64-bit integer posed no special problem; the high-order half of the even-odd register pair was simply set to zero. When V_1 is negative, or, more generally, when its sign is not known in advance by the programmer, care must be taken to ensure that the sign bit is extended into each of the bits of the even-numbered register. The situations in Case 1 and 2 illustrate this.

Case 1. V_1 is positive or zero

decimal number	hexadecimal 32-bit representation				hexadecimal 64-bit representation			
0	00	00	00	00	0000	0000	0000	0000
12	00	00	00	0C	0000	0000	0000	000C
32,767	00	00	7F	FF	0000	0000	0000	7FFF
2,147,483,647	7F	FF	FF	FF	0000	0000	7FFF	FFFF

Case 2. V_1 is negative

decimal number	hexadecimal 32-bit representation				hexadecimal 64-bit representation			
-12	FF	FF	FF	F4	FFFF	FFFF	FFFF	FFF4
-32,767	FF	FF	80	01	FFFF	FFFF	FFFF	8001
-2,147,483,647	80	00	00	01	FFFF	FFFF	8000	0001

Creating a 64-Bit Dividend

The correct 64-bit representation of any 32-bit binary integer can be obtained by multiplying the 32-bit integer by the full-word representation of $+1$. Either the M or the MR instruction (but not MH) can be used for this. The product, as we have seen, is represented in 64 bits. The value of the multiplicand, of course, remains unchanged when multiplying it by $+1$.

To ensure that the proper 64-bit representation of a dividend is in an even-odd register pair before executing a binary integer division instruction, you can therefore proceed as in the following examples:

To divide 7 by 2:

```
L   9,=F'7'
M   8,=F'1'
D   8,=F'2'
```

To divide -7 by 2:

```
L   9,=F'-7'
M   8,=F'1'
D   8,=F'2'
```

In the previous two examples, use of Registers 8 and 9 isn't necessary: any even-odd register pair will serve the same purpose. What IS necessary, however, is that the Load (L) instruction copy the multiplicand into the *odd*-numbered register of the pair, and the Multiply (M) and Divide (D) instructions refer to the *even*-numbered register of the pair.

Exceptions

There are two other precautions to observe when using either of the two divide instructions. First, division by zero ($V_2 = 0$) is not valid. If attempted, the program is automatically interrupted by the hardware and terminated by the operating system. And, second, a divide instruction that attempts to generate a quotient larger than $2^{31} - 1$ or smaller than -2^{31} is not valid. The program is interrupted by the hardware and terminated by the operating system. Each of these situations is known as a **fixed-point divide exception.**

5.4 CONDITIONAL BRANCHES

It is frequently necessary, and quite easy, to determine whether the result of an add, subtract, multiply, or divide instruction is positive, negative, or zero. This is done by determining the setting of the condition code via conditional branch instructions.

Condition Code

As mentioned in the discussion of the add instructions, the condition code is a number stored in a hardware indicator to record the nature of a result. This is done whenever an add or subtract instruction is executed. The meaning of the number that is stored in the condition code indicator, that is, the meaning of the condition code itself, depends on what instruction was executed. In the IBM 360 and 370 systems, more than half of the available instructions generate conditions that are recorded in the condition code indicator. Since there is only one condition code indicator used during the execution of a program, *the condition code is changed each time an instruction that sets it is executed.* In other words, the condition code reflects only the result of the most recently executed code-setting instruction.

Code-Setting Instructions

A list of all the nonprivileged instructions that set the condition code, together with the corresponding meanings of the codes, is given in Figure 8.5a (see Chap. 8). Included in this list, of course, are the add and subtract instructions. But notably missing are the multiply and divide instructions. We will learn how to deal with this discrepancy shortly.

There are six RX-type conditional branch instructions that can be used to determine whether the condition code is set to reflect a zero, a positive, or a negative result. The assembly language opcodes for these instructions are

opcode	meaning
BZ	branch if result was zero
BNZ	branch if result was not zero
BM	branch if result was minus (i.e., negative)
BNM	branch if result was not minus (i.e., was positive or zero)
BP	branch if result was positive
BNP	branch if result was not positive (i.e., was negative or zero)

Unlike other RX instructions, these six conditional branch instructions are written with only one operand field, for reasons that will be explained in Chapter 8. The single operand designates the address of the instruction to which a branch is to be made if the condition being tested is true. If the condition being tested is *not* true, then no branch is made; instead, execution of the program continues with the instruction that immediately follows the conditional branch instruction. A simple example should serve to illustrate this capability:

```
       L      3,X          copy an integer from symbolic address X into Register 3
       S      3,=F'7'      subtract +7 from Register 3
       BZ     ZERO         branch to symbolic address ZERO if the result was zero
       BP     POS          branch to symbolic address POS if it was positive

       :                   } section of the program that is executed
                           } when the difference computed above was negative

POS    :                   } section of the program that is executed
                           } when the difference was positive

ZERO   :                   } section of the program that is executed
                           } when the difference was zero
```

Note that the test for a positive result is independent of the test for a zero result, and vice versa. This is because there is a separate condition code setting for a positive result and for a zero result—and for a negative result, as well.

The conditional branch instructions themselves do not set the condition code; they merely test it. Therefore, the setting that resulted from the subtract instruction in the example cited exists not only when the BZ instruction is executed but also when the BP instruction is executed. The setting of the condition code remains unchanged until an instruction that changes it is executed. The generally accepted practice is to follow a code-setting instruction with one or more conditional branch instructions whenever one wants to determine the nature of a result. This practice avoids the possibility that another code-setting instruction will be executed before the intended conditional branches.

In the preceding section, the meanings of the condition codes for the A, AR, and AH add instructions and the S, SR, and SH subtract instructions were given. From these, it may be seen that any of the six conditional branch instructions may be used to determine the nature of the result following one of the six add or subtract instructions. But it is a design property of the IBM 360 and 370 systems that none of the multiply or divide instructions set the condition code. So the question is, How can we determine whether the result of a multiply or divide instruction is positive, negative, or zero? The answer lies in the use of another instruction, Load and Test Register (LTR).

The LTR instruction is an RR-type instruction. Its format is as follows:

opcode	operand
LTR	R1,R2

The purpose of the LTR instruction is to set the condition code according to the contents of a register—zero, positive, or negative. Once set by this instruction, the condition code, and thus the nature of the number that was tested, can be determined via a conditional branch instruction. The LTR works as follows: the number in the register designated by the second operand (R2) is copied into the register designated by the first operand (R1), and the condition code is set according to whether the number that was copied is zero, positive, or negative. R1 and R2 may designate the same register.

The following two examples illustrate the use of LTR to determine whether a product is zero, negative, or positive.

If we know that the product is within the range of a 32-bit integer, then we can test it as follows:

```
        L       7,V1    R7 = MULTIPLICAND
        M       6,V2    R6 & R7 = 64-BIT PRODUCT
        LTR     7,7     TEST LOW-ORDER 32 BITS OF PRODUCT
        BM      NEG     BRANCH IF PRODUCT WAS NEGATIVE
        BZ      ZRO     BRANCH IF ZERO
        B       POS     BRANCH IF POSITIVE
```

If the range of the product is not known, the test is a little more complex, since the LTR only allows testing the contents of one register at a time:

```
        L       7,V1    R7 = MULTIPLICAND
        M       6,V2    R6 & R7 = 64-BIT PRODUCT
        LTR     6,6     TEST HIGH-ORDER 32 BITS OF PRODUCT
        BM      NEG     <0 IF HI-ORDER NEGATIVE.
        BNZ     POS     >0 IF HI-ORDER NOTNEG,NOTZRO:
        LTR     7,7     ELSE,MUST TEST LO-ORDER 32 BITS
        BNZ     POS     >0 IF LOW-ORDER NOT ZERO,
        BZ      ZRO     =0 IF LOW-ORDER IS ZERO.
```

In this sequence, a negative product will cause a branch to location NEG, a positive product will cause a branch to POS, and a product of zero will cause a branch to ZRO; however, no distinction is made for products outside the range of 32-bit integers.

For division, the sign of the quotient can be determined as follows:

```
        L       7,V1    R6 & R7 = DIVIDEND
        M       6,-F'1' TO ENSURE PROPER SIGN
        D       6,V2    R6 = REMAINDER,R7 = QUOTIENT
        LTR     7,7
        BM      NEG     BRANCH IF QUOTIENT NEGATIVE
        BZ      ZRO     BRANCH IF QUOTIENT ZERO
        B       POS     OTHERWISE IT'S POSITIVE
```

The nature of the remainder can be determined in similar fashion.

5.5 COMPARING INTEGERS

Any binary integer can be algebraically compared to any other binary integer without having to subtract one from the other. One of the two integers being compared must be in a register; the other can either be in a register or in a memory location, depending on the compare instruction that is used. *Neither integer is changed by a compare instruction.*

There are three algebraic compare instructions for binary integers: C, CR, and CH. To describe these instructions, we will continue to use the notation introduced earlier:

V_1 = the integer whose address is specified by the first operand of the instruction
V_2 = the integer whose address is specified by the second operand of the instruction

opcode	meaning	type
C	COMPARE Compares V_1 to V_2. V_1 is in a register; V_2 is a 32-bit integer in a memory location.	RX
CR	COMPARE REGISTERS Compares V_1 to V_2. Both V_1 and V_2 are in registers.	RR
CH	COMPARE HALF WORD Compares V_1 to V_2. V_1 is in a register; V_2 is a 16-bit integer in a memory location.	RX

In algebraic comparisons, the two quantities, V_1 and V_2, are compared as signed 32-bit integers, and the rules of algebra are used: V_1 is considered to be less than V_2 if there is a positive integer N such that $V_1 + N = V_2$. For the half-word comparison CH, V_2 is expanded to 32 bits for purposes of the comparison but is not altered in its memory location. The expansion, performed by propagating the sign bit of V_2 into the high-order 16 bits of a 32-bit word, takes place in a register that is unavailable to programmers.

Each execution of a compare instruction sets the condition code as indicated in the following table:

instruction	condition code and its meanings			
	0	1	2	3
C, CR, CH	$V_1 = V_2$	$V_1 < V_2$	$V_1 > V_2$	- - -

To determine the result of a comparison, we can use one of the following six RX-type conditional branch instructions:

opcode	meaning	
BE	branch if V_1 equals V_2	$V_1 = V_2$
BNE	branch if V_1 is not equal to V_2	$V_1 \neq V_2$
BL	branch if V_1 is less than V_2	$V_1 < V_2$
BNL	branch if V_1 is not less than V_2	$V_1 \geq V_2$
BH	branch if V_1 is higher than V_2	$V_1 > V_2$
BNH	branch if V_1 is not higher than V_2	$V_1 \leq V_2$

The use of these instructions is analogous to that of the six arithmetic conditional branch instructions described in the previous section. Each of these six instructions is written with only one operand field. That field designates the address of the instruction to which a branch is made if the condition being tested is true. If the condition being tested is *not* true, then no branch is made; instead, execution of the program continues with the instruction that immediately follows the conditional branch instruction.

Examples 1 through 3 serve to illustrate the use of the compare and conditional branch instructions. As with the arithmetic conditional branch instructions, the instructions used here do not set the condition code; they merely test it.

Example 1. Algebraic comparison of two 32-bit binary integers, one of which is in a register, the other in memory

L	3,X	copy an integer from symbolic address X into Register 3
C	3,=F'9'	compare Register 3's contents to +9
BE	EQUAL	branch to symbolic address EQUAL if the integers were equal
BH	HIGH	branch to symbolic address HIGH if the contents of Register 3 were algebraically greater than +9

             ⋮   } section of the program that is executed when the contents of Register 3 were algebraically less than +9

HIGH   ⋮   } section of the program that is executed when the contents of Register 3 were algebraically greater than +9

EQUAL   ⋮   } section of the program that is executed when the contents of Register 3 were equal to +9

Example 2. Algebraic comparison of two 32-bit integers, both of which are in registers

L	3,X	copy an integer from symbolic address X into Register 3
L	4,=F'9'	copy the integer +9 into Register 4
CR	3,4	compare the contents of Register 3 to that of Register 4
BNH	LE	branch to symbolic address LE if Register 3's contents
B	GT	were not greater than Register 4's; otherwise branch to symbolic address GT

LE   ⋮   } section of the program that is executed when Register 3's contents were not greater than Register 4's

GT   ⋮   } section of the program that is executed when Register 3's contents were greater than Register 4's

---

Example 3. Algebraic comparison of two integers, one a 32-bit integer in a register, the other a 16-bit integer in memory

L	5,X	copy an integer from symbolic address X into Register 3
CH	5,=H'-1'	compare the contents of Register 5 to −1
BNE	NEQ	branch to symbolic address NEQ if the two integers were not equal

             ⋮   } section of program that is executed when the two integers were equal

             ⋮

NEQ   ⋮   } section of the program that is executed when the two integers were not equal

5.6 CHANGING SIGN AND GENERATING ABSOLUTE VALUES

Use of the instructions described here makes it easy for programmers to deal with two's complement representation when an integer's sign must be changed or made positive or negative. The three instructions in this group are all RR-type instructions, so that in each instruction both operand fields must specify register addresses. As before, we use the notation V_1 and V_2 to describe the effect of the instructions.

opcode	meaning	type
LCR	LOAD COMPLEMENT FROM REGISTER Copies the negative of V_2—i.e., its two's complement —into the register occupied by V_1; the result replaces V_1.	RR
LPR	LOAD POSITIVE ABSOLUTE VALUE FROM REGISTER Copies the positive absolute value of V_2 into the register occupied by V_1; the result replaces V_1.	RR
LNR	LOAD NEGATIVE ABSOLUTE VALUE FROM REGISTER Copies the negative absolute value of V_2 into the register occupied by V_1; the result replaces V_1.	RR

Each of the three instructions sets the condition code as indicated in the following table. Consequently, the nature of the result may be determined by use of the conditional branch instructions BZ, BNZ, BM, BNM, BP, and BNP.

instruction	condition code and its meanings			
	0	1	2	3
LCR	result was zero	result was negative	result was positive	overflow occurred
LPR	result was zero	- - -	result was positive	overflow occurred
LNR	result was zero	result was negative	- - -	- - -

The occurrence of overflow, illustrated in Examples 2 and 5, usually causes the hardware to interrupt execution of the program, with consequent termination by the operating system. This can be prevented by use of the "program mask," as will be discussed in Chapter 11.

Example 1.

			Reg 3
LCR	3,3	before execution:	FFFFFFFA
		*after execution:	00000006

Typical Use of LCR to Change the Sign

* When both register addresses are the same, the result replaces the number that was in that register before execution of the LCR.

Example 2.

			Reg 3	Reg 4
LCR	3,4	before execution:	87654321	80000000
		*after execution:	80000000	80000000

LCR Overflow

* The two's complement of -2^{31} is still -2^{31}. The number $+2^{31}$ cannot be represented in 32 bits. Therefore, when $V_2 = -2^{31}$, the LCR instruction generates an overflow error condition.

Example 3.

				Reg 4	Reg 5
LPR	5,4	before execution:		FFFFFFFA	000000AB
		after execution:		FFFFFFFA	00000006

Example 4.

				Reg 4	Reg 5
LPR	4,5	before execution:		FFFFFFFA	000000AB
		*after execution:		000000AB	000000AB

* The positive absolute value of a positive number is that positive number.

Example 5.

LPR Overflow

				Reg 7	Reg 8
LPR	8,7	before execution:		80000000	12345678
		*after execution:		80000000	80000000

*The positive absolute value of -2^{31} cannot be represented in 32 bits. When $V_2 = -2^{31}$, execution of an LPR instruction generates an overflow error condition.

Example 6.

*Typical Use of
LNR: Generates
Negative Absolute
Value*

				Reg 4	Reg 5
LNR	4,5	before execution:		FFFFFFFA	000000AB
		after execution:		FFFFFF55	000000AB

Example 7.

*Zero Is Neither
Positive Nor
Negative*

				Reg 4	Reg 5
LNR	5,4	before execution:		FFFFFFFA	000000AB
		*after execution:		FFFFFFFA	FFFFFFFA

* The negative absolute value of a negative number is that negative number. However, it should be noted that the negative absolute value of 0 (zero) is 0. In the IBM 360 and 370 systems, the binary integer representations of -0 and $+0$ are the same, that is, all bits in the representation are zeroes.

5.7 INTEGER ARITHMETIC EXAMPLES

In the following programs, and in those of all subsequent chapters, the technique of indexing and loop control described in Chapter 4 is used. The best way to understand these programs, and the best way to learn how the instructions work together to produce the desired result, is to manually trace the execution of each program, statement by statement. This requires patience and a systematic method of recording the results of each instruction. The first example is traced in detail to illustrate the concept. For the others, only the important aspects are summarized; you may trace them for your own experience.

The problems to be considered are:

1. Compute the sum of N integers.
2. Compute the average value of N integers.
3. Multiply each integer in an array by a constant.
4. Count the number of positive integers that occur in an array of N integers.
5. Replace each integer in an array by its absolute value.
6. Determine the largest and the smallest integers in an array of N integers.

Solutions to these problems, shown in Figures 5.2 through 5.7, are explained in the discussion of the examples. Since it is assumed that the statements shown in the figures represent part of a larger program, the CSECT, END, and BALR-USING base-register statements are not included.

The programming solutions given for each problem are valid for any integers that do not cause overflow, but no data are included in the solutions. Instead, memory space for the data is reserved by means of the DS directive. This directive has an effect similar to that of a Fortran DIMENSION statement: Space is reserved, but no data are placed in that space by the directive. Use of the DS directive will be described in the next chapter; for the purposes of the present chapter, all that is required is to understand the meaning of a DS directive in this form:

name field	opcode	operand
X	DS	nF

This statement reserves n consecutive full words, each on a full-word boundary, and assigns the address of the first word that is reserved to the symbol X; n can be any unsigned decimal integer. If n is omitted, its value is assumed to be 1.

DS Reserves Space for Data and Results

The reason for excluding data from the solutions is to emphasize that the solutions are not dependent on any particular data. For the solutions to be run in a computer system, however, you would have to add statements whose purpose is to place data into the reserved memory areas. This could be done by reading the data and converting it to binary integer format, as discussed in Chapter 4. The sample program given at the end of this chapter provides a further illustration of the techniques required to do this.

Example 1. Compute the sum of N integers
(See Figure 5.2.)

The solution shown in Figure 5.2 is valid for any N integers, for N between 1 and 100 inclusive. The limit of 100 is set by the operand in Statement 14, which reserves 100 full words for the integers. The lower limit of 1 is set by the loop-control mechanism of the program—in particular, the BCT instruction in Statement 9—which requires that there be at least one integer in the array.

The program begins with three loop-initialization instructions. The Load Address (LA) instruction of Statement 2 puts the address of the first integer—symbolic address ARRAY, defined by Statement 14—into Register 8. During each iteration of the loop, Register 8 will contain the address of the integer that is to be added to the sum during that iteration. The Load (L) instruction of Statement 3 puts the count of the number of integers in the array into Register 9. This count will determine how many iterations of the loop will be performed at run time. The Subtract Register (SR) instruction of Statement 5 puts a zero into Register 10, by subtracting whatever number was in that register from itself. Register 10 is initialized to zero because it will be used to accumulate the sum during each loop iteration.

Initializing the Loop's Counter and the Result

Following these loop-initialization instructions, the loop is executed N times. Each time it is executed a different integer component of the array is added to the sum in Register 10. The possibility that an addition would generate a number outside the range of allowable full-word integers (greater than $2^{31}-1$ or less than -2^{31}) is not considered; it is assumed that this will not happen, but, if it did, the program would be terminated by the operating system because of an overflow error condition.

Figure 5.2   Compute the sum of N integers.

```
1         * INITIALIZATION
2         START   LA    8,ARRAY       R8 = ADDR OF FIRST INTEGER
3                 L     9,N           R9 = NUMBER OF INTEGERS
4                 SR    10,10         R10 = SUM BEING ACCUMULATED
5         * COMPUTE SUM
6         ADD     A     10,0(8)       ADD CURRENT INTEGER TO R10
7         * LOOP CONTROL
8                 LA    8,4(8)        R8 = ADDR OF NEXT INTEGER
9                 BCT   9,ADD         DECR # INTEGERS BY 1 & REPEAT
10        * SAVE FINAL RESULT
11                ST    10,SUM        COPY ACCUMULATED SUM INTO MEMORY
                        .
                        .
                        .
12        SUM     DS    F             FULL WORD FOR FINAL SUM
13        N       DS    F             FULL WORD FOR NO. OF INTEGERS
14        ARRAY   DS    100F          100 FULL WORDS FOR ARRAY
                        .
                        .
                        .
```

Execution of the loop proceeds as follows. The Add (A) instruction of Statement 6 adds the integer whose address is in Register 8 to the sum being accumulated in Register 10. The Load Address (LA) instruction of Statement 8 increases the address in Register 8 by the constant 4 given in its displacement field. This is done as preparation for the next loop iteration; an increase of 4 adjusts the address to the next integer in the array, as shown in this diagram:

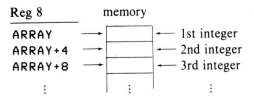

Loop Control Via
BCT

The Branch on Count (BCT) instruction of Statement 9 determines whether the loop should be repeated. The BCT reduces the count that is in Register 9 by +1, and, if the reduced count is not zero, the BCT branches to the instruction whose symbolic address is ADD. If the reduced count *is* zero, the BCT instruction does not branch, thereby terminating the loop. As explained in Chapter 4, this technique of loop control depends on the fact that the initial loop-control counter, in this case, the number of integers in the array, is at least 1.

A different array component is added to the sum in Register 10 during each iteration of the loop. When the loop-control counter in Register 9 is finally reduced to zero, the loop is terminated with the total sum of the array's integers in Register 10. At this point, the Store (ST) instruction of Statement 11 copies the sum from Register 10 into a memory location for subsequent use by other portions of the program (not shown).

In order to trace the execution of the program, let us assume the following addresses have been assigned, and that the data are as shown:

symbolic address	numeric address	number stored at that address	
		hex	decimal
N	500	0000 0003	3
ARRAY	504	0000 000A	10
	508	FFFF FFF2	-14
	50C	0000 000C	12

In other words, the assumptions are that there are three integers in the array, that the array begins at address 504, and that the integers stored in the array are 0000000A, FFFFFFF2, and 0000000C. The trace is as follows (underlined numbers indicate changes to previous numbers in the respective registers).

	statement	Reg 8	Reg 9	Reg 10
initialization	#2	000504		
	#3	000504	00 00 00 03	
	#4	000504	00 00 00 03	00 00 00 00
first iteration	#6	000504	00 00 00 03	00 00 00 0A
	#8	000508	00 00 00 03	00 00 00 0A
	#9	000508	00 00 00 02	00 00 00 0A
second iteration	#6	000508	00 00 00 02	FF FF FF FC
	#8	00050C	00 00 00 02	FF FF FF FC
	#9	00050C	00 00 00 01	FF FF FF FC
third iteration	#6	00050C	00 00 00 01	00 00 00 08
	#8	000510	00 00 00 01	00 00 00 08
	#9	000510	00 00 00 00	00 00 00 08

At this point, the loop-control counter in Register 9 has been reduced to zero by the BCT in Statement 9, so there is no branch to continue the loop. Instead, the sum 00000008 in Register 10 is stored into symbolic address SUM, which is numeric address 4FC, since SUM just precedes N in memory (see Figure 5.2).

Example 2. **Compute the average of N integers**
(See Figure 5.3.)

This solution is a modification of the previous one, since to compute the average it is necessary to first determine the sum. The modification consists of Statements 11.1 through 11.7.

To compute the average, the sum must be divided by the number of integers, N. The divide instruction requires that the dividend be a 64-bit integer in a pair of consecutively numbered registers, the first of which must be an even-numbered register. This means that for the divide instruction of Statement 11.3, namely D 10,N, Registers 10 and 11 must contain the dividend as a 64-bit binary integer, and symbolic memory location N must contain the divisor as a 32-bit binary integer. As discussed earlier, the multiply (M) instruction in Statement 11.2 generates the appropriate representation of the 64-bit dividend.

When the division instruction is executed, the 64-bit dividend is replaced by two 32-bit quantities, the quotient and the remainder. Remember that the remainder always has the same sign as the dividend (unless the remainder is zero), whereas the sign of the quotient is determined by the rules of algebra. Also remember that both the remainder and the quotient are integers. As an illustration, consider four simple cases: $12/3$, $12/(-3)$, $13/3$, and $(-13)/3$.

divisor		← dividend →		remainder		quotient	
		Reg 10		Reg 11		Reg 10		Reg 11
0000	0003	0000	0000	0000	000C	0000	0000	0000	0004
FFFF	FFFD	0000	0000	0000	000C	0000	0000	FFFF	FFFC
0000	0003	0000	0000	0000	000D	0000	0001	0000	0004
0000	0003	FFFF	FFFF	FFFF	FFF3	FFFF	FFFF	FFFF	FFFC

In Chapters 12 and 13, other methods for performing arithmetic calculations will be described. Those methods allow integers and mixed numbers in all calculations, and, in particular, the methods of Chapter 13 allow a quotient to be computed as a mixed number rather than by generating a separate integer remainder. However, the use of those methods requires different instructions and different representations of data.

Figure 5.3   Compute the average of N integers.

```
              .
              .
              .
   1    * INITIALIZATION
   2    START    LA    8,ARRAY        STATEMENTS #1 - #11 AND
   3             L     9,N            #12 - #14 ARE SIMILAR
   4             SR    11,11          TO THOSE IN FIG. 5.2
   5    * COMPUTE SUM
   6    ADD      A     11,0(8)
   7    * LOOP CONTROL
   8             LA    8,4(8)
   9             BCT   9,ADD
  10    * SAVE FINAL RESULT
  11             ST    11,SUM
  11.1  * COMPUTE AVERAGE            FIRST, CREATE SIGNED DOUBLE-WORD
  11.2            M     10,=F'1'       DIVIDEND IN EVEN-ODD REG PAIR
  11.3            D     10,N           THEN DIVIDE BY NO. OF INTEGERS
  11.4            ST    11,QUOTIENT   SAVE INTEGER QUOTIENT Q
  11.5            ST    10,REMNDR     SAVE INTEGER REMAINDER R
                  .
                  .
                  .
  11.6  QUOTIENT DS    F             FULL-WD FOR Q
  11.7  REMNDR   DS    F             FULL-WD FOR R
  12    SUM      DS    F
  13    N        DS    F
  14    ARRAY    DS    100F
                  .
                  .
                  .
```

Example 3.   Multiply each integer in an array by a constant
(See Figure 5.4.)

The heart of this solution is the following three-instruction sequence:

```
        MULT      L      11,0(8)
                  MR     10,5
                  ST     11,0(8)
```

The first operand of the MR instruction designates the even-odd register pair that contains the 32-bit multiplicand and will contain the 64-bit product. The second operand of the MR designates the 32-bit multiplier. The multiplier is placed into Register 5 by Statement 4; the multiplicand is placed into Register 11 by Statement 6. The product replaces the multiplicand, via Statement 7.

32- vs. 64-Bit Products
The solution given in Figure 5.4—in particular, Statement 8—assumes that the magnitude of each product will not require more than 32 bits. A product requiring more than 32 bits would be generated whenever the two factors, multiplicand and multiplier, were such that the product exceeded $2^{31} - 1$ or was less than -2^{31}.

Fundamental Techniques

Figure 5.4   Multiply each integer in an array by a constant.

```
                .
                .
                .

1     * INITIALIZATION
2              LA     8,ARRAY              R8 = ADDR OF FIRST INTEGER
3              L      9,N                  R9 = NUMBER OF INTEGERS
4              L      5,CONSTANT           R5 = MULTIPLIER, A CONSTANT
5     * COMPUTE PRODUCT =  CURRENT INTEGER X CONSTANT . . . PRODUCT < 2**31
6     MULT     L      11,0(8)              R11=MULTIPLICAND=CURRENT INTEGER
7              MR     10,5                 R11 X R5 = PRODUCT IN R10 & R11
8              ST     11,0(8)              REPLACE INTEGER BY PRODUCT
9     * LOOP CONTROL
10             LA     8,4(8)               R8 = ADDR OF NEXT INTEGER
11             BCT    9,MULT               DECR # INTEGERS BY 1 & REPEAT
                .
                .
                .

12    N        DS     F                    SPACE FOR NO. OF INTEGERS
13    CONSTANT DS     F                    SPACE FOR CONSTANT MULTIPLIER
14    ARRAY    DS     50F                  SPACE FOR 50-INTEGER ARRAY
                .
                .
                .
```

Figure 5.5   Count the number of positive integers in an array.

```
1     * INITIALIZATION
2              LA     8,ARRAY              R8 = ADDR OF FIRST INTEGER
3              L      9,N                  R9 = NUMBER OF INTEGERS
4              SR     10,10                R10 = COUNT OF POSITIVE INTEGERS
5     * DETERMINE WHICH INTEGERS ARE POSITIVE, AND COUNT THOSE
6     POSCHK   L      11,0(8)              R11 GETS CURRENT INTEGER
7              LTR    11,11                LTR ESTABLISHES SIGN CONDITION
8              BNP    LOOPCTL              IF NOT POSITIVE, DON'T COUNT IT
9              A      10,=F'1'             ELSE, ADD 1 TO COUNT IN R10
10    * LOOP CONTROL
11    LOOPCTL  LA     8,4(8)               R8 = ADDR OF NEXT INTEGER
12             BCT    9,POSCHK             DECR # INTEGERS BY 1 & REPEAT
13             ST     10,POSCTR            SAVE COUNT OF POSITIVE INTEGERS
                .
                .
                .

14    POSCTR   DS     F                    SPACE FOR NO. POS INTEGERS
15    N        DS     F                    SPACE FOR NO. OF INTEGERS
16    ARRAY    DS     200F                 SPACE FOR 200-INTEGER ARRAY
```

Example 4.   Count the number of positive integers in an array
    (See Figure 5.5.)

The heart of this solution is given by the following three statements:

```
         POSCHK     L      11,0(8)
                    LTR    11,11
                    BNP    LOOPCTL
```

To determine whether an integer is positive, use either the BP or BNP conditional branch instructions, as in Statement 8. Since all conditional branch instructions depend on the most-recent result or, more precisely, on the most-recent setting of the condition code, it is necessary to set the condition code before using a conditional branch instruction. It is a property of the design of the IBM 360 and 370 computer systems that the Load (L) instruction does not set the condition code, whereas the Load and Test Register (LTR) instruction does. Therefore the LTR is used in Statement 7 to set the condition code depending on whether the integer that had just been loaded via L 11,0(8) is positive, negative, or zero. This enables the BNP instruction following the LTR instruction to correctly determine whether that integer is not positive, i.e., is zero or negative.

Example 5. **Replace integers by their absolute values**
(See Figure 5.6.)

LPR and Overflow

This solution is similar to that of Figure 5.5. Statement 6, the LPR instruction, generates the positive absolute value of the integer that was placed into Register 10 by Statement 5. Statement 7 copies the positive absolute value into the memory location that had been occupied by the original integer. It should be noted that the solution assumes that none of the integers is equal to -2^{31}; if any integer were equal to -2^{31}, its positive absolute value, $+2^{31}$, would be outside the range of integers that can be represented in 32 bits and the LPR instruction would cause an overflow.

Example 6. **Determine the algebraically largest and smallest integers in an array**
(See Figures 5.7 and 5.8.)

One way to solve this problem is to arrange all the integers in order, from the smallest to largest. The desired result would then be obtained by choosing the first and last integers in the rearranged set. Such a procedure, known as *sorting,* is not necessary for this problem. Instead, the following simpler technique is used.

Establishing
Initial Values

Each integer in the array is examined, one by one. Each time an integer is examined, it is compared to the largest integer of all those previously examined. If the integer is larger than the currently largest integer, it clearly must replace the largest integer of all those examined so far. If the integer being examined is *not* larger than the currently largest integer, it is compared to the currently smallest integer to see if it is smaller than it. After all integers have been examined in this way, the two desired results will have been established without having rearranged the integers. The technique just outlined is illustrated in the pseudocode of Figure 5.7.

Figure 5.6   Replace integers by their absolute values.

```
 1    * INITIALIZATION
 2             LA     8,ARRAY              R8 = ADDR OF FIRST INTEGER
 3             L      9,N                  R9 = NUMBER OF INTEGERS
 4    * REPLACE EACH INTEGER BY ITS (POSITIVE) ABSOLUTE VALUE
 5    ABSVAL   L      10,0(8)              R10 = CURRENT INTEGER
 6             LPR    10,10                LPR GENERATES POS. ABS. VAL.
 7             ST     10,0(8)              REPLACE CURRENT INTEGER
 8    * LOOP-CONTROL
 9             LA     8,4(8)               R8 = ADDR OF NEXT INTEGER
10             BCT    9,ABSVAL             DECR # INTEGERS BY 1 & REPEAT
                 .
                 .
                 .
11    N        DS     F
12    ARRAY    DS     200F
                 .
                 .
                 .
```

Figure 5.7   Pseudocode for Figure 5.8.

```
MAX_AND_MIN:

    address of current integer := ARRAY;   {address of 1st integer}
    loop-control counter := N;
    current largest integer := 1st integer;
    current smallest integer := 1st integer;

    REPEAT UNTIL loop-control counter = 0

      IF current largest integer < current integer
      THEN
        replace current largest integer by current integer;
      ELSE
        IF current smallest integer > current integer
        THEN
          replace current smallest integer by current integer;
        END IF;
      END IF;
      adjust address of current integer to next integer;
      decrement loop-control counter;

    END UNTIL;

    MAX := current largest integer;
    MIN := current smallest integer;

EXIT MAX_AND_MIN.
```

Figure 5.8   Determine the algebraically largest and smallest integers in an array. (See also Figure 5.7.)

```
 1     * INITIALIZATION
 2            LA     5,ARRAY               R5 = ADDR OF FIRST INTEGER
 3            L      6,N                   R6 = NUMBER OF INTEGERS
 4            L      7,0(5)                R7 = CURRENT SMALLEST INTEGER
 5            L      8,0(5)                R8 = CURRENT LARGEST INTEGER
 6     * SEE IF CURRENT INTEGER IS LARGER THAN CURRENT LARGEST INTEGER
 7     *     OR IS SMALLER THAN CURRENT SMALLEST INTEGER
 8     MAXTEST C     8,0(5)                CUR. LARGEST VS CUR. INTEGER
 9            BNL    MINTEST               IF STILL LARGEST,DONT REPLACE IT
10            L      8,0(5)                OTHERWISE, GET NEW LARGEST INT.
11            B      LOOPCTL
12     MINTEST C     7,0(5)                CUR. SMALLEST VS CUR. INTEGER
13            BNH    LOOPCTL               IF STILL SMALLEST,DONT REPLACE
14            L      7,0(5)                OTHERWISE, GET NEW SMALLEST INT.
15     * LOOP CONTROL
16     LOOPCTL LA    5,4(5)                INCR ADDR TO NEXT INTEGER
17            BCT    6,MAXTEST             DECR # INTEGERS BY 1 & REPEAT
18     * SAVE RESULTS
19            ST     8,MAX                 MAX = LARGEST INTEGER
20            ST     7,MIN                 MIN = SMALLEST INTEGER
                .
                .
                .
21     MAX    DS     F                     RESVD FOR LARGEST INTEGER
22     MIN    DS     F                     RESVD FOR SMALLEST INTEGER
23     N      DS     F                     NO. OF INTEGERS
24     ARRAY  DS     500F                  SPACE FOR 500-INTEGER ARRAY
                .
                .
                .
```

Figure 5.9   Memory allocation for M × N array in column-major form.

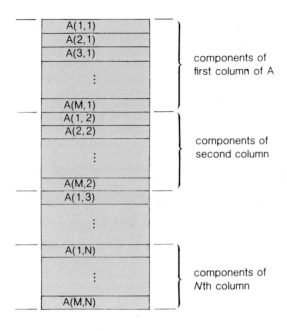

Note that in the initialization steps, the first array entry is used to establish the initial values of the current largest and smallest integers. This is preferable to attempting to estimate these initial values, since by not estimating, the procedure remains independent of the data in the array. Note also that the current largest and smallest integers are held in registers until all integers in the array have been examined. This makes it easy for the program to compare and replace them.

5.8   TWO-DIMENSIONAL ARRAYS

Address of a Two-Dimensional Array Component

A two-dimensional array consisting of M rows and N columns is stored in memory according to the pattern shown in Figure 5.9. The components of the array, assumed to be full-word integers, are stored consecutively, column by column. The last component of any column, K, is followed immediately by the first component of column $K+1$, for $K = 1,2,...,N-1$. This is known as **column-major form.** The address of the full-word integer in the Jth row and Kth column of an array, A, stored in column-major form is

$$\{\text{address of A(J,K)}\} = \{\text{address of A(1,1)}\} + \{4*(J-1)\} + \{4*M*(K-1)\}$$

When processing a two-dimensional array in Fortran, it is usually necessary to use two subscript variables in nested DO-loops. For example, to set each component of a two-dimensional integer array, A, to zero in Fortran, it is common practice to write statements like these:

```
       DO   20   J=1,M
       DO   10   K=1,N
       A(J,K) = 0
  10   CONTINUE
  20   CONTINUE
```

In assembly language, we must also use two nested loops, but as with one-dimensional arrays it is convenient to separate the loop-control variables from the index needed to successively address each component. The statements in Figure 5.10 illustrate how the problem of setting each component to zero might be programmed in assembly language. A similar procedure can be used to add the corresponding components of two arrays.

Figure 5.10   Set an M × N array to zero.

```
*    STATEMENTS TO SET EACH COMPONENT OF AN M × N ARRAY TO ZERO
*      ARRAY NAME   IS    A
*      A  CONTAINS  FULL-WORD  INTEGERS
*
*    NUMBER OF ROWS ASSUMED STORED AT SYMBOLIC ADDRESS  M
*    NUMBER OF COLUMNS ASSUMED STORED  AT SYMBOLIC ADDRESS   N
*
*    INITIALIZATION OF OUTER LOOP CONTROL VARIABLE (REGISTER 6)
*      AND INDEX   (REGISTER 7)
*
           L       6,N           R6 = NUMBER OF COLUMNS FOR OUTER LOOP CTL
           LA      7,0           R7 = INDEX FOR ACCESSING COMPONENTS
           L       8,=F'0'       R8 = ZERO, TO BE STORED INTO ARRAY  A
*
*    BEGIN OUTER LOOP BY INITIALIZING INNER LOOP CONTROL VARIABLE
OUTER      L       9,M           R9 = NUMBER OF ROWS FOR INNER LOOP CONTROL
*    INNER LOOP SETS EACH COMPONENT OF A COLUMN TO ZERO
INNER      ST      8,A(7)        STORE 0 INTO CURRENT ROW OF CURRENT COL.
           LA      7,4(7)        INCREASE INDEX TO NEXT COMPONENT
           BCT     9,INNER       COUNT DOWN # ROWS REMAINING IN COLUMN
           BCT     6,OUTER       COUNT DOWN # COLUMNS REMAINING IN A
            .
            .
            .
M          DS      F             RESERVED FOR # ROWS
N          DS      F             RESERVED FOR # COLUMNS

A          DS      (20*20)F      SPACE FOR UP TO  20 × 20  ARRAY
```

When the number of rows equals the number of columns, the address formula given previously shows that the difference between the addresses of any two consecutive diagonal components $A(J,J)$ and $A(J+1,J+1)$ is $4 + 4*M$, where $M = N =$ number of rows and columns. Therefore, to sum up the diagonal components of an M×M array, as in this Fortran sequence

```
        ISUM = 0
        DO  20  J=1,M
        ISUM = ISUM + A(J,J)
   20   CONTINUE
```

we need simply start with A(1,1) and increment the index by an amount equal to $4 + 4*M$ for each iteration of the loop. The statements in Figure 5.11 illustrate how this might be accomplished in assembly language. As in previous examples, it is assumed that there will be no overflow.

5.9   SUMMARY

The instructions discussed in this chapter are summarized in Figure 5.12, except for the instructions for converting between binary integer and text format, which will be described in Section 12.8.

The instructions treat all binary data as integers. We have therefore referred to them as "integer arithmetic" instructions. It should be noted that they are also known as "fixed-point" arithmetic instructions, since, in general, they can be used to process noninteger data, as will be discussed briefly in Chapter 11. A binary integer in the IBM 360 and 370 systems is usually represented and processed as a 32-bit quantity, including one bit for its algebraic sign. However, the division instructions require that the dividend be 64 bits, and two of the multiply instructions generate 64-bit products. Also, 16-bit integers can be processed by using the half-word instructions LH, STH, AH, SH, MH, and CH. In all cases, two's complement arithmetic is employed. Other methods of representing and processing numeric data, nonintegers as well as integers, will be discussed in Chapters 11 through 13.

Figure 5.11 *Sum the diagonal components of an M × M array.*

```
*   STATEMENTS TO SUM UP THE DIAGONAL COMPONENTS OF AN  M × M  ARRAY
*
*   ARRAY  A  CONTAINS FULL-WORD INTEGERS
*
*   NUMBER OF ROWS AND COLUMNS ASSUMED STORED AT SYMBOLIC ADDRESS  M
*
*   INITIALIZATION OF LOOP CONTROL VARIABLE (REGISTER 6)
*
          L      6,M              R6 = NUMBER OF ROWS AND COLUMNS
*
*   COMPUTE  4*M  FOR USE AS PART OF INDEX  4+4*M
*
          L      5,=F'4'          R5 IS ODD-NUMBERED REGISTER FOR MULTIPLY
          MR     4,6              R4 AND R5 CONTAIN PRODUCT 4*M
*   ASSUME  4*M  IS  LESS THAN  2**31
*    SO THAT CORRECT REPRESENTATION OF 4*M IS IN REGISTER 5
*    AND INITIAL VALUE OF SUM (ZERO) IS IN R4
*
* INITIALIZE INDEX TO ZERO (REGISTER 8)
          LA     8,0              R8 = INDEX TO ACCESS A(J,J)
*   LOOP TO ACCUMULATE SUM OF DIAGONAL COMPONENTS IN  REGISTER 4
*
TRACE     A      4,A(8)           R4 = SUM + A(J,J)
          LA     8,4(8,5)         INCR INDEX BY 4 + 4*M, WHERE R5 = 4*M
          BCT    6,TRACE          COUNT DOWN # ROWS
*
*   STORE SUM AT SYMBOLIC ADDRESS 'ISUM'
*
          ST     4,ISUM
           .
           .
           .
M         DS     F                RESERVED FOR # ROWS AND COLUMNS
ISUM      DS     F                RESERVED FOR SUM OF DIAGONAL COMPONENTS
A         DS     (30*30)F         SPACE FOR UP TO 30 × 30 ARRAY
```

Each of the integer arithmetic instructions operates on either one or two quantities, one or both of which must be in registers. Consequently, included among the instructions are some that copy data from memory into a register, others that copy data from a register into memory, and still others that copy data from one register to another. Among the latter are instructions that will change a number's sign (LCR), create its positive or negative absolute value (LPR, LNR), and test to see if a number is zero, positive, or negative (LTR). The result of the LTR test can be determined by means of one of the conditional branch instructions, e.g., BZ, BP, or BM.

Two integers may be algebraically compared without altering either integer by means of the C, CR, and CH instructions. The result of the comparison can be determined by one of the conditional branch instructions, e.g., BE, BH, or BL.

The addition, subtraction, multiplication, and division instructions each operate on two integers. Arithmetic combinations of more than two integers must be programmed as appropriate sequences of these four fundamental operations. There is no instruction that will raise an integer to an arbitrary power.

Three types of error conditions can arise during execution of certain binary arithmetic instructions. These are known as fixed-point overflow, fixed-point divide, and specification errors. The situations that can cause these errors and the instructions in which they can occur are summarized in Appendix D. The occurrence of a fixed-point divide or a specification error will result in the program's being interrupted and terminated. Unless specifically prohibited by the Set Program Mask (SPM) instruction, this will also happen if fixed-point overflow occurs (described in Chap. 11).

In the IBM 360, it is imperative that 32-bit integers be aligned on full-word memory boundaries and that 16-bit integers be aligned on half-word boundaries. In the 370, this is not required; but the 370's arithmetic operations are faster on integers that are so aligned than they are on integers that are not.

Figure 5.12   Summary of integer arithmetic instructions.

opcode	name	type	section	condition codes	summary of action taken
A	Add	RX	5.3	0,1,2,3	V_1 replaced by $V_1 + V_2$
AH	Add Half Word	RX	5.3	0,1,2,3	V_1 replaced by $V_1 + V_2$; V_2 is a half word
AL	Add Logical	RX	5.3	0,1,2,3	V_1 replaced by $V_1 + V_2$; overflow ignored
ALR	Add Logical Registers	RR	5.3	0,1,2,3	V_1 replaced by $V_1 + V_2$; overflow ignored
AR	Add Registers	RR	5.3	0,1,2,3	V_1 replaced by $V_1 + V_2$
C	Compare	RX	5.5	0,1,2,3	$V_1 : V_2$
CH	Compare Half Word	RX	5.5	0,1,2,3	$V_1 : V_2$; V_2 is a half word
CR	Compare Registers	RR	5.5	0,1,2,3	$V_1 : V_2$
D	Divide	RX	5.3		$V_1 / V_2 = Q + R / V_2$; R_1 replaced by R, and $R_1 + 1$ by Q
DR	Divide Registers	RR	5.3		$V_1 / V_2 = Q + R / V_2$; R_1 replaced by R, and $R_1 + 1$ by Q
L	Load	RX	5.2		V_1 replaced by V_2
LCR	Load Complement from Registers	RR	5.6	0,1,2,3	V_1 replaced by $-V_2$
LH	Load Half Word	RX	5.2		V_1 replaced by V_2; V_2 is a half word
LM	Load Multiple	RS	5.2		$R_1, R_1 + 1, \ldots$ replaced by $V_2, \ldots$ (up to 16 consecutive words)
LNR	Load Negative Absolute Value	RR	5.6	0,1	V_1 replaced by $-\text{ABS}(V_2)$
LPR	Load Positive Absolute Value	RR	5.6	0,2,3	V_1 replaced by $+\text{ABS}(V_2)$
LR	Load Registers	RR	5.2		V_1 replaced by V_2
LTR	Load and Test Registers	RR	5.6	0,1,2,3	V_1 replaced by V_2
M	Multiply	RX	5.3		bits 0–63 of R_1 and $R_1 + 1$ replaced by $V_1 \times V_2$
MH	Multiply Half Word	RX	5.3		bits 0–31 of R_1 replaced by $V_1 \times V_2$; V_2 is a half word
MR	Multiply Registers	RR	5.3		bits 0–63 of R_1 and $R_1 + 1$ replaced by $V_1 \times V_2$
S	Subtract	RX	5.3	0,1,2,3	V_1 replaced by $V_1 - V_2$
SH	Subtract Half Word	RX	5.3	0,1,2,3	V_1 replaced by $V_1 - V_2$; V_2 is a half word
SL	Subtract Logical	RX	5.3	1,2,3	V_1 replaced by $V_1 - V_2$; overflow ignored
SLR	Subtract Logical Registers	RR	5.3	1,2,3	V_1 replaced by $V_1 - V_2$; overflow ignored
SR	Subtract Registers	RR	5.3	0,1,2,3	V_1 replaced by $V_1 - V_2$
ST	Store	RX	5.2		V_2 replaced by V_1
STH	Store Half Word	RX	5.2		V_2 replaced by bits 16–31 of R_1; V_2 is a half word
STM	Store Multiple	RS	5.2		$V_2, \ldots$ replaced by $V_1, \ldots$ (up to 16 consecutive words)

Note: V_1 denotes the quantity whose address is specified by the first operand,
V_2 denotes the quantity whose address is specified by the second operand,
R_1 denotes the register specified in the first operand.

Meanings of the condition codes are summarized in the indicated sections and in Fig. 8.5a.

Binary Integers   In the IBM 360 and 370 systems, the maximum positive value that a binary integer can have is $2^{k-1} - 1$, where k is the number of bits used to represent the integer. The minimum negative value is -2^{k-1}. In the IBM 360 and 370, $k = 32$ for a full-word integer, and $k = 16$ for a half-word integer. Thus the maximum positive full-word integer is $2^{31} - 1 = 2,147,483,647$; the maximum positive half-word integer is $2^{15} - 1 = 32,767$.

Overflow   Overflow occurs when an attempt is made to compute a full-word binary integer that either exceeds the maximum allowable positive number or is less than the minimum allowable negative number. In most situations, overflow causes termination of your program at run time.

Two's Complement   Binary integers are represented in two's complement form in the IBM 360 and 370 systems. In this form the sign bit (bit b_0) is 0 (zero) for positive numbers and 1 for negative numbers, and it participates in all arithmetic operations with a positional value of $-b_0 \times 2^{k-1}$. Except when overflow occurs, the correct two's complement representation of an integer is generated by all the binary arithmetic instructions, in accordance with the rules of algebra.

RX-Type Arithmetic Instructions   These instructions require that one operand be in a register and the other in a memory location. The register is specified in the first operand field; the memory location's address is specified via the second operand field.

RR-Type Arithmetic Instructions   These instructions require that each operand be in a register. The register addresses are specified in the first and second operand fields of the instruction. The two register addresses need not be different.

Algebraic Versus Logical Instructions   In algebraic instructions, the sign bit is used to produce a result consistent with the laws of algebra for signed numbers. In logical instructions, plus and minus signs are not involved in the operations; instead, the bit that would otherwise be called the sign bit is simply the high-order numeric bit of the quantity: e.g., a logical full word has 32 numeric bits, whereas an algebraic full word has 31 numeric bits and 1 sign bit.

Full-Word Versus Half-Word Arithmetic   The full-word binary arithmetic instructions operate on two full words. The half-word instructions operate on one full word and one half word.

Even-Odd Register Pair   This is two consecutively numbered registers, the first of which must be an even-numbered register.

Condition Code   This is a hardware indicator that records the nature of the result of the most recently executed code-setting instruction. Many but not all instructions are code-setting instructions (see below). When tested by a conditional branch instruction, the value of the condition code determines whether or not the branch is taken.

Code-Setting Instructions   A variety of instructions—among them, all adds, subtracts, compares, and sign operations, but NOT multiply or divide operations—set the condition code. Each time it is set, its previous setting is lost.

Conditional Branch Instructions   These come in two principal categories—those that test whether the result of the most recently executed arithmetic code-setting instruction was zero, negative, or positive; and those that test whether the result of the most recently executed compare instruction was equal, less than, or greater than. Conditional branch instructions can also test combinations of these conditions, e.g., a zero-or-negative result, or a less-than-or-equal result. See Chapter 8 or Appendix B and C for further details.

Column-Major Versus Row-Major Form   In column-major form, the elements of column J in an $M \times N$ two-dimensional array A are stored consecutively in memory: A(1,J), A(2,J), . . ., A(M,J). The first element of column $J+1$—namely, A(1,J+1)—is stored immediately after A(M,J). In row-major form, the elements of row K in A are stored consecutively in memory: A(K,1), A(K,2), . . ., A(K,N). The first element of row $K+1$—namely, A(K+1,1)—is stored immediately after A(K,N).

1. Load (L) and Store (ST) are indispensable instructions for addition, subtraction, multiplication, and division of binary integers. Why?

2. Under what circumstances would it be correct to use half-word binary integer instructions instead of full-word instructions? What would be the advantage of doing so?

3. What is "overflow," and what situation (or situations) cause it to occur? What usually happens when it does occur? What happens when an attempt is made to divide by zero?

4. Of the four main arithmetic operations—the full-word add, subtract, multiply, and divide instructions—only one will never result in an overflow condition, no matter what its operands are. Which operation is it, and why doesn't it result in overflow?

5. When multiplying two full-word binary integers, why is it important to know—or at least to be able to determine—whether the product is within the range of a 32-bit integer? (See also Exercise 10 at the end of this chapter.)

6. If the Divide (D) instruction is used to divide -29 by $+13$, what two numbers are produced for the result? Which one is the remainder, and which the quotient? What two numbers are produced if the D instruction divides $+13$ by -29? Again, which is the remainder, and which is the quotient? What is the general rule governing the algebraic sign of the remainder and quotient that are produced by the Divide (D) instruction?

7. Each of the following pairs of Load and Divide instructions can produce incorrect results at run time. Why?

```
   L   9,=F'-29'     L   8,=F'-29'     L   8,=F'-29'     L   9,=F'-29'
   D   8,=F'13'      D   9,=F'13'      D   8,=F'13'      D   9,=F'13'
```

8. What is the fundamental purpose of multiplying the dividend by $+1$ as part of the instruction sequence for dividing two binary integers?

9. For each of the following conditional branch instructions, name the condition or conditions which cause it to branch: BZ, BM, BP, BNZ, BNM, BNP. (**Note:** If you didn't distinguish between zero, positive, and negative conditions—e.g., if you assumed that negative meant not positive—you were wrong. Why?)

10. The Load and Test (LTR) instruction sets the condition code but does not change the value or sign of the number it is testing. Normally, it only tests numbers that are in registers. Nevertheless, there is a way that LTR can be used to test a binary integer that is in a memory location. How? (**Hint:** See Figure 5.5.)

11. What is the fundamental difference between these two sequences of instructions:

```
   L    8,X              L    8,X
   S    8,Y              C    8,Y
   BP   XGREATER         BH   XGREATER
```

12. The three instructions that perform sign operations (LCR, LPR, and LNR) only do so on a number that's in a register. Except when the number is 0 (zero), LCR changes its sign, LPR forces its sign to be positive, and LNR forces its sign to be negative. For each of these three instructions, what is the result when the number it operates on is 0 (zero)?

13. How should the program segment in Figure 5.8 be changed so that instead of determining the algebraically largest and smallest integers in an array, it would determine the maximum and minimum values of the array components?

14. How should the program segment in Figure 5.8 be changed so that in addition to determining the algebraically largest and smallest values in an array, it also determines how many of the integers were equal to the largest value, and how many were equal to the smallest value?

15. The following two instructions each put a full-word binary 0 (zero) into a register. Explain the difference between the two instructions, and explain why each of them succeeds at what it does.

```
   LA   7,0
   L    8,=F'0'
```

16. Which of the following two instructions loads the contents of symbolic location *N?* What does the other one do?

```
LA    7,N
L     7,N
```

17. In Figure 5.11 the heart of the "trace" loop contains this instruction:

```
LA    8,4(8,5)
```

Explain how it achieves its stated purpose, namely, explain how this one instruction is able to increase the index by 4 + 4*M for this program segment, where *M* is the number of rows and columns in a matrix.

Problem Statement

Write a program that will read employee time records, each record containing two clock times in hours and minutes in the format described below. For each, the program is to compute and print the elapsed time, together with the given input data.

The two clock times are assumed to be within 24 hours of one another but not necessarily on the same day. They represent the time an employee's work started and the time it ended. The earlier time is in columns 20–23, and the later time in columns 30–33; both times are given in so-called military format (e.g., 11:30 A.M. = 1130, 11:30 P.M. = 2330).

Each line of printed output should contain the given input data together with the elapsed time in hours and minutes, as in these examples:

start time	stop time	elapsed hrs	mins
0830	1700	08	30
1700	2400	07	00
2000	0330	07	30
0330	2000	16	30

Solution Procedure

The procedure (Figs. 5.13a–5.13b) depends on being able to treat each clock time as two two-digit integers and on being able to convert each two-digit integer to its binary integer representation. Once that is done for each of the four two-digit integers, we can assume that they are symbolically defined as follows:

$$HH = \text{stopping hour}, \quad MM = \text{stopping minute}$$
$$hh = \text{starting hour}, \quad mm = \text{starting minute}$$

The decisions that govern how to compute the elapsed time are depicted in the accompanying pseudocode. Note that the underlying assumption that the elapsed time is less than 24 hours means that we do not need any dates associated with the times. But the assumption that the work may start on one day and end on the next means that the stopping time may be numerically smaller than the starting time. The procedure recognizes this, and accounts for it by adding 24 hours to the stop time.

Figure 5.13a   Pseudocode for sample problem solution in Figure 5.13b.

```
COMPUTE_ELAPSED_TIME:

  open input and output files;
  print heading line;

  REPEAT WHILE there is more data to read

    read one input record;
    convert start_hour and start_minute to binary;
    convert stop_hour and stop_minute to binary;

    IF stop_minute < start_minute
    THEN {borrow}
      add 60 to stop_minute;
      subtract 1 from stop_hour;
    END IF;

    IF stop_hour < start_hour
    THEN {next day}
      add 24 to stop_hour;
    END IF;

    elapsed_hours := stop_hour - start_hour;
    elapsed_minutes := stop_minutes - start_minutes;
    convert elapsed_hours and elapsed_minutes to EBCDIC;
    print start_time, stop_time, elapsed_hours, elapsed_minutes;

  END WHILE;

  close all files;

EXIT COMPUTE_ELAPSED_TIME.
```

Figure 5.13b Solution to sample problem.

```
FLAG LOCTN OBJECT CODE    ADDR1 ADDR2 STMNT M SOURCE STATEMENT

     000000                         3 SPCH5    CSECT
                                    4 *
                                    5 * SPCH5   READS INPUT DATA CARDS CONTAINING EMPLOYEE 'TIME CARDS'.
                                    6 *    EACH CARD CONTAINS THE CLOCK TIMES FOR START AND
                                    7 *    TERMINATION OF A WORK SHIFT FOR ONE EMPLOYEE.
                                    8 *    THE PROGRAM COMPUTES THE ELAPSED WORK TIME
                                    9 *    (IN HOURS AND MINUTES) FOR THAT EMPLOYEE, AND PRINTS
                                   10 *    THE GIVEN START AND STOP TIMES TOGETHER WITH THE ELAPSED TIME.
                                   11 *    IT DOES THIS FOR AS MANY INPUT CARDS AS THERE ARE.
                                   12 *
                                   13 *    THE INPUT DATA FORMAT IS AS FOLLOWS
                                   14 *
                                   15 *        COLS  20-23    HHMM    START TIME, IN HOURS AND MINUTES
                                   16 *              30-33    HHMM    STOP TIME, IN HOURS AND MINUTES
                                   17 *
                                   18 * ALL TIMES ARE MILITARY TIMES    0000 = MIDNIGHT; 2359 = 11 59 PM
                                   19 * THE ELAPSED TIME IS ASSUMED TO BE LESS THAN 24 HOURS, BUT
                                   20 *    THE STOP TIME MAY OCCUR ON THE DAY FOLLOWING THE START TIME.
                                   21 *
000000 90 EC D00C                  22           STM   14,12,12(13)        STANDARD ENTRY
000004 05 C0                       23           BALR  12,0
000006                             24           USING *,12
000006 50 D0 C35E     000364       25           ST    13,SAVE+4
00000A 41 D0 C35A     000360       26           LA    13,SAVE
                                   27 *
                                   28 * OPEN INPUT AND OUTPUT FILES, AND PRINT HEADING LINE.
                                   29 *
00000E                             30           OPEN  (SYSIN,(INPUT))      INPUT IS 'SYSIN' DATA STREAM
00001A                             36           OPEN  (SYSPRNT,(OUTPUT))   OUTPUT IS 'SYSOUT' PRINTER

                                   42 * DOS *******
                                   43 *         OPEN  SYSIN
                                   44 *         OPEN  SYSPRNT
                                   45 ****************

000026                             46           PUT   SYSPRNT,HEADING
                                   51 *
                                   52 * MAIN PROCESSING LOOP ...
                                   53 *         READS ONE INPUT CARD
                                   54 *         CONVERTS START HOUR AND START MINUTE TO BINARY INTEGERS
                                   55 *         CONVERTS STOP HOUR AND STOP MINUTE TO BINARY INTEGERS
                                   56 *         COMPUTES ELAPSED TIME IN HOURS AND MINUTES
                                   57 *         CONVERTS ELAPSED HOURS AND ELAPSED MINUTES TO TEXT (EBCDIC)
                                   58 *         PRINTS THE START AND STOP TIMES, AND ELAPSED HRS & MINS
                                   59 *         REPEATS THE LOOP UNTIL END-OF-DATA
                                   60 *         WHEN END-OF-DATA IS REACHED, THE PROGRAM IS TERMINATED.
                                   61 *
000034                             62 LOOP     GET   SYSIN,INAREA              GET AN INPUT CARD
                                   67 *
000042 F2 71 C122C155 000128 00015B 68          PACK  BCD,STARTHR         CONVERT START HOUR TO BINARY
000048 4F 30 C122        000128    69           CVB   3,BCD
00004C 50 30 C12A        000130    70           ST    3,STARTHH
000050 F2 71 C122C157 000128 00015D 71          PACK  BCD,STARTMIN        CONVERT START MINUTE TO BINARY
000056 4F 30 C122        000128    72           CVB   3,BCD
00005A 50 30 C12E        000134    73           ST    3,STARTMM
00005E F2 71 C122C15F 000128 000165 74          PACK  BCD,STOPHR          CONVERT STOP HOUR TO BINARY
000064 4F 30 C122        000128    75           CVB   3,BCD
000068 50 30 C132        000138    76           ST    3,STOPHH
00006C F2 71 C122C161 000128 000167 77          PACK  BCD,STOPMIN         CONVERT STOP MINUTE TO BINARY
000072 4F 30 C122        000128    78           CVB   3,BCD
000076 50 30 C136        00013C    79           ST    3,STOPMM
                                   80 *
                                   81 * ADJUST START AND STOP TIMES FOR BORROWING AND FOR NEXT DAY IF NEED BE
                                   82 *
00007A 58 60 C136        00013C    83           L     6,STOPMM           SEE IF STOP MIN LESS THAN START MIN
00007E 59 60 C12E        000134    84           C     6,STARTMM
000082 47 B0 C094        00009A    85           BNL   NOBORROW           BRANCH IF BORROW NOT NECESSARY
                                   86 *
000086 5A 60 C3A2        0003A8    87           A     6,=F'60'           TO BORROW, ADD 60 MINS TO STOPMM
00008A 50 60 C136        00013C    88           ST    6,STOPMM
00008E 58 60 C132        000138    89           L     6,STOPHH           AND SUBT 1 HOUR FROM STOPHH
000092 5B 60 C3A6        0003AC    90           S     6,=F'1'
000096 50 60 C132        000138    91           ST    6,STOPHH
                                   92 *
00009A 58 60 C132        000138    93 NOBORROW L 6,STOPHH                SEE IF STOP HOUR LESS THAN START HOUR
00009E 59 60 C12A        000130    94           C     6,STARTHH
0000A2 47 B0 C0A8        0000AE    95           BNL   ELAPSED            BRANCH IF BOTH HOURS ARE IN SAME DAY
                                   96 *
0000A6 5A 60 C3AA        0003B0    97           A     6,=F'24'           IF STOP HOUR IS IN NEXT DAY,
0000AA 50 60 C132        000138    98           ST    6,STOPHH               INCREASE IT BY 24 HOURS
                                   99 *
                                  100 * COMPUTE ELAPSED TIME
                                  101 *
0000AE 58 60 C132        000138   102 ELAPSED  L     6,STOPHH           COMPUTE ELAPSED HOURS
0000B2 5B 60 C12A        000130   103           S     6,STARTHH
0000B6 50 60 C13A        000140   104           ST    6,ELAPSHH
0000BA 58 60 C136        00013C   105           L     6,STOPMM           COMPUTE ELAPSED MINUTES
0000BE 5B 60 C12E        000134   106           S     6,STARTMM
0000C2 50 60 C13E        000144   107           ST    6,ELAPSMM
                                  108 *
                                  109 * CONVERT ELAPSED TIME TO EBCDIC (TEXT) FORM FOR PRINTING
                                  110 *
```

Figure 5.13b   continued

```
FLAG LOCTN OBJECT CODE     ADDR1 ADDR2  STMNT M SOURCE STATEMENT

     0000C6 58 60 C13A      000140        111           L     6,ELAPSHH
     0000CA 4E 60 C122      000128        112           CVD   6,BCD
     0000CE F3 17 C1ECC122 0001F2 000128  113           UNPK  ELAPSHR,BCD      ELAPSHR IS 2-DIGIT FIELD
     0000D4 96 F0 C1ED      0001F3        114           OI    ELAPSHR+1,X'F0'
     0000D8 58 60 C13E      000144        115           L     6,ELAPSMM
     0000DC 4E 60 C122      000128        116           CVD   6,BCD
     0000E0 F3 17 C1EFC122 0001F5 000128  117           UNPK  ELAPSMIN,BCD     ELAPSMIN IS 2-DIGIT FIELD
     0000E6 96 F0 C1FD      0001F6        118           OI    ELAPSMIN+1,X'F0'
                                          119    *
                                          120    * PRINT START TIME, STOP TIME, AND ELAPSED TIME, AND GO GET NEXT CARD.
                                          121    *
     0000EA D2 4F C19CC142 0001A2 000148  122           MVC   OUTLINE,INAREA   MOVE INPUT CARD TO OUTPUT LINE AREA
     0000F0                               123           PUT   SYSPRNT,OUTAREA
     0000FE 47 F0 C02E      000034        128           B     LOOP
                                          129    * WHEN END-OF-DATA IS REACHED, CONTROL IS TRANSFERRED HERE
                                          130    *
     000102                               131    EOD    CLOSE (SYSIN)
     00010E                               137           CLOSE (SYSPRNT)
     00011A 58 D0 C35E      000364        143           L     13,SAVE+4                    STANDARD EXIT
     00011E 98 EC D00C                    144           LM    14,12,12(13)
     000122 07 FE                         145           BR    14

                                          146    *  DOS  *******
                                          147    *EOD    CLOSE SYSIN
                                          148    *       CLOSE SYSPRNT
                                          149    *       EOJ
                                          150    ***************

                                          151    *
                                          152    * CONSTANTS AND DATA AREAS
                                          153    *
     000128                               154    BCD      DS    D              SPACE FOR DECIMAL FORM OF HRS & MINS
     000130                               155    STARTHH  DS    F              START HOUR IN BINARY
     000134                               156    STARTMM  DS    F              START MINUTE IN BINARY
     000138                               157    STOPHH   DS    F              STOP HOUR IN BINARY
     00013C                               158    STOPMM   DS    F              STOP MINUTE IN BINARY
     000140                               159    ELAPSHH  DS    F              ELAPSED HOURS IN BINARY
     000144                               160    ELAPSMM  DS    F              ELAPSED MINUTES IN BINARY
                                          161    *
                                          162    * INPUT CARD AREA
                                          163    *
     000148                               164    INAREA   DS    0CL80          DEFINITION OF INPUT AREA ...
     000148                               165             DS    CL19           COLS 1-19    UNUSED
     00015B                               166    STARTHR  DS    CL2            20-21        START HOUR
     00015D                               167    STARTMIN DS    CL2            22-23        START MINUTE
     00015F                               168             DS    CL6            24-29        UNUSED
     000165                               169    STOPHR   DS    CL2            30-31        STOP HOUR
     000167                               170    STOPMIN  DS    CL2            32-33        STOP MINUTE
     000169                               171             DS    CL47           34-80        UNUSED
                                          172    *
                                          173    * OUTPUT PRINT AREA
                                          174    *
     000198                               175    OUTAREA  DS    0CL132         DEFINITION OF OUTPUT AREA ...
     000198 4040404040404040              176             DC    CL10' '        COLS 1-10    BLANKS
     0001A2                               177    OUTLINE  DS    CL80           11-90        CARD INPUT DATA
     0001F2                               178    ELAPSHR  DS    CL2            91-92        ELAPSED HOURS
     0001F4 40                            179             DC    CL1' '         93           BLANK-
     0001F5                               180    ELAPSMIN DS    CL2            94-95        ELAPSED MINUTES
     0001F7 4040404040404040              181             DC    CL37' '        96-132       BLANKS
                                          182    *
                                          183    * HEADING LINE FOR BEGINNING OF PRINTED OUTPUT
                                          184    *
     00021C                               185    HEADING  DS    0CL132         DEFINITION OF HEADING ...
     00021C 4040404040404040              186             DC    CL26' '        COLS 1-26    BLANKS
     000236 E2E3C1D9E340E3C9              187             DC    CL11'START TIME'   27-37    START TIME HEADING
     000241 E2E3D6D740E3C9D4              188             DC    CL11'STOP TIME'    38-48    STOP TIME HEADING
     00024C 4040404040404040              189             DC    CL42' '         49-90       BLANKS
     000276 C5D3C1D7E2C5C440              190             DC    CL12'ELAPSED TIME'  91-102  ELAPSED TIME HEADING
     000282 4040404040404040              191             DC    CL30' '         103-132     BLANKS
                                          192    * DCB'S FOR INPUT AND OUTPUT FILES
                                          193    *
     0002A0                               194    SYSIN    DCB   DSORG=PS,MACRF=(GM),DDNAME=SYSIN,EODAD=EOD,        X
                                          195                   RECFM=FB,LRECL=80,BLKSIZE=4080
                                          247    *
     000300                               248    SYSPRNT  DCB   DSORG=PS,MACRF=(PM),DDNAME=SYSPRINT,               X
                                          249                   RECFM=FB,LRECL=132,BLKSIZE=4092

                                          301    *  DOS  *******
                                          302    *SYSIN   DTFCD DEVADDR=SYSIPT,WORKA=YES,IOAREA1=INBUF,EOFADDR=EOD, X
                                          303    *              DEVICE=2540
                                          304    *SYSPRNT DTFPR DEVADDR=SYSLST,WORKA=YES,IOAREA1=OUTBUF,BLKSIZE=132, X
                                          305    *              DEVICE=1403
                                          306    *
                                          307    *INBUF   DS    CL80
                                          308    *OUTBUF  DC    CL132' '
                                          309    ***************

                                          310    *
                                          311    * SAVE AREA
```

Figure 5.13b continued

```
FLAG LOCTN OBJECT CODE    ADDR1  ADDR2  STMNT M SOURCE STATEMENT

                                        312   *
       000360                           313   SAVE      DS     18F

                                        314   *  DOS  *******
                                        315   *SAVE     DS     9D
                                        316   ***************

                                        317   * LITERALS
       0003A8 0000003C                  319                    =F'60'
       0003AC 00000001                  320                    =F'1'
       0003B0 00000018                  321                    =F'24'
                                        322             END
```

CROSS-REFERENCE

```
SYMBOL    LEN   VALUE   DEFN    REFERENCES

BCD       00008 000128  00154   00068  00069  00071  00072  00074  00075  00077  00078  00112  00113  00116  00117
ELAPSED   00004 0000AE  00102   00095
ELAPSHH   00004 000140  00159   00104  00111
ELAPSHR   00002 0001F2  00178   00113  00114
ELAPSMIN  00002 0001F5  00180   00117  00118
ELAPSMM   00004 000144  00160   00107  00115
EOD       00004 000104  00133   00216
HEADING   00084 00021C  00185   00048
INAREA    00050 000148  00164   00064  00122
LOOP      00004 000034  00063   00128
NOBORROW  00004 00009A  00093   00085
OUTAREA   00084 000198  00175   00125
OUTLINE   00050 0001A2  00177   00122
SAVE      00004 000360  00313   00025  00026  00143
SPCH5     00001 000000  00003
STARTHH   00004 000130  00155   00070  00094  00103
STARTHR   00002 00015B  00166   00068
STARTMIN  00002 00015D  00167   00071
STARTMM   00004 000134  00156   00073  00084  00106
STOPHH    00004 000138  00157   00076  00089  00091  00093  00098  00102
STOPHR    00002 000165  00169   00074
STOPMIN   00002 000167  00170   00077
STOPMM    00004 00013C  00158   00079  00083  00088  00105
SYSIN     00004 0002A0  00195   00034  00063  00135
SYSPRNT   00004 000300  00249   00040  00047  00124  00141
```

1. Suppose that Registers 2 and 3 and symbolic memory location X contain the following hexadecimal integers:

Register 2:	0000A000
Register 3:	FFFF6000
Location X:	00000002

What integers exist in Registers 2 and 3 after each of the following instructions is executed? Assume that, for each instruction, the integers given above exist just prior to the execution of that instruction.

a. A 2,X	d. D 2,X	g. SR 3,2	
b. S 3,X	e. AR 2,3	h. MR 2,3	
c. M 2,X	f. AR 3,2	i. DR 2,3	
		j. SH 3,X	

2. Suppose that Registers 2, 3, and 4 and symbolic memory locations X, X+4, and X+8 contain the following hexadecimal integers:

Register 2:	0000A000	Location X:	02040608
Register 3:	FFFF6000	Location X+4:	0A0B0C0D
Register 4:	00000000	Location X+8:	FFFFFFFF

What integers exist in Registers 2, 3, and 4 and at addresses X, X+4, and X+8 after each of the following instructions is executed? Assume that for each instruction, the integers given above exist just prior to the execution of that instruction.

a. LM 2,4,X	d. LNR 3,4	g. LR 4,2
b. LCR 3,4	e. LR 2,4	h. LTR 3,3
c. STM 3,4,X	f. LPR 4,3	i. LH 3,X+4
		j. STH 3,X+8

3. Suppose that Registers 8 and 9 and symbolic memory locations Y and Y+4 contain the following hexadecimal integers:

Register 8:	00000123	Location Y:	0000A000
Register 9:	FFFFF123	Location Y+4:	FFFF6000

What condition—high, equal, or low—results from each of the following compare instructions? Assume that for each instruction, the integers given above exist just prior to execution of that instruction.

a. CR 8,9	c. CH 8,Y+4	e. C 9,Y
b. C 8,Y	d. CR 9,8	f. CH 9,Y+4

4. The Load Multiple (LM) and Store Multiple (STM) instructions each have the following property: if the address of the register designated by the R2 field is less than that designated by the R1 field, the registers that participate in the execution of the instruction are R1, R1+1,...,15, 0, 1,...,R2. For example, in the instruction

$$STM   14,12,12(13)$$

the contents of registers 14,15,0,1,...,12 are stored in the 15 consecutive full words beginning at the address designated by the third operand field 12(13). Given this property of the LM and STM instructions, what can be said about the contents of all 16 registers immediately after execution of the following standard program exit sequence?

```
L        13,SAVE+4
LM       14,12,12(13)
BR       14
```

5. Write an assembly language program that will divide each of the integers in a one-dimensional array, L, by an integer constant, K. The integer quotient of each division should replace the dividend L(J); the integer remainder from each division should be stored in the corresponding position, M(J), of the one-dimensional integer array, M. The following Fortran segment illustrates the computations that are to be performed:

```
          DIMENSION L(100),M(100)
          N = ...
          K = ...
             .
             .
             .
          DO 10 J = 1,N
          IQUO = L(J)/K
          IREM = L(J) - IQUO * K
          L(J) = IQUO
          M(J) = IREM
   10     CONTINUE
```

Your solution should be valid for any integers, N and K, provided that $1 \leq N \leq 100$, and $-2^{31} \leq K \leq 2^{31} - 1$, with $K \neq 0$.

6. Write an assembly language program to determine how many integers in a one-dimensional array, M, are greater than some given integer, K. In Fortran, this might be accomplished as follows:

```
          DIMENSION M(200)
          LM = ...
          K = ...
             .
             .
             .
          J = 0
          DO 10 N = 1,LM
          IF ( M(N) .GT. K ) J = J + 1
   10     CONTINUE
```

7. Write an assembly language program segment that will copy each of the integers from a two-dimensional array, L, into a two-dimensional array, M. In Fortran, this segment might be accomplished as follows:

```
          DIMENSION L(25,25),M(25,25)
          LM = ...
             .
             .
             .
          DO 20 J = 1,LM
          DO 10 K = 1,LM
          M(J,K) = L(J,K)
   10     CONTINUE
   20     CONTINUE
```

8. Write an assembly language program segment to determine how many integers in a two-dimensional array, M, are less than some given integer, K. In Fortran, this segment might be accomplished as follows:

```
          DIMENSION M(50,50)
          LM = ...
          K = ...
               .
               .
               .
          N = 0
          DO 10 J1 = 1,LM
          DO 20 J2 = 1,LM
          IF ( M(J1,J2) .LT. K ) N = N+1
    20    CONTINUE
    10    CONTINUE
```

9. Write an assembly language program segment that will put any arbitrary set of 25 integers into ascending numerical sequence. The segment can use the logic illustrated in this Fortran sequence:

```
          DIMENSION M(100)
          N = 25
               .
               .
          DO 20 J = 1,N-1
          DO 10 K = J,N
          IF ( M(J) .LE. M(K) ) GOTO 10
          L = M(J)
          M(J) = M(K)
          M(K) = L
    10    CONTINUE
    20    CONTINUE
```

10. Write a program segment that will multiply any two full-word integers together, and determine whether the product exceeds $+2^{31}-1$, is less than -2^{31}, or is in the range -2^{31} to $+2^{31}-1$.

If the product exceeds $+2^{31}-1$, the program should substitute $+2^{31}-1$ for the product.

If the product is less than -2^{31}, the program should substitute -2^{31} for the product.

If the product is in the range -2^{31} to $+2^{31}-1$, the program should not substitute any integer for the product.

11. Write a program segment that will calculate the scalar product of two one-dimensional integer arrays, M and N, each consisting of K components. The scalar product is formed by summing the products of corresponding components, as shown in this Fortran segment:

```
          DIMENSION M(10),N(10)
          K = 10
               .
               .
               .
          ISUM = 0
          DO 10 J = 1,K
          ISUM = ISUM + M(J)*N(J)
    10    CONTINUE
```

12. Write a program segment that will calculate the product of two M×M integer arrays, M and N. The product is itself an M×M array, MN, each component MN(J,K) being the scalar product of the Jth row of M and the Kth column of N, as shown in this Fortran segment:

```
        DIMENSION M(10,10),N(10,10),MN(10,10)
        MNSIZE = 10
            .
            .
            .
        DO 30 J = 1,MNSIZE
        DO 20 K = 1,MNSIZE
        MN(J,K) = 0
        DO 10 L = L,MNSIZE
        MN(J,K) = MN(J,K) + M(J,L)*N(L,K)
    10      CONTINUE
    20      CONTINUE
    30      CONTINUE
```

13. The sum of the first N positive integers, $1 + 2 + 3 + ... + N$, which can be written as Σn, is $N \cdot (N+1)/2$. The sum of their squares, Σn^2, is $N \cdot (N+1) \cdot (2N+1)/6$; and the sum of their cubes, Σn^3, is $N^2 \cdot (N+1)^2/4$.

    a. Using the above formulas, write a set of assembly language statements that will compute each of the three sums for any given integer, N.

    b. Modify your solution to Exercise 13a so that it will compute any one (but only one) of the three sums, the sum to be computed being determined by a parameter, K: If $K = 1$, compute the sum of the integers; if $K = 2$, compute the sum of their squares; and if $K = 3$, the sum of their cubes.

    c. What is the largest integer, N, for which the sum of the cubes can be represented as a 32-bit binary integer (including sign)? Modify your solutions to Exercises 13a and 13b so that they print an appropriate message when a sum is too large to be represented in 32 bits.

14. Write a set of assembly language statements that will compute the factorial function of N for any positive integer, N. (The factorial function of a positive integer, N, is the product of the first N integers, $1 \times 2 \times 3 \times ... \times N$, commonly written as $N!$) Modify your solution so that it prints an appropriate message when $N!$ exceeds 32 bits. What is the smallest N for which this is the case? How might $N!$ be calculated for integers greater than this using binary integer arithmetic?

15. Suppose there is a one-dimensional array, A, consisting of no more than 100 full-word integers. Write the assembly language statements that will create another integer array, B, that consists of all the integers in A but stored in reverse order. For example, if A consists of the five integers $-1, 2, 3, -4, 5$, then B would consist of the five integers $5, -4, 3, 2, -1$.

16. The concept of the transpose of an M×M array, A, is simply that each component of the transposed array, B, is obtained from the array A by the following rule: B(J,K) = A(K,J) for each pair of subscripts, K and J. In Fortran, the transpose of an array, A, can be created like this:

```
        DO 20 K=1,M
        DO 10 J=1,M
        B(J,K) = A(K,J)
    10      CONTINUE
    20      CONTINUE
```

Write a set of assembly language statements that will create the transpose of an M×M integer array, A. Your program should work correctly for any M such that $M \leq 30$.

CHAPTER

6

Constants and Data Areas

An assembly language programmer can specify two categories of constants in a source module: constants to be used by the program at run time, and constants to be used by the assembler at assembly time.

Run-time constants can be specified in two ways: (1) as defined constants, specified by means of the DC directive or (2) as value-based constants, specified either by use of "literals" or by use of "self-defining terms."

An **assembly-time constant** is represented by a symbol whose value is the value of the constant. There are two main classes of such symbols: (1) symbols that are part of the assembly language itself and (2) symbols that are defined by the EQU directive.

In addition to the distinction between assembly-time constants and run-time constants, all constants are classified as being either relocatable or absolute. An **absolute constant** is one that is independent of any factor affecting, or affected by, the location of a program in memory. A **relocatable constant** is one that depends on the location of a program in memory.

As will be discussed in Section 6.4, **data areas** are memory locations that are reserved by DS (Define Storage) directives for specific types of data. The assembler assigns addresses to the areas, but does not put any data into them; it is up to your program to do so at run time.

The beginning address of each run-time constant and data area is known as its **address boundary.** Each run-time constant and data area is said to be aligned on its boundary. The most elementary type of boundary is a byte boundary; other types are half-word, full-word, and double-word boundaries. In Section 6.4 we shall see what boundaries are ordinarily assigned by the assembler for the various types of run-time constants and data areas. Section 6.5 will show you how to override the assembler's ordinary boundary assignments.

6.1 RELOCATABLE AND ABSOLUTE CONSTANTS

Every assembly language constant consists of an algebraic expression containing one or more terms. A term is the smallest element of the language that can be used to represent a distinct and separate value. Each term that appears in an expression is itself either absolute or relocatable: it is relocatable if, and only if, it is a symbol used to represent a memory address; otherwise it is absolute. The integer +1 used to increment a counter is an example of an absolute term. An example of a relocatable term is any symbol used as the symbolic address of an instruction.

A constant consisting of a single term is relocatable if that term is relocatable; under all other conditions, it is absolute. A constant consisting of an algebraic combination of absolute and relocatable terms is considered to be either absolute, relocatable, or invalid according to the following rules:

1. Any algebraic combination of two absolute terms is an absolute constant. In addition, the difference between two relocatable terms is an absolute constant.
2. If an absolute term is added to or subtracted from a relocatable term, the result is a relocatable constant.
3. A unary plus or minus operator may be used to emphasize or change the sign of an absolute or relocatable term without changing the nature of that term.
4. Constants formed in accordance with the previous three rules may themselves be algebraically combined to form another constant. The rules used to combine terms are also used to combine constants: the resulting constant is either absolute or relocatable.
5. No other algebraic combination of absolute or relocatable terms or constants is permitted. If such combinations are used, the result is an invalid constant; in particular, the sum, product, or quotient of two relocatable terms or constants is an invalid constant.

Relocatable Constants Are Main Memory Addresses

The distinction between absolute and relocatable terms and constants is important because the value of a relocatable term or constant may be different at run time than it is at assembly time since it depends on where the loader places a program in memory. The value of an absolute term or constant is the same at run time as at assembly time since it is independent of the location of a program in memory.

To illustrate these rules, let R, S, and T be nonnegative relocatable constants, and let A, B, and C be any absolute constants.

```
valid absolute constants:      -A, A+B, A-B, A*B, A/B, (A+B)/C, R-S
valid relocatable constants:   R+A, R-A, R+(S-T), R-(S-T), -R
invalid constants:             R+S, R*S, R/S, R+(S-A)
```

6.2 RUN-TIME CONSTANTS

Run-time constants occupy memory locations when a program is being executed. Like all other information in memory, run-time constants are represented by sequences of bits. However, the length of the bit sequence and the combination of bits used to represent a constant depend on the type of constant involved.

"Type" Determines Representation

For example, the integer constant +3 is represented differently from the floating-point constant +3, and both are different from the text character 3 that might occur, say, in a telephone number. The integer +3 is represented like this:

```
0000  0000  0000  0000  0000  0000  0000  0011
```

the floating-point representation of +3 is

```
0100  0001  0011  0000  0000  0000  0000  0000
```

and the character representation of 3 is

```
1111  0011
```

Figure 6.1 Data type terminology.

Assembly Language	FORTRAN	COBOL
Text	enclosed in quotes	USAGE IS DISPLAY
Binary integers	INTEGER (full-word integer)	USAGE IS COMPUTATIONAL
Floating-point single-precision double-precision	REAL DOUBLE-PRECISION	USAGE IS COMPUTATIONAL-1 USAGE IS COMPUTATIONAL-2
Decimal	--	USAGE IS COMPUTATIONAL-3
Hexadecimal	--	--
Binary digits	--	--
Addresses	program names variable names statement labels	program names elementary, group, and record names paragraph and section names

The representation of a constant in memory contains no indication of the type of constant it is. A constant's type is implied by context only. When a constant is used at run time, the type of use to which it is put must necessarily be in agreement with the type of constant it is, otherwise invalid results may occur.

In the IBM 360 and 370 Assembly Language, there are seven principal types of run-time constants. Some of these may also be represented in Fortran and Cobol, though the terminology is different in these languages (Fig. 6.1). In IBM 360 and 370 Assembly Language, the seven types of run-time constants are:

1. Text, or "characters"
2. Binary integers, either full-word or half-word
3. Floating-point numbers, either single-precision, double-precision, or extended precision
4. Decimal numbers, also called packed-decimal numbers and binary-coded decimal numbers
5. Hexadecimal digits
6. Binary digits
7. Addresses, either full-word or half-word

Types of Constants (margin)

Defined Constants

The **Define Constant (DC) directive** causes the assembler to generate an appropriate machine language representation of one or more constants. These constants can be specified in a variety of ways: as decimal numbers, hexadecimal numbers, binary numbers, character data, and, in a few cases, as symbols that the assembler translates into their numeric equivalences. Each specification of a constant must be preceded by a type code identifying the form in which the constant is being specified. And each specification is subject to certain rules governing the size and other characteristics of the data and determining the machine language representation that will be generated.

Each use of a DC directive is written as a single assembly language statement, with the same fields as other statements: name field, opcode, operand, comments, continuation, and identification. As with other statements, the comments, continuation, and identification fields may optionally be blank. The name field, opcode, and operand have the following general form in a DC directive:

name field	opcode	operand
{ any symbol or blank }	DC	{ one or more subfields, separated by commas }

Each subfield in the operand has up to four components, two of which are required and two of which are optional:

DC operand subfield components

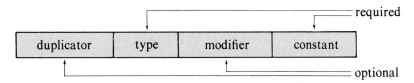

The components are written in the order depicted in the diagram, without any separation between them. For example,

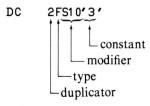

When one or both optional components are omitted, no indication is made of their omission:

```
DC     F'3'
```

There can be more than one subfield in a DC operand, and more than one constant in a subfield, as these examples indicate:

```
DC     F'3',F'4'        two subfields, separated by a comma

DC     F'3,4'           two constants in a subfield, separated by a comma
```

The two required subfield components—type and constant—have provisions that allow an assembly language programmer to specify every representation of data that is possible in the IBM 360 and 370 computer systems. A list of the permissible type codes, and some information pertinent to their meanings, is given in Figure 6.2.

When a symbol is used in the name field of a DC directive statement, that symbol becomes the symbolic address of the first constant that occurs in the operand of the statement. As such, the symbol can be used in instructions to refer to the constant, as, for example:

```
           L     5,FCON
FCON       DC    F'3'
```

Here, the Load instruction L 5,FCON will, at run time, copy the binary representation of the decimal integer $+3$ into Register 5, as was discussed in the preceding chapter.

The **duplicator** designates how many consecutive representations of the constant or constants are to be generated by the assembler. If the duplicator is omitted, its value is assumed to be 1. For example:

```
DC     F'3'             generates one representation of the integer +3

DC     2F'3'            generates two consecutive representations of +3
```

The duplicator may also be written as an arithmetic expression enclosed in parentheses; this expression may include symbols, provided that they were defined in statements prior to their use in the duplicator. For example,

```
DC     (8*16)F'3'       generates 128 consecutive representations of +3

DC     (N)F'3'          generates N consecutive representations of +3,
                        if the value of N had been previously defined
```

Figure 6.2   *Types of constants for DC directive.*

type code	meaning	see also	examples	comments	alignment
C	text or "characters"	Chapter 7	C'ABC:123'	Each character is converted to its 8-bit EBCDIC representation. The characters are stored in consecutive bytes.	byte
F	binary integer (full word)	Chapters 5,6	F'3' F'−3'	The number is converted to its 32-bit binary integer representation (including sign). Maximum number = 2,147,483,647.	full-word
H	binary integer (half word)		H'3' H'−3'	The number is converted to its 16-bit binary integer representation (including sign). Maximum = 32,767.	half-word
E	floating-point (short form)	Chapter 13	E'3' E'−3.5'	The number is converted to its floating-point representation. Maximum approximately 7.2×10^{75}; accuracy about seven digits.	full-word
D	floating-point (long form)		D'3' D'−3.5'	Maximum approx. 7.2×10^{75}, with about 16-digit accuracy.	double-word
L	floating-point (extended form)		L'3' L'−3.5'	Maximum approx. 7.2×10^{75}, with about 32-digit accuracy.	double-word
P	decimal numbers (packed form)	Chapter 12	P'3.5' P'−3'	Each digit is converted to a 4-bit binary integer. Maximum = 31 digits. Decimal point is ignored, e.g., P'3.5' is same as P'35'.	byte
Z	decimal numbers (zoned form)		Z'3' Z'−3.5'	Each digit is converted to its 8-bit EBCDIC representation. Maximum = 16 digits. Decimal point is ignored, as in P-type constants.	byte
X	hexadecimal	Chapter 8	X'12AC'	Each digit must be one of the 16 hexadecimal digits. Each is represented by an equivalent 4-bit binary number. Decimal point not allowed.	byte
B	bit sequence	Chapter 8	B'11001'	The bits are represented as given, 8 bits per byte.	byte
A	address	Chapter 9	A(SYMBOL)	Value of the symbol as a binary integer.	full-word
V		Chapter 10	V(SYMBOL)	Space reserved for an external address.	
Y S Q	address	--		These three types of address constants are not discussed in this text.	

The **modifier**, when present, can consist of from one to three factors. These are known as the length modifier, the scale modifier, and the exponent modifier. If more than one of these factors is present in a modifier, they must be written in the order just stated.

The purpose of the **length modifier (Ln)** is to specify that n bytes of memory are to be used for the representation of the constant. If n is larger than the number of bytes the constant would ordinarily require, the constant may be extended (*padded*) on the left or right by the assembler, depending on the constant's type. If n is smaller than what would ordinarily be required, the assembler will truncate the constant on the left or right, depending on its type. For example, with $n = 1$,

        DC   FL1'3'   generates a 1-byte binary integer representation of $+3$

Figure 6.3 *Specifying constants for full- and half-word data.*

```
FLAG LOCTN OBJECT CODE      ADDR1   ADDR2  STMNT M SOURCE STATEMENT

                                      4   * FULL-WORD CONSTANTS
                                      5   *                          NUMBER OF BYTES
      000000 0000000A                 6        DC    F'10'            4
      000004 FFFFFFF6                 7        DC    F'-10'           4
      000008 0000000A                 8        DC    2F'10'           2 X 4
             0000000A
      000010 FFFFFFF6                 9        DC    2F'-10'          2 X 4
             FFFFFFF6
      000018 0000000A0000000A        10        DC    F'10,10'         1 X (4 + 4)
      000020 0000000A0000000A        11        DC    2F'10,10'        2 X (4 + 4)
             0000000A0000000A
      000030 0000000A                12        DC    F'10',F'10'      4 + 4
      000034 0000000A
      000038 0000000A                13        DC    3F'10',2F'10'    3 X 4  +  2 X 4
             0000000A
             0000000A
      000044 0000000A
             0000000A
      00004C 7FFFFFFF                14        DC    F'2147483647'    4
      000050 80000000                15        DC    F'-2147483648'   4

                                     16   * IF NUMBER OUTSIDE RANGE, CONSTANT IS INCORRECT
      000054 7FFFFFFF                17        DC    F'-2147483649'   (LESS THAN  -2**31 )
      000058 80000000                18        DC    F'2147483648'    (EXCEEDS  2**31 - 1 )

                                     19   * HALF-WORD CONSTANTS
      00005C 000A                    20        DC    H'10'            2
      00005E FFF6                    21        DC    H'-10'           2
      000060 000A                    22        DC    2H'10'           2 X 2
             000A
      000064 FFF6                    23        DC    2H'-10'          2 X 2
             FFF6
      000068 000A000A                24        DC    H'10,10'         1 X (2 + 2)
      00006C 000A000A                25        DC    2H'10,10'        2 X (2 + 2)
             000A000A
      000074 000A                    26        DC    H'10',H'10'      2 + 2
      000076 000A
      000078 000A                    27        DC    3H'10',2H'10'    3 X 2  +  2 X 2
             000A
             000A
      00007E 000A
             000A
      000082 7FFF                    28        DC    H'32767'         2
      000084 8000                    29        DC    H'-32768'        2

                                     30   * IF NUMBER OUTSIDE RANGE, CONSTANT IS INCORRECT
      000086 7FFF                    31        DC    H'-32769'        (LESS THAN  -2**15 )
      000088 8000                    32        DC    H'32768'         (EXCEEDS  2**15 - 1 )
```

The **scale modifier (Sn)** specifies that the constant is to be multiplied by 2^n or by 16^n before its binary representation is generated by the assembler. The factor 2^n is used for F- and H-type constants; in this case, n must be in the range of from -187 through $+346$. The factor 16^n is used for D-, E-, and L-type constants: $0 \leq n \leq 14$ for D and E, and $0 \leq n \leq 28$ for L. For example, with $n = 10$:

```
DC      FS10'3'
```
generates a full-word binary integer representation of $3 \times 2^{10} = 3072$

The **exponent modifier (En)** specifies that an H-, F-, D-, E-, or L-type constant is to be multiplied by 10^n before its representation is generated by the asembler. In this case, n must be in the range of from -85 through $+75$. For example, with $n = 5$,

```
DC      FE5'3'
```
generates a full-word binary integer representation of $3 \times 10^5 = 300,000$

F- and H-type constants are always specified as signed or unsigned decimal integers, *without commas or decimal points*. In the absence of a length modifier, an F-type constant generates a full-word binary integer. The constant must, therefore, be in the range of from -2^{31} through $2^{31}-1$, i.e., $-2,147,483,648$ through $+2,147,483,647$. Similarly, in the absence of a length modifier, an H-type constant generates a half-word binary integer. Such a constant must be in the range of from -2^{15} through $2^{15}-1$, i.e., $-32,768$ through $+32,767$.

Unless a length modifier is specified, F-type constants are aligned on full-word boundaries and H-type constants are aligned on half-word boundaries. If a length modifier is specified, alignment is on a byte boundary. The scale and exponent modifiers do not affect the boundary alignments.

Examples of the use of a DC directive for F- and H-type constants are shown in Figure 6.3. These examples do not include the use of modifiers; we leave that to you as an exercise. Examples of most of the other types of constants will be given in subsequent chapters.

Value-Based Constants

The use of value-based constants allows a programmer to specify a constant in an operand without having to define that constant elsewhere in the program. There are two types of value-based constants that can be used to create data for use at run time: literals and self-defining terms.

Literals. A *literal* is a symbolic representation of a constant to which the assembler assigns an address. When a single constant is needed in the operand of certain instructions, the programmer can use a literal to designate that constant without having to define the constant with a DC directive. The following three statements illustrate this:

```
Statement 1    FCON    DC    F'1'
Statement 2            L     5,FCON
Statement 3            L     5,=F'1'
```

At run time, the second and third statements would produce exactly the same result. Each would load the full-word binary integer +1 into Register 5. However, Statement 2 requires that Statement 1 be included; Statement 3 does not require Statement 1. The operand =F'1' is a literal designating the constant +1.

When the assembler processes Statement 3, it generates the binary integer representation of +1, assigns an address to it, and creates the appropriate base-displacement form of its address in the assembled Load instruction. It does this in response to the presence of the F-type literal, =F'1'. As may be inferred, the format of a literal is, with one major exception, nearly identical to that of an operand in a DC directive. The exception is the presence of the equals sign (=), which must precede the subfields as shown here:

format of a literal

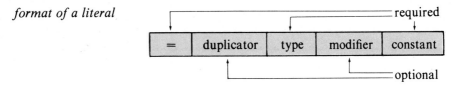

Thus, in Statement 3 above, the literal =F'1' does not include the two optional fields.

In addition to the mandatory presence of the equals sign, there are a few other differences, all minor, between the format of a literal and that of an operand in a DC directive. The most important of these is that one cannot specify more than one operand in a literal. For example, =F'1',F'2' is not valid. Except for these differences, all the rules for forming an operand in a DC directive also apply to literals and any of the data type codes listed in Figure 6.2 can be used in the specification of a literal.

Restrictions on Literals

Certain restrictions govern the use of literals. These derive from the fact that the assembler assigns a memory address to each literal and substitutes the base-displacement form of that address in the instruction in which the literal is used. The restrictions are: literals cannot be used to designate a register address in any instruction, to specify the immediate data or mask fields in any instruction, or to specify the length fields (L, L1, or L2) in any instruction. *They can, however, be specified in the second operand of any Load, Add, Subtract, Multiply, Divide, and Move instruction that is not an RR or SI instruction.* Literals can also be specified in the second operand of most Compare instructions and of a few other instructions to be covered in Chapter 12. Note in particular that a literal should not be used as the second operand in a Store instruction nor as the destination of other copy-type operations.

The reason for these restrictions is twofold. First, as was mentioned, the assembler places the address of a literal, not the constant that it represents, into a machine language instruction. Length fields, mask fields, immediate data fields, and register addresses cannot be represented by memory

Figure 6.4   Types of self-defining terms.

type of term	method of representation	comments	examples
decimal integer	unsigned decimal integer	maximum, OS: $2^{31} - 1$ DOS: $2^{24} - 1$	3 12
binary integer	B'⌣' binary digits	maximum, OS: 32 bits DOS: 24 bits	B'0001' B'11' B'1011'
hexadecimal integer	X'⌣' hexadecimal digits	maximum, OS: 8 hex digits DOS: 6 hex digits	X'4A' X'6D' X'4100'
sequence of text characters	C'⌣' text characters	maximum, OS: 4 chars. DOS: 3 chars.	C'Z' C'CAT' C'A=B'

Note: Two of the text characters that can be used in a C-type term require special treatment: the apostrophe (') and the ampersand (&). Two consecutive apostrophes and two consecutive ampersands must be written in the character sequence whenever one apostrophe or one ampersand is wanted, e.g., in the term C'&&', the two ampersands represent one ampersand.

addresses. Second, when the same literal is used more than once in a program, as for example in the instructions

```
L    5,=F'2'
M    4,=F'2'
```

only one representation of that literal is created by the assembler, and the assembled instructions referring to that literal will all contain the same memory address. Therefore, if we were to store or otherwise copy data into the memory area reserved by the assembler for the literal, the execution of the other instructions that refer to the literal could be adversely affected.

Despite what may seem like a rather lengthy list of restrictions, literals are exceptionally useful, for their use removes the necessity to define a constant via a DC directive when that constant is needed for the operand of an instruction.

Self-Defining Terms.   A *self-defining term* is an absolute constant that can be written in one of four ways: as a decimal integer, a binary integer, a hexadecimal integer, or a sequence of text characters. The formats for writing self-defining terms are shown in Figure 6.4. Although the notation used for self-defining terms is similar to that used for literals, sometimes causing problems for beginning programmers, the distinction between the two is of critical importance. In contrast to the use of literals in instructions, the use of self-defining terms has the following property: when a self-defining term is used in an instruction, the assembler substitutes the binary representation of that term, *not* its address. The assembler distinguishes a self-defining term from a literal by the absence or presence of an equals sign.

As can be seen from Figure 6.4, self-defining decimal integers are not written in the F-notation that is used with literals. This is because they are used so extensively in source modules. For example, in the statement

```
L    5,FCON
```

the 5 is a self-defining decimal integer. The assembler substitutes its 4-bit binary representation, 0101, when it assembles the Load instruction.

Self-defining terms are frequently used to specify the immediate data fields in instructions, as well as the mask fields, length fields, and register addresses. For example, consider the SI instruction Compare Logical Immediate (CLI):

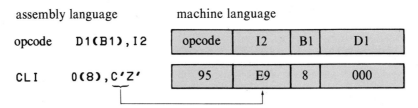

assembly language	machine language
opcode D1(B1),I2	opcode | I2 | B1 | D1
CLI 0(8),C'Z'	95 | E9 | 8 | 000

The immediate data field, the I2 field, is specified in this CLI instruction as the self-defining term C'Z'. This term represents the text character Z. In machine language, the binary representation used to represent the Z in the assembled instruction is the EBCDIC code for Z, 1110 1001, which in hexadecimal notation is E9. (See Fig. 7.1 for the EBCDIC codes for all the printable characters.) It would be incorrect to write CLI 0(8),=C'Z' since a literal cannot be specified in the immediate data field of any instruction. Specifying a self-defining term causes the assembler to generate the binary representation of that term, not its address.

6.3 ASSEMBLY-TIME CONSTANTS

Assembly-time constants do not occupy memory locations in a user's program, i.e., they are not in memory when a program is being executed. Instead, their values can be used by the assembler as part of the assembly process, when generating instructions and defined constants and when processing directives.

There are two main classes of assembly-time constants: those represented by symbols that are part of the assembly language itself, and those represented by user-defined symbols. The most important symbol that is part of the assembly language and is used as an assembly-time constant is the memory location symbol, an asterisk (∗). User-defined symbols that are to be used as assembly-time constants must be defined by means of the EQU directive.

Memory Location Symbol (∗)

In Chapter 3, we saw that when the assembler generates the object code corresponding to an instruction or defined constant, it assigns a memory address to that code. In general, the assembler associates a memory address with each source-language statement that it processes. The memory address associated with a statement is determined by the following formula:

$$
\left\{ \begin{array}{c} \text{address associated} \\ \text{with a statement} \end{array} \right\} = \left\{ \begin{array}{c} \text{address associated} \\ \text{with the preceding} \\ \text{statement} \end{array} \right\} + \left\{ \begin{array}{c} \text{number of bytes} \\ \text{generated or reserved} \\ \text{by preceding statement} \end{array} \right\}
$$

In this formula, the address associated with the first statement of a program is 0000.

The memory address associated with a statement is, with a few exceptions (such as the EQU to be described in the following section), the value that the assembler assigns to the symbol appearing in the name field of that statement. In addition, this value is always assigned to another symbol, the memory location symbol. Thus, *the value of the memory location symbol depends on the statement in which it is used.* In the IBM 360 and 370 Assembly Language, the memory location symbol is always represented by a single character, the asterisk (∗). The asterisk can be used in the operand field of most instructions and in the operand field of some directives. However, it cannot be used in the name field of any statement. Its most frequent and perhaps most important use is in the EQU and USING directives.

Consider the following sequence of statements, the statements required at the beginning of every source module:

```
SUB     CSECT
        STM       14,12,12(13)
        BALR      12,0
        USING     *,12
        ST        13,SAVE+4
        LA        13,SAVE
```

Let us assume that the assembler associates memory address 0000 with the CSECT directive. This assumption determines the memory addresses associated with all subsequent statements shown. It, therefore, also determines the value assigned to the memory location symbol (*) appearing in the operand of the USING directive.

The value assigned to the symbol SUB is 0000, since that is the address that is associated with the CSECT directive. The CSECT directive, like most other directives, does not cause any bytes to be generated or reserved in the object module. Therefore, the address associated with the statement following the CSECT directive, namely with the STM instruction, is also 0000. Since the STM instruction is an RS-type instruction, 4 bytes are generated for it. Consequently, the address associated with the statement following the STM, namely the BALR instruction, is 0004. Two bytes are generated by the BALR instruction (an RR-type instruction), so that the memory address associated with the USING directive that follows it is 0006. This example can be summarized as follows:

source language statement			address associated with the statement	generated object code	number of bytes generated
SUB	CSECT		0000	none	none
	STM	14,12,12(13)	0000	90ECD00C	4
	BALR	12,0	0004	05C0	2
	USING	*,12	0006	none	none
	ST	13,SAVE+4	0006	50D0C---	4
	LA	13,SAVE	000A	41D0C---	4

Since the address associated with the USING directive is 0006, the value of the memory location symbol (*) appearing in the operand of that USING directive is also 0006. In other words, the following two statements are interchangeable:

```
                    USING    *,12
```

and

```
          HERE    USING    HERE,12
```

The memory location symbol (*) is therefore a convenient shorthand notation that can be used in a statement's operand field to represent the address associated with that statement. According to the definitions given at the beginning of this chapter, the memory location symbol is a relocatable constant.

Equivalence Constants (EQU)

The concept of equivalence constants allows a programmer to define a value for a symbol and use that symbol whenever he or she wishes to employ that value in the operand of a source language statement. The value of the symbol is defined by means of the **Equivalence (EQU) directive.**

The symbol being defined is placed in the name field of the EQU statement; the value of the symbol is the value of the operand field of that statement. However, its value cannot be changed by any other statement in the program.

A major reason for using the EQU directive is to provide an easy means of changing the value of an assembly-time constant whenever the program is reassembled. No matter how many times that symbol is used in the program, the only statement that needs to be changed in order to change its value is the EQU statement that defines it.

There are other important reasons for using the EQU directive. The required value may not be known by the programmer when writing the program; the required value is too tedious to compute by hand; the required value would change if a change is made in the program; or the required value is easier to use symbolically than numerically. Moreover, all uses of a symbol defined by an EQU directive will appear in the cross-reference listing produced by the assembler. These concepts are illustrated in the discussions and examples that follow.

The general format of the EQU directive is the same as that of any other directive: name field, opcode field, operand field, comment field, continuation field, and identification field. But, unlike the DC directive that defines a run-time constant, *the EQU does not cause any bytes to be generated in the object module.* Instead, the constant defined by an EQU directive is used by the assembler at assembly time.

To illustrate one use of the EQU directive, consider the example used in the preceding subsection, modified to include an EQU:

```
SUB     CSECT
        STM     14,12,12(13)
        BALR    12,0
BASE    EQU     *
        USING   BASE,12
        ST      13,SAVE+4
        LA      13,SAVE
```

The memory address associated with each statement is determined by the formula given earlier:

$$\left\{ \begin{array}{c} \text{address associated} \\ \text{with a statement} \end{array} \right\} = \left\{ \begin{array}{c} \text{address associated} \\ \text{with the preceding} \\ \text{statement} \end{array} \right\} + \left\{ \begin{array}{c} \text{number of bytes} \\ \text{generated or reserved} \\ \text{by preceding statement} \end{array} \right\}$$

Thus, the memory address associated with the EQU statement is 0006, as the following summary indicates.

source language statement			address associated with the statement	generated object code	number of bytes generated
SUB	CSECT		0000	none	none
	STM	14,12,12(13)	0000	90ECD00C	4
	BALR	12,0	0004	05C0	2
BASE	EQU	*	0006	none	none
	USING	BASE,12	0006	none	none
	ST	13,SAVE+4	0006	50D0C--	4
	LA	13,SAVE	000A	41D0C--	4

Since the memory address associated with the EQU statement is 0006, the value of the memory location symbol is also 0006. Therefore the value of the operand in the EQU directive is 0006. But since the value assigned to the symbol in the name field of any EQU directive is always equal to the value of the operand in that directive, the value of the symbol BASE is 0006. In the example, the value of BASE happens to coincide with the value of the address associated with the EQU statement. But, because the operand in an EQU statement can include any symbol defined in statements preceding that EQU statement, and since the symbols in the operand can be combined algebraically, this need not always be the case. This is shown in some of the following examples.

Example 1.   Value not known in advance by programmer

```
HERE    EQU     *
```

The symbol HERE is assigned the current value of the memory location symbol. This value is not known in advance by the programmer. Note that HERE is a relocatable constant since it represents a memory address.

Example 2. Value too tedious to compute by hand

```
MSG1       DC    C'SAMPLE USE OF THE EQU.'
TLNG1      EQU   *-MSG1
```

The symbol TLNG1 is assigned the value computed by subtracting the value that was assigned to the symbol MSG1 from the current value of the memory location symbol. This value will be exactly equal to the number of bytes reserved by the above DC directive, namely 22. Use of the EQU removes the tedium of having to count the number of characters should the message length be needed as a value elsewhere in the program. If the text message is changed by the programmer, the value of TLNG1 will automatically be changed when the program is reassembled. Note that TLNG1 is an absolute constant, since it equals the difference of two relocatable constants.

Example 3. Value can change if program is changed

```
TABLE2     DC    F'1'
           DC    F'2'
           DC    F'3'
           DC    F'4'
           DC    F'5'
TLNG2      EQU   *-TABLE2
```

The value of TLNG2 is 20. This is the number of bytes reserved for the above table of integers (4 bytes per integer). Although it is easy enough for a programmer to compute the value 20, it is advantageous to let the assembler compute it using the EQU directive. Then, if statements are added to or deleted from the TABLE2 table, for example when modifying or correcting a program, the value of TLNG2 will be recomputed by the assembler. The following illustrates this:

```
TABLE2     DC    F'1'
           DC    F'2'
           DC    F'3'
           DC    F'4'
           DC    F'5'
           DC    F'6'       NEW STATEMENT ADDED
TLNG2      EQU   *-TABLE2   NOW THE VALUE OF TLNG2 IS 24
```

Example 4. Value used symbolically

```
STATUS     DS    CL1        DEVICE STATUS BYTE
OFF        EQU   X'00'      DEVICE IS OFF
ON         EQU   X'FF'      DEVICE IS ON
```

To illustrate the use of these three statements, assume that the byte reserved for the symbol STATUS records the fact of whether or not an I/O device connected to the computer is "off" (without power) or "on." Then, elsewhere in a program, we can determine that device's status before attempting to use it, by means of a compare instruction such as

```
CLI    STATUS,ON
BE     POWERON
```

This is equivalent to writing

```
CLI    STATUS,X'FF'
BE     POWERON
```

but the use of ON has two advantages: (1) each use of ON will be recorded in the cross-reference listing by the assembler and (2) a change can be made to the value of ON without having to change any statements in the program except the EQU that defines ON. Since the cross-reference listing can be of significant help in debugging or modifying programs and since it does not include references to self-defining terms such as X'FF', it is good practice to use symbols that are equated to self-defining terms. Moreover, if the need to record status information other than the ON/OFF status indicated here arose, it would be a simple matter to do so if EQU's were being used, and not so simple if they were not. For example,

```
STATUS   DS    CL1            DEVICE STATUS BYTE
OFF      EQU   X'00'          DEVICE IS OFF
ON       EQU   X'0F'          DEVICE IS ON BUT NOT IN USE
INUSE    EQU   X'FF'          DEVICE IS ON AND BEING USED
```

Now the CLI instruction given earlier to test the device's status *does not have to be changed* to reflect the change in meaning of the symbol ON, for now

```
CLI   STATUS,ON
BE    POWERON
```

is equivalent to

```
CLI   STATUS,X'0F'
BE    POWERON
```

If the symbolic definition ON had not been used, the CLI instruction, and all other instructions in the program that were testing for X'FF' under the previous definition, would have had to have been changed to test for X'0F'. This might have required a tedious and error-prone set of changes. As it is, only the EQU had to be changed.

Example 5.   Use of symbolic register addresses and symbolic displacements

Example 4 showed two advantages of symbolically defining self-defining terms. Similar advantages can be gained from symbolically defining the addresses of the general registers and the values of displacement constants. As an example, suppose OFFSET is defined by EQU as follows:

```
OFFSET   EQU   12
```

and suppose the 16 general register addresses are defined symbolically, as shown in Figure 6.5. Then the following two instructions are equivalent:

```
STM   14,12,12(13)
```

and

```
STM   R14,R12,OFFSET(R13)
```

At first glance this may not appear to be of much use. But the symbolic register addresses and all their uses in a source module are printed in the cross-reference listing by the assembler. So, of course, are the symbolic displacement constants. Since no uses of the self-defining decimal integers 0,1,2,3,... are printed in the cross-reference listing, the advantages gained from the use of symbols should be clear at this point: with symbols, it is easy to determine whether (and where) a given register and/or displacement is used in a program. This, in turn, can be of significant help in debugging a program, and it can make program modification less prone to error than it would be without symbolic constants.

Figure 6.5 *Symbolic register addresses.*

```
R0     EQU     0
R1     EQU     1
R2     EQU     2
R3     EQU     3
R4     EQU     4
R5     EQU     5
R6     EQU     6
R7     EQU     7
R8     EQU     8
R9     EQU     9
R10    EQU     10
R11    EQU     11
R12    EQU     12
R13    EQU     13
R14    EQU     14
R15    EQU     15
```

Example 6.   Invalid use of EQU

```
SPLNG     EQU     *-SPCHAR
SPCHAR    DC      C'@#$%c&&*()+-=:;?/,.'
```

This EQU is an invalid attempt to define SPLNG as the number of characters in the SPCHAR constant. A valid definition would be

```
SPCHAR    DC      C'@#$%c&&*()+-=:;?/,.'
SPLNG     EQU     *-SPCHAR
```

The reason the first is invalid and the second is not is that *all symbols appearing in the operand of an EQU directive must have been defined prior to their appearance in that operand.* The reason for this restriction will be explained in the discussion of two-pass assemblers in Chapter 23. (It should also be noted that if the first definition of SPLNG above *was* valid, the value of SPLNG would then be zero.)

Example 7.   Relocatable versus absolute constants

A memory-address field of an instruction operand is in implicit form if and only if it is a relocatable constant or a literal.

```
        L      4,Y      IMPLICIT: USES IMPLIED BASE REGISTER
        LA     5,Y          "          "              "
        LA     6,W          "          "              "
        LA     7,Z      EXPLICIT: SAME AS LA 7,4(0,0)
        L      8,Z          "          "      L  8,4(0,0)
        ...
Y       DC     F'4'     Y IS A RELOCATABLE CONSTANT (A SYMBOLIC ADDRESS)
Z       EQU    4        Z IS AN ABSOLUTE CONSTANT
W       EQU    Y        W IS A RELOCATABLE CONSTANT (EQUAL TO AN ADDR)
```

Note that the instruction L 8,Z would load the contents of the location whose address is 000004; i.e., it does *not* load the *value* of Z, it loads the *contents* of Z. On the other hand, the LA 7,Z instruction loads the value of Z as discussed in Section 4.5.

6.4 DATA AREAS

The **Define Storage (DS) directive** is used to reserve an area of memory for future data. This directive causes a designated amount of memory space to be reserved in the program but *does not place any data into the reserved area.*

When using the DS directive, we must specify how much memory space is to be reserved as well as the type of boundary alignment that is required for the data that will eventually be placed in the area. The area that is reserved may be subdivided into smaller areas of varying length, and each of the subdivisions may be assigned symbolic addresses. The entire area and/or any subdivision of the area may be duplicated. The duplication process reserves consecutive areas or subdivisions with the same characteristics as the original.

The manner in which the DS directive is used in conjunction with instructions will be described in subsequent chapters. In this section, attention is focused on the DS directive itself: (1) general format, (2) examples, and (3) subdivisions.

General Format

The DS directive consists of the same fields as other assembly language directives: name, opcode, operand, comments, continuation, and identification. The general format of the name, opcode, and operand fields is

name	opcode	operand
{a symbol,} {or blank }	DS	{one or more subfields,} {separated by commas}

Each operand subfield of a DS directive can contain from one to four components, arranged as shown below without any intervening blanks or other separators:

DS operand subfield components

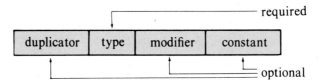

As an example of this arrangement, the following DS directive will reserve two consecutive 8-byte areas, each aligned on a byte boundary, with the first byte of the first area having the symbolic address DATE:

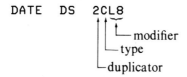

Other examples will be given later.

It should be apparent that the operand format of the DS directive is identical to that of the DC directive, except that the required and the optional subfield components are different. But, aside from this, there are important differences in the ways in which the subfield components are interpreted.

Constant. Since the DS directive does not cause any data to be placed in memory, the constant is not required. However, we may wish to specify a constant for either of two reasons. First, for documentation purposes the specification of a typical constant indicates on the listing the kind of data that will occupy the area at run time. Second, if a typical constant is specified without specifying a length modifier, the assembler will compute the length of the area as being equal to the number of

length modifier	type code	constant	boundary alignment	length
length modifier is used in the operand	any valid type code	either no constant, or any valid constant	byte boundary	determined via length modifier
length modifier is not used in the operand	B, C, P, X, or Z	any valid constant	byte boundary	determined via constant
		no constant	byte boundary	1
	H or Y	either no constant, or any valid constant	half-word boundary	2
	E or F A, Q, or S	either no constant, or any valid constant	full-word boundary	4
	D or L	either no constant, or any valid constant	double-word boundary	8

bytes that would be required for that typical constant. Thus, the example given previously for two consecutive 8-byte areas would have the same effect as the DS directive

```
DATE    DS    2C'06/07/80'
```

Modifier.   The only modifier allowed in a DS directive is the length modifier. This may be written either as Ln where n is a nonnegative, unsigned decimal integer or as L(x) where x is any valid arithmetic expression whose value is a nonnegative decimal integer and an absolute rather than re-locatable constant.

The value of n or x is the number of bytes—the length—reserved for the area that is associated with the symbol appearing in the name field. Thus in the first example given earlier, the length of the area associated with DATE is 8. It can also be stated as the **length attribute** of DATE is 8. Note that although the amount of space reserved is 16 bytes, for two consecutive 8-byte areas, only the length of the first of these areas is associated with the symbol DATE. Figure 6.6 shows the relationship of the length modifier to the constant and type components of a DS operand.

The length attribute of a symbol has the following importance: *if a programmer omits a length field when specifying a symbolic address in an SS$_1$ or SS$_2$ instruction, the assembler uses the length attribute of that symbol for the omitted length-field specification.* Thus, for the definition of DATE given previously, the following two instructions are equivalent to one another:

```
        MVC    DATE(8),=C'06/07/80'
        MVC    DATE,=C'06/07/80'         ⎰ length omitted, so
               └──────────────────      ⎱ length attribute of DATE
DATE    DS     2CL8                        is used by assembler
```

Type.   The only required subfield component in a DS directive's operand is *type*. Any type code shown in Figure 6.2 may be specified in a DS directive. The type code determines the boundary alignment of the first byte of the reserved area unless the length modifier is specified. If the length modifier is specified, then alignment is on a byte boundary, irrespective of the type code. In the absence of a length modifier, the type code also determines the length of the area and the length attribute of the symbol associated with the area (Fig. 6.6).

Duplicator.   The optional duplicator component of a DS operand is used to specify the number of consecutive areas to be reserved. When the duplicator is omitted, its value is assumed to be 1. When present, it must be written either as an unsigned nonnegative decimal integer or as (x), where x is any valid arithmetic expression whose value is a nonnegative decimal integer; x must be an absolute constant.

If the duplicator's value is 0 (zero), no memory space is reserved, but the alignment and length attribute of the area are determined as shown in Figure 6.6. This fact is used as a means of defining subdivisions within an area.

Examples.   The examples that follow illustrate the relationships among the type, modifier, and constant components of a DS operand, which are given in Figure 6.6. They also illustrate one other rule, that for determining the total number of bytes reserved for a memory area. The total number of bytes reserved may be called the *size* of an area and is computed by multiplying the duplicator by the area's length attribute:

$$\left\{\begin{array}{c} \text{size of} \\ \text{memory area} \\ \text{in number} \\ \text{of bytes} \end{array}\right\} = \{\text{duplicator}\} \times \left\{\begin{array}{c} \text{length attribute of} \\ \text{memory area} \\ \text{in number} \\ \text{of bytes} \end{array}\right\}$$

If the duplicator is not present in an operand, its value is assumed to be 1. Note that although the size and length attribute of an area are equal when the duplicator is 1, *the size and length attribute are conceptually different aspects of an area.* Of course, when the duplicator is not 1, the size and length attribute are numerically different as well. For brevity, we will use the word *length* instead of *length attribute* when no ambiguity exists.

Example 1.   One full-word area

$$\text{EG1 \quad DS \quad F}$$

Duplicator not present, so assumed value is 1.
Length modifier not present, so length is 4, determined by type code F; alignment is on a full-word boundary.
Size = Duplicator × Length = 1 × 4 = 4 bytes.

Example 2.   Two 3-byte areas

$$\text{EG2 \quad DS \quad 2CL3}$$

Duplicator is 2.
Length modifier specifies that length is 3; alignment is on a byte boundary.
Size = Duplicator × Length = 2 × 3 = 6 bytes.

Example 3.   Eighty 1-byte areas

$$\text{EG3 \quad DS \quad 80C}$$

Duplicator is 80.
Length modifier not present, no constant specified; thus length is 1, determined by type code C. C gives byte-boundary alignment.
Size = Duplicator × Length = 80 × 1 = 80 bytes.

Example 4.   One 80-byte area

$$\text{EG4 \quad DS \quad CL80}$$

Duplicator is 1 (by omission).
Length modifier specifies that length is 80; alignment is on a byte boundary.
Size = Duplicator × Length = 1 × 80 = 80 bytes.

Example 5. Double-word areas

```
EG5   DS   4D
```

Duplicator is 4.
Length modifier not present, so length is 8, determined by type code D; alignment is on a double-word boundary.
Size = Duplicator × Length = 4 × 8 = 32 bytes.

Example 6. No space reserved

```
EG6   DS   0H
```

Duplicator is 0 (zero).
Length modifier not present, so length is 2, determined by type code H; alignment is on a half-word boundary.
Size = Duplicator × Length = 0 × 2 = 0 bytes.

Subdivisions

It is sometimes desirable to define areas within an area. In Cobol, this facility is provided through the technique of group items. In Fortran, the EQUIVALENCE statement is used. In assembly language, the following procedure is used.

Suppose we want to reserve an 8-byte area for a calendar date, in the form month/day/year where month, day, and year are each 2 bytes, e.g., 06/07/83. Suppose also that the entire calendar date area is to be given the name DATE, and that the month, day, and year subfields are to be given the names MONTH, DAY, and YEAR, respectively. To accomplish this, we use a duplication factor of zero for the overall area:

```
DATE    DS   0CL8     8 BYTES FOR DATE, BUT NONE RESERVED
MONTH   DS   CL2      2 BYTES FOR MONTH
        DS   C        1 BYTE FOR /
DAY     DS   CL2      2 BYTES FOR DAY
        DS   C        1 BYTE FOR /
YEAR    DS   CL2      2 BYTES FOR YEAR
```

The length attribute of DATE is 8, so that it can be used to refer to the 8 bytes beginning at the address assigned to DATE. But the size of the area associated with DATE is zero. *Therefore, both DATE and MONTH will be assigned the same address.* This appears in memory as

The result is that both DATE and MONTH refer to the same byte position. But DATE is associated with an 8-byte field, whereas MONTH is associated with a 2-byte field.

These subdivisions could be defined in a Cobol data division by the statements

```
01    DATE.

      02    MONTH    PICTURE    XX.
      02    FILLER   PICTURE    X.
      02    DAY      PICTURE    XX.
      02    FILLER   PICTURE    X.
      02    YEAR     PICTURE    XX.
```

As another example of subdividing an area, the statements given below will assign symbolic addresses to each of the data fields shown in the diagram and also assign the symbolic address STMT with length attribute 80 to the entire area:

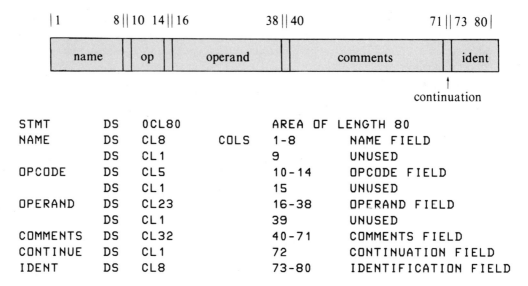

continuation

```
STMT       DS    0CL80              AREA OF LENGTH 80
NAME       DS    CL8     COLS  1-8      NAME FIELD
           DS    CL1           9        UNUSED
OPCODE     DS    CL5           10-14    OPCODE FIELD
           DS    CL1           15       UNUSED
OPERAND    DS    CL23          16-38    OPERAND FIELD
           DS    CL1           39       UNUSED
COMMENTS   DS    CL32          40-71    COMMENTS FIELD
CONTINUE   DS    CL1           72       CONTINUATION FIELD
IDENT      DS    CL8           73-80    IDENTIFICATION FIELD
```

6.5 BOUNDARY ALIGNMENTS

As was shown in Figure 6.6, boundary alignment, which assures that a constant or memory area begins at a half-word, full-word, or double-word address, is always performed by the assembler when an H-, F-, D-, or related type of constant or data area is defined without a length modifier. However, full-word, half-word, and double-word boundary alignment is often needed for data constants or data areas even when the data is byte-oriented data, such as characters, bits, and decimal numbers. For these types of data, the assembler will not provide the desired alignment unless it is explicitly designated in the program. If the desired alignment is not explicitly designated, the assembler provides only the alignments shown in Figure 6.6. A method for explicitly designating the desired data alignment is described in the material that follows.

The most straightforward way to force alignment to the desired boundary for any constant or data area is to immediately precede the DC or DS directive that defines it with one of these three statements:

```
DS        0H
DS        0F
DS        0D
```

The DS 0H statement forces alignment of the following data constant or data area to be on a half-word boundary; DS 0F forces it to a full-word boundary; and DS 0D forces it to a double-word boundary.

For example, the statement

```
DC        X'80000000'
```

does not guarantee alignment of the hexadecimal constant X'80000000' on a full-word boundary; it only guarantees alignment on a byte boundary. If alignment on a full-word boundary is desired, this pair of statements will guarantee it:

```
DS        0F
DC        X'80000000'
```

Similarly, the following pair guarantees alignment of the packed-decimal constant P'2.84' on a double-word boundary:

```
DS        0D
DC        P'2.84'
```

Figure 6.7a   Illustration of forced and natural alignment.

```
LOCTN OBJECT CODE SOURCE STATEMENT

001000                        DS    0F         FORCE ALIGNMENT TO FULL-WD BDY
001000 80            A         DC    X'80'      1-BYTE CONSTANT
001004 00000001      B         DC    F'1'       4-BYTE CONST, ON FULL-WD BDY
001008               C         DS    CL25       25 BYTES RESERVED
001028                         DS    0D         FORCE ALIGNMENT TO DBL-WD BDY
001028 F1F2F3        D         DC    X'F1F2F3'   3-BYTE CONST
00102C 0002          E         DC    H'2'       2-BYTE CONST, ON HALF-WD BDY
001030               F         DS    18F        18 FULL WORDS RESERVED
001078 C5D5C4        G         DC    C'END'     3-BYTE CONST, ON BYTE BDY
00107B FF            H         DC    X'FF'      1-BYTE CONST, ON BYTE BDY
```

Figure 6.7b   Memory allocation for statements of Figure 6.7a.

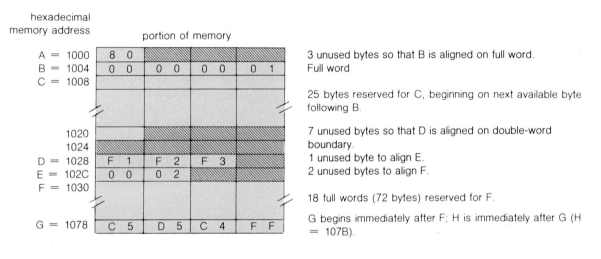

And this pair guarantees alignment of the memory area CARD on a half-word boundary:

```
                    DS        0H
          CARD      DS        CL84
```

There are thus two ways in which half-word, full-word, and double-word alignment can take place: (1) through use of the H-, F-, or D-type codes in a DC or DS statement, as shown in the preceding sections of this chapter; or (2) by forcing alignment with duplication factors of 0 (zero), as shown earlier.

One small fact should be noted: whenever alignment takes place, the assembler may leave some memory bytes unused in order to place a constant or data area at the next available boundary of the desired type. The unused byte positions are included in the memory of the program in which they occur, but no data are placed in these positions. The statements of Figure 6.7a, together with the corresponding diagram of Figure 6.7b, illustrate these concepts.

6.6   SUMMARY

Every constant that appears in an assembly language source module statement is either a relocatable constant or an absolute constant and is either a run-time or an assembly-time constant. A relocatable constant is one whose value depends on the location of a program in main memory. For example, all symbols used to represent memory addresses, including the memory location symbol (*), are relocatable constants. An absolute constant is one whose value is independent of any factor affecting or affected by the location of a program in memory. For example, all self-defining terms are absolute constants. Certain algebraic combinations of absolute and relocatable constants yield relocatable constants, other combinations yield absolute constants, and still others are invalid.

A run-time constant is one whose value is represented in memory at the time a program is being executed or run. For example, all data generated by a DC directive are run-time constants. An assembly-time constant is one whose value is not represented in memory when a program is being run but is available for use by the assembler when a source module is being assembled. For example, all constants defined by the EQU directive are assembly-time constants.

The length of the bit sequence and the combination of bits used to represent a run-time constant depend on three factors: (1) the constant's type, as specified by the type code in a DC operand, a literal, or a self-defining term; (2) the modifier in a DC operand or literal; and (3) the value that is specified. In addition, the memory address assigned to a run-time constant generated by a literal or DC directive depends on the type of boundary alignment indicated in the constant. If a length modifier is used in the specification of the constant, alignment is simply on the byte boundary corresponding to the current value of the memory location counter. If no length modifier is specified, alignment is dictated by the type code, as indicated in Figure 6.6.

Memory areas may be reserved for use at run time by means of the DS directive. The operand of the DS directive is identical in format to that of the DC directive; but, unlike the DC directive, the DS directive does not cause the assembler to generate constants. The amount of memory space and the type of boundary alignment is determined from the operand of a DS directive, and the address of the first byte reserved is assigned to the name-field symbol (if any) in that directive.

To force the assembler to align a defined constant or reserved memory area on a boundary other than that dictated by the type code or length modifier, you can precede the DC or DS directive with a DS directive whose duplicator is zero and whose type code specifies the desired alignment. Thus, DS 0D would force the memory location counter to be adjusted to the next double-word boundary if it were not already at such a boundary. Similarly, DS 0H and DS 0F can be used to force half- and full-word boundary alignment, respectively. Whenever the memory location counter is adjusted to force alignment, there may be one or more unused bytes in the resulting object module.

6.7   REVIEW

Relocatable Constants   A relocatable constant is essentially the address of some main memory location within a program. Therefore, its value depends on the location of a program in main memory at run time. Since a program will usually be at a different location in memory each time it is run, the value of a relocatable constant will usually be different each time the program is run.

Absolute Constants   Unlike relocatable constants, the value of an absolute constant is independent of the location of a program in main memory. Its value will therefore be the same each time a program is run.

Run-Time Constants   These constants occupy memory locations when a program is being executed. Constants specified by the DC directive, or as literals, or as the one-byte "immediate data" field of SI-type instructions, are run-time constants. A run-time constant can be either relocatable or absolute.

Assembly-Time Constants   These do not occupy memory locations when a program is being executed. Instead, they are declared in the source module and used by the assembler when it translates source code into object code. In this chapter, the only way to specify an assembly-time constant is via an EQU directive. Other ways to specify them will be discussed in Chapters 16 and 17. An assembly-time constant can be either relocatable or absolute.

DC Directive   DC defines constants for use by a program at run time. Each constant must be of a specified type (see Fig. 6.2). Constants defined by DC are subject to the same boundary alignment constraints as areas defined by a DS (see Fig. 6.6).

Literals   Literals are constants that can be specified in the second operand field of some instructions. The format of a literal differs from that of constants in a DC directive chiefly by the presence of an equals sign (=). Like DC constants, a literal is assigned to a memory location by the assembler. If the same literal is specified in more than one instruction, all uses of it will refer to the same memory location. For that reason, you should not store any data into a literal.

Memory Location Symbol (∗)   This symbol's value is the address of the statement in which it appears. It is therefore a relocatable constant.

EQU Directive   EQU defines a constant for use by the assembler at assembly time. The value of a constant defined by an EQU directive cannot be changed by any other statement in the program.

DS Directive   DS reserves a memory area for use by your program at run time. The DS operand must specify the type of constant that will be placed in that area. The area is subject to certain boundary alignment constraints (see Fig. 6.6).

Length Attribute   A length is associated with each symbol defined in the name field of a DC or DS directive. That length is known as the symbol's "length attribute". The value of the length attribute is the length of the area (not including duplicates) addressed by the symbol.

Data Alignment   Half-word, full-word, or double-word boundary alignment for a constant can be guaranteed, independently of the constant's type, by preceding the constant with a DS 0H, 0F, or 0D directive. The same is true for data areas.

6.8   REVIEW QUESTIONS

1. In a DC or DS directive, what is the purpose of the "duplicator"? What happens if the duplicator is omitted from a DC or DS operand?
2. What is the difference in purpose between the duplicator and the length (L) modifier when used in the operand of a DC directive? What happens if the length modifier is omitted from a DC or DS operand?
3. What is the difference in purpose between the scale (S) and exponent (E) modifiers when used in the operand of a DC directive? What decimal integer is specified by this DC directive: DC FS10E3'2' ?
4. When a literal is specified in the operand of an instruction, the assembler assigns the literal to a memory location and assembles the base-displacement form of its address into the instruction. Does the assembler do the same for self-defining terms that occur in instruction operands? If not, what does it do for self-defining terms?
5. Why is the memory location symbol (∗) equal to 6 when it is used in the standard BALR-USING sequence required at the beginning of each source module?
6. What is the size (in bytes as well as in words) of the register save area as defined by either of these two directives:

```
        SAVE    DS  18F       or      SAVE    DS  9D
```

7. What is wrong with this sequence of statements:

```
        LENGTH  EQU *-TEXT
        TEXT    DC  C'TEXT LENGTH'
```

8. When we define symbolic register addresses as in Figure 6.5, are the symbols R0, R1, . . . , R15 relocatable constants or are they absolute constants? Are they run-time constants or are they assembly-time constants? What would be loaded into Register 1 by the following instruction at run time:

```
        LA      R1,R1
```

9. What would be loaded at run time by each of the Load (L) and Load Address (LA) instructions shown in Example 7 near the end of Section 6.3?
10. In the second part of Example 6 near the end of Section 6.3, the symbol SPLNG is defined correctly. What is its value? Why is it useful to define SPLNG this way?
11. What is the length attribute of each of the symbols defined in Examples 1 through 6 of Section 6.4?
12. What is the length attribute of each of the symbols defined in the STMT example at the end of Section 6.4? What statement is needed to guarantee that the STMT area in that example will begin on a half-word boundary? Without that guarantee, what type of boundary will the STMT area definitely begin on?

1. What is the fundamental difference between a DC and a DS directive? What other differences and similarities exist between these two directives?

2. What is the fundamental difference between the following two directives:

```
X       DC      X'40'
Y       EQU     X'40'
```

Is X a relocatable or an absolute symbol? What about Y? State the reasons for your answers.

3. Consider the purpose and effect of the following directives. How do they differ? How are they similar?

```
D       DC      X'0001'
E       DC      H'0001'
```

4. Assume that the address assigned to the symbol DATA in the following set of statements is 000500_{16}. What address would the assembler assign to each of the other name-field symbols if this sequence appeared in a source module exactly as shown?

```
DATA        DS      F
MSG1        DC      C'PROBLEM #4'
MSG2        DS      2F
MSG3        DC      X'0087000041'
MSG4        DC      CL132
```

5. Write an appropriate DS or DC directive for each of the following requirements:

   a. Define an area of memory that contains 200 blanks.
   b. Define an area of memory that contains 200 bytes of binary zeroes.
   c. Reserve an area of memory for a one-dimensional integer array consisting of at most 100 components.
   d. Reserve an area of memory for a two-dimensional integer array consisting of at most 20 rows and 30 columns.
   e. Reserve 18 consecutive full words, with the symbolic address of the first of these being SAVE.
   f. Reserve 132 bytes beginning on a double-word boundary.

6. What DC and/or DS directives are required to achieve the same purpose as these Cobol data division statements?

```
01   HEADING.
     02   FILLER     PICTURE   X(50)    VALUE SPACES.
     02   FILLER     PICTURE   X(50)    VALUE 'YEAR-END REPORT'.
     02   FILLER     PICTURE   X(6)     VALUE 'PAGE'.
     02   PAGE       PICTURE   9999.
     02   FILLER     PICTURE   X(22)    VALUE SPACES.
```

7. Convert each of the following two sets of assembly language statements into machine language, giving the address associated with each statement as well as the object code (in hex) corresponding to each instruction and defined constant. Assume that, in each case, the address to be assigned to the symbol TEST is 000000.

a. TEST	CSECT		b. TEST	CSECT	
	STM	14,12,12(13)		STM	14,12,12(13)
	BALR	12,0		BALR	12,0
	USING	*,12		USING	*,12
	ST	13,SAVE+4		ST	13,SAVE+4
	LA	13,SAVE		LA	13,SAVE
	L	5,CON5		LA	8,AREA
	MH	5,Z		L	9,CON5
*			LOOP	MVC	0(5,8),PATTERN
	ST	5,P		LA	8,5(8)
	L	13,SAVE+4		BCT	9,LOOP
	LM	14,12,12(13)		L	13,SAVE+4
	BR	14		LM	14,12,12(13)
CON5	DC	F'5'		BR	14
CON6	DC	F'6'	CON5	DC	F'5'
P	DS	F	PATTERN	DC	X'0102030405'
Z	DC	H'20'	AREA	DS	5CL5
SAVE	DS	18F	SAVE	DS	18F
	END			END	

8. What object code would be generated for each of these DC directives?

a. DC FS10'2'
b. DC FE2'10'
c. DC 4X'4'
d. DC XL4'4'
e. DC F'2',F'100'
f. DC F'2,100'
g. DC 4XL4'4'
h. DC 80CL80' '

9. What is the relationship between the length modifier specified in a DC or DS directive and the length field in the operand of an SS_1 or SS_2 instruction when that length field is implied? What length-field contents would be assembled for this SS_1 instruction,

```
MVC     PRINTER,RECORD
```

for each of the following pairs of DS directives?

a. PRINTER DS 132C
   RECORD   DS 80C
b. PRINTER DS CL132
   RECORD   DS CL80
c. PRINTER DS 2CL60
   RECORD   DS CL80
d. PRINTER DS 0CL132
   RECORD   DS 0CL80

10. In addition to the use of the exponent modifier (En) following the type code in a DC directive, we can specify a power of ten by which a constant is to be multiplied through use of the exponent notation *following* the constant. For example, DC F'1E5' is equivalent to DC F'100000'. The difference between use of the exponent notation as a modifier and its use following a constant is that the modifier applies to all the constants specified in a given operand subfield, whereas, when it follows a constant, the exponent applies only to that constant. If both are specified, their algebraic sum is the exponent that is applied. The sum must be in the range of from -85 through 75. For example,

```
DC   FE5'2E2,3E-1,4E0'
```

specifies constants of 2×10^7, 3×10^4, and 4×10^5, respectively. What decimal constants are specified by each of these DC directives?

a. DC   F'1E2'
b. DC   FE3'2E4,4E2,1E-3'
c. DC   HS3'1E3,2E2'
d. DC   FE6'5',F'6E7'

11. Suppose there is a set of input data in which each record contains the name, ID, and course grades for a student in the following format: student name in columns 1–25, student ID in columns 30–38, course ID's in columns 40–45, 50–55, 60–65, and 70–75, with corresponding course grades in columns 46–49, 56–59, 66–69, and 76–79. Write a sequence of directives that will reserve an area of memory for an input record and assign symbolic addresses to each of its fields.

12. Draw a diagram similar to that of Figure 6.7b to represent the memory allocations that would result from the following set of directives. Assume that the address assigned to the symbol AREAS is 000EF4.

```
AREAS        DS      0F
A1           DC      CL5'X'
A2           DC      XL5'C'
A3           DC      F'12'
A4           DC      2H'12'
A5           DS      11CL11
A6           DS      3D
A7           DS      0H
A8           DS      CL80
```

What is the length attribute of each of the symbols in these statements?

13. Suppose that the results of a questionnaire are recorded on a set of input records. The questionnaire consisted of six questions, each requiring a *yes, no,* or *undecided* response. The responses are coded as integers, 0 = no, 1 = yes, and 2 = undecided, columns 12, 24, 36, 48, 60, 72 being used for questions 1, 2, 3, 4, 5, 6, respectively. Write an assembly language program that will read all the input records; calculate the number of *yes, no,* and *undecided* responses to each question; and print the results in a suitably readable format.

14. Write an assembly language program that will calculate and print the integers 2^n through 10^n for $n = 1,2,...,9$. Each line of output should contain all the integers calculated for a given n.

7

Byte and String Manipulations

As discussed previously, the word **byte** refers to any addressable 8-bit quantity. In the IBM EBCDIC code scheme, many of the 256 possible 8-bit quantities are used to represent characters that can be typed or displayed at a terminal or printer. The printable characters in the EBCDIC code scheme are shown in Figure 7.1.

A sequence of bytes is called a **string.** Sometimes the terms *character string* or *text string* are used to emphasize that the bytes represent printable characters. The number of bytes in a string is called the **string length.** Thus, the terms *byte manipulations* and *string manipulations* are essentially interchangeable; both refer to the following types of operations on one or more consecutive bytes: copying bytes, comparing two sequences of bytes, and searching a sequence of bytes for the occurrence of specific values. In this chapter, the instructions used to accomplish these operations will be described and illustrated with several examples.

Byte-manipulation instructions have three general characteristics. (1) All byte-manipulation instructions operate on two strings. One of the strings is always in memory; the other may be in memory or in a register, depending on the instruction itself. (2) All byte-manipulation instructions require that the number of bytes being operated on—the length of the strings—be specified either explicitly or implicitly. (3) All the byte-manipulation instructions described in this chapter treat bytes as 8-bit nonalgebraic quantities: the high-order bit is not considered to be a sign bit but is treated in the same way as the other bits.

See Summary in Figure 7.12

Figure 7.1 *Printable characters in the EBCDIC code scheme. (Note: Each 8-bit EBCDIC code is shown as a two-digit hexadecimal number.)*

SPECIAL GRAPHIC CHARACTERS

hex code	character symbol & name	hex code	character symbol & name	hex code	character symbol & name	hex code	character symbol & name	hex code	character symbol & name
40	blank space	50	& ampersand	60	– hyphen	79	` grave accent	A1	~ tilde
4A	¢ cent sign	5A	! exclamation	61	/ slash	7A	: colon	C0	{ left brace
4B	. period	5B	$ dollar	6A	¦ vertical bars	7B	# number sign	CC	♪ hook
4C	< less than	5C	* asterisk	6B	, comma	7C	@ commercial at	CE	⊢ fork
4D	(left paren	5D	) right paren	6C	% percent	7D	' apostrophe	D0	} right brace
4E	+ plus	5E	; semicolon	6D	_ underline	7E	= equals	E0	\ reverse slash
4F		logical OR	5F	¬ logical NOT	6E	> greater than	7F	" quotation mark	EC	⊣ chair
				6F	? question mark			FA		long vertical bar

LOWERCASE ALPHABET

hex		hex		hex	
81	a	91	j		
82	b	92	k	A2	s
83	c	93	l	A3	t
84	d	94	m	A4	u
85	e	95	n	A5	v
86	f	96	o	A6	w
87	g	97	p	A7	x
88	h	98	q	A8	y
89	i	99	r	A9	z

UPPERCASE ALPHABET

hex		hex		hex	
C1	A	D1	J		
C2	B	D2	K	E2	S
C3	C	D3	L	E3	T
C4	D	D4	M	E4	U
C5	E	D5	N	E5	V
C6	F	D6	O	E6	W
C7	G	D7	P	E7	X
C8	H	D8	Q	E8	Y
C9	I	D9	R	E9	Z

DECIMAL DIGITS

hex	
F0	0
F1	1
F2	2
F3	3
F4	4
F5	5
F6	6
F7	7
F8	8
F9	9

7.1 CHARACTER CONSTANTS

C-Type Constants To define a data constant as a sequence of characters, we use the C data-type code. This code may be used in the DC directive, in literals, and in self-defining terms. The C code requires that each character be specified just as it would be written (including the blank character), with two exceptions: (1) to specify an apostrophe (') we must write two consecutive apostrophes ('') so that the assembler can distinguish the specified apostrophes from the delimiting apostrophes and (2) to specify an ampersand (&) we must write two consecutive ampersands (&&).

One byte is always allotted for each specified character. The maximum number of characters that can be specified for a single DC or literal constant is 256; for self-defining terms, the maximum is four characters.

Figure 7.2 illustrates the usual methods of specifying constants as character sequences. It also illustrates what happens in two special situations: truncation and padding.

When the length modifier Ln specifies *fewer* bytes than are needed to contain the binary representation of the data constant given in a C-type DC directive, the assembler deletes characters from the right. It accepts only the number of characters specified in the length modifier. This is called *truncation* on the right.

When the length modifier Ln specifies *more* bytes than are needed to contain the binary representation of the data constant given in a C-type DC directive, the assembler adds blank characters on the right to fill the length that was specified. This is called *padding* with blanks.

7.2 COPYING BYTES

There are two sets of byte-copying instructions: (1) those that copy bytes from memory into a register or from a register into memory, and (2) those that copy bytes from one area of memory to another area of memory. The former are called INSERT and STORE instructions, respectively; the latter are called MOVE instructions. (Strictly speaking, the word MOVE is a slight misnomer, since it implies erasure of the bytes from their original position. The MOVE instructions would be more

Figure 7.2   *Character constants and data areas.*

```
FLAG LOCTN OBJECT CODE     ADDR1  ADDR2  STMNT M SOURCE STATEMENT

                                     5  * CHARACTER CONSTANTS, VIA 'DC'
       000000 C1                     6          DC    3C'A'      1 'A' REPEATED 3 TIMES
              C1
              C1
       000003 C1C1C1                  7          DC    C'AAA'     1 SET OF 3 A'S
       000006 C140C2C5E3              8          DC    C'A BET'   1 5-BYTE CONSTANT
                                     9  * SELF-DEFINING TERMS
       00006F                        10  E1      EQU   C'?'       ONE BYTE, HEX 6F
       00007D                        11  E2      EQU   C''''      ONE APOSTROPHE = HEX 7D
       0000C1                        12  E3      EQU   C'A'       ONE BYTE, HEX C1

                                     13  * RESERVING DATA AREAS FOR CHARACTERS, ALIGNED ON
                                     14  *  BYTE BDY UNLESS PRECEDING  DS SAYS OTHERWISE.
       00000B                        15          DS    CL77
       000058                        16          DS    CL2
       00005A                        17          DS    0H         ON HALF-WORD BOUNDARY
       00005A                        18          DS    CL40
       000084                        19          DS    0F         ON FULL-WORD BOUNDARY
       000084                        20          DS    133C
       000110                        21          DS    0D         ON DOUBLE-WD BOUNDARY
       000110                        22  X       DS    CL20

                                     23  * TRUNCATION ON THE RIGHT TO FIT LENGTH
       000124 C1C2                    24          DC    CL2'ABCD'  1 CONST, LENGTH = 2 BYTES
       000126 E7                      25          DC    3CL1'XYZ'  3 CONSTS, EACH OF LNG = 1
              E7
              E7
                                     26  * PADDING ON THE RIGHT WITH BLANKS
       000129 C1C240                  27          DC    CL3'AB'    1 CONST, LENGTH = 3 BYTES
       00012C E740                    28          DC    2CL2'X'    2 CONSTS, EACH OF LNG = 2
              E740

                                     29  * LITERALS
       000130 D2 00 C110C140 000110 000140  30   MVC   X(1),=C'&&'  ONE AMPERSAND (&) = HEX 50
       000136 D2 01 C110C141 000110 000141  31   MVC   X(2),=C'ZZ'  TWO Z'S  ( Z = HEX E9 )
                                     32          LTORG

       000140 50
       000141 E9E9
```

accurately named COPY, since they produce a duplicate of the original byte string without erasing the original. However, the name MOVE is preserved for historical reasons.)

Copying Bytes to and from Registers

opcode	meaning	type
IC	INSERT CHARACTER Copies 1 byte from memory into the 8 right-most bits of a register, without altering the other bits in that register.	RX
STC	STORE CHARACTER Copies 1 byte—the 8 right-most bits of a register—into memory.	RX
ICM	INSERT CHARACTERS UNDER MASK Copies N bytes, $N \le 4$, from memory into a register. The number of bytes copied and their relative positions in the register are specified in the second operand of the instruction.	RS
STCM	STORE CHARACTERS UNDER MASK Copies N bytes, $N \le 4$, from a register into memory. The number of bytes copied and their relative positions in the register are specified in the second operand of the instruction.	RS

Note that the ICM and STCM instructions are available on the IBM 370 but not on the IBM 360. The letter M in these instructions refers to the fact that the second operand of the ICM and STCM constitutes a **mask** rather than a register address or a length. In these two instructions the mask is a 4-bit field that has a dual purpose. First, the number of bytes that are inserted or stored is equal to the number of 1's in the 4-bit mask. And second, the relative position of the bytes in the register is determined by the relative position of the 1's in the mask, the correspondence being from left to right, one for one.

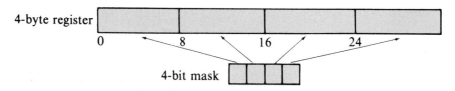

In the examples that follow, it is assumed that symbolic address A is 1000 (hex). The examples are not necessarily related to one another.

Example 1.

			Reg 6	memory location 1000
IC	6,A	before execution:	01 23 AB CD	E1 E2 E3 E4
		after execution:	01 23 AB E1	E1 E2 E3 E4

As in the LOAD instructions, the source field in an INSERT instruction is designated by the second operand, the destination by the first.

Example 2.

			Reg 6	memory location 1000
STC	6,A	before execution:	01 23 AB CD	E1 E2 E3 E4
		after execution:	01 23 AB CD	CD E2 E3 E4

In all STORE instructions, the source field is designated by the first operand, the destination by the second.

Example 3.

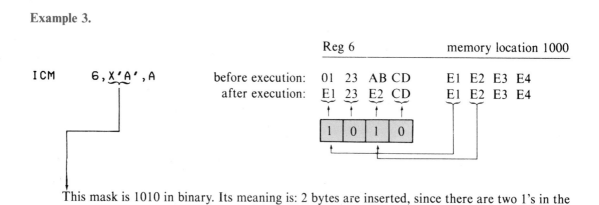

This mask is 1010 in binary. Its meaning is: 2 bytes are inserted, since there are two 1's in the mask; the relative byte positions *in the register* are the first and third, as shown in the diagram.

Example 4.

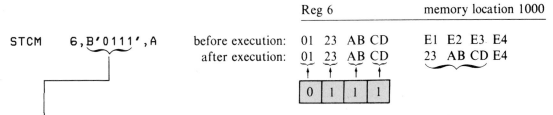

STCM   6,B'0111',A

	Reg 6	memory location 1000
before execution:	01 23 AB CD	E1 E2 E3 E4
after execution:	01 23 AB CD	23 AB CD E4

This mask is given in binary rather than hex. Its meaning is: 3 bytes are stored, since there are three 1's in the mask; the relative byte positions *in the register* are the second, third, and fourth, as shown in the diagram.

Copying Bytes from One Area of Memory to Another

opcode	meaning	type
MVI	MOVE IMMEDIATE Copies 1 byte *from* I2 field of MVI instruction *to* memory location designated by first operand.	SI
MVC	MOVE CHARACTERS	SS_1
MVCIN	MOVE INVERSE Copies L bytes, $L \leq 256$, *from* memory location designated by second operand *to* memory location designated by first operand. (L = value of length field in first operand.)	SS_1
MVCL	MOVE CHARACTERS LONG Copies L bytes, $L \leq 2^{24}$, *from* memory location designated by bits 8–31 of the general register specified in the second operand *to* memory location designated by bits 8–31 of the general register specified in the first operand. (L = value of length field associated with the first operand.)	RR

Note that the MVCL and MVCIN instructions are available on the IBM 370 but not the IBM 360. A discussion of MVCL will be presented in Section 7.8.

In the examples of MVI and MVC that follow, it is assumed that symbolic address A is 1000 (hex), and that B is 2000 (hex).

Example 1.

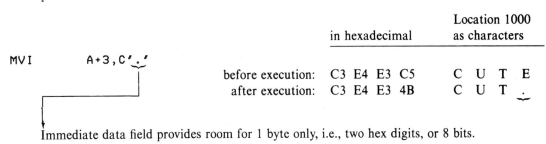

MVI   A+3,C'.'

	in hexadecimal	Location 1000 as characters
before execution:	C3 E4 E3 C5	C U T E
after execution:	C3 E4 E3 4B	C U T .

Immediate data field provides room for 1 byte only, i.e., two hex digits, or 8 bits.

Example 2.

	Location 2000 as characters	Location 1000 as characters
`MVC      B(4),A`		
before execution:	P O R T	T A L K
after execution:	T A L K	T A L K

Length field specifies how many bytes are to be copied.

Example 3.

	Location 1000 as characters
`MVC      A+1(3),A`	
before execution:	T E L E
after execution:	T T T T

Sending field 1000–1002 overlaps receiving field 1001–1003. What happens is the following. First, a byte is copied from 'A' to 'A+1', i.e., from address 1000 to address 1001, with the result that the character E at 1001 is replaced by the character T copied from 1000. Then, since the second of the three bytes in the sending field is at 1001, the character T is copied from 1001 to 1002, replacing the L that was there. Finally, the T is copied from 1002 to 1003, with the result shown above: TTTT has replaced TELE.

MVCIN (Move Inverse)

The MVCIN instruction is available as a special feature rather than as a standard instruction on most IBM 370 systems. As in the MVC instruction, MVCIN can copy from 1 to 256 bytes from one location to another. The sending location's address is specified in the second operand field, and the receiving location's address and length are specified in the first operand field. However, MVCIN differs from MVC in two important respects: (1) the first operand address in MVCIN designates the *right*-most byte of the receiving location (not the left-most byte); and (2) in the receiving location the left-to-right sequence of bytes is reversed from what it was in the sending location.

For example, if as in the MVC instruction of Example 2 above these are the *sending* location's bytes for MVCIN,

T A L K   second operand designates the address of this byte

then the *receiving* location's bytes will be these:

K L A T   first operand designates the address of this byte

Using the notation of Example 2, the MVCIN that would accomplish this is MVCIN B+3(4),A. Obviously, the MVCIN is useful only in situations—such as the use of special input/output devices—that require reversal of the normal character sequence.

7.3   COMPARING BYTES

In comparing any two bytes, the contents of each byte are treated as unsigned 8-bit numbers. An unsigned quantity such as a byte contents is called a **logical quantity,** whereas signed quantities such as integers are *arithmetic* quantities. To emphasize this distinction, all byte comparison instructions begin with the letters CL, meaning *Compare Logical*.

See Figure 7.1 or Appendix F

The smallest byte contents is 0000 0000; the largest is 1111 1111 (FF in hex notation). Any of the 256 possible 8-bit patterns is allowed in a byte. In the IBM Systems 360 and 370, the correspondence between bytes and characters given by the EBCDIC coding scheme determines whether one character is greater than or less than another character. For example, A is less than B since an A is represented as 1100 0001, which is less (numerically) than the representation of a B, namely 1100 0010. Notice that the blank (0100 0000) is less than any other printable character.

In comparing two byte strings of equal length, the comparison starts at the left-hand (high-order) end of each string and proceeds byte by byte to the right, comparing the bytes from corresponding positions, until one of two situations occurs: (1) either two bytes (one from each string) are found to be unequal or (2) the strings are exhausted and all pairs of bytes are found to be equal.

In the first situation, the relative value of the first pair of unequal bytes determines which string is the greater and which the lesser. In the second situation, the strings are considered equal. These two situations are illustrated in Examples 1–3.

Example 1.

First string: WILY
Second string: WARD

Result: First string is greater than the second string, since I is greater than A.

Example 2.

First string: STRIPE
Second string: STRUNG

Result: First string is less than the second string, since I is less than U.

Example 3.

First string: VALUE
Second string: VALUE

Result: Both strings are equal, since each corresponding pair of bytes is equal.

There are six instructions in the IBM Systems 360 and 370 that compare byte strings. In all but one of these, the two strings must be of equal length, i.e., consist of an equal number of bytes. The exception, the CLCL instruction, permits comparison of unequal-length strings by momentarily filling, or padding, the shorter string with a pad character designated by the second operand of the instruction.

The six byte-comparison instructions fall naturally into two groups: (1) instructions in which one of the strings must be in a register and (2) instructions in which both of the strings are in memory locations.

Comparing Bytes When One of the Strings Is in a Register

opcode	meaning	type
CL	COMPARE LOGICAL Compares two 4-byte strings: *first string* is in the register designated by the first operand. *Second string* is in the memory location designated by the second operand.	RX

CLR	COMPARE LOGICAL REGISTERS	RR
	Compares two 4-byte strings: *first string* is in the register designated by the first operand. *Second string* is in the register designated by the second operand.	
CLM	COMPARE LOGICAL UNDER MASK	RS
	Compares two N-byte strings, $N \leq 4$: *first string* is in the register designated by the first operand. *Second string* is in the memory location designated by the second operand.	

Note that the CLM instruction is available on the IBM 370 but not on the IBM 360. The letter *M* in this instruction refers to the fact that the second operand is a *mask*. The CLM mask functions in a manner similar to that in the ICM and STCM instructions discussed previously: the number of 1's in the mask is the number of bytes that are compared, and the relative position of the 1's determines which bytes in the register are used in the comparison.

Comparing Bytes When Both Strings Are in Memory Locations

opcode	meaning	type
CLI	COMPARE LOGICAL IMMEDIATE	SI
	Compares two 1-byte strings: *first string* is in the memory location designated by the first operand. *Second string* is in the immediate data field of the instruction itself.	
CLC	COMPARE LOGICAL CHARACTERS	SS$_1$
	Compares two N-byte strings, $N \leq 256$: *first string* is in the memory location designated by the first operand. *Second string* is in the memory location designated by the second operand. (N = value of length field in first operand.)	
CLCL	COMPARE LOGICAL CHARACTERS LONG	RR
	Compares two possibly unequal-length strings, maximum length $= 2^{24}-1$: *first string* is in the memory location designated by bits 8–31 of the general register specified in the first operand. *Second string* is in the memory location designated by bits 8–31 of the general register specified in the second operand.	

Note that the CLCL instruction is available on the IBM 370 but not the IBM 360. A discussion of the CLCL is presented in Section 7.8.

instruction	condition code and its meaning			
	0	1	2	3
CL,CLC,CLCL, CLI,CLM,CLR	first string equal to second string	first string less than second string	first string greater than second string	---

All the compare instructions mentioned up to this point set the condition code as shown in the table above. This provides the means by which the result of a comparison can be determined, as discussed in the next section.

7.4 DETERMINING THE RESULT OF A STRING COMPARISON

Whichever compare instruction is used, the result of the comparison may be determined by means of a conditional branch instruction. The same conditional branch instructions used in determining the result of an algebraic comparison are used in determining the result of a string comparison. If V_1 denotes the string whose address is specified by the first operand in a compare instruction, and

V_2 the string specified by the second operand, then the six RX-type conditional branch instructions can be used as follows:

opcode	meaning	
BE	Branch if V_1 equals V_2	$V_1 = V_2$
BNE	Branch if V_1 is not equal to V_2	$V_1 \neq V_2$
BL	Branch if V_1 is less than V_2	$V_1 < V_2$
BNL	Branch if V_1 is not less than V_2	$V_1 \geq V_2$
BH	Branch if V_1 is higher than V_2	$V_1 > V_2$
BNH	Branch if V_1 is not higher than V_2	$V_1 \leq V_2$

As discussed in Chapter 5, each of these six instructions is written with only one operand field. That field designates the address of the instruction to which a branch is made if the condition being tested is true. If the condition is *not* true, then no branch is made, instead, execution of the program continues with the instruction that immediately follows the conditional branch instruction. Examples illustrating the use of the conditional branch instructions with string comparisons are given in the sections that follow.

7.5 STRING-PROCESSING EXAMPLES

The byte-manipulation instructions described in the preceding sections are sufficient to enable many string processing problems to be programmed efficiently in assembly language. From a problem-solving standpoint, the key aspect of these instructions is that they allow a programmer to deal with strings of arbitrary length, provided their length is known at the time the program is written. The examples considered in this section illustrate this. However, if a string's length is not known at the time a program is written, the solutions presented here would not be valid. This type of problem will be discussed in Sections 7.7 and 7.8.

Consider the following elementary but typical string-handling tasks:

1. Fill an area of memory with blank spaces.
2. Search a string for all occurrences, if any, of the exclamation point character "!"; replace each occurrence with the period ".".
3. Search a string for the first occurrence of either a blank or a comma, and determine how many characters in the string preceded the first blank or comma that was found.
4. Compare an arbitrary 5-byte string with the value "END " (the letters *E N D* followed by two blanks) to see if it is equal to it or not.
5. Compare an arbitrary 5-byte string with each of the three 5-byte strings "END ", "STOP ", "FINIS" and determine which, if any, of these it is equal to.

The assembly language statements to perform each of these tasks are given in Figures 7.3 through 7.7 and are explained in the examples that follow. In all of these examples, it is assumed that the statements shown represent part of a program, not the whole program. Consequently, the CSECT, END, and BALR-USING base register statements are not shown.

Example 1. Fill an area with blanks
(See Figure 7.3.)

To fill an area of memory with blanks, two things must be known: (1) the address of the area and (2) the number of bytes in the area, i.e., the area's length. The address can be written either symbolically or in base-displacement form. The area's length, an unsigned integer, can be written symbolically or numerically, or can be omitted and implied by the length attribute of the area.

The simplest method of filling an area with blanks is to define one area that always contains blanks and copy that to the area that is to be filled. For the definitions of TEMP and BLANKS given,

```
TEMP    DS    CL80            LENGTH ATTRIBUTE OF 'TEMP' IS 80
BLANKS  DC    CL80' '         80 BLANK CHARACTERS
```

Figure 7.3   Fill an area with blanks.

```
1               MVI     TEMP,C' '                    PUT A BLANK INTO FIRST BYTE
2    *                                               OF AREA NAMED 'TEMP'
3               MVC     TEMP+1(79),TEMP              PROPAGATE BLANK INTO REMAINING
4    *                                               79 POSITIONS OF 'TEMP' AREA
                         .
                         .
                         .
5    TEMP       DS      CL80                          RESERVE 80 BYTES FOR TEMP
                         .
                         .
                         .
```

either of the following two MVC instructions will copy 80 blanks into the area named TEMP:

```
MVC    TEMP(80),BLANKS      EXPLICIT LENGTH FIELD
MVC    TEMP,BLANKS          LENGTH FIELD IMPLIED
```

*Destructive
Overlap Example*
In Figure 7.3, a different method is used. This illustrates the concept of **destructive overlap**, created by an MVC when two conditions exist simultaneously: (1) the sending area designated by the second operand *overlaps* the receiving area designated by the first operand, and (2) the first byte of the receiving area is *within* the sending area.

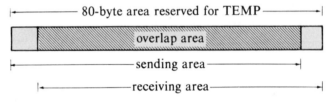

Destructive Overlap

In Figure 7.3, Statement 5 defines the area, giving it a symbolic name and a size of 80 bytes. Statements 1 and 3 utilize the destructive overlap concept as follows: Statement 1 puts a blank into the first byte of the area; Statement 3 causes that blank to be propagated into the remaining bytes of the area. This propagation is a form of destructive overlap.

A trace of the execution of the two instructions in Figure 7.3 shows the following sequence of events:

MVI moves blank into first byte.

MVC propagates first byte in 79 distinct steps, successively replacing the sending area bytes, one at a time, before they are copied into the receiving area.

Figure 7.4   Replace exclamation points with periods.

```
1    *   INITIALIZATION
2    START    LA    4,STRING          R4=ADDR OF FIRST BYTE OF STRING
3             LA    5,LENGTH          R5=LENGTH OF STRING
4    * SEARCH FOR ALL EXCLAMATION POINTS
5    COMPARE  CLI   0(4),C'!'         COMPARE CURRENT BYTE TO '!'
6             BNE   NEXT              IF NOT EQUAL, ATTEMPT NEXT BYTE
7             MVI   0(4),C'.'         IF EQUAL, REPLACE IT WITH '.'
8    * LOOP CONTROL
9    NEXT     LA    4,1(4)            R4=ADDR OF NEXT BYTE OF STRING
10            BCT   5,COMPARE         DECR STR LNG BY 1,REPEAT LOOP
11   * END OF PROCEDURE
                        .
                        .
                        .
12   STRING   DC    C'TEST! WILL IT WORK? YES!'
13   LENGTH   EQU   *-STRING
                        .
                        .
                        .
```

Two things should be noted. First, whereas the method of propagation illustrated here can be useful, it can also be disastrous if the programmer is unaware of the destructive overlap potential of the sending and receiving fields. Thus, each use of the MVC must be carefully planned. Second, if the first byte of the receiving area is *not* within the sending area, destructive overlap cannot occur. If, in this situation, the two areas partially overlap, they are said to overlap nondestructively. This is illustrated by this diagram:

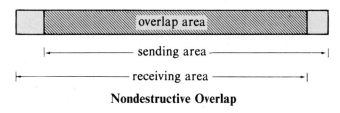

Nondestructive Overlap

Example 2.   Replace exclamation points with periods
(See Figure 7.4.)

In this solution, each repetition of the loop examines one byte of the string; the address of the byte being examined is in Register 4, initialized to the beginning (left end) of the string by Statement 2 and incremented to the next consecutive byte by Statement 9. The number of loop repetitions, i.e., the loop-control counter, is the string length, defined by Statements 12 and 13. Statement 3 initializes the loop-control counter, placing the string length into Register 5. The BCT instruction in Statement 10 reduces the loop-control counter by one; if the result of this reduction is not zero, the BCT branches to the statement named COMPARE to continue the search. When the counter reaches zero, no branch is made and the search is terminated.

Statements 5 and 6 determine whether the byte whose address is in Register 4 is an exclamation point or not. Since only one byte is being examined, the CLI instruction is used. Its first operand, 0(4), is in base-displacement form D1(B1) and means "a displacement of zero bytes beyond the address given in Register 4." (This phrase is usually stated as "zero beyond 4.") In other words, Statement 4 compares the byte whose address is in Register 4 with the exclamation point in the immediate data field of the CLI. Statement 5 determines what the result of that comparison is: when the result is equal, that is, when an exclamation point is found, no branch occurs. The BNE only branches when the result of the comparison is not equal.

For Loops, the Effective Address Is in a Register

```
1     * INITIALIZATION
2     START   LA    4,STRING          R4=ADDR OF FIRST BYTE OF STRING
3             LA    5,LENGTH          R5=LENGTH OF STRING
4     * SEARCH FOR FIRST BLANK OR COMMA
5     COMPARE CLI   0(4),C','         COMPARE CURRENT BYTE TO COMMA
6             BE    DONE              IF COMMA, TERMINATE SEARCH
7             CLI   0(4),C' '         IF NOT, COMPARE TO BLANK
8             BE    DONE              IF BLANK, TERMINATE SEARCH
9     * LOOP CONTROL
10            LA    4,1(4)            R4=ADDR OF NEXT BYTE OF STRING
11            BCT   5,COMPARE         DECR STR LNG BY 1,REPEAT LOOP
12    * COMPUTE NUMBER OF BYTES PRECEDING THE BLANK OR COMMA
13    DONE    LA    4,LENGTH          ORIGINAL LENGTH MINUS REMAINING
14            SR    4,5                LENGTH IS RESULT DESIRED
15    * END OF PROCEDURE
16    EXIT    STH   4,POSIT           R4=LENGTH UP TO COMMA OR BLANK
                    .
                    .
                    .
17    STRING  DC    C'FIND COMMA, OR BLANK'
18    LENGTH  EQU   *-STRING          ASSBLR COMPUTES #BYTES IN STRING
19    POSIT   DS    H                 HALF-WORD FOR PTR TO ' ' OR ','
                    .
                    .
                    .
```

Statement 7 is executed whenever an exclamation point is found. It moves (copies) a period from its immediate data field to the same location, designated as 0(4), at which the exclamation point is found, thereby replacing the exclamation point.

Statement 13 illustrates a useful way to let the assembler calculate the length of a string: the assembler calculates the difference of two addresses—the address of the byte following the last byte of the string, minus the address of the first byte of the string—and assigns this value to the symbol LENGTH. (The EQU pseudo-op and the memory location symbol ($*$) were described in Chapter 6.)

Example 3. Find first comma or blank in a string and compute length
(See Figure 7.5.)

This solution is similar to that of Example 2. The differences are that: (1) the search is terminated *either* when a comma or blank is found *or* when there are no more bytes to be examined, and (2) when the search is terminated, the number of bytes that precede the first comma or blank is calculated and stored in the location named POSIT. Note that it always requires at least two types of statements to examine a string: the first is a comparison, the second is a conditional branch determining the results of the comparison.

Statements 13 and 14 calculate the number of bytes that precede the first comma or blank in the string. For the sample string of Statement 17, this number is four; i.e., the program finds the blank following the D in FIND. However, the program shown will work for *any* string, provided its address is STRING and that it consists of at least 1 byte. For example,

sample string	string length	number of bytes preceding the first comma or blank
C'DEAR JOHN,'	10	4 (blank in 5th position)
C'DEARJOHN,'	9	8 (comma in 9th position)
C' DEAR JOHN,'	11	0 (blank in 1st position)
C'DEARJOHN'	8	8 (no blank or comma found)

Figure 7.6   *Compare 5-byte string to C'END   '.*

```
1              CLC    COMMAND(5),STRING        COMPARE 5-BYTE STRINGS
2              BE     FOUND                    BRANCH IF EQUAL
               .
               .
               .
3   STRING DS         CL5                      5-BYTE AREA RESERVED FOR STRING
4   COMMAND DC         CL5'END'                'END' IS PADDED ON RIGHT
               .
               .
               .
```

Since it is inconceivable that any string would have a length for which the binary representation would require more than 15 bits ($2^{15} = 32{,}768$), only a half word was reserved for the computed value stored in POSIT. Thus, in Statement 16, the half-word store instruction STH is used in conjunction with the half word reserved by Statement 19.

Example 4.   Compare 5-byte string to C'END   '
(See Figure 7.6.)

Since both strings are in memory and are of length greater than four, the CLC instruction is used. If the string lengths were greater than 256, or if the strings were of unequal length, the CLCL instruction would have to be used instead of the CLC.

Example 5.   Compare 5-byte string with strings in a table
(See Figure 7.7.)

A **table** is a set of related items stored in memory. In the case at hand, each of the items is a 5-byte string; the strings are stored consecutively in memory. An item in a table is almost always called a **table entry**, the terminology used in Figure 7.7.

The number of entries in a table depends on two things: the length of each entry and the amount of space available for the table. In Figure 7.7, there are three entries, given by Statements 14 through 16. But, instead of using the number three in the program, Statement 17 lets the assembler calculate the number and assign it to the symbol ENTRIES. In this way, if the programmer wanted to insert more entries, he or she would not have to change any of the statements in the program, not even Statement 17.

Statements 5, 8, and 12 require comment. Statement 5 compares the 5-byte string located at the current table-entry address given in Register 4 with the 5-byte string located at the symbolic address STRING. Statement 8 increments the table-entry address in Register 4 by five (the length of each table entry) so that the second iteration of the loop will examine the second entry, and the third iteration will examine the third entry. This is illustrated in the diagram.

address in Reg 4:			+1	+2	+3	+4
1st iteration:	TABLE	→	E	N	D		
2nd iteration:	TABLE + 5	→	F	I	N	I	S
3rd iteration:	TABLE + 10	→	S	T	O	P	

The search is terminated when a match is found *or* when no match is found and there are no more entries to be examined. In the first case, the address of the matching entry is stored in symbolic location POSIT for possible future use. If no match is found, a zero is stored in POSIT to indicate

Figure 7.7   Compare 5-byte string with strings in a table.

```
1      * INITIALIZATION
2      START   LA    4,TABLE             R4=ADDR OF FIRST ENTRY IN TABLE
3              LA    5,ENTRIES           R5=NUMBER OF ENTRIES
4      * COMPARE STRING TO EACH ENTRY (STRING LENGTH IS 5)
5      LOOK    CLC   0(5,4),STRING       COMPARE CURRENT ENTRY TO STRING
6              BE    EXIT                TERMINATE PROCEDURE WHEN FOUND
7      * LOOP CONTROL
8              LA    4,5(4)              IF NOT FOUND, ADV TO NEXT ENTRY
9              BCT   5,LOOK              DECR #ENTRIES BY 1,REPEAT LOOP
10     * END OF PROCEDURE                WHEN SEARCH IS COMPLETE,EITHER
11             SR    4,4                 R4=0 IF NOT FOUND IN TABLE, OR
12     EXIT    ST    4,POSIT             R4=ADDR OF ENTRY THAT WAS FOUND
                     .
                     .
                     .
13     STRING  DS    CL5                 5-BYTE AREA RESERVED FOR STRING
14     TABLE   DC    CL5'END'            TABLE WITH 3 5-BYTE ENTRIES
15             DC    CL5'FINIS'
16             DC    CL5'STOP'
17     ENTRIES EQU   (*-TABLE)/5         ASSBLR COMPUTES NO.ENTRIES
18     POSIT   DS    F                   FULL-WD FOR ADDR OF FOUND ENTRY
                     .
                     .
                     .
```

"no match." Other actions would be equally valid. The point is that some action is advisable to indicate, for subsequent portions of the program, what the result of the search is. Since an address of zero cannot be the address of any table entry within a program, the use of zero for "no match" is unambiguous. In this type of programming technique, the symbolic location POSIT is called a **flag** or **switch.**

POSIT requires only 3 bytes when addresses are 24-bit numbers. Nevertheless, a full word was reserved for POSIT so that the straightforward store instruction ST could be used in Statement 12. Alternatively, 3 bytes could have been reserved for POSIT and the STCM instruction used to select the low-order (right-most) 3 bytes from Register 4, as follows:

```
EXIT    STCM    4,B'0111',POSIT
           .
           .
           .
POSIT   DS      CL3                 3 BYTES FOR ADDR OF FOUND ENTRY
```

This is an illustration of a situation that arises again and again in assembly language programming: we must select an instruction that is compatible with the type and length of the data being operated on, and we must be certain that the data area is properly aligned in memory and of sufficient size for the instruction that is selected.

7.6   SUBSTRING OPERATIONS

In some types of programming applications, it is necessary to process strings that exist within other, larger strings. The smaller strings are known as **substrings** of the larger ones, as in this example:

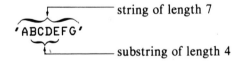

We frequently need to be able to determine if a given substring, say S, exists within some string T. Among the operations we may wish to perform on S are those of **deleting** each occurrence of S from T; **replacing** S by another string, S1; or of **inserting** a string, S2, immediately following S in T. For example, suppose we are given these definitions of T, S, S1, and S2:

```
T:         'A NOT SO TYPICAL STRING NAMED T'
S:         'NOT SO '
S1:        'VERY '
S2:        'UNUSUAL BUT RATHER '
```

Then, each of the three operations named previously can be illustrated as follows:

1. Deleting S from T would yield a new string, TNEW (say):

```
        TNEW: 'A TYPICAL STRING NAMED T'
```

2. Replacing S in T by S1 would yield this new string:

```
        TNEW: 'A VERY TYPICAL STRING NAMED T'
```

3. Inserting S2 immediately following S in T would give this:

```
    TNEW: 'A NOT SO UNUSUAL BUT RATHER TYPICAL STRING NAMED T'
```

Figure 7.8 summarizes the sequence of steps required for each of these three string-editing operations. An obvious point to note is that each operation—delete, replace, insert—can change the length of the string being edited. A perhaps not so obvious observation is that the CLC and MVC instructions are not well designed for these types of problems because the length fields in the CLC and MVC instructions must be specified at assembly time. For these types of problems, this would mean that different-length substrings S, S1, and S2 could not be processed at run time by the same MVC and CLC instructions. For example, if we had written the following sequence of statements:

```
       .....
       LA     3,N           R3 = NUMBER OF ITERATIONS OF LOOP TO
       SH     3,=H'6'            SEARCH FOR 7-CHAR SUBSTR IN T
       LA     2,T           R2 = ADDR OF CURRENT SUBSTR IN T
       LA     1,S           R1 = ADDR OF SUBSTRING S
LOOP   CLC    0(7,1),0(2)   COMPARE 7 BYTES OF S TO SUBSTR IN T
       BE     EQUAL         BRANCH WHEN SUBSTRING S FOUND IN T
NOTEQ  EQU    *             BEGIN UPDATING TO NEXT CHAR POSIT
        .
        .
        .
EQUAL  EQU    *             BEGIN STRING EDITING FUNCTION
       ......
S      DC     C'NOT SO '
T      DC     C'A NOT SO TYPICAL STRING NAMED T'
N      EQU    *-T           LENGTH OF STRING NAMED T
```

both the length of string T and the length of substring S are, so to speak, "baked in" to the program. Once assembled, the program will not run for any other lengths of S and T than those shown.

We do not need any new techniques to remove the dependence on the length of the string T: we can simply replace the statements defining T and its length by the two statements

```
T      DS     CL256         SPACE RESERVED FOR MAX LENGTH STRING T
N      DS     H             SPACE RESERVED FOR LENGTH OF T
```

and replace the statement that initializes the loop-control counter with this one:

```
       LH     3,N           R3 = NUMBER OF ITERATIONS OF LOOP
```

Figure 7.8   Pseudocode for string-editing procedures DELETE, REPLACE, and INSERT.

```
STRING_EDIT:

  REPEAT UNTIL number of remaining comparisons <= 0

    IF current substring in T = S
    THEN
      IF operation = replace
      THEN
        copy S1 to current position in TNEW;
        increase length of TNEW by length of S1;
        adjust current position in TNEW by length of S1;
      ELSE
        IF operation = insert
        THEN
          copy S followed by S2 to current position in TNEW;
          increase length of TNEW by length of S plus length of S2;
          adjust current position in TNEW by length of S plus length of S2;
        END IF;
      END IF;
      { the following steps are done for all three operations }
      adjust current position in T by length of S;
      reduce number of remaining comparisons by length of S;

    ELSE { current substring of T did not match S }
      copy one character from current position in T
        to current position in TNEW;
      increase length of TNEW by 1;
      adjust current position in TNEW by +1;
      adjust current position in T by +1;
      reduce the number of remaining comparisons by 1;

    END IF;

  END UNTIL;

  copy remaining characters (if any) from T to TNEW
    and increase length of TNEW accordingly;

EXIT STRING_EDIT.
```

```
NOTATION:

T        string to be edited
TNEW     resulting (edited) string
S        substring in T that is object of delete, replace, or insert operation
S1       replaces each occurrence of S in T (replace operation)
S2       inserted after each occurrence of S in T     (insert operation)
```

But the problem is, how can we remove the dependence on the length of the substring S? In the previous sequence of statements, this dependence shows itself in two forms. First, the number of comparisons required to search for a substring of length M is obtained by subtracting $M-1$ from the length of the string being examined. This is illustrated by the following diagram, in which $M = 7$ and the length of T = 31, so that the number of comparisons is $31 - (7 - 1) = 25$:

A NOT SO TYPICAL STRING NAMED T

1st comparison
2nd comparison
3rd comparison

last (25th) comparison

The second, and more critical, way in which the dependence on the length of substring S shows itself in the sequence of statements is in the length field of the CLC instruction:

```
LOOP    CLC    0(7,1),0(2)    COMPARE 7 BYTES OF S TO SUBSTR IN T
```

Substituting a symbol for the numeric length will not remove the dependence:

```
LOOP    CLC    0(M,1),0(2)
                .
                .
S       DC     C'NOT SO '
M       EQU    *-S            LENGTH OF STRING NAMED S
```

Dependence is still "baked in" at assembly time because the symbol M, like the self-defining term 7, can have only one value at assembly time. So the question remains: how can we remove the dependence on the length of substring S in such a way that a single sequence of statements can be used to examine an arbitrary string T for the occurrence of an arbitrary substring S without having to reassemble the statements for each different string T and substring S? The answer is to be found in the use of other instructions: the Execute (EX) instruction, described in Section 7.7; and the CLCL and MVCL instructions, described in Section 7.8.

7.7 THE EXECUTE INSTRUCTION

The **Execute (EX)** instruction is an RX-type instruction. When executed at run time, it causes the CPU to execute another instruction, called the "target" instruction, located at the address given in the second operand field of the EX instruction. Its format is

opcode	operand
EX	R1,D2(X2,B2)

address of target instruction
designated by second operand

One of the main uses of the EX instruction depends on its capability for effectively but not actually changing the second byte (bits 8–15) of the target instruction before the target instruction is executed. This capability makes it possible to vary the length-field contents of SS_1 and SS_2 instructions and to vary the mask-field contents in certain RS and SI instructions. The following specifications govern use of the EX instruction:

1. The target instruction can be any valid instruction except an EX instruction.
2. When the target instruction is executed by the EX, it is executed just as though it were located where the EX itself is located, with one additional characteristic (see specification 3).

   If the target instruction is anything other than one of the conditional or unconditional branch instructions, then, after the target instruction is executed by the EX, the instruction following the EX in memory will be the next one performed by the CPU. If the target instruction is a conditional branch, the branch will be made if the condition being tested is true. If the condition being tested is not true, the branch will not be made and the instruction following the EX will be the next one performed by the CPU. If the target instruction is an unconditional branch, the branch will be made. If the target is a branch and link instruction (BAL or BALR, to be discussed further in Chaps. 9 and 10), the address placed into the register designated by the first operand field of these instructions will be the address of the instruction that follows the EX, *not* the address of the instruction following the BAL or BALR. Similarly, if the target instruction is a supervisor call instruction (SVC, to be discussed in Chap. 19), the address transmitted to the operating system will be the address of the instruction following the EX, *not* the address of the instruction following the SVC.

3. The register designated by the first operand of the EX instruction plays a special role, depending on whether it is Register 0 or some other general register.

If the register designated by the first operand of an EX instruction is Register 0, that register is not used in the execution of the EX instruction. If the register designated by the first operand is any general register *other than* Register 0, the target instruction is executed as though its second byte contained the result of the Boolean OR operation

$$\left\{ \begin{array}{c} \text{bits 24--31} \\ \text{of designated} \\ \text{register} \end{array} \right\} \quad \text{OR} \quad \left\{ \begin{array}{c} \text{second byte} \\ \text{of target} \\ \text{instruction} \end{array} \right\} = \left\{ \begin{array}{c} \text{effective contents} \\ \text{of second byte} \\ \text{of target instruction} \end{array} \right\}$$

Neither the contents of the designated register nor the contents of the target instruction are changed by this operation. The Boolean OR is carried out by the CPU in a register unavailable to programmers.

Target's Length Field (Bits 8–15) Should Be Zero

In this context, the Boolean OR is **an operation on pairs of bits:** bit 24 of the register operates on bit 8 of the target, bit 25 operates on bit 9 of the target, and so forth, up to bit 31 operating on bit 15 of the target. *If both bits of a pair are '0', the resulting bit is a '0'; otherwise, the resulting bit is a '1'.* The following examples illustrate this:

bits 24–31 of register		bits 8–15 of target		resulting bits
00001111	OR	00110011	=	00111111
00001100	OR	00110011	=	00111111
00001111	OR	00000000	=	00001111
00001100	OR	00000000	=	00001100

The last two examples illustrate an important, frequent use of the EX instruction: *if the second byte of the target instruction contains all 0's, then the result of the OR operation will always be just the contents of bits 24–31 of the designated register.*

With the EX instruction, we can now resolve the problem posed in the preceding section: how to remove the dependence of a CLC instruction and, by analogy, of a MVC instruction, on the length field assembled into that instruction. Remember that in the preceding section we presented a sequence of assembly language statements that included the following compare instruction:

```
LOOP      CLC    0(7,1),0(2)    COMPARE 7 BYTES OF S TO SUBSTR IN T
```

where Register 1 contained the address of the current substring in the string T and Register 2 contained the address of a 7-byte string S. Now, if we assume that the length of S is stored as a halfword binary integer at symbolic address M, we can replace the compare instruction with the following statements:

```
          LH     4,M            R4 = LENGTH OF S, MINUS 1
          SH     4,=H'1'        (ONE LESS IS NEEDED FOR EX)
LOOP      EX     4,COMPARE      COMPARE S TO SUBSTRING IN T
          .
          .
          .
M         DS     H              SPACE FOR LENGTH OF S
COMPARE   CLC    0(0,1),0(2)    LENGTH FLD OF ZERO FOR EX INSTR.
```

Figure 7.9   The string-editing DELETE procedure. (See also Figure 7.8.)

```
              .
              .
              .
* THE FOLLOWING STATEMENTS CAN BE USED TO DELETE EACH OCCURRENCE OF AN
*  ARBITRARY-LENGTH SUBSTRING  S  FROM ANOTHER STRING  T .  THE RESULT
*  IS STORED AT SYMBOLIC ADDRESS 'TNEW' .
* THE LENGTH OF  T  IS GIVEN AS A HALF-WORD BINARY INTEGER AT  'N' .
* THE LENGTH OF  S  IS A HALF-WORD BINARY INTEGER AT  'M' .
* THE LENGTH OF THE RESULTING STRING  'TNEW'  DEPENDS ON THE NUMBER OF
*  OCCURRENCES OF  S  IN  T .  THIS LENGTH IS COMPUTED AND STORED AS
*  A HALF-WORD BINARY INTEGER AT  'NN' .
* THE GIVEN STRINGS  S  AND  T  ARE NOT ALTERED.  THEIR LENGTHS ARE
*  RESTRICTED TO BE LESS THAN OR EQUAL TO 256 , AND GREATER THAN 0 .

* INITIALIZATIONS
              LA    1,S           R1 = ADDR OF  S
              LA    2,T           R2 = ADDR OF CURRENT POSITION IN  T
              LA    9,TNEW        R9 = ADDR OF CUR. POSITION IN  TNEW
              LH    10,=H'0'      R10 = COMPUTED LNG OF  TNEW (INITIALLY 0)
              LH    3,N           R3 = NUMBER OF COMPARISONS REMAINING TO
              SH    3,M               BE MADE. INITIALLY, EQUAL TO
              AH    3,=H'1'           N - ( M - 1 )
              BNP   MOVE              IF N < M THEN MAKE NO COMPARISONS
              LH    4,M           R4 = LENGTH OF  S , MINUS 1
              SH    4,=H'1'            +1  IS SUBTRACTED FOR EX INSTR

* COMPARE   S  TO SUBSTRING OF SAME LENGTH IN  T
LOOP          EX    4,COMPARE         COMPARISON  OF   M  BYTES
              BE    EQUAL             BRANCH IF SUBSTRING  S  IS FOUND
NOTEQUAL      MVC   0(1,9),0(2)   COPY ONE CHAR FROM  T  TO  TNEW
              AH    10,=H'1'      INCR LNG OF  TNEW  BY  +1
              LA    9,1(9)        ADJ CUR POSIT IN  TNEW  BY  +1
              LA    2,1(2)        ADJ CUR POSIT IN   T   BY  +1
              BCT   3,LOOP        REDUCE #REMAINING COMPARISONS BY  +1
              B     MOVE          IF NO MORE COMPARISONS, GO COPY REST OF T

* DELETE OPERATION AVOIDS MOVING  S  FROM  T  TO  TNEW
EQUAL         AH    2,M           ADJ CUR POSITION IN  T  BY LENGTH OF  S
              SH    3,M           REDUCE # REMAINING COMPARISONS BY LNG OF S
              BP    LOOP          IF MORE COMPARISONS REMAIN, DO THEM

* COPY REMAINING CHARACTERS (IF ANY) FROM  T  TO  TNEW
MOVE          LA    5,T           COMPUTE # CHARACTERS REMAINING IN  T , BY
              AH    5,N               SUBTRACTING CUR. POSIT. IN T FROM ADDR
              SR    5,2           OF FIRST BYTE BEYOND  T
              BNP   NOMORE        NO MORE CHARS IF  S  OCCUPIED LAST  M
              AR    10,5          BYTES OF  T .  OTHERWISE, INCR LNG OF
              SH    5,=H'1'       TNEW, AND PREPARE TO MOVE REMAINING
              EX    5,MOVEX       CHARS TO  TNEW  VIA  EX  INSTR
NOMORE        STH   10,NN         STORE COMPUTED LENGTH OF  TNEW
              .
              .
              .
T             DS    CL256         SPACE FOR MAX LENGTH   T   STRING
S             DS    CL256         SPACE FOR MAX LENGTH   S   STRING
TNEW          DS    CL256         SPACE FOR MAX LENGTH  TNEW  STRING
N             DS    H             SPACE FOR LENGTH OF  T   ( 0<LNG≤256 )
M             DS    H             SPACE FOR LENGTH OF  S   ( 0<LNG≤256 )
NN            DS    H             SPACE FOR LENGTH OF  TNEW
* FOLLOWING ARE TARGET INSTRS FOR   EX   INSTRUCTIONS IN ABOVE PROCEDURE
COMPARE       CLC   0(0,1),0(2)   R1=ADDR OF S; R2= CUR POSIT IN T
MOVEX         MVC   0(0,9),0(2)   R9= CUR POSIT IN TNEW; R2 = POSIT IN T
```

There are two important points to be noted. First, *it is necessary that the length that is placed into the register for use by the EX instruction be one less than the length desired.* This is because in machine language, the length-field content of an SS_1 or SS_2 instruction is always one less than the actual length; a machine language length of L corresponds to an actual length of $L+1$, so that an 8-bit length field can represent the 2^8 possible lengths 1,2,3,...,256 rather than 0,1,2,...,255, and, similarly, a 4-bit length field represents the 2^4 possible lengths 1,2,3,...,16 rather than 0,1,...,15.

Second, *the target instruction should be removed from the sequence of instructions that includes the EX instruction;* i.e., the target may be considered as a kind of data on which the EX operates.

Using the previous five statements instead of the single CLC demonstrated previously, the EX instruction will cause a string of arbitrary length (not exceeding 256 bytes) to be compared to a substring in T. For example, if the length of S is 7, then, when the EX is executed, bits 24–31 of Register 4 will contain 00000110, i.e., a binary 6 ($= 7 - 1$), so that the CLC instruction is executed *as though* it were written as CLC 0(7,1),0(2).

As a further illustration of the capabilities of the EX instruction, Figure 7.9 shows a set of statements that will delete all occurrences of an arbitrary string, S (of length less than or equal to 256 bytes), from an arbitrary string, T. The processing logic is as given in Figure 7.8 for the 'DELETE' operation.

As noted, the main restriction on the arbitrariness of the length field when the EX instruction is used as described is that the length be less than or equal to 256. This is because the length fields in MVC and CLC instructions are similarly restricted; the EX is designed to operate within this restriction. When a length field is greater than 256 bytes, then there are two alternatives available: we can use a sequence of EX's (with a corresponding sequence of MVC's or CLC's) so that all the bytes are accounted for; or we can use the MVCL or CLCL instructions. The latter instructions are not available on the IBM 360, only on the IBM 370. They will be discussed in the next section.

7.8 THE CLCL AND MVCL INSTRUCTIONS

The Compare Logical Characters Long (CLCL) and Move Logical Characters Long (MVCL) are so named because, in both of these instructions, the number of bytes operated on is not restricted to be less than or equal to 256, as is the case in the CLC and MVC instructions. In CLCL and MVCL, the number of bytes can be from 0 to $2^{24}-1$. Since the latter number is one less than the maximum number of addressable bytes in a 16-megabyte memory, there is no real length restriction at all. To accommodate such a numeric range, CLCL and MVCL were designed as RR-type instructions. The following descriptions explain how the contents of the designated registers are interpreted in each of these instructions.

CLCL

For its execution, the CLCL instruction utilizes two even-odd pairs of registers. As discussed earlier, an even-odd register pair is two consecutively numbered registers in which the address of the first register is an even number and that of the second an odd number. An even-odd register pair is specified by its even-numbered register address. For the CLCL instruction, one register pair contains the address and length of one of the strings to be compared, while the other register pair contains the address and length of the other string. Moreover, for the CLCL instruction *the lengths of the two strings need not be the same.* To compensate for strings of unequal length, a **padding character** must be in one of the registers at the time of execution. The padding character is used during execution to temporarily lengthen the shorter string so that it is the same length as the longer one during the comparison. This lengthening, done in a register unavailable to the programmer, does not alter the strings in memory. Most often, the padding character is chosen to be a blank (X'40') if the strings contain nothing but printable characters, or a binary zero (X'00') for arbitrary strings. These choices will ensure that the shorter string will be less than the longer string, if it is not equal to it.

The format of the CLCL instruction and the meaning attached to the even-odd register pairs are as follows:

opcode   operand

CLCL   R1,R2   (both R1 and R2 are even-numbered registers)

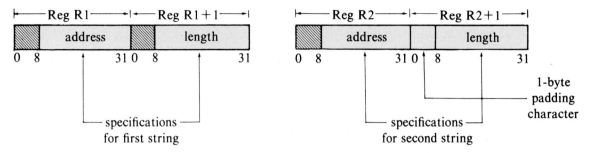

Clearly, the string addresses and lengths as well as the padding character must be loaded into the registers before the CLCL is executed. The result of the comparison may be tested in the usual manner by one of the conditional branch instructions: the string specified by the first operand field (R1) is determined to be equal, less than, or greater than the string specified by the second operand field. For example, consider the following EBCDIC strings, and assume that the padding character is X'00':

first string	second string	result of comparison
EQ	EQU	1st < 2nd
ABCD	ABC	1st > 2nd
102400	1024	1st > 2nd

In the third example, the strings are not equal because the padding character is a binary zero (X'00') not an EBCDIC zero (X'F0'). Note, however, that if we compare the two hexadecimal strings X'1024' and X'102400', the strings would be considered equal if the padding character were X'00'.

By using the CLCL instruction, we can resolve the problem posed at the end of Section 7.6: how to avoid having a string's length being "baked in" to a program at assembly time so that it cannot be altered at run time. The CLCL can be used to compare two arbitrary strings as follows:

```
          LA    2,S        PUT ADDR OF 1ST STRING IN EVEN# REG
          L     3,M        PUT LENGTH OF 1ST STR IN NEXT ODD# REG
          LA    4,T        PUT ADDR OF 2ND STR IN EVEN# REG
          LR    5,3        USE LNG OF 1ST STR, WITH PAD CHAR = X'00'
          CLCL  2,4        COMPARE STR SPECIFIED IN R2 & R3
                           WITH STR SPECIFIED IN R4 & R5

          .
          .
          .
S         DS    CL1000     SPACE FOR UP TO 1000-BYTE STRING
T         DS    CL2000     SPACE FOR UP TO 2000-BYTE STRING
M         DS    F          SPACE FOR LENGTH OF STRING S
```

In these statements, the space reserved for the two strings depends on the problem in which the strings occur. There is no restriction other than memory size. Similarly, in order to accommodate any allowable length, the space reserved for the string length is a full word. If we wanted to compare two strings of unequal length, we would replace the LR 5,3 instruction with L 5,N where N is the symbolic address of the full word whose content is the second string's length. If we wanted to use a padding character other than X'00', we could follow the LR 5,3 or L 5,N instruction with ICM 5,X'8',PAD where PAD is the symbolic address of the desired padding character.

One other characteristic of the CLCL instruction's execution significantly affects the way in which the instruction must be used in loops: *the contents of the two pairs of registers are altered during the execution of the instruction.* If the result of the comparison is that the two strings are not equal, the length and address fields of each register pair identify the bytes that caused the unequal result. In this case, the two lengths are decreased by the number of bytes that were equal, and the addresses point to the first unequal bytes in the respective strings. (If the two strings were unequal in *length,* the length field of the shorter operand is set to zero and the address field of the shorter operand is increased by the length of that operand.) Similarly, if the result of the comparison is that the two strings are equal, including the padding character, if necessary, both length fields are set to zero and the addresses are incremented by the corresponding lengths. In all cases, bits 0–7 of the even-numbered registers are set to zero, and bits 0–7 of the odd-numbered registers (and hence the padding character) are unchanged. Further details are given in the IBM 370 *Principles of Operation* manual (GA22–7000). One consequence of the register alterations just described is that if the CLCL is to be used in a loop, the length fields must be reloaded before each execution of the CLCL, and, depending on the locations of the strings being compared, the address fields may also have to be reloaded into the registers.

MVCL

The MVCL instruction, like the CLCL instruction, utilizes two even-odd pairs of registers during its execution. The format of MVCL and the meaning of the contents of the register pairs are similar to those of the CLCL:

opcode   operand

MVCL   R1,R2   (both R1 and R2 designate even-numbered registers)

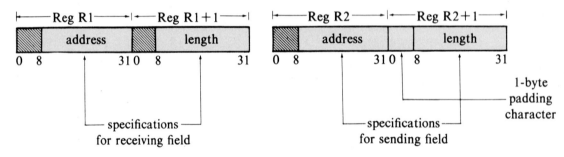

The number of bytes specified by the length field in Register R1+1 is copied into the receiving field, beginning at the address designated in Register R1. The bytes are copied from the sending field, starting from the address designated in Register R2. If the sending-field length is less than the receiving-field length, the remaining bytes of the receiving field are filled with the padding character. If the receiving-field length is specified as zero, no bytes are copied.

The contents of the two pairs of registers are altered during the execution of a MVCL instruction, as follows: at the completion of execution, the length field in Register R1+1 is zero and the address in Register R1 has been incremented by the original length in R1+1. The length field in Register R2+1 has been decreased by the number of bytes copied from the receiving field and the address in Register R2 has been incremented by the same amount. Bits 0–7 of the even-numbered registers are set to zero; bits 0–7 of the two odd-numbered registers (and hence the padding character) are unchanged. One consequence of these register-content changes is that if the MVCL is to be used in a loop, the length fields (and possibly the address fields) will have to be reloaded into the respective registers before each execution of MVCL. Further details of the execution of the MVCL can be found in the IBM 370 *Principles of Operations* manual (GA22–7000).

One other point deserves mention before concluding this discussion: *no bytes are copied if the sending and receiving fields overlap destructively.* Instead, condition code 3 is set and the situation may be detected with the **Branch on Overlap (BO)** conditional branch instruction. The conditions defining destructive overlap were described in Section 7.5; a complete discussion of the condition code will be found in Section 8.4.

It should be clear from this discussion that the MVCL instruction can be used instead of the combination of EX and MVC whenever it is desirable to postpone specification of a field length until run time. Details of how to accomplish this are left as an exercise.

7.9 THE TR AND TRT INSTRUCTIONS

The Translate (TR) and Translate and Test (TRT) instructions are specifically designed to help reduce the size and running time of programs that perform the following types of recurring string operations: (1) replacing some, but not necessarily all, bytes in a string with other predetermined bytes, and (2) searching a string from left to right for the first occurrence of any one of some predetermined set of bytes.

The **TR instruction** can be used in any situation where it is desirable to **replace** certain bytes in a string with other bytes. For example, it can be used to replace all exclamation points with periods, all commas with semicolons, and all other punctuation characters with question mark characters; change all lowercase letters in a string to uppercase letters; and translate a string from the EBCDIC codes in which it is represented to some other code scheme, such as ASCII.

The **TRT instruction** can be used in any situation where we want to **find** one of a number of different characters in a string. For example, it can be used to find the first occurrence of any punctuation character; find the first occurrence of any mathematical operator + − * / ; or find the first occurrence of a nonprinting character, i.e., a character that does not produce a symbol on a printer or terminal.

The discussion that follows describes how the TR and TRT instructions can be used for tasks similar to those mentioned.

General Description

Both the TR and TRT instructions operate on two strings. For purposes of discussion, one of the two strings is called the **argument string** and the other is called the **function string.** The bytes in the argument string are generally not known to the programmer, for it is the bytes in the argument string that are replaced by the action of the TR and searched by the action of the TRT. The bytes of the function string *are* known to the programmer; the programmer defines them in such a way as to cause the desired result to be achieved by the TR or TRT instructions. This will be illustrated in the discussion that follows.

In the TR and TRT instructions, the argument string and its length are designated by the first operand and the function string is designated by the second operand. However, the length of the function string, which is usually 256 bytes, is not specified in either instruction. Both the TR and TRT instructions are SS$_1$-type instructions:

opcode	operand
TR	D1(L,B1),D2(B2)
TRT	D1(L,B1),D2(B2)

                     argument   function
                       string   string

Each of the two instructions works on the following principles. The CPU examines each of the bytes of the argument string one by one, from left to right. Immediately after examining a byte of the argument string, and before examining the next byte in that string, the CPU selects one of the bytes in the function string. The position of the byte that is selected depends on the value of the argument byte that was just examined.

In the TR instruction, the function byte that is selected replaces the argument byte that was just examined. Then the next argument byte (if any) is examined. If there are no more argument bytes to be examined, the execution of the TR instruction is terminated.

In the TRT instruction, the selected function byte is tested to see if it is either X'00' or not X'00'. If the selected function byte is not X'00', a copy of that byte is inserted into bit positions 24–31 of Register 2, the address of the corresponding argument byte is inserted into bit positions 8–31 of Register 1, execution of the instruction is terminated, and a condition code is set. *Condition code 1*

TRT May Alter Registers 1 and 2. It Also Sets the Condition Code. TR Doesn't.

is set if one or more argument bytes still remain to be examined when the nonzero function byte is found; *condition code 2 is set* when no more argument bytes remain to be examined when the nonzero function byte is found.

If a function byte selected during the execution of a TRT instruction is X'00', no further action is taken with that byte. Instead, the next argument byte (if any) is examined. If there are no more argument bytes to be examined, the execution of the TRT instruction is terminated and *condition code 0 is set.*

The condition code setting generated by a TRT instruction can be determined by following the TRT instruction with a conditional branch instruction, as described in Section 8.4. For example, if FN2 is the table defined in Figure 7.11 and ARG2 is the symbolic address of any 8-byte string, then the following sequence will find the left-most math operator (if any) in the ARG2 string:

```
* BRANCH TO 'NONE' IF NO MATH OPERATOR IS FOUND IN ARG2
* BRANCH TO 'MORE' IF A MATH OPERATOR IS FOUND IN ANY BYTE OF ARG2
*  EXCEPT THE LAST (RIGHTMOST) BYTE
* BRANCH TO 'ONE' IF THE LEFTMOST OPERATOR FOUND IS IN THE LAST
*  (RIGHTMOST) BYTE OF 'ARG2'
*
         TRT     ARG2(8),FN2   LOOK FOR A MATH OPERATOR IN 'ARG2'
         BC      8,NONE        BRANCH IF NONE FOUND
         BC      4,MORE        BRANCH IF FOUND PRIOR TO LAST BYTE
         BC      2,ONE         BRANCH IF FOUND ONLY IN LAST BYTE
```

In both the TR and TRT instructions, the CPU determines the position of the function byte that is to be selected by adding the 8-bit value of the corresponding argument byte to the address of the beginning of the function string:

$$
\left\{ \begin{array}{c} \text{position, or} \\ \text{address, of} \\ \text{the function byte} \\ \text{to be selected} \end{array} \right\} = \left\{ \begin{array}{c} \text{address of} \\ \text{the first byte} \\ \text{of the function} \\ \text{string} \end{array} \right\} + \left\{ \begin{array}{c} \text{8-bit value} \\ \text{of the} \\ \text{corresponding} \\ \text{argument byte} \end{array} \right\}
$$

For example, if the function string begins at location 1004 (hex) and the argument byte that was just examined is X'5A', the position of the function byte that is selected is computed to be 1004 + 5A = 105E. Whenever an argument byte is a X'5A', the address of the function byte that is selected will be 5A bytes beyond the beginning of the function string. Another way of expressing this is to say that the first byte of the function string is selected if the corresponding argument byte is X'00', the second byte is selected if the argument byte is X'01', the third if the argument byte is X'02', and so forth. Thus an argument byte of X'FF', i.e., the largest possible byte, will cause the 256th byte to be selected from the function string. Since the programmer, in general, does not know what bytes will be in the argument string, it is always advisable to make the function string 256 bytes long.

The remaining question is, what should the bytes in a function string be? The answer depends on which instruction—TR or TRT—is used and for what specific purpose the instruction is to be used.

Function String for TR Instruction

The function string for the TR instruction consists of 256 bytes, chosen as follows: for each byte of the argument string that is to be replaced, the position in the function string corresponding to that argument-byte value must contain the byte that is to replace that argument byte. For any byte of the argument string that is not to be replaced, the position in the function string corresponding to that argument-byte value must contain a duplicate of the byte that caused that position to be selected.

Lowercase to Uppercase

For example, if we wanted to change all lowercase letters in a string to uppercase letters, without changing any of the other characters in the string, the function string would consist of the 256 EBCDIC codes X'00', X'01', ...X'FF', except for the following (see Fig. 7.1): the 130th through 138th bytes (corresponding to lowercase *a* = X'81' through lowercase *i* = X'89') would be the representations of uppercase *A* through *I,* namely X'C1', X'C2',...,X'C9'; the 146th through 154th bytes (lowercase *j* through *r*) would be the representations of uppercase *J* through *R,* namely X'D1', X'D2',...,X'D9'; and the 163rd through 170th bytes (lowercase *s* through *z*) would be the representations of uppercase

```
*    FUNCTION STRING USED WITH  TR  INSTRUCTION TO REPLACE ALL LOWERCASE
*    LETTERS IN AN ARGUMENT STRING WITH UPPERCASE LETTERS, WITHOUT
*    ALTERING THE OTHER BYTES IN THE ARGUMENT STRING.
*
FN1        DS        0CL256     DEFINE BEGINNING & LENGTH OF FUNCTION STRING.

*    FIRST 129 BYTES,  X'00'  THROUGH  X'80'
           DC        X'00,01,02,03,04,05,06,07,08,09,0A,0B,0C,0D,0E,0F'
           DC        X'10,11,12,13,14,15,16,17,18,19,1A,1B,1C,1D,1E,1F'
           DC        X'20,21,22,23,24,25,26,27,28,29,2A,2B,2C,2D,2E,2F'
           DC        X'30,31,32,33,34,35,36,37,38,39,3A,3B,3C,3D,3E,3F'
           DC        X'40,41,42,43,44,45,46,47,48,49,4A,4B,4C,4D,4E,4F'
           DC        X'50,51,52,53,54,55,56,57,58,59,5A,5B,5C,5D,5E,5F'
           DC        X'60,61,62,63,64,65,66,67,68,69,6A,6B,6C,6D,6E,6F'
           DC        X'70,71,72,73,74,75,76,77,78,79,7A,7B,7C,7D,7E,7F,80'

*    130TH  THRU  138TH  BYTES REPLACE LOWERCASE  A THRU I
*                                     WITH  UPPERCASE  A THRU I
           DC        X'C1,C2,C3,C4,C5,C6,C7,C8,C9'

*    139TH THRU 145TH BYTES,  X'8A'  THRU X'90'
           DC        X'8A,8B,8C,8D,8E,8F,90'
*    146TH  THRU  154TH  BYTES REPLACE LOWERCASE  J THRU R
*                                     WITH  UPPERCASE  J THRU R
           DC        X'D1,D2,D3,D4,D5,D6,D7,D8,D9'

*    155TH THRU 162ND BYTES,  X'9A'  THRU X'A1'

           DC        X'9A,9B,9C,9D,9E,9F,A0,A1'

*    163RD  THRU  170TH  BYTES REPLACE LOWERCASE  S THRU Z
*                                     WITH  UPPERCASE  S THRU Z
           DC        X'E2,E3,E4,E5,E6,E7,E8,E9'

*    REMAINING 86 BYTES,  X'AA'  THRU X'FF'
           DC        X'AA,AB,AC,AD,AE,AF'
           DC        X'B0,B1,B2,B3,B4,B5,B6,B7,B8,B9,BA,BB,BC,BD,BE,BF'
           DC        X'C0,C1,C2,C3,C4,C5,C6,C7,C8,C9,CA,CB,CC,CD,CE,CF'
           DC        X'D0,D1,D2,D3,D4,D5,D6,D7,D8,D9,DA,DB,DC,DD,DE,DF'
           DC        X'E0,E1,E2,E3,E4,E5,E6,E7,E8,E9,EA,EB,EC,ED,EE,EF'
           DC        X'F0,F1,F2,F3,F4,F5,F6,F7,F8,F9,FA,FB,FC,FD,FE,FF'
```

S through *Z,* namely X'E2', X'E3',...,X'E9'. Figure 7.10 shows how the function string could be defined. It begins at symbolic address FN1 and occupies 256 consecutive bytes. If we assume that the argument string—the one whose lowercase letters are to be changed to uppercase letters—is located at symbolic address ARG1 and consists of 30 characters, then the following single TR instruction will accomplish the desired result:

```
        TR  ARG1(30),FN1
```

```
before execution:    ARG1  DC  C'This is a 30-character string'
after execution:     ARG1  DC  C'THIS IS A 30-CHARACTER STRING'
```

Function String for TRT Instruction

The function string for the TRT instruction consists of 256 bytes, chosen as follows: for each byte of the argument string that is to cause the search to stop, the position in the function string corresponding to that argument-byte value must contain a nonzero byte. For each byte of the argument string that is not to cause the search to stop, the position in the function string corresponding to that argument-byte value must contain X'00'.

*Figure 7.11 Function string to search for occurrences of mathematical operators +, −, *, and /.*

```
*   FUNCTION STRING FOR USE WITH  TRT  INSTRUCTION TO SEARCH FOR
*   OCCURRENCES OF ANY ONE OF THE FOUR MATHEMATICAL OPERATORS
*            +    ( X'4E')
*            -    ( X'60')
*            *    ( X'5C')
*            /    ( X'61')
*
FN2      DS    0CL256    DEFINE BEGINNING & LENGTH OF FUNCTION STRING
*  FIRST 78 BYTES ARE  X'00'
         DC    78X'00'
*  79TH BYTE IS  X'4E', FOR THE PLUS SIGN
         DC    X'4E'
*  80TH THRU 92ND BYTES ARE  X'00'
         DC    13X'00'
*  93RD BYTE IS  X'5C', FOR THE ASTERISK
         DC    X'5C'
*  94TH THRU 96TH BYTES ARE  X'00'
         DC    3X'00'
*  97TH AND 98TH BYTES ARE X'60', X'61'   FOR THE MINUS AND SLASH
         DC    X'60,61'
*  REMAINING 158 BYTES ARE X'00'
         DC    158X'00'
```

Find Math Operators

For example, if we wanted to search for the first occurrence of any one of the four mathematical operators $+$, $-$, $*$, $/$, then all bytes in the function string should be X'00' *except these four:* the 79th byte, corresponding to C'+' = X'4E'; the 93rd byte, corresponding to C'*' = X'5C'; the 97th byte, corresponding to C'−' = X'60'; and the 98th byte, corresponding to C'/' = X'61'. Figure 7.11 shows how the function string for this example could be defined. It begins at symbolic address FN2 and occupies 256 consecutive bytes. If we assume that the argument string is located at symbolic address ARG2 and consists of 8 bytes:

```
ARG2   DC   C'A=X+Y**2'
```

then the following single TRT instruction will determine the position of the first occurrence of a mathematical operator in the ARG2 string:

```
TRT  ARG2(8),FN2
```

Neither string is altered by the TRT instruction, but Registers 1 and 2 and the condition code are altered. To illustrate this, suppose the following conditions exist before the TRT is executed.

	location 1004								Reg 1	Reg 2	condition code
hex →	C1	7E	E7	4E	E8	5C	5C	F2	12 34 56 78	87 65 43 21	0
chars →	A	=	X	+	Y	*	*	2			

After execution of the TRT instruction the following conditions would exist:

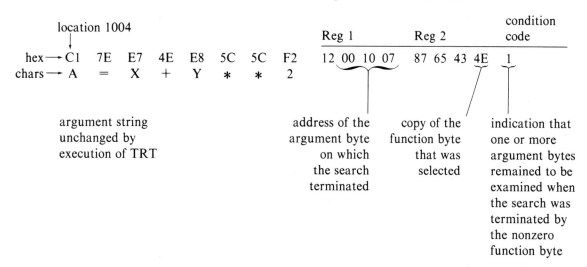

	location 1004								Reg 1	Reg 2	condition code
hex →	C1	7E	E7	4E	E8	5C	5C	F2	12 00 10 07	87 65 43 4E	1
chars →	A	=	X	+	Y	*	*	2			

argument string unchanged by execution of TRT

address of the argument byte on which the search terminated

copy of the function byte that was selected

indication that one or more argument bytes remained to be examined when the search was terminated by the nonzero function byte

Further Observations

Using EX with TRT

Two further observations may be helpful. First, since at assembly time the programmer generally does not know the lengths of the argument strings that will be processed at run time, he or she usually uses the EX instruction in conjunction with TR and TRT. For the example of the TRT instruction illustrated in the previous section, the following statements would be more generally useful:

```
        LA    4,ARG2        R4 = ADDR OF START OF ARG STRING
        LH    5,LARG2       R5 = LENGTH OF ARG STRING
LOOP    SH    5,=H'1'       SUBTRACT +1 FOR 'EX' INSTR
        EX    5,TRTFN2      TRT FOR ARG STRING VIA 'FN2'
        BZ    NONE          BRANCH IF NO MATH OPERATOR FOUND
        .             process the operator whose address is in Reg 1
        .
        .
        LA    5,0(5,4)      R5 = ADDR OF LAST BYTE IN ARG STRING
        SR    5,1           R5 = LNG OF REMAINDER OF ARG STRING
        BZ    NOMORE        BRANCH IF NO MORE ARG BYTES TO EXAMINE
        LA    4,1(1)        R4 = ADDR OF START OF REMAINING ARG STRG
        B     LOOP          GO EXAMINE REMAINING ARG STRING
        .
        .
        .
ARG2    DS    CL256         SPACE FOR MAX LNG ARG STRING
LARG2   DS    H             SPACE FOR ACTUAL LNG OF ARG STRING
TRTFN2  TRT   0(0,4),FN2    TRT FOR ANY STRING USING 'FN2'
FN2     DS    0CL256        START & LENGTH OF FUNCTION STRING FOR
                            MATHEMATICAL OPERATORS
        .
        .
        .
```

Note that this sequence depends on two properties of the TRT instruction: (1) the TRT sets condition code 0 if no argument-string bytes match any of the nonzero function-string bytes, and (2) the TRT sets Register 1 (bits 8–31) equal to the address of the first argument-string byte found that matches a nonzero function byte. The first property is used by the BZ NONE instruction, as will be explained further in Section 8.4; the second property is used by the SR 5,1 instruction to compute the number of bytes remaining to be examined by the TRT instruction, and by the LA 4,1(1) instruction to determine the address at which the TRT is to begin its next search. Thus, the combination of EX and TRT can be used in a loop to find, successively, all occurrences of a mathematical operator in the given argument string.

Creating a Function String with a Macro

The second observation concerns the tedium of preparing a function string such as the one in Figure 7.10. In some cases the tedium can be relieved by creating the function string at run time; in other cases, a macro that will cause the assembler to generate the desired function string at assembly time can be defined. Macros are discussed in Chapter 17. Here we merely wish to point out that with an appropriately defined macro named FN, we could create the function string of Figure 7.10 with the following seven statements:

name field	opcode	operand			
FN1	FN	X'00',X'80'	FIRST 129 BYTES, X'00' THROUGH X'80'		
	FN	X'C1',X'C9'	130TH	THRU	138TH
	FN	X'8A',X'90'	139TH	THRU	145TH
	FN	X'D1',X'D9'	146TH	THRU	154TH
	FN	X'9A',X'A1'	155TH	THRU	162ND
	FN	X'E2',X'E9'	163RD	THRU	170TH
	FN	X'AA',X'FF'	171ST	THRU	256TH

Creating a Function String with Run-Time Instructions

Alternatively, we could create the function string of Figure 7.10 by means of a run-time procedure such as this one:

```
* CREATE FUNCTION STRING TO REPLACE LOWERCASE LETTERS
*   IN AN ARGUMENT STRING WITH UPPERCASE LETTERS.
* 'LOOP' SETS THE  (N+1)ST  BYTE TO THE HEX REPRESENTATION OF N,
        LH    2,=H'255'            FOR N = 255,254,253,..., 2,1.
LOOP    STC   2,FN1(2)    EFFECTIVE ADDR CALCULATED VIA INDEX REG 2.
        BCT   2,LOOP            AT CONCLUSION OF LOOP, INITIALIZE
        MVI   FN1,X'00'         FIRST BYTE TO X'00'.
        MVC   FN1+129(9),=C'ABCDEFGHI'   130TH-138TH BYTES (A-I)
        MVC   FN1+145(9),=C'JKLMNOPQR'   146TH-154TH BYTES (J-R)
        MVC   FN1+162(8),=C'STUVWXYZ'    163RD-170TH BYTES (S-Z)
        .
        .
        .
FN1     DS    CL256       RESERVE 256 BYTES FOR FUNCTION STRING TO
*                         REPLACE LOWERCASE LETTERS WITH UPPERCASE
*                         LETTERS. CONTENTS CREATED AT 'LOOP'.
```

It should be clear that such a run-time procedure will find its greatest utility when the large majority of function bytes can be generated via a loop. Moreover, it should be adequately documented, as should the area reserved for the function string itself, to avoid any doubt about the purpose of the procedure and the contents of the function string.

7.10 SUMMARY

The byte and string manipulation instructions discussed in this chapter are summarized in Figure 7.12. With but one exception, these instructions involve the operations of copying and/or comparing byte strings. The exception is the Execute (EX) instruction, which has been included here because of its frequent use in enabling variable-length strings to be operated on.

Figure 7.12 *Summary of byte manipulation instructions.*

opcode	name	type	section	condition codes	summary of action taken
CL	Compare Logical	RX	7.3	0,1,2	$V_1{:}V_2$ (compares 4 bytes)
CLC	Compare Logical Characters	SS$_1$	7.3	0,1,2	$V_1{:}V_2$ (compares L bytes, $L \leq 256$)
CLCL	Compare Logical Characters Long	RR	7.8	0,1,2	$V_1{:}V_2$ (compares L bytes with padding, $L \leq 2^{24}-1$)
CLI	Compare Logical Immediate	SI	7.3	0,1,2	$V_1{:}I2$ (compares 1 byte to I2 field)
CLM	Compare Logical under Mask	RS	7.3	0,1,2	$V_1{:}V_2$ (compares 0 to 4 bytes, via M1 field)
CLR	Compare Logical Registers	RR	7.3	0,1,2	$V_1{:}V_2$ (compares 4 bytes)
EX	Execute	RX	7.7		executes target instr; uses bits 24–31 of $R1$ if $R1 \neq 0$
IC	Insert Character	RX	7.2		bits 24–31 of $R1$ replaced by V_2
ICM	Insert Characters under Mask	RS	7.2	0,1,2	selected bytes of $R1$ replaced by V_2, via M1 field
MVC	Move Characters	SS$_1$	7.2		L bytes of V_1 replaced by V_2, $L \leq 256$
MVCIN	Move Inverse	SS$_1$	7.2		L bytes of V_1 ($L \leq 256$) replaced by V_2 in reverse sequence
MVCL	Move Characters Long	RR	7.8	0,1,2,3	L bytes of V_1 replaced by V_2 + padding, $L \leq 2^{24}-1$
MVI	Move Immediate	SI	7.2		V_1 replaced by I2 field
STC	Store Character	RX	7.2		V_2 replaced by bits 24–31 of $R1$
STCM	Store Characters under Mask	RS	7.2		V_2 replaced by selected bytes of $R1$, via M1 field
TR	Translate	SS$_1$	7.9		L bytes of V_1 replaced by selected bytes of V_2
TRT	Translate and Test	SS$_1$	7.9	0,1,2	L bytes of V_1 searched via string V_2

Note: The meanings of the condition codes for individual instructions are summarized in Figure 8.5a. In the action summaries given, V_1 denotes the quantity whose address is specified by the first operand of an instruction, and V_2 denotes the quantity whose address is specified by the second operand of an instruction.

The instructions that copy bytes fall into two categories: (1) those that copy bytes to or from a register, and (2) those that copy bytes from one main memory location to another. In the first category are the IC, ICM, STC, and STCM instructions; in the second are the MVI, MVC, and MVCL instructions.

The instructions that compare byte strings also fall into two categories: (1) those in which one or both strings are in registers (CL, CLM, CLR), and (2) those in which both strings are in memory locations (CLI, CLC, CLCL). The result of any of these comparisons may be determined by use of a conditional-branch instruction: the string designated by the first operand of a compare instruction will always be equal to, less than, or greater than the string designated by the second operand.

The Translate (TR) and Translate and Test (TRT) instructions are specially designed for two particular types of string-searching operations. TR examines each byte of a string and, depending on its value, either replaces it with some predetermined byte or leaves it unchanged. TRT examines each byte of a string from left to right and stops the search when it finds the first occurrence of any one of some predetermined set of values. The TR is aptly named, since it translates any given string into a (possibly) different string. The TRT is not so aptly named, since no translation takes place; instead, the condition under which its search is terminated is reflected in the condition code and the contents of Registers 1 and 2, as described in Section 7.9.

The EX instruction provides a means of varying the quantity in the length fields of SS$_1$ and SS$_2$-type instructions. This permits strings whose lengths are not known until run time to be processed by the MVC, CLC, TR, and TRT instructions, provided that the lengths do not exceed 256 bytes. Use of the EX instruction also enables the immediate data field of SI-type instructions, such as MVI, CLI, and TM (the latter to be discussed in Chap. 8), to be varied at run time. In all cases, the instruction that is executed via EX is not changed in memory; instead, its length or immediate data field (bits 8–15) is modified in a register not available to programmers.

The instructions summarized are used primarily for nonarithmetic operations such as determining the contents of a string, searching for a particular substring within a given string, replacing one string with another, and inserting or deleting a string within another string. The need for these types of operations arises whenever text must be processed, for example, when printing messages and when performing the operations inherent in text-editing and word-processing systems.

7.11   REVIEW

Printable Characters   Any character that can be displayed on a terminal or printer is known as a printable character. In the EBCDIC scheme, each character is identified by a unique 8-bit code. See Figure 7.1.

Strings   Any sequence of consecutive characters is known as a string, or character string, or text string. The number of characters in a string is known as its length. Any character, printable or nonprintable, can be included in the string; but usually a string consists only of printable characters.

C-Type Constants   These are character constants. One byte is allocated for each specified character, except that two consecutive ampersands (& &) are required to specify a single ampersand, and two consecutive apostrophes (' ') are required to specify a single apostrophe. Note that two apostrophes are not the same as a single quotation mark (").

Masks   A mask is used to select certain objects and reject others. In the ICM, STCM, and CLM instructions, a mask consisting of 4 bits is used to select from one to four bytes of a register. Any of the four bits may be "on" (1) or "off" (0), so that any of the four bytes in the register may be selected or not.

SI-Type Instructions   In the two SI-type byte instructions (MVI, CLI), one of the operands is a single character in the "I2" field of the instruction; the other operand is a single character in memory.

SS$_1$-Type Instructions   In the SS$_1$-type byte instructions (MVC, MVCIN, CLC, TR, TRT), both strings being operated on are in memory locations. Both must be of the same length, and that length must be specified either explicitly or implicitly in the first operand field of the instructions. The maximum length is 256.

Effective Addresses   In SI- and SS$_1$-type instructions, there is no provision for indexing. For these instructions, to obtain effective addresses during execution of a loop, an initial address must first be loaded into a register and then incremented during each loop iteration. Explicit operand formats must be used in the loop. See Figure 7.4.

Destructive Overlap   When bytes are copied from one memory area to another, they are copied one byte at a time. If the start of the receiving area is within the sending area, then some sending bytes become receiving bytes and are replaced before they are sent, a condition known as destructive overlap. See Example 1 of Section 7.5.

Substring Operations   Deleting, replacing, and inserting substrings (i.e., strings within strings) are very common operations in text editors and word processors. The EX instruction is very useful for these operations.

EX Instruction Among other things, EX provides run-time lengths for CLC and MVC. One less than the length's value must be in a register other than Register 0 when EX is executed. EX must refer to that register as well as to its target CLC or MVC instruction. The target instructions should have an explicit length field of zero.

CLCL, MVCL These RR-type instructions operate on two strings of essentially any length. The lengths of the strings can be input at run time and need not be equal. Two even-odd register pairs (four registers) are required for execution of these instructions. The EX instruction is not needed with CLCL or MVCL.

TR, TRT These SS$_1$-type instructions perform useful string searches. TR can replace any set of characters in a string with another set, e.g., lowercase with uppercase. TRT can search a string for the occurrence of any characters, e.g., math operators. Run-time string lengths can be handled by TR and TRT via the EX instruction.

7.12 REVIEW QUESTIONS

1. When using the DC directive to define a character constant, what will cause the constant to be *truncated?* If truncated, what will be the resulting constant's length, and which characters from the DC operand will be lost? Give an example of a character constant that results in truncation, and one that doesn't.

2. When using the DC directive to define a character constant, what will cause the constant to be *padded?* If padded, what will be the resulting constant's length? Give an example of a character constant that results in padding, and state what the padded constant would be.

3. What are the two SI-type string-handling instructions, and what distinguishes them from the other string-handling instructions?

4. What are the two SS$_1$-type counterparts of the SI-type string-handling instructions, and what restrictions (if any) are placed on their use?

5. What is the maximum-length string that can be processed by an SI-type string-handling instruction? By an SS$_1$-type instruction? By an RX-type instruction? By an RR-type instruction?

6. If a program compared lowercase 'z' to uppercase 'A', would 'z' be equal to, less than, or greater than 'A'? Why? In general, what determines whether one character is equal to, less than, or greater than another character? What printable character is less than all other printable characters? (**Hint:** See Figure 7.1.)

7. In comparing two equal-length strings, what determines the outcome of the comparison, i.e., what determines whether the strings are equal or not, and if they're not equal then what determines which of the two is less than the other?

8. Both the IC and ICM instructions replace certain bytes of a register with characters obtained from memory. Which bytes does each instruction replace? What happens to the bytes in the register that are not replaced by characters?

9. Why would the "move" instructions (MVI, MVC, MVCIN, and MVCL) have been more appropriately named "copy" instructions?

10. If a length field is specified in an SI-type instruction—e.g., MVI X(1),C'+'—will this cause a run-time error, an assembly-time error, or no error? Why?

11. If a literal is specified in an SI-type instruction—for example, MVI X,=C'+'—will this cause a run-time error, an assembly-time error, or no error? Why?

12. If the length field is implied in an SS$_1$-type instruction—e.g., MVC X,Y instead of MVC X(5),Y—what length is supplied by the assembler, and where is that length defined in the program?

13. In the program segment of Figure 7.5, could the Load Address (LA) instruction in statement #3 be replaced by a Load (L) instruction? For example, could LA 5,LENGTH be replaced by L 5,LENGTH if no changes were made to the other statements in the figure? Why or why not?

14. What is the purpose of a function string when used with a TR instruction, and what is its purpose when used with a TRT instruction? What should the length of a function string be, and why?

Problem Statement

Write a program that will read student grade point average (GPA) data and compute and print a distribution of GPA's by giving the total number of students for which data were read and the number of students whose GPA's lie in one of each of these eight ranges: 0.00–0.99, 1.00–1.49, 1.50–1.99, 2.00–2.49, ..., 3.50–3.99, and exactly 4.00. We assume that each input record contains the GPA of one student in columns 30–33, including a decimal point in column 31. The range of GPA's is assumed to be from 0.00 to 4.00; anything outside this range is counted as an error.

Solution Procedure

The procedure, as outlined in Figures 7.13a and 7.13b, is to read each record, determine the appropriate range for the GPA, and add +1 to the counter that is defined for that range. When end-of-data is reached, all the counters are converted to EBCDIC format and printed, one per line, with an accompanying text message that identifies the range corresponding to that counter. After all the counters have been printed, the total number of students is also printed, the total having been obtained by counting the number of input records that were read.

Figure 7.13a   Pseudocode for sample problem solution in Figure 7.13b.

```
GPA_DISTRIBUTION:

    open input and output files;

    REPEAT FOR j := 1, 2, ..., 10
        set tally DISTR[j] to zero
    END FOR;

    REPEAT WHILE there is more data to read

        read one input record

        IF  GPA  < 0.00  THEN  add 1 to DISTR[1];  {data error}
        IF  GPA  is in  [ 0.00 ... 0.99 ]  THEN  add 1 to DISTR[2];
        IF  GPA  is in  [ 1.00 ... 1.49 ]  THEN  add 1 to DISTR[3];
        IF  GPA  is in  [ 1.50 ... 1.99 ]  THEN  add 1 to DISTR[4];
        IF  GPA  is in  [ 2.00 ... 2.49 ]  THEN  add 1 to DISTR[5];
        IF  GPA  is in  [ 2.50 ... 2.99 ]  THEN  add 1 to DISTR[6];
        IF  GPA  is in  [ 3.00 ... 3.49 ]  THEN  add 1 to DISTR[7];
        IF  GPA  is in  [ 3.50 ... 3.99 ]  THEN  add 1 to DISTR[8];
        IF  GPA  = 4.00  THEN  add 1 to DISTR[9];
        IF  GPA  > 4.00  THEN  add 1 to DISTR[1];  {data error}

        add 1 to DISTR[10];  {total number of records}

    END WHILE;

    print heading line;

    REPEAT FOR  j := 1, 2, ..., 10
        convert DISTR[j] to EBCDIC;
        print range message and distribution data;
    END FOR;

    close all files;

    EXIT GPA_DISTRIBUTION.
```

Figure 7.13b   *Solution to sample problem.*

```
FLAG LOCTN OBJECT CODE     ADDR1  ADDR2  STMNT M SOURCE STATEMENT

     000000                                   3 SPCH7    CSECT
                                              4 *
                                              5 * SPCH7  READS INPUT DATA CARDS, EACH CONTAINING A STUDENT
                                              6 *    GRADE POINT AVERAGE (GPA) IN THE FORMAT GIVEN BELOW.
                                              7 *
                                              8 *    THE PROGRAM COMPUTES A DISTRIBUTION OF ALL GPA'S, IN THE
                                              9 *    FOLLOWING RANGES ...
                                             10 *
                                             11 *       0.00-0.99, 1.00-1.49, 1.50-1.99, 2.00-2.49,
                                             12 *                  2.50-2.99, 3.00-3.49, 3.50-3.99, 4.00-4.00
                                             13 *       AND ALSO ANY GPA OUTSIDE THE RANGE 0.00-4.00 IS
                                             14 *       COUNTED AS INVALID.
                                             15 *
                                             16 * EACH INPUT RECORD CONTAINS A GPA IN COLS 30-33, INCLUDING
                                             17 *       THE DECIMAL POINT, E.G.  2.49
                                             18 *
000000 90 EC 000C                            19          STM   14,12,12(13)          STANDARD ENTRY
000004 05 C0                                 20          BALR  12,0
000006                                       21          USING *,12
000006 50 D0 C40E         000414             22          ST    13,SAVE+4
00000A 41 D0 C40A         000410             23          LA    13,SAVE
                                             24 *
                                             25 * OPEN INPUT AND OUTPUT FILES
                                             26 *
00000E                                       27          OPEN  (SYSIN,(INPUT))      INPUT IS 'SYSIN' DATA STREAM
00001A                                       33          OPEN  (SYSPRNT,(OUTPUT))   OUTPUT IS 'SYSOUT' PRINTER

                                             39 * DOS *******
                                             40 *    OPEN  SYSIN
                                             41 *    OPEN  SYSPRNT
                                             42 ***************

                                             43 *
                                             44 * INITIALIZE DISTRIBUTION COUNTERS
                                             45 *
000026 41 50 C132         000138             46          LA    5,DISTR               GET ADDR OF COUNTER ARRAY
00002A 58 60 C106         00010C             47          L     6,N                   GET SIZE OF ARRAY
00002E 58 70 C452         000458             48          L     7,=F'0'               GET ZERO FOR INITIALIZATIONS
000032 50 75 0000         000000             49 INIT     ST    7,0(5)                JTH COUNTER = 0,  J=1,2,...,N
000036 41 55 0004         000004             50          LA    5,4(5)                INCR TO NEXT COUNTER
00003A 46 60 C02C         000032             51          BCT   6,INIT                COUNT DOWN ARRAY COMPONENTS
                                             52 *
                                             53 * MAIN PROCESSING LOOP ...
                                             54 *       READS AN INPUT CARD
                                             55 *       DETERMINES THE RANGE OF GPA
                                             56 *       ADDS +1 TO THE COUNTER FOR THAT RANGE
                                             57 *       REPEATS THE PROCEDURE FOR EACH INPUT CARD UNTIL END-OF-DATA
                                             58 *       WHEN END-OF-DATA IS REACHED, CONTROL IS TRANSFERRED TO 'EOD'
                                             59 *
00003E                                       60 LOOP     GET   SYSIN,INAREA          GET AN INPUT CARD
00004C 41 50 C132         000138             65          LA    5,DISTR               SET UP COUNT ARRAY ADDRESS
000050 41 60 C10A         000110             66          LA    6,RANGE               SET UP RANGE ARRAY ADDRESS
000054 58 70 C106         00010C             67          L     7,N                   GET SIZE OF COUNT ARRAY
000058 05 03 C20D6000 000213                 68 COMP     CLC   GPA,0(6)              COMPARE GPA TO RANGE IN ARRAY
00005E 47 40 C06C         000072             69          BL    COUNTIT               BRANCH IF IN RANGE.
000062 41 55 0004         000004             70          LA    5,4(5)                INCR COUNT ARRAY ADDR
000066 41 66 0004         000004             71          LA    6,4(6)                INCR RANGE ARRAY ADDR
00006A 46 70 C052         000058             72          BCT   7,COMP                COMP NEXT RANGE, IF ANY
00006E 41 50 C132         000138             73          LA    5,DISTR               ELSE IT IS 'OUTSIDE RANGE'

000072 58 A5 0000         000000             74 COUNTIT  L     10,0(5)               WHEN RANGE KNOWN, GET COUNTER
000076 5A A0 C456         00045C             75          A     10,=F'1'              AND INCREASE IT.
00007A 50 A5 0000         000000             76          ST    10,0(5)
00007E 47 F0 C038         00003E             77          B     LOOP
                                             78 *
                                             79 * WHEN END-OF-DATA IS SENSED DURING 'GET', CONTROL IS TRANSFERRED HERE.
                                             80 *
000082                                       81 EOD      PUT   SYSPRNT,HEADING       PRINT HEADING LINE
                                             86 *
                                             87 * INITIALIZE ARRAY ADDRESSES AND LOOP COUNTER FOR CONVERSION TO EBCDIC
000090 41 50 C132         000138             88          LA    5,DISTR               GET ADDR OF COUNT ARRAY
000094 41 60 C15A         000160             89          LA    6,RANGEMSG            GET ADDR OF RANGE MESSAGE ARRAY
000098 58 70 C106         00010C             90          L     7,N                   GET SIZE OF COUNT ARRAY
                                             91 *
                                             92 * 'CONVT' LOOP CONVERTS EACH COUNTER TO ECBDIC, THEN PRINTS IT & RANGE
00009C 58 A5 0000         000000             93 CONVT    L     10,0(5)               CONVERT JTH COUNT TO EBCDIC TEXT
0000A0 4E A0 C0F2         0000F8             94          CVD   10,BCD
0000A4 F3 97 C0FAC0F2 000100 0000F8          95          UNPK  EBCDIC,BCD
0000AA 96 F0 C103         000109             96          OI    EBCDIC+9,X'F0'
                                             97 *
                                             98 * PRINT CURRENT DISTRIBUTION DATA
0000AE D2 0E C2456000 00024B                 99          MVC   MSG,0(6)              COPY RANGE MESSAGE TO OUTPUT LINE
0000B4 D2 09 C254C0FA 00025A 000100         100          MVC   AMOUNT,EBCDIC         COPY COUNT TO OUTPUT LINE
0000BA                                      101          PUT   SYSPRNT,OUTAREA       PRINT ONE LINE WITH RANGE & COUNT
                                            106 *
                                            107 * INCREASE TO NEXT DISTR RANGE AND COUNT
0000C8 41 55 0004         000004            108          LA    5,4(5)                INCR COUNT ARRAY ADDR
0000CC 41 66 000F         00000F            109          LA    6,15(6)               INCR RANGEMSG ARRAY ADDR
0000D0 46 70 C096         00009C            110          BCT   7,CONVT               GO CONVT AND PRINT NEXT LINE, IF ANY
                                            111 *
                                            112 * WHEN ALL RANGES AND DISTRIBUTIONS HAVE BEEN PRINTED, TERMINATE.
```

Figure 7.13b   continued

```
FLAG LOCTN OBJECT CODE     ADDR1 ADDR2 STMNT M SOURCE STATEMENT

     000004                                113           CLOSE (SYSIN)
     00000E                                119           CLOSE (SYSPRNT)
     0000EA 58 D0 C40E      000414         125           L      13,SAVE+4              STANDARD EXIT
     0000EE 98 EC D00C                     126           LM     14,12,12(13)
     0000F2 07 FE                          127           BR     14

                                           128    * DOS *******
                                           129    *        CLOSE SYSIN
                                           130    *        CLOSE SYSPRNT
                                           131    *        EOJ
                                           132    ***************

                                           133    *
                                           134    * CONSTANTS AND DATA AREAS
                                           135    *
     0000F8                                136    BCD      DS     D              DECIMAL FORM OF DISTR COUNTER
     000100                                137    EBCDIC   DS     CL10               TEXT FORM OF DISTR COUNTER
                                           138    * TABLES FOR RANGES AND DISTRIBUTIONS
                                           139    *
     00010C 0000000A                       140    N        DC     F'10'          NUMBER OF RANGES IN TABLE
                                           141    *
     000110 F04BF0F0                        142    RANGE    DC     CL4'0.00'      NOT  0.00-4.00  = DISTR(1)
     000114 F14BF0F0                        143             DC     CL4'1.00'           0.00-0.99  = DISTR(2)
     000118 F14BF5F0                        144             DC     CL4'1.50'           1.00-1.49  = DISTR(3)
     00011C F24BF0F0                        145             DC     CL4'2.00'           1.50-1.99  = DISTR(4)
     000120 F24BF5F0                        146             DC     CL4'2.50'           2.00-2.49  = DISTR(5)
     000124 F34BF0F0                        147             DC     CL4'3.00'           2.50-2.99  = DISTR(6)
     000128 F34BF5F0                        148             DC     CL4'3.50'           3.00-3.49  = DISTR(7)
     00012C F44BF0F0                        149             DC     CL4'4.00'           3.50-3.99  = DISTR(8)
     000130 F44BF0F1                        150             DC     CL4'4.01'      EQUAL TO 4.00    = DISTR(9)
     000134 00000000                        151             DC     XL4'0000'      DUMMY  FOR TOTALS = DISTR(10)
                                           152    *
     000138                                153    DISTR    DS     10F            SPACE FOR 10 DISTRIBUTION COUNTS
                                           154    *
                                           155    * RANGE MESSAGE TABLE FOR OUTPUT PRINT LINES  (SEE 'RANGE' TABLE ABOVE)
                                           156    *
     000160 D5D6E340F04BF0F0                157    RANGEMSG DC     CL15'NOT 0.00-4.00'
     00016F F04BF0F060F04BF9                158             DC     CL15'0.00-0.99'
     00017E F14BF0F060F14BF4                159             DC     CL15'1.00-1.49'
     00018D F14BF5F060F14BF9                160             DC     CL15'1.50-1.99'
     00019C F24BF0F060F24BF4                161             DC     CL15'2.00-2.49'
     0001AB F24BF5F060F24BF9                162             DC     CL15'2.50-2.99'
     0001BA F34BF0F060F34BF4                163             DC     CL15'3.00-3.49'
     0001C9 F34BF5F060F34BF9                164             DC     CL15'3.50-3.99'
     0001D8 F44BF0F040404040                165             DC     CL15'4.00'
     0001E7 4040E3D6E3C1D3E2                166             DC     CL15'  TOTALS'
                                           167    *
                                           168    * INPUT CARD AREA
                                           169    *
     0001F6                                170    INAREA   DS     0CL80          DEFINITION OF INPUT AREA ...
     0001F6                                171             DS     CL29           COLS 1-29   UNUSED
     000213                                172    GPA      DS     CL4                 30-33   GPA  AS   X.XX
     000217                                173             DS     CL47                34-80   UNUSED
                                           174    *
                                           175    * OUTPUT PRINT AREA
                                           176    *
     000246                                177    OUTAREA  DS     0CL132         DEFINITION OF OUTPUT AREA ...
     000246 4040404040                     178             DC     CL5' '         COLS 1-5    BLANKS
     00024B                                179    MSG      DS     CL15                6-20    SPACE FOR RANGE MESSAGE
     00025A                                180    AMOUNT   DS     CL10                21-30   SPACE FOR DISTR COUNT
     000264 40404040404040 40              181             DC     CL102' '            31-132  BLANKS
                                           182    *
                                           183    * HEADING LINE
                                           184    *
     0002CA                                185    HEADING  DS     0CL132         DEFINITION OF HEADING LINE ...
     0002CA 40404040404040 40              186             DC     CL10' '        COLS 1-10   BLANKS
     0002D4 D9C1D5C7C5404040                187             DC     CL10'RANGE'         11-20   RANGE HEADING
     0002DE C3D6E4D5E3404040                188             DC     CL10'COUNT '        21-30   COUNT  HEADING
     0002E8 40404040404040 40              189             DC     CL102' '            31-132  BLANKS
                                           190    * DCB'S FOR INPUT AND OUTPUT FILES
                                           191    *
     00034E                                192    SYSIN    DCB    DSORG=PS,MACRF=(GM),DDNAME=SYSIN,EODAD=EOD,        X
                                           193                    RECFM=FB,LRECL=80,BLKSIZE=4080
     0003B0                                245    SYSPRNT  DCB    DSORG=PS,MACRF=(PM),DDNAME=SYSPRINT,               X
                                           246                    RECFM=FB,LRECL=132,BLKSIZE=4092

                                           298    * DOS *******
                                           299    *SYSIN   DTFCD  DEVADDR=SYSIPT,WORKA=YES,IOAREA1=INBUF,EOFADDR=EOD, X
                                           300    *               DEVICE=2540
                                           301    *SYSPRNT DTFPR  DEVADDR=SYSLST,WORKA=YES,IOAREA1=OUTBUF,BLKSIZE=132, X
                                           302    *               DEVICE=1403
                                           303    *
                                           304    *INBUF   DS     CL80
                                           305    *OUTBUF  DC     CL132' '
                                           306    ***************

                                           307    *
     000410                                308    SAVE     DS     18F            SAVE AREA
```

Figure 7.13b   continued

```
                                    309    *  DOS  ******
                                    310    *SAVE    DS    9D
                                    311    ***************

                                    312    * LITERALS
000458 00000000                     314                      =F'0'
00045C 00000001                     315                      =F'1'
                                    316            END
```

CROSS-REFERENCE

SYMBOL	LEN	VALUE	DEFN	REFERENCES			
AMOUNT	0000A	00025A	00180	00100			
BCD	00008	0000F8	00136	00094	00095		
COMP	00006	000058	00068	00072			
CONVT	00004	00009C	00093	00110			
COUNTIT	00004	000072	00074	00069			
DISTR	00004	000138	00153	00046	00065	00073	00088
EBCDIC	0000A	000100	00137	00095	00096	00100	
EOD	00004	000082	00082	00214			
GPA	00004	000213	00172	00068			
HEADING	00084	0002CA	00185	00083			
INAREA	00050	0001F6	00170	00062			
INIT	00004	000032	00049	00051			
LOOP	00004	00003E	00061	00077			
MSG	0000F	00024B	00179	00099			
N	00004	00010C	00140	00047	00067	00090	
OUTAREA	00084	000246	00177	00103			
RANGE	00004	000110	00142	00066			
RANGEMSG	0000F	000160	00157	00089			
SAVE	00004	000410	00308	00022	00023	00125	
SPCH7	00001	000000	00003				
SYSIN	00004	000350	00193	00031	00061	00117	
SYSPRNT	00004	0003B0	00246	00037	00082	00102	00123

1. Suppose that a character constant is defined by

```
CON   DC   C'ASSEMBLY'
```

What condition—high, low, or equal—would result from execution of each of the following compare instructions:

   a. CLI   CON,C'C'
   b. CLI   CON,C' '
   c. CLC   CON,=C'ASSEMBLE'
   d. CLC   CON(5),=C'EMBLY'

2. Suppose that a character constant is defined by

```
          DS   0F
SYMBOL    DC   CL10'CONSTANT'
```

Describe the result that would be produced by execution of each of the following instructions:

   a. IC   4,SYMBOL
   b. ICM   5,X'9',SYMBOL
   c. L   6,SYMBOL
   d. MVC   SYMBOL+1(9),SYMBOL
   e. MVI   SYMBOL,C' '
   f. MVC   SYMBOL,=10C' '

3. Write an assembly language program that will read a set of input records and print them one per line, with a blank character separating columns 4 and 5, 8 and 9, 12 and 13, and so on. For example, input like this

```
ABCDEFGHIJKLMNOPQRSTUVWXYZ
```

would be printed like this

```
ABCD EFGH IJKL MNOP QRST UVWX YZ
```

4. Write an assembly language program that will read a set of input records and print only those that contain an asterisk (*) in column 1.

5. Write an assembly language program that will read a set of input records and print only those that contain no characters other than letters, digits, and blanks.

6. Write an assembly language program that will read a set of input records that consist of assembly language statements, and print the statements one per line except as follows: any statement that contains the directive SPACE in its opcode field should not be printed. In its place, the program should print n consecutive blank lines where the value of n is specified as an unsigned decimal integer in the statement's operand field. Assume that $1 \leq n \leq 9$; also assume that all input statements are in standard fixed format.

7. Write an assembly language program in accordance with the same criteria as those given in Exercise 6, except that the input statements may be in free format (see Section 2.2 for a definition of free format).

8. Suppose there is a set of input records that describe characteristics of persons you know, as follows: In each record, columns 1–10 contain someone's first name, columns 11–20, 21–30, and 31–40 contain three one-word characteristics that describe that person. For example,

1st record	AL	POPULAR	TALL	STRONG
2nd record	JAN	SMART	OUTGOING	POPULAR
3rd record	BILL	STRONG	QUIET	SMART

Write an assembly language program that will print all the different characteristics that appear in the input, together with the names of those persons described by a characteristic. Each characteristic should appear only once in the printed output. For example, if the input consisted of only the above three records, the output would consist of these lines:

```
POPULAR       AL        JAN
TALL          AL
STRONG        AL        BILL
SMART         JAN       BILL
OUTGOING      JAN
QUIET         BILL
```

9. Write an assembly language program that will read a set of input records that contains any arbitrary text, and perform the following task: count the number of occurrences of each letter of the alphabet, and the number of occurrences of each of these pairs of consecutive letters: EI, IE, OU, TH. Print the results in some appropriate format.

10. Assume that there is a string of n characters ($1 \leq n \leq 256$) at symbolic address T, and that the value of n is given as a half-word binary integer at symbolic address N. Write assembly language statements that could be used to replace each occurrence of the three-character string C'###' with the three characters C'...'.

11. Assume that there is a set of input records and that all but the first contain any arbitrary text. Assume that the first record contains a string, S, beginning in column 13, and that the length of S is given as an unsigned decimal integer, right-justified, in columns 1–12. Incorporate the statements of Figure 7.9 into a program that deletes all occurrences of S from the text in each of the input records and prints the results. Each line of output should correspond to an input record.

12. Analogous to the program statements of Figure 7.9, write a set of statements that will perform the string-editing REPLACE operation depicted for arbitrary strings in Figure 7.8. Then, incorporate these statements into a program that will replace a given string, S, with another given string, S1, in text that is read as input records, as in Exercise 11. Print the resulting text, one line per input record.

13. Suppose there is an arbitrary string at address STR, whose length is given as a half-word binary integer at address N. Write a set of assembly language statements that will examine this string one character at a time, left to right, and perform the following deletion operation: for each occurrence of the EBCDIC backspace character (X'16'), delete that character *and the one preceding it* before examining the next character in the string. (The string may contain several consecutive backspaces, such as might be created when correcting text typed at a terminal.)

For example, if we let a back-arrow ← denote the backspace character, then, if the given string is

```
A FEWW← ERTOR←←←RORS
```

the resulting string would be

```
A FEW ERRORS
```

14. Suppose there is a 10-byte string that represents an integer in EBCDIC code. Write a set of assembly language statements that will examine this string, one character at a time, left to right, and replace all leading zeroes by blanks. Write a program that calculates and prints the numbers 2^n through 5^n for $n = 1,2,...,10$ in the tabular form shown below, with leading zeroes replaced by blanks.

2	3	4	5
4	9	16	25
8	27	64	125
..	...	...	....
256	6561	65536	390625
512	19683	262144	1953125
1024	59049	1048576	9765625

15. Modify your program solution to Exercise 14 so that the results are printed with appropriate punctuating commas. For example, the last line (for $n = 10$) would be printed

1,024	59,049	1,048,576	9,765,625

(**NOTE:** The ED and EDMK instructions described in Section 12.9 provide an easier solution to the problems of suppressing leading zeroes and providing punctuating commas than solutions based solely on the instructions described in Chaps. 4 through 7.)

16. Analogous to the program statements of Figure 7.9, write a set of statements that will perform the string-editing INSERT operation depicted for arbitrary strings in Figure 7.8. Then, incorporate these statements into a program that will insert a given string, S2, after each occurrence of another given string, S, in text that is read as input records. Print the resulting text, one line per input record. The two strings, S and S2, together with their lengths, can be read from the first input record.

17. Define a function string that could be used by the TR instruction to translate any argument string of up to 256 characters from EBCDIC code to ASCII code. EBCDIC characters that have no representation in the ASCII scheme might be translated into the question mark (?) character or some other appropriate character.

18. Define a function string that could be used by the TRT instruction to find occurrences of left and right parentheses in any argument string. Then write an assembly language program that uses the TRT and your function string to determine how many left parentheses there are in a given string, whether the number of left parentheses is the same as the number of right parentheses, and what the deepest level of nested pairs of parentheses is.

19. Rework Exercise 5, using the TRT instruction with an appropriate function string to determine whether a record should be printed or not.

8

Bit Manipulations

The term **bit manipulations** includes several types of instructions that operate on one or more con- *See Summary in* secutive bits: (1) **shifting** a bit sequence to the right or left, (2) **altering** individual bits, (3) **testing** *Figure 8.11* individual bits, and (4) testing the **condition code**.

Since bits are not individually addressable by a base-displacement address (the smallest unit of addressable information being a byte), the bits that are operated on must be *selected* from within one or more bytes. Except for the shift instructions, the selection is accomplished by means of a *mask,* a sequence of 4, 8, or 32 consecutive bits that are matched one for one to the sequence of bits from which the selected bits are chosen. The manner in which the selection takes place, and the result of the selection process, depends on the instruction being used. In shift instructions, either 32 or 64 bits are always selected.

Analogous to the concept of a byte or character string, a sequence of consecutive bits is often called a **bit string.** To avoid confusion with the word *string* in its meaning of a sequence of bytes, the full phrase *bit string* is usually used to refer to a sequence of bits.

To define a data constant as a sequence of bits, we can use the *B* or the *X* data-type code. These *B-Type and X-* may be used in the DC directive, in literals, and in self-defining terms. The *B* code requires that the *Type Constants* bits be specified in binary notation; the *X* requires hexadecimal notation, 4 bits for each hex digit.

One byte is always used for each consecutive 8 bits. If an integral multiple of 8 bits is not specified, the left-most byte used by the bit sequence is padded on the left with binary zeroes. The maximum number of bytes that can be specified for a single DC or literal constant is 256; for self-defining terms, the maximum is 4 bytes.

Figure 8.1 illustrates the methods of specifying constants as bit sequences.

To reserve data areas for bit sequences, we can use the B or X data-type codes in the DS directive. However, only an integral multiple of bytes can be reserved, no matter what code is used.

Figure 8.1 'B' and 'X' constants.

```
FLAG LOCTN OBJECT CODE      ADDR1   ADDR2  STMNT M SOURCE STATEMENT

                                            5    * DEFINED CONSTANTS                    COMMENTS

       000000 0F0F                           6              DC    B'111100001111'    0000 1111 0000 1111
       000002 F0                             7              DC    B'11110000'        1111 0000
       000003 0F                             8              DC    B'1111'            0000 1111
       000004 07                             9              DC    B'111'             0000 0111
       000005 03                            10              DC    B'11'              0000 0011
       000006 01                            11              DC    B'1'               0000 0001
       000007 FFFF                          12              DC    X'FFFF'            1111 1111 1111 1111
       000009 0FFF                          13              DC    X'FFF'             0000 1111 1111 1111
       00000B FF                            14              DC    X'FF'              1111 1111
       00000C 0F                            15              DC    X'F'               0000 1111

                                           16    * EQU CONSTANTS

       000001                               17    E1         EQU   B'1'              0000 0001
       000003                               18    E2         EQU   B'11'             0000 0011
       000007                               19    E3         EQU   B'111'            0000 0111
       00000F                               20    E4         EQU   B'1111'           0000 1111
       00001F                               21    E5         EQU   B'11111'          0001 1111
       00003F                               22    E6         EQU   B'111111'         0011 1111
       00007F                               23    E7         EQU   B'1111111'        0111 1111
       0000FF                               24    E8         EQU   B'11111111'       1111 1111
       000100                               25    E9         EQU   B'100000000'      0000 0001 0000 0000

                                           26    * SELF-DEFINING TERMS

       00000E 95 01 C066     000066         27              CLI   LO,B'1'            0000 0001
       000012 95 01 C066     000066         28              CLI   LO,X'1'            0000 0001
       000016 95 03 C066     000066         29              CLI   LO,B'11'           0000 0011
       00001A 95 11 C066     000066         30              CLI   LO,X'11'           0001 0001
       00001E 95 E9 C066     000066         31              CLI   LO,B'111 01001'    1110 1001
       000022 95 E9 C066     000066         32              CLI   LO,X'E9'           1110 1001
       000026 95 E9 C066     000066         33              CLI   LO,C'Z'            1110 1001

                                           34    * LITERALS

       00002A D2 00 C066C060 000066 000060  35              MVC   LO,=B'1'           0000 0001
       000030 D2 00 C066C060 000066 000060  36              MVC   LO,=X'1'           0000 0001
       000036 D2 00 C066C061 000066 000061  37              MVC   LO,=B'11'          0000 0011
       00003C D2 00 C066C062 000066 000062  38              MVC   LO,=X'11'          0001 0001
       000042 D2 00 C066C063 000066 000063  39              MVC   LO,=B'1111'        0000 1111
       000048 D2 00 C066C063 000066 000063  40              MVC   LO,=X'F'           0000 1111
       00004E D2 00 C066C063 000066 000063  41              MVC   LO,=X'0F'          0000 1111
       000054 D2 00 C066C064 000066 000064  42              MVC   LO,=X'F0'          1111 0000
       00005A D2 00 C066C065 000066 000065  43              MVC   LO,=X'FF'          1111 1111
                                           44              LTORG
       000060 01
       000061 03
       000062 11
       000063 0F
       000064 F0
       000065 FF

       000066                              45    LO         DS    XL1
```

8.1 SHIFTING BITS

The 32 bits in a general register and the 64 bits in an even-odd pair of general registers can be simultaneously shifted to the right or to the left by means of the RS-type shift instructions described in this section. There are no instructions available to shift a bit string in memory; all shifting takes place in registers.

There are two categories of shift instructions: arithmetic and logical. In **arithmetic shifts,** the sign bit of the register or register pair is treated differently from the other bits, and the condition code will be set to reflect the nature of the result. In **logical shifts,** the sign bit is treated in the same manner as all other bits, and the condition code is not set.

Arithmetic Shift Instructions

There are two pairs of arithmetic shift instructions. One pair is used for shifting the 32 bits in a single register, and the other pair is used for shifting the 64 bits in a double register. In each pair, one of the instructions is used when shifting right, and the other when shifting left. All four instructions are **RS-type instructions,** but instead of the usual RS operand format—R1,R2,D3(B3)—the second operand, R2, is not written in assembly language and is not used in machine language. The first field,

R1, designates the register or register pair whose contents are to be shifted. The second field, D3(B3), specifies the number of positions to be shifted. *The number of positions shifted,* N, *is the value of the low-order 6 bits of the effective address designated by the D3(B3) field.* N is always considered to be nonnegative. Therefore its value is in the range $0 \leq N \leq 63$. (If $N = 0$, the instruction is executed but no shift occurs.)

The four arithmetic shift instructions are

opcode	meaning	type
SRA	SHIFT RIGHT SINGLE ARITHMETIC	RS
SLA	SHIFT LEFT SINGLE ARITHMETIC	RS

The 32-bit quantity in the register designated by the first operand is arithmetically shifted right (or left) N bit positions.

SRDA	SHIFT RIGHT DOUBLE ARITHMETIC	RS
SLDA	SHIFT LEFT DOUBLE ARITHMETIC	RS

The 64-bit quantity in the even-odd register pair designated by the first operand is arithmetically shifted right (or left) N bit positions. The first operand must designate the even-numbered register of the register pair.

The arithmetic shift instructions have the following properties:

1. When the contents of a register or register pair are shifted N bits to the *right,* the N right-most bits are lost, and the sign bit (bit 0) that existed before the shift began is inserted into each of the N left-most vacated positions, i.e., into bit positions 1 through N. The sign bit itself remains unchanged.

   Right Shift: Sign Bit Propagated

2. When the contents of a register or register pair are shifted N bits to the *left,* zeroes are inserted into the N right-most vacated positions, the N left-most bits (not including the sign bit) are lost, and condition code 3—the overflow indicator—is set if a bit value different from that of the sign bit was among those that were lost. The sign bit itself remains unchanged.

   Left Shift: Overflow Possible

3. If the overflow indicator is not set as the result of an arithmetic shift instruction, condition code 0, 1, or 2 is set depending on the resulting single- or double-register contents—zero, negative, or positive.

There are several consequences of these properties. In the single-register shifts, SRA and SLA, all arithmetic bits (bits 1–31) will be lost if $N \geq 31$. When $N \geq 31$ for SRA, the sign bit replaces bits 1–31; when $N \geq 31$ for SLA, a 0-bit replaces bits 1–31. In the double-register shifts, SRDA and SLDA, the sign bit is bit 0 of the even-numbered register; all the other bits, numbered from 1–63, are arithmetic bits. Therefore, in double-register shifts all arithmetic bits will be lost only when $N = 63$; they are replaced by the sign bit in right shifts and by a 0-bit in left shifts.

Because of the special handling given to the sign bit, it follows that a left shift of N positions multiplies the number in the register or register pair by 2^N, preserving the correct algebraic sign for the product. The result will be correct unless the left shift generates an overflow condition. It also follows that a right shift of N positions divides the number in the register or register pair by 2^N, preserving the correct algebraic sign for the quotient but discarding the remainder. For positive numbers, shifting right to divide by 2^N gives the same quotient as ordinary division. For example, $(+7)/2 = 3$, and $+7$ shifted right one place is also 3. But for negative numbers, shifting right can give a quotient different from that of division. For example, $(-7)/2 = -3$, whereas -7 shifted right one place is -4. In other words, truncation is towards minus infinity, not towards zero as in division.

Finally, it should be noted that, since the condition code is set by the arithmetic shift instructions, the conditional branch instructions can be used to determine whether the result was zero, negative, or positive unless there was an overflow. If an arithmetic left shift causes an overflow, the program will be interrupted and terminated by the operating system unless the Set Program Mask (SPM) instruction is used to prohibit interruption (see Section 11.4). In the latter case, the **Branch on Overflow (BO)** conditional branch instruction can be used to detect the overflow condition.

The examples that follow and those in Figures 8.2a through 8.2c illustrate these properties of arithmetic shifts.

Figure 8.2a Arithmetic shifts of a 32-bit positive number.

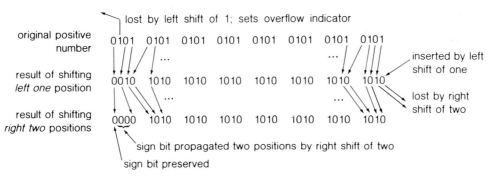

Figure 8.2b Arithmetic shifts of a 32-bit negative number.

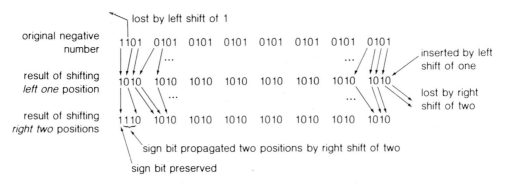

Figure 8.2c Arithmetic shifts of a 64-bit negative number.

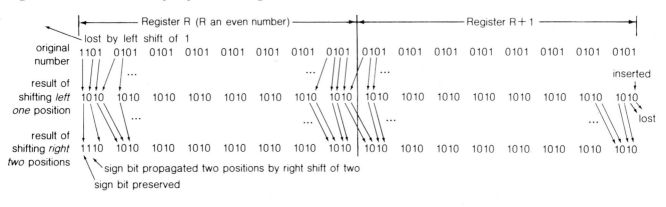

Example 1.   Result is zero

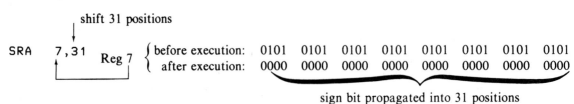

Example 2. Negative result

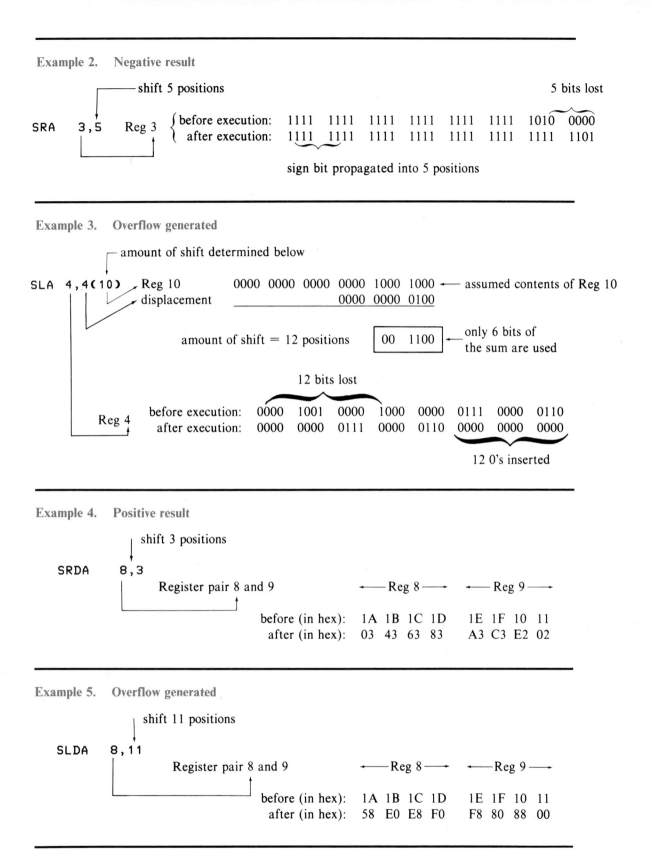

shift 5 positions   5 bits lost

```
SRA   3,5   Reg 3 { before execution:  1111  1111  1111  1111  1111  1111  1010  0000
                  { after execution:   1111  1111  1111  1111  1111  1111  1111  1101
```

sign bit propagated into 5 positions

Example 3. Overflow generated

amount of shift determined below

```
SLA  4,4(10)  Reg 10       0000 0000 0000 0000 1000 1000  ← assumed contents of Reg 10
              displacement                 0000 0000 0100
```

amount of shift = 12 positions | 00   1100 | ← only 6 bits of the sum are used

12 bits lost

```
        Reg 4   before execution:  0000  1001  0000  1000  0000  0111  0000  0110
                after execution:   0000  0000  0111  0000  0110  0000  0000  0000
```

12 0's inserted

Example 4. Positive result

shift 3 positions

```
SRDA   8,3
            Register pair 8 and 9        ← Reg 8 →    ← Reg 9 →
                        before (in hex):  1A  1B  1C  1D   1E  1F  10  11
                        after (in hex):   03  43  63  83   A3  C3  E2  02
```

Example 5. Overflow generated

shift 11 positions

```
SLDA   8,11
            Register pair 8 and 9        ← Reg 8 →    ← Reg 9 →
                        before (in hex):  1A  1B  1C  1D   1E  1F  10  11
                        after (in hex):   58  E0  E8  F0   F8  80  88  00
```

Logical Shifts

Logical shifts are used in conjunction with other bit- and byte-manipulation instructions to separate or join sequences of bits. Like arithmetic shifts, there are four logical shift instructions, two for single-register shifts and two for double-register shifts. The register address and the number of positions to be shifted are specified in the same way as for arithmetic shifts. The four instructions are

opcode	meaning	type
SRL	SHIFT RIGHT SINGLE LOGICAL	RS
SLL	SHIFT LEFT SINGLE LOGICAL	RS

The 32-bit quantity in the register designated by the first operand is logically shifted right (or left) N bit positions.

opcode	meaning	type
SRDL	SHIFT RIGHT DOUBLE LOGICAL	RS
SLDL	SHIFT LEFT DOUBLE LOGICAL	RS

The 64-bit quantity in the even-odd register pair designated by the first operand is logically shifted right (or left) N bit positions. The first operand must designate the even-numbered register of the register pair.

The logical shift instructions have the following properties:

Sign Bit Is Shifted, Not Propagated

1. When the contents of a register or register pair are shifted N bits to the *right,* the N right-most bits are lost, and zeroes are inserted into the N left-most vacated positions. The sign bit position (bit 0) is treated in the same manner as the other bit positions; it is not propagated as it is in arithmetic shifts.

Overflow Is Not Possible

2. When the contents of a register or register pair are shifted N bits to the *left,* the N left-most bits are lost, and zeroes are inserted into the N right-most vacated positions. The sign bit position is treated in the same manner as the other bit positions; an overflow condition is never generated.
3. Regardless of the nature of the result of a logical shift instruction, the condition code is not set.

Since vacated positions at the right or left ends are always filled with zeroes, the result will always be zero in single-register shifts if the number of bits shifted exceeds 31. But a double-register shift will not necessarily produce a result of zero, since N is always less than 64.

Example 1.

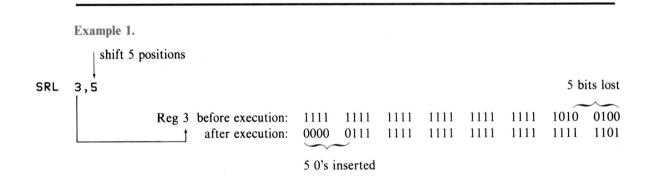

```
              shift 5 positions
                    |
                    ↓
  SRL  3,5                                                          5 bits lost
    |
    |          Reg 3  before execution:  1111 1111 1111 1111 1111 1111 1010 0100
    |_____↑   after execution:   0000 0111 1111 1111 1111 1111 1111 1101
                                         ‾‾‾‾
                              5 0's inserted
```

Example 2.

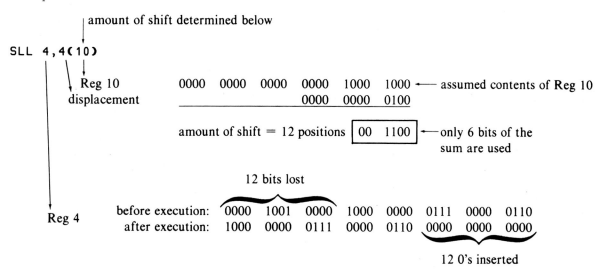

Reg 4

Example 3.

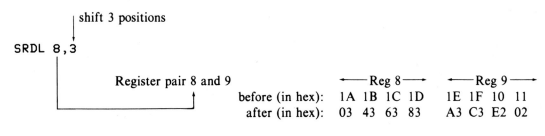

```
SRDL 8,3
```

shift 3 positions

Register pair 8 and 9

	Reg 8	Reg 9
before (in hex):	1A 1B 1C 1D	1E 1F 10 11
after (in hex):	03 43 63 83	A3 C3 E2 02

Example 4.

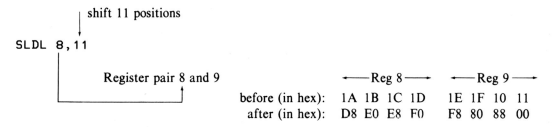

```
SLDL 8,11
```

shift 11 positions

Register pair 8 and 9

	Reg 8	Reg 9
before (in hex):	1A 1B 1C 1D	1E 1F 10 11
after (in hex):	D8 E0 E8 F0	F8 80 88 00

8.2 ALTERING BITS

Some assembly language programs use the individual bits in a bit string to represent status information. This type of information can be used to control the flow of a program and to keep a succinct
record of events that occur during the execution of a program. For example, the status of a file could
be recorded in this bit string:

*Use of Bits as
Indicators*

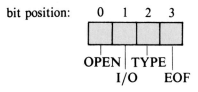

Each bit in this bit string has a value of 0 or 1. These values could imply the status of a file as follows:

bit	value		meaning
OPEN bit	0	=	file not opened
	1	=	file opened
I/O bit	0	=	if opened, file is used for input only
	1	=	if opened, file is used for output only
TYPE bit	0	=	sequential file
	1	=	indexed sequential file
EOF bit	0	=	file has not reached end-of-file
	1	=	file has reached end-of-file

A single bit is often not enough for a given situation. In that case, two or more bits can be used. Because there are only two possibilities in each case, a single bit is sufficient for the OPEN and EOF situations. But two bits each for the I/O and TYPE information would allow four possibilities for these entities:

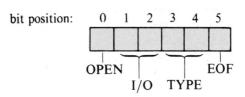

These bits could have the following meanings:

bit	value		meaning
OPEN bit	0	=	file not opened
	1	=	file opened
I/O bits	00	=	no meaning
	01	=	opened for input only
	10	=	opened for output only
	11	=	opened for input and output
TYPE bits	00	=	none of the standard types
	01	=	sequential
	10	=	indexed sequential
	11	=	direct
EOF bit	0	=	not yet end-of-file
	1	=	end-of-file

In general, n consecutive bits will provide for 2^n possible meanings. By using bits instead of bytes or larger units to record status information, programmers can be frugal in their use of available memory space.

Then the problem becomes the ability to alter and test the values of individual bits or bit strings. There are two instructions that *test* bits on the IBM Systems 360 and 370, the Test under Mask (TM) and Test and Set (TS) instructions. These are described in Section 8.3. The instructions that *alter* bits are the Boolean operations OR, AND, and EXCLUSIVE-OR.

The Boolean operations OR, AND, and EXCLUSIVE-OR have three characteristics in common:

1. They operate on two bit strings, each of the same length.
2. Only one of the bit strings, the *target,* is altered. The other bit string, the *mask,* selects the individual bits that are to be altered in the target bit string. Each bit in the mask that is a "1" selects the correspondingly positioned bit in the target, regardless of whether that target bit is a "0" or a "1."
3. The mask bit string is matched, bit for bit, with the target bit string: each bit in the mask operates on the corresponding bit in the target.[1] The sign bit is not given any special treatment.

Fundamental Techniques

Figure 8.3a   *The Boolean OR operation.*

mask bit	target bit	resulting bit	
0	0	0	} mask bit = 0
0	1	1	target bit *unchanged*
1	0	1	} mask bit = 1
1	1	1	target bit *set to 1*

Figure 8.3b   *The Boolean AND operation.*

mask bit	target bit	resulting bit	
0	0	0	} mask bit = 0
0	1	0	target bit *reset to 0*
1	0	0	} mask bit = 1
1	1	1	target bit *unchanged*

Figure 8.3c   *The Boolean EXCLUSIVE-OR operation.*

mask bit	target bit	resulting bit	
0	0	0	} mask bit = 0
0	1	1	target bit *unchanged*
1	0	1	} mask bit = 1
1	1	0	target bit *reversed*

OR

The Boolean OR operation **sets** the selected target bits to 1, regardless of what the previous values of those bits were. Bits not selected by the mask are not changed.

AND

The Boolean AND operation **preserves** the value of the selected target bits and **resets** the remaining bits to zero, regardless of what the previous values of those bits were.

EXCL-OR

The Boolean EXCLUSIVE-OR operation **reverses** the value of the selected target bits: if a selected bit was 0, it is set to 1; if it was 1, it is reset to 0. Bits not selected by the mask are not changed.

These three operations are depicted in Figures 8.3a through 8.3c.

There are four OR instructions, four AND instructions, and four EXCLUSIVE-OR instructions on the IBM Systems 360 and 370. Within each set of four, the instructions are distinguished by the length and location of the mask and target bit strings. Figure 8.4 summarizes these distinctions.

The bit string resulting from an OR, AND, or EXCLUSIVE-OR operation is considered to be either zero or nonzero, and the condition code is set accordingly. No distinction is made between positive and negative results. Thus the only conditional branch instructions that should be used following Boolean instructions are BZ, BZR, BNZ, and BNZR.

1. In the IBM Systems 360 and 370, the emphasis on mask and target bit strings is valid because the result always replaces the target. Bits in the target bit string are selected and altered *in place*. However, in many electronic applications of the Boolean operations, the result does not replace the target; instead, it is generated as a separate quantity. In these instances, the use of the mask and target nomenclature is not appropriate; there are simply two operands that obey the rules of combination given in Figures 8.3a through 8.3c.

Figure 8.4   Boolean instructions on IBM Systems 360 and 370.

opcode	op-name	op-type	location of MASK	location of TARGET	length of mask and target
O N X	OR AND EXCLUSIVE-OR	RX	in full-word memory location designated by second operand	in register designated by first operand	32 bits
OR NR XR	OR Registers AND Registers EXCLUSIVE-OR Regs.	RR	in register designated by second operand	in register designated by first operand	32 bits
OI NI XI	OR Immediate AND Immediate EXCLUSIVE-OR Immed.	SI	in immediate data field (second operand)	in 1-byte memory location designated by first operand	8 bits
OC NC XC	OR Characters AND Characters EXCLUSIVE-OR Chars.	SS$_1$	in L-byte* memory location designated by second operand	in L-byte* memory location designated by first operand	$8 \times L$ bits*

*The value of L is specified in the length field of the first operand: $1 \leq L \leq 256$

Example 1.

```
          | target operand
          ↓ ↓ mask operand
OR   5,6
```

before execution:
Reg 6	=	1111	1111	1111	1111	0000	0000	0000	0000
Reg 5	=	0101	0101	0101	0101	0101	0101	0101	0101

after execution:
Reg 5	=	1111	1111	1111	1111	0101	0101	0101	0101

set to 1's   unchanged

Example 2.

```
          | target operand
          ↓ ↓ mask operand
NR   5,6
```

before execution:
Reg 6	=	1111	1111	1111	1111	0000	0000	0000	0000
Reg 5	=	0101	0101	0101	0101	0101	0101	0101	0101

after execution:
Reg 5	=	0101	0101	0101	0101	0000	0000	0000	0000

unchanged   set to 0's

Example 3.

```
    | target operand
    |  | mask operand
XR  5,6
```

before execution:	Reg 6	=	1111	1111	1111	1111	0000	0000	0000	0000
	Reg 5	=	0101	0101	0101	0101	0101	0101	0101	0101

after execution:	Reg 5	=	1010	1010	1010	1010	0101	0101	0101	0101

                               each bit reversed   unchanged

8.3   TESTING BITS

Two instructions test individual bits to determine whether their values are 0 or 1. Both of these test the bits of a byte in memory. In the IBM Systems 360 and 370, there is no instruction that tests individual bits in a bit string whose length is greater than eight; but this can be accomplished by using Boolean operations, as will be shown in Section 8.5, Example 2. The instructions testing individual bits should not be confused with the *byte compare* instructions (CL, CLR, CLI, CLM, CLC, CLCL). The latter compare the values of two byte strings; the former determine whether individually selected bits are 0 or 1.

The two instructions that test individual bits in a byte are (1) Test under Mask (TM) and (2) Test and Set (TS). TM is the more generally useful of the two. It tests up to 8 bits at once, without altering the bits that are tested. TS tests only 1 bit—the high-order or "sign" bit of a byte—and then sets all the bits in the tested byte to 1. Its use is restricted to certain special situations, which will be described shortly.

Test Under Mask

The TM instruction tests any subset of the 8 bits in a byte. The byte whose bits are tested—the target byte—can be located in any addressable memory position. The bits to be tested in the target byte are selected by a 1-byte mask located in the immediate data field of the TM instruction.

The TM is an SI-type instruction:

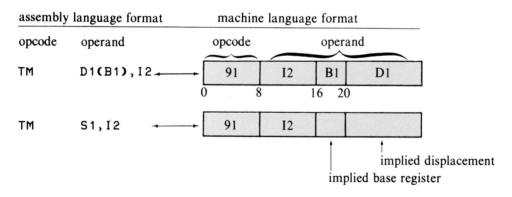

The 8 bits in the I2 mask field correspond, one for one, left to right, with the 8 bits in the target byte (addressed by the first operand field). Each 1-bit in the mask causes the corresponding bit in the target byte to be selected for testing. Each 0-bit in the mask causes the corresponding bit in the target byte *not* to be selected for testing.

Mask Bits in "I2" Field

The result of the TM instruction can be determined by means of conditional branch instructions:

> BZ Branch if Zeroes
>> branches if all tested bits are 0's, or if all *mask* bits are 0's

> BO Branch if Ones
>> branches if all tested bits are 1's

> BM Branch if Mixed Zeroes and Ones
>> branches if some tested bits are 0's and the other tested bits are 1's

Examples of the use of the TM are given following the next section.

Test and Set

The TS instruction tests the high-order, or "sign," bit of a byte in memory; after testing that bit, it replaces the entire byte with 1's (B'11111111'). Thus, the TS behaves as though it were two consecutive instructions built into one:

```
TM    BYTE,B'10000000'
MVI   BYTE,B'11111111'
```

The TS is an S-type instruction: it requires only a single operand field. As shown below, no mask is necessary because the TS always tests the high-order bit of a byte.

The result of the test made by the TS instruction can be determined by means of conditional branch instructions:

> BZ Branch if Zero
>> branches if the tested bit had a value of 0

> BNZ Branch if Not Zero
>> branches if the tested bit had a value of 1

The unusual nature of the TS instruction, i.e., the fact that after it tests the high-order bit it sets all the bits in the byte to 1's, is specifically designed for multiprogramming and multiprocessing systems in which two or more programs are contending for use of a nonsharable component of the computer system. Such a component, also called a nonsharable computer system *resource,* could be a printer, a terminal, a portion of memory, or the like. A computer system resource is said to be nonsharable if only one program can use it at a time.

It is a common practice for the program that controls the use of a nonsharable resource to do so by utilizing one bit or byte to record the instantaneous status of the resource, similar to the file status bits mentioned earlier. The most important status information with which we are concerned is whether the nonsharable resource is in use or not. This could be recorded as

> STATUS-BYTE: value 0 = not in use
>> value 1 = in use

The TS instruction permits such a status byte to be tested and then immediately set to the "in-use" mode, so that no other program can gain access to that byte while its status is being tested by the first program. This is necessary for the following reason: if, instead of a TS instruction, a program used the two-instruction sequence TM followed by MVI, another program could gain access to that byte during the instant between the completion of the TM and the beginning of the MVI's execution. The second program would then find that byte set to 0 (not in use) even though the first program was about to set it to 1 (in use). Both programs might then attempt to use the nonsharable resource simultaneously without being aware of one another's actions. This would violate the integrity of the computer system. Use of the TS instruction can prevent this from happening.

Example 1.

```
TM    ALPHA,X'F0'
```

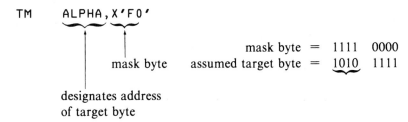

mask byte = 1111 0000
assumed target byte = 1010 1111

Result of TM: some tested bits are 0's, others are 1's. BM will branch, BO and BZ won't.

Example 2.

```
TM    ALPHA,X'0F'
```

mask byte = 0000 1111
assumed target byte = 1010 1111

Result of TM: all tested bits are 1's. BO will branch, BM and BZ won't.

Example 3.

```
TM    ALPHA,B'01010000'
```

mask byte = 0101 0000
assumed target byte = 1010 1111

Result of TM: all tested bits are 0's. BZ will branch, BM and BO won't.

Example 4.

```
TS    ALPHA
```

	byte at ALPHA	
before execution:	0111	1111
after execution:	1111	1111

Result of TS: tested bit was 0. BZ will branch, BNZ won't.

Example 5.

```
TS    ALPHA
```

	byte at ALPHA
before execution:	1000 0000
after execution:	1111 1111

Result of TS: tested bit was 1. BNZ will branch, BZ won't.

8.4 THE CONDITION CODE

The condition code is a hardware indicator that records the nature of the result of certain instructions. Since the indicator consists of only two bits, only four possible conditions can be recorded. These are known as the *condition code settings:*

$$00 = \text{Condition Code } 0$$
$$01 = \text{Condition Code } 1$$
$$10 = \text{Condition Code } 2$$
$$11 = \text{Condition Code } 3$$

The specific meaning of each of these four condition code settings depends on the instruction that generated the condition. Not all of the instructions available on the IBM Systems 360 and 370 cause the condition code to be set, but more than half of them do. The condition code is always set to one of its four possible values whenever one of the code-setting instructions is executed. However, the condition code is not affected by any of the instructions that are not code-setting instructions.

Each BC and BCR Mask Bit Selects a Condition Code Value

The setting of the condition code can be examined and its value determined by two instructions designed for this purpose: (1) Branch on Condition (BC), and (2) Branch on Condition via Register (BCR). *Both of these instructions are conditional branch instructions.* The setting of the condition code when either of these instructions is executed determines whether or not a branch is made. More precisely, the bits in a 4-bit mask field within the BC and BCR instruction determine which setting or settings of the condition code will cause a branch. The mask field occupies bits 8–11 of a machine language BC and BCR instruction. Each of the 4 bits in the mask field denotes a different one of the four possible settings of the condition code:

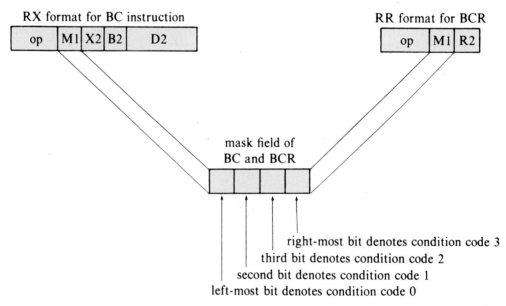

right-most bit denotes condition code 3
third bit denotes condition code 2
second bit denotes condition code 1
left-most bit denotes condition code 0

When any of these bits is set to the value 1, the corresponding condition code setting will cause the BC and BCR instructions to branch. For example:

mask field	meaning
1000	If the condition code is 0, the BC and BCR will branch.
1100	If the condition is either 0 or 1, the BC and BCR will branch.
1010	If the condition code is either 0 or 2, the BC and BCR will branch.
0011	If the condition code is either 2 or 3, the BC and BCR will branch.
1111	Whatever the condition code setting is, the BC and BCR will branch (thereby constituting an unconditional branch).
0000	Whatever the condition code setting is, the BC and BCR will not branch (thereby constituting a so-called "no-op," or no operation, instruction).

Any of the sixteen possible 4-bit mask-field contents is allowed. Each has a precise meaning, as indicated by the preceding examples and (later) in Figures 8.6a and 8.6b.

In previous sections, it was stated that the nature of the result of certain instructions, for example, *compare* instructions, *arithmetic* instructions, *Boolean* instructions, and so forth, could be determined by means of conditional branch instructions such as BE, BH, BL, BZ, BP, BM, and their negative counterparts BNE, BNH, BNL, BNZ, BNP, BNM. Now a more precise statement can be made: each conditional branch instruction just mentioned is a variation of the BC instruction. The variations are created by different values of the mask field and are often called **extended mnemonics** since they are all based on the same actual opcode, namely that of the BC.

Extended mnemonics are used so that we need not remember the appropriate mask field. For example, the instruction

                    BE   FOUND

is identical to the instruction

                    BC   8,FOUND

The first operand in the BC instruction is the mask-field value:

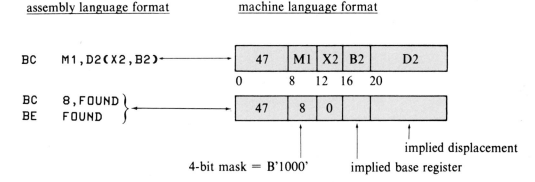

However, as shown, a mask field of B'1000' means that condition code 0 causes a branch. So the immediate question is, what does condition code 0 mean? *The meaning of each condition code setting depends on the instruction that caused the code to be set.* Figure 8.5a summarizes the meanings of the condition code settings for all nonprivileged instructions. (Some privileged instructions also set the condition code, but they are not discussed in this text.)

Figure 8.5a shows that condition code 0 is set by any compare instruction when the two quantities being compared are equal: that is why BC 8,FOUND is identical to BE FOUND.

Figure 8.5a Condition code settings for nonprivileged instructions.

			condition code setting depends on the instruction and its result			
	instruction		condition code 0	condition code 1	condition code 2	condition code 3
INTEGER OPERATIONS	Add Subtract	A, AR, AH S, SR, SH	result is 0	result is negative	result is positive	operation generated an overflow
	Add Subtract	AL,ALR SL,SLR	result is 0, with no carry (AL, ALR only)	result is not 0, with no carry	result is 0, with carry	result is not 0, with carry
	Compare	C, CR, CH	both operands are equal	first operand less than second	first operand greater than second	---
	Load	LCR	result is 0	result is negative	result is positive	overflow generated
		LNR	result is 0	result is negative	---	---
		LPR	result is 0	---	result is positive	overflow generated
		LTR	result is 0	result is negative	result is positive	---
	Shift	SLA, SLDA	result is 0	result is negative	result is positive	overflow generated
		SRA, SRDA	result is 0	result is negative	result is positive	---
BYTE OPERATIONS	Insert	ICM	all inserted bits 0, or all mask bits 0	1st inserted bit is 1	1st inserted bit is 0 but not all are 0	---
	Compare	CL, CLR CLC,CLI	both operands are equal	first operand less than second	first operand greater than second	---
		CLCL	operands are equal, or have zero lengths	first operand less than second	first operand greater than second	---
		CLM	bytes selected are equal or mask bits are all 0	first operand field less than second	first operand field greater than second	---
	Copy	MVCL	first operand length equals second operand's	first operand length less than second	first operand length greater than second	destructive overlap (no bytes copied)
	Translate	TRT	all argument bytes tested; all function bytes 0	one or more argument bytes not tested	search stopped on last argument byte	---
BIT OPERATIONS	AND OR EXCL-OR	N,NC,NI,NR O,OC,OI,OR X,XC,XI,XR	result is 0 result is 0 result is 0	result is not 0 result is not 0 result is not 0	--- --- ---	--- --- ---
	Test	TM	all selected bits 0 or all mask bits 0	some sel. bits are 0 and some bits are 1	---	all selected bits are 1's
		TS	left-most bit of tested byte is 0	left-most bit of tested byte is 1	---	---
DECIMAL	Add Subtract	AP, ZAP SP	result is 0	result is negative	result is positive	operation generated an overflow
	Compare	CP	both operands are equal	first operand less than second	first operand greater than second	---
	Shift	SRP	result is 0	result is negative	result is positive	overflow generated
FLOATING POINT	Add	AE,AER,AD, ADR,AU,AUR, AW,AWR,AXR	mantissa of result is 0	result is negative	result is positive	---
	Subtract	SE,SER,SD, SDR,SU,SUR, SW,SWR,SXR	mantissa of result is 0	result is negative	result is positive	---
	Load	LCER,LCDR	result mantissa is 0	result is negative	result is positive	---
		LNER,LNDR	result mantissa is 0	result is negative	---	---
		LPER,LPDR	result mantissa is 0	---	result is positive	---
		LTER,LTDR	result mantissa is 0	result is negative	result is positive	---
	Compare	CE, CER CD, CDR	both operands are equal	first operand less than second	first operand greater than second	---
MISCELLANEOUS	Compare and swap	CS, CDS	compared operands equal, second one is replaced	compared operands not equal, first is replaced	---	---
	Set pgm mask	SPM	(the condition code is set to the value of bits 2 and 3 of the designated register)			
	Store clock	STCK	clock in set state	clock in not-set state	clock in error state	clock in stopped state or not-operational
	Editing	ED, EDMK	last edited field is 0	last edited field is negative	last edited field is positive	---

Figure 8.5b   *Nonprivileged instructions that do not set the condition code.*

Branches	Branch and Link	BAL	BALR	BAS	BASR		
	Branch on Condition	BC	BCR				
	Branch on Count	BCT	BCTR				
	Branch on Index	BXH	BXLE				
Integer operations	Multiply	M	MR	MH			
	Divide	D	DR				
	Load	L	LM	LH			
	Store	ST	STM	STH			
Byte operations	Copy	IC	STC	STCM	MVC	MVI	MVCIN
	Translate	TR					
Bit operations	Shift Logical	SRL	SRDL				
		SLL	SLDL				
Decimal operations	Multiply	MP					
	Divide	DP					
	Copy	MVN	MVO	MVZ			
Floating-point operations	Multiply	ME	MER	MD	MDR	MXD	MXDR	MXR
	Divide	DE	DER	DD	DDR		
	Halve	HER	HDR				
	Round	LRER	LRDR				
	Load	LE	LER	LD	LDR		
	Store	STE	STD				
Miscellaneous operations	Decimal-binary Conv.	CVB	CVD				
	Decimal-EBCDIC Conv.	PACK	UNPK				
	Execute	EX					
	Load Address	LA					
	Monitor Call	MC					
	Supervisor Call	SVC					

Figure 8.5b shows that none of the multiply or divide instructions sets the condition code, and that none of the logical shift instructions sets the condition code. To determine whether the result of a multiply, divide, or logical shift is positive, negative, or zero, we must therefore use the Load and Test Register (LTR) instruction. For logical shifts, the determination could be made like this:

```
SLL    4,8      SHIFT REG 4 CONTENTS LEFT 8 BITS
LTR    4,4      SEE IF THE RESULT OF THE SHIFT IS ZERO
BZ     ZERO
```

The complete set of correspondences between the extended mnemonic conditional branch instructions and the BC instruction is shown in Figure 8.6a. Note that the unconditional branch B is actually a BC that *always* branches; similarly, the no-op instruction NOP is a BC that *never* branches.

The BC is an RX-type instruction. Its counterpart, the BCR, is an RR-type instruction. In the BC instruction, the second operand designates the address of the instruction to which the branch is to be made if the condition code is set to one of the values selected by the mask:

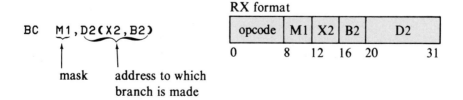

Figure 8.6a   RX-type conditional branch instructions.

extended mnemonic	equivalent BC		mask bits	condition codes designated by mask bits
BE	BC	8,	1000	0
BNE	BC	7,	0111	1, 2, and 3
BL	BC	4,	0100	1
BNL	BC	11,	1011	0, 2, and 3
BH	BC	2,	0010	2
BNH	BC	13,	1101	0, 1, and 3
BZ	BC	8,	1000	0
BNZ	BC	7,	0111	1, 2, and 3
BM	BC	4,	0100	1
BNM	BC	11,	1011	0, 2, and 3
BP	BC	2,	0010	2
BNP	BC	13,	1101	0, 1, and 3
BO	BC	1,	0001	3
BNO	BC	14,	1110	0, 1, and 2
NOP	BC	0,	0000	none
B	BC	15,	1111	0, 1, 2, and 3
--	BC	12,	1100	0 and 1
--	BC	3,	0011	2 and 3
--	BC	10,	1010	0 and 2
--	BC	5,	0101	1 and 3
--	BC	9,	1001	0 and 3
--	BC	6,	0110	1 and 2

Figure 8.6b   RR-type conditional branch instructions.

extended mnemonic	equivalent BCR		mask bits	condition codes designated by mask bits
BER	BCR	8,	1000	0
BNER	BCR	7,	0111	1, 2, and 3
BLR	BCR	4,	0100	1
BNLR	BCR	11,	1011	0, 2, and 3
BHR	BCR	2,	0010	2
BNHR	BCR	13,	1101	0, 1, and 3
BZR	BCR	8,	1000	0
BNZR	BCR	7,	0111	1, 2, and 3
BMR	BCR	4,	0100	1
BNMR	BCR	11,	1011	0, 2, and 3
BPR	BCR	2,	0010	2
BNPR	BCR	13,	1101	0, 1, and 3
BOR	BCR	1,	0001	3
BNOR	BCR	14,	1110	0, 1, and 2
NOPR	BCR	0,	0000	none
BR	BCR	15,	1111	0, 1, 2, and 3
--	BCR	12,	1100	0 and 1
--	BCR	3,	0011	2 and 3
--	BCR	10,	1010	0 and 2
--	BCR	5,	0101	1 and 3
--	BCR	9,	1001	0 and 3
--	BCR	6,	0110	1 and 2

In the BCR instruction, the second operand field designates a register address, not a memory address. The designated register must contain the address of the instruction to which the branch is to be made if the condition code is set to one of the values selected by the mask:

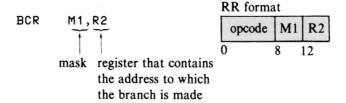

No Branch If R2=0

The BCR gets its name, Branch on Condition via Register, from the fact that the branch is made to the address contained in the designated register. There is one exception, however: if the designated register is zero, no branch is made regardless of the contents of the mask field M1.

An extended mnemonic conditional branch instruction is defined for most of the sixteen possible mask fields of the BCR instruction. These are summarized in Figure 8.6b. Although not discussed in preceding chapters, an RR-type conditional branch may be used in any situation in which its corresponding RX-type branch would be used. One of the most important instructions in this group is the unconditional branch, Branch via Register (BR). The BR is used to return from a subroutine to a calling program, as will be discussed in the next chapter. The instruction BCR with M1=0 is the counterpart of the BC with M1=0: both are no-op instructions. The BCR no-op, written mnemonically as NOPR, is the instruction that is generated by the CNOP directive.

8.5 BIT MANIPULATION EXAMPLES

The bit manipulation instructions described in the preceding sections provide capabilities needed in a variety of problems and situations. For example:

1. Shift instructions, in addition to their obvious use as a succinct method of multiplying and dividing by powers of two, enable a program to separate and link adjacent bit strings.
2. Boolean instructions enable a program to isolate bits, to set individual bits to 0 or 1, and to reverse the setting of bits.
3. The TM instruction provides an easy method for testing the values of individual bits, thereby facilitating the use of status indicators and switches.
4. The BC and BCR operations underlie the conditional branch instructions, without which decisions could not be made by programs.

The four examples that follow illustrate how these capabilities are used in conjunction with other instructions.

Example 1.   Use of a status byte
(See Figure 8.7.)

Suppose that the instantaneous status of a file is to be recorded in a single status byte, as follows:

bit name	bit position within byte	value of bits		meaning
OPEN	0	0	=	file is closed
		1	=	file is opened
IO	1,2	00	=	no meaning
		01	=	opened for input only
		10	=	opened for output only
		11	=	opened for input and output
TYPE	3,4	00	=	none of the standard types
		01	=	sequential
		10	=	indexed sequential
		11	=	direct
EOF	5	0	=	not yet end-of-file
		1	=	end-of-file

Schematically, this can be represented as

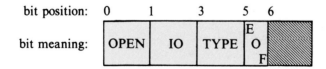

In a program, it can be defined as in Figure 8.7. The definition requires a number of statements; one virtue of this is that the status byte is fully documented within the program in which it is defined.

Note that a whole byte is used for the status information, even though there are two unused bits in the byte. This serves two purposes: (1) it leaves a little room for defining other status bits at a later time, and (2) it facilitates use of the bit manipulation instructions that can only address a whole byte.

Note also that the EQU directive is used to assign *names* to the bits and to the various states, and that the DC directive gives a name to the status byte and sets its initial value. All names used in a program are listed in the cross-reference table produced by the assembler; therefore, the use of names for the status bits and for the various states facilitates any debugging and modifying that might have to be done.

Figure 8.7   Definitions for a file-status byte.

```
 1    * FILE STATUS INFORMATION
 2    FILESTAT DC    B'00000000'    FILE STATUS INITIALLY 0'S
 3    OPEN     EQU   B'10000000'    BIT 0     0=CLOSED, 1=OPEN
 4    IO       EQU   B'01100000'    BIT 1,2   FOR I/O STATE:
 5    IOIN     EQU   B'00100000'              01=INPUT ONLY
 6    IOOUT    EQU   B'01000000'              10=OUTPUT ONLY
 7    IOINOUT  EQU   B'01100000'              11=INPUT & OUTPUT
 8    TYPE     EQU   B'00011000'    BIT 3,4   FOR FILE TYPE
 9    TYPSAM   EQU   B'00001000'              01=SEQTL (SAM)
10    TYPISAM  EQU   B'00010000'              10=INDEXED (ISAM)
11    TYPBDAM  EQU   B'00011000'              11=DIRECT (BDAM)
12    EOF      EQU   B'00000100'    BIT 5     0=NOT EOF, 1=EOF
```

Several situations arise in connection with the use of such a status byte. Using the definitions of Figure 8.7, some of them could be handled in the following manner:

1. When the file is opened,

```
        OI    FILESTAT,OPEN        SET OPEN BIT TO '1'
```

2. If the file is opened as an indexed sequential file,

```
        OI    FILESTAT,TYPISAM     SET ISAM BIT TO '1'
```

3. If it is necessary to determine whether the file is opened for output or input,

```
        TM    FILESTAT,IOOUT       SEE IF OUTPUT BIT IS '1'
        BO    OUTPUT               BRANCH IF IT IS '1'
        TM    FILESTAT,IOIN        SEE IF INPUT BIT IS '1'
        BO    INPUT                BRANCH IF IT IS '1'
        .................
OUTPUT  EQU   *                    file is opened for output
        .
        .
INPUT   EQU   *                    file is opened for input
        .
        .
```

4. If it is necessary to determine whether the file is opened both for input and for output,

```
        TM    FILESTAT,IOINOUT     TEST I/O BITS
        BO    BOTH                 BRANCH IF BOTH ARE 1's
```

5. If it is necessary to reset the "open" status bit to zero, indicating the file has been closed,

```
        NI    FILESTAT,X'FF'-OPEN  SET OPEN BIT TO '0'
```

In all cases, the assembler substitutes the value of the symbol that is used for each status bit. For example, based on the definitions of Figure 8.7, the following three statements are equivalent to one another:

```
        TM    FILESTAT,IOIN
        TM    FILESTAT,B'00100000'
        TM    FILESTAT,X'20'
```

Figure 8.8   Test the value of the Nth bit in a word.

```
 1  * THIS SET OF STATEMENTS TESTS THE NTH BIT OF A STATUS WORD
 2  *  (N IS BETWEEN 0 AND 31, INCLUSIVE)
 3  *
 4  *  IF THE BIT'S VALUE IS 0, CONTROL GOES TO STMT NAMED 'OFF'  'OFF''
 5  *  IF THE BIT'S VALUE IS 1, CONTROL GOES TO STMT NAMED 'ON'   'ON.''
 6  *
 7  *  THE STATUS WORD IS LOCATED AT STMT NAMED 'STATUS' TUS''
 8  *
 9  *
10           LH      2,BITN          R2=VALUE OF N (BIT POSITION)
11           L       3,STATUS        R3=WORD CONTAINING BIT TO TEST
12           SLL     3,0(2)          MOVE BIT TO POSITION 0
13           N       3,PATTERN       ISOLATE TESTED BIT
14           BZ      OFF             RESULT=0 IF TESTED BIT WAS 0
15           B       ON
                 .
                 .
                 .
16  BITN     DS      H               HALF WORD FOR N (BIT POSITION)
17  STATUS   DS      F               FULL WORD FOR STATUS BITS
18  PATTERN  DC      X'80000000'     BIT 0 OF PATTERN IS A 1
                 .
                 .
                 .
```

In Situation 5, to reset a bit to zero, the mask must be set up so that all bits are preserved (unchanged) except the one to be reset. The operand X'FF'-OPEN has the value B'01111111'. The result of this value ANDed to the file-status byte value is that all bits in the file-status byte are preserved except the OPEN bit, bit 0. That one is set to 0. The operand X'FF'-{any mask} always reverses each bit of an 8-bit mask. We can see from the example that such a reversal is precisely what is needed to reset a bit.

Example 2.   Use of a status word
(See Figure 8.8.)

Sometimes 8 bits are not enough to represent the status of a situation. In such cases, we use either several bytes in the manner described in the previous section, or a full word or several full words. To use full words, the techniques of setting, testing, resetting, and inverting status bits can be handled as follows.

Suppose that a full word is used to record the status of up to 32 terminals connected to the computer. Each bit corresponds to a terminal, the bits are numbered from left to right 0, 1, 2, 3,...,31, and these numbers correspond to the terminal numbers. Each bit records the state of one terminal: if bit N is a 0, then terminal N is not in use; if bit N is a 1, then terminal N is being used.

Testing or Resetting Bit N.   To test or reset the Nth bit in the status word, that word can be placed into a register and the Nth bit isolated from the other bits. The isolation is achieved by SHIFT and AND instructions (see Figure 8.8):

```
     LH      2,BITN       R2=VALUE OF N
     L       3,STATUS     R3=STATUS WORD
     SLL     3,0(2)       MOVE BIT N TO POSITION 0
     N       3,PATTERN    SET ALL BUT BIT #0 TO '0'.
```

It is assumed that BITN is the half-word location that has the value of N, that STATUS is the location of the status word, and that PATTERN is a location that contains a 1-bit in position 0 and 0-bits everywhere else:

```
PATTERN   DC   X'80000000'
```

The amount of the left shift is in Register 2; that is what the operand 0(2) of the SLL instruction produces. For example, if $N=8$, then SLL 3,0(2) is interpreted as though it were SLL 3,8. The effect of the left shift is to move bit N into position 0 of Register 3. (Recall that N is in the range 0–31; if N is 0, then SLL 3,0(2) causes no shift.) Once bit N is in position 0, it is isolated by the AND instruction using the PATTERN word. At this point, bit N is in a known position. It can easily be tested, reset, set, or inverted.

To test bit N after it has been isolated by this procedure, we follow the AND instruction with a conditional branch instruction as shown in Statement 14 of Figure 8.8.

To reset bit N to 0, the procedure of Figure 8.8 can be replaced by these seven statements:

```
LH      2,BITN      R2= VALUE OF N
L       3,STATUS    R3= WORD CONTAINING BIT TO TEST
SLL     3,0(2)      MOVE BIT TO POSITION #0
N       3,PATTERN   ISOLATE TESTED BIT
SRL     3,0(2)      MOVE BIT BACK TO POSITION #N
X       3,STATUS    FORCE BIT #N TO BE 0, AND PUT
ST      3,STATUS     RESULT BACK INTO STATUS WORD
```

Setting or Inverting Bit N.   To illustrate how to set and invert a bit in a word, we once again use the areas and the constant defined in Figure 8.8.

To set bit N to 1, these five statements are sufficient:

```
LH      2,BITN      R2=VALUE OF N
L       3,PATTERN   R3='1' IN POSITION #0
SRL     3,0(2)      MOVE '1' TO POSITION #N
O       3,STATUS    'OR' THE STATUS BITS INTO R3,
ST      3,STATUS    PUT RESULT BACK INTO STATUS WORD
```

To invert bit N, from 0 to 1 or vice versa, these five statements suffice:

```
LH      2,BITN      R2=VALUE OF N
L       3,PATTERN   R3='1' IN POSITION #0
SRL     3,0(2)      MOVE '1' TO POSITION #N
X       3,STATUS    REVERSE BIT #N, PRESERVE OTHERS
ST      3,STATUS    PUT RESULT BACK INTO STATUS WORD
```

Trace these four situations for two different cases: (1) in which the Nth bit is originally 0, and (2) in which it is originally 1.

Example 3.   Convert hex digits to EBCDIC codes
(See Figure 8.9.)

To print a hex digit on an IBM terminal or line printer, the digit must be represented in the EBCDIC character scheme. Each EBCDIC code requires 8 bits, whereas a hex digit requires only 4. Thus a full word of hex digits requires two words of EBCDIC bytes. This is shown in the accompanying diagrams, together with the EBCDIC code for each hex digit.

Figure 8.9   Convert eight hex digits to EBCDIC codes.

```
                 .
                 .
                 .
 1   * THIS SET OF STATEMENTS GENERATES EIGHT CONSECUTIVE BYTES IN
 2   * EBCDIC CODE FORMAT CORRESPONDING TO EIGHT CONSECUTIVE HEX DIGITS.
 3   *
 4   *   THE HEX DIGITS ARE ASSUMED TO BE IN THE FULL WORD NAMED 'DIGITS'
 5   *   THE EBCDIC BYTES ARE PLACED IN THE AREA NAMED 'RESULT'
 6   *
 7           LA    1,EBCDIC            R1=ADDR OF EBCDIC CODE TABLE
 8           LA    2,RESULT            R2=ADDR OF FIRST RESULT BYTE
 9           L     3,=F'8'             R3=LOOP-CONTROL COUNTER
10           L     7,DIGITS            R7=HEX DIGITS
11   * GENERATE AN EBCDIC BYTE
12   NEXT    LH    6,=H'0'             R6 IS CLEARED, THEN NEXT HEX
13           SLDL  6,4                   DIGIT IS SHIFTED INTO IT, AND
14           LA    8,0(6,1)            IS USED TO COMPUTE ADDR OF
15           MVC   0(1,2),0(8)         CORRESPONDING EBCDIC CODE.
16   * LOOP-CONTROL
17           LA    2,1(2)              ADJUST ADDR TO NEXT RESULT BYTE
18           BCT   3,NEXT              REPEAT TILL EIGHT DIGITS DONE
                 .
                 .
                 .
19   DIGITS  DS    F                   HEX DIGITS (FULLWORD) TO BE CONV
20   RESULT  DS    CL8                 AREA FOR RESULT BYTES
21   EBCDIC  DC    C'0123456789ABCDEF' EBCDIC CODES FOR HEX DIGITS
                 .
                 .
                 .
```

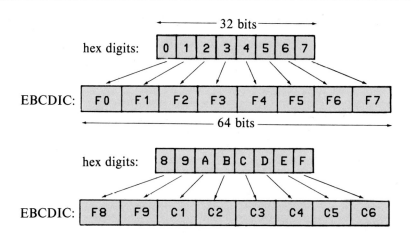

In this example, the goal is to convert a sequence of eight arbitrary hex digits into their EBCDIC codes. The program in Figure 8.9 does this. Two things should be noticed in this solution: the use of the double logical left shift in Statement 13 to isolate a hex digit in a register and simultaneously position the next hex digit for its eventual isolation; and (2) the use of the LA instruction in Statement 14 to compute the address of the correct EBCDIC byte, based on the numeric value of the hex digit.

The techniques used are illustrated by the trace that follows, which assumes that the hex digits to be converted are X'C0F9A6B4'. The other assumptions are merely address assumptions, namely:

$$RESULT = 4020, \qquad EBCDIC = 4028$$

The program will work, however, for any hex digits and any valid addresses.

In the trace, the values shown are those that exist immediately *after* Statement 15 is executed during each iteration of the loop:

contents of registers shown in hex

iteration	Reg 2	Reg 3	Reg 6	Reg 7 ·	Reg 8	bytes moved to RESULT
1st	4020	8	0000000C	0F9A6B40	4034	C3
2nd	4021	7	00000000	F9A6B400	4028	C3 F0
3rd	4022	6	0000000F	9A6B4000	4037	C3 F0 C6
4th	4023	5	00000009	A6B40000	4031	C3 F0 C6 F9
5th	4024	4	0000000A	6B400000	4032	C3 F0 C6 F9 C1
6th	4025	3	00000006	B4000000	402E	C3 F0 C6 F9 C1 F6
7th	4026	2	0000000B	40000000	4033	C3 F0 C6 F9 C1 F6 C2
8th	4027	1	00000004	00000000	402C	C3 F0 C6 F9 C1 F6 C2 F4

The number in Register 8 that is computed by Statement 14,

$$\text{LA} \quad 8,0(6,1)$$

is the address of the 8-bit EBCDIC code that corresponds to the hex digit in Register 6. For example, in the first iteration the hex digit is C. The LA instruction adds this to the number in Register 1, i.e., it adds it to the address of the beginning of the EBCDIC code table, 4028, and thereby generates the address of the desired 8-bit code: 4028 + C = 4034.

Example 4. Translate from decimal to binary integer
(See Figure 8.10.)

When data enter a computer's memory from an I/O device such as a terminal or card reader, they are stored in the format in which the device transmitted them. For IBM devices, this format is the EBCDIC code scheme. If the data are numeric, they must be translated into their appropriate internal format—binary integer, floating-point, or packed-decimal—before they can be used in arithmetic calculations. This example shows one way to translate a positive decimal integer from its EBCDIC representation to its internal binary integer format.

To understand the concepts involved, recall that a decimal integer's value is determined by means of the positional notation method:

$$1358 = 1 \times 10^3 + 3 \times 10^2 + 5 \times 10^1 + 8 \times 10^0$$
$$= 1000 \quad + 300 \quad + 50 \quad + 8$$

In EBCDIC format, the number 1358 is represented as a 4-byte binary quantity whose hex representation is

and whose binary representation is

1111 0001	1111 0011	1111 0101	1111 1000

To convert this to a binary integer, these steps must be followed:

1. The so-called *zone bits* 1111 of the EBCDIC scheme must be removed for each digit.
2. The remaining bits of each digit, i.e., the bits that represent each digit in binary form, must be multiplied by the appropriate power of 10.
3. Each of the products in Step 2 must be added together to form the binary integer result.

Figure 8.10   *Translating a nonnegative integer from EBCDIC to binary.*

```
           .
           .
           .
 1   * THIS SET OF STATEMENTS TRANSLATES A NONNEGATIVE INTEGER
 2   * FROM ITS EBCDIC REPRESENTATION TO ITS FULL-WORD BINARY REPRESENTATION
 3   *
 4   *
 5   * THE EBCDIC REPRESENTATION IS ASSUMED TO BE EIGHT BYTES LONG, RIGHT-
 6   * JUSTIFIED, BEGINNING AT SYMBOLIC ADDRESS 'INT10'. IT MAY HAVE
 7   * LEADING ZEROES OR LEADING BLANKS
 8   *
 9   * THE RESULTING BINARY REPRESENTATION WILL BE STORED AT 'INT2'.
10   *
11   *    INITIALIZATION
12            LA    2,INT10X      R2 = ADDR OF LOW-ORDER BYTE
13            LA    3,P10         R3 = ADDR OF TABLE OF  10**N
14            LH    4,=H'8'       R4 = MAX # DIGITS TO BE TRANSLATED
15            LH    5,=H'0'       R5 = ACCUMULATED RESULT (INITIALLY ZERO)
16   *
17   NEXT     CLI   0(2),X'F0'    IF CURRENT BYTE VALUE NOT BETWEEN
18            BL    DONE            0 AND 9 (IN EBCDIC) THEN A LEADING
19            CLI   0(2),X'F9'    BLANK HAS BEEN REACHED.
20            BH    DONE
21   *                          MULTIPLY CURRENT DIGIT BY 10**N :
22            IC    7,0(2)          PUT EBCDIC DIGIT INTO ODD-NUMBERED
23            N     7,PATTERN     REGISTER, AND REMOVE ITS ZONE BITS.
24            M     6,0(3)        THEN MPY BY CURRENT POWER OF 10, AND
25            AR    5,7           ADD PRODUCT TO RESULT IN REG 5.
26   *
27            SH    2,=H'+1'      FOR LOOP CONTROL, ADJUST BYTE ADDRESS
28            AH    3,=H'+4'        TO NEXT DIGIT, AND TABLE ADDR TO NEXT
29            BCT   4,NEXT          10**N; THEN REPEAT UP TO EIGHT TIMES.
30   *
31   DONE     ST    5,INT2        SAVE RESULTING BINARY INTEGER
                    .
                    .
                    .
32   INT2     DS    F             BINARY INTEGER RESULT (FULL WORD)
33   INT10    DS    CL8           EIGHT EBCDIC DIGITS, RIGHT-JUSTIFIED
34   INT10X   EQU   *-1           ADDR OF LEAST SIGNIFICANT EBCDIC DIGIT
35   PATTERN  DC    X'0000000F'   MASK PRESERVES RIGHT-MOST FOUR BITS
36   *
37   P10      DC    F'1,10,100,1000'      TABLE OF POWERS OF 10,  I.E.
38            DC    F'1E4,1E5,1E6,1E7'     10**N  FOR  N = 0,1,2,...,7
                    .
                    .
                    .
```

For the number 1358, this works as follows:

Step 1: $\underbrace{1111\ 0001}$ $\underbrace{1111\ 0011}$ $\underbrace{1111\ 0101}$ $\underbrace{1111\ 1000}$

                 0001   0011   0101   1000

Step 2:   Since $10^3 = 0011\ 1110\ 1000$ in binary

$10^2 =$ $0110\ 0100$ in binary

$10^1 =$ 1010 in binary

$10^0 =$ 0001 in binary

then, for the number 1358,

$$1 \times 10^3 = 0001 \times 0011\ 1110\ 1000 = 0011\ 1110\ 1000 = 3E8 \text{ in hex}$$
$$3 \times 10^2 = 0011 \times \quad\quad 0110\ 0100 = 0001\ 0010\ 1100 = 12C \text{ in hex}$$
$$5 \times 10^1 = 0101 \times \quad\quad\quad\quad 1010 = \quad\quad 0011\ 0010 = 32 \text{ in hex}$$
$$8 \times 10^0 = 1000 \times \quad\quad\quad\quad 0001 = \quad\quad\quad\quad 1000 = 8 \text{ in hex}$$

Step 3: The resulting binary integer is the sum of the products just formed, namely 0101 0100 1110, or 54E in hex.

This three-step procedure forms the basis for the programming solution in Figure 8.10. However, there is one main difference between the program's design and the three steps: the program does the three steps for each digit in turn, *accumulating* the sum of Step 3 as it goes, and processing the digits from *right to left* (low order to high order). A maximum of eight digits is allowed; the program stops when it reaches this limit or when it finds a nondigit character such as a blank in the EBCDIC representation.

Let us illustrate how the program works, with a trace for the number 1358. We make the following address assumption:

$$\text{INT10} = 4000_{16}$$

All other addresses shown in the trace can be derived from this one. In the trace, the numbers shown are those that exist *immediately after Statement 25 is executed* during each iteration of the loop.

	contents of registers shown in hexadecimal					
iteration	Reg 2	Reg 3	Reg 4	Reg 5	Reg 6	Reg 7
1st	4007	400C	8	0000 0008	0	0000 0008
2nd	4006	4010	7	0000 003A	0	0000 0032
3rd	4005	4014	6	0000 0166	0	0000 012C
4th	4004	4018	5	0000 054E	0	0000 03E8

At this point the program has completed its calculations, the result being in Register 5.

There are several things to notice about the program:

1. The number 1358 is assumed to exist in symbolic location INT10, i.e., memory location 4000, like this:

40	40	40	40	F1	F3	F5	F8

The program, however, will work equally well for any positive integer that contains no more than 8 digits.

2. The digits are processed right to left, so the initial address in Register 2, namely 4007, is the address of the right-most digit. This address is decreased by 1 in Statement 27, once during each iteration of the loop. This decrease allows the right-to-left processing.

3. Statement 22 places the current EBCDIC digit in Register 7, and Statement 23 removes all but the low-order 4 bits from Register 7.

4. Statement 24 multiplies the low-order 4 bits of the current digit by the appropriate power of 10, as was done in the hand calculations of Step 2. Statement 24 gets the appropriate power of 10 from the table located at symbolic address P10; this table is accessed via Register 3.

5. Statement 25 adds the result of the multiplication to the sum being accumulated in Register 5.

Because we frequently need to convert a number from EBCDIC format to binary integer format, the instruction set of the IBM 360 and 370 systems contains two instructions designed for this purpose. These are the PACK and CVB instructions, which were briefly introduced in Chapter 4 and will be discussed more extensively in Chapter 12. Correspondingly, we can perform the reverse translation from binary integer to EBCDIC format with the CVD instruction, in conjunction with either the UNPK, the ED, or the EDMK instructions. See Chapter 12 for the necessary details.

The instructions classified as bit manipulation instructions are summarized in Figure 8.11. Since individual bits are not addressable in the IBM 360 and 370 systems, all but two of the instructions must specify the address of a register and/or memory location that contains the bits to be operated on. The two exceptions are the BC and BCR instructions. In these, the bits that are tested are not explicitly addressed; instead they are always understood to be the two condition code bits.

The eight shift instructions are distinguished from one another by the direction of the shift (right or left), the length and location of the quantity being shifted (32 bits in any general register, or 64 bits in an even-odd pair of registers), and the manner in which the sign bit and the result are handled (arithmetically or logically). *Logical shifts* are useful in separating and linking bit strings, as in the examples of Figures 8.8 and 8.9. Logical shifts treat the sign bit the same as any other bit and do not set the condition code. *Arithmetic shifts* are useful in situations where the sign bit must be propagated, for example in extending a full-word integer to a double-word representation; they are also useful as a means of multiplying or dividing by powers of two. Arithmetic right shifts cause the sign bit to be propagated to the right; arithmetic left shifts compare the sign bit (bit 0) to each bit shifted out of bit position 1 and set the condition code to 3 (overflow) if any such pair of bits is unequal. Except in the case of overflow, arithmetic shifts set the condition code to 0, 1, or 2, depending on whether the result is zero, negative, or positive, respectively.

The Boolean instructions OR, AND, and EXCLUSIVE-OR allow individual bits to be set to 1, reset to 0, or inverted. The address of the register or memory location containing the bits must be specified in the instruction, and the bits to be set or reset must be selected by a mask field. The mask field is in a general register when an RR-type Boolean instruction is used; it is in a memory location when an RX- or SS_1-type Boolean instruction is used; and it is in the immediate data field for SI-type instructions. Boolean instructions are especially useful for the control of bits that represent the occurrence of events or other status information.

Of the two bit-testing instructions Test Under Mask (TM) and Test and Set (TS), the TM is more frequently used because it allows the setting of one or more bits in a byte to be tested. The TS tests only the left-most bit of a byte, and, unlike the TM, it sets all the bits in that byte to 1's. Both TM and TS set the condition code, so that the result of the test can be determined by a conditional branch instruction.

The BC and BCR instructions test the current setting of the condition code and branch if the setting matches one or more of the settings selected by the mask field of the instruction. Since the condition code records the nature of the result of the most recently executed code-setting instruction, as defined in Figure 8.5, the BC and BCR instructions provide the means by which conditional branches (IF-type instructions) are executed at run time. The so-called extended mnemonics—BE, BER, BZ, BZR, etc.—are nothing but convenient abbreviations, as it were, of particular BC or BCR instructions. It is the mask-field contents, not the machine language opcode, that distinguish one RX- or RR-type extended mnemonic instruction from another.

8.7 REVIEW _____

Selecting Bits   Individual bits do not have memory addresses; the smallest addressable memory unit is a byte. Operations on bits therefore must either select bits from within bytes or words or operate on all the bits in a byte or word. Bit selection in most cases is done by means of a mask.

B- and X-Type Constants   These types of constants specify the value of bits in one or more bytes via a DC operand, a literal, or a self-defining term. In X-type constants, each hex digit (0 thru F) represents four consecutive bits (0000 thru 1111), as defined in Figure 1.5 of Chapter 1.

Shifting   Any register's contents, as well as the contents of an even-odd register pair, can be shifted (i.e., moved) N bits to the left or right by instructions designed for that purpose. There are no instructions that shift bits in memory.

Arithmetic Shifts   In these shifts, the sign bit is not shifted; only the numeric bits are. But the sign bit fills vacated bit positions in right shifts, and it is used to detect overflow in left shifts. The condition code is set to reflect the nature of the result: zero, negative, positive, or overflow.

Logical Shifts   In these shifts, the sign bit is shifted the same number of positions as all other bits are. Vacated bit positions are always filled with zeroes. An overflow cannot occur (i.e., it is irrelevant), and the condition code is not set.

Figure 8.11 Summary of bit manipulation instructions.

opcode	name	type	section	condition codes	summary of action taken
BC	Branch on Condition	RX	8.4		branches to addr of V_2, if cond. codes selected by M1
BCR	Branch on Condition via Register	RR	8.4		branches to addr in R1, if cond. codes selected by M1
N	AND	RX	8.2	0,1	V_1 replaced by AND of V_1 and V_2 (32 bits)
NC	AND Characters	SS$_1$	8.2	0,1	V_1 replaced by AND of V_1 and V_2 (L bytes, $L \le 256$)
NI	AND Immediate	SI	8.2	0,1	V_1 replaced by AND of V_1 and I2 (1 byte)
NR	AND Registers	RR	8.2	0,1	V_1 replaced by AND of V_1 and V_2 (32 bits)
O	OR	RX	8.2	0,1	V_1 replaced by OR of V_1 and V_2 (32 bits)
OC	OR Characters	SS$_1$	8.2	0,1	V_1 replaced by OR of V_1 and V_2 (L bytes, $L \le 256$)
OI	OR Immediate	SI	8.2	0,1	V_1 replaced by OR of V_1 and I2 (1 byte)
OR	OR Registers	RR	8.2	0,1	V_1 replaced by OR of V_1 and V_2 (32 bits)
SLA	Shift Left Single Arithmetic	RS	8.1	0,1,2,3	V_1 arithmetically shifted left N bits, $N \le 31$
SLDA	Shift Left Double Arithmetic	RS	8.1	0,1,2,3	V_1 arithmetically shifted left N bits, $N \le 63$
SLDL	Shift Left Double Logical	RS	8.1		V_1 logically shifted left N bits, $N \le 63$
SLL	Shift Left Single Logical	RS	8.1		V_1 logically shifted left N bits, $N \le 31$
SRA	Shift Right Single Arithmetic	RS	8.1	0,1,2	V_1 arithmetically shifted right N bits, $N \le 31$
SRDA	Shift Right Double Arithmetic	RS	8.1	0,1,2	V_1 arithmetically shifted right N bits, $N \le 63$
SRDL	Shift Right Double Logical	RS	8.1		V_1 logically shifted right N bits, $N \le 63$
SRL	Shift Right Single Logical	RS	8.1		V_1 logically shifted right N bits, $N \le 31$
TM	Test under Mask	SI	8.3	0,1,3	tests bits in V_1 selected by M1 mask field
TS	Test and Set	S	8.3	0,1	tests high-order bit of V_1 and sets all V_1 bits to 1
X	EXCLUSIVE-OR	RX	8.2	0,1	V_1 replaced by EXCL-OR of V_1 and V_2 (32 bits)
XC	EXCLUSIVE-OR Characters	SS$_1$	8.2	0,1	V_1 replaced by EXCL-OR of V_1 and V_2 (L bytes, $L \le 256$)
XI	EXCLUSIVE-OR Immediate	SI	8.2	0,1	V_1 replaced by EXCL-OR of V_1 and I2 (1 byte)
XR	EXCLUSIVE-OR Registers	RR	8.2	0,1	V_1 replaced by EXCL-OR of V_1 and V_2 (32 bits)

Note: V_1 denotes the quantity whose address is specified via the first operand of the instruction; V_2 denotes the quantity whose address is specified via the second operand.

Boolean Operations The Boolean "and," "or," and "not" operations are provided by the AND, OR, and EXCLUSIVE-OR instructions. These instructions depend on a mask to select the target bits that are operated on. AND preserves the selected bits; OR sets the selected bits; and EXCL-OR reverses the selected bits. See Figures 8.3a-c.

Bit Testing The value of bits can be tested via the Test under Mask (TM) instruction. The tested bits must all be in the same memory byte. TM's mask selects the bits to be tested; bits not selected are not tested. The result can be determined by conditional branch instructions.

Condition Code The condition code is a 2-bit hardware indicator whose value and meaning is determined by the most recently executed code-setting instruction. Many but not all instructions set the condition code (see Figs. 8.5a and 8.5b). The value of the code can be determined only by executing conditional branch instructions.

Conditional Branch Instructions The BC (Branch on Condition) instruction underlies the extended mnemonic conditional branch instructions such as BZ, BE, etc. See Figure 8.6a. Each binary "1" in the 4-bit mask of a BC's operand selects a different value of the condition code. This permits any combination of condition code values to be simultaneously tested by a BC instruction. The BCR instruction is analogous to the BC instruction (see Fig. 8.6b), except that the BCR operand must specify a register that contains the address to which it branches.

Unconditional Branches The Branch (B) instruction is a BC that branches no matter what the condition code is. Analogously, the BR (Branch via Register) is a BCR; it is used when returning from a subroutine.

NOP A No-Operation (NOP) instruction is a BC that doesn't branch, no matter what the condition code is. Analogously, the NOPR is a BCR. NOP's do what their names imply: no operation is performed; instead, the CPU proceeds to the next instruction.

8.8 REVIEW QUESTIONS

1. What bit strings are represented by these literals: =X'7F', =X'AAA', =B'1010', =B'111'? By these 4-bit masks: X'8', X'1', B'01', B'10'?
2. What happens to the vacated bit positions when an arithmetic right or left shift is executed? What happens to the vacated positions when a logical right or left shift is executed?
3. Explain the conditions under which a left-shift instruction can be used as an alternative to a multiply instruction. Can a right shift be similarly used as an alternative to a divide instruction? Why or why not?
4. If the value of the target byte at symbolic address BYTE is X'77' before execution of each of the following instructions, what is its value after each one is executed:

```
    OI   BYTE,X'78'      NI   BYTE,X'78'      XI   BYTE,X'78'
```

5. If the value of the target byte at symbolic address BYTE is X'77', which of the following pairs of instructions will cause a branch to location TRUE, and why:

```
TM   BYTE,X'78'      TM   BYTE,'78'      TM   BYTE,X'78'
BZ   TRUE            BM   TRUE           BO   TRUE
```

6. What is the value of the condition code when the result of any compare instruction is equal? Less than? Greater than? (See Fig. 8.5a.)
7. What is the value of the condition code when the result of any code-setting integer arithmetic instruction is zero? Negative? Positive? (See Fig. 8.5a.)
8. What integer arithmetic instructions do not set the condition code? What byte manipulation instructions do not set it? What bit manipulation instructions do not set it? (See Fig. 8.5b.)
9. Other than the instruction type and length, what is the only difference between the RX-type conditional branch instructions and the RR-type ones?
10. Why must hex digits be converted to EBCDIC format in order to be printed?
11. After examining the program segment of Figure 8.9, explain exactly what is accomplished by the SLDL instruction in Statement #13, the LA instruction in Statement #14, and the MVC instruction in Statement #15.

Problem Statement

Write a program that will read an arbitrary number of input records and print an encoded version of them, one line per record. The encoded version is to be obtained by interchanging the high-order four bits in each EBCDIC character with the low-order four bits of that character, and then inverting each of the four new high-order bits. For example, the letter 'A' is represented as hexadecimal C1 (1100 0001) in the input data and would be encoded to hexadecimal EC (1110 1100) since X'C1' becomes X'1C' when the high- and low-order bits are interchanged, and then the four new high-order bits, 0001, when inverted become 1110.

This encoding scheme has the advantage of being simple to implement and of being invertible; it has the disadvantage of being exceptionally easy to decipher.

Solution Procedure

The procedure (Figs. 8.12a–8.12b) for each input record that is read is to encode each character in a register, using the SHIFT, OR, and EXCLUSIVE-OR instructions, and then move the encoded character to its appropriate position in the output line area. When all the characters of a given input record have been encoded and moved to the output area, the line is printed.

Note that some of the encoded characters may not be among those that are printable, as described in Figure 7.1 of the preceding chapter. In that case, the printer or terminal will most likely print a blank in the character's stead. Some printers, however, will not print anything (i.e., the unprintable character will be treated as a null character), and some printers will not accept the unprintable character, causing the program to be terminated with an output data error. You will have to determine what the response of your printer or terminal is by running the program solution given in Figure 8.12b.

Figure 8.12a   Pseudocode for sample problem solution in Figure 8.12b.

```
ENCODE:

   open input and output files;

   REPEAT WHILE there is more data to read

      read one input record;

      REPEAT FOR i := 1, 2, ..., 80
        encode ith character;
      END FOR;

      print encoded record;

   END WHILE;

   close all files;

EXIT ENCODE.
```

Figure 8.12b   Solution to sample problem.

```
 000000                                          3  SPCH8     CSECT
                                                 4  *
                                                 5  * SPCH8  READS AN ARBITRARY NUMBER OF INPUT DATA CARDS
                                                 6  *    AND PRINTS AN ENCODED VERSION OF THEM, ONE CARD PER LINE.
                                                 7  *
                                                 8  *    THE ENCODED VERSION IS OBTAINED BY INTERCHANGING THE HIGH-ORDER
                                                 9  *    FOUR BITS WITH THE LOW ORDER FOUR BITS OF EACH EBCDIC CHARACTER
                                                10  *    AND THEN INVERTING EACH OF THE FOUR NEW HIGH-ORDER BITS.
                                                11  *
                                                12  *    E.G.,  THE LETTER 'A'  IS X'C1' AND WOULD BECOME X'EC',
                                                13  *    SINCE X'C1' IS FIRST TRANSFORMED TO X'1C', AND
                                                14  *    THEN THE '1' (B'0001') IS TRANSFORMED INTO 'E' (B'1110').
                                                15  *
 000000 90 EC 000C                             16            STM    14,12,12(13)        STANDARD ENTRY
 000004 05 C0                                  17            BALR   12,0
 000006                                        18            USING  *,12
 000006 50 D0 C22E        000234               19            ST     13,SAVE+4
 00000A 41 D0 C22A        000230               20            LA     13,SAVE
                                               21  *
                                               22  * OPEN INPUT AND OUTPUT FILES
                                               23  *
 00000E                                        24            OPEN   (SYSIN,(INPUT))     INPUT IS 'SYSIN' DATA STREAM
 00001A                                        30            OPEN   (SYSPRNT,(OUTPUT))  OUTPUT IS 'SYSOUT' PRINTER

                                               36  *  DOS  *******
                                               37  *         OPEN   SYSIN
                                               38  *         OPEN   SYSPRNT
                                               39  ***************

                                               40  *
                                               41  * MAIN PROCESSING LOOP ...
                                               42  *        READS AN INPUT DATA CARD
                                               43  *        TRANSFORMS IT AS DESCRIBED IN COMMENTS ABOVE
                                               44  *        WRITES THE TRANSFORMED DATA ONTO PRINTER FILE
                                               45  *        CONTINUES READING, TRANSFORMING, AND WRITING TILL END-OF-DATA
                                               46  *        END-OF-DATA ROUTINE IS AT 'EOD', JUST TO TERMINATE PROGRAM.
                                               47  *
 000026                                        48  LOOP      GET    SYSIN,INAREA        GET AN INPUT DATA CARD
                                               53  *
 000034 41 50 C096        00009C               54            LA     5,INAREA            INITIALIZE CHARACTER ADDRESS
 000038 58 60 C272        000278               55            L      6,=F'80'            INITIALIZE CHARACTER COUNT
                                               56  *
                                               57  * TRANSFORM EACH INPUT CHARACTER ONE AT A TIME
                                               58  *
 00003C 58 80 C276        00027C               59  TRANS     L      8,=F'0'             CLEAR R8 TO ZEROS
                                               60  *
 000040 43 85 0000        000000               61            IC     8,0(5)   R8 BITS 24-31 GET EBCDIC BITS 0-7.
 000044 88 80 0004        000004               62            SRL    8,4      RIGHT SHIFT PUTS EBCDIC BITS 0-3 INTO
                                               63  *                         R8 BITS 28-31 AND 0'S INTO R8 BITS 24-27
                                               64  *
 000048 43 95 0000        000000               65            IC     9,0(5)   R9 BITS 24-31 GET EBCDIC BITS 0-7.
 00004C 89 90 0004        000004               66            SLL    9,4      LEFT SHIFT PUTS EBCDIC BITS 4-7 INTO
                                               67  *                         R9 BITS 24-27 AND 0'S INTO R9 BITS 28-31
                                               68  *
 000050 16 89                                  69            OR     8,9      R8 BITS 24-27 GET EBCDIC BITS 4-7 FROM R9.
                                               70  *
 000052 42 85 0000        000000               71            STC    8,0(5)   STORE REPLACES EBCDIC BITS 0-3 & 4-7
                                               72  *                         WITH EBCDIC BITS 4-7 & 0-3, RESPECTVLY.
                                               73  *
 000056 97 F0 5000                             74            XI     0(5),X'F0'    INVERT NEW EBCDIC BITS 0-3 IN MEMORY
                                               75  *
 00005A 41 55 0001        000001               76            LA     5,1(5)              INCR TO NEXT CHAR
 00005E 46 60 C036        00003C               77            BCT    6,TRANS             REPEAT TILL NO MORE CHARS
                                               78  *
                                               79  * COPY INPUT DATA TO OUTPUT LINE AND PRINT IT
                                               80  *
 000062 D2 4F C0F0C096 0000F6 00009C           81            MVC    OUTLINE,INAREA
 000068                                        82            PUT    SYSPRNT,OUTAREA
 000076 47 F0 C020        000026               87            B      LOOP
                                               88  *
                                               89  * END-OF-DATA TRANSFERS CONTROL HERE TO TERMINATE PROGRAM.
                                               90  *
 00007A                                        91  EOD       CLOSE  (SYSIN)
 000086                                        97            CLOSE  (SYSPRNT)
 000092 58 D0 C22E        000234              103            L      13,SAVE+4           STANDARD EXIT
 000096 98 EC 000C                           104            LM     14,12,12(13)
 00009A 07 FE                                105            BR     14
                                             106  *  DOS  *******
                                             107  *EOD       CLOSE SYSIN
                                             108  *          CLOSE SYSPRNT
                                             109  *          EOJ
                                             110  ***************

                                             111  *
                                             112  * INPUT CARD AREA
                                             113  *
 00009C                                      114  INAREA    DS     0CL80               INPUT AREA DEFINITION ...
 00009C                                      115            DS     CL80                COLS 1-80  INPUT CARD
```

Figure 8.12b   continued

```
FLAG LOCTN OBJECT CODE    ADDR1  ADDR2  STMNT M SOURCE STATEMENT

                                         116   *
                                         117   * OUTPUT PRINT AREA
                                         118   *
    0000EC                                119   OUTAREA  DS   0CL132              OUTPUT AREA DEFINITION ...
    0000EC 4040404040404040               120            DC   CL10' '             COLS 1-10  BLANKS
    0000F6                                121   OUTLINE  DS   CL80                      11-90  INPUT DATA
    000146 4040404040404040               122            DC   CL42' '                  91-132 BLANKS
                                         123   *
                                         124   *
                                         125   * DCB'S FOR INPUT AND OUTPUT FILES
                                         126   *
    000170                                127   SYSIN    DCB  DSORG=PS,MACRF=(GM),DDNAME=SYSIN,EODAD=EOD,        X
                                         128            RECFM=FB,LRECL=80,BLKSIZE=4080
                                         180   *
    0001D0                                181   SYSPRNT  DCB  DSORG=PS,MACRF=(PM),DDNAME=SYSPRINT,               X
                                         182            RECFM=FB,LRECL=132,BLKSIZE=4092
                                         234   *  DOS  *******
                                         235   *SYSIN   DTFCD DEVADDR=SYSIPT,WORKA=YES,IOAREA1=INBUF,EOFADDR=EOD, X
                                         236            DEVICE=2540
                                         237   *SYSPRNT DTFPR DEVADDR=SYSLST,WORKA=YES,IOAREA1=OUTBUF,BLKSIZE=132, X
                                         238   *        DEVICE=1403
                                         239   *
                                         240   *INBUF   DS   CL80
                                         241   *OUTBUF  DC   CL132' '
                                         242   ***************
                                         243   *
                                         244   * SAVE AREA
                                         245   *
    000230                                246   SAVE     DS   18F
                                         247   *  DOS  *******
                                         248   *SAVE    DS   9D
                                         249   ***************
                                         250   * LITERALS
    000278 00000050                       252                 =F'80'
    00027C 00000000                       253                 =F'0'
                                         254            END
```

```
          CROSS-REFERENCE


SYMBOL    LEN   VALUE  DEFN   REFERENCES

EOD      00004 00007C 00093  00149
INAREA   00050 00009C 00114  00050  00054  00081
LOOP     00004 000026 00049  00087
OUTAREA  00084 0000EC 00119  00084
OUTLINE  00050 0000F6 00121  00081
SAVE     00004 000230 00246  00019  00020  00103
SPCH8    00001 000000 00003
SYSIN    00004 000170 00128  00028  00049  00095
SYSPRNT  00004 0001D0 00182  00034  00083  00101
TRANS    00004 00003C 00059  00077
```

1. What would be the contents of Registers 6 and 7 after each of the following shift instructions was executed? Assume that *before* each instruction is executed, the contents of Registers 6 and 7 are as follows:

   Reg 6: X'01234567'   Reg 7: X'89ABCDEF'

a. SRA	6,4	**e.** SLA	6,6	**i.** SLDL	6,63
b. SRA	7,8	**f.** SLDA	6,6	**j.** SRDL	6,63
c. SRL	6,4	**g.** SLL	6,8	**k.** SLL	7,31
d. SRL	7,8	**h.** SLDL	6,8	**l.** SRDA	6,32

2. Assume that before each of the following instructions is executed, the contents of the memory location whose symbolic address is Y is as follows:

   Y   DC   X'0189'

   What would be the contents of location Y after each of the following instructions was executed?

a. NI	Y,X'F0'	**e.** XC	Y,=X'0189'	**i.** NC	Y,=X'FFFF'
b. NI	Y,X'00'	**f.** OC	Y,=X'0189'	**j.** OC	Y,=X'FFFF'
c. OI	Y,X'F0'	**g.** NC	Y,=X'FF00'	**k.** XC	Y,=X'FFFF'
d. OI	Y,X'0F'	**h.** XC	Y,=X'FF00'	**l.** XI	Y,X'89'

3. Suppose that, as in Chapter 5, we represent the kth bit in a register with the symbol b_k, $k = 0,1,2,...,31$, where b_0 represents the sign bit. Then the contents of a register can be represented as $b_0 b_1 b_2...b_{31}$. Write a sequence of instructions that will interchange bits $b_0 b_1... b_n$ of a register with bits $b_{n+1} b_{n+2}...b_{31}$, for any n such that $0 \leq n \leq 30$. For example, if the register contents exist as

   0000 0001 0010 0011 0100 0101 0110 0111

   and if $n = 15$, then the resulting register contents would be

   0100 0101 0110 0111 0000 0001 0010 0011

4. It is sometimes desirable to convert a byte string to some other byte string, in such a manner that reconversion to the original string is possible. This is known as *encoding* the original string, the reconversion being *decoding*. Assume that an arbitrary byte string (of length less than or equal to 256 bytes) exists at the memory location whose symbolic address is STR. The string's length is stored as a half-word integer at location LNG.

   For each of the following encoding schemes, write a sequence of instructions that will replace the string at STR with its encoded version. Also, for each of the schemes write a sequence of instructions that will decode the encoded version of a string.

   a. Interchange bits 0–3 of each byte with bits 4–7 of that byte.
   b. Shift the entire string right 4 bits, with the original right-most 4 bits becoming the new left-most 4 bits.
   c. Generate the bit-by-bit complement of each byte in the string.
   d. For each 4 consecutive bytes in the string, generate the complement of just those bits whose relative positions correspond to the 1's in an arbitrary full-word integer. If when the string's length is divided by 4, the remainder is $N \neq 0$, then use the first N bytes of the integer to encode the last N bytes of the string.
   e. For each K consecutive bytes in the original string, generate the complement of just those bits whose relative positions correspond to the 1's in an arbitrary K-byte string. If, when the original string's length is divided by K, the remainder is $N \neq 0$, use the first N bytes of the arbitrary K-byte string to encode the last N bytes of the original string.

5. Write a sequence of instructions that will determine the relative position, k ($k = 0,1,2,...,31$), of the left-most 1-bit in any nonzero full-word integer, and store the result as a 1-byte nonnegative integer whose value is $4*k$. For example, if the arbitrary full-word integer is

$$0000\ 0001\ 0010\ 0011\ 0100\ 0101\ 0110\ 0111$$

then $k = 7$, and the 1-byte result is 0001 1100.

6. Rewrite the program statements given in Figure 8.10 so that if the value of the decimal integer
$d_0 d_1 d_2 ... d_7$ (where d_n is a decimal digit) is

$$d_0 \times 10^7 + d_1 \times 10^6 + ... + d_6 \times 10^1 + d_7 \times 10^0$$

then your conversion algorithm computes this value by effectively grouping terms and performing the arithmetic as follows:

$$(...((d_0 \times 10 + d_1) \times 10 + d_2) \times 10 + ... + d_6) \times 10 + d_7$$

7. Suppose there exists an arbitrary bit string of 1024 bits (32 full words) at the memory location whose symbolic address is BITS. Write assembly language statements that can be used to search this bit string for all occurrences of a 4-bit string given (right-justified) in location PAT, and replace each occurrence with a 4-bit string of all 0's.

8. Suppose, as in Exercise 7, that an arbitrary 1024-bit string exists at symbolic address BITS. Write the assembly language statements that can be used to replace each occurrence of m consecutive 0's—for any m such that $8 \le m \le 256$—with 16 bits, the first 8 of which are all 0's, and the last 8 of which are the binary representation of $m-1$. For example, if the original string consisted of 1024 0's, the resulting string would consist of just 64 bits, as follows:

$$00000000\ 11111111\ 00000000\ 11111111\ 00000000\ ...\ 11111111$$

9. Suppose that a bit string has been transformed by the procedure described in Exercise 8, and that the transformed string is at symbolic address NEWBITS, its length (in numbers of bits) being stored as a half-word integer at symbolic address NEWLNG. Write the assembly language statements that can be used to recreate the original bit string from the transformed string.

10. In the IBM 360 and 370 systems, main memory addresses that end in three hex zeroes are said to define a page boundary. A main memory page consists of 4096 ($=1000_{16}$) consecutive bytes, beginning at a page boundary. If main memory addresses consist of 24 bits, then each page is identified by the high-order 12 bits of its page boundary address. This quantity is known as the page number. If there are $4 \times N \times 2^{10}$ bytes of main memory, then there are N pages of main memory ($N=1,2,...,4096$).

Suppose that $N = 1024$—a 4 megabyte main memory—and suppose that an N-bit string has been defined so that there is a one-to-one correspondence between bits of the string and pages of main memory, bit k corresponding to page k. Suppose also that when bit k is a 0, page k is not in use at the moment, and that when bit k is a 1, page k is in use by some program.

   a. Write the assembly language statements that will count the number of pages that are not in use at any given moment.
   b. Write assembly language statements that will change the status bit for page k to "in use," for any k such that $0 \le k \le 1023$.
   c. Write assembly language statements that will change the status bit for page k to "not in use."
   d. Write assembly language statements that will determine the largest page number, m, such that page m is not in use.

11. In the terminology of Exercise 10, suppose that instead of an N-bit string that records the status of each main memory page as being "in use" or "not in use," there is an N-*byte* string that records the status of each memory page, one byte per page. Assume that the bits of each page-status byte have the following meaning:

Bit 0	0 = "not in use,"	1 = "in use"
Bit 1	0 = "system page,"	1 = "user page"
Bit 2	0 = "read-only page,"	1 = "writable page"
Bit 3	(not used for any purpose)	
Bits 4–7	4-bit priority number, 0000–1111_2	

a. Write the assembly language statements that will count the number of user pages with priority number greater than eight that are not in use at any given moment.

b. Write assembly language statements that will determine the largest page number, m, such that page m is a "read-only user page" that has a priority number greater than eight and is not in use.

c. Write assembly language statements that will determine the number of user pages that are read-only and the number that are writable.

d. Write assembly language statements that will determine how many in-use pages exist for each of the sixteen possible priority numbers.

CHAPTER

9

Internal Subroutines

Introductory Concepts

A **subroutine** is a set of statements that may be used at one or more points in a computer program to perform some task at the request of that program. An **internal subroutine** is one whose statements are contained within the requesting program at assembly time. By contrast, an **external subroutine**—to be discussed in the next chapter—is one whose statements are assembled separately from the requesting program.

Alternate names for the concept of a subroutine are subprogram and procedure. Thus, Pascal procedures are subroutines, as are Fortran subprograms. Cobol's "Perform" verb jumps to what is in effect an internal subroutine, as does Basic's "GoSub" verb. In this book we will use the term subroutine to include all such examples, the prefix *sub* meaning "subordinate to the requesting program," and the word *routine* being synonymous with the idea of a "method of performing a commonly needed task."

Although a subroutine produces specific results for specific data, it is usually written so that it is capable of producing results for a wide range of data values. Therefore we can say that a subroutine can be a general programming solution to a specific problem.

The primary purpose of this chapter is to explain how a program makes a request to and receives results from an internal subroutine. As we shall also see, subroutines allow us to modularize the programming solution to a problem. That is, we can divide the problem into a number of manageably small and related subproblems, each with its own programming solution.

9.1   TERMINOLOGY

When a program requests that a subroutine perform its task, it is said to **call** that subroutine. The program making the request is known as the **caller.** The subroutine requested to perform the task is known as the **called program.** The address of the first instruction executed by a subroutine when it is called is the subroutine's **entry point.** The address of the instruction to which a subroutine branches when it returns to the caller is the caller's **reentry point.** These concepts are depicted in Figure 9.1.

Figure 9.1 Calling and called programs.

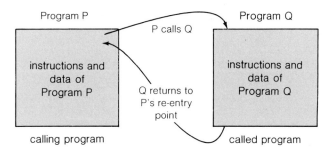

Figure 9.2 Sequence of called programs.

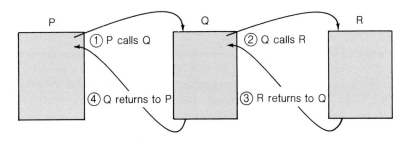

A **closed subroutine** is one written in such a way that a single copy of it is all that is required, no matter how many places it is used in a program. That is the type of subroutine under consideration in this chapter and also in Chapter 10. In contrast to a closed subroutine, an **open subroutine** must be inserted at each place it is used in a program. A macro's expansion, discussed in Chapter 17, is in effect an open subroutine.

There is no restriction on the number of times a program may call a subroutine, nor is there any restriction on the number of different places within a program from which a call may be made to a subroutine. Moreover, a called program may in turn call another program. If it does so, it becomes the caller for that encounter. However, a called program normally returns to the program that calls it. For example, in the sequence of Figure 9.2, Program P calls Program Q, and before Q returns to P it calls Program R. Only after R returns to Q does Q return to P.

9.2 LINKAGE

Since a closed subroutine can be called from any number of different places within a program, the caller has to be able to specify the reentry point to which the subroutine will return. In the IBM 360 and 370 systems, there are two instructions that do this: an RR-type Branch and Link via Register (**BALR**), and an RX-type Branch and Link (**BAL**) instruction. Both BALR and BAL do what their names imply: they branch to a subroutine and simultaneously provide the required link back to the caller, i.e., the reentry point address.

Calling a Subroutine

The RR-type BALR instruction will be needed when calling *ex*ternal subroutines, as will be seen in Chapter 10. For *in*ternal subroutines, we shall need only the RX-type BAL instruction.

To use BAL, the subroutine's entry point is specified symbolically in the second operand:

```
BAL     R1,symbol
```

BAL branches to the location specified by *symbol,* but before doing so it puts the address of the instruction that follows it into the register designated in its first operand. Let us assume that the BAL is at location A. Then, since the BAL is an RX-type instruction, its length is four bytes and the address it puts into the R1 register is A+4.

[Some models of the IBM 370 systems include the BAS (Branch and Save) instruction as an alternative to BAL. The only difference between BAL and BAS occurs when the reentry address is loaded into bits 8–31 of the R1 register: BAL puts the instruction length code in bits 0–1, the condition code in bits 2–3, the program mask bits in bits 4–7, and the reentry address in bits 8–31; BAS just puts X'00' in bits 0–7 and the reentry address in bits 8–31.]

The address placed into the first-operand register by a caller's BAL instruction is the caller's reentry point. Thus, both the entry point and the reentry point are specified by a single Branch and Link instruction. The reentry point is at the instruction following the BAL that calls the subroutine.

Returning from a Subroutine

It should now be clear how the called subroutine returns to the appropriate reentry point. In order to do so, the subroutine simply has to branch to the address that's in the register specified by the BAL that called it. As you may have guessed, there is an RR-type Branch via Register (**BR**) instruction that's designed to do just that:

$$\text{BR} \qquad \text{R1}$$

The BR instruction branches to the address contained in the register specified in its operand. By using this instruction, a subroutine is able to branch to whatever reentry point had been loaded into that register by the caller.

RR-Type Branches

You should recall that the BR and other extended mnemonic RR-type conditional branch instructions were discussed in Section 8.4 (see Fig. 8.6b). Among them were BER, BLR, and BHR, and their negative counterparts BNER, BNLR, and BNHR. For example, the BNER 14 instruction in the SKIP subroutine of Figure 9.3b in the next section branches to the address in Register 14 if the result of the CLI comparison is "not-equal." BR itself is an RR-type "Branch on Condition" instruction, BCR; but the condition it branches on is always true, so it always branches.

To summarize: An internal subroutine's entry point and the caller's reentry point are specified via a BAL instruction. The subroutine can return to the reentry point via a BR or other RR-type branch instruction, provided both the BAL and the RR-type branch use the same register for the reentry point address.

BAL's Reentry Register

Although there is no standardized register for the reentry point when calling an internal subroutine, the author recommends using Register 14, since that's the standard reentry-point register when calling external subroutines, and since it still leaves Registers 2 through 11 available for unrestricted use. However, this practice requires a word of caution: if a subroutine contains any I/O or other supervisor macro (such as OPEN, CLOSE, GET, PUT) or if a subroutine in turn calls another subroutine, then the contents of Register 14 need to be saved and restored by the subroutine.

Finally, note two subtle but interesting facts:

1. **Caller's perspective** If you look at the segment within the calling program where a BAL instruction is, and if you are unaware of what the BAL does or what is taking place in the subroutine that it is calling, then it could appear that the BAL does the subroutine's computations all by itself—the actual instructions that are doing the work are not immediately apparent. This is similar to the use of I/O macros that branch to other locations, including ones within the operating system, to carry out an I/O request.
2. **Subroutine's perspective** The person who programs a subroutine need not know what a caller's reentry point is. The subroutine itself doesn't know until the reentry point is passed to it at run time. And as we shall see in the next section, neither the programmer nor the subroutine needs to know what data is going to be operated on by the subroutine until that data is made available at run time.

9.3 ADDRESS CONSTANTS

Addresses are basic to the use of subroutines. We have already seen how important they are to the BAL instruction, which loads the caller's reentry point into a register just prior to branching to a subroutine's entry point. We now need to digress slightly to explain what an address constant is, since it is used by a caller as well as by a subroutine.

An **address constant** is a constant whose value is the value of an expression that can contain one or more name-field symbols. Like other constants in assembly language, an address constant can be specified either in a DC directive or as a literal. For example, the literal $=A(X)$ designates a full-word binary integer whose value is the value of the name-field symbol X. And for the same X, the value of the constant generated by the directive DC A(X) is the same as the value of the literal constant $=A(X)$.

To illustrate the concept of a symbol's value in relation to the contents of a memory location, consider this example:

```
          L     2,X
          LA    3,X
          L     4,=A(X)
              . . .
      X   DS    F
```

In this example, X is, of course, a symbolic address. Register 2 gets the number stored at the location whose symbolic address is X; i.e., it gets the contents of location X. But Register 3 and Register 4 each get the value of the symbol X, i.e., the numeric address of location X.

Notice that in address constants, you use a left and right parenthesis rather than apostrophes to enclose the expression: in other words, A(X) instead of A'X'.

Notice also that if W is defined by the EQU directive

```
          W     EQU   5
```

then an appropriate run-time constant involving W can be defined at assembly time as an A-type constant either by a literal or by a DC directive: $=A(W)$ or DC A(W). Thus, even though W does not represent a memory address, in other words even though it is an absolute rather than a relocatable constant, it can nevertheless be used in an address constant. But neither W nor any other symbol can occur in an F-type constant or in any of the other numeric constants; e.g., F'W' is not a valid assembly language constant.

One type of address constant that is sometimes useful involves the length attribute of a symbol. Recall from Chapter 6 that the **length attribute** of a symbol is the number of bytes that the assembler assigns to the memory area associated with the symbol. Recall also that a memory area is associated with a symbol when that symbol appears in the name field of a statement for which memory is allocated, such as an instruction or a DC or DS directive.

The notation for the length attribute of a symbol Z is L'Z. For any symbol Z the value of its length attribute, i.e., the value of L'Z, depends on the type of statement on which Z is defined, as follows:

1. If Z is defined in the name field of an instruction, then L'Z = 2, 4, or 6, depending on the instruction's length (2, 4, or 6 bytes).
2. If Z is defined in the name field of a DC or DS directive containing a length modifier L*n*, then L'Z = *n*.
3. If Z is defined in the name field of a DC or DS directive *not* containing a length modifier, then L'Z is the length of the constant: L'Z=2 for H-type constants, L'Z=4 for F-type constants, etc.

An A-type constant whose value is the value of L'Z is specified simply as A(L'Z).

Address constants can contain more than one field separated by commas: for example, A(X,Y,Z) is the same as three consecutive full-word address constants, the first being A(X), the second A(Y), and the third A(Z).

Finally, we should mention that in addition to A-type address constants, there are several other data-type codes for address constants, each with a specific purpose and meaning: V-, Y-, S-, and Q-. All but Q-type constants are available in both OS and DOS; the Q-type is available only in OS. In this chapter, we are concerned only with A-type constants; in Chapter 10 we shall also be concerned with V-type constants. The other types will not be discussed in this text.

To be of general use, a subroutine usually obtains specific data from the caller. It also puts its results in areas accessible to and usually designated by the caller. The data and the result areas are the subroutine's **parameters.**

We speak of formal parameters and actual parameters. The **actual parameters** are the ones that are specified by the caller when it calls a subroutine. The **formal parameters** are the ones that are referred to from within the subroutine so that the assembler can generate the instructions needed to access the actual parameters.

Parameter Requirements

The order in which the actual parameters are specified when a subroutine is called must be the same as the order in which the subroutine expects to receive them. Similarly, the data type of each actual parameter must be the same as the data type of the corresponding formal parameter. In short, the design of a subroutine dictates the manner in which it is called, not vice versa.

Specifying Parameters

We obviously need some way for the caller to specify the data and result areas. In other words, we need some way for the subroutine to know what its actual parameters are each time it is called. There are three methods:

1. The subroutine can specify symbolic addresses for its input data as well as for its output results.
2. The caller can specify either the address or the value of the parameters when it calls the subroutine, so that the subroutine does not need to specify symbolic addresses.
3. Some combination of Methods 1 and 2 can be used.

As an example to illustrate these methods, consider the following problem: Given the memory address of a character string, determine the address of the first nonblank character in the string.

Method 1 is shown in Figure 9.3a. In it, the subroutine gets the location of the string from the symbolic address STRING, and puts its result in the fixed location named BLANKADR. Neither of these symbols is defined by the internal subroutine. They are defined in another part of the calling program. The subroutine, being a segment within the calling program, has access to those symbols without their having to be defined by the subroutine itself.

Note from Figure 9.3a that the SKIP subroutine expects that the caller will use Register 14 for the reentry address, i.e., the caller's BAL instruction is expected to be BAL 14,SKIP because the subroutine returns to the caller via the address in Register 14. The same is true in the other solutions.

Method 2 is in Figure 9.3b. In it, the subroutine assumes that the address of the string has been placed in Register 2 by the caller, and it puts its results in Register 3. In this method, the caller is said to pass the parameter to the subroutine.

Note that in Method 2 both caller and subroutine MUST be in agreement about which registers are used for the parameters, and what the data type (in this case, A-type data) of each parameter is. In other words, the caller has to pass data and receive results in the precise manner dictated by the design of the subroutine.

Method 3 is in Figure 9.3c. In it, the data is obtained as in Method 1, and the result is returned as in Method 2.

Method 2 Revisited

Of the three methods, Method 2 is the most general, but it may also be the most obscure at this point. It is the most general because the addresses of the parameters that it uses are not determined at assembly time; instead they are determined at run time when the subroutine is called. This means that its data and results can be anywhere in memory, depending on the needs of the caller, and not just at the symbolic addresses STRING and BLANKADR.

On the other hand, Method 1 is the least general of the three methods, since its parameter addresses are definitely determined at assembly time. But probably Method 1 is the easiest to understand. So it may therefore be instructive to see how Method 1 is transformed into Method 2. The essential task in the transformation is to eliminate symbolic address references to the parameters.

Converting a Segment to a Subroutine

The author suggests that the best way to begin the process of writing a subroutine is to write it—or at least think of it—as a program segment instead of as a subroutine.

After you are convinced that your segment is correct, the next step is to decide what within the segment should be the subroutine's parameters, in other words, what should be allowed to vary each time the subroutine is called. When that is determined, then you can eliminate symbolic address

Figure 9.3a   *Internal subroutine with assembly-time parameters.*

```
* DETERMINE ADDR OF 1ST NON-BLANK CHARACTER IN A STRING
* CALLED VIA  BAL  14,SKIP
* PARAMETERS:   STRING = ADDR OF STRING
*               BLANKADR = ADDR OF 1ST NON-BLANK CHAR
*
SKIP      ST    3,SKIPR           SAVE REG 3 CONTENTS
          LA    3,STRING          GET ADDR OF STRING
SKIPL     CLI   0(3),C' '         LOOK FOR BLANKS
          BNE   SKIPX             STOP LOOP WHEN NON-BLANK FOUND
          LA    3,1(3)            ELSE, ADVANCE TO NEXT CHAR.
          B     SKIPL
SKIPX     ST    3,BLANKADR        STORE RESULT FOR CALLER
          L     3,SKIPR           RESTORE REG 3 CONTENTS
          BR    14                RETURN TO CALLER
SKIPR     DS    F                 RESERVED FOR REG 3
*------------------------------------------------------------
```

Figure 9.3b   *Internal subroutine with run-time parameters.*

```
* CALLED VIA  BAL  14,SKIP
* PARAMETERS:  R2 = ADDR OF STRING
*              R3 = ADDR OF RESULT
*
SKIP      LR    3,2               R3 = ADDR OF STRING
SKIPL     CLI   0(3),C' '         LOOK FOR BLANKS
          BNER  14                RETURN WHEN NON-BLANK FOUND
          LA    3,1(3)            ELSE, ADVANCE TO NEXT CHAR.
          B     SKIPL
*------------------------------------------------------------
```

Figure 9.3c   *Internal subroutine with assembly-time and run-time parameters.*

```
* CALLED VIA  BAL  14,SKIP
* PARAMETERS:   STRING = ADDR OF STRING
*               R3 = ADDR OF RESULT
*
SKIP      LA    3,STRING          R3 = ADDR OF STRING
SKIPL     CLI   0(3),C' '         LOOK FOR BLANKS
          BNER  14                RETURN WHEN NON-BLANK FOUND
          LA    3,1(3)            ELSE, ADVANCE TO NEXT CHAR.
          B     SKIPL
*------------------------------------------------------------
```

references to those items. In some cases this may require changing a symbolic address into an explicit base-displacement address. In other cases, it may require that a Load Address instruction be eliminated, since the address that it would have loaded will in fact be obtained from the caller. Other possibilities also exist and must be determined on a case-by-case basis.

The final step is to introduce appropriate "entry" and "exit" statements to complete the transformation from segment to subroutine.

Note that the subroutine in Figure 9.3a is almost a segment. In fact, if we were to omit the ST 3,SKIPR instruction at the beginning and the L 3,SKIPR and BR 14 instructions at the end, then it would indeed be a segment. If we were to start with this segment, then to change it into a Method 1 subroutine would just require us to put in the "entry" and "exit" statements.

Now look at Figure 9.3a and compare it to Figure 9.3b. You'll see that in Figure 9.3b we removed the LA 3,STRING instruction that was in Figure 9.3a. This was done because in Figure 9.3b the address of the string is obtained from the caller in Register 2 and simply copied into Register

3 by the LR 3,2 instruction. We also removed the ST 3,BLANKADR instruction, because the result is being returned to the caller in Register 3, not in a memory location. With these two changes, the dependence of the Method 1 solution on symbolic addresses for its parameters has been completely removed.

Our last observation is that in Figure 9.3b, since Register 3 is the only register being used by the subroutine, and since it is also being used to pass the result back to the caller, then there is no need to save and restore its contents as had been done in Figure 9.3a and as is discussed further below. With the inclusion of the "exit" statements (BNER 14 and BR 14), the transformation from Method 1 to Method 2 is completed.

Saving and Restoring Registers

Since there is only one set of registers, both caller and subroutine will often need to use the same registers. The simplest way to avoid register usage conflicts between caller and subroutine is this: Before it uses registers for its own needs, the subroutine should store the contents of all the registers that it is going to use. Then, just before returning to the caller, the subroutine should reload the contents of those registers that it had stored. In this way, the register contents needed by the caller will be the same after the subroutine has completed its work as they were before it began.

The process of storing and reloading register contents is known as "saving and restoring" the registers. This is what was done for Register 3 in Figure 9.3a. If this hadn't been done, and if the calling program depended on not having Register 3's contents changed by the subroutine, then upon return from the subroutine the calling program would very likely not work correctly.

The examples in the next section illustrate a fairly easy way to save and restore more than one register.

9.5   EXAMPLES

In Figures 9.4 and 9.5 we present internal subroutines, CVE and CVX, that could be called from more than one place in a program. Consequently, when passing parameters we use Method 2 from the previous section.

The CVE subroutine converts an integer from its full-word binary representation to its EBCDIC character representation. CVX converts from the EBCDIC representation of a hex integer (e.g., C'1A') to its equivalent full-word binary representation (in this case, B'00 ... 011010').

As can be seen from the figures, several registers need to have their contents saved and restored, and this is done via the STM and LM instructions. As you will recall from Chapter 5, the Store Multiple (**STM**) instruction is specifically designed to save the contents of *consecutive* registers, and the Load Multiple (**LM**) instruction is designed to restore them.

Calling Sequence

The arrangement of the instructions and parameters when calling a subroutine is known as the subroutine's *calling sequence*. Because of the design of CVE, the calling sequence for the CVE subroutine would be written as follows:

```
        LM      2,4,=A(X,E,N)
        BAL     14,CVE
```

The symbols X, E, and N represent memory areas defined as follows:

```
X       DS      F
E       DS      CL10
N       DC      A(L'E)
```

Similarly, the calling sequence for CVX would be this:

```
        LM      2,3,=A(G,Y)
        BAL     14,CVX
```

Figure 9.4   Convert binary integer to EBCDIC.

```
* CONVERTS FULLWORD BINARY INTEGER X TO N-BYTE EBCDIC INTEGER E
*  WITH LEADING ZEROES REPLACED BY BLANKS, AND SIGN PRECEDING
*   MOST SIGNIFICANT DIGIT: BLANK IF POSITIVE, DASH IF NEGATIVE.
* N MUST NOT EXCEED 16, AND MUST INCLUDE ONE POSITION FOR THE
*  SIGN CHARACTER.
* E.G.,   IF N=8 AND X=F'-12195', THEN E=C'  -12195'
*
* CALLED VIA  BAL  14,CVE  WITH R1 CONTAINING ADDR OF =A(X,E,N)
*
CVE        STM      0,4,CVESAVE      SAVE REGS 0...4
           LM       2,4,0(1)         R2=A(X), R3=A(E), R4=A(N)
*
* CONVERT FROM BINARY TO EBCDIC
           L        0,0(2)           R0=X  (FULLWORD BINARY INTEGER)
           CVD      0,CVEBCD         CONVERT TO BCD FORM OF  X
           L        4,0(4)           R4=N  (LENGTH OF EBCDIC FIELD)
           SH       4,=H'1'          R4=N-1 FOR 'EX' & LOOP-CTRL
           SLL      4,4              UNPK'S "L1" IS BITS 8-11 ONLY
           EX       4,CVEUNPK        CONVERT TO EBCDIC FORM OF  X
           SRL      4,4              RECOVER N-1
           LA       1,0(4,3)         R1= ADDR OF LEAST SIGNIF DIGIT
           OI       0(1),X'F0'       ELIMINATE SIGN IN LO-ORDER BYTE
*
* REPLACE LEADING ZEROES WITH BLANKS
CVELOOP    CLI      0(3),C'0'        A LEADING ZERO IS A ZERO TO LEFT
           BNE      CVELOOPX          OF LEFT-MOST NON-ZERO DIGIT
           MVI      0(3),C' '        REPLACE EACH ONE WITH A BLANK
           LA       3,1(3)           ADVANCE TO NEXT EBCDIC DIGIT
           BCT      4,CVELOOP        CONTINUE TILL NO MORE DIGITS
*
* INSERT MINUS SIGN (IF NEEDED) NEXT TO LEADING DIGIT
CVELOOPX   SH       3,=H'1'          BACK UP TO SIGN POSITION
           LTR      0,0              DETERMINE SIGN OF  X
           BNM      CVELOOPZ         BRANCH IF POSITIVE OR ZERO
           MVI      0(3),C'-'        ELSE PUT SIGN AT LEADING DIGIT
*
* EXIT FROM CVE
CVELOOPZ   LM       0,4,CVESAVE      RESTORE REGS 0...4
           BR       14               RETURN TO CALLER
*
* CVE'S DATA AREAS
CVEBCD     DS       D                DOUBLE WORD FOR BCD FORM OF  X
CVESAVE    DS       5F               AREA FOR SAVED REGS
CVEUNPK    UNPK     0(0,3),CVEBCD    EXECUTED UNPK INSTRUCTION
*-----------------------------------------------------------------
```

Here, the symbols G and Y represent memory areas defined as follows:

```
          Y        DS       F
          G        DS       CL10
```

In each call, the symbols used for the addresses of the actual parameters are not important. What IS important is the order in which they occur, the fact that the addresses and not the data itself are passed, the type of data that each address represents, and the registers used for the addresses and for the reentry point.

Figure 9.5   Convert hex integer from EBCDIC to binary.

```
*
* CONVERTS EBCDIC HEX INTEGER AT LOCATION  E  TO FULLWORD BINARY
*  INTEGER AT LOCATION  X.  HEX INTEGER'S LENGTH ASSUMED NOT TO
*  EXCEED 8 DIGITS, EXCLUSIVE OF LEADING BLANKS AND/OR SIGN.
*
* CALLED VIA  BAL  14,CVX  WITH R1 CONTAINING ADDR OF =A(E,X)
*
CVX        STM     14,3,CVXSAVE         SAVE REGS 14,15,0,1,2,3
           LM      2,3,0(1)             R2=A(E), R3=A(X)
           BAL     14,SKPBLK            SKIP PAST LEADING BLANKS
*
* REMEMBER HEX NUMBER'S SIGN
           MVI     CVXFLG,0(2)          SAVE 1ST NON-BLANK CHAR
           CLI     0(2),C'-'            LOOK FOR LEADING SIGN
           BE      CVXSGN
           CLI     0(2),C'+'
           BNE     CVXHEX
CVXSGN     LA      2,1(2)               ADVANCE PAST SIGN CHARACTER
*
* CONVERT EBCDIC HEX INTEGER TO FULLWORD BINARY INTEGER
CVXHEX     MVC     0(4,3),=F'0'         INITIALIZE BINARY INTEGER X
           LH      1,=H'8'              INITIALIZE HEX DIGIT COUNT
CVXHEXL    BAL     14,HEXCHK            SEE IF IT'S A VALID DIGIT
           LTR     15,15                R15 >= 0  => HEX DIGIT IN R15
           BM      CVXHEXX              R15 < 0   => NOT A HEX DIGIT
           BAL     14,HEXCON            ADD DIGIT TO BASE-2 INTEGER
           BCT     1,CVXHEXL            CONTINUE UP TO 8 DIGITS
*
* EXIT FROM CVX
CVXHEXX    CLI     CVXFLG,C'-'          SEE IF HEX NUMBER WAS NEGATIVE
           BNE     CVXHEXZ
           L       1,0(3)               IF SO, MAKE BINARY INTGR NEGTV
           LNR     1,1
           ST      1,0(3)
CVXHEXZ    LM      14,3,CVXSAVE         RESTORE REGS 14,15,0,1,2,3
           BR      14
*
* CVX'S DATA AREAS
CVXFLG     DS      C                    FLAG REMEMBERS SIGN
CVXSAVE    DS      6F                   REGISTER SAVE AREA
*-------------------------------------------------------------------
```

It should also be noted that in each call, the LM instruction is equivalent to consecutive LA instructions, as shown by this equivalent call to CVE:

```
           LA      2,X
           LA      3,E
           LA      4,N
           BAL     14,CVE
```

As discussed earlier, the A-type literal in the operand of the LM 2,4,=A(X,E,N) instruction is an address constant for which the assembler creates consecutive full-word addresses, as shown here:

Figure 9.6   Low-level subroutines for CVX. (See Figure 9.5.)

```
         *
         * SKIP TO FIRST NON-BLANK, NON-ZERO CHARACTER IN STRING
         * CALLED VIA  BAL  14,SKPBLK   WITH  R2 = A(STRING)
SKPBLK    CLI    0(2),C' '
          BE     SKPBLKL
          CLI    0(2),C'0'
          BNER   14              RETURN WHEN SIGNIF DIGIT FOUND
SKPBLKL   LA     2,1(2)          ELSE, ADVANCE TO NEXT CHAR.
          B      SKPBLK
         *-------------------------------------------------------------
         *
         * CONVERT CURRENT HEX CHARACTER FROM EBCDIC TO HEX DIGIT
         * RETURNS BINARY EQUIV OF HEX DIGIT IN R15 IF & ONLY IF
         *  CHAR IS VALID HEX DIGIT; OTHERWISE, R15=-1
         *
         * CALLED VIA  BAL  14,HEXCHK   WITH  R2 = A(HEX CHARACTER)
         *  RESULT DEPENDS ON EBCDIC CODE SCHEME.
HEXCHK    IC     15,0(2)            GET HEX CHARACTER AND ISO-
          N      15,=X'0000000F'     LATE ITS RIGHT-MOST 4 BITS
          CLI    0(2),C'0'
          BL     HEXCHKA           USE EBCDIC CODE SCHEME
          CLI    0(2),C'9'          TO SEE IF IT'S 0,1,...,9
          BH     HEXCHKN
          BR     14                O.K. IF IT'S IN [0,9]
         *
HEXCHKA   CLI    0(2),C'A'         ELSE SEE IF IT'S IN  [A,F]
          BL     HEXCHKN           USE EBCDIC CODE SCHEME
          CLI    0(2),C'F'          TO SEE IF IT'S  A,B,...,F
          BH     HEXCHKN
          AH     15,=H'9'          IF VALID, CREATE BINARY
          BR     14                (RECALL C'A'=X'C1', ETC)
         *
HEXCHKN   LH     15,=H'-1'         INVALID => RETURN CODE = -1
          BR     14
         *-------------------------------------------------------------
         *
         * MULTIPLY PARTIALLY CONVERTED BASE-2 INTEGER BY 16,
         *   AND ADD CURRENT HEX DIGIT TO IT, IGNORING ANY OVERFLOW.
         * E.G.,  2AF5 = ( (2*16 + 10)*16 + 15 )*16 + 5
         *
         * CALLED VIA  BAL  14,HEXCON  WITH  R3=A(RESULT), R15= CURRENT DIGIT
HEXCON    L      0,0(3)            GET PARTIALLY CONVERTED RESULT
          SLL    0,4               MPY BY 16=2**4
          ALR    0,15              ADD CURRENT DIGIT TO IT
          ST     0,0(3)            THIS GIVES NEW PARTIAL RESULT
          BR     14
         *-------------------------------------------------------------
```

The LM 2,4,=A(X,E,N) instruction therefore loads the first of these full-word addresses into Register 2, the second into Register 3, and the third into Register 4. That of course gives the exact same result as the previous three consecutive LA instructions. It should be clear that in situations where more than one parameter is needed, the technique of using an LM instruction with A-type literals is clearer than using a sequence of LA instructions. It is also more compact.

Note that CVX itself calls three other internal subroutines: SKPBLK, HEXCHK, and HEXCON. These are shown in Figure 9.6. The first of these (SKPBLK) is a slightly modified version of the SKIP subroutine of Figure 9.3b. The modification is that **SKPBLK** skips past leading zeroes as well as leading blanks, and passes its result back to the caller using the same register that passed the string's address.

HEXCHK converts a valid hex digit from its EBCDIC character representation to its 4-bit binary integer representation and returns the result in Register 15.

HEXCON is called once for each 4-bit hex digit, and it adds that digit to the partially completed binary representation of the original hex number. For example, to convert from hex 2AF5 to binary, the HEXCON subroutine is called four times and successively computes the following binary integers (shown here with their hex and decimal equivalents):

```
                    0010              2      2
               0010 1010             2A      2*16 + 10
          0010 1010 1111            2AF      (2*16 + 10)*16 + 15
     0010 1010 1111 0101           2AF5      ((2*16 + 10)*16 + 15)*16 + 5
```

Data Versus Addresses

Accessing Data

Note that the calling sequence for HEXCON passes the address of the partially completed result, so that HEXCON's first instruction must load that result into a register in order to do the computation. The instruction that does that, L 0,0(3), is similar to the L 0,0(2) instruction near the beginning of the CVE subroutine itself. Both of these use the explicit base-displacement form to access data from a location whose address isn't known until it is passed to the subroutine, i.e., until run time.

In other words, when an address is passed but a data value is needed, that address must be used as an explicit base address via an explicit base register.

9.6 MODULARIZATION

In this section we show how the BAL instruction and internal subroutines can be used to organize an assembly language program into relatively small segments, or **modules.** The approach is similar to what one would take in organizing a program written in a high-level language.

Sample Problem Definition

Consider the following problem: Design and write a program that will read an input character string consisting of hexadecimal digits and write the equivalent output string of decimal digits. For example, if the input is 2AF5 then the output would be 10997, since $2AF5_{16} = 10997_{10}$.

Based on the work that we've done in the preceding section, we have two principal subroutines—CVE and CVX—to help us solve this problem. The question is, how should we organize our solution around these two subroutines? Our approach to resolving this question uses a top-down design and makes ample use of internal subroutines and the BAL instruction.

For the following discussion, refer to Figure 9.7.

Level 0: From the top-most level's perspective, the only tasks to be done besides the standard entry and standard exit are initializations, the main steps of the solution, and proper program termination. So, the top-most level's solution is relatively easy: it just calls lower-level routines to carry out the details.

Level 1: The initialization task in this problem need only consist of opening two files: the input data file and the output result file. The three main processing steps are reading the hex data, converting it to decimal, and writing it to the output file. The program termination task need only consist of closing the input and output files.

BAL's Reentry Register

At this level, our subroutines are calling other subroutines—either the I/O routines provided by the system or our own Level 2 CONVERT routine. Therefore either the reentry point for the caller to each Level 1 subroutine must be saved and restored, or we must use a different register when calling Level 2 subroutines. Since using different reentry registers for different levels is unwieldy and error-prone, it is best to use the same reentry register at each level. This in turn requires us to save and restore the reentry points.

We could use a memory location for this, but as an alternative we've saved each reentry point in another register, one that is not part of the calling sequence, and that will be saved and restored by lower-level subroutines on an as-needed basis. In each of the subroutines at this level, an LR 2,14 instruction saves a reentry point in Register 2, and an LR 14,2 instruction restores it to Register 14.

Level 2: At this level, the task is to convert a single hex input integer, which is given in EBCDIC format, to its equivalent representation as a decimal integer, also in EBCDIC format. The task is accomplished in two steps: (1) convert EBCDIC hex to internal binary format, and then (2) convert internal binary to EBCDIC decimal format.

As can be seen in Figure 9.7, the first task is done via a call to our 'CVX' routine and the second is done via a call to our 'CVE' routine. The reentry point for the caller to the Level 2 CONVERT subroutine is saved before calling the Level 3 routines.

Levels 3 and 4: Our CVX and CVE subroutines are at Level 3, and the subroutines called by them—SKPBLK, HEXCHK, and HEXCON—are at Level 4.

Level 5: Since there are no more tasks needed to solve this problem, we can put the I/O data areas, DCB's (or DTF's), and constants at Level 5, which is the lowest level in our organization.

9.7 MULTIPLE BASE REGISTERS

Displacement Limit

Sometimes use of internal subroutines rather than external ones leads to program sizes exceeding 4096 bytes. In such cases, more than one implied base register may have to be used in order that all implicit operands can be correctly represented in base-displacement form by the assembler. The problem, of course, is that every displacement must be less than or equal to $4095_{10} = FFF_{16}$. If there is only one implied base register, then, by the conventions we have been using, the implied base address will be 000006; thus, the largest address that could be specified in base-displacement form would be $000006 + FFF = 001005_{16} = 4101_{10}$. This is slightly larger than 4096, but certainly not enough larger to eliminate the problem. With more than one implied base register, we could use one of these with a base address of 000006; another with a base address of 001006; a third, if necessary, with a base address of 002006; and so forth. It is a fairly simple matter to establish more than one implied base register, and, once that has been done, the assembler will choose the base register whose base address requires the smallest implied displacement for each implicit operand. Thus, different operands may be represented in base-displacement form with different implied base registers.

Assembly Time

To establish more than one implied base register, each register and its base address must be designated via a USING directive to fulfill the assembly-time requirements. For each such register, there must also be an instruction placing the appropriate base address in that register at run time. This is identical to the requirement for a single implied base register, but the method of accomplishing it is somewhat different. The BALR 12,0 instruction is insufficient by itself. One method, shown in Figure 9.8, relies on a property of the USING directive summarized in Figure 9.9. That property means, for example, that this single directive,

```
USING      *,12,11,10
```

is equivalent to these three consecutive directives,

```
USING      *,12
USING      *+4096,11
USING      *+8192,10
```

In each of these operands, the symbol * is the memory location symbol, not the multiplication operator.

This property of the USING directive makes it easy to satisfy the assembly-time requirement. To satisfy the run-time requirement we must be a bit more careful, as demonstrated by the statements in Figure 9.8.

Run-Time Rule

To use implicit addressing at all, we must designate at least one implied base register and base address, and each implicit address must, at run time as well as at assembly time, be in the range of at least one of the implied base registers. In Figure 9.8 the implicit addresses SAVE+4 and SAVE are in the range of base register 10 only, due to the USING directive. So before the respective ST

Figure 9.7   Convert hex input to decimal output.

```
*-------------------------------------------------------------------
*                 LEVEL   0
*                 --------
*
HEXTODEC CSECT
*
* READS HEX INTEGERS IN EBCDIC FORMAT AND WRITES THE EQUIVALENT
*  DECIMAL INTEGERS, ALSO IN EBCDIC FORMAT.
*
         STM   14,12,12(13)        STANDARD ENTRY
         BALR  12,0
         USING *,12
         ST    13,SAVE+4
         LA    13,SAVE
*
* OVERALL PROGRAM STRUCTURE
         BAL   14,INITIAL          INITIALIZATIONS
         BAL   14,PROCESS          MAIN PROCESSING
         BAL   14,STOPRUN          END-OF-JOB
*
         L     13,SAVE+4
         LM    14,12,12(13)
         BR    14                  STANDARD EXIT
*-------------------------------------------------------------------
*                 LEVEL   1
*                 --------
*
* INITIALIZATIONS
INITIAL  LR    2,14                SAVE REENTRY ADDR
         OPEN  (DATA,(INPUT))      OPEN INPUT DATA FILE
         OPEN  (RESULT,(OUTPUT))   OPEN OUTPUT RESULT FILE
         LR    14,2                RESTORE REENTRY ADDR
         BR    14                  RETURN TO CALLER
*
* MAIN PROCESSING STRUCTURE
PROCESS  LR    2,14                SAVE REENTRY ADDR
PROCESSL GET   DATA,INAREA         GET ONE HEX INPUT NUMBER
         BAL   14,CONVERT          CONVERT HEX TO DECIMAL
         PUT   RESULT,OUTAREA      WRITE RESULTS
         B     PROCESSL            CONTINUE TILL END-OF-FILE
PROCESSX LR    14,2                END-OF-FILE TRANSFERS HERE
         BR    14                  RETURN TO REENTRY POINT
*
* END-OF-JOB PROCESSING
STOPRUN  LR    2,14                SAVE REENTRY ADDR
         CLOSE (DATA)              CLOSE INPUT DATA FILE
         CLOSE (RESULT)            CLOSE OUTPUT RESULT FILE
         LR    14,2                RECOVER REENTRY ADDR
         BR    14                  RETURN TO CALLER
*-------------------------------------------------------------------
```

Figure 9.7 continued

```
*------------------------------------------------------------
*                   LEVEL  2
*                   --------
*
*  'CONVERT' SUBROUTINE CONVERTS HEX INPUT TO DECIMAL OUTPUT
*     CALLS 'CVX' TO CONVERT EBCDIC HEX INPUT TO BINARY INTEGER
*     CALLS 'CVE' TO CONVERT BINARY INTEGER TO DECIMAL OUTPUT
*  INPUT IS OBTAINED FROM INPUT AREA FIELD NAMED 'HEXNUM'
*  RESULT IS PLACED IN OUTPUT AREA FIELD NAMED 'DECNUM'
*
CONVERT  ST    14,CONVSAVE                SAVE REENTRY POINT
         LM    2,3,=A(HEXNUM,BINARY)
         BAL   14,CVX                     CONVT HEXNUM TO BINARY
         LM    2,4,=A(BINARY,DECNUM,DECNUML)
         BAL   14,CVE                     CONVT BINARY TO DECNUM
         L     14,CONVSAVE
         BR    14                         RETURN TO CALLER
CONVSAVE DS    F                          RESERVED FOR REG 14
*------------------------------------------------------------
*                   LEVEL  3
*                   --------
*
*  CVX  &  CVE  routines go here.  See Figs. 9.4 & 9.5
*------------------------------------------------------------
*                   LEVEL  4
*                   --------
*
*  SKPBLK, HEXCHK, &  HEXCON  routines go here.  See Fig. 9.6
*------------------------------------------------------------
*                   LEVEL  5
*                   --------
*
* INPUT RECORD AREA
INAREA   DS    0CL80
HEXNUM   DS    CL80            HEX NUMBER; LEADING BLANKS/ZEROES O.K.
*
* OUTPUT RECORD AREA
OUTAREA  DS    0CL133
         DC    X'40'           SINGLE-SPACE CARRIAGE CONTROL
DECNUM   DS    CL12            SIGNED DECIMAL NUMBER FIELD
         DC    CL120' '
*
* CONSTANTS, ETC.
DECNUML  DC    A(L'DECNUM)     LENGTH OF DECIMAL FIELD
BINARY   DS    F               INTERMEDIATE BINARY INTEGER
SAVE     DS    18F             REGISTER SAVE AREA
*
* DCB'S FOR INPUT AND OUTPUT FILES
*
DATA     DCB   ...
RESULT   DCB   ...
         END
```

Figure 9.8   Example of the USING directive.

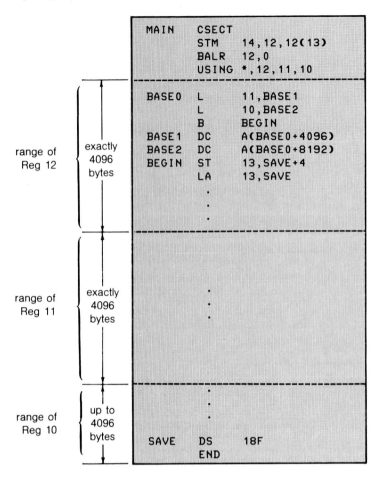

```
            MAIN     CSECT
                     STM      14,12,12(13)
                     BALR     12,0
                     USING    *,12,11,10
          ─────────────────────────────────────
            BASE0    L        11,BASE1
                     L        10,BASE2
                     B        BEGIN
            BASE1    DC       A(BASE0+4096)
            BASE2    DC       A(BASE0+8192)
            BEGIN    ST       13,SAVE+4
                     LA       13,SAVE
                      .
                      .
                      .
          ─────────────────────────────────────
                      .
                      .
                      .
          ─────────────────────────────────────
                      .
                      .
            SAVE     DS       18F
                     END
```

range of Reg 12 — exactly 4096 bytes

range of Reg 11 — exactly 4096 bytes

range of Reg 10 — up to 4096 bytes

Figure 9.9   The USING directive.

opcode	operand
USING	$B_0,R_0,R_1,R_2,\ldots,R_n$

where B_0 and the R_k's are defined and related as follows:

B_0 = symbol whose value is assumed by the assembler to be the base address in Register R_0.

R_k = address of any one of the general registers.

The *base address* in Register R_k and the *range* of R_k are assumed by the assembler to be related to those of Register R_0 as follows:

register	base address	range
R_0	B_0	B_0 through $B_0 + 4095$
R_1	$B_1 = B_0 + 4096$	B_1 through $B_1 + 4095$
R_2	$B_2 = B_0 + 8192$	B_2 through $B_2 + 4095$
.	.	.
.	.	.
R_n	$B_n = B_0 + 4096 \cdot n$	B_n through $B_n + 4095$

and LA instructions can be executed at run time, the base address that corresponds to the USING declaration must be loaded into base register 10. The rule is that *when an instruction is executed at run time, any base address required for its execution must already be in the appropriate base register.* We can also apply this rule to the two load instructions that follow the USING directive in Figure 9.8 and thereby see why the two respective address constants must be in the range of base register 12.

Once an implied base register is declared by a USING directive, the assembler will use it as needed until a subsequent DROP directive specifies that register. The purpose of the DROP directive is simply to inform the assembler that a register previously declared by a USING directive is no longer to be used for implicit addresses. By judicious combinations of USING and DROP directives we can therefore reduce the number of registers committed to base addresses at any one time. The format of the DROP directive is

opcode	operand
DROP	$R_0, R_1, \ldots, R_n$

where the operand contains a list of one or more register addresses. An example and further discussion of the DROP and USING directives are given in Chapter 23.

9.8 SUMMARY

A subroutine is a set of statements that may be called from one or more points in a computer program to perform some task at the request of that program. An internal subroutine is one whose statements are contained within the requesting program at assembly time.

An internal subroutine has access to the same symbolic addresses as the portion of the program that calls it. Therefore it can obtain its parameters from fixed locations via symbolic addresses. However, if more generality is desired, its parameters can be passed to it via numeric addresses or data provided by the caller. The sequence of instructions that load the parameter data or addresses, establish the reentry point, and branch to a subroutine is known as the subroutine's "calling sequence." The parameters must be passed in the same order and be of the same data types as the subroutine expects.

The Branch and Link (BAL) instruction does two essential things when it calls an internal subroutine: it places the caller's reentry point address in a register available to the subroutine, and it then branches to the entry point of the subroutine. The RR-type extended mnemonic branch instructions (BR, BER, etc.) provide a simple means of returning to the reentry point of the caller.

To avoid register usage conflicts between caller and subroutine, an internal subroutine should save the contents of any registers that it is going to use, and restore their contents just prior to returning to the caller.

Internal subroutines can be used to organize a program into a number of relatively small modules. When this is done, the principles of top-down design used in high-level languages can therefore also be applied to the design of assembly language programs.

The use of internal subroutines may result in an object module longer than 4096 bytes; this could require the use of more than one implied base register, thereby reducing the number of registers available for general use.

9.9 REVIEW

Subroutine   A set of statements that may be called from one or more points in a computer program to perform some task at the request of that program.

Internal Subroutine   A subroutine whose statements are contained within the requesting program at assembly time.

Closed Subroutine   A subroutine written in such a way that a single copy of it is all that's required no matter how many times it is called.

Open Subroutine   A subroutine written in such a way that a copy of it must be inserted at each place that it is used.

Entry Point   In a subroutine, the first instruction executed when it is called.

Reentry Point   In a caller, the first instruction executed after returning from a called subroutine.

Calling Sequence   The sequence of instructions, and the sequence and types of parameters, that are used in calling a subroutine.

BAL Instruction   The RX-type Branch and Link instruction that puts the caller's reentry point in a register just prior to branching to a subroutine's entry point.

BR Instruction   The extended mnemonic RR-type branch instruction that branches to the address that's in the register designated in its operand.

Subroutine Parameter   A variable that identifies (or has the value of) data operated on by a subroutine, or one that identifies a result determined by the subroutine.

A-Type Constant   Used in the operand of a DC directive or as a literal, this type of constant is distinguished from H-, F-, and other types of numeric constants not merely by the letter "A," but mainly because its defining expression may include one or more symbols as well as self-defining terms, and is enclosed within parentheses. The result of assembling a valid A-type constant is a binary integer whose value is the value of the expression.

Length Attribute of a Symbol   The number of bytes that the assembler assigns to the memory area associated with the symbol. Denoted by L'X for any valid symbol X. See Section 9.3.

Range of a Base Register   The 4096 bytes beginning at the base address contained in that register.

USING Directive   The directive that establishes one or more implied base addresses and their corresponding base registers for use by the assembler when it converts symbolic memory addresses into base-displacement form. See Section 9.7.

Range of a USING Directive   The $4096 \times N$ bytes beginning at the base address indicated in the USING's operand, where N is the number of base registers specified in that operand.

DROP Directive   The directive that removes one or more base registers and their associated base addresses from the set established by a prior USING directive. See Section 9.7.

9.10   REVIEW QUESTIONS

1. What is the fundamental difference between using a Branch (B) instruction to call a subroutine and using a Branch and Link (BAL) to do so?
2. Using the BAL instruction in the manner described in this chapter always puts the caller's reentry point immediately after the BAL instruction. But suppose that the set of instructions that you intend to have the CPU execute when a subroutine returns to the reentry point does not begin immediately following the BAL instruction that called the subroutine. What is the simplest way to ensure that the intended instructions will be executed after the subroutine returns?
3. What is evidently incorrect about this instruction?

```
LM    2,4,=A(W,X,Y,Z)
```

4. Explain why it is necessary for a subroutine to save and restore the contents of registers that it uses. Show what statements are needed to do this in a subroutine if the only four registers it uses are 2, 4, 6, and 9. What statements would be needed for the save and restore operations in the subroutine if the only four registers it uses are 2, 3, 4, and 5? (**Note:** The difference between the answers to these two questions should lead you to a conclusion about the use of registers in a subroutine.)

5. What are the registers whose contents are stored by this STM instruction: STM 14,12,12(13) ?

6. What is the difference in purpose between an LR 2,14 instruction and an LR 14,2 instruction?

7. Suppose the symbols U, V, and W are defined by these statements:

```
W    DS    4F
V    DC    CL10' '
U    DC    X'2AF5'
```

What is the length attribute of each of the three symbols? What is the value of the A-type constant A(L'DECNUM) that is specified in the operand of a DC directive near the end of Figure 9.7?

8. Each of the three "SKIP" subroutines in Figures 9.3a–c contains a loop that doesn't terminate until a nonblank character is found. It would be better if each subroutine had a counter to control the number of loop iterations, especially if a string being examined consisted of nothing but blanks. Would the counter have to be passed to the subroutines as a parameter? If so, how should this be done in each of the three cases, and what changes would have to be made to each subroutine?

9. What aspects of the CVE subroutine of Figure 9.4 make it fairly general and useful? How could the CVE subroutine be simplified, perhaps at the expense of its generality, and still be useful to some degree?

10. What aspects of the CVX subroutine of Figure 9.5 make it fairly general and useful? How could the CVX subroutine be simplified, perhaps at the expense of its generality, and still be useful to some degree?

11. Should we have used an internal closed subroutine for the standard entry shown in the Level 0 portion of Figure 9.7? Why or why not? Should we have done so for the standard exit? Why or why not?

12. What is the difference in purpose between these two USING directives: USING *,12,11 and USING *,11,12? Which one of these should follow the BALR 12,0 instruction in the standard entry, and why?

13. If we use two implied base registers as shown in the USING directive below, why can we not just follow the USING with two BALR instructions, like this:

```
USING  *,12,11
BALR   12,0
BALR   11,0
```

Would the above sequence of statements cause an assembly-time error or a run-time error, or neither type of error, or both types? Explain your answer.

14. If we use two implied base registers as shown in the USING directive below, why can we not just follow the USING with two LA instructions, like this:

```
USING  *,12,11
LA     12,*
LA     12,*+4096
```

Would the above sequence of statements cause an assembly-time error or a run-time error, or neither type of error, or both types? Explain your answer.

1. Rewrite the program segment of Figure 8.9 in Chapter 8 so that it is an internal subroutine that converts 8 hex digits to EBCDIC codes. The parameters should be passed to your subroutine in a manner similar to what was described as Method 2 in the present chapter.

2. Rewrite each of the program segments in the figures listed below so that each is an internal subroutine that performs the same task that the segment does. For each subroutine, the parameters should be passed in a manner similar to what was described as Method 2 in the present chapter.

   a. Fig. 5.2: Compute the sum of N integers.
   b. Fig. 5.4: Multiply each integer in an array by a constant.
   c. Fig. 5.5: Count the number of positive integers in an array.
   d. Fig. 5.8: Determine the algebraically largest and smallest integers in an array.

3. Write an internal subroutine that will copy all the components of a one-dimensional integer array into another array. The information needed to specify each array should be passed to your subroutine as parameters.

4. Write an internal subroutine that will convert a decimal (not hexadecimal) integer from its n-byte EBCDIC representation to its representation as a 32-bit binary integer. Your subroutine should permit the EBCDIC number to contain leading blanks as well as leading zeroes, and a sign (plus, minus, or omitted) to the left of the most significant digit.

5. Rewrite the SKPBLK subroutine of Figure 9.6 so that in addition to what it now does, it gets the string's length as a parameter from the caller and uses that length to control the number of loop iterations.

6. Modify your solution to Exercise 5 so that the subroutine returns some true/false indicator (e.g., 1 or 0) to the caller, depending on whether or not the string contains any characters other than blanks or zeroes. (**Hint:** The indicator is an additional result parameter.)

7. Write an internal subroutine that will print a blank line that causes the printer to skip to the top of a new page. (**Note:** Your subroutine will have to use the same printer DCB, or DTF, that the rest of the program uses.)

8. Write an internal subroutine that will examine the characters in an arithmetic expression and tell the caller whether or not the number of left parentheses is the same as the number of right parentheses in the expression. The address and length of the string containing the arithmetic expression should be passed as parameters to your subroutine.

9. Write an internal subroutine that will examine a string one character at a time, left to right, and perform the following delete operation: for each occurrence of the EBCDIC backspace character (X'16'), delete that character and the one preceding it before examining the next character in the string. Both the address and the length of the string should be passed as parameters to your subroutine. Note that the string may contain several consecutive backspaces, such as might be created when correcting text typed at a terminal. (This is the same problem as Exercise 13 in Chapter 7, the only difference being that here it is to be solved with an internal subroutine.)

10

External Subroutines

The primary purpose of this chapter is to explain the requirements for interfacing a calling program to an external subroutine and to explain how those requirements are conventionally programmed in the IBM 360 and 370 systems. Other related materials are discussed in Sections 10.5 through 10.7.

This chapter is based on most of the terminology and concepts that were introduced in Chapter 9 on internal subroutines. Therefore, you may find it useful to review the relevant portions of Chapter 9, especially Sections 9.8 and 9.9, for a summary and review of the material.

10.1 TERMINOLOGY AND LINKAGE REQUIREMENTS

The one thing that determines whether a subroutine is external or internal is this: an external subroutine is assembled separately from the program that calls it, whereas an internal subroutine is assembled as part of the same program that calls it. This difference affects the manner in which parameters are obtained by an external subroutine, and it also affects the manner in which a caller branches to an external subroutine's entry point.

As in Chapter 9, we shall only be concerned with closed subroutines, i.e., subroutines written in such a way that only one copy of them is needed at run time, no matter how many places they are used in a program.

Remember that when a program requests that a subroutine perform a task, it is said to **call** that subroutine. The program making the request is known as the **calling program,** whereas the subroutine requested to perform the task is known as the **called program.** The address of the first instruction executed by a subroutine when it is called is known as the subroutine's **entry point.** Correspondingly, the address of the instruction to which a subroutine branches when it returns to a calling program is known as the calling program's **reentry point.**

Since a closed subroutine can be called from any number of different places within a program, there needs to be some mechanism by which the calling program can specify the appropriate reentry point to which the subroutine will return. Moreover, since each subroutine is assumed to be written as a general solution to a particular problem, there needs to be some mechanism by which the calling program can specify the data that the subroutine is to operate on and the memory areas that are to be used for the results. These last two types of information—the data and the areas for the results—are the values of the subroutine's **parameters**, i.e., the values of the variables that must be specified when the subroutine is called, without which the subroutine cannot perform its task satisfactorily. The calling program is said to **pass** the values of the parameters to the subroutine.

It should be noted that the parameter values must be passed in the exact order the subroutine expects to receive them. Moreover, the data must be of the type expected by the subroutine—integer, character data, etc.—and the areas reserved for the results must be consistent with the type and number of results. In short, the design of a subroutine determines the nature of the information that is passed to that subroutine. The programmer cannot write a program to call a subroutine unless he or she knows the number and types of data and results to specify, and the order in which to specify them. The programmer usually determines these things by reading the documentation about the subroutine.

We may summarize the discussion by saying that, in order to call a closed subroutine, certain requirements must be met. These requirements are known as the **linkage requirements,** since they are what is needed to interface, or link, a calling program to a called program. The linkage requirements are: (1) passing the values of the parameters, (2) passing the address of the reentry point, and (3) branching to the entry point. The mechanism by which these requirements are met is known as the **calling sequence,** a set of statements in the calling program that fulfill the requirements. In many computer systems, the calling sequence has been standardized, especially for calls to external subroutines. The standard calling sequence in the IBM 360 and 370 Assembly language, together with standard procedures to be followed within subroutines, will be described in Section 10.3. These standards, known as the **linkage conventions**, depend on certain addressing considerations.

10.2 ADDRESSING AND ADDRESS CONSTANTS

Two facts about the execution of computer programs should be abundantly clear at this point: (1) whenever data is to be obtained from or placed into memory, the address of the memory location of that data must be specified via the operand of the instruction; and (2) whenever one instruction is to branch to another instruction, the address of the new instruction must be specified via the operand of the branch instruction.

Assembly-Time Addresses vs. Run-Time Addresses

In machine language, a memory address is an unsigned integer that denotes the number of bytes from the beginning of the real, hardware main memory of the computer. The beginning of real main memory is a particular byte designated by the hardware designers as having an address of zero. However, a programmer is rarely concerned with real memory and real memory addresses. Instead, his or her concern is primarily with the set of memory addresses assigned to a program by the assembler. These addresses will ultimately be transformed, or mapped, into real memory addresses by the combined actions of the operating system and the CPU, but, until that happens, they do not refer to physical locations in main memory. Therefore, although two programs may be assigned the same memory addresses at assembly time, there will be no conflict when they are run because their respective addresses can be mapped into different real memory addresses.

The distinction between the set of addresses assigned at assembly time and the set of real memory addresses into which these are mapped is important because it enables programmers to write programs independent of one another without worrying about memory address conflicts. For example, if Program P has an instruction that, when assembled, branches to memory address 000500, that means address 000500 in Program P, and that particular address is independent of address 000500 in any other program. Nor is it necessarily address 000500 in real memory.

Internal vs. External Addresses

We can say that the addresses assigned to a program at assembly time are *internal* to that program. We can also say that addresses that are internal to one program are *external* to all other programs. Figure 10.1 shows the addresses assigned to two programs, Program P and Program Q, that were assembled separately from one another. The assembler assigned addresses beginning at zero for each program; all addresses assigned in Q are external to those assigned in P (and vice versa).

Figure 10.1   *Memory addresses assigned by the assembler.*

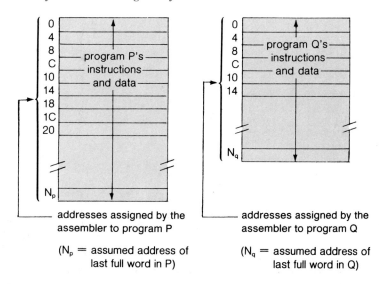

addresses assigned by the
assembler to program P

(N_p = assumed address of
last full word in P)

addresses assigned by the
assembler to program Q

(N_q = assumed address of
last full word in Q)

This obviously means that if an instruction in Q branches to address 10, that instruction refers to address 10 in Q only, not to address 10 in P. Clearly, some addresses in Q conflict with (are identical with) some addresses in P.

Now, suppose Q is an external subroutine, and suppose that when P is running, P wants to request that Q perform calculations using P's data. The linkage requirements listed at the end of the previous section give rise to these questions:

1. How does Q gain access to the data and result areas that are in the calling program, P?
2. How can P specify the entry point in Subroutine Q in order to branch to it at run time?
3. How will Q specify the reentry point in order to return to the calling program, P, at run time?

It should be clear that the answer to each question involves external addresses: Q needs the addresses of P's data, of P's result areas, and of the instruction in P to which it should return when it finishes its calculations. Also, P needs the address of the first instruction in Q, in order to branch to it.

But, as was pointed out, some of the addresses of Q and P are identical. How, for example, can address 000000 in Q be distinguished from address 000000 in P? The answer is, it can't. In order for P and Q to be able to communicate information to one another, their addresses must not be in conflict. Some mechanism is required to ensure that, when an address is specified at run time in either Program P or Subroutine Q, the CPU will be able to determine to which of the two programs that address refers. One of the mechanisms most commonly used for this purpose is provided by the linkage editor program.

The linkage editor program has an intermediary role between the assembler and the loader. It produces what is known as a **load module,** a combination of all the object modules required to run a given program, such as Program P. In the load module, there are no address conflicts: each object module has been relocated by an amount just sufficient to render its addresses distinct from those of all the other object modules in that load module. A simple case is depicted in Figure 10.2, in which it is assumed that in order for Program P to run, only Subroutine Q and no other subroutine is required. Thus, the load module consists of both P and Q, with Q relocated as shown. In order to run Program P, it is the load module consisting of P together with its subroutine Q that is loaded. Loading P's object module alone is insufficient; loading both P's and Q's object modules could produce address conflicts between P and Q. Because all address conflicts and all references from P to Q (and vice versa) have been resolved in the load module, it is the load module that is loaded.

Resolving Address Conflicts

Figure 10.2   Memory addresses in a load module.

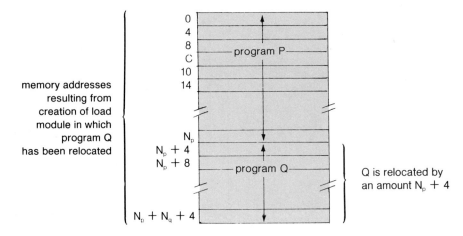

Having briefly outlined why address conflicts are resolved by the linkage editor, we will now learn how a program, such as P, can specify the entry point of Q (an external address) at assembly time so that the appropriate branch from P to Q's entry point will be assembled. When the assembler assembles the branch instruction, it does not, indeed cannot, include the assembled entry-point address in that branch instruction. It leaves this task to the linkage editor. When the linkage editor creates the load module, it will, in effect, complete the assembled branch instruction and thereby *bind* the subroutine to the calling program.

In the IBM 360 and 370 systems, references from any program to an external program are accomplished by means of "external address constants." An **external address constant** symbolically specifies an address that is in some other program than the one in which it is specified. The letter *V* is used to denote an external address constant; it may appear either in the operand of a DC directive or as a literal, as in

```
DC        V(symbol)
L         15,=V(symbol)
```

The parentheses, which are required, are used instead of apostrophes. The *symbol* enclosed in parentheses is the symbolic address of an entry point in another program. Its value, as mentioned, is determined by the linkage editor, not by the assembler. The assembler will, however, reserve a full word for each V-type constant and inform the linkage editor of it. The details of how this is done are not important at this point; they will be discussed in Chapter 23. What is important is that, *through the V-type constant, a program can refer symbolically to the entry point of another program.* It is this facility that enables a program to branch to an external subroutine's entry point.

Specifying External Addresses

10.3   LINKAGE CONVENTIONS

The conventions used to satisfy the linkage requirements in the IBM 360 and 370 systems are divided very naturally into two groups: (1) those that are used in the calling program and (2) those that are used in the called program. The conventions used in these programs are intimately related, of course, and constitute the interface between the two programs.

To the set of three linkage requirements described in Section 10.1, a fourth requirement is added in IBM systems and in many other computer systems. This is the requirement that the data contained in the registers at the time a call is made to a subroutine *be preserved by the subroutine* so that upon return to the calling program the registers have the same contents as when the subroutine was entered. The manner in which this is done for external subroutines is prescribed by the linkage conventions. (The usefulness of this requirement from a programming standpoint should be evident since it is simpler not to have to save and restore register contents in the calling program.)

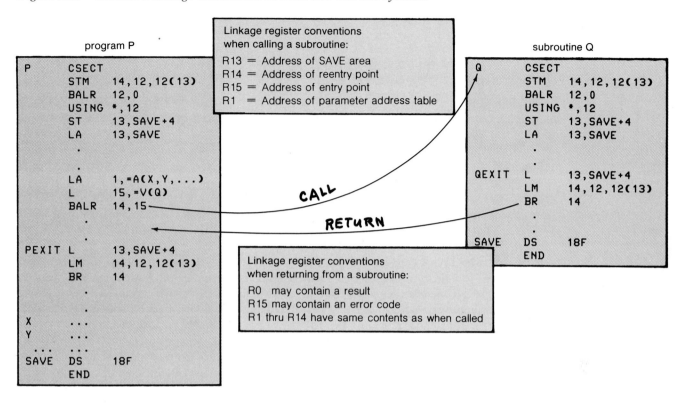

Figure 10.3   Standard linkage conventions in IBM 360 and 370 systems.

An overview of the standard linkage conventions in the IBM 360 and 370 systems is provided in Figure 10.3. Refinements and extensions will be discussed shortly, but, from the standard set of conventions, we can observe the following:

1. Every program, be it a called or calling program, begins and ends its execution in the same manner.
2. The values of the parameters and the addresses of the result areas are passed indirectly through Register 1.
3. The conventions dictate how certain registers shall be used when calling or returning from a subroutine.
4. Certain registers may be used to pass results back to the calling program.

Beginning and Ending Execution: The SAVE Areas

As shown in Figure 10.3, every assembly language subroutine begins with a sequence of statements like this:

```
X       CSECT                   ESTABLISH NAME OF PROGRAM
        STM     14,12,12(13)    SAVE REGISTERS 14,15,0,1,2,...,12
        BALR    12,0            ESTABLISH BASE ADDRESS IN REG 12
        USING   *,12
        ST      13,SAVE+4       SAVE CALLER'S SAVE AREA ADDRESS
        LA      13,SAVE         LOAD OWN SAVE AREA ADDRESS
```

Similarly, the last three instructions executed by a subroutine at run time are defined by these statements:

```
        L       13,SAVE+4       RESTORE CALLER'S SAVE AREA ADDRESS
        LM      14,12,12(13)    RESTORE CALLER'S REGS 14,15,0,...,12
        BR      14              BRANCH TO ADDRESS GIVEN IN REG 14
```

And, supplementing these statements is the definition of SAVE, as follows:

```
SAVE    DS      18F              RESERVE 18 CONSECUTIVE FULL WORDS
```

> **NOTE:** You will recall from Section 2.3 that these requirements are the same as those required in OS for *all* programs, whether or not they are subroutines. In DOS, the requirements for subroutines are as shown previously with but one difference: the SAVE area must begin on a double-word boundary:
>
> ```
> SAVE     DS       9D        'DOS' SAVE AREA = 18 FULLWDS ON DBLWD BDY
> ```

Register 13 and Save Areas

From Figure 10.3, we see that one of the conventions used when calling a subroutine is to have the address of the calling program's SAVE area in Register 13. Thus, when Subroutine Q begins execution, its STM instruction stores the contents of Registers 14,15,0,1,2,...,12 into the calling program's SAVE area, specifically, beginning at the fourth word (twelfth byte) of that area. It then stores the address of the calling program's SAVE area in its own (Q's) SAVE area via the ST 13,SAVE+4 instruction. It does this for two reasons. First, the calling program's SAVE area address must be saved somewhere, because Subroutine Q must be able to use Register 13 for its *own* SAVE area address whenever it calls another program or executes a system input/output or other macro. Second, since the contents of Register 13 must be saved and since they will be needed when restoring the other register contents, they had better be saved in an area from which they can be recovered prior to returning to the calling program. There are only three alternatives: save Register 13's contents in another register, save them in the calling program's memory area, or save them in Q's own memory area. The first alternative is unsatisfactory since it would preempt a register from further use. The second alternative is unsatisfactory since it would require that yet another address be saved by Subroutine Q—namely, the address where Register 13's contents were stored in the calling program. So the only satisfactory alternative is to store the calling program's SAVE area address in Q's own memory area. Then it is accessible through a base address internal to Q and can easily be recovered. By convention, the second word of Q's own SAVE area is used to store the address of the calling program's SAVE area (Fig. 10.4).

Standard vs. Complete Save Area Conventions

Figure 10.5a depicts the contents of the SAVE areas of three programs: Program P, Subroutine Q (called by P), and Subroutine R (called by Q). This illustrates the manner in which the areas are used under the standard linkage conventions described previously. However, the standard linkage convention has one further refinement, as illustrated in Figure 10.5b: the third word of each calling program's SAVE area contains the address of the SAVE area in the program that it has called. This is put there by the called program, through the sequence of statements at the beginning of the called program:

```
STM     14,12,12(13)    SAVE REGS 14,15,0,1,...,12 IN CALLER'S AREA
BALR    12,0            ESTABLISH BASE ADDRESS IN REG 12
USING   *,12
ST      13,SAVE+4       SAVE CALLER'S SAVE AREA ADDRESS IN OWN AREA
LR      2,13            COPY CALLER'S ADDR TO REG 2 FOR SUBSEQ STORE
LA      13,SAVE         LOAD OWN SAVE AREA ADDRESS
ST      13,8(2)         SAVE OWN SAVE AREA ADDR IN CALLER'S AREA
```

One advantage to having both SAVE area addresses stored in this fashion is that it can be of assistance during debugging sessions. However, we will employ only the standard convention of Figures 10.3 and 10.5a. The complete convention and various aspects of its use are fully described in *OS/VS1 Supervisor Services and Macro Instructions* (IBM Publication GC24–5103) and in *DOS/VS Supervisor and I/O Macros* (GC33–5373).

Figure 10.4   Format of register SAVE area.

The description shown here is for the SAVE area in program P after P calls program Q, and before it calls another program. It is assumed that P was called by program X. If P were a main program, X would be the operating system (see also figs. 10.5a and 10.5b).

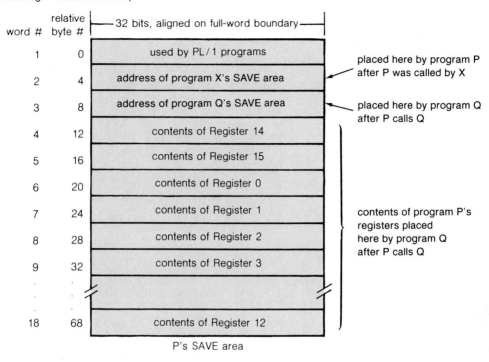

Figure 10.5a   SAVE area contents with standard conventions (assuming P called Q and Q called R).

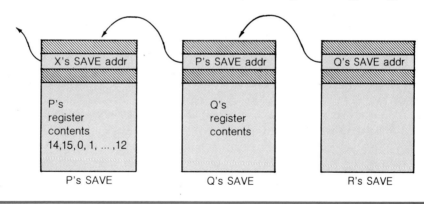

Figure 10.5b   SAVE area contents with complete conventions (assuming P called Q and Q called R).

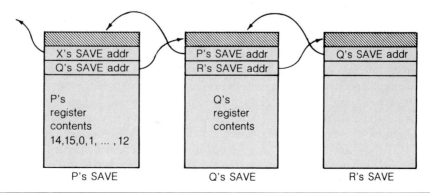

Figure 10.6 *Passing parameter addresses through Register 1.*

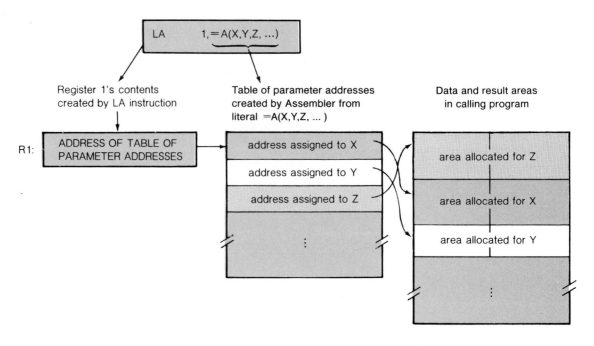

Passing Values of Parameters

Assuming that the contents of Register 13 had been correctly set to the address of the SAVE area at the beginning of a program's execution and had not been changed from that value, the conventional calling sequence for external subroutines in the IBM 360 and 370 systems consists of these instructions (see Fig. 10.3):

```
LA       1,=A(X,Y,...)
L        15,=V(Q)
BALR     14,15
```

The first instruction enables the values of the parameters to be passed to the subroutine. It works as follows: The literal constant =A(X,Y,...) is a table of address constants, similar in format to the V-type address constant required for external addresses, but with the difference that the list of one or more symbols enclosed in parentheses in the A-type address constant *all represent addresses internal to the calling program*. The three dots simply indicate that there may be more symbols included; their number depends, as has been mentioned, on the requirements of the subroutine. For any given A-type constant, the assembler creates a table of full-word addresses, one word for each symbol specified in the constant. This is shown in Figure 10.6; the table consists of consecutive full words, in which bits 8–31 of each word contain the address assigned to the corresponding symbol by the assembler and bits 0–7 of each word are 0's.

Parameter Address Table

Note that the linkage convention's method of passing parameters to an external subroutine is different from the method introduced in Chapter 9 for internal subroutines. What is passed to an external subroutine is the address of the table: not the values of the parameters, not the addresses of the parameters, but the address of a table that contains the addresses of the parameters. It is worth noting that it does not matter how many or what type of data or results must be exchanged between the calling and the called program; the calling sequence enables all situations to be handled with a single address, namely, the address of the parameter address table. It is also worth noting that the order in which the parameter addresses must appear in this table is dictated by the subroutine's design; it is not a decision that can be made by the calling program.

Corresponding to each symbol listed in the A-type literal operand, there must be a statement defining that symbol. This statement will usually be either a DC or DS directive, i.e., it will either define the symbol as the symbolic address of a constant defined at assembly time or as the symbolic

Figure 10.7   Illustration of linkage conventions.

```
P       CSECT                          VABS        CSECT
        STM   14,12,12(13)             *
        BALR  12,0                     *  SUBROUTINE VABS(K,N)  REPLACES EACH COMPONENT OF THE INTEGER
        USING *,12                     *  ARRAY   K   WITH ITS ABSOLUTE VALUE.    'N'  IS THE NUMBER
        ST    13,SAVE+4                *  OF COMPONENTS IN    K .
        LA    13,SAVE                  *
         .                                         STM    14,12,12(13)        SAVE CALLER'S REGS 14,15,0,1,...,12
         .                                         BALR   12,0                ESTABLISH BASE ADDRESS IN REG 12
         .                                         USING  *,12
        LA    1,=A(M,MN)                            ST     13,SAVE+4           SAVE CALLER'S SAVE AREA ADDRESS
        L     15,=V(VABS) }  CALL                   LA     13,SAVE             LOAD SUBR'S SAVE AREA ADDRESS
        BALR  14,15      }                 *
         .                              *  OBTAIN PARAMETERS FROM CALLING PROGRAM
         .                              *
        L     13,SAVE+4                            LM     7,8,0(1)            R7 = ADDRESS OF ARRAY  K
        LM    14,12,12(13)                         L      9,0(8)              R8 = ADDRESS OF PARAMETER N
        BR    14                       *                                      R9 = N
         .                              *  COMPUTE ABSOLUTE VALUES
M       DS    100F                     *
MN      DC    F'100'                   LOOP        L      5,0(7)              R5 = K(J), J=1,2,...,N
SAVE    DS    18F                                  LPR    5,5                 R5 = ABS(K(J))
        END                                        ST     5,0(7)              K(J) = ABS(K(J))
                                        *
                                        *  LOOP CONTROL
                                                   LA     7,4(7)              INCR ADDR TO NEXT COMPONENT
                                                   BCT    9,LOOP              REPEAT IF STILL MORE COMPONENTS
                                        *  EXIT FROM SUBROUTINE
                                                 { L      13,SAVE+4           RESTORE CALLER'S SAVE AREA ADDR.
                                          RETURN { LM     14,12,12(13)        RESTORE REGS 14,15,0,1,2,...,12
                                                 { BR     14                  BRANCH TO RE-ENTRY POINT
                                        *
                                        SAVE        DS     18F                SUBROUTINE'S SAVE AREA
                                                    END
```

address of a memory area whose data is to be supplied at run time. In either case, the subroutine needs the address at run time in order to obtain the data from the calling program's memory or to store the results in that memory. Therefore, one of the first instructions that the subroutine will execute after it has stored the register contents and the caller's SAVE area address is one that will obtain one or more parameter addresses from the table.

For example, to copy the first parameter address into Register 2, this instruction is sufficient:

Accessing the Parameter Address Table

```
L          2,0(1)
```

To copy the first two parameter addresses into Registers 2 and 3, respectively, these two instructions can be used:

```
L          2,0(1)
L          3,4(1)
```

or this single instruction can be used:

```
LM         2,3,0(1)
```

The significance of this technique is that, without having specified its parameters as external addresses at assembly time, for example, without specifying them as V-type constants, the subroutine has, at run time, obtained the external memory addresses of data and/or result areas in the calling program. The technique works no matter how large or small the calling program is, no matter where in its memory the table of parameter addresses is, and no matter where the data and/or result areas are. Thus, the subroutine is truly independent of the calling program. All that is required is that the linkage conventions be followed and that the calling program specify the correct number, type, and order of the parameters.

To illustrate these concepts, consider the external subroutine VABS in Figure 10.7 and the skeletal calling program accompanying it. The subroutine's purpose, as shown in the figure, is to replace each component of an integer array with its absolute value. Although the comments in the subroutine refer to an array named K and to its size, the variable N, there is, in fact, no directive or operand that specifies K or N. Indeed, in the calling program, the actual variable names are M and MN, respectively. This makes no difference. What the subroutine needs in order to complete its task is the address of the array and the number of components in it. In accordance with the linkage convention, this information is obtained as follows: the calling program's instruction LA 1,=A(M,MN) puts the address of the parameter address table into Register 1. In this case, the parameter address table consists of two addresses, in this order:

address assigned to M
address assigned to MN

The subroutine's instruction LM 7,8,0(1) copies the first of these two parameter addresses into Register 7 and the second into Register 8. This is followed by the instruction L 9,0(8), which loads Register 9 with the contents of the word whose address is in Register 8, i.e., with the size of the array. At this point, the subroutine has all the information it needs to complete its task.

Branching to and Returning from an External Subroutine

The branch to an external subroutine and the subroutine's branch back to the calling program both depend on the properties of the Branch and Link via Register (**BALR**) instruction. The primary property, as its name implies, is its ability to establish the necessary link between subroutine and calling program, namely, the reentry point. Generally, the properties of the BALR instruction are these:

opcode	operand	type
BALR	R1,R2	RR

When the BALR instruction is executed, a branch is made to the address contained in bits 8–31 of the register designated by the R2 field, unless that register is Register 0. If R2 designates Register 0, no branch is made. Regardless of whether or not R2 designates Register 0, execution of the BALR instruction places the address of the BALR instruction *plus two* into bits 8–31 of the R1 register. (Execution of the BALR instruction also copies certain data from the program status word into bits 0–7 of the R1 register: bits 0–1 = the instruction length code; bits 2–3 = the condition code; bits 4–7 = the program mask. The contents of the R1 register are not changed, however, until either the address to which the BALR branches is obtained from the R2 register, or it is determined that the R2 register is Register 0. Some models of the IBM 370 include the instruction BASR, Branch and Save via Register, as an alternative to BALR. The only difference between BASR and BALR is that BASR puts X'00' into bits 0–7 of the R1 register instead of the instruction length code, condition code, and program mask.)

For example, suppose the address of a BALR 12,0 instruction is 005432_{16}. When this instruction is executed, 005434 will be placed into bits 8–31 of Register 12, but no branch will be made. However, if, instead of BALR 12,0, the instruction at 005432 was BALR 14,15, then its execution would cause a branch to whatever address was in Register 15 and would also cause 005434 to be placed into bits 8–31 of Register 14.

Register 14
Register 15

Thus it should be clear that in the IBM 360 and 370 systems, the combined effect of the two instructions

```
L       15,=V(Q)
BALR    14,15
```

is that the BALR 14,15 branches to the external entry point designated by the literal =V(Q) after placing the reentry point address into Register 14. In other words, the reentry point is at the instruction that immediately follows the BALR instruction.

Note that since the contents of Register 14 are saved by the subroutine, then in the sequence of instructions that constitutes the return from the subroutine, namely

```
L       13,SAVE+4
LM      14,12,12(13)
BR      14
```

the BR 14 instruction branches to the reentry point that was established by the calling program's BALR 14, 15. That address is not known at assembly time, of course; it is not known until the subroutine is called at run time.

Passing Results Back to the Calling Program

As in high-level languages, results from assembly language subroutines are almost invariably passed back to the calling program via one or more of the parameters specifically understood to be result variables. Although the results replaced the data in the 'VABS' subroutine of Figure 10.7, this need not have been the case. The subroutine could have been designed so that the resulting array was separate from the original array; this would have meant that three parameters would have been required, not two.

Register 0
Register 15

However, there are two situations in which results may be passed back via registers rather than parameters: (1) when the result consists entirely of a single quantity, such as would be produced for a mathematical function, the linkage conventions permit the result to be passed back via Register 0; and (2) when the subroutine is designed to detect errors in the parameters (for example, a request to compute the square root of -1 would not be acceptable to most square root routines), the linkage conventions permit an error code to be returned via Register 15.

Error Detection

As a matter of principle, all programs should include instructions that detect and reject invalid data. This is even more important for subroutines than for main programs. A programmer using an external subroutine written by someone else should not be expected to have to deal with invalid results that come up due to invalid data. Consider, for example, the VABS subroutine of Figure 10.7. This subroutine does not test the value of N, the number of components in the array; it assumes this value will be positive. What would happen if the calling program unwittingly passed a negative or zero value of N? At best the subroutine would get hung up in a long loop, due to the way the BCT instruction works. Worse things could happen, however, especially if during this long loop the address in Register 7 was incremented to a point where the Load and Store sequence disrupted some instructions in the program. The subroutine also fails to test any integer whose absolute value is being computed. Thus, if any integer were exactly equal to -2^{31}, the LPR instruction would cause an overflow with probable program termination.

Other Standard Exits

Figure 10.8 shows how the VABS subroutine might be rewritten to detect and process an invalid value of N: it returns a code in Register 15 indicating whether the value of N was valid or not. (Detection and processing of a potential overflow situation is left as an exercise.) Note that once the decision to return some quantity in either Register 0 or Register 15 is made, the standard sequence for returning to the calling program has to be amended. The act of restoring the calling program's Register 0 and/or Register 15 contents would void the result and/or code that had been placed in those registers by the subroutine. Consequently, there are four cases to be considered when returning from a subroutine: (1) restore all registers, (2) restore all but Register 0, (3) restore all but Register 15, and (4) restore all but Registers 0 and 15. Figure 10.8 illustrates the use of one of these and also illustrates how the calling program might be programmed to determine whether the subroutine accepted or rejected its data. Figure 10.9 gives the sequences of instructions required to handle each of the four return situations mentioned. The displacements in the various LM instructions are derived from the format of the SAVE area (see Fig. 10.4).

Call by Reference Versus Call by Value

As we have seen, the parameter addresses passed to the subroutine point to—i.e., *refer* to—memory locations in the calling program. Some of those locations contain data the subroutine is to operate on (its *input*) and the others contain the results (*output*) of the subroutine's operations. A calling sequence that passes addresses of data instead of data values is known as a *call by reference*. Other types of calling sequences are possible, one of the most common being *call by value*. In a call-by-value sequence, data values rather than addresses are passed to the subroutine.

There are certain advantages and disadvantages to each method; we will briefly mention two. A more complete discussion is in James L. Peterson's book, *Computer Organization and Assembly Language Programming* (Academic Press, 1978).

Figure 10.8 *Linkage conventions with error codes.*

```
P       CSECT                          VABS      CSECT
        STM    14,12,12(13)            *
        BALR   12,0                    * SUBROUTINE VABS(K,N) REPLACES EACH OF  N   INTEGERS IN
        USING  *,12                    *   THE ARRAY  K   WITH ITS ABSOLUTE VALUE.    A CODE IS
        ST     13,SAVE+4               *   RETURNED IN REGISTER 15 AS FOLLOWS:
        LA     13,SAVE                 *          REG 15 = 0   IF  N  IS POSITIVE
                                       *          REG 15 = 4   IF  N  NOT POSITIVE
          .                            *
          .                                     STM    14,12,12(13)       SUBROUTINE ENTRY PROCEDURE
          .                                     BALR   12,0
        LA     1,=A(M,MN)                        USING  *,12
        L      15,=V(VABS)                       ST     13,SAVE+4
        BALR   14,15                             LA     13,SAVE
        LTR    15,15                   *                    GET PARAMETERS AND TEST  N
        BZ     OK                               LM     7,8,0(1)           R7 = ADDRESS OF ARRAY  K
BAD     ...                                      L      9,0(8)             R9 = N
                                                 LTR    9,9                TEST  N  TO SEE IF IT'S POSITIVE
OK      ...                                      BNP    ERR                IF NOT, SET ERROR CODE AND EXIT.
                                                 LH     15,=H'0'           IF POSITIVE, SET RETURN INDICATOR.
        L      13,SAVE+4              *                    COMPUTE ABSOLUTE VALUES
        LM     14,12,12(13)          LOOP       L      5,0(7)             R5 = K(J),  J=1,2,...,N
        BR     14                               LPR    5,5                R5 = ABS(K(J))
                                                 ST     5,0(7)             K(J) = ABS(K(J))
          .                          *                    LOOP CONTROL
          .                                     LA     7,4(7)             INCR ADDR TO NEXT COMPONENT
          .                                     BCT    9,LOOP             REPEAT IF STILL MORE COMPONENTS
                                       *                    EXIT FROM SUBROUTINE
M       DS     100F                   EXIT      L      13,SAVE+4          RESTORE CALLER'S SAVE AREA ADDR.
MN      DC     F'100'                            L      14,12(13)          RESTORE REG 14 BUT NOT REG 15
SAVE    DS     18F                               LM     0,12,20(13)        RESTORE REGS 0,1,2,...,12
        END                                      BR     14                 BRANCH TO RE-ENTRY POINT
                                       *                    ERROR DETECTED
                                       ERR       LH     15,=H'4'           SET RETURN CODE TO  4
                                                 B      EXIT               EXIT WITHOUT PROCESSING ARRAY DATA
                                       *                    SUBR REGISTER SAVE AREA
                                       SAVE      DS     18F
                                                 END
```

Figure 10.9 *Restoring registers when returning from a subroutine.*

to restore all registers:

```
L     13,SAVE+4
LM    14,12,12(13)
BR    14
```

to restore all but register 15:

```
L     13,SAVE+4
L     14,12(13)
LM    0,12,20(13)
BR    14
```

to restore all but register 0:

```
L     13,SAVE+4
LM    14,15,12(13)
LM    1,12,24(13)
BR    14
```

to restore all but registers 0 and 15:

```
L     13,SAVE+4
L     14,12(13)
LM    1,12,24(13)
BR    14
```

The main advantage of call by reference is that it can easily be adapted for use with any type or amount of data. Whatever the data—large arrays, character strings, complex data structures—a single address gives the data's location and another may point to its length or other descriptive information. Another advantage is that a single uniform method is used whether a calling program is passing data to the subroutine or is receiving the subroutine's output data.

Clearly this advantage of call by reference can be a corresponding disadvantage of call by value. For example, it would be quite cumbersome and time-consuming to pass all the values of a large array rather than its address. The values would have to be passed either through the registers or in some memory area or file common to both the calling and called programs; otherwise the subroutine would not be able to gain access to the data.

Yet there are cases where call by value is justified. This occurs when there is a single value (or just a few values) to be passed. The calling program can use registers to pass input data to the subroutine, and the subroutine can pass its results back to the calling program in similar fashion. A good example of this is a subroutine that computes the square root of a number: there is only one input and one output data value.

In simple situations the appeal of call by value is usually outweighed by its lack of generality. That is why call by reference is used in the IBM linkage conventions.

10.4 COMMENTS ON THE LINKAGE CONVENTIONS

There are several reasons for the use of conventional methods of interfacing to external subroutines. Among the most important are:

1. A subroutine written by one person can be called by a program written by someone else. If the subroutine's method of return is clear to both persons, neither has to investigate the details of the other's program.
2. The passing of parameters is done in a single consistent manner, whether the data and results are integers, characters, or of any other type or length.
3. If all compilers generate the same standard code for the equivalent of the subroutine call and return operations, then programs written in Fortran, Cobol, and other high-level languages can be interfaced to one another and to assembly language programs.
4. Benefits 1–3 are increased in importance when a person wishes to transfer a program from one computer installation to another, if the same conventional methods are used at both sites.

This is not to say that every external subroutine conforms to the conventions, or that every compiler produces code that conforms to the conventions. But it is a goal worth striving toward. To determine the differences between the conventions and code produced by any given compiler, it is necessary to read the relevant documentation, e.g., an IBM Programmer's Guide, for that compiler. To determine the differences between the conventions and the code used in another assembly language program, it may be necessary to obtain a listing of that program.

As previously discussed, each external subroutine must establish its own implied base register and not rely on the base register established in a calling program. The reason for this is that no external address will, at run time, be compatible with the implied displacements generated by the assembler. However, part of the convention is that the calling program pass the entry-point address to the subroutine in Register 15. For this reason, some programmers establish Register 15, rather than Register 12, as the base register in a subroutine. This proves unsatisfactory in two important situations: (1) when the subroutine calls another subroutine, and (2) when the subroutine returns an error code in Register 15. As a general rule, therefore, Register 15 should not be used as the base register.

Registers 0, 1, 13, 14, and 15 are known as the **linkage registers.** This is because they are used in fixed ways as part of the subroutine linkage conventions and because they are used in fixed ways when system macro instructions are executed. System macro instructions, such as the I/O macros OPEN, CLOSE, GET, and PUT, result in calls either to subroutines provided from the system subroutine library as an extension of the operating system capabilities or as calls directly to the operating system itself. In either case the linkage registers are used by system macros to pass information in a manner virtually identical to that of the subroutine linkage conventions. In particular, all system macros depend on there being a register-save-area address in Register 13. For this reason it is good practice to load the save-area address into Register 13 as part of the instruction sequence that begins program execution and not change the contents of Register 13 thereafter.

10.5 EXTERNAL VERSUS INTERNAL SUBROUTINES

Making the Choice

Writing an external subroutine is not much different from writing an internal one. The choice of which type to write depends to a great extent on how many different programmers and/or programs can make use of the subroutine. Another but less important factor is the subroutine's size.

If a subroutine is likely to be called by many different programs, it is best to write it as an external subroutine and store it, in object module format, in a subroutine library. From a library it can be linked into other programs by the linkage editor. Of course, each program that calls it must know what the calling sequence is. But by using the standard linkage conventions and providing adequate documentation about the parameters, the subroutine will be accessible to others.

If a subroutine is very small—i.e., if it only requires a few instructions—it may be advisable to have it be internal rather than external. In this way, the number of statements that call, enter, and return from the subroutine can be reduced so that they don't outweigh the computer time and/or space used by the rest of the subroutine.

But smallness alone isn't enough to affect the decision. For example, computing an absolute value requires no more than three instructions (Load, Load Positive, and Store). Yet the ABS function available in many high-level languages has been written and stored as an external subroutine. The reason is that ABS is used in many different programs.

Writing a Subroutine

Perhaps the best way to write a subroutine—internal or external—is to begin it as an ordinary program segment and then generalize it so that its variable data are passed to it as actual parameters rather than being accessed symbolically. This is the approach we took in Chapter 9, and we now take it again in order to show the similarities and differences between the design and use of an internal subroutine and the design and use of an external one.

Consider the program segment in Figure 10.10. This segment determines the three-letter abbreviation for the name of a month that is given as two digits. For example, given 07, the segment produces JUL; given 11, it produces NOV.

If there is a need by many programmers for this segment, it would be worthwhile to rewrite it as an external subroutine. If you need it at several different places in your program but hardly any other programs need it, it could be coded as an internal subroutine. And if it's only needed once in your program but not by any other programs, there's no need to make it into a subroutine at all; just use it as a segment.

To see the differences in design and usage, we have rewritten the segment both as an internal subroutine and as an external one.

Differences

As an internal subroutine, its calling sequence and its entry and exit statements are rather minimal, as shown in Figure 10.11a. This reduces the overhead: only the registers being used are stored and saved. The addresses of the parameters are passed in registers rather than as in the standard linkage conventions.

As an external subroutine, the standard linkage conventions are used as shown in Figure 10.11b. This adds to the overhead, but it makes the subroutine callable by any program that uses the linkage conventions.

Similarities

Despite the linkage differences, there are basic similarities between the two subroutine solutions. One similarity is that the table of months occurs in all three solutions; it need not be a parameter, since it never changes. The other similarities occur in accessing the parameters. From the segment in Figure 10.10 you should be able to see that the parameters are these:

1. The 2-digit month (MMNUM)
2. The resulting abbreviation (MMLETR)
3. The resulting error code (MMERR)

In the internal subroutine (Fig. 10.11a), we've left the error code in a fixed location since it is accessible to all other parts of the calling program. But we've allowed the 2-digit month and the result to be in variable locations by having the caller pass their locations to the subroutine. The caller passes the addresses of the parameters themselves, rather than the address of the parameter address table. And the subroutine saves and restores only those registers that it uses.

```
MMCONV    LA    4,MMTBL        R4 = ADDR OF MONTH ABBREV TABLE
          LH    5,=H'12'       R5 = # ENTRIES IN TABLE
MMCONVL   CLC   MMNUM,0(4)     FIND NUMERIC MONTH IN TABLE
          BE    MMCONVX        BRANCH WHEN FOUND
          LA    4,6(4)         ELSE INCR TO NEXT TABLE ENTRY
          BCT   5,MMCONVL      KEEP LOOKING
          MVI   MMERR,MMNG     SET X'FF' CODE FOR INVALID DIGITS
          B     MMEXIT
MMCONVX   MVI   MMERR,MMOK     ERR CODE IS X'00' WHEN FOUND
          MVC   MMLETR,2(4)    GET ABBREVIATION FROM TABLE
MMEXIT    ...                  CONTINUE OTHER PROCESSING
          ...
*
*   TABLE OF 2-DIGIT MONTHS AND CORRESPONDING ABBREVIATIONS
MMTBL     DC    C'01JAN,02FEB,03MAR,04APR,05MAY,06JUN'
          DC    C'07JUL,08AUG,09SEP,10OCT,11NOV,12DEC'
*
MMNUM     DS    CL2            RESERVED FOR GIVEN 2-DIGIT MONTH
MMLETR    DS    CL3            RESERVED FOR RESULTING 3-LETTER ABBREV
MMERR     DS    CL1            ERR CODE FOR RESULT OF TABLE SEARCH
MMOK      EQU   X'00'          X'00' CODE = SEARCH SUCCESSFUL
MMNG      EQU   X'FF'          X'FF' CODE = UNSUCCESSFUL
```

Figure 10.11a   *Internal subroutine: converts numeric month to its three-letter abbreviation.*

```
* CONVERTS 2-CHARACTER NUMERIC MONTH TO 3-LETTER ABBREVIATION
* CALLED VIA  LM    2,3,=A(DIGITS,RESULT)
*             BAL   14,MMCONV
* ERRCODE RETURNED IN  MMERR:  X'00' IF SUCCESSFUL, X'FF' IF NOT
*
MMCONV    STM   4,5,MMSAVE     SAVE REGS 4,5 ONLY
          LA    4,MMTBL        R4 = ADDR OF MONTH ABBREV TABLE
          LH    5,=H'12'       R5 = # ENTRIES IN TABLE
MMCONVL   CLC   0(2,2),0(4)    R2 = ADDR OF 2-DIGIT NUMERIC MONTH
          BE    MMCONVX        BRANCH WHEN NUMERIC MONTH FOUND
          LA    4,6(4)         ELSE INCR TO NEXT TABLE ENTRY
          BCT   5,MMCONVL      KEEP LOOKING
          MVI   MMERR,MMNG     SET X'FF' CODE FOR INVALID DIGITS
          B     MMEXIT
MMCONVX   MVI   MMERR,MMOK     ERR CODE IS X'00' WHEN FOUND
          MVC   0(3,3),2(4)    R3 = ADDR OF RESULT FROM TABLE
MMEXIT    LM    4,5,MMSAVE     RETURN TO CALLER
          BR    14
*
*   TABLE OF 2-DIGIT MONTHS AND CORRESPONDING ABBREVIATIONS
MMTBL     DC    C'01JAN,02FEB,03MAR,04APR,05MAY,06JUN'
          DC    C'07JUL,08AUG,09SEP,10OCT,11NOV,12DEC'
*
MMERR     DS    CL1            ERR CODE FOR RESULT OF TABLE SEARCH
MMOK      EQU   X'00'          X'00' CODE = SEARCH SUCCESSFUL
MMNG      EQU   X'FF'          X'FF' CODE = UNSUCCESSFUL
MMSAVE    DS    2F             MMCONV REGISTER SAVE AREA
```

Figure 10.11b   External subroutine: converts numeric month to its three-letter abbreviation.

```
* 'MMCONV' SUBROUTINE
* CONVERTS 2-CHARACTER NUMERIC MONTH TO 3-LETTER ABBREVIATION
* CALLED VIA STANDARD LINKAGE CONVENTIONS
*        WITH ADDR OF  =A(DIGITS,RESULT)  IN REGISTER 1
* RETURNS ERR CODE IN R15
*        0 IF SUCCESSFUL, -1 IF NOT
*
MMCONV     CSECT
           STM    14,12,12(13)   STD ENTRY
           BALR   12,0
           USING  *,12
           ST     13,SAVE+4
           LA     13,SAVE
           LM     2,3,0(1)       R2 = A(DIGITS)
*                                R3 = A(RESULT)
           LA     4,MMTBL        R4 = ADDR OF MONTH ABBREV TABLE
           LH     5,=H'12'       R5 = # ENTRIES IN TABLE
*
MMCONVL    CLC    0(2,2),0(4)    LOOK FOR NUMERIC MONTH IN TABLE
           BE     MMCONVX        BRANCH WHEN FOUND
           LA     4,6(4)         ELSE INCR TO NEXT TABLE ENTRY
           BCT    5,MMCONVL      KEEP LOOKING
           LH     15,=H'-1'      SET ERR CODE FOR INVALID DIGITS
           B      MMEXIT
MMCONVX    LH     15,=H'0'       SET ERR CODE WHEN SUCCESSFUL
           MVC    0(3,3),2(4)    R3 = ADDR OF RESULT FROM TABLE
*
MMEXIT     L      13,SAVE+4      STD EXIT, BUT PRESERVE REG 15
           L      14,12(13)
           LM     1,12,24(13)
           BR     14
*
*  TABLE OF 2-DIGIT MONTHS AND CORRESPONDING ABBREVIATIONS
MMTBL      DC     C'01JAN,02FEB,03MAR,04APR,05MAY,06JUN'
           DC     C'07JUL,08AUG,09SEP,10OCT,11NOV,12DEC'
*
SAVE       DS     18F            MMCONV REGISTER SAVE AREA
           END
```

In the external subroutine (Fig. 10.11b), the caller passes the address of the parameter address table, as required by the linkage conventions. The subroutine saves and restores all but Register 13 in the caller's SAVE area. The error code is returned in Register 15, rather than in a memory area.

Error Code

Note, however, that if an external assembly language subroutine is to be called from a high-level language, then the error code (if any) should be returned in a variable rather than in a register. This is because most high-level languages do not provide an explicit mechanism to test the contents of a hardware register.

For the MMCONV subroutine in Figure 10.11b, this would mean adding a parameter comparable to the MMERR symbol in the segment of Figure 10.10 and changing the two LH instructions to MVI instructions whose destination address was in explicit base-displacement form. Those changes are left as exercises.

10.6   ENTRY, EXTRN, COM, AND DSECT DIRECTIVES

Related to the use of subroutines are several techniques for allowing symbolic references between separately assembled modules. Among these are the following: (1) external addresses: ENTRY, EXTRN, (2) common addresses: COM, and (3) dummy addresses: DSECT.

External Addresses: ENTRY, EXTRN

As has been shown, the V-type address constant is used to symbolically reference an external address, i.e., an address that is defined outside the program in which it is referenced. In order for that to be

Figure 10.12 Illustration of ENTRY and EXTRN directives.

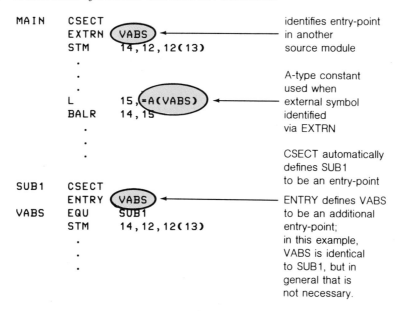

possible, the external address must be an *entry point* of the program in which it is defined. In the examples, the entry point has identified the first instruction to be executed in a subroutine, i.e., it has always been the symbol appearing in the name field of a subroutine's CSECT directive. In addition to symbols defined by a CSECT directive, any other symbol defined in a source module can be referenced by V-type constants from a different source module. For this to be accomplished, the module in which the symbol is *defined* must include an ENTRY statement whose operand contains the symbol. The ENTRY statement essentially declares that the symbol or symbols in its operand field can be referenced by a V-type constant in another program. ENTRY is a directive, not an instruction. No memory locations are reserved for this directive in the object module.

Under two conditions we can reference an external address by means of an A-type constant instead of using a V-type constant to reference an external address. First, the external symbol referred to in the A-type constant must not appear in the name field of any statement within the program that is referencing it as an external address. And second, the external symbol referred to in the A-type constant must appear in the operand field of an EXTRN directive in the same program in which it is referenced as an external address. In other words, the EXTRN directive essentially declares that the symbol or symbols in its operand field represent external addresses. When EXTRN is used to identify an external symbol, the symbol is referenced with an A-type constant; when EXTRN is not used, the symbol is referenced with a V-type constant. No memory locations are reserved for an EXTRN statement. Figure 10.12 illustrates the ENTRY and EXTRN directives.

Common Addresses: COM

When a programmer subdivides a large program into two or more modules, one of these modules constitutes the main program, the program in which the major logic decisions are made, and the others are internal or external subroutines. As has been pointed out, there are several advantages to such a modular approach, but sometimes there is also an added problem: it may happen that two or more of the external subroutines must refer to many of the same constants and memory areas. This could mean that many parameters have to be passed from one program to another, creating a programming burden. To avoid this, an area of memory common to all the programs can be defined. Parameters, data, and results can be stored into and loaded from this area by any of the programs, *as though the area were internal to each program.* By using this technique, we can avoid passing parameters and using V-type or EXTRN/A-type constants.

To use this technique, each source module must include a set of identical statements describing the organization of data in the common memory. This set of statements begins with the COM directive and usually contains only DS directives. The order of the DS directives, the amount of storage

Figure 10.13   Illustration of COM.

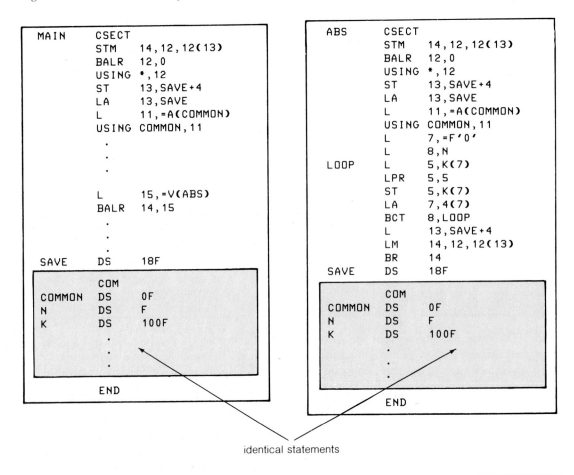

```
MAIN      CSECT
          STM     14,12,12(13)
          BALR    12,0
          USING   *,12
          ST      13,SAVE+4
          LA      13,SAVE
          L       11,=A(COMMON)
          USING   COMMON,11
          .
          .
          .

          L       15,=V(ABS)
          BALR    14,15
          .
          .
          .
SAVE      DS      18F
          COM
COMMON    DS      0F
N         DS      F
K         DS      100F
          .
          .
          .
          END
```

```
ABS       CSECT
          STM     14,12,12(13)
          BALR    12,0
          USING   *,12
          ST      13,SAVE+4
          LA      13,SAVE
          L       11,=A(COMMON)
          USING   COMMON,11
          L       7,=F'0'
          L       8,N
LOOP      L       5,K(7)
          LPR     5,5
          ST      5,K(7)
          LA      7,4(7)
          BCT     8,LOOP
          L       13,SAVE+4
          LM      14,12,12(13)
          BR      14
SAVE      DS      18F
          COM
COMMON    DS      0F
N         DS      F
K         DS      100F
          .
          .
          .
          END
```

identical statements

that each reserves, and the name-field symbols in each statement must be identical in each source module. At execution time, any of the programs can use these symbols to place data into the common memory for it and the other programs to use. The only requirement is that each source module designate an implied base register whose purpose is to provide addressability for the symbols in the common memory. The assembler must be informed of this through the USING directive, and the base address must be loaded at run time before instructions that symbolically referred to the common memory are executed. This is illustrated in Figure 10.13.

It should be noted that, although the area of memory defined by a COM directive is external to all the programs that use it at run time, it is made to appear to be internal to each program through the use of identical symbols (Fig. 10.13). Because of this, it is sometimes difficult to determine the cause of programming errors involving the use of common memory.

Dummy Addresses: DSECT

The major reason that one program, Program A, passes a parameter to another program, Program B, is that the memory area in A, which is addressed by that parameter, becomes accessible to B. Now, it may happen that there are several subareas within that area; for example, fields within a personnel record or columns within an array. How can B gain access to each subarea? One way would be for A to pass a separate parameter for each subarea, but that would be awkward. Another, much better way, would be for B to reference each subarea in terms of its distance, or displacement, from the beginning of the area that the subareas belong to. This is easy to do, since the address of the beginning of the area is passed to B as a parameter. The use of the DSECT directive allows the displacements to be symbolic rather than numeric. Symbolic displacements provide greater flexibility and result in fewer programming errors than do numeric displacements.

DSECT defines the beginning of a **dummy section.** A dummy section is not translated into machine language data or instructions and therefore occupies no memory space at run time. Instead, the statements within a dummy section are used solely as symbolic descriptions of the logical structure of a memory area. Symbols defined within a dummy section can be used at assembly time to process data from any memory area that has the same logical structure as is described by the dummy section. The reason for this is as follows.

A relocatable symbol defined in the name field of a dummy section statement is assigned a value relative to the beginning of the dummy section. Moreover, the assembler always assigns the value 000000 to the beginning of a dummy section. When a dummy section symbol is used in the operand of an instruction, the assembler does not use the implied base register or base address of the section in which the instruction appears. Instead, it uses the dummy section's implied base register and base address. This, in turn, requires that there be a USING directive and an appropriate load-type instruction that establishes an implied base register and base address for the dummy section and that these appear in the section containing the instruction.

But since a dummy section occupies no memory space at run time, the fundamental question is, "What address should be used as the base address for a dummy section?" Not surprisingly, there are two aspects to the answer: one applies to assembly-time processing, the other to run-time processing.

At *assembly time,* the USING directive should specify the name of the dummy section (the name-field symbol of the DSECT directive) in its base-address field, and it should specify a register other than 0, 1, 12, 13, 14, or 15 as the implied base register. This establishes a base address of zero and an implied base register that is not in conflict with other register usage. For example, see the USING DAREA,11 directive in Figure 10.14. In that figure, the base-displacement address field of the assembled CLI OTCODE,C'X' instruction will refer to Register 11, with a displacement of 032_{16}. This is because OTCODE is defined as byte position 50_{10}, relative to the beginning of the dummy section, and the base address (DAREA) is zero since DAREA is at the beginning of the dummy section. Thus the assembler translates the CLI instruction as though it were addressing a byte in the dummy section. *Assembly-Time Base Address*

But note what happens at *run time* for the programs in Figure 10.14. The address of the beginning of the area named AREA is passed from the calling program to the subroutine in the conventional manner, and the called subroutine loads that address into the same register that had been declared as the implied base register for the dummy section. Therefore when the assembled CLI instruction is executed at run time, the effective address computed by the CPU for symbolic address OTCODE is not 000032_{16}, but 032_{16} plus the address in Register 11. In other words, it is the real memory address of a byte in the calling program, namely, the byte that is in the fiftieth position beyond the beginning of the area named AREA. Thus the CPU processes the CLI instruction as though it were addressing a byte in the calling program, even though it was not assembled that way. *Run-Time Base Address*

Further study of Figure 10.14 will reveal the three-fold advantage gained from the use of dummy sections:

1. The elements in the area named AREA can be referred to symbolically even though their addresses are not known at assembly time and even though they are not part of the PAYROLL subroutine that refers to them.
2. If a change is made to the logical structure of AREA, that change must also be made to the dummy section, but no such change has to be made to instructions that refer to dummy section symbols: all that is required is a reassembly of the modules.
3. Although the dummy section of Figure 10.14 describes just one employee record, the LA 11,DLNG(11) instruction that increments the run-time base address permits each entry in a table of identically structured employee records to be processed symbolically.

The distinction between addresses assigned at assembly time and those used at run time is obviously of crucial importance to the understanding of the DSECT directive. Further examples of the use of DSECT will be given in the discussion on recursive subroutines in the next section, and also in Chapters 15, 20, 21, and 23.

Figure 10.14   Illustration of DSECT.

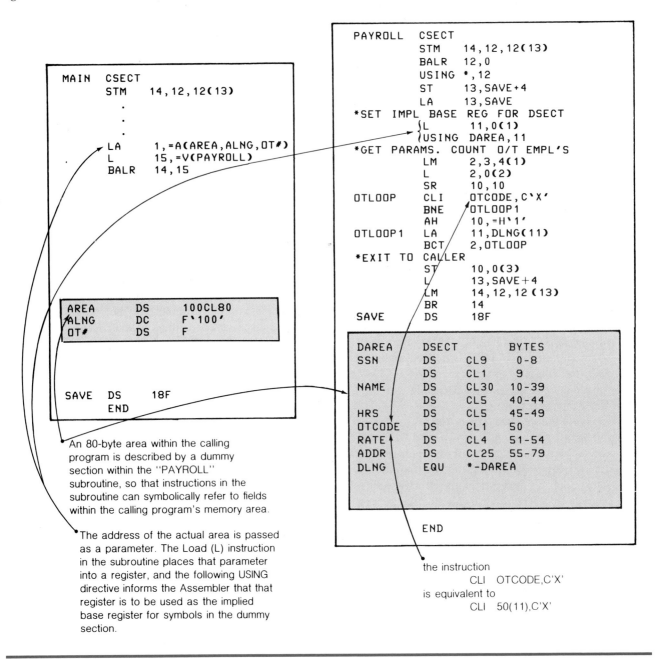

```
MAIN   CSECT
       STM    14,12,12(13)
       .
       .
       .
       LA     1,=A(AREA,ALNG,OT#)
       L      15,=V(PAYROLL)
       BALR   14,15
```

```
AREA        DS     100CL80
ALNG        DC     F'100'
OT#         DS     F
```

```
SAVE   DS   18F
       END
```

An 80-byte area within the calling
program is described by a dummy
section within the "PAYROLL"
subroutine, so that instructions in the
subroutine can symbolically refer to fields
within the calling program's memory area.

The address of the actual area is passed
as a parameter. The Load (L) instruction
in the subroutine places that parameter
into a register, and the following USING
directive informs the Assembler that that
register is to be used as the implied
base register for symbols in the dummy
section.

```
PAYROLL  CSECT
         STM    14,12,12(13)
         BALR   12,0
         USING  *,12
         ST     13,SAVE+4
         LA     13,SAVE
*SET IMPL BASE REG FOR DSECT
        {L     11,0(1)
        {USING DAREA,11
*GET PARAMS. COUNT O/T EMPL'S
         LM     2,3,4(1)
         L      2,0(2)
         SR     10,10
OTLOOP   CLI    OTCODE,C'X'
         BNE    OTLOOP1
         AH     10,=H'1'
OTLOOP1  LA     11,DLNG(11)
         BCT    2,OTLOOP
*EXIT TO CALLER
         ST     10,0(3)
         L      13,SAVE+4
         LM     14,12,12(13)
         BR     14
SAVE     DS     18F
```

```
DAREA    DSECT          BYTES
SSN      DS     CL9      0-8
         DS     CL1      9
NAME     DS     CL30     10-39
         DS     CL5      40-44
HRS      DS     CL5      45-49
OTCODE   DS     CL1      50
RATE     DS     CL4      51-54
ADDR     DS     CL25     55-79
DLNG     EQU    *-DAREA
```

```
         END
```

the instruction
```
      CLI   OTCODE,C'X'
```
is equivalent to
```
      CLI   50(11),C'X'
```

10.7   RECURSIVE SUBROUTINES

A *recursive subroutine* is one that may be used as a subroutine of itself at run time, either by calling itself directly or being called by a subroutine that it has called. When it calls itself, or when it is called by a subroutine that it has called, it is said to be called recursively. By a **"recursive call"** we also mean this: each such call enters the same copy of the subroutine as all the other calls. Thus, no matter how many times a recursive subroutine is called recursively, there is only one copy of it in memory at run time.

Recursive subroutines have applications in many problems that arise in computer science. However, discussion of these problems and their solutions is beyond the scope of this text. We will restrict our discussion to a brief overview of the mechanism that underlies recursive subroutines written in assembly language. The mechanism can be used to write either an internal recursive subroutine or an external recursive subroutine.

When a recursive subroutine calls itself, it must not only pass some parameters to itself, but it must also establish a reentry point so that it can return to itself. The call and the return to itself are written like the call and return in any other subroutine. What is different in a recursive subroutine is what happens just after entering the subroutine, and just prior to returning from it.

Let us assume that Program A calls recursive Subroutine B. Clearly, B is obligated to return to A's reentry point. But suppose that before returning to A, Subroutine B calls itself recursively. The first rule of recursive subroutine calls is this: before B can return to A, it must return to itself from its recursive call. By repeated applications of this rule, we then obtain this general rule:

If B has been called recursively *N* consecutive times, it must return to the *N* callers in the reverse order in which they called B.

Thus, a recursive subroutine B always returns to its most recent caller's reentry point.

Note that since there is only one copy of a recursive subroutine in memory, then in order for it to execute correctly, it is necessary that a complete record of the status of its unfinished work be saved when it calls itself or calls another subroutine. The status information—which includes the contents of registers and the values of all parameters and other variables—must be saved in such a way that it can be restored when the subroutine resumes its unfinished work.

An outline of the essential steps required when entering and returning from a recursive subroutine is shown in Figure 10.15. Referring to that figure, the steps can be summarized as follows:

When a recursive subroutine is entered at run time, it requests that the operating system allocate a memory area large enough to contain all the status information that it may need to save. The request is made via a macro: **GETMAIN** in OS, and **GETVIS** in DOS. After allocating the memory area, the operating system tells the subroutine what the beginning address of the allocated area is. In Figure 10.15, that address is returned in Register 1 by the GETMAIN and GETVIS macros. You should consult the appropriate OS or DOS macro manual for alternative methods of using GETMAIN or GETVIS.

A different status area is allocated via GETMAIN (or GETVIS) each time the subroutine is called, and only one status area is in use by the subroutine while it is processing a call. In this way no two calls to the subroutine will have their status information stored in the same area. For each call to a recursive subroutine, all status data, including the register save area, are stored in the areas allocated at run time via the GETMAIN (or GETVIS) macros. Status data is *not* stored in areas reserved by DS directives, because DS areas occupy the same memory locations each time the subroutine is called.

The beginning address of the allocated memory area is used as the base address for all references to that area. Symbolic references are achieved by using a DSECT directive to describe the structure of the information in the allocated area. A USING directive specifies the DSECT's name and the register that will contain the area's base address.

After obtaining the address of the status area, the subroutine then obtains the parameters from the caller and executes whatever instructions are necessary for its task, including recursively calling itself.

At some point prior to returning, the subroutine must pass its results back to the caller. Then, immediately prior to returning, the allocated memory area is released by a macro: **FREEMAIN** in OS, and **FREEVIS** in DOS. All the status data stored in that area are lost when the area is released, but it is no longer needed, since the results have already been passed back to the caller. Moreover, by releasing the area each time it returns, the subroutine ensures that the number of allocated areas always equals the number of unfinished calls. It also helps ensure that the total amount of memory the operating system can allocate to the program is not likely to be exceeded.

Note that when a status area is acquired, the address of the previous area is stored in the new area's STATSAVE+4 word. Later, just prior to releasing the current area, the address of the previous area is recovered from the STATSAVE+4 word. In other words, the areas are connected via their STATSAVE+4 words. The most recent area allocated is always the area that is released first. In computer science, we say that the areas are connected in a last-in, first-out (LIFO) sequence. Because of the LIFO sequence, the set of all status areas that have not yet been released is said to constitute a stack of status areas. The status areas are said to be items on the stack. See Figure 10.16.

Figure 10.15   Entering and returning from an external recursive subroutine.

```
RECURSE  CSECT
         STM     14,12,12(13)             STANDARD ENTRY
         BALR    12,0
         USING   *,12
         ST      13,SAVE+4                SAVE CALLER'S STATUS AREA ADDR
         LA      13,SAVE
*
* GET ADDR OF NEW STATUS AREA VIA GETMAIN (OR GETVIS).
         LR      2,1                      SAVE CALLER'S ADDR OF PARAM ADDRS
         L       0,=A(AREASIZE)           R0 = REQUESTED STATUS AREA'S SIZE
         GETMAIN R,LV=(0)                 REQUEST MEMORY FOR STATUS AREA
*        GETVIS                           DOS REQUEST
         LR      13,1                     R1 = ADDRESS OF NEW STATUS AREA
         USING   STATAREA,13              R13= BASE REG FOR 'DSECT' AREA
         MVC     STATSAVE+4(4),SAVE+4     PUT CALLER'S STATUS AREA ADDRESS
*                                         INTO NEW STATUS AREA
*
* PROCESS MOST RECENT CALLER'S REQUEST
         LR      1,2                      RECOVER CALLER'S ADDR OF PARAM ADDRS
         LM      ...,0(1)                 GET CALLER'S PARAMETER ADDRESSES
         .....          PROCESS CALLER'S REQUEST, INCLUDING RECURSIVE CALLS
         .....                            GIVE RESULTS TO CALLER
*
*   RETURN TO MOST RECENT CALLER
         MVC     SAVE+4(4),STATSAVE+4 RECOVER CALLER'S STATUS AREA ADDR
         DROP    13                       RELEASE R13 FROM BASE REGISTER
         L       0,=A(AREASIZE)           TELL FREEMAIN (FREEVIS) SIZE AND
         LR      1,13                     LOCATION OF AREA TO BE RELEASED,
         LA      13,SAVE                  AND GIVE IT A REG SAVE AREA.
         FREEMAIN                         RELEASE MOST RECENT STATUS AREA
*        FREEVIS                          DOS REQUEST
         L       13,SAVE+4                GET CALLER'S STATUS AREA ADDRESS
         LM      14,12,12(13)             RESTORE CALLER'S REGS
         BR      14                       RETURN TO CALLER
*
*   DSECT STATEMENTS NAME AND DESCRIBE VARIABLE DATA IN STATUS AREA
STATAREA DSECT
STATSAVE DS      18F          REGISTER SAVE AREA WITHIN STATUS AREA
         ........             VARIABLES & DESCRIPTIONS IN STATUS AREA
AREASIZE EQU     *-STATAREA   LAST STMT IN DSECT GIVES SIZE OF STATUS AREA
*
RECURSE  CSECT        , RESUME RECURSIVE SUBROUTINE'S FIXED AREAS
SAVE     DS      18F   REGISTER SAVE AREA WITHIN RECURSIVE SUBROUTINE
         END
```

One final note: In the statements of Figure 10.15, the address of the subroutine's ordinary register save area (SAVE) is loaded just prior to executing the GETMAIN or GETVIS system macro. The reason is that each time GETMAIN or GETVIS is executed, there is no other area available; the macro is about to get an area, but meanwhile there needs to be a save-area address in Register 13 for the GETMAIN and GETVIS system procedures. With FREEMAIN or FREEVIS, the situation is similar: these macros are going to release the area that would normally contain the register save area, so they too need the address of a different area.

10.8   SUMMARY

A subroutine is a set of statements that constitute a programming solution to a particular problem; it may be used any number of times by one or more computer programs. Subroutines may be either internal to the programs that call them, or external to those programs. If external, they need not be written in the same language as the programs that use them. A program uses a subroutine by means of a specially adapted sequence of statements known as the "calling sequence." This sequence satisfies

Figure 10.16   Recursive subroutine concepts.

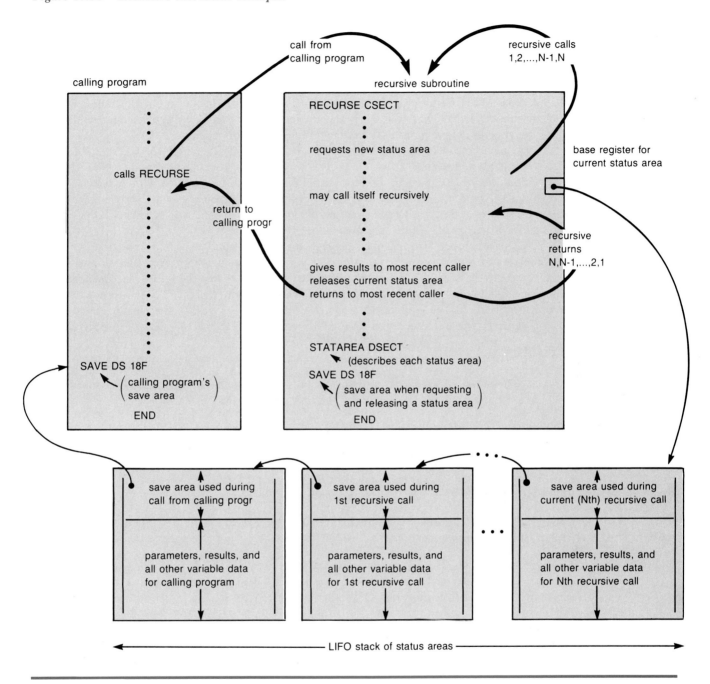

the linkage requirements of branching to the subroutine's entry point, of designating the reentry point of the calling program, and of passing to the subroutine the parameters that it was designed to process.

Each computer system usually has a conventional method of calling and returning from external subroutines. These almost always include a method of saving the contents of registers so that the calling program will remain unaffected by the subroutine's use of registers. In the IBM 360 and 370 systems, the conventions require that upon entry to a subroutine, Register 1 must contain the address of a parameter address table, Register 13 the address of the calling program's register save area, Register 14 the reentry address, and Register 15 the entry address. Upon return from a subroutine, the contents of the registers must be the same as when the subroutine was entered, except that Register 0 may contain a result and Register 15 may contain an error code. The subroutine returns to the reentry address specified by the calling program.

Internal and external subroutines both have advantages and disadvantages. Internal subroutines have the advantage of sharing the same set of symbolic and real memory addresses as the portion of the program that calls them, so that it may be unnecessary to pass as many parameters as with external subroutines. It may also be convenient to relax the linkage requirements and thereby reduce the overhead associated with calling and returning. The use of internal subroutines may result in an object module longer than 4096 bytes; this could require the use of more than one base register, thereby reducing the number of registers available for general use.

An advantage of external subroutines is that they can be written and tested separately from other portions of an overall programming solution, can be used in the solution of more than one problem without having to be rewritten or reassembled, and can even be written in languages different from those used in the programs that call them or are called by them.

Some important additional facilities are provided by the ENTRY, EXTRN, COM, and DSECT directives. ENTRY identifies symbols that are to be *accessible from* other programs. EXTRN identifies symbols *defined in* other programs and permits them to be specified with A-type constants rather than V-type constants. COM defines the beginning of a memory area to be shared by more than one program. DSECT allows a programmer to define symbolic displacements for which the base address is not specified until run time.

A recursive subroutine in assembly language must include a mechanism to do two things: (1) put the complete status of the parameters and other variable data on a stack each time the subroutine is called recursively, and (2) restore the most recent status data from the stack when the subroutine returns to itself from a recursive call. The mechanism for doing this involves run-time requests to the operating system: The GETMAIN and GETVIS macros request that a memory area for the current status data be allocated; the FREEMAIN and FREEVIS macros release an allocated area.

10.9 REVIEW

External Subroutine   A separately assembled set of statements that may be called from one or more points in a computer program to perform some task at the request of that program.

Entry Point   In a subroutine, the first instruction executed when it is called.

Reentry Point   In a caller, the first instruction executed after returning from a subroutine.

Subroutine Parameter   A variable that identifies (or has the value of) data that will be operated on by a subroutine, or that identifies a result determined by the subroutine.

Calling Sequence   The sequence of instructions, and the sequence and types of parameters, that are used in calling a subroutine.

Linkage Conventions   The calling sequence standards that dictate how parameters are to be passed to external subroutines, and what registers are to be used when calling and returning from an external subroutine and when executing an I/O or other system macro.

Linkage Registers   Registers 0, 1, 13, 14, and 15, used in fixed ways as part of the linkage conventions. These registers should not ordinarily be used for any other purpose.

BALR Instruction   The RR-type Branch and Link instruction that puts the caller's reentry point in a register just prior to branching to a subroutine's entry point.

BR Instruction   The extended mnemonic RR-type branch instruction that branches to the address that's in the register designated in its operand.

Address Constant   A DC or literal constant whose value can be a relocatable address.

A-Type Constant   An address constant whose defining expression may include internal symbols as well as external symbols designated by EXTRN directives. See also Chapter 9.

V-Type Constant   An address constant whose defining expression consists of a single relocatable symbol declared as an entry point in another, separately assembled program.

ENTRY, EXTRN Directives   ENTRY identifies symbols known as "entry points" that are to be accessible from other programs. EXTRN identifies symbols known as "external addresses" that are defined as entry points in other programs but are to be referenced with A-type rather than V-type constants.

COM, DSECT Directives   COM describes and creates a data area that at run time will be shared by two or more separately assembled programs. DSECT describes but does not create a data area whose address will be passed to the program at run time.

Recursive Subroutine   A subroutine programmed in such a way that it can call itself any number of times while processing a calling program's request. A recursive subroutine always returns to the reentry point of its most recent caller.

10.10   REVIEW QUESTIONS

1. What is the principal difference between an A-type address constant and a V-type address constant? Why can't all address constants simply be A-type constants?
2. Why must we use the RR-type BALR (or BASR) instruction instead of the RX-type BAL (or BAS) instruction to call an external subroutine?
3. Explain why the L 9,0(8) instruction is needed in the VABS subroutine of Figure 10.7 to obtain one of the parameters from the calling program.
4. When using the instruction LA 1,=A(X,Y, . . .) to load the address of the parameter address table, is it necessary for the parameters X,Y, . . . to be defined by statements that are in the same order in which they appear in the A-type constant? Why or why not?
5. Why doesn't an external subroutine store the contents of Register 13 in the calling program's save area, instead of storing it in its own save area?
6. Explain how the values of the displacements in each of the LM instructions of Figure 10.9 were determined.
7. Why does an *external* subroutine need to establish an implied base address and base register via the standard BALR-USING sequence, whereas an *in*ternal subroutine does not need to do so?
8. What base-displacement address does the assembler generate when it assembles an operand symbol such as OTCODE in Figure 10.14 that is defined within a dummy section?
9. Why is it necessary to have a different implied base register than Register 12 for the symbols that are defined within a dummy section?
10. What would be the consequence of omitting the BALR instruction from the standard BALR-USING sequence that establishes Register 12 as the implied base register in an external subroutine?
11. What would be the consequence of omitting the instruction that loads a base address into a dummy section's implied base register? (For a specific example, consider what would happen if the L 11,0(1) instruction that's near the beginning of the PAYROLL program in Figure 10.14 were omitted.)
12. Explain why a different status area is needed for each of the N consecutive recursive calls to a recursive subroutine.
13. Explain why a register save area is used in each status area of a recursive subroutine. (**Hint:** Explain why a recursive subroutine cannot use the same register save area for each of the recursive calls.)
14. Explain the advantage of having a recursive subroutine request status areas from the operating system at run time instead of reserving them at assembly time.

1. What would be the effect at run time in an external subroutine that began its execution with the instructions corresponding to these statements:

    a.
```
A      CSECT
       STM      14,12,12(13)
       BALR     12,0
       USING    *,12
       LA       13,SAVE
```

    b.
```
B      CSECT
       BALR     12,0
       USING    *,12
       STM      14,12,12(13)
       ST       13,SAVE+4
       LA       13,SAVE
```

    c.
```
C      CSECT
       USING    *,15
       STM      14,12,12(13)
       ST       13,SAVE+4
       LA       13,SAVE
```

2. What would be the effect at run time if an external subroutine ended its execution with the instructions corresponding to these statements:

    a.
```
LM      14,12,12(13)
L       13,SAVE+4
BR      14
```

    b.
```
L       13,SAVE+4
LM      12,14,12(13)
BR      14
```

    c.
```
LA      13,SAVE+4
LM      14,12,12(13)
BR      14
```

3. There are two IBM system macros that can be used to simplify the process of saving and restoring registers. These are the SAVE and RETURN macros, described in the *OS/VS1 Supervisor Services and Macro Instructions* manual, #GC24–5103. Using this manual or simply by experimenting with the SAVE and RETURN macros, determine the expansion that is generated for each of the following statements:

```
a. SAVE        (14,12)
b. SAVE        (14,12),,*
c. SAVE        (12,14)
d. RETURN      (14,12)
e. RETURN      (14,12),RC=15
f. RETURN      (14,12),RC=(15)
g. RETURN      (14,12),T,RC=0
h. SAVE        (14,12),T
```

4. Write an external subroutine that will convert a 32-bit binary integer to its EBCDIC character representation. Make whatever assumptions seem reasonable about the format of the result.

5. Rewrite the program segment of Figure 8.9 in Chapter 8 so that it is an external subroutine that converts 8 hex digits to EBCDIC codes.

6. Rewrite each of the program segments in the figures listed below so that it is an external subroutine that performs the same task that the segment does.

   a. Fig. 5.2: Compute the sum of N integers.
   b. Fig. 5.4: Multiply each integer in an array by a constant.
   c. Fig. 5.5: Count the number of positive integers in an array.
   d. Fig. 5.8: Determine the algebraically largest and smallest integers in an array.

7. Write an external subroutine that will print the contents of the sixteen general registers in hexadecimal notation, in a suitably readable format (similar to that which appears in a memory dump).

8. Referring to the string-editing operations depicted in Figure 7.8, what parameters would have to be passed to a subroutine that performed the DELETE operation? To a subroutine that performed the INSERT operation? The REPLACE operation? Write three external subroutines, one for each of the three string-editing operations of Figure 7.8.

9. Write an external subroutine named MATMPY that will compute the product of an $M \times N$ array and an $N \times K$ array (in that order), the result being an $M \times K$ array. Assume that the arrays are integer arrays and that the product is computed as in this Fortran subroutine:

```
      SUBROUTINE MATMPY (JA,M,N,JB,K,JC)
      DIMENSION JA(50,50),JB(50,50),JC(50,50)
      DO 40 KROW = 1,M
      DO 30 KCOL = 1,K
      JC(KROW,KCOL) = 0
      DO 20 KK = 1,N
      JC(KROW,KCOL) = JC(KROW,KCOL) + JA(KROW,KK)*JB(KK,KCOL)
20    CONTINUE
30    CONTINUE
40    CONTINUE
      RETURN
      END
```

10. Write an external subroutine that, for any given 32-bit binary integer J, will determine the largest value of n such that J can be expressed as an integral multiple of 2^n. For example, if $J = 1024$, then $n = 10$ since $J = 1 \times 2^{10}$. If $J = 1025$, then $n = 0$. The subroutine should return the value of n as a binary integer in Register 0.

11. a. Write an external subroutine that will print the contents of memory from address $A - a$ to address B, where A and B are specified as parameters, and a is calculated by the subroutine so that $a < 8$ and $A - a$ is a double-word boundary. The memory contents should be printed in hexadecimal notation, in a suitably readable format (similar to that which appears in a memory dump).

    b. Modify your Exercise 11a subroutine so that $A - a$ is exactly divisible by 32, and $a < 32$. The first line printed should contain blanks instead of the contents of locations $A - a$, $A - a + 1, ..., A - 1$.

    c. Modify your Exercise 11b subroutine so that it will also print the contents of the sixteen general registers that are passed to it. It can do this by calling the external subroutine written as the solution to Exercise 7.

    d. Modify your Exercise 11c solution so that it will print the memory contents, the register contents, or both, depending on the value of a parameter passed to the subroutine.

12. Write an external subroutine that will examine a string one character at a time, left to right, and perform the following delete operation: for each occurrence of the EBCDIC backspace character (X'16'), delete that character and the one preceding it before examining the next character in the string. Both the address and the length of the string should be passed as parameters to your subroutine. Note that the string may contain several consecutive backspaces, such as might be created when correcting text typed at a terminal. (This is the same problem as #13 in Chapter 7, and #9 in Chapter 9, the difference being that it is now to be solved with an external subroutine.)

13. Write a main program (not a subroutine) that will copy all the components of a 50×50 two-dimensional integer array A into another 50×50 integer array B. Explain why more than one implied base register is needed. How many implied base registers would be needed if this were a subroutine rather than a main program? How many implied base registers would be needed if this were a main program and the arrays were 30×30 instead of 50×50?

PART

III

Noninteger Arithmetic

11

Introductory Concepts

Problems that involve computations with mixed numbers—numbers that may contain both an integer portion and a fractional portion—are almost invariably programmed in Fortran or some other high-level language rather than in assembly language. Nevertheless, an understanding of how these computations are handled at the assembly language or machine language level is important for at least two reasons: (1) to enable programmers to understand the limitations inherent in computer arithmetic when mixed numbers are processed, and (2) to enable programmers to understand how computations specified in high-level languages are implemented at the level of machine language.

Implied Decimal Point

In the IBM 360 and 370 systems, and in virtually all other present-day computer systems, the position of the decimal point in arithmetic operations is not explicitly represented. Its position is implied. This poses no serious problem when handling integers, since the decimal point's position is always to the right of the right-most digit and it would be superfluous to represent it explicitly. Even with integers, however, the lack of an explicit decimal point poses somewhat of a problem in division; the solution is to represent the result in two parts: an integer quotient and an integer remainder. With mixed numbers, the lack of a decimal point is more serious; we can't ignore the decimal point, since its position determines the value of a number. We cannot, for example, add two numbers such as 0.15 and 1.5 unless we can align the decimal points before doing the addition.

Hardware Solutions

There are two principal hardware solutions to this problem. One is known as floating-point arithmetic, the other as decimal (or packed-decimal) arithmetic. In **floating-point arithmetic,** the hardware aligns the position of the decimal point during the execution of instructions. In **decimal arithmetic,** all numbers are represented as integers and the programmer has the responsibility of aligning the implied decimal point positions in every arithmetic operation. Because of its added complexity and cost, floating-point hardware and decimal hardware are not available on some computers. However, both are available on the IBM 360 and 370 systems.

Before discussing the instructions required for utilizing these hardware capabilities, the following introductory concepts are presented: methods of converting mixed numbers from one base to another, problems inherent in the use of mixed numbers in computer systems, and methods for preventing certain numerical errors from terminating a program in the IBM 360 and 370 systems.

11.1 A QUESTION OF ACCURACY

The fractional portion of a mixed decimal number can be represented as a sequence of decimal digits, d_j, preceded by a decimal point, as follows:

$$0 . d_1 d_2 d_3 ...$$

Except for the representation of some rational fractions p/q (where p and q are both integers, and $p < q$), the fractional portion must be truncated to whatever accuracy is desired. When performing arithmetic with pencil and paper, we always have the option of including as many digits to the right of the decimal point as we wish. In computer systems, increasing the number of digits beyond the capacity of a word usually requires additional hardware, additional software, or both. Even then there is an upper limit to how many digits can be incorporated, so that what results is the representation of a rational fraction that only approximates the desired number.

Loss of Accuracy

For example, when we write 0.33333... we understand that we can write as many three's as we please in order to better approximate the rational fraction ⅓. But in computer systems, a fixed upper limit on the number of digits that can be accommodated is imposed by the hardware and software. If the limit is six, then our best approximation would be 0.333333. Further, if during the course of a computation we were to attempt to compute the quantity $(A-B)*C$, where $C=30$ and $A-B = 1/10,000,000$, the correct result of 0.000003 would be incorrectly represented as 0.000000, since to six places the value of $A-B$ is 0.000000. If the same $(A-B)*C$ were multiplied by another factor, D, the result would be zero *no matter what the value of D is*. Note that the exact value of $(A-B)*C$ required only six digits to the right of the decimal point, yet, because of the sequence in which it was computed, it could not be represented accurately. Worse, the result of subsequent calculations such as $(A-B)*C*D$ could be greatly in error.

It is not the purpose of this textbook to discuss methods for handling such problems; this falls under the topic of numerical analysis. But you should be aware that the problems exist and should consult a numerical analysis text for further information (see references in Section 11.5).

11.2 CONVERSION FROM ONE BASE TO ANOTHER

In base 10, the value of the decimal fraction represented as

Positional Notation for Fractions

$$0 . d_1 d_2 d_3 ... d_m$$

may be computed as

$$d_1 \times 10^{-1} + d_2 \times 10^{-2} + ... + d_m \times 10^{-m}$$

In base P, the value of the fraction consisting of the base digits p_j,

$$0 . p_1 p_2 p_3 ... p_k$$

can be computed as

$$p_1 \times P^{-1} + p_2 \times P^{-2} + ... + p_k \times P^{-k}$$

For example, in base 2, the representation 0.110011 has the value

$$1 \times 2^{-1} + 1 \times 2^{-2} + 0 \times 2^{-3} + 0 \times 2^{-4} + 1 \times 2^{-5} + 1 \times 2^{-6}$$

$$= \frac{1}{2} + \frac{1}{4} + 0 + 0 + \frac{1}{32} + \frac{1}{64}$$

$$= \frac{51}{64}$$

To convert from the representation of a fraction in one base, P, to another base, Q, the required calculations depend on whether they are done in the base P system (the old base) or in the base Q system (the new base). We would ordinarily like to perform the calculations in whichever system is the easiest to manipulate.

To convert a base P representation, $0 . p_1 p_2 p_3 ... p_k$, to a base Q representation, $0 . q_1 q_2 q_3 ... q_m$, calculations in the base P system are performed iteratively. The value of the number can be expressed either in the old system as

$$J = p_1 \times P^{-1} + p_2 \times P^{-2} + ... + p_k \times P^{-k}$$

or in the new system as

$$J = q_1 \times Q^{-1} + q_2 \times Q^{-2} + ... + q_m \times Q^{-m}$$

Therefore the iteration proceeds as follows:

$$
\begin{aligned}
\text{Let} \quad N_1 &= Q \times J &&= q_1 + q_2 \times Q^{-1} + q_3 \times Q^{-2} + ... + q_m \times Q^{-m+1} \\
N_2 &= Q \times (N_1 - q_1) &&= q_2 + q_3 \times Q^{-1} + ... + q_m \times Q^{-m+2} \\
N_3 &= Q \times (N_2 - q_2) &&= q_3 + q_4 \times Q^{-1} + ... + q_m \times Q^{-m+3}
\end{aligned}
$$

and so forth. Note that the quantity $N_i - q_i$ that appears in the calculation of N_{i+1} is simply the fractional portion of N_i. In other words, the ith step of the iteration procedure produces a number, N_i, whose integer portion is q_i and whose fractional portion, $N_i - q_i$, is used in the next step. In general, the number of digits, q_i, that are determined by this process depends on the accuracy that is desired.

For example, to convert the number one-half from its decimal representation 0.5 to its binary representation, we have P=10 and Q=2, and

$$N_1 = 2 \times 0.5 = 1.0, \text{ so } q_1 = 1, \text{ and } N_1 - q_1 = 0$$

$0.5_{10} = 0.1_2$

Thus, $N_2 = N_3 = ... = N_j = 0$ for all $j > 1$. The binary representation of one-half is thus 0.1_2.

However, to convert the number one-tenth from its decimal representation 0.1_{10} to its binary representation, we find

$$
\begin{aligned}
N_1 &= 2 \times 0.1 = 0.2, \text{ so } q_1 = 0, \text{ and } N_1 - q_1 = 0.2 \\
N_2 &= 2 \times 0.2 = 0.4, \text{ so } q_2 = 0, \text{ and } N_2 - q_2 = 0.4 \\
N_3 &= 2 \times 0.4 = 0.8, \text{ so } q_3 = 0, \text{ and } N_3 - q_3 = 0.8 \\
N_4 &= 2 \times 0.8 = 1.6, \text{ so } q_4 = 1, \text{ and } N_4 - q_4 = 0.6 \\
N_5 &= 2 \times 0.6 = 1.2, \text{ so } q_5 = 1, \text{ and } N_5 - q_5 = 0.2
\end{aligned}
$$

$0.1_{10} = 0.1999..._{16}$

At this point, notice that $N_5 - q_5 = N_1 - q_1$, so the binary representation of one-tenth is a never-ending sequence of bits, 0.000110011001100110011....

When converting a base P representation, $0 . p_1 p_2 p_3 ... p_k$, to a base Q representation, $0 . q_1 q_2 q_3 ... q_m$, calculations in the base Q system are most easily performed as follows. Let $J = 0 . p_1 p_2 p_3 ... p_k$, and define the integer K by the equation $J = K \times P^{-k}$. In other words, K is the integer represented by the digits $p_1 p_2 p_3 ... p_k$. We can convert K to the base Q system by the methods used for conversion of integers (as described in Chap. 1) and then divide the result by P^k, doing the computations in the base Q system.

For example, to convert 0.110011_2 to its equivalent decimal representation, we have P=2, Q=10, and

$$J = 110011_2 \times (2^{-6})_{10}$$

But,

$0.110011_2 =$
0.796875_{10}

$$
\begin{aligned}
110011_2 &= 1 \times 2^5 + 1 \times 2^4 + 0 \times 2^3 + 0 \times 2^2 + 1 \times 2^1 + 1 \times 2^0 \\
&= 32 + 16 + 0 + 0 + 2 + 1 \\
&= 51_{10}
\end{aligned}
$$

and $2^{-6} = 1/64$. Thus, in the base 10 system the number 0.110011_2 is represented as $51/64 = 0.796875_{10}$.

Similarly, to convert $0.C1_{16}$ to its decimal representation, we have P=16, Q=10, and

$$J = C1_{16} \times (16^{-2})_{10}$$

But,

$$Cl_{16} = 12 \times 16^1 + 1 \times 16^0$$
$$= 193_{10}$$

Thus, in the base 10 system the number $0.Cl_{16}$ is represented as $(193)_{10} \times (16^{-2})_{10}$, i.e.,

$$\frac{193}{16^2} = \frac{193}{256} = 0.75390625_{10}$$

$0.Cl_{16} = 0.75390625_{10}$

11.3   REPRESENTATION OF MIXED NUMBERS

Binary Representation

One way to represent mixed numbers in a 32-bit word is to let a certain number of low-order bits be used for the fractional portion and the remaining high-order bits for the sign and integer portion. For example, if we choose 12 bits for the fractional portion, then a 32-bit word could be considered to represent a mixed number in the following fashion:

Fixed-Point Representation

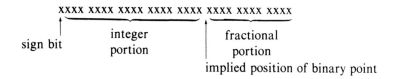

xxxx xxxx xxxx xxxx xxxx xxxx xxxx xxxx

sign bit   integer portion   fractional portion

implied position of binary point

Using this scheme to represent the decimal number 1.5, we would have

0000 0000 0000 0000 0001 1000 0000 0000

\+ sign   integer $+1$ binary one-half

With twelve bits for the fractional portion in a 32-bit word, the magnitude of the smallest fraction that can be represented is 2^{-12} (approximately 2×10^{-4}) and that of the largest integer is $2^{19} - 1$ (i.e., about 5×10^5). Thus, neither the range of numbers nor the accuracy that can be attained for fractions is very great, and we can increase one only at the expense of the other.

Range and Accuracy

It should be noted that if we use the integer arithmetic instructions to process mixed numbers represented by the above scheme in the IBM 360 and 370 systems, the implied position of the binary point would have to be explicitly adjusted via arithmetic shift instructions to retain the desired accuracy in multiplication or division. To illustrate this, let us continue the previous example and suppose that we wish to multiply 1.5_{10} by 1.5_{10}. Since the representation of 1.5 is indistinguishable from the integer representation of 3×2^{11}, the integer multiply instruction would yield the following 32-bit product of 1.5×1.5, namely the representation of 9×2^{22}:

0000 0010 0100 0000 0000 0000 0000 0000

To recover the desired representation of 2.25, we would have to shift the integer product right 12 bits (or divide it by 2^{12}), the correct result being

Shifting

0000 0000 0000 0000 0010 0100 0000 0000

\+ sign   integer $+2$ fraction ¼

implied position of binary point

Thus, we see that the integer arithmetic instructions can be used to perform arithmetic on mixed numbers, provided that shifting is employed. There are, however, two limitations: (1) we cannot easily provide for both a wide range of numbers and a sufficient degree of accuracy in a fixed number of bits, e.g., in a full word of 32 bits; and (2) unless there are a sufficient number of bits for the fractional portion, fractions such as one-tenth will be represented with relatively poor accuracy due to the incommensurability of the decimal and binary systems. (For example, one-tenth would be represented in this scheme as

$$\underset{\substack{\uparrow \\ + \text{ sign}}}{} \underbrace{0000\ 0000\ 0000\ 0000\ 0000}_{\text{integer } 0}\ \underbrace{0001\ 1001\ 1010}_{\text{fraction one-tenth, rounded to twelve bits}}$$

But, $.0001\ 1001\ 1010_2 = .1000\ 9765\ 625_{10}$, clearly a poor approximation.) To overcome these limitations, the decimal method and floating-point method of representing mixed numbers is more commonly employed.

Decimal Representation

This method employs the decimal number system in the hardware. In the IBM 360 and 370 systems, this is done with a method of representation known as packed-decimal format. In this format, integers and mixed numbers are represented as decimal (not binary) integers. Each decimal digit is represented by 4 bits in what is known as the **binary-coded decimal,** or BCD, code scheme: 0, 1, 2,..., 9 are represented, respectively, as 0000, 0001, 0010, ..., 1001. A mixed number, F, is represented as the integer $N = F \times 10^n$, where n is the number of digits to the right of the decimal point in F. For example, the number 1.5 might be represented by the integer $N = 15 = 1.5 \times 10^1$, and the number 0.1 by the integer $N = 1 = 0.1 \times 10^1$. The factor 10^n is called the **scale factor.** Different scale factors may be used for different numbers.

The sign of a number in the packed-decimal format is represented by 4 bits, 1100 for plus and 1101 for minus. The sign bits are placed to the right of the low-order digit. For example, the product of $(+1.5) \times (-1.5)$ would be the product of these numbers:

BCD Representation

$$\underbrace{(0001}_{(1}\ \underbrace{0101}_{5}\ \underbrace{1100)}_{+)}\ \times\ \underbrace{(0001}_{(1}\ \underbrace{0101}_{5}\ \underbrace{1101)}_{-)}$$

the result being (0000 0010 0010 0101 1101), namely, the representation of $0225-$, or -2.25×10^2. Notice that the representation of the product is obtained by treating the two factors as decimal numbers and performing the arithmetic using the rules of the decimal number system. This is done by the hardware in the IBM 360 and 370 systems. Notice also that there is no problem of incommensurability, for decimal fractions are represented as decimal integers and there need be no approximation that wouldn't also be made with pencil and paper. The only restriction is that no packed-decimal number may consist of more than thirty-one decimal digits.

As will be discussed in Chapter 12, a set of instructions explicitly designed for decimal arithmetic is used to process packed-decimal numbers. These include add, subtract, multiply, divide, compare, and shift instructions. Neither the decimal point nor the scale factor is represented in a packed-decimal number. Instead, shifting, i.e., effectively multiplying or dividing by powers of ten, enables us to make explicit adjustments of the position of the implied decimal point so that numbers with different scale factors can be arithmetically combined.

Floating-Point Representation

Scientific vs. Floating-Point Notation

Perhaps the most common method of representing mixed numbers in computers is known as the floating-point method. In this method, numbers are represented and processed as a fraction times a scale factor. The method is conceptually similar to that of scientific notation, where for example 1.5 can be written as 0.15×10^1. But in floating-point format, unlike scientific notation, the complete scale factor is not represented; only its exponent is represented. Moreover, the base of the scale factor is usually a power of two, say 2^m, rather than ten. We will first consider a base of 2 (i.e., $m = 1$), and then a base of $2^4 = 16$. The latter base is employed in the IBM 360 and 370 systems, the former in some other computer systems.

With a scale factor base of 2, the fraction is represented with n bits, e.g., $b_1b_2b_3...b_n$, its value being $b_1 \times 2^{-1} + b_2 \times 2^{-2} + b_3 \times 2^{-3} + ... + b_n \times 2^{-n}$. For example, since $0.15 \times 10^1 = 0.15 \times 1.25 \times 2^3 = 0.1875 \times 2^3$, and since $0.1875_{10} = 0.0011_2$, the decimal number 1.5 would be represented in floating-point format by the equivalent of $(0.0011)_2 \times 2^3$, the fraction bits being $b_1b_2b_3...b_n = 0011000...0$, and the exponent being 3. The base of the scale factor 2^3—the 2 itself—would not be represented explicitly; its value would be implied in all computations.

In a k-bit word, the sign, exponent, and fraction bits are often arranged as follows:

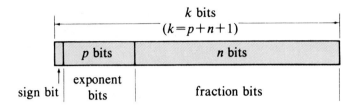

The sign bit represents the sign of the fraction, not the sign of the exponent. Thus, if we assume that $k = 32$ with $p = 7$ and $n = 24$, we might expect that $(0.0011) \times 2^3$ would be represented in floating-point format as

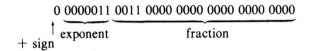

$1.5_{10} = 0.15 \times 10^1$
$= 0.0011_2 \times 2^3$

Normalized Form

However, this is not quite the way it's done, for two reasons. First, there must be a provision for representing negative exponents. Second, the two leading zeroes in the fraction are in a sense "wasted," since we can write $(0.0011) \times 2^3 = (0.11)_2 \times 2^1$. In other words, leading zeroes can be absorbed into the exponent, thereby providing additional bit positions for increased accuracy. This may be of no consequence for a number such as 0.0011, which is the exact equivalent of 0.1875, but it *is* of some consequence for a number such as 0.000110011001100110011..., which must be truncated to an approximate representation of one-tenth. Thus, the generally preferred form of a fraction is with its leading bit nonzero (unless of course the number is exactly zero). This is known as the **normalized form** of the fraction.

Representing Exponents

Turning to the problem of the exponent's sign, how might a negative exponent be represented? One way, of course, is to use the first exponent bit as its sign bit and to represent the exponent in sign-magnitude form, e.g., 0000011 for $+3$ and 1000011 for -3. Another way is to represent the exponent in p-bit two's complement form, e.g., (with $p = 7$) 0000011 for $+3$ and 1111101 for -3. A third way is to represent an exponent m by an unsigned binary integer, $q + m$. This is known as **excess-q notation.** For a 7-bit exponent, $q = \frac{1}{2} \times 2^7$; for a p-bit exponent, $q = \frac{1}{2} \times 2^p$. Thus, in 7 bits $q = 64$; the exponent $+3$ would be represented as $64 + 3 = 67_{10} = 1000011_2$, and the exponent -3 would be $64 + (-3) = 61_{10} = 0111101_2$. The advantage of this latter method over the sign-magnitude and two's complement methods is that the exponent is always represented by a nonnegative integer and its sign is implied, not explicit. Adjustments of an exponent required for normalizing a fraction and for doing arithmetic on two floating-point numbers therefore need not be concerned with the sign of the exponent.

Range vs. Accuracy

Now the remaining question is, what should be the number of bits allotted for the exponent portion of a floating-point number? Clearly, the more bits, the greater the range of numbers that can be represented. But in a k-bit word, we must have $k = p + n + 1$, where p is the number of exponent bits and n the number of fraction bits. Clearly, the larger p is, the smaller n—and hence the accuracy—will be. If k is large, then both p and n can be reasonably large so that both range and accuracy can be of acceptable size. But in the IBM 360 and 370 systems $k = 32$, which is not an especially large word length. For accuracy to about six decimal digits, we need an n of at least 24, leaving $p = 7$. But with a scale factor base of 2, a 7-bit exponent gives a range of from 2^{-64} to 2^{63} for the scale factor, not an especially large range, since $2^{63} \approx 10^{19}$. In the IBM 360 and 370 systems, this limitation is overcome as follows.

The number of exponent bits is seven, but the base of the scale factor is 16 ($= 2^4$), not 2. Thus the range of the exponents is from 16^{-64} to 16^{63}, i.e., from 2^{-256} to 2^{252}. This is comfortably large enough to handle the vast majority of computational needs, since $2^{252} \approx 10^{76}$. Note that with a scale factor base of 16, the fraction bits must be treated as hexadecimal fractions rather than binary fractions. In other words, the 24 bits allotted for the fraction are treated as six hexadecimal digits. For example, the representation of the number 1.5 can be determined as follows:

$$0.15 \times 10^1 = 0.15 \times 0.625 \times 16^1 = 0.09375 \times 16^1$$
$$\text{but since } 0.09375_{10} = 0.18_{16}$$
$$\text{then } 0.15 \times 10^1 = 0.18_{16} \times 16^1$$

Thus, in the floating-point format of the IBM 360 and 370 systems, 1.5 is represented as

$$0 \; 1000001 \; 0001 \; 1000 \; 0000 \; 0000 \; 0000 \; 0000$$

$+$ sign $\qquad$ fraction $= 0.18_{16}$

$41_{16} = 65_{10} = 64 + 1$, i.e., 16^1

This is the normalized form of the fraction, even though the leading bit is zero, the reason being that as a hexadecimal fraction the leading *digit* is not zero. Thus, we are back to the "wasted bits," so to speak. But we have gained considerably in the range of numbers that can be represented. To provide for more accuracy when needed, the floating-point format in the IBM 360 and 370 systems can be processed either as a full word, a double word, or a quadruple word. These three possibilities are known as single-precision, double-precision, and extended-precision, respectively. The double-precision form provides slightly more than twice the accuracy of single-precision, and the extended-precision format provides twice the accuracy of the double-precision format. In all three cases, however, the exponent occupies only 7 bits, is represented in **excess-64** notation, and corresponds to a power of 16.

To summarize briefly: in all floating-point formats, in whatever computer system is being used, the principle of separating the order of magnitude of a number from its significant digits—similar to scientific notation—allows a wider range of numbers to be represented in a fixed number of bits than any other method in use. This, together with the fact that the hardware performs all the adjustments of exponents when two floating-point numbers are arithmetically combined, makes the use of this format attractive for a large class of problems.

As will be shown in Chapter 13, a set of instructions explicitly designed for floating-point arithmetic is used to process floating-point numbers. These include add, subtract, multiply, divide, and compare instructions, as well as instructions that test and/or change the sign of a floating-point number. Normalization of fractions is accomplished by the hardware during the execution of most instructions; there are no shift instructions to normalize a fraction.

11.4 OVERFLOW, UNDERFLOW, AND SIGNIFICANCE ERRORS: THE SPM INSTRUCTION

As in integer arithmetic, arithmetic with mixed numbers may produce a result that cannot be represented in the number of bits allowed. If the magnitude of the number is too large for the range permitted, the condition is called **overflow.** If the magnitude of the number is too small for the range (but not 0), the condition is called **underflow.** In floating-point addition and subtraction, if the resulting fraction is 0 but the exponent isn't, all significant bits have been lost and the condition is termed a **significance error.**

In the IBM 360 and 370 systems, the occurrence of any of these conditions normally causes program interruption:

1. Overflow in fixed-point operations (integer arithmetic and arithmetic left shifts)
2. Overflow in packed-decimal operations
3. Underflow in floating-point operations
4. Significance error in floating-point operations

When a program is interrupted, control of the CPU is given to the operating system and the program's execution is usually terminated. In order to prevent interruption in any of these situations, the SPM (Set Program Mask) instruction must be executed at some point *before* the arithmetic operation is executed.

The SPM instruction sets the condition code and a 4-bit program-mask field. It is an RR-type instruction in which only the R1 field is specified:

opcode	operand
SPM	R 1

Bits 2 through 7 of the register designated by the R1 field are used to *replace* the 2-bit condition code and the 4-bit program mask that exist in the program status word. Bits 2 and 3 pertain to the condition code, bits 4 through 7 to the program mask. Bits 0, 1, and 8–31 of the register are ignored during execution of the SPM instruction, and the entire contents of the register are unchanged by the instruction. Bits 2 through 7 have the meaning shown in this diagram:

The Program Mask Bits

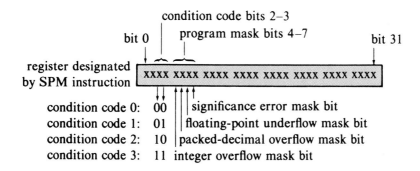

If a mask bit is set to 0, the program will not be interrupted when the corresponding error condition arises. If it is set to 1, the program will be interrupted when that error arises. *All mask bits are set each time the SPM is executed.* If the SPM is not executed in a program, the initial settings of these mask bits—established by the operating system—will prevail.

11.5 SUMMARY

In most computer systems, the representation and processing of noninteger quantities demand special consideration. This may take the form of software to simulate noninteger arithmetic even though the quantities are represented as integers, or it may take the form of hardware and associated software instructions that are separate and distinct from the facilities for operating on integers. One of the problems posed by noninteger arithmetic operations in computer systems is the incommensurability of the decimal and binary number systems: there can be a loss of accuracy when a fixed number of bits is used to represent noninteger decimal numbers in the binary system, no matter how many bits are used. Another problem arises from the need to align the decimal point positions of two numbers before they may be added or subtracted and to ensure that a sufficient number of digit positions to the right and/or left of the decimal point are reserved for arithmetic results. Yet a third problem is due to the fact that there must be some realistic upper limit on the number of bits used to represent numbers, whether they be integers or mixed numbers: the more of these bits used for the fractional portion of a number, the less that can be used for the integer portion, and vice versa. Too severe a restriction on the number of integer bits may reduce the range of representable numbers below acceptable limits.

One of the commonly implemented methods of dealing with these problems is that of floating-point format. Conceptually this format is similar to the use of scientific notation in hand calculations. Each number in floating-point format—integer or noninteger—is represented in a fixed number of bits that consist of three components: a fraction, which represents the most significant digits of the number; an exponent, which represents the power to which some fixed integer base is raised; and a sign, which represents the algebraic sign of the fraction. The product of two factors, the fraction and the base raised to the power represented by the exponent, represents the magnitude of the floating-point number; the sign of the fraction is the sign of that number. In all calculations, the fraction is considered to be a number from 0 to 1 (including 0 but not 1); it is scaled to its appropriate magnitude by increasing or decreasing the exponent. In the IBM 360 and 370 systems, the exponent is in excess-64 notation. This means that the quantity 64_{10} must be subtracted from the exponent to obtain the integer power of 16 that it represents.

As will be discussed in Chapter 13, a special set of instructions and registers is available in the IBM 360 and 370 systems to facilitate the processing of floating-point numbers. Many other computer systems have similar instruction sets. The use of these instructions eliminates the need for the programmer to align decimal point positions prior to or following a calculation. This is done by the hardware. The principle of separating the order of magnitude of a number from its significant digits allows for a wide range of numbers to be represented in a relatively small number of bits, while providing for a fixed number of significant digits in each number.

An alternative method of dealing with the problems posed by noninteger arithmetic is embodied in the number format known as packed-decimal representation. This format, and associated instructions, is available on the IBM 360 and 370 systems. In it, all numbers are represented as decimal integers (each digit being represented in 4-bit binary-coded decimal form), and all calculations are performed according to the rules of decimal arithmetic. Numbers with up to thirty-one significant digits can be represented. However, as will be discussed in Chapter 12, the position of the decimal point is not represented. Instructions that explicitly handle decimal point alignment must be used whenever necessary to ensure correct results.

In all methods of representing numbers, a calculation may produce a result that is too large for the range of numbers that can be accommodated. When this happens, the condition known as *overflow* usually results in interruption of program execution. In using floating-point format, two other error conditions can arise. One, known as *underflow*, occurs when the magnitude of a result is too small (but not zero) to be represented; the other, a *significance error*, occurs when all significant bits of a sum or difference are zero but the exponent is not. As with overflow, the occurrence of either of these two conditions usually results in program interruption. However, program interruption can be prevented in the IBM 360 and 370 systems by use of the SPM instruction. When the SPM is used, it is up to the user's program to detect the error and take appropriate action. The conditions for which SPM can be used are overflow in fixed-point arithmetic, overflow in packed-decimal arithmetic, underflow, and significance errors. Overflow in floating-point operations always results in program interruption.

For further study of numerical analysis, you may wish to consult:

Burden, Richard L., et al. *Numerical Analysis*. 3rd ed. Boston: Prindle, Weber, and Schmidt, 1985.

Conte, S.D., and deBoor, Carl. *Elementary Numerical Analysis: An Algorithmic Approach*. 3rd ed. New York: McGraw-Hill, 1980.

Forsythe, George E. *Computer Methods for Mathematical Computations*. Englewood Cliffs, N.J.: Prentice-Hall, 1977.

Johnson, Lee W., and Riess, R. Dean. *Numerical Analysis*. 2nd ed. Reading, Mass.: Addison Wesley, 1982.

Spencer, Donald D. *Computer Science Mathematics*. Columbus, Ohio: Merrill, 1976.

11.6 REVIEW

Mixed Numbers   Arithmetic with mixed numbers—numbers with both an integer and a fractional component—is qualitatively different from arithmetic with integers. This is because of the need to properly account for the position of the decimal point and the number of digits to the right and left of it.

Accuracy   Many fractions, e.g., ⅓, must be approximated when a fixed number of digits (or bits) are used to represent them. The fewer the digits or bits that are used, the poorer the approximations. In the worst case, a small but nonzero fraction such as 0.000000001 may have to be represented as zero—not an insignificant problem, since multiplying a number by zero is obviously not the same as multiplying it by a small but nonzero number.

Fixed-Point Representation   In this technique, a fixed number of bits in a computer word is reserved for the fractional portion of a number; the remaining bits are used for the sign and the integer portion. The decimal (really, binary) point is assumed to be in the same fixed position for all numbers. The trade-off is between accuracy of the fraction and range of the integer portion. The better the accuracy, the poorer the range of numbers.

Decimal Representation   In this technique, a variable number of digits is reserved for a mixed number. Arithmetic is done by the hardware in the decimal number system, and all numbers are assumed to be integers. Scaling (accounting for the decimal point's position) is done by the software.

Floating-Point Representation   This technique emulates scientific notation in order to be able to represent a large range of numbers with acceptable accuracy using relatively few digits. But instead of being based on powers of ten as in scientific notation, numbers in floating-point notation are based on powers of 2^m. Integers, fractions, and mixed numbers are all represented as fractions times a power of 2^m. During arithmetic operations, scaling is done by the hardware.

Normalized Form   If the fractional portion of a nonzero floating-point number has no leading zeroes, this is the normalized form of the number.

Excess-q Notation   If it's necessary to subtract q from the exponent portion of a floating-point number in order to determine its true value, the exponent is said to be represented in excess-q notation.

Program Mask   These four bits in the IBM 360 and 370 systems control whether or not a program is interrupted when a fixed-point overflow, decimal overflow, floating-point underflow, or floating-point significance error occurs. The bits can be individually set on or off via the SPM (Set Program Mask) instruction.

11.7   REVIEW QUESTIONS

1. What additional considerations must be dealt with when doing arithmetic with mixed numbers that do not arise when doing arithmetic with integers?
2. What is meant by the "range" of a number? What determines the "accuracy" of a number?
3. What are the inherent limitations as well as the advantages in the use of the fixed-point representation of mixed numbers? Of decimal representation? Of floating-point representation?
4. What is the base of floating-point numbers in the IBM 360 and 370 systems? What is the approximate range of numbers that can be represented by this method?
5. In the IBM 360 and 370 systems, what is meant by "single-precision" floating-point numbers? By "double-precision"?
6. What is meant by the term "overflow" when it is applied to arithmetic operations? By "underflow"? By "significance error"?
7. What important function does the SPM instruction perform, and why is it important?

11.8   EXERCISES

1. Convert the following decimal numbers to a 32-bit binary representation in which the low-order 12 bits represent the fraction:

a. 3.125	**d.** 0.99	**g.** 0.333333
b. 0.03125	**e.** 0.999	**h.** 0.75390625
c. 31.25	**f.** 0.9999	**i.** 7539.0625

2. Convert the following numbers from base 2 or base 16 (as indicated) to base 10:

a. 0.111_2	**d.** 0.01010101_2	**g.** 0.01110111_2
b. $0.E_{16}$	**e.** 8.6_{16}	**h.** 0.1110111_2
c. $0.AA_{16}$	**f.** 0.86_{16}	**i.** $3.B8_{16}$

3. What is the 7-bit excess-64 exponent that represents the power of 16 in each of the following terms:

a. 16^3

b. 16^{-3}

c. 16^2

d. 16^{30}

e. 16^{-30}

f. 16^{-2}

g. 16^{60}

h. 16^{-60}

i. 16^0

4. Each of the following is the hexadecimal representation of a floating-point number in the IBM 360 and 370 systems. What is the representation of that number in scientific notation in the decimal system?

a. 40400000

b. C1C20000

c. 3F3F0000

d. 40800000

e. 41100000

f. 46000001

g. C0333333

h. 00000001

i. 7FFFFFFF

5. Whenever we compute a number in floating-point format, the calculation may cause an exponent overflow error condition or an exponent underflow error condition. If we write that number as

$$a \times 16^b$$

with $16^{-1} \le a < 1$, what determines the smallest positive value of b for which exponent overflow would occur? What is that value in the IBM 360 and 370 systems? (Note that if B is a value of b for which exponent overflow will occur, $B + n$ for all positive n is also such a value.)

6. In the notation of Exercise 5, with $16^{-1} \le a < 1$, what determines the algebraically largest value of b for which exponent underflow will occur? What is that value in the IBM 360 and 370 systems?

7. One major difference between the packed-decimal method of representing numbers and the floating-point method of representing numbers is that in the former the scale factor is implied, not explicitly represented, whereas in the latter, the scale factor is represented. What are some of the consequences of this difference from a programming standpoint?

8. Imagine a computer system in which the floating-point representation is based on the decimal system instead of the binary or hexadecimal system, i.e., each digit of the fraction is represented in 4-bit BCD code, the base of the scale factor is ten, and all computations are performed in accordance with the rules of decimal arithmetic. How might the exponent be represented in order to allow a range of positive numbers from approximately 10^{-99} to 10^{99}?

12

Packed-Decimal Operations

In addition to the *binary* integer arithmetic operations described in Chapters 4 and 5, the IBM 360 and 370 systems provide a capability for *decimal* integer arithmetic. It is based on a representation of numbers called **packed-decimal format.** Constants can be defined for this format by the DC directive and by literals, and there is a set of instructions that perform decimal arithmetic and that convert numbers between EBCDIC character format and packed-decimal format.

See Summary in Figure 12.6

There are two main reasons for the use of packed-decimal format:

Rationale

1. To reduce the amount of memory space that would be required in EBCDIC format to store simple integers, such as inventory part numbers and telephone numbers
2. To provide a method of processing decimal fractions without the loss of accuracy that could occur if they were processed as binary numbers

The reduction in memory space is the reason this format is called "packed." As will be seen, two digits can be stored in a byte with packed format rather than the one digit per byte that EBCDIC requires.

However, it is the consideration of accuracy that dictates the use of packed-decimal operations when performing calculations in banking and related business applications, as the following discussion illustrates.

In the decimal system, fractions are represented in terms of negative powers of ten, as this example illustrates:

$$\text{three-fourths} = 0.75 = 7 \times 10^{-1} + 5 \times 10^{-2}$$
$$= 7/10 + 5/100$$

In the binary system, fractions are represented in terms of negative powers of two:

$$\text{three-fourths} = .11 = 1 \times 2^{-1} + 1 \times 2^{-2}$$
$$= \frac{1}{2} + \frac{1}{4}$$

The problem this presents is not in converting from one representation to the other but rather the possible loss of accuracy in converting from a decimal fraction to a binary fraction. This is because the set of numbers expressible in a finite number of binary digits is not in one-to-one correspondence with the set of numbers expressible in a finite number of decimal digits.

For example, consider the fraction 1/10 (one-tenth). In the decimal system, this is

$$\text{one-tenth} = 0.1 = 1 \times 10^{-1}$$

In the binary system, however, this is a never-ending sequence of bits:

$$\text{one-tenth} = .00011001100110011...$$
$$= 1 \times 2^{-4} + 1 \times 2^{-5} + 1 \times 2^{-8} + 1 \times 2^{-9} + ...$$

Inherent Errors   As a consequence, we obtain different results when, for example, we multiply 1/10 by ten in the decimal system and in the binary system. In the decimal system, $10 \times 0.1 = 1.0$. In the binary system, this is

$$(1010) \times (0.00011001100110011...)$$
$$= .1111111111...$$

i.e., not quite 1.0. In problems involving a large number of calculations, this type of discrepancy may lead to cumulative rounding errors that may not be tolerable, particularly in banking and related business applications.

The use of packed-decimal operations can avoid these errors. Nevertheless, since the decimal arithmetic instructions operate only on integers, it is necessary to represent fractions and mixed numbers as integers with an implied decimal point position. For example, 1.43 would be represented and processed as 143. It is up to the programmer to properly account for the decimal point's implied position. We shall indicate how this is done after describing the directives and instructions that are used to define and process packed-decimal integers. (It should be noted that in IBM Cobol, packed-decimal format is specified by the clause USAGE IS COMPUTATIONAL-3. This format is not readily available to Fortran programmers.)

12.1   DATA FORMATS

BCD Representation   In the data formats referred to as packed-decimal in IBM terminology, and more generally as binary-coded decimal (BCD) format, each of the ten decimal digits is represented by 4 bits:

decimal digit	packed-decimal representation
0	0000
1	0001
2	0010
3	0011
4	0100
5	0101
6	0110
7	0111
8	1000
9	1001

As should be obvious, these 4-bit representations are simply those of the respective digits in the binary number system. However, they are manipulated as *decimal* digits during all arithmetic operations.

For example, the number 10 (ten) is represented as two digits (8 bits), not as a binary ten (4 bits). The following examples illustrate this difference.

decimal	packed decimal	binary integer
10	0001 0000	1010
32	0011 0010	100000
432	0100 0011 0010	110110000
5432	0101 0100 0011 0010	1010100111000

Range
The maximum number of digits allowable in a packed-decimal number is thirty-one. This gives a range of $-10^{31}+1$ through $10^{31}-1$. Since each digit requires 4 bits, the maximum packed-decimal number requires 16 bytes.

Note that the binary integer format generally requires fewer bits to represent a value than does the packed-decimal format. For example, with 32 bits, the maximum packed-decimal number is 10^7-1, whereas the maximum binary integer is $2^{31}-1$, or approximately 2.1×10^9. Although less economical in bits, packed-decimal accuracy is more suitable for some applications than binary, especially when dealing with fractions.

Sign
The *sign* of a packed-decimal number is always represented by 4 bits (not by one bit, as in binary numbers). These 4 bits always occupy the right-most bit positions in the low-order byte, as follows:

decimal	packed decimal			
+325	0011	0010	0101	$\overline{1100}$
	3	2	5	C
−789	0111	1000	1001	$\overline{1101}$
	7	8	9	D

sign bits

The plus sign (+) is almost always represented by 1100 (X'C') and the minus sign (−) by 1101 (X'D'). The hardware also accepts X'A', X'E', and X'F' for plus and X'B' for minus, but the preferred codes, X'C' and X'D', are generated by all arithmetic and shift instructions in accordance with the rules of algebra.

There is one additional observation to be made: each packed-decimal number is always represented in an integral number of bytes. The number of bytes required depends on the number of digits. If N is the number of digits, then the number of bytes is $\frac{N+1}{2}$ if N is odd, and $\frac{N+2}{2}$ if N is even. (This rule includes allowance for the bits required for the sign, which are stored in the right half of the right-most byte.) For example,

decimal number	number of digits	packed decimal (in hex)	number of bytes
+2	1	2C	1
−32	2	032D	2
+432	3	432C	2
+5432	4	05432C	3
−65432	5	65432D	3
−765432	6	0765432D	4

Note that when the number of digits is even, a leading 0 (zero) is supplied to fill the left-most byte. Note also that the sign bits serve as a delimiter for a packed-decimal number: that is, the sign bit identifies the byte position of the low-order digit.

Figure 12.1 Defining packed-decimal constants.

```
FLAG LOCTN OBJECT CODE       ADDR1   ADDR2   STMNT M SOURCE STATEMENT

     000000 325C                              5          DC   P'+3.25'        DECIMAL POINT IGNORED

     000002 000000325C                        6          DC   PL5'+325'       PADDING ON LEFT SINCE LNG L = 5
                                              7    *                          EXCEEDS NUMBER OF BYTES RE-
                                              8    *                          QUIRED FOR THE CONSTANT

     000007 5C                                9          DC   PL1'+325'       TRUNCATION ON LEFT SINCE
                                             10    *                          L = 1 IS LESS THAN NUMBER
                                             11    *                          OF BYTES REQD FOR CONSTANT.

     000008 120C                             12          DC   2P'1.20'        TWO CONSECUTIVE COPIES OF
            120C
                                             13    *                          +120 (PLUS ASSUMED IN AB-
                                             14    *                          SENCE OF MINUS SIGN.)

     00000C 034D567C                         15          DC   P'-34,567'      MULTIPLE OPERANDS ALLOWED IN 'DC'

     000010                                  16    X     DS   PL8
     000018 F8 22 C010C048 000010 000048     17          ZAP  X(3),=P'1258'
     00001E F8 22 C010C04B 000010 00004B     18          ZAP  X(3),=P'-1258'
     000024 F8 00 C010C04E 000010 00004E     19          ZAP  X(1),=P'-1'
     00002A F8 00 C010C04F 000010 00004F     20          ZAP  X(1),=P'+1'
     000030 F8 11 C010C050 000010 000050     21          ZAP  X(2),=P'+0.1'
     000036 F8 11 C010C052 000010 000052     22          ZAP  X(2),=P'15'     NOTE FROM LITERAL TABLE THAT
     00003C F8 11 C010C052 000010 000052     23          ZAP  X(2),=P'1.5'    P'15', P'1.5'  AND  P'0.15'
     000042 F8 11 C010C052 000010 000052     24          ZAP  X(2),=P'0.15'   ARE ONE AND THE SAME LITERAL.

                                             25    * P-TYPE LITERALS ARE ALIGNED ON BYTE BOUNDARY

     000048 01258C
     00004B 01258D
     00004E 1D
     00004F 1C
     000050 001C
     000052 015C
```

P-Type Constants

In assembly language, packed-decimal constants are distinguished from other constants by the letter *P*. For example, DC P'5' defines a 1-byte packed-decimal representation of the decimal integer +5. Figure 12.1 illustrates a few other typical P-type constants. There are several observations to be made:

Length Modifier

1. In the DC directive, the only permissible modifier for P-type constants is the length modifier, Ln. The value of n is the number of *bytes,* not digits, and must be less than or equal to sixteen.

Padding

2. In P-type constants, padding is always on the left with zeroes. Truncation is also always at the left and can result in a loss of the most significant digits.

Truncation

3. Truncation can always be avoided by a reasonable choice of the length modifier Ln or by omitting the length modifier.

To reserve data areas for packed-decimal data, we can use the P-type operand with a length modifier or the P-type operand with a typical value to imply the length. For example,

```
AREA1     DS     PL5               RESERVES 5 BYTES
AREA2     DS     P'+123456789'     RESERVES 5 BYTES
```

Alignment

In both methods, alignment is always on a byte boundary.

12.2 INSTRUCTION FORMATS

Unlike the operations on binary integers described in Chapter 5, the operations on packed-decimal numbers do not take place in registers; they take place in main memory. There are four categories of packed-decimal operations:

1. Arithmetic—add, subtract, multiply, divide, shift-and-round
2. Comparison of two numbers
3. Copying a number from one memory location to another
4. Conversion to and from packed-decimal format

All but two of the instructions in these categories are either SS_1-type or SS_2-type instructions. In SS_1-type instructions there are two operand fields; each field specifies the memory address of the data being operated on, and the length of each data item is specified in the first operand:

        D1(L,B1),D2(B2)   [SS₁ operand]
        with $1 \leq L \leq 256$

In SS_2-type instructions, there are also two operand fields that specify the memory addresses of data items, but the length of each item is specified separately in each operand:

        D1(L1,B1),D2(L2,B2)   [SS₂ operand]
        with $1 \leq L1 \leq 16$
             $1 \leq L2 \leq 16$

Length Field

Thus, one critical factor in packed-decimal operations is the length of each data item. In the IBM 360 and 370 systems, *this length is always specified in number of bytes, not digits*. So, unlike binary integers, which are always 2 or 4 bytes long, a packed-decimal number can consist of from 1 to 16 bytes. Programmers must therefore assure that each number's length is correctly specified each time it is referred to in an instruction. This can be done either explicitly or implicitly. You should recall from Chapters 3 and 6 that when an implicit length is used, the operand length field is the length attribute of the operand symbol and is supplied by the assembler. But to enable the assembler to do this correctly, the desired data length must be specified correctly in a DC or DS directive.

Thus, each P-type *data area* must be defined with a length modifier. For example, in this statement the length attribute of X is 8:

        X   DS   PL8

In other words, the value of the length modifier is the implicit length that the assembler uses when X is an operand in a packed-decimal instruction.

Similarly, each P-type *constant* may but need not be defined with a length modifier; if the length modifier for a P-type constant is omitted, the assembler calculates the number of bytes—and hence the length attribute—required for the constant. For example, either of the following two statements gives the same length attribute for Y, because the number of bytes required for the constant is 3:

        Y   DC   P'12.875'
        Y   DC   PL3'12.875'

*Implicit vs.
Explicit Lengths*

Use of implicit lengths is to be preferred over use of explicit lengths. As an example, consider the SS_2-type ZAP (Zero and Add Packed) instruction, which will be described in the next section. Based on the definitions of X and Y above, it is much better to write this

        ZAP   X,Y

instead of this

        ZAP   X(8),Y(3)

As can be seen, both ZAP instructions will give the same result. But you are more likely to make an error when using explicit lengths (as in the second ZAP instruction above) than when using implicit lengths, because of the additional information that you must be aware of when typing the operand. For similar reasons, use of explicit lengths almost always makes program debugging and maintenance significantly more difficult and time-consuming than use of implicit lengths does. Consequently, use of explicit lengths is NOT recommended. Nevertheless, in this chapter we shall almost always specify the length explicitly in order to emphasize what length is being used.

12.3 ARITHMETIC OPERATIONS

In this section, we will discuss the five packed-decimal arithmetic operations

> Zero and Add Packed (ZAP)
> Add Packed (AP)
> Subtract Packed (SP)
> Multiply Packed (MP)
> Divide Packed (DP)

The section concludes with a discussion of the decimal overflow, decimal divide, and data error conditions.

All five instructions are of SS$_2$-type format. Each instruction requires two operands, and each operand designates the address and length of a packed-decimal number in memory. The result of each arithmetic operation replaces the number specified by the first operand. Thus, the first operand is the destination; the second is the source.

Zero and Add Packed

```
ZAP     D1(L1,B1),D2(L2,B2)
```

address and length (in bytes) of source

address and length (in bytes) of destination

Zero and Add Packed (ZAP) copies a packed-decimal number from one memory location to another, after filling the destination area with zeroes. The destination can be of greater length than the number copied from the source field. This makes it possible to extend a number on the left with zeroes in preparation for any of the other arithmetic operations. Such an extension can avoid the possibility of overflow.

When L1 > L2, the result in the destination area will contain at least L1-L2 bytes of leading zeroes. If L1 < L2, and if there is not enough room in the destination area to accommodate all the significant digits of the number in the source field, a decimal overflow occurs (condition code 3 is set). In all other cases, the condition code is set according to whether the result is zero, negative, or positive.

Example 1.

			A	B
Padding	ZAP B(8),A(4)	before execution:	0023456C	any 8 bytes
		*after execution:	0023456C	00000000 0023456C

*L1-L2 = 4 = number of bytes of leading zeroes.

Example 2.

			A	B
Overflow	ZAP B(2),A(4)	before execution:	0023456C	any 2 bytes
		*after execution:	0023456C	456C

*L1 < L2 and loss of significant digits causes decimal overflow.

Example 3.

			A	B	
ZAP	B(3),A(4)	before execution:	0023456C	any 3 bytes	*Exact Fit*
		*after execution:	0023456C	23456C	

*Although L1 < L2, there is no decimal overflow since no significant digits were lost.

Add Packed

AP   D1(L1,B1),D2(L2,B2)

When this instruction is executed, the number whose address and length are specified by the second operand is algebraically added to the number whose address and length are specified by the first operand. The sum replaces the number specified by the first operand, and the condition code is set to 0, 1, or 2 when the sum is zero, negative, or positive, respectively. However, the number of byte positions, L1, must be large enough to contain all the significant digits of the result and its sign. If not, an overflow error condition occurs, condition code 3 is set, and the program may be automatically interrupted and terminated.

Example 1.

			X1	Y1
AP	X1(3),Y1(2)	before execution:	03214C	010C
		after execution:	03224C	010C

Example 2.

			X2	Y2
AP	X2(2),Y2(3)	before execution:	099C	00001C
		after execution:	100C	00001C

Example 3.

			X3	Y3
AP	X3(2),Y3(3)	before execution:	999C	00001C
		*after execution:	000C	00001C

*A carry out of the high-order digit causes an overflow error condition.

Example 4.

			X4	Y4
AP	X4(3),Y4(3)	before execution:	00123D	00123C
		*after execution:	00000C	00123C

*A result of zero is always positive.

Subtract Packed

$$SP \quad D1(L1,B1),D2(L2,B2)$$

When this instruction is executed, the number whose address and length are specified by the second operand is algebraically subtracted from the number whose address and length are specified by the first operand. The resulting difference replaces the number specified by the first operand, and the condition code is set to 0, 1, or 2 according to whether the difference is zero, negative, or positive.

As in packed-decimal additions, there is one precaution to observe: *the number of byte positions, L1, must be large enough to contain all the significant digits of the result and its sign.* If not, an overflow error condition occurs, condition code 3 is set, and the program may be automatically interrupted and terminated.

Example 1.

			X1	Y1
SP	X1(3),Y1(2)	before execution:	03214C	010C
		after execution:	03204C	010C

Example 2.

			X2	Y2
SP	X2(2),Y2(3)	before execution:	099D	00001C
		after execution:	100D	00001C

Example 3.

			X3	Y3
SP	X3(2),Y3(3)	before execution:	999D	00001C
		*after execution:	000D	00001C

*A carry out of the high-order digit causes an overflow error condition.

Example 4.

			X4	Y4
SP	X4(3),Y4(3)	before execution:	00123D	00123D
		*after execution:	00000C	00123D

*A result of zero is always positive.

Multiply Packed

$$MP \quad \underbrace{D1(L1,B1)}_{\text{multiplicand}},\underbrace{D2(L2,B2)}_{\text{multiplier}}$$

When this instruction is executed, the number whose address and length are specified by the first operand is multiplied by the number whose address and length are specified by the second operand. The resulting product, its sign determined by the rules of algebra, replaces the multiplicand in memory, *but the condition code is not set.* However, the Compare Packed (CP) instruction can be used to determine the sign of the product.

Due to the fact that the number of significant bytes in the product is the sum of the number of significant bytes in the multiplier and multiplicand, there are several precautions to observe:

1. $L2 < L1$: the number of bytes in the multiplier must be less than the number of bytes in the multiplicand.
2. $1 \leq L2 \leq 8$: the number of bytes in the multiplier must not exceed 8.
3. In order that there will always be enough room to contain the product, whatever its value might be, the multiplicand (the number specified by the first operand) must have at least L2 bytes of high-order zeroes.

When these precautions are observed, there will be no product overflow and no specification error (see discussion of errors at end of this section). Moreover, the leading digit of the product will always be zero.

Example 1.

			V1	W1
MP	V1(4),W1(2)	before execution:	0000999C	999D
		after execution:	0998001D	999D

Example 2.

			V2	W2
MP	V2(3),W2(2)	before execution:	00999C	999D
		*after execution:	98001D	999D

*Overflow error condition: not enough high-order zeroes in V2.

Example 3.

			V3	W3
MP	V3(2),W3(2)	before execution:	012C	012C
		*after execution:	012C	012C

*The operation is not carried out since L2 is not less than L1.

Example 4.

			V4
MP	V4(4),V4+2(2)	before execution:	0000256D
		*after execution:	0065536C

*A number can be multiplied by itself if all the precautions discussed are observed. In this example, the second operand address and length denote the last 2 bytes of V4, namely 256D, while the first operand address and length denote the entire field, 0000256D.

Divide Packed

$$\text{DP} \quad \underbrace{\text{D1(L1,B1)}}_{\text{dividend}},\underbrace{\text{D2(L2,B2)}}_{\text{divisor}}$$

When this instruction is executed, the number whose address and length are specified by the first operand is divided by the number whose address and length are specified by the second operand. The result consists of two components: (1) Q, the integer quotient, of length L1-L2 *bytes;* and (2) R, the integer remainder, of length L2 bytes. The quotient and the remainder are stored side-by-side as packed-decimal integers in the memory location that had been occupied by the dividend, as indicated in this diagram:

$$\frac{X}{Y} = Q + \frac{R}{Y}$$

X Is Dividend.
Y Is Divisor.
Q Is Quotient.
R Is Remainder.

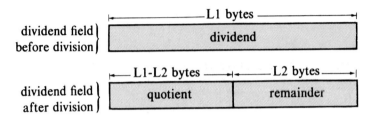

The sign of the quotient is determined by the rules of algebra; the sign of the dividend is the same as that of the remainder even if the remainder is zero. The condition code is not set by the DP instruction, so the nature of the quotient—zero, negative, or positive—must be determined by a separate test (for example, via the compare instruction, CP).

DP Length Requirements

To avoid any error condition that could interrupt the program, several precautions must be observed:

1. L2 < L1: the number of digits in the divisor must be less than the number of digits in the dividend, including leading zeroes.
2. 1 ≤ L2 ≤ 8: the number of digits in the divisor must be less than sixteen.
3. The number of significant digits in the quotient must be smaller than the number of digits that can be stored in the L1-L2 bytes allowed for the quotient. This will always be the case if the dividend—the number specified by the first operand—has at least L2 bytes of leading zeroes.
4. The value of the divisor must not be zero.

Example 1.

			V1	W1
DP	V1(4),W1(2)	before execution:	0000999C	998D
		after execution:	001D001C	998D

L1-L2 = 2 = length of quotient   remainder

Example 2.

			V2	W2
DP	V2(4),W2(1)	before execution:	0000999C	3C
		after execution:	00333C0C	3C

L1-L2 = 3 = length of quotient   remainder

Example 3.

			V3	W3
DP	V3(2),W3(1)	before execution:	999C	3C
		after execution:	999C	3C

L1-L2 = 1 = insufficient length for the quotient 333C, an error condition known as *divide exception.*

Example 4.

			V4	W4
DP	V4(2),W4(3)	before execution:	999C	00003C
		after execution:	999C	00003C

L1-L2 = −1 = an impossible length for the quotient, an error condition known as *specification exception.*

Error Situations

Several types of error situations can be detected during execution of a packed-decimal arithmetic instruction:

1. **Decimal overflow** occurs when the length of the result of an AP, SP, SRP, or ZAP instruction is too long to fit into the number of bytes specified in the first operand. (Leading zeroes cannot cause overflow; only significant digits can.)
2. **Data exception** occurs in any of four situations:
   a. The sign or digit codes of a packed-decimal number are invalid.
   b. The operands of AP, SP, MP, DP, or CP overlap without having identical right-most bytes.
   c. The operands of ZAP overlap with the right-most byte of the second operand to the right of that of the first operand.
   d. The first operand of an MP instruction does not have a sufficient number of high-order zeroes.
3. **Specification exception** occurs when the operand lengths of an MP or a DP instruction are incompatible. Either the multiplier or divisor exceeds fifteen digits and sign (i.e., $L2 > 8$), or the multiplier or divisor has the same number or more digits than the multiplicand or dividend (i.e., $L2 \geq L1$).
4. **Divide exception** occurs when the quotient would be too large for the operand field, as would be the case in an attempt to divide by zero.

When one of these errors is detected, execution of the program is interrupted by the hardware and terminated by the operating system. The only exception is that interruptions due to decimal overflow can be prevented by resetting the appropriate program mask bit to zero, as discussed in Chapter 11. Whether or not the decimal overflow interrupt has been prohibited by the SPM instruction, the occurrence of decimal overflow causes condition code 3 to be set so that it may be detected by a subsequent Branch on Overflow (BO) instruction.

Combined Multiply and Divide Example

Suppose we want to compute $(a \cdot b)/c$. We first need to determine how many bytes should be allocated for $a \cdot b$ and for $(a \cdot b)/c$, in order to assure that the answer is correctly represented. This depends on the number of bytes in each of the factors $a, b,$ and c, which we can assume are as follows:

factor	number of bytes
a	k
b	m
c	p

The rules for the multiply instruction MP require that the multiplier contain no more than 8 bytes, that the number of bytes in the multiplicand exceed that of the multiplier, and that the product contain no more than thirty-one significant digits (16 bytes). We will therefore assume that b is the multiplier with $m \leq 8$ and that $k + m \leq 16$. We can then satisfy all the rules for MP by putting a in a multiplicand field that is $k + m$ bytes long.

For example, if $a = 999$ in a 2-byte field and $b = 9$ in a 1-byte field, then $k = 2$ and $m = 1$ so that $k + m = 3$. The corresponding instructions are these:

```
        ZAP     X,A         PUT 999 IN A 3-BYTE MULTIPLICAND FIELD
        MP      X,B         MULTIPLY BY 9, A 1-BYTE MULTIPLIER
        ...
A       DC      PL2'999'
B       DC      PL1'9'
X       DS      PL3
```

The product $999 \times 9 = 8991$ is then represented correctly as a 3-byte packed-decimal number, 08991C.

The rules for the divide instruction DP require that the number of bytes in the divisor not exceed 8 and also be less than that of the dividend. We therefore assume that $p \leq 8$, and we must assure that the dividend field satisfies two criteria: (1) it must be more than p bytes long and (2) it must be long enough to contain all the significant digits of the quotient. Both of these criteria will be satisfied if the dividend contains p bytes of leading zeroes.

$$\frac{a \cdot b}{c} = Q + \frac{R}{c}$$

To continue the example, let us assume that $c = 5$ in a 1-byte field, so that $p = 1$. Since our previous result was $a \cdot b = 8991$ in a 3-byte field, so that $k + m = 3$, we need to put $a \cdot b$ in a 4-byte field with 1 byte of leading zeroes. The corresponding instructions are these:

```
        ZAP     Y,X         PUT 8991 IN A 4-BYTE DIVIDEND FIELD
        DP      Y,C         DIVIDE BY +5, A 1-BYTE DIVISOR
        ...
X       DS      PL3
Y       DS      PL4
C       DC      P'5'
```

The result, $8991 \div 5 = 1798 + 1/5$, is correctly represented in the 4-byte dividend field, Y, as two consecutive packed-decimal numbers, a 3-byte quotient and a 1-byte remainder: 01798C1C.

This analysis illustrates that if we had defined XX as a 4-byte field we could have computed $(a \cdot b)/c$ in three instructions:

```
    ZAP    XX,A      PUT 999 IN A 4-BYTE MULTIPLICAND FIELD
    MP     XX,B      MULTIPLY BY 9, A 1-BYTE MULTIPLIER
    DP     XX,C      DIVIDE BY 5, A 1-BYTE DIVISOR
    ...
XX  DS     PL4       RESULT IS 01798C1C
```

12.4 COMPARISONS

Any two packed-decimal numbers can be algebraically compared without changing either number. This is accomplished by means of the Compare Packed (CP) instruction, an SS_2-type instruction. Note that the character compare instructions (CLC, etc.) cannot be used because they do not interpret the sign bits algebraically and do not properly account for operands of unequal length.

If we let

$$V_1 = \text{The number specified by the address and length}$$
$$\text{of the first operand D1(L1,B1)}$$
$$V_2 = \text{The number specified by the address and length}$$
$$\text{of the second operand D2(L2,B2)}$$

then the instruction

$$\text{CP} \quad \text{D1(L1,B1),D2(L2,B2)}$$

sets the condition code as follows:

condition	condition code
$V_1 = V_2$	0
$V_1 < V_2$	1
$V_1 > V_2$	2

The comparison is made as though both V_1 and V_2 were equal in length, though they need not be. *CP Length* The only restrictions on length are that both L1 and L2 be less than or equal to sixteen. *Requirements*

As with any other comparison instruction, RX-type conditional branch instructions may be used to determine the result of a comparison:

BE	branches if $V_1 = V_2$
BNE	branches if $V_1 \neq V_2$
BH	branches if $V_1 > V_2$
BNH	branches if $V_1 \leq V_2$
BL	branches if $V_1 < V_2$
BNL	branches if $V_1 \geq V_2$

Alternatively, the RR-type conditional branch instructions, BER, BNER, etc., may be used.

Example 1.

		V1	V2
CP	V1(2),V2(3)	012C	00345D
	result: $V_1 > V_2$		

Example 2.

		V1	V2
CP	V1(3),V2(2)	00345C	345C
	result: $V_1 = V_2$		

Example 3.

		V1	V2
CP	V1(4),V2(1)	1234567D	0C
	result: $V_1 < V_2$		

The CP instruction is especially useful when it is necessary to determine if a number is zero prior to using it as a divisor. It can also be used to determine the nature of the result of an MP or DP instruction, by comparing the result to =P'0'. No distinction is made between a positive and a negative zero by the CP instruction.

12.5 DECIMAL POINT ALIGNMENT: SHIFTING ON THE IBM 370

To illustrate the problem of decimal point alignment, consider the problem of computing A*B+C for various values of A, B, and C as illustrated in the examples.

Example 1.

	assembly language		machine language
A	DC	P'+2.5'	025C
B	DC	P'+3.5'	035C
C	DC	P'+1.0'	010C

In machine language, the three numbers are all integers. The position of the decimal point does not affect the machine language representation. In other words, +2.5 is represented the same as +25 and as +0.25.

Consequently, the value A*B = 8.75 is represented as 875C; this is indistinguishable from +0.875, +8.75, and +87.5. So the immediate question is, how can we add +1.0 to +8.75? Since both numbers are treated as integers, we would have

$$
\begin{array}{r}
875C \\
+\ 010C \\
\hline
885C
\end{array}
$$

This is clearly wrong, for the correct answer, +9.75, would be represented as 975C.

Shifting Example   The resolution of the dilemma is embodied in the concept of **shifting.** To align the implied decimal points so that addition can take place properly, we shift one of the factors right or left. If we shift to the **left,** we cause zeroes to be inserted on the right and a corresponding number of digits to be deleted from the left. If we shift to the **right,** we cause zeroes to be inserted on the left and a corresponding number of digits to be deleted from the right. For example, if we shift P'+1.0' *left* one position, then 010C becomes 100C. The addition in this example can now be performed correctly. We use the caret (^) to indicate the position of the implied decimal point:

$$
\begin{array}{r}
8_\wedge 7\ 5\ C \\
+\ 1_\wedge 0\ 0\ C \\
\hline
9_\wedge 7\ 5\ C
\end{array}
$$

— zero inserted on right to align implied decimal points

In ordinary arithmetic, we would do exactly the same thing when adding 8.75 and 1.0:

$$\begin{array}{r} 8.75 \\ +\ 1.00 \\ \hline 9.75 \end{array}$$

— zero inserted on right to align explicit decimal points

Note that we ordinarily would not consider shifting 8.75 right to align it with 1.0, because to do so would result in a loss of accuracy. In shifting a number to the right, we drop the least significant digits. For example, in a right shift of one position, 8.75 becomes 8.7 (or 8.8, if rounded), so that 8.75 + 1.0 becomes

either
$$\left\{ \begin{array}{cc} 8.7 & 0\ 8\ 7\ C \\ +\ 1.0 & 0\ 1\ 0\ C \\ \hline 9.7 & 0\ 9\ 7\ C \end{array} \right.$$
or
$$\left\{ \begin{array}{cc} 8.8 & 0\ 8\ 8\ C \\ +\ 1.0 & 0\ 1\ 0\ C \\ \hline 9.8 & 0\ 9\ 8\ C \end{array} \right.$$

But despite this loss of accuracy, there are times when a shift to the right is quite appropriate, as the next example illustrates.

Example 2.

assembly language			machine language
A	DC	P'+2.5'	0 2ʌ5 C
B	DC	P'+3.14159'	0 3ʌ1 4 1 5 9 C
C	DC	P'+1.0'	0 1ʌ0 C

Here, the number at B is an approximation to the number $\pi = 3.14159265....$ If the result of calculating A*B+C is desired to two decimal positions, we must shift both A*B and C, as follows:

$$\begin{array}{rl} A*B\ = & (0\ 2_\wedge 5\ C) * (0\ 3_\wedge 1\ 4\ 1\ 5\ 9\ C) = 7_\wedge 8\ 5\ 3\ 9\ 7\ 5\ C \rightarrow 7_\wedge 8\ 5\ C \\ C\ = & 0\ 1_\wedge 0\ C \longrightarrow 1_\wedge 0\ 0\ C \\ A*B+C\ = & \longrightarrow 8_\wedge 8\ 5\ C \end{array}$$

If the result had been desired to three decimal positions, we would have *rounded* A*B before shifting:

$$\begin{array}{rl} A*B\ = & 7_\wedge 8\ 5\ 3\ 9\ 7\ 5\ C \longrightarrow 0\ 7_\wedge 8\ 5\ 4\ C \\ C\ = & 0\ 1_\wedge 0\ C \longrightarrow 0\ 1_\wedge 0\ 0\ 0\ C \\ A*B+C\ = & \longrightarrow 0\ 8_\wedge 8\ 5\ 4\ C \end{array}$$

Rounding Example

In general, we always round when shifting to the right in order that the resulting number be the best approximation possible for the number of digits that remain after the shift. In the IBM 370 (but *not* the 360), the instruction used to shift and round a packed-decimal number is Shift and Round Packed (SRP). This instruction is discussed below. Instructions needed to accomplish shifting and rounding on the IBM 360, where the SRP is not available, will be described in Section 12.6.

Shift and Round Packed Instruction

The SRP instruction is a modified SS₁-type instruction, with the following assembly language and machine language formats:

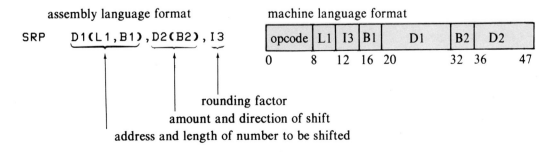

As indicated, the first operand specifies the packed-decimal number's location in memory and its length in bytes. However, the number computed as the effective address from the second operand, namely,

$$\{\text{displacement D2}\} + \{\text{base address in Register B2}\}$$

is *not used as an address*. Instead, its low-order 6 bits denote the number of digit positions to be shifted and the direction of the shift: if the low-order 6 bits represent a nonnegative integer n, then the packed-decimal number is shifted n positions to the left; if those 6 bits represent a negative integer $-n$, the number is shifted n positions to the right. The sign of the number is not shifted, and vacated digit positions are filled with zeroes. For right shifts of n digits, the negative integer $-n$ is assumed by the hardware to be in two's complement form. Since the assembler does not translate $-n$ to its 6-bit two's complement representation, you should, as in the examples that follow, write $64-n$ rather than $-n$.

Although *rounding occurs only during right shifts,* a valid decimal digit must always be specified for I3, regardless of the shift direction. Before a right shift is completed, the integer specified by the I3 field is added to the left-most digit that is to be shifted out. Therefore, to round while shifting right, the I3 field should be 5; to avoid rounding, it should be 0. (Note that a number is rounded as though it were positive. In a right shift of n positions, the rounding factor is added to the nth digit from the right, and the resulting carry digit (0 or 1) is added to the $(n+1)$ digit from the right, with further carries (if any) propagated as required by the rules of addition. Then the right shift is performed and the nth digit and all lower-order digits are discarded.)

Example 1.

```
                                           symbolic
                                           address A
                                           _____
  SRP    A(4),64-4,5
         ‿‿      ↑ ↑            before execution:   7853975C
          |      | |            after execution:    0000785C
          |      | rounding factor                        ↑
          |      right shift of four positions      sign not shifted
          symbolic address and length
          of packed-decimal number
          to be shifted
```

Example 2.

```
                                           symbolic
                                           address A
                                           _____
  SRP    A(4),64-3,5           before execution:   7853975D
                              *after execution:    0007854D
                                                          ↑
        *Note that the number is rounded as though it were positive.|
```

Example 3.

```
                                           symbolic
                                           address B
                                           _____
  SRP    B(2),1,5             before execution:   010C
         ↑↑                   after execution:    100C
         | rounding factor
         | (present but not used in left shifts)
         left shift of one position
```

Example 4.

| | symbolic |
| | address B |

```
SRP    B(2),2,0
          ↑
       left shift of two positions
```

before execution:	010C
*after execution:	000C

*This example generates an *overflow error condition* because a significant digit (i.e., a nonzero digit) has been shifted out during the left shift. When this occurs, condition code 3 is set, and the program may be automatically interrupted and terminated.

Example 5.

| | symbolic |
| | address C |

```
SRP    C(5),0(8),5
            ⌣     ↑
            ↑  rounding factor
         amount and direction of shift
         is determined by the low-order
         6 bits in Reg 8
```

before execution:	031415926C
after execution:	000031416C

In this example, it was assumed that Register 8 contains X'FFFFFFFD', i.e., -3. Thus, the amount of shift is three positions and the direction is to the right, as illustrated. The rounding factor is added to the left-most digit shifted out (the 9 in this example), and the carry is added to the lowest-order digit that remains, thus increasing the 5 to a 6.

Multiplication and Division

The requirements for assuring a sufficient number of significant digits in the result of a multiplication or division were described in Section 12.4 for integer computations. Those same requirements must be met when one or more factors contain implied decimal points, but there is also an additional requirement. *We must assure that a product and quotient contain an appropriate number of significant digits to the left and right of the implied decimal point.*

To illustrate this requirement, consider this multiplication: P'60'∗P'5' = P'300'. Since decimal arithmetic instructions ignore implied decimal points and treat all packed-decimal numbers as integers, then in the computer we also get P'60'∗P'.5' = P'300' and P'6.0'∗P'5' = P'300', whereas obviously 60∗0.5 = 30 and 6.0∗5 = 30. Similarly in divisions: in the computer, P'60' ÷ P'5' = P'12', P'60' ÷ P'.5' = P'12', and P'6.0' ÷ P'5' = P'12', whereas in fact 60 ÷ 0.5 = 120 and 6.0 ÷ 5 = 1.2.

To assure an appropriate number of significant digits to the left and right of the implied decimal point in a product or quotient, we can proceed as follows.

Multiplication. If p and q are the number of digits to the right of the implied decimal point (i.e., the number of fraction digits) in the multiplicand and multiplier, respectively, then the result of a multiply (MP) instruction will always contain $p + q$ fraction digits. Therefore, to assure that there are just k fraction digits in the product, we can shift the MP's result $p + q - k$ digits to the right.

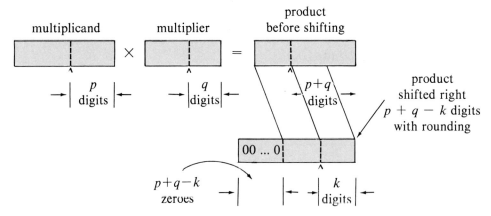

For example, if we want no fraction digits in the result of P'60'*P'.5', then $k = 0$ with $p = 0$ and $q = 1$. Thus we must shift the MP result $p + q - k = 1$ digit to the right:

```
        ZAP     X,=P'60'        CREATE 3-BYTE MULTIPLICAND
        MP      X,=P'.5'        MULTIPLY BY 1-BYTE MULTIPLIER
        SRP     X,64-1,5        SHIFT RESULT RIGHT 1 DIGIT
        ...
X       DC      PL3             CORRECT PRODUCT = 00030C
```

Division. If p and q are the number of fraction digits in the dividend and divisor, respectively, and if $p \geq q$, then the quotient resulting from a divide instruction (DP) always contains $p - q$ fraction digits. If $p < q$, then $q - p$ low-order digits of the quotient will be truncated. To assure that there will be k fraction digits in the quotient, we can shift the *dividend* $q + k$ digits to the left before dividing, and shift the DP's quotient p digits to the right after dividing.

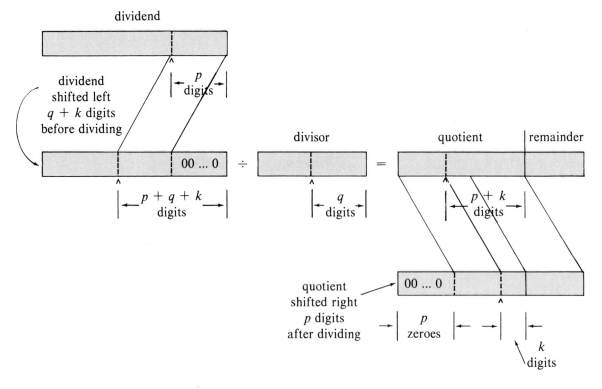

For example, if we want one fraction digit in the result of P'6.0' ÷ P'5', then $k = 1$ with $p = 1$ and $q = 0$:

```
        ZAP     X,=P'6.0'       CREATE 4-BYTE DIVIDEND
        SRP     X,1,0           SHIFT DIVIDEND LEFT 1 DIGIT
        DP      X,=P'5'         CREATE DP'S 3-BYTE QUOTIENT
        SRP     X(3),64-1,5     SHIFT QUOTIENT RIGHT 1 DIGIT
        ...
X       DS      PL4             CORRECT RESULT = 00012C0C
```

Since it is imperative to avoid loss of significant digits when shifting left, the dividend should have $q + k$ leading zero digits in addition to what it would require in simple integer division. That is why we created a 4-byte dividend rather than a 3-byte dividend in the previous example.

NOTE: The previous general procedures are not necessary if we already know the value of each factor. But they or similar procedures are required when the values of the factors are not known at assembly time. In general we don't know those values, since they are likely to be either input data or the results of other calculations. Therefore, we should always estimate the *maximum* number of significant digits that are expected to occur to the right and left of the implied decimal point in each factor and make the appropriate decisions for space allocation and shifting. As a simple example of this, we can safely estimate that monthly salaries require no more than two digits to the right and five digits to the left of the implied decimal point: P'99999.99', or PL4.

12.6 COPYING A NUMBER: SHIFTING ON THE IBM 360

Although any packed-decimal number can be copied from one main memory location by means of the MVC, MVCL, or ZAP instructions, there are three instructions that are especially designed for certain copying operations intrinsic to packed-decimal numbers. These are

MVO	Move with Offset	(SS$_2$-type)
MVN	Move Numerics	(SS$_1$-type)
MVZ	Move Zones	(SS$_1$-type)

The MVO instruction copies a number from one memory location to another, but the result is *shifted left 4 bits* (half a byte) from what the original number was. This instruction makes it possible to shift a packed-decimal number on the IBM 360.

The MVN instruction copies the *right-most 4 bits* of one or more consecutive bytes. This makes it easy to set or alter the sign bits of a packed-decimal number, for example, to create an absolute value.

The MVZ instruction copies the *left-most 4 bits* of one or more consecutive bytes. It is used primarily to set the sign bits in a number represented in EBCDIC format (so-called zoned-decimal format, to be discussed in Section 12.8).

In each of these three instructions, the field being copied (the source) is specified by the second operand, and the destination is specified by the first operand. The following examples illustrate these concepts. This section concludes with a discussion of shifting packed-decimal numbers on the IBM 360.

Move with Offset

$$\underbrace{\text{MVO D1(L1,B1)}}_{\text{destination}},\underbrace{\text{D2(L2,B2)}}_{\text{source}}$$

All bytes of the source field are copied from right to left, but they are all shifted left 4 *bits* and replace the digits, but not the sign, of the destination field. If L2 < L1, the source field is extended left with enough high-order zeroes to fill the destination field. If L2 ≥ L1, the source field is truncated on the left in order to fit into the destination field. The condition code is *not* set if overflow occurs.

Example 1.

	A	B
MVO A(4),B(4) before execution:	2468135D ⌐	6314159C
after execution:	314159CD⌐	6314159C

Number copied from **B** is offset 4 bits to the left, but its leading digit is lost since there is not enough room for it.

Example 2.

	A	B
MVO A(5),B(2) before execution:	123456789D ⌐	987C
after execution:	00000987CD⌐	987C

Copied number is offset 4 bits to the left, and leading zeroes are inserted to fill the remaining space.

Move Numerics

$$\text{MVN} \quad \underbrace{\text{D1(L,B1)}}_{\text{destination}},\underbrace{\text{D2(B2)}}_{\text{source}}$$

This is similar to the MVC instruction, except that *only the right-most 4 bits of each source byte are copied.* The left-most 4 bits of each destination byte are not altered.

Example 3.

	A
MVN A+3(1),=P'-1' before execution:	0135792C
after execution:	0135792D

sign copied from $=P'-1'$

Move Zones

$$\text{MVZ} \quad \underbrace{\text{D1(L,B1)}}_{\text{destination}},\underbrace{\text{D2(B2)}}_{\text{source}}$$

This is similar to the MVC instruction, except that *only the left-most 4 bits of each source byte are copied.* The right-most 4 bits of each destination byte are not altered.

Example 4.

```
MVZ     A+3(1),=X'D0'
```

	A
before execution:	F1F2F3F4
after execution:	F1F2F3D4

copied from =X'D0'

Shifting Packed-Decimal Numbers on the IBM 360

Since the Shift and Round Packed (SRP) instruction is not available on the IBM 360, the problem of aligning the implied decimal point in packed-decimal numbers must be resolved by means of other instructions.

Shifting without SRP

One way to shift a packed-decimal number to the left N digits is to multiply it by 10^N. Similarly, to shift a packed-decimal number *right* N digits, we can divide it by 10^N. Both multiplication and division are fairly time-consuming instructions; the multiply instruction is essentially a sequence of successive additions, the divide a sequence of successive subtractions. Moreover, there is no simple way to round when doing right shifts by means of a division instruction. Consequently, shifting is usually done as a combination of instructions based on the MVO. There are many ways to do this, and it is suggested that you devise your own methods as a way of learning how to use the MVO, MVN, MVZ, and ZAP instructions. In addition, you are urged to study Figures 12.2a–d, in which solutions to the four main shifting problems are presented: (1) shift left an odd number of digits; (2) shift left an even number of digits; (3) shift right an odd number of digits, with rounding; and (4) shift right an even number of digits, with rounding. In each of the solutions, it is assumed that the packed-decimal number to be shifted is at symbolic location Q, and consists of L bytes, $L \leq 16$. The condition code will not necessarily reflect the result of the shifts.

Figure 12.2a   Shifting left an odd number of digits. (L is an absolute constant, equal to the length in bytes of the number at location Q.)

```
* SHIFT 1 DIGIT LEFT          * SHIFT 3 DIGITS LEFT         * SHIFT 5 DIGITS LEFT
    ZAP   W(16),Q(L)              ZAP   W(16),Q(L)              ZAP   W(16),Q(L)
    MVN   W+15(1),=X'00'          MVN   W+15(1),=X'00'          MVN   W+15(1),=X'00'
    MVO   Q(L),W(16)              MVO   Q(L),W+1(16)            MVO   Q(L),W+2(16)
    ...                          ...                          ...
W   DC    32X'00'            W   DC    32X'00'            W   DC    32X'00'
```

Figure 12.2b   Shifting left an even number of digits. (L is an absolute constant, equal to the length in bytes of the number at location Q.)

```
* SHIFT 2 DIGITS LEFT         * SHIFT 4 DIGITS LEFT         * SHIFT 6 DIGITS LEFT
    MVO   W(16),Q(L)              MVO   W(16),Q(L)              MVO   W(16),Q(L)
    MVC   W+15(1),=X'00'          MVC   W+15(1),=X'00'          MVC   W+15(1),=X'00'
    MVO   Q(L),W(16)              MVO   Q(L),W+1(16)            MVO   Q(L),W+2(16)
    ...                          ...                          ...
W   DC    32X'00'            W   DC    32X'00'            W   DC    32X'00'
```

Figure 12.2c Shifting right an odd number of digits—with rounding. (L is an absolute constant, equal to the length in bytes of the number at location Q.)

```
* SHIFT 1 DIGIT RIGHT          * SHIFT 3 DIGITS RIGHT         * SHIFT 5 DIGITS RIGHT
      ZAP    W(16),Q(L)              ZAP    W(16),Q(L)              ZAP    W(16),Q(L)
      MVN    W+15(1),=P'0'           MVN    W+15(1),=P'0'           MVN    W+15(1),=P'0'
      AP     W(16),=P'5'             AP     W(16),=P'500'           AP     W(16),=P'50000'
      MVO    Q(L),W(15)              MVO    Q(L),W(14)              MVO    Q(L),W(13)
      ...                           ...                           ...
W     DC     16X'00'           W     DC     16X'00'           W     DC     16X'00'
```

Figure 12.2d Shifting right an even number of digits—with rounding. (L is an absolute constant, equal to the length in bytes of the number at location Q.)

```
* SHIFT 2 DIGITS RIGHT         * SHIFT 4 DIGITS RIGHT         * SHIFT 6 DIGITS RIGHT
      MVN    W+15(1),=P'0'           MVN    W+15(1),=P'0'           MVN    W+15(1),=P'0'
      MVO    W(16),Q(L-1)            MVO    W(16),Q(L-1)            MVO    W(16),Q(L-1)
      AP     W(16),=P'5'             AP     W(16),=P'500'           AP     W(16),=P'50000'
      MVO    Q(L),W(15)              MVO    Q(L),W(14)              MVO    Q(L),W(13)
      ...                           ...                           ...
W     DC     16X'00'           W     DC     16X'00'           W     DC     16X'00'
```

12.7 APPLYING PACKED-DECIMAL OPERATIONS

To illustrate the use of packed-decimal operations, two small but typical business-oriented problems will now be described and solved.

The first problem is to calculate the amount, A, of interest earned on a principal of P dollars compounded at an annual interest rate, I, for a period of N years:

$$A = P(1 + I)^N - P$$

The second problem is to convert a date (given as month/day/year) into its so-called Julian date, namely, the number that indicates how many days have elapsed from the beginning of the year to that date.

Computation of Interest

The solution to this problem (Fig. 12.3) illustrates the types of decisions that a programmer has to make when doing calculations that involve decimal point positioning. These decisions are: (1) How many digit positions, both to the right and to the left of the decimal point, should be provided for the results of intermediate calculations? and (2) In what order should the calculations be performed?

In deciding how many digit positions should be provided to the *left* of the implied decimal point, simply estimate the largest number that is likely to be calculated, and be certain to allow enough leading zeroes to avoid the possibility of overflow. The descriptions of the MP and DP instructions are helpful in deciding the number of leading zeroes for which to provide space.

In deciding how many digit positions should be provided to the *right* of the implied decimal point, remember that when two numbers are multiplied, the number of digits to the right of the decimal point in the product is the sum of the number of digits to the right of the decimal point in each factor.

Finally, in deciding the order in which calculations are to be performed, you must take care to minimize the possibility of cumulative round-off errors, or errors due to approximations.

Figure 12.3   Computation of $A = P(1 + I)^N - P$.

```
* CALCULATION USING PACKED-DECIMAL OPERATIONS
*             A = P * (1 + I) ** N - P
*
* P = PRINCIPAL IN DOLLARS AND CENTS          P'XXXXX.XX'
* I = ANNUAL INTEREST, E.G.:    0.0950  (9.5%)   P'X.XXXX'
* N = NUMBER OF YEARS                              P'XX'
* A = INTEREST EARNED                        P'XXXXXX.XX'
*
* INITIALIZATION
          ZAP    X(4),I(3)             INITIALLY,
          AP     X(4),=P'10000'          X=1+I = 1.XXXX
          ZAP    Y(8),P(4)               Y=P WITH LEADING ZEROES
          ZAP    CTR(8),N(2)           CTR=N, FOR LOOP-CONTROL
          CVB    5,CTR                 CONVERT N TO BINARY INTEGER
* COMPUTE   Y = ((P*(1+I))*(1+I))*...*(1+I)
LOOP      MP     Y(8),X(4)             GENERATES SIX DECIMAL PLACES
          SRP    Y(8),64-4,0           TRUNCATE TO TWO PLACES
          BCT    5,LOOP                REPEAT N-1  TIMES
* COMPUTE     A = Y - P
          ZAP    A(5),Y(8)             MOVE Y AND REMOVE LEADING ZEROES
          SP     A(5),P(4)             A = XXXXXX.XX
          .
          .
X         DS     PL4                   1 + I             X.XXXX
Y         DS     PL8                   P*(1+I)**N   XX...XXXX.XX
CTR       DS     D                     N (FOR CVB)     000000XX.
P         DS     PL4                   P                XXXXX.XX
A         DS     PL5                   A              XXXXXX.XX
N         DS     PL2                   N                     XX.
I         DS     PL3                   I                 X.XXXX
          .
          .
```

In the solution shown in Figure 12.3, the following decisions can be seen:

1. In the computation of $P \times (1 + I)$, a total of 16 digit positions were reserved: six to the right of the decimal, since $1 + I$ had four to the right and P had two; and ten to the left in order to take care of the assumed worst-case conditions of $P = \$100,000$, $I = 20\%$, and $N = 25$ years.

2. In the computation of the result, the amount of money on hand *at the end of each year* was truncated (not rounded) to dollars and cents before the calculation for the next year was made. This method is one way to avoid the accumulation of unearned money through round-off.

Note that the CVB instruction in Figure 12.3 converts the packed-decimal number N (number of years) to a binary integer for loop control. The CVB is described in the next section.

The following data can be used to trace through the program of Figure 12.3 to see how the decimal point alignment problem is handled:

$$P = \$10,000.00 \qquad (10000.00)*(1.0850) = 10850.000000$$
$$I = 8.5\% \qquad (10850.00)*(1.0850) = 11772.250000$$
$$N = 5 \text{ years} \qquad (11772.25)*(1.0850) = 12772.891250$$
$$(12772.89)*(1.0850) = 13858.585650$$
$$(13858.58)*(1.0850) = 15036.559300$$

so that $A = \$15,036.55 - \$10,000.00 = \$5,036.55$.

Figure 12.4   Calculation of Julian date.

```
* CALCULATING JULIAN DATE J CORRESPONDING TO CALENDAR DATE M/D/Y:
*                J = (M-1)*30.57 + D - X
*       WHERE    X = 0  IF M ≤ 2
*                X = 1  IF M > 2 AND Y IS A LEAP YEAR
*                X = 2  IF M > 2 AND Y NOT A LEAP YEAR
*
          ZAP    JD(3),M(2)              ADD LEADING ZEROES TO MONTH
          SP     JD(3),=P'1'            M-1
          MP     JD(3),=P'30.57'       (M-1)*30.57
          SRP    JD(3),64-2,5           ROUND OFF TO AN INTEGER
          AP     JD(3),D(2)            (M-1)*30.57 + D
          CP     M(2),=P'2'             IS M > 2 ?
          BNH    DONE                   BRANCH IF EITHER JAN OR FEB
          ZAP    YX(3),Y(2)             ADD LEADING ZEROES TO YEAR,
          DP     YX(3),=P'4'            THEN TEST FOR LEAP YEAR.
          CP     YXR(1),=P'0'           IS REMAINDER ZERO ?
          BE     LEAP                   IF SO, IT'S LEAP YEAR
          SP     JD(3),=P'2'            IF NOT LEAP YEAR, J= (M-1)*30.57+D-2
          B      DONE
LEAP      SP     JD(3),=P'1'            IF LEAP YEAR, J= (M-1)*30.57+D-1
DONE      ZAP    J(2),JD(3)             REMOVE UNNEEDED LEADING ZEROES
            .
            .
            .
M         DS     PL2                    MONTH               XX.
D         DS     PL2                    DAY                 XX.
Y         DS     PL2                    YEAR                XX.
J         DS     PL2                    JULIAN              XXX.
JD        DS     PL3                    FOR CALCULATING  (M-1)*30.57  XXX.XX
YX        DS     PL3                    FOR CALCULATING  Y/4
YXR       EQU    YX+2                   REMAINDER OF Y/4  IS ONE BYTE LONG
            .
            .
            .
```

Calculation of Julian Date

The Julian date of any day of the year is the number that indicates how many days have elapsed from the beginning of the year, up to and including that day. For example, the Julian date of January 1 is 1, that of February 1 is 32, and that of December 31 is 365 (366 in leap years).

The Julian date is useful in cost accounting and related business applications where it is necessary to compute elapsed time in days and/or weeks. It is much simpler to subtract two Julian dates to arrive at the result than it is to subtract two calendar dates. For these types of applications, it is convenient to have an algorithm that converts a calendar date given as month/day/year to its equivalent Julian date. The purpose of this problem is to describe such an algorithm and to show how it might be programmed using the packed-decimal arithmetic instructions.

To convert a calendar date, mm/dd/yy, to its Julian date, the algorithm is as follows:

$$\text{Let } M = \text{mm} \quad \text{the two-digit number representing the month}$$
$$\text{Let } D = \text{dd} \quad \text{the two-digit date of the month}$$
$$\text{Let } Y = \text{yy} \quad \text{the last two digits of the year}$$

Calculate $J_1 = (M-1)*30.57$, and *round it off to an integer*. Then the Julian date J corresponding to the calendar date $M/D/Y$ is given by one of these three expressions:

$$J = J_1 + D \qquad \text{if } M \leq 2$$
$$J = J_1 + D - 1 \qquad \text{if } M > 2 \text{ and } Y \text{ is a leap year}$$
$$J = J_1 + D - 2 \qquad \text{if } M > 2 \text{ and } Y \text{ is not a leap year}$$

In addition to its dependence on the values of *M, D,* and *Y,* the algorithm is clearly dependent on the value of the constant 30.57, the concept of rounding, and the calculation that determines whether or not *Y* is a leap year. Except when $Y = 00$, *Y* is a leap year if it is exactly divisible by 4. (If $Y = 00$, the full four-digit year must be exactly divisible by 400 in order for it to be a leap year. But since the year 2000 is exactly divisible by both 4 and 400, this case won't be considered in the program solution of Fig. 12.4.)

The concept of rounding is quite straightforward in this problem. The product $(M-1)*30.57$ will always have two digits implied to the right of the decimal point, so that a right shift of two positions, with rounding, is all that is required.

The constant 30.57 is, to two decimal places, the average of the ten Julian dates corresponding to March 1, April 1, May 1,..., December 1, when these dates are leap year dates. Thus, the product $(M-1)*30.57$ rounded off to an integer gives the Julian date of the first day of March, April, May,..., December in a leap year. Once these Julian dates are determined, the remaining calculation simply adds the date of the month, and subtracts 2 or 1 depending on whether the year is or is not a leap year.

A program segment to accomplish these calculations is given in Figure 12.4. On the IBM 360, the SRP instruction would have to be replaced by the following sequence (see also Fig. 12.2d). In this sequence, W would be defined by the DC directive

```
        W   DC   16X'00'

MVN     W+15(1),=P'0'      INITIALIZE W TO P'+0'
MVO     W(16),JD(2)        TRUNCATE TO 1 DECIMAL PLACE, AND OFFSET
AP      W(16),=P'5'        ROUND BY ADDING 5 TO LOW-ORDER DIGIT
MVO     JD(3),W(15)        TRUNCATE RESULTING LOW-ORDER DIGIT
```

12.8   CONVERSION TO AND FROM PACKED-DECIMAL FORMAT

Three different methods of representing numbers in the IBM 360 and 370 systems have been described: (1) EBCDIC format, (2) binary integer format, and (3) packed-decimal format. In addition, as will be shown in Chapter 13, there is a fourth method of representation: floating-point format. A natural question arises: Are these formats interchangeable? That is, can we easily change a number from one format to another?

The answer is *yes* for the first three formats and *no* (at least, not easily) for floating-point format. The conversions among EBCDIC, binary integer, and packed-decimal formats are made quite easy by two sets of instructions:

1. Instructions for converting between binary and packed-decimal:

> CVD converts binary to packed-decimal
> CVB converts packed-decimal to binary

2. Instructions for converting between packed-decimal and EBCDIC:

> PACK converts EBCDIC to packed-decimal
> UNPK converts packed-decimal to EBCDIC

There is no single instruction for converting from binary to EBCDIC (or vice versa), but it is a simple matter to do so by using two instructions from the sets just mentioned:

> CVD
> UNPK } converts binary to EBCDIC in two steps

> PACK
> CVB } converts EBCDIC to binary in two steps

The methods of using these instructions will now be described. Two important limitations of PACK and UNPK will be discussed at the end of this section.

Packed-Decimal/Binary Conversions

opcode	meaning	type
CVD	CONVERT TO DECIMAL Converts a 32-bit binary integer into an 8-byte packed-decimal number.	RX
CVB	CONVERT TO BINARY Converts an 8-byte packed-decimal number into a 32-bit binary integer.	RX

For these two instructions, the following hold true:

Restrictions and Rules for CVD, CVB

1. The RX formats of the CVD and CVB are

$$\text{CVD R1,D2(X2,B2)}$$
$$\text{CVB R1,D2(X2,B2)}$$

2. The location of the 32-bit binary integer is specified by the first operand field, which is a register address. Thus, when using CVD, the binary integer must already be in that register; when using CVB, the resulting integer will be placed in that register.
3. The location of the 8-byte packed-decimal number *must be on a double-word boundary in the IBM 360.* Its address is specified by the second operand field.
4. The packed-decimal number that is converted by the CVB cannot be greater than P'2147483647' or less than P'−2147483648'. This is because numbers outside this range cannot be represented as 32-bit signed integers. If an attempt is made to convert a number outside this range, a fixed-point divide exception occurs and the program is interrupted.

CVD and CVB Examples

			Reg 5	memory location A
CVB	5,A	before execution: after execution:	any number 00 00 00 10	00 00 00 00 00 00 01 6C 00 00 00 00 00 00 01 6C

			Reg 5	memory location A
CVB	5,A	before execution: after execution:	any number FF FF FF F0	00 00 00 00 00 00 01 6D 00 00 00 00 00 00 01 6D

			Reg 5	memory location A
CVD	5,A	before execution: after execution:	7F FF FF FF 7F FF FF FF	←——— any number ——→ 00 00 02 14 74 83 64 7C

			Reg 5	memory location A
CVD	5,A	before execution: after execution:	80 00 00 00 80 00 00 00	←——— any number ——→ 00 00 02 14 74 83 64 8D

Packed-Decimal/EBCDIC Conversions

opcode	meaning	type
PACK	Converts numbers from EBCDIC to packed-decimal format.	SS$_2$
UNPK	Converts packed-decimal numbers to EBCDIC format (see note 3, which follows).	SS$_2$

For these two instructions, the following hold true:

1. The first operand specifies the result field; the second, the field used to create the result:

Restrictions and Rules of Thumb for PACK, UNPK

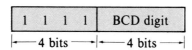

$$\text{PACK} \quad \underbrace{\text{D1(L1,B1)}}_{\text{packed-decimal field}}, \underbrace{\text{D2(L2,B2)}}_{\text{EBCDIC field}}$$

$$\text{UNPK} \quad \underbrace{\text{D1(L1,B1)}}_{\text{EBCDIC}}, \underbrace{\text{D2(L2,B2)}}_{\text{packed-decimal}}$$

2. L1 and L2 are *byte* counts; each is required to be less than or equal to 16. The counts need not be equal, but care must be taken to avoid loss of the most significant digits during the conversion process. Such loss will not occur if we use a slightly conservative rule of thumb, namely, that every byte of a packed-decimal number corresponds to 2 bytes of an EBCDIC number. For PACK, this rule leads us to choose $L1 > \frac{1}{2} * L2$; for UNPK, it leads us to choose $L1 \geq 2 * L2$.

3. The EBCDIC data format used by these two instructions is a slight but important variation of the standard EBCDIC format. This variation is known as the **zoned-decimal format.** In standard EBCDIC, every digit is represented in 8 bits:

1	1	1	1	BCD digit

|← 4 bits →|← 4 bits →|

The left half of this byte is called the **zone portion;** the right half, the **numeric portion.** In a standard EBCDIC number each zone portion consists of four binary 1's (a hex F), as shown above. In the variation of EBCDIC processed by the PACK and UNPK instructions, *the zone portion of the right-most byte contains the sign of the number:*

BCD vs. EBCDIC Signs

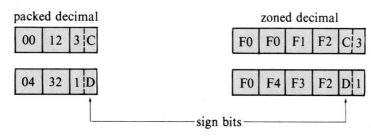

The bits recognized as valid sign bits in zoned-decimal format are the same as those in packed-decimal format: X'A', X'C', X'E', or X'F' for plus; X'B' or X'D' for minus. The UNPK instruction always copies the sign bits unchanged from the low-order 4 bits of the packed-decimal number to the zone bits of the low-order byte in the receiving EBCDIC field. PACK always copies the sign bits unchanged from the low-order EBCDIC byte to the low-order packed-decimal byte, as shown in the diagram. Whether the numbers being converted are positive or negative, there are certain inherent limitations to this treatment of the sign bits. These limitations will be discussed further at the end of this section.

Sign Bits

PACK and UNPK Examples

			B	A
PACK	A(4),B(4)	before execution:	F1 F2 F3 C4	any 4 bytes
	result source field field	after execution:	F1 F2 F3 C4	00 01 23 4C

L1=4,L2=4: more than enough space in result field, so leading
BCD zeroes are generated as needed.

			B	A
PACK	A(2),B(4)	before execution:	F1 F2 F3 D4	any 2 bytes
		after execution:	F1 F2 F3 D4	23 4D

L1=2,L2=4: insufficient space in result field to contain entire source
field: one high-order digit is not converted.

			Y	X
UNPK	X(4),Y(4)	before execution:	12 34 56 7C	any 4 bytes
	result source field field	after execution:	12 34 56 7C	F4 F5 F6 C7

L1=L2=4: not enough space in result field to hold all the digits of
source field: three high-order digits are not converted.

			Y	X
UNPK	X(8),Y(4)	before execution:	12 34 56 7D	any 8 bytes
		after execution:	12 34 56 7D	F0 F1 F2 F3 F4 F5 F6 D7

L1=8, L2=4: more than enough space in result field, so leading
EBCDIC zeroes are generated as needed.

Neither PACK nor UNPK sets the condition code, and neither causes an error condition when there is insufficient space in the result field.

Further, in the PACK instruction the low-order 4 bits of each byte are not checked for valid codes; they are simply copied unchanged into their respective positions in the packed-decimal representation. This is also true of the zone bits in the right-most byte of the EBCDIC field. The zone bits of the other EBCDIC bytes are ignored.

Similarly, in the UNPK instruction, neither the digits nor the sign bits of the packed-decimal field are checked for validity. They are copied unchanged into their respective positions in the EBCDIC field.

Limitations of PACK and UNPK

The limitation of the PACK instruction becomes apparent when we wish to convert negative numbers to packed-decimal format. PACK only recognizes the sign coded in the zone bits of the right-most byte. Therefore, a negative number such as -1234 must be represented as 123M in EBCDIC notation, since the hex code for the letter M is X'D4'. In IBM punched-card code, this corresponds to punching the minus sign (an "11-zone" punch) in the same column as the low-order digit. It is an awkward requirement, especially when using a terminal instead of punched cards for input data. Therefore, to convert a negative integer that is entered in the usual way, e.g., as -1234 instead of 123M, we need more than just the PACK instruction. We need a set of instructions to correctly process the minus sign. The sequence of instructions below will convert a twelve-character EBCDIC integer field to its 32-bit two's complement binary representation. The twelve characters can include leading blanks or leading zeroes, with the algebraic sign being one of the twelve characters to the left of the leading digit: plus represented by a blank, minus represented by a hyphen (-). For example,

| | 2 | 1 | 4 | 7 | 4 | 8 | 3 | 6 | 4 | 7 | | | | - | 2 | 1 | 4 | 7 | 4 | 8 | 3 | 6 | 4 | 8 | | | | | | | | - | 1 | 0 | 0 | | | | | | | | | | 0 | 1 | 0 | 0 | etc. |

```
             PACK   NPACKED,NEBCDIC       CONVERT TO PACKED DECIMAL
             MVN    NPACKED+7(1),=P'-1'   ASSUME IT'S NEGATIVE
             LA     5,LNG                 INITIALIZE LOOP COUNT
             LA     6,NEBCDIC             INITIALIZE FIELD ADDRESS
LOOP         CLI    0(6),C'-'             LOOK FOR MINUS SIGN
             BE     FINIS                 IF FOUND, SEARCH NO MORE
             LA     6,1(6)                INCREASE ADDRESS TO NEXT BYTE
             BCT    5,LOOP                REPEAT TILL ALL BYTES EXAMINED
             MVN    NPACKED+7(1),=P'+1'   IF NOT NEGATIVE, THEN POSITIVE
FINIS        CVB    5,NPACKED             CONVERT TO BINARY
             ST     5,NBINARY             STORE RESULT
               .
               .
               .
LNG          EQU    12                    LENGTH OF EBCDIC FIELD
NEBCDIC      DS     CL(LNG)               SPACE FOR EBCDIC FIELD
NPACKED      DS     D                     SPACE FOR PACKED-DECIMAL FIELD
NBINARY      DS     F                     SPACE FOR BINARY RESULT
```

Converts Signed Integer From EBCDIC to Binary

There is a similar limitation to the use of the UNPK instruction: UNPK places the sign in the zone bits of the low-order byte of the EBCDIC field, so that, for example, the packed-decimal number P'-1234' will be converted to an EBCDIC field such as C'123M'. Positive numbers are also inappropriately represented after the conversion. For example, P'$+1234$' will be converted to an EBCDIC field such as C'123D', since the hex code for the letter D is X'C4'. If we want to print the results of a conversion in a more appropriate form, e.g., as -1234 or 1234, we need more than just the UNPK instruction. This is why, in Chapter 4, we introduced the OI instruction: it eliminates the sign code created by UNPK in the low-order byte. In the next section, we will discuss how the Edit (ED) and Edit and Mark (EDMK) instructions can be used to produce an appropriate EBCDIC representation for printed output. See especially Example 6 at the end of the next section.

12.9 CREATING READABLE OUTPUT

The PICTURE clause in Cobol contains a number of editing options for producing readable numeric output on a printed page. Among these options are:

1. Insertion of a decimal point in the appropriate position
2. Replacement of leading zeroes by blank spaces, except after the decimal point
3. Insertion of commas or spaces to make large numbers easier to read
4. Use of a blank space instead of a plus sign for positive numbers
5. Use of either a CR suffix or a minus-sign prefix for negative numbers

Cobol provides these and similar options for obvious reasons; but they would be rather cumbersome to program in assembly language were it not for two quite remarkable instructions in the IBM 360 and 370 systems—Edit (ED) and Edit and Mark (EDMK). Each of these instructions converts packed-decimal numbers into EBCDIC code, and *simultaneously* performs a number of other operations designed to achieve the types of editing results just listed.

One concept needs to be emphasized in order to understand the underlying principle of the ED and EDMK instructions. As shown in earlier chapters, a line of printed output is produced by transmitting each line from main memory to the printer device, character by character. This means that each line must be completely set up in main memory—blanks, punctuation marks, digits, etc.—in exactly the form that is to appear on the printed page. This is what the ED and EDMK are designed to do. They do it by means of a concept known as a *pattern*.

Patterns

A few illustrations will serve to indicate the types of results that can be achieved by the ED and EDMK instructions:

packed-decimal number	edited result
00 01 23 45 6C	1,234.56
00 01 23 45 6D	1,234.56-
00 12 34 56 7D	$ 12,345.67-
00 12 34 56 7D	$ 12,345.67CR
00 09 05 10 0C	$****9,051.00

The variations are numerous. For example, the dollar sign can be *floated* so that it just precedes the first significant digit, and instead of commas we could use spaces. Also, for use in European systems, we can interchange the comma and period and substitute a different currency symbol. How is such flexibility achieved in a single instruction? The answer is that each printed output format must be precisely described by a sequence of bytes called a **pattern.** The pattern contains the punctuation in the desired positions and contains information that dictates where *in the pattern* each significant digit is to be placed.

For example, a pattern that would produce the first edited result just shown would be this:

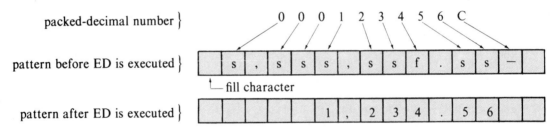

Each byte in a pattern can consist of any 8 bits, but there are three particular 8-bit combinations that have a special purpose when used in a pattern:

$$X'20' = \text{digit selector}$$
$$X'21' = \text{significance starter}$$
$$X'22' = \text{field separator}$$

How Patterns Work

The **digit selector,** denoted by "s" in the previous diagram, causes the current digit to be taken from the packed-decimal number being processed. If that digit is considered to be significant, it replaces the digit selector; if it is not significant, it is discarded and the digit selector is replaced by the fill character.

The **significance starter,** denoted by "f" in the diagram, selects the current digit just as the digit selector does, but, in addition, *it forces all subsequent digits to be considered significant*. If the digit selected by the significance starter was a significant digit, it replaces the significance starter. Otherwise, the significance starter is replaced by the **fill character.**

The **field separator,** used in multiple-field editing, will not be discussed in this text.

Note that the number of digit selectors and significance starters should be equal to the number of digits in the packed-decimal number and that the key concept for understanding how patterns work is that of **significant digit.** Since each packed-decimal number is always considered to be an integer, it should be clear that all of its digits are significant except the leading zeroes. These are all nonsignificant.

The ED and EDMK instructions can detect the difference between significant and nonsignificant digits, i.e., between leading and nonleading zeroes. It is this capacity that allows leading zeroes to be suppressed, currency and/or algebraic signs to be floated, and the other niceties indicated at the beginning of this section.

When a significant digit is detected, or when a significance starter forces significance, an indicator is turned on. Until that event, the indicator remains off. This indicator, known appropriately as the **significance indicator,** is the means by which the ED and EDMK instructions "know" whether a zero is significant or not.

ED and EDMK Instructions: Format and Meaning

Both ED and EDMK are SS_1-type instructions. Their operands have identical meanings:

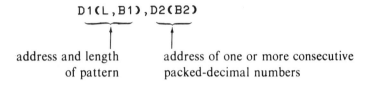

```
D1(L,B1),D2(B2)
```

    address and length   address of one or more consecutive
       of pattern   packed-decimal numbers

The only difference between ED and EDMK is that EDMK makes it possible to float a currency and/or algebraic sign, whereas ED does not. In all other aspects, they both work as follows.

The pattern and the packed-decimal number are processed left to right, 1 byte at a time. Each byte of the pattern either is left unchanged or is replaced. If replaced, it is replaced either by the current packed-decimal digit (expanded to EBCDIC format) or by the first character in the pattern, called the *fill character.* The decision as to which of these actions takes place is governed by three factors: (1) the state of the significance indicator (either *on* or *off*), (2) the value of the pattern byte being examined, and (3) the value of the current packed-decimal digit being examined. These factors, and their effect on the pattern byte being examined, are summarized in Figure 12.5. *After all digits of a packed-decimal number have been processed, the significance indicator is used to record the sign of the number:*

indicator *off* = sign is positive
indicator *on* = sign is negative

This makes it possible for the negative sign condition to be printed to the *right* of the number, since the remaining pattern bytes will not be changed when the indicator is on (see the ED and EDMK examples).

As shown in Figure 12.5, the EDMK instruction causes one other action to take place: when the significance indicator is off and a significant digit is detected, the address of the corresponding *pattern* byte is placed into Register 1. This address can then be used to insert a floating currency and/or algebraic sign into the pattern, as in Example 3. There are, however, two somewhat tedious requirements:

Difference between ED and EDMK

1. The address of the pattern byte immediately following the significance starter should be placed into Register 1 *before* the EDMK instruction is executed. This is because EDMK records the address of the first significant digit only when that digit turns on the significance indicator, not when the significance starter turns on the indicator.
2. *After* EDMK is executed, the address in Register 1 must be reduced by +1 in order for the ensuing MVI instruction to place the floating symbol in the pattern byte preceding the first significant digit.

Figure 12.5 Actions taken during execution of ED and EDMK instructions. (The significance indicator is always off before execution of ED and EDMK.)

	values being examined		action taken	
	pattern byte	packed-decimal digit	new pattern byte	new state of significance indicator
when the SIGNIFICANCE INDICATOR is *off*	digit selector	0	fill character	off
		1–9	digit (in EBCDIC)	on • ‡
	significance starter	0	fill character	on •
		1–9	digit (in EBCDIC)	on • ‡
	field separator	none	fill character	off
	any other byte	none	fill character	off
when the SIGNIFICANCE INDICATOR is *on*	digit selector	0–9	digit (in EBCDIC)	on •
	significance starter	0–9	digit (in EBCDIC)	on •
	field separator	none	fill character	off
	any other byte	none	pattern byte not changed	on

• If the packed-decimal digit being examined is the right-most digit of the number and if the sign code is plus, the new state of the significance indicator will be *off*. If it is the right-most digit and the sign code is not plus, the new state of the significance indicator will be *on*.

‡When the significance indicator is *off* and detection of a significant digit turns it *on*, the address of that significant digit is placed into bits 8–31 of Register 1 by EDMK.

Both ED and EDMK set the condition code. This allows the conditional branch instructions BZ, BM, BP, etc., to be used following ED or EDMK to determine the algebraic sign (if any) that should be moved into the pattern (see Example 4). The condition code is set to 0 if all source digits are zero; it is set to 1 if the source digits are not all zero and their sign is negative; or it is set to 2. No condition causes the code to be set to 3. But if the pattern has no digit selectors or significance starters, the condition code is set to 0. And if the pattern includes one or more field separators, these rules apply only to the last source field and corresponding pattern bytes. A program's execution will be interrupted by the hardware and terminated by the operating system if an ED or EDMK instruction encounters an invalid decimal digit or invalid sign code in a packed-decimal field.

ED and EDMK Examples

Note that in the examples given, the pattern bytes are replaced when the ED or EDMK instructions are executed. One way to preserve a pattern for subsequent use with other decimal numbers is to define it via a DC directive and copy it to the area specified as the pattern in the ED and EDMK instruction being executed. This is illustrated in Examples 5 and 6.

Note also that the significance starter X'21' is placed *two* positions to the left of the decimal point, rather than one. This is so that if the integer portion of a number is identically zero, a single zero will appear to the left of the decimal point in the result, as in Example 5. (Recall that the significance starter forces all *subsequent* digits to be considered significant, but does not by itself force the *current* digit to be considered significant.)

Since there are no C-type constants corresponding to X'20',X'21',X'22', we must use X-type constants in a DC directive to generate the desired bytes in patterns. Therefore, it helps to become familiar with the following EBCDIC character codes:

X'40' = C' '	X'4E' = C'+'
X'4B' = C'.'	X'60' = C'-'
X'5B' = C'$'	X'6C' = C'%'
X'6B' = C','	X'C3' = C'C'
X'5C' = C'*'	X'D9' = C'R'

Example 1.

`ED    P(12),X`

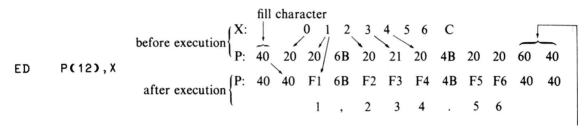

fill character

	X:			0	1	2	3	4	5	6	C		
before execution	P:	40	20	20	6B	20	21	20	4B	20	20	60	40
after execution	P:	40	40	F1	6B	F2	F3	F4	4B	F5	F6	40	40
				1	,	2	3	4	.	5	6		

Fill character replaced these pattern bytes since sign of number is positive.

Example 2.   Fixed dollar sign ($) and trailing minus sign (−), if negative

```
ED   P(15),Y
MVI  P,C'$'
```

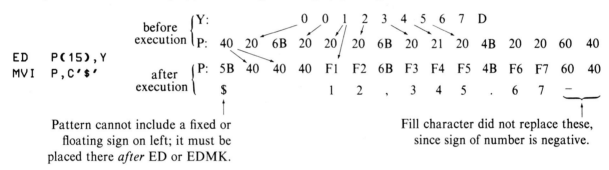

	Y:			0	0	1	2	3	4	5	6	7	D		
before execution	P:	40	20	6B	20	20	20	6B	20	21	20	4B	20	20	60	40
after execution	P:	5B	40	40	40	F1	F2	6B	F3	F4	F5	4B	F6	F7	60	40
		$				1	2	,	3	4	5	.	6	7	−	

Pattern cannot include a fixed or floating sign on left; it must be placed there *after* ED or EDMK.

Fill character did not replace these, since sign of number is negative.

Example 3.   Floating dollar sign ($) and trailing CR, if negative

```
LA    1,P+10      ADDR OF BYTE BEYOND SIGNIF. STARTER
EDMK  P(15),Z     EDIT AND CAPTURE ADDR OF 1ST SIGNIFICANT DIGIT
SH    1,=H'1'     REDUCE ADDR IN REGISTER #1 BY ONE
MVI   0(1),C'$'   PLACE FLOATING SIGN IN FRONT OF 1ST SIGNIF DIGIT
```

	Z:			0	0	1	2	3	4	5	6	7	D		
before execution	P:	40	20	6B	20	20	20	6B	20	21	20	4B	20	20	C3	D9
after execution	P:	40	40	40	5B	F1	F2	6B	F3	F4	F5	4B	F6	F7	C3	D9
					$	1	2	,	3	4	5	.	6	7	C	R

Fill character did not replace these, since sign of number is negative.

Example 4. Floating minus sign (−), if negative

```
         LA    1,P+10       ADDR OF BYTE BEYOND SIGNIF. STARTER
         EDMK  P(15),Z      EDIT AND CAPTURE ADDR OF 1ST SIGNIFICANT DIGIT
         BNM   CONTINUE     BRANCH IF EDITED RESULT NOT NEGATIVE
         SH    1,=H'1'      OTHERWISE, REDUCE ADDR IN REG 1 BY +1,
         MVI   0(1),C'-'    AND INSERT FLOATING MINUS SIGN
CONTINUE EQU   *
```

before execution
$\begin{cases} Z: \qquad\qquad\quad 0\ \ 0\ \ 1\ \ 2\ \ 3\ \ 4\ \ 5\ \ 6\ \ 7\ \ D \\ P:\ \ 40\ \ 20\ \ 6B\ \ 20\ \ 20\ \ 20\ \ 6B\ \ 20\ \ 21\ \ 20\ \ 4B\ \ 20\ \ 20\ \ \underbrace{40\ \ 40} \end{cases}$

after execution
$\begin{cases} P:\ \ 40\ \ 40\ \ 40\ \ 60\ \ F1\ \ F2\ \ 6B\ \ F3\ \ F4\ \ F5\ \ 4B\ \ F6\ \ F7\ \ 40\ \ 40 \\ \qquad\quad\ \ -\ \ \ 1\ \ \ 2\ \ \ ,\ \ \ 3\ \ \ 4\ \ \ 5\ \ \ .\ \ \ 6\ \ \ 7 \end{cases}$

Fill character did not replace these,
since sign of number is negative.

Example 5. Floating asterisk (∗) and trailing minus sign (−), if negative. Fixed dollar sign ($) precedes the asterisks

```
         MVC   P(15),PSAVE   MOVE SAVED PATTERN TO EDITING PATTERN FIELD
         ED    P(15),W       EDIT THE PACKED-DECIMAL NUMBER AT 'W'
         BM    MINUS         BRANCH IF EDITED NUMBER WAS NEGATIVE
         MVC   P+13(2),=C' ' OTHERWISE MOVE BLANK TO COVER UP FILL CHAR.
MINUS    MVI   P,C'$'        THEN MOVE $ INTO 1ST BYTE OR EDITED RESULT
*              FOLLOWING 15 BYTES ARE A PATTERN THAT CAN BE REUSED
PSAVE    DC    X'5C'         FILL CHARACTER IS C'*'
         DC    X'206B'       ONE DIGIT SELECTOR, ONE COMMA
         DC    X'2020206B'
         DC    X'2020214B'   TWO DIGIT SEL, ONE SIGNIF STARTER, ONE DEC. PT.
         DC    X'2020'       TWO DIGIT SELECTORS
         DC    X'6040'       MINUS AND BLANK, IN CASE NUMBER IS NEGATIVE
W        DC    P'000000.05'  TEST DATA
```

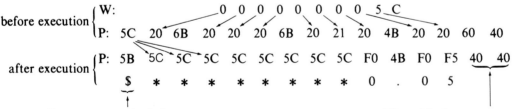

before execution
$\begin{cases} W: \qquad\qquad 0\ \ 0\ \ 0\ \ 0\ \ 0\ \ 0\ \ 0\ \ 5\ \ C \\ P:\ \ 5C\ \ 20\ \ 6B\ \ 20\ \ 20\ \ 20\ \ 6B\ \ 20\ \ 21\ \ 20\ \ 4B\ \ 20\ \ 20\ \ 60\ \ 40 \end{cases}$

after execution
$\begin{cases} P:\ \ 5B\ \ 5C\ \ 5C\ \ 5C\ \ 5C\ \ 5C\ \ 5C\ \ 5C\ \ 5C\ \ F0\ \ 4B\ \ F0\ \ F5\ \ 40\ \ 40 \\ \qquad\quad \$\ \ *\ \ \ *\ \ \ *\ \ \ *\ \ \ *\ \ \ *\ \ \ *\ \ \ *\ \ \ 0\ \ \ .\ \ \ 0\ \ \ 5 \end{cases}$

Pattern cannot include
a fixed or floating sign
on left; it must be placed
there after ED or EDMK.

These blanks were *not* placed here by ED;
they were placed here by MVC following ED
after testing the condition code to determine that the number's sign was not
negative. Note that since in this example the number wasn't negative, the
ED instruction caused the X'6040' to be
replaced by the fill character. Thus,
the MVC covered up the fill characters.

Example 6. Convert 32-bit binary integer to 12-character EBCDIC, without commas, but with leading zeroes replaced by blanks, and a floating minus sign if the number is negative

```
          L     1,NBINARY              GET BINARY INTEGER
          CVD   1,NPACKED              CONVERT TO PACKED DECIMAL
          MVC   NEBCDIC,PATTERN        MOVE 12-CHAR PATTERN TO RESULT FIELD
          LA    1,NEBCDIC+11           GET ADDR OF BYTE BEYOND SIGNIF STARTER
          EDMK  NEBCDIC,NPACKED+2      EDIT LOW-ORDER 6 BYTES OF PACKED-DECIMAL FIELD
          BNM   CONTINUE               PLUS SIGN REPRESENTED BY BLANK
          SH    1,=H'1'                OTHERWISE, REDUCE ADDR IN REG 1, AND
          MVI   0(1),C'-'               INSERT FLOATING MINUS SIGN
CONTINUE  EQU   *
                .
                .
                .
NEBCDIC   DS    CL12                   SPACE FOR RESULT FIELD
NPACKED   DS    D                      SPACE FOR PACKED-DECIMAL INTERMED RESULT
NBINARY   DS    F                      LOCATION OF 32-BIT BINARY INTEGER
PATTERN   DC    X'402020202020202020202120'  PATTERN FOR INTEGER WITHOUT COMMAS
```

When Editing n *Digits,* n *Should Be an Odd Number*

Example 6 points out one further consideration: If n digit positions are specified in the pattern (via X'20' or X'21'), and if the field separator X'22' is not used (as is the case in all the examples of this chapter), then n should be an odd number and the length of the packed-decimal field being edited should be $(n+1)/2$ bytes. For if the length is greater than $(n+1)/2$, then one or more low-order digits will not be matched to any pattern bytes. And if it is less than that, then the CPU will attempt to match some pattern bytes with whatever data follows the packed-decimal field in memory.

How to Determine the Packed-Decimal Operand Address for ED and EDMK

Recall that the sign in a packed-decimal number requires half a byte, so that there are $2Q-1$ digits in Q bytes. If $2Q-1 = n$ digits, then $Q = (n+1)/2$ bytes. Note that under almost all circumstances, the n digits that we want to edit will be the n low-order digits of the number. Therefore the ED or EDMK operand needs the address of the $Q = (n+1)/2$ low-order bytes of a packed-decimal number.

Now, if the symbolic address of the packed-decimal number is NPACKED, and if the length of the packed-decimal number is L bytes, then the symbolic address of the Q low-order bytes is NPACKED $+ L - Q$. But since $Q = (n+1)/2$, then the desired address is NPACKED $+ L - (n+1)/2$.

We can now see why the EDMK in Example 6 refers to NPACKED+2 instead of to NPACKED: the length of the packed-decimal number at NPACKED was $L = 8$, and there were $n = 11$ digit positions in the pattern so that $(n+1)/2 = 6$. Thus NPACKED $+ L - (n+1)/2 =$ NPACKED $+ 8 - 6$.

12.10 SUMMARY

In the packed-decimal format, signed decimal numbers with up to 31 significant digits can be processed using the decimal number system's rules of arithmetic. Each digit of a decimal number is represented in 4-bit binary-coded decimal format: $0_{10} = 0000_2$, $1_{10} = 0001_2,..., 9_{10} = 1001_2$. The sign is represented by 4 bits to the right of the right-most digit: plus $(+)$ as 1100_2, minus $(-)$ as 1101_2.

Using decimal arithmetic rather than binary arithmetic, results achieved in the computer can be exactly equal to results achievable by hand calculation even when noninteger quantities are involved. This avoids the differences in accuracy that can arise when a fixed number of bits is used to represent noninteger decimal numbers in the binary system. It is especially useful in banking and related business computer applications.

In the IBM 360 and 370 systems, there are instructions to add, subtract, multiply, divide, and compare two numbers represented in packed-decimal format. There are also instructions to affix leading zeroes to a packed-decimal number, to convert between packed-decimal and EBCDIC representation and between packed-decimal and binary representation, and to change a single digit or sign. Shifting left or right—effectively multiplying or dividing by powers of 10 in order to align decimal points—is easily accomplished in the IBM 370 by means of the SRP instruction; in the IBM 360, this can be accomplished by a combination of instructions dependent on MVO. See Figure 12.6 for a summary of these instructions.

Unlike the integer arithmetic instructions described in Chapter 5 or the floating-point instructions to be described in Chapter 13, almost all packed-decimal instructions are either SS_1 or SS_2 format. The only exceptions are CVB and CVD, RX-type instructions for converting to and from binary format. In SS_1- and SS_2-type instructions, the number of bytes to be processed must be specified, explicitly or implicitly. This in turn requires some care to ensure that there have been a sufficient number of bytes allocated for the sum, difference, product, or quotient of two packed-decimal numbers.

In assembly language, packed-decimal constants can be generated by means of the data-type code P. This can be used in the DC directive and in literals. The P code also can be used in the DS directive to reserve the number of bytes required by a constant; e.g., in the formulation DS P'99.99', three bytes are reserved.

Finally, it was shown that the ED and EDMK instructions provide exceptionally useful mechanisms for translating packed-decimal numbers into formats suitable for printing. There are no comparable instructions for use directly with either binary or floating-point number representations, although binary integers can be converted to packed-decimal representation via the CVD instruction. (Methods for converting floating-point numbers will be discussed in the next chapter.) For conversion from EBCDIC input format to the packed-decimal format, we can use the PACK instruction; to convert from EBCDIC to binary integer, we can use PACK followed by CVB. As discussed in Section 12.8, additional instructions are required to process negative numbers so that the sign can be represented separately from the digits in EBCDIC format.

12.11 REVIEW

Packed-Decimal Numbers In machine language, each decimal digit is represented by its equivalent 4-bit binary digit. The algebraic sign is represented by four bits in the right-most bit positions of the low-order byte (hex A, C, E, or F for plus; B or D for minus). Arithmetic operations use the rules of decimal arithmetic and assume that the numbers are integers. Each operand is always in memory instead of in a register, and its length (number of bytes) must be indicated whenever the operand is referred to. The maximum length is 16 bytes (31 digits).

Decimal Points The position of the decimal point—and therefore the actual value of any packed-decimal number—is implied rather than explicitly represented. Numbers may need to be shifted before and/or after an arithmetic operation for the result to be consistent with other numbers.

P-Type Constants Decimal points can be used in assembly language constants (e.g., P'3.5'), but they are ignored in machine language. The optional length modifier (e.g., PL4'3.5') specifies the number of *bytes,* not the number of digits.

Arithmetic Operations When adding or subtracting two packed-decimal numbers, the result replaces the first operand, so its length must be long enough to avoid overflow. In multiplication and division, the result also replaces the first operand; the second operand's length must not exceed 8 bytes and must be less than the first operand's.

SS_1-Type Instructions In these (ED, EDMK, MVN, MVZ, SRP), the first operand's length (in bytes) is the only one that's indicated. For an implicit length, the assembler supplies the length attribute of the symbol. The second operand's length is determined from the first operand's.

SS_2-Type Instructions In SS_2-type instructions (AP, CP, DP, MP, SP, ZAP, PACK, UNPK), each operand's length (in bytes) must be indicated either explicitly or implicitly. For an implicit length, the assembler supplies the length attribute of the symbol.

Figure 12.6 Summary of packed-decimal instructions.

opcode	name	type	section	condition codes	summary of action taken
AP	Add Packed Decimal	SS_2	12.3	0,1,2,3	V_1 is replaced by $V_1 + V_2$.
CP	Compare Packed Decimal	SS_2	12.4	0,1,2	V_1 is compared to V_2; the lengths L_1 and L_2 need not be the same.
DP	Divide Packed Decimal	SS_2	12.3		V_1 is replaced by $L_1 - L_2$ quotient bytes and L_2 remainder bytes of V_1/V_2; $L_2 < L_1$ and $1 \leq L_2 \leq 8$.
ED	Edit	SS_1	12.9	0,1,2	L-byte V_1 pattern is replaced by edited EBCDIC representation of packed-decimal field V_2.
EDMK	Edit and Mark	SS_1	12.9	0,1,2	Same as ED, but Reg 1 also gets address of most significant edited digit if that digit is detected while the significance indicator is *off*.
MP	Multiply Packed Decimal	SS_2	12.3		V_1 is replaced by $V_1 \times V_2$, with $L_1 < L_2$ and $1 \leq L_2 \leq 8$.
MVN	Move Numerics	SS_1	12.6		The 4 low-order bits of each byte in V_1 are replaced by the 4 low-order bits of corresponding V_2 bytes.
MVO	Move with Offset	SS_2	12.6		All except the sign bits of V_1 are replaced by all the bits of V_2, from right to left. If $L_2 < L_1$, the remaining high-order V_1 bits are set to zero; if $L_2 > L_1$, the result is truncated at the high-order end to fit the V_1 field.
MVZ	Move Zones	SS_1	12.6		The 4 high-order bits of each byte in V_1 are replaced by the 4 high-order bits of corresponding V_2 bytes.
PACK	Pack	SS_2	12.8		V_1 is replaced by the L_1-byte packed-decimal representation of the L_2-byte EBCDIC field, V_2. If $L_1 > \frac{1}{2}(L_2)$, no truncation can occur.
SP	Subtract Packed Decimal	SS_2	12.3	0,1,2,3	V_1 is replaced by $V_1 - V_2$.
SRP	Shift and Round Packed Decimal	SS_1	12.5	0,1,2,3	V_1's digits are shifted n places right or left and rounded during a right shift (see note below).
UNPK	Unpack	SS_2	12.8		V_1 is replaced by the L_1-byte EBCDIC representation of the L_2-byte packed-decimal field, V_2. If $L_1 \geq 2(L_2)$, no truncation can occur.
ZAP	Zero and Add Packed Decimal	SS_2	12.3	0,1,2,3	V_1 is replaced by V_2, with $L_1 - L_2$ bytes of leading zeroes.

Notes: V_1 is the quantity whose address is specified by the first operand, with length L in SS_1 instructions and L_1 in SS_2 instructions.

V_2's address is specified by the second operand; its length is L in SS_1 instructions and L_2 in SS_2 instructions.

SRP is a modified SS_1 instruction, with operand $D_1(L_1,B_1),D_2(B_2),I_3$, and $L_1 \leq 8$. The rounding factor is given by I_3; the number of positions and direction of shift by the low-order six bits of $D_2(B_2)$: negative (in two's complement notation)=right shift, positive=left shift.

The SRP Instruction Shifting is used to adjust the implied decimal point's position. For consistency, always round when shifting right. Rounding does not occur when shifting left, but a rounding factor must nevertheless be specified.

The ZAP Instruction Use this instruction to increase the length of a number preparatory to doing other arithmetic operations. In effect, ZAP increases the length by appending zeroes to the high-order end of the result.

The CP Instruction When comparing two numbers via the CP instruction, the hardware does the comparison as though both were integers. If the lengths of the numbers are not equal, the hardware temporarily makes them equal by padding the high-order end of the shorter number with zeroes before doing the comparison.

The PACK and UNPK Instructions These are convenient for converting a number between EBCDIC and packed-decimal. However, neither instruction processes the number's algebraic sign in a satisfactory manner, and neither one checks to see if high-order digits are lost during the conversion process.

The ED and EDMK Instructions These are very useful for converting a packed-decimal number into an EBCDIC output format designed for human readability. The exact output format of each number must be specified by a pattern that is used by ED and EDMK during the conversion process. Both instructions use the pattern's "fill" character to replace unnecessary punctuation and insignificant zeroes in the result. The difference between the two instructions is that EDMK marks the position of the first significant output digit by putting its address into Register 1, whereas ED doesn't.

Patterns A pattern is an n-byte constant that specifies the position of the digits, commas, and decimal point (if any) in an n-byte numeric output field. By means of the "significance starter," a pattern can also specify the position where suppression of leading zeroes is to cease.

Run-Time Errors *Overflow* occurs during execution of AP, SP, SRP, and ZAP when the number of significant digits in a result exceeds the number of digit positions specified for the result field. A *divide error* occurs when dividing by zero and when the length of the quotient field is insufficient. A *data error* occurs when the sign of an operand is not in the range of hex A through F or when one of its digits is not in the range of hex 0 through 9. (For other instances of data errors, see Appendix D.) A *specification error* occurs when the rules for operand lengths in an MP or DP instruction are violated.

12.12 REVIEW QUESTIONS

1. What are the preferred sign codes for packed-decimal numbers?
2. How many bytes are allocated for an n-digit P-type constant?
3. What are the rules that the assembler follows when deciding whether to pad a P-type constant? What are the rules for truncation of P-type constants?
4. What are the rules for operand lengths in an MP instruction? In a DP instruction?
5. Under what conditions can overflow occur when doing packed-decimal arithmetic?
6. What happens when a packed-decimal operand does not have any sign in the right-most four bits of its low-order byte? As an example, consider a 6-digit number in 3 bytes (e.g., X'123456') rather than in 4 bytes (X'0123456C').
7. What SRP instruction is needed to correctly add P'+0.250' and P'−360'?
8. After multiplying P'+0.250' and P'−360', what SRP instruction will make the implied decimal point's position be the same as in the constant P'−90'?
9. What instructions are needed to divide P'+360' by P'+125' and produce a 2-byte integer and 2-byte remainder? What P-type constants accurately represent the result of the division? (**Hint:** By hand calculation, the answer is exactly 2.88.)
10. What MVN instruction will make the sign of an n-byte packed-decimal number be positive?
11. What combination of the CP and MVN instructions can be used to change the sign of an n-byte packed-decimal number (i.e., if the number was positive, make it negative; if negative, make it positive)?
12. What specific characteristic of the PACK instruction makes it unsatisfactory for converting EBCDIC numbers that are signed in the usual way, e.g., −1234 or +1234? Explain.

13. What specific characteristic of the UNPK instruction makes it unsatisfactory for converting negative packed-decimal numbers? Explain.
14. In patterns used with ED and EDMK, what is the purpose of the digit selector? Of the significance starter? Of the fill character?
15. What are the differences between the significance *starter* and the significance *indicator?*
16. In the program segment of Example 6 at the end of Section 12.9, explain what the error would have been if the EDMK instruction had referred to NPACKED instead of to NPACKED+2.
17. What changes are necessary to the program segment in Example 6 of Section 12.9 in order to create an EBCDIC integer with punctuating commas? In other words, as it now stands, the packed-decimal number P'1234567890' would be printed as C'   1234567890' with two blanks preceding the first significant digit. What changes are necessary to print that number as C'   1,234,567,890' with two blanks preceding the first significant digit?

12.13 SAMPLE PROBLEM AND SOLUTION

Problem Statement

Write a program that will read an arbitrary number of input records containing student grades (one record per course, one or more consecutive records per student), and compute and print each student's grade point average (GPA). The input records have the following format:

columns		
1–20:	student name	
21–29:	student i.d.	
31–36:	course i.d.	
40–45:	course units	(a nonnegative integer)
50–52:	student grade	(in the form of 3.2 on a scale of from 0.0 to 4.0)

Solution Procedure

The procedure (Figures 12.7a and 12.7b) will use the well-known formula for computing a grade point average,

$$GPA = \frac{\Sigma U_i G_i}{\Sigma U_i}$$

where U_i is the number of units for course i, and G_i is the numerical grade for that course. (If all the U_i are zero, then the GPA is zero.)

Since all the records for any one student occur consecutively in the input data, the procedure will be to print each student's records as received from the input data stream, and to follow the last record for each student with a line containing the total number of units, ΣU_i, and the GPA.

```
COMPUTE_GPAS:

   open input and output files;
   read first input record;
   end_of_data_switch := off;

   REPEAT UNTIL end-of-data-switch is on

      current_id := student I.D. from input record;
      total_units := 0;
      total_grade_points := 0;

      REPEAT UNTIL ( I.D. from input record <> current_id )
               OR ( end-of-data-switch is on )

         convert units to packed decimal;
         convert grade to packed decimal;
         add units to total_units;
         add units*grade to total_grade_points;

         print this input record;

         IF there is more data to read
         THEN
           read next input record;
         ELSE
           end-of-data-switch := on;
         END IF;

      END UNTIL;  { stay in this loop if new input record for same student }

      calculate GPA;
      print GPA and total_units;

   END UNTIL;  { stay in this loop until data runs out }

   close input and output files;

EXIT COMPUTE_GPAS.
```

Figure 12.7b Solution to sample problem.

```
FLAG LOCTN OBJECT CODE      ADDR1   ADDR2   STMNT M SOURCE STATEMENT

      000000                                   3   SPCH12    CSECT
                                               4   *
                                               5   * SPCH12   READS INPUT DATA CARDS CONTAINING STUDENT GRADES
                                               6   *      (SOME UNSPECIFIED NUMBER OF CONSECUTIVE CARDS PER STUDENT)
                                               7   *      IN WHICH EACH CARD CONTAINS THE STUDENT'S NAME & I.D.
                                               8   *      AND ONE OF HIS OR HER COURSES TOGETHER WITH THE COURSE I.D.
                                               9   *      AND COURSE UNITS, AND THE GRADE POINTS (0.00-4.00) EARNED
                                              10   *      BY THAT STUDENT IN THAT COURSE.  THE INPUT FORMAT IS THIS...
                                              11   *
                                              12   *          COLS 1-20   STUDENT NAME
                                              13   *               21-29   STUDENT I.D.
                                              14   *               31-36   COURSE I.D.
                                              15   *               40-45   # UNITS        ( U )
                                              16   *               50-53   GRADE POINTS  (GP)
                                              17   *
                                              18   * THE PROGRAM COMPUTES AND PRINTS EACH STUDENT'S GRADE POINT AVERAGE
                                              19   *     (GPA)  USING THIS FORMULA ...
                                              20   *
                                              21   *        GPA = (  SUM OF  (GP * U)  ) / ( SUM OF  (U)  )
                                              22   *
      000000 90 EC D00C                       23             STM    14,12,12(13)          STANDARD ENTRY
      000004 05 C0                            24             BALR   12,0
      000006                                  25             USING  *,12
      000006 50 D0 C4D2       0004D8          26             ST     13,SAVE+4
      00000A 41 D0 C4CE       0004D4          27             LA     13,SAVE
                                              28   *
                                              29   * OPEN INPUT AND OUTPUT FILES, AND READ THE FIRST INPUT CARD
                                              30   *
      00000E                                  31             OPEN   (SYSIN,(INPUT))       INPUT IS 'SYSIN' DATA STREAM
      00001A                                  37             OPEN   (SYSPRNT,(OUTPUT))    OUTPUT IS 'SYSOUT' PRINTER

                                              43   *  DOS  *******
                                              44   *        OPEN    SYSIN
                                              45   *        OPEN    SYSPRNT
                                              46   ****************
      000026                                  47             GET    SYSIN,INAREA          READ FIRST INPUT CARD
                                              52   *
                                              53   * MAIN PROCESSING LOOP ...
                                              54   *
                                              55   *   WHEN BEGINNING A NEW STUDENT ...
                                              56   *      SETS CURRENT STUDENT I.D. EQUAL TO INPUT I.D.
                                              57   *      SETS CURRENT TOTAL UNITS (U) AND TOTAL GRADE POINTS (GP) TO ZERO.
                                              58   *      PRINTS A HEADING LINE FOR OUTPUT LISTING
                                              59   *
      000034 D2 08 C18EC1BF 000194 0001C5     60   LOOP      MVC    CSID,SID              SET CURRENT STUDENT I.D.
      00003A F8 10 C197C51A 00019D 000520     61             ZAP    TU,=P'0'              SET CURRENT TOTAL UNITS TO ZERO
      000040 F8 30 C199C51A 00019F 000520     62             ZAP    TGP,=P'0'             SET CURRENT TOTAL GP TO ZERO
      000046                                  63             PUT    SYSPRNT,HEADING       PRINT HEADING LINE
                                              68   *
                                              69   *   WHEN THE NEXT INPUT CARD IS STILL FOR THE CURRENT STUDENT ...
                                              70   *      ACCUMULATE UNITS (U) AND GRADE POINTS (GP) FOR THIS STUDENT
                                              71   *      AND PRINT THIS INPUT CARD.
                                              72   *      THEN READ THE NEXT CARD TO SEE IF IT'S FOR THE SAME STUDENT.
                                              73   *
      000054 F2 15 C19DC1D2 0001A3 0001D8     74   REPEAT    PACK   BCDU,SU               CONVT STUDENT UNITS TO PKD-DEC
      00005A F2 30 C19FC1DC 0001A5 0001E2     75             PACK   GP,SGPINT             CONVT INTEGER PART OF GP TO PKD-DEC
      000060 F2 11 C1A3C1DE 0001A9 0001E4     76             PACK   GPDEC,SGPDEC          CONVT FRACTIONAL PART OF GP  "  "
                                              77   *
                                              78   *           SRP    GP,2,0              SHIFT INTEGER GP (MPY BY 100), AND
      000066 F1 F3 C16EC19F 000174 0001A5     79             MVO    XX,GP
      00006C D2 00 C17DC51B 000183 000521     80             MVC    XXS(1),=X'00'
      000072 F1 3F C19FC16E 0001A5 000174     81             MVO    GP,XX
      000078 FA 31 C19FC1A3 0001A5 0001A9     82             AP     GP,GPDEC              ADD FRACTIONAL GP TO INTEGER GP.
                                              83   *
      00007E FC 31 C19FC19D 0001A5 0001A3     84             MP     GP,BCDU               MPY GP BY UNITS
      000084 FA 33 C199C19F 00019F 0001A5     85             AP     TGP,GP                AND ADD PRODUCT TO TOTAL GP.
                                              86   *
      00008A FA 11 C197C19D 00019D 0001A3     87             AP     TU,BCDU               ACCUMULATE TOTAL UNITS.
                                              88   *
                                              89   * PRINT STUDENT'S INPUT DATA CARD
                                              90   *
      000090 D2 4F C205C1AB 00020B 0001B1     91             MVC    OUTLINE,INAREA        MOVE CARD TO OUTPUT AREA
      000096                                  92             PUT    SYSPRNT,OUTAREA       PRINT IT.
                                              97   *
                                              98   * READ NEXT STUDENT DATA CARD AND SEE IF IT'S FOR CURRENT STUDENT
                                              99   *
      0000A4                                 100             GET    SYSIN,INAREA
      0000B2 D5 08 C18EC1BF 000194 0001C5    105             CLC    CSID,SID              IS NEXT STUDENT = CURRENT STUDENT
      0000B8 47 80 C04E       000054         106             BE     REPEAT                IF SO, CONTINUING ACCUMULATIONS.
                                             107   *
```

Figure 12.7b   continued

```
FLAG LOCTN OBJECT CODE     ADDR1  ADDR2  STMNT M SOURCE STATEMENT

                                         108    * WHEN NEXT STUDENT IS DIFFERENT FROM CURRENT STUDENT,
                                         109    *  CALCULATE CURRENT STUDENT'S GPA AND PRINT IT WITH TOTAL UNITS.
                                         110    *
0000BC F8 20 C1A5C51A 0001AB 000520      111  CALC  ZAP  GPAQUO,=P'0'          INITIALIZE GPA TO ZERO
0000C2 F9 10 C197C51A 00019D 000520      112        CP   TU,=P'0'             IS TOTAL UNITS ZERO
0000C8 47 80 C0FC     000102             113        BE   CALCX                IF SO, THEN GPA = 0
                                         114    *
0000CC F8 43 C1A5C199 0001AB 00019F      115        ZAP  GPA,TGP              COPY TOTAL GRADE POINTS TO GPA
                                         116    *   SRP  GPA,1,0              SHIFT LEFT 1 DIGIT PRIOR TO DIVN
0000D2 F8 F4 C16EC1A5 000174 0001AB      117        ZAP  XX,GPA
0000D8 D1 00 C17DC51B 000183 000521      118        MVN  XXS(1),=X'00'
0000DE F1 4F C1A5C16E 0001AB 000174      119        MVO  GPA,XX
                                         120    *
0000E4 FD 41 C1A5C197 0001AB 00019D      121        DP   GPA,TU              (TOTAL GRADE POINTS) / (TOTAL UNITS)
                                         122    *
                                         123    *   SRP  GPAQUO,64-1,5       ROUND QUOTIENT TO 3 SIGNIF DIGITS
0000EA F8 F2 C16EC1A5 000174 0001AB      124        ZAP  XX,GPAQUO
0000F0 D1 00 C17DC51A 000183 000520      125        MVN  XXS(1),=P'0'
0000F6 FA F0 C16EC51C 000174 000522      126        AP   XX,=P'5'
0000FC F1 2E C1A5C16E 0001AB 000174      127        MVO  GPAQUO,XX(15)
                                         128    *
000102 D2 06 C3C1C51D 0003C7 000523      129  CALCX MVC  PGPA,=X'4020202148B2020'  GPA PATTERN = XXX.XX
000108 DE 06 C3C1C1A5 0003C7 0001AB      130        ED   PGPA,GPAQUO
00010E D2 03 C3BAC524 0003C0 00052A      131        MVC  PUNITS,=X'4020202120'   UNIT PATTERN =   XXXX
000114 DE 03 C3BAC197 0003C0 00019D      132        ED   PUNITS,TU
                                         133    *
00011A                                   134        PUT  SYSPRNT,BLANKS          PRINT ONE BLANK LINE
000128                                   139        PUT  SYSPRNT,TOTALS          FOLLOWED BY TOTALS
000136                                   144        PUT  SYSPRNT,BLANKS
                                         149    *
                                         150    * DETERMINE WHETHER TO PROCESS NEXT STUDENT OR TO TERMINATE
                                         151    *
000144 95 FF C1AA     0001B0             152        CLI  EODSW,ON             WAS END-OF-DATA REACHED
000148 47 70 C02E     000034             153        BNE  LOOP                 IF NOT, GO PROCESS NEXT STUDENT
                                         154    *
                                         155    * END OF JOB PROCESSING
                                         156    *
00014C                                   157        CLOSE (SYSIN)
000156                                   163        CLOSE (SYSPRNT)
000162 58 D0 C4D2     0004D8             169        L    13,SAVE+4            STANDARD EXIT
000166 98 EC D00C                        170        LM   14,12,12(13)
00016A 07 FE                             171        BR   14
                                         
                                         172    * DOS *******
                                         173    *     CLOSE SYSIN
                                         174    *     CLOSE SYSPRNT
                                         175    *     EOJ
                                         176    ***************
                                         
                                         177    *
                                         178    * END-OF-DATA REQUIRES SETTING A SWITCH SO THAT TOTALS FOR THE
                                         179    * LAST CURRENT STUDENT CAN BE COMPUTED AND PRINTED.
                                         180    *
00016C 92 FF C1AA     0001B0             181  EOD   MVI  EODSW,ON             SET 'EODSW' TO 'ON' POSITION
000170 47 F0 C0B6     0000BC             182        B    CALC                 THEN CALCULATE HIS/HER TOTALS
                                         183    *
                                         184    *
                                         185    * CONSTANTS AND DATA AREAS
                                         186    *
000174 0000000000000000                  187  XX     DC   2XL16'00'           TEMPORARY FOR IBM360 SHIFTS
000183                                   188  XXS    EQU  XX+15               16TH BYTE OF XX
000194                                   189  CSID   DS   CL9                 CURRENT STUDENT'S I.D.
00019D 000C                              190  TU     DC   P'000'              TOTAL UNITS FOR CURRENT STUDENT
00019F 0000000C                          191  TGP    DC   P'00000.00'         TOTAL GRADE POINTS FOR CUR. STUDENT
0001A3 000C                              192  BCDU   DC   P'00'               ONE COURSE'S UNITS
0001A5 0000000C                          193  GP     DC   P'0000.00'          ONE COURSE'S GRADE POINTS * UNITS
0001A9 000C                              194  GPDEC  DC   P'0.00'             ONE COURSE'S GRADE POINTS (FRACTL PART)
0001AB                                   195  GPA    DS   0P'00000.000'        GPA FOR CURRENT STUDENT
0001AB 00000C                            196  GPAQUO DC   P'00000'            QUOTIENT
0001AE 000C                              197  GPAREM DC   P'000'              REMAINDER
0001B0 00                                198  EODSW  DC   X'00'               END-OF-DATA SWITCH, AS FOLLOWS ...
0000FF                                   199  ON     EQU  X'FF'               EODSW = X'FF' IF AT END-OF-DATA
000000                                   200  OFF    EQU  X'00'               EODSW = X'00' IF NOT AT END-OF-DATA
                                         201    * INPUT CARD AREA
                                         202    *
0001B1                                   203  INAREA DS   0CL80               DEFINITION OF INPUT AREA ...
0001B1                                   204        DS   CL20                COLS 1-20  STUDENT NAME
0001C5                                   205  SID    DS   CL9                 21-29  STUDENT I.D.
0001CE                                   206        DS   CL1                 30     UNUSED
0001CF                                   207        DS   CL6                 31-36  COURSE I.D.
0001D5                                   208        DS   CL3                 37-39  UNUSED
0001D8                                   209  SU     DS   CL6                 40-45  # COURSE UNITS
0001DE                                   210        DS   CL4                 46-49  UNUSED
0001E2                                   211  SGP    DS   0CL4                50-53  GRADE PTS FOR THIS COURSE
                                         212    *
0001E2                                   213  SGPINT DS   CL1                 50     INTEGER PORTION
0001E3                                   214        DS   CL1                 51     DECIMAL POINT
0001E4                                   215  SGPDEC DS   CL2                 52-53  FRACTIONAL PORTION
                                         216    *
0001E6                                   217        DS   CL27                54-80  UNUSED
```

334   Noninteger Arithmetic

Figure 12.7b   continued

```
FLAG LOCTN OBJECT CODE     ADDR1 ADDR2  STMNT M SOURCE STATEMENT

                                          218  * OUTPUT PRINT AREA
                                          219  *
      000201                               220  OUTAREA  DS    OCL132         DEFINITION OF OUTPUT AREA ...
      000201 4040404040404040             221           DC    CL10' '        COLS 1-10   BLANKS
      00020B                               222  OUTLINE  DS    CL80           11-90   INPUT CARD DATA
      00025B 4040404040404040             223           DC    CL42' '        91-132  BLANKS
                                          224  *
                                          225  * BLANK LINE FOR OUTPUT
                                          226  *
      000285                               227  BLANKS   DS    OCL132
      000285 4040404040404040             228           DC    CL132' '       COLS 1-132  BLANKS
                                          229  *
                                          230  * HEADING LINE FOR OUTPUT
                                          231  *
      000309                               232  HEADING  DS    OCL132         DEFINITION OF HEADING ...
      000309 4040404040404040             233           DC    CL10' '        COLS 1-10   BLANKS
      000313 E2E3E4C4C5D5E340             234           DC    CL20'STUDENT NAME'  11-30   STUDENT NAME
      000327 C94BC44B7B404040             235           DC    CL9'I.D.#'     31-39   STUDENT I.D.
      000330 40                            236           DC    CL1' '         40      BLANKS
      000331 C3D6E4D9E2C5                 237           DC    CL6'COURSE'     41-46   COURSE I.D.
      000337 404040                        238           DC    CL3' '         47-49   BLANKS
      00033A E4D5C9E3E240                 239           DC    CL6'UNITS'      50-55   # UNITS
      000340 40404040                      240           DC    CL4' '         56-59   BLANKS
      000344 C7D9C1C4C5                   241           DC    CL5'GRADE'      60-64   GRADE POINTS
      000349 4040404040404040             242           DC    CL68' '        65-132  BLANKS
                                          243  *
                                          244  * AREA FOR PRINTED TOTALS
                                          245  *
      00038D                               246  TOTALS   DS    OCL132         DEFINITION OF TOTALS ...
      00038D 4040404040404040             247           DC    CL39' '        COLS 1-39   BLANKS
      0003B4 E2E4D4D4C1D9E840             248           DC    CL12'SUMMARY'   40-51   C'SUMMARY'
      0003C0                               249  PUNITS   DS    CL4            51-55   TOTAL UNITS
      0003C4 404040                        250           DC    CL3' '         56-58   BLANKS
      0003C7                               251  PGPA     DS    CL7            59-65   GPA
      0003CE 4040404040404040             252           DC    CL67' '        66-132  BLANKS
                                          253  *
                                          254  * DCB'S FOR INPUT AND OUTPUT FILES
                                          255  *
      000411                               256  SYSIN    DCB   DSORG=PS,MACRF=(GM),DDNAME=SYSIN,EODAD=EOD,      X
                                          257                  RECFM=FB,LRECL=80,BLKSIZE=4080
                                          309  *
      000474                               310  SYSPRNT  DCB   DSORG=PS,MACRF=(PM),DDNAME=SYSPRINT,             X
                                          311                  RECFM=FB,LRECL=132,BLKSIZE=4092

                                          363  * DOS  *******
                                          364  *SYSIN   DTFCD DEVADDR=SYSIPT,WORKA=YES,IOAREA1=INBUF,EOFADDR=EOD,  X
                                          365                  DEVICE=2540
                                          366  *SYSPRNT DTFPR DEVADDR=SYSLST,WORKA=YES,IOAREA1=OUTBUF,BLKSIZE=132,  X
                                          367                  DEVICE=1403
                                          368  *
                                          369  *INBUF   DS    CL80
                                          370  *OUTBUF  DC    CL132' '
                                          371  ***************

                                          372  *
                                          373  * SAVE AREA
                                          374  *
      0004D4                               375  SAVE     DS    18F

                                          376  * DOS  *******
                                          377  *SAVE    DS    9D
                                          378  ***************

                                          379  * LITERALS
      000520 0C                            381                              =P'0'
      000521 00                            382                              =X'00'
      000522 5C                            383                              =P'5'
      000523 402020214B2020               384                              =X'402020214B2020'
      00052A 4020202120                   385                              =X'4020202120'
                                          386           END
```

CROSS-REFERENCE

```
SYMBOL     LEN   VALUE   DEFN    REFERENCES

BCDU       00002 0001A3  00192   00074   00084   00087
BLANKS     00084 000285  00227   00136   00146
CALC       00006 0000BC  00111   00182
CALCX      00006 000102  00129   00113
CSID       00009 000194  00189   00060   00105
EOD        00004 00016C  00181   00278
EODSW      00001 0001B0  00198   00152   00181
GP         00004 0001A5  00193   00075   00079   00081   00082   00084   00085
GPA        00005 0001AB  00195   00115   00117   00119   00121
```

Figure 12.7b continued

GPAQUO	00003	0001AB	00196	00111	00124	00127	00130			
GPAREM	00002	0001AE	00197							
GPDEC	00002	0001A9	00194	00076	00082					
HEADING	00084	000309	00232	00065						
INAREA	00050	0001B1	00203	00049	00091	00102				
LOOP	00006	000034	00060	00153						
OFF	00001	000000	00200							
ON	00001	0000FF	00199	00152	00181					
OUTAREA	00084	000201	00220	00094						
OUTLINE	00050	00020B	00222	00091						
PGPA	00007	0003C7	00251	00129	00130					
PUNITS	00004	0003C0	00249	00131	00132					
REPEAT	00006	000054	00074	00106						
SAVE	00004	0004D4	00375	00026	00027	00169				
SGP	00004	0001E2	00211							
SGPDEC	00002	0001E4	00215	00076						
SGPINT	00001	0001E2	00213	00075						
SID	00009	0001C5	00205	00060	00105					
SPCH12	00001	000000	00003							
SU	00006	0001D8	00209	00074						
SYSIN	00004	000414	00257	00035	00048	00101	00161			
SYSPRNT	00004	000474	00311	00041	00064	00093	00135	00140	00145	00167
TGP	00004	00019F	00191	00062	00085	00115				
TOTALS	00084	00038D	00246	00141						
TU	00002	00019D	00190	00061	00087	00112	00121	00132		
XX	00010	000174	00187	00079	00081	00117	00119	00124	00126	00127	00188
XXS	00010	000183	00188	00080	00118	00125				

12.14 EXERCISES

1. What is the packed-decimal representation of the following constants? (Write your answers in hexadecimal notation.)

   a. P'-10'   d. P'1000'   g. P'-99.999'
   b. P'-0.065'   e. PL4'1'   h. P'-99,999'
   c. P'+6.5'   f. PL1'4'   i. P'999.999'

2. Write the packed-decimal representation (in hexadecimal notation) of the result of each of the following SRP instructions, if each instruction were executed at run time with this number stored at location X:

   X   DC PL5'-246.75'

   a. SRP   X,4,0   c. SRP   X,64-3,5   e. SRP   X,64-5,5
   b. SRP   X,64-4,5   d. SRP   X,3,5   f. SRP   X,5,0

3. Suppose that the following statement defines a memory location with symbolic address PD:

   PD   DS PL10

   What packed-decimal number would be stored at PD after each of the following sets of instructions were executed?

   a. ZAP   PD,=P'10'
      AP   PD,=P'1.0'

   b. ZAP   PD,=P'6.25'
      MP   PD,=P'2.5'

   c. ZAP   PD,=P'+30.57'
      DP   PD,=P'-4.3'

   d. ZAP   PD,=P'-12345.67890'
      MP   PD,=P'+0.0002'

   e. ZAP   PD,=P'200'
      AP   PD,=P'1'
      MP   PD,=P'200'
      DP   PD,=P'2'

4. Suppose that a valid packed-decimal number exists at symbolic address R. Write the assembly language statements (not an entire program; just enough statements) needed to accomplish each of the following tasks:

    a. Compute the area of a circle whose radius is given at R.

    b. Compute the volume of a sphere whose radius is given at R.

    c. Calculate the amount $A = (1 + r)^n$, where r is the number at R, and $n = 5$, with $0.000001 \leq r \leq 0.999999$.

    d. Calculate the amount $P = \dfrac{r}{1 - (1 + r)^{-n}}$, where r is the number at R, and $n = 5$, with $0.000001 \leq r \leq 0.999999$.

5. Since there are no instructions explicitly designed to change the sign of a packed-decimal number, to generate its positive absolute value, or to generate its negative absolute value, what instructions can be used to accomplish each of these tasks for an arbitrary packed-decimal number that occupies N bytes at symbolic address Y?

6. Assume that the packed-decimal representation of PL10'149.95' is stored at symbolic memory location Q. Trace the twelve instruction sequences given in Figures 12.2a through 12.2d, and show the hexadecimal number that would be produced by the execution of each instruction in each of the twelve sequences. Note that in each sequence, it is assumed that location W initially contains all zeroes.

7. Convert the program statements of Figure 12.3 to a subroutine that will compute the amount $A = P(1+I)^N - P$ for arbitrary P, I, and N such that $0 \leq P < 10^5$, $0 < I < 0.20$, and $0 \leq N \leq 25$ (all quantities in packed-decimal format). What changes, if any, would have to be made to your subroutine to extend the permissible range of P to 10^7, and that of N to 40?

8. Convert the program statements of Figure 12.4 to a subroutine that will compute the Julian date for any day of the year.

9. Write a subroutine that will compute the elapsed time in hours and minutes between any two clock times that are less than 24 hours apart. For example, if the earlier time is 12:48 P.M. and the later time 01:30 A.M. the next morning, the elapsed time would be 12 hours, 42 minutes.

10. Write a subroutine that will determine the largest value and the smallest value in an array of N packed-decimal numbers. Assume that each number in the array occupies L bytes, with $0 < L \leq 16$. N and L must both be passed to your subroutine. (Hint: You will need to use the execute (EX) instruction discussed in Chapter 7.)

11. As was discussed in Chapter 11 (Section 11.4) and in Section 12.3, the SPM instruction can be used to prohibit program interruption when a decimal overflow error occurs. Write the instructions (including the SPM) that would prohibit interruption from a decimal overflow error condition. What instructions are required to *remove* the prohibition of a decimal overflow interrupt?

12. What error condition, if any, would be caused by execution of each of the following sets of instructions in which each operand length field is implied?

```
a.        DP        X,N
          .
          .
          .
   X      DC        P'5'
   N      DC        P'2'

b.        DP        U,V
          .
          .
          .
   U      DC        P'5000'
   V      DC        P'2'
```

```
c.          DP       Z,Y
                     .
                     .
                     .
    Y       DC       P'40'
    Z       DC       P'0'
d.          MP       X,=P'128'
                     .
                     .
                     .
    X       DC       P'64'
e.          MP       Q,=P'128'
                     .
                     .
                     .
    Q       DC       P'64'
f.          MP       Q,Q
                     .
                     .
                     .
    Q       DC       PL10'128'
g.          ZAP      Q,P
            AP       Q,X
                     .
                     .
                     .
    Q       DS       PL3
    P       DC       P'54321'
    X       DC       P'12345'
h.          ZAP      R,S
            SRP      R,4,0
                     .
                     .
                     .
    R       DS       PL3
    S       DC       P'97351'
```

13. Based on the set of instructions given near the end of Section 12.8, write a subroutine that will convert an integer from its EBCDIC representation to its packed-decimal representation, under the following conditions:

a. the EBCDIC representation contains from 1 to 12 bytes, and the sign of the integer immediately precedes the first significant digit (plus represented by a blank, minus by a minus sign C'—');

b. the address and length of the EBCDIC representation, and the address and length of the resulting packed-decimal representation, are parameters that must be passed to your subroutine.

14. Based on the set of instructions given in Example 6 of Section 12.9, write a subroutine that will convert an integer from its packed-decimal representation to its EBCDIC representation, under the following conditions:

   a. in the resulting EBCDIC representation, leading zeroes should be replaced by blanks, the sign of a positive number should be represented by a blank to the left of the most significant digit, and the sign of a negative number should be represented by a minus sign to the left of the most significant digit;

   b. the address and length of the packed-decimal representation, and the address and length of the resulting EBCDIC representation, are parameters that must be passed to your subroutine.

15. In IBM Cobol, the USAGE clause for numeric items is optional, and if it is omitted then the corresponding numeric data is represented in either zoned-decimal or EBCDIC format, depending on whether or not the picture clause designates an algebraic sign. For example,

Cobol	representation (in hex)
02 X PICTURE 999 VALUE 200.	F2F0F0
02 Y PICTURE S999 VALUE -150.	F1F5D0

Since there are no instructions to do arithmetic on either zoned-decimal or EBCDIC number representations, computations involving such numbers must include conversion to and from a format suitable for computation.

Write a set of instructions and appropriate DC and/or DS directives that will accomplish the same purpose as the following Cobol sentences, if X and Y were defined as above:

```
ADD X TO Y.
MULTIPLY Y BY -1.
```

16. For each of the packed-decimal numbers given below, define a pattern that could be used by an ED instruction to create the EBCDIC representation shown to the right of the number.

packed-decimal (given)		EBCDIC (desired)	
Assembly	Hexadecimal	Assembly	Hexadecimal
P'999'	999C	C' 999'	4040F9F9F9
P'99.9'	999C	C' 99.9'	40F9F94BF9
P'9.99'	999C	C' 9.99'	40F94BF9F9
P'.999'	999C	C'0.999'	F04BF9F9F9
PL2'9'	009C	C' 9'	40404040F9

17. For each of the packed-decimal numbers given below, define a pattern that could be used by an EDMK instruction to create the EBCDIC representation shown to the right of the number.

packed-decimal (given)		EBCDIC (desired)	
Assembly	Hexadecimal	Assembly	Hexadecimal
P'12345'	12345C	C'+12345'	4EF1F2F3F4F5
P'-123.45'	12345D	C'-123.45'	60F1F2F34BF4F5
PL3'3.87'	00387C	C' 3.87'	404040F34BF8F7
PL4'-19.95'	0001995D	C' -19.95'	4060F1F94BF9F5
PL4'-99999'	0099999D	C'-99,999'	60F9F96BF9F9F9

18. Change the instructions given in Examples 1 through 4 of Section 12.9 so that the patterns given there are reusable.

19. Make whatever changes are necessary to the instructions and directives of Example 6 in Section 12.9 so that the resulting EBCDIC representation will contain an appropriate number of commas, in addition to having leading zeroes replaced by blanks and a floating minus sign if the number is negative.

20. The equation below gives the amount of each monthly payment, $p(r)$, required for an n-year mortgage of d dollars, at a fixed annual interest of r%:

$$p(r) = \frac{d * r/1200}{1 - (1 + r/1200)^{-12n}}$$

For example, if a $50,000 mortgage is to be paid off in 30 years at 9% annual interest, the monthly payments according to the formula would be

$$p(9) = \frac{50000 * .09/12}{1 - (1 + .09/12)^{-360}} = \$402.31$$

   a. Write a subroutine that uses packed-decimal arithmetic to calculate the monthly payments, $p(r_j)$, for any given values of d, n, and r, with $r_j = r + \frac{1}{4}j$ and $j = 0,1,2,3$. Thus, for the previous example, your subroutine would calculate these four quantities:

   $$p(9) = 402.31, \quad p(9.25) = 411.34, \quad p(9.5) = 420.43, \quad p(9.75) = 429.58$$

   b. Write a main program that calls your subroutine for various values of d, n, and r, and prints the results in a suitably edited format.

21. Based on the formula in Exercise 20, write a subroutine that will calculate the total of all monthly payments, $P(r) = 12n*p(r)$, and the ratios, $R(r) = P(r)/d$, for any given d, n, and r. Thus, for $d = 50,000$, $n = 30$, and $r = 9$, your subroutine would calculate $P(r) = 360*402.31 = 144,831.60$ and $R(r) = 2.8966$. Write a main program that calls your subroutine for various values of d, n, and r and prints the results in a suitably edited format.

13

Floating-Point Operations

The concept, format, and use of numbers written in *floating-point* notation are similar to that of numbers written in so-called scientific notation. But, as will be seen, floating-point operations provide an important simplification for the problem of decimal-point alignment; alignment is performed by the hardware during the execution of floating-point instructions.

In scientific notation, a number is written as $\pm D \times 10^N$. N can be a positive or negative integer, or zero, and D is a decimal number, usually between 0 and 10. D is called the **mantissa,** or fraction, N is called the **characteristic,** or exponent, and 10 is the **base.** In order to add or subtract two numbers in scientific notation, we must first adjust their characteristics so that they are equal. For example, to add 2.99776×10^{10} and 3.876×10^6, we can perform the addition only after adjusting the characteristic of the smaller number:

Scientific vs. Floating-Point Notation

$$
\begin{array}{r}
2.99776\ \ \times 10^{10} \\
+\ 0.0003876 \times 10^{10} \\
\hline
+\ 2.9981476 \times 10^{10}
\end{array}
$$

This adjustment of characteristics is, of course, necessary in order to align the decimal points. In multiplication, the characteristics are added, and in division, they are subtracted:

$$(a \times 10^n) \times (b \times 10^m) = (a \times b) \times 10^{n+m}$$
$$(a \times 10^n) \div (b \times 10^m) = (a \div b) \times 10^{n-m}$$

Through an option available on most models of the IBM 360 and 370 systems, use of scientific notation is emulated by floating-point notation in which a base of sixteen instead of ten is used; and the mantissa is a hexadecimal fraction between 0 and $+1$, rather than a decimal number between 0 and 10.[1] We can therefore write a floating-point number as

$$\pm\, H \times 16^{K}$$

where K = a positive or negative integer, or zero, and

$$H = 0.h_1h_2h_3h_4...$$
$$= H_1 \times 16^{-1} + H_2 \times 16^{-2} + H_3 \times 16^{-3} + H_4 \times 16^{-4}+...$$

(The h_j are hexadecimal digits; the H_j are their decimal representations.)

When adding, subtracting, multiplying, or dividing two floating-point numbers in the IBM 360 and 370 systems, *the process of adjusting the characteristics is performed by the hardware.* This is one of the major advantages of using floating-point numbers: *decimal-point alignment is a hardware function.*

It might be instructive to look at the floating-point representations of a few decimal numbers:

decimal system	floating-point, base 16
1.0	0.1×16^{1}
0.5	0.8×16^{0}
1.225×10^{1}	$0.C4 \times 16^{1}$
2.9976×10^{10}	$0.6FAB576 \times 16^{9}$

The first two are fairly obvious: 0.1 as a hexadecimal fraction has a value of 1×16^{-1}, or one-sixteenth, so that $0.1 \times 16^{1} = (1 \times 16^{-1}) \times 16^{1} = 1$; and 0.8 has a value of 8×16^{-1}, or one-half. The floating-point representation of the third number is less obvious, though still manageable:

$$0.C4 \times 16^{1} = (12 \times 16^{-1} + 4 \times 16^{-2}) \times 16^{1}$$
$$= 12 + \frac{1}{4}$$
$$= 1.225 \times 10^{1}$$

The representation of the fourth number, however, is not as obvious. This number is nevertheless accurate to five decimal places, as you can easily verify. Since it is not necessarily a simple matter to convert a number into its hexadecimal floating-point representation, we almost always relegate this chore to a computer program.

At this point we wish to observe a few important properties of floating-point numbers.

1. **Shifting** Just as moving the decimal point right or left corresponds to multiplying or dividing by *ten,* so moving the hexadecimal point right or left corresponds to multiplication or division by *sixteen.* For example, consider these numbers:

> decimal: $1.225 \times 10^{1} = 12.25 \times 10^{0} = 0.1225 \times 10^{2}$
> hexadecimal: $C.4 \times 16^{0} = C4.0 \times 16^{-1} = 0.C4 \times 16^{1}$

Through these and similar examples, we see that the movement of the hexadecimal or decimal point, which is equivalent to keeping the point fixed while shifting the digits, is always compensated for by a change in the characteristic, and vice versa. This elementary fact is critical to an understanding of floating-point operations.

---

1. Floating-point representation is also used by Fortran and Cobol programs. In Fortran, "real" variables and constants are in short-format, "double-precision" in long-format. In IBM Cobol, USAGE IS COMPUTATIONAL-1 yields short-format representation, and USAGE IS COMPUTATIONAL-2 yields long-format representation. Both short- and long-format representation are defined in the next section.

2. Normalized form As previously mentioned, the mantissa of a floating-point number, $\pm H \times 16^K$, is a hexadecimal fraction less than 1 in magnitude:

$$H = 0.h_1h_2h_3h_4...$$

where each h_j is a hexadecimal digit. A nonzero floating-point number is said to be **normalized** when $h_1 \neq 0$, and **unnormalized** when $h_1 = 0$. An unnormalized number can always be normalized by shifting it to the left and reducing the characteristic by an appropriate amount equal to the number of positions shifted. For example,

unnormalized form	normalized form
$0.00C4 \times 16^3$	$0.C4 \times 16^1$
$0.08 \quad \times 16^1$	$0.8 \quad \times 16^0$

In the IBM 360 and 370 systems, and in most other computer systems, floating-point numbers are normalized by the hardware during the execution of most floating-point arithmetic instructions. Although deliberate exceptions to this rule occur in a few floating-point instructions, there are no shifting instructions available for normalization; normalization must be accomplished via other instructions. The advantage of normalized form is that as many significant digits as possible are retained in the available number of bits; in other words, leading zeroes are absorbed into the characteristic. Unnormalized form is useful primarily when converting numbers to and from floating-point format.

3. Accuracy A hexadecimal floating-point number may be only a very good approximation to the decimal number we want to represent. For example, the number 0.1 (one-tenth) is a never-ending fraction in hexadecimal:

$$0.1 \text{ (decimal)} = 0.1999999...\text{(hexadecimal)}$$
$$= 1 \times 16^{-1} + 9 \times 16^{-2} + 9 \times 16^{-3} + 9 \times 16^{-4} +...$$

No approximation in hexadecimal is exactly one-tenth. For example,

$$0.2 \text{ hex} = 2 \times 16^{-1} = 0.125 \text{ decimal}$$
$$0.1A \text{ hex} = 1 \times 16^{-1} + 10 \times 16^{-2}$$
$$\approx 0.10156 \text{ decimal}$$
$$0.19A \text{ hex} = 1 \times 16^{-1} + 9 \times 16^{-2} + 10 \times 16^{-3}$$
$$\approx 0.100098 \text{ decimal}$$

In other words, the more hexadecimal digits we use, the better the approximation. But it is still an approximation. The same is true for many other rational numbers, such as 1/3, 1/5, 1/7, and 1/9 for which there are no exact floating-point representations.

There are also many *integers* for which no exact floating-point representation exists. For example, the only ones that can be exactly represented in short format are of the form $K \times 16^N$, where $|K| < 16^6 = 16,777,216$ and $0 \leq N \leq 63$. This range includes all integers whose magnitudes are less than 2^{24}, but no *odd* integers and only some *even* integers with magnitudes greater than 2^{24}.

The significance of these limitations is that results obtained via hand calculations or even from binary integer calculations may be slightly different from those obtained via floating-point calculations. To reduce and in some cases eliminate these types of discrepancies, normalized form is almost always used, and long or extended formats may have to be used.

4. **Magnitude** The approximate magnitude of a floating-point number is essentially independent of the number of bits required to represent the number: magnitude depends primarily on the value of the characteristic. In the IBM 360 and 370 systems, the maximum allowable value for a characteristic is 63 ($=2^6-1$), and the minimum value is -64. Thus the magnitude of normalized floating-point numbers in the 360 and 370 ranges approximately from 16^{-65} to 16^{63} for positive numbers and from about -16^{-65} to -16^{63} for negative numbers. We can translate this into more familiar terms by noting that in the equation

$$16^n = 10^x$$

the value of x corresponding to a known value of n is given by

$$x = n \log_{10} 16$$
$$\approx n \, (1.20412)$$

Thus, a good approximation is that

$$16^{-65} \approx 10^{-78.2678} \approx 5.4 \times 10^{-79}$$

and

$$16^{63} \approx 10^{75.8596} \approx 7.2 \times 10^{75}$$

In other words, the range of normalized floating-point numbers in the IBM 360 and 370 systems is from approximately

$$5.4 \times 10^{-79} \quad to \quad 7.2 \times 10^{75}$$

in magnitude. Yet *only 32 bits are used to represent any six-digit number in this range.* Remember that 32 bits limit the maximum value to about 2.1×10^9 in binary integer format, and 32 bits limit the maximum value to about 10^7 in packed-decimal format. Consequently, a far greater range in magnitude is attainable for a given number of bits in floating-point format than in either binary integer or packed-decimal format. This is one of two important reasons for the use of floating-point numbers; the other reason, as previously mentioned, is the hardware's alignment of the decimal point.

13.1 MACHINE LANGUAGE REPRESENTATION

In the IBM 370 system, a floating-point number, $\pm H \times 16^K$, can be represented in three types of fixed-length formats: **short** format, **long** format, and **extended** format. Short and long formats are also available in the IBM 360; extended format is not. In each format, the first bit represents the sign of the floating-point number: 0 for plus, 1 for minus. The next 7 bits represent the characteristic, K, coded in what is known as **excess-64 binary notation.** The remaining bits represent the mantissa, H: six hex digits in short format, fourteen in long format, and twenty-eight in extended format. The base (16) is not represented; its value is implied.

short format (single-precision)

sign bit ⟶

| K | H |

01   8   31

long format (double-precision)

sign bit ⟶

| K | H |

01   8   63

extended format (extended-precision)

sign bit ⟶

| K | high-order 14 digits of *H* |

01   8   63

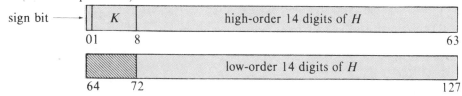

| | low-order 14 digits of *H* |

64   72   127

A short-format number occupies 4 bytes, and in the IBM 360 (but not the 370) it must be stored on a full-word boundary. A long-format number occupies 8 bytes; in the 360 it must be stored on a double-word boundary. An extended-format number is stored as two consecutive long-format numbers. The characteristic of the high-order part of an extended-format number is the characteristic of that extended number, and the sign of the high-order part is the sign of the extended number. Thus, bits 64 through 71 are in effect ignored and the mantissa of an extended number is considered to be 28 hex digits, occupying bits 8–63 and 72–127 of the number. (Additional information about bits 64 through 71 is given in Exercise 17 at the end of this chapter.)

In the representation of the mantissa,

$$H = 0.h_1h_2h_3h_4\ldots$$

The value of H is always less than 1. The hexadecimal point is considered to be between bits 7 and 8 in each of the formats but is not represented; its position is implied. The digit h_1 occupies bits 8–11; h_2, bits 12–15; and so forth. The sign of the mantissa is not represented in the bits occupied by the mantissa's digits. The sign is represented in bit 0 of each format. Thus, we speak of the **sign-magnitude representation,** since it is the absolute value, or magnitude, of the mantissa represented in each of the formats.

As mentioned earlier, the characteristic is represented in excess-64 notation. This means that the true value of characteristic K is represented as a 7-bit binary integer whose value is 64 more than that of K:

Representation of Characteristics

true value K (decimal integer)	excess-64 representation of K (7 bits)	hex equivalent of 7-bit excess-64 notation
-64	0000000	00
-63	0000001	01
-62	0000010	02
.	.	.
.	.	.
.	.	.
-1	0111111	3F
0	1000000	40
+1	1000001	41
+2	1000010	42
.	.	.
.	.	.
.	.	.
+62	1111110	7E
+63	1111111	7F

The following floating-point representations illustrate these concepts.

decimal number in scientific notation	equivalent number written as hexadecimal fraction times power of 16	representation of decimal number in short format

sign bit   characteristic (7 bits)   mantissa (24 bits)

decimal	equivalent	representation
1.0×10^0	0.1×16^1	`0 4 1 1 0 0 0 0`
-0.5×10^0	-0.8×16^0	`1 4 0 8 0 0 0 0`
1.225×10^1	$0.C4 \times 16^1$	`0 4 1 C 4 0 0 0`
2.9976×10^{10}	$0.6FAB57 \times 16^9$	`0 4 9 6 F A B 5 7`
-2.9976×10^{10}	$-0.6FAB57 \times 16^9$	`1 4 9 6 F A B 5 7`
1.674×10^{-24}	$0.20613F \times 16^{-19}$	`0 2 D 2 0 6 1 3 F`
-1.674×10^{-24}	$-0.20613F \times 16^{-19}$	`1 2 D 2 0 6 1 3 F`

In each of the last four numbers, the short-format representation is accurate to six hex digits although it is not the precise value represented by the corresponding decimal number at the left. This loss of accuracy, due to the incommensurability of the decimal and hexadecimal number systems, can become a serious problem when propagated and accumulated in a series of computations. As a partial compensation for this, the long or extended formats can be used. With a greater number of digits in the mantissa, the loss of accuracy can be confined to digits beyond the seventh significant place, sufficient for almost all calculations. The precision provided by the three formats is:

	number of hex digits	maximum number of decimal digits
short format	6	7
long format	14	16
extended format	28	33

Conversion from one format to another is a simple matter since instructions are provided for this purpose. Conversion from decimal notation to floating-point format (and vice versa) requires some calculations that, while straightforward, are usually accomplished by a subroutine. This will be described in Section 13.8.

13.2 ASSEMBLY LANGUAGE REPRESENTATION

Corresponding to the three types of machine language representation of floating-point numbers, there are three types of floating-point constants in assembly language. These are distinguished by the data-type code:

E = short format (single-precision)
D = long format (double-precision)
L = extended format (quadruple-precision).

Examples are shown in Figure 13.1. The important things to observe are these: (1) boundary alignment, (2) use of scale and exponent modifiers, S*n* and E*n*, to multiply the mantissa by a power of 16 and 10, respectively, and (3) use of the decimal point to distinguish the integer and fractional components of the number.

For the short format, **alignment** is always on a full-word boundary; for the long and extended formats, on a double-word boundary. Use of the length modifier L*n* is not recommended.

The **scale modifier** S*n* is used only when we want to create an unnormalized floating-point number. The value of *n* is the number of hex zeroes that are to precede the first significant digit in the mantissa. Obviously, the value of *n* must be positive and consistent with the length of the mantissa.

Figure 13.1   *Defining floating-point constants.*

```
FLAG LOCTN OBJECT CODE     ADDR1  ADDR2  STMNT M SOURCE STATEMENT

                                         4     * E = SHORT, D = LONG
      000000 41100000                    5           DC    E'1.0'
      000008 4110000000000000            6           DC    D'1.0'
      000010 4019999A                    7           DC    E'0.1'
      000018 4019999999999999A           8           DC    D'0.1'

                                         9     * EXPONENT FACTOR GIVES POWER OF 10
      000020 496FAB57                    10          DC    E'2.9976E+10'
      000024 C96FAB57                    11          DC    E'-2.9976E+10'
      000028 496FAB5760000000            12          DC    D'2.9976E+10'

      000030 2D20613F                    13          DC    E'1.674E-24'
      000034 AD20613F                    14          DC    E'-1.674E-24'

                                         15    * SCALE FACTOR CREATES UN-NORMALIZED NUMBER
      000038 450000C4                    16          DC    ES4'12.25'
      00003C 41C40000                    17          DC    E'12.25'

      000040 4C0006FB                    18          DC    ES3'2.9976E+10'
      000044 496FAB57                    19          DC    E'2.9976E+10'

                                         20    * APPROX SMALLEST AND LARGEST NUMBERS
      000048 001001D1                    21          DC    E'5.4E-79'
      00004C 7FFEB0E4                    22          DC    E'7.2E+75'

                                         23    * MULTIPLE CONSTANTS PERMISSIBLE
      000050 4110000041200000            24          DC    E'1,2,3'        IN SHORT FORMAT
             41300000
      00005C 41100000                    25          DC    E'1',E'2',E'3'
      000060 41200000
      000064 41300000
      000068 41100000                    26          DC    E'1',2E'2,3'
      00006C 4120000041300000
             4120000041300000

      000080 4019999999999999A           27          DC    D'0.1,0.2'     IN LONG FORMAT
             4033333333333333
      000090 4019999999999999A           28          DC    D'0.1',D'0.2'
      000098 4033333333333333
      0000A0 4019999999999999A           29          DC    2D'0.1,0.2'
             4033333333333333
             4019999999999999A
             4033333333333333
```

The **exponent modifier** En can be used to express the constant in scientific notation. The value of n is the power of 10; the permissible range is from -85 through $+75$.

In addition to defining floating-point constants by means of the DC directive, we also can define the floating-point **literals** in short (E), long (D), and extended (L) format.

To reserve memory space for floating-point data, we can use either the E- or the F-type codes for short format, since each results in alignment on a full-word boundary. But for long and extended formats, always use the D- and L-type codes, respectively. For example,

DS   4F   }   Each reserves space for four single-precision (short-format)
DS   4E   }   floating-point numbers, correctly aligned on full-word boundaries.

DS   30D   Reserves space for 30 double-precision (long-format) floating-point numbers, each on a double-word boundary.

DS   10L   Reserves space for 10 extended-precision floating-point numbers, each on a double-word boundary. (The L-type code can only be used for the IBM 370.)

13.3   FLOATING-POINT INSTRUCTIONS: OVERVIEW AND REGISTER USAGE

There are 44 instructions in what is known as the Floating-point Arithmetic Instruction Set of the IBM 360 and 370 and an additional 7 instructions in the Extended-precision Instruction Set of the IBM 370. The 44 instructions are evenly divided into two classes: 22 that process short-format numbers and 22 that process long-format numbers. The remaining 7 instructions are designed for use with extended-precision numbers. All 51 instructions are either RX- or RR-type instructions. We will simply refer to them collectively as *the* floating-point instructions.

See Summary in Figure 13.9

The opcodes of these instructions are summarized in Figure 13.2. This figure also shows the functional correspondence that exists between the floating-point instructions and the integer arithmetic instructions studied in previous chapters. Notice that in addition to the types of operations familiar from integer arithmetic—load, store, add, subtract, and so forth—there are two types of operations that have no counterpart in the integer arithmetic instructions set: halve and round. Notice also the absence of shift instructions, as has already been mentioned, and the absence of any instructions converting numbers between floating-point and any other format.

The 51 floating-point instructions will be described in the sections that follow. What needs to be pointed out here are the following register usage constraints. In the IBM 360 and 370 systems, all floating-point operations are carried out in a special set of registers, the floating-point registers. There are only four floating-point registers. Each is 64 bits long. Their addresses are 0, 2, 4, and 6. These registers cannot be used for indexing, base registers, or other similar purposes, but only for floating-point operations.

The constraints associated with the use of the floating-point registers are these:

1. **Short-format numbers** Numbers that are represented in the 32-bit short format and processed by the short-format instructions are manipulated in the high-order 32 bits of a floating-point register. Any of the four floating-point registers may be designated.
2. **Long-format numbers** Numbers that are represented in the 64-bit long format and processed by the long-format instructions are manipulated in the entire 64 bits of a floating-point register. Any of the four floating-point registers may be designated.
3. **Extended-format numbers** Numbers that are represented in the 128-bit extended-precision format and processed by the extended-precision instructions are always manipulated in two consecutive floating-point registers; these are always either registers 0 and 2, or registers 4 and 6. When registers 0 and 2 are used, they must be referred to by designating register 0; when registers 4 and 6 are used, they must be referred to by designating register 4.

In RX-type floating-point instructions, the first operand field must designate an appropriate floating-point register address. In RR-type floating-point instructions, both operands must designate appropriate floating-point register addresses. As mentioned, these addresses may be either 0, 2, 4, or 6 in short- or long-format instructions but must be either 0 or 4 in extended-precision instructions. Any other register address will cause a "specification error" to occur, i.e., the program will be interrupted by the hardware and terminated by the operating system.

13.4 LOAD AND STORE OPERATIONS

Any short- or long-format number can be copied from memory into a floating-point register by means of the Load Short (LE) or Load Long (LD) instructions. Similarly, a short- or long-format number can be copied from a floating-point register to a main memory location by means of the two respective store instructions, Store Short (STE) and Store Long (STD). The LE, LD, STE, and STD instructions are all RX-type instructions. No corresponding load or store instructions exist for extended-format numbers; we must use two consecutive LD's or STD's.

To simplify the descriptions of floating-point instructions in this chapter, the following notation will be used:

V_1 = the floating-point number whose address is designated by the *first* operand field in an instruction
V_2 = the floating-point number whose address is designated by the *second* operand field in an instruction

With this notation, the four LOAD and STORE instructions mentioned can be described as follows:

opcode	meaning
LE	LOAD (short) [RX instruction] Copies the short-format number V_2 from memory into the high-order 32 bits of the register designated by the first operand field. The low-order 32 bits of that register are not changed.

	name	type	integer instructions			floating-point instructions — short format		long format		extended format
Load into registers	Load	RX	L	LH	LM	LE		LD		
	Load Registers	RR	LR			LER		LDR		
Store into memory	Store	RX	ST	STH	STM	STE		STD		
Compare or test	Compare	RX	C	CH		CE		CD		
	Compare Registers	RR	CR			CER		CDR		
	Load and Test	RR	LTR			LTER		LTDR		
Sign	Load Complement	RR	LCR			LCER		LCDR		
	Load Negative	RR	LNR			LNER		LNDR		
	Load Positive	RR	LPR			LPER		LPDR		
Arithmetic operations	Add	RX	A, AL	AH		AE	AU	AD	AW	
	Add Registers	RR	AR, ALR			AER	AUR	ADR	AWR	AXR
	Subtract	RX	S, SL	SH		SE	SU	SD	SW	
	Subtract Registers	RR	SR, SLR			SER	SUR	SDR	SWR	SXR
	Multiply	RX	M	MH		ME		MD		MXD
	Multiply Registers	RR	MR			MER		MDR		MXR, MXDR
	Divide	RX	D			DE		DD		
	Divide Registers	RR	DR			DER		DDR		
	Halve	RR				HER		HDR		
	Round	RR								LRER, LRDR

LD   **LOAD** (long)   [RX instruction]
Copies the long-format number V_2 from memory into the register designated by the first operand.

STE   **STORE** (short) [RX instruction]
Copies the short-format number V_1 from the high-order 32 bits of the register designated by the first operand to the memory location designated by the second operand.

STD   **STORE** (long)   [RX instruction]
Copies the long-format number V_1 from the register designated by the first operand to the memory location designated by the second operand.

A short- or long-format number can also be copied from one floating-point register to another by means of RR-type instructions, LER for short format and LDR for long format. There is no corresponding extended-format register-to-register copy instruction; two consecutive LDR's must be used.

opcode	meaning
LER	LOAD REGISTER (short) [RR instruction] Copies the short-format number V_2 into the high-order 32 bits of the register designated by the first operand field. The low-order bits of that register are not changed.
LDR	LOAD REGISTER (long) [RR instruction] Copies the long-format number V_2 into the register designated by the first operand field.

None of the load, load register, or store instructions just described sets the condition code. As mentioned earlier, however, a specification error and program interruption will occur if floating-point register addresses 0, 2, 4, or 6 are not specified in the first operand field of the RX instructions and in both operand fields of the RR instructions. (In the LER and LDR instructions, it is permissible for both operand fields to designate the same register.)

13.5   COMPARING AND TESTING FLOATING-POINT NUMBERS

As in packed-decimal and integer arithmetic, it is often useful to compare two floating-point numbers algebraically without altering either one. One reason for making such a comparison is to determine whether a number is positive, negative, or zero; for example, to determine the nature of a product or quotient or to prevent division by zero. Another reason is to put a set of floating-point numbers into increasing or decreasing numerical sequence, i.e., to sort them.

Two types of instructions for accomplishing these tasks are available in the IBM 360 and 370 systems. One type can be used to compare algebraically any two short- or long-format floating-point numbers, provided at least one of them is in a floating-point register; the other can be used to determine whether a short- or long-format number is greater than, less than, or equal to zero. Both types of instructions set the condition code as noted in the descriptions below, so that a subsequent conditional branch instruction can be used to determine the nature of the result. A summary of the instructions discussed in this section is given in Figure 13.3.

To describe these instructions, we once again use the notation

V_1 = the floating-point number whose address is designated by the *first* operand field
V_2 = the floating-point number whose address is designated by the *second* operand field

Compare Instructions: CE, CER, CD, CDR

For comparing two *short*-format numbers:

opcode	meaning	type
CE	Compares V_1 to V_2, where V_1 is in a floating-point register and V_2 is in memory.	RX
CER	Compares V_1 to V_2, where both are in floating-point registers.	RR

For comparing two *long*-format numbers:

opcode	meaning	type
CD	Compares V_1 to V_2, where V_1 is in a floating-point register and V_2 is in memory.	RX
CDR	Compares V_1 to V_2, where both are in floating-point registers.	RR

Figure 13.3   Floating-point Load, Store, Compare, Test, and Sign.

name	mnemonic opcode	type RX	type RR	condition code 0	1	2	3
Single-precision Instructions							
Load	LE	X		---	---	---	---
Load Registers	LER		X	---	---	---	---
Store	STE	X		---	---	---	---
Compare	CE	X		$V_1 = V_2$	$V_1 < V_2$	$V_1 > V_2$	---
Compare Registers	CER		X	$V_1 = V_2$	$V_1 < V_2$	$V_1 > V_2$	---
Load and Test	LTER		X	$V_2 = 0$	$V_2 < 0$	$V_2 > 0$	---
Load Complement	LCER		X	$V_2 = 0$	$V_2 > 0$	$V_2 < 0$	---
Load Negative	LNER		X	$V_2 = 0$	$V_2 \neq 0$	---	---
Load Positive	LPER		X	$V_2 = 0$	---	$V_2 \neq 0$	---
Double-precision Instructions							
Load	LD	X		---	---	---	---
Load Registers	LDR		X	---	---	---	---
Store	STD	X		---	---	---	---
Compare	CD	X		$V_1 = V_2$	$V_1 < V_2$	$V_1 > V_2$	---
Compare Registers	CDR		X	$V_1 = V_2$	$V_1 < V_2$	$V_1 > V_2$	---
Load and Test	LTDR		X	$V_2 = 0$	$V_2 < 0$	$V_2 > 0$	---
Load Complement	LCDR		X	$V_2 = 0$	$V_2 > 0$	$V_2 < 0$	---
Load Negative	LNDR		X	$V_2 = 0$	$V_2 \neq 0$	---	---
Load Positive	LPDR		X	$V_2 = 0$	---	$V_2 \neq 0$	---

Notes: 1. There are no extended-precision instructions for comparing, testing, or performing sign operations on extended-precision numbers.

2. None of these instructions can cause an exponent overflow, exponent underflow, significance exception, or divide exception at run time.

3. V_1 designates the number referred to by the first operand in a floating point instruction, and
   V_2 designates the number referred to by the second operand in a floating point instruction.

4. In these instructions, V_j (j = 1 or 2) is considered to be zero if its mantissa is zero, irrespective of its sign or characteristic.

5. In these instructions, $V_1 = V_2$ if they would be equal when both were in normalized form.

All four instructions set the condition code:

code	meaning
0	$V_1 = V_2$
1	$V_1 < V_2$
2	$V_1 > V_2$

Therefore, the appropriate conditional branch instructions are:

BER	or	BE	branches if $V_1 = V_2$
BNER	or	BNE	branches if $V_1 \neq V_2$
BHR	or	BH	branches if $V_1 > V_2$
BNHR	or	BNH	branches if $V_1 \leq V_2$
BLR	or	BL	branches if $V_1 < V_2$
BNLR	or	BNL	branches if $V_1 \geq V_2$

When the CE, CER, CD, or CDR instructions are executed, V_1 and V_2 are normalized by the hardware during the comparison operation without changing their respective representations in the register or memory location. The examples illustrate this.

Example 1.

	V_1 floating-point register 0	V_2 memory location X
CE 0,X	450000C4	41C40000

result: $V_1 = V_2$, i.e., $12.25 = 12.25$

Example 2.

	V_1 floating-point register 2	V_2 memory location Y
CD 2,Y	AD20613F1B000000	3300000020613F1B

result: $V_1 < V_2$, i.e., $-1.674 \times 10^{-24} < +1.674 \times 10^{-24}$

Example 3.

	V_1 floating-point register 2	V_2 floating-point register 4
CDR 2,4	4F0000006FAB5760	C96FAB5760000000

result: $V_1 > V_2$, i.e., $+2.9976 \times 10^{10} > -2.9976 \times 10^{10}$

Load and Test Instructions: LTER, LTDR

To determine whether a short or long number is positive, negative, or zero, we can use a load-and-test instruction, LTER or LTDR.

opcode	meaning	type
LTER	Tests a *short*-format number V_2, and simultaneously loads it into the register occupied by V_1.	RR
LTDR	Tests a *long*-format number V_2, and simultaneously loads it into the register occupied by V_1.	RR

Both of these set the condition code:

code	meaning
0	the mantissa of V_2 is zero
1	$V_2 < 0$ and its mantissa is not zero
2	$V_2 > 0$ and its mantissa is not zero

Therefore, the appropriate conditional branch instructions to use following either LTER or LTDR are:

BZR	or	BZ	branches if $V_2 = 0$
BNZR	or	BNZ	branches if $V_2 \neq 0$
BMR	or	BM	branches if $V_2 < 0$
BNMR	or	BNM	branches if $V_2 \geq 0$
BPR	or	BP	branches if $V_2 > 0$
BNPR	or	BNP	branches if $V_2 \leq 0$

There is one precaution to be observed: when using LTER or LTDR, V_2 *is considered to be zero if its mantissa is zero;* the characteristic is not examined by the hardware in making the determination.

Example 1.

			floating-point register 0

LTER   0,0

before execution: 41 00 00 00
after execution: 41 00 00 00

specifies the floating-point register containing V_2

specifies the floating-point register into which V_2 is to be copied

result: $V_2 = 0$, since $0 \times 16^1 = 0$.

Example 2.

	floating-point register 0	floating-point register 2
LTER 0,2 before execution:	AB123456	7F9812AB
after execution:	7F9812AB	7F9812AB

result: $V_2 > 0$, since sign bit $= 0$, and mantissa $\neq 0$.

Example 3.

	floating-point register 4	floating-point register 6
LTDR 4,6 before execution:	4110000000000000	C110000000000000
after execution:	C110000000000000	C110000000000000

result: $V_2 < 0$, since sign bit $= 1$, and mantissa $\neq 0$.

13.6 CHANGING SIGNS

It is a particularly simple matter to change the sign of a floating-point number when that number is in memory, for only one bit must be changed. If the number is at location A, we can use simple Boolean instructions to set the sign bit to 0 or 1 or to reverse it:

```
* MAKE SIGN OF A POSITIVE:
    NI A,X'7F'
* MAKE SIGN OF A NEGATIVE:
    OI A,X'80'
* CHANGE SIGN OF A:
    XI A,X'80'
```

However, Boolean operations, which apply only to general registers, cannot be used when a number is in a floating-point register. Consequently, three sets of instructions are provided for the three sign operations. All are RR-type load-register instructions, similar to those used with integers in general registers, although designed specifically for short- and long-format floating-point numbers.

To copy the *positive absolute value of V_2* from floating-point register R2 into floating-point $+ |V_2|$ register R1, we use

```
    LPER        R1,R2        for short-format numbers
    LPDR        R1,R2        for long-format numbers
```

To copy the *negative absolute value* of V_2 from floating-point register R2 into floating-point $- |V_2|$ register R1, we use

```
    LNER        R1,R2        for short-format numbers
    LNDR        R1,R2        for long-format numbers
```

To copy the *negative* of V_2 from floating-point register R2 into floating-point register R1, we $- V_2$ use

```
    LCER        R1,R2        for short-format numbers
    LCDR        R1,R2        for long-format numbers
```

In each of these instructions, it is of course permissible for R1 and R2 to designate the same register. If that is the case, the instructions simply make the sign of V_2 positive or negative or change it.

Each of the six instructions mentioned sets the condition code so that the conditional branch instructions may be used to determine the nature of the result:

code	meaning
0	mantissa of result is zero
1	sign of result is < 0, and mantissa $\neq 0$
2	sign of result is > 0, and mantissa $\neq 0$

The only precaution to be observed is that although all six instructions *always* set or change the sign, even when the mantissa is zero, the conditional branch instructions cannot be used to distinguish a positive zero from a negative zero. This is because condition code 0 is always set when the mantissa is zero, regardless of the sign of the number.

A summary of the instructions discussed in this section was given in Figure 13.3.

13.7 ARITHMETIC OPERATIONS

There are six types of floating-point arithmetic operations: add, subtract, multiply, divide, halve, and round. The assembly language opcodes for these instructions are summarized in Figure 13.4. They have the following general properties:

1. All the single-precision instructions operate on short-format numbers. All except the two multiply instructions produce short-format results. Both ME and MER generate double-precision (long-format) products.

2. All the double-precision instructions operate on long-format numbers. These instructions all generate double-precision (long-format) results.

3. Of the extended-precision instructions, AXR, SXR, and MXR operate on extended-precision numbers and produce extended-precision results. MXD and MXDR do not operate on extended-precision numbers; they each multiply two double-precision numbers to produce an extended-precision result. Of the two round instructions, LRER rounds a double-precision number to single-precision format and LRDR rounds an extended-precision number to double-precision format.

The result of any multiply, divide, or halve instruction is always in normalized form, whether or not the factor or factors being operated on are normalized. The same is true of the Add Normalized instructions and the Subtract Normalized instructions. The remaining instructions—the two round instructions and the Add Unnormalized and Subtract Unnormalized instructions—do not force the result to be normalized.

The manner in which these instructions are processed by the hardware is summarized in the following paragraphs. Error conditions that can occur because of the limitations of the floating-point formats are discussed at the end of this section.

The ADD and SUBTRACT Instructions

Addition and subtraction are performed in identical fashion to one another except that in subtraction, V_2—the quantity addressed by the second operand field—participates with its sign bit reversed. In all addition and subtraction operations, the sum or difference replaces V_1, and V_2 is left unchanged.

The hardware computes the sum or difference by means of the following sequence of steps:

1. The characteristics of V_1 and V_2 are compared. Denoting their difference by N, the mantissa accompanying the smaller characteristic is shifted right N hexadecimal digits and its characteristic is increased by N. The result of this step is that the two quantities to be added or subtracted have equal characteristics, i.e., the hexadecimal points have been aligned.

2. The left-most digit shifted out during the alignment of Step 1 is retained as an extra low-order digit so that accuracy can be preserved to 6, 14, or 28 digits. The retained digit is called the *guard* digit. The mantissa that was not shifted during Step 1 is extended on the right with one low-order zero digit, and the two 7-, 15-, or 29-digit

Figure 13.4 *Floating-point arithmetic instructions.*

Single-precision Instructions

Except for ME and MER, these all operate on short-format numbers and produce short-format results.	mnemonic opcode	RX	RR	exponent overflow	exponent underflow	significance	divide by zero	specification	condition code
Add normalized	AE	X		X	X	X		X	X
	AER		X	X	X	X		X	X
Add unnormalized	AU	X		X		X		X	X
	AUR		X	X		X		X	X
Subtract normalized	SE	X		X	X	X		X	X
	SER		X	X	X	X		X	X
Subtract unnormalized	SU	X		X		X		X	X
	SUR		X	X		X		X	X
Multiply (short to long format)	ME	X		X	X			X	
(short to long format)	MER		X	X	X			X	
Divide	DE	X		X	X		X	X	
	DER		X	X	X		X	X	
Halve	HER		X		X			X	

Double-precision Instructions

All these operate on long-format numbers and produce long-format results.	mnemonic opcode	RX	RR	exponent overflow	exponent underflow	significance	divide by zero	specification	condition code
Add normalized	AD	X		X	X	X		X	X
	ADR		X	X	X	X		X	X
Add unnormalized	AW	X		X		X		X	X
	AWR		X	X		X		X	X
Subtract normalized	SD	X		X	X	X		X	X
	SDR		X	X	X	X		X	X
Subtract unnormalized	SW	X		X		X		X	X
	SWR		X	X		X		X	X
Multiply	MD	X		X	X			X	
	MDR		X	X	X			X	
Divide	DD	X		X	X		X	X	
	DDR		X	X	X		X	X	
Halve	HDR		X		X			X	

Extended-precision Instructions

operation	operand	result	mnemonic	RX	RR	exponent overflow	exponent underflow	significance	divide by zero	specification	condition code
Add	extended	extended	AXR		X	X	X	X		X	X
Subtract	extended	extended	SXR		X	X	X	X		X	X
Multiply	extended	extended	MXR		X	X	X			X	
	long	extended	MXD	X		X	X			X	
	long	extended	MXDR		X	X	X			X	
Round	long	short	LRER		X	X	X			X	
	extended	long	LRDR		X	X	X			X	

Note: The condition code is set by all add and subtract instructions as follows:

0 = mantissa of result is zero
1 = result negative, mantissa ≠ zero
2 = result positive, mantissa ≠ zero

mantissas are added or subtracted, the sign and magnitude of the result being determined in accordance with the rules of algebra. The result of this step is called the *intermediate* sum or difference. (If the intermediate sum or difference includes a carry out of the high-order digit, one more shift takes place: the mantissa of the intermediate result is shifted *right* one digit, and its characteristic is increased by one.)

3. At this point, normalization takes place in Add Normalized and Subtract Normalized instructions; the characteristic of the intermediate result is decreased by the number of positions shifted. Vacated positions on the right are filled with zeroes, and the normalized result is truncated to 6, 14, or 28 digits, depending on the particular instruction that was executed. (This normalization step does not take place in the Add Unnormalized and Subtract Unnormalized instructions. Instead, the mantissa of the intermediate result computed in Step 2 is simply truncated to 6, 14, or 28 digits.)

The result of Step 3 is the result of the instruction's execution, except when any one of three possible error situations is detected: exponent underflow, exponent overflow, or loss of all significant digits. These error situations will be discussed separately at the end of this section.

The MULTIPLY Instruction

In multiplication, the normalized product of V_1 and V_2 replaces V_1, and V_2 is left unchanged. The length of the product's mantissa is as follows (see Fig. 13.4):

opcodes	mantissas of V_1 and V_2	mantissa of $V_1 \times V_2$
ME, MER	6 hex digits (short)	14 hex digits (long)
MD, MDR	14 hex digits (long)	14 hex digits (long)
MXD, MXDR	14 hex digits (long)	28 hex digits (extended)
MXR	28 hex digits (extended)	28 hex digits (extended)

For the instructions in which the product's mantissa is 28 digits (i.e., is in extended format), there is an additional constraint on the use of floating-point registers: V_1—the quantity addressed by the first operand field—must either be in floating-point register 0 or in floating-point register 4.

The hardware computes the product by means of the following sequence of steps, provided V_1 and V_2 are each different from zero (if either is zero, the result is immediately set to zero without further calculation):

1. The numbers V_1 and V_2 are normalized and an intermediate product is computed by multiplying the normalized mantissas and adding their characteristics. Because of the preliminary normalization of V_1 and V_2, the intermediate product is either already in normalized form or requires but one shift left (with compensating decrease in characteristic) to be normalized. If the left shift is required, it is done. The normalized intermediate product is then used as the basis for Step 2.
2. The sum of the characteristics computed in Step 1 is reduced by 64. The mantissa of the normalized intermediate product is adjusted to a length of 14 or 28 digits, depending on the instruction. In ME and MER, the product's mantissa has two low-order zero digits appended, to make 14 digits in all; in MD and MDR, the product's mantissa is truncated to 14 digits; in MXD and MXDR, the product's mantissa is not changed since exactly 28 digits were developed in Step 1; and in MXR, the product's mantissa is truncated to 28 digits.

The result of Step 2 is the result of the instruction's execution, except when either of two possible error situations is detected: exponent underflow or exponent overflow. These error situations will be discussed separately.

The DIVIDE Instruction

In division, the normalized quotient of V_1 divided by V_2 replaces V_1, and V_2 is left unchanged. Unlike integer division and packed-decimal division, *no remainder is preserved in floating-point division.* The quotient has the same number of digits as each of its two factors does, and its sign is determined by the rules of algebra. Referring to the opcodes in Figure 13.4, it should be noted that there is no instruction for dividing two extended-precision numbers.

The hardware computes the quotient by means of the following sequence of steps, provided V_1 and V_2 are each different from zero (if $V_1=0$ and $V_2\neq0$ the result is immediately set to zero without further calculation):

1. V_1 and V_2 are normalized and an intermediate quotient is computed by dividing the normalized mantissa of V_1 by that of V_2, and subtracting their characteristics. The intermediate quotient is either already in normalized form, or else a right shift of one digit (with compensating increase in characteristic) is necessary to produce a mantissa less than 1 in magnitude. If a right shift is required, it is done.
2. The difference of the characteristics computed in Step 1 is increased by 64, and the mantissa of the intermediate quotient is truncated to 6 or 14 digits (depending on the instruction).

The result of Step 2 is the result of the instruction's execution, except when one of three possible error conditions is detected: exponent underflow, exponent overflow, or a divisor (V_2) of zero. These error situations will be discussed later.

The HALVE Instructions

The two instructions that *halve* a value are equivalent in effect to division by 2: V_2 is effectively divided by 2, and the result replaces V_1. If $V_2=0$, the result is zero without further calculation. The execution time of a halve instruction is appreciably shorter than it would be in a division instruction, since an actual division is not performed: when $V_2\neq0$, halving is accomplished by shifting the mantissa right 1 *bit* position (not one digit) and then normalizing the result if necessary. As in addition and subtraction, a guard digit is used to preserve accuracy: the low-order bit that is shifted out becomes the high-order bit of the guard digit (its other bits being zeroes), and this digit participates in the normalization.

The only error condition that can occur is exponent underflow. This will be discussed later.

The ROUND Instructions

The two instructions that *round* are considered to be part of the extended-precision feature. LRDR rounds the number V_2 from extended to long format; LRER rounds V_2 from long to short format. In both cases, the rounded result replaces V_1, which may be in any floating-point register (0, 2, 4, or 6). When using the LRER instruction, V_2 may be in any floating-point register; when using LRDR, V_2 must either be in floating-point register 0 or in floating-point register 4.

The instructions round by adding a hex 8 to the high-order digit of the low-order half of the mantissa of V_2 and propagating the carry to the left. The sign of V_2 is ignored in this addition process.

Normalization does not take place during rounding. But if rounding generates a carry out of the high-order digit of the mantissa, the mantissa is shifted right one digit (with compensating increase in characteristic) so that the mantissa of the result is less than 1 in magnitude.

The only error condition that can occur is exponent overflow. This will be discussed later.

Example

To compute $-\frac{1}{2}\pi(a+4)$ where a is a floating-point quantity and $\pi = 3.1415926535897932...$, we can do the following:

```
*  FOR SHORT FORMAT                        *  FOR LONG FORMAT
       LE    4,EPI         π                     LD    4,DPI
       HER   4,4           ½π                     HDR   4,4
       LE    0,A           a                      LD    0,AA
       AE    0,=E'4'       a+4                     AD    0,=D'4'
       MER   4,0           ½π(a+4)                 MDR   4,0
       LCER  4,4          -½π(a+4)                 LCDR  4,4
       STE   4,X                                  STD   4,XX

          ...                                         ...
 EPI   DC    E'3.141593'                    DPI   DC    D'3.141592653589793'
 A     DC    E'0.740486'                    AA    DC    D'0.740486292941931'
 X     DS    E                              XX    DS    D
```

Error Conditions

Four types of error situations can be detected when a floating-point arithmetic instruction is executed:

1. **Exponent overflow** Occurs when the magnitude of a result is equal to or greater than 16^{64}, i.e., its characteristic exceeds 127, and its mantissa is not zero
2. **Exponent underflow** Occurs when the magnitude of a normalized result is equal to or less than 16^{-65}, i.e., its characteristic is less than zero, and its mantissa is not zero
3. **Significance exception** Occurs when the *mantissa* of the intermediate sum or difference resulting from any add or subtract operation is zero
4. **Divide exception** Occurs when the mantissa of a divisor (V_2) in any floating-point divide instruction is zero

Not all of these situations can occur in all arithmetic operations. The errors detectable in each type of operation are summarized in Figure 13.4. When one of these errors is detected during floating-point arithmetic operations, the action taken by the computer hardware depends on two things: (1) the type of error and (2) the provisions specified in the program mask.

The **program mask** (discussed in Chap. 11) can be used to prohibit program interruption when an exponent underflow or significance error occurs. If the appropriate program mask bit is set to 0, then whenever an underflow or significance error occurs, the result of the offending instruction is forced to be a *true zero,* i.e., a number whose mantissa and characteristic are both zero and whose sign is plus. If the appropriate program mask bit is a 1 when an underflow or significance error occurs, the program is interrupted and execution may be terminated by the operating system.

The program mask cannot be used to prohibit program interruption when an exponent overflow or divide exception error occurs. When either of these errors occurs, the program is interrupted and execution is terminated by the operating system.

Further details concerning these error conditions can be found in the IBM publications, *Principles of Operation for the IBM System 360* and *Principles of Operation for the IBM System 370.*

13.8 CONVERSION TO AND FROM FLOATING-POINT FORMAT

Two main types of conversions are of interest: (1) that between floating-point and fixed-point integers, and (2) that between floating-point and EBCDIC text in the form $\pm$ x.xxx...E$\pm$n.

The first of these is what is required when floating an integer by means of a Fortran statement such as

$$X = FLOAT(I)$$

or when converting a real number to an integer with a Fortran statement such as

$$I = IFIX(X)$$

The second type of conversion is what is needed for input and output. It is somewhat more complex than the first not only because of the I/O format requirements, but also because it can involve conversion of a fraction as well as an integer and conversion of a power of 10 to or from a power of 16.

Single-precision floating-point numbers will be used to illustrate the conversion techniques. This has three consequences:

1. In converting from floating-point to integer format, the value of the integer cannot exceed $2^{31}-1$, or be less than -2^{31}.
2. In converting from integer to floating-point format, the value of the integer should not exceed $2^{24}-1$ (16,777,215) since only 24 bits are provided in the short-format mantissa; if the integer value exceeds $2^{24}-1$, the resulting representation may not be exactly equal to the integer value.
3. In converting to and from text format, only seven significant digits are used since an eight-digit decimal number cannot in general be accurately represented in the six available hex digits.

Conversions that allow for more than seven significant digits and conversions between floating-point and packed-decimal format will not be discussed.

Conversion between Floating-Point and Fixed-Point Integer

The essential aspect of the conversion technique is to recognize that an integer can easily be converted in two steps: (1) between short-normalized and long-unnormalized format and (2) between long-unnormalized and fixed-point format. In other words, for any eight-digit integer, the conversion sequence is

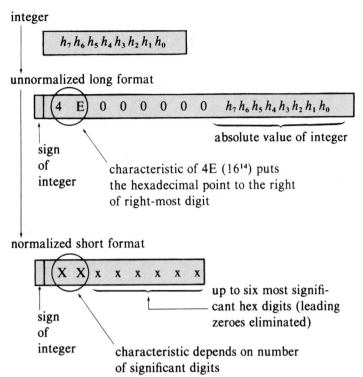

For example, for the integer 100:

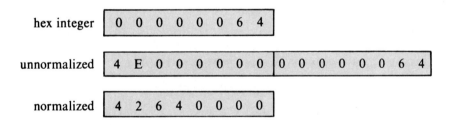

The subroutine in Figure 13.5 converts from integer to floating-point. Any integer greater than *XFLOAT* 16,777,315 ($= 16^6 - 1$) is truncated, resulting in a loss of either 1 or 2 low-order hex digits (maximum value lost is therefore less than one part in 16^5). The subroutine in Figure 13.6 converts from floating- *XFIX* point to integer, provided the integer is representable in 32 bits. In both subroutines, provisions for converting negative integers as well as positive ones are included.

Figure 13.5   Convert integer to floating-point format.

```
FLAG LOCTN OBJECT CODE    ADDR1 ADDR2 STMNT M SOURCE STATEMENT

                                      3   * SUBROUTINE XFLOAT(J,X)
                                      4   *    CONVERTS A FULLWORD INTEGER  J  TO NORMLZD SHORT-FORMAT NUMBER  X
                                      5   * PARAMETERS
                                      6   *    1ST PARAMETER = ADDRESS OF J
                                      7   *    2ND PARAMETER = ADDRESS OF X

   000000                             8   XFLOAT  CSECT
   000000 90 EC D00C                  9           STM    14,12,12(13)       STANDARD ENTRY
   000004 05 C0                       10          BALR   12,0
   000006                             11          USING  *,12
   000006 50 D0 C05E    000064        12          ST     13,SAVE+4
   00000A 41 D0 C05A    000060        13          LA     13,SAVE
   00000E 60 00 C04A    000050        14          STD    0,TEMP2            SAVE CONTENTS OF F.P. REG#0

   000012 98 23 1000                  15          LM     2,3,0(1)           GET PARAMETERS
                                      16   *                               R2 = ADDRESS OF INTEGER J
                                      17   *                               R3 = ADDRESS OF RESULT X
                                      18   * CREATE UN-NORMALIZED X IN R6,R7 AND STORE IT TEMPORARILY IN 'TEMP1'

   000016 58 22 0000    000000        19          L      2,0(2)             R2 = J
   00001A 10 72                       20          LPR    7,2                R7 = ABS(J)

   00001C 58 60 C052    000058        21          L      6,FCON             R6 = 0 * (16**14)
   000020 54 20 C056    00005C        22          N      2,SIGN             ISOLATE J'S SIGN BIT, AND
   000024 16 62                       23          OR     6,2                   AFFIX IT TO UN-NORMLZD X
   000026 90 67 C042    000048        24          STM    6,7,TEMP1          STORE UN-NORMLZD LONG-FORMAT X

                                      25   * NORMALIZE BY MULTIPLYING UN-NORMALIZED  X  BY  +1

   00002A 68 00 C042    000048        26          LD     0,TEMP1            FPR#0 = UN-NORMLZD X
   00002E 6C 00 C0A2    0000A8        27          MD     0,=D'1'               * FLO-PT 1
   000032 70 03 0000    000000        28          STE    0,0(3)             STORE NORMLZD SHORT-FRMAT VIA R3

                                      29   * RESTORE REGISTERS AND RETURN TO CALLING PROGRAM

   000036 68 00 C04A    000050        30          LD     0,TEMP2            F.P.REG #0
   00003A 58 D0 C05E    000064        31          L      13,SAVE+4          STANDARD EXIT
   00003E 98 EC D00C                  32          LM     14,12,12(13)
   000042 07 FE                       33          BR     14

   000048                             34   TEMP1   DS     D                 TEMP SPACE FOR UN-NORMLZD VALUE
   000050                             35   TEMP2   DS     D                 TEMP SPACE FOR F.P.REG #0
   000058 4E000000                    36   FCON    DC     X'4E000000'       SHORT FORMAT UN-NORMLZD 0 16**14
   00005C 80000000                    37   SIGN    DC     X'80000000'       SIGN BIT
   000060                             38   SAVE    DS     18F

   0000A8 4110000000000000            39
                                      40           END
```

Conversion between Floating-Point and EBCDIC Text String

As has already been mentioned, the general format of an EBCDIC floating-point number is

$$\underbrace{\pm}_{\text{sign}} \quad \underbrace{xxx.....xx}_{\substack{\text{integer} \\ \text{portion}}} . \underbrace{xx.....xx}_{\substack{\text{fraction} \\ \text{portion}}} \quad \underbrace{E \pm n}_{\text{power of ten}}$$

It will be assumed that the fraction and integer portions each consist of seven or fewer digits.

When converting from EBCDIC text to floating-point format, the text string is scanned from left to right to determine four things: (1) the sign of the number, (2) the digits in the integer portion, (3) the digits in the fraction portion, and (4) the power of ten, including its sign. The integer portion, fraction portion, and power of ten are each considered to be integers, which we shall denote by J, K, and N, respectively. The floating-point number represented in EBCDIC format by this scheme can thus be evaluated from the expression

$$\left(J + \frac{K}{10^7}\right) \times 10^N$$

where $N = \pm n$, and $K < 10^7$.

TXTFP   The problem of scanning the text string and converting the three integers to full-word binary format will not be discussed since it does not involve any new concepts or techniques. Consequently the subroutine TXTFP shown in Figure 13.7 starts with the assumption that J, K, and N are given

Figure 13.6 *Convert floating-point to integer format.*

```
FLAG LOCTN OBJECT CODE     ADDR1  ADDR2  STMNT M SOURCE STATEMENT

                                          3    * SUBROUTINE  XFIX(X,J)  CONVERTS SHORT FLO-PT  X  TO INTEGER  J
                                          4    * CODE RETURNED IN REGISTER 15
                                          5    *      R15 = 0  IF  X  IS IN RANGE OF FULL-WORD INTEGER VALUES
                                          6    *      R15 = 4  IF  X  NOT IN FULL-WORD INTEGER RANGE
                                          7    *
     000000                               8    XFIX      CSECT
     000000 90 EC D00C                     9              STM     14,12,12(13)          STANDARD ENTRY
     000004 05 C0                         10              BALR    12,0
     000006                               11              USING   *,12
     000006 50 D0 C086     00008C         12              ST      13,SAVE+4
     00000A 41 D0 C082     000088         13              LA      13,SAVE
     00000E 60 00 C062     000068         14              STD     0,TEMP2               SAVE F.P.REG #0

                                         15    * GET PARAMETERS FROM CALLING PROGRAM
     000012 98 23 1000                    16              LM      2,3,0(1)              R2= ADDRESS OF SHORT-FORMAT  X
                                         17    *                                       R3= ADDRESS OF RESULT  J
                                         18    * DETERMINE RANGE OF  X
     000016 68 00 C0CA     000000         19              LD      0,=D'0'               LOWER-HALF OF F.P.REG#0 IS 0
     00001A 78 02 0000     000000         20              LE      0,0(2)                UPPER-HALF OF F.P.REG#0 IS X
     00001E 32 00                         21              LTER    0,0                   DETERMINE SIGN OF  X
     000020 47 40 C02A     000030         22              BM      XNEG
     000024 79 00 C07E     000084         23              CE      0,FCONP               IF  X > 0  COMPARE IT TO LARGEST
     000028 47 20 C056     00005C         24              BH      XFIXERR                 SHORT-FORMAT INTGR  < 2**31
     00002C 47 F0 C032     000038         25              B       XFIXOK
     000030 79 00 C07A     000080         26    XNEG      CE      0,FCONM               IF  X < 0 COMPARE IT TO -2**31
     000034 47 40 C056     00005C         27              BL      XFIXERR                 X < -2**31 NOT CONVERTIBLE

                                         28    * CONVERT X   (ALREADY IN FPR#0)   TO INTEGER FORMAT
     000038 6E 00 C072     000078         29    XFIXOK    AW      0,FCON2               UN-NORMLZE, COMPLEMENT IF NEGTVE
     00003C 60 00 C06A     000070         30              STD     0,TEMP1               STORE INTEGER IN 'TEMP1+4'
     000040 D2 03 3000C06E        000074  31              MVC     0(4,3),TEMP1+4        COPY IT TO RESULT J, VIA R3
     000046 48 F0 C0D2     0000D8         32              LH      15,=H'0'              SET RETURN CODE FOR VALID X

                                         33    * NORMAL EXIT
     00004A 68 00 C062     000068         34    XFIXX     LD      0,TEMP2               RESTORE FPR#0
     00004E 58 D0 C086     00008C         35              L       13,SAVE+4
     000052 58 ED D00C     00000C         36              L       14,12(13)             RESTORE ALL BUT R15
     000056 98 0C D014                    37              LM      0,12,20(13)
     00005A 07 FE                         38              BR      14

                                         39    * SET ERROR CODE IN R15 WHEN  X  NOT IN FULL-WD INTGR RANGE
     00005C 48 F0 C0D4     0000DA         40    XFIXERR   LH      15,=H'4'
     000060 47 F0 C044     00004A         41              B       XFIXX

     000068                               42    TEMP2     DS      D                     TEMP SPACE FOR F.P.REG#0
     000070                               43    TEMP1     DS      D                     TEMP SPACE FOR UN-NORMLZD INTGER
     000078 4E00000100000000              44    FCON2     DC      X'4E00000100000000'   UN-NORMALIZED  2**32
     000080 C8800000                      45    FCONM     DC      X'C8800000'           NORMALIZED  -2**31
     000084 487FFFFF                      46    FCONP     DC      X'487FFFFF'            NORMALIZED  2**31 - 256
                                         47    * NOTE   2**31 - 256  IS LARGEST SHORT FORMAT INTGR LESS THAN  2**31
     000088                               48    SAVE      DS      18F
     0000D0 000000000000000D              49
     0000D8 0000
     0000DA 0004
                                         50              END
```

as binary integers. The previously mentioned subroutine (XFLOAT, in Fig. 13.5) is used to convert J and K to floating-point format, and the floating-point representation of 10^N is determined from tables.

Similarly, for the problem of converting from floating-point to EBCDIC text, the subroutine FPTXT in Figure 13.8 computes the integers J, K, and N but does not create the actual text strings. A subsequent conversion (not shown) via the CVD and UNPK, ED, or EDMK instructions is required to produce the EBCDIC text strings once the binary representations of J, K, and N are known. It should be noted that the FPTXT subroutine creates full-word representations of J, K, and N with $-9 \leq J \leq +9$, $-9999999 \leq K \leq +9999999$, and $-75 \leq N \leq +75$.

FPTXT

You are urged to study the two subroutines in detail by tracing their execution with a few representative numbers. The method used to convert from powers of 10 to powers of 16 is but one of many possible methods; this is true for the reverse conversions from powers of 16 to powers of 10. Both methods use tables to accomplish the conversions. This has the advantage of relative simplicity over most other methods, but it has two disadvantages: (1) a somewhat longer execution time than might be achieved with more sophisticated methods and (2) a possible loss of accuracy in the least significant digit due to the multiplications and divisions used in achieving the results.

Figure 13.7 Convert mixed number to floating-point format.

```
FLAG LOCTN OBJECT CODE      ADDR1  ADDR2  STMNT M SOURCE STATEMENT

                                      3    * SUBROUTINE TXTFP(J,K,N,X)
                                      4    *
                                      5    * CONVERTS  (J,K,N)  TO SINGLE-PRECISION FLO-PT NUMBER  X
                                      6    *    (J,K,N) CONSISTS OF THREE INTEGERS  J, K, N
                                      7    *   WHICH CORRESPOND TO EXTERNAL FLO-PT FORMAT  J.K*10**N
                                      8    * NO MORE THAN 7 SIGNIFICANT DIGITS ADVISED FOR J AND K
                                      9    *
                                     10    *  CONSTRAINTS ... ABS(N) <= 75,  ABS(K) < 10**7,  J & K SAME SIGN
                                     11    * RETURN CODE IN REG 15 ... = 0 IF BOTH  N  AND  K  ARE WITHIN LIMITS
                                     12    *                          = 4 IF EITHER  N  OR  K  NOT WITHIN LIMITS

000000                               13    TXTFP   CSECT
000000 90 EC D00C                    14            STM    14,12,12(13)        STANDARD ENTRY
000004 05 C0                         15            BALR   12,0
000006                               16            USING  *,12
000006 50 D0 C236           00023C   17            ST     13,SAVE+4
00000A 41 D0 C232           000238   18            LA     13,SAVE
00000E 60 00 C202           000208   19            STD    0,TEMP              SAVE FPR#0

                                     20    * GET CALLING PROGRAM'S PARAMETERS

000012 98 25 1000                    21            LM     2,5,0(1)            R2= ADDR OF J
                                     22    *                                 R3= ADDR OF K
                                     23    *                                 R4= ADDR OF N
                                     24    *                                 R5= ADDR OF RESULT X
000016 45 E0 C0B8           0000BE   25            BAL    14,TXTTEST          SEE IF  K  AND  N  WITHIN LIMITS
00001A 49 F0 C2AE           0002B4   26            CH     15,=H'4'            INVALID IF RETURN CODE = 4
00001E 47 80 C086           00008C   27            BE     TXTFPXX

                                     28    * CONVERT  J  TO SHORT-FORMAT

000022 D2 07 C21A2000       000220   29            MVC    TEMPJ,0(2)          PUT  J  IN TEMP AREA
000028 41 10 C27A           000280   30            LA     1,=A(TEMPJ,XJ)      CALL 'XFLOAT' SUBROUTINE AND
00002C 58 F0 C282           000288   31            L      15,=V(XFLOAT)       HAVE RESULT STORED IN 'XJ'
000030 05 EF                         32            BALR   14,15

                                     33    * CONVERT  K  TO SHORT-FORMAT

000032 D2 07 C2223000       000228   34            MVC    TEMPK,0(3)          PUT  K  IN TEMP AREA
000038 41 10 C286           00028C   35            LA     1,=A(TEMPK,XK)      CALL 'XFLOAT' SUBROUTINE AND
00003C 58 F0 C282           000288   36            L      15,=V(XFLOAT)       HAVE RESULT STORED IN 'XK'
000040 05 EF                         37            BALR   14,15

                                     38    * COMPUTE FLOATING-POINT VALUE  J + ( K / 10**7 )

000042 78 00 C216           00021C   39            LE     0,XK                TEST  K
000046 79 00 C28E           000294   40            CE     0,=E'0'             IF  K = 0
00004A 47 70 C054           00005A   41            BNE    TXTFP1                 AND
00004E 79 00 C212           000218   42            CE     0,XJ                IF  J = 0
000052 47 80 C05C           00005C   43            BE     TXTFP3                 THEN BYPASS ADDITION
000056 47 F0 C058           00005E   44            B      TXTFP2
00005A 7D 00 C292           000298   45    TXTFP1  DE     0,=E'1E7'           COMPUTE  K / 10**7
00005E 7A 00 C212           000218   46    TXTFP2  AE     0,XJ                THEN ADD  J
000062 70 00 C22A           000230   47    TXTFP3  STE    0,XTEMP             STORE RESULT TEMPORARILY
                                     48    * COMPUTE  ( J + K/10**7 ) * 10**N

000066 58 44 0000           000000   49            L      4,0(4)              R4 = N
00006A 12 44                         50            LTR    4,4                 DETERMINE SIGN OF  N
00006C 47 80 C07E           000084   51            BZ     TXTFPX              IF N = 0, THEN  10**N = 1
000070 41 A0 C296           00029C   52            LA     10,=A(P1,P2)        IF N > 0, USE TABLES  P1,P2
000074 47 20 C076           00007C   53            BP     TXTFP4
000078 41 A0 C29E           0002A4   54            LA     10,=A(M1,M2)        IF N < 0, USE TABLES  M1,M2
00007C 45 E0 C098           00009E   55    TXTFP4  BAL    14,TENN             DETERMINE  10**N  FROM TBLS
000080 7C 00 C22A           000230   56            ME     0,XTEMP            10**N  *  ( J + ( K/10**7 ) )

000084 70 05 0000           000000   57    TXTFPX  STE    0,0(5)              SAVE SHORT-FORMAT ANSR FOR CALLR
000088 48 F0 C2B0           0002B6   58            LH     15,=H'0'            RETURN CODE = 0 SINCE PARAMS OK

00008C 68 00 C202           000208   59    TXTFPXX LD     0,TEMP              RESTORE FPR#0
000090 58 D0 C236           00023C   60            L      13,SAVE+4           RESTORE GENERAL REGISTERS
000094 58 ED 000C           00000C   61            L      14,12(13)               (BUT NOT REG 15)
000098 98 0C D014                    62            LM     0,12,20(13)
00009C 07 FE                         63            BR     14

                                     64    * INTERNAL SUBROUTINE TO DETERMINE  10**N  FROM TABLES
                                     65    *
                                     66    * UPON ENTRY,   R4 = N
                                     67    *              R10 = ADDR OF TWO TABLE ADDRESSES
                                     68    *                    1ST ADDR IS TABLE #1   P1 IF N>0,  M1 IF  N<0
                                     69    *                    2ND ADDR IS TABLE #2   P2 IF N>0,  M2 IF  N<0
```

Figure 13.7   continued

```
FLAG LOCTN OBJECT CODE      ADDR1  ADDR2  STMNT M SOURCE STATEMENT

                                           70  *
                                           71  * UPON EXIT,   F.P.REG#0  CONTAINS  10**N
       00009E 98 89 A000                    72  TENN     LM     8,9,0(10)           GET ADDRS FOR TABLES #1 & #2
       0000A2 10 64                         73           LPR    6,4         GET ABS(N)
       0000A4 8C 60 0003     000003         74           SRDL   6,3                 ABS(N)/8, SAVE REMAINDER IN R7
       0000A8 89 60 0003     000003         75           SLL    6,3                 USE QUOTIENT AS INDEX FOR TBL #2
       0000AC 68 06 9000                    76           LD     0,0(6,9)            GET 10**N1, N1=0,8,16,... OR 72
       0000B0 48 60 C2B0     0002B6         77           LH     6,=H'0'             CLEAR REG 6
       0000B4 8D 60 0006     000006         78           SLDL   6,6                 USE REMAINDER AS INDEX TO TBL #1
       0000B8 6C 06 8000                    79           MD     0,0(6,8)            10**N = 10**N1 * 10**N2, N2=0,1..OR 7
       0000BC 07 FE                         80  TENNX    BR     14

                                           81  * INTERNAL SUBROUTINE TO DETERMINE IF ABS(N) <= 75  AND  ABS(K) < 10**7
                                           82  *              ENTERED WITH  R3 = ADDR OF  K
                                           83  *                            R4 = ADDR OF  N
                                           84  *              EXIT WITH   R15  = 4  IF EITHER RANGE NOT O.K.
       0000BE 58 84 0000     000000         85  TXTTEST  L      8,0(4)      GET N
       0000C2 10 88                         86           LPR    8,8         ABS(N)
       0000C4 59 80 C2A6     0002AC         87           C      8,=F'75'
       0000C8 47 20 C0D6     0000DC         88           BH     TXTTESTX    ERROR IF  ABS(N) > 75
       0000CC 58 83 0000     000000         89           L      8,0(3)      GET  K
       0000D0 10 88                         90           LPR    8,8         ABS(K)
       0000D2 59 80 C2AA     0002B0         91           C      8,=F'1E7'
       0000D6 47 B0 C0D6     0000DC         92           BNL    TXTTESTX    ERROR IF  ABS(K) NOT < 10**7
       0000DA 07 FE                         93           BR     14
       0000DC 48 F0 C2AE     0002B4         94  TXTTESTX LH     15,=H'4'
       0000E0 07 FE                         95           BR     14          ERROR CODE IS  R15 = 4
                                           96  * FOLLOWING TWO TABLES --- P1  AND  P2 --- USED WHEN  N > 0

                                           97  * TABLE OF  10**N, FOR N = 0,1,2,3,...,7

       0000E8 4110000000000000              98  P1       DC     D'1'
       0000F0 41A0000000000000              99           DC     D'1E1,1E2,1E3,1E4,1E5,1E6,1E7'

                                          100  * TABLE OF  10**N, FOR  N = 0,8,16,24,...,72

       000128 4110000000000000             101  P2       DC     D'1,1E8'
       000138 4E2386F26FC10000             102           DC     D'1E16,1E24,1E32,1E40'
       000158 68AF298D050E4396             103           DC     D'1E48,1E56,1E64,1E72'


                                          104  * FOLLOWING TWO TABLES --- M1  AND  M2 --- USED WHEN  N < 0

       000178 4110000000000000             105  M1       DC     D'1E0,1E-1,1E-2,1E-3,1E-4'
       0001A0 3CA7C5AC471B4784             106           DC     D'1E-5,1E-6,1E-7'

       0001B8 4110000000000000             107  M2       DC     D'1E0,1E-8,1E-16,1E-24,1E-32'
       0001E0 1F8B61313BBABCE3             108           DC     D'1E-40,1E-48,1E-56,1E-64,1E-72'

                                          109  * OTHER CONSTANTS AND TEMPORARY AREAS

       000208                              110  TEMP     DS     D                   FOR FPR#0
       000210                              111  TEMP1    DS     D                   FOR 10**ABS(N)
       000218                              112  XJ       DS     F                   INTEGER J
       00021C                              113  XK       DS     F                   INTEGER  K
       000220                              114  TEMPJ    DS     D                   FLO-PT  J
       000228                              115  TEMPK    DS     D                   FLO-PT   K
       000230                              116  XTEMP    DS     D                   J + ( K / 10**7 )
       000238                              117  SAVE     DS     18F                 REGISTER SAVE AREA

       000280 0000022000000218             118
       000288 00000000
       00028C 000002280000021C
       000294 00000000
       000298 46989680
       00029C 000000E800000128
       0002A4 0000017800000188
       0002AC 0000004B
       0002B0 00989680
       0002B4 0004
       0002B6 0000
                                          119           END
```

Figure 13.8 *Convert floating-point format to mixed number.*

```
FLAG LOCTN OBJECT CODE     ADDR1  ADDR2  STMNT M SOURCE STATEMENT

                                          3    * SUBROUTINE FPTXT (X,J,K,N)
                                          4    *
                                          5    * CONVERTS A SHORT-FORMAT NORMALIZED FLOATING POINT NUMBER X
                                          6    *    INTO THREE INTEGERS  J, K, N
                                          7    *    CORRESPONDING TO EXTERNAL FLO-PT FORMAT  J.K*10**N
                                          8    * ABS(J) IS ALWAYS LESS THAN 10.
                                          9    * BOTH J AND K HAVE THE SAME SIGN
                                          10   *    IF NEGATIVE, BOTH ARE IN 2'S COMPLEMENT FORM.
                                          11   *
     000000                               12   FPTXT    CSECT
     000000 90 EC D00C                    13            STM    14,12,12(13)             STANDARD ENTRY
     000004 05 C0                         14            BALR   12,0
     000006                               15            USING  *,12
     000006 50 D0 C302     000308         16            ST     13,SAVE+4
     00000A 41 D0 C2FE     000304         17            LA     13,SAVE
     00000E 60 00 C2BA     0002C0         18            STD    0,FPR0                   SAVE FLO-PT REGS
     000012 60 20 C2C2     0002C8         19            STD    2,FPR2
     000016 60 40 C2CA     0002D0         20            STD    4,FPR4
     00001A 60 60 C2D2     0002D8         21            STD    6,FPR6
     00001E D2 0B C2DAC352 0002E0 000358  22            MVC    INT(12),=F'0,0,0'        (J,K,N) = (0,0,0)  INITIALLY
                                          23   *
                                          24   * GET PARAMETERS FROM CALLING PROGRAM
     000024 98 25 1000                    25            LM     2,5,0(1)                 R2= ADDRESS OF X
                                          26   *                                       R3= ADDR OF J
                                          27   *                                       R4= ADDR OF K
                                          28   *                                       R5= ADDR OF N

                                          29   * DETERMINE WHETHER  X = 0, OR IF  ABS(X) > 1 , < 1 , OR = 1

     000028 68 00 C34A     000350         30            LD     0,=D'0'                  CLEAR LOWER-HALF OF FPR#0
     00002C 78 02 0000     000000         31            LE     0,0(2)                   PUT  X  IN UPPER-HALF OF FPR#0
     000030 20 40                         32            LPDR   4,0                      FPR#4 = ABS(X)
     000032 20 60                         33            LPDR   6,0                      FPR#6 = ABS(X)
     000034 47 80 C0CC     0000D2         34            BZ     FPTXTX                   IF X=0, (J,K,N) = (0,0,0)
     000038 79 40 C35E     000364         35            CE     4,=E'1'                  TEST ABS(X)
     00003C 47 40 C048     00004E         36            BL     FPTXT0                   IF < 1, MUST FIND 10**(-N)
     000040 47 20 C05C     000062         37            BH     FPTXT1                   IF > 1, MUST FIND 10**(+N)
     000044 D2 03 C2DAC362 0002E0 000368  38            MVC    TEMPJ,=F'1'              IF = 1, (J,K,N) = (1,0,0)
     00004A 47 F0 C0CC     0000D2         39            B      FPTXTX

                                          40   * ABS(X) < 1

     00004E 41 A0 C366     00036C         41   FPTXT0   LA     10,=A(M1,M2,BH)          PARAMS FOR 'PTEN'
     000052 45 E0 C0F8     0000FE         42            BAL    14,PTEN                  DETERMINE  N  AND  10**N
     000056 11 00                         43            LNR    0,0                      ABS(N)  RETURNED IN RO
     000058 50 00 C2E2     0002E8         44            ST     0,TEMPN                  STORE  -N
     00005C 2D 40                         45            DDR    4,0                      FLO-PT 10**N RETURNED IN FPR#0
     00005E 47 F0 C06A     000070         46            B      FPTXT2                   FPR#4 NOW HAS  ABS(X) / 10**N

                                          47   * ABS(X) > 1

     000062 41 A0 C372     000378         48   FPTXT1   LA     10,=A(P1,P2,BL)          PARAMS FOR 'PTEN'
     000066 45 E0 C0F8     0000FE         49            BAL    14,PTEN                  DETERMINE  N  AND  10**N
     00006A 50 00 C2E2     0002E8         50            ST     0,TEMPN                  ABS(N)  RETURNED IN RO
     00006E 2D 40                         51            DDR    4,0                      FPR#4 = ABS(X)/10**N
                                          52   * DETERMINE INTEGER  (J)  AND FRACTIONAL  (K)  COMPONENTS
                                          53   *   OF ABS(X)/10**N  IN SHORT-FORMAT.

     000070 79 40 C35E     000364         54   FPTXT2   CE     4,=E'1'                  IF ABS(X)/10**N  < 1 ,
     000074 47 40 C088     00008E         55            BL     FPTXT2A                  THEN INTEGER 'J'  IS ZERO.
     000078 70 40 C2DA     0002E0         56            STE    4,TEMPJ                  SAVE  ABS(X)/10**N  (TEMPORARY)
     00007C D4 03 C2DAC2FA 0002E0 000300  57            NC     TEMPJ(4),FCON1           ERASE THE FRACTIONAL 'K' PORTION
                                          58   *                                        LEAVING FLO-PT 'J'
     000082 79 40 C2DA     0002E0         59            CE     4,TEMPJ                  IF DIFFERENCE IS ZERO
     000086 47 80 C0AA     0000B0         60            BE     FPTXT3A                  THEN FRACTION IS ZERO.
     00008A 7B 40 C2DA     0002E0         61            SE     4,TEMPJ                  COMPUTE FRACTIONAL PORTION 'K'
     00008E 70 40 C2DE     0002E4         62   FPTXT2A  STE    4,TEMPK                  SAVE FRACTIONAL PORTION
     000092 94 00 C2DE     0002E4         63            NI     TEMPK,X'00'              ERASE CHARACTERISTIC AND SIGN

                                          64   * CONVERT FRACTIONAL PORTION TO FIXED-POINT INTEGER RESULT  K

     000096 58 90 C2DE     0002E4         65            L      9,TEMPK                  GET FRACTL PORTION AS INTEGER
     00009A 5C 80 C37E     000384         66            M      8,=F'1E7'                MULTIPLY BY  10**7
     00009E 8F 80 0008     000008         67            SLDA   8,8                      SHIFT PRODUCT INTO  R8
     0000A2 91 80 2000                    68            TM     0(2),X'80'               TEST SIGN BIT OF  X
     0000A6 47 80 C0A6     0000AC         69            BZ     FPTXT3                   IF SIGN BIT 0, K IS POSITIVE
     0000AA 11 88                         70            LNR    8,8                      OTHERWISE, MAKE K NEGATIVE
     0000AC 50 80 C2DE     0002E4         71   FPTXT3   ST     8,TEMPK                  'TEMPK' = K

                                          72   * CREATE FIXED-POINT INTEGER RESULT  J

     0000B0 68 00 C34A     000350         73   FPTXT3A  LD     0,=D'0'
     0000B4 78 00 C2DA     0002E0         74            LE     0,TEMPJ                  FPR#0 = J AS FLO-PT NUMBER
     0000B8 6E 00 C2F2     0002F8         75            AW     0,FCON2                  UN-NORMLZE, COMPLEMENT IF NEGTVE
     0000BC 60 00 C2EA     0002F0         76            STD    0,FCON3                  LOWER-HALF OF FPR#0 IS J
     0000C0 58 90 C2EE     0002F4         77            L      9,FCON3+4                GET INTEGER REPRESENTING J
     0000C4 91 80 2000                    78            TM     0(2),X'80'               TEST SIGN OF X
```

Figure 13.8   continued

```
FLAG LOCTN OBJECT CODE      ADDR1  ADDR2  STMNT M SOURCE STATEMENT

     0000C8 47 80 C0C8      0000CE          79          BZ    FPTXT4              IF SIGN BIT ZERO,  J IS POSITIVE
     0000CC 11 99                           80          LNR   9,9                 OTHERWISE, MAKE J NEGATIVE
     0000CE 50 90 C2DA      0002E0          81   FPTXT4 ST    9,TEMPJ             'TEMPJ' = J

                                            82   * EXIT FROM  'FPTXT'  SUBROUTINE

     0000D2 D2 03 3000C2DA         0002E0   83   FPTXTX MVC   0(4,3),TEMPJ        GIVE RESULTS TO CALLING PROGRAM
     0000D8 D2 03 4000C2DE         0002E4   84          MVC   0(4,4),TEMPK
     0000DE D2 03 5000C2E2         0002E8   85          MVC   0(4,5),TEMPN
     0000E4 68 00 C2BA      0002C0          86          LD    0,FPR0              RESTORE FLO-PT REGISTERS
     0000E8 68 20 C2C2      0002C8          87          LD    2,FPR2
     0000EC 68 40 C2CA      0002D0          88          LD    4,FPR4
     0000F0 68 60 C2D2      0002D8          89          LD    6,FPR6
     0000F4 58 D0 C302      000308          90          L     13,SAVE+4           RESTORE GENERAL REGISTERS
     0000F8 98 EC D00C                      91          LM    14,12,12(13)
     0000FC 07 FE                           92          BR    14
                                            93   * INTERNAL SUBROUTINE TO DETERMINE INTEGER POWER OF 10 CORRESPONDING TO
                                            94   *    CHARACTERISTIC OF VALUE GIVEN IN FPR#6 UPON ENTRY TO THIS ROUTINE
                                            95   *
                                            96   * UPON ENTRY,  F.P.REG #6 = ABS(X)
                                            97   *              GENL REG 10 = ADDR OF PARAMETERS (SEE COMMENTS BELOW)
                                            98   *
                                            99   * UPON EXIT,   F.P.REG #0 = 10**N
                                           100   *             GENL REG 0 = ABS(N)
                                           101   *    WHERE  N  IS THE INTEGER POWER OF 10 THAT WAS TO BE DETERMINED
                                           102   *

     0000FE 98 8A A000                     103   PTEN   LM    8,10,0(10)          R8 = ADDR OF TABLE #1
                                           104   *                               R9 = ADDR OF TABLE #2
                                           105   *                               R10 = ADDR OF CONDTL BRANCH TBL
     000102 48 70 C382      000388         106          LH    7,=H'0'             R7 = INITIAL VALUE OF  N

                                           107   * ASSUME ABS(N) = P + Q, WHERE P AND Q ARE NON-NEG INTGRS &  Q < 10
                                           108   *
                                           109   *    FIRST, DETERMINE VALUE OF P FROM TABLE #1

     000106 69 68 0008      000008         110   PTEN1  CD    6,8(8)              COMPARE ABS(X) TO VALUES IN TBL1
     00010A 44 0A 0000      000000         111          EX    0,0(10)             BRANCH WHEN RANGE FOUND
     00010E 41 88 0008      000008         112          LA    8,8(8)              INCR ADDR TO NEXT ENTRY IN TBL 1
     000112 4A 70 C384      00038A         113          AH    7,=H'10'            INCR VALUE OF  P BY 10
     000116 47 F0 C100      000106         114          B     PTEN1               CONTINUE SEARCH
     00011A 6D 68 0000      000000         115   PTEN1X DD    6,0(8)              FACTOR OUT 10**P FROM ABS(X)

                                           116   *    THEN, DETERMINE VALUE OF  Q  FROM TABLE #2

     00011E 69 69 0008      000008         117   PTEN2  CD    6,8(9)              COMPARE ABS(X)/10**P  TO EACH
     000122 44 0A 0004      000004         118          EX    0,4(10)                VALUE IN TBL 2; BRANCH WHEN
                                           119   *                                   RANGE IS FOUND
     000126 41 99 0008      000008         120          LA    9,8(9)              INCR ADDR TO NEXT ENTRY IN TBL 2
     00012A 4A 70 C386      00038C         121          AH    7,=H'1'             INCR VALUE OF  P+Q  BY 1
     00012E 47 F0 C118      00011E         122          B     PTEN2

                                           123   * FINALLY, COMPUTE  10**N

     000132 68 08 0000      000000         124   PTEN2X LD    0,0(8)              GET      10**P
     000136 6C 09 0000      000000         125          MD    0,0(9)              FPR#0 = 10**N = 10**P * 10**Q
     00013A 18 07                          126          LR    0,7                 R0 = ABS(N)
     00013C 07 FE                          127          BR    14

                                           128   * CONDITIONAL BRANCH TABLES
                                           129   *    BH   USED WHEN   ABS(X) < 1 I.E.,  N < 0
                                           130   *    BL   USED WHEN   ABS(X) > 1 I.E.,  N > 0

     00013E 47 20 C114      00011A         131   BH     BH    PTEN1X
     000142 47 20 C12C      000132         132          BH    PTEN2X
     000146 47 40 C114      00011A         133   BL     BL    PTEN1X
     00014A 47 40 C12C      000132         134          BL    PTEN2X
                                           135   * FOLLOWING TWO TABLES  --- P1  AND P2  --- USED WHEN  N > 0.

                                           136   * TABLE #1  LONG FLO-PT  10**P, P = 0,10,20,30,...,70,80

     000150 4110000000000000              137   P1     DC    D'1E0,1E10,1E20,1E30,1E40,1E50,1E60,1E70'
     000190 7FFFFFFFFFFFFFFF              138          DC    X'7FFFFFFFFFFFFFFF'

                                           139   * TABLE #2  LONG FLO-PT  10**Q, Q = 0,1,2,3,...,8,9,10

     000198 4110000000000000              140   P2     DC    D'1E0,1E1,1E2,1E3,1E4,1E5,1E6,1E7,1E8,1E9,1E10'

                                           141   * FOLLOWING TWO TABLES  --- M1  AND M2  --- USED WHEN  N < 0.

                                           142   *TABLE #1 FOR NEGATIVE VALUES OF  P  I.E.,
                                           143   *         10**P FOR P  = 0,-10,-20,-30,...,-70

     0001F0                               144   M1     DS    0D
     0001F0 4110000000000000              145          DC    D'1E0,1E-10,1E-20,1E-30,1E-40'
     000218 173BDCF495A9703E              146          DC    D'1E-50,1E-60,1E-70'
     000230 0000000000000000              147          DC    X'0000000000000000'

                                           148   *TABLE #2 FOR NEGATIVE Q ---
                                           149   *         10**Q FOR Q = 0,-1,-2,-3,...,-16
```

Floating-Point Operations   365

Figure 13.8   *continued*

```
FLAG LOCTN OBJECT CODE      ADDR1  ADDR2  STMNT M SOURCE STATEMENT

     000238 4110000000000000          150  M2      DC      D'1E0,1E-1,1E-2,1E-3,1E-4,1E-5'
     000268 3C10C6F7A0B5ED8D          151          DC      D'1E-6,1E-7,1E-8,1E-9,1E-10'
     000290 37AFEBFF0BCB24AB          152          DC      D'1E-11,1E-12,1E-13,1E-14,1E-15,1E-16'
                                      153  *
                                      154  * CONSTANTS AND TEMPORARY AREAS

     0002C0                           155  FPR0    DS      D              F.P.REG#0
     0002C8                           156  FPR2    DS      D              F.P.REG#2
     0002D0                           157  FPR4    DS      D              F.P.REG#4
     0002D8                           158  FPR6    DS      D              F.P.REG#6
     0002E0                           159  INT     DS      0F
     0002E0                           160  TEMPJ   DS      F              INTEGER RESULT J
     0002E4                           161  TEMPK   DS      F              INTEGER RESULT K
     0002E8                           162  TEMPN   DS      F              INTEGER RESULT N
     0002F0                           163  FCON3   DS      D              TEMP SPACE FOR J
     0002F8 4E00000100000000          164  FCON2   DC      X'4E00000100000000'  UNNORMALIZED  2**32
     000300 FFF00000                  165  FCON1   DC      X'FFF00000'          SIGN, CHAR, AND 1ST HEX DIGIT
     000304                           166  SAVE    DS      18F            GENERAL REGISTERS
     000350 0000000000000000          167
     000358 000000000000000
     000364 41100000
     000368 00000001
     00036C 000001F000000238
     000378 0000015000000198
     000384 00989680
     000388 0000
     00038A 000A
     00038C 0001

                                      168          END
```

Converting by Hand

    In hand calculations, unlike the method used in the accompanying programs, conversion of a number from decimal scientific notation $(P \times 10^N)$ to hexadecimal floating-point representation consists of three steps.

Step 1   Convert $P \times 10^N$ to $(P \times 16^W) \times 16^K$,
         where $W + K = N/(\log_{10}16)$, with $|W| < 1$ and $K =$ an integer.

Step 2   Convert $P \times 16^W$ to $0.H_{16} \times 16^M$,
         where M is an integer, and $0.H_{16}$ is in normalized form.

Step 3   Combine the results of Steps 1 and 2 to obtain the answer:
         $P \times 10^N = 0.H_{16} \times 16^{M+K}$.

To illustrate, suppose $P \times 10^N$ is 3.4×10^2. Then from Step 1 we find that $W + K = 2/1.204120 = 1.660964$, so $K = 1$ and $W = 0.660964$. In other words, $3.4 \times 10^2 = (3.4 \times 16^{0.660964}) \times 16^1$. Applying Step 2, we find that $3.4 \times 16^{0.660964} = 3.4 \times 6.25 = 21.25_{10} = 15.4_{16} = 0.154_{16} \times 16^2$, so that $0.H_{16} = 0.154_{16}$ and $M = 2$. From Step 3 the result is then found to be

$$3.4 \times 10^2 = 0.154_{16} \times 16^3$$

This procedure is of course valid for any N: positive, negative, or zero. For example, it can be used to show that $3.4 \times 10^{-2} = 0.8B439581..._{16} \times 16^{-1}$, which in hexadecimal short-format notation is 3F8B4396. Similarly, $3.4 \times 10^0 = 0.36666666..._{16} \times 16^1$, i.e., 41366666 in short format.

13.9 SUMMARY

The advantages of using the floating-point instructions and data formats are that (1) the range of numbers that may be represented and operated on is far greater than that attainable with the integer or packed-decimal representations for a given number of bits, and (2) the execution of floating-point instructions frees the programmer from having to align hexadecimal points or other fractional indicators. The range of numbers includes zero and all 6-, 14-, and 28-digit hexadecimal integers as well as mixed numbers whose magnitude is in the approximate range of from 5.4×10^{-79} to 7.2×10^{75}. The instruction set consists of operations analogous to those available for integer arithmetic: loading, storing, and comparing floating-point numbers, testing and/or changing the sign of floating-point numbers, and adding, multiplying, subtracting, and dividing two floating-point numbers. Supplementing these instructions are two special instructions: *halve* (division by two via shifting) and *round* (transforming from long to short or from extended to long formats with the lowest-order digit of the result rounded).

The short, long, and extended formats all consist of a mantissa, a characteristic, and a sign. The characteristic is expressed in 7-bit, excess-64 notation (X'00' through X'7F') representing the decimal integers -64 through $+63$; this is the power of 16 by which the mantissa is multiplied. The mantissa is the magnitude of a 6-, 14-, or 28-digit hexadecimal number always considered to be less than 1 (6 digits in short format, 14 in long format, and 28 in extended). The sign is a single bit representing the algebraic sign of the mantissa.

When adding, subtracting, multiplying, or dividing two floating-point numbers, and when halving a floating-point number, a nonzero result is always expressed in normalized form unless the unnormalized add or subtract instructions are used. (In normalized form, the leading mantissa digit is nonzero, i.e., X'1' through X'F'.) With the unnormalized add and subtract instructions, the result need not be normalized; its form depends on the relative magnitudes and forms of the numbers being added or subtracted. The result of a load or store operation is in the same form—normalized or unnormalized—as the number that is being loaded or stored. Similarly, no normalization takes place in the round instructions. However, when comparing two floating-point numbers, the comparisons take place as though the numbers were both in normalized form, even though the forms of the numbers are not changed by the comparisons.

All floating-point instructions (Fig. 13.9) are of either RR-type or RX-type format. In RR format, both operands designate floating-point registers; in RX format, the first operand designates a floating-point register, the second a main memory address. There are four floating-point registers, each 64 bits long. Their addresses are 0, 2, 4, and 6. The upper half (left-most 32 bits) of each register is used for short-format numbers, the full 64 bits are used for long-format numbers, and the two pairs of registers—0 and 2, and 4 and 6—are used for extended-precision numbers. In the latter case, the address of the first pair is 0, and that of the second is 4. A summary of the instructions that operate on short, long, and extended numbers is given in Figures 13.2 through 13.4. The names and mnemonic opcodes of these instructions bear an obvious and useful similarity to those of the integer instruction set described in Chapter 5.

Floating-point constants can be generated in assembly language with the DC directive and via literals. The E-, D-, and L- data type codes generate the short, long, and extended formats, respectively. However, unlike the provisions for converting numbers between the integer and packed-decimal formats via the CVB and CVD instructions, no comparable instructions exist for converting between integer and floating-point formats, or between packed-decimal and floating-point format. These conversions must be handled via subroutines. Similarly, there are no instructions comparable to PACK, UNPK, ED, or EDMK for converting numeric data between its input or output character representation and its main memory floating-point representation. These operations must be handled via subroutines.

13.10 REVIEW

Floating-Point Numbers In IBM 360 and 370 machine language, each floating-point number is represented as a hexadecimal fraction times a power of 16. The fraction (known also as the *mantissa*) is in sign-magnitude form; the power of 16 (known as the *exponent,* or *characteristic*) is a 7-bit, excess-64 number. The base of 16 itself isn't represented; it's implied.

Excess-64 In excess-64 notation, an exponent of k is represented as $k+64_{10}$.

Range The absolute value of a floating-point number is either zero or is in the range from 16^{-64} to 16^{63}; i.e., approximately 5.4×10^{-79} to 7.2×10^{75}.

Accuracy The fraction portion of a single-precision (short-format) number has 6 hex digits; a double-precision number, 14 hex digits; and an extended-precision number, 28 hex digits. This translates roughly into 7, 16, and 33 decimal digits, respectively.

Normalized Form In this form, a nonzero hex fraction has no leading zeroes. This is similar to scientific notation in the decimal system, in which a number such as 0.00035 is represented at 0.35×10^{-3}. Most floating-point instructions produce results in normalized form (see Fig. 13.9).

Figure 13.9 Summary of floating-point instructions.

opcode and type RX	RR	instruction name	section	cond code	div-chk	exp-ovfl	exp-und	signif	V_1	V_2	result		
AD	ADR	Add normalized (long)	13.7	X		X	X	X	long	long	long	normalized	$V_1 + V_2$
AE	AER	Add normalized (short)	13.7	X		X	X	X	short	short	short	normalized	$V_1 + V_2$
AU	AUR	Add unnormalized (short)	13.7	X		X		X	short	short	short	unnormalized	$V_1 + V_2$
AW	AWR	Add unnormalized (long)	13.7	X		X		X	long	long	long	unnormalized	$V_1 + V_2$
	AXR	Add normalized (extended)	13.7	X		X	X	X	extended	extended	extended	normalized	$V_1 + V_2$
CD	CDR	Compare (long)	13.5	X					long	long	---	---	V_1 vs. V_2
CE	CER	Compare (short)	13.5	X					short	short	---	---	V_1 vs. V_2
DD	DDR	Divide (long)	13.7		X	X	X		long	long	long	normalized	V_1 / V_2
DE	DER	Divide (short)	13.7		X	X	X		short	short	short	normalized	V_1 / V_2
	HDR	Halve (long)	13.7			X			---	long	long	normalized	$\frac{1}{2}(V_2)$
	HER	Halve (short)	13.7			X			---	short	short	normalized	$\frac{1}{2}(V_2)$
	LCDR	Load complement (long)	13.7	X					---	long	long	(unchanged)	$-V_2$
	LCER	Load complement (short)	13.7	X					---	short	short	(unchanged)	$-V_2$
LD	LDR	Load (long)	13.4						---	long	long	(unchanged)	V_2
LE	LER	Load (short)	13.4						---	short	short	(unchanged)	V_2
	LNDR	Load negative (long)	13.7	X					---	long	long	(unchanged)	$-|V_2|$
	LNER	Load negative (short)	13.7	X					---	short	short	(unchanged)	$-|V_2|$
	LPDR	Load positive (long)	13.7	X					---	long	long	(unchanged)	$+|V_2|$
	LPER	Load positive (short)	13.7	X					---	short	short	(unchanged)	$+|V_2|$
	LRDR	Load rounded (ext'd to long)	13.7	X		X			---	extended	long	unnormalized	V_2 rounded
	LRER	Load rounded (long to short)	13.7	X		X			---	long	short	unnormalized	V_2 rounded
	LTDR	Load and test (long)	13.7	X					---	long	long	(unchanged)	V_2
	LTER	Load and test (short)	13.7	X					---	short	short	(unchanged)	V_2
MD	MDR	Multiply (long)	13.7			X	X		long	long	long	normalized	$V_1 \times V_2$ truncated
ME	MER	Multiply (short)	13.7			X	X		short	short	long	normalized	$V_1 \times V_2$
MXD	MXDR	Multiply (long to extended)	13.7			X	X		long	long	extended	normalized	$V_1 \times V_2$
	MXR	Multiply (extended)	13.7			X	X		extended	extended	extended	normalized	$V_1 \times V_2$ truncated
SD	SDR	Subtract normalized (long)	13.7	X		X	X	X	long	long	long	normalized	$V_1 - V_2$
SE	SER	Subtract normalized (short)	13.7	X		X	X	X	short	short	short	normalized	$V_1 - V_2$
STD		Store (long)	13.4						long	---	long	(unchanged)	V_2
STE		Store (short)	13.4						short	---	short	(unchanged)	V_2
SU	SUR	Subtract unnormalized (short)	13.7	X		X		X	short	short	short	unnormalized	$V_1 - V_2$
SW	SWR	Subtract unnormalized (long)	13.7	X		X		X	long	long	long	unnormalized	$V_1 - V_2$
	SXR	Subtract normalized (extended)	13.7	X		X	X	X	extended	extended	extended	normalized	$V_1 - V_2$

Notes: V_1 is the floating point number whose address is specified by the first operand.
V_2 is the floating point number whose address is specified by the second operand.

A result is considered to be zero if its mantissa is zero, irrespective of its characteristic.

Registers There are four 64-bit floating-point registers (addresses 0, 2, 4, and 6) specifically designed for use in floating-point operations.

Instructions Separate from but similar to binary integer instructions, these are divided into three categories: short-format, long-format, and extended-format instructions (see Fig. 13.4). The category of an instruction must match that of the data being operated on. All of the floating-point instructions are either RX-type or RR-type instructions.

Constants Use E-type constants for short-format floating-point numbers, D-type for long-format, and L-type for extended-format. Scale (Sn) and Exponent (En) modifiers are permitted; see also Chapter 6. Length (Ln) modifiers should not be used.

Run-Time Errors *Overflow* occurs if a result exceeds the maximum value that can be represented. *Underflow* occurs if a result is less than the minimum possible value, but not zero. A *divide error* occurs when attempting to divide by zero. A *significance error* occurs if during an addition or subtraction operation, the fraction portion of the sum or difference becomes zero. See also Chapter 11, on the SPM instruction.

Input/Output Operations There are no special instructions available for conversion to and from floating-point format. Subroutines must be used. The fact that the floating-point exponent base is 16 rather than 10 makes such conversions relatively time-consuming.

13.11 REVIEW QUESTIONS

1. From a programming standpoint, what are the advantages of using floating-point numbers?
2. What determines the range of numbers that can be represented in floating-point format? What determines the accuracy?
3. Using hex instead of binary notation, what are the 7-bit excess-64 representations of each of these exponents: -3, -2, -1, 0, $+1$, $+2$, $+3$?
4. What floating-point register addresses are valid for use with single-precision instructions? With double-precision? Extended-precision?
5. What is the advantage (if any) to using a HALVE instruction (HER or HDR) instead of just dividing a number by $+2$?
6. Which floating-point instructions do NOT set the condition code?
7. In what way or ways is the SPM (Set Program Mask) instruction that was discussed in Chapter 11 related to floating-point operations?
8. In short format (single-precision), it is not possible to represent with complete accuracy any *odd* integers with magnitudes greater than 2^{24}. Why is this so? What can be said about the representation of *even* integers greater than 2^{24}?
9. Using the hand calculation method presented at the end of Section 13.8, determine the single-precision floating-point representation of 3.14159265 and of 2.71828183.

Problem Statement

Write an assembly language program that will find the real roots (if any) of a quadratic equation with integer coefficients:

$$M x^2 + Nx + P = 0$$

where M, N, and P are arbitrarily given integers.

The three coefficients are given as input data in integer format, as follows:

$$\text{input record columns}\quad 1\text{--}10 : M$$
$$21\text{--}30 : N$$
$$41\text{--}50 : P$$

The results are to be printed on a single line of output for each set of coefficients that are read, with M, N, and P printed in integer format and the two roots X_1 and X_2 printed in external floating-point format.

For example, if the equation is $3x^2 - 6x + 2 = 0$, then the results would be printed as

M	N	P	X_1	X_2
3	-6	2	1.57735E 00	0.422650E 00

Solution Procedure

The procedure (Figures 13.10a and 13.10b) will use the well-known formulas for finding the real roots of any quadratic equation whose coefficients are as defined above, namely

$$X_1 = \frac{-N + \sqrt{N^2 - 4MP}}{2M} \qquad X_2 = \frac{-N - \sqrt{N^2 - 4MP}}{2M}$$

doing the calculations with short-format numbers and considering these cases separately: (1) $M=N=0$; (2) $M=0$ and $N\neq0$; (3) $M\neq0$ and $N=0$; (4) $M\neq0$ and $N\neq0$. In the latter two cases, if the discriminant N^2-4MP is negative, there are no real roots and a message to that effect will be printed.

We will assume that there exists an external subroutine named SQRT that we can call, with the result being returned in floating-point register 0. We also will assume an arbitrary number of input records, each with a set of integer coefficients representing an equation for which the real roots (if any) are to be determined.

And, finally, we assume the existence of external subroutines to convert a number from its external floating-point format to its internal single-precision format, and vice versa.

(Under certain conditions the solution presented here may not give answers with acceptable accuracy. A discussion of the types of conditions for which this may happen may be found in *Computer Methods for Mathematical Computations* by George E. Forsythe et al. [Englewood Cliffs, N.J.: Prentice-Hall, 1977].)

Figure 13.10a   Pseudocode for sample problem solution in Figure 13.10b.

```
FIND_ROOTS:

  open input and output files;

  REPEAT WHILE there is more data to read

    read one input record;
    convert coefficients M, N, and P to floating-point (short) format;

    IF M = 0  { leading coefficient is zero }
    THEN
      IF N=0
      THEN
        IF P=0
        THEN
          { any number is a solution of 0x² + 0x + 0 = 0 }
        ELSE
          { 0x² + 0x + P = 0 has no solution }
        END IF;
      ELSE
        X1 := -P/N;  { only solution of 0x² + Nx + P = 0 }
      END IF;
    ELSE  { leading coefficient non-zero }
      D := N² - 4MP;  { discriminant }
      IF D < 0
      THEN
        { no real solution }
      ELSE
        IF N = 0
        THEN  { simple formula can be used: Mx² + P = 0 }
          root := square root of -P/M;
          X1 := root;
          X2 := - root;
        ELSE  { use full version of quadratic formula }
          root := square root of D;
          X1 := (- N + root)/2M;
          X2 := (- N - root)/2M;
        END IF;
      END IF;
    END IF;

    print M, N, P, X1, X2;

  END WHILE;

  close input and output files;

EXIT FIND_ROOTS.
```

Figure 13.10b   Solution to sample problem.

```
FLAG LOCTN OBJECT CODE    ADDR1  ADDR2  STMNT M SOURCE STATEMENT

     000000                                 3    SPCH13   CSECT
                                            4    *
                                            5    * SPCH13  USES SHORT-FORMAT FLOATING-POINT ARITHMETIC TO
                                            6    *    FIND THE REAL ROOTS OF A QUADRATIC EQUATION WITH INTEGER
                                            7    *    COEFFICIENTS  M, N, AND P ...
                                            8    *
                                            9    *         M * (X**2)  +  N * X  +  P  =  0
                                           10    *
                                           11    *    IF TWO REAL ROOTS EXIST AND NEITHER  M  NOR  N  IS ZERO,
                                           12    *    THE ROOTS ARE
                                           13    *              X1  =  ( -N  +  (N**2 - 4*M*P)**(1/2) ) / (2*M)
                                           14    *              X2  =  ( -N  -  (N**2 - 4*M*P)**(1/2) ) / (2*M)
                                           15    *
                                           16    *    IF TWO REAL ROOTS EXIST AND N = 0  BUT  M  IS NOT ZERO,
                                           17    *    THE ROOTS ARE
                                           18    *              X1  =  + ( -P/M )**(1/2)
                                           19    *              X2  =  - ( -P/M )**(1/2)
                                           20    *
                                           21    *    IF ONLY ONE REAL ROOT EXISTS (I.E., IF M=0 AND N IS NOT 0) THEN
                                           22    *    THAT ROOT IS
                                           23    *              X1  =  -P / N
                                           24    *
                                           25    *    OTHERWISE THE ROOTS ARE EITHER TRIVIALLY ZERO  (M = N = P = 0),
                                           26    *    OR DO NOT EXIST  (M = N = 0,  BUT  P  IS NOT 0),
                                           27    *    OR ARE COMPLEX (WHEN   (N**2 - 4*M*P)  IS NEGATIVE).
                                           28    *
                                           29    * THE COEFFICIENTS  M, N, AND P ARE READ FROM INPUT DATA CARDS
                                           30    *    (ONE CARD PER EQUATION TO BE SOLVED) IN THE FOLLOWING FORMAT...
                                           31    *
                                           32    *         COLS  1-10    M
                                           33    *               21-30   N
                                           34    *               41-50   P
                                           35    *
                                           36    * EACH COEFFICIENT SHOULD BE IN THE RANGE  -2**24  TO  2**24 - 1.
                                           37    * THE COEFFICIENTS AND THE ROOTS (IF ANY) WILL BE PRINTED ON'SYSOUT'.
                                           38    *
                                           39    *
                                           40    * THE FOLLOWING SYMBOLS ARE USED FOR THE FLOATING POINT REGISTERS
                                           41    *
     000000                                42    FR0      EQU   0          FLO-PT REG #0
     000002                                43    FR2      EQU   2          FLO-PT REG #2
     000004                                44    FR4      EQU   4          FLO-PT REG #4
     000006                                45    FR6      EQU   6          FLO-PT REG #6
                                           46    *
                                           47    *
     000000 90 EC D00C                     48             STM   14,12,12(13)        STANDARD ENTRY
     000004 05 C0                          49             BALR  12,0
     000006                                50             USING *,12
     000006 50 D0 C35A      000360         51             ST    13,SAVE+4
     00000A 41 D0 C356      00035C         52             LA    13,SAVE
                                           53    *
     00000E 58 10 C1BA      0001C0         54             L     1,MASK     SET PROGRAM MASK TO PROHIBIT INT-
     000012 04 10                          55             SPM   1          ERRUPTS FROM SIGNIF & UNDERFLOWS
                                           56    * OPEN INPUT AND OUTPUT FILES
                                           57    *
     000014                                58             OPEN  (SYSIN,(INPUT))     INPUT IS 'SYSIN' INPUT DATA STREAM
     00001E                                64             OPEN  (SYSPRNT,(OUTPUT))  OUTPUT IS 'SYSOUT' PRINTER

                                           70    *  DOS  *******
                                           71    *       OPEN  SYSIN
                                           72    *       OPEN  SYSPRNT
                                           73    ***************

                                           74    *
                                           75    * MAIN PROCESSING LOOP ...
                                           76    *       READS ONE INPUT DATA CARD
                                           77    *       CONVERTS THE THREE INTEGER COEFF'S TO SHORT-FORMAT FLO-PT
                                           78    *       DETERMINES THE NATURE OF THE SOLUTION (AS DESCRIBED ABOVE)
                                           79    *       CALCULATES THE SOLUTION WHEN IT EXISTS
                                           80    *       PRINTS THE COEFF'S AND THE SOLUTION, OR THE COEFF'S AND
                                           81    *          AN APPROPRIATE MESSAGE WHEN NO SOLUTION EXISTS
                                           82    *       REPEATS THE ABOVE PROCEDURE TILL END-OF-DATA IS REACHED.
                                           83    *
     00002A                                84    LOOP     GET   SYSIN,INAREA        GET COEFF'S FROM INPUT DATA
                                           89    *
     000038 45 E0 C152      000158         90             BAL   14,CONVERT          CONVERT THE COEFF'S TO FLO-PT
                                           91    *
                                           92    * SEE IF THERE ARE TWO NON-TRIVIAL ROOTS
                                           93    *
     00003C 78 00 C19E      0001A4         94             LE    FR0,FM     IF  M = 0  THEN TWO NON-TRIVIAL
     000040 32 00                          95             LTER  FR0,FR0        ROOTS DO NOT EXIST.
     000042 47 80 C0D0      0000D6         96             BZ    MZERO
                                           97    *
                                           98    * IF TWO NON-TRIVIAL ROOTS EXIST, SEE IF THEY ARE COMPLEX OR REAL.
                                           99    *
     000046 7C 00 C1A6      0001AC        100             ME    FR0,FP     LET  D = N**2 - 4*M*P
     00004A 7C 00 C3A2      0003A8        101             ME    FR0,=E'4'           D'S SIGN DETERMINES ROOT'S NATURE.
                                          102    *
     00004E 78 20 C1A2      0001A8        103             LE    FR2,FN
```

Figure 13.10b   continued

```
FLAG LOCTN OBJECT CODE      ADDR1 ADDR2 STMNT M SOURCE STATEMENT

      000052 3C 22                        104          MER    FR2,FR2
      000054 3B 20                        105          SER    FR2,FR0           FR2 = N**2 - 4*M*P
      000056 70 20 C1B2      0001B8       106          STE    FR2,FD     LET D = N**2 - 4*M*P
                                          107   *
      00005A 32 22                        108          LTER   FR2,FR2           IS  D  NEGATIVE
      00005C 47 B0 C064      00006A       109          BNM    REAL             IF NOT THEN ROOTS ARE REAL
                                          110   *
      000060 D2 27 C21EC3E2 000224 0003E8 111  COMPLEX MVC    MSG,=CL40'COMPLEX ROOTS'
      000066 47 F0 C11A      000120       112          B      PRINT
                                          113   *
                                          114   * WHEN THE ROOTS ARE REAL AND NON-TRIVIAL, DETERMINE HOW TO FIND THEM.
                                          115   *
      00006A 78 40 C1A2      0001A8       116  REAL    LE     FR4,FN           IF  N = 0 THEN USE SIMPLER FORMULA.
      00006E 32 44                        117          LTER   FR4,FR4
      000070 47 80 C0A6      0000AC       118          BZ     NZERO
                                          119   * IF NEITHER  M  NOR  N  IS  ZERO, THEN USE STANDARD QUADRATIC FORMULA
                                          120   *
      000074 41 10 C3A6      0003AC       121          LA     1,=A(FD)         COMPUTE  SQRT(D)
      000078 58 F0 C3AA      0003B0       122          L      15,=V(SQRT)
      00007C 05 EF                        123          BALR   14,15
      00007E 70 00 C1B6      0001BC       124          STE    FR0,SQRTFD       RESULT RETURNED IN FLO-PT REG #0
                                          125   *
      000082 7B 00 C1A2      0001A8       126          SE     FR0,FN           COMPUTE  X1 = (-N+SQRT(D))/(2*M)
      000086 7D 00 C19E      0001A4       127          DE     FR0,FM
      00008A 34 00                        128          HER    FR0,FR0
      00008C 70 00 C1AA      0001B0       129          STE    FR0,FX1
      000090 78 00 C1B6      0001BC       130          LE     FR0,SQRTFD       COMPUTE  X2 = (-N-SQRT(D))/(2*M)
      000094 7A 00 C1A2      0001A8       131          AE     FR0,FN
      000098 33 00                        132          LCER   FR0,FR0
      00009A 7D 00 C19E      0001A4       133          DE     FR0,FM
      00009E 34 00                        134          HER    FR0,FR0
      0000A0 70 00 C1AE      0001B4       135          STE    FR0,FX2
      0000A4 45 E0 C17A      000180       136          BAL    14,REVERT        CONVERT  X1 & X2  TO EXTERNAL FORMAT
      0000A8 47 F0 C11A      000120       137          B      PRINT            AND GO PRINT RESULTS.
                                          138   *
                                          139   *  WHEN  M  IS NOT ZERO  BUT  N = 0  THEN USE SIMPLER FORMULA.
                                          140   *
      0000AC 78 00 C1A6      0001AC       141  NZERO   LE     FR0,FP           COMPUTE  -P/M
      0000B0 7D 00 C19E      0001A4       142          DE     FR0,FM
      0000B4 33 00                        143          LCER   FR0,FR0
      0000B6 70 00 C1B2      0001B8       144          STE    FR0,FD
      0000BA 41 10 C3A6      0003AC       145          LA     1,=A(FD)         COMPUTE  SQRT(-P/M)
      0000BE 58 F0 C3AA      0003B0       146          L      15,=V(SQRT)
      0000C2 05 EF                        147          BALR   14,15            RESULT RETURNED IN FLO-PT REG #0
      0000C4 70 00 C1AA      0001B0       148          STE    FR0,FX1          X1 = + SQRT(-P/M)
      0000C8 33 00                        149          LCER   FR0,FR0
      0000CA 70 00 C1AE      0001B4       150          STE    FR0,FX2          X2 = - SQRT(-P/M)
      0000CE 45 E0 C17A      000180       151          BAL    14,REVERT        CONVERT  X1 & X2  TO EXTERNAL FORMAT
      0000D2 47 F0 C11A      000120       152          B      PRINT            AND GO PRINT RESULTS.
                                          153   *
                                          154   *  WHEN  M = 0  THEN TWO NON-TRIVIAL ROOTS DO NOT EXIST.
                                          155   *
                                          156   *    THERE ARE THREE POSSIBILITIES ...
                                          157   *    (1)  X1 = -P/N    IF  M = 0  AND  N  IS NOT ZERO,
                                          158   *             WITH NO SECOND SOLUTION.
                                          159   *    (2)  X1 = X2 = 0  IF  M = N = P = 0  (THE  TRIVIAL SOL'N).
                                          160   *    (3)  NO SOLUTION  IF  M = N = 0  BUT  P  IS NOT ZERO.
                                          161   *
      0000D6 78 00 C1A2      0001A8       162  MZERO   LE     FR0,FN           IS  N = 0
      0000DA 32 00                        163          LTER   FR0,FR0
      0000DC 47 70 C0F8      0000FE       164          BNZ    CASE1            IF NOT, THEN ONLY ONE ROOT.
                                          165   *
      0000E0 78 00 C1A6      0001AC       166          LE     FR0,FP           IS  N = P = 0
      0000E4 32 00                        167          LTER   FR0,FR0
      0000E6 47 80 C0EE      0000F4       168          BZ     CASE2            IF SO, THEN TRIVIAL SOLUTION.
                                          169   *
      0000EA D2 27 C21EC40A 000224 000410 170  CASE3   MVC    MSG,=CL40'NO SOLUTION'
      0000F0 47 F0 C11A      000120       171          B      PRINT
      0000F4 D2 27 C21EC432 000224 000438 172  CASE2   MVC    MSG,=CL40'TRIVIAL SOLUTION'
      0000FA 47 F0 C11A      000120       173          B      PRINT
      0000FE D2 03 C1AEC3AE 0001B4 0003B4 174  CASE1   MVC    FX2,=E'0'
      000104 78 00 C1A6      0001AC       175          LE     FR0,FP
      000108 7D 00 C1A2      0001A8       176          DE     FR0,FN
      00010C 33 00                        177          LCER   FR0,FR0
      00010E 70 00 C1AA      0001B0       178          STE    FR0,FX1          X1 = -P/N
      000112 45 E0 C17A      000180       179          BAL    14,REVERT        CONVERT  X1 TO EXTERNAL FORMAT
      000116 D2 13 C232C45A 000238 000460 180          MVC    PX2,=CL20'ONLY ONE SOLUTION'
      00011C 47 F0 C11A      000120       181          B      PRINT            GO PRINT RESULTS.
                                          182   *
                                          183   * PRINT THE COEFFICIENTS AND THE ROOTS
                                          184   *
      000120 D2 4F C1CCC246 0001D2 00024C 185  PRINT   MVC    OUTLINE,INAREA   MOVE  M, N, AND P TO PRINT LINE
                                          186   *
      000126                              187          PUT    SYSPRNT,OUTAREA
                                          192   *
      000134 47 F0 C024      00002A       193          B      LOOP             GO GET NEXT INPUT CARD, IF ANY.
                                          194   *
                                          195   * WHEN END-OF-DATA IS REACHED, TERMINATE THE PROGRAM .
                                          196   *
```

Figure 13.10b continued

```
FLAG LOCTN OBJECT CODE      ADDR1 ADDR2  STMNT M SOURCE STATEMENT

     000138                              197   EOD      CLOSE (SYSIN)
     000142                              203            CLOSE (SYSPRNT)
     00014E 58 D0 C35A       000360      209            L     13,SAVE+4         STANDARD EXIT
     000152 98 EC D00C                   210            LM    14,12,12(13)
     000156 07 FE                        211            BR    14

                                         212   *  DOS *******
                                         213   *        CLOSE SYSIN
                                         214   *        CLOSE SYSPRNT
                                         215   *        EOJ
                                         216   ***************

                                         217   *
                                         218   *   INTERNAL SUBROUTINE ...
                                         219   *
                                         220   *        'CONVERT'       CONVERTS  M, N, P  TO SHORT-FORMAT FLO-PT
                                         221   *
     000158 50 E0 C1BE       0001C4      222   CONVERT  ST    14,CONVTX         SAVE RETURN ADDR
     00015C 41 10 C3B2       0003B8      223            LA    1,=A(M,FM)        CONVERT 1ST COEFF, M
     000160 58 F0 C3BA       0003C0      224            L     15,=V(CONVT)
     000164 05 EF                        225            BALR  14,15
     000166 41 10 C3BE       0003C4      226            LA    1,=A(N,FN)        CONVERT 2ND COEFF, N
     00016A 58 F0 C3BA       0003C0      227            L     15,=V(CONVT)
     00016E 05 EF                        228            BALR  14,15
     000170 41 10 C3C6       0003CC      229            LA    1,=A(P,FP)        CONVERT 3RD COEFF, P
     000174 58 F0 C3BA       0003C0      230            L     15,=V(CONVT)
     000178 05 EF                        231            BALR  14,15
     00017A 58 E0 C1BE       0001C4      232            L     14,CONVTX         RETURN TO CALLER.
     00017E 07 FE                        233            BR    14
                                         234   * INTERNAL SUBROUTINE ...
                                         235   *
                                         236   *        'REVERT'        CONVERTS X1 & X2  TO EXTERNAL FORMAT
                                         237   *
     000180 50 E0 C1BE       0001C4      238   REVERT   ST    14,CONVTX         SAVE RETURN ADDR
     000184 D2 27 C21EC46E 000224 000474 239            MVC   MSG,=CL40' '      CLEAR THE PRINT AREAS
     00018A 41 10 C3CE       0003D4      240            LA    1,=A(FX1,PX1)     CONVERT 1ST ROOT, X1
     00018E 58 F0 C3D6       0003DC      241            L     15,=V(DECONVT)
     000192 05 EF                        242            BALR  14,15
     000194 41 10 C3DA       0003E0      243            LA    1,=A(FX2,PX2)     CONVERT 2ND ROOT, X2
     000198 58 F0 C3D6       0003DC      244            L     15,=V(DECONVT)
     00019C 05 EF                        245            BALR  14,15
     00019E 58 E0 C1BE       0001C4      246            L     14,CONVTX         RECOVER RETURN ADDR
     0001A2 07 FE                        247            BR    14
                                         248   *
                                         249   *   CONSTANTS  AND  DATA AREAS
                                         250   *
     0001A4                              251   FM       DS    E                 SPACE FOR FLO-PT  M
     0001A8                              252   FN       DS    E                 SPACE FOR FLO-PT  N
     0001AC                              253   FP       DS    E                 SPACE FOR FLO-PT  P
     0001B0                              254   FX1      DS    E                 SPACE FOR ROOT  X1
     0001B4                              255   FX2      DS    E                 SPACE FOR ROOT  X2
     0001B8                              256   FD       DS    E                 SPACE FOR FLO-PT  D = N**2 - 4*M*P
     0001BC                              257   SQRTFD   DS    E                 SPACE FOR SQRT(D)
     0001C0                              258            DS    0F
     0001C0 0C000000                     259   MASK     DC    X'0C000000'       MASK FOR SIGNIF AND UNDERFLOW ERRS
     0001C4                              260   CONVTX   DS    F                 SAVE AREA FOR REG 14 DURING CONV'N.
                                         261   *
                                         262   * OUTPUT AREA
                                         263   *
     0001C8                              264   OUTAREA  DS    0CL132            DEFINITION OF OUTPUT AREA
     0001C8 4040404040404040             265            DC    CL10' '           COLS 1-10   BLANKS
     0001D2                              266   OUTLINE  DS    CL80              11-90   INPUT DATA CARD
     000222 4040                         267            DC    CL2' '            91-92   BLANKS
     000224                              268   MSG      DS    0CL40             93-132  ROOT MESSAGE AREA
     000224                              269   PX1      DS    CL20              93-112  1ST ROOT AREA
     000238                              270   PX2      DS    CL20              113-132 2ND ROOT AREA
                                         271   *
                                         272   * INPUT AREA
                                         273   *
     00024C                              274   INAREA   DS    0CL80             DEFINITION OF INPUT AREA ...
     00024C                              275   M        DS    CL10              COLS 1-10    1ST COEFF,  M
     000256                              276            DS    CL10              11-20   UNUSED
     000260                              277   N        DS    CL10              21-30   2ND COEFF,  N
     00026A                              278            DS    CL10              31-40   UNUSED
     000274                              279   P        DS    CL10              41-50   3RD COEFF,  P
     00027E                              280            DS    CL30              51-80   UNUSED
                                         281   *
                                         282   * DCB'S FOR INPUT AND OUTPUT FILES
                                         283   *
     00029C                              284   SYSIN    DCB   DSORG=PS,MACRF=(GM),DDNAME=SYSIN,EODAD=EOD,        X
                                         285                  RECFM=FB,LRECL=80,BLKSIZE=4080
                                         337   *
     0002FC                              338   SYSPRNT  DCB   DSORG=PS,MACRF=(PM),DDNAME=SYSPRINT,               X
                                         339                  RECFM=FB,LRECL=132,BLKSIZE=4092
                                         391   * DOS *******
                                         392   *SYSIN   DTFCD DEVADDR=SYSIPT,WORKA=YES,IOAREA1=INBUF,EOFADDR=EOD, X
                                         393   *             DEVICE=2540
                                         394   *SYSPRNT DTFPR DEVADDR=SYSLST,WORKA=YES,IOAREA1=OUTBUF,BLKSIZE=132, X
                                         395   *             DEVICE=1403
```

Figure 13.10b   continued

```
FLAG LOCTN OBJECT CODE      ADDR1  ADDR2  STMNT M SOURCE STATEMENT

                                          396    *
                                          397    *INBUF    DS    CL80
                                          398    *OUTBUF   DC    CL132' '
                                          399    ***************

                                          400    *
                                          401    * SAVE AREA
                                          402    *
        00035C                            403    SAVE     DS    18F

                                          404    *  DOS *******
                                          405    *SAVE     DS    9D
                                          406    ***************

                                          407    * LITERALS
        0003A8 41400000                   409             =E'4'
        0003AC 000001B8                   410             =A(FD)
        0003B0 00000000                   411             =V(SQRT)
        0003B4 00000000                   412             =E'0'
        0003B8 0000024C000001A4           413             =A(M,FM)
        0003C0 00000000                   414             =V(CONVT)
        0003C4 00000260000001A8           415             =A(N,FN)
        0003CC 00000274000001AC           416             =A(P,FP)
        0003D4 000001B000000224           417             =A(FX1,PX1)
        0003DC 00000000                   418             =V(DECONVT)
        0003E0 000001B400000238           419             =A(FX2,PX2)
        0003E8 C3D6D4D7D3C5E740           420             =CL40'COMPLEX ROOTS'
        000410 05D640E2D6D3E4E3           421             =CL40'NO SOLUTION'
        000438 E3D9C9E5C9C1D340           422             =CL40'TRIVIAL SOLUTION'
        000460 D6D5D3E84DD6D5C5           423             =CL20'ONLY ONE SOLUTION'
        000474 4040404040404040           424             =CL40' '
                                          425             END
```

CROSS-REFERENCE

```
SYMBOL    LEN   VALUE  DEFN   REFERENCES

CASE1     00006 0000FE 00174  00164
CASE2     00006 0000F4 00172  00168
CASE3     00006 0000EA 00170
COMPLEX   00006 00006D 00111
CONVERT   00004 000158 00222  00090
CONVT     00004 000000 00414  00224  00227  00230
CONVTX    00004 0001C4 00260  00222  00232  00238  00246
DECONVT   00004 000000 00418  00241  00244
EOD       00004 000138 00199  00306
FD        00004 0001B8 00256  00106  00121  00144  00145  00410
FM        00004 0001A4 00251  00094  00127  00133  00142  00223  00413
FN        00004 0001A8 00252  00103  00116  00126  00131  00162  00176  00226  00415
FP        00004 0001AC 00253  00100  00141  00166  00175  00229  00416
FR0       00001 000000 00042  00094  00095  00095  00100  00101  00105  00124  00126  00127  00128  00128  00129  00130
                              00131  00132  00132  00133  00134  00134  00135  00141  00142  00143  00143  00144  00148
                              00149  00149  00150  00162  00163  00163  00166  00167  00167  00175  00176  00177  00177
                              00178
FR2       00001 000002 00043  00103  00104  00105  00105  00106  00108  00108
FR4       00001 000004 00044  00116  00117  00117
FR6       00001 000006 00045
FX1       00004 0001B0 00254  00129  00148  00178  00240  00417
FX2       00004 0001B4 00255  00135  00150  00174  00243  00419
INAREA    00050 00024C 00274  00086  00185
LOOP      00004 00002A 00085  00193
M         0000A 00024C 00275  00223  00413
MASK      00004 0001C0 00259  00054
MSG       00028 000224 00268  00111  00170  00172  00239
MZERO     00004 000006 00162  00096
N         0000A 000260 00277  00226  00415
NZERO     00004 0000AC 00141  00118
OUTAREA   00084 0001C8 00264  00189
OUTLINE   00050 0001D2 00266  00185
P         0000A 000274 00279  00229  00416
PRINT     00006 000120 00185  00112  00137  00152  00171  00173  00181
PX1       00014 000224 00269  00240  00417
PX2       00014 000238 00270  00180  00243  00419
REAL      00004 00006A 00116  00109
REVERT    00004 000180 00238  00136  00151  00179
SAVE      00004 00035C 00403  00051  00052  00209
SPCH13    00001 000000 00003
SQRT      00004 000000 00411  00122  00146
SQRTFD    00004 0001BC 00257  00124  00130
SYSIN     00004 00029C 00285  00062  00085  00201
SYSPRNT   00004 0002FC 00339  00068  00188  00207
```

1. Convert each of the following numbers from its short-format floating-point representation (shown here) to its representation in the decimal system's scientific notation. No more than six significant digits are necessary (e.g., $41100000 = 1.0 \times 10^0$).

   a. 41800000   **e.** 42880000   **i.** 4E000001
   b. C1800000   **f.** BE880000   **j.** C8800000
   c. 3F800000   **g.** 00000000   **k.** 7FFFFFFF
   d. 40400000   **h.** 00000001   **l.** FFFFFFFF

2. For each of the following questions, assume that W, X, Y, and Z are defined as follows:

```
W   DC   E'2'     SHORT-FORMAT REPRESENTATION OF DECIMAL 2
X   DS   E        ARBITRARY NUMBER IN SHORT FORMAT
Y   DC   D'0.1'   LONG-FORMAT REPRESENTATION OF DECIMAL 0.1
Z   DS   D        ARBITRARY NUMBER IN LONG FORMAT
```

   a. Write the floating-point instructions that will add the number at symbolic address W to that at X, and store the result at X.
   b. Write the floating-point instructions that will square the number at symbolic address Y, and store the result at Z.
   c. Write the floating-point instructions that will determine whether the number at symbolic address Y is positive, negative, or zero.
   d. Write the floating-point instructions that will determine whether the number at symbolic address Z is greater than 4096.
   e. Write the floating-point instructions that will round the long-format representation of 0.1 to short format, and store the result at X.

3. Suppose that symbolic address R contains a nonnegative short-format floating-point number. Write the instructions (and constants, if necessary) to calculate the following quantities:

   a. The area of a circle whose radius is given at R
   b. The volume of a sphere whose radius is given at R
   c. The amount $A = (1 + r)^n$, where r is the number at R and $n = 5$

   d. The amount of $P = \dfrac{r \times 10^5}{1 - (1 + r)^{-n}}$, where r is the number at R, and $n = 5$

4. Assume that X is the symbolic address of an arbitrary short-format floating-point number. What run-time error conditions would or might occur when each of the following sets of instructions was executed? Why?

```
a. LE    0,=E'0'          d. LE    0,X
   SE    0,X                 SE    0,=E'1'
b. LE    4,X              e. LE    6,X
   ME    4,=E'16'            HER   6,6
c. LE    2,=E'1'          f. LE    4,X
   DE    2,X                 MER   4,4
```

5. Assume that Z is the symbolic address of an arbitrary long-format floating-point number. What run-time error conditions would or might occur when each of the following sets of instructions was executed? Why?

```
a. LD    0,=D'10'         d. LD    4,Z
   AD    0,Z                 DDR   4,4
b. LD    2,Z              e. LD    4,Z
   LPDR  0,2                 LRER  0,4
c. LD    6,=D'1E10'       f. LD    6,Z
   DD    6,Z                 MER   6,6
```

6. As discussed in Sections 11.4 and 13.7, the Set Program Mask instruction can be used to prohibit program interruption when an exponent underflow or significance error occurs. Write the instructions (including the SPM) that would prohibit interruption from an exponent underflow error condition, and write the instructions that would prohibit interruption from a significance error condition. What instructions are required to simultaneously prohibit both these error conditions from causing a program interruption? What instructions are required to *remove* the prohibition of interrupts occurring in either of these two error situations?

7. What would be the result if each of the following sets of instructions were executed while interrupts for exponent underflow and significance errors were prohibited? What would be the effect if they were executed while those interrupts were *not* prohibited?

```
a. LE   2,=E'1'              c. LD   2,=D'1'
   SE   2,=E'1'                 AD   2,=D'-1'
b. LD   4,=D'1E-40'          d. LD   6,=D'1E-40'
   MDR  4,4                     DD   6,=D'-1E40'
```

8. When m and n are integers such that $0 \leq m \leq n$, then the coefficient B_{mn} of the mth term in the binomial expansion of $(x+a)^n$ is known as the *binomial* coefficient; it is usually written as $\binom{n}{m}$. Thus,

$$(x + a)^n = \sum_{m=0}^{n} B_{mn} x^{n-m} a^m = \sum_{m=0}^{n} \binom{n}{m} x^{n-m} a^m$$

It is known that $B_{mn} = \binom{n}{m} = n!/[(n-m)!m!]$, where $n!$ is the notation for "factorial n," and is evaluated as $n! = n(n-1)(n-2)...(2)(1)$ for positive integers n, with the added definition that $0! = 1$. For example,

$$\binom{2}{0} = \frac{2!}{2!0!} = 1 \; ; \binom{2}{1} = \frac{2!}{1!1!} = 2 \; ; \binom{2}{2} = \frac{2!}{0!2!} = 1$$

a. Write a subroutine that will calculate the binomial coefficient $\binom{n}{m}$ for arbitrary integers m and n satisfying the relationship $0 \leq m \leq n \leq 20$, assuming that both m and n are passed to your subroutine as short-format floating-point numbers. Do your calculations with single-precision arithmetic instructions.

b. Rewrite your solution to Exercise 8a, this time doing the calculations with double-precision instructions. Compare the results achieved using the two solutions for $\binom{n}{m} = \binom{10}{5}$ and for $\binom{n}{m} = \binom{20}{10}$. Note that both $\binom{10}{5}$ and $\binom{20}{10}$ can be represented *exactly* in short format, since $\binom{10}{5} = 252_{10} = FC_{16}$, and $\binom{20}{10} = 184756_{10} = 2D1B4_{16}$. What accounts for the discrepancy between the two solutions for these quantities?

9. The Newton-Raphson method for finding the real roots of an equation yields an especially simple iterative method for determining the positive square root of any positive real number x. If a_o is a good first approximation to the square root of x, then successively better approximations a_j are given by this recurrence relation:

$$a_{n+1} = \frac{1}{2}\left(a_n + \frac{x}{a_n}\right), \text{ for } n = 0,1,2,...$$

Using single-precision floating-point instructions, write a subroutine that will determine the square root of a nonnegative short-format number using this recurrence relation. Stop the iteration at the first value of n such that $|a_{n+1} - a_n| < 10^{-5}$. A simple first approximation is to let $a_o = \frac{1}{2}(x+1)$ when $x > 1$, and $a_o = 1$ when $x < 1$. How many iterations are required when $x = 10$? When $x = 100$? 1000? 10,000? How might a_0 be chosen so that the number of iterations is not so large when x is large?

10. The series expansions

$$\sin x = x - \frac{x^3}{3!} + \frac{x^5}{5!} - \frac{x^7}{7!} + \frac{x^9}{9!} - \cdots$$

$$\cos x = 1 - \frac{x^2}{2!} + \frac{x^4}{4!} - \frac{x^6}{6!} + \frac{x^8}{8!} - \cdots$$

are useful for computing the trigonometric sine and cosine functions of an angle x given in radians, when $0 \leqslant x < 1$. (x radians $= 180x/\pi$ degrees, where $\pi = 3.1415926\ldots$). When $1 \leqslant x \leqslant \pi/2$, the same series can be used provided x is replaced by $\pi/2 - x$, since $\sin(\pi/2 - x) = \cos x$, and $\cos(\pi/2 - x) = \sin x$.

Using single-precision floating-point instructions, write a subroutine that will compute the sine or cosine function for any x such that $0 \leqslant x \leqslant \pi/2$, with accuracy to at least five decimal digits.

11. Modify the subroutine written for Exercise 10 so that it will compute the sine or cosine for any angle x that is given as a short-format floating-point number. (Hint: Make use of these formulas: $\sin(\pi - x) = \sin x$, $\sin(3\pi/2 - x) = -\cos x$, $\sin(2\pi - x) = -\sin x$, and $\sin(2k\pi + x) = \sin x$ for all integers k.)

12. The sum of the first N positive integers, $1 + 2 + 3 + \ldots + N$ is $N(N+1)/2$. Derive a formula for the sum of the positive integers M through N: $M + (M+1) + (M+2) + \ldots + N$, and write a subroutine that will calculate this sum using your formula.

13. For the solution to Exercise 12, you obviously have the choice of using the integer arithmetic instructions of Chapter 5, or the short-, long-, or extended-format floating-point instructions. What criteria should govern your choice?

14. One of the more rapidly converging formulas for computing π to an arbitrary number of decimal digits was derived in 1706 by John Machin:

$$\frac{\pi}{4} = 4\left(\frac{1}{5} - \frac{1}{3 \cdot 5^3} + \frac{1}{5 \cdot 5^5} - \cdots\right) - \left(\frac{1}{239} - \frac{1}{3 \cdot 239^3} + \frac{1}{5 \cdot 239^5} - \cdots\right)$$

Write a program that uses this formula to compute π with double-precision instructions. What criteria should determine when the calculations should be terminated? (For further information on Machin's formula and other methods of calculating π, see *A History of π* by Petr Beckmann [New York: St. Martin's Press, 1971].)

15. At C cents per gallon, it costs P dollars to purchase an amount of gasoline that is just sufficient to drive 100 miles in an automobile that gets M miles per gallon. What is the equation relating C and M to P? Suppose that 10 different values of C and 10 different values of M are given as short-format floating-point numbers in respective one-dimensional arrays, $C(J)$ and $M(J)$. Write a subroutine that will calculate the 100 values of P and store them in a two-dimensional array, $P(J,K)$. The arrays C, M, and P are to be passed to your subroutine.

16. A simple (though inefficient) sort routine is based on the principle of successively finding the nth smallest number in an array of N numbers, for $n = 1,2,\ldots,N$. The routine is known as an "exchange," or "bubble" sort, and can be represented by this Fortran subroutine:

```
                  SUBROUTINE XSORT(A,N)
                  DIMENSION A(1000)
                  M=N-1
                  DO 50 J=1,M
                  L=J+1
                  DO 40 K=L,N
                  IF ( A(J) .LE. A(K) ) GO TO 40
                  X = A(J)
                  A(J) = A(K)
                  A(K) = X
         40       CONTINUE
         50       CONTINUE
                  RETURN
                  END
```

   a. Write an assembly language subroutine that will sort *N* short-format floating-point numbers into ascending sequence, using the bubble sort algorithm described by the previous Fortran subroutine.

   b. Modify your sort subroutine so that it will process long-format numbers instead of short-format numbers.

17. The instructions for processing extended-precision floating-point numbers include the arithmetic operations of add, subtract, multiply, and round, but do not include counterparts of any other single- or double-precision instructions. For each of the following double-precision instructions, write the combination of instructions that will accomplish the same purpose for extended-precision numbers: LD, LDR, STD, LTDR, LCDR, LNDR, LPDR, CD, CDR. (**Note:** In an extended-format number, the low-order 64 bits are formatted like a double-precision number: the first low-order bit is a sign bit, the next 7 bits are the low-order characteristic, and the remaining 56 bits are the low-order mantissa. The sign bit is the same as the sign bit of the full extended-format number, but the characteristic is 14 less than the characteristic contained in the high-order 64 bits. Moreover, if subtracting 14 from the high-order characteristic would cause the low-order characteristic to be negative, then the low-order characteristic is forced (by the hardware) to be 128 more than its correct value.)

18. Provisions for simulating the extended-precision instructions on those IBM 360 and 370 systems that do not have this set as a hardware feature are described in IBM Publication OS/VS1 *Supervisor Services and Macro Instructions* (#GC24-5103). The same publication describes a method for dividing two extended-format numbers using a macro named DXR. Using the DXR macro and whatever other facilities are required, rework Exercise 14 to compute π in extended-precision arithmetic.

IV

Directives

14

Cosmetic Directives

D irectives that provide control over the appearance of source language statements on the listing, and over certain aspects of the validity of source language statements, will be referred to as *cosmetic directives*. Although the use of this term is not standard terminology, it is introduced here as a way to group the directives in this chapter under an appropriate heading.

Cosmetic directives can be used for the following purposes:

1. To begin a new page at any point on the listing (EJECT)
2. To put a title on each page of the listing (TITLE)
3. To create line spacing that visually separates adjacent bodies of statements on the listing (SPACE)
4. To suppress the printing of selected portions of a listing (PRINT)
5. To define additional mnemonic opcodes in terms of existing ones and to declare specific mnemonic opcodes to be invalid (OPSYN)
6. To require sequence checking of source language statements (ISEQ)
7. To define a nonstandard statement format (ICTL)

Summary in Figure 14.2

Skillful use of cosmetic directives is an art, and the technique is difficult to verbalize. But a skillful use of these directives in conjunction with comment statements significantly improves the readability and usefulness of a listing. The rules for using these directives are described in this chapter and are summarized in Figure 14.2 at the end of the chapter. An example of the use of most of these directives is given in Figure 14.1.

14.1 EJECT: BEGIN A NEW PAGE

The EJECT directive causes the line following it to be printed on a new page of the listing. Its format is

opcode	operand
EJECT	blank

An EJECT directive may appear anywhere in the source program and may be used any number of times. It is not printed on the listing. Its purpose is to separate different portions of the listing from one another, thereby enhancing the readability of the listing.

14.2 TITLE: DEFINE A TITLE LINE FOR EACH PAGE

The TITLE directive causes the first line of each page to be printed with a heading, or title, of up to 100 characters. The heading characters are specified in the operand field of the TITLE directive:

opcode	operand
TITLE	a text string of up to 100 characters, enclosed in apostrophes

The text string in the operand field may contain any printable characters, including blanks and punctuation marks. The string is printed beginning at the left margin at the top of each page of the listing. A TITLE directive may appear anywhere and any number of times in the source code, but it is not printed on the listing. For each occurrence of a TITLE directive, the assembler begins a new page of the listing, using the text string from the operand of that TITLE directive for the heading line. The same heading line is used on each subsequent page until a new TITLE directive is found by the assembler.

Two points should be noted. First, the TITLE and EJECT directives should not be used in consecutive statements, since each one causes a skip to a new page. And, second, two consecutive apostrophes or ampersands must be used to represent a single apostrophe or ampersand in a TITLE operand. Two consecutive apostrophes are used to distinguish the apostrophe to be printed from the ones that delimit the text string; two consecutive ampersands are used to distinguish the ampersand to be printed from the one that denotes the start of a variable symbol. For example:

source code	printed heading
TITLE 'MAIN PROGRAM'	MAIN PROGRAM
TITLE ' ''PUSH'' && ''POP'' ROUTINES'	'PUSH' & 'POP' ROUTINES

14.3 SPACE: INSERT BLANK LINES

The SPACE directive causes one or more blank lines to be inserted in the listing at the point where the SPACE directive exists in the source code. The number of blank lines to be inserted is specified in the operand field either as a self-defining decimal term or as a blank. A blank operand causes one blank line to be inserted. Thus, the format is

opcode	operand
SPACE	a self-defining decimal term or blank

A SPACE directive may appear anywhere and any number of times in the source code; it is not printed on the listing. If the operand specifies more blank lines than there is room for on the page to which the SPACE directive pertains, the blank lines are not continued onto the next page.

The SPACE directive is useful for separating minor sections of source code on a listing whenever a page break is not warranted. This greatly enhances the readability of the listing. For example:

source code			printed listing		
SEARCH	CSECT		SEARCH	CSECT	
	STM	14,12,12(13)		STM	14,12,12(13)
	BALR	12,0		BALR	12,0
	USING	*,12		USING	*,12
	ST	13,SAVE+4		ST	13,SAVE+4
	LA	13,SAVE		LA	13,SAVE
	SPACE				
	LM	2,4,0(1)		LM	2,4,0(1)
	L	2,0(2)		L	2,0(2)
	.			.	
	.			.	
	.			.	

14.4 PRINT: CONTROL THE AMOUNT OF DETAIL PRINTED

The PRINT directive controls the type and amount of detail printed in any portion of the listing. The control information is specified in the operand field by means of certain key words:

opcode	operand
PRINT	one or more key words, separated by commas

PRINT Options

In the IBM 360 and 370 Assembly language, there are three levels of detail that can be controlled by the key words. There are, correspondingly, three pairs of key words that can be used in the operand field:

key words	meaning
ON or OFF	whether or not any lines following the PRINT directive are printed on the listing
GEN or NOGEN	whether or not the statements generated in a macro expansion are printed
DATA or NODATA	whether the object code of a constant is printed in its entirety, or whether only the first 8 bytes of each constant's object code are printed

PRINT Defaults

When the assembler begins to assemble a source module, it assumes that the ON, GEN, and NODATA key words are in effect for the listing. These are known as the *default* values of the key words. Each default remains in effect until explicitly changed by a PRINT directive in the source module, with these exceptions: the key word OFF overrides the key words GEN and DATA, NOGEN overrides both DATA and NODATA within macro expansions, and both DATA and NODATA apply to macro expansions (as well as to other object-code constants) when GEN is in effect. Further details are given in the following descriptions:

source code	effect on printed listing
PRINT OFF	*No statement following this PRINT directive, up to and including the next PRINT ON directive in the source code, will be printed on the listing.*
PRINT ON	All statements following this PRINT directive, except those affected by NOGEN and NODATA, will be printed on the listing. The previous setting of the other two keyword pairs remains in effect.

PRINT GEN	If ON is in effect from a previous PRINT directive or from the default value, macro expansions will be printed on the listing in all statements following this PRINT directive (up to a subsequent PRINT NOGEN, if any).
PRINT NOGEN	If ON is in effect, macro expansions that follow this PRINT directive will not be printed until a subsequent PRINT GEN directive occurs.
PRINT DATA	If ON is in effect, the object code of each constant defined by a DC directive is printed in its entirety up to the point where a subsequent PRINT NODATA directive occurs.
PRINT NODATA	If ON is in effect, only the first 8 object-code bytes of a subsequent DC constant are printed. (NOGEN overrides both DATA and NODATA for macro expansions; but, when GEN is in effect, both DATA and NODATA apply to macro expansions as well as to other object-code constants.)

Key words can be combined in a single PRINT directive. For example,

```
PRINT   ON,NOGEN,NODATA
```

is equivalent to the following three directives, in the order given here:

```
PRINT   ON
PRINT   NOGEN
PRINT   NODATA
```

The PRINT directive may appear anywhere and any number of times in a source module. The occurrence of a key word in a PRINT directive cancels the effect of the opposite key word in that pair that may have occurred in a previous PRINT directive. Thus, PRINT ON cancels a previous PRINT OFF, PRINT GEN cancels a previous PRINT NOGEN, and PRINT DATA cancels a previous PRINT NODATA. To restore a previous setting, the programmer must know what that previous setting was and use the appropriate key word in a PRINT directive. In this way, portions of a listing may be put under control of one key word setting while other portions are under control of its opposite.

To facilitate switching from one key word of a pair to its opposite, the IBM 370 Assembly language has two other directives, **PUSH** and **POP.** (These are available in OS Assembly Language but not in DOS.) The PUSH directive allows the setting of a key word to be temporarily suspended while its opposite is in effect; the POP directive allows the effect of the suspended key word to be restored without having to respecify it. This removes the requirement that a programmer know the settings that are in effect at each point of the source module and is especially useful in macro definitions. (PUSH and POP can also be used to temporarily suspend and then restore the base register and base address information supplied by USING directives. We will not explore this capability further.)

To suspend the most recently established key words of a PRINT directive, the format of the PUSH directive is simply

opcode	operand
PUSH	PRINT

To restore the key words of the most recently suspended PRINT directive, the format of the POP directive is

```
POP      PRINT
```

Between any given PUSH directive and its matching POP directive, the programmer would normally have one or more PRINT directives to institute temporary settings of the key words. Additional PUSH and POP pairs can also be used between other PUSH and POP pairs. Up to four levels of pairs (a limit set by the assembler) may be nested.

In addition to the PRINT, PUSH, and POP directives in assembly language, the job control language contains options that can be used to control the amount of printed detail on a listing. These options are described in the *Assembler Programmer's Guide*, in the section on Assembler Options, and will not be pursued here.

14.5 OPSYN: DEFINE A NEW MNEMONIC OPCODE

The OPSYN directive establishes a new mnemonic opcode in terms of an existing opcode. It can also be used to remove an existing opcode from the set of allowable opcodes. Available in OS Assembly Language but not in DOS, it has the following formats:

name field	opcode	operand
a new opcode	OPSYN	an existing opcode
an existing opcode	OPSYN	blank

The first format defines the opcode given in the name field to have all the properties of the opcode given in the operand field. The second format removes the opcode given in the name field from the set of allowable opcodes. The effect of both these formats is of course limited to the source module in which they occur. For example,

source code	effect
BLE OPSYN BNH	The new opcode Branch if Less than or Equal (BLE) is defined to be equivalent to Branch if Not High (BNH).
ISEQ OPSYN	Any subsequent occurrence of the ISEQ directive will be considered invalid.

Note that too extensive use of the OPSYN directive would make the program difficult for anyone other than the programmer to understand. For this reason, the OPSYN directive should be used sparingly, if at all, within a program; or it should be used for the same opcodes by everyone in a programming shop so that the newly defined opcodes are available to and understood by all the programmers in that shop.

14.6 ISEQ: SOURCE-STATEMENT SEQUENCE CHECKING

The ISEQ directive is used to cause the assembler to verify that the statements in a source module are in the sequence in which they were intended to be. The verification depends upon sequence numbers that the programmer has placed in the identification field of each source statement. Although the identification field normally occupies positions 73 through 80 in standard format, its positions must be specified in the ISEQ directive. This allows nonstandard formats, or fewer than eight positions in standard format, to be sequence-checked.

The ISEQ directive is used in pairs; the first ISEQ of the pair initiates sequence checking, the second terminates it. The format for initiating sequence checking is

opcode	operand
ISEQ	p,q

The format for terminating sequence checking is

opcode	operand
ISEQ	blank

The sequence number of each statement is assumed to begin in position p and end in position q.

While the ISEQ directive is in effect, the assembler compares the sequence number of each line of code in the source module, including that of a continuation line, to that of the immediately preceding line of code. If the two sequence numbers are not in increasing sequence, a warning is printed on the listing. A line with only blanks in the identification field is excluded from the sequence-checking operation. For example,

source code	effect
ISEQ 73,80	Sequence checking of source statements begins with the line following this ISEQ directive. The assembler uses positions 73 through 80 for the identification field.
ISEQ	The blank operand signals the assembler to terminate sequence checking. Checking may be resumed at a subsequent point in the source module by a statement of the form ISEQ p,q.

The values of p and q must satisfy the constraint $p \leq q$ or the ISEQ statement is incorrect. Note that if there is no ISEQ directive to terminate sequence checking in a source module, sequence checking continues to the end of the module.

Other exceptions are discussed in the *Assembler Language Reference Manual*.

14.7 ICTL: DEFINE NONSTANDARD STATEMENT FORMAT

As mentioned in Chapter 2, there are two essentially different statement formats allowable in the IBM 360 and 370 Assembly language: standard format and nonstandard format. If you wish to use a nonstandard format, the first statement of a source module must be an ICTL directive (itself in standard format). All statements following will be in the format described by that ICTL directive. No other ICTL directives are permitted in the source module.

Using the ICTL directive, a programmer can specify the beginning position, the ending position, and the continuing position of the statements appearing in a source module. Remember that the *beginning* position is the position that is used as the first position of the name field; the *ending* position is the last position of the comment field; and the *continuing* position is the first position that can be used in a continuation line.

The Beginning, Ending, and Continuing Positions

In standard format, these three positions are defined as

$$
\begin{aligned}
b &= \text{beginning position} &= \text{position 1} \\
e &= \text{ending position} &= \text{position 71} \\
c &= \text{continuing position} &= \text{position 16}
\end{aligned}
$$

To change one or more of these defined positions, the ICTL directive must be written in one of the following three formats:

opcode	operand
ICTL	b
ICTL	b,e
ICTL	b,e,c

In each of these formats, the letters b, e, and c represent decimal integers whose values obey the following constraints: $1 \leq b \leq 40$, $2 \leq c \leq 40$, $41 \leq e \leq 80$ and $b < c < e$, $b + 5 \leq e$.

Constraints on b, c, and e

If the first form—ICTL b—is used, the assembler assumes that the value of e is 71, as it is in standard format. Moreover, if either the first or the second forms—ICTL b or ICTL b,e—are used, the assembler assumes that continuation lines are not allowed, regardless of the values of b and e.

If the third form is used, the continuation field—position 72 in standard format—is redefined to be the position immediately following the ending position e. (If $e = 80$, there will be no continuation field and thus no continuation lines.)

Figure 14.1 *TITLE, PRINT, and ISEQ.*

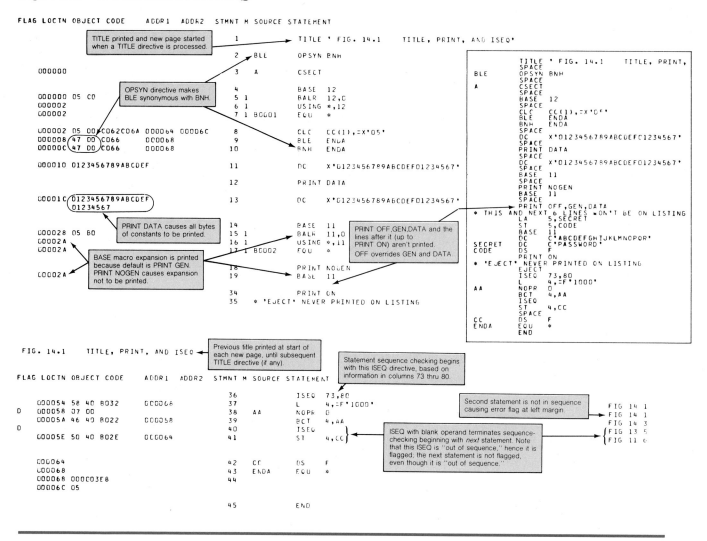

Figure 14.1 *TITLE, PRINT, and ISEQ.*

As Examples 1 and 2 show, an obvious purpose of the ICTL directive is to allow the use of statements in which the identification field occurs first, rather than last, in a line of source code. This facility could be useful if the source code were created with an on-line text editor that placed a line number in the first 8 bytes of each line of code.

Example 1.

source statement: ICTL 9,80,24

effect: $b=9$, $e=80$, $c=24$

Positions 1 through 8 are no longer available for the statement name field. The name field is redefined to begin in position 9. But positions 1 through 8 can be used for the identification field. A subsequent ISEQ directive such as

ISEQ   1,8

could invoke sequence checking using positions 1 through 8 as the identification field.

Note, however, that since $e=80$, there can be no continuation lines in the nonstandard format defined by this example.

Figure 14.2 Summary of cosmetic directives.

statement format			meaning	constraints
	EJECT		begins a new page at the point in the listing at which the EJECT directive occurs	operand must be blank
	ICTL	b,e,c	defines the nonstandard format to be used by all remaining statements in the source module; b identifies the beginning position, e the ending position, and c the continuing position	must be the first statement in source module, with $b<c<e$, $b+5\leq e$, and $1\leq b\leq 40$, $2\leq c\leq 40$, $41\leq e\leq 80$
	ISEQ	p,q	specifies that sequence checking of source statements is to begin, using the text string in positions p thru q; if p, q omitted, sequence-checking is terminated	$1\leq p\leq q\leq 80$
a	OPSYN	b	defines the new opcode a to be equivalent to the existing opcode b, unless b is omitted; if b is omitted, the existing opcode a is defined as invalid	if present, b must be a valid opcode; if b is omitted, a must be a valid opcode
	POP	d	restores the PRINT and/or USING directive operands that were saved by the most recently occurring PUSH directive	d must be one of these: PRINT USING PRINT,USING USING,PRINT
	PRINT	k	the printing of subsequent statements and object code on the listing is controlled by the keyword k until the occurrence of a PRINT or POP directive that overrides k	k must be one of these: GEN or NOGEN DATA or NODATA ON or OFF
	PUSH	d	causes the assembler to remember the operands in the most recent PRINT and/or USING directive	same constraints as in POP directive
	SPACE	n	causes n blank lines to be inserted in the listing at the point at which the SPACE directive occurs; if n omitted, one blank line is inserted	if not omitted, n must be a decimal self-defining term
	TITLE	'...'	begins a new page on the listing and causes the text string (indicated here by ...) to be printed at the top of the new and subsequent pages until another TITLE directive occurs	the text string cannot contain more than 100 characters

Note: PUSH, POP, and OPSYN are available in OS assembly language but not in DOS assembly language.

Example 2.

$$\text{source statement:} \quad \texttt{ICTL 9,79,24}$$
$$\text{effect:} \quad b=9, e=79, c=24$$

The effect is the same as in the previous example except that the continuation field position is 80 ($= e+1$) since $e=79$. Thus continuation lines may be used, each beginning in position 24.

14.8 SUMMARY

The directives listed in Figure 14.2 provide control over the appearance of the listing, the sequence and format of statements, and the use of opcodes. They have been grouped by the author under the term *cosmetic directives* for pedagogical reasons even though the term is not widely used.

Directives   Directives are requests to the assembler to perform some task at assembly time. A directive's mnemonic name is specified in a statement's opcode field. Each directive may have its own operand format.

SPACE, EJECT, TITLE   These three directives affect the appearance of the listing produced by the assembler, by determining where blank lines should be inserted and new pages begun.

PRINT   This affects the content of the listing by determining what is and isn't printed under certain conditions.

PUSH, POP (only in OS)   These work together to preserve and restore previously specified PRINT and/or USING operands. Their principal use is within macro definitions (see Chap. 17).

ICTL   The statement format defined by the ICTL directive must be used throughout the source module in which ICTL appears, except that ICTL itself must be in standard format, and when used it must be the first statement in the source module.

ISEQ   This causes the data in the identification fields of successive source statements to be compared, so that the assembler can ascertain whether the statements are in or out of sequence.

OPSYN (only in OS)   OPSYN has two uses—to make certain opcodes unavailable for use, and to define synonyms for some opcodes so that they will be easier to use. The OPSYN specifications, however, apply only to the source module in which they occur.

14.10   REVIEW QUESTIONS

1. What restrictions govern the title that can be used in TITLE directives?
2. Under what conditions is it advisable to use the SPACE directive?
3. What is the difference between a PRINT NODATA directive and a PRINT DATA directive? Between PRINT NOGEN and PRINT GEN? PRINT ON and PRINT OFF?
4. What is the effect of a PRINT DATA,OFF directive? PRINT NODATA,ON?
5. What OPSYN directive will replace the Branch if Not Low opcode (BNL) by a Branch if Greater or Equal opcode (BGE)?
6. What position (i.e., column) within a source module statement in standard format is defined by each of the following terms: *beginning* position, *ending* position, *continuing* position? What is the significance (or meaning) of each of these three positions?

14.11   EXERCISES

1. What rules or constraints, if any, exist at your programming center to standardize the use of each of the cosmetic directives mentioned in this chapter?

2. As a general rule of thumb, the directive PRINT ON,GEN,DATA would have the most utility in a source module that was being debugged or modified, while the PRINT ON,NOGEN,NODATA directive would be more appropriate in a source module that was a finished product, so to speak. If these rules were followed, would you have to specify all three key word options? Why or why not?

3. What would be the effect of two consecutive TITLE directives in a source module?

4. What would be the effect of two consecutive EJECT directives in a source module?

5. What would be the effect of a TITLE directive followed immediately by an EJECT directive or vice versa?

6. What would be the effect of the following TITLE directive:

```
TITLE 'MNEMONIC OPCODES FOR IBM'S 360 & 370 SYSTEMS'
```

7. What would be the effect of the following SPACE directive:

```
SPACE 500
```

8. Formulate and experiment with some rules of thumb concerning use of the SPACE and EJECT directives. Select the one that seems the most effective. Then use your rule in several of your programs, and reevaluate it at a later date, modifying it if necessary. Compare your rule with the rules used by other programmers.

9. If the OPSYN directive is used in a source module, it must appear before any assembly language instruction, and may be preceded only by the following directives: ICTL, EJECT, ISEQ, OPSYN, PRINT, SPACE, and TITLE. In view of this, what would be the effect if the following three statements were the first three statements in a source module:

```
                    ISEQ        73,80
         ISEQ       OPSYN
         OPSYN      OPSYN
```

10. As mentioned in the text, the ICTL directive makes it possible to have source modules in which the identification field occurs first, rather than last, in a line of source code. Describe at least two other situations in which the use of the ICTL directive could be of some benefit in writing source code.

15

Pseudo-ops

Pseudo-ops, directives that can affect the value of the memory location counter at assembly time, may be used for the following purposes:

1. To define the beginning of a control section (CSECT, START, DSECT, COM)
2. To specify the end of a source module (END)
3. To identify the entry points and external references occurring in a source module (ENTRY, EXTRN)
4. To define constants, reserve data areas, and ensure proper boundary alignments (DC, DS, CNOP)
5. To designate implied base registers (USING, DROP)
6. To change the memory location counter (ORG)
7. To cause the assembler to assemble the literal constants it has accumulated in the literal pool (LTORG)

Summary in Figure 15.5

In this chapter, descriptions of the CSECT, START, ORG, LTORG, and END pseudo-ops will be given. The others mentioned in the list will not be reviewed, since they were discussed in previous chapters (see Fig. 15.5). Since all five pseudo-ops to be discussed at this time are in some way directly dependent on the notion of a control section, we begin with a brief description of the concepts that will be needed.

Figure 15.1 *Relationship of control sections to source and object modules.*

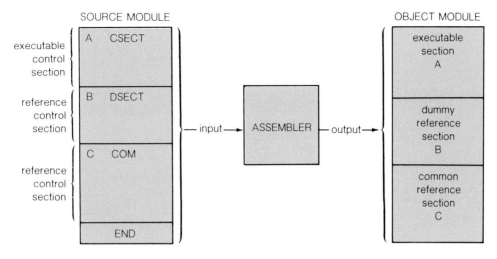

15.1 CONTROL SECTIONS

Each assembly language source module consists of one or more relocatable subdivisions known as control sections. There are two types of control sections: **executable control sections,** initiated by CSECT or START directives, and **reference control sections,** initiated by DSECT or COM directives. An executable control section can contain instructions, constants, and data areas. A reference control section contains neither instructions nor constants; it merely describes or reserves memory areas for use by executable control sections at run time.

The use of reference control sections was described briefly in Chapter 10, but the use of more than one executable control section has not been discussed. Such use provides an alternative to writing separate source modules when we wish to segment a large program into separate relocatable sections. Instead of being in separate modules, the executable sections can be within the same source module. However, since each section is still separately relocatable, it must be written in such a way that control passes properly to another section regardless of the relative physical position of the sections in main memory at run time.

As indicated by Figure 15.1, all the control sections of a source module are assembled into a single object module that is the machine language counterpart of the source module. Figure 15.1 illustrates a simple situation; there are only three control sections organized in a straightforward manner, although the capability to intermix statements from different sections in somewhat arbitrary fashion exists (as will be shown). Too arbitrary an organization can render a source module virtually unreadable and difficult to modify, so it is perhaps wisest to employ several simple conventions regarding control section layout and organization.

From the standpoint of this chapter, the most important point about control sections is this: *the assembler maintains a separate memory location counter (MLC) for each control section in a source module.* This means, of course, that the addresses assigned to symbols defined in one control section are independent of the addresses assigned to symbols defined in any other control section. Therefore, a separate implied base register (or registers) should be established for each of the control sections of a source module.

Control Section MLC's

In addition to establishing base registers for the addressability of control sections, a programmer must inform the assembler on the key issue of which symbols are to be defined in which control sections. The CSECT, START, DSECT, and COM pseudo-ops are the means by which this is done.

Figure 15.2   Continuing a control section.

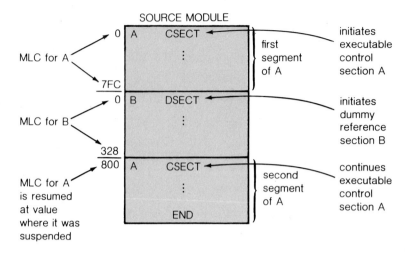

15.2   CSECT

The Control Section (CSECT) pseudo-op is used to specify the beginning of an executable control section in a source module. In those situations where statements from other control sections are intermingled with those of a given control section, CSECT must also be used to indicate the point at which any previously initiated executable control section is to be resumed. Figure 15.2 illustrates a simple case of initiating and continuing an executable control section.

The format of the CSECT pseudo-op is

name field	opcode	operand
{any symbol} {or blank}	CSECT	blank

The symbol (if any) appearing in the name field of a CSECT directive is the name of the control section. This symbol is always considered to be a control section entry point, i.e., it may be referred to as an external symbol from within other source modules. If the name field is blank, the control section is said to be unnamed or private. Because unnamed sections cannot be referenced by other control sections, their use is generally not recommended.

Resuming a Suspended Control Section

In Figure 15.2 the reference section named "B" is placed somewhere in the middle of the source module rather than at the end. To indicate where dummy section B ends and where executable section A resumes, there is a second CSECT with the same name-field symbol as that which initiated the executable section. When continuing a control section with the CSECT directive, the same symbol must be placed in the name field as that which was used to initiate the section. This identifies which control section is being continued; it does not result in a multiply-defined symbol. Note that when A is suspended by initiating B, the value of the memory location counter for Section A is remembered by the assembler. Section B is assigned its own memory location counter with initial value zero. When section A is continued, its MLC is resumed by the assembler at the value where it left off. In Figure 15.2, this is assumed to be location 800_x. For another example, see Figure 15.4.

15.3   START

Difference between START and CSECT

The START pseudo-op has only one purpose: to denote the beginning of the *first* executable control section in a source module. In this respect, it is not as flexible as the CSECT pseudo-op since the CSECT can be used to denote the beginning of *any* executable control section, including the first one. The main advantage of using START instead of CSECT is that START provides a clear-cut indication of where the first executable section begins.

The format of the START pseudo-op is

name field	opcode	operand
{any symbol or blank}	START	a self-defining term or blank

The symbol in the name field is the symbolic name of the control section being initiated. It is always considered to be an entry point of the control section. It is permissible to leave the name field blank, as in the CSECT, the result being an unnamed executable section that cannot be referred to from other sections.

The value of the self-defining term in the operand (if present) designates the initial value for the memory location counter of the control section. If the operand is blank, this initial value is zero.

Note that the START pseudo-op cannot be used to resume an executable control section; CSECT must be used for this purpose, even if START was used to initiate the control section.

15.4   ORG

The Origin (ORG) pseudo-op instructs the assembler to change the value of the memory location counter of the control section in which the ORG occurs. The format of ORG is

name field	opcode	operand
{any symbol or blank}	ORG	a relocatable expression or blank

If the operand field contains a relocatable expression, the memory location counter is set to the value of that expression. If the operand field is blank, the counter is set to the smallest address that has not been previously assigned to any constant, data area, or instruction in the control section. In either case, the new value of the memory location counter is assigned to the symbol (if any) that appears in the name field of the ORG directive.

The value of the relocatable expression can be equal to, greater than, or less than the location counter value that it replaces. If it is equal to that value, there is essentially no effect other than to assign the value to the name-field symbol. If it is greater than the current location counter value, the assembler skips over the intervening addresses and the corresponding bytes are unused.

Perhaps the most frequent use of ORG is to set the location counter back to a previous value *ORG's Main Use* in order to redefine an area of memory. The following example illustrates this:

source statement			effect
A	DS	50F	reserves 50 full words for area A
	ORG	A	sets value of location counter to value of A
B	DS	20F	reserves 20 full words for B, beginning at location A
	ORG	A	sets value of location counter to value of A
C	DS	16F	reserves 16 full words for C, beginning at location A
D	ORG		sets location counter to be 1 byte beyond the area reserved for A

The result is that the three reserved areas of memory—A, B, and C—each begin at the same address, as this diagram illustrates:

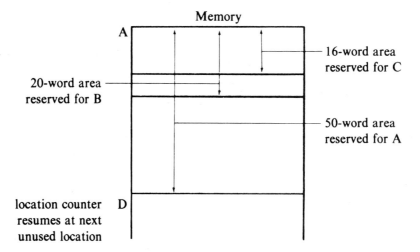

In Fortran, a result identical to that depicted in this assembly language example would be achieved by the following two statements:

```
DIMENSION A(50),B(20),C(16)
EQUIVALENCE ( A(1),B(1),C(1) )
```

As another example, consider this sequence of statements:

```
DATE      DS      CL6
          ORG     DATE
YEAR      DS      CL2
MONTH     DS      CL2
DAY       DS      CL2
          ORG
```

In this sequence, DATE is a six-character field, and YEAR, MONTH, and DAY are two-character fields superimposed on the DATE field as the next diagram illustrates.

The same result would be achieved by Cobol data division statements such as

```
02  DATE.
    03  YEAR        PICTURE 99.
    03  MONTH       PICTURE 99.
    03  DAY         PICTURE 99.
```

One final observation: unlike the CSECT and START pseudo-ops (and the LTORG described in the next section), the ORG pseudo-op may be used in reference control sections as well as in executable control sections. It may be used any number of times in a source module.

15.5 LTORG

The LTORG pseudo-op causes the assembler to assemble all the literal constants it has accumulated. The phrase "assemble the literal constants" means that each constant in the literal pool is removed from that pool and assigned a memory location in the control section in which the LTORG occurs. The memory location counter for that control section is increased accordingly. (The first literal assembled each time a LTORG is processed is assembled on a double-word boundary.)

Although the LTORG pseudo-op is not required in a source module, its use is recommended in any source module containing more than one executable control section, because the assembler always places all literals (from all the executable control sections in a module) into a single literal pool. If the LTORG is omitted, the assembler will not assemble the literals until it reaches the end of the first executable control section. When this is allowed to happen, a literal from one executable section may be assembled in a different executable section! To prevent this from happening, these rules should be observed:

1. If there is more than one executable control section in a source module, there should be a LTORG directive at the end of each of the sections.   *Rules for LTORG*
2. If statements from different control sections are intermingled in a source module, i.e., if one or more sections are "continued" as described in Section 15.2, a LTORG directive should occur at the end of each segment of each control section.

Except for these rules, there are no restrictions on the use of the LTORG directive. It may be used whenever you want the literal constants to be assembled in an executable control section.

The format for the LTORG pseudo-op is simply

name field	opcode	operand
{any symbol or blank}	LTORG	blank

If there is a symbol in the name field, its value is the address the assembler would assign to the first literal (if any) that is assembled when the LTORG is processed.

15.6 END

The END directive indicates to the assembler that there are no more statements to be processed in the source module. It is, therefore, the physically last statement in the module. The format is

opcode	operand
END	a relocatable expression or blank

The operand is used to designate the first instruction that is to be executed at run time. If the operand is blank, the assembler assumes that the first instruction to be executed is the first one of the first executable control section in the module. If the operand contains a relocatable expression, the value of that expression is the address of the first instruction to be executed.

When the END directive is processed by the assembler, all control sections except the first executable section in the source module are terminated. Any literals remaining in the literal pool are then assembled into the first executable section, and that section is terminated. These concepts are illustrated in Figures 15.3 and 15.4.

Figure 15.3 ORG's and DSECT's.

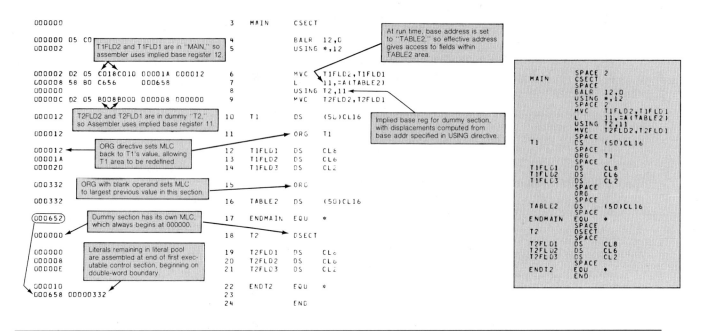

Figure 15.4 CSECT's and LTORG's.

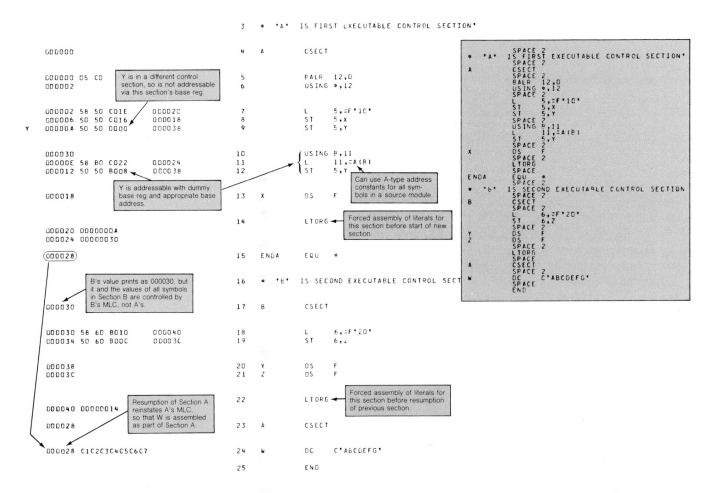

Figure 15.5   Summary of pseudo-ops.

name field	opcode	operand	meaning	section
symbol	COM		initiate or continue a common reference control section	10.6
	CNOP	*b,w*	insert RR-type no-ops if necessary to force alignment of MLC to a specific half word within a full or double word (not discussed in this text)	(none)
symbol	CSECT		initiate or continue an executable control section	15.2
symbol	DC	see section 6.2	define one or more constants for use at run time	6.2
	DROP	r_n	inform the assembler that one or more registers, r_n, are no longer to be used as implied base registers	9.7
symbol	DS	see section 6.4	reserve one or more memory areas for use at run time	6.4
symbol	DSECT		initiate or continue a dummy reference control section	10.6
	END	*d*	mark the physical end of a source module; *d* optionally specifies address of first instruction to be executed	15.6
	ENTRY	s_n	identify one or more symbols, s_n, that may be referred to from within other source modules	10.6
	EXTRN	s_n	identify one or more symbols, s_n, that are defined in other source modules and may be referenced in this source module	10.6
symbol	LTORG		instruct the assembler to assemble all literal constants from the literal pool	15.5
symbol	ORG	*e*	force the MLC in this section to be set to *e*; if *e* omitted, force the MLC to be the largest address not previously assigned in the section	15.4
symbol	START	*t*	initiate the first executable control section, and set its MLC to *t*; if *t* omitted, set its MLC to zero	15.3
	USING	e,r_n	inform the assembler that one or more registers, r_n, are to be used as implied base registers with respective base addresses *e*, $e+4096, \ldots$	3.5; 9.7 10.6 10.7

NOTE: *symbol* = any valid name-field symbol
b,w = one of these pairs: 0,4; 2,4; 0,8; 2,8; 4,8; 6,8
d = any valid relocatable expression, or blank
e = any valid relocatable or absolute expression, or blank
r_n = a list of valid absolute expressions with values 0–15
s_n = a list of symbols
t = a self-defining term or blank

15.7   SUMMARY

The term *pseudo-op* is used in this text to denote directives that affect or depend on the memory location counter. As indicated in Figure 15.5, many of the pseudo-ops described have been covered in previous chapters, and five—CSECT, START, ORG, LTORG, and END—have been discussed in this chapter. Each of these five pseudo-ops is in some way directly related to the concept of a control section.

A control section is a relocatable subdivision of a source module. Each control section may be given a name that must be unique within the source module and that constitutes an entry point of that section. CSECT or START may be used to define the beginning of executable control sections, but the use of START is restricted to denoting the beginning of the first executable control section in a source module. DSECT or COM directives are used to define the beginning of reference control sections, DSECT being used for dummy sections and COM for common sections.

When there is more than one control section in a source module, each section must begin with the appropriate directive and must be resumed with an appropriate directive if resumption is desired. When resuming a section, its name (if any) must be respecified in the name field of the directive.

Within a control section, the memory location counter may be changed by the ORG directive. The new value is specified by the expression in the ORG's operand field. This capability is especially useful for redefining existing data areas with concurrent but different logical structures and names.

The LTORG directive causes the assembly of all literals existing in the literal pool. Once assembled, a literal is removed from the pool so that it will not be assembled again. Appropriate use of LTORG can assure that literals will be within the range of a particular implied base register. This can prevent literals that are referenced in one control section from being assembled in a separately relocatable section.

The END directive denotes the physical end of a source module. Its occurrence causes all literals remaining in the literal pool to be assembled. It also can be used to specify the address of the first instruction that is to be executed at run time.

15.8   REVIEW

Pseudo-op   This type of directive can affect the current value of the assembler's memory location counter—i.e., the address to be assigned to an instruction, constant, or memory area.

Control Section   This term refers to any relocatable unit within a source module. The assembler maintains a separate memory location counter for each control section: addresses in each control section are independent of those in all other control sections. The two types of control sections are known as executable sections and reference sections.

Executable Control Section   This type of control section must be initiated by a CSECT or START directive. Unlike reference control sections, executable control sections can contain instructions, constants, and data areas.

Reference Control Section   This type of control section must be initiated by a DSECT or COM directive. If initiated by DSECT, its purpose is to describe the structure of a memory area without reserving any memory space for that area. If initiated by COM, its purpose is not only to describe the structure of a data area, but also to reserve memory space for that area. A reference control section cannot contain any instructions or constants.

Literal Pool   Constants defined as literals are kept by the assembler in a "pool" or table until one of two things occurs: either the end of the source module is reached, or a LTORG directive is processed. At that time, the constants are assembled.

15.9   REVIEW QUESTIONS

1. What is the minimum number of control sections that can occur in a source module?
2. What would be the effect of having the following two consecutive CSECT directives at the beginning of a source module:

```
        CSECT
MYPROGR CSECT
```

3. What are the three significant differences between the START directive and the CSECT directive? What do START and CSECT have in common?
4. What determines which control section literals are assembled into? If there are any literals remaining in the literal pool when the assembler reaches the end of the source module, into what control section are those literals assembled?
5. If there are no literals in the literal pool when a LTORG directive is processed by the assembler, what will happen? (Try it and see.)
6. What would be the result of having a LTORG directive immediately precede the END directive?

7. What is the major difference between use of ORG with a relocatable expression in its operand field and use of ORG with a blank operand field?

8. When using ORG to redefine an area of memory, why is it good practice to follow the redefinition with an ORG directive that has a blank operand, as in the examples of Section 15.4?

9. Of the fourteen pseudo-ops described in Figure 15.5, which ones can cause the assembler to change the value of the memory location counter?

15.10   EXERCISES

1. What are the differences between the CSECT and START directives?

2. What are the differences between an executable control section and a dummy control section?

3. Suppose a source module consists of two control sections, namely an executable control section named MAIN and a dummy control section named DUM. What statements are required in the executable section to allow symbolic references to areas defined within the dummy section?

4. There are three ways in which the end of a control section may be specified in a source module. One of these is simply to resume, i.e., continue, a previously defined control section with an appropriate directive. What are the two other ways of ending a control section?

5. In the following statements, the first occurrence of the ORG directive sets MLC back to the beginning of the area named TABLE1 in order to redefine the TABLE1 area with symbolically named fields. What is the purpose of the second ORG that occurs? What would be the effect if this second ORG were omitted without changing the other statements?

```
TABLE1     DS      (50)CL16
           ORG     TABLE1
FLD1       DS      CL8
FLD2       DS      CL6
FLD3       DS      CL2
           ORG
TABLE2     DS      (40)CL8
                     .
                     .
                     .
```

6. When data are organized into a table, it is often convenient to refer to the fields of any one table entry symbolically. The DSECT directive can be used to define the fields in a typical table entry; suitable instructions in the program can then allow one to symbolically reference any particular table entry. For example, in the preceding exercise, TABLE1 consists of up to 50 16-byte entries. If this table is defined in an executable control section named MAIN, the fields of each entry in the table could be defined by a dummy section as follows:

```
TABLE1         DS      (50)CL16
T1ENTRY        DSECT
FLD1           DS      CL8
FLD2           DS      CL6
FLD3           DS      CL2
MAIN           CSECT
```

What statements are required in the executable section MAIN to permit references via FLD1, FLD2, and FLD3 to the kth entry in TABLE1 for any integer k such that $1 \leq k \leq 50$? How does this technique differ from the use of ORG to define the fields, as in Exercise 5?

7. Write the assembly language statements that would result in memory being reserved in a manner analogous to the effect of these Fortran statements:

    a. `DIMENSION X(40), Y(40), Z(80)`
       `EQUIVALENCE ( X(1), Y(1), Z(1) )`

    b. `DIMENSION X(5,5), Y(5,5), Z(10,10)`
       `EQUIVALENCE ( X(1,1), Y(1,1), Z(1,1) )`

    c. `DIMENSION X(5,5), Y(5,5), Z(10,10)`
       `EQUIVALENCE ( X(1,1), Y(2,1), Z(5,1) )`

    d. `DIMENSION X(10), Y(20)`
       `EQUIVALENCE (X(1), Y(10), W)`
       (assume that W is a scalar variable; i.e., it is not dimensioned)

8. Write the assembly language statements that would result in memory being reserved in a manner analogous to the effect of these Cobol statements:

```
a. 02       STUDENT.
            03 NAME          PICTURE X(40).
            03 I-D           PICTURE 9(9).

b. 02       ADDRESS          PICTURE X(80).
   02       MAIL-ADDR REDEFINES ADDRESS.
            03 STREET        PICTURE X(35).
            03 FILLER        PICTURE X(5).
            03 CITY-ST       PICTURE X(30).
            03 FILLER        PICTURE X(5).
            03 ZIP           PICTURE 9(5).

c. 01       TITLE.
            02 FILLER        PICTURE X(40) VALUE SPACES.
            02 FILLER        PICTURE X(50) VALUE 'STUDENTS ON DEANS LIST'.
            02 FILLER        PICTURE X(5) VALUE 'PAGE'.
            02 PAGE          PICTURE 999.

d. 02       SALARY           PICTURE 9(5) USAGE IS COMPUTATIONAL-3.
   02       SALARY-X         REDEFINES SALARY PICTURE X(3).
            88 NO-SALARY VALUE SPACES.
```

9. Compare the technique of including more than one executable control section in a source module to that of placing each executable control section in a separate source module. What are the advantages of the former over the latter? What are the disadvantages?

10. Under what circumstances could literals be assigned to memory locations whose addresses are beyond the range of all the implied base registers that were specified by USING directives? How could this be avoided without using LTORG? How could it be avoided by means of LTORG?

11. An ORG directive that is used to redefine a previously defined area, as in the solutions to Exercises 7 and 8, can be followed by any valid statements. But you should generally avoid following such an ORG directive with an instruction or with a directive that causes object code to be generated, if that object code would overlay previously generated object code. For example, what would be assembled into the object module as the result of the following two sets of statements? What problems might this cause at run time?

```
a. A1    DC      C'ABCD'
         ORG     A1
   A2    DC      X'ABCD'
         ORG
```

```
  b. B1      DC      A(B1)
             ORG     B1
     B2      DC      F'4'
             ORG
```

12. Prepare a source module consisting of the following statements and assemble (but do not execute) the module. Note what happens to the address constants. Formulate a rule for address constants that contain symbols defined in dummy sections. Insert other address constants and reassemble the module to verify your rule. Is A(DY-DX) a relocatable or an absolute address constant?

```
     A       CSECT
             BALR    12,0
             USING   *,12
             L       1,X
             L       2,Y
     X       DC      A(DY)
     Y       DC      A(DY-DX)
     Z       DC      A(DX+DZ)
     B       DSECT
     DX      DS      CL3
     DY      DS      CL6
     DZ      EQU     DY-DX
             END
```

13. When writing a subroutine, one can include DSECT's to describe the parameters that are passed by the calling program, and the fields (if any) within the data areas that the calling program specifies with its parameters. With this in mind, suppose there is a need for a subroutine to compute the batting averages of baseball players, based on information passed via a table. Suppose also that the table is defined in the calling program as follows:

```
PLAYERS     DS      (50)CL22     Space for up to 50 player entries
            ORG     PLAYERS      Typical table entry:
NAME        DS      CL15           Bytes    0–14 player's name (given)
ATBATS      DS      P'+999'              15–16 # times at bat (given)
HITS        DS      P'+999'              17–18 # hits (given)
AVG         DS      P'9.999'             19–21 batting average (computed)
            ORG
```

Write a subroutine that will calculate the batting average of each player in such a table. Define a suitable set of parameters to be passed to your subroutine and define these parameters and the typical table entry by means of DSECT's so that the data can be referred to symbolically from within the subroutine. (**Note:** By definition, batting average = # hits / # at-bats, with $0 \le$ # hits $\le$ # at-bats.)

14. Suppose there is a need for a subroutine that will compute the percentage of *yes* votes and the percentage of *no* votes on each of several ballot propositions in a local election. Suppose that the calling program passes the number of votes cast and space reserved for the percentages, as defined in the following table:

```
VOTES       DS      (30)CL16     Space for up to 30 propositions
            ORG     VOTES        Typical table entry:
PROPNO      DS      CL2            Bytes    0–1 prop. I.D. # (given)
NYES        DS      P'9999999'            2–5 # yes votes (given)
NNO         DS      P'9999999'            6–9 # no votes (given)
PYES        DS      P'999.99'            10–12 % yes votes (computed)
PNO         DS      P'999.99'            13–15 % no votes (computed)
            ORG
```

Write a subroutine that will calculate the percentage of *yes* and *no* votes for each proposition in such a table. As in Exercise 13, define a suitable set of parameters to be passed to your subroutine and define these parameters and the typical table entry by means of DSECT's so that the data can be referred to symbolically from within the subroutine.

15. Write a main program (and create suitable test data) to call the subroutine that is written for the solution to Exercise 13. Then change the source module that contains your main program so that it includes the subroutine of Exercise 13 as a second executable control section.

16. Write a main program (and create suitable test data) to call the subroutine that is written for the solution to Exercise 14. Then change the source module that contains your main program so that it includes the subroutine of Exercise 14 as a second executable control section.

16

Conditional Assemblies

Although the assembler normally processes the statements of a source module in the order in which they exist, this normal processing sequence can be altered by the use of certain directives. Also, instead of being fixed at the time they are written, the content of statements in the source module can be made to depend on the value of certain variables. If either of these conditions exists during the assembly of a source module, we have what is known as a **conditional assembly.**

In this book, we will use the term **control directives** to denote the directives used to affect the outcome of conditional assemblies. These directives may be grouped conveniently according to their function:

1. Directives that enable the assembler to skip over some specific statements in a source module—AGO, AIF, and ANOP directives
2. Directives that create or modify variables whose values are used by the assembler to determine whether and/or how to process a statement—GBLx, LCLx, and SETx directives

Before describing the format and purpose of each control directive, we will discuss certain concepts that underlie the use of these directives: sequence symbols, and assembly variables and their scope.

16.1 SEQUENCE SYMBOLS

Purpose Like an ordinary symbol, a **sequence symbol** identifies a source module statement by its appearance in the name field of that statement. But unlike an ordinary symbol, a sequence symbol is not assigned an address when processed by the assembler. Instead, sequence symbols simply indicate the position of statements in the source module, so that the AGO and AIF directives can cause the assembler to skip to certain statements during conditional assemblies and thereby select some for processing and reject others.

Requirements In order to distinguish a sequence symbol from an ordinary symbol (and from variable symbols, discussed in the next section), the first character of a sequence symbol must be a period (.). Of the remaining one to seven characters, the first must be a letter and the others, if any, must be either letters or digits. Examples of valid sequence symbols are

Examples
```
.A
.B1
.SEQ3
.XY31AB
.W100004
```

The following are invalid sequence symbols for the reasons stated:

```
B1            first character not a period
.1B           second character not a letter
.SEQUENCE     more than eight characters
.A B C        blanks not allowed
.X(3)         parentheses not allowed
```

A sequence symbol can appear in the name field of any statement except the following:

Exceptions
GBLx and LCLx directives
ISEQ, ICTL, and OPSYN directives
EQU directives
ACTR directives (not discussed in this text)
COPY directives (not discussed in this text)
DSECT directives in DOS (but not in OS)
MACRO directives, and the macro prototype statement
   (see Chap. 17)
Any other statement in which an ordinary symbol or
   variable symbol already appears in the name field

16.2 ASSEMBLY VARIABLES AND THEIR SCOPE: GBLx, LCLx, SETx

An **assembly variable** is a symbol whose value can be used by the assembler to determine whether and/or how to process a statement in the source module. The value of an assembly variable is not assembled into the object module; it is used only by the assembler. (In most textbooks and reference manuals, assembly variables are called **SET symbols** because the SETx directive assigns values to them. This terminology is unsatisfactory in the author's opinion. Since we are talking about variables whose values are used by the assembler while it assembles a source module, the term *assembly variable* seems more descriptive and useful.)

Variable Symbols In assembly language, an assembly variable is always represented by a **variable symbol,** which is a string of from two to eight characters, the first of which must be an ampersand (&). Of the remaining one to seven characters, the first must be a letter and the others (if any) must be either letters or digits. Examples of valid variable symbols are

Examples
```
&A
&B1
&VAR3
&XY31AB
&W100004
```

In addition to the rules just mentioned for writing variable symbols, there is one other rule: the first three characters following the ampersand cannot be the letters "SYS." Symbols that begin with the characters &SYS are used as system variables (see Section 16.4). Therefore, examples of invalid variable symbols include

B1	first character not an ampersand
&1B	second character not a letter
&VARIABLE	more than eight characters
&A B C	blanks not allowed
&SYS2	can't begin with &SYS

There are three distinct types of assembly variables: *Types*

1. **A**rithmetic variables—values must be integers in the range from -2^{31} through $+2^{31} - 1$
2. **B**oolean variables (also known as logical variables)—values are always either 1 (true) or 0 (false)
3. **C**haracter variables—values are strings of from 0 to 255 characters

As will be seen, an assembly variable's type is always specified in the opcode of the directives   *"x" Is A, B, or C* GBLx, LCLx, and SETx: (1) GBLA, LCLA, SETA for *a*rithmetic assembly variables, (2) GBLB, LCLB, SETB for *B*oolean assembly variables, and (3) GBLC, LCLC, SETC for *c*haracter assembly variables. We will use the generic forms GBLx, LCLx, and SETx when the context is clear, and the specific forms GBLA, GBLB, GBLC, LCLA,..., SETC when it is necessary to make the distinction as to type.

In addition to its type, each assembly variable must be declared as having either global scope or local scope. GBLx directives are used to declare those variables whose scope is global, and LCLx those whose scope is local. Thus, *the declaration via GBLx or LCLx simultaneously determines both the scope and the type of an assembly variable.* No assembly variable can be declared as being both global and local, nor can it be classified as being of more than one type.

The scope of an assembly variable determines the set of source module statements in which   *Scope* *the value of that assembly variable is available to the assembler.* An assembly variable whose scope is *global* is one whose value is available to the assembler in all statements that follow the first GBLx declaration for that variable. An assembly variable whose scope is *local* is one whose value is available to the assembler either in the macro definition in which it was declared, or, if it was declared outside all macro definitions, in those statements that are outside macro definitions, i.e., in so-called **open**   *Open Code* **code.** Since the concept of local scope is directly related to that of macro definitions, we will restrict our discussions and examples in this chapter to global variables. Macros and local variables will be discussed in Chapter 17. Nevertheless, the following observations can be made (see Fig. 16.1):

1. The initial values of global and local assembly variables are assigned by the assembler according to the variable's type:

type	initial value
arithmetic	0
Boolean	0
character	null string (a string of length zero)

2. The value of a global assembly variable is initialized the *first* time it is declared by a GBLx directive. Thereafter, its value can only be changed by a SETx directive.
3. The value of a local assembly variable is initialized *each* time it is declared by a LCLx directive. It also can be changed by a SETx directive within the variable's scope.
4. In DOS macros and DOS open code, GBLx directives must precede LCLx ones. Moreover, GBLx and LCLx directives in DOS open code must precede the first CSECT or START directive in a source module.

Figure 16.1 *Global and local scope of assembly variables.*

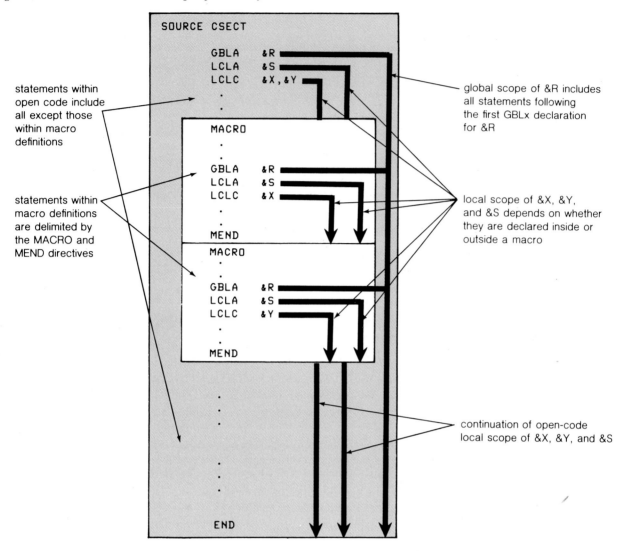

GBLx
LCLx

The formats for the GBLx and LCLx directives are similar to one another:

name field	opcode	operand
blank	$\begin{cases} \text{GBLA} \\ \text{GBLB} \\ \text{GBLC} \end{cases}$	one or more variable symbols separated by commas
blank	$\begin{cases} \text{LCLA} \\ \text{LCLB} \\ \text{LCLC} \end{cases}$	one or more variable symbols separated by commas

For example,

source statement		meaning
GBLA	&X,&Y	declares &X and &Y to be global arithmetic assembly variables, each with initial value 0
LCLC	&UN,&L,&CHAR	declares &UN, &L, and &CHAR to be local character assembly variables, each with initial value null

name field	opcode	operand
variable symbol	`SETA`	an arithmetic expression
variable symbol	`SETB`	a Boolean expression
variable symbol	`SETC`	a character expression

The opcode must be in agreement with the type of assembly variable identified in the name field. A SETx directive can be used any number of times in a source module, but only after the corresponding GBLx or LCLx directive has declared the name, scope, and type of the assembly variable identified in the SETx name field. To be valid, a SETx directive must be within the scope of that assembly variable. The following examples illustrate this:

source statement			meaning
`&X`	`SETA`	`&X+1`	The operand is computed to be 1 more than the current value of the variable &X; the resulting sum is the new value of &X. &X must have been previously declared by a GBLA or LCLA directive.
`&UN`	`SETC`	`'XYZ'`	The three-character string XYZ becomes the value of the variable &UN, which must have been declared by a GBLC or LCLC directive.

It might be helpful if we illustrate the use of assembly variables in a simple setting: that in which a single global assembly variable is used to change the content of any number of source module statements.

Example: Assembly Variables

Let us suppose that we have a source module in which there are statements containing the name of a university or college. The school's name might, for example, occur in a character string defined by a DC directive such as

```
SCHOOL    DC        C'UNIVERSITY OF SAN FRANCISCO'
```

It also might occur in the operand of a TITLE directive

```
          TITLE    'ASSEMBLED AT THE UNIVERSITY OF SAN FRANCISCO'
```

If we wanted the school name to be a variable instead of a fixed string, so that the name could easily be changed whenever it appeared throughout the source module, we could define a global character assembly variable to represent the name, as follows:

```
          GBLC    &UNIV
&UNIV     SETC    'UNIVERSITY OF SAN FRANCISCO'
```

The GBLC directive declares that we want &UNIV to be a global character assembly variable. The SETC directive assigns the value UNIVERSITY OF SAN FRANCISCO to the variable &UNIV. The assembler will substitute the value of &UNIV for every occurrence of &UNIV in the source module. We would therefore write the following statements in place of those given earlier:

```
SCHOOL    DC        C'&UNIV'
          TITLE    'ASSEMBLED AT THE &UNIV'
```

Now, whenever we want to change the name of the university in the source module, all we have to do is change one statement, namely the SETC directive that assigns a value to &UNIV. We would not have to change the DC statement or the TITLE statement or any other statement in which the school's name is represented by the variable symbol &UNIV. In other words, those statements would be assembled *as though* they contained whatever character string we put in the SETC operand.

This extremely simple example should help explain the power of assembly variables: by changing one statement in a source module, we can cause many statements to be effectively changed. When this capability is combined with that of the AIF and AGO directives, the advantages are increased considerably.

16.3   CONDITIONAL ASSEMBLIES: AIF, AGO, ANOP

In addition to being able to substitute the values of assembly variables into statements at the time they are assembled, the assembler can test the value of an assembly variable and make processing decisions based on the test's outcome. The tests are described in the operand of the Assembler IF (AIF) directive. The decisions are yes-no decisions; the assembler either processes the statement following the AIF or skips to another statement whose sequence symbol is given in the AIF's operand.

The format for the AIF directive is

name field	opcode	operand
{ sequence symbol or blank }	AIF	(logical expression) sequence symbol

AIF Processing

The logical expression represents the condition being tested and must be enclosed in parentheses. If the value of the logical expression is true, then the next statement the assembler processes is the one identified by the sequence symbol in the operand of the AIF directive. If the value of the logical expression is false, the next statement that the assembler processes is the one immediately following

AIF Purpose

the AIF. Thus, *the AIF directive is used to cause the assembler to alter its normal statement-by-statement processing sequence, provided that the condition being tested is true.* We can say that the assembler *conditionally branches* to the statement identified by the sequence symbol in the operand of the AIF directive. Note that it is the assembler that conditionally branches at assembly time: the AIF directive is not assembled into the object module; therefore, it does not cause the program to branch at run time. Consequently, the logical expression in an AIF directive must contain only terms that can be evaluated at assembly time.

The logical expression states a relationship that will be either true or false. The relationship is a comparison of two expressions to determine whether the value of one of the expressions is equal to, less than, greater than, greater than or equal to, or less than or equal to the value of the other expression. Each of the two expressions can include assembly variables and constants that may be combined arithmetically ($+$, $-$, $*$, $/$) or logically (AND, OR, AND NOT, OR NOT). The following examples illustrate some of these concepts:

source statement	meaning
AIF (&X EQ 1).X	If the value of the variable symbol &X is equal to 1, the assembler branches to the statement identified by the variable symbol .X.
AIF ('&U' NE 'USF').W	If the value of the string represented by the variable symbol &U is not equal to the string USF, the assembler branches to the statement identified by .W. Note the apostrophes around the assembly variable when it is a character variable.
AIF ((&X EQ 1) AND ('&U' NE 'USF')).T	If both conditions are true—&X = 1 and &U ≠ USF—the assembler branches to statement .T.

Each of the six arithmetic relations

EQ	(equal)	LT	(less than)	LE	(less than or equal)
NE	(not equal)	GT	(greater than)	GE	(greater than or equal)

must be preceded and followed by a single blank character. Similarly, each of the four logical relations

AND   OR   AND NOT   OR NOT

must be preceded and followed by a single blank character. A blank must also precede the word NOT.

The Assembler GOTO (AGO) directive causes the assembler to alter its normal processing sequence by directing it to branch to another statement without testing any condition. Its format is *AGO Purpose*

name field	opcode	operand
{sequence symbol} or blank	AGO	sequence symbol

The sequence symbol in the operand identifies the next statement that the assembler is to process. For example, the statement

AGO   .V

will cause the assembler to skip to the statement identified by the sequence symbol .V.

The Assembler No-Op (ANOP) directive provides a means of identifying a statement (and hence a position in the source module) without causing any action to be taken by the assembler. Its format is *ANOP Purpose*

name field	opcode	operand
{sequence symbol} or blank	ANOP	blank

Example: Conditional Assemblies

Suppose that we have an assembly language program that is to be used on several different IBM System 370 computer systems. Suppose that on some of those systems, the high-speed printer prints the symbol $\div$ for the division operator and that on the others it prints the symbol /. Also suppose that the EBCDIC codes for these two symbols differ from one another; for the symbol $\div$ it is X'5A', for the symbol / it is X'61'.

One way to guarantee that the program will print the appropriate divide symbol is simply to write two separate source modules, one for each of the two types of printers. Another way would be to write only one source module that includes control directives that cause the appropriate divide symbol to be assembled. An outline of how this might be done is shown in Figure 16.2.

In Figure 16.2, the GBLC &DIVIDE statement declares that the variable symbol &DIVIDE is to be used as a character-type assembly variable throughout the source module. The GBLC directive also causes the assembler to assign an initial value of null—a zero-length string—to the &DIVIDE variable. The statement following the GBLC directive

&DIVIDE SETC   '/'

will be included in the source module only for those computer systems whose printer prints the symbol /. For the other systems, the previous SETC statement is not included in the source module. The value of the symbol &DIVIDE will therefore be either '/' or '' (null) depending on whether or not the SETC is included. None of the other statements in the source module have to be changed to accommodate the needs of the printers because of the manner in which the AIF directive is processed.

Figure 16.2 Example of use of AIF, AGO, and ANOP directives.

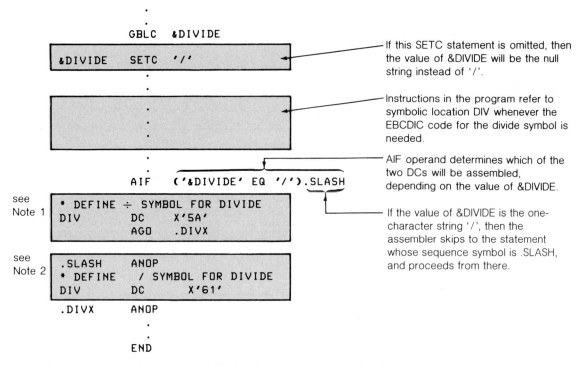

```
                    .
                    .
         GBLC    &DIVIDE                          ┌──── If this SETC statement is omitted, then
                                                  │     the value of &DIVIDE will be the null
 &DIVIDE    SETC   '/'          ◄─────────────────┘     string instead of '/'.
                    .
                    .
                    .                             ┌──── Instructions in the program refer to
                                ◄─────────────────┘     symbolic location DIV whenever the
                    .                                   EBCDIC code for the divide symbol is
                    .                                   needed.
                    .
                    .                             ┌──── AIF operand determines which of the
         AIF    ('&DIVIDE' EQ '/').SLASH ─────────┘     two DCs will be assembled,
                                                        depending on the value of &DIVIDE.

 see     * DEFINE ÷ SYMBOL FOR DIVIDE             ┌──── If the value of &DIVIDE is the one-
 Note 1  DIV       DC      X'5A'                  │     character string '/', then the
                   AGO     .DIVX    ──────────────┘     assembler skips to the statement
                                                        whose sequence symbol is .SLASH,
 see     .SLASH    ANOP                                 and proceeds from there.
 Note 2  * DEFINE  / SYMBOL FOR DIVIDE
         DIV       DC      X'61'

         .DIVX     ANOP
                    .
                    .
         END
```

Note 1: The three statements that include DIV DC X'5A' are processed by the assembler only if the value of the global character assembly variable &DIVIDE is *not* equal to the one-character string '/'.

Note 2: The three statements that include DIV DC X'61' are processed only if the value of &DIVIDE is equal to '/'.

The AIF directive in Figure 16.2 contains the condition that the assembler will test: whether or not the value of the variable &DIVIDE is equal to the slash character, /. If it is equal to the slash character, the assembler skips over the three statements that follow the AIF and resumes its processing at the statement whose name field contains the sequence symbol .SLASH. There it will process the statement

```
        DIV   DC   X'61'
```

which creates the constant needed for the symbol / on the printer. But if the variable &DIVIDE represents the null string instead of the single character /, the AIF condition will be false, and the assembler will process the statement

```
        DIV   DC   X'5A'
```

and then skip down to the .DIVX statement. Therefore, only one statement would be assembled with the symbolic address DIV; it would be the statement that defines the appropriate divide symbol.

16.4 SYSTEM VARIABLE SYMBOLS

System variable symbols are variable symbols whose values are assigned by the assembler. All system variable symbols are character variables; three are global variables, and three are local. A system variable symbol can be used in the operand of any source module statement in which it is permissible to use a character assembly variable, subject to the restrictions governing use of global and local variables. However, the value of a system variable symbol cannot be changed by a SETx directive.

Global System Variables

The three global system variable symbols are &SYSDATE, &SYSTIME, and &SYSPARM. All are available in OS, but only &SYSPARM is available in DOS.

The value of **&SYSDATE** is the date on which the source module in which it appears is assembled. The date is represented by eight characters in the form mm/dd/yy, for example, 03/31/80 for March 31, 1980.

The value of **&SYSTIME** is the time at which the source module is assembled. The time is represented by five characters in the form hh.mm, for example, 13.30 for 1:30 P.M., and 01.30 for 1:30 A.M.

The value of **&SYSPARM** is the character string established by the PARM parameter of the EXEC command in job control language. Its length may be from 0 to 57 characters in OS, and 0 to 8 in DOS. For example, the following JCL

```
in OS:    //STEP      EXEC    ASMFC,PARM=SYSPARM(SLASH)
in DOS:   // OPTION           SYSPARM='SLASH'
```

assigns the five-character string SLASH to the system variable &SYSPARM.

To illustrate the use of &SYSDATE and &SYSTIME, suppose that the date and time of assembly were March 31, 1980, at 1:30 P.M. Then the statement

```
          DC      C'ASSEMBLED ON &SYSDATE AT &SYSTIME'
```

would be assembled as though it were written as

```
          DC      C'ASSEMBLED ON 03/31/80 AT 13.30'
```

To illustrate the use of &SYSPARM, suppose that the EXEC command were the one given above, namely,

```
    //STEP       EXEC    ASMFC,PARM=SYSPARM(SLASH)
```

Then the example of Figure 16.2 could be simplified by eliminating the GBLC and SETC directives used for &DIVIDE and by replacing the AIF directive by the following directive:

```
    AIF     ('&SYSPARM' EQ 'SLASH').SLASH
```

The effect would be the same as that previously described for the situation depicted in Figure 16.2. The advantage of using &SYSPARM is that the source module would not have to be changed at all, just reassembled.

Local System Variables

The three local system variable symbols are &SYSECT, &SYSLIST, and &SYSNDX.

The value of **&SYSECT** is the name of the control section in which &SYSECT is used. Its length is therefore from 0 to 8 characters.

The value of **&SYSLIST** is the value of a positional parameter in a macro instruction. Its length may be 0, 1, or more characters.

The value of **&SYSNDX** is a four-digit character string, 0001 through 9999.

The three local system variable symbols can be used only inside macro definitions. Consequently, further discussion will be postponed until Chapter 17.

16.5 ARITHMETIC, BOOLEAN, AND CHARACTER EXPRESSIONS

As discussed in the preceding sections, expressions are used in the operands of SETx and AIF directives. There are three distinct types of expressions, each with its own rules of syntax and evaluation. In this section, we describe some of these rules so that somewhat more sophisticated conditional assembly situations can be considered. However, a complete discussion of the rules for forming and evaluating expressions is beyond the scope of this textbook and you are referred to the relevant portions of the *Assembler Language Reference Manual* for further information.

Arithmetic Expressions

An arithmetic expression can contain one or more variable symbols and self-defining terms that are combined by the operations of addition (+), subtraction (−), multiplication (∗), and division (/). The variable symbols that appear in arithmetic expressions must have been declared in prior statements by the GBLA or LCLA directives. The value of an arithmetic expression is always either a signed integer or zero. Parentheses can be used within the expression to indicate the order in which operations are to be performed. If parentheses are omitted, the operations are performed from left to right, with multiplications and divisions being performed before additions and subtractions. In divisions, the quotient is always truncated to an integer, the fractional portion being dropped.

The following are examples of valid arithmetic expressions:

&X+&Y	the value of this expression is the sum of the values of the variable symbols &X and &Y
&Z*10	the value is ten times the value of &Z
-&Z	the value is the negative of the value of &Z
&A+&B/10	the integer portion of the value of &B/10 is added to the value of &A; the resulting sum is the value of the expression
(&A+&B)/10	the sum of the values of &A and &B is divided by 10; the integer portion of the resulting quotient is the value of the expression

Boolean Expressions

A Boolean, or logical, expression can be used to assign a value of 0 or 1 to a Boolean assembly variable. But its most frequent use in a source module is as the condition that is tested in the operand of an AIF directive.

A Boolean expression is always enclosed in parentheses, and it always has the value of 1 (true) or 0 (false). Although a Boolean expression can be simply a Boolean assembly variable, it is more frequently made up of a relation—EQ, NE, GT, LT, LE, or GE—between two arithmetic expressions or two character expressions. It can also consist of one or more logical combinations of such relations.

The following are examples of valid Boolean expressions:

(&X NE 100)	If the value of &X is different from 100, the value of this expression will be 1 (true); otherwise it will be 0.
('&UNIV' EQ '')	If the value of &UNIV is the null string, the value of this expression is 1; otherwise it is 0.
((&X NE 100) OR (&X EQ &Y))	If the value of &X is either different from 100 or equal to the value of &Y, or both, the value of this expression is 1; otherwise it is 0.
((&X EQ 100) AND (&X LT &Y))	If the value of &X is equal to 100 and is also less than the value of &Y, the value of this expression will be 1; otherwise it will be 0.

Character Expressions

Concatenation

A character expression can have one of two forms. It can be either a string enclosed in apostrophes or it can be the concatenation of two or more strings, each of which is enclosed in apostrophes. In the latter case, the concatenation operator—a period (.)—must be used to separate the apostrophe that ends one string from the apostrophe that begins the next one.

A string in a character expression may contain variable symbols. The assembler replaces each variable symbol in a character expression with the value of that symbol when it evaluates the expression. The variable symbol may be a character variable, a Boolean variable, or an arithmetic variable. In a character expression, the value of a variable symbol is always a character string. Therefore, the value of a Boolean variable appearing in a character expression will be either the character "1" or the character "0" and not the number 1 or 0. Similarly, the value of an arithmetic variable appearing in a character expression will be the characters that represent the numeric value of that arithmetic variable (except that the sign and any leading zeroes are not represented).

The value of a character expression is always a character string of from 0 to 255 characters. The examples shown below illustrate this. For these examples, we shall assume that &SYSDATE, &A, &B, and &C have had these values and types assigned to them:

```
&SYSDATE  =  03/31/80   (character variable)
      &A  =  4096        (arithmetic variable)
      &B  =  1           (Boolean variable)
      &C  =  USF         (character variable)
```

character expression	value of expression	explanation
'USF'	USF	The value of an expression consisting of a character string is just that string.
'&C'	USF	The value of an expression containing a variable symbol is the string that results after the value of that variable has been substituted in the expression.
'&A + 1'	4096 + 1	The value of an expression containing a variable symbol and a string is the string that results after the value of that variable has been substituted in the expression. *Note that no arithmetic is performed.* The value of &A is represented as a string, not as a numeric quantity.
'&A'.' + 1'	4096 + 1	The result of concatenation is a single string, as though both strings were inside the same pair of apostrophes.
'&A.&B' '&A&B'	40961 40961	Concatenation can occur within a pair of apostrophes. The concatenation operator may be omitted if there would be no ambiguity.
'&A..1'	4096.1	The first of the two periods is the concatenation operator; the second is part of the string being concatenated. The result is the same as though it were written as '&A'.'.1'.
'&A.1'	40961	The concatenation operator is used to avoid ambiguity.
'&C'.'&SYSDATE'	USF03/31/80	The value of the system variable &SYSDATE is substituted before the concatenation takes place.
'&C '.'&SYSDATE' '&C'.' &SYSDATE' '&C &SYSDATE'	USF 03/31/80 USF 03/31/80 USF 03/31/80	When a blank space is desired, it must be explicitly represented. The three expressions shown have the same value.
&A.X	4096X	When a variable symbol is concatenated with an ordinary symbol (X, in this example), the result is the string consisting of the value of that variable symbol immediately followed by the ordinary symbol.
X&A	X4096	The concatenation operator is not used to concatenate an ordinary symbol with a variable symbol.

Figure 16.3 *Use of expressions in a conditional assembly.*

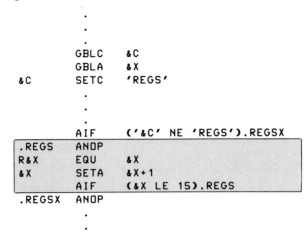

```
                    .
                    .
                    .
            GBLC    &C
            GBLA    &X
    &C      SETC    'REGS'
                    .
                    .
                    .
            AIF     ('&C' NE 'REGS').REGSX
    .REGS   ANOP
    R&X     EQU     &X
    &X      SETA    &X+1
            AIF     (&X LE 15).REGS
    .REGSX  ANOP
                    .
                    .
                    .
```

Some of these aspects of expressions are illustrated in Figure 16.3. Other examples will be given in Chapter 17.

In Figure 16.3, the value of the character variable &C is used to determine whether or not to include the statements that are in the box following the AIF directive. The value of &C is established by the GBLC and SETC directives. The SETC directive would be omitted if the boxed statements were not to be included. (Alternatively, as discussed previously, the system variable &SYSPARM could be used to accomplish the same purpose.) The statements within the box cause the assembler to generate these 16 consecutive EQU directives:

```
            R0      EQU     0
            R1      EQU     1
            R2      EQU     2
            R3      EQU     3
            R4      EQU     4
            R5      EQU     5
            R6      EQU     6
            R7      EQU     7
            R8      EQU     8
            R9      EQU     9
            R10     EQU     10
            R11     EQU     11
            R12     EQU     12
            R13     EQU     13
            R14     EQU     14
            R15     EQU     15
```

A Loop at Assembly Time Note that the AIF directive within the box causes the assembler to skip *back* to a statement it has already processed. Since the value of &X is changed before each such skip, a different EQU is generated each time the AIF condition is true. (Remember that the initial value of an arithmetic variable is 0.)

16.6 ADDITIONAL CAPABILITIES

In this section we will mention briefly two other capabilities available in the IBM 360 and 370 Assembly language: subscripted assembly variables, and the substring notation for character variables.

Subscripted Assembly Variables

Assembly variables can be subscripted, provided they are appropriately dimensioned. The dimension must be declared in the GBLx or LCLx directive. All components of a subscripted assembly variable are of the same type and are assigned the initial value appropriate to that type. For example,

GBLA	&X(10)	declares that &X is a global subscripted arithmetic assembly variable with up to ten components; the names of the components are &X(1), &X(2),..., &X(10)
LCLB	&Y(5)	declares that &Y is a local subscripted Boolean assembly variable with up to five components named &Y(1),..., &Y(5)
GBLC	&Z(3)	declares that &Z is a global subscripted character assembly variable with up to three components, &Z(1), &Z(2), and &Z(3)

Subscript Rules

The dimension in the GBLx and LCLx directives must be an unsigned decimal integer (but not 0). The maximum dimension allowed is 32767 (4095 in DOS). If a variable symbol is dimensioned, it must always be used as a subscripted variable. The subscript can be any valid arithmetic expression whose value is positive but not greater than the dimension size. The following statements illustrate these concepts.

	GBLA	&X(10),&W	declares that &X has ten components, and &W has one
	GBLB	&Y(5)	declares that &Y has five components
	GBLC	&Z(5)	declares that &Z has five components
&X(2)	SETA	3	assigns the value 3 to the second component of &X
&Y(3)	SETB	(&X(2) EQ 3)	assigns the value 1 to the third component of &Y
&Z(5)	SETC	'&X(1)+&X(2)'	assigns the string value 0+3 to the fifth component of &Z
&Z(1)	SETC	'&W.(1)'	assigns the string 0(1) to the first component of &Z

Note that the concatenation operator *must* be used to distinguish subscripting from concatenation.

Substring Notation

One or more consecutive characters within a character string can be referred to by using the substring notation. This notation can be used only in the operand of AIF, SETB, and SETC directives. The notation consists of two arithmetic expressions separated by commas and enclosed in parentheses and is written immediately after the character expression that identifies the string. The first arithmetic expression in parentheses designates the position of the first character in the substring; the second arithmetic expression designates the number of characters in the substring. A substring's length can be from 0 to 255 characters in OS and from 0 to 8 characters in DOS. For example,

Substring Rules

'THIS'(3,2)   designates the substring IS
     ↑ ↑
     | substring is two characters long
   substring begins at third position in the string

'&C'(1,1)   designates the substring consisting of the first character of the value of &C
    ↑ ↑
    | substring is one character long
  substring begins at first position in the string

'&Z(5)'(2,2)   designates the substring consisting of the second and third characters of the string represented by the subscripted variable symbol &Z(5)

Substring notation is particularly useful for selecting and testing characters within a string, as in the following AIF directive:

```
AIF ('&C'(1,1) EQ '(').P1
```

If the first character of the string represented by &C is a left parenthesis, the assembler skips to the statement identified by the sequence symbol .P1.

16.7 SUMMARY

The assembler's usual processing sequence, in which it processes statements in the order in which they occur in a source module, can be altered by the use of the AIF and AGO directives. To do this, use sequence symbols to identify statements to which the assembler is to skip; use assembly variables to specify the conditions (if any) under which the skipping is to occur.

A sequence symbol is a string of from two to eight characters: the first is a period, the second a letter, and the remaining ones (if any) may be letters or digits. When placed in the name field of a statement, the sequence symbol identifies that statement for use by the assembler at assembly time.

An assembly variable is a symbol whose value can be established and changed by appropriate directives and used by the assembler at assembly time. It is represented by a variable symbol, a string whose rules of formation are identical to those of a sequence symbol, except that the first character must be an ampersand instead of a period.

There are three distinct types of assembly variables: arithmetic, Boolean, and character. Any valid variable symbol can be used for any type of assembly variable, but once an assembly variable's type has been established it cannot be changed within its scope. Both type and scope are established by means of either the GBLx or LCLx directives: GBLx for variables of global scope, and LCLx for those of local scope, where the "x" stands for type—x = A for arithmetic, B for Boolean, and C for character variables.

An assembly variable's type determines the manner in which its value is represented and processed. Its value can be changed by appropriate use of a SETx directive of the same type. Its scope determines the set of source module statements in which its value is available to the assembler at assembly time.

The assembler substitutes the value of an assembly variable for that variable before evaluating an expression in which it appears. This capability, together with that of the AIF directive, provides a useful means for varying the object code and/or listing produced by the assembler with a minimum of changes to the source module.

Supplementary facilities exist for enhancing the usefulness of these capabilities. For example, the global system variables &SYSDATE, &SYSTIME, and &SYSPARM are character variables whose values are always available at assembly time. &SYSDATE provides the date of assembly, &SYSTIME the time of assembly, and &SYSPARM the string specified in the PARM= parameter of the OS job-control EXEC command or of the SYSPARM= parameter of the DOS OPTION command. Other facilities include subscripting of assembly variables and processing of substrings contained within the values of character assembly variables.

16.8 REVIEW

Conditional Assembly   The result of assembling a statement, and even whether or not a statement is assembled, can be made to depend on the inclusion of certain directives—AGO, AIF, ANOP, GBLx, LCLx, and SETx—and the value of their associated assembly variables. When this happens, we have what is known as a conditional assembly.

Sequence Symbol (.X)   The purpose of a sequence symbol is to identify a statement so that it can be referred to in the operand of an AGO, AIF, or ANOP directive. A sequence symbol may therefore be thought of as a symbolic statement identifier. It is NOT a symbolic memory address.

Variable Symbol (&X)   Each variable symbol is the name of an assembly variable. Its value is used by the assembler when it assembles a statement that contains the symbol.

Open Code   This term refers to statements that are not included in any macro definition.

Scope of an Assembly Variable The scope of an assembly variable is the set of statements in which its value is available to the assembler, and it depends on two things: (a) whether the variable was first declared in open code or in a macro's definition, and (b) whether it was declared as a global variable or as a local one. See Figure 16.1.

GBLx and LCLx Directives The scope of an assembly variable that is declared by a GBLx directive is global. The scope of an assembly variable that is declared by a LCLx directive is local. The letter "x" represents the variable's type, and can be "A" (arithmetic), "B" (Boolean), or "C" (character).

SETx Directive This directive assigns the value of its operand expression to the variable symbol appearing in its name field. The name-field symbol must have been previously declared by a GBLx or LCLx directive of the same type as the SETx directive.

Arithmetic Assembly Variables These must be declared either by GBLA or LCLA directives and are assigned an initial value of 0 (zero). Their values, which are integers in the range -2^{31} to $+2^{31}-1$, can only be changed by a SETA directive.

Boolean Assembly Variables These must be declared either by GBLB or LCLB directives and are assigned an initial value of 0 (zero). Their values, which are always either 0 (false) or 1 (true), can only be changed by a SETB directive.

Character Assembly Variables These must be declared either by GBLC or LCLC directives and are assigned an initial value of "null" (a string of length zero). Their values, which are character strings whose length can be from 0 to 255, can only be changed by a SETC directive.

System Variables Symbols beginning with the letters "&SYS" are part of the assembly language. Therefore, symbols declared by GBLx and LCLx directives must not begin with "&SYS". See Sections 16.4 and (in the next chapter) 17.6.

Expressions Corresponding to the three types of assembly variables, there are three types of conditional assembly expressions: arithmetic, Boolean, and character. Each has its own rules of syntax and evaluation. See Section 16.5.

AIF Directive The operand of each AIF directive contains two main components: (1) a Boolean expression that is evaluated by the assembler at assembly time, and (2) a sequence symbol that identifies the statement the assembler will skip to if the Boolean expression is true. AIF directives can appear in open code as well as within macro definitions.

16.9 REVIEW QUESTIONS

1. What are the rules for writing a sequence symbol? A variable symbol?
2. Most texts and reference manuals do not mention the term "assembly variable." Instead, they use a different term to mean the same thing. What is that term?
3. For which of the following directives can a sequence symbol NOT identify the statement (i.e., not appear in the name field of the statement) in which the directive appears: CSECT, LTORG, EQU, LCLA, GBLB, SETC, END?
4. If a variable symbol is used to declare an assembly variable of local scope in open code, can the same symbol also be used to declare an assembly variable of local scope within a macro definition? Are those two local declarations related or unrelated? (**Hint:** See Fig. 16.1.)
5. Repeat Question #4, but substitute the word "global" for "local."
6. Despite the rule given in Chapter 14 (Section 14.2) about consecutive ampersands (&) in a TITLE operand, consecutive ampersands were not used in the TITLE operand in the example near the end of Section 16.2. Why is the example correct despite the rule, and why is the rule correct despite the example?
7. Consider the following statement that appears in Figure 16.2:

```
AGO     .DIVX
```

Could the "AGO" opcode be replaced by a "B" (Branch) opcode in that statement? Why or why not?

8. Consider the following two statements that appear in Figure 16.2:

```
        AGO     .DIVX
        . . .
.DIVX   ANOP
```

   a. Could we have replaced ".DIVX" by "DIVX" in both statements? Why or why not?
   b. Could we have replaced the "ANOP" opcode by a "NOP" opcode? Why or why not?
9. Suppose that without changing anything else in Figure 16.2, we were to replace the following statement in that figure:

```
&DIVIDE    SETC    '/'
```

with this statement:

```
&DIVIDE    SETC    '!'
```

   Which (if any) of the two DC directives in that figure would be assembled, and why?
10. Consider the following statement from Figure 16.3:

```
AIF     ('&C' NE 'REGS').REGSX
```

   a. Suppose that without changing any other statements in that figure, we changed the "NE" relation in the above AIF operand to "EQ". How would that affect the analysis given for Figure 16.3 in the text?
   b. Suppose that without changing any other statements in Figure 16.3, we changed the .REGSX symbol in the above AIF operand to .REGS. How would that affect the analysis given for Figure 16.3 in the text?
11. Suppose that &C is a character variable whose value is ASSEMBLER. What is the value of the substring represented by these notations: '&C'(1,8), '&C'(8,1), '&C'(1,1), '&C'(8,8)?
12. What is the major difference between the &SYSTIME variable and either the TIME macro in OS systems or the GETIME macro in DOS systems?

16.10 EXERCISES

1. Which of the following are valid sequence symbols? Which are valid variable symbols? Which are valid ordinary symbols?

a. ABLE	k. .*
b. .X3	l. *.
c. .3X	m. &&X
d. .&ABC	n. &L
e. &.ABC	o. (&L)
f. &ABLE	p. GBLC
g. .ABLE	q. &GBLC
h. ABLE.	r. .GBLC
i. ZETA2	s. .XX
j. &ZETA2	t. &XX

2. What is the fundamental purpose of sequence symbols? How does this differ from the purpose of ordinary symbols?

3. Which of the following two statements is invalid, and why?

```
.X4    ANOP
X4     ANOP
```

4. The principal differences among arithmetic assembly variables, Boolean assembly variables, and character assembly variables are based on the manner in which their values are represented and used by the assembler. What are the restrictions on the manner in which the values of these three types of assembly variables are represented?

5. What is meant by the term "open code"?

6. What initial values would be assigned to each of the assembly variables occurring in the following statements:

```
GBLC        &A,&B
LCLA        &XYZ,&ZYX
LCLC        &STRING,&NUMBER
GBLB        &EVEN,&ODD
```

7. For each of the following AIF directives, determine what values of the arithmetic assembly variable &X will make the logical expression true:

```
a. AIF    ((4*(&X/4) NE &X) AND (8*(&X/8) EQ &X)).DA
b. AIF    (&X/4 LE 4).DB
c. AIF    (((&X GE 1) AND (&X LT 16)) AND (&X NE 12)).DC
```

8. Assume that &X is an arithmetic assembly variable and that &B is a Boolean assembly variable whose value is determined by the statement

```
&B    SETB    ((&X/2)*2 EQ &X)
```

For what values of &X will the following AIF directive cause the assembler to branch to .DD?

```
AIF    (&B).DD
```

9. What is meant by the term *null string?* Write a valid SETC directive that will assign the null string to the character variable &C.

10. Write the conditional assembly statements that will generate the following four EQU's:

```
FPR0    EQU    0
FPR2    EQU    2
FPR4    EQU    4
FPR6    EQU    6
```

11. Write the conditional assembly statements that will generate the following table of 256 EBCDIC character codes:

```
EBCDIC    DC    FL1'01'
          DC    FL1'02'
          DC    FL1'03'
           .
           .
           .
          DC    FL1'255'
          DC    FL1'256'
```

12. Suppose there are two subroutines, named PRINT and PUNCH, respectively. Suppose also that a source module is to be written in such a way that it will call either the PRINT subroutine or the PUNCH subroutine, but not both. Write the conditional assembly statements (and any other statements that are necessary) to enable the module to be assembled with the desired subroutine's name wherever it is needed in the source module, under the constraint that only one statement need be changed to change the subroutine name in the module.

13. Suppose that a source module is to be written in such a way that certain floating-point constants are to be either in short format (single precision) or in long format (double precision). How could this be accomplished via conditional assembly statements?

14. In the example given for Section 16.2, the character assembly variable &UNIV was used to specify the name of a university for substitution in statements such as

```
       TITLE    'ASSEMBLED AT THE &UNIV'
```

Suppose instead that the TITLE operand is written as follows:

```
       TITLE    'ASSEMBLED AT &THE &UNIV'
```

Write the conditional assembly statements that will assign the null string to &THE unless the first seven letters in the value of &UNIV are either UNIVERS or COLLEGE. In the latter cases, assign the string THE to the variable &THE.

15. Suppose that an assembly is initiated by the job control language statement

```
   //STEP        EXEC       ASFMC,PARM=SYSPARM(NOSEQ)
```

What would be the effect of the following statements in the source module:

```
                 AIF        ('&SYSPARM' NE 'NOSEQ').OK
   ISEQ          OPSYN
   .OK           ANOP
```

16. Write the conditional assembly language statements that will generate a table of twelve constants that can be used as patterns with the ED and EDMK instructions to convert packed-decimal numbers to the equivalent of Fortran In format, for $n = 1,2,..., 12$. (Patterns are discussed in Section 12.9.)

17

Macros

A **macro** is an opcode that represents a set of one or more assembly language instructions, directives, or other macros. As such, it is a kind of high-level extension of assembly language. The set of statements that a macro represents must be defined before the macro can be used in a source module. Some macros, such as the GET and PUT I/O macros, are defined by system programmers and may be used by any assembly language programmers. Other macros are defined by programmers for use in their own or their colleagues' source modules. In this chapter, we will describe how to define and use macros. It will be apparent that macros are a significant extension of the concept of conditional assemblies discussed in Chapter 16. The use of variable symbols together with the SETx and AIF directives in macro definitions provides capabilities that can make assembly language programming simpler, less error prone, more structured, and more like that in a high-level language without sacrificing the capabilities of assembly language.

17.1 A SAMPLE MACRO

Before describing the mechanisms available for defining macros, we will illustrate the use of a macro with a simple example.

Suppose that there is a macro named ADD with the following property: whenever the statement

opcode	operand
ADD	X , Y

is written in a source module, the effect is equivalent to these three statements:

```
L     5,X
A     5,Y
ST    5,X
```

But more than this, we can write

```
ADD     ALPHA,BETA
```

and get the same effect as if we wrote

```
L     5,ALPHA
A     5,BETA
ST    5,ALPHA
```

In fact, the ADD macro is such that we can write any two valid symbols in place of ALPHA and BETA. All that is required is that we understand three things about the ADD macro:

1. It always causes Register 5 to be used, so that the previous number in that register is replaced by the result of the ADD macro.
2. There must be exactly two symbols in the operand, and they must designate full-word integers.
3. The number whose address is represented by the second symbol is added to the number whose address is represented by the first symbol; the sum is stored at the address represented by the first symbol.

Once these facts are understood, we can write any of the following source code statements with the knowledge that each will be equivalent to those shown on the right:

source code statements		equivalent statements	
ADD	X1,X2	L	5,X1
		A	5,X2
		ST	5,X1
ADD	Z,=F'15'	L	5,Z
		A	5,=F'15'
		ST	5,Z
ADD	Y,X	L	5,Y
		A	5,X
		ST	5,Y
ADD	0(4),0(6)	L	5,0(4)
		A	5,0(6)
		ST	5,0(4)

If we were to use the ADD macro in a source module in any of the ways just illustrated, the assembler would insert the three equivalent statements at the point where the ADD macro was used. The inserted statements are known as the **macro's expansion.** It is the expansion statements that are executed at run time, not the ADD macro. The ADD macro does not have a corresponding machine language format into which it is translated at assembly time. Instead, the ADD macro represents the expansion statements, and it is these statements that get translated into their corresponding machine language formats.

When the ADD macro or any other macro is used in a source module, we say that the macro is being **invoked.** This means that the assembler is called upon to insert the appropriate expansion. This capability is made possible through the mechanism of macro definitions.

17.2 DEFINING MACROS

The definition of a macro can be included in the source module in which it is invoked, or it can be placed in a separate file that is accessible to the assembler while it is assembling that source module. When included in a source module, a macro definition must occur before the first CSECT or START directive in that module and after any ICTL or OPSYN directives. When included in a separate file, the name of the file must be specified in a job control statement. In either case, a macro definition must consist of three types of information:

1. The *name* of the macro—the opcode that will be used to invoke it
2. The format of the operand field of the macro
3. The sequence of instructions, directives, comments, or other macros that the macro opcode represents.

The first statement of a macro definition must be a MACRO directive. This is known as the *header* statement and has the format

MACRO Directive

name field	opcode	operand
blank	MACRO	blank

The second statement of the definition must describe the name, opcode, and operand fields of the macro. This statement is known as the **prototype statement,** or sometimes as the *model* statement; it defines the syntax to be used when the macro is invoked in a source module. Its format is

Macro Prototype

name field	opcode	operand
$\begin{Bmatrix} \text{variable symbol} \\ \text{or blank} \end{Bmatrix}$	$\begin{Bmatrix} \text{macro's} \\ \text{name} \end{Bmatrix}$	$\begin{Bmatrix} \text{a list of positional parameters} \\ \text{and/or keyword parameters} \end{Bmatrix}$

The macro's name must be present in the opcode field of the prototype statement. This name must be different from the names of all mnemonic instructions, directives, and other macros. The name-field symbol and the parameters in the operand are not required; their presence depends on the other statements in the definition. Each **positional parameter** is represented by a variable symbol; each **keyword parameter** is represented by a variable symbol followed immediately by an equal sign (=) and the default value of that symbol. In OS, keyword and positional parameters may be intermixed in the operand. In DOS, all positional operands must precede all keyword ones. In both systems, the parameters must be separated by commas. Blanks are not permitted as separators. The following prototype statements should help clarify these concepts:

Macro Parameters

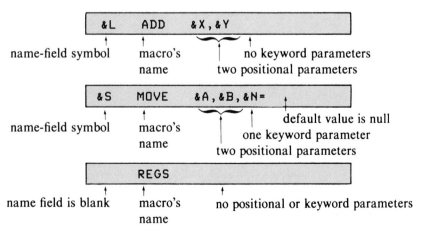

Immediately following the prototype statement is a set of one or more statements known as the **body** of the macro definition. The statements in the body of the definition define the manner in which the macro is to be processed by the assembler when the macro is invoked. The body may include any valid assembly language statement except a MACRO, ICTL, OPSYN, or MEND directive. (In DOS but not OS, one other directive is not permitted: END .)

The last statement of the definition must be a MEND directive. Known as the *trailer* statement, its format is

name field	opcode	operand
sequence symbol or blank	MEND	blank

These concepts are illustrated in Figures 17.1 and 17.2. Figure 17.2 shows how the ADD macro described in the preceding section is defined. In addition to the facts that the MACRO directive must occur first, the prototype second, and the MEND last, the following rule is essential: *the variable symbols appearing in the prototype statement represent values that are substituted in the statements of the body when the macro is invoked.*

The variable symbols used in the prototype statement have the following properties:

1. They are character assembly variables whose scope is local, i.e., restricted to the statements in the definition.
2. They must be different from all global and other local assembly variables that are declared by GBLx or LCLx statements in the definition.
3. Their values are determined when the macro is invoked.

For example, suppose the ADD macro of Figure 17.2 is invoked by the statement

```
LOOP        ADD         X,Y
```

Then, at assembly time, the assembler will compare this statement to the corresponding prototype statement in the definition of the ADD macro,

```
&L          ADD         &A,&B
```

The assembler then makes the following assignments of string values:

```
&L    =    'LOOP'
&A    =    'X'
&B    =    'Y'
```

It substitutes these values into the statements of the body of the definition, namely,

```
&L          L           5,&A
            A           5,&B
            ST          5,&A
```

and thereby produces the expansion

```
LOOP        L           5,X
            A           5,Y
            ST          5,X
```

Notice that the relative position of X and Y in the operand of the statement that invokes the ADD macro is of crucial importance. In other words, ADD X,Y would produce a different expansion than ADD Y,X.

Name-Field Parameter

Notice also that the variable symbol &L in the name field of the prototype statement allows the programmer to specify a name-field symbol when invoking the macro. The macro definition—statements in the body of the macro—defines the statement of the expansion that is to be associated with the name-field symbol used when the macro is invoked. Thus, we could have other statements that branch to the statement that invokes the macro in our source module, as in the sequence

```
LOOP        ADD         X,Y
            ---         ---
            ---         ---
            BCT         5,LOOP
```

Figure 17.1   Schematic representation of a macro's definition.

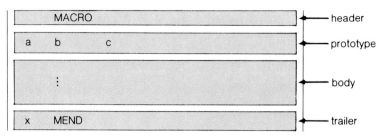

a = an optional variable symbol designating the name-field
    symbol that may be associated with the macro when it
    is invoked

b = the macro's name, or opcode

c = the specifications of the operand

x = an optional sequence symbol identifying the MEND
    statement

Figure 17.2   Definition of ADD macro.

The manner in which the value of a variable symbol is determined thus depends on whether the symbol is the name-field symbol, a positional parameter, or a keyword parameter. *In all three cases, however, the value is a character string.*

The value of the prototype's name-field symbol is the string that exists in the name field of the statement that invokes the macro. This string consists of from 0 to 8 characters, i.e., it can be null.

The values of the prototype's positional parameters are the strings that occupy the corresponding positions in the operand of the statement that invokes the macro. There is a one-to-one correspondence between the positional parameters in the prototype and the values of these parameters in the invoking statement.

The values of the prototype's keyword parameters (if any) are the strings defined for each keyword parameter in the prototype's operand. These are known as the *default values*. A keyword parameter's default value will be overridden by any value specified for that keyword in the operand of the invoking statement.

It should be noted that *an expansion will be generated whether or not it consists of valid assembly language statements.* Only after it has been generated, not before, will the assembler flag a statement that is in error.

A few examples should help clarify these concepts. In the prototype statement of Figure 17.3, namely,

```
&S        MOVE         &A,&B,&N=
```

the default value of &N is the null string. To override this or any keyword's default value, you must specify that keyword and its desired value, leaving off the ampersand (&). Thus, if the invoking statement is

```
X         MOVE         HERE,THERE,N=10
```

Figure 17.3   Definition of MOVE macro.

```
              MACRO
      &S      MOVE      &A,&B,&N=
              AIF       ('&N' EQ '').M1
      &S      MVC       &B.(&N),&A
              AGO       .M2
      .M1     ANOP
      &S      MVC       &B,&A
      .M2     MEND
```

then the value of the keyword parameter &N will be the character string 10. But if the invoking statement is

```
      X       MOVE      HERE,THERE
```

the value of the keyword parameter &N will be its default, the null string. And, finally, if the invoking statement is

```
      X       MOVE      HERE
```

not only will the value of &N be null, but so will the value of &B. The expansions generated for these three statements are these:

source statement			expansion statement		
X	MOVE	HERE,THERE,N=10	X	MVC	THERE(10),HERE
X	MOVE	HERE,THERE	X	MVC	THERE,HERE
X	MOVE	HERE	X	MVC	,HERE

In the third case, the expansion generated is an invalid assembly language statement and will be so flagged by the assembler.

REGS Macro: Conditional Assembly

As another example, consider the prototype statement of Figure 17.4. This prototype contains no parameters and no name-field symbol. This means that the only statement that should be used to invoke the REGS macro is one whose opcode contains the macro name REGS and whose name and operand fields are blank. Comparing Figure 17.4 to Figure 16.3 of the preceding chapter, we see that the REGS macro definition incorporates the statements that generate the 16 consecutive EQU directives discussed in Section 16.5. In other words, the concept of the conditional assembly has been placed inside a macro definition. If the REGS macro is not invoked, its EQU directives will not be generated. If it is invoked, the value of the local arithmetic variable &X will be initialized by the assembler to be 0 at the time REGS is invoked and the remaining statements in the definition will be processed until the value of &X exceeds 15. For each value of &X less than or equal to 15, the macro definition causes the corresponding EQU directive

```
      R&X     EQU       &X
```

to be generated.

17.3   USE OF CONTROL DIRECTIVES

The statements in the body of a macro's definition can include any of the control directives—GBLx, LCLx, SETx, AIF, AGO, ANOP. In order to illustrate the additional capabilities in which this results consider the following problem.

Figure 17.4   *Definition of REGS macro.*

```
           MACRO
           REGS
           LCLA    &X
    .REGS  ANOP
    R&X    EQU     &X
    &X     SETA    &X+1
           AIF     (&X LE 15).REGS
           MEND
```

Suppose a programmer would like to have a macro to use whenever he or she must write the statements needed to return from a subroutine. The macro would have to represent each of the four standard return sequences (see Chap. 10):

```
L      13,SAVE+4
LM     14,12,12(13)        restore all registers
BR     14
----------------------
L      13,SAVE+4
L      14,12(13)           restore all but R15 and R0
LM     1,12,24(13)
BR     14
----------------------
L      13,SAVE+4
L      14,12(13)           restore all but R15
LM     0,12,20(13)
BR     14
----------------------
L      13,SAVE+4
LM     14,15,12(13)        restore all but R0
LM     1,12,24(13)
BR     14
```

One way to accomplish this would simply be to define four separate macros, one for each situation. But the preferable way to accomplish it is by defining one macro that could be used in all four situations. This is preferable because it is easier to understand and easier to use, even though it is more difficult to define.

The problem of designing such a macro has two parts: (1) what the macro prototype should be and how to invoke it, and (2) what statements should be in the body of the definition in order for the assembler to process the macro as intended when it is invoked.

Our choice of prototype is

```
&L    RETRN    &R1,&R2
```

(This prototype differs from that of the IBM system macro RETURN, even though both RETRN and RETURN have essentially the same purpose. The IBM macro is more generally useful than the one described here.) The meaning of the RETRN macro is *Return to the calling program after restoring all registers except the registers (if any) designated in the operand.* The exceptions can only be Register 0, Register 15, or both Register 0 and Register 15. Thus, there are four essentially different ways to invoke the RETRN macro:

```
RETRN              restores all registers
RETRN  0,15        restores all but R15 and R0
RETRN  15          restores all but R15
RETRN  0           restores all but R0
```

Each of these invoking statements will cause the assembler to generate the corresponding expansion for the return sequence as given earlier in this section.

Clearly, the definition of the RETRN macro must be able to distinguish among different values of the parameters &R1 and &R2. This is done by using AIF directives in the macro definition. For example, to determine whether any values are present in the operand when RETRN is invoked, a statement such as this AIF can be used:

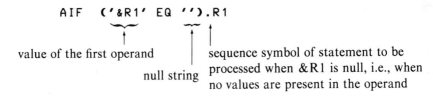

The other three situations can be similarly tested.

A possible definition of the RETRN macro that always produces the desired expansion is shown in Figure 17.5. To understand this definition, you must keep two things clearly in mind:

1. The prototype statement (line 2) identifies the name of the RETRN macro and the variable symbols whose values can be specified when the RETRN macro is invoked.
2. The statements in the body of the definition are processed at assembly time each time the RETRN macro is invoked. It is during this assembly time processing of the definition that the expansion is generated by the assembler. The expansion is not executed until run time.

In the remainder of this section, we will discuss the definition of the RETRN macro.

Statements 3–7 enable the assembler to determine the subsequent statements of the definition that should be processed when the macro is invoked and one of the following situations exists: (1) no values are specified in the operand of the invoking statement; (2) one value (either 0 or 15) is specified in the operand; (3) two values are specified in the operand (either 0,15 or 15,0); or (4) one or more unacceptable values are specified in the operand. This is done as follows:

The RETRN Macro

statement number	statement		explanation
3	AIF	('&R1' EQ '').R1	This determines whether the first operand field is present. If not, the assembler skips to Statement 10, identified by the sequence symbol .R1.
4	AIF	(('&R1' NE '0') AND ('&R1' NE '15')).RERR	When the first operand field is present, this determines whether its value is acceptable.
5	AIF	('&R2' EQ '').R3	When the first operand is present and its value is either 0 or 15, this determines whether the second operand is present. If it is not, the assembler skips to Statement 25, identified by the sequence symbol .R3.
6	AIF	(('&R2' NE '0') AND ('&R2' NE '15')).RERR	This determines whether the value in the second operand is acceptable.
7	AGO	.R2	When both operands are present and valid, the assembler skips to Statement 17, identified by the sequence symbol .R2.

Figure 17.5 Definition of RETRN macro.

```
 1              MACRO
 2   &L         RETRN       &R1,&R2
 3              AIF         ('&R1' EQ '').R1
 4              AIF         (('&R1' NE '0') AND ('&R1' NE '15')).RERR
 5              AIF         ('&R2' EQ '').R3
 6              AIF         (('&R2' NE '0') AND ('&R2' NE '15')).RERR
 7              AGO         .R2
 8   .*
 9   .*   &R1 NOT PRESENT, THEREFORE &R2 ASSUMED NOT PRESENT
10   .R1        ANOP
11   &L         L           13,SAVE+4
12              LM          14,12,12(13)        RESTORE ALL REGISTERS
13              BR          14
14              MEXIT
15   .*
16   .*   &R1 IS PRESENT, AND &R2 IS PRESENT, AND BOTH ARE VALID
17   .R2        ANOP
18   &L         L           13,SAVE+4
19              L           14,12(13)           RESTORE ALL BUT R15 AND R0
20              LM          1,12,24(13)
21              BR          14
22              MEXIT
23   .*
24   .*   &R1 IS PRESENT, BUT &R2 IS NOT PRESENT
25   .R3        ANOP
26              AIF         ('&R1' EQ '0').R3A
27   &L         L           13,SAVE+4
28              L           14,12(13)           RESTORE ALL BUT R15
29              LM          0,12,20(13)
30              BR          14
31              MEXIT
32   .*
33   .R3A       ANOP
34   &L         L           13,SAVE+4
35              LM          14,15,12(13)        RESTORE ALL BUT R0
36              LM          1,12,24(13)
37              BR          14
38              MEXIT
39   .*
40   .*   INVALID VALUES OF &R1 OR &R2
41   .RERR      ANOP
42              MNOTE       9,'&R1 OR &R2 NOT VALID. EXPANSION NOT GENERATED.'
43   .*
44              MEND
```

Thus, when the condition tested in Statement 3 is true, the only other definition statements processed by the assembler are

```
10   .R1        ANOP
11   &L         L           13,SAVE+4
12              LM          14,12,12(13)   restore all registers
13              BR          14
14              MEXIT
```

The MEXIT directive instructs the assembler to stop its assembly-time processing of the RETRN macro. This directive is equivalent to an unconditional skip (AGO) to the MEND directive. Its format is

name field	opcode	operand
{ sequence symbol or blank }	MEXIT	blank

When the condition tested in Statement 3 is not true, Statement 4 is processed. If the value of &R1 is neither 0 nor 15, the only other definition statements processed by the assembler are

```
41   .RERR   ANOP
42           MNOTE   9,'&R1 OR &R2 NOT VALID. EXPANSION NOT GENERATED.'
43   .*
44           MEND
```

MNOTE Directive

The MNOTE directive specifies a message that is printed on the listing and a **severity code** (9, in this case). Its format is

name field	opcode	operand
{ sequence symbol or blank }	MNOTE	n,'...'

where n is the severity code and '...' is the character string, to be printed on the listing

A severity code value greater than eight usually causes run-time execution to be suppressed. A code less than or equal to eight simply generates a warning message. In either case, the MNOTE directive is printed when it is part of the expansion and its position in the listing is cross-referenced at the end of the listing. The values of any variable symbols appearing in the MNOTE character string are substituted by the assembler before the string is printed.

Macro Comment .

Statement 3 (and a few other statements in the definition) begins with the two characters '.*' in positions 1 and 2. This identifies the statement as an *internal macro comment statement*. Such statements are never printed in the expansion; their purpose is to serve as documentation or to provide spacing for readability of the definition on the listing.

When the conditions tested in both Statements 3 and 4 are not true, Statement 5 is processed. This AIF statement determines whether the second operand (the value of &R2) is present when the macro is invoked. If the macro is invoked by either of these two statements:

```
RETRN   0
RETRN   15
```
nonnull value for &R1; null value for &R2

the second operand will not be present. When the value of &R2 is null, the assembler determines which of the two acceptable values of &R1 is present in the invoking statement. It does this via Statement 26. Depending on the value of &R1, either Statements 27–31 or Statements 33–38 are processed. You can verify that these correspond to the cases &R1 = 15 and &R1 = 0, respectively.

Note that when both &R1 and &R2 are present in the operand of the statement that invokes the RETRN macro, the statement can be written as either

```
RETRN   0,15
```
or
```
RETRN   15,0
```

In both cases, the correct expansion for restoring all but Registers 0 and 15 is generated; these are generated by Statements 17–22.

In summary, the RETRN macro definition causes the assembler to generate the correct expansion for a standard subroutine return in each of the four situations shown here:

source statement	expansion generated

```
RETRN              L     13,SAVE+4
                   LM    14,12,12(13)      RESTORE ALL REGISTERS
                   BR    14


RETRN 0,15   ⎫     L     13,SAVE+4
    or       ⎬     L     14,12(13)         RESTORE ALL BUT R15 AND R0
RETRN 15,0   ⎭     LM    1,12,24(13)
                   BR    14


RETRN 15           L     13,SAVE+4
                   L     14,12(13)         RESTORE ALL BUT R15
                   LM    0,12,20(13)
                   BR    14


RETRN 0            L     13,SAVE+4
                   LM    14,15,12(13)      RESTORE ALL BUT R0
                   LM    1,12,24(13)
                   BR    14
```

17.4   CONCATENATION: AN EXAMPLE

Corresponding to the RETRN macro of the preceding section, we can define a CALL macro that will generate the standard set of statements required when calling a subroutine. As discussed in Chapter 10, this set consists of the statements

```
        LA          1,=A(X,Y,...)
        LA          13,SAVE
        L           15,=V(SUBR)
        BALR        14,15
```

Since the statements we have been using to begin an executable control section include LA 13,SAVE, that instruction usually is not needed when calling a subroutine. But if we had not included that instruction when beginning a section, or if the contents of Register 13 had been altered prior to a subroutine call, the instruction would be required in the call.

The definition of the CALL macro in Figure 17.6 generates the correct statements for any subroutine name and any number of parameters X,Y,.... It also permits the invoking statement to specify whether or not the address of the register save area should be loaded into Register 13 and, if so, what that address should be. It is a simple definition because it relies on the principle of string concatenation discussed in Chapter 16. The definition also illustrates the type of situation in which a keyword parameter is to be preferred over a positional parameter: namely, one in which the default is frequently the value that is desired for the parameter.

CALL Macro

The prototype statement in Figure 17.6 contains two positional parameters and one keyword parameter. The keyword parameter's default value is used to decide whether or not to generate the instruction that loads Register 13 with the save-area address. The first positional parameter is the name of the subroutine to be called; the second is the set of parameters to be used in the call. For example, if this were the statement invoking the CALL macro,

```
        CALL        SQRT,(X)
```

the expansion generated would be

```
        LA          1,=A(X)
        L           15,=V(SQRT)
        BALR        14,15
```

Figure 17.6   Definition of CALL macro.

```
1               MACRO
2       &L      CALL        &SUBR,&PARAM,&SAVE=
3       &L      LA          1,=A&PARAM
4               AIF         ('&SAVE' EQ '').C1
5               LA          13,&SAVE
6       .C1     L           15,=V(&SUBR)
7               BALR        14,15
8               MEND
```

The expansion is generated by the assembler after it substitutes the following values for the parameters and name-field symbol in the body of the definition:

&L	= null string
&SUBR	= SQRT
&PARAM	= (X)
&SAVE	= null string

Since each of the variable symbols that occurs in a prototype statement is a local character variable, the values given are character strings available to the assembler only while it generates the expansion for the CALL SQRT,(X) statement. A subsequent CALL statement will cause a possibly different expansion to be generated, depending on the values given in that CALL statement.

There are two important things to note: First, the value of &SAVE that was generated is the default value specified in the prototype. This is because the invoking CALL statement did not specify that the default should be overridden. To override the default, we would have to specify a value for the keyword SAVE as in the statement

```
CALL    SQRT,(X),SAVE=MAINAREA
```

If this were done, the expansion would be

```
LA      1,=A(X)
LA      13,MAINAREA
L       15,=V(SQRT)
BALR    14,15
```

Concatenation   The second point to note is the manner in which the value of &PARAM is used in the definition. Statement 3 of Figure 17.6,

```
&L      LA      1,=A&PARAM
```

causes the assembler to concatenate the string value of &PARAM to the letter A. Thus the second operand in Statement 3,

```
=A&PARAM
```
becomes
```
=A(X)
```

You can verify that for each of the source statements on the left, the expansion generated is the one given on the right:

source statement			expansion		
LOOP	CALL	SEARCH,(A,N,X)	LOOP	LA	1,=A(A,N,X)
				L	15,=V(SEARCH)
				BALR	14,15
	CALL	CALL,(PARAM),SAVE=SAVE		LA	1,=A(PARAM)
				LA	13,SAVE
				L	15,=V(CALL)
				BALR	14,15
	CALL	HELP		LA	1,=A
				L	15,=V(HELP)
				BALR	14,15

In the expansion for the CALL HELP statement, the assembler has assigned the null string to the variable symbol &PARAM. This is because no value for &PARAM was specified in the CALL HELP statement. As was indicated earlier, the absence of a string value for *any* positional parameter causes the null string to be assigned as the value for that parameter. The assembler does not check for inconsistencies or errors of this type unless the macro definition explicitly provides for such checks (via AIF directives). The erroneous statement in the expansion

$$\text{LA} \quad 1,=A$$

will be flagged by the assembler as an error when it tries to assemble that statement.

17.5   USE OF PARAMETER SUBLISTS

A **parameter sublist** is a set of one or more values specified for a positional or keyword parameter when invoking a macro. The values must be separated by commas and enclosed in parentheses. Statements in the body of the definition can refer to any of the values in the sublist by means of subscripts. *The subscript designates the position of the value within the sublist.* The subscript must therefore be greater than or equal to 1.

For example, when invoking the CALL macro that was defined in Figure 17.6, the value of the second parameter &PARAM is specified by a parameter sublist. In the CALL SQRT,(X) example discussed earlier, the sublist consisted of only a single value, X, but it is a sublist because it is enclosed in parentheses and represents the value of a macro parameter. In the definition, &PARAM could have been subscripted in the form &PARAM(1) to refer to the value X. The subscript of 1 is used because X is the first value in the sublist. Similarly, for the CALL statement

$$\text{CALL} \quad \text{SEARCH,(A,N,X)}$$

the value of &PARAM is the string (A,N,X) as before, but &PARAM can also be subscripted to refer to individual values in the sublist:

$$\&PARAM(1) \ = \ A$$
$$\&PARAM(2) \ = \ N$$
$$\&PARAM(3) \ = \ X$$

A subscript greater than the number of values in the sublist corresponds to a value of null. For the above CALL statement, the value of &PARAM(k) for any k greater than 3 is the null string.

We will illustrate the use of sublists by describing the BASE macro defined in Figure 17.7. The purpose of the BASE macro is to provide an easy means of establishing *one or more* implied base registers in a source module. The positional parameter &R in the prototype

BASE Macro

$$\&L \qquad \text{BASE} \qquad \&R$$

Figure 17.7 *Definition of BASE macro.*

```
 1                MACRO
 2     &L         BASE       &R
 3                LCLA       &X,&Y              &Y WILL BE MULTIPLE OF 4096
 4     &X         SETA       1                  &X IS SUBSCRIPT FOR SUBLIST VALUES
 5     .*
 6     .*   ESTABLISH FIRST BASE REGISTER VIA 'BALR'
 7     .*
 8     &L         BALR       &R(1),0
 9                USING      *,&R(1)
10     B&SYSNDX   EQU        *
11     .*
12     .*   DETERMINE WHETHER THERE ARE ANY MORE SUBLIST ENTRIES
13     .*
14     .B1        ANOP
15     &X         SETA       &X+1
16                AIF        ('&R(&X)' EQ '').B2
17     .*
18     .*   ESTABLISH ALL BUT FIRST BASE REGISTER VIA 'LA' INSTRUCTIONS
19     .*
20                LA         &R(&X),2048(&R(&X-1))
21                LA         &R(&X),2048(&R(&X))
22     &Y         SETA       4096*&X-4096
23                USING      B&SYSNDX+&Y,&R(&X)
24                AGO        .B1
25     .*
26     .B2        MEND
```

Sublist Example   will be specified as a sublist when invoking the BASE macro. For example,

```
           BASE        (12,11)
```

will cause the assembler to generate an expansion that will establish Register 12 as the first base register and Register 11 as the second. The expansion generated in this case will be

```
           BALR        12,0
           USING       *,12
B0001      EQU         *
           LA          11,2048(12)
           LA          11,2048(11)
           USING       B0001+4096,11
```

The first two statements of this expansion need no explanation, but perhaps the remaining ones do. The second implied base register, Register 11, will be loaded with an address that is 4096 greater than that in the first base register. This address is placed into Register 11 at run time by the combined effect of the two LA instructions. (We cannot write LA 11,4096(12) because the hexadecimal equivalent of 4096_{10} is 1000_{16}, i.e., more than the three hex digits permitted in a displacement.) The assembler is informed of the base address for Register 11 by the USING B0001+4096,11 directive. The symbol B0001 is generated by the assembler through the concatenation of the value of &SYSNDX (assumed to be 0001 in this case) with the letter *B*. The use of the system variable &SYSNDX will be discussed further in Section 17.6.

Statements 3 and 4 in Figure 17.7 establish &X and &Y as local arithmetic variables with initial values 1 and 0, respectively. &X will be used as the subscript when referring to a sublist value, e.g., &R(&X). &Y will be used as a multiple of 4096, i.e., 4,096; 8,192; 12,288,...; depending on how many sublist values are specified when the BASE macro is invoked.

Statements 8 and 9 establish the implied base register whose address is given by the first sublist value &R(1) when the macro is invoked. Statement 10 creates a symbol whose value is the base address in Register &R(1); this symbol is created by concatenating the letter *B* with the value of the system variable &SYSNDX. The value of &SYSNDX is generated by the assembler; it is a four-digit string that does not change during a macro's expansion but is different for each expansion. For the first macro expanded in a source module, &SYSNDX is 0001, for the second, it is 0002, and so forth. Thus, if we were to invoke the BASE macro more than once in a source module, the symbol represented by B&SYSNDX would be different each time BASE was invoked. This avoids the possibility of generating a symbol that would be multiply-defined.

Statement 15 increases the subscript value by 1, and Statement 16 tests the corresponding sublist value to see if it is or is not the null string. If the value of &R(&X) is the null string, this simply means that the end of the sublist has been reached and the expansion is terminated. If &R(&X) is not null, its value is the register address to be used for the next implied base register in the expansion.

Statements 20 and 21 generate the Load Address instructions that will place the appropriate base address into Register &R(&X) at run time, when $\&X > 1$. If we return to our earlier example,

```
BASE          (12,11)
```

then, when &X = 2, we have, from Statements 20 and 21, these LA instructions:

```
                    sublist value corresponding
                    to &R(&X) when &X=2

                              sublist value corresponding
                              to &R(&X−1) when &X=2

LA       11,2048(12)
LA       11,2048(11)
```

Statement 22 computes the current multiple of 4096 to be used in the USING directive, and assigns the computed value to &Y. Statement 23 generates the required USING directive. Continuing the example, we see that with &X=2,

```
&Y = 4096*2-4096 = 4096.
```

So, if we assume that &SYSNDX = 0001, the generated USING directive is

```
USING     B0001+4096,11
```

The expansion is generated in similar fashion for three or more sublist values. Statement 24 causes the assembler to skip back to Statement 14, whence it will increase the subscript value and repeat the described processing for the next sublist value, if any. For example, if the BASE macro is invoked by the statement

```
BASE          (10,11,12)
```

the expansion generated is

```
          BALR     10,0
          USING    *,10
B0002     EQU      *
          LA       11,2048(10)
          LA       11,2048(11)
          USING    B0002+4096,11
          LA       12,2048(11)
          LA       12,2048(12)
          USING    B0002+8192,12
```

If only a single base register is desired, say Register 12, we can write either BASE (12) or BASE 12. In other words, if a sublist contains only one value, the parentheses are not required. In the BASE macro definition, the use of subscripts will work as desired: &R(1) will refer to the first and only sublist value, and &R(2) will refer to the null string. The expansion generated for either BASE (12) or BASE 12 will be

```
        BALR     12,0
        USING    *,12
B0003   EQU      *
```

The third statement is "wasted," but there is no harm done since B0003 will not be generated again for any macro expansion in that source module.

17.6 &SYSNDX, &SYSLIST, AND &SYSECT

&SYSNDX, &SYSLIST, and &SYSECT are local system variable symbols whose values are assigned by the assembler. They may not be declared by GBLx or LCLx directives, and their values may not be changed by SETx directives. They can be used only in macro definitions, not in open code.

&SYSNDX

The value assigned to &SYSNDX is, as discussed, the character string representation of a four-digit decimal integer, from 0001 to 9999. The integer (and hence the string) is not changed during the expansion of a macro but is increased by +1 each time any macro is invoked. This provides an important capability for use in macro definitions for the following reason.

It is often necessary to generate a statement with a name-field symbol so that that statement can be referred to from within the macro expansion. This was done, for example, in the definition of the BASE macro of Figure 17.7. But, if a given macro is invoked more than once in a source module, and if that macro's expansion includes a name-field symbol generated by the definition of the macro, it is necessary to find some means of avoiding generation of the *same* name-field symbol each time the macro is invoked. If this were not done, the symbol would be multiply-defined. The &SYSNDX symbol provides the means for avoiding this. In the macro's definition, we simply concatenate &SYSNDX to a string of from one to four characters, the first being a letter, the others being letters or digits, as was done for the BASE macro. Then, each time the macro is invoked, the concatenation of the string with the value of &SYSNDX will result in the generation of a symbol that is unique for all expansions of that macro and unique for all expansions of any other macro. (You should, of course, avoid defining symbols in open code that end in four digits.)

&SYSLIST

The &SYSLIST symbol can be used to denote the value of any positional operand. Because &SYSLIST refers to the operands in a statement that invokes the macro, not to the parameters in the prototype, it is not necessary to define corresponding positional parameters in the prototype when &SYSLIST is used in a definition. However, &SYSLIST cannot be used for keyword operands.

When &SYSLIST is used, it must always be subscripted. The subscript indicates the relative position of an operand in the statement that invokes the macro. We could, for example, have defined the ADD macro discussed at the beginning of this chapter as

```
        MACRO
&L      ADD
&L      L        5,&SYSLIST(1)
        A        5,&SYSLIST(2)
        ST       5,&SYSLIST(1)
        MEND
```

Had we done so, &SYSLIST(1) would refer to the first operand specified when ADD was invoked and &SYSLIST(2) would refer to the second operand. Not much may have been gained in such a simple example, but suppose we wanted an ADD macro that would add two or more integers, the exact number being determined by the statement that invokes ADD. We could then redefine the ADD macro as

&SYSLIST
Example

```
          MACRO
&L        ADD
          LCLA      &K
&K        SETA      1
&L        L         5,&SYSLIST(&K)
.A        ANOP
&K        SETA      &K+1
          A         5,&SYSLIST(&K)
          AIF       ('&SYSLIST(&K+1)' NE '').A
          ST        5,&SYSLIST(1)
          MEND
```

We could then invoke the ADD macro to add two integers, or three, or however many we cared to, as the following statements illustrate:

source statement	expansion	
ADD X,Y,Z	L	5,X
	A	5,Y
	A	5,Z
	ST	5,X

&SYSLIST can also be used to refer to sublist values *within* a positional operand. To do this, two subscripts are used. The first subscript indicates the relative position of the operand; the second indicates the relative position of a sublist value within that operand. Thus, **&SYSLIST(m,n)** refers to the nth sublist value in the mth positional operand of the statement that invokes a macro. An example will be given in Section 17.7. Note that the subscripts used in &SYSLIST can be any valid arithmetic expressions whose values are positive integers. There are also two special cases: &SYSLIST(0), which refers to the value of the symbol in the name field when a macro is invoked, and &SYSLIST(k,0), which is invalid for all k.

&SYSECT

The value of &SYSECT is the name of the control section in which the macro containing &SYSECT in its definition is invoked. The assembler substitutes the control section's name for &SYSECT when it generates an expansion. The need for this capability arises in a macro definition that generates a dummy section (DSECT) and then must resume the control section in which that macro is invoked.

Note that the values of all three local system variables are affected by nesting (described in the next section).

17.7 NESTED MACROS

A **nested macro** is a macro instruction that is invoked in the body of a macro definition. It is also known as an inner macro, and its expansion is known as the inner expansion of the macro in which it appears. Correspondingly, a macro definition that includes a nested macro is known as an outer macro. The expansion of the outer macro might or might not invoke the inner expansion, depending on the dictates of AIF directives that appear in the definition.

Inner and Outer
Macros

The definition of the BEGIN macro in Figure 17.8 illustrates a simple nesting situation. The REGS macro (defined in Fig. 17.4) is nested within the BEGIN macro. When the BEGIN macro is invoked, its expansion will include that of the REGS macro.

The values that are specified in the operand of a nested macro can include any of the parameters specified in the prototype of the outer macro. They also can include any of the variables declared by GBLx or LCLx directives in the outer macro as well as any of the system variables. The parameters or variables of the outer macro are said to be *passed* to the inner macro. In the INIT macro of Figure 17.9, the value of &R is passed as a character string from the outer macro to the inner BASE macro.

Passing
Parameters

Figure 17.8   Definition of BEGIN macro.

Figure 17.9   Definition of INIT macro.

```
        MACRO
&L      BEGIN
&L      CSECT
        REGS
        STM     R14,R12,12(R13)
        BALR    R12,0
        USING   *,R12
        ST      R13,SAVE+4
        LA      R13,SAVE
        MEND
```

```
        MACRO
&L      INIT    &R,&SAVE=SAVE
&L      CSECT
        STM     14,12,12(13)
        BASE    &R
        ST      13,&SAVE+4
        LA      13,&SAVE
        MEND
```

The value of &R used for the expansion of the BASE macro will be the value appearing in the statement that invokes the INIT macro. For example, the expansion of the statement:

```
        MAIN        INIT        12
```

consists of these statements:

```
        MAIN        CSECT
                    STM     14,12,12(13)
                    BALR    12,0
                    USING   *,12
        B0001       EQU     *
                    ST      13,SAVE+4
                    LA      13,SAVE
```

(The BASE macro in Fig. 17.9 was discussed in the previous section.)

XSRP Macro
A similar use of nested macros is illustrated by the XSRP macro defined in Figure 17.10. XSRP invokes two other macros, Shift Left Packed-Decimal (SLPD) and Shift Right Packed-Decimal (SRPD). But not only are the prototype parameters passed to the nested macros, the name-field symbol and the value of the local variable &ROUND also are passed. The SLPD macro is defined in Figure 17.11; the expansions it generates are equivalent to the code shown in Figures 12.2a and 12.2b. The definition of SRPD is left as an exercise.

The prototype of the Shift and Round Packed (XSRP) macro is modeled after the format of the IBM 370 SRP instruction. However, XSRP does not possess the full range of capabilities that SRP does; the number of digits that can be shifted by XSRP must be less than or equal to six and must be specified as a decimal integer, and the rounding factor—also required to be a decimal integer—can be only 0 or 5. Compare these limitations with the capabilities of SRP described in Chapter 12; verification is left as an exercise.

Nested Macros and &SYSLIST &SYSNDX &SYSECT
The values of the local system variables &SYSLIST, &SYSNDX, and &SYSECT are affected by nested macros in the following manner. &SYSLIST always refers to the positional operands in the macro instruction that invokes a definition containing it. When a macro definition that contains &SYSLIST is invoked as an outer macro, each occurrence of &SYSLIST in that definition refers to the outer macro instruction's positional operands. When invoked as an inner macro, each occurrence of &SYSLIST refers to the operands of the inner macro instruction.

&SYSNDX is assigned a different value for each inner macro that is invoked. The value is not changed during the expansion of an inner macro, but reverts to its previous value when the expansion of the inner macro is completed. Each new value assigned to &SYSNDX is a number that is one more than the previous highest value of &SYSNDX.

&SYSECT always refers to the name of the control section in which a macro containing &SYSECT is invoked. Therefore, the value of &SYSECT can change only if a macro definition contains a START, CSECT, DSECT, or COM directive, or if an open code statement contains one

Figure 17.10 Definition of XSRP macro for the IBM 360.

```
              MACRO
&L            XSRP       &X,&N,&R
              LCLC       &ROUND
.*
.* THE XSRP (SHIFT AND ROUND PACKED) MACRO PROVIDES A
.*  LIMITED CAPABILITY FOR SHIFTING PACKED-DECIMAL NUMBERS
.*  ON THE IBM 360.
.*
.*      &X DESIGNATES THE ADDRESS OF THE PACKED-DECIMAL NUMBER.
.*
.*      &N  MUST BE A DECIMAL INTEGER IN THE RANGE -6 TO +6 .
.*          IT REPRESENTS THE NUMBER OF DIGITS TO BE SHIFTED,
.*          AND THE DIRECTION OF SHIFT:
.*              RIGHT SHIFT IF &N IS NEGATIVE
.*              LEFT SHIFT IF &N IS POSITIVE
.*
.*      &R  DETERMINES WHETHER ROUNDING IS TO BE SUPPRESSED
.*          DURING A RIGHT SHIFT:
.*              NO ROUNDING IF   &R = 0
.*              ROUNDING IF &R IS NOT EQUAL TO 0
.*
.*  A RIGHT SHIFT IS ACCOMPLISHED BY INVOKING THE   SRPD   MACRO;
.*  A LEFT SHIFT, BY INVOKING THE   SLPD   MACRO.
.*
.*
.*
.*
              AIF        ('&N'(1,1) EQ '-').SRP2
.*
&L            SLPD       &X,&N
              MEXIT
.*
.SRP2         ANOP
&ROUND        SETC       'YES'
              AIF        ('&R' NE '0').SRP3
&ROUND        SETC       'NO'
.SRP3         ANOP
.*
&L            SRPD       &X,&N,RND=&ROUND
              MEND
```

of those directives. When a control section is initiated or continued in open code, the value of &SYSECT is set equal to the name of that section. But when a control section is initiated in a macro expansion, the value of &SYSECT continues to be the name of the previous section unless either of two conditions occur. First, if a subsequent macro is invoked as an inner macro in the expansion, then for that inner expansion &SYSECT is the name of the newly initiated control section. Second, if the expansion of the outer macro terminates without resuming the previous control section, &SYSECT becomes the name of the new control section. For example, assume that the macro DUMMY is defined in terms of another macro, DATA, and assume that DATA does not initiate a new control section:

```
              MACRO
&L            DUMMY      &A,&B
&L            DSECT
              DATA       &A,&B
&SYSECT       CSECT
              MEND
```

&SYSECT
Example

Figure 17.11   *Definition of SLPD macro for the IBM 360.*

```
                MACRO
&L              SLPD        &P,&D
                LCLA        &A,&B
                LCLB        &EVEN
                LCLC        &W
&B              SETA        &D
&A              SETA        &B/2
&EVEN           SETB        (&A*2 EQ &B)
&W              SETC        'W&SYSNDX'
.*
.*      THE SLPD (SHIFT LEFT PACKED-DECIMAL) MACRO SHIFTS
.*        THE PACKED DECIMAL NUMBER WHOSE ADDRESS IS GIVEN
.*        BY THE VALUE OF  &P  TO THE LEFT  N  DIGITS,
.*        WHERE N  IS GIVEN BY THE VALUE OF &D .
.*
.*        &D  MUST BE WRITTEN AS AN UNSIGNED DECIMAL DIGIT
.*            IN THE RANGE  FROM  1  TO  6 .
.*
.*        (THE POSSIBLE EXPANSIONS ARE SHOWN IN FIGS.12.2A
.*            AND 12.2B .)
.*
                AIF         (&EVEN).EVEN
.*
&L              ZAP         &W.(16),&P
                MVN         &W+15(1),=X'00'
                MVO         &P,&W+&A.(16)
                B           S&SYSNDX
                AGO         .COMMON
.*
.EVEN           ANOP
&A              SETA        &A-1
&L              MVO         &W.(16),&P
                MVC         &W+15(1),=X'00'
                MVO         &P,&W+&A.(16)
                B           S&SYSNDX
.*
.COMMON         ANOP
&W              DC          32X'00'
.*
S&SYSNDX        DS          0H
                MEND
```

During the expansion of the outer macro, DUMMY, the value of &SYSECT will be the name of the control section in which DUMMY is invoked. But during the expansion of the inner macro, DATA, the value of &SYSECT will be the name of the section in which DATA is invoked, represented as &L. When the inner expansion is completed, &SYSECT reverts to its previous value. Thus, the statement

```
        &SYSECT     CSECT
```

in this example will result in the continuation of the section in which DUMMY was invoked. If no CSECT directive had been included in the definition of DUMMY, then, when the expansion of DUMMY had been completed, the value of &SYSECT would have become the value of &L, i.e., the name of the section initiated by the DSECT within the expansion.

Six different attributes, or characteristics, of a symbol or of the data or data areas represented by symbols can be specified in the operands of SETx and AIF directives. One of the six attributes—the length attribute—also can be specified in the operand of a DC, DS, or EQU directive and in the operand of any instruction.

The attributes are specified with a notation that consists of two characters prefixed to an ordinary or variable symbol. The two characters are a letter followed by an apostrophe ('), as follows:

T'	type attribute
K'	count attribute
S'	scaling attribute
I'	integer attribute
L'	length attribute
N'	number attribute

For example, N'&X denotes the number attribute of the variable symbol &X.

The use of attributes provides additional capabilities in macro definitions and conditional assemblies. We will not illustrate all these capabilities, nor will we discuss all the rules and restrictions pertaining to the use of attributes. What follows is merely a summary of the main uses of attributes and a few illustrative examples. Consult the IBM assembly language reference manual for a complete discussion.

Type Attribute

The value of the type attribute T' of a symbol is a single letter that designates the type of data or data area that the symbol represents. The set of attribute values corresponding to different data types is summarized in Figure 17.12. For example, if X were defined by the statement

```
X    DS    3CL5
```

T'X would have the value C, i.e., X represents character data.

Count Attribute

Substring Notation

The value of the count attribute K' is an integer that equals the number of characters constituting the value of a variable symbol. (The count attribute cannot be used with ordinary symbols.) For example, if &X is a variable symbol whose value is 100, then K'&X = 3, i.e., three characters are required to represent the value of 100 as a character string. Similarly, if &A is the seven-character string (ALPHA), then K'&A = 7, K'&A–2 = 5, and, using the substring notation introduced in Chapter 16, we have

```
'&A'(2,K'&A-2)  =  ALPHA.
```

In other words, the count attribute can be used to perform string operations on strings whose length is not known to the programmer.

Scaling Attribute

The scaling attribute S' can be used only with symbols that refer to fixed-point (F,H), floating-point (E,D,L), or decimal (P,Z) constants. For fixed-point and floating-point constants, the value of S' is simply the value of n in the scale modifier Sn used to define the constant. For packed-decimal constants, the value of S' is simply the number of digits to the right of the implied decimal point. The following examples illustrate this:

```
X    DC    FS2'300'      S'X = 2
Y    DC    ES1'3.142'    S'Y = 1
Z    DC    P'3.142'      S'Z = 3
W    DC    F'10'         S'W = 0
```

Figure 17.12   Type attributes of ordinary symbols.

If X is an ordinary symbol that is defined in the name field of a DC or DS directive, then the type attribute T'X is a single character whose value depends on the type of data or data area defined by X.

T'X	type of data or data area defined by X
A	A-type address constant
B	Binary constant
C	Character constant
D	Long-format floating-point constant
E	Short-format floating-point constant
F	Full-word binary integer constant
G	Full-word binary integer constant, with explicit length
H	Half-word binary integer constant
K	Any floating-point constant with explicit length
L	Extended-format floating-point constant
P	Packed decimal constant
Q	Q-type address constant
R	A-,S-,Q-,V-, or Y-type address constant with explicit length
S	S-type address constant
V	V-type address constant
X	Hexadecimal constant
Y	Y-type address constant
Z	Zoned decimal constant

Note: For the following type attributes, the length of the defined constant or data area is understood to have been implied, not explicitly given:

A-, S-, Q-, V-, and Y-type address constants
D-, E-, and L-type floating point constants
F- and H-type binary integer constants

If X is an ordinary symbol that is *not* defined in the name field of a DC or DS directive, then the type attribute T'X is a single character whose value depends on the type of statement in which X is defined.

T'X	type of statement in which X is defined
I	assembly language instruction
J	CSECT, DSECT, START, COM directive
M	statement invoking a macro
N	a macro instruction operand that is a self-defining term
O	a macro instruction operand that is omitted (null value)
T	EXTRN
U	LTORG, EQU, and certain other types
W	CCW
$	WXTRN

Integer Attribute

The integer attribute I' can only be used with symbols that refer to fixed-point, floating-point, or decimal constants. The value of I' is the number of positions occupied by the integer portion of such a constant. For fixed-point constants, the word *positions* means bits; for floating-point constants, it means hex digits in the mantissa; and for decimal constants, it means decimal digits. The following examples illustrate this. The formulas at the right show precisely how the integer attribute is calculated, L' being the length attribute.

```
X   DC   FS2'300'        I'X = 29      I' = 8*L' - 1 - S'
Y   DC   ES1'3.142'      I'Y =  5      I' = 2*L' - 2 - S'
Z   DC   P'3.142'        I'Z =  2      I' = 2*L' - 1 - S'
```

Length Attribute

The length attribute L' of an ordinary symbol is the number of bytes of memory occupied by the data or data area represented by that symbol. If the symbol represents an instruction, the length attribute of that symbol is the length of that instruction. If the symbol is defined by a DS or DC directive, the length attribute of that symbol is the value n specified by the length modifier, Ln, if any; and, if no length modifier is used in the definition, the length attribute of the symbol is the implied length of the constant or data area. It should be noted that the length attribute is independent of the duplication factor in a DC or DS directive. For example, if V were defined by this statement:

```
V   DC   3CL8'LENGTH'
```

L'V would have the value 8. Similarly, for the symbols X, Y, and Z defined in the discussion of integer attributes, L'X=4, L'Y=4, and L'Z=3. From its definition, we see that the length attribute of a symbol is an absolute constant, i.e., it is independent of the location of a program in memory at run time.

The length attribute also can be specified for variable symbols, e.g., L'&X. When this is done, the value of that variable symbol must be an ordinary symbol defined by a statement in open code. Otherwise, the assembler cannot evaluate its length attribute at assembly time. For example, consider this macro definition:

```
        MACRO
&L      MOVER     &A,&B
&L      MVC       &B.(L'&A),&A
        MEND
```

When invoked, the length field in the MVC instruction of the expansion will contain the length attribute of the ordinary symbol designated in the first operand of MOVER. Thus,

```
MOVER     HERE,THERE
```

generates the instruction

```
MVC       THERE(L'HERE),HERE.
```

HERE is the value of the variable symbol &A. For this definition and expansion to be valid, HERE must be the name-field symbol of some open code statement. Other restrictions on the use of L' with variable symbols will not be discussed.

Number Attribute

The value of the number attribute N' is equal to the number of values in a parameter sublist of a statement that invokes a macro. Note that according to its definition, the number attribute can be specified only inside macro definitions, and can be specified only with variable symbols that represent parameters in a macro's prototype.

Examples. To conclude this brief discussion of attributes, we present two examples of the use of the number attribute, N'. The first example is rather elementary; the second illustrates the power of N' when combined with the system variable &SYSLIST.

According to the definition of the BASE macro of Figure 17.7, in order to determine how many sublist values are specified in the operand, we must look for the occurrence of a null sublist value. This concept was embodied in Statement 16 of that definition, namely,

```
AIF       ('&R(&X)' EQ '').B2
```

An alternate way of achieving the same objective would be to use the number attribute N'&R, and rewrite Statement 16 as

```
AIF       (&X GT N'&R).B2
```

Figure 17.13a   HEDIT macro, illustrating use of &SYSLIST(M,N).

```
FLAG LOCTN OBJECT CODE    ADDR1  ADDR2  STMNT M SOURCE STATEMENT

                                         3              MACRO
                                         4    &L        HEDIT    &N,&PN
                                         5    .*    'HEDIT' CONVERTS ONE OR MORE HALF-WORD INTEGERS TO THEIR
                                         6    .*         6-CHARACTER EBCDIC REPRESENTATIONS.  SIX CHARS IS
                                         7    .*         SUFFICIENT SINCE THE RANGE IS -32,768 TO +32,767 .
                                         8    .*
                                         9    .*  IN EACH EBCDIC STRING, THE FIRST CHAR IS THE SIGN (BLANK
                                        10    .*         FOR +) AND THE REMAINING CHARS REPRESENT THE INTEGER
                                        11    .*         WITH LEADING ZEROES REPLACED BY BLANKS.
                                        12    .*
                                        13    .*  THE SYMBOLIC ADDR OF EACH INTEGER AND ITS CORRESPONDING
                                        14    .*         EBCDIC STRING AREA MUST BE SPECIFIED AS THE 1ST AND
                                        15    .*         2ND SUBLIST VALUES OF A POSITIONAL OPERAND.
                                        16    .*
                                        17    .*  FOR EXAMPLE, TO CONVERT 3 HALF-WD INTEGERS WGHOSE SYMBOLIC
                                        18    .*         ADDRS ARE L, M, AND N INTO 6-CHAR EBCDIC STRINGS AT
                                        19    .*         SYMBOLIC ADDRS PL, PM, AND PN, USE 'HEDIT' THIS WAY
                                        20    .*
                                        21    .*              HEDIT    (L,PL),(M,PM),(N,PN)
                                        22    .*
                                        23             LCLA  &K          SUBSCRIPT FOR &SYSLIST
                                        24    &K       SETA  1
                                        25    &L       ST    5,A3&SYSNDX    SAVE REG 5 CONTENTS TEMPORARILY
                                        26    .AO      ANOP
                                        27    .*
                                        28    .*  GET KTH HALF-WD INTEGER AND CONVT TO PACKED DECIMAL
                                        29    .*
                                        30             LH    5,&SYSLIST(&K,1)
                                        31             CVD   5,A2&SYSNDX
                                        32    .*
                                        33    .*  MOVE PATTERN INTO 6-BYTE AREA SPECIFIED BY KTH OPERAND
                                        34    .*         AND EDIT LOW-ORDER 3 BYTES OF PACKED DECIMAL NUMBER
                                        35    .*
                                        36             MVC   &SYSLIST(&K,2).(6),=X'402020202120'
                                        37             ED    &SYSLIST(&K,2).(6),A2&SYSNDX+5
                                        38    .*
                                        39    .*  INSERT MINUS SIGN IF NUMBER WAS NEGATIVE
                                        40    .*
                                        41             BNM   B&K.&SYSNDX
                                        42             MVI   &SYSLIST(&K,2),C'-'
                                        43    B&K.&SYSNDX    EQU   *
                                        44    .*
                                        45    .*  REPEAT CONVERT AND EDIT STEPS FOR EACH OPERAND
                                        46    .*
                                        47    &K       SETA  &K+1
                                        48             AIF   (&K LE N'&SYSLIST).AO
                                        49             B     A4&SYSNDX
                                        50    .*
                                        51    A2&SYSNDX    DS    D       STORAGE FOR PACKED DECIMAL NUMBER
                                        52    A3&SYSNDX    DS    F       STORAGE FOR REG 5 CONTENTS
                                        53    A4&SYSNDX    L     5,A3&SYSNDX   RESTORE REG 5 CONTENTS
                                        54             MEND
```

With this statement, the assembler would skip to the statement identified by the sequence symbol .B2 if the value of &X were greater than the number of values specified in the sublist denoted by &R. For example, if the BASE macro were invoked by the statement

```
BASE          (12,11)
```

the value of N'&R would be 2, and the expansion would be terminated after Register 11 had been processed.

When used with the system variable &SYSLIST, the number attribute N' is defined as follows: (!) N'&SYSLIST is the number of positional operands specified or specifically omitted when invoking a macro, and (2) N'&SYSLIST(k) is the number of sublist values specified or specifically omitted in the kth positional operand when invoking a macro. We illustrate the use of &SYSLIST and its number attribute N'&SYSLIST with the macro HEDIT defined in Figure 17.13a. In the AIF directive near the end of the definition, namely,

```
AIF           (&K LE N'&SYSLIST).AO
```

N'&SYSLIST will be the number of half-word integers to be converted to EBCDIC representation when HEDIT is invoked. Thus, if HEDIT is invoked by the statement

```
HEDIT         (N,PN),(M,PM),(L,PL)
```

then N'&SYSLIST = 3. You should verify that the definition of Figure 17.13a produces the expansions shown in Figure 17.13b.

Figure 17.13b   Expansions of HEDIT macro. (See Figure 17.13a.)

```
FLAG LOCTN OBJECT CODE     ADDR1  ADDR2   STMNT M SOURCE STATEMENT

     000000                              56      HEDIT   CSECT
     000000 90 EC D00C                   57              STM     14,12,12(13)
     000004 05 C0                        58              BALR    12,0
     000006                              59              USING   *,12
     000006 50 D0 C12E          000134   60              ST      13,SAVE+4
     00000A 41 D0 C12A          000130   61              LA      13,SAVE
                                         62      *


                                         63              HEDIT   (X,PX)
     00000E 50 50 C03A          000040   64  1           ST      5,A30001     SAVE REG 5 CONTENTS TEMPORARILY
     000012 48 50 C10C          000112   65  1           LH      5,X
     000016 4E 50 C032          000038   66  1           CVD     5,A20001
     00001A D2 05 C112C172 000118 000178 67  1           MVC     PX(6),=X'402020202120'
     000020 DE 05 C112C037 000118 00003D 68  1           ED      PX(6),A20001+5
     000026 47 B0 C028          00002E   69  1           BNM     B10001
     00002A 92 60 C112          000118   70  1           MVI     PX,C'-'
     00002E                              71  1 B10001    EQU     *
     00002E 47 F0 C03E          000044   72  1           B       A40001
     000038                              73  1 A20001    DS      D       STORAGE FOR PACKED DECIMAL NUMBER
     000040                              74  1 A30001    DS      F         STORAGE FOR REG 5 CONTENTS
     000044 58 50 C03A          000040   75  1 A40001    L       5,A30001    RESTORE REG 5 CONTENTS


                                         76              HEDIT   (Y,PY),(Z,PZ)
     000048 50 50 C08A          000090   77  1           ST      5,A30002     SAVE REG 5 CONTENTS TEMPORARILY
     00004C 48 50 C10E          000114   78  1           LH      5,Y
     000050 4E 50 C082          000088   79  1           CVD     5,A20002
     000054 D2 05 C11AC172 000120 000178 80  1           MVC     PY(6),=X'402020202120'
     00005A DE 05 C11AC087 000120 00008D 81  1           ED      PY(6),A20002+5
     000060 47 B0 C062          000068   82  1           BNM     B10002
     000064 92 60 C11A          000120   83  1           MVI     PY,C'-'
     000068                              84  1 B10002    EQU     *
     000068 48 50 C110          000116   85  1           LH      5,Z
     00006C 4E 50 C082          000088   86  1           CVD     5,A20002
     000070 D2 05 C122C172 000128 000178 87  1           MVC     PZ(6),=X'402020202120'
     000076 DE 05 C122C087 000128 00008D 88  1           ED      PZ(6),A20002+5
     00007C 47 B0 C07E          000084   89  1           BNM     B20002
     000080 92 60 C122          000128   90  1           MVI     PZ,C'-'
     000084                              91  1 B20002    EQU     *
     000084 47 F0 C08E          000094   92  1           B       A4C002
     000088                              93  1 A20002    DS      D       STORAGE FOR PACKED DECIMAL NUMBER
     000090                              94  1 A30002    DS      F         STORAGE FOR REG 5 CONTENTS
     000094 58 50 C08A          000090   95  1 A40002    L       5,A30002    RESTORE REG 5 CONTENTS
                                         96              HEDIT   (X,PX),(Y,PY),(Z,PZ)
     000098 50 50 C0FA          000100   97  1           ST      5,A30003     SAVE REG 5 CONTENTS TEMPORARILY
     00009C 48 50 C10C          000112   98  1           LH      5,X
     0000A0 4E 50 C0F2          0000F8   99  1           CVD     5,A20003
     0000A4 D2 05 C112C172 000118 000178 100 1           MVC     PX(6),=X'402020202120'
     0000AA DE 05 C112C0F7 000118 0000FD 101 1           ED      PX(6),A20003+5
     0000B0 47 B0 C0B2          0000B8   102 1           BNM     B10003
     0000B4 92 60 C112          000118   103 1           MVI     PX,C'-'
     0000B8                              104 1 B10003    EQU     *
     0000B8 48 50 C10E          000114   105 1           LH      5,Y
     0000BC 4E 50 C0F2          0000F8   106 1           CVD     5,A20003
     0000C0 D2 05 C11AC172 000120 000178 107 1           MVC     PY(6),=X'402020202120'
     0000C6 DE 05 C11AC0F7 000120 0000FD 108 1           ED      PY(6),A20003+5
     0000CC 47 B0 C0CE          0000D4   109 1           BNM     B20003
     0000D0 92 60 C11A          000120   110 1           MVI     PY,C'-'
     0000D4                              111 1 B20003    EQU     *
     0000D4 48 50 C110          000116   112 1           LH      5,Z
     0000D8 4E 50 C0F2          0000F8   113 1           CVD     5,A20003
     0000DC D2 05 C122C172 000128 000178 114 1           MVC     PZ(6),=X'402020202120'
     0000E2 DE 05 C122C0F7 000128 0000FD 115 1           ED      PZ(6),A20003+5
     0000E8 47 B0 C0EA          0000F0   116 1           BNM     B30003
     0000EC 92 60 C122          000128   117 1           MVI     PZ,C'-'
     0000F0                              118 1 B30003    EQU     *
     0000F0 47 F0 C0FE          000104   119 1           B       A40003
     0000F8                              120 1 A20003    DS      D       STORAGE FOR PACKED DECIMAL NUMBER
     000100                              121 1 A30003    DS      F         STORAGE FOR REG 5 CONTENTS
     000104 58 50 C0FA          000100   122 1 A40003    L       5,A30003    RESTORE REG 5 CONTENTS
                                         123     *
     000108 58 D0 C12E          000134   124             L       13,SAVE+4
     00010C 98 EC D00C                   125             LM      14,12,12(13)
     000110 07 FE                        126             BR      14
                                         127     *
     000112 0000                         128     X       DC      H'0'
     000114 8000                         129     Y       DC      H'-32768'
     000116 7FFF                         130     Z       DC      H'+32767'
     000118                              131             DS      0D
     000118                              132     PX      DS      CL6
     000120                              133             DS      0D
     000120                              134     PY      DS      CL6
     000128                              135             DS      0D
     000128                              136     PZ      DS      CL6
     000130                              137     SAVE    DS      18F
     000178 402020202120                 138
                                         139             END
```

A macro is an opcode that can be used as a kind of high-level directive to represent a set of one or more instructions, directives, and previously defined macros. The definition of each macro invoked in a source module must either be included in that source module or reside in a file accessible to the assembler when the source module is being assembled.

Each time a macro is invoked, the assembler generates an expansion by processing the macro's definition. The statements generated are inserted at the point immediately following the statement invoking the macro and are then assembled as though they were part of the original source module.

All macro definitions must begin with a header (the MACRO directive), end with a trailer (the MEND directive), and contain a prototype statement as well as one or more statements that constitute the body of the definition. The prototype must immediately follow the header. It defines the macro's name and the parameters whose values may be specified when invoking the macro. The body must immediately follow the prototype. It includes the statements that will be generated and may also include control directives to provide conditional assembly capabilities at the time the expansion is generated.

All parameters included in the prototype are processed as local character assembly variables; their scope is limited to the statements in the definition. The values of these parameters are specified when a macro is invoked and are substituted for the respective prototype parameters during the generation of the expansion at assembly time.

Global assembly variables can be passed from open code to macro definitions, and local assembly variables can be declared within the body of the definition. Appropriate SETx directives can be used in the body to change the values of these variables. The variables also can be used in expressions, e.g., in AIF and SETx operands, to control the processing of the definition. Thus, the statements in the body can specify decisions to be made at assembly time in order to dictate to the assembler the statements and/or variable values that shall be represented in the expansion.

The examples given in this chapter illustrated the following capabilities that can be used in macro definitions: substitution of values for parameters; decision making during the expansion process, concatenation, sublists, nested macros, substring evaluation, and the use of &SYSNDX, &SYSLIST, MNOTE, MEXIT, and the special comment statement denoted by '.*' in its first two positions. Also discussed and briefly illustrated was the mechanism of data attributes: T' (type), K' (count), S' (scaling), I' (integer), L' (length), and N' (number). A complete discussion of all the rules relating to the IBM 360 and 370 macro facilities can be found in the *Assembler Reference Manual*.

17.10   REVIEW

Macro   A macro is a programmer-defined opcode that represents a set of one or more instructions, directives, or other macros.

Macro Definition   The definition of a macro is a set of statements that begins with a MACRO directive, ends with an MEND directive, and includes a prototype that defines the macro opcode, name field, and operand parameters. Between the prototype and the MEND are statements—the "body" of the definition—that tell the assembler what to do when it processes the opcode of an invoked macro.

Macro Parameters   Parameters can be defined in the prototype of a macro definition and must be either positional or keyword. They are denoted by variable symbols that represent character strings. Thus, when a macro is invoked the value of each parameter is a character string.

Invoking a Macro   A macro is said to be "invoked" when it is the opcode in a source statement outside of its definition.

Macro Expansion   These are the statements that are generated by the assembler when it processes the opcode of an invoked macro. The statements in a macro expansion are derived from those in the macro's definition, and they may depend on the parameter values (if any) that are specified when the macro is invoked.

Nested (Inner) Macro   A nested or "inner" macro is a macro that is invoked in the body of another macro's definition. In effect, when you invoke a macro, that macro may in turn invoke another macro, and so on. Parameter values specified when invoking a macro can be passed to an inner macro.

Conditional Assembly   The occurrence and/or contents of statements in a macro expansion can be made to depend on the inclusion of certain directives—AGO, AIF, ANOP, GBLx, LCLx, and SETx— and on the value of their associated assembly variables and macro parameters. When this happens, we have what is known as a conditional assembly.

Sequence Symbol (.X)   The purpose of a sequence symbol is to identify a statement so that it can be referred to in the operand of an AGO, AIF, or ANOP directive. A sequence symbol may therefore be thought of as a symbolic statement number. It is NOT a symbolic memory address. (See Chap. 16, Sect. 16.1.)

Variable Symbol (& X)   Each variable symbol is the name of an assembly variable. Its value is used by the assembler when it assembles a statement that contains the symbol. (See Chap. 16, Sect. 16.2.)

GBLx and LCLx Directives   The scope of an assembly variable that is declared by a GBLx directive includes all macro definitions in which that variable is declared by GBLx. The scope of an assembly variable that is declared by a LCLx directive within a macro definition is limited to the statements within that macro definition. The letter x represents the variable's type, and can be "A" (arithmetic), "B" (Boolean), or "C" (character).

SETx Directive   This directive assigns the value of its operand expression to the variable symbol appearing in its name field. The name-field symbol must have been previously declared by a GBLx or LCLx directive of the same type as the SETx directive.

MEXIT Directive   This directive is equivalent to an unconditional skip to the MEND directive.

MNOTE Directive   When it is part of a macro's expansion, this directive causes a programmer-defined message to appear on the assembler listing at assembly time. (It does NOT generate a run-time message.)

&SYSNDX   The value of this system variable is the string representation of a four-digit decimal integer, from 0001 to 9999. The integer is increased by +1 each time any macro is invoked. When concatenated with an appropriate string, &SYSNDX can be used within a macro definition to define a symbol whose value is different each time the macro is invoked within a source module.

&SYSLIST(k)   This system variable represents the value of the kth positional parameter in the statement that invokes a macro. &SYSLIST(0) refers to the name-field parameter.

&SYSLIST (k,n)   This system variable represents the value of the nth sublist parameter within the kth positional parameter of the statement that invokes a macro. &SYSLIST(k,0) is undefined for all k.

&SYSECT   This system variable represents the name of the control section in which a macro containing &SYSECT is invoked. It is designed for use within macros that initiate other control sections. (See Sect. 17.7.)

Attributes   Certain characteristics (attributes) of a symbol, or of the data or data area that the symbol represents, can be obtained at assembly time by use of a special notation (see Sect. 17.8) prefixed to the symbol. Restrictions on the use of this notation include the following: the count and number attributes can only be used with variable symbols, the scaling and integer attributes with symbols that represent numeric data, and the length attribute with symbols that represent object code or data areas.

String Concatenation   Two strings are said to be concatenated when one of them is appended to the end of the other one, with the result being a single string whose length equals the sum of the lengths of the two strings. The concatenation operator is a period (.), and is normally placed between the two strings, as in A.B, but is omitted when the appended string is a variable symbol, as in A&B.

1. What must be included in a macro definition's prototype statement, and what can either be included or omitted from it?

2. What are the principal differences between a positional parameter and a keyword parameter? Can a keyword parameter be used in the name field of the prototype?

3. When a macro is invoked, does the name of a keyword parameter have to be specified? If the name of your register save area was MYAREA, how would you invoke the INIT macro of Figure 17.9? What would be its expansion?

4. There's something wrong with each of the following two alternative definitions of the ADD macro (Fig. 17.2). Which definition could cause an assembly-time error? A run-time error? Explain.

```
        MACRO                           MACRO
&L      ADD     &A,&B                   ADD     &A,&B
        L       5,&A            &L      L       5,&A
        A       5,&B                    A       5,&B
        ST      5,&A                    ST      5,&A
        MEND                            MEND
```

5. Explain why the variable symbol &S occurs three times in the MOVE macro definition of Figure 17.3.

6. In the definition of the REGS macro of Figure 17.4, there is no SETA directive to initialize &X. Why doesn't there have to be?

7. Revise the REGS macro of Figure 17.4 so that it also generates appropriate symbolic names for the four floating-point registers.

8. Would it be valid to replace the AGO directive in statement number 7 of Figure 17.5, namely

```
            AGO     .R2
```

with this branch (B) instruction:

```
            B       .R2
```

Why or why not?

9. What would happen if the macro comment statements of Figure 17.5 (e.g., Statements 8 and 9, 15 and 16, etc.) were replaced by ordinary comment statements? In other words, suppose each '.*' string in positions 1 and 2 of those statements was replaced by '*.'. Would that cause an assembly-time error? A run-time error? Or what?

10. Under what conditions would the MNOTE directive near the end of Figure 17.5 be part of the expansion when the RETRN macro is invoked?

11. If a particular subroutine were used often in a program, it would be possible to define a macro in which that subroutine's name were the opcode. This could be done by nesting a slight variation of the CALL macro (Fig. 17.6) within the new macro's definition. With this in mind, define a SQRT macro so that the square root of a number whose symbolic address is X could be obtained with this single statement:

```
            SQRT    X
```

12. In the discussion about &SYSNDX in Section 17.6, you are told to avoid defining symbols in open code that end in four digits. Why?

13. What are the alternatives to using the sublist notation such as &R(1) in the definition of the BASE macro in Figure 17.7? Are there any advantages or disadvantages of the sublist notation compared to those alternatives? If so, what are they? (**Hint:** &SYSLIST.)

14. In the substring notation '&A'(m,n), what do the letters m and n represent? In particular, if &A = COMPUTER then what is '&A'(1,5)? '&A'(5,1)? '&A'(1,1)? '&A'(5,5)?

15. As in Question #14, suppose &A = COMPUTER. What is the value (if any) of K'&A? Of N'&A? Of T'&A? Of L'&A?

16. Suppose X is defined by this statement:

```
            X       DS      10F
```

What is the value (if any) of K'X? Of N'X? Of T'X? Of L'X?

1. The assembly language instruction Load and Test Register (LTR) is an RR-type instruction that sets the condition code according as the number that is loaded is zero, negative, or positive. Although there is no comparable RX-type instruction, the macro named Load and Test (LT), defined here, will generate an expansion that in effect would be the RX-type counterpart of LTR.

```
             MACRO
   &L    LT       &R,&M
   &L    L        &R,&M
         LTR      &R,&R
         MEND
```

Define macros that would in effect be the RX-type counterparts of the LCR, LNR, and LPR assembly language instructions.

2. The assembly language instruction Branch Not High (BNH) is a conditional branch instruction that branches if the condition code is any value except '2'. It would perhaps have been more appropriately named Branch Less than or Equal (BLE). The macro defined here makes the opcode BLE the equivalent of the opcode BNH. Define other macros named BGE, BLT, and BGT that would be equivalent to the instructions BNL, BL, and BH, respectively.

```
             MACRO
   &L    BLE      &M
   &L    BNH      &M
         MEND
```

3. What is the purpose of the MEXIT directive? If there were no MEXIT directive, how could its purpose be achieved through the use of other directives?

4. A macro's expansion can include constants and storage areas as well as instructions. In the following macro definition, a full word is generated to serve as a temporary storage area for general Register 5 in order that the register can be used to add +1 to an integer stored in memory.

```
                 MACRO
      &L    BUMP       &M
      &L    ST         5,B&SYSNDX
            L          5,&M
            AH         5,=H'1'
            ST         5,&M
            L          5,B&SYSNDX
            B          B&SYSNDX+4
B&SYSNDX DS F
            MEND
```

   a. Why is the symbol B&SYSNDX used in the BUMP macro instead of B alone?
   b. Why is the instruction   B   B&SYSNDX+4   included in the definition of the BUMP macro?
   c. Define a macro named SWAP that will interchange the contents of two full words in memory.

5. One way to copy more than 256 bytes from one memory location to another is to use the MVCL instruction. Another way (often used in the IBM 360, which has no MVCL instruction) is to code consecutive MVC instructions. The following macro definition will cause the required number of MVC instructions to be generated regardless of the number of bytes that are to be copied. The number of bytes to be copied must be specified by the keyword parameter &N or the default of 1 byte will be copied.

```
              MACRO
&L            XMVC        &A,&B,&N=1
              LCLA        &X,&Y
              AIF         ('&L' EQ '').X0
&L            EQU         *
.X0           ANOP
&X            SETA        &N
.X1           AIF         (&X LE 256).X2
              MVC         &A+&Y.(256),&B+&Y
&Y            SETA        &Y+256
&X            SETA        &X-256
              AGO         .X1
.X2           MVC         &A+&Y.(&X),&B+&Y
              MEND
```

Define a macro named XCLC for the IBM 360 that will compare an arbitrary number of bytes at one location in memory to the same number of bytes at another memory location. The condition code must reflect the result of the comparison so that a subsequent conditional branch instruction can be used.

6. Answer the following questions for the XMVC macro defined in Exercise 5:

   a. What expansion would be generated if XMVC were invoked by the statement

   XMVC   THERE,HERE,N=800

   b. What is the purpose of the first AIF directive occurring in the definition of XMVC? Why is this directive necessary in the XMVC definition?

   c. Note that &A and &B must be specified as relocatable expressions; they cannot be specified as explicit base-displacement addresses. Why is this so?

7. The HEDIT macro of Figure 17.13 converts a half-word binary integer to the EBCDIC form that is suitable for printing. Define a macro named FEDIT that will convert a full-word binary integer to a suitable EBCDIC form. Note that the largest decimal integer that can be represented as a full-word binary integer consists of ten significant digits. (**Hint:** See Section 12.9.)

8. Define a macro that will convert an integer from its 12-byte EBCDIC representation to its full-word binary representation. (**Hint:** See Section 12.8.)

9. Complete the definition of the XSRP macro of Figure 17.10 by defining an SRPD macro analogous to the SLPD macro of Figure 17.11.

10. One of the instructions in the optional extended-precision floating-point instruction set is Load Rounded, Long to Short (LRER). Since this instruction, described in Section 13.7, would be useful even in systems that do not have the extended-precision feature, define a macro, say XLRER, that will duplicate the function of LRER for systems lacking extended-precision hardware.

11. Rewrite the definition of the BASE macro given in Figure 17.7 so that it is not necessary to enclose the register addresses within parentheses when invoking the macro, no matter how many registers are specified. (**Hint:** Use the system variable &SYSLIST in your definition.)

12. Suppose that the BASE macro of Figure 17.7 were invoked by the statement

                        BASE   16

Would an expansion containing the invalid register address be generated? If so, when would the error be detected?

13. Suppose that the REGS macro of Figure 17.4 were invoked by the statement

        START   REGS   0,15

How would the symbol START be processed by the assembler? What effect would the operand have on the expansion of the macro?

14. Suppose that the HEDIT macro of Figure 17.13a were invoked by the statement

                HEDIT   X,PX

Why wouldn't this produce the same expansion as HEDIT (X,PX)? What is the expansion of HEDIT X,PX? What would be the effect at run time?

15. By means of the substring notation introduced in Section 16.6, and used in Figure 17.10, it is possible to examine any subset of consecutive characters comprising a macro operand. In particular, a macro operand can be examined one character at a time and thus affect the course of the expansion generated. Using the substring notation, define a macro named PIC that will cause an appropriate editing pattern to be generated for use with the ED and EDMK instructions. For example, if the PIC prototype is

        &L   PIC   &P

then the expansion generated for the statement

        P1   PIC   999,999.99

should be

        P1   DC   X'402121216B2121214B2020'

(Refer to Section 12.9 for definitions and examples of patterns.) This is not a particularly easy problem; you may wish to establish some conditions on the permissible forms of the operand specified when PIC is invoked.

16. The substring notation (see Exercise 15) can be used to allow a revised definition of the CALL macro of Figure 17.6. The revision is as follows: instead of requiring the subroutine name and parameter list to be separated by a comma, let the statement invoking the CALL macro be written like a CALL in Fortran, e.g., like this:

            CALL   SUBR(X,Y,Z)

Write a definition of the CALL macro that will accomplish this.

17. What are the similarities and differences between the use of macros and the use of subroutines? What guidelines, if any, can you formulate to help you decide when to define a macro for a given task and when to write a subroutine for that task? Can you conceive of any tasks for which a macro whose expansion calls a subroutine might be appropriate?

V

Input/Output

18

I/O Hardware Concepts

For a program to be run, it must be in main memory, as must the data on which it operates. Secondary memory is a passive storage device for programs and data not in use. It can store many thousands of times as much information as main memory, yet it is much less costly per unit of information. A major reason for the cost difference is that since programs are not run in secondary memory, access to information stored in secondary memory need not be as uniformly fast as to data and instructions in main memory. Whereas access to information in main memory is accomplished in speeds of the order of one microsecond (10^{-6} seconds) per byte independently of the byte's physical location, access to information in secondary memory is accomplished in speeds of the order of one millisecond (10^{-3} seconds) per byte or more, depending on the physical location of the bytes being accessed. The lower cost of secondary memory per unit of information makes large storage capacities economically feasible. The slower access to information is partly compensated for by a variety of software techniques, many of which will be discussed in the remaining chapters.

Two main classes of secondary memory used by applications programmers are magnetic tapes and magnetic disks. In both, data are stored on magnetized surfaces that move past data-sensing and data-recording mechanisms called **read/write heads.** The amount of data that can be stored on a tape or disk, the data blocksizes that best match the physical characteristics of these devices, and the speed with which data can be transferred between main memory and the devices are all important concerns in input/output programming. These are discussed in the following sections. Other I/O hardware concepts, such as the methods by which the CPU communicates with I/O devices and secondary memory, the role of I/O processors and so-called "channel programming," and the characteristics of magnetic drum memory devices, will not be discussed in this text.

Figure 18.1 Magnetic tape concepts.

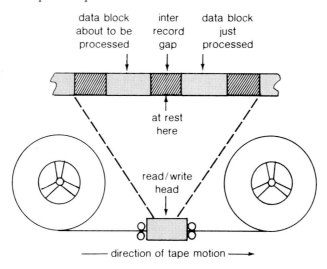

18.1   MAGNETIC TAPES

In a tape device, data can be recorded and sensed only while a magnetized tape surface passes under a stationary read/write head. To position the data that is at point *B*, say, under the read/write head, all the data before point *B* is reached must also pass under the read/write head. (Tape cassettes used for sound recordings provide a good analogy in this respect.) The tape must be accelerated from rest to its normal processing speed before any data can be sensed, recorded, or skipped over. The acceleration time, known as the **start time,** is of the order of 10 milliseconds. The **data-transfer time** is of the order of 100,000 to 500,000 bytes per second, or from 2 to 10 microseconds per byte. Data on tape is usually recorded at a density of 800 or 1600 bytes per inch, but both higher-density and lower-density tapes are in use. Whatever the density, the data is recorded in physical blocks that are separated by gaps. When a tape is at rest, a **gap** (not data) is positioned under the read/write head; thus, a gap allows the tape to accelerate and decelerate without having to sense or record data in the process. These concepts are illustrated in Figure 18.1. *Tape Characteristics*

The ratio of total gap space to the length of a tape provides a useful measure of the efficiency with which a tape is used to store data. Each gap is approximately one-half inch long. The more blocks there are, the more gaps there are. The number of blocks is determined both by the length of the tape and by the **blocksize,** i.e., the number of bytes in a block. At 1600 BPI (bits per inch), a 3200-byte physical block (2 inches) results in 20% gap space (i.e., half-inch gaps constitute 20% of the total tape length), and a 6400-byte block results in 10% gap space.

A good approximation to the total number of bytes that can be stored on a reel of magnetic tape in which the size of all data blocks is the same can be calculated from the formula *Tape Capacity*

$$\{\text{tape capacity}\} = \frac{L \times B}{G + \dfrac{B}{D}}$$

where L = tape length in inches
            B = blocksize in bytes

            D = tape density in bytes per inch
            G = gap space in inches

From this formula, it can be seen that the total capacity is dependent on the length, density, and gap size, all of which are given physical characteristics of a tape, and also on the blocksize and on the ratio of blocksize to density. Choice of blocksize is a programmer's option, and the decision should *Tape Blocksize*

Figure 18.2   Effect of blocksize on tape capacity (for 3600-foot reel with gap size ½ inch).

	capacity (no. of bytes)	
blocksize	800 BPI	1600 BPI
80	5.76×10^6	6.28×10^6
800	23.0×10^6	34.6×10^6
1600	27.6×10^6	46.1×10^6
3200	30.7×10^6	55.3×10^6
6400	32.5×10^6	61.4×10^6

capacity (in bytes) given by

$$\frac{L \times B}{G + \dfrac{B}{D}}$$

with $L = 3600 \times 12$ inches
$G = $ ½ inch
$D = $ density
$B = $ blocksize

Figure 18.3   Effect of blocksize on tape transfer time.

	transfer time overhead	
blocksize	$T = 2 \times 10^{-3}$ ms/byte	$T = 10 \times 10^{-3}$ ms/byte
80	98.4 %	92.6 %
800	86.2 %	55.5 %
1600	75.6 %	38.5 %
3200	60.1 %	23.8 %
6400	43.9 %	13.5 %

overhead percent given by

$$\left(\frac{S}{S + B \times T}\right) \times 100$$

with $S = $ 10 ms start time
$T = $ transfer rate
$B = $ blocksize

be made with care. In order not to let the gap space dominate the utilization of the tape reel, we should choose B so that B/D is reasonably larger than G. This is illustrated by the data in Figure 18.2.

There is another reason for careful selection of blocksize. This has to do with the rate at which data is transferred between tape and main memory. We have already mentioned that this rate is usually from 2 to 10 microseconds per byte, after an initial start time of 10 milliseconds. Thus, the total time required to transfer a block of data between tape and main memory is given by the formula

$$\text{transfer time} = \text{start time} + (\text{blocksize})(\text{transfer rate})$$

Blocksize vs. Transfer Time

The larger the blocksize, the less the effect of start time on total transfer time. If $T = $ transfer rate in milliseconds per byte, and S is start time in milliseconds, then we should choose a blocksize so that the overhead due to start time, as measured by the ratio $S / (S + B \times T)$, is reasonably small. As can be seen from the data in Figure 18.3, the choice of blocksize to reduce data-transfer overhead is consistent with that required to reduce total gap space; we want large blocksizes in both cases.

Since it may be necessary to pass over some tape (perhaps a significant amount of tape) in order to reach some desired data record, the total time required to access a data record on tape can be fairly long compared to CPU processing speeds. In the worst case, it may take a few minutes to reach data that is at the end of a 3600-foot reel, if we start our search at the beginning of the tape. This is in sharp contrast to disk devices, discussed in the next section, in which worst-case access times are on the order of a hundred milliseconds.

18.2   MAGNETIC DISKS

In disk packs such as those used in the IBM 3330 disk system, there are a number of continuously rotating coaxial plates called **disks.** Data are stored on the surfaces of the disks in such a way that to access data on any one surface, we need not read past data on other surfaces. Mechanisms allow us to skip directly to the position on a surface where the desired data are stored. As with tape reels,

Figure 18.4   IBM disk pack concepts.

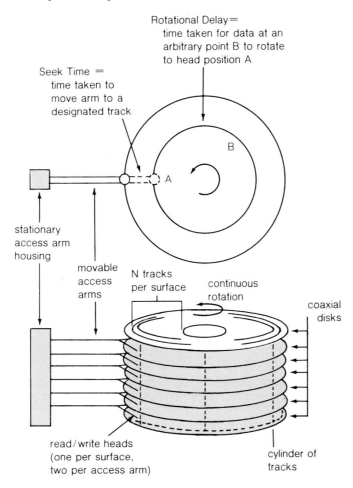

each disk pack can be easily removed from the unit that houses it and be replaced by another pack. When removed, a pack (like a tape reel) is said to be **offline,** i.e., disconnected from the computer system; when placed in the unit and connected to the computer system, it is said to be **online.**

The diagram in Figure 18.4 depicts a disk pack of the type used in IBM 3330 systems. In this type of pack, data are stored in concentric circular **tracks** on the surfaces of the disks. Each track of any one surface is vertically aligned with the correspondingly positioned tracks of all other surfaces, thereby forming a cylinder of tracks. Each surface has the same number of tracks, *N,* so that there are *N* cylinders. There is usually one read/write head per surface; the head must be positioned to the desired track before data can be sensed or recorded. When an access arm is moved to a track, all the other access arms are simultaneously moved to the tracks of the cylinder to which that track belongs. The positioning motion is called **seeking;** the time required for seeking is called **seek time.** Once an arm is positioned at a desired track, the read/write head cannot sense or record data at an arbitrary point *B* on the track until that point has rotated around to a position directly under the head. The time required for this rotation is called **rotational-delay time.** The worst case for seeking occurs when the read/write heads are positioned at the innermost track and the desired data record is positioned in the outermost track (or vice versa). The worst case for rotational delay occurs when the desired data are just past the read/write head, so that a full rotation is required before data can be sensed or recorded. The maximum time required for worst-case seeking and worst-case rotational delay is on the order of a hundred milliseconds.

Designs other than that depicted in Figure 18.4 exist for a number of other manufacturers' disk devices. In some of these, there is one read/write head for each track of a surface, so that seeking is not required. This is called a fixed head or "head-per-track" disk system. In other designs, each

Disk Characteristics

Figure 18.5   Count-Data format: track utilization for IBM 3330 disk system with $N = 13{,}165/(135 + B)$. (See also Figure 18.9.)

N = number of data blocks per track	B = maximum possible blocksize for the indicated number of data blocks	maximum number of bytes per track	percent of maximum capacity
1	13030	13030	100 %
2	6447	12894	98.96
3	4253	12759	97.92
4	3156	12624	96.88
5	2498	12490	95.86
6	2059	12354	94.81
7	1745	12215	93.74
8	1510	12080	92.71
9	1327	11943	91.66
10	1181	11810	90.64
15	742	11130	85.42
20	523	10460	80.28
25	391	9775	75.02
30	303	9090	69.76
35	241	8435	64.74
40	194	7760	59.55
45	157	7065	54.22
50	128	6400	49.11
55	104	5720	43.90
60	84	5040	38.68

access arm can be moved independently of the other arms, so that at different instants different access arms can be positioned at different cylinders. And in still others, the concentric circular track technique is not used; instead, data are stored in discrete sectors of a surface, the number and position of the sectors varying with distance from the center of the surface. Various combinations of these design techniques also exist. However, in the discussions that follow and in those of the remaining chapters, we will be concerned only with the type of disk pack depicted in Figure 18.4, since that is the type currently in use on most IBM 360 and 370 systems.

Data on a track are recorded in one or more physical blocks separated by **gaps,** analogous to interrecord gaps on tape. As with tapes, the more blocks there are on a disk track, the more gaps there are as well. The more gaps, the less room there is for data. Since each track has a fixed circumference and data density, the number of bytes that can be stored on a track depends on the blocksize.

Blocksize vs. Track Capacity

The relationship between blocksize and track capacity is usually determined by consulting tables, such as the one in Figure 18.5 for the IBM 3330 disk system. There are two critically important consequences of the data shown in the table:

1. *Blocksizes of less than about 1,000 bytes make inefficient use of the available space.* For example, if each block held only one record (80 bytes), there would be over 60 blocks on the track and over 60% of the available space would be wasted due to the gaps. If each block held 20 records, there would still be almost 10% wasted space.

Choosing a Blocksize

2. *A blocksize exactly equal to or slightly smaller than one of the blocksizes shown in the table should be chosen.* To do otherwise can result in considerably more wasted space than is shown in the table. For example, if a blocksize of 6450 bytes is chosen instead of 6447, then only one such block would fit on a track. This means that the attained capacity would be $\frac{6450}{13030}$, or approximately 50% of maximum capacity. If the blocksize

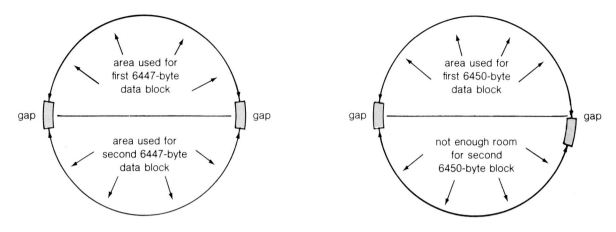

were 6447, then two such blocks could fit on a track, and the attained capacity would be $\frac{2\times6447}{13030}$, i.e., greater than 98.9% of maximum capacity. This concept is illustrated in Figure 18.6. The formula at the top of Figure 18.5, N = 13165/(135+B), gives the number of data blocks that can fit on an IBM 3330 track for a given blocksize B. The constants represent the space required for gaps and other hardware-dependent information. When using the formula, you must discard the decimal portion of the quotient, since only whole blocks (not portions of blocks) can be stored on a track. For example, if B = 84, then 13165/219 = 60.114..., so N = 60.

The choice of an appropriate blocksize is also important from the standpoint of the time required to transfer data between disk and main memory. As mentioned earlier, two mechanical motions are involved in positioning a desired data block under a read/write head: head positioning and disk rotation. In the IBM 3330 disk storage system, the rotation rate of the disks is about 16.7 milliseconds per revolution so that the average rotational delay (sometimes referred to as average *latency*) is just half this, or 8.4 ms. The seek time of the 3330 system varies from 0 to 55 ms; it is zero if no seeking is required, 10 ms if seeking to an adjacent cylinder, and 55 ms if seeking from the innermost to the outermost cylinder (or vice versa). The average seek time cited in IBM publications is 30 ms. The total time required to position a data block under a read/write head is known as the disk **access time;** this is equal to the sum of the rotational delay time and the seek time. Once positioned, the data is transferred at a rate of 806,000 bytes per second or 1.24 microseconds per byte.

If we define a data-transfer overhead factor, *X,* as

$$X = \left(\frac{\text{access time}}{(\text{access time}) + (\text{data-transfer time})}\right)(100)$$

where access time is 8.4 plus seek time (in milliseconds), and data-transfer time is

$$(\text{blocksize}) (1.24 \times 10^{-3} \text{ ms per byte})$$

the dependence of *X* on blocksize for various values of seek time is as shown in Figures 18.7 and 18.8. It should be clear from these figures that a significant reduction in the overhead factor, *X,* is achieved when the blocksize is greater than about 2000 bytes, and that the best possible reductions are achieved when the seek time is zero. It also should be clear that the ratio of data-transfer time to access time is quite small except for the largest blocksizes and the smallest seek times.

The attainable capacity of a track in the IBM 3330 disk system depends not only on blocksize, but also on the method of formatting data on the track. There are two methods that may be used: count-data format and count-key-data format. In **count-data format,** each data block is preceded by

Figure 18.7 Data-transfer overhead for IBM 3330 disk system.

blocksize (number of bytes)	data transfer overhead			
	seek time 0	seek time 10 ms (1 cyl)	seek time 30 ms (pack avg)	seek time 55 ms (worst case)
13030	34.2 %	53.2 %	70.4 %	79.7 %
6447	51.2	69.7	82.8	88.8
4253	61.4	77.7	87.9	92.3
3156	68.2	82.5	90.7	94.2
2498	73.1	85.6	92.5	95.3
1181	85.1	92.6	96.3	97.7
742	90.1	95.2	97.7	98.6
523	92.8	96.6	98.3	99.0
391	94.5	97.4	98.7	99.2
303	95.7	98.0	99.0	99.4
241	96.6	98.4	99.2	99.5

$$\text{overhead} = \frac{\text{(access time)}}{\text{(access time)} + \text{(transfer time)}} \times 100$$

Figure 18.8 Data-transfer overhead for IBM 3330 disk system.

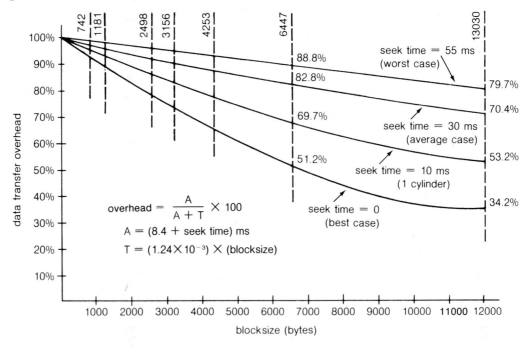

a short (12-byte) count block, used by the hardware and operating system to specify the data block-size and certain other information. The data block and its count block are separated by a small gap; together they constitute what is known as a *data record:*

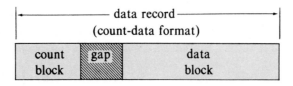

Figure 18.9   Count-Key-Data format: track utilization for IBM 3330 disk system with N = 13165/ (191 + DL + KL). (See also Figure 18.5.)

N = number of data blocks per track	maximum possible value of DL+KL (blocksize + key length) for the indicated number of data blocks	maximum number of bytes per track	percent of maximum capacity
1	12974	12974	99.57%
2	6391	12782	98.10
3	4197	12591	96.63
4	3100	12400	95.16
5	2442	12210	93.71
6	2003	12018	92.23
7	1689	11823	90.74
8	1454	11632	89.27
9	1271	11439	87.79
10	1125	11250	86.34
15	686	10290	78.97
20	631	9340	71.68
25	335	8375	64.27
30	247	7410	56.87
35	185	6475	49.69
40	138	5520	42.36
45	101	4545	34.88
50	72	3600	27.63

In **count-key-data format,** each data block is preceded by two blocks: a count block and a key block. The key block contains an alphanumeric character string, called the *key,* that identifies the data block. The count block contains the data-block length, the length of the key, and other information used by the system. Together, the three blocks constitute a data record:

Clearly, the presence of the key block and the accompanying additional gap reduce the amount of space available on a track for data blocks. The track capacities given in Figure 18.5 are valid for the count-data format, but not for the count-key-data format. The capacities for count-key-data format are shown in Figure 18.9. Comparing these data with those of Figure 18.5, it will be noted that the track capacities are systematically less in count-key-data format than in count-data format, the difference becoming progressively worse as more blocks are added to each track. However, the differences are generally small for reasonably large blocksizes, and there is an advantage—the ability to search for data blocks by key rather than by physical position. Count-key-data format is used for indexed sequential files.

The main point to note is that the second column in Figure 18.9 represents the sum of the key length and the blocksize, not solely the blocksize as in Figure 18.5. The larger the key length, the smaller the permissible blocksize for a given entry in the table. Therefore, from the standpoint of space utilization, the data blocksizes chosen for count-key-data format may not be compatible with those for count-data format. For example, if you choose a blocksize of 2000 bytes (i.e., DL=2000), then in count-data format this results in six blocks per track and a utilization ratio of 6×2000/13030, or about 92.1%. But in count-key-data format a DL of 2000 and a key length of 8 amounts to KL+DL=2008; this means only five blocks per track are possible. The space utilization ratio is then 5×2008/13030, or only about 77%.

Key Length and Data Length

Figure 18.10 *Disk track formats (IBM 3330).*

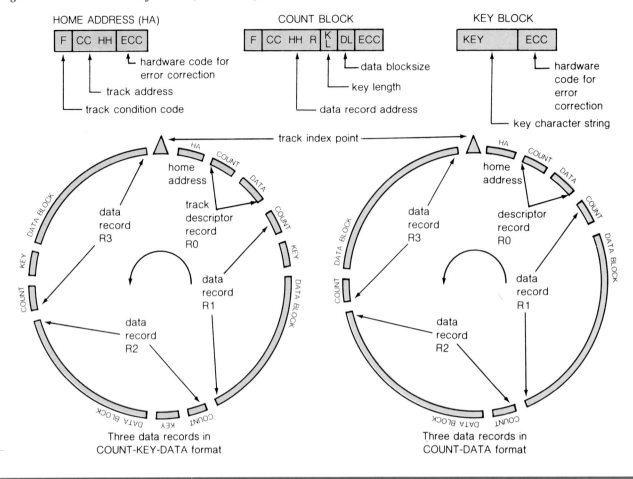

Three data records in COUNT-KEY-DATA format

Three data records in COUNT-DATA format

Track Format Details

There are a few other details about track space utilization worth noting. Each track has a beginning and ending point, known as the *index* point. Following the index point are two records used by the system: the "home-address" record (HA), and the track-descriptor record (R0). The user data records, denoted by R1 through Rn, follow the track-descriptor record and may be in either count-data or count-key-data format. This is illustrated in Figure 18.10.

The physical position of a data record in a disk pack is denoted by an address consisting of three components: a 2-byte cylinder number (CC), a 2-byte track or head number (HH), and a 1-byte number (R) indicating the relative position of the record on that track. A typical CCHHR record address would be

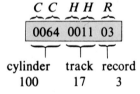

This address is stored in the count block of the third data record on track 17 of cylinder 100. Since programmers do not ordinarily know the address of a data block in the form CCHHR, they must supply some other information that the operating system can translate into the absolute address. This information is either a relative address that indicates the position of a data block relative to the beginning of a particular collection of data blocks, or the key that uniquely identifies a data block.

Note that several tracks may be needed to contain a collection of data whose total size exceeds the maximum track capacity. The best arrangement, from the standpoint of minimizing seek time, would be to store the data on consecutive tracks within a cylinder and to use adjacent cylinders when more than one cylinder was required. This arrangement is known as **contiguous space allocation.** However, due to the competing needs of the many data collections sharing the memory space of a disk pack, contiguous space is not always available for an entire data collection. Therefore, it often happens that only portions of a data collection are stored contiguously, the separate portions being scattered in a somewhat nonregular fashion throughout the disk pack.

18.3 TAPE AND DISK COMPARISON

In the IBM 3330 disk system, there are 19 tracks per cylinder. Thus, the maximum capacity of a cylinder is approximately a quarter of a million bytes: 247,570 bytes if all tracks are formatted in count-data format, and 246,506 bytes if count-key-data format is used. The maximum capacity of a disk pack in the IBM 3330 system depends on the pack model that is used. As this is written, two models are available: Model 1 contains 404 cylinders and Model 11 contains 808 cylinders. The maximum capacity of a Model 1 pack then is approximately 100 million bytes and that of a Model 11 pack approximately 200 million bytes. For the Model 1, this is roughly equivalent to the capacity of 1.7 tape reels at 1600 BPI (assuming 3600-foot reels and 6400-byte blocks); for the Model 11, it is roughly equivalent to 3.5 such tape reels.

However, it should be clear that the sequence of records on a tape must match the sequence required by programs that process the records. Otherwise, an undue amount of time could be spent moving the tape forward or backward while searching for some desired data record. This would be the case, for example, if tapes were used to store flight information for an airline reservation system. Since the time required to locate an arbitrarily positioned record would be unacceptably long, tapes are not used for such situations. Disks are used instead, because they provide not only the ability to process records sequentially, but also the ability to process records in what is essentially random order. For this reason, the discussions in subsequent chapters will be oriented toward disk input and output.

18.4 SUMMARY

The principal concept discussed in this chapter is that of blocksize and its effect on memory space utilization and data-transfer times in the IBM 3330 disk system.

The choice of blocksize for a given application is usually made by the programmer. For the IBM 3330, reasonably efficient space utilization can be achieved by choosing blocksizes of approximately 2000 bytes or more, the choice being dependent on the data format (count-data or count-key-data) and on the corresponding track capacities shown in Figures 18.5 and 18.9. The choice of data format is made indirectly by the programmer when he or she chooses a data-set organization, as will be discussed in Chapters 19 through 22.

Blocksizes of 2000 bytes or more are also effective in reducing total data-transfer time, although the principal means of reducing the transfer time is to reduce the seek time by requesting that data be stored in contiguous fashion (i.e., on consecutive tracks within a cylinder, and on consecutive cylinders).

Blocksize has such a significant effect on space utilization because each disk track's capacity is fixed by the physical characteristics of the disk device: track circumference, data density, space required for control information such as the home address, and space required by gaps between data blocks. The more data blocks there are, the more gaps there will be, and the less space will be available for data. Larger blocksizes can result in fewer blocks, and, therefore, in fewer gaps. This in turn can make more track space available for data. However, to realize these advantages, you must choose a blocksize with care. As illustrated in Figure 18.6 and discussed in the text, an uninformed choice of blocksize can result in considerable unused track space.

Blocksize has an effect on the total data-transfer time, because each data-transfer operation transfers an entire data block and is almost invariably preceded by data-transfer delays due to seek motion and rotational positioning of the data. The relative importance of these delays can be reduced if larger blocksizes are used. As will be discussed in the next chapter, blocksizes of sufficient size to achieve the desired efficiencies are obtained by the technique of blocking logical records.

Further information on the IBM 3330 disk system can be found in IBM Publication GA26–1615. For the IBM 3350, see GA26–1638; for the IBM 3380, see GA26–4193. Information on other IBM disk systems can be found in publications listed in the IBM System/360 and System/370 Bibliography, Publication GA22–6822.

Tape Capacity   This is the number of bytes that can be stored on a reel of magnetic tape. The capacity depends on the length of the tape, the density of recorded information, the size of each data block, and the size of the gaps.

Blocksize   This is the number of bytes in a data block, i.e., the number of bytes in a physical record as measured from the end of one gap to the beginning of the next.

Gap   This is an area of a magnetic tape or disk track where no data is stored. One such area follows each data block. On disks, each gap is used by the electronics to sense that a record has begun or ended. On tapes, a gap is the area that is passed over while the tape is starting or stopping.

IBM 3330 Disk Drive   This type of disk drive (and its successors, such as the IBM 3350) is notable for its relatively fast average access time, and for its access arms that move in unison. Disk packs used with these drives are removable. (See Fig. 18.4.)

Seek Time   This is the amount of time it takes for a disk access arm to move from its current position to the position of a designated track.

Rotational Delay   This is the amount of time it takes for a continuously rotating disk to be positioned so that the sought-after data block is accessible to the read/write head of an access arm.

Access Time   This is the amount of time it takes to get a read/write head positioned at the beginning of a designated data block. It is calculated as the sum of seek time and rotational delay.

Count-Data Format   In this format, each data block on a track is preceded by a short count block that contains, among other things, the blocksize of the data block. See Figure 18.10.

Count-Key-Data Format   In this format, each data block on a track is preceded by two blocks: a short count block and a key block. The count block is the same as in count-data format. The key block contains a character string that the disk's electronics can examine when searching for a particular data block that contains that string. The string is known as the data block's "key." See Figure 18.10.

18.6   REVIEW QUESTIONS _____

1. How many milliseconds are there in a second? How many microseconds in a second? How many microseconds in a millisecond?
2. What is the average seek time, average rotational delay, and average access time for IBM 3330 disk systems?
3. Consider a 2400-foot tape reel in which the gap space is one-half inch and the density is 1600 bytes/inch. What is the tape capacity on such a reel if the blocksize is 80 bytes? 800 bytes? 2000 bytes?
4. What is the maximum number of bytes that can be stored in count-data format on an IBM 3330 Model 1 disk pack if the blocksize on every track is 80 bytes? 800 bytes? 2000 bytes? 13030 bytes? (**Hint:** There are 404 cylinders in an IBM 3330 Model 1 disk pack, and each cylinder contains 19 tracks.)
5. Compare your answers to Questions #3 and #4. Under the conditions stated in those problems, how many tape reels does it take to back up all the data stored on a Model 1 disk pack?
6. If count-key-data format were used instead of count-data format, what would be the answers to Questions #4 and #5? (See Fig. 18.9.)
7. Clearly, the data transfer overhead as defined in Figures 18.7 and 18.8 depends on the ratio of transfer time to access time: The larger this ratio is, the smaller the overhead will be. What factors does transfer time depend on? What factors does access time depend on? Which of these factors (if any) does a programmer have some control over?
8. Based on the data in Figures 18.7 and 18.8, what is the data-transfer overhead when the blocksize is 80 bytes? 800 bytes? 2000 bytes?

1. The data in the first two columns of Figure 18.5 for track capacities in count-data format on a disk pack in the IBM 3330 disk system can be derived from the formula

$$N = \frac{13165}{135 + B} = \text{number of blocks per track for blocksize } B$$

   When computing N by this formula, the remainder must be discarded. For example, for blocksize $B = 84$ we have

$$\frac{13165}{135 + 84} = 60.11..., \text{ so } N = 60$$

   Using this formula, compute the maximum number of bytes per track, and the percent of maximum track capacity, corresponding to blocksizes of $B = 80$, $B = 800$, $B = 4000$, and $B = 8000$ in count-data format.

2. Analogous to the formula given in Exercise 1 for count-data format is that for computing track capacities in count-key-data format on a disk pack in the IBM 3330 disk system:

$$N = \frac{13165}{191 + DL + KL} = \text{number of blocks per track for blocksize DL and key length KL}$$

   For example, for $DL = 64$ and $KL = 8$ we have

$$\frac{13165}{191 + 64 + 8} = 50.057..., \text{ so } N = 50$$

   Using this formula, compute the maximum number of bytes per track, and the percent of maximum track capacity, corresponding to blocksizes of $DL = 80$, $DL = 800$, $DL = 4000$, and $DL = 8000$, and $KL = 8$ in count-key-data format.

3. How many 80-byte records can be stored on an IBM 3330 disk system with Model 1 disk packs, under each of the following sets of conditions:

   a. count-data format, 1 record per block
   b. count-data format, 10 records per block
   c. count-data format, 50 records per block
   d. count-data format, 100 records per block

4. How many 80-byte records can be stored on a 3600-foot reel of magnetic tape if the gap size is a half inch, under each of the following sets of conditions:

   a. 800 BPI, 1 record per block
   b. 800 BPI, 10 records per block
   c. 1600 BPI, 1 record per block
   d. 1600 BPI, 10 records per block
   e. 6250 BPI, 1 record per block
   f. 6250 BPI, 10 records per block

5. Suppose that your computer installation were to limit disk blocksizes to a maximum of 4096 bytes. What would be the actual maximum blocksize for 80-byte records? For 132-byte records? For 2500-byte records? In an IBM 3330 disk system, what would be the percent of maximum disk capacity utilized in each of these three cases? Assume that count-data format is used.

6. If your computer installation does not use an IBM 3330 disk system, prepare track capacity tables comparable to those in Figures 18.5 and 18.9 for the disk system in use in your installation.

7. Determine the following characteristics of the magnetic tapes used in your computer installation: recording density, gap size, reel length, transfer rate, and start time. If any of these characteristics differ from those given in Figures 18.2 and 18.3, determine the effects of blocksize on tape capacity and tape-transfer time for your computer installation's tapes.

8. How many microseconds are required to transfer 1 byte between secondary memory and main memory if the transfer rate of the secondary memory device is 312,000 bytes per second? 192,000 bytes per second? 9600 bytes per second? 30 bytes per second?

9. What is the minimum time required to read all the data stored on a 3600-foot reel of magnetic tape under each of the following sets of conditions. The gap size is one-half inch, the transfer rate 192,000 bytes per second, and the start time 10 milliseconds.

    a. 800 BPI, blocksize = 1600 bytes
    b. 800 BPI, blocksize = 6400 bytes
    c. 1600 BPI, blocksize = 1600 bytes
    d. 1600 BPI, blocksize = 6400 bytes
    e. 6250 BPI, blocksize = 1600 bytes
    f. 6250 BPI, blocksize = 6400 bytes

10. What is the minimum time required to read all the data stored on an IBM 3330 disk system Model 1 disk pack, if the records are stored in count-data format with blocksize = 12000 bytes? Blocksize = 6400 bytes? 1600 bytes? (**Hint:** Assume that all the tracks of one cylinder are read before those of another cylinder are read, and that the cylinders are read consecutively, i.e., with minimum seek time between cylinders.)

11. What would be the average time required to read all the data stored on an IBM 3330 disk system Model 1 disk pack, if the records are stored in count-data format with blocksize = 12000 bytes? 6400 bytes? 1600 bytes? (**Hint:** Compute the average time by assuming that the average access time for each data block is 38.4 milliseconds, i.e., 30 ms seek and 8.4 ms rotational delay.)

12. At 2400 cards per minute, a card reader reads data at the rate of 3200 bytes per second. How long would it take such a card reader to read one box of punched cards (2000 cards)? What is the minimum time to read the same amount of data from an IBM 3330 disk system Model 1 disk pack, if the blocksize were 80 bytes?

19

I/O Software Concepts

In IBM 360 and 370 Assembly language programs, all user-program input and output processing is accomplished by means of macro instructions. Most of the macros generate executable statements, including calls to the operating system; others generate data and/or data areas that are used by the operating system. Macros such as OPEN, GET, PUT, and CLOSE that generate executable statements are known as *imperative* macros; the others are *declarative* macros.

Though their purpose is generally the same, most macros that are used in OS systems differ in substantial detail from those used in DOS systems. Except for VSAM macros (to be discussed in Chap. 22), I/O macros constitute the one major area where the two versions of IBM 360 and 370 Assembly language are essentially incompatible. The job control language statements that describe files in each of the two systems are also incompatible, although here too the purpose is generally the same in both systems.

This chapter provides an overview of the main concepts involved in using I/O macros for sequential and indexed sequential files in both OS and DOS systems. The purpose as well as many of the details of the macros will be described, but programming examples will not be given until Chapters 20 and 21. Although most of the concepts to be discussed are needed for an understanding of those chapters, you may wish to read through the present chapter rapidly and return to it when needed. A comprehensive summary at the end of the chapter will help you assimilate the various concepts.

Fixed- vs. Variable-Length

As has been discussed in Chapter 18, efficient use of disk and tape storage devices requires reasonably large blocksizes of the order of a few thousand bytes. To achieve such large blocksizes, a technique known as blocking is used. In blocking, a sufficient number of records to be processed by a program, such as 80-byte input data records or 132-byte print-line data records, are positioned end-to-end in a data block. Such records are called **logical records.** If the logical records being processed all have the same length, they are known as *fixed-length records,* and the data blocks that contain them are known as *fixed-length blocks.* If the logical records do not all have the same length (for example, if they represent lines that were typed at a terminal), they are known as *variable-length records,* and the blocks containing them are *variable-length blocks.*

A fixed-length block that contains N fixed-length logical records has the structure shown here:

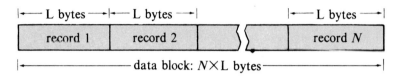

Variable-Length Data Block Format

In variable-length blocks, the length of each logical record is placed in a *record descriptor word* (RDW) that is prefixed to that record in the block, and the length of the block is similarly placed in a *block descriptor word* (BDW) that is prefixed to the entire block, as shown here:

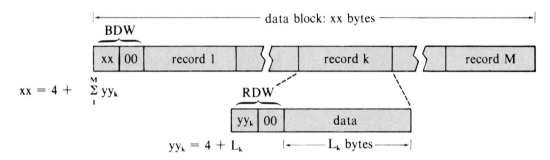

As shown, both the RDW and the BDW are 4 bytes; the lengths occupy the first 2 bytes and the remaining 2 bytes are reserved for other system use. The length in each RDW includes the 4 bytes of the RDW itself, and the length in the BDW is the sum of the lengths in each RDW plus the 4 bytes for the BDW. No block can contain both variable- and fixed-length records; either one or the other format must be used.

The sequence of the logical records in a data block is the sequence in which they are transferred to or from main memory. When a data block is transferred to main memory, it remains there until all the logical records contained in it are processed or are no longer needed. When a data block is being constructed for output, it is also kept in main memory until it contains all the records that can be fit into it. Then it is written to secondary memory. In this way, each read or write operation benefits from a large blocksize, since the transfer time overhead percentage is less than it would be if logical records were read or written one at a time.

The process of extracting logical records from a data block is known as **deblocking,** that of adding records to a data block is known as **blocking.** These concepts are illustrated in Figure 19.1.

Choice of Blocksize

As described in Chapter 18, larger blocksizes make more efficient use of disk storage than do smaller ones. But they obviously require more main memory buffer space, and this in turn makes less efficient use of main memory. From the standpoint of CPU processing, the most natural blocksize to use would be 4096 bytes, since this is exactly the amount of main memory that can be covered by a single base register; 4096 bytes is also the unit of space used by some versions of the operating system when allocating main memory to user programs. Consequently, a compromise between efficient secondary memory utilization and efficient main memory utilization is usually made: blocksizes as near to (but not greater than) 4096 bytes are chosen. In count-data format and in count-key-data format with key lengths not greater than 100 bytes, three 4096-byte data blocks will fit on an IBM 3330 disk track, resulting in about 94% space utilization (see Figs. 18.5 and 18.9).

Figure 19.1   Blocking and deblocking.

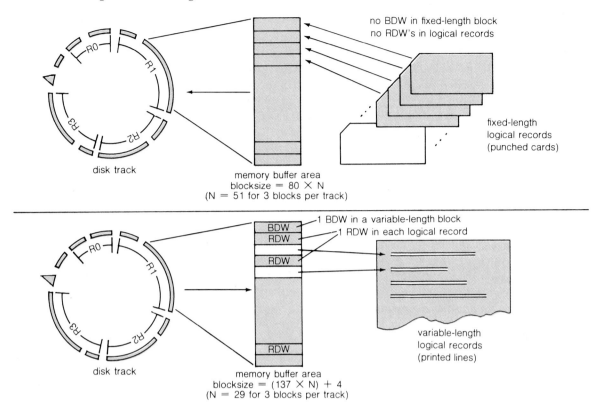

Figure 19.1   Blocking and deblocking.

Note that two additional provisions exist in some versions of the IBM 360 and 370 systems for further optimal use of track space. One is known as *track overflow,* an optional hardware feature in which a data block can be continued from one track to the next. The other involves the use of so-called *variable-length spanned records,* an optional software feature that allows variable-length records to be partly in one data block and partly in the next. Neither of these two provisions will be discussed further in this text.

19.2   DATA SET ORGANIZATION

A collection of logical records that have some useful relationship to one another is generally known as a **file** or **data set.** We will use the terms interchangeably. Each data set stored in secondary memory must be assigned a name at the time it is created, and its name must be unique among all names used for data sets on a disk pack. Each data set name (abbreviated as "dsname") must consist of one or more component names, each of from one to eight alphanumeric characters. The components are separated by periods, and the total number of characters in the name, including periods, must not exceed 44. For example: MDK.SOURCE.CREATE might be the name of a source module used to create other data sets.

Filenames

There are four methods of organizing the logical records of a data set for processing by a program. These are known as sequential organization, indexed sequential organization, direct organization, and partitioned organization. All four methods are available in OS systems, and all but partitioned organization are available in DOS. In addition, the Virtual Storage Access Method (VSAM)—available in both OS/VS and DOS/VS systems—provides mechanisms for the equivalent of sequential, indexed sequential, and direct organizations. In VSAM these are known as entry-sequenced, key-sequenced, and relative-record data sets. VSAM data sets are described in Chapter 22.

In **sequential organization,** the logical records must be processed in the order in which they exist in the data set. The Nth record can only be processed after the $(N-1)$st record has been processed, and before the $(N+1)$st is processed. Sequential organization is probably the simplest of the four organizations for writing programs and provides a relatively efficient means of processing logical records that are in some prespecified sequence. Sequentially organized data sets are always stored in count-data format.

In **indexed sequential organization,** the logical records can be processed either as though they were sequentially organized or in a random order. To process records randomly, the key of the desired logical record must be specified when requesting input or output from the operating system. The key—consisting of from 1 to 255 alphanumeric characters—must uniquely identify that record, distinguishing it from all other logical records in the data set. The key must be part of the data in each record. The operating system maintains an *index* that correlates each logical record key with the data block in which that logical record is located. The index is stored in a separate portion of the data set. Indexed sequential data sets are always stored in count-key-data format.

In **direct organization,** the logical records can be processed either sequentially or in random order, but to process a logical record the relative position of the data block containing it must be specified by the user's program when requesting input or output. The operating system does not maintain an index; instead, it is the responsibility of the user's program to determine the data block in which a given logical record is stored. Data sets organized by the direct method are stored either in count-data format or in count-key-data format, depending on whether or not the data blocks are to be identified by keys. The two formats cannot be intermixed within a single data set.

In **partitioned organization,** the data set is divided into one or more sequential data sets called *members* of the partitioned data set. Each member is identified by a unique name that is stored in a *directory* that is also part of the partitioned data set. The logical records of each member must be processed sequentially; however, the records of any one member can be processed without having to process the records of any other member. Each member is stored in count-data format; the directory is stored in count-key-data format.

Figures 19.2 through 19.5 illustrate the four different data set organizations in schematic fashion. Neither direct organization nor partitioned organization will be discussed in detail in this text. (Partitioned organization is used extensively for maintaining library files, e.g., source module libraries, object module libraries, and macro libraries. Direct organization can be used to circumvent some of the constraints associated with indexed sequential organization.)

One essential point should be noted: a file's organization must be defined when the file is first created. Thereafter, its organization cannot be changed.

19.3   ACCESS METHODS

An *access method* is a set of system procedures (programs) that carry out a user program's I/O requests. Some of the programs that constitute each access method reside within the operating system, and some are system subroutines—also known as logic modules—that are linked to a program at load time or run time.

The access method that is used depends on the organization of the file for which the I/O request is made. It is necessary for the user's program to declare which access method is to be used for each file that it processes, and it is necessary for the I/O macros in the program to conform to the rules of that access method.

In OS systems there are seven access methods; in DOS systems there are four:

file organization	OS access method	DOS access method
sequential	QSAM or BSAM	SAM
indexed sequential	QISAM or BISAM	ISAM
direct	BDAM	DAM
partitioned	BPAM	- - -
virtual storage	VSAM	VSAM

Queued vs. Basic   The letters "AM" above mean simply Access Method; SAM is, for example, Sequential Access Method. In OS, the initial letter Q or B refers to the *technique,* Queued or Basic, that is used with the access method. In queued techniques, the file's records must be processed sequentially, and the

Figure 19.2 Overview of sequential data set format.

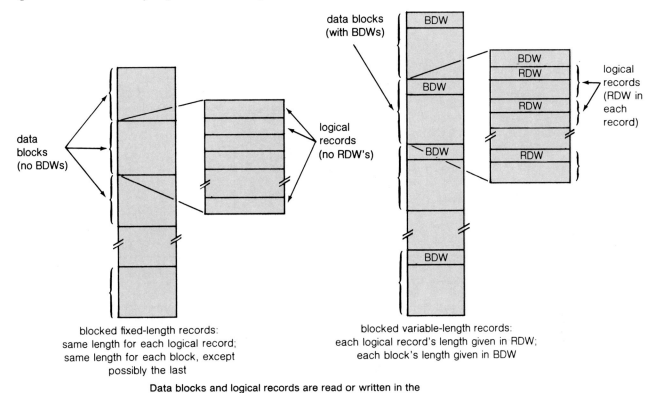

blocked fixed-length records:
same length for each logical record;
same length for each block, except
possibly the last

blocked variable-length records:
each logical record's length given in RDW;
each block's length given in BDW

**Data blocks and logical records are read or written in the
sequence in which they exist. No index or directory is kept.**

Figure 19.3 Overview of indexed sequential data set format.

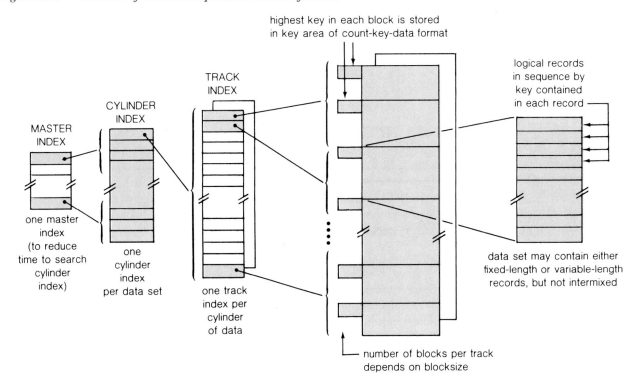

Figure 19.4   Overview of direct data set format.

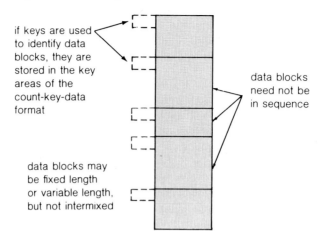

if keys are used to identify data blocks, they are stored in the key areas of the count-key-data format

data blocks need not be in sequence

data blocks may be fixed length or variable length, but not intermixed

Figure 19.5   Overview of partitioned data set format.

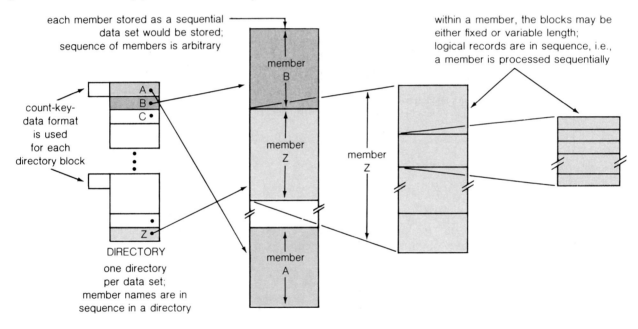

each member stored as a sequential data set would be stored; sequence of members is arbitrary

within a member, the blocks may be either fixed or variable length; logical records are in sequence, i.e., a member is processed sequentially

count-key-data format is used for each directory block

member B

member Z

member Z

member A

DIRECTORY

one directory per data set; member names are in sequence in a directory

access method performs all blocking, deblocking, and I/O synchronization. In basic techniques, the records may but need not be processed sequentially; and with some exceptions, the user's program must perform all blocking, deblocking, and I/O synchronization.

19.4   I/O MACROS

In assembly language, every operation that is associated with input and output of files is accomplished by means of macros. The macros can be considered as extensions of assembly language that generate the required instructions, constants, and control information needed to perform the I/O operations.

The macros that are used in OS systems differ in detail from those used in DOS systems, but in general both sets of macros are designed for the same purposes. In each system, the macros that are used depend on a file's organization and access method (see Figs. 19.6a and 19.6b).

Most of the I/O macros are **executable,** or imperative, macros. That is, at run time they result in calls to the operating system or to system-supplied subroutines. The other I/O macros are **nonexecutable,** or declarative, macros that create constants and control information used at run time.

Since executable I/O macros result in calls to system routines, it is important to be aware of the register linkage conventions that are used. These are as follows:

Register Linkage Conventions

1. Register 13 must contain the address of the user program's register save area when an I/O macro is executed. That is why it is good practice to load Register 13 with the save-area address when a program is first entered and not use the register for any other purpose.
2. The contents of Registers 14 and 15 will be changed when an I/O macro is executed. After executing an I/O macro, Register 14 will usually contain the address of the instruction that immediately follows the macro in the source module, and Register 15 may contain a completion code or error code whose meaning depends on the macro that was executed.
3. The contents of Registers 0 and 1 may also be changed when an I/O macro is executed. These registers are used to pass parameters to and from the user's program.
4. The contents of Registers 2 through 12 are not changed when an I/O macro is executed.

SVC Instruction

It is also useful to be aware of the mechanism by which executable I/O macros call the operating system, since this will appear as part of the assembly listing whenever the PRINT GEN directive is in effect. *The mechanism used is the Supervisor Call (SVC) instruction.* SVC is an RR-type instruction in which the two register address fields are not utilized for register addresses, but instead contain a 1-byte numeric code N that identifies the purpose of the SVC:

assembly language	machine language
SVC N	opcode N
↑decimal integer, from 0 to 255	⊢— 2 bytes —⊣

The numeric code specified in the operand of the assembly language instruction is represented as an unsigned 8-bit integer in the second byte of the machine language instruction. When SVC is executed, four things happen: (1) control is transferred to a fixed location within the operating system; (2) the address of the instruction following the SVC is preserved so that the operating system can return control to the user program following completion of the task being requested; (3) the state of the computer system is set to supervisor mode so that privileged instructions may be executed while the operating system is performing the task; and (4) the SVC operand is made available to the operating system through the interruption code field of the program status word. The operating system determines the purpose of the SVC by examining the SVC operand code and proceeds accordingly.

19.5 DECLARATIVE MACROS: DCB AND DTFxx

The Data Control Block (DCB) macro in OS systems and the Define File (DTFxx) macro in DOS systems create a data area containing parameters that describe certain characteristics of a data set. These characteristics are specified by keyword parameters whose names and general purposes are summarized in Figures 19.7a and 19.7b. The operating system and access methods use the information provided by the DCB or DTFxx macros to control the processing of a data set at run time. Therefore there must be one DCB or DTFxx macro in a source module for each data set that is to be processed.

The Data Definition (DD) statement of OS job control language, and correspondingly the ASSGN, DLBL, and EXTENT statements of DOS job control language, also describe various characteristics of a data set. These supplement the information provided by the DCB and DTFxx macros and provide a means of defining some data set characteristics outside a source module. These characteristics and the names of the corresponding keyword parameters are briefly summarized in Figures 19.8a and 19.8b.

Figure 19.6a I/O macros in OS systems.

macro name	QSAM	BSAM	QISAM	BISAM	BDAM	BPAM	macro function
BLDL						X	build a directory entry list
BSP		X					backspace a physical record
BUILD	X	X	X	X	X	X	build a buffer pool in area reserved at assembly time
BUILDRCD	X						build a buffer pool and a record area
CHECK		X		X	X	X	wait for and test completion of a READ or WRITE
CHKPT	X	X	X	X	X	X	create a checkpoint record
CLOSE	X	X	X	X	X	X	logically disconnect a data set
CNTRL	X	X					control online input/output devices
DCB	X	X	X	X	X	X	construct a data control block
DCBD	X	X	X	X	X	X	create a dummy section for data control blocks
ESETL			X				end sequential retrieval
FEOV	X	X					force end of volume
FIND						X	find the beginning of a BPAM member
FREEBUF		X		X	X	X	return a buffer to a buffer pool
FREEDBUF				X	X		return a dynamically obtained buffer
FREEPOOL	X	X	X	X	X	X	release a buffer pool
GET	X		X				obtain next logical record from input buffer
GETBUF		X		X	X	X	obtain a buffer area from a buffer pool
GETPOOL	X	X	X	X	X	X	build a buffer pool in area acquired at run time
NOTE		X				X	obtain relative position of last block read or written
OPEN	X	X	X	X	X	X	logically connect a data set
PDAB	X						construct a parallel data access block
PDABD	X						create a dummy section for parallel data access blocks
POINT		X				X	establish relative position of block for next read/write
PRTOV	X	X					test for printer carriage overflow
PUT	X		X				move next logical record to output buffer
PUTX	X		X				rewrite updated record or copy an existing record
READ		X		X	X	X	read a block of records
RELEX					X		release exclusive control of data block
RELSE	X		X				release an input buffer
SETL			X				set lower limit for sequential retrieval
SETPRT	X	X					set printer control information
STOW						X	update a BPAM directory
SYNADAF	X	X	X	X	X	X	analyze permanent input/output errors
SYNADRLS	X	X	X	X	X	X	release SYNADAF buffer and save areas
TRUNC	X						truncate an output buffer
WAIT		X		X	X	X	wait for one or more I/O data transfers to be completed
WRITE		X		X	X	X	write a block of records
XLATE	X	X					translate to and from ASCII code

Figure 19.6b *I/O macros in DOS systems.*

macro name	card reader	printer	any device	SAM disk	ISAM	DAM	macro function
CHECK				X			wait for and test completion of a READ or WRITE
CLOSE	X	X	X	X	X	X	logically disconnect a data set
CNTRL	X	X		X		X	control on-line input-output devices
DTFxx	X	X	X	X	X	X	construct a file control area to define the file
xxMOD	X	X	X	X	X	X	generate an I/O processing module (logic module)
ENDFL					X		terminate file load-mode begun by SETFL
ERET					X		return to access method for error-handling options
ESETL					X		terminate sequential mode begun by SETL
FEOVD				X			force end-of-volume for disk files
GET	X		X	X	X		obtain next logical record from input buffer
LBRET				X		X	return (i.e., exit) from label-handling routines
NOTE				X			obtain address of most recently processed data block
OPEN	X	X	X	X	X	X	logically connect a file to the user's program
POINTx				X			prepare to read or write a specific data block
PRTOV		X					respond to printer carriage overflow
PUT		X	X	X	X		move next logical record to output buffer
READ				X	X	X	read a data block into I/O buffer
RELSE				X			release an input buffer
SETFL					X		initiate load-mode for creating ISAM files
SETL					X		set lower limit to begin ISAM sequential retrieval
TRUNC				X			truncate an output buffer
WAITF					X	X	wait for I/O data transfer completion
WRITE				X	X	X	write a data block from I/O buffer

Note: Device-dependent macros for magnetic tape, paper tape, diskette, optical character readers, and magnetic ink character readers are not shown.
The declarative macros are DTFxx and xxMOD, where xx = CD for cards, PR for printer, DI for device independence, SD for sequential disk files, IS for indexed sequential files, and DA for direct access. All the other macros listed above are imperative (executable).

Not all parameters need be specified in any one DCB or DTFxx macro or in any one job control statement. Some are applicable only in certain cases, e.g., for certain types of devices, and for others there are default values that adequately cover most processing needs. The choice of what to specify and how to specify it depends on the keyword, the access method, and the device containing the data set. We will enumerate only those choices we will be using. Descriptions also can be found in the IBM manuals listed at the end of the chapter.

OS Systems

As is shown in Figure 19.7a, there are 37 DCB keyword parameters: 16 may be specified in either the DCB macro or DD statement, and of the remainder, 11 may be specified only in the DCB macro and 10 may be specified only in the DD statement. When there is a choice, it is preferable to use the DD statement, since more run-time processing flexibility is thereby gained.

DCB Keywords

Figure 19.7a *DCB keyword parameters in OS systems.*

DCB keyword	permitted as DCB macro parameter	permitted as DCB subparameter in DD statement	description	QSAM	BSAM	QISAM	BISAM	BDAM	BPAM
BFALN	X	X	buffer-boundary alignment	X	X	X	X	X	X
BFTEK	X	X	buffer-processing technique	X	X			X	
BLKSIZE	X	X	physical blocksize	X	X	X		X	X
BUFCB	X		buffer control-block address	X	X	X	X	X	X
BUFL	X	X	buffer length	X	X	X	X	X	X
BUFNO	X	X	number of buffers in buffer pool	X	X	X	X	X	X
BUFOFF	X	X	ASCII-tape block prefix length	X	X				
CODE		X	paper-tape code scheme	X	X				
CYLOFL	X	X	number of tracks in cylinder overflow area			X			
DDNAME	X		name of DD statement	X	X	X	X	X	X
DEN		X	magnetic tape density	X	X				
DEVD	X		device-dependent parameters	X	X				
DIAGNS		X	trace option for debugging	X	X	X	X	X	X
DSORG	X	X	data set organization	X	X	X	X	X	X
EODAD	X		address of end-of-input-data routine	X	X	X			X
EROPT	X	X	system error option	X					
EXLST	X		address of special processing routine	X	X	X	X	X	X
FRID		X	optical character reader record i.d.			X			
FUNC		X	type of data set for IBM 3525 card punch	X	X				
KEYLEN	X	X	length of record key			X	X	X	X
LIMCT		X	block or track search limit					X	
LRECL	X	X	length of logical record	X	X	X			X
MACRF	X		I/O macro specifications	X	X	X	X	X	X
MODE		X	card reader/punch mode	X	X				
MSHI	X		address of highest-level master index area				X		
MSWA	X		address of work area for new records				X		
NCP	X	X	number of chained channel programs		X		X		X
NTM	X	X	number of tracks for a master index level			X			
OPTCD	X	X	optional processing functions	X	X	X		X	X
PRTSP		X	printer line spacing	X	X				
RECFM	X	X	record format	X	X	X		X	X
RKP	X	X	position of record key			X			
SMSI	X		length of highest-level master index area				X		
SMSW	X		length of MSWA work area				X		
STACK		X	card-punch stacker-bin number	X	X				
SYNAD	X		address of user error-analysis routine	X	X	X	X	X	X
TRTCH		X	seven-track tape recording technique	X	X				

The DSORG and MACRF parameters are required in each DCB macro. DSORG specifies the data set's organization. MACRF specifies the type of data-transfer macros that will be used when processing the data set and also specifies certain I/O processing options whose use depends on the access method.

For DSORG, there are only four choices:

`DSORG=PS`	sequential organization
`DSORG=IS`	indexed sequential organization
`DSORG=DA`	direct organization
`DSORG=PO`	partitioned organization

For MACRF, there are a large number of choices because of the large number of possible I/O processing options. For example, when using QSAM we might write the MACRF= parameter as follows:

```
dcbname   DCB   DSORG=PS,MACRF=(GM),...        QSAM input via GET macro in MOVE mode
```

Figure 19.7b DTFxx keyword parameters in DOS systems.

DTF keyword	SAM	ISAM	DAM	keyword function
AFTER=YES			X	formatted WRITE erases a track's unused space
BLKSIZE	XX		XX	physical blocksize
CISIZE	X			control interval size for Fixed Block Architecture (FBA)
CONTROL=YES	X		X	CNTRL macro used for this file
CYLOFL		X		number of tracks in cylinder overflow areas
DELETFL=NO	X			work file labels will not be erased
DEVADDR	X		X	symbolic unit identifier, e.g. SYSxxx
DEVICE	X	X	XX	IBM device i.d., e.g. 3330
DSKXTNT		XX	X	maximum number of disk extents for this file
EOFADDR	XX			name of end-of-input-data routine
ERRBYTE			XX	name of two-byte I/O error indicator area
ERREXT=YES	X	X	X	requests indicators for irrecoverable I/O errors
ERROPT	X			IGNORE, SKIP, or process I/O errors via named routine
FEOVD=YES	X		X	read and write disk end-of-volume records
HINDEX		X		i.d. of IBM device (e.g., 3330) containing highest level index
HOLD=YES	X	X	X	track protection via exclusive control during I/O
IDLOC			X	name of area that gets CCHHR of data block
INDAREA		X		name of cylinder index buffer area
INDSKIP=YES		X		bypass unneeded portions of cylinder index
INDSIZE		X		size (in bytes) of cylinder index buffer area
IOAREA1	XX		XX	name of required I/O buffer area
IOAREA2	X	X		name of optional second I/O buffer area
IOAREAL		X		name of I/O buffer area for file creation or extension
IOAREAR		X		name of I/O buffer area for random processing
IOAREAS		X		name of I/O buffer area for sequential processing
IOREG	X	X		locate mode register address (any register 2 thru 12)
IOROUT		XX		LOAD/ADD/RETRVE/ADDRTR designates file processing mode
IOSIZE		X		size (in bytes) of IOAREAL
KEYARG		X	X	name of key field area
KEYLEN		XX	X	length (in bytes) of key field
KEYLOC		X		relative position of key in each logical record
LABADDR	X		X	name of user's label-handling routine
MODNAME	X	X	X	name of xxMOD logic module
MSTIND=YES		X		a master index is used
NRECDS		XX		number of records per block when RECFORM=FIXBLK
NOTEPNT=YES	X			NOTE or POINTx macro will be used
PWRITE=YES	X			data blocks written even if control interval buffer not full
RDONLY=YES	X	X	X	user source module is Read-Only
READID=YES			X	READ macro refers to CCHHR (i.e., to record i.d.)
READKEY=YES			X	READ macro refers to record KEY
RECFORM	X	XX	X	record format
RECSIZE	X	XX	X	logical record length
RELTYPE			X	DECimal or HEXadecimal record i.d. in IDLOC and SEEKADR areas
SEEKADR			XX	name of field containing track location of record
SEPASMB=YES	X	X	X	DTFxx assembled into separate module
SRCHM=YES			X	system searches for record on more than one track
TRLBL=YES			X	user standard trailer-label records are read/written
TRUNCS=YES	X			TRUNC macro may be used with this file
TYPEFLE	X	X	XX	file's OPEN mode
UPDATE=YES	X			INPUT or WORK file is to be updated
VARBLD	X			reg. addr. (2–12) for buffer space remaining in locate mode
VERIFY=YES	X	X	X	records are checked for parity error after being written
WLRERR	X			name of user's wrong-length-record error-handling routine
WORKA=YES	X			move mode is used, so GET/PUT specifies I/O record area
WORKL		X		name of I/O record area when creating or extending file
WORKR		X		name of I/O record area when processing randomly
WORKS=YES		X		move mode for sequential processing (like WORKA=YES)
WRITEID=YES			X	WRITE macro refers to CCHHR (i.e., to record i.d.)
WRITEKY=YES			X	WRITE macro refers to record KEY
XTNTXIT			X	name of user's routine that processes extent labels

Note: XX means the parameter is required, X that it is optional. Some DTFCD and DTFPR parameters are not included in the above list.

Figure 19.8a   DD statements for OS systems.

General Data Set Characteristics

DCB	one or more attributes of the data set, as noted in Figure 19.7a
DISP	present and future status of the data set
DSNAME	the name of the data set
LABEL	expiration date, retention period, passwords, and the type of label used
VOLUME	used for data sets on private, multiple, and/or specific volumes

Space Allocation Requests

SPACE	space allocation for one new data set
SPLIT	space allocation for two or more new data sets, sharing cylinders
SUBALLOC	space allocation for two or more new data sets, not sharing cylinders

Input Data Stream

*	input data follows this statement; delimiter is /*, //, or end of-file
DATA	input data follows this statement; delimiter is /* or end-of-file
DLM	changes the /* delimiter to some other character string

Output Data Stream

HOLD	defers sending the output data set to an output device
OUTLIM	specifies a maximum number of logical records for the output data set
SYSOUT	designates the class of device the output data set is to be sent to

General Hardware-dependent Information

AFF	gives same I/O channel separation as specified by SEP in another DD statement
SEP	separates I/O transmission channel of this data set from those of others
UNIT	specifies types and numbers of devices for the data set

Printer and Punch Characteristics

BURST	printer paper output is to be separated (i.e., 'bursted')
CHARS	identifies character arrangements for IBM 3800 printer subsystem
COPIES	number of copies of the data set that is to be printed
FCB	forms control information
FLASH	forms overlay frame specifications for IBM 3800 printer subsystem
MODIFY	identifies a copy modification module (IBM 3800 printer subsystem)
UCS	identifies character set for printing on an IBM 1403, 3203-4, or 3211

Remote Workstation Specifications

COMPACT	specifies whether and how data sent to a remote workstation is compacted
DEST	specifies a remote workstation for an output data set
TERM	specifies that a remote unit record device is in use

Miscellaneous Capabilities

AMP	program processing attributes for a VSAM data set
CHKPT	requests checkpoints be taken at end-of-volume for QSAM and BSAM data sets
DDNAME	identifies a subsequent DD statement that defines this data set
DSID	specifies the identifier of a data set residing on diskette (IBM 3540)
DUMMY	suppresses I/O, space allocation, and disposition (QSAM or BSAM only)
MSVGP	identifies a group of mass storage volumes on a Mass Storage System device
QNAME	routes teleprocessing messages to an applications program (TCAM only)

NOTE: All the above are optional keyword parameters except *, DATA, and DUMMY. The latter are optional positional parameters. The values and/or subparameters that can be specified by the keyword parameters are described in the JCL manuals referenced at the end of this chapter. Except for DCB, DISP, and SPACE, these will not be discussed in this text.

Figure 19.8b   File parameters in job control statements for DOS systems.

Note: The general formats of the three DOS file JCL statements are:
```
/ / DLBL    dtfname,'filename',date,xx,DSF,BUFSP=,CAT=,BLKSIZE=,CISIZE=
/ / EXTENT SYSxxx,volser#,type,seq#,track#,space, split
/ / ASSGN  SYSxxx,unit,options . . .
```
For comparison with OS, the following summary parallels Figure 19.8a

General File Characteristics			
/ / DLBL		dtfname	identity of user program DTFxx macro
		filename	the name of the actual file
		date	expiration date or retention period
		xx	SD, DA, DU, ISC, ISE, or VSAM
		DSF	data-secured file
		BUFSP	VSAM buffer size
		CAT	name of DLBL statement for VSAM catalog
		BLKSIZE	block size, for sequential disk files (DTFSD) only
		CISIZE	control-interval size for DTFSD files on FBA devices
Space Allocation Requests			
/ / EXTENT		SYSxxx	overrides units specified by DEVADDR= in DTFxx macro
		volser#	i.d. of volume on which space is requested
		type	type of extent: data, independent overflow, or index
		seq#	0 for ISAM master index; *n* for *n*th extent
		track#	relative CKD track or FBA block where extent begins
		space	number of tracks or blocks in this extent
		split	highest track # in each cylinder of a shared CKD extent
Input Data Stream			
/ / EXTENT		SYSxxx	SYSIPT designates primary input data stream
Output Data Stream			
/ / EXTENT		SYSxxx	SYSLST designates primary output data stream
Hardware-dependent Information			
/ / ASSGN		SYSxxx	symbolic unit identified by / / EXTENT or by DEVADDR= in DTFxx
		unit	cuu: channel and unit address
			unit is unavailable (UA) or is to be ignored (IGN)
			SYSyyy: refers to SYSxxx of a previous / / ASSGN
			class: READER, PRINTER, PUNCH, TAPE, DISK, CKD, FBA, DISKETTE
			type: IBM model #, e.g. 2560, 1403, 3330, . . .
		options	TEMP: assignment is temporary
			PERM: assignment is permanent
			VOL=: volume serial number if device is tape, disk, or diskette
			SHR: disk device is shared with other files
			ss: magnetic tape characteristics, e.g. 9-track vs. 7-track
			ALT: magnetic tape is alternate unit
			H1: use card reader input hopper #1
			H2: use card reader input hopper #2

(The MOVE mode used in this form is a buffer processing option that will be discussed later in this chapter.) When using BISAM, we might write the MACRF= parameter as shown here:

$$\text{dcbname   DCB   DSORG=IS,MACRF=(R),...}\qquad\text{BISAM input via READ macro}$$

Note that the combination of codes specified for the DSORG and MACRF parameters defines the access method to be used for processing; organization is specified by DSORG and access technique is implied via MACRF. It is implied because, as can be seen from the I/O macro summary of Figure 19.6a, the GET macro can be used only with the queued access technique, whereas the READ macro can be used only with the basic access technique. A similar distinction exists for PUT and PUTX (queued output) and WRITE (basic output).

As can be seen in the previous examples, the rules for coding the DCB parameters are designed not only to provide the operating system with the information it needs to process a data set, but also to serve as abbreviated reminders to the programmer as to the purpose of the parameters.

The RECFM, LRECL, and BLKSIZE parameters designate the record format, logical record length, and data block size, respectively. *Record format* refers to whether the logical records are of fixed or variable length, and whether they are blocked or unblocked. In this text, we will almost always use one of the following two codes for RECFM:

RECFM=FB   each data block contains one or more fixed-length records
RECFM=VB   each data block contains one or more variable-length records

For LRECL and BLKSIZE, the values specified must conform to the following rules:

LRECL=m where m is the number of bytes in each fixed-length record if RECFM=FB, or the number of bytes in the largest variable-length record if RECFM=VB. For variable-length records, m must include the 4 bytes of the record descriptor word.

BLKSIZE=n where n is an integral multiple of m for blocks containing fixed-length records, and is equal to (4 + an integral multiple of m) for blocks containing variable-length records.

For example, if the data set consisted of fixed-length 80-byte records, we could write LRECL=80, RECFM=FB, BLKSIZE=4080. This would give 51 records per block. If the data set consisted of variable-length records, the largest of which was 137 bytes (including the record descriptor word), we could write LRECL=137,RECFM=VB,BLKSIZE=3977. This would give 29 records per block, plus a 4-byte block-descriptor word. These blocksize choices are the largest that would contain an integral number of records and still be less than or equal to 4096, as discussed earlier in Section 19.1.

DOS Systems

The DTFxx macro that is used in DOS systems designates either a device or an access method for disk files. The principal DTFxx macros are these:

DTFCD   card reader/punch file
DTFPR   printer file
DTFDI   device-independent file
DTFSD   sequential disk file
DTFIS   indexed sequential file
DTFDA   direct access file

Other DTFxx macros are available for use with specific devices and will not be considered in this text. These include DTFMT (magnetic tape), DTFPT (paper tape), DTFDU (diskette unit), DTFMR (magnetic ink reader), DTFOR (optical reader), and DTFCN (console). Information about these macros can be found in the DOS macro reference manuals listed at the end of this chapter.

dtfname

The name-field symbol of a DTFxx macro is used in all other I/O macros that refer to the same file as that DTFxx macro. As discussed in the next section, we will use the term "dtfname" when speaking of this name-field symbol. *There is one important constraint to remember:* the dtfname must not be more than seven characters long, because the DTFxx macro expansion includes symbols that consist of the dtfname suffixed with a single letter. For example, if dtfname=CARD, then symbols such as CARDC, CARDS, and CARDL may be created within the CARD DTFxx macro.

Figure 19.8b lists most of the DTFxx parameters for SAM, ISAM, and DAM disk files. Parameters for DTFCD and DTFPR (as well as for DTFSD) will be discussed in Chapter 20; those for DTFIS, in Chapter 21. Comparison of Figure 19.8b with Figure 19.8a shows similarities in purpose but differences in detail between OS and DOS systems.

DTF Keywords

The access method and file organization are specified via the letters *xx* in the DTFxx macro name. A file's processing mode is designated by the TYPEFLE= or IOROUT= parameter, and the record processing mode (*move* mode vs. *locate* mode) is specified, respectively, by the mutually exclusive WORKA= and IOREG= parameters.

Figure 19.9 *Merging the DSCB, DD, and DCB macro information.*

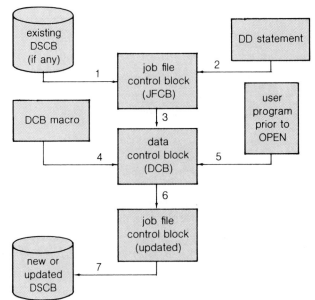

1. The existing data set control block (DSCB), if any, is used to initialize the Job File Control Block (JFCB).
2. The DD statement supplements and overrides the information that was obtained from the DSCB.
3. The JFCB is used to initialize the data control block (DCB).
4. The DCB macro's information supplements and overrides that which was obtained from the JFCB.
5. Run-time modifications may be made to the DCB by the user program prior to completion of the OPEN process.

   The information contained after completion of Step 5 is the information that is used when any I/O-related macro is invoked. (In a few cases, that information may subsequently be modified by the user's program.)

6. The manner in which the JFCB is updated depends on whether the data set was opened for output or not. If it was opened for output, the DCB information replaces that which was in the JFCB. If it was opened for input or update, no existing JFCB information is replaced, but new information is added.
7. If the data set was opened for output, then the updated JFCB is written as the new DSCB.

Record format, logical record length, and data blocksize are specified by the RECFORM, RECSIZE, and BLKSIZE parameters. For example:

RECFORM=FIXBLK — Each data block contains one or more fixed-length records, BLK meaning "blocked."

RECFORM=VARUNB — Each data block contains exactly one variable-length record, UNB meaning "unblocked."

RECSIZE=m — m is the number of bytes in each fixed-length record if RECFORM=FIXBLK or =FIXUNB; and m is the number of bytes, plus 4, in the largest variable-length record if RECFORM= VARBLK or =VARUNB. (The extra 4 bytes is for the record descriptor word that precedes each record.)

BLKSIZE=n — n is an integer multiple of m for blocks containing fixed-length records and is equal to (4 + an integer multiple of m) for blocks containing variable-length records.

19.6 OPEN AND CLOSE

The operating system maintains the information necessary to characterize a data set while it is being stored or processed. Some of the information is stored on disk in the data set's control block (DSCB), also known as the file's *label,* but most is provided through job control statements and the DCB or DTFxx macros. The information from these sources is merged at run time when a data set is opened via the OPEN macro, as shown in Figure 19.9 for OS systems. A similar merge process, not shown here, takes place in DOS systems. Note that the DSCB or label is created by the merge process when a new data set is being created. Thereafter, the DSCB or label is updated.

The connection between a file, job control statements, and DCB or DTFxx macros is established by parameters:

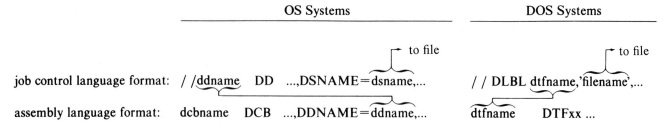

Within an assembly language program, all references to a data set are made by references to the *dcbname* or *dtfname*. In OS systems, the DDNAME= parameter of the DCB macro identifies the corresponding DD statement, and the DD statement in turn identifies the actual data set. In DOS systems, the DLBL statement identifies the DTFxx macro. The DLBL also identifies the actual file, as shown above. It should be noted that most books and reference manuals use the term "filename" where we have used "dtfname." The latter is more accurate, since the actual name of a file need not be identical with the dtfname.

The formats for the OPEN and CLOSE macros depend on whether you are using OS or DOS.

OS Systems

To open an OS data set, the address of the DCB macro and one of several possible processing options must be specified in the OPEN macro. Its format is

        OPEN   (dcb-address,(processing option))

The seven principal processing options are defined in Figure 19.10a. The dcb-address may be specified symbolically or may be contained in a register whose address is enclosed in parentheses. For example, to open a data set whose DCB macro's dcbname is TRANS, to be processed for input, we could write

        OPEN   (TRANS,(INPUT))

Alternatively, if the address of the DCB macro TRANS were in Register 3, we could write

        OPEN   ((3),(INPUT))

at the time the OPEN were invoked. The latter form is not often used with the OPEN macro, but in the use of some other macros being able to specify a parameter via a general register gives added flexibility to the use of the macro.

When processing of a data set is completed, it must be logically disconnected from the program before the program's execution is terminated. This is called *closing* a data set. It is accomplished by the CLOSE macro, whose simplest form is

        CLOSE   (dcb-address)

More than one data set can be closed with a single execution of the CLOSE macro, provided that the dcb-addresses for each data set are listed in the operand, separated by commas:

        CLOSE   (dcb-address-1,dcb-address-2,...)

As with the OPEN macro, the dcb-addresses may be contained in general registers. Thus, to close the TRANS data set, we could write CLOSE (TRANS), or, if Register 3 contained the address of the TRANS DCB macro, CLOSE ((3)).

When a data set is closed, the fields of the DCB macro are restored to the setting that existed before the OPEN macro was invoked. Because of this, a data set can be reopened for subsequent processing before program execution is terminated. We might do this, for example, to create a data set in OUTPUT mode and then process it during the same run in INPUT mode.

Figure 19.10a Processing options with the OPEN macro in OS systems.

processing option	meaning	QSAM	BSAM	QISAM	BISAM	BDAM	BPAM
EXTEND	An existing data set is to be processed by adding records to its end. No records already in the data set may be changed or deleted, and no records may be inserted at any point in the existing data set.	X	X	X	•		
INPUT	An existing data set is to be used for retrieval of information. No records in the data set will be changed or deleted, and no records will be added or inserted.	X	X	•	•	X	X
INOUT	The data set is first used for INPUT and then without closing or reopening it, for OUTPUT.		X		•		
OUTPUT	A new data set is to be created or the information in an existing data set is to be entirely replaced by new records.	X	X	X	•	X	X
OUTIN	The data set is first used for OUTPUT and then, without closing or reopening it, it is used for INPUT.		X		•		
OUTINX	The data set is processed like an OUTIN data set, except that in the OUTPUT mode processing, the records are added to the end of the data set as in EXTEND.		X		•		
UPDAT	The information in an existing data set is to be used for retrieval and existing logical records may be changed, but records may not be inserted, added, or deleted.	X	X	•	•	X	X

• Note: Except when creating or extending an indexed sequential data set using QISAM, the processing options for indexed sequential data sets are not specified in the OPEN macro for QISAM or BISAM. Instead, they are specified in the MACRF= parameter of the DCB macro.

DOS Systems

To open a DOS file, the address of the DTFxx macro must be specified in the OPEN macro, and one of several processing options must be given by the TYPEFLE= or IOROUT= parameter of the DTFxx macro. The format of OPEN is

        OPEN   dtf-address

The dtf-address may be specified symbolically—in which case it is just the dtfname—or it may be contained in a register whose address is enclosed in parentheses. For example, to open a file whose dtfname is TRANS, we could write

        OPEN   TRANS

Alternatively, if the address of the TRANS DTFxx macro were in Register 3, we could write

        OPEN   (3)

The processing options are defined in Figure 19.10b. As can be seen, the choice of options depends on the access method (more specifically, on the DTFxx macro). For SAM and DAM disk files, the options are specified by the TYPEFLE= parameter and also (in one case only) by the UPDATE= parameter. For ISAM files, they are specified by the IOROUT= parameter, with TYPEFLE= indicating whether sequential or random processing is to be used.

Each file that has been opened must be closed, i.e., logically disconnected from the program, before terminating run-time execution. This is done by the CLOSE macro. Its format is

        CLOSE   dtf-address

processing option	meaning	SAM	ISAM	DAM
TYPEFLE=INPUT	For SAM files, an existing file is to be used for retrieval of information; no records in the file can be changed or deleted, and no new records can be added or inserted. For DAM files, label records will be read; data records can be read or written.	X		X
TYPEFLE=INPUT UPDATE=YES	An existing SAM file is to be used for retrieval of information and for changing (i.e., updating) selected records. No records can be deleted, added, or inserted.	X		
TYPEFLE=OUTPUT	For SAM files, a new file is to be created, or an existing file is to be entirely replaced by new records. For DAM files, label records will be written; data records can be written or read.	X		X
TYPEFLE=WORK	A SAM file is to be used first for output, and then for input or output.	X		
IOROUT=RETRVE, TYPEFLE=x	An existing ISAM file is to be used for retrieval and/or updating. No records in the file can be deleted, and no new records can be added or inserted. x can be RANDOM, SEQNTL, or RANSEQ.		X	
IOROUT=ADDRTR, TYPEFLE=x	An existing ISAM file is to be used for retrieval and updating of existing records and for insertion of new records. x can be RANDOM, SEQNTL, or RANSEQ.		X	
IOROUT=ADD	New records can be inserted into an existing ISAM file.		X	
IOROUT=LOAD	A new ISAM file is to be created (i.e., loaded), or an existing ISAM file is to be extended by adding new records in sequence beyond the end of the file.		X	

More than one file can be closed with a single execution of CLOSE, provided the dtf-addresses for each file are listed in the operand:

         CLOSE   dtf-address-1,dtf-address-2,...

As with the OPEN macro, a dtf-address can be specified via a register. For example, to close the TRANS file, we could write either CLOSE TRANS or CLOSE (3). In the latter case, the dtf-address TRANS must be in Register 3. After a file is closed, it can be reopened with the same DTF macro or with a different one.

19.7   GET, PUT, AND PUTX

I/O via GET and PUT

When processing sequential or indexed sequential files, logical records are read and written one at a time, in sequence, by means of the GET, PUT, and PUTX macros.[1]

In OS systems, GET reads a logical record, PUT writes a new logical record, and PUTX rewrites a record that was read via GET.

In DOS, GET reads a logical record and PUT writes a new record or rewrites a record that was read via GET. The PUTX macro is not available in DOS.

In both OS and DOS, the rewrite function is used to change, i.e., update, the contents of a logical record; the record that is rewritten *replaces* the record that had been read from disk.

The operand of GET, PUT, and PUTX must specify the name of the file's DCB or DTFxx macro. The operand of GET or PUT (but not PUTX) may also specify the name of the I/O area that is used for the logical record. Whether or not we specify the name of that I/O area depends on whether we are using *move* mode or *locate* mode, as discussed on the next page.

The fundamental concept embodied in the GET, PUT, and PUTX macros—the concept that distinguishes these macros from the READ and WRITE macros to be discussed in the next section—is that *logical records, not data blocks, are being transferred.* The GET macro does not necessarily cause a data block to be read from secondary memory, and the PUT and PUTX macros do not necessarily cause a data block to be written to secondary memory. Instead, with the GET macro the

---

1. There is one exception to this. In DOS, it is the WRITE macro rather than the PUT macro that is used to create an ISAM file, even though the records must be written in sequence.

Figure 19.11 Move mode and locate mode.

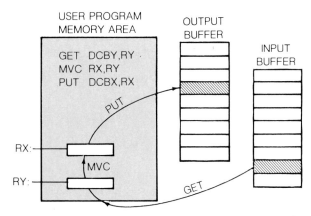

In *move mode*, a GET or PUT macro causes the logical record to be copied from input buffer to logical record area, or vice versa.

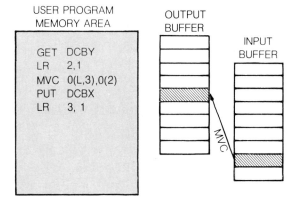

In *locate mode*, the address of the logical record in the input or output buffer is returned in Register 1 following a GET or PUT macro. The logical record is not copied to or from a logical record area in the user's program.

---

sequentially next logical record is obtained from the data block that may already have been read into main memory when a previous GET was invoked. This is the process of deblocking discussed earlier. Similarly, with the PUT and PUTX macros, the logical record is placed into a data block that will not be written until it can contain no more records. This is the process of blocking. The processes of blocking and deblocking are performed by the access methods and are transparent to the user's program.

Move Mode Versus Locate Mode

Two main logical record processing modes are available in OS and DOS. In **move mode,** the access method copies a logical record from the input buffer area to the user's logical record area when a GET macro is executed, and copies a logical record from the user's logical record area to the output buffer area when a PUT macro is executed. In **locate mode,** logical records are not copied to or from the buffer area. Instead, the access method gives the user's program the address of the logical record, while the record remains in the buffer area so that the user program can process the record directly from that buffer area. Locate mode can save processing time and memory space; move mode is somewhat simpler to program. Either (but not both) of the modes can be used for a file at run time.

The concepts of move mode and locate mode are depicted in the diagrams of Figure 19.11 for OS systems. In these diagrams, it is assumed that a logical record is being copied from a file identified by a DCB macro named DCBY to a file identified by a DCB macro named DCBX. In move mode the logical record areas (RY for input and RX for output) are specified in the GET and PUT macros, respectively. In locate mode, the logical record areas are not specified in the GET and PUT macros; instead, the address of each logical record is in Register 1 (placed there by the access method), and the program uses that address to copy the record from input to output buffer.

In OS, the MACRF= parameter of the DCB macro must specify whether move mode or locate mode is to be used. For example, MACRF=(GM) specifies move mode for the input file, and MACRF=(PM) specifies move mode for the output file. Similarly, MACRF=(GL) and MACRF=(PL) would specify locate mode for input and output files.

In DOS, move mode is specified by WORKA=YES for sequential files, and WORKS=YES for indexed sequential files. Locate mode is specified by IOREG=(n), $2 \leq n \leq 12$, where n is the address of the register in which the access method places the logical record's address. If IOREG= is specified, then neither WORKA= nor WORKS= can be specified, and vice versa. All three, of course, are parameters in the DTFxx macro.

End-of-File

If there are N logical records in a file, the end-of-file condition occurs when a GET macro is executed for the $(N+1)$st time. If this happens, the operating system does not return control to the instruction following the GET macro. Instead, it returns control to the instruction whose address is specified by the EODAD= parameter of the DCB macro for OS and the EOFADDR= parameter of the DTFxx macro for DOS. If no EODAD= or EOFADDR= parameter is specified and an end-of-file condition occurs, then the user program is terminated. Note that this corresponds to the END= parameter in a Fortran READ statement and to the AT END clause in a Cobol READ statement.

19.8 READ AND WRITE

I/O via READ and WRITE

In some situations, input and output must be accomplished by the READ and WRITE macros instead of the GET, PUT, or PUTX macros.

In OS, READ and WRITE must be used with the basic access methods BSAM, BISAM, BDAM, and BPAM. In DOS, they must be used with SAM work files, with all DAM files, and with ISAM files when processing randomly and when adding or inserting new records. The OS formats and other considerations for READ and WRITE are different from those of DOS.

OS Systems

When processing data sets with any of the basic access methods, data-transfer operations are accomplished by means of the READ and WRITE macros:

READ	reads a data block
WRITE	writes a data block

The general formats for these macros depend on which access method is being used, as shown in the following representations:

for BSAM and BPAM:

$$\begin{Bmatrix} READ \\ WRITE \end{Bmatrix} \text{decb-name,type,dcb-addr,buffer-addr,buffer-length,} \begin{Bmatrix} MF=E \\ MF=L \end{Bmatrix}$$

for BISAM:

$$\begin{Bmatrix} READ \\ WRITE \end{Bmatrix} \text{decb-name,type,dcb-addr,buffer-addr,buffer-length,key-addr,} \begin{Bmatrix} MF=E \\ MF=L \end{Bmatrix}$$

for BDAM:

$$\begin{Bmatrix} READ \\ WRITE \end{Bmatrix} \text{decb-name,type,dcb-addr,buffer-addr,buffer-length,key-addr,track-addr,} \begin{Bmatrix} MF=E \\ MF=L \end{Bmatrix}$$

The *decb-name* parameter points to an area generated within the expansion of a READ or WRITE macro. This area, known as the **data event control block** (decb), always begins on a fullword boundary within the macro expansion. It is used by the operating system to store the information given by the macro's parameters and to pass back to the user's program indicators that describe the reasons for the failure, if any, of the I/O operation. These indicators are known as *exception codes*. The format of the data event control block depends on the access method (Fig. 19.12a).

READ and WRITE Parameters in OS

The *type* parameter specifies certain variations of the READ or WRITE macro that characterize the type of processing to be performed. The variations depend on the access method as well as on whether it is a READ or WRITE macro. Most of the codes that can be specified are summarized in Figure 19.12b.

The *dcb-addr* parameter identifies the address of the DCB macro that is associated with the READ or WRITE macro being executed. The *buffer-addr* parameter identifies the buffer area to be used, and the *buffer-length* parameter specifies the number of data bytes to be read or written. The *key-addr* parameter points to the memory area that contains the key that identifies data blocks stored in count-key-data format, and the *track-addr* parameter points to the memory area that contains the relative or absolute disk track address of the data block to be read or written.

Figure 19.12a   Data event control block formats for OS systems.

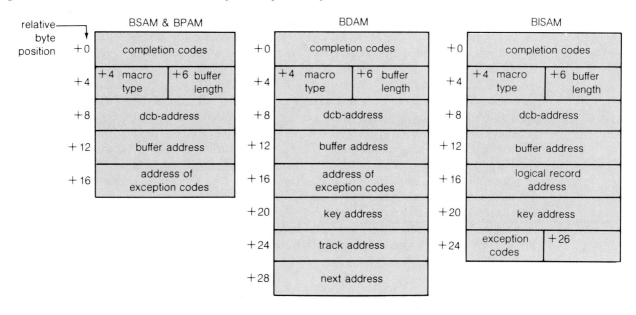

Figure 19.12b   Type parameter codes used in READ and WRITE macros for OS systems. (Note: Not all BDAM codes are shown.)

BSAM/BPAM read		BSAM/BPAM write	
SF	read the data set sequentially	SF	write the data set sequentially
SB	read a mag tape data set backwards (BSAM only)	SD	write a fixed-length dummy record in count-key-data format (BSAM only)
		SZ	write a dummy track-descriptor record to fill the track to capacity (BSAM only)

BISAM read		BISAM write	
K	read a block for retrieval, not for update	KN	write a new record, or rewrite a variable-length record whose length has been changed
KU	read a block for possible updating	K	rewrite a block that has been updated

BDAM read		BDAM write	
DI	read the data block (and key block, if any) from the track address given with the READ	DI	write the data block (and key block, if any) at the track address given with the WRITE
DK	read the data block from the track position identified by the key given with the READ	DK	write the data block into the track position identified by the key given with the WRITE
DIF DKF	same as DI or DK, but also requests the track address of the block that is read	DIF DKF	same as DI or DK, but also requests the track address of the block that is written
		DA	write a new data block in the first available track position
		DAF	same as DA, but also requests the track address of the block that is written

The need to specify the buffer-address and buffer-length reflects the fact that the operating system does not perform blocking or deblocking functions. In addition, when processing blocks in random order, the operating system does not know which block is to be read or where to insert a block that is to be written until the block's position is identified by the user's program. BISAM requires that the position be identified by a key; the key is used to determine the disk track address via the index maintained by the operating system. BDAM requires that the block's position be identified either by a key or by its track address, or both.

The MF=E and MF=L keyword parameters in the READ and WRITE macros are not always used. When both are omitted, the macro is said to be in *standard form*. MF=E is the *execute form* and MF=L the *list form* of the macro. In the standard and list forms, the macro's expansion includes a data event control block, and the decb-name parameter is the name of that decb. In the execute form, the expansion does not include a decb; instead, the decb-name parameter refers to a decb in some other standard or list form of the macro. There are two major uses for the execute and list forms: (1) the decb in a list-form macro can be shared by two or more execute-form macros, and (2) when a list-form macro is in an erasable area of memory, execute forms that refer to it can be used for I/O from within reentrant programs or in programs that are executed in a read-only portion of memory. In Chapter 21, we will encounter instances in which shared decb's are required for BISAM. We will not, however, have occasion to illustrate reentrant or read-only situations.

DOS Systems

The formats for the READ and WRITE macros in DOS depend on the access method as follows:

for SAM work files:

$$\left\{ \begin{matrix} \text{READ} \\ \text{WRITE} \end{matrix} \right\} \quad \text{dtf-address,type,buffer-address,buffer-length}$$

for ISAM and DAM files:

$$\left\{ \begin{matrix} \text{READ} \\ \text{WRITE} \end{matrix} \right\} \quad \text{dtf-address,type}$$

READ and WRITE Parameters in DOS

In all the formats, the *dtf-address* parameter identifies the DTFxx macro for the file that is being read or written, and the *type* parameter specifies certain variations of the macro that characterize the type of processing to be performed, as shown in Figure 19.13.

For SAM work files, the *buffer-address* and *buffer-length* parameters designate, respectively, the I/O buffer area to be used and the number of bytes to be read or written. The buffer-address must be specified because unlike most of the other DTFxx macros the DTFSD for SAM work files does not permit IOAREA1 or IOAREA2 to designate the buffer. The buffer-length must be specified in the READ or WRITE macro when the record format is undefined, but is not specified there for unblocked record formats. In the latter case, the buffer-length is the value of the BLKSIZE= parameter in the DTFSD.

For DAM files, like SAM work files, the record format must be either unblocked or undefined. However for DAM READ or WRITE macros, the buffer-*address* is specified by the IOAREA1= parameter of the DTFDA macro. The DAM READ macro assumes that the buffer-*length* is the value of the BLKSIZE= parameter, but the WRITE macro requires that for unblocked records the user's program must put the length into the record descriptor word, and for undefined record formats it must put it in the register specified by the RECSIZE= parameter of DTFDA.

For ISAM files, the requirements are as follows. The buffer-length is specified by the IOSIZE= parameter of DTFIS. The buffer-address for a READ is specified by IOAREAR= in DTFIS. The buffer-address for a WRITE is specified by IOAREAL= when creating a new file or adding new records to a file; but it is specified by IOAREAR= when updating existing records, since the records are rewritten from the same area into which they were read.

Further details for ISAM files will be given in Chapter 21. DAM files and SAM work files will not be covered in this text. It should be noted however that unlike OS, there is no data event control block associated with a DOS READ or WRITE macro. Consequently, if you are interested in using SAM work files or DAM files, you must be able to process I/O error exception conditions as described in the IBM reference manuals listed at the end of this chapter.

SAM read		SAM write	
SQ	read the file sequentially	SQ	write in count-key-data format
		UPDATE	rewrite a data block but not the count or key blocks
ISAM read		ISAM write	
KEY	read the record whose key is in the KEYARG area	KEY	rewrite a record that has been updated
		NEWKEY	write a new record
DAM read		DAM write	
ID	read the data block and key block from the track address specified in the SEEKADR field	ID	write the key and data blocks to the track address specified in the SEEKADR field
KEY	read the data block whose key matches that in the KEYARG field	KEY	write the data block to the track position whose key matches the one in the KEYARG field
		AFTER	same as ID, except that a new record is written following the previously last record on the track
		AFTER,EOF	same as AFTER, except that an end-of-file record is written following the last record on the track
		RZERO	erase the track whose address is specified in the SEEKADR field

19.9   I/O SYNCHRONIZATION

When a data block is read or written, a certain amount of time will elapse (access time plus data-transfer time) before the data transfer is completed. The user's program must be delayed during that time; otherwise the data in the buffer area may be invalid or incomplete. *The process of delaying execution is known as I/O synchronization.*

OS Systems

In the queued access methods, the delays are performed by the operating system before it returns control to the user's program following a GET, PUT, or PUTX macro. In the basic access methods, a CHECK or WAIT macro must follow each READ or WRITE in order to cause the requisite delay. CHECK must always be used with BSAM and BPAM operations; either CHECK or WAIT can be used with BISAM and BDAM.

The simplest formats of the CHECK and WAIT macros are

CHECK	decb-address	for BSAM, BPAM, BDAM
CHECK	decb-address,DSORG=IS	for BISAM only
WAIT	ECB=decb-address	for BISAM & BDAM only

The decb-address in the operand of these macros is simply the address of the data event control block used in the corresponding READ or WRITE macro.

The main difference between the CHECK and WAIT macros has to do with the manner in which the operating system returns control to the user's program upon completion of the I/O operation. Control is always returned to the instruction immediately following the WAIT macro, regardless of whether or not any errors occurred during the I/O operation. Control is returned to the instruction immediately following the CHECK macro only if no errors or end-of-data condition occurred during the I/O operation. If end-of-data was detected, control is returned to the address specified by the EODAD parameter in the DCB macro. If errors were detected, control is returned to the address specified by the synchronization error address (SYNAD) parameter in the DCB macro.

When control is returned to the SYNAD routine or to the instruction following a WAIT macro, the user's program must examine the exception codes (and certain other information provided by the operating system) to determine the cause of the error, if any, and take appropriate action. In general, the alternatives are to accept the fact that the block was read or written with an error, to skip that block and resume processing at the next data block, or to abnormally terminate the program with an ABEND macro.

Error-Handling Options in OS

A SYNAD routine also can be specified when queued access methods are used. Although neither the CHECK nor WAIT macro is used with queued access methods, the operating system will return control to the SYNAD routine if a data error is detected during execution of an I/O macro. Since there is no data event control block, the exception codes are made available in one of two ways: (1) with QISAM, they are stored in two bytes within the DCB macro expansion; (2) with QSAM, they are stored in an area whose address is specified in Register 0 upon entry to the SYNAD routine.

With the basic access methods, the user's program is terminated if an error occurs while a CHECK macro is being executed and no SYNAD routine had been specified. With the queued access methods, absence of a SYNAD routine causes user-program termination whenever an error occurs during an I/O operation, except under these two conditions for sequential data sets: (1) Data blocks causing I/O errors on a *printer* data set opened for OUTPUT can be ignored by coding EROPT=ACC in the DCB macro. In this case, each offending data block is written (i.e., "accepted") despite the I/O error. (2) Data blocks causing I/O errors on *any* sequential data set opened either for INPUT or UPDAT can be either accepted or skipped by coding EROPT=ACC or EROPT=SKP, respectively, in the DCB macro. If accepted, each offending block is read (GET) or rewritten (PUTX) despite the error; if skipped, each offending block is bypassed, i.e., not read or rewritten.

DOS Systems

In DOS, the I/O delays are performed by the operating system before it returns control to the user's program following a GET or PUT macro. But a CHECK or WAITF macro must follow each READ or WRITE in order to cause the requisite delay. CHECK is used only with SAM work files; WAITF is used with ISAM and DAM files.

The formats of the two macros are

```
CHECK      dtf-address          for SAM work files only
WAITF      dtf-address          for ISAM or DAM files
```

The main difference between CHECK and WAITF has to do with the manner in which the operating system returns control to the user's program upon completion of the I/O operation. Control is always returned to the instruction following the WAITF macro, regardless of whether or not any I/O errors occurred. But control is returned to the instruction immediately following a CHECK macro only if no errors or end-of-file condition occurred. If end-of-file was detected, control is returned to the address specified by the EOFADDR= parameter of the DTFSD macro. If errors were detected, then the option specified in the ERROPT= parameter is processed.

Error-Handling Options in DOS

When control is returned to the user's ERROPT routine or to the instruction following a WAITF macro, the user's program must examine the exception codes provided by the operating system to determine the cause of the error, if any, and take appropriate action. It should be noted, however, that the ERROPT= parameter need not specify the address of an error-processing routine. Instead, it can specify action that the operating system is to take before it returns control to the instruction that follows a CHECK macro. Thus, for SAM input work files, we can specify ERROPT=IGNORE or ERROPT=SKIP, and an error will either be ignored or the entire block skipped. (For SAM output work files, ERROPT=IGNORE is permissible, but not ERROPT=SKIP.) Similar options exist for card and printer files.

19.10 BUFFER AREAS

As has been discussed, data blocks read into main memory are read into buffer areas; data blocks written from main memory are written from buffer areas. Each buffer area must be large enough to contain the largest data block (including BDW's and RDW's) that will be processed in the data set for which it is being used.

Figure 19.14   Use of two input buffer areas.

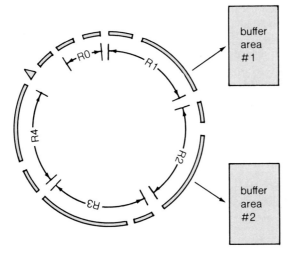

buffer area #1

buffer area #2

Area #1 will contain data blocks from disk data records R1, R3, R5, . . . Area #2 will contain data blocks from disk data records R2, R4, R6, . . . While R1 is being processed from area #1, R2 is read into area #2. While R2 is being processed, R3 is read into area #1, and so forth, with processing from area #1 while reading into area #2, and vice versa.

There may be one or more buffer areas associated with a data set. In the IBM 360 and 370 systems, there are several ways of specifying the size and number of buffer areas, defining the buffer areas, and using the buffer areas during input/output operations. Essentially, the alternatives involve the following two concepts:

1. Buffers may be in memory areas that are either defined at assembly time or are acquired at run time.
2. When more than one buffer area is acquired at run time, it is usually part of a *buffer pool,* a set of contiguous buffer areas.

Double Buffering

When processing a data set sequentially, it is advantageous to use two buffers. When processing in random fashion, there is usually little advantage gained from using more than one buffer. The reason for this difference is the following: when processing sequentially, the order in which the data blocks are read or written is determined by the sequence of the logical records in the data set. The Nth block must be processed after the $(N-1)$st block and before the $(N+1)$st block. Therefore, during input operations the $(N+1)$st block can be transferred from secondary memory to main memory while the Nth block is simultaneously being processed by the CPU. Similarly, during output operations the $(N-1)$st block can be transferred from main memory to secondary memory while the Nth block is being processed. This is illustrated in Figure 19.14 for input operations on sequential data sets. Note, however, that when processing records randomly, it is not so simple to predict which data block is needed next; the decision depends on the data and on the manner in which it is being processed.

The possibility for simultaneous I/O and CPU processing operations is due to the manner in which the hardware is designed and will not be discussed here. However, it should be clear that because of the relatively long access times and data-transfer times required to copy data blocks to or from secondary memory, simultaneous use of two buffers can reduce the amount of time a program must wait for each data block transfer to be completed.

As may be expected, the methods for acquiring and utilizing buffer areas depend on whether we are using OS or DOS systems.

OS Buffer Options in Queued Access Methods

The principal buffer utilization technique used with queued access methods is known as **simple buffering.** Another technique, known as *exchange buffering,* also can be used. This technique, which is more complex and less generally applicable than simple buffering, will not be discussed in this text.

If simple buffering is used, and if the buffer pool area is acquired at the time the data set is opened, a programmer need not be concerned with the details of how the buffers are assigned or utilized. The number of buffers in the pool is automatically set to 2, and the synchronization of the use of the buffers is performed by the operating system. Each buffer area in the pool is associated with the same opened data set; the pool has the format shown in Figure 19.15a.

In addition to being able to automatically create a buffer pool at open time, two other methods are available: (1) by executing a GETPOOL macro prior to opening a data set, or (2) by executing a BUILD macro prior to opening a data set. The BUILD macro creates the pool in an area that had been reserved at assembly time by a DS directive. The GETPOOL macro creates the pool in an area acquired at run time. Except in special processing circumstances, neither BUILD nor GETPOOL need be used. Automatic acquisition of a buffer pool at open time provides sufficient capabilities for most processing needs.

OS Buffer Options in Basic Access Methods

Three buffer utilization procedures are available with basic access methods: dynamic buffering, direct buffering, and user-controlled buffering.

In **dynamic buffering,** the buffer pool area is obtained and structured by the OPEN macro. The number of buffers in the pool is specified by the BUFNO parameter in the DCB macro. A buffer is selected from the pool each time a READ macro is executed, and the same area can be used by a subsequent WRITE macro when updating. Dynamic buffering, which is only available for use with BDAM and BISAM when a data set is opened for input or updating, simplifies I/O programming by placing the responsibility for control of the buffers in the operating system (see Chap. 21).

In **direct buffering,** the buffer pool area may be created by the BUILD, GETPOOL, or OPEN macros as in the queued access methods. The structure of the pool area is the same as that shown in Figure 19.15a for the queued methods. But, unlike the queued methods, a buffer area must be selected from the pool before it can be used in a READ or WRITE macro. This is done by executing a GETBUF macro. When no longer needed (for example, when a data set is closed), the buffer area can be returned to the pool by a FREEBUF macro and be used for other purposes.

In **user-controlled** buffering, the user's program is entirely responsible for reserving and using buffer areas. A buffer pool area is not created by the operating system; instead, buffer areas are reserved at assembly time and utilized by the user's program at run time in whatever way best suits the processing needs.

The three buffering methods are not mutually exclusive; they may all be used with a single data set. It is up to the user's program to designate which buffer area is being used with a given READ or WRITE macro instruction.

DOS Buffer Options

All I/O buffer areas in DOS must be reserved at assembly time. They are part of the user-program's memory area and are not supplied by the operating system. For sequential processing, either one or two buffers may be reserved. For random processing, only one buffer is reserved.

For SAM files (but not SAM work files), the names of the buffer areas must be specified by the IOAREA1= parameter (and optionally the IOAREA2= parameter) of the DTFSD macro. The areas must be reserved by DS directives. For SAM work files, the buffers must be reserved by DS directives and their addresses specified in READ and WRITE macros.

For DAM files, the name of the buffer area is specified by the IOAREA1= parameter and the buffer area must be reserved by the DS directive.

For ISAM files, two buffers can be used when creating (i.e., loading) a file or when sequentially retrieving from it. The optional second area's name must be specified by the IOAREA2= parameter in the DTFIS, but the required first area's name is specified by IOAREAL= for file creation, and by IOAREAS= for sequential retrieval. Only one buffer is used when randomly processing an ISAM file. Its name is specified by the IOAREAR= parameter in the DTFIS. In all cases, the areas must be reserved by DS directives.

The formats of the I/O areas depend on the access method. In Figure 19.15b we show the formats to be used with ISAM files. These and the formats for the other access methods are explained in detail in the *DOS/VS Supervisor and I/O Macros* reference manual, IBM# GC33–5373.

Figure 19.15a   Format of buffer pool area for OS systems.

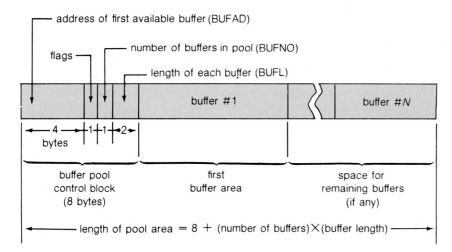

The beginning of each buffer area in the pool is aligned on a double-word boundary unless BFALN=F is specified in the DCB macro.

BFALN=F causes buffers to be aligned on a full-word boundary that is not also a double-word boundary.

Figure 19.15b   ISAM buffer area formats for DOS systems.

Note: These formats assume that RECFORM=FIXBLK, i.e., fixed-length logical records with two or more records per data block. See also "I/O Areas" in *DOS/VS Supervisor and I/O Macros*, IBM #GC33–5373.

1. Format of the area specified by IOAREAL= and IOAREA2= , with IOROUT=LOAD or IOROUT=ADD.

   Used when loading (i.e., creating or extending) an ISAM file, and when inserting new records into an ISAM file.

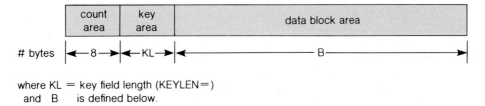

   where KL = key field length (KEYLEN=)
   and   B   is defined below.

   Each logical record in the data block area must contain that record's key.

2. Format of the area specified by IOAREAS= and IOAREA2= , with IOROUT=RETRVE and TYPEFLE=SEQNTL; and by IOAREAR= with IOROUT=RETRVE and TYPEFLE=RANDOM.

   Used when processing sequentially or randomly for retrieval and updating of existing records in an ISAM file.

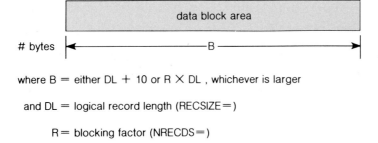

   where B = either DL + 10 or R × DL , whichever is larger

   and DL = logical record length (RECSIZE=)

      R = blocking factor (NRECDS=)

   Each logical record in the data block area will contain that record's key.
   Note: When a record is retrieved from the ISAM overflow area, the first 10 bytes of the data block area will contain the record's *sequence link* (SL), a system pointer used for maintaining logical sequence of overflow records. There is always only one overflow record per data block, even though RECFORM=FIXBLK.

Since the operating system controls all input/output operations, it is not possible to do I/O without properly describing the data sets and the operations to be performed. Two mechanisms exist for this purpose: job control language (JCL) and assembly language macro instructions.

JCL is used to describe certain characteristics of a data set to be processed at run time. Assembly language macros are used to provide additional information about the data set, to characterize the I/O operations to be performed, and to initiate I/O data transfer and related control operations performed by the operating system at run time. The JCL statements and macro instructions that are used for sequential and indexed sequential files in OS systems differ in most details from those used in DOS systems, but their overall purposes are the same in both systems.

Before processing of a data set can begin, it must be opened (i.e., logically connected to the user's program) through execution of the OPEN macro at run time. It is at this time that the descriptions in the JCL statements, the declarative macros (DCB or DTFxx), and the data set's control block or label are merged (see Fig. 19.9). Among the characteristics obtained by the operating system at open time are these: the physical space requirements for the data set in secondary memory, the organization of the data set's records and the method by which they will be accessed, and descriptions of the buffer and record areas. Still other characteristics are passed to the operating system at the time that an I/O operation is initiated. After all I/O operations have been completed, the data set is logically disconnected from the program by the CLOSE macro. After it has been closed, the data set's future availability is determined by information supplied in JCL statements.

Although these remarks apply to all data sets processed at run time, there are an appreciable number of details that may differ from one data set to another. These details depend primarily on three factors: (1) the type of device on which the data set is stored, (2) the data set's organization, and (3) the I/O access method to be used. The type of device in turn determines the data set organizations that are permitted, and the data set organization determines the access methods that are permitted. For storage devices in which random access is not physically practicable, such as magnetic tape, paper tape, cards, printers, and so forth, only the sequential organization is permitted. For disk and other direct-access storage devices, any of the data set organizations that are supported by the operating system are permissible.

The organization of a data set must be established at the time the data set is created, and thereafter it cannot be changed. In OS systems, organization is specified by the DSORG= parameter in the DCB macro; in DOS systems it is specified by the letters *xx* in the DTFxx macro.

The access method used with a data set at run time is a set of system procedures that carry out the I/O operations requested by the user's program. The access method must be established at the time a data set is opened. In OS, this is done through the combined values of the DSORG= and MACRF= parameters in the DCB macro. In DOS systems, the data set organization as specified by the DTFxx macro determines the access method. Once an organization and access method are specified in either OS or DOS, the user's program is constrained to use only certain I/O macros and DCB or DTFxx parameters. Perhaps the most important constraint concerns the choice of GET/PUT macros vs. READ/WRITE macros.

In OS, GET must be used for input, and PUT (or PUTX) for output whenever a queued access technique—QSAM or QISAM—is used with a sequential or indexed sequential data set. With the basic access techniques—BSAM, BISAM, BDAM, and BPAM—READ is used for input and WRITE for output.

In DOS, GET and PUT are used for SAM files (other than work files), READ and WRITE for DAM and for SAM work files. ISAM files require GET for sequential retrieval and PUT for updating existing records when processing sequentially; but READ is used for random retrieval, and WRITE is used to add or insert new records into a file.

Among the other concepts presented in this chapter, perhaps the most important are those associated with handling the end-of-data condition, synchronizing I/O with CPU operations, and designating buffer and record areas.

End-of-Data

In the OS queued techniques (QSAM and QISAM), and in one of the basic techniques (BSAM), end-of-data will cause the program to be terminated unless the EODAD= parameter in the DCB macro specifies a user routine to handle this condition. In all other basic techniques, end-of-data is not a meaningful concept since the records are being processed randomly.

In DOS, the EOFADDR= parameter in the DTFxx macro plays the same role that EODAD= does in OS.

Synchronization

Synchronization is essentially a delay in program execution whenever this is necessary to ensure that a data-transfer operation has been completed before any further attempt is made to use the buffer associated with that transfer. Moreover, if transmission (or other) errors are detected by the operating system, synchronization involves action to resolve the errors by terminating the program, by ignoring the errors, or by bypassing the block that caused the errors.

In OS queued techniques, the delays are an inherent part of the execution of the GET, PUT, and PUTX macros; in the basic techniques, the delays must be explicitly requested via the CHECK or WAIT macros following execution of a READ or WRITE macro. For resolution of I/O errors, there are three options from which to choose in the queued techniques and three in the basic techniques. The OS options, which must be specified via the DCB macro at the time a data set is opened, are as follows.

For OS queued access:

1. Let the operating system terminate the program.
2. If the data set is the printer or is any sequential input data set, let the operating system bypass the data block or accept it with errors by coding EROPT=SKP or EROPT=ACC, respectively.
3. For any data set, let the user program handle the errors via a subroutine whose entry point is designated in the SYNAD= parameter.

For OS basic access:

1. Use the CHECK macro and let the operating system terminate the program if errors are detected.
2. Use the CHECK macro and let the user program handle the errors by designating an error subroutine entry point via the SYNAD= parameter.
3. Use the WAIT macro and let the user program handle the errors when the operating system returns control to the instruction following WAIT.

In DOS, the options available for handling I/O errors depend on whether we are using the GET/PUT macros or the READ/WRITE macros.

For DOS GET/PUT:

1. Let the operating system terminate the program if an I/O error occurs.
2. Let the operating system ignore an error or skip past a data block that is in error, by coding ERROPT=IGNORE or ERROPT=SKIP in the DTF macro.
3. Let the user program handle the error by coding the name of the error-handling routine in the ERROPT= parameter.

For DOS READ/WRITE:

1. With SAM work files, use the CHECK macro and let the operating system handle the error according to the ERROPT= parameter specification (IGNORE, SKIP, or user-routine-address).
2. With ISAM and DAM files, use the WAITF macro and process the error when the operating system returns control to the instruction that follows WAITF.

Buffers

Buffers are the main memory areas used for transfer of data blocks to and from secondary memory. The methods available for allocating and using buffers depends on which access methods are specified.

In OS, there are two different buffering techniques with queued access methods, "simple" and "exchange." The simple buffering technique is the default (i.e., it need not be explicitly requested), and may be used with either QSAM or QISAM. The exchange buffering technique must be explicitly requested via the BFTEK parameter in the DCB macro but may be used only with QSAM. In certain cases (primarily those involving input and output of the same logical records) exchange buffering can improve I/O efficiency, but in order to concentrate on more fundamental processes it will not be discussed further in this text.

Simple buffering can take place without executing any buffer-related macros and without specifying any buffer-related DCB parameters. In this approach, a buffer pool consisting of two buffer areas is allocated by the operating system at open time. Or, you can explicitly request buffer allocation via the GETPOOL macro before opening a data set or request that your own (user-program) buffers be used via the BUILD macro. Whichever approach is used, the buffers are properly used by the operating system whenever a GET, PUT, or PUTX macro is executed.

With OS basic access methods, three buffering techniques are available: "dynamic," "direct," and "user-controlled" buffering. The READ and WRITE macros cause data blocks, not logical records, to be transferred.

Direct buffering is like simple buffering in that the buffer pool may be allocated either at open time or via the GETPOOL or BUILD macros. However, unlike simple buffering, the number of buffer areas in each pool must be designated by the BUFNO= parameter of the DCB macro. A buffer area must also be selected from the pool via the GETBUF macro and its address must be designated in each READ or WRITE macro.

Dynamic buffering is restricted to use with BDAM and BISAM. The buffer pool is allocated at open time by the operating system and a buffer area is selected by the operating system each time a READ or WRITE macro is executed. The use of dynamic buffering with BISAM processing will be discussed in Chapter 21.

User-controlled buffering requires the user's program to handle all functions related to reserving buffer space and designating buffer-addresses.

In DOS, all buffer areas must be reserved by the user's program at assembly time. Thus, in a sense, the only buffering technique available is akin to the OS "user-controlled" buffering.

Record Areas

The principal methods for accessing logical records are known as move mode and locate mode. In move mode, each logical record is moved by the operating system from buffer area to record area (or vice versa) when an input (or output) macro is executed. In locate mode, logical records are not so moved; instead, they are processed directly from their locations in the buffer area. The two modes are mutually exclusive; one or the other must be designated. In OS, the designation is made via the MACRF= parameter; in DOS, move mode is designated by the WORKA= or WORKS= parameters and locate mode by the IOREG= parameter.

Other Considerations

A number of other I/O software concepts and mechanisms are provided for in the IBM 360 and 370 systems in addition to those mentioned. One of the main reasons for such diversity of capabilities is the desire to be able to increase I/O processing efficiency in programs that are run frequently, especially when large data sets are processed. The disparity between I/O access times and data-transfer times on the one hand and main memory access times and processing speeds on the other make such improvements worthwhile. You can pursue these additional topics through the references listed in the next section.

Further details on the material summarized in this chapter, and information on other I/O processing options not covered, can be found in the reference manuals cited in this section.

For comprehensive discussions and examples of the I/O software facilities:

OS	*Data Management Services Guide*	DOS/VS	*Data Management Guide*
	VS1 IBM Publication GC26–3874		IBM #GC33–5372
	VS2 IBM Publication GC26–3875		
OS/VS1	*JCL Services*	DOS/VS	*System Management Guide*
	IBM Publication GC24–5100		IBM #GC33–5371

For detailed explanations of macro and job control formats:

OS	*Data Management Macro Instructions*	DOS/VS	*Supervisor and I/O Macros*
	VS1 IBM Publication GC26–3872		IBM #GC33–5373
	VS2 IBM Publication GC26–3873		
OS	*JCL Reference*	DOS/VS	*System Control Statements*
	VS1 IBM Publication GC24–5099		IBM #GC33–5376
	VS2 IBM Publication GC28–0692		

It will also help to be familiar with the types of utility programs available for certain often-needed data set operations, such as printing or punching a data set, creating a copy of a data set, and maintaining partitioned data sets. Information about utility programs can be found in

OS	*Utilities*	DOS/VS	*System Utilities*
	VS1 IBM Publication GC26–3901		IBM #GC33–5381
	VS2 IBM Publication GC26–3902		

19.13 REVIEW _____

You may find it useful to review I/O software concepts by rereading the Summary in Section 19.11. Here we simply list the principal terms that have been introduced in this chapter. The definitions of these as well as other terms can also be found in the *IBM Data Processing Glossary,* Pub. #GC20–1699.

Record   A collection of related data items that is treated as a unit.

Logical Record   A record that's independent of its physical environment.

Physical Record or **Data Block**   A record whose length and other characteristics depend on the storage mechanism, i.e., on the I/O device. A data block may contain all or part of one or more logical records.

Blocking   The act of combining two or more logical records into one data block.

Deblocking   The act of making each logical record of a data block available for processing, one record at a time.

I/O Buffer   An area of main memory used for reading or writing a data block. A buffer's size should equal the maximum blocksize of the file that it's being used for.

Blocksize   The number of bytes allocated for a data block.

Fixed-Length Record   A record having the same length as all other records with which it is associated.

Variable-Length Record   A record whose length is independent of the lengths of other records with which it is associated.

RDW (Record Descriptor Word)   A full word prefixed to a variable-length record and containing a number equal to 4 plus the length of that record.

BDW (Block Descriptor Word)   A full word prefixed to a variable-length data block and containing a number equal to 4 plus the length of that block.

Data Set   A named set of related records treated as a unit. Synonymous with **file.**

End-of-File Condition   When a file's records are being processed sequentially, the end-of-file condition is the event that occurs when an attempt is made to read beyond the last record in the file. Synonymous with **End-of-Data** condition.

Sequential Organization   An arrangement of logical records in a data set such that the records must be processed in the order in which they exist in the data set.

Indexed Sequential Organization   A sequenced arrangement of logical records in a data set. The sequence is determined by a key field in each record, and an index of keys is maintained by the operating system to enable each record to be accessed by the key that identifies it.

Direct Organization   An arrangement of records in which the relative position of each data block must be specified in order to access it.

Partitioned Organization   An arrangement of records whereby the data set is subdivided into sequential subfiles known as "members." Each member is identified by its name, and a directory of the members' names is maintained by the operating system to enable each member to be accessed by its name. In effect, a partitioned data set is a library file.

Access Method   A set of system procedures that carry out a program's I/O request in response to an executable I/O macro. Access method procedures are dependent on the organization of the file being accessed; different procedures are used for different file organizations. See Section 19.3.

SVC Instruction   The instruction that transfers control to the operating system, i.e., to the "supervisor" program, at run time (SVC=Supervisor Call). See Section 19.4.

Executable Macro   A macro whose expansion includes instructions that may be executed by the CPU at run time. An executable I/O macro—also known as an *imperative* macro—often includes an SVC instruction to request an I/O operation from the operating system.

I/O Macro   An opcode whose purpose is to communicate information about input and/or output operations to the operating system at run time. See Figures 19.6a and 19.6b.

Move Mode   A record processing mode in which an input record is moved from an I/O buffer to a program's work area, and an output record is moved from a work area to an I/O buffer.

Locate Mode   The record processing mode in which a logical record's location (address) in an I/O buffer is made available to a program, so that no program work area is needed to process the record.

DCB and DTFxx   These *nonexecutable,* or *declarative,* I/O macros create a data area whose contents describe certain characteristics about a file or data set. See Figures 19.7a and 19.7b.

DSCB (Data Set Control Block)   A record or records stored with a file and containing descriptive information about the file. Synonymous with **file label.**

dcbname   The symbol that appears in the name field of a DCB macro.

dcb-address   Depending on the context, this term can either be a synonym for dcbname or can refer to the value of dcbname.

dtfname   The symbol that appears in the name field of a DTFxx macro.

dtf-address Depending on the context, this term can either be a synonym for dtfname or can refer to the value of dtfname.

dsname In OS, an abbreviation for data set name. Synonymous with DOS **filename.**

ddname In OS job control language, the name assigned to a Data Definition (DD) statement.

DECB (Data Event Control Block) In OS, an area within the expansion of a READ or WRITE macro. The area is used by the operating system to store one or more macro parameters and to pass back exception codes that identify the cause of an I/O failure if any occurs.

I/O Synchronization The process of delaying a program's execution until a requested I/O operation has been completed.

19.14 REVIEW QUESTIONS

1. What is the principal difference between an executable (i.e., imperative) macro and a nonexecutable (i.e., declarative) macro?
2. What is the principal difference between a logical record and a physical record?
3. Is it necessary to "open" the system printer file? Is it necessary to "close" it? What about the system's standard input file?
4. What type of record does the GET macro read, a logical record or a physical record? What type of record does the PUT macro write, a logical record or a physical record?
5. a. What must be in Register 13 when an executable I/O macro (such as OPEN and CLOSE, or GET and PUT) is invoked at run time?
   b. What registers are likely to have their contents changed when an executable I/O macro is invoked at run time?
6. What are the purposes of the following macro parameters:
   in OS, the DCB parameters RECFM, LRECL, BLKSIZE;
   in DOS, the DTF parameters RECFORM, RECSIZE, BLKSIZE?
7. In OS, what is the difference between a *dsname* and a *ddname?* In DOS, what is the difference between a *dtfname* and a *filename?*
8. How should you specify that "move mode" is to be used when processing the records in a file?
9. a. Can the end-of-file condition occur when attempting to write to a file, or only when attempting to read from a file?
   b. How should you specify what you want the operating system to do when it detects the end-of-file condition on a sequential file?
10. a. What is the purpose of the CHECK macro?
    b. What is the difference in purpose between the CHECK macro and either the WAIT macro in OS or the WAITF macro in DOS?
    c. What will happen at run time if you do not use the CHECK macro or the WAIT or WAITF macros?
11. If you are writing output to the printer, it's possible that the printer could detect an error in the data; for example, you may have written a control character that cannot be processed by the printer.
    a. What options are provided by the DCB EROPT (or DTF ERROPT) parameter to give your program some control over this type of error situation?
    b. What will happen if this error situation occurs when you have not specified any EROPT (or ERROPT) option at all?
12. What job control language statements (if any) are required for I/O operations in the computer system that you use? In what way are those statements connected or related to your DCB or DTF macros?
13. When using "simple buffering" in OS, or when doing I/O in DOS, where are the I/O buffers and what (if anything) must be included in a program to reserve and/or request memory space for those buffers?

1. What, if any, rules or restrictions govern the choice of blocksize for data sets stored on disk in your computer installation?

2. What is the purpose of the technique known as *blocking?* What is the purpose of *deblocking?* Under what condition is blocking and deblocking not required?

3. What are the consequences of specifying RECFM=FB in a DCB macro for a data set? What are the consequences of specifying RECFM=VB in a DCB macro for a data set?

4. If a sequential data set consists of no more than N fixed-length logical records, each of length L bytes, determine the maximum value of the BLKSIZE parameter that is less than or equal to 4096, for each of the following values of $L : L = 80$, $L = 132$, $L = 256$, $L = 2500$. (Assume that the data set is to reside on a disk pack in the IBM 3330 disk system.) How many tracks would be required to store a sequential data set under each of the four conditions? (Assume that $N = 10,000$.)

5. If a sequential data set consists of no more than N variable-length logical records, the maximum record length being L bytes, determine the maximum value of the BLKSIZE parameter that is less than or equal to 4096, for each of the following values of $L : L = 80$, $L = 132$, $L = 256$, $L = 2500$. (Assume that the data set is to reside on a disk pack in the IBM 3330 disk system.) How many tracks would be required to store a sequential data set under each of the four conditions? (Assume that $N = 10,000$.)

6. Write an appropriate form of the //EXTENT statement or SPACE= parameter of the JCL DD statement to reserve a sufficient amount of disk space for each of the four situations given in Exercise 4.

7. Write an appropriate form of the //EXTENT statement or SPACE= parameter of the JCL DD statement to reserve a sufficient amount of disk space for each of the four situations given in Exercise 5.

8. Of the four data-set organizations mentioned in this chapter—sequential, indexed sequential, partitioned, and direct—only one can be used for data sets stored on magnetic tape. Which one is it and why are none of the others permitted to be used with tape data sets?

9. Define what is meant by the "end-of-data" condition for sequential data sets. Under what OPEN processing options (defined in Fig. 19.10) can the end-of-data condition occur? How is the EODAD= or EOFADDR= parameter used in conjunction with the end-of-data condition? What happens at run time when end-of-data occurs if no EODAD= or EOFADDR= parameter has been specified?

10. Each access method is in a sense a set of subroutines that exist as part of the operating system. These subroutines are *called* by the SVC instruction that is generated as part of the expansion of each executable I/O macro. What are the similarities between the SVC instruction and the BALR 14,15 instruction used to call user-defined subroutines? What are the differences between the SVC and the BALR 14,15 instructions?

11. As discussed in Section 19.4, Register 13 must contain the address of the user-program's register save area each time an I/O macro is executed at run time. What other constraints do the I/O macro register conventions place on user programs? How do these conventions differ from and how are they similar to the conventions that exist for calls to user-defined subroutines?

12. Write a DCB or DTFPR macro for a sequential data set whose contents are to be sent to a high-speed printer. (The length of a printed line can be no more than 132 characters and the number of lines to be printed should be assumed to be no more than 5000.) Explain each DCB or DTFPR parameter that you use and explain the value assigned to that parameter.

13. Write a DCB or DTFxx macro for a sequential input data set whose contents are some arbitrary number of 80-byte records. Explain each parameter that you use and explain the value assigned to that parameter.

14. Write appropriate OPEN and CLOSE macros for each of the data sets described in Exercises 12 and 13.

15. The GET macro obtains the sequentially next logical record from a data block. If we assume that only one input buffer had been requested, and if either (1) no previous GET macro had been executed or (2) the previous GET had obtained the last logical record from a data block, then execution of a GET macro causes the operating system to read the next data block (if any) and then obtain the first logical record from that block. Explain how this sequence of events might be modified to minimize the delay inherent in reading a data block if there were two input buffers instead of one.

16. The READ macro causes the operating system to read the sequentially next data block from secondary memory. It is up to the user's program to obtain the sequentially next logical record from that data block.

a. Write a subroutine named DEBLOCK that will obtain the sequentially next logical record from a data block that had been read via a READ macro. Assume that the records are fixed length. The parameters that should be passed to your subroutine are these:

—the address of the input buffer, as had been specified in the READ macro
—the address of the logical record area into which the sequentially next logical record should be moved (as in move mode)
—the address of the logical record length
—the address of the data blocksize
—the address of a full-word binary integer N, which is the number that identifies the relative position within the data block of the record to be obtained within that block ($N = 0,1,2,..., M$, where M identifies the last record in the block; $N=0$ means it is a new data block)

Your DEBLOCK subroutine must move the entire logical record to the calling program's logical record area, and increase the value of N by $+1$, returning the increased value to the calling program. However, if there were no more logical records in the data block at the time the call to DEBLOCK was made, your subroutine should return a value of $N = 0$.

b. Write a main program that will test your DEBLOCK subroutine. Your main program need not execute a READ macro; instead, it can simply contain a simulated data block, for example, one that is created by the following set of directives:

```
BLOCK       DC    CL20'RECD 1'
            DC    CL20'RECD 2'
            DC    CL20'RECD 3'
            DC    CL20'RECD 4'
LRECL       DC    F'20'
BLKSIZE     DC    F'80'
RECDAREA    DC    CL20
N           DC    F'0'
```

17. In a sequential data set with fixed-length records, every data block except possibly the last one contains the same number of bytes, i.e., the same number of logical records. The last data block may or may not contain the same number of logical records as do the other data blocks.

a. Since there is no record descriptor word or block descriptor word with fixed-length data blocks, how might the length of the sequentially last data block be indicated in the data set?

b. Modify your DEBLOCK subroutine of Exercise 16 to allow for the possibility that the last data block is not as long as the others.

18. Modify your DEBLOCK subroutine of Exercise 16 so that instead of moving the sequentially next logical record to the calling program's logical record area, it returns the address of that record in Register 1. (This is then analogous to locate mode.)

19. In move mode, the PUT macro places the designated logical record into the next available position in the output buffer, provided that there is room for the record. The data block is not written from the output buffer until either (1) a PUT macro would cause the number of bytes in the data block to exceed the value of BLKSIZE or (2) the data set is closed, whichever occurs first.

    a. Assume that only one output buffer had been requested. Depict the sequence of events that occur when a PUT macro is executed in move mode, as described above.
    b. Explain how this sequence of events might be modified to minimize the delay inherent in writing a data block if there were two output buffers instead of one.

20. The WRITE macro causes the operating system to write a data block from a designated buffer area to the next available secondary memory location allocated for the data set. It is up to the user's program to move logical records into the buffer area before executing a WRITE macro.

    a. Write a subroutine named BLOCKING that will move a designated logical record into the next available position in a buffer area. Assume that the records are fixed length. The parameters that should be passed to your subroutine are these:

    —the address of the output buffer, as would be specified in the WRITE macro
    —the address of the logical record area containing the logical record to be moved to the output buffer (as in move mode)
    —the address of the logical record length
    —the address of the data blocksize
    —the address of a full-word binary integer N, which is the number that identifies the relative position within the data block of the logical record that is about to be moved to the data block ($N = 0,1,2,...,M$, where M identifies the last record in the block, and $N=0$ means that it is a new data block)

    Your BLOCKING subroutine must move the entire logical record to the appropriate position within the data block and increase the value of N by $+1$, returning the increased value to the calling program. However, if there was no more room in the data block at the time the call to BLOCKING was made, your subroutine should return a value of $N = 0$.

    b. Write a main program that will test your BLOCKING subroutine. Create a simulated set of logical records with DC directives, as in Exercise 16b.

21. Modify your BLOCKING subroutine of Exercise 20 so that instead of moving the logical record to the output buffer, it returns the address of the next position in the buffer in Register 1 and increases N by $+1$. However, if there is no more room in the buffer, your subroutine should return a value of $N = 0$ and the address (in Register 1) of the first position in the buffer. This is then analogous to locate mode.

22. Modify your BLOCKING subroutine of Exercise 20 so that the record that is moved to the buffer area *replaces* the record that had most recently been moved to that area. In this case, your subroutine must not increase the value of N. The new subroutine is analogous to updating records in move mode.

23. What is the purpose of the SYNAD parameter in the DCB macro? How does its use differ for sequential access methods as opposed to basic access methods? (Further information about SYNAD can be found in the descriptions of the DCB macro for each of the access methods in the *Data Management Macro Instructions* reference manual.)

20

Sequential Organization

The processing of sequential data sets always involves at least three distinct phases: an initialization phase, a main processing phase, and an end-of-data phase. In the initialization phase, each data set is opened and perhaps the first record is read. In the main processing phase, each record is processed according to whatever criteria are appropriate to the problem. In the end-of-data phase, the last output record (if any) remaining in main memory has to be written and the data sets must be closed.

We will begin with a discussion of several processing considerations for two of the most frequently used sequential data sets. Following this discussion, the problems of creating, updating, and retrieving information from a sequential data set will be discussed, using as an example a fictitious dormitory room master file. Note that the topics presented in this chapter build upon the sequential file concepts discussed in Chapter 19. Both OS and DOS processing techniques will be covered, but in OS we will consider only QSAM and not BSAM. BSAM is usually reserved for special needs such as creating data sets that are processed via BDAM.

20.1   THE SYSTEM INPUT AND OUTPUT DATA SETS

The system input data set contains what is known as the **input data stream.** In OS, it is referred to as SYSIN; in DOS, as SYSIPT. The **system output data set** contains information to be printed. In OS, it is referred to as SYSOUT; in DOS, as SYSLST.

All data read from SYSIN or SYSIPT are in EBCDIC format (C-type data). If the data are to be used for numeric calculations, they must be converted to an appropriate numeric format (e.g., F-, P-, or E-). Similarly, all data written to the SYSOUT or SYSLST files must be in EBCDIC format. Numeric data calculated in a program must be converted to EBCDIC before they are written. Elementary conversion procedures were described in Chapter 4; more complete procedures were explained in Chapters 12 and 13.

SYSIN and SYSOUT in OS Systems

The SYSIN data set is a sequential data set created by the operating system. A special form of the DD statement, either DD * or DD DATA, identifies the SYSIN data. Neither SPACE= nor DISP= can be specified for SYSIN, and only a few DCB subparameters—BLKSIZE, LRECL, and BUFNO—are permitted.

Like SYSIN, the SYSOUT data set is a sequential data set created by the operating system. It is identified on a DD statement by the parameter SYSOUT=. Neither SPACE= nor DISP= can be specified for SYSOUT.

Both SYSIN and SYSOUT data sets are opened and closed in the same way as any other data set, and the DCB macro must be used to designate organization (DSORG), macro format (MACRF), and the DD statement pertaining to it (DDNAME). Examples of opening and closing SYSIN and SYSOUT, together with appropriate DCB macros, are given in Figures 20.1 and 20.2. In this text, we will assume that the respective DD statements have the forms

```
for SYSIN:       //SYSIN      DD *
for SYSOUT:      //SYSPRINT   DD SYSOUT=A
```

The corresponding DDNAME parameters for the DCB macro, as shown in Figures 20.1 and 20.2, are DDNAME=SYSIN and DDNAME=SYSPRINT.

You can designate the blocksize for SYSIN and SYSOUT, choosing a value consistent with the device characteristics. However, some computer installations use default values of blocksizes for both these data sets. You should determine what blocksizes should be specified at your computer installation. Unless stated otherwise, these values (for the IBM 3330 disk system) will be coded for SYSIN and SYSOUT in this text:

```
for SYSIN:    RECFM=FB,LRECL=80,BLKSIZE=4080         (51 records per block)
              RECFM=VB,LRECL=84,BLKSIZE=4036         (48 records per block)

for SYSOUT:   RECFM=FB,LRECL=132,BLKSIZE=4092        (31 records per block)
              RECFM=VB,LRECL=136,BLKSIZE=4084        (30 records per block)
```

SYSIPT and SYSLST in DOS Systems

The SYSIPT data set needs no job control statements unless it is assigned to a device other than the system card reader. When it's the card reader, the data records described by the DTFCD macro simply follow the // EXEC command for the program that reads those data.

Similarly, SYSLST needs no job control statements unless it is assigned to a device other than the system printer. When it's the printer, the output records defined by DTFPR are printed on the system printer.

We will consider only the customary assignments of card reader and system printer.

The simplest form of the DTFCD macro is as follows:

```
dtfname      DTFCD      DEVADDR=SYSIPT,WORKA=YES,IOAREA1=INBUF,         -
                        EOFADDR=EOJ,DEVICE=2540
```

This specifies that SYSIPT data records will be read from an IBM 2540 card reader, with a single I/O buffer named INBUF, and that the name of the user's end-of-file routine is EOJ. Move mode is used due to the WORKA=YES parameter. Several parameters that are important for sequential disk (DTFSD) files are not specified in DTFCD, because they have default values that ordinarily should not be overridden. These include TYPEFLE=INPUT, BLKSIZE=80, RECFORM=FIXUNB; in other words, SYSIPT records are unblocked, of fixed length (80 bytes), and are used for input. Other parameters may be specified, but they depend on properties of the input card reader (e.g., whether it also has a card punch component) and will not be discussed in this text.

Figure 20.1   Move mode with SYSIN and SYSOUT.

```
EG1          CSECT
*
*   THIS PROGRAM READS RECORDS FROM THE 'SYSIN' DATA SET
*   AND WRITES THEM ONTO THE 'SYSOUT' DATA SET
*
*   QSAM PROCESSING IS USED IN MOVE MODE, WITH FIXED-LENGTH RECORDS
*
             STM     14,12,12(13)       STANDARD ENTRY
             BALR    12,0
             USING   *,12
             ST      13,SAVE+4
             LA      13,SAVE
*
*   THE 'SYSIN' DATA SET IS OPENED FOR INPUT USING THE 'TRANSIN' DCB
*   THE 'SYSOUT' DATA SET IS OPENED FOR OUTPUT USING THE 'TRANSOU' DCB
*
             OPEN    (TRANSIN,(INPUT))
             OPEN    (TRANSOU,(OUTPUT))
*            OPEN    TRANSIN,TRANSOU  OPEN SYSIPT & SYSLST
*
*   A LOGICAL INPUT RECORD IS MOVED FROM THE SYSTEM'S INPUT BUFFER TO THE
*    PROGRAM'S LOGICAL INPUT RECORD AREA NAMED 'CARD', VIA THE GET MACRO.
*   THEN THE RECORD IS MOVED TO THE LOGICAL OUTPUT RECORD AREA NAMED
*    'LINE' VIA THE  MVC  INSTRUCTION.
*   AND FINALLY IT IS MOVED FROM THE LOGICAL OUTPUT RECORD AREA TO THE
*    SYSTEM'S OUTPUT BUFFER VIA THE  PUT  MACRO.
*
COPYLOOP     GET     TRANSIN,CARD       OBTAIN A LOGICAL INPUT RECORD
             MVC     LINE(80),CARD      MOVE IT TO LOGICAL OUTPUT AREA
             PUT     TRANSOU,LINE       MOVE IT TO SYSTEM OUTPUT BUFFER
             B       COPYLOOP           GO GET NEXT INPUT RECORD
*
*   WHEN THE END-OF-DATA CONDITION IS REACHED ON THE INPUT DATA SET, THE
*   OPERATING SYSTEM TRANSFERS CONTROL TO THE ADDRESS DESIGNATED BY
*   THE EODAD= PARAMETER IN THE DCB MACRO, NAMELY 'EOJ'.
*
EOJ          CLOSE   (TRANSIN)          CLOSE THE 'SYSIN' DATA SET
             CLOSE   (TRANSOU)          CLOSE THE 'SYSOUT' DATA SET
             L       13,SAVE+4          STANDARD EXIT
             LM      14,12,12(13)
             BR      14
*EOJ         CLOSE   TRANSIN,TRANSOU  CLOSE SYSIPT & SYSLST
*            EOJ                        TERMINATE
*
*   'TRANSIN' IS DCB FOR 'SYSIN'; 'TRANSOU' FOR 'SYSOUT'
*   'CARD' IS RECORD AREA FOR 'SYSIN';  'LINE' FOR 'SYSOUT'
*
TRANSIN      DCB     DSORG=PS,MACRF=(GM),DDNAME=SYSIN,EODAD=EOJ,RECFM=FB,  X
                     LRECL=80,BLKSIZE=4080
TRANSOU      DCB     DSORG=PS,MACRF=(PM),DDNAME=SYSPRINT,RECFM=FB,         X
                     LRECL=132,BLKSIZE=4092
*TRANSIN     DTFCD   DEVADDR=SYSIPT,WORKA=YES,IOAREA1=INBUF,EOFADDR=EOJ,   X
*                    DEVICE=2540
*TRANSOU     DTFPR   DEVADDR=SYSLST,WORKA=YES,IOAREA1=OUTBUF,BLKSIZE=132,  X
*                    DEVICE=1403
CARD         DS      CL80             LOGICAL INPUT RECORD AREA
LINE         DC      CL132' '         LOGICAL OUTPUT RECORD AREA
SAVE         DS      18F              REGISTER SAVE AREA
*SAVE        DS      9D
*INBUF       DS      CL80
*OUTBUF      DC      CL132' '
             END
```

Figure 20.2   Locate mode with SYSIN and SYSOUT.

```
EG2           CSECT
*
*   THIS PROGRAM READS RECORDS FROM THE 'SYSIN' DATA SET
*   AND WRITES THEM ONTO THE 'SYSOUT' DATA SET
*
*   QSAM PROCESSING IS USED IN LOCATE MODE, WITH FIXED-LENGTH RECORDS
*
              STM    14,12,12(13)       STANDARD ENTRY
              BALR   12,0
              USING  *,12
              ST     13,SAVE+4
              LA     13,SAVE
*
*   OPEN 'SYSIN' FOR INPUT VIA 'TRANSIN' DCB
*     AND 'SYSOUT' FOR OUTPUT VIA 'TRANSOU' DCB
*
              OPEN   (TRANSIN,(INPUT))
              OPEN   (TRANSOU,(OUTPUT))
*             OPEN   TRANSIN,TRANSOU   OPEN SYSIPT & SYSLST
GREG          EQU    1                 LOCATE MODE RECD ADDR FOR 'GET'
*GREG         EQU    2
PREG          EQU    1                 LOCATE MODE RECD ADDR FOR 'PUT'
*PREG         EQU    2
*
*   OBTAIN ADDRESS OF FIRST LOGICAL RECORD AREA IN OUTPUT BUFFER AREA
*
              PUT    TRANSOU           ADDRESS IS RETURNED IN REG 1
              LR     8,PREG            SAVE IT IN REG 8
*
*   OBTAIN ADDRESS OF LOGICAL RECORD IN INPUT BUFFER,
*     MOVE THE RECORD FROM THE INPUT BUFFER TO THE OUTPUT BUFFER,
*     AND THEN OBTAIN ADDRESS OF NEXT LOGICAL RECORD IN OUTPUT BUFFER.
*
COPYLOOP      GET    TRANSIN           ADDRESS IS RETURNED IN REG 1
              LR     9,GREG            SAVE IT IN REG 9
              MVC    0(80,8),0(9)      MOVE RECORD FROM INPUT TO OUTPUT
              PUT    TRANSOU             AREAS, AND OBTAIN ADDRESS OF NEXT
              LR     8,PREG              OUTPUT RECORD.  SAVE IT IN REG 8,
              B      COPYLOOP          AND THEN GET NEXT INPUT RECD ADDR.
*
*   'SYSIN' END-OF-DATA CONDITION CAUSES CONTROL TO BE TRANSFERRED
*     TO 'EOJ' ROUTINE, VIA  EODAD=  PARAMETER IN DCB MACRO
*
EOJ           CLOSE  (TRANSIN)         CLOSE 'SYSIN' DATA SET
              CLOSE  (TRANSOU)         CLOSE 'SYSOUT' DATA SET
              L      13,SAVE+4         STANDARD EXIT
              LM     14,12,12(13)
              BR     14
*EOJ          CLOSE  TRANSIN,TRANSOU   CLOSE SYSIPT & SYSLST
*             EOJ                      TERMINATE
*
*   'TRANSIN' IS DCB FOR 'SYSIN';  'TRANSOU', FOR 'SYSOUT'
*   NO LOGICAL RECORD AREAS ARE DEFINED WHEN USING LOCATE MODE
*
TRANSIN       DCB    DSORG=PS,MACRF=(GL),DDNAME=SYSIN,EODAD=EOJ,RECFM=FB,    X
                     LRECL=80,BLKSIZE=4080
TRANSOU       DCB    DSORG=PS,MACRF=(PL),DDNAME=SYSPRINT,RECFM=FB,           X
                     LRECL=132,BLKSIZE=4092
SAVE          DS     18F
*TRANSIN      DTFCD  DEVADDR=SYSIPT,IOREG=(2),IOAREA1=INBUF,EOFADDR=EOJ,     X
*                    DEVICE=2540
*TRANSOU      DTFPR  DEVADDR=SYSLST,IOREG=(2),IOAREA1=OUTBUF,BLKSIZE=132,    X
*                    DEVICE=1403
*SAVE         DS     9D
*INBUF        DS     CL80
*OUTBUF       DC     CL132' '
              END
```

The simplest form of the DTFPR macro is as follows:

```
dtfname     DTFPR     DEVADDR=SYSLST,WORKA=YES,IOAREA1=OUTBUF,      -
                      BLKSIZE=132,DEVICE=1403
```

This specifies that SYSLST records will be printed on an IBM 1403 printer, with a single I/O buffer named OUTBUF. Move mode is used due to the WORKA=YES parameter. The BLKSIZE= parameter states that the I/O buffer is 132 characters long. There is no TYPEFLE=OUTPUT parameter permitted; the printer is always an output file. There is no REC-FORM= parameter because the default is RECFORM=FIXUNB, and FIXBLK is not permitted. Other parameters may be specified; some of these depend on the properties of the printer, but a few are important because they determine how the user program will control printer line-spacing. The latter include CTLCHR=, CONTROL=, and PRINTOV=. Of these, only the CTLCHR= parameter will be discussed in this text (see Sect. 20.4). Absence of all three of these parameters, as in the previous example, indicates that control of printer line-spacing will be done independently of the printer's carriage-control mechanism. This was the case in Figure 2.4b of Chapter 2.

Input/Output Example

Move Mode

To read data from the system input file and write the 80-byte records on the system output file, the simplest procedure is that shown in Figure 20.1, using move mode (see Sect. 19.7). Each execution of the GET macro causes a record to be moved from the input buffer into the logical record area named CARD, and each execution of the PUT macro causes the record to be moved from the logical record area named LINE to the output buffer. An MVC instruction moves the record from the CARD area to the LINE area. (This is essentially the procedure that was depicted in Fig. 19.11.)

You will see that in Figure 20.1 we have written the program to run in an OS system but have shown the substitutions that are required to convert the program to DOS. We will follow this practice throughout the remainder of the text.

Locate Mode

Instead of using move mode, it is possible to use locate mode with either or both of the system input/output files. Three important characteristics of locate mode should be noted:

1. The address of the logical record area is not specified in the GET or PUT macro when locate mode is used for input or output, because the logical record areas are not defined in the user's program at assembly time.
2. The address of the logical record obtained via the GET macro is returned in a register following execution of the GET macro. In OS, that address is always returned in Register 1. In DOS, it is always returned in the register whose address n is specified by the IOREG=(n) parameter in the DTFCD macro. The value of n must be in the range 2 through 12.
3. The address of the *next* logical record area to be used by the PUT macro is returned in a register following execution of PUT. As with GET, the register used with PUT in OS is Register 1, and in DOS it is Register n, where n is specified by IOREG=(n) in DTFPR, and $2 \leq n \leq 12$. Since it is the *next* logical record whose address is returned, this means that when PUT is executed, the operating system has remembered where the *current* logical record area is. It also means that the first execution of PUT in locate mode is in the nature of an initialization procedure; it simply returns the address of the first logical record area, but doesn't assume that there is a record to be processed.

Note that if there are N records to be written, there must be N executions of the PUT macro. But the Kth execution writes the $(K-1)$st record, since the first execution of PUT does not write a record at all. Therefore, since the Nth execution writes the next-to-last record, a natural question is, "When does the last record get written?" The answer is that it gets written by the operating system when the data set is closed. In effect, the operating system executes the PUT that is required to write the last record.

These observations are illustrated in the program of Figure 20.2. The address returned by the GET macro is used by the source operand of the MVC instruction, and the address returned by the PUT macro is used by the destination operand of that instruction. In this way the logical record is moved from the input buffer to the output buffer. Note that to make the transition between OS and DOS easier, we have used symbolic register addresses GREG and PREG instead of numeric register addresses.

Move Mode

To process fields in a record—using *move* mode, the logical record area should be subdivided into named areas, each area corresponding in length and relative position to a field of the logical record. For example, consider this input record:

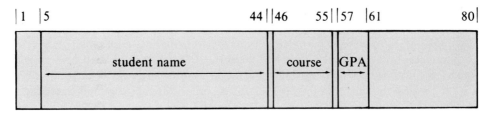

We could define a logical input record area for this record as follows:

```
CARD     DS    CL80     RESERVE 80 POSITIONS FOR INPUT RECORD
         ORG   CARD     SET MEMORY LOCATION COUNTER TO 'CARD'
         DS    CL4      COLUMNS 1- 4    UNUSED
NAME     DS    CL40        "    5-44    FOR STUDENT NAME
         DS    CL1         "    45      UNUSED
COURSE   DS    CL10        "    46-55   FOR COURSE TAKEN
         DS    CL1         "    56      UNUSED
GPA      DS    CL4         "    57-60   FOR GPA (AS 'X.XX')
         ORG            SET MEM LOC CTR TO FIRST BYTE BEYOND 'CARD'
```

With the definition shown, each field of the record can be referred to in the operand of an instruction or directive. If we wanted to modify the program of Figure 20.1 to print the records for only those students with a GPA of 3.50 or better, we would simply insert these two statements immediately after the GET macro:

```
CLC   GPA,=C'3.50'       COMPARE GPA TO 3.50
BL    COPYLOOP           READ NEXT RECORD IF GPA LESS THAN 3.5
```

Locate Mode

To process fields within a logical record in *locate* mode, a DSECT defining the logical record fields must be established at assembly time. A dummy base register that points to the beginning of the DSECT area must also be established by means of a USING directive at assembly time, and the logical record address received from the GET macro should be loaded into the dummy base register at run time. For example, the record shown earlier would be defined like this:

```
CARD     DSECT            BEGIN DUMMY SECTION NAMED 'CARD'
         DS    CL4
NAME     DS    CL40
         DS    CL1        SAME AS IN ABOVE MOVE MODE DEFINITIONS
COURSE   DS    CL10
         DS    CL1
GPA      DS    CL4
EG2      CSECT            RESUME CONTROL SECTION NAMED 'EG2'
```

If this dummy-section definition is inserted in the program of Figure 20.2, then to print the records for just those students with a GPA of 3.50 or better, we would add the following three statements (or statements similar to them) immediately following the GET macro:

```
USING    CARD,11
LR       11,GREG
CLC      GPA,=C'3.50'
BL       COPYLOOP
```

Any available register can be used as the dummy base register. The point to be noted is that both the USING directive that establishes the dummy base register and the load instruction that places the appropriate address into that register at run time must designate the same register, and they must both occur before any instruction that refers to fields within the dummy section.

In Figures 20.1 and 20.2, the MVC instruction was used to move a logical record from an input area to an output area. The length of the record was known to be 80 characters, so the length of 80 could be coded in the MVC in the source module. However, when processing variable-length records, the length of a record is not necessarily known until it is processed at run time. However, the record length can be obtained at run time from the record descriptor word. Once the record length is obtained, the record can be moved with an Execute instruction. We will illustrate this procedure first for move mode and then for locate mode. Although the system input and system output data sets are not likely to contain variable-length records, we will continue to use our example, making whatever changes are necessary to accommodate variable-length records.

The logical record area must be defined to include the record descriptor word (RDW). At the least, the area should begin on a half-word boundary, to make the count field in the RDW accessible to LH and STH instructions. This can be accomplished, of course, by preceding the DS directive that defines the area with a DS 0H directive: *Using the RDW*

```
              DS    0H
      CARD    DS    CL84
```

Note that the definition of the record area now includes 4 bytes for the RDW; it also assumes that the largest variable-length record will be 80 bytes. (Remember that the area reserved must always be large enough to contain both the RDW and the largest variable-length record in the data set.) The modifications to Figure 20.1 necessary to process variable-length records in move mode can then be coded like this:

```
COPYLOOP    GET     TRANSIN,CARD    OBTAIN A LOGICAL RECORD        Move Mode
            LH      10,CARD         LOAD RECORD LENGTH FROM RDW
            SH      10,=H'1'        SUBT +1 FOR EXECUTE INSTR
            EX      10,VMVC         MOVE RECORD FROM INPUT TO OUTPUT
            PUT     TRANSOU,LINE      AREAS, AND PUT IT INTO OUTPUT
            B       COPYLOOP          BUFFER. THEN GET NEXT RECORD.
VMVC        MVC     LINE(0),CARD    MVC FOR VAR-LNG MOVE.
                    .
                    .
                    .
TRANSIN     DCB     ...,RECFM=VB,LRECL=84,BLKSIZE=4036
TRANSOU     DCB     ...,RECFM=VB,LRECL=136,BLKSIZE=4084
*TRANSIN    DTFCD   ...,RECFORM=VARUNB,BLKSIZE=84
*TRANSOU    DTFPR   ...,RECFORM=VARUNB,BLKSIZE=136
*INBUF      DS      CL84
*           DS      CL136
            DS      0H
CARD        DS      CL84
            DS      0H
LINE        DC      CL136' '
```

In locate mode, a similar procedure can be followed, but the process of obtaining the record length should be modified: the record length must be obtained from the record descriptor word (RDW) of the logical record, i.e., from the first 2 bytes of the logical record area.

We will show how to do this for the general case of blocked records (RECFM=VB or RECFORM=VARBLK) even though the DOS SYSIPT and SYSLST files do not permit blocked records. The same method can then be used for any file (DOS or OS) in which blocked records are permitted. The method consists of moving the first 2 bytes of the RDW to a temporary area that is aligned on a half-word boundary, so that the LH (Load Half Word) instruction can be used whether we have an IBM 360 or IBM 370. In the IBM 360 this is necessary because LH requires half-word alignment of the data being loaded and because there is no guarantee that the beginning of each logical record in the I/O buffer will be on a half-word boundary. The reason that there is no such guarantee is that even if the first record in a buffer is aligned on a half-word boundary, a subsequent

Figure 20.3 *Control characters for printer line-spacing in OS and DOS.*

action taken before line is printed	control character	action taken	control character if action taken after line is printed	control character if action taken without printing the line
single space	X'40' (blank)	single space	X'09'	X'0B'
double space	X'F0' (zero)	double space	X'11'	X'13'
triple space	X'60' (minus)	triple space	X'19'	X'1B'
suppress space	X'4E' (plus)	suppress space	X'01'	(none)
skip to new page	X'F1' (one)	skip to new page	X'89'	X'8B'
ANSI control characters		IBM machine code control characters		

record in the buffer need not be so aligned unless every record's length is a multiple of two. Clearly, with variable-length records, this cannot be assumed to be true. Thus the modifications are as follows:

Locate Mode

```
COPYLOOP   GET    TRANSIN        OBTAIN ADDRESS OF LOGICAL RECORD
           LR     9,GREG         USE REG 9 TO SAVE INPUT RECD ADDR
           MVC    VRECL,0(9)     GET LENGTH FROM RDW IN I/O BUFFER
           LH     10,VRECL       LOAD RECD LNG FROM HALF-WORD AREA
           SH     10,=H'1'       SUBT +1 FOR EXECUTE INSTR
           EX     10,VMVC        MOVE RECORD FROM INPUT TO OUTPUT
           PUT    TRANSOU         AREAS, AND OBTAIN ADDRESS OF NEXT
           LR     8,PREG         OUTPUT RECORD. SAVE THIS IN REG 8
           B      COPYLOOP       AND THEN GET NEXT INPUT RECD ADDR.
VMVC       MVC    0(0,8),0(9)    MVC FOR VAR-LNG MOVE.
VRECL      DS     H              HALF WORD FOR RECORD LENGTH
```

20.4 PRINTER OUTPUT: PAGE AND LINE SPACING; DATE AND TIME MACROS

The first character of each logical record written to the system output data set can be used to control printer line-spacing. The most common space-control functions are to single space, double space, triple space, suppress spacing, and skip to a new page. Each of these, and others not to be discussed here, is designated by a control character, which is simply one of the 256 EBCDIC characters. There are two different sets of control characters to choose from: the American National Standards Institute (ANSI) characters and the IBM machine code characters. In the ANSI set, the spacing action is taken before the line is printed; in the IBM set, the action is taken either after the line is printed or without printing the line at all. The control characters that must be used are shown in Figure 20.3.

Carriage Control
 In OS, the choice of control character set is designated in the RECFM= parameter of the DCB macro. The ANSI set is designated by the letter "A," the IBM set by the letter "M": RECFM=FBA or VBA, or RECFM=FBM or VBM.

In DOS, we must specify CTLCHR= ASA for the ANSI set and CTLCHR= YES for the IBM set. (The CTLCHR= parameter is specified in the DTFPR macro.) Unlike in OS, the record format parameter (RECFORM=) in DOS plays no role in designating the control character set.

Once one of these designations is made, it is the user program's responsibility to place the desired control character into the first character of *each* logical record. (If using variable-length records, the control character is placed in the first position following the record descriptor word.)

To illustrate these concepts, we use the ANSI set and move mode for SYSIN and SYSOUT with fixed-length records. The procedure is readily adaptable to locate mode and/or variable-length records, and to DOS.

The program shown in Figure 20.4 reads records from SYSIN and writes them onto SYSOUT. Beginning with the first record, every fiftieth record is written so that it will be printed at the top of a new page. Intervening records are single-spaced in sets of five; every fifth record is double-spaced. Note that since every record that is written must contain a control character, the SYSIN records are moved to the second position of the SYSOUT records, not to the first as in the preceding examples in this chapter. The control character itself is not printed; it simply controls the spacing. Thus, though the length of the record area is 133 characters, the length of the printed line remains at 132 characters. (Note, however, that in order to keep the blocksize within 4096 bytes a 133-byte logical record results in a blocksize of 3990, instead of 4092 as with 132-byte records.)

Title Lines

If a title line with the date of the report and a page number is desired at the top of each page, the following types of modifications must be made:

1. A logical record area must be defined to include the title, space for the date and page number, and the top-of-page control character.
2. The date of the report must be obtained from the operating system, and it must be suitably formatted for printing.
3. A page-number counter must be maintained and converted to EBCDIC format each time a new page is to be started.
4. The title line must be printed each time the line-number counter reaches the limit established for number of lines per page.

The logical record area for the title could be defined as follows:

```
TITLE     DS    CL133       SPACE FOR TITLE LINE
          ORG   TITLE       BEGIN REDEFINITION FOR FIELDS
          DC    X'F1'       ANSI CTL CHAR FOR TOP OF NEW PAGE
          DC    CL14' '     BLANKS TO CENTER THE TITLE
*FOLLOWING IS SOME APPROPRIATE TITLE, WITH TRAILING BLANKS
          DC    CL90'   LISTING OF SYSIN DATA'
MONTH     DS    CL2         SPACE FOR TWO-DIGIT MONTH
          DC    C'/'
DAY       DS    CL2         TWO-DIGIT DAY OF MONTH
          DC    C'/'
YEAR      DS    CL2         TWO-DIGIT YEAR
          DC    CL11' '     SPACING FOR READABILITY
          DC    C'PAGE '
PAGE      DC    CL4' '      UP TO FOUR-DIGIT PAGE NUMBER
          ORG
```

Date and Time in OS: The TIME Macro

To obtain the date and time of the report at run time, the simplest form of the TIME macro that can be used is

opcode	operand
TIME	blanks

(The general format of the TIME macro, and a number of other useful macros, can be obtained from the publication *OS/VS1 Supervisor Services and Macro Instructions,* IBM Publication GC24–5103.)

Figure 20.4 *Printer line-spacing example.*

```
EG3         CSECT
*
*    THIS PROGRAM READS RECORDS FROM SYSIN AND WRITES THEM TO SYSOUT.
*    EVERY FIFTIETH RECORD IS WRITTEN SO THAT IT WILL BE PRINTED AT
*    THE TOP OF A NEW PAGE.  INTERVENING RECORDS ARE SINGLE-SPACED
*    IN SETS OF FIVE: EVERY FIFTH RECORD IS FOLLOWED BY A BLANK LINE.
*
*    ANSI PRINTER CONTROL CHARACTERS ARE USED, WITH FIXED-LENGTH
*     RECORDS IN QSAM MOVE MODE.
*
            STM      14,12,12(13)          STANDARD ENTRY
            BALR     12,0
            USING    *,12
            ST       13,SAVE+4
            LA       13,SAVE
*
            OPEN     (TRANSIN,(INPUT))     OPEN 'SYSIN'
            OPEN     (TRANSOU,(OUTPUT))    OPEN 'SYSOUT'
*           OPEN     TRANSIN,TRANSOU       OPEN SYSIPT & SYSLST
*
COPYLOOP    GET      TRANSIN,CARD          MOVE CARD TO RECORD AREA
            BAL      14,SPACING            GO SET UP PRINT CONTROL CHAR
            MVC      PRINT2(80),CARD       MOVE CARD TO OUTPUT LINE AREA
            PUT      TRANSOU,LINE          MOVE PRINT LINE TO OUTPUT BUF-
            B        COPYLOOP              FER, AND GO GET NEXT CARD RECD
*
EOJ         CLOSE    (TRANSIN)             CLOSE SYSIN
            CLOSE    (TRANSOU)             CLOSE SYSOUT
            L        13,SAVE+4             STANDARD EXIT
            LM       14,12,12(13)
            BR       14
*EOJ        CLOSE    TRANSIN,TRANSOU       CLOSE SYSIPT & SYSLST
*           EOJ                            TERMINATE
*
*    INTERNAL SUBROUTINE TO SET UP PRINT CONTROL CHARACTER BASED ON NUMBER
*    OF LINES THAT HAVE BEEN PRINTED.  CALLED VIA R14, WITH NO PARAMETERS.
*
SPACING     LH       5,SETCTR              DETERMINE IF FIVE CONSEC LINES
            SH       5,=H'1'               HAVE BEEN PRINTED.
            BP       SPACE1                IF NOT, CONTINUE SINGLE-SPACING
               LH       5,LINECTR          DETERMINE IF 50 LINES HAVE
               SH       5,=H'1'            BEEN PRINTED. IF NOT, JUST
               BP       SPACE2             SET UP DOUBLE SPACE.
                  MVI      PRINT1,NEWPAGE  OTHERWISE, SET CTL CHAR
                  MVC      LINECTR,MAXLINE FOR NEW PAGE AND RESET
                  MVC      SETCTR,MAXSET   LINE COUNTERS.
                  B        EXIT
SPACE2      STH      5,LINECTR             WHEN DOUBLE-SPACING, SET CTL
            MVI      PRINT1,DBLSPACE       CHAR AND RESET 5-LINE CTR.
            MVC      SETCTR,MAXSET
            B        EXIT
SPACE1      STH      5,SETCTR              WHEN SINGLE-SPACING, JUST SET
            MVI      PRINT1,SGLSPACE       CTL CHAR AND REDUCE LINE CTRS.
            LH       5,LINECTR
            SH       5,=H'1'
            STH      5,LINECTR
EXIT        BR       14
*
*    CONSTANTS AND DATA AREAS FOR PRINTER LINE SPACING EXAMPLE
*
TRANSIN     DCB      DSORG=PS,MACRF=(GM),DDNAME=SYSIN,EODAD=EOJ,RECFM=FB,   X
                     LRECL=80,BLKSIZE=4080
```

Figure 20.4   continued

```
TRANSOU    DCB     DSORG=PS,MACRF=(PM),DDNAME=SYSPRINT,RECFM=FBA,       X
                   LRECL=133,BLKSIZE=3990
*TRANSIN   DTFCD   DEVADDR=SYSIPT,WORKA=YES,IOAREA1=INBUF,EOFADDR=EOJ,  X
*                  DEVICE=2540
*TRANSOU   DTFPR   DEVADDR=SYSLST,WORKA=YES,IOAREA1=OUTBUF,BLKSIZE=133, X
*                  DEVICE=1403
*
CARD       DS      CL80              CARD INPUT AREA
*
LINE       DS      CL133             PRINTER OUTPUT AREA
           ORG     LINE
PRINT1     DS      CL1               SPACE FOR PRINT CONTROL CHARACTER
PRINT2     DC      CL132' '          PRINT LINE AREA, INITIALLY BLANK
           ORG
*
LINECTR    DC      H'0'              NUMBER OF LINES PRINTED, EACH PAGE
MAXLINE    DC      H'50'             MAX NUMBER OF LINES PER PAGE
*
SETCTR     DC      H'0'              NUMBER OF CONSEC SINGLE-SPACED LINES
MAXSET     DC      H'5'              MAX NUMBER OF CONSEC SGL-SP LINES
*
NEWPAGE    EQU     X'F1'             ANSI CTL CHAR FOR TOP OF NEW PAGE
SGLSPACE   EQU     X'40'             ANSI CTL CHAR FOR SINGLE-SPACING
DBLSPACE   EQU     X'F0'             ANSI CTL CHAR FOR DOUBLE-SPACING
*
SAVE       DS      18F
*SAVE      DS      9D
*INBUF     DS      CL80
*OUTBUF    DC      CL133' '

           END
```

When the TIME macro is invoked, the operating system returns the date in Register 1 and the time of day in Register 0 in the following formats:

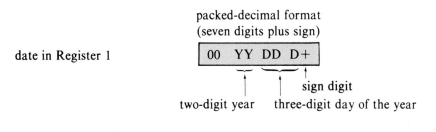

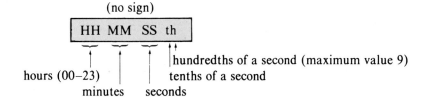

The three-digit day of the year must be converted to month, day, and year in EBCDIC format in order to be printed in the form shown in the previous TITLE area. This and the other changes listed are left as exercises.

Date and Time in DOS: The COMRG and GETIME Macros

To obtain the date and time in DOS, two separate macros are required. Each macro returns a result in Register 1. In their simplest forms, the operand field should be blank:

```
opcode          operand

GETIME
COMRG
```

(Other aspects of these macros, as well as other useful macros, are described in the IBM Publication *DOS/VS Supervisor and I/O Macros,* GC33–5373.)

Response from GETIME Macro in DOS

In the above form, the GETIME macro returns the time of day in Register 1 as a signed packed-decimal number, in the following format:

time in Register 1 | 0 | H | H | M | M | S | S | + |

HH is hours (00–23), MM is minutes, and SS is seconds.

Response from COMRG Macro

The COMRG macro returns the *address* of the date rather than the date itself. The address is returned in Register 1, and the field that it points to is known as the *communication region,* of which the first 8 bytes contain the calendar date in EBCDIC format, stored as mm/dd/yy. Thus it is a simple matter in DOS to put the date in a title line. For example, using the title-line definition given earlier, just move the date from communication region to title line as follows:

```
COMRG
MVC     MONTH(8),0(1)
```

To put the time of day in the title line, we would first have to convert it from packed-decimal to EBCDIC. This and the other changes listed above are left as exercises.

20.5 DORMITORY ROOM MASTER FILE: PROBLEM STATEMENT

In this and the next chapter, we will illustrate the use of the I/O macros by considering the following problem: *a data set is to be created, maintained, and used to provide information about dormitory room occupancy on a university campus. The information to be maintained for each dorm room is the dorm identity and room number, and the names of the students (if any) who are assigned to that room.*

Since the data set will contain all the information we want to know and maintain about dorm room occupancy, it is known as a **master file.** The data set used to create or update the master file records is known as a **transaction file.** We will use the system input data set for the transaction file.

The dorm room master file, like other master files used in computer data processing, will be assumed to be stored on disk for some indefinite length of time. Whenever new information is to be added to it or existing information is to be changed or deleted, a program to make the additions, changes, and deletions is executed, using the information in the transaction file records as the basis for the adjustments to the master file records. Whenever a report giving room occupancy data is desired, a program that produces the report is executed. Programs that will accomplish these functions are described in the sections that follow.

Record Sequence

To process the master file as a sequential data set, we require that its logical records be in some useful sequence and that the logical records of the transaction file be in the same sequence. Since the problem statement is oriented around dormitory rooms rather than students, we will require that the records be in sequence by dorm and room number within dorm. The dorm field in each record is thus referred to as the **major field** for sequencing and the room number field as the **minor field.**

Figure 20.5   Transaction record format.

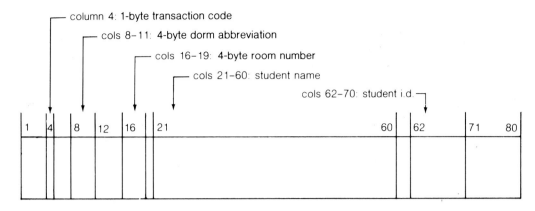

The following assumptions are made about the nature of the data:

1. Each dormitory is identified by a one- to four-character abbreviation, all of which must be letters. If fewer than four letters are used, the field is padded on the right with blanks. For example,

HH	=	Hayes-Healy Hall
PHE	=	Phelan Hall
INTL	=	International House

2. Each dormitory room number consists of one to four letters or digits. If fewer than four letters and digits are used, the field is padded on the left with blanks. For example,

304	=	room number 304
1202	=	room number 1202
2A	=	room number 2A

3. There are no more than two students assigned to a room, but there may be only one student assigned to some rooms, and no students assigned to others.

4. Each student is identified by his or her name in a forty-character field, and by his or her student i.d. number in a nine-character field.

20.6   TRANSACTION RECORD FORMAT

We will assume that each transaction record is a fixed-length, 80-byte record stored on the system input data set. The format of each record is shown in Figure 20.5. The transaction code field (column 4) identifies the purpose of the transaction in the following manner:

code	meaning
1	Add a record for this dorm and room number to the master file. (No student name or i.d. will appear on records bearing transaction code 1. Its purpose is to add a record for a dorm room to which no student has been assigned.)
2	Add the student identified in this transaction record to the master file record identified by the dorm and room number field given in the transaction.
3	Delete the student identified in this transaction record from the master file record identified by the dorm and room number in the transaction.
4	Delete the master file record that is identified by the dorm and room number in the transaction. (No student name or i.d. will appear on records bearing transaction code 4.)

For a given dorm and room number, it will be assumed that the transaction records are in sequence by transaction code. Thus, the transaction code is a second minor field, subordinate to the room number.

Note that we are assuming "perfect" data in the transaction file. We assume first of all that the records are in proper sequence; second, that every "add" and "delete" request is a correct one in the sense that there is no transaction to add a student or a room if that student or room already exists in the master file and there is no request to delete a student or room if there is no master file record for that student or room; and third, that there are no duplicate records in the transaction file and no records with invalid transaction codes. Although these may seem like reasonable assumptions, in practice, mistakes can be made by whomever prepares the transaction data. It is up to the program to detect and reject erroneous data and to produce a printed report describing the errors. But, since the purpose of this example is to demonstrate correct use of I/O macros, handling of data errors will not be dealt with in the discussions that follow. This will be left as an end-of-chapter exercise.

20.7 MASTER FILE RECORD FORMAT

For the master file record format, we will require that there be one record per dorm room. As mentioned earlier, the records will be in sequence by dorm (major) and room number (minor). Each record will contain and be identified by the dorm abbreviation and room number, the values of these two fields thereby serving as each record's **key.**

To simplify the processing descriptions given in the sections that follow, we shall use a fixed-length record format, as shown in Figure 20.6a. This requires that space be reserved in each record for the identities of the two students who might be assigned to the room to which that record pertains. If fewer than two students are assigned to a room, space reserved but not used is filled with blanks.

Note that instead of fixed-length records we could choose to use variable-length records, as shown in Figure 20.6b. This can result in a saving of storage space at the expense of some additional programming steps required when adding students to a record or deleting students from a record. For, instead of filling unused space with blanks, the unused area simply does not exist in the record; its length is null. When using variable-length records, it is often convenient to have a count of the number of students that are represented in the record. This count can either be derived from the record length stored in the record descriptor word or can be explicitly stored in the record, as shown in Figure 20.6b. However, except for the discussion of space allocation in the next section, we will not describe the procedures required for processing the variable-length format.

20.8 MASTER FILE SPACE ALLOCATION

Space allocation for the master file is required only when the file is created. The amount of space requested as primary allocation is acquired at that time; if more space is needed subsequently—because either more students are added or more rooms are added—the space is acquired by the operating system in amounts equal to the secondary allocation request.

The simplest procedure for determining how much primary space should be requested for a sequential data set is to determine a blocksize, estimate the number of records that will be in the data set, and request space for the number of blocks required to contain the estimated number of records. Since additional space will be granted each time it is required—up to 15 times in all—a secondary allocation of 10% of the primary allocation will usually be ample. If we estimate R records will be in the data set, with S bytes per record, and if we choose a blocksize of B bytes, then the number of blocks that should be requested as a primary allocation is $(R \times S)/B$.

Since sequentially organized data sets are stored in count-data format, we base the choice of blocksize on the data that was given in Figure 18.5. For fixed-length records (106 bytes per record), a blocksize of 4028 bytes will contain 38 records and result in track-space utilization of 92.7%. For variable-length records (maximum record length of 112 bytes per record), a blocksize of 4036 bytes would contain at least 36 records and result in track-space utilization of 92.9%. In the present problem,

Figure 20.6a   Fixed-length master file record format.

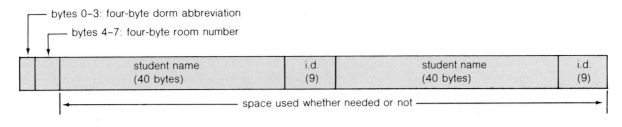

— bytes 0–3: four-byte dorm abbreviation
— bytes 4–7: four-byte room number

| | | student name (40 bytes) | i.d. (9) | student name (40 bytes) | i.d. (9) |

← ——————————— space used whether needed or not ——————————— →

Figure 20.6b   Variable-length master file record format.

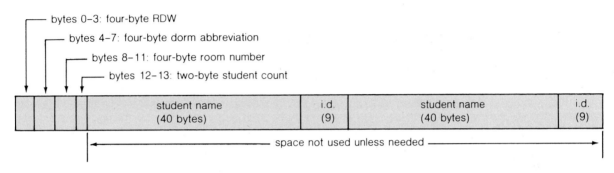

— bytes 0–3: four-byte RDW
— bytes 4–7: four-byte dorm abbreviation
— bytes 8–11: four-byte room number
— bytes 12–13: two-byte student count

| | | | | student name (40 bytes) | i.d. (9) | student name (40 bytes) | i.d. (9) |

← ——————————— space not used unless needed ——————————— →

we can estimate the number of records that will be contained in the master file by estimating the number of dorm rooms. If we assume that there are 5000 dorm rooms, the primary allocation request is determined as follows:

for fixed-length records:

$$
\begin{aligned}
R &= 5000 \text{ records} \\
S &= 106 \text{ bytes per record} \\
B &= 4028 \text{ bytes per block} \\
(R \times S)/B &= 132 \text{ blocks}
\end{aligned}
$$

for variable-length records:

$$
\begin{aligned}
R &= 5000 \text{ records} \\
S &= 112 \text{ bytes per record} \\
B &= 4036 \text{ bytes per block} \\
(R \times S)/B &= 139 \text{ blocks}
\end{aligned}
$$

The number of blocks determined for variable-length record format is an upper limit: it assumes that each variable-length record will contain the identities of two students. (Note that these blocksizes were chosen assuming that the secondary memory device is an IBM 3330 disk system. Appropriate adjustments would have to be made if a different disk system were used or if the computer installation management staff had established other criteria for determining blocksizes.)

20.9   CREATING A SEQUENTIAL DATA SET

One way of creating a sequential data set is simply to copy records, one at a time, from one data set to another. The first data set could be opened for INPUT; the one being created, for OUTPUT. Programs to accomplish this were given in Figures 20.1 and 20.2. The sequential data set being created in those programs was the system output file. But a simple change to the job control statements, DCB or DTF macros, and logical record area definitions is all that would be needed to adapt those programs to the problem of creating other sequential data sets.

The cited method, simple as it is, is not sufficient for all problems. The dorm room master file presents a good example of the need for a different procedure. For instance, if two consecutive transaction records were for the same dorm and room, but for different students, as in this situation,

```
HH  310  H.A. WHITTAKER    123456789
HH  310  A.H. STONEWOOD    234567890
```

copying them one at a time to the output data set would create *two* records for that dorm room, not one as required by the problem statement. Therefore, we need a method to create the following record for the above transaction records:

```
HH  310 HA WHITTAKER   123456789   A.H. STONEWOOD   234567890
```

The method needed requires that the master file record be constructed in the logical record area and *not be moved to the output buffer until both student transaction records have been read from the transaction file.* In more general cases, we would have to construct the master file record based on *N* transaction records. (For example, instead of dorm rooms, we can imagine classrooms with *N* students for arbitrary *N*.)

An outline of the program required to create a sequential data set under the general conditions just mentioned is given in Figure 20.7. The steps depicted assume that the sequential input file is in the same sequence as that desired for the output file. Because of the nature of sequential files, this must always be the case; if it is not the case, the file that is created will not be of much use for the purposes of making future additions or changes.

Main Processing

As mentioned earlier, the processing steps are organized into three phases: initialization, main processing, and end-of-data. In the main processing phase, the PUT macro needed to move a logical record into the output buffer will not be invoked until a complete logical record has been constructed. For our dorm room master file, a complete logical record will consist of the dorm abbreviation, the room number, and zero, one, or two sets of student identities. The number of students identified in a logical output record will depend on the number of students assigned to that dorm room. This in turn will depend on the data that exists in the transaction file. Since the transaction records are in sequence by dorm and room number, all records for a given dorm and room will occur consecutively in the transaction file. If fewer than two students are assigned to a room, the master file record area will be padded with blanks before the record is moved to the output buffer.

To determine when all transaction records for a given dorm and room number have been processed, each transaction record must be compared to the previous transaction record that was processed. Or, each transaction record can be compared to the logical record being constructed in the output area. The two records will be considered equal as long as they both refer to the same master file record—in our example, to the same dorm and room number. When the two records are not equal, the processing for the master file record identified in the output record area has been completed and it can be moved to the output buffer via a PUT macro. The construction of a new output record can then begin.

End-of-Data Processing

When the end-of-data condition is reached on the transaction file, there will still be one master file record remaining in the output record area. This is because we cannot in general anticipate whether end-of-data or simply another transaction record will be obtained when the GET macro is invoked. Therefore, at end-of-data, the record still remaining in the output record area must be moved to the output buffer before closing the data sets.

The sequence of processing steps just described, and outlined in Figure 20.7, is accomplished for the dorm room master file by the program in Figure 20.8. A few typical transaction records and the resulting output master file records are shown in Figure 20.9. In studying the program, note that the assumption of "perfect" data eliminates the need to check for duplicate transaction records, or for data that incorrectly assigns more than two students to a room, or for data that is out of sequence. None of these checks is included in the program of Figure 20.8.

DOS Considerations

DOS programmers should note two important aspects of the program in Figure 20.8. They both concern the output buffer area. For a sequential disk file this area must include space for an 8-byte field that the operating system uses for the "count" field when writing the buffer in count-data format. The field occupies the first 8 bytes of the buffer, and its length must be included in the BLKSIZE= parameter of the DTFSD macro. This field is not present in input buffers, only in output buffers.

Figure 20.7   *Overview of steps to create a sequential data set.*

```
CREATE:

    INITIALIZATION;
    MAIN_PROCESSING;
    END_OF_DATA;

EXIT CREATE.



INITIALIZATION:

    open transaction file;
    open master file;
    get first transaction record;
    begin constructing first output record;

EXIT INITIALIZATION.



MAIN_PROCESSING:

    REPEAT WHILE there is more data to read
       read next transaction record;
       IF construction of output record has been completed
       THEN
          move output record (if any) to output buffer;
          begin constructing new output record,
                using data from transaction record;
       ELSE
          continue constructing output record,
                using data from transaction record;
       END IF;
    END WHILE;

EXIT MAIN_PROCESSING;



END_OF_DATA:

    move last-constructed output record to output buffer;
    close files;

EXIT END_OF_DATA.
```

Moreover, the presence of a large buffer area in the user's program presents an addressability problem when using a single implied base register as we have done. The problem is that memory addresses that are more than 4095 bytes beyond the single implied base address cannot be represented in base-displacement form. This is why we have placed the DOS buffer area at the very end of the source module and used the LTORG directive before defining the buffer area. As discussed in Chapter 15, LTORG causes all literals to be assembled beginning at the point where the LTORG occurs. If there had been any literals used in the program (there weren't) their addresses would have been representable in base-displacement form, since they would have been within the range of the single implied base address. They wouldn't have been within that range if we had allowed the assembler to place them *after* the buffer area, as it would have done had there been no LTORG.

Figure 20.8   Creating the dorm room master file via QSAM.

```
FLAG LOCTN OBJECT CODE     ADDR1  ADDR2  STMNT M SOURCE STATEMENT

     000000                               3     CREATE  CSECT
                                          4     *
                                          5     * THIS PROGRAM CREATES A SEQUENTIAL DATA SET USING QSAM..
                                          6     * TRANSACTION DATA IS IN 'SYSIN' DATA SET, OPENED IN MOVE MODE.
                                          7     *OUTPUT DATA SET CONTAINS ONE RECORD PER DORM ROOM, IN SEQUENCE
                                          8     * BY DORM AND ROOM NUMBER.  EACH RECORD CONTAINS NAMES AND I.D.'S
                                          9     * OF UP TO TWO STUDENTS ASSIGNED TO THE ROOM WHICH THAT RECORD
                                         10     * REPRESENTS.
                                         11     *OUTPUT DATA SET RECORDS ARE FIXED-LENGTH, PROCESSED IN MOVE MODE.
                                         12     *
                                         13             PRINT NODATA,NOGEN
     000000 90 EC D00C                   14             STM   14,12,12(13)      STANDARD ENTRY
     000004 05 C0                        15             BALR  12,0
     000006                              16             USING *,12
     000006 50 D0 C292        000298      17             ST    13,SAVE+4
     00000A 41 D0 C28E        000294      18             LA    13,SAVE
                                         19     *
                                         20     * INITIALIZATIONS
                                         21     *
     00000E                              22             OPEN  (MASTER,(OUTPUT)) OPEN MASTER FILE
     00001A                              28             OPEN  (TRANS,(INPUT))   OPEN 'SYSIN' TRANSACTION FILE

                                         34     *  DOS *******
                                         35     *       OPEN  MASTER
                                         36     *       OPEN  TRANS
                                         37     ***************

     000026                              38             GET   TRANS,INAREA      GET FIRST TRANSACTION RECORD
     000034 45 E0 C0A2        0000A8     43             BAL   14,CONSTRCT       BEGIN CONSTRUCTING FIRST OUTPUT RECD
                                         44     *
                                         45     * MAIN PROCESSING
                                         46     *
     000038                              47     READ    GET   TRANS,INAREA      GET NEXT TRANS RECD (IF ANY)
     000046 D5 03 C0E9C132 0000EF 000138 52             CLC   TDORM,MDORM       IF THE DORM AND ROOM OF TRANS RECD
     00004C 47 70 C05C        000062     53             BNE   WRITE             ARE NOT EQUAL TO THAT OF OUTPUT
     000050 D5 03 C0F1C136 0000F7 00013C 54             CLC   TROOM,MROOM       RECD, THEN MOVE OUTPUT RECD TO OUT-
     000056 47 70 C05C        000062     55             BNE   WRITE             PUT BUFFER AND BEGIN NEW RECD.
     00005A 45 E0 C0C2        0000C8     56             BAL   14,UPDATING       OTHERWISE, CONTINUE CONSTRUCTING THE
     00005E 47 F0 C032        000038     57             B     READ             OUTPUT RECD VIA 'UPDATING' ROUTINE.
                                         58     *
     000062                              59     WRITE   PUT   MASTER,OUTAREA    MOVE OUTPUT RECD TO OUTPUT BUFFER.
     000070 45 E0 C0A2        0000A8     64             BAL   14,CONSTRCT       BEGIN CONSTRUCTING NEXT OUTPUT RECD.
     000074 47 F0 C032        000038     65             B     READ             THEN GET NEXT TRANS RECD.
                                         66     *
                                         67     * END-OF-DATA PROCESSING
                                         68     *
     000078                              69     EOJ     PUT   MASTER,OUTAREA    MOVE LAST OUTPUT RECD TO OUTPUT BUF-
     000086                              74             CLOSE (MASTER)          FER, THEN CLOSE ALL FILES.
     000092                              80             CLOSE (TRANS)
     00009E 58 D0 C292        000298     86             L     13,SAVE+4        STANDARD EXIT.
     0000A2 98 EC D00C                   87             LM    14,12,12(13)
     0000A6 07 FE                        88             BR    14
                                         89     *  DOS *******
                                         90     *       CLOSE MASTER
                                         91     *       CLOSE TRANS
                                         92     *       EOJ
                                         93     ***************

                                         94     * INTERNAL SUBROUTINE WITH TWO ENTRY POINTS, 'CONSTRCT' & 'UPDATING'
                                         95     * BOTH ENTERED WITH  BAL  14,... WITH NO PARAMETERS.
                                         96     *
                                         97     *'CONSTRCT' BEGINS CONSTRUCTION OF A NEW OUTPUT MASTER RECD.
                                         98     *'UPDATING' CONTINUES CONSTRUCTION OF AN EXISTING OUTPUT MASTER RECD.
                                         99     *
                                        100     * TRANSACTION CODE 'TTYPE' DETERMINES UPDATING ACTION
                                        101     *    TTYPE = C'1' ... ADD A NEW ROOM WITH NO STUDENTS
                                        102     *          = C'2' ... ADD A STUDENT NAME & I.D.
                                        103     *          = C'3' ... DELETE A STUDENT NAME & I.D.
                                        104     *          = C'4' ... DELETE ENTIRE MASTER RECD.
                                        105     *
     0000A8 D2 03 C132C0E9 000138 0000EF 106     CONSTRCT MVC  MDORM,TDORM       WHEN CONSTRUCTING A NEW RECD, MOVE
     0000AE D2 03 C136C0F1 00013C 0000F7 107             MVC   MROOM,TROOM       DORM AND ROOM NUMBER FROM TRANS TO
     0000B4 D2 30 C13AC19C 000140 0001A2 108             MVC   MDATA1,BLANKS     OUTPUT AREA, AND BLANK OUT STUDENT
     0000BA D2 30 C16BC19C 000171 0001A2 109             MVC   MDATA2,BLANKS     DATA AREAS.
     0000C0 95 F2 C0E5        0000EB     110             CLI   TTYPE,C'2'        IF TRANS CODE IS '2' INSTEAD OF '1',
     0000C4 47 70 C0E0        0000E6     111             BNE   EXIT              CONTINUE CONSTRUCTION. ELSE, EXIT.
                                        112     *
     0000C8                             113     UPDATING EQU  *
     0000D0                             114             USING SDAREA,11          SET UP DUMMY BASE REGISTER TO ACCESS
     0000C8 41 B0 C13A        000140    115             LA    11,MDATA1          FIELDS IN STUDENT DATA AREA BY NAME.
     0000CC D5 08 B028C19C 000028 0001A2 116            CLC   MID,BLANKS         IF FIRST STUDENT AREA IS BLANK, MOVE
     0000D2 47 80 C0D4        0000DA    117             BE    ADD1               NAME & I.D. TO THAT AREA.
     0000D6 41 BB 00 31       000031    118             LA    11,DATALNG(11)     OTHERWISE, INCR ADDR TO SECOND AREA.
     0000DA D2 27 B000C0F6 000000 0000FC 119     ADD1    MVC  MNAME,TNAME        MOVE STUDENT NAME & I.D. INTO APPRO-
     0000E0 D2 08 B028C11F 000028 000125 120            MVC   MID,TID            PRIATE STUDENT DATA AREA.
     0000E6 07 FE                        121     EXIT    BR   14                 THEN EXIT TO CALLING ROUTINE.

                                        122     * TRANSACTION INPUT RECORD AREA
```

Figure 20.8   continued

```
FLAG LOCTN OBJECT CODE     ADDR1 ADDR2  STMNT M SOURCE STATEMENT

                                         123   *
      0000E8                              124   INAREA   DS    CL80              RESERVE 80 BYTES FOR CARD IMAGE.
      0000E8                    000138    125            ORG   INAREA            BEGIN REDEFINITION OF INPUT AREA.
      0000E8                              126            DS    CL3               COL 1-3   UNUSED
      0000EB                              127   TTYPE    DS    CL1                   4     TRANS TYPE CODE
      0000EC                              128            DS    CL3                  5-7    UNUSED
      0000EF                              129   TDORM    DS    CL4                  8-11   DORM ABBREVIATION
      0000F3                              130            DS    CL4                 12-15   UNUSED
      0000F7                              131   TROOM    DS    CL4                 16-19   DORM ROOM NUMBER
      0000FB                              132            DS    CL1                  20     UNUSED
      0000FC                              133   TNAME    DS    CL40                21-60   STUDENT NAME
      000124                              134            DS    CL1                  61     UNUSED
      000125                              135   TID      DS    CL9                 62-70   STUDENT I.D.
      000138                    00012E    136            ORG
                                         137   * MASTER FILE OUTPUT RECORD AREA
                                         138   *
      000138                              139   OUTAREA  DS    CL106             RESERVE 106 BYTES FOR RECORD.
      000138                    0001A2    140            ORG   OUTAREA           BEGIN REDEFINITION OF OUTPUT AREA.
      000138                              141   MDORM    DS    CL4               BYTES 0-3   DORM ABBREVIATION
      00013C                              142   MROOM    DS    CL4                    4-7    DORM ROOM NUMBER
      000140                              143   MDATA1   DS    CL49                   8-56    1ST STUDENT DATA AREA
      000171                              144   MDATA2   DS    CL49                  57-105   2ND STUDENT DATA AREA
      0001A2                    0001A2    145            ORG
                                         146   *
                                         147   * DUMMY SECTION FOR PROCESSING FIELDS WITHIN STUDENT DATA AREAS BY NAME
                                         148   *
      000000                              149   SDAREA   DSECT
      000000                              150   MNAME    DS    CL40              NAME FIELD AREA
      000028                              151   MID      DS    CL9               I.D. FIELD AREA
      000031                              152   DATALNG  EQU   *-MNAME           LENGTH OF STUDENT DATA AREA
      0001A2                              153   CREATE   CSECT
                                         154   *
                                         155   * BLANKS USED TO INITIALIZE STUDENT DATA AREAS
                                         156   *
      0001A2 40                          157   BLANKS   DC    (DATALNG)C' '      'DATALNG' IS SIZE OF STUDENT DATA AREA
                                         158   *
                                         159   * DCB'S FOR TRANSACTION FILE AND OUTPUT MASTER FILE
                                         160   *
      0001D3                              161   TRANS    DCB   DSORG=PS,MACRF=(GM),DDNAME=SYSIN,EODAD=EOJ,            X
                                         162                  RECFM=FB,LRECL=80,BLKSIZE=4080
                                         214   *
      000234                              215   MASTER   DCB   DSORG=PS,MACRF=(PM),DDNAME=DORMS,                     X
                                         216                  RECFM=FB,LRECL=106,BLKSIZE=4028

                                         268   *  DOS  *******
                                         269   *TRANS    DTFCD DEVADDR=SYSIPT,WORKA=YES,IOAREA1=INBUF,EOFADDR=EOJ,  X
                                         270   *                DEVICE=2540
                                         271   *INBUF    DS    CL80
                                         272   *
                                         273   *MASTER   DTFSD DEVADDR=SYSO15,DEVICE=3330,TYPEFLE=OUTPUT,WORKA=YES, X
                                         274   *                RECFORM=FIXBLK,RECSIZE=106,BLKSIZE=4036,IOAREA1=OUTBUF
                                         275   ***************

                                         276   *
                                         277   * REGISTER SAVE AREA
                                         278   *
      000294                              279   SAVE     DS    18F

                                         280   *  DOS  *******
                                         281   *SAVE     DS    9D
                                         282   *         LTORG
                                         283   *         DS    0D
                                         284   *OUTBUF   DS    CL4036
                                         285   ***************

                                         286            END
```

CROSS-REFERENCE

```
SYMBOL     LEN    VALUE   DEFN    REFERENCES

ADD1       00006  0000DA  00119   00117
BLANKS     00001  0001A2  00157   00108   00109  00116
CONSTRCT   00006  0000A8  00106   00043   00064
CREATE     00001  000000  00153
DATALNG    00001  000031  00152   00118   C0157
EOJ        00004  000078  00070   00183
EXIT       00002  0000E6  00121   00111
INAREA     00050  0000E8  00124   00040   00049  30125
MASTER     00004  000234  00216   00026   00060  00070  00078
MDATA1     00031  000140  00143   00108   00115
```

Figure 20.8 continued

```
MDATA2    00031 000171 00144   00109
MDORM     00004 000138 00141   00052 00106
MID       00009 000028 00151   00116 00120
MNAME     00028 000000 00150   00119 00152
MROOM     00004 00013C 00142   00054 00107
OUTAREA   0006A 000138 00139   00061 00071 00140
READ      00004 000038 00048   00057 00065
SAVE      00004 000294 00279   00017 00018 00086
SDAREA    00001 000000 00149   00114
TDORM     00004 0000EF 00129   00052 00106
TID       00009 000125 00135   00120
TNAME     00028 0000FC 00133   00119
TRANS     00004 000104 00162   00032 00039 00048 00084
TROOM     00004 0000F7 00131   00054 00107
TTYPE     00001 0000EB 00127   00110
UPDATING  00001 0000C8 00113   00056
WRITE     00004 000062 00060   00053 00055
```

Figure 20.9 Typical transactions and resulting sequential master file.

transaction records

```
2 HH     310 H.A. WHITTAKER  123456789
2 HH     310 A.H. STONEWOOD  234567890
2 HH     320 B.L. CARVER     345678901
1 HH     330
2 INTL  101 S.S. PINAFORE    456789012
2 INTL  102 Q.R. LANCELOT    246835790
2 INTL  102 X.A. CAMELOT     135792468
```

TRANSACTION
FILE

CREATE
program

MASTER
FILE

master file records

```
HH    310 H.A. WHITTAKER  123456789 A.H. STONEWOOD  234567890
HH    320 B.L. CARVER     345678901
HH    330
INTL 101 S.S. PINAFORE    456789012
INTL 102 Q.R. LANCELOT    246835790 X.A. CAMELOT     135792468
```

The process of updating a sequential data set includes four possible actions:

Action 1: Add records to the end of the data set.

Action 2: Change or delete some of the data in existing records without deleting any records and without changing the length of any records.

Action 3: Insert new records in their proper sequence within the data set, or change the length of one or more existing records by adding new data to them or deleting data from them.

Action 4: Delete one or more existing records from the data set.

In the context of the dorm room master file example, these four actions could stem from the following situations:

1. Records would be added to the end of the data set if a new dorm, with a four-letter abbreviation that was alphabetically greater than those of existing dormitories, were built. Adding such records to the end of the data set would not alter the sequence of the master file records.

2. Since fixed-length records are used, data in existing records could be changed or deleted without altering the records' lengths, whenever a new student was assigned to a room or a student was transferred from one room to another.

3. New records would be inserted if new rooms became available in existing dorms or if a new dorm with a four-letter abbreviation that was not alphabetically greater than those of existing dormitories was built. (If variable-length records were used, the length of an existing record could be changed by adding or removing a student's name and i.d.)

4. Records would be deleted from the data set if the corresponding rooms were no longer available for some reason or if a mistake had been made in dorm abbreviation or room number when a record was added to the master file.

In the most general case, transaction records representing all four possible actions may exist in the transaction file. In such a case, the entire existing master file must be examined, one record at a time. Records for which no changes are to be made are copied to a new master file. Records for which one or more changes are to be made are copied to the new master file after the changes are made. Records that are to be deleted are not copied. And insertions and additions are written onto the new master file in their proper sequence.

In two special cases, the existing master file need not be copied, thereby saving processing time. In one of these cases, described as Action 1, the transaction records must represent only additions to the end of the data set. In the other case, described as Action 2, the transaction records must represent only changes or deletions to existing records without changing their lengths.

Action 1: EXTEND Mode (OS Only)

To add records to the end of an existing OS sequential data set, the data set can be opened in EXTEND mode. The records may be processed either in move mode or locate mode, and the record format may be either fixed or variable length. The processing steps are the same as those required for creating a sequential data set. Thus, the only change to the program shown in Figure 20.8 would be to replace the master file OPEN macro with this macro

```
OPEN   (MASTER,(EXTEND))
```

The author knows of no comparable capability in DOS for sequential disk files.

Action 2: UPDAT Mode (Figs. 20.10 and 20.11)

To make changes or deletions in existing records without changing their lengths, and without performing any of the other three updating actions listed earlier, a sequential data set can be opened for updating only. In OS, this is done by specifying UPDAT in the OPEN macro. In DOS, it is done by specifying UPDATE=YES together with TYPEFLE=INPUT in the DTFSD macro.

Figure 20.10   Overview of UPDAT procedures for sequential data sets.

```
UPDAT:

   INITIALIZATIONS;
   MAIN_PROCESSING;
   END_OF_DATA;

EXIT UPDAT.



INITIALIZATIONS:

   open transaction file;
   get first transaction record;
   open master file;
   get first master record;

EXIT INITIALIZATIONS.



MAIN_PROCESSING:

   REPEAT UNTIL there is no more transaction data to process

     IF transaction record updates this master record
     THEN
       make changes to master record;
       get next transaction record (if any);
     ELSE
       IF changes were made to master record
       THEN
         rewrite master record;
       END IF;
       get next master record;
     END IF;

   END REPEAT;

EXIT MAIN_PROCESSING;



END_OF_DATA:

   IF changes were made to master record
   THEN
     rewrite master record;
   END IF;

   close all data sets;

EXIT END_OF_DATA.
```

Figure 20.11 Updating the dorm room master file via QSAM (UPDAT).

```
FLAG LOCTN OBJECT CODE     ADDR1 ADDR2 STMNT M SOURCE STATEMENT

     000000                                3    UPDAT   CSECT
                                           4    *
                                           5    *THIS PROGRAM UPDATES THE DORM ROOM MASTER FILE IN 'UPDAT' MODE,
                                           6    * USING QSAM PROCESSING WITH FIXED-LENGTH RECORDS AND LOCATE-
                                           7    * MODE BUFFERING.
                                           8    *
                                           9    *NO RECORDS ARE ADDED, DELETED, OR INSERTED, BUT EXISTING RECORDS
                                          10    * MAY BE MODIFIED BY THE ADDITION OR DELETION OF STUDENT NAMES AND
                                          11    * I.D.'S.  WHEN A NAME AND I.D. IS DELETED, IT IS SIMPLY REPLACED
                                          12    * BY BLANKS.  WHEN A NAME AND I.D. IS ADDED TO A RECORD, IT IS PUT
                                          13    * INTO THE STUDENT DATA AREA THAT IS BLANK.  IT IS  ASSUMED THAT THE
                                          14    * INPUT TRANSACTION DATA ARE 'PERFECT'   NO ERRORS, NO DUPLICATES,
                                          15    * NO INVALID TRANSACTIONS.
                                          16    *
     000000 90 EC D00C                    17            STM     14,12,12(13)        STANDARD ENTRY.
     000004 05 C0                         18            BALR    12,0
     000006                               19            USING   *,12
     000006 50 D0 C24E      000254        20            ST      13,SAVE+4
     00000A 41 D0 C24A      000250        21            LA      13,SAVE
     000000                               22            USING   OUTAREA,11          DUMMY BASE REG FOR OUTPUT AREA
                                          23    *
     00000E                               24            OPEN    (TRANS,(INPUT))     OPEN 'SYSIN' DATA SET.
     00001A                               30            OPEN    (MASTER,(UPDAT))    OPEN MASTER FILE

                                          36    *  DOS  *******
                                          37    *       OPEN  TRANS
                                          38    *       OPEN  MASTER
                                          39    ***************

     000026                               40            GET     TRANS,INAREA        GET FIRST TRANSACTION RECORD.
     000034 45 E0 C0AE      0000B4        45            BAL     14,GETMSTR          GET FIRST MASTER RECORD
                                          46    *
                                          47    * MAIN PROCESSING PROCEDURES
                                          48    *
     000038 D5 03 C10FB000 000115 000000  49    MAINLOOP CLC    TDORM,MDORM         IF DORM AND ROOM OF TRANS RECD ARE
     00003E 47 70 C05C      000062        50            BNE     REWRITE             NOT EQUAL TO THOSE OF MASTER RECD,
     000042 D5 03 C117B004 00011D 000004  51            CLC     TROOM,MROOM         THEN RE-WRITE MASTER (IF NECESSARY)
     000048 47 70 C05C      000062        52            BNE     REWRITE             AND THEN GET NEXT MASTER RECD.
     00004C 45 E0 C0C4      0000CA        53            BAL     14,UPDATING         OTHERWISE, GO DO UPDATING, AND THEN
     000050                               54            GET     TRANS,INAREA        GET NEXT TRANS RECD AND REPEAT THE
     00005E 47 F0 C032      000038        59            B       MAINLOOP            PROCESS TILL END-OF-DATA.
                                          60    *
     000062 95 FF C189      00018F        61    REWRITE CLI     MFLAG,BYP           MFLAG NOT 'BYP' IF CHANGES HAD BEEN
     000066 47 80 C070      000076        62            BE      BYPASS              MADE TO MASTER RECORD.
     00006A                               63            PUTX    MASTER              WHEN THAT IS THE CASE, RE-WRITE IT.
                                          67    *  DOS  *******
                                          68    *       PUT   MASTER
                                          69    ***************

     000076 45 E0 C0AE      0000B4        70    BYPASS  BAL     14,GETMSTR          IN EITHER CASE, GET NEXT MASTER RECD,
     00007A 47 F0 C032      000038        71            B       MAINLOOP            AND CONTINUE PROCESSING.
                                          72    * END-OF-DATA PROCESSING
                                          73    *
     00007E 95 FF C189      00018F        74    EOJ     CLI     MFLAG,BYP           BEFORE CLOSING, SEE IF MASTER RECD
     000082 47 80 C08E      000094        75            BE      EOJX                MUST BE RE-WRITTEN.
     000086                               76            PUTX    MASTER              IF SO, REWRITE IT.
                                          80    *  DOS  *******
                                          81    *       PUT   MASTER
                                          82    ***************

     000092                               83    EOJX    CLOSE   (TRANS)             THEN CLOSE ALL DATA SETS, AND EXIT.
     00009E                               89            CLOSE   (MASTER)
     0000AA 58 D0 C24E      000254        95            L       13,SAVE+4
     0000AE 98 EC D00C                    96            LM      14,12,12(13)
     0000B2 07 FE                         97            BR      14

                                          98    *  DOS  *******
                                          99    *EOJX    CLOSE TRANS
                                         100    *        CLOSE MASTER
                                         101    *        EOJ
                                         102    ***************

                                         103    * INTERNAL SUBROUTINE 'GETMSTR' ENTERED VIA BAL 14,GETMSTR
                                         104    * GETS NEXT MASTER RECD IN LOCATE MODE, AFTER RESETTING RECD-CHGD FLAG.
                                         105    *
     0000B4 18 2E                        106    GETMSTR LR      2,14                SAVE RETURN ADDRESS
     0000B6 92 FF C189      00018F       107            MVI     MFLAG,BYP           RESET RECORD-CHANGED FLAG, TO INDI-
     0000BA                              108            GET     MASTER              CATE NO CHANGES HAVE YET BEEN MADE.
     0000C4 18 B1                        112            LR      11,REGX             SAVE ADDR OF LOGICAL RECD AREA IN
     0000C6 18 E2                        113            LR      14,2                REG 11, THEN RETURN TO CALLER.
     0000C8 07 FE                        114            BR      14
                                         115    *
                                         116    * SYMBOLIC REGISTER ADDRESS FOR LOCATE MODE
     000001                              117    REGX    EQU     1                   OS SYSTEMS
                                         118    *REGX    EQU     9                   DOS SYSTEMS

                                         119    * INTERNAL SUBROUTINE 'UPDATING' ENTERED VIA  BAL 14,... WITH
                                         120    * LOGICAL RECORD ADDRESS IN REGISTER 11, FOR DUMMY BASE REGISTER.
                                         121    * ADDS OR DELETES STUDENT NAME & I.D. FROM STUDENT DATA AREA
                                         122    *  IN MASTER RECD.  SETS FLAG INDICATING MSTR RECD HAS BEEN CHANGED.
                                         123    *
```

Figure 20.11 continued

```
FLAG LOCTN OBJECT CODE      ADDR1   ADDR2   STMNT M SOURCE STATEMENT

                                            124   * TRANSACTION CODE 'TTYPE' DETERMINES UPDATING ACTION
                                            125   *    TTYPE = C'1' ... ADD A NEW ROOM WITH NO STUDENTS
                                            126   *          = C'2' ... ADD A STUDENT NAME & I.D.
                                            127   *          = C'3' ... DELETE A STUDENT NAME & I.D.
                                            128   *          = C'4' ... DELETE ENTIRE MASTER RECD.
                                            129   *
       0000CA                               130   UPDATING EQU   *
       0000CA 18 AB                         131            LR    10,11            SAVE LOGICAL RECD AREA ADDR IN REG 10
       0000CC 95 F2 C10B      000111        132            CLI   TTYPE,C'2'       TRANS CODE '2' MEANS ADD STUDENT
       0000D0 47 80 C0E6      0000EC        133            BE    ADD
       0000D4 D5 08 B030C145 000030 00014B  134   DEL      CLC   MID,TID          OTHERWISE, ASSUME IT'S CODE '3' AND LOOK
       0000DA 47 80 C0DC      0000E2        135            BE    DEL1             FOR STUDENT I.D. IN 1ST & 2ND DATA AREAS
       0000DE 41 BB 0031      000031        136            LA    11,DATALNG(11)   IF NOT IN 1ST, MUST BE IN 2ND   INCR ADDR
       0000E2 D2 30 B008C158 000008 00015E  137   DEL1     MVC   MDATA1,BLANKS    REPLACE NAME & I.D. WITH BLANKS WHEN DE-
       0000E8 47 F0 C100      000106        138            B     EXIT             LETING.
       0000EC D5 08 B030C158 000030 00015E  139   ADD      CLC   MID,BLANKS       WHEN ADDING, LOOK FOR VACANT STUDENT DATA
       0000F2 47 80 C0F4      0000FA        140            BE    ADD1             AREA.  IF NOT 1ST ONE, THEN ASSUME THAT
       0000F6 41 BB 0031      000031        141            LA    11,DATALNG(11)   2ND AREA IS VACANT, AND INCR ADDR TO IT.
       0000FA D2 27 B008C11C 000008 000122  142   ADD1     MVC   MNAME,TNAME      MOVE NAME & I.D. FROM TRANS RECD TO STU-
       000100 D2 08 B030C145 000030 00014B  143            MVC   MID,TID          DENT DATA AREA.
       000106 92 00 C189      00018F        144   EXIT     MVI   MFLAG,REWR       BEFORE RETURNING, SET FLAG TO INDICATE
       00010A 18 BA                         145            LR    11,10            THAT RECD WAS CHGD, AND RESTORE DUMMY
       00010C 07 FE                         146            BR    14               BASE REG CONTENTS


                                            147   * TRANSACTION INPUT RECORD AREA
                                            148   *
       00010E                               149   INAREA   DS    CL80             RESERVE 80 BYTES FOR CARD IMAGE.
       00010E              00015E           150            ORG   INAREA           BEGIN REDEFINITION OF INPUT AREA.
       00010E                               151            DS    CL3              COL 1-3    UNUSED
       000111                               152   TTYPE    DS    CL1              4          TRANS TYPE CODE
       000112                               153            DS    CL3              5-7        UNUSED
       000115                               154   TDORM    DS    CL4              8-11       DORM ABBREVIATION
       000119                               155            DS    CL4              12-15      UNUSED
       00011D                               156   TROOM    DS    CL4              16-19      DORM ROOM NUMBER
       000121                               157            DS    CL1              20         UNUSED
       000122                               158   TNAME    DS    CL40             21-60      STUDENT NAME
       00014A                               159            DS    CL1              61         UNUSED
       00014B                               160   TID      DS    CL9              62-70      STUDENT I.D.
       00015E              000154           161            ORG
                                            162   *
                                            163   * MASTER FILE LOGICAL RECORD AREA VIA 'DSECT' (FIXED LENGTH RECDS)
                                            164   *
       000000                               165   OUTAREA  DSECT
       000000                               166   MDORM    DS    CL4              BYTES 0-3  DORM ABBREVIATION
       000004                               167   MROOM    DS    CL4              4-7        DORM ROOM NUMBER
       000008                               168   MDATA1   DS    CL49             8-56       1ST STUDENT DATA AREA
       000039                               169   MDATA2   DS    CL49             57-105     2ND STUDENT DATA AREA
       000008              00006A           170            ORG   MDATA1           REDEFINE STUDENT DATA AREA
       000008                               171   MNAME    DS    CL40             8-47       STUDENT NAME FIELD
       000030                               172   MID      DS    CL9              48-56      STUDENT I.D. FIELD
       000031                               173   DATALNG  EQU   *-MNAME          LENGTH OF STUDENT AREA
       00015E                               174   UPDAT    CSECT
                                            175   *
                                            176   * BLANKS USED TO INITIALIZE STUDENT DATA AREAS
                                            177   * MFLAG INDICATES WHEN A MASTER RECD MUST BE REWRITTEN.
                                            178   *
       00015E 40                            179   BLANKS   DC    (DATALNG)C' '    'DATALNG' IS SIZE OF STUDENT DATA AREA
       00018F FF                            180   MFLAG    DC    X'FF'            X'FF' = DON'T REWRITE; X'00' = REWRITE
       000000                               181   REWR     EQU   X'00'            REWR = RECORD HAS BEEN CHGD, REWRITE OK
       0000FF                               182   BYP      EQU   X'FF'            BYP = RECD NOT CHGD, DONT REWRITE
                                            183   * DCB'S FOR TRANSACTION FILE AND OUTPUT MASTER FILE
                                            184   *
       000190                               185   TRANS    DCB   DSORG=PS,MACRF=(GM),DDNAME=SYSIN,EODAD=EOJ,         X
                                            186                  RECFM=FB,LRECL=80,BLKSIZE=4080
                                            238   *
       0001F0                               239   MASTER   DCB   DSORG=PS,MACRF=(GL,PL),DDNAME=DORMS,               X
                                            240                  RECFM=FB,LRECL=106,BLKSIZE=4028

                                            292   * DOS *******
                                            293   *TRANS    DTFCD DEVADDR=SYSIPT,WORKA=YES,IOAREA1=INBUF,EOFADDR=EOJ, X
                                            294   *               DEVICE=2540
                                            295   *INBUF    DS    CL80
                                            296   *
                                            297   *MASTER   DTFSD DEVADDR=SYS015,DEVICE=3330,TYPEFLE=INPUT,UPDATE=YES, X
                                            298   *               RECFORM=FIXBLK,RECSIZE=106,BLKSIZE=4028,IOAREA1=OUTBUF, X
                                            299   *               IOREG=(REGX)
                                            300   ***************

                                            301   *
                                            302   * REGISTER SAVE AREA
                                            303   *
       000250                               304   SAVE     DS    18F

                                            305   * DOS *******
                                            306   *SAVE     DS    9D
                                            307   *        LTORG
                                            308   *        DS    0D
                                            309   *OUTBUF   DS    CL4028
                                            310   ***************

                                            311            END
```

Figure 20.11 **continued**

CROSS-REFERENCE

SYMBOL	LEN	VALUE	DEFN	REFERENCES			
ADD	00006	0000EC	00139	00133			
ADD1	00006	0000FA	00142	00140			
BLANKS	00001	00015E	00179	00137	00139		
BYP	00001	0000FF	00182	00061	00074	00107	
BYPASS	00004	000076	00070	00062			
DATALNG	00001	000031	00173	00136	00141	00179	
DEL	00006	0000D4	00134				
DEL1	00006	0000E2	00137	00135			
EOJ	00004	00007E	00074	00207			
EOJX	00004	000094	00085	00075			
EXIT	00004	000106	00144	00138			
GETMSTR	00002	0000B4	00106	00045	00070		
INAREA	00050	00010E	00149	00042	00056	00150	
MAINLOOP	00006	000038	00049	00059	00071		
MASTER	00004	0001F0	00240	00034	00064	00077	00093 00109
MDATA1	00031	000008	00168	00137	00170		
MDATA2	00031	000039	00169				
MDORM	00004	000000	00166	00049			
MFLAG	00001	00018F	00180	00061	00074	00107	00144
MID	00009	000030	00172	00134	00139	00143	
MNAME	00028	000008	00171	00142	00173		
MROOM	00004	0000C4	00167	00051			
OUTAREA	00001	0000C0	00165	00022			
REGX	00001	000001	00117	00112			
REWR	00001	000000	00181	00144			
REWRITE	00004	000062	00061	00050	00052		
SAVE	00004	000250	00304	00020	00021	00095	
TDORM	00004	000115	00154	00049			
TID	00009	00014B	00160	00134	00143		
TNAME	00028	000122	00158	00142			
TRANS	00004	000190	00186	00028	00041	00055	00087
TROOM	00004	00011D	00156	00051			
TTYPE	00001	000111	00152	00132			
UPDAT	00001	000000	00174				
UPDATING	00001	0000CA	00130	00053			

In the processing steps that are used when a data set is opened for updating, each updated record is rewritten to the same relative position in the data set that it occupied before the updating occurred. For this reason, the process is known as **updating in place.** In OS, it is the PUTX macro (not PUT) that is used to rewrite a record; in DOS, PUT is used.

No record can be rewritten unless it is the most recently read record. The GET macro is used in both OS and DOS to read each record. But, as in the process of creating a sequential data set, there may be any number of consecutive transaction records that are used to update a given master record. Accordingly, a master record is not rewritten until all updating changes have been made to it. (It is not rewritten at all if *no* updating changes are made to it since rewriting would only incur an unnecessary waste of processing time.)

When the end-of-data condition is reached on the transaction file, there may still be a master record that was in the process of being updated in main memory. If so, this master record must be rewritten before closing the data sets. The decision of whether or not to rewrite is controlled by a flag, or switch, that is reset each time a new master record is read, and set whenever a change is made to that record.

These processing concepts are outlined in Figure 20.10. A program that updates the dorm room master file in UPDAT mode is given in Figure 20.11. In studying that program, note that the logical record area for the master record is defined by a DSECT directive, since the logical record is not moved to or from the buffer in locate mode.

Actions 1 through 4: INPUT and OUTPUT Modes (Figs. 20.12a–c and 20.13)

In the general updating situation, the transaction file may contain records representing any of the four updating actions listed earlier. Neither the EXTEND mode nor the UPDAT mode can be used. Instead, the existing sequential master file is opened in INPUT mode and a new sequential master file is opened in OUTPUT mode. The existing master file is not altered in any way; the new master file is an updated version of the existing file, including new records, changed records, and unchanged records, but excluding deleted records.

The General Case

```
SEQUENTIAL_UPDATE:

  INITIALIZATION;  { see below }
  MAIN_PROCESSING;  { see figure 20.12b ]
  end-of-data procedures;  { see figure 20.12c }
  END_OF_JOB;  { see below }

EXIT SEQUENTIAL_UPDATE.


INITIALIZATION:

  open transaction data set in INPUT mode;
  get first transaction record;
  open existing master data set in INPUT mode;
  get first master record;
  open new master data set in OUTPUT mode;

EXIT INITIALIZATION.


END_OF_JOB:

  move output master record to output buffer;
  close all data sets;

EXIT END_OF_JOB.
```

In this updating procedure, two sets of records are merged to produce the new master records. One set consists of the transaction records; the other, of the existing master records. Each step of the merge process is designed to construct an output master record in its proper sequence. The steps involved are outlined in Figures 20.12a–20.12c.

When the construction of an output master record has been completed, the master record is moved to the output buffer and one of the two input records is used to begin construction of the next output master record. Unless the transaction record currently being processed is lower in sequence than the master, the record chosen to begin the construction is the existing master record.

However, while the construction is in progress, one or more transaction records may contain information pertaining to the new master record. Each of these must be processed before the new master record can be moved to the output buffer. If one of the transaction records for the new master record is a 'delete record' transaction, a flag is set so that the new master record will not be moved to the output buffer.

End-of-Data Considerations

In general, we cannot predict which input data set—transaction or master—will reach end-of-data first. Therefore, the procedure includes provisions for either event. If end-of-data occurs on the transaction data set first, the remaining input master records must be copied to the new output master. If the end-of-data condition occurs on the input master data set first, the remaining transaction records must be processed as though it were in EXTEND mode, i.e., the transaction records are simply added to the end of the new master.

Finer details of the procedure outlined in the preceding paragraphs are given in the program of Figure 20.13, which updates the dorm room master file discussed in preceding sections. As in the previous programs, the updating procedure presented assumes that the input transaction data contain no errors or duplicates and that they are in the same dorm and room number sequence as the existing master data set. In addition, it is assumed that when there is more than one transaction record for a given dorm and room number, these are in sequence by the transaction code number.

Figure 20.12b   Main processing procedure for updating sequential data sets.

```
MAIN_PROCESSING:

  REPEAT UNTIL (transaction data set runs out of records)
               OR (input master data set runs out of records)

    IF input transaction lower in sequence than input master record
    THEN
      begin construction of output master record using transaction record;
      get next transaction record;
    ELSE
      begin construction of output master record using input master record;
      get next master record;
    END IF;

    REPEAT UNTIL (output master record lower in sequence than transaction)
               OR (transaction data set is empty)

      IF output master record lower in sequence than transaction record
      THEN
        IF master record deleted
        THEN
          reset record-deleted flag;
        ELSE
          move master record to output buffer;
        END IF;
        { exit from UNTIL loop will occur }
      ELSE
        IF output master record equal in sequence to transaction record
        THEN
          IF transaction record a delete request
          THEN
            set record-deleted flag;
          ELSE
            continue construction of output master;
          END IF;
          get next transaction record;
        ELSE
          { transaction data is out of sequence -- stop processing }
        END IF;
      END IF;

    END UNTIL;

  END UNTIL;

EXIT MAIN_PROCESSING.
```

The program shown in Figure 20.13 uses move mode for all three data sets. In practice, it would reduce processing time to use locate mode with both the input and output master files, since this would eliminate moving records from the input buffer to the logical record area and from the record area to the output buffer. Use of locate mode is left as an exercise.

20.11   RETRIEVING FROM A SEQUENTIAL DATA SET

Retrieval, in the context of this section, means extracting data from the records of a data set for the purpose of producing printed reports based on the data. Clearly, whatever data is extracted must be obtained by sequentially reading one logical record at a time. Data need not be extracted from all the records, but each record must be read and examined to see if it meets the criteria governing selection of data.

Figure 20.12c End-of-data procedures for updating sequential data sets.

```
END_OF_TRANSACTION_DATA:

   WHILE there is more data in input master data set

      move output master record to output buffer;
      move input master record to output record area;
      get next master record;

   END WHILE;

EXIT END_OF_TRANSACTION_DATA.



END_OF_INPUT_MASTER_DATA:

   WHILE there is more data in transaction data set

      IF output master record lower in sequence than transaction record
      THEN
        move output master record to output buffer;
        use transaction record to begin construction of output master record;
      ELSE
        continue construction of output master;
      END IF;
      get next transaction record;

   END WHILE;

EXIT END_OF_INPUT_MASTER_DATA.
```

There are three main types of reports commonly produced:

Type 1: A report listing all or some portion of the data in a data set in the sequence in which the records are read.

Type 2: A report listing all or some portion of the data in a sequence other than that in which the records are read.

Type 3: A report giving some information derived from the data set but not stored as data in that data set.

For our dorm room master file, the following reports exemplify the cited categories:

1. A report listing the names and i.d.'s of all students in a given dorm in numerical order by room number.
2. A report listing the names and i.d.'s of all students in a given dorm in alphabetical order by student name.
3. A report showing the number and/or percent of rooms that are vacant in a given dorm.

To produce the first type of report, the fields in each record are tested to see if they meet the criteria established for the report and, if so, the desired data are extracted and written to the system output file. Page and line spacing, a title line with date and page number, and column headings are usually inserted in the report to improve readability.

To produce the second type of report, we must extract the desired data from the existing records, but instead of writing the extracted information to the system output file, it is written to a new data set. After all the desired information has been extracted, the new data set is sorted into the sequence needed for the report, and the sorted data set is then processed as when producing a report of the first type.

To produce the third type of report, totals or other derived data must be accumulated until all the records that can contribute data to the report have been read. At that point, the derived data are printed.

Figure 20.13   Updating the dorm room master file via QSAM.

```
FLAG  LOCTN  OBJECT CODE     ADDR1  ADDR2  STMNT M SOURCE STATEMENT

      000000                                3     UPDATE   CSECT
                                            4     *
                                            5     * THIS PROGRAM UPDATES THE DORM ROOM MASTER FILE, USING QSAM PROCESSING
                                            6     * AND MOVE MODE BUFFERING FOR FIXED-LENGTH RECORDS.
                                            7     *
                                            8     * THE UPDATING PROCEDURE PERMITS ADDITIONS, INSERTIONS, AND DELETIONS
                                            9     * OF MASTER FILE RECORDS, AND CHANGES TO EXISTING RECORDS.  (RECORD-
                                           10     * LENGTHS CANNOT BE CHANGED SINCE THEY ARE FIXED-LENGTH RECORDS.)  IT
                                           11     * IS ASSUMED THAT THE INPUT TRANSACTION DATA ARE 'PERFECT', I.E., NO
                                           12     * ERRORS, NO DUPLICATES, NO INVALID TRANSACTIONS.
                                           13     *
      000000 90 EC D00C                    14              STM    14,12,12(13)        STANDARD ENTRY
      000004 05 C0                         15              BALR   12,0
      000006                               16              USING  *,12
      000006 50 D0 C472     000478         17              ST     13,SAVE+4
      00000A 41 D0 C46E     000474         18              LA     13,SAVE
                                           19     *
                                           20     * INITIALIZATION PROCEDURES
                                           21     *
      00000E                               22              OPEN   (TRANS,(INPUT))    OPEN TRANS FILE
      00001A                               28              OPEN   (MSTRIN,(INPUT))   OPEN EXISTING MASTER FILE
      000026                               34              OPEN   (MSTROUT,(OUTPUT)) OPEN NEW OUTPUT MASTER FILE

                                           40     *  DOS  ******
                                           41     *        OPEN   TRANS
                                           42     *        OPEN   MSTRIN
                                           43     *        OPEN   MSTROUT
                                           44     ***************
      000032                               45              GET    TRANS,TAREA        GET FIRST TRANSACTION RECORD
      000040                               50              GET    MSTRIN,OLDAREA     GET FIRST INPUT MASTER RECORD
                                           55     *
                                           56     * MAIN PROCESSING PROCEDURES
                                           57     *
      00004E D5 03 C1FBC244 000201 00024A  58     MAINLOOP CLC    TDORM,OLDMDORM     IF TRANS RECD IS LOWER IN SEQUENCE
      000054 47 40 C078     00007E         59              BL     TRANSLO            THAN INPUT MASTER RECD, USE TRANS
      000058 47 70 C060     000066         60              BNE    MASTERLO           RECD TO BEGIN CONSTR OF OUTPUT RECD.
      00005C D5 03 C203C248 000209 00024E  61              CLC    TROOM,OLDMROOM     IF DORMS ARE EQUAL, THEN TEST ROOM#
      000062 47 40 C078     00007E         62              BL     TRANSLO            USE TRANS IF IT'S LOWER, ELSE ...
      000066 D2 69 C2AEC244 0002B4 00024A  63     MASTERLO MVC    NEWAREA,OLDAREA    BEGIN CONSTR OF OUTPUT RECD USING
      00006C                               64              GET    MSTRIN,OLDAREA     INPUT MASTER RECD.  THEN GET NEXT
      00007A 47 F0 C08A     000090         69              B      PROCESS            MASTER RECD BEFORE PROCESSING OUTPUT
                                           70     *
      00007E 45 E0 C17A     000180         71     TRANSLO  BAL    14,CONSTRCT        GO CONSTRUCT OUTPUT RECD USING TRANS
      000082                               72              GET    TRANS,TAREA        RECD, AND GET NEXT TRANS RECD BEFORE
                                           77     *                                  PROCESSING OUTPUT.
                                           78     *
      000090 D5 03 C2AEC1FB 0002B4 000201  79     PROCESS  CLC    NEWMDORM,TDORM     IF OUTPUT MASTER RECD IS LOWER IN SEQ
      000096 47 70 C0B4     0000BA         80              BNE    COMPLETE           THAN TRANS RECD, THEN CONSTR OF OUT-
      00009A D5 03 C2B2C203 0002B8 0002C9  81              CLC    NEWMROOM,TROOM     PUT RECD HAS BEEN COMPLETED. (IF
      0000A0 47 70 C0B4     0000BA         82              BNE    COMPLETE           HIGHER, TRANS DATA IS OUT OF SEQ )

                                           83     *                                  IF OUTPUT MSTR = TRANS RECD ...
      0000A4 45 E0 C19E     0001A4         84              BAL    14,UPDATING        UPDATE THE RECD, AND THEN
      0000A8                               85              GET    TRANS,TAREA        GET NEXT TRANS RECD.
      0000B6 47 F0 C08A     000090         90              B      PROCESS            SEE IF NEXT TRANS = OUTPUT MSTR.
                                           91     *
      0000BA 45 E0 C15A     000160         92     COMPLETE BAL    14,PUTMSTR         WHEN CONSTR COMPLETED, MOVE RECD TO
      0000BE 47 F0 C048     00004E         93              B      MAINLOOP           OUTPUT BUFFER, AND GO DETERMINE HOW
                                           94     *                                  TO BEGIN CONSTR OF NEXT OUTPUT RECD.
                                           95     *
                                           96     * END-OF-DATA PROCEDURES
                                           97     *                                  WHEN END OF TRANSACTION DATA OCCURS
      0000C2 95 FF C349     00034F         98     ENDTRANS CLI    EODSW,EOF          FIRST, SEE IF MASTER INPUT HAD AL-
      0000C6 47 80 C12A     000130         99              BE     EOJ                READY REACHED END-OF-DATA. IF SO,
      0000CA 92 FF C349     00034F        100              MVI    EODSW,EOF          GO TO 'EOJ'. OTHERWISE, SET FLAG
      0000CE 45 E0 C15A     000160        101     COPYLOOP BAL    14,PUTMSTR         AND COMMENCE COPYING INPUT MASTER
      0000D2 D2 69 C2AEC244 0002B4 00024A 102              MVC    NEWAREA,OLDAREA    RECDS TO OUTPUT MASTER FILE, TILL
      0000D8                              103              GET    MSTRIN,OLDAREA     INPUT MASTER END-OF-DATA IS REACHED
      0000E6 47 F0 C0C8     0000CE        108              B      COPYLOOP
                                          109     *                                  WHEN END OF INPUT MASTER OCCURS,
      0000EA 95 FF C349     00034F        110     ENDMSTR  CLI    EODSW,EOF          SEE IF TRANS INPUT HAD ALREADY
      0000EE 47 80 C12A     000130        111              BE     EOJ                REACHED END-OF-DATA. IF SO,
      0000F2 92 FF C349     00034F        112              MVI    EODSW,EOF          GO TO 'EOJ'. OTHERWISE, SET FLAG.
      0000F6 D5 03 C2AEC1FB 0002B4 000201 113     ADDLOOP  CLC    NEWMDORM,TDORM     COMMENCE ADDING TRANS RECDS TO END
      0000FC 47 40 C110     000116        114              BL     ADDPUT             OF NEW MASTER.
      000100 47 70 C108     00010E        115              BNE    ADDLOOPX
      000104 D5 03 C2B2C203 0002B8 000209 116              CLC    NEWMROOM,TROOM     WHEN ADDING RECDS, ALLOW FOR MORE
      00010A 47 40 C110     000116        117              BL     ADDPUT             THEN ONE TRANS PER DORM ROOM SO
      00010E 45 E0 C19E     0001A4        118     ADDLOOPX BAL    14,UPDATING        THAT TWO STUDENTS CAN BE ADDED.
      000112 47 F0 C118     00011E        119              B      ADDGET
                                          120     *
      000116 45 E0 C15A     000160        121     ADDPUT   BAL    14,PUTMSTR         WHEN FINISHED CONSTR OF OUTPUT RECD,
      00011A 45 E0 C17A     000180        122              BAL    14,CONSTRCT        MOVE IT TO OUTPUT BUFFR, THEN BEGIN
                                          123     *                                  CONSTR OF NEXT OUTPUT RECD.
      00011E                              124     ADDGET   GET    TRANS,TAREA        CONTINUE GETTING TRANS RECDS TILL
      00012C 47 F0 C0F0     0000F6        129              B      ADDLOOP            END-OF-DATA REACHED.
                                          130     *
                                          131     *
                                          132     * END-OF-JOB PROCEDURE
                                          133     *
```

Figure 20.13   continued

```
FLAG LOCTN OBJECT CODE      ADDR1 ADDR2  STMNT M SOURCE STATEMENT

    000130 45 E0 C15A       000160        134  EOJ      BAL    14,PUTMSTR        MOVE LAST MASTER OUTPUT RECD TO BUF-
    000134                                135           CLOSE  (MSTROUT)         FER. THEN CLOSE FILES AND TERMINATE
    00013E                                141           CLOSE  (MSTRIN)          PROGRAM.
    00014A                                147           CLOSE  (TRANS)
    000156 58 D0 C472       000478        153           L      13,SAVE+4
    00015A 98 EC D00C                     154           LM     14,12,12(13)
    00015E 07 FE                          155           BR     14

                                         156  *   DOS  *******
                                         157  *        CLOSE MSTROUT
                                         158  *        CLOSE MSTRIN
                                         159  *        CLOSE TRANS
                                         160  *        EOJ
                                         161  **************
                                         162  * INTERNAL SUBROUTINE TO MOVE NEW MSTR RECD TO OUTPUT BUFFER,
                                         163  *    PROVIDED THAT IT HASN'T BEEN DELETED.
                                         164  *
    000160 95 FF C34A       000350        165  PUTMSTR  CLI    MFLAG,BYP         DID TRANS RECD DELETE IT
    000164 47 80 C174       00017A        166           BE     BYPASS            ...YES
    000168 18 2E                          167           LR     2,14              IF NOT, SAVE RETURN ADDR,
    00016A                                168           PUT    MSTROUT,NEWAREA    AND MOVE RECD TO OUTPUT BUFFER.
    000178 18 E2                          173           LR     14,2              THEN RECOVER RETURN ADDR,
    00017A 92 00 C34A       000350        174  BYPASS   MVI    MFLAG,WR          RESET DELETE FLAG,
    00017E 07 FE                          175           BR     14                AND RETURN TO CALLER.
                                         176  *
                                         177  *
                                         178  * INTERNAL SUBROUTINE WITH TWO ENTRY POINTS, 'CONSTRCT' & 'UPDATING'
                                         179  * BOTH ENTERED WITH BAL 14,... WITH NO PARAMETERS.
                                         180  *
                                         181  * TRANSACTION CODE 'TTYPE' DETERMINES UPDATING ACTION
                                         182  *    TTYPE = C'1' ... ADD A NEW ROOM WITH NO STUDENTS
                                         183  *          = C'2' ... ADD A STUDENT NAME & I.D.
                                         184  *          = C'3' ... DELETE A STUDENT NAME & I.D.
                                         185  *          = C'4' ... DELETE ENTIRE MASTER RECD.
                                         186  *
                                         187  *'CONSTRCT' BEGINS CONSTRUCTION OF NEW OUTPUT MASTER RECD USING TRANS
                                         188  * RECD.  'UPDATING' CONTINUES CONSTRUCTION OF NEW OUTPUT MASTER RECD.
                                         189  *
    000180 D2 03 C2AEC1FB 0002B4 000201  190  CONSTRCT MVC    NEWMDORM,TDORM    WHEN CONSTRUCTING A NEW RECD, MOVE
    000186 D2 03 C2B2C203 0002B8 000209  191           MVC    NEWMROOM,TROOM    DORM AND ROOM NUMBER FROM TRANS
    00018C D2 30 C2B6C318 0002BC 00031E  192           MVC    NEWDATA1,BLANKS   TO OUTPUT AREA, AND BLANK OUT STU-
    000192 D2 30 C2E7C318 0002ED 00031E  193           MVC    NEWDATA2,BLANKS   DENT DATA AREAS.
    000198 95 F2 C1F7       0001FD        194           CLI    TTYPE,C'2'        IF TRANS CODE IS '2', INSTEAD OF '1',
    00019C 47 80 C1AE       0001B4        195           BE     OKUPDATE          CONTINUE CONSTRUCTION.
    0001A0 47 F0 C1F2       0001F8        196           B      EXIT              OTHERWISE, EXIT.
                                         197  *
    0001A4                                198  UPDATING EQU    *
    0001A4 95 F4 C1F7       0001FD        199           CLI    TTYPE,C'4'        IS THIS A DELETE REQUEST
    0001A8 47 70 C1AE       0001B4        200           BNE    OKUPDATE          ...IF NOT, GO DO UPDATING.
    0001AC 92 FF C34A       000350        201           MVI    MFLAG,BYP         IF SO, SET DELETE FLAG TO BY-
    0001B0 47 F0 C1F2       0001F8        202           B      EXIT              PASS WRITING TO NEW MASTER.
                                         203  *
    0001B4                                204  OKUPDATE EQU    *
    000000                                205           USING  SDAREA,11         SET UP DUMMY BASE REGISTER TO ACCESS
    0001B4 41 B0 C2B6       0002BC        206           LA     11,NEWDATA1       FIELDS IN STUDENT DATA AREA BY NAME.
    0001B8 95 F2 C1F7       0001FD        207           CLI    TTYPE,C'2'        IF TRANS CODE = '2', THEN ADD STUDENT
    0001BC 47 80 C1D8       0001DE        208           BE     ADD               NAME AND I.D.
    0001C0 D5 08 B028C231 000028 000237  209  DEL      CLC    NEWMID,TID        OTHERWISE, ASSUME CODE = '3', AND
    0001C6 47 80 C1C8       0001CE        210           BE     DEL1              DELETE EITHER 1ST OR 2ND NAME & I.D.
    0001CA 41 BB 0031       000031        211           LA     11,DATALNG(11)    IF NOT 1ST, MUST BE 2ND  INCR ADDR.
    0001CE D2 27 B000C318 000000 00031E  212  DEL1     MVC    NEWMNAME,BLANKS   DELETE BY REPLACING NAME & I.D. WITH
    0001D4 D2 08 B028C318 000028 00031E  213           MVC    NEWMID,BLANKS     BLANKS.
    0001DA 47 F0 C1F2       0001F8        214           B      EXIT
    0001DE D5 08 B028C318 000028 00031E  215  ADD      CLC    NEWMID,BLANKS     WHEN ADDING, SEE WHICH STUDENT DATA
    0001E4 47 80 C1E6       0001EC        216           BE     ADD1              AREA IS BLANK, AND MOVE NAME & I.D.
    0001E8 41 BB 0031       000031        217           LA     11,DATALNG(11)    INTO THAT AREA.  IF NOT 1ST AREA,
    0001EC D2 27 B000C208 000000 0002CE  218  ADD1     MVC    NEWMNAME,TNAME    THEN ASSUME IT'S 2ND AREA.
    0001F2 D2 08 B028C231 000028 000237  219           MVC    NEWMID,TID
    0001F8 07 FE                          220  EXIT     BR     14                EXIT TO CALLING ROUTINE.
                                         221  * TRANSACTION INPUT AREA
                                         222  *
000 0001FA                                223  TAREA    DS     CL80              RESERVE 80 BYTES FOR CARD IMAGE.
000 0001FA            00024A             224           ORG    TAREA             BEGIN REDEFINITION OF INPUT AREA.
000 0001FA                                225           DS     CL3               COL 1-3   UNUSED
000 0001FD                                226  TTYPE    DS     CL1               4         TRANS TYPE CODE
000 0001FE                                227           DS     CL3               5-7       UNUSED
    000201                                228  TDORM    DS     CL4               8-11      DORM ABBREVIATION
    000205                                229           DS     CL4               12-15     UNUSED
000 000209                                230  TROOM    DS     CL4               16-19     DORM ROOM NUMBER
000 00020D                                231           DS     CL1               20        UNUSED
000 00020E                                232  TNAME    DS     CL40              21-60     STUDENT NAME
000 000236                                233           DS     CL1               61        UNUSED
000 000237                                234  TID      DS     CL9               62-70     STUDENT I.D.
000 00024A            000240             235           ORG
000                                      236  *
000                                      237  * INPUT MASTER RECORD AREA
000                                      238  *
000 00024A                                239  OLDAREA  DS     CL106             RESERVE 106 BYTES  (FIXED-LNG RECDS).
000 00024A            0002B4             240           ORG    OLDAREA           BEGIN REDEFINITION OF OUTPUT AREA.
```

Figure 20.13   continued

```
FLAG LOCTN OBJECT CODE    ADDR1  ADDR2  STMNT M SOURCE STATEMENT

     00024A                             241 OLDMDORM DS   CL4              BYTES 0-3   DORM ABBREVIATION
     00024E                             242 OLDMROOM DS   CL4                   4-7   DORM ROOM NUMBER
     000252                             243 OLDDATA1 DS   CL49                  8-56   1ST STUDENT DATA AREA
     000283                             244 OLDDATA2 DS   CL49                 57-105  2ND STUDENT DATA AREA
     0002B4              0002B4         245          ORG
                                        246 *
                                        247 * OUTPUT MASTER RECORD AREA
                                        248 *
     0002B4                             249 NEWAREA  DS   CL106            RESERVE 106 BYTES  (FIXED-LNG RECDS).
     0002B4              00031E         250          ORG  NEWAREA          BEGIN REDEFINITION OF OUTPUT AREA.
     0002B4                             251 NEWMDORM DS   CL4              BYTES 0-3   DORM ABBREVIATION
     0002B8                             252 NEWMROOM DS   CL4                   4-7   DORM ROOM NUMBER
     0002BC                             253 NEWDATA1 DS   CL49                  8-56   1ST STUDENT DATA AREA
     0002ED                             254 NEWDATA2 DS   CL49                 57-105  2ND STUDENT DATA AREA
     00031E              00031E         255          ORG
                                        256 *
                                        257 * DSECT TO DEFINE FIELD NAMES WITHIN STUDENT DATA AREAS
                                        258 *
     000000                             259 SDAREA   DSECT
     000000                             260 NEWMNAME DS   CL40             BYTES 0-39  STUDENT NAME FIELD
     000028                             261 NEWMID   DS   CL9                  40-48  STUDENT I.D. FIELD
     000031                             262 DATALNG  EQU  *-NEWMNAME       LENGTH OF STUDENT DATA AREA
     00031E                             263 UPDATE   CSECT
                                        264 *
                                        265 * BLANKS USED TO INITIALIZE STUDENT DATA AREAS
                                        266 * EODSW USED TO SIGNAL WHEN END-OF-DATA REACHED.
                                        267 * MFLAG USED TO SIGNAL THAT CURRENT MASTER RECD IS DELETED
                                        268 *
     00031E 40                          269 BLANKS   DC   (DATALNG)C' '    'DATALNG' IS SIZE OF STUDENT DATA AREA
                                        270 *
     00034F 00                          271 EODSW    DC   X'00'            X'00'=NEITHER FILE AT END; X'FF'=ONE AT END.
     0000FF                             272 EOF      EQU  X'FF'            X'FF' = FLAG FOR END-OF-DATA ON EITHER FILE
     000350 00                          273 MFLAG    DC   X'00'            X'00'=OK TO WRITE;X'FF'=DONT WRITE
     000000                             274 WR       EQU  X'00'            X'00' = RECD NOT DELETED, WRITE OK
     0000FF                             275 BYP      EQU  X'FF'            X'FF' = RECD DELETED, DONT WRITE IT
                                        276 * DCB'S FOR TRANS FILE, INPUT MASTER FILE, AND OUTPUT MASTER FILE
                                        277 *
     000351                             278 TRANS    DCB  DSORG=PS,MACRF=(GM),DDNAME=SYSIN,EODAD=ENDTRANS,       X
                                        279               RECFM=FB,LRECL=80,BLKSIZE=4080
                                        331 *
     0003B4                             332 MSTRIN   DCB  DSORG=PS,MACRF=(GM),DDNAME=OLDDORM,EODAD=ENDMSTR,      X
                                        333               RECFM=FB,LRECL=106,BLKSIZE=4028
                                        385 *
     000414                             386 MSTROUT  DCB  DSORG=PS,MACRF=(PM),DDNAME=NEWDORM,                    X
                                        387               RECFM=FB,LRECL=106,BLKSIZE=4028

                                        439 *  DOS  ******
                                        440 *TRANS    DTFCD DEVADDR=SYSIPT,WORKA=YES,IOAREA1=INBUF,EOFADDR=ENDTRANS, X
                                        441 *               DEVICE=2540
                                        442 *INBUF    DS   CL80
                                        443 *
                                        444 *MSTRIN   DTFSD DEVADDR=SYS015,DEVICE=3330,TYPEFLE=INPUT,WORKA=YES,     X
                                        445 *               RECFORM=FIXBLK,RECSIZE=106,BLKSIZE=4028,IOAREA1=OLDBUF, X
                                        446 *               EOFADDR=ENDMSTR
                                        447 *
                                        448 *MSTROUT DTFSD DEVADDR=SYS016,DEVICE=3330,TYPEFLE=OUTPUT,WORKA=YES,    X
                                        449 *               RECFORM=FIXBLK,RECSIZE=106,BLKSIZE=4036,IOAREA1=NEWBUF
                                        450 ****************

                                        451 * REGISTER SAVE AREA
                                        452 *
     000474                             453 SAVE     DS   18F

                                        454 *  DOS  ******
                                        455 *SAVE     DS   9D
                                        456 *         LTORG
                                        457 *         DS   0D
                                        458 *OLDBUF   DS   CL4028
                                        459 *NEWBUF   DS   CL4036
                                        460 ****************

                                        461          END
```

CROSS-REFERENCE

```
SYMBOL     LEN   VALUE  DEFN   REFERENCES

ADD       00006 0001DE 00215   00208
ADDGET    00004 00011E 00125   00119
ADDLOOP   00006 0000F6 00113   00129
ADDLOOPX  00004 0001DE 00118   00115
ADDPUT    00004 000116 00121   00114  00117
ADD1      00006 0001EC 00218   00216
BLANKS    00001 00031E 00269   00192  00193  00212  00213  00215
```

Figure 20.13   continued

```
BYP       00001 0000FF 00275   00165   C0201
BYPASS    00004 00017A 00174   00166
COMPLETE  00004 0000BA 00092   00080   C0082
CONSTRCT  00006 000180 00190   00071   C0122
COPYLOOP  00004 0000CE 00101   00108
DATALNG   00001 000031 00262   00211   00217   00269
DEL       00006 0001C0 00209
DEL1      00006 0001CE 00212   00210
ENDMSTR   00004 0000EA 00110   00354
ENDTRANS  00004 0000C2 00098   00300
EODSW     00001 00034F 00271   00098   C0100   00110   00112
EOF       00001 0000FF 00272   00098   C0100   00110   00112
EOJ       00004 000130 00134   00099   C0111
EXIT      00002 0001F8 00220   00196   C0202   00214
MAINLOOP  00006 00004E 00058   00093
MASTERLO  00006 000066 00063   00060
MFLAG     00001 000350 00273   00165   C0174   00201
MSTRIN    00004 0003B4 00333   00032   C0051   00065   00104   00145
MSTROUT   00004 000414 00387   00038   00139   00169
NEWAREA   0006A 0002B4 00249   00063   C0102   00170   00250
NEWDATA1  00031 0002BC 00253   00192   C0206
NEWDATA2  00031 0002ED 00254   00193
NEWMDORM  00004 0002B4 00251   00079   00113   00190
NEWMID    00009 000028 00261   00209   00213   00215   00219
NEWMNAME  00028 000000 00260   00212   00218   00262
NEWMROOM  00004 0002B8 00252   00081   00116   00191
OKUPDATE  00001 0001B4 00204   00195   C0200
OLDAREA   0006A 00024A 00239   00052   00063   00066   00102   00105   00240
OLDDATA1  00031 000252 00243
OLDDATA2  00031 000283 00244
OLDMDORM  00004 00024A 00241   00058
OLDMROOM  00004 00024E 00242   00061
PROCESS   00006 000090 00079   00069   00090
PUTMSTR   00004 000160 00165   00092   C0101   00121   00134
SAVE      00004 000474 00453   00017   00018   00153
SDAREA    00001 000000 00259   00205
TAREA     00050 0001FA 00223   00047   00074   00087   00126   00224
TDORM     00004 000201 00228   00058   00079   00113   00190
TID       00009 000237 00234   00209   00219
TNAME     00028 00020E 00232   00218
TRANS     00004 000354 00279   00026   C0046   00073   00086   00125   00151
TRANSLO   00004 00007E 00071   00059   C0062
TROOM     00004 000209 00230   00061   00081   00116   00191
TTYPE     00001 0001FD 00226   00194   C0199   00207
UPDATE    00001 000000 00263
UPDATING  00001 0001A4 00198   00084   C0118
WR        00001 000000 00274   00174
```

To illustrate some of the processes involved, consider the following problem of producing a report based on data in the dorm room master file: *For a given dorm, the report is to list all the rooms that are unoccupied or have only one student assigned to them. If a student is assigned, his or her name is also to be listed. At the end of the report, the total number of rooms in the dorm, together with the percent of rooms unoccupied, with only one student assigned to them, and fully occupied, is to be printed. The format of the report is to be as shown here.*

DORM OCCUPANCY REPORT			PAGE 3
DORM	**ROOM**	**ROOM OCCUPANT**	
HH	320	B.L. CARVER	345678901
HH	330	----	
HH	335	A.A. SAMPEN	235689013
HH	420	X.J. WASHBOURN	098765432

TOTAL NUMBER OF ROOMS	% FULL	% HALF FULL	% EMPTY
225	72.4%	25.6%	2.0%

Figure 20.14a   Overview of dorm file report procedure.

```
DORM_FILE_REPORT:

   INITIALIZATION;
   MAIN_PROCESSING;
   END_OF_DATA;

EXIT DORM_FILE_REPORT.



   INITIALIZATION:

      open transaction file;
      open master file;
      open report file;
      get transaction record;
      print title and heading at top of new page;

   EXIT INITIALIZATION.



   MAIN_PROCESSING:

      REPEAT UNTIL master record key is higher than transaction record key

         get next master record;
         IF master record key is equal to transaction record key
         THEN
            increase total room count;
            IF this room does not have two students
            THEN
               DETAILED_PROCESSING;   { see figure 20.14b }
            END IF;
         END IF;

      END UNTIL;

   EXIT MAIN_PROCESSING;



   END_OF_DATA:

      calculate percentages;
      print derived data;

   EXIT END_OF_DATA.
```

To designate the dorm for which the report is to be produced, we can use a transaction record similar to the ones used in creating and updating the dorm room file, but containing no information other than the dorm abbreviation and a transaction code of '5'.

A procedure for producing this report is outlined in Figures 20.14a and 20.14b. Note that since the dorm identity is the major sequencing field in the dorm room master file, the records in the master file are read until the first one that matches the given dorm identity is found. From that point on, the desired information is extracted from each master record that is read until either the end-of-data condition is reached on the master, or a record for a different dorm is encountered. In either case, the extraction process is terminated when that point is reached in the master file, and the total number of rooms and percentages is then printed. It is left as an exercise to write the program that will produce the desired report.

Figure 20.14b   Detailed processing for dorm file report.

```
DETAILED_PROCESSING:

   move room number to print line;

   IF this room has 1 student
   THEN
      increase half-full room count;
      move name and i.d. to print line;
   ELSE
      increase empty room count;
      move blanks to print line;
   END IF;

   IF there is not enough room for another line on this page
   THEN
      print title and heading at top of a new page;
   END IF;

   print data line;

EXIT DETAILED_PROCESSING.
```

20.12   SUMMARY

To summarize the procedures involved in processing a sequential data set, we have seen that in creating, updating, or retrieving information, we must process the records in the sequence in which they exist.

Due to the sequential nature of the data, we ordinarily should not write or rewrite a record until it has been determined that the construction of that record has been completed. In the simplest cases, a single transaction record will suffice to construct a record. But in more general cases, more than one transaction record, occurring consecutively in the transaction file, will be used in the construction process.

There are four possible updating actions and three possible methods for updating a sequential data set. When the only updating action consists of adding records to the end of an existing data set, the data set can be opened in EXTEND mode. None of the existing records of the data set are processed; only new records are added. When the only updating action consists of making changes or deletions in existing records without changing their length, the data set can be opened in UPDAT mode. All the records in the data set, up to and including the last one to be changed, must be read via the GET macro. Only those that are to be changed are rewritten. The records are updated in place.

When any combination of the four updating actions may occur in the transaction file, the existing master data set must be opened in INPUT mode and a new data set, opened in OUTPUT mode, must be created. All the records in the existing data set must be processed, even those for which no changes are to be made. The existing data set is not altered in any way. The new data set is an updated version of the existing set, including new records, changed records, and unchanged records, but excluding deleted records.

When retrieving information from a sequential data set, each record must be examined to see if its data meets the criteria established for retrieval. If the report produced by the retrieval process is to be in a different sequence than that of the records in the data set, the extracted information must be sorted before it can be printed. If the sequence for the report matches that of the data set, the extracted information can be printed after each record has been read.

SYSIN, SYSIPT   The name of the system input data set in OS is SYSIN; in DOS it is SYSIPT. The data in this sequential input file is in EBCDIC format.

SYSOUT, SYSLST   The name of the system output data set in OS is SYSOUT; in DOS it is SYSLST. This sequential output file contains printer listings, in EBCDIC format.

Move Mode   A record-processing mode in which an input record is moved from an I/O buffer to a program's work area, and an output record is moved from a work area to an I/O buffer. (See also Chap. 19.)

Locate Mode   A record-processing mode in which a logical record's location (address) in an I/O buffer is made available to a program, so that no program work area is needed to process the record. (See also Chap. 19.)

Fixed-Length Record   A record having the same length as all other records with which it is associated.

Variable-Length Record   A record whose length is independent of the lengths of other records with which it is associated.

Carriage-Control Character   A character that controls line-spacing on a printer. It does so only if it is the first character of a print record and if the appropriate parameter has been specified for the print file: for the ANSI control characters, the parameter is RECFM=FBA or RECFM=VBA in OS, and CTLCHR=ASA in DOS. See Figure 20.3.

Master File   A file that contains all the pertinent information about a set of related records, and which may be periodically updated to reflect current conditions.

Transaction File   A file containing the data that's used to update or retrieve from a master file.

INPUT Mode   The "open" mode that a program uses when it wants to read records from an existing file, without updating existing records or adding new records.

OUTPUT Mode   The "open" mode that a program uses to create a new file, or to replace all the records in an existing file with new records.

Update Mode   The "open" mode that a program uses to update or delete existing sequential file records "in place," provided no record's length is changed. In OS, this mode is specified in the OPEN macro by the word UPDAT; in DOS, it is specified in the DTF macro by the parameter UPDATE=YES.

EXTEND Mode (OS only)   The "open" mode that a program uses when it wants to add records to the end of a sequential file without having to create a new file in order to do so.

End-of-Data Condition   When a data set's records are being processed sequentially, the end-of-data condition is the event that occurs when an attempt is made to read beyond the last record in the data set. Synonymous with "End-of-File" condition.

Retrieval   The act of obtaining specific data from an existing file. The term has the same meaning as the phrase "information retrieval."

20.14   REVIEW QUESTIONS

1. What is the name of the file that contains the system input data stream? What is the name of the system output file?
2. What are the assembly language differences between "move mode" processing for a sequential file as shown in Figure 20.1 and the corresponding "locate mode" processing in Figure 20.2?
3. In the program in Figure 20.2, a PUT macro occurs before any record has been read by a GET macro. Explain the purpose of that PUT macro.

4. In Section 20.3, it is shown how to obtain the length of a variable-length record from the record descriptor word prior to moving that record to an output area. Why is it necessary to use the EX instruction when moving the record, and why is it necessary to subtract +1 from the record length when using that EX instruction?

5. One of the requirements when using printer carriage-control characters involves a specification in the DCB or DTF macro. What is that specification (in OS or in DOS), and what are the other requirements?

6. In OS, why should you use the TIME macro instead of the &SYSDATE system variable when obtaining the date for your printer output report?

7. What were the factors used in Section 20.8 to determine an appropriate blocksize for the dorm room master file?

8. a. Why is it that the procedure for creating the dorm room master file could not simply read each input transaction record and write it onto the master file?
    b. In the main processing logic of Figure 20.7 and in the corresponding program statements in Figure 20.8, what is happening when a master file output record is being "constructed"?

9. What is meant by the process of "updating in place," and how does this process differ from the process used in the general updating procedure depicted in Figures 20.12a through 20.12c for sequential data sets?

10. How do you specify that updating in place is being used in an assembly language program? How do you specify that the general updating process is being used in an assembly language program?

11. a. Why are two separate end-of-data procedures used in Figures 20.12c and 20.13 for updating a sequential data set?
    b. In the end-of-transaction-data procedure, why isn't it necessary to "construct" the output master record as is done in the end-of-input-master procedure?

12. Of the three types of reports outlined in Section 20.11, which type (or types) best describes the sample report that is illustrated in that section? Explain.

20.15 EXERCISES

1. Determine what conventions and restrictions, if any, exist at your computer installation with regard to the use of SYSIN and SYSOUT, or SYSIPT and SYSLST.

2. What statements in the programs of Figures 20.1 and 20.2 would have to be changed if either (a) the input data were other than SYSIN or (b) the output data set were other than SYSOUT? What would the changes be?

3. Compare the programs of Figures 20.1 and 20.2. What are the advantages of using locate mode over using move mode? What are the disadvantages?

4. Change the programs of Figures 20.1 and 20.2 so that both the input and output data sets contain variable-length records (RECFM=VB in OS, RECFORM=VARUNB in DOS).

5. Suppose that the input data records for the program of Figure 20.1 contained the following information:

> columns 5–44 = student name
> columns 46–55 = course identification
> columns 57–60 = course grade points, from 0.00 to 4.00

Write a program that will read an arbitrary number of such input records and compute and print the percentage of records with grade points between n and $n+1$, for $n = 0,1,2,3$.

6. Write a subroutine that will convert the date returned by the TIME macro (as discussed in Section 20.4) to 8-byte EBCDIC format as mm/dd/yy. For example, if the date returned is X'0080038C', the 8-byte EBCDIC representation would be C'02/07/80'.

7. Modify the program given in Figure 20.4 so that the first line printed on each page of output contains a title, the page number, and the date on which the program is run. The date should be in the format mm/dd/yy, which can be generated either by the subroutine written for Exercise 6 or by any similar subroutine or macro already existing for this purpose at your computer installation.

8. What are the corresponding assembly language statements and/or DCB or DTFxx macro parameters for each of the following IBM Cobol clauses?

   a. BLOCK CONTAINS 4000 CHARACTERS
   b. RECORD CONTAINS 80 CHARACTERS
   c. RECORDING MODE IS FB
   d. READ filename AT END STOP RUN
   e. WRITE record AFTER ADVANCING 2 LINES
   f. OPEN INPUT filename

9. Prepare suitable test data to create a sequential dorm room master file in accordance with the specifications given in this chapter. Ensure that your test data covers at least the following situations: no students assigned to a room, one student assigned to a room, two students assigned to the same room. Ensure that the transaction records are in proper sequence by sorting them via the IBM Sort/Merge program (see IBM Publication SC33–4035, *Sort/Merge Programmer's Guide*).

10. Using the test data from Exercise 9 and the program in Figure 20.8, create a sample dorm room master file. To verify that its contents are correct, print the master file via the IBM OS utility program IEBPTPCH (see IBM Publication GC26–3901, *Utilities*) or the corresponding DOS utility program (see Publication GC33–5381).

11. What specific types of possible data errors have been avoided in this chapter by the assumption of "perfect" data in the transaction file that is input to the program of Figure 20.8? Modify the program of Figure 20.8 so that it would detect and reject all such errors and print them on the system output data set. Prepare test data that would force your modified program to encounter these errors.

12. Under what conditions can the open-mode processing option known as EXTEND be used to update a sequential data set? What would be the advantage of using this processing option rather than the more general procedures depicted in Figures 20.12 and 20.13? Why couldn't the UPDAT mode (as shown in Figs. 20.10 and 20.11) be used as an alternative to the EXTEND mode?

13. a. What specific types of possible data errors have been avoided in this chapter by the assumption of "perfect" data in each of the following updating situations: EXTEND mode, UPDAT mode, and the general updating procedures of Figure 20.12?
    b. Assume that a transaction file processed by the program of Figure 20.13 inadvertently contained records for three different students to be assigned to the same dorm room. What would be the result when these records were processed by the program?
    c. Assume that a transaction file processed by the program of Figure 20.13 inadvertently contained a record to delete a student from a dorm room to which he or she had never been assigned. What would be the result when this record was processed by the program?
    d. What changes would have to be made to the program of Figure 20.13 to enable it to detect and reject the data errors described in Exercises 13b and 13c?

14. a. What changes would have to be made to the program of Figure 20.13 to enable it to process the input transaction file in locate mode rather than move mode?
    b. What changes would have to be made to the program of Figure 20.13 to enable it to process both the input and output master files in locate mode rather than move mode?

15. Write a program that will print the entire contents of the dorm room master file in some suitably readable format. Your program should be written to allow for an arbitrary number of records on the master file with no more than 50 lines printed per page and with an appropriate title line including date and page number on each page.

16. Write a program that will create a sequential file consisting of just those dorm room master file records containing less than two students per room.

17. Write a program that will produce the dorm room occupancy report described in Section 20.11, based on the procedures depicted in Figures 20.14a and 20.14b.

18. Using the solutions to Exercises 16 and 17, suitably modified if necessary, describe how the dorm room occupancy report could be produced in such a way that all the rooms to which no students were assigned were printed before all the rooms to which one student was assigned. Implement your solution to this problem. (**Hint:** You may wish to use the IBM Sort/Merge program described in IBM Publication SC33–4035.)

19. A high school district has decided to convert its teacher assignment records to a form suitable for computer processing and maintenance. The records presently exist on paper. Each teacher's record contains the teacher's name, the name of the school to which the teacher is currently assigned, from one to three subjects that the teacher is qualified to teach, and the year in which the teacher first was employed by the school district.

    a. Design a transaction record format that can be used to create a sequential master file consisting of all the current manually maintained teacher assignment records, and design a master file format for these records.
    b. Design a transaction record format that can be used to update the teacher assignment master file, with capabilities to add new teachers, delete teachers who have retired or left the district, change any or all of the subjects that a teacher is qualified to teach, and change the school to which the teacher is assigned.
    c. Write a program to create the teacher assignment master file.
    d. Write a program to update the teacher assignment master file, allowing for the possibility of transaction data errors.
    e. Write a program (or programs) that will produce each of the following reports:

       1. A report giving all the information in the master file, listed in ascending sequence by year of first assignment (so-called "seniority" sequence)
       2. A report giving all the information about teachers who are qualified to teach a given subject, the subject being identified by a transaction record that is read by the retrieval program

    f. Create appropriate test data to verify that each of the programs in Exercises 19c, 19d, and 19e work correctly.

21

Indexed Sequential Organization

E ach record of an indexed sequential data set must be uniquely identified by the value of a key field that is part of the record. The records must be maintained in ascending sequence by key values, i.e., the record with the lowest key must occur first, and the key field of each record must begin in the same relative position and have the same length as the key fields of the other records of the data set.

Use of indexed sequential organization provides one significant advantage over that of sequential organization: not only may the logical records be processed sequentially, but they may also be processed randomly. In OS, the QISAM access method is used for sequential processing, and the BISAM access method for random processing. In DOS, the ISAM access method is used for both sequential and random processing.

To enable random processing to be accomplished without requiring a user's program to determine the position of records within the data set, the operating system maintains an index that associates each key value with the position of the record identified by that value. In simplest terms, the user program presents a key to the operating system, and the operating system finds and reads that record (if it exists) or writes it into its logically correct sequential position.

In this chapter, we will discuss several aspects of indexed sequential processing, beginning with an overview. Space allocation considerations will then be discussed as will the processes of creating, updating, and retrieving from an indexed sequential data set. These processes will be illustrated with the dorm room master file introduced in Chapter 20. You may therefore find it useful to review the concepts presented in Chapters 19 and 20, especially Figures 19.6 (I/O macros), 19.7 (DCB and DTFIS parameters), and 19.10 (OPEN options).

21.1 INTRODUCTORY CONCEPTS

Although the concepts are essentially the same whether we are using OS or DOS systems, the processing details for indexed sequential data sets are significantly different between the two systems. We have already mentioned one major difference: the use of two access methods (QISAM and BISAM) in OS, but only one (ISAM) in DOS. But there are other major differences. One is the manner in which I/O error conditions are communicated to the user's program from the operating system. Another is the manner in which buffers are allocated. A third is the way in which buffers are used by the GET, PUT, READ, and WRITE macros. And a fourth, though not strictly an assembly language consideration, is the manner in which space is allocated by the job control language statements. Because of these and other differences, it is probably fair to say that in indexed sequential processing we have the most pronounced instance of incompatibility between OS Assembly Language and DOS Assembly Language.

QISAM

The **queued indexed sequential access method** (QISAM) must be used to create an indexed sequential data set in OS. It can also be used when updating in place via PUTX in UPDAT mode and when adding records to the end of a data set via PUT in EXTEND mode. It cannot, however, be used to insert new records into an existing data set (see Section 21.4).

QISAM vs. QSAM

The processing steps used with QISAM are similar to those described in the preceding chapter for QSAM. Buffer allocation and I/O synchronization are performed as in QSAM. Records must be read or written in their correct logical key sequence. There are, however, a number of differences between the two access methods, two of them quite significant. One significant difference is that *sequential processing can begin at any arbitrary record in the data set* when updating or retrieving records in an indexed sequential data set using QISAM. The record at which processing begins must be identified by its key and specified in a Set Location (SETL) macro before invoking a GET macro. Any number of SETL macros can be invoked at run time; thus, in effect, we can sequentially process the records in one or more separate sections of an indexed sequential data set without having to process the entire data set. In order to stop retrieval from one section before beginning a new section of the data set, we simply invoke the End SETL (ESETL) macro. This can be done before or after the end-of-data condition is reached.

"Deleted" Records

The other significant difference between QISAM and QSAM processing is that in QISAM *records can be deleted when updating in place.* This is accomplished by using the first byte of each logical record (or the first byte immediately following the record descriptor word if using variable-length records) as a **delete flag.** The user's program must set this byte to X'FF' if the record is to be deleted, and to X'40' (a blank) if it is not to be deleted. Any record flagged for deletion in this manner will not be retrievable via QISAM in subsequent processing. Note that the programmer must declare his or her intention of using the first byte as a delete flag at the time an indexed sequential data set is created; once this is done, the first byte should not be used for any other purpose. (The method of declaring this is to specify OPTCD=L in the DCB macro or DD statement.)

Other differences between QISAM and QSAM processing methods include:

DSORG

1. The DSORG parameter must always be coded as DSORG=IS for QISAM. The RECFM, LRECL, and BLKSIZE parameters should be coded only when creating the data set, not when updating or retrieving from it.
2. Move mode or locate mode buffering can be used, but the other buffering options available with QSAM processing—data mode, substitute mode, and exchange buffering—are not permitted with QISAM.

MACRF

3. When retrieving records in INPUT mode, we must specify in the MACRF parameter whether or not the SETL macro will be used by coding MACRF=(GM,SK) or (GL,SK) instead of MACRF=(GM) or (GL). If SETL is not going to be used, sequential retrieval will begin at the first record in the data set and proceed from there as in QSAM processing.
4. When updating records in UPDAT mode, locate mode buffering must be used, but PU rather than PL is coded in the MACRF parameter and use of the SETL macro must be indicated: MACRF=(GL,PU) or (GL,SK,PU).

See Section 21.3 for further details of QISAM.

BISAM

The OS **basic indexed sequential access method** (BISAM) cannot be used to create an indexed sequential data set, but it can be, and frequently is, used to update or retrieve records. (The use of BISAM corresponds to the clause "access is random" in IBM Cobol, whereas the use of QISAM corresponds to "access is sequential.")

"Deleted" Records

When updating an indexed sequential data set using BISAM, new records may be added or inserted and existing records may be changed or deleted. Deletion is accomplished by the same delete-flag method used in QISAM. However, when using BISAM, it is important to be aware that records that are flagged for deletion—whether by QISAM or by BISAM—may still physically be in the data set. (The reason for this, which has to do with the way the operating system processes such records, will be discussed in the next section when the concept of prime and overflow areas is described.) Unlike QISAM, the BISAM READ macro ignores the delete flag; it will retrieve a logical record whether it has been flagged for deletion or not, provided it is still physically in the data set. On the other hand, a record flagged for deletion will be physically replaced when BISAM is used to write a new record with the same key as the flagged record. Thus, there will never be two records with the same key in the data set.

Synchronization

Remember that the use of the READ or WRITE macros requires that the user program perform certain buffer-related functions. For BISAM, these include I/O synchronization via the CHECK or WAIT macros, buffer allocation via direct or dynamic buffering, and I/O error processing. The

Invalid Keys

principal I/O error that must be processed is known as an **invalid key condition.** An invalid key during a READ would occur if there were no record in the data set corresponding to the record key designated via the READ macro. An invalid key during a WRITE would occur if there were already a record in the data set corresponding to the designated record key when an attempt was being made to write a new record. These conditions can be detected by examining certain control bits in the data event control block after a CHECK or WAIT macro has been invoked.

In addition to these considerations, there are two other points to be noted:

1. The OPEN macro is not used to designate the processing mode when using BISAM. We simply write

```
OPEN  (dcb-address)
```

and specify the processing mode via the MACRF parameter.

2. Certain DCB parameters are never specified when using BISAM; among these are BLKSIZE, LRECL, RECFM, KEYLEN, and RKP. The values of these parameters are specified only when an indexed sequential data set is created. Thereafter, they are obtained from the data set control block at open time.

Further details of BISAM will be discussed in Section 21.5.

ISAM

As mentioned earlier, both sequential-mode processing and random-mode processing are accomplished by the same access method, ISAM, in DOS systems. The main differences between the two modes are designated in the DTFIS macro.

To **create** an indexed sequential file in DOS, we must use the WRITE macro with IOAREAL= buffer area and specify IOROUT=LOAD in the DTFIS macro. In addition, we must follow the OPEN macro with a SETFL (Set File Load Mode) macro and precede the CLOSE macro with an ENDFL (End SETFL) macro. Records must be written in ascending key sequence.

To **extend** an indexed sequential file, i.e., to add records in ascending key sequence beyond the previous last record of the file, we use the same procedures and parameters as when creating the file. The difference between creating and extending is not indicated in the user's program; instead, it is specified in the // DLBL job control statement via a code (ISC or ISE) following the expiration date field, as follows (see also Fig. 19.8b):

```
to create a file:   // DLBL dtfname,'filename',date,ISC,...
to extend a file:   // DLBL dtfname,'filename',date,ISE,...
```

To **update** an indexed sequential file, we can use either sequential-mode processing or random-mode processing. In **sequential mode,** we can choose between updating in place and the general updating procedures. Updating in place is restricted to changing data field contents (but not the key field), and is specified via IOROUT=ADDRTR and TYPEFLE=SEQNTL in the DTFIS macro. It uses the GET macro to retrieve a record and the PUT macro to rewrite a record that has been retrieved. Generalized updating permits all possible changes to a record (except that once again we cannot change the key field), requires that the file to be updated be opened for retrieval (IOROUT=RETRVE), and a new file—the updated file—created as described previously. The only way to change a key field in a record is to delete that record and add a new record with the correct key field.

To **update in random mode,** generalized updating is permitted by specifying IOROUT=ADDRTR and TYPEFLE=RANDOM. In this mode, records can be updated in place, and new records can be inserted in their proper key-sequenced position without having to create a new file. However, there is no provision for deleting records in random mode (and none when updating in place in sequential mode). In particular, the delete-flag mechanism of OS does not exist in DOS. The only way to delete a record is via the generalized sequential-mode procedures (i.e., by not copying an input record to the output file), or via a mock delete-flag mechanism that you must program yourself.

In addition to the above considerations, there are several other points to be noted:

1. The logical record format must be either fixed-blocked or fixed-unblocked (RECFORM=FIXBLK or =FIXUNB).
2. When loading or adding new records onto a file, the buffer must include a count area and a key area, as was depicted in Figure 19.15b.
3. When retrieving or updating an existing record the buffer must be 10 bytes longer than the length of a record in order to accommodate the sequence link field used in overflow records. This was also depicted in Figure 19.15b and will be discussed further in the next section.
4. The SETL (Set Location) and ESETL (End SETL) macros can be used to skip to any desired position in an indexed sequential file before processing subsequent records sequentially.

21.2 SPACE ALLOCATION

Secondary memory space for an indexed sequential data set is generally allocated in three distinct areas: the prime data area, the independent overflow area, and the cylinder index area.

In OS systems, there are a number of ways in which the allocated space can be arranged. These depend on the manner in which the SPACE= parameter of the DD statement is coded, as shown in Figure 21.1a. In DOS systems, there is essentially only one way in which the space can be arranged, and this is done by // EXTENT statements as shown in Figure 21.1b.

In addition to the prime, overflow, and index areas just mentioned, there are two other areas (both optional) that can be allocated. Of the two the most frequently used is the cylinder overflow area. This area occupies tracks within each cylinder of the prime data area and is allocated through the CYLOFL= parameter of the DCB or DTFIS macro. The other area is the **master index area,** which is allocated only for exceptionally large files. In OS it is requested by the OPTCD= and NTM= parameters of the DCB macro, and in DOS by the MSTIND=YES parameter of the DTFIS macro together with an // EXTENT statement.

The **prime data area** contains blocks written at the time the data set was created. The data blocks in this area are stored in ascending sequence, sequenced by the highest key of the logical records in each block. The logical records within each data block are also in ascending key sequence. In addition to containing records written by a user program, each cylinder of the prime data area contains a **track index** written and maintained by the operating system. The track index contains one pair of entries for each prime data track in the cylinder. Each pair of index entries contains four items: (1) the address of the prime data track to which it refers, (2) the key of the highest record in that track, (3) the address of the lowest overflow record associated with that track, and (4) the key of the highest overflow record associated with that track. These entries are used by the operating system to determine the track on which a given logical record is or should be stored. The format of the track-index entries is depicted in Figure 21.2.

Figure 21.1a   Requesting and arranging space for an indexed sequential data set in OS systems.

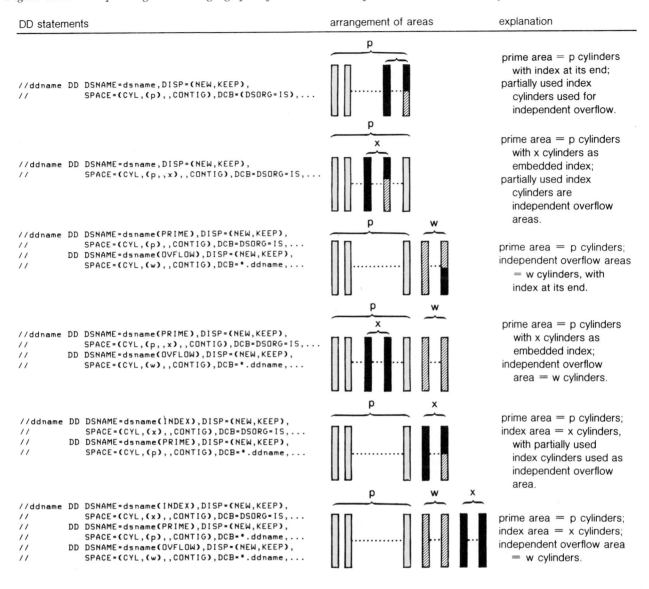

DD statements	arrangement of areas	explanation

```
//ddname DD DSNAME=dsname,DISP=(NEW,KEEP),
//          SPACE=(CYL,(p),,CONTIG),DCB=(DSORG=IS),...
```
prime area = p cylinders with index at its end; partially used index cylinders used for independent overflow.

```
//ddname DD DSNAME=dsname,DISP=(NEW,KEEP),
//          SPACE=(CYL,(p,,x),,CONTIG),DCB=DSORG=IS,...
```
prime area = p cylinders with x cylinders as embedded index; partially used index cylinders are independent overflow areas.

```
//ddname DD DSNAME=dsname(PRIME),DISP=(NEW,KEEP),
//          SPACE=(CYL,(p),,CONTIG),DCB=DSORG=IS,...
//       DD DSNAME=dsname(OVFLOW),DISP=(NEW,KEEP),
//          SPACE=(CYL,(w),,CONTIG),DCB=*.ddname,...
```
prime area = p cylinders; independent overflow areas = w cylinders, with index at its end.

```
//ddname DD DSNAME=dsname(PRIME),DISP=(NEW,KEEP),
//          SPACE=(CYL,(p,,x),,CONTIG),DCB=DSORG=IS,...
//       DD DSNAME=dsname(OVFLOW),DISP=(NEW,KEEP),
//          SPACE=(CYL,(w),,CONTIG),DCB=*.ddname,...
```
prime area = p cylinders with x cylinders as embedded index; independent overflow area = w cylinders.

```
//ddname DD DSNAME=dsname(INDEX),DISP=(NEW,KEEP),
//          SPACE=(CYL,(x),,CONTIG),DCB=DSORG=IS,...
//       DD DSNAME=dsname(PRIME),DISP=(NEW,KEEP),
//          SPACE=(CYL,(p),,CONTIG),DCB=*.ddname,...
```
prime area = p cylinders; index area = x cylinders, with partially used index cylinders used as independent overflow area.

```
//ddname DD DSNAME=dsname(INDEX),DISP=(NEW,KEEP),
//          SPACE=(CYL,(x),,CONTIG),DCB=DSORG=IS,...
//       DD DSNAME=dsname(PRIME),DISP=(NEW,KEEP),
//          SPACE=(CYL,(p),,CONTIG),DCB=*.ddname,...
//       DD DSNAME=dsname(OVFLOW),DISP=(NEW,KEEP),
//          SPACE=(CYL,(w),,CONTIG),DCB=*.ddname,...
```
prime area = p cylinders; index area = x cylinders; independent overflow area = w cylinders.

Figure 21.1b   Requesting space for an indexed sequential data set in DOS systems.

Note: The statements below must be given in the sequence shown here. (See also Fig. 19.8b)

```
// DLBL dtfname,'filename',date,ISC
// EXTENT ,,4,0,a,n  — optional master index area
// EXTENT ,,4,1,b,r  — required cylinder index area
// EXTENT ,,1,2,c,s  — required prime data area
// EXTENT ,,2,3,d,t  — optional independent overflow area
```

extent type ⟶
extent seq# ⟶
⟶ *relative track number* where space allocation begins
⟶ *number of consecutive tracks* in the space allocation

The areas a thru a+n, b thru b+r, c thru c+s, and d thru d+t must not contain any tracks in common with one another.

Figure 21.2   Record formats in prime data area.

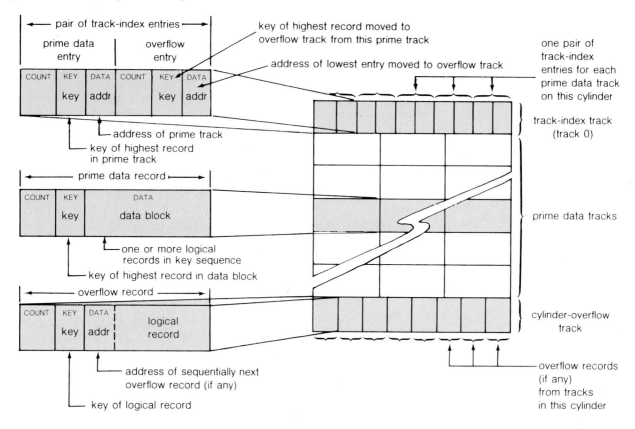

The **independent** and **cylinder overflow areas** are used to contain logical records forced off prime data area tracks when new records are inserted in ascending sequence. The process is illustrated in Figure 21.3. Note that when a record flagged for deletion is forced off a prime data track, it is not moved to the overflow area; instead, it is discarded. This is the only way that such records can be physically removed from the data set without re-creating the data set. Note also that records in the overflow area are unblocked and are not stored in key sequence; they are stored in the sequence in which they are placed there. The intended processing sequence is maintained in a next-record-address field (sequence link) that is prefixed to each logical record, as shown in Figure 21.3. Thus, overflow track space is used inefficiently, both for storage and for searching. The inefficiencies can be eliminated only by re-creating the data set, for example, by opening it for sequential input and copying it to a new data set. This process is known as **reorganizing the data set**: in the new data set, all records will be blocked and in sequence in the prime data area, and the overflow areas will be empty.

The **index area** of an indexed sequential data set contains a cylinder index and the optional master index. It does not contain the track indexes, which as we have seen, are part of the prime data area. There is only one cylinder index for the data set. Each entry in the **cylinder index** is associated with one of the cylinders of the prime data area. An entry contains the address of the track index in that prime cylinder and the highest key that is stored in that track index. Cylinder index entries are used by the operating system to determine the prime data cylinder on which a logical record is, or should be, stored. Once this has been determined, the track index in that prime cylinder is searched to determine the address of the record; this search hierarchy is depicted in Figure 21.4. The **master index** shown in the figure is optional and is used only with large data sets, e.g., those requiring at least 40 cylinders of prime area on an IBM 3330. Each entry in the master index contains the address of a track in the cylinder index together with the highest key stored in that cylinder index track. Thus, the master index adds another level to the search hierarchy.

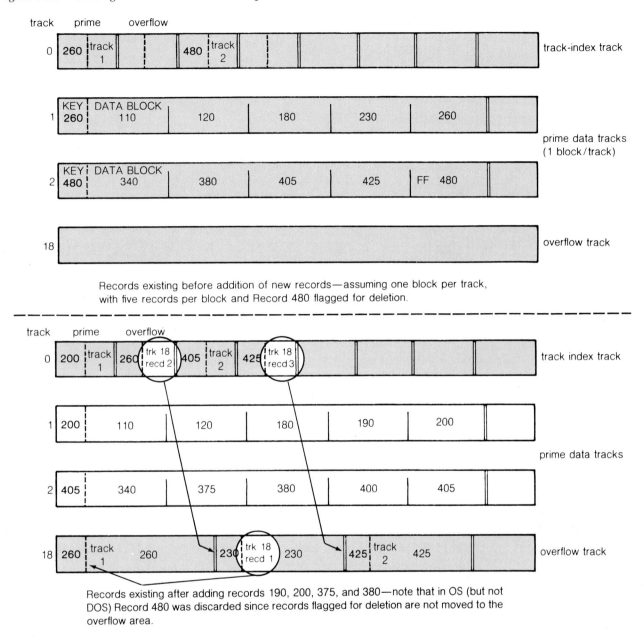

Figure 21.3   Adding records to an indexed sequential data set.

Records existing before addition of new records—assuming one block per track, with five records per block and Record 480 flagged for deletion.

Records existing after adding records 190, 200, 375, and 380—note that in OS (but not DOS) Record 480 was discarded since records flagged for deletion are not moved to the overflow area.

To visualize the concepts of prime, index, and overflow areas, it may be helpful to consider the following analogy. Suppose that a multivolume set of encyclopedias is like an indexed sequential data set; the articles in the encyclopedias are data blocks, the pages are tracks, and the volumes are cylinders. If this is the case, the titles printed at the beginning of each article are keys; the set of all keys printed at the top of each page in a volume together with the page number for each key may be thought of as an index to that volume (a "track" index); and the set of all keys printed on the volume bindings together with the volume numbers may be thought of as a cylinder index.

If we want to find an article, we look first at the cylinder index to find the correct cylinder (i.e., the volume in which the article appears), then at the track index (the titles at the top of each page), and finally at the article titles (the keys) printed at the beginning of each article on the page. If we were the publishers and wanted to add an article to the encyclopedias, we would either have to reprint

Analogy with Encyclopedias

Figure 21.4   Hierarchy of indexes in indexed sequential data set.

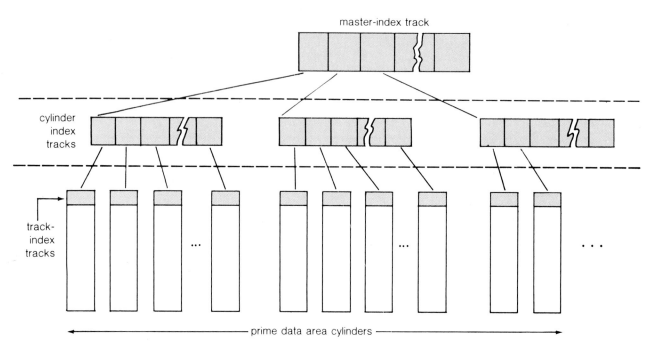

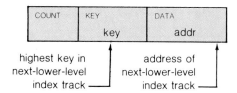

the volumes in order to maintain alphabetical sequence of articles or we could publish a supplementary volume or volumes. A single supplementary volume containing all new articles would correspond to an independent overflow area; a supplement to each existing volume would correspond to a cylinder overflow area. (The existing volumes themselves correspond to the prime data area.) When the supplements had gotten reasonably fat, we would reprint the encyclopedias, putting everything in its proper sequential position, thereby eliminating the supplements. This corresponds to the process of reorganization of an indexed sequential data set. Finally, we may note that if we had a very large number of volumes, stored in several rooms of a library, we might want to create a short document giving the identity of the highest volume in each room. This corresponds to the master index.

The problem of determining how many cylinders to allocate for an indexed sequential data set can now be seen to depend on how much space is required for each of the following: prime area data blocks, prime area track indexes, prime area cylinder overflow records, index area master and cylinder index entries, and independent overflow records. Since all the data in these various areas is stored in count-key-data format, we should use the information that was given in Figure 18.9 for the IBM 3330 disk system (or similar data for whatever storage device is being used). Alternatively, we can use the track capacity formulas from which those data are derived, since the formulas allow us to consider various key-lengths and data block lengths more easily. For the IBM 3330 system, the track capacity formula is[1]

$$\left\{ \begin{matrix} \text{number of blocks} \\ \text{per track} \end{matrix} \right\} = \frac{13165}{191 + \text{KL} + \text{DL}}$$

1. The numerical factors in this formula include allowances for the home address, the various gap spaces, and other overhead considerations. Capacity formulas for other IBM direct access devices can be found in *OS/VS1 Data Management Services Guide,* IBM Publication GC26–3874, in the section on Space Allocation or in *DOS/VS Data Management Guide,* GC33–5372.

where KL and DL represent the key-length and data block length, respectively. KL is defined by the KEYLEN= parameter in the DCB or DTFIS macro and is the same for all data in the prime, index, and overflow areas; it is simply the length of the key area in the count-key-data format. The quantity DL depends on whether we are calculating the number of blocks per track in the prime data area, the overflow area, or the track, cylinder, and master indexes. For the prime data area, DL is simply the blocksize. For the overflow areas, DL is 10 plus the logical record length (the factor 10 accounts for the next-record address prefixed to each overflow record; see Fig. 21.3). For each of the indexes, $DL = 10$.

Index Space Requirements

It is fairly easy to obtain an estimate of the amount of space needed for the various indexes. If we assume that key-length KL is less than or equal to 128 bytes (a reasonable assumption), this formula shows that, with $DL=10$, the number of blocks that can be stored on an index track ranges from 40 for $KL=128$ to 64 for $KL=2$. Therefore, since there are only 19 pairs of entries (one pair for each track in a prime data cylinder, or 38 track index entries in each track index), *only one track is needed for each track index.* Similarly, since each track of the cylinder index will account for 40 to 64 prime data area cylinders, a safe estimate is that *only one track of cylinder index is needed for every 10,000,000 bytes of prime data blocks* (remember that, in the IBM 3330 disk system, each cylinder can contain about a quarter of a million bytes). This rationale also shows that a master index is not needed except for unusually large data sets: each track of a master index will account for 40 to 64 tracks of a cylinder index, or 40×40 to 64×64 cylinders of the prime data area. For the IBM 3330 disk system, 1600 cylinders would entail either two or four disk *packs,* depending on whether a Model 11 or a Model 1 pack was being used. It should be stressed that these conclusions are based on the IBM 3330 disk system and the assumption that the key-length does not exceed 128 bytes. For situations other than these, you should make your own calculations.

Prime Space Requirements

The remaining task is to determine the amount of space needed for the prime data blocks and for the overflow records. To do this, we must estimate the total size of the data set to be created and estimate the number of overflow records that can be expected to occur. Suppose that the logical record length is denoted by L, the blocksize by B, and the estimated number of logical records in the data set by R. Then, the number of prime data blocks required will be $(L\times R)/B = N$. If the blocksize and key-length permit M blocks per track and if there are P prime data tracks per cylinder, the number of cylinders required for the prime data area will be given by the formula

$$\{\text{number of cylinders for prime data}\} = C = \frac{N}{M \times P} = \frac{L \times R}{B \times M \times P}$$

Dorm File Example

For example, if the dorm room master file defined in Chapter 20 were to be created as an indexed sequential data set, the calculations would be as follows:

$$L = 106 \text{ bytes per record}$$
$$B = 4028 \text{ bytes per block for fixed-length records}$$
$$R = 5000 \text{ records per data set (estimated number of dorm rooms)}$$
$$N = \frac{L \times R}{B} = 132 \text{ blocks per data set}$$
$$M = \frac{13165}{191 + KL + DL} = \frac{13165}{191 + 8 + 4028} = 3 \text{ blocks per track}$$

In the formula for M, the value chosen for KL, key-length, was 8 bytes, since we would want to use the dorm abbreviation and dorm room (4 bytes each) as the key of each record. The value of DL, data length, was simply the blocksize, B. To calculate the number of cylinders required, we must decide how many prime data tracks are available per cylinder. We have already seen that one of the prime data tracks will be used for the track index. And, as we will suggest below, two of the tracks in each prime data area cylinder should be reserved for cylinder overflow. Therefore, the number of prime data tracks per cylinder, P, is given by

$$P = \left\{ \begin{array}{c} \text{total} \\ \text{number of} \\ \text{tracks per} \\ \text{cylinder} \end{array} \right\} - \left\{ \begin{array}{c} \text{number of} \\ \text{tracks for} \\ \text{track index} \end{array} \right\} - \left\{ \begin{array}{c} \text{number of} \\ \text{tracks for} \\ \text{cylinder} \\ \text{overflow} \end{array} \right\}$$

$$= \{19\} - \{1\} - \{2\}$$
$$= 16 \text{ prime data tracks per IBM 3330 cylinder.}$$

Thus, the number of cylinders required for the dorm room master file using indexed sequential organization is

$$C = \frac{N}{M \times P} = 3 \text{ cylinders}$$

Since no additional seek time is required to access a record when it is placed in the cylinder overflow area (the access arm already being positioned at that prime data cylinder), it is good practice to always reserve tracks for cylinder overflow. Independent overflow can also be reserved, should more space be needed. The use of independent overflow has another advantage: in some data sets, the records added after the data set is created are often clustered around some key value. For example, the i.d.'s assigned to new students may be consecutive numbers, the dorm room numbers in a new dorm will be consecutive, etc. Thus, some cylinders will experience more overflow than others. Rather than reserving more cylinder overflow space—the same number of tracks always being reserved for each cylinder—we should reserve independent overflow space. A common practice is to reserve about 10% of the tracks for cylinder overflow, and, if warranted, about 10% additional space for independent overflow. When these areas are filled (or sooner), the data set should be reorganized.

Dorm Room Master File in OS

For the dorm room master file, two tracks for cylinder overflow areas per prime data cylinder and one cylinder for independent overflow area would be ample. If we knew that there was a record for each dorm room in the file and that no new dorms would be built in the near future, no overflow areas would need to be reserved: the operating system could allocate whatever was needed when it was needed. Thus, when creating the dorm room master file as an indexed sequential data set, we could code the DD statement as shown below. In both cases, we would also code CYLOFL=2 in the DCB macro. The CYLOFL= parameter must be used to reserve tracks for cylinder overflow; the DD statement SPACE= parameter is not used for this purpose. In addition, we would use the OPTCD= parameter of the DCB macro to designate independent and/or cylinder overflow usage.

1. To request three contiguous cylinders, letting the operating system subdivide it:

```
//ddname      DD      DSNAME=dsname,DCB=(DSORG=IS),
//                    SPACE=(CYL,(3),,CONTIG),DISP=(NEW,KEEP),...
```

2. To request three contiguous prime area cylinders, and one cylinder for independent overflow:

```
//ddname      DD      DSNAME=dsname(PRIME),DCB=(DSORG=IS),
//                    SPACE=(CYL,(3),,CONTIG),DISP=(NEW,KEEP),...
//            DD      DSNAME=dsname(OVFLOW),DCB=(*.ddname),
//                    SPACE=(CYL,(1)),DISP=(NEW,KEEP),...
```

Dorm Room Master File in DOS

As in OS, two tracks for cylinder overflow areas per prime data cylinder and one cylinder for independent overflow area is ample. But in DOS, space must be reserved not in units of cylinders but in units of tracks. The IBM 3330 has 19 tracks per cylinder, so it is a simple matter to convert from cylinders back to tracks. The prime and independent overflow areas can be reserved as follows. The cylinder overflow area must be reserved via the CYLOFL= parameter of the DTFIS macro.

```
// DLBL    dtfname,'filename',,ISC
// EXTENT  SYS001,volser#,4,1,190,1    one track for cylinder index
// EXTENT  ,,1,2,133,57                57 tracks for prime data area
// EXTENT  ,,2,3,209,19                19 tracks for ind. overflow
```

The processing logic required to create an indexed sequential data set is essentially the same as that for creating a sequential data set, described in Section 20.9 and Figures 20.7 and 20.8. However, certain additional parameters must be included in the DCB and DTFIS macros, and in DOS two additional imperative macros (SETFL and ENDFL) must be executed.

In both OS and DOS, the length and position of the key field must be the same in all logical records of the data set. Moreover, the blocksize must reflect the fact that count-key-data format is used when data blocks are written to the disk storage unit. If we again let DL denote blocksize and KL the key-length, then the track capacity formula for the IBM 3330 disk system in count-key-data format is $13165/(191+KL+DL)$. If we decide that we want three data blocks per track, then from this formula we find the maximum possible blocksize is

Blocksize (IBM 3330)

$$DL = \frac{13165}{3} - (191 + KL)$$
$$= 4388 - 191 - KL$$
$$= 4197 - KL$$

As in sequential data sets, the actual blocksize must be a multiple of the record length for fixed-length records and a multiple of the largest record length, plus 4 bytes for the block descriptor word, when using variable-length records. Before calculating the blocksize for the dorm room master file, we first discuss the DCB and DTFIS parameters that we will need.

DCB Parameters

Figure 21.5a describes the principal DCB parameters for indexed sequential data sets. The length and position of the key field must be indicated by KEYLEN= and RKP=, respectively. RKP=0 designates the first position in a record. For fixed-length records, RKP can be 0 or greater. For variable-length records, RKP must be 4 or greater, since the record descriptor word occupies bytes 0–3. In either case KEYLEN can be from 1 to 255 bytes. The record length, denoted by LRECL, must include the key-length since the key is part of each record; it must include the byte reserved for the delete flag, if any; and if variable-length records are used, it must include the 4 bytes reserved for the record descriptor word.

OS Record Key Parameters

The OPTCD parameter designates certain optional functions that may be requested. The functions are specified by one-letter codes concatenated in any order. The most important of these are I, L, M, and Y.

Note that if OPTCD=I is specified, we must also have requested a space allocation for an independent overflow area in the job control language. If OPTCD=M is specified, we must also use the NTM parameter to define the condition under which a master index is created. If OPTCD=Y is specified, we must also use the CYLOFL parameter to specify the number of tracks to be reserved for cylinder overflow in each prime data area cylinder. And, if OPTCD=L is specified, 1 byte must be reserved for the delete flag in the first position of each fixed-length record and in the fourth position of each variable-length record (i.e., just after the record descriptor word). Moreover, if OPTCD=L is specified, the record key cannot begin in the position used for the delete flag, so that RKP must be 1 or greater for fixed-length records and 5 or greater for variable-length records.

OPTCD and Its Implications

It is generally good practice to specify the delete-flag option unless we know that records are not going to be deleted. For, if OPTCD=L is not specified, the only way to delete a logical record is with the general updating procedures described for sequential files, i.e., the entire data set must be processed in input mode (using QISAM) and a new data set, which does not include the deleted records, would have to be created. Given that the delete-flag option exists, this would be an unnecessarily time-consuming process.

OS Delete Flag

Figure 21.5a *Principal DCB parameters when creating an indexed sequential data set in OS systems.*

parameter	meaning
BLKSIZE = n	blocksize of n bytes, including 4 bytes for the block descriptor word (if any)
CYLOFL = c	c tracks in each prime data cylinder are to be used as cylinder overflow area (see OPTCD = Y below)
DDNAME = ddname	identifies the DD statement that describes the data set
DSORG = IS	specifies that organization is indexed sequential
KEYLEN = k	k bytes is the length of the key field in each logical record (see RKP below)
LRECL = m	m bytes in each logical record, if RECFM = FB; if RECFM = VB, $m = 4 + \{$ maximum record length $\}$
MACRF = $\left\{ \begin{array}{l} \text{(PM)} \\ \text{(PL)} \end{array} \right\}$	(PM) for PUT macro in move mode, (PL) for PUT macro in locate mode
NTM = t	if the cylinder index requires more than t tracks, then a master index will be created provided that OPTCD = M is specified; if after it is created the master index requires more than t tracks, then a higher level master index will be created; if the higher level requires more than t tracks, then a still higher level master index will be created, but no more than three levels are created
OPTCD = ...	OPTCD = I specifies that independent overflow area is to be used; OPTCD = L, that the delete flag option will be used; OPTCD = M, that a master index is to be created; OPTCD = Y, that cylinder overflow areas are to be used
RECFM = $\left\{ \begin{array}{l} \text{FB} \\ \text{VB} \end{array} \right\}$	FB for blocked fixed-length records, VB for blocked variable-length records
RKP = p	p is the relative position of the first byte in the key field; $p = 0$ designates the first byte position in the record

NOTE: BLKSIZE, CYLOFL, KEYLEN, LRECL, NTM, OPTCD, RECFM, and RKP *can only be specified when creating an indexed sequential data set. They cannot be specified when updating or retrieving from the data set.*

DTFIS Parameters

DOS Record Key Parameters

Figure 21.5b describes the principal DTFIS parameters. The length and position of the key field are given by KEYLEN = and KEYLOC =, respectively. KEYLOC = 1 denotes the first position in a record. The key-length can be from 1 to 255 bytes. The record length, denoted by RECSIZE, must include the key-length since the key is part of each record.

There is no parameter for blocksize. Instead, the *blocking factor,* i.e., the number of records per block, is specified by NRECDS =. Thus, blocksize = NRECDS×RECSIZE. Variable-length records are not permitted; either blocked or unblocked fixed-length records must be designated.

Record, Block, and File Size Parameters

To reserve n tracks in each prime data area cylinder for the cylinder overflow area, we write CYLOFL = n. To indicate that a master index is to be used, we need MSTIND = YES. In addition it is mandatory that the DSKXTNT = x parameter specify the total number of extents that are allocated via //EXTENT job control statements. The minimum value of x is 2, since there must be at least one prime data extent and one cylinder index extent.

Input/Output

parameter	meaning
CYLOFL=*c*	*c* tracks in each prime data cylinder are to be used as cylinder overflow area
DEVICE=*device#*	*device#* is the identity assigned by IBM to the unit that contains the *prime data area*. For example, for the IBM 3330 disk system, specify DEVICE=3330
DSKXTNT=*x*	*x* extents have been allocated, including all index, overflow, and prime data extents.
HINDEX=*device#*	*device#* is the identity assigned by IBM to the unit that contains the *highest level index*. For example, DEVICE—3330 designates the IBM 3330 disk system.
IOAREAL=*buffername*	name of the I/O buffer area for file creation
KEYLEN=*k*	*k* bytes is the length of the key field in each record
KEYLOC=*p*	*p* is the relative position of the first byte in the key field; $p = 1$ designates the first byte position in the record
MSTIND=YES	specifies that a master index is to be used
NRECDS=*n*	*n* is the number of records in a data block. If RECFORM=FIXBLK, then $n > 1$; if RECFORM=FIXUNB, $n=1$.
RECFORM= $\left\{ \begin{matrix} \text{FIXBLK} \\ \text{FIXUNB} \end{matrix} \right\}$	FIXBLK for blocked fixed-length records FIXUNB for unblocked fixed-length records
RECSIZE=*m*	*m* bytes in each logical record, so that blocksize = RECSIZE×NRECDS = *m·n*
WORKL=*workareaname*	name of logical record area used for file creation (i.e., move mode is mandatory)

It is also mandatory to specify IOROUT=LOAD and IOAREAL=*buffername* when creating   *Buffers*
an indexed sequential file. And, we must specify WORKL=*workareaname*. Both the buffer and the
work area must be reserved via DS directives. The buffer must include space for the count and key
fields used in count-key-data format, as was depicted in Figure 19.15b. The work area must include
space for those count and key fields *only* if the records are *un*blocked.

As mentioned earlier, DOS makes no provision for a delete-flag option. Therefore it is not nec-   *DOS Delete Flag*
essary to reserve a delete-flag byte at the beginning of each logical record. Nevertheless, it is good
practice to do so, for two reasons: (1) the file can then be processed in OS systems as well as DOS
systems; and (2) the user's program then has an easy-to-use mechanism for marking and recognizing
records that are in effect deleted even though they still physically exist in the file.

The Dorm Room Master File in OS Systems

To illustrate these concepts, we will now describe the changes needed to create the dorm room master
file of Chapter 20 as an indexed sequential data set. Only a few changes are needed. The record
format must be redefined to include the delete-flag byte position, and the DCB macro must be appropriately coded. Figures 21.6a and 21.6b depict the revised record formats. The corresponding
logical record area description for the fixed-length format is as shown here:

```
* MASTER FILE RECORD AREA
*
OUTAREA   DS     CL107   RESERVE 107 BYTES FOR THE RECORD
          ORG    OUTAREA BEGIN REDEFINITION OF RECORD AREA
MDELETE   DC     CL1' '  BYTE 0    DELETE FLAG (INITIALLY BLANK)
MDORM     DS     CL4        1-4    DORM ABBREVIATION
MROOM     DS     CL4        5-8    DORM ROOM
*   NOTE:  BYTES 1-8 CONSTITUTE THE RECORD KEY FIELD
MDATA1    DS     CL49       9-57   1ST STUDENT DATA AREA
MDATA2    DS     CL49       58-106 2ND STUDENT DATA AREA
          ORG
```

Figure 21.6a   Fixed-length master file record format.

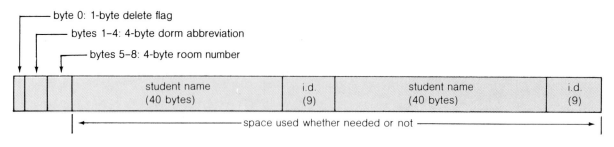

Figure 21.6b   Variable-length master file record format.

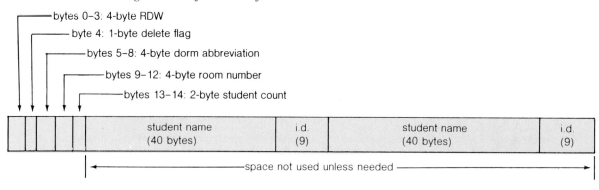

This description should be compared to the one given in Figure 20.8. The only change is the inclusion of the delete-flag byte position and the corresponding increase in record length from 106 to 107 bytes.

Given this record description, the DCB macro required to create the dorm room master file as an indexed sequential data set would be written as shown below. The designation OPTCD=ILY assumes that independent overflow may be needed when updating the master file. If not, OPTCD=LY would be sufficient.

```
MASTER      DCB    DSORG=IS,MACRF=(PM),DDNAME=DORMS,              X
                   RECFM=FB,LRECL=107,BLKSIZE=4066,               X
                   KEYLEN=8,RKP=1,CYLOFL=2,OPTCD=ILY
```

The value of BLKSIZE, 4066, is the largest value that is a multiple of 107 (the record length) without being greater than 4096. It accommodates 38 records per block and provides for three blocks per track on the IBM 3330. The track-space utilization is thus $3\times(KL+DL)/13060$, or about 93.8%, in the prime data area. In the overflow areas, however, the track-space utilization is only about 40%, since the overflow records are unblocked 107-byte records.

If these changes are made to the program that was given in Figure 20.8, the master file will be created as an indexed sequential data set. No other changes are required in the program. (The DD statements, however, must also be appropriately changed.)

OS Error Conditions

However, it must be stressed that the records written onto the new data set must be in ascending key sequence and no two records can contain the same record key. If the first of these conditions is violated, a "sequence check" error will occur; if the second is violated, a "duplicate record" error condition will occur.

The Dorm Room Master File in DOS Systems

The record area description given previously for OS systems is also valid for DOS, provided we decide to use blocked records. That of course is what we will do, since it is a much more efficient way to utilize disk space than unblocked records. The blocksize (4066 bytes) calculated for OS is equally valid for DOS. Given this, plus the fact that we will not use a master index (the file simply not being large enough to warrant that), the DTFIS macro for the dorm room master file is this:

```
MASTER    DTFIS DSKXTNT=3,IOROUT=LOAD,WORKL=OUTAREA,              X
                IOAREAL=MSTBUF,RECFORM=FIXBLK,RECSIZE=107,        X
                NRECDS=38,HINDEX=3330,KEYLEN=8,KEYLOC=2,CYLOFL=2, X
                DEVADDR=SYS001,DEVICE=3330
```

If this DTFIS replaces the DTFSD macro that was used in Figure 20.8, and if two other changes are made to the program of Figure 20.8, then the master file will be created as an indexed sequential file. (The job control statements must of course also be changed appropriately.) One change that is required in the program of Figure 20.8 is the insertion of two macros, SETFL and ENDFL. The SETFL macro establishes that the file is to be processed in **"load mode,"** i.e., for file creation, and must immediately follow the OPEN macro. The ENDFL macro simply ends the load mode and must immediately precede the CLOSE macro. The formats of the two macros are identical:

opcode	operand
SETFL	dtf-address
ENDFL	dtf-address

The other change that is required in the program of Figure 20.8 in order to create an indexed sequential file in DOS is to replace the PUT macro with a WRITE macro. Its format is this:

opcode	operand
WRITE	dtf-address,NEWKEY

The second parameter in the operand must be NEWKEY. Of course, before the WRITE macro is executed the logical record must exist in the work area identified by the WORKL= parameter of DTFIS. The access method moves that record to the buffer specified by IOAREAL= when the WRITE macro is executed.

The above changes to Figure 20.8 are left as exercises for you. Note that the records that are written to the indexed sequential data set when creating it must be in ascending key sequence and that no two records can contain the same record key. If the first of these conditions is violated, a "sequence-check" error will occur; if the second is violated, a "duplicate-record" error will occur.

21.4 UPDATING IN SEQUENTIAL MODE

The process of updating an indexed sequential data set in sequential mode includes the same four possible updating actions as those listed in Section 20.10 for sequential data sets:

Action 1: Add records to the end of the data set.
Action 2: Change or delete some of the data in existing records without deleting any records and without changing the length of any records.
Action 3: Insert new records in their proper sequence within the data set, or change the length of one or more existing records by adding new data to them or deleting data from them.
Action 4: Delete one or more existing records from the data set.

Because it requires that the entire data set be re-created, Action 3 is not usually performed sequentially unless there is a substantially large number of new records to be inserted. That is, *new records cannot be inserted into an existing data set using sequential mode.* This is because insertion of new records may require that a record be added to an overflow area, and the sequential-processing mode is not designed to do this. Instead, random-mode processing must be used. However, sequential-mode processing can be used for Actions 1, 2, and 4.

Sequential Mode in OS Systems

Extending

To add records to the end of an indexed sequential data set (Action 1), the processing logic required is almost identical to that used for creating such data sets. There are only two differences: (1) the data set must be opened in EXTEND mode rather than OUTPUT mode and (2) DISP=(MOD,KEEP) must be coded on the DD statement rather than DISP=(NEW,KEEP). The records that are added must be in ascending key sequence and must all have a key that is greater than the highest key in the existing data set. If either condition is violated, a "sequence check" error or a "duplicate record" error will occur. Note that it is prime data area space that is used for the added records, not overflow space. Therefore, if not enough prime space was initially allocated to anticipate the addition of records in EXTEND mode, a "space-not-found" error condition would occur. To utilize the overflow areas, we would have to add new records in random mode.

Updating

For Action 2, the data set is opened without specifying the processing mode in the OPEN macro. Instead, the MACRF parameter is used to indicate that updating is to be performed:

```
        OPEN    (MASTER)
                .
                .
                .
        MASTER  DCB     DSORG=IS,MACRF=(GL,PU),DDNAME=DORMS,EODAD=EOJ
```

Note that we must provide for an end-of-data routine, since the data set is to be read sequentially. We must also use PUTX to rewrite records that are being updated and locate mode buffering; PUT cannot be used, and neither can move mode. The processing logic is the same as that depicted in Figure 20.10.

Deleting

If the OS delete-flag option is specified (OPTCD=L), Action 4 can be combined with Action 2. To delete a record, we must move X'FF' into the delete-flag byte position *and rewrite the record.* Otherwise, the processing logic is again the same as that depicted in Figure 20.10.

Sequential Mode in DOS Systems

Extending

To add records to the end of an indexed sequential data set (Action 1), the processing logic is identical to that used for creating such data sets. There is no difference between a DOS Assembly Language program that creates an indexed sequential data set and one that extends it. The difference is in the job control statements, specifically in the //DLBL statement, as was described in Section 21.1: To create such a data set, we must code ISC in the appropriate //DLBL field; to extend or otherwise update such a data set, we must code ISE in that field.

Updating

For Action 2 (updating existing records), there are a number of differences to be aware of. They are almost all confined to the DTFIS macro, as shown below. But in addition, the imperative macros SETFL and ENDFL are not used for updating, and the PUT macro rather than the WRITE macro is used for rewriting an updated record.

The DTFIS macro must be coded as follows for sequential-mode updating:

```
MASTER  DTFIS DSKXTNT=3,IOROUT=ADDRTR,WORKS=OUTAREA,               X
              IOAREAS=MSTBUF,RECFORM=FIXBLK,RECSIZE=107,           X
              NRECDS=38,HINDEX=3330,KEYLEN=8,KEYLOC=2,CYLOFL=2,    X
              DEVADDR=SYS001,DEVICE=3330,TYPEFLE=INPUT,EOFADDR=EOJ
```

In this, we have used the dorm room file definitions for concreteness. But what is important to note is the inclusion of the TYPEFLE=INPUT parameter, the replacement of IOROUT=LOAD with IOROUT=ADDRTR, and the change from WORKL= to WORKS= and IOAREAL= to IOAREAS=. These changes constitute the mechanism by which the DOS access method is informed that sequential-mode updating is to take place, regardless of whether it's the dorm room file or any other indexed sequential file.

Deleting

Finally, it should be noted that Action 4 (deleting existing records) is not supported by DOS access methods. This is because there is no delete-flag option as there is in OS and no other mechanism other than user-program awareness. In other words, a user program can of course put X'FF' into the first byte of a record to flag it for deletion as is done in OS systems, and this is recommended. But any DOS Assembly Language program that reads that record will have to recognize the X'FF' code and ignore the record.

The SETL Macro in OS and DOS

The speed of the updating process for Actions 2 and 4 can be increased by use of SETL and ESETL, provided these macros are not executed too frequently. SETL enables updating to take place in any arbitrary data block without having to read preceding blocks in sequence. As mentioned in Chapter 19, one advantage of sequential access methods is that of being able to use two buffers: one to contain the logical records being processed and the other to allow the next data block to be read or the previous one written while processing of logical records takes place. Too-frequent use of SETL and ESETL can negate this advantage. Each execution of SETL may require access to the cylinder and track indexes, and each execution of ESETL may cause the most recently changed data block to be rewritten, even if the next transaction is for a record in that same block. One compromise is to use SETL once, at the beginning of execution, and then process the remaining records sequentially.

The format of the ESETL macro is simply

in OS:	ESETL	dcb-address
in DOS:	ESETL	dtf-address

The format of the SETL macro is

in OS:	SETL	dcb-address,option-code,key-address
in DOS:	SETL	dtf-address,option-code

The **key-address** field in the OS SETL macro designates the location of the key field that is to be used to identify the record at which sequential updating is to begin. In DOS, this key-address is specified by the KEYARG= parameter in the DTFIS macro instead of in the SETL macro. The **option-code** parameter indicates whether the key-address points to a complete record key or to a partial record key, i.e., a *key class,* also known as a *generic* key. It can also be used to indicate that retrieval is to begin at the first nondeleted record in the data set; in the latter case, the key-address parameter is omitted. The codes and their meanings are

DOS option code	OS option code	meaning
KEY	K	Start retrieval at the first non-deleted record whose key matches the key given at key-address.
---	KH	Start retrieval at the first non-deleted record whose key is equal to or greater than the key given at key-address.
GKEY	KC	Start retrieval at the first non-deleted record whose key class is equal to or greater than the key class given at key-address.
BOF	B	Start retrieval at the first non-deleted record in the data set.

(By *non-deleted record* we mean a record whose delete-flag byte position does not contain X'FF'. However, if using DOS, or if the delete option was not selected when the OS data set was created, all records are considered to be non-deleted.)

The concept of a *key class* can be very useful. A **key class** is defined by specifying the first n characters of a key, $1 \leq n \leq$ KEYLEN, and setting the remaining characters to *binary* zeroes. For example, in our dorm room file, a 4-byte dorm abbreviation could constitute a key class within the 8-byte record key. It could be specified as shown here:

```
         MVC      KEYCLASS,=8X'00'
         GET      TRANS,INAREA
         MVC      KEYCLASS(4),TDORM
         SETL     MASTER,KC,KEYCLASS      OS ONLY
         SETL     MASTER,GKEY             DOS ONLY
         GET      MASTER
           .
           .
           .
KEYCLASS DS       CL8                     8 BYTES NEEDED SINCE KEYLEN=8
```

In OS, the DCB macro indicates that SETL processing is to be used, by the way in which the MACRF= parameter is coded: MACRF=(GL,SK,PU). Otherwise, the DCB is coded the same as for other sequential-mode updating.

In DOS, the DTFIS macro doesn't specifically indicate that SETL processing is to be used, but the KEYARG= parameter must designate the name of the field that will contain the search key when SETL is executed: KEYARG=KEYCLASS in the previous example. Given this procedure, if the 4-byte dorm abbreviation in the TDORM field were C'HH   ', processing would begin with the first non-deleted record whose 8-byte key was C'HH   xxxx' or higher, regardless of the value of the room number xxxx.

There is, however, one precaution to observe: *a "record-not-found" error condition will occur if the specified key or key class is higher than any key or key class in the data set, or if there is not a matching key or key class in the data set.*

Figures 21.7 and 21.8
The processing logic that may be used when updating sequentially in conjunction with the SETL macro is outlined in Figure 21.7. Except for the inclusion of the SETL step during the initialization procedures, this outline is identical to that given in Figure 20.10 for sequential updating. Thus, as mentioned earlier, SETL is executed only once; thereafter the master file records are processed sequentially. The program of Figure 21.8 illustrates how this logic might be applied to the problem of updating the dorm room master file. As in the preceding chapter, it is assumed that the transaction data are "perfect": no transaction will request that a student be added to a room to which he or she has already been assigned or which is already full, and none will request that a student be deleted from a room to which he or she has not been assigned. In addition, it is assumed that the SETL does not result in a "record-not-found" condition.

21.5 OS RANDOM-MODE PROCESSING CONSIDERATIONS

As mentioned in the opening section of the chapter, BISAM is used for random updating and retrieval of logical records in an existing indexed sequential data set. It cannot be used to create a data set.

We will cover five main aspects of the use of OS macros and buffers: dynamic buffering, the READ and WRITE macro formats, the MACRF parameter, I/O synchronization, and invalid key conditions.

Dynamic Buffering

In dynamic buffering, the operating system allocates a buffer pool at open time. The DCB macro should include the BUFNO=1 parameter to indicate that only one buffer area is needed in the buffer pool. The operating system uses this buffer area each time a READ macro is invoked. The user program need not reserve space for the buffer pool or buffer area.

Data blocks are always read into the buffer area and, except in two situations, they are written from the same area. The exceptions occur when a new logical record is to be added to the data set and when the length of an existing variable-length record is to be changed. In both these situations, the user program's WRITE macro must designate the address of an area within the program that contains the logical record to be written.

In the other two possible updating situations—when updating an existing record without changing its length or when deleting an existing record via the delete-flag option—*the record must be changed in the buffer area* and rewritten from that area. This is similar to the use of locate mode in sequential processing. Unlike locate mode, however, the address of the logical record in the buffer area is not returned in Register 1 following a READ macro. Instead, it is stored in the data event control block, as shown in Figure 21.9.

READ and WRITE Macros and the MACRF Parameter

When we update an *existing* record in an indexed sequential data set, we must first read the data block containing the desired logical record. The key of that record must be specified by a parameter in a version of the READ macro known as READ KU. After modifying the record, it must be rewritten by a version of the WRITE macro known as WRITE K. When a *new* record is added to the data set, we must use a version of the WRITE macro known as WRITE KN.

Figure 21.7   Overview of sequential-mode updating via SETL.

```
UPDATE_WITH_SETL:

  INITIALIZATIONS;
  MAIN_PROCESSING;
  END_OF_DATA;

EXIT UPDATE_WITH_SETL.



INITIALIZATIONS:

  open transaction file;
  get first transaction record;
  open master file in UPDAT mode;
  SETL using key of first transaction record;
  get first master record;

EXIT INITIALIZATIONS.


MAIN_PROCESSING:

  REPEAT UNTIL (there is no more transaction data to process)
             OR (there is no more master data to process)

    IF transaction record key = master record key
    THEN
      IF transaction is delete
      THEN
        set delete flag;
        rewrite master record;
        get next master record;
      ELSE  { transaction is change }
        make changes to master record;
      END IF;
      get next transaction record;
    ELSE
      IF changes were made to master record
      THEN
        rewrite master record;
      END IF;
      get next master record;
    END IF;

  END UNTIL;

EXIT MAIN_PROCESSING.



END_OF_DATA:

  IF changes were made to master record
  THEN
    rewrite master record;
  END IF;

  close all data sets;

EXIT END_OF_DATA.
```

Indexed Sequential Organization   561

Figure 21.8   Updating the dorm room master file via QISAM and SETL.

```
FLAG LOCTN OBJECT CCDE      ADDR1  ADDR2  STMNT M SOURCE STATEMENT

     000000                                3   QISAM      CSECT
                                           4   *
                                           5   * THIS PROGRAM UPDATES THE DORM ROOM MASTER FILE USING QISAM IN
                                           6   *   LOCATE MODE.  TRANSACTIONS ARE IN SEQUENCE BY DORM AND ROOM
                                           7   *   NUMBER, CORRESPONDING TO MASTER FILE KEY SEQUENCE.
                                           8   *
                                           9   * THE FIRST TRANSACTION'S KEY IS USED TO START RETRIEVAL VIA SETL
                                          10   *   MACRO.  THEREAFTER PROCESSING IS DONE AS IN SEQTL FILES, EXCEPT
                                          11   *   THAT RECORDS MAY BE DELETED VIA DELETE FLAG OPTION (OPTCD=L) ES-
                                          12   *   TABLISHED WHEN MASTER FILE WAS CREATED.
                                          13   *
     000000 90 EC D00C                    14              STM    14,12,12(13)        STANDARD ENTRY.
     000004 05 C0                         15              BALR   12,0
     000006                               16              USING  *,12
     000006 50 D0 C32A      000330        17              ST     13,SAVE+4
     00000A 41 D0 C326      00032C        18              LA     13,SAVE
     000000                               19              USING  MAREA,11            DUMMY BASE REG FOR LOGICAL RECD
                                          20   *
                                          21   * INITIALIZATIONS
                                          22   *
     00000E                               23              OPEN   (MASTER,(UPDAT))    OPEN MASTER FOR UPDAT IN LOCATE MODE
     00001A                               29              OPEN   (TRANS,(INPUT))     OPEN TRANSACTIONS IN MOVE MODE
                                          35   *  DOS  *******
                                          36   *          OPEN  MASTER
                                          37   *          OPEN  TRANS
                                          38   ****************
     000026                               39              GET    TRANS,TAREA         GET FIRST TRANSACTION RECORD
     000034 D2 03 C19EC155 0001A4 00015B  44              MVC    KDORM,TDORM         MOVE 1ST TRANS KEY TO KEY AREA FOR
     00003A D2 03 C1A2C15D 0001A8 000163  45              MVC    KROOM,TROOM         USE IN 'SETL' MACRO
                                          46   *  DOS  *******
                                          47   *          SETL  MASTER,GKEY
                                          48   ****************
     000040                               49              SETL   MASTER,K,KAREA      START MASTER FILE RETRIEVAL AT RECD
     000058 45 E0 C0D2      0000D8        57              BAL    14,GETMSTR          WHOSE KEY MATCHES 1ST TRANS KEY.
                                          58   *
                                          59   * MAIN PROCESSING
                                          60   *
     00005C 05 03 B001C155 000001 00015B  61   MAINLOOP   CLC    MDORM,TDORM         IF KEY FIELD IN TRANS RECD DIFFERS
     000062 47 70 C080      000086        62              BNE    REWRITE             FROM THAT IN MASTER RECD, THEN GO
     000066 05 03 B005C15D 000005 000163  63              CLC    MROOM,TROOM         SEE IF MASTER RECD HAS HAD CHANGES
     00006C 47 70 C080      000086        64              BNE    REWRITE             MADE TO IT, AND IF SO REWRITE IT.
     000070 45 E0 C0E8      0000EE        65              BAL    14,UPDATING         IF TRANS KEY EQUALS MASTER KEY, CON-
     000074                               66              GET    TRANS,TAPEA         TINUE TO UPDATE THAT MASTER RECD,
     000082 47 F0 C056      00005C        71              B      MAINLOOP            GET NEXT TRANS RECD, AND REPEAT.
                                          72   *
     000086 95 FF C1D7      0001DD        73   REWRITE    CLI    MFLAG,BYP           WERE CHANGES MADE TO MASTER RECD
     00008A 47 80 C094      00009A        74              BE     BYPASS              IF NOT, BYPASS REWRITING IT.
     00008E                               75              PUTX   MASTER              IF SO, REWRITE IT (UPDATE IN PLACE).
                                          79   *  DOS  *******
                                          80   *          PUT   MASTER
                                          81   ****************
     00009A 45 E0 C0D2      0000D8        82   BYPASS     BAL    14,GETMSTR          THEN GET NEXT MASTER RECD,
     00009E 47 F0 C056      00005C        83              B      MAINLOOP            AND REPEAT THE MAIN PROCESSING LOOP.
                                          84   * END-OF-DATA
                                          85   *
     0000A2 95 FF C1C7      0001DD        86   EOJ        CLI    MFLAG,BYP           IF CHANGES WERE MADE TO MASTER
     0000A6 47 80 C0B2      0000B8        87              BE     EOJX                RECD, REWRITE IT VIA 'PUTX'.
     0000AA                               88              PUTX   MASTER
                                          92   *  DOS  *******
                                          93   *          PUT   MASTER
                                          94   ****************
     0000B6                               95   EOJX       CLOSE  (TRANS)             CLOSE DATA SETS
     0000C2                              101              CLOSE  (MASTER)
     0000CE 58 D0 C32A      000330       107              L      13,SAVE+4
     0000D2 98 EC D00C                   108              LM     14,12,12(13)        STANDARD EXIT
     0000D6 07 FE                        109              BR     14
                                         110   *  DOS  *******
                                         111   *EOJX       CLOSE TRANS
                                         112   *          CLOSE MASTER
                                         113   *          EOJ
                                         114   ****************
                                         115   * INTERNAL SUBROUTINE TO GET NEXT MASTER RECD IN LOCATE MODE.
                                         116   *  ENTERED VIA  BAL 14,GETMSTR .  RETURNS ADDR OF RECD IN R11 .
                                         117   *
     0000D8 18 2E                        118   GETMSTR    LR     2,14                SAVE RETURN ADDRESS
     0000DA 92 FF C1C7      0001DD       119              MVI    MFLAG,BYP           RESET RECORD-CHANGED FLAG.
     0000DE                              120              GET    MASTER              GET ADDR OF NEXT LOGICAL RECD IN R1.
     0000E8 18 B1                        124              LR     11,REGX             COPY ADR INTO DUMMY BASE REG, R11.
     0000EA 18 E2                        125              LR     14,2                RETURN TO CALLER.
     0000EC 07 FE                        126              BR     14
                                         127   *
                                         128   * SYMBOLIC REGISTER ADDRESS FOR LOCATE MODE
     000001                              129   REGX       EQU    1                   OS SYSTEMS
                                         130   *REGX       EQU    9                   DOS SYSTEMS
```

Figure 21.8   continued

```
FLAG LOCTN OBJECT CODE     ADDR1  ADDR2  STMNT M SOURCE STATEMENT

                                          131  * INTERNAL SUBROUTINE TO UPDATE AN EXISTING MASTER RECD.
                                          132  *   ENTERED VIA  BAL 14,UPDATING  WITH ADDR OF MASTER RECD IN R11.
                                          133  *
                                          134  * TRANSACTION CODE 'TTYPE' DETERMINES UPDATING ACTION
                                          135  *   TTYPE = C'1' ... ADD A NEW ROOM WITH NO STUDENTS
                                          136  *         = C'2' ... ADD A STUDENT NAME & I.D.
                                          137  *         = C'3' ... DELETE A STUDENT NAME & I.D.
                                          138  *         = C'4' ... DELETE ENTIRE MASTER RECD.
                                          139  *
000EE 95 F4 C151           000157        140  UPDATING CLI   TTYPE,C'4'         DETERMINE WHETHER IT'S A DELETE OR A
0000F2 47 70 C10A          000110        141           BNE   CHANGE               CHANGE REQUEST.
0000F6 18 4E                             142           LR    4,14               IF DELETE, SAVE R14 TO ALLOW 'PUTX'
0000F8 92 FF B000          000000        143           MVI   MDELETE,X'FF'       TO REWRITE THE RECD, AFTER FLAGGING
0000FC                                   144           PUTX  MASTER              IT FOR DELETION.
                                          148  *   DOS  *******
                                          149  *         PUT   MASTER
                                          150  ****************
000108 45 E0 C0D2          000008        151           BAL   14,GETMSTR         AFTER REWRITING, GET NEXT MASTER RECORD
00010C 18 E4                             152           LR    14,4               THEN RECOVER R14 AND EXIT TO CALLER.
00010E 07 FE                             153           BR    14
                                          154  *
000110 18 AB                             155  CHANGE   LR    10,11              SAVE LOGICAL RECD ADDR IN REG 10.
000112 95 F2 C151          000157        156           CLI   TTYPE,C'2'         ADD A STUDENT IF TTYPE = '2'
000116 47 80 C12C          000132        157           BE    ADD
00011A D5 08 B031C18B 000031 000191      158  DEL      CLC   MID,TID            OTHERWISE ASSUME IT'S CODE '3' AND LOOK
000120 47 80 C122          000128        159           BE    DEL1                FOR I.D. IN 1ST & 2ND DATA AREAS
000124 41 BB 0031          000031        160           LA    11,DATALNG(11)     IF NOT IN 1ST, MUST BE IN 2ND  INCR ADDR
000128 D2 30 B009C1A6 000009 0001AC      161  DEL1     MVC   MDATA1,BLANKS      REPLACE NAME & I.D. WITH BLANKS WHEN
00012E 47 F0 C146          00014C        162           B     EXIT                DELETING A STUDENT.
000132 D5 08 B031C1A6 000031 0001AC      163  ADD      CLC   MID,BLANKS         WHEN ADDING LOOK FOR VACANT STUDENT DATA
000138 47 80 C13A          000140        164           BE    ADD1                AREA.  IF NOT 1ST ONE, THEN ASSUME THAT
00013C 41 BB 0031          000031        165           LA    11,DATALNG(11)     2ND AREA IS VACANT, AND INCR ADDR.
000140 D2 27 B009C162 000009 000168      166  ADD1     MVC   MNAME,TNAME        MOVE NAME & I.D. FROM TRANS RECD TO STU-
000146 D2 08 B031C18B 000031 000191      167           MVC   MID,TID            DENT DATA AREA.
00014C 92 00 C1D7          00010D        168  EXIT     MVI   MFLAG,REWR         BEFORE RETURNING, SET RECD-CHGD FLAG AND
000150 18 BA                             169           LR    11,10               RESTORE DUMMY BASE REG CONTENTS.
000152 07 FE                             170           BR    14                 EXIT TO CALLER.


                                          171  * MASTER FILE LOGICAL RECORD AREA (VIA DUMMY SECTION)
                                          172  *
000000                                   173  MAREA    DSECT
000000                                   174  MDELETE  DS    CL1       BYTES 0       DELETE FLAG
000001                                   175  MDORM    DS    CL4             1-4     DORM ABBREVIATION
000005                                   176  MROOM    DS    CL4             5-8     DORM ROOM
000009                                   177  MDATA1   DS    CL49            9-57    1ST STUDENT DATA AREA
00003A                                   178  MDATA2   DS    CL49            58-106  2ND STUDENT DATA AREA
000009                      00006B       179           ORG   MDATA1    REDEFINE STUDENT DATA AREA
000009                                   180  MNAME    DS    CL40            9-48    STUDENT NAME FIELD
000031                                   181  MID      DS    CL9             49-57   STUDENT I.D. FIELD
000031                                   182  DATALNG  EQU   *-MNAME                 LENGTH OF STUDENT AREA
000154                                   183  QISAM    CSECT
                                          184  *
                                          185  *
                                          186  * TRANSACTION INPUT AREA
                                          187  *
000154                                   188  TAREA    DS    CL80      RESERVE 80 BYTES FOR CARD IMAGE
000154                      0001A4       189           ORG   TAREA     BEGIN REDEFINITION OF INPUT AREA
000154                                   190           DS    CL3       COL 1-3   UNUSED
000157                                   191  TTYPE    DS    CL1             4     TRANS TYPE CODE
000158                                   192           DS    CL3             5-7   UNUSED
00015B                                   193  TDORM    DS    CL4             8-11  DORM ABBREVIATION
00015F                                   194           DS    CL4             12-15 UNUSED
000163                                   195  TROOM    DS    CL4             16-19 DORM ROOM NUMBER
000167                                   196           DS    CL1             20    UNUSED
000168                                   197  TNAME    DS    CL40            21-60 STUDENT NAME
000190                                   198           DS    CL1             61    UNUSED
000191                                   199  TID      DS    CL9             62-70 STUDENT I.D.
0001A4                      00019A       200           ORG
                                          201  * KEY AREA, AND OTHER CONSTANTS
                                          202  *
0001A4                                   203  KAREA    DS    CL8       RESERVE 8 BYTES FOR RECORD KEY
0001A4                      0001AC       204           ORG   KAREA
0001A4                                   205  KDORM    DS    CL4       BYTES 0-3 DORM ABBREVIATION
0001A8                                   206  KROOM    DS    CL4             4-7 DORM ROOM NUMBER
0001AC                      0001AC       207           ORG
                                          208  *
0001AC 40                                209  BLANKS   DC    (DATALNG)C' '  DATALNG IS LENGTH OF STUDENT DATA AREA
0001DD FF                                210  MFLAG    DC    X'FF'          X'FF'=DON'T REWRITE;X'00'=DO REWRITE.
0000FF                                   211  BYP      EQU   X'FF'          BYP = RECD NOT CHGD, DONT REWRITE IT.
000000                                   212  REWR     EQU   X'00'          REWR = RECD CHGD, REWRITE IT.


                                          213  * DCB'S FOR TRANSACTION FILE ('SYSIN')
                                          214  *   AND MASTER FILE WITH FIXED-LENGTH RECORDS, IN LOCATE MODE.
                                          215  *
0001DE                                   216  TRANS    DCB   DSORG=PS,MACRF=(GM),DDNAME=SYSIN,EODAD=EOJ,          X
                                          217                RECFM=FB,LRECL=80,BLKSIZE=4080
                                          269  *INBUF   DS    CL80
```

Indexed Sequential Organization   563

Figure 21.8   continued

```
FLAG LOCTN OBJECT CODE    ADDR1  ADDR2  STMNT M SOURCE STATEMENT

                                          270   *
        000240                             271   MASTER    DCB    DSORG=IS,MACRF=(GL,SK,PU),DDNAME=DORMS,EODAD=EOJ

                                          338   *   DOS  *******
                                          339   *TRANS     DTFCD  DEVADDR=SYSIPT,WORKA=YES,IOAREA1=INBUF,EOFADDR=EOJ,     X
                                          340   *                 DEVICE=2540
                                          341   *
                                          342   *MASTER    DTFIS  DEVADDR=SYS001,DEVICE=3330,DSKXTNT=3,HINDEX=3330,       X
                                          343   *                 RECFORM=FIXBLK,RECSIZE=107,NRECDS=38,IOAREAS=MSTBUF,    X
                                          344   *                 KEYLEN=8,KEYLOC=2,CYLOFL=2,IOREG=(REGX),                X
                                          345   *                 IOROUT=ADDRTR,TYPEFLE=SEQNTL,EOFADDR=EOJ,KEYARG=KAREA
                                          346   ***************

                                          347   *
                                          348   * REGISTER SAVE AREA
                                          349   *
        00032C                             350   SAVE      DS     18F

                                          351   *  DOS  *******
                                          352   *SAVE      DS     9D
                                          353   *         LTORG
                                          354   *         DS     0D
                                          355   *MSTBUF    DS     CL4066
                                          356   ***************

                                          357             END
```

CROSS-REFERENCE

```
SYMBOL     LEN   VALUE  DEFN    REFERENCES

ADD        00006 000132 00163   00157
ADD1       00006 000140 00166   00164
BLANKS     00001 0001AC 00209   00161   00163
BYP        00001 0300FF 00211   00073   00086   00119
BYPASS     00004 00009A 00082   00074
CHANGE     00002 000110 00155   00141
DATALNG    00001 000031 00182   00160   00165   00209
DEL        00006 00011A 00158
DEL1       00006 000128 00161   00159
EOJ        00004 0000A2 00086   00238   00291
EOJX       00004 0000B8 00097   00087
EXIT       00004 00014C 00168   00162
GETMSTR    00002 0000C8 00118   00057   00082   00151
KAREA      00008 0001A4 00203   00051   00204
KDORM      00004 0001A4 00205   00044
KROOM      00004 0001A8 00206   00045
MAINLOOP   00006 00005C 00061   00071   00083
MAREA      00001 000000 00173   00019
MASTER     00004 000230 00273   00027   00050   00076   00089   00105   00121   00145
MDATA1     00031 000009 00177   00161   00179
MDATA2     00031 00003A 00178
MDELETE    00001 000000 00174   00143
MDORM      00004 000001 00175   00061
MFLAG      00001 0001DD 00210   00073   00086   00119   00168
MID        00009 000031 00181   00158   00163   00167
MNAME      00028 000009 00180   00166   00182
MROOM      00004 000005 00176   00063
QISAM      00001 000000 00183
REGX       00001 0000C1 00129   00124
REWR       00001 000000 00212   00168
REWRITE    00004 000086 00073   00062   00064
SAVE       00004 00032C 00350   00017   00018   00107
TAREA      00050 000154 00188   00041   00068   00189
TDORM      00004 00015B 00193   00044   00061
TID        00009 000151 00199   00158   00167
TNAME      00028 000168 00197   00166
TRANS      00004 0001E0 00217   00033   00040   00067   00099
TROOM      00004 030163 00195   00045   00063
TTYPE      00001 000157 00191   00140   00156
UPDATING   00004 0000EE 00140   00065
```

Figure 21.9 BISAM data event control block format.

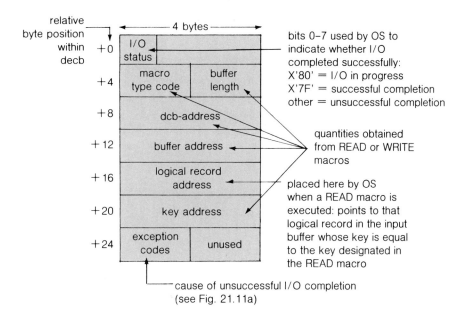

The general form of the READ and WRITE macros is as shown below. The *type* parameter is coded as K, KU, or KN to designate the version of the macro being used.

$$\begin{Bmatrix} \text{READ} \\ \text{WRITE} \end{Bmatrix} \text{decb-name,type,dcb-address,buffer-address,buffer-length,key-address,} \begin{Bmatrix} \text{MF=E} \\ \text{MF=L} \end{Bmatrix}$$

The keyword parameters MF=E and MF=L identify what is known as the *execute* and *list* forms of these macros. The use of the list and execute forms is necessary in order to be able to read and write from the same buffer area using the same data event control block. The list form (MF=L) must be placed in a data area of the source module, not intermixed among instructions to be executed at run time. The execute form (MF=E) *is* placed among instructions to be executed, just as a GET or PUT or standard READ or WRITE would be. Whenever the execute form is processed at run time, the data event control block created by the macro expansion of the corresponding list form is used *as though it were part of the expansion of the execute form.* The correspondence between the two forms is identified by the decb-name parameter.

MF=E and MF=L

As an example of these concepts, consider the following statements.

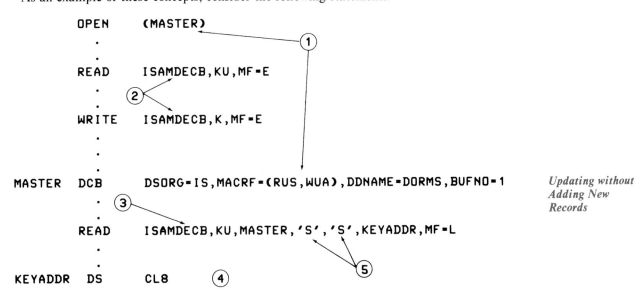

Updating without Adding New Records

① *Open Mode*	There are several points to be noted. First, the OPEN macro does not indicate the processing mode; the MACRF parameter is used for this purpose. In this example, it indicates that the dataset will be opened to enable updating using dynamic buffering with BISAM:

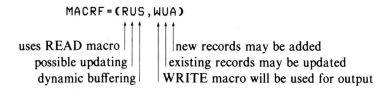

Other possible MACRF codes are summarized in Figure 21.10.

② *MF=E*   Second, to update existing records, execution of the READ KU macro must be followed by execution of the WRITE K macro; both must refer to the same data event control block by means of the execute form MF=E.

③ *MF=L*   Third, the information in the data event control block named ISAMDECB is initialized by the expansion of the list form of the READ macro. Figure 21.9 indicates the information that is initially placed in that control block: type, dcb-address, buffer-address, buffer-length, and key-address. Thus, the execute forms do not have to respecify these items unless they are to be changed or were changed by another macro. The execute form of the READ macro specifies type KU because the execute form of the WRITE refers to the same data event control block and specifies a different type, K. Since the other parameters are not changed by any macro, they need not be respecified.

④ *Symbolic Key*   Fourth, the area designated by the key-address field must contain the key of the record to be read. This must also be the key of the record that is being updated. The key-address area must be separate from the buffer area.

⑤ *Dynamic Buffering*   Fifth, the use of 'S' (enclosed in apostrophes) in the buffer-address and buffer-length fields of the READ and WRITE macros has the following meanings:

   with READ macro:
      buffer-address = 'S' means that dynamic buffering is to be used.
      buffer-length = 'S' means that the number of bytes to be read is to be taken from the count field of the record (for blocked records, 'S' must be coded).

   with WRITE macro:
      buffer-address = 'S' means that the data block is in the same dynamic buffer used in the previous READ KU macro.
      buffer-length = 'S' is always specified in a WRITE macro unless a variable-length record is being rewritten with a length different from its previous length.

Adding New Records   If we were adding new records instead of or in addition to updating existing records, a WRITE KN macro would have to be used to add the new records. To do so, the following rule should be observed: *all records or blocks of records read using a READ KU macro with a given data control block macro (DCB) must be written back with a WRITE K macro before a new record can be added, unless the READ KU and the WRITE KN that are used to add a record refer to the same data event control block.*

Following this rule, it is most often simplest to let the READ KU, WRITE K, and WRITE KN macros all refer to the same data event control block. However, dynamic buffering (buffer-address = 'S') cannot be specified for the WRITE KN macro because the new record is not in the dynamic buffer: it is in some logical record area within the user's program. The record area must include a 16-byte prefix used by the operating system. The logical record itself begins in the 17th byte of the area, as shown below. (It is not blocked, since it will either be written onto an overflow track or will replace an existing record in a prime data block.)

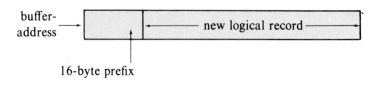

Figure 21.10   Principal MACRF code combinations for BISAM.

intended processing mode	WAIT macro		CHECK macro		code	meaning
	dynamic buffering	direct buffering	dynamic buffering	direct buffering		
input only	(RS)	(R)	(RSC)	(RC)	A	new records are to be added (WRITE KN)
output only	----	(WA)	-----	(WAC)	C	CHECK macro is used to test for I/O completion (if C not coded, then WAIT must be used)
updating existing records	(RUS,WU)	(RU,WU)	(RUSC,WUC)	(RUC,WUC)	R	READ macro is used
					S	dynamic buffering is requested in READ macros
updating, and/or adding new records	(RUS,WUA)	(RU,WUA)	(RUSC,WUAC)	(RUC,WUAC)	U	existing records will be updated (when U is combined with R, it must also be combined with W)
					W	WRITE macro is used

As an illustration of this rule, consider these statements:

```
          OPEN      (MASTER)
                .
          READ      ISAMDECB,KU,,'S',MF=E
                .
                .
          WRITE     ISAMDECB,K,,'S',MF=E
                .
                .
          WRITE     ISAMDECB,KN,,BUFFER,MF=E
                .
MASTER    DCB       DSORG=IS,MACRF=(RUS,WUA),DDNAME=DORMS,BUFNO=1
          READ      ISAMDECB,KU,MASTER,'S','S',KEYADDR,MF=L
KEYADDR   DS        CL8             SPACE FOR RECORD KEY
BUFFER    DS        CL123           SPACE FOR OUTPUT AREA
          ORG       BUFFER
          DS        CL16            16-BYTE SYSTEM PREFIX
NEWRECD   DS        CL107           107-BYTE LOGICAL RECORD
          ORG
```

With these statements, either of the two WRITE macros can be executed following the READ KU macro; the choice depends on processing logic not shown. The important point is that all three macros use the same data event control block. Following the execution of the READ KU macro, either the WRITE K, the WRITE KN, or the READ KU will be the next read or write request executed. This will release the data block that was being held by the operating system pending possible update, and it will thereby satisfy the requirements of the rule. Note that even when adding a new record, the separate key-address area must contain the key of that record.

I/O Synchronization and Invalid Key Conditions

In BISAM processing, as in all basic access methods in the IBM 360 and 370 systems, there must be a provision to delay execution of the user's program until the I/O data transfer has been completed. This is the I/O synchronization function discussed in Chapter 19. In addition, there must be a provision for detecting when an invalid key condition has occurred during a READ or WRITE operation. Both of these provisions can be accomplished through the use of the CHECK macro or the WAIT macro.

We cannot intermix the use of CHECK and WAIT with a given data set: the choice must be designated in the MACRF parameter. Use of the CHECK macro also requires that the user program include an internal subroutine whose purpose is to process any invalid key or other error conditions

exception code bit position	--- source ---		meaning when bit is set to '1'
	READ	WRITE	
0	X	type K	logical record not found in data set
1	X	X	record length invalid
2		type KN	space not found for new record in overflow areas
3	X	type K	dynamic buffering request invalid or update WRITE request invalid
4	X	X	uncorrectable I/O data transfer error
5	X	X	unreachable block
6	X		record just read was in overflow area
7		type KN	duplicate record detected: the new record to be added has same key as an existing record
8-15			used by operating system

occurring during a READ or WRITE operation. The address of this subroutine must be designated by the SYNAD= parameter in the DCB macro: when an error condition occurs, the operating system transfers control to the SYNAD subroutine. If no error condition occurs, control is transferred to the instruction immediately following the CHECK macro.

I/O Synchronization

The use of the WAIT macro does not depend on the SYNAD address: control is always transferred to the instruction immediately following the WAIT macro, and it is then up to the user's program to determine what further action should be taken. Since the WAIT macro is simpler to use, we will focus on it and not discuss the CHECK macro further.

The simplest form of the WAIT macro is

```
WAIT    ECB=decb-name
```

OS Status Byte

The name of the data event control block in the operand must be the same as the name in the corresponding READ or WRITE macro. When WAIT is executed, the user's program will be delayed until the I/O data transfer is completed. When control is returned to the instruction following WAIT, the user's program must test the exception code bits in the data event control block to determine the cause of completion: successful or unsuccessful, and, if unsuccessful, why. The exception code bits are stored in byte positions 24 and 25 of the data event control block (see Figs. 21.9 and 21.11a) and may be tested with a TM instruction.

I/O Error-Handling

If all the exception bits are zero, or if all but bit 6 are zero, the I/O data transfer was completed successfully. (Bit 6 merely records the fact that a record was read from an overflow area and is not, properly speaking, an error condition.) If any of the other bits are not zero, the corresponding error condition indicated in Figure 21.11a occurred during the I/O operation and the user program must take some appropriate action. Ordinarily, there is not much that can be done except to terminate the program by means of the abnormal end (ABEND) macro, perhaps preceding that by writing an error message. However, two of the eight exception code bits correspond to invalid key conditions; the user's program need not be terminated when these occur.

Invalid Key Conditions

If bit 0 (**record not found**) is on, this may simply have been caused by a transaction request to update a record that does not exist in the data set. The invalid transaction can be written to an error message file and the program can process the next transaction. Similarly, if bit 7 (**duplicate record**) is on, it may be due to a request to add a new record to the data set when a record with that key already exists in the data set. After writing an appropriate error message, the program can process the next transaction. The processing steps that will accomplish these procedures are presented in Section 21.7.

21.6 DOS RANDOM-MODE PROCESSING CONSIDERATIONS

As mentioned in Section 21.1, the ISAM access method is used for both sequential and random processing in DOS. But as can be expected there are a number of differences between the two processing modes. In this section we will cover five main aspects of DOS random-mode processing: buffering, DTFIS parameters, READ and WRITE macros, I/O synchronization, and invalid key conditions.

Buffering

As in all DOS access methods, the user's program must reserve buffer space via the DS directive and designate the buffer that is to be used by specifying an IOAREAx parameter in the DTFIS macro. In ISAM random-mode processing, there are two different types of buffers that must be reserved: one for adding new records to a file and one for retrieving and updating existing records from the file. In the following discussion, we will assume that the record format is defined as RECFORM=FIXBLK. The considerations for buffering are slightly different if unblocked records are processed and will not be discussed in this text.

Buffer for Adding New Records

The buffer used for adding new records is designated by the IOAREAL= parameter. A work area for new records must be designated by WORKL=, because locate mode is not permitted when adding or inserting new records. The IOAREAL buffer must, just as when creating a file, include space for three consecutive fields: the count and key fields that are used by the access method when writing in count-key-data format, and the data block field:

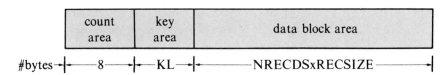

The length of the data block area must be at least 10 bytes longer than the length of one logical record, in order to provide space for the 10-byte next-record-address field (sequence link) in records that are added to the overflow area.

Buffer for Retrieval and Updating

The buffer used for retrieving and updating existing records is designated by the IOAREAR= parameter, and the corresponding logical record work area is designated by the WORKR= parameter unless locate mode is used. (Locate mode can be used when retrieving or updating, but we will not consider it. As will be recalled, it is designated by the IOREG=(n) parameter, with $2 \le n \le 12$, where n is the address of the register in which the operating system returns a logical record's address.)

The IOAREAR= buffer must *not* include space for the count and key fields; space is reserved only for the data block. But as with IOAREAL=, the data block area must be at least 10 bytes longer than the length of a logical record to accommodate the sequence link field in overflow records.

Thus, a DTFIS macro for the random-mode updating of the dorm room master file would contain at least the following parameters: IOAREAL=, IOAREAR=, WORKL=, WORKR=; and each of the four areas would be defined by suitable DS directives. The program of Figure 20.14 shows how this would be done.

DTFIS Parameters

In addition to the buffering parameters mentioned above, and in addition to the parameters mentioned in the section on creating indexed sequential files, the DTFIS macro must also include the following parameters for random-mode processing:

IOROUT=ADDRTR	specifies that retrieval, updating of existing records, and insertion of new records may take place at run time
TYPEFLE=RANDOM	specifies that the ADDRTR functions will be done via random-mode processing
KEYARG=keyfieldname	specifies the symbolic address of the area in which the key of a record must be placed in order to perform random retrieval or updating

The KEYARG= parameter is the same one used in sequential-mode processing with the SETL macro. In both that situation and in the present one the operating system uses the key that is stored in the KEYARG field to search its indexes for the location of the data block that contains the logical record whose key matches the one in the KEYARG field. The user's program must know what that key is; it will usually obtain it from a transaction record. If it doesn't know the key, the record cannot be retrieved or updated.

READ and WRITE Macros

The READ and WRITE macros must be used with random-mode processing; GET and PUT are not permitted. The macros have simple formats:

To retrieve existing records
```
READ      dtf-address,KEY
```

To update the most recently retrieved record
```
WRITE     dtf-address,KEY
```

To insert or add a new record
```
WRITE     dtf-address,NEWKEY
```

The READ KEY and WRITE KEY macros use the IOAREAR buffer area and the WORKR record area. The key of the record that is to be retrieved or updated must be stored in the KEYARG field before a READ KEY or WRITE KEY is executed.

The WRITE NEWKEY macro uses the IOAREAL buffer area and the WORKL record area. The key of the record being written need not be placed in the KEYARG field before executing a WRITE NEWKEY.

Note that a record that is to be updated must first be read via READ KEY, and it must be written via WRITE KEY before another READ or WRITE macro is executed. It is not, however, necessary to update every record that is read. If a record is not to be updated, then the READ KEY macro can be followed by another READ KEY for a different record or by a WRITE NEWKEY for a different record.

All READ and WRITE macros must be immediately followed by a WAITF macro, as described below.

I/O Synchronization and Invalid Key Conditions

I/O Synchronization

The I/O synchronization requirements discussed in Chapter 19 are achieved via the WAITF macro, whose format is

opcode	operand
WAITF	dtf-address

Execution of WAITF ensures that the I/O data-transfer operation has either been completed or has been prematurely terminated due to an error condition. The WAITF macro must therefore be executed immediately after each READ or WRITE macro so that further processing is not attempted on an incomplete or nonexistent record.

DOS Status Byte

When the user program regains control following the WAITF macro, it can determine whether or not an error occurred by testing bits stored by the operating system in the DTFIS macro expansion area. These bits are in a single status byte whose symbolic address is always the dtfname suffixed with the letter C. For example, for our MASTER DTFIS the status byte's name is MASTERC.

The meaning of the bits in the status byte depends on whether or not we are in LOAD mode, because the operating system uses the same byte to record error status information when in LOAD mode *and* when not in LOAD mode. Thus, there are two sets of bits, as shown in Figures 21.11b and 21.11c. We will consider only the IOROUT=ADDRTR case, i.e., Figure 21.11b.

I/O Error-Handling

If all the bits in the status byte are zero, or if all but bit 7 is zero, the I/O data-transfer operation was completed successfully. If any of the other bits are not zero, the corresponding error condition indicated in Figure 21.11b occurred during the I/O operation and the user program must take some appropriate action.

Figure 21.11b   Error code bits if IOROUT=ADD, RETRVE, or ADDRTR in DOS. (See also DOS/VS Supervisor & I/O Macros, *IBM Publication GC33-5373.)*

error code bit position	meaning when bit is set to '1'
0	an uncorrectable I/O error other than those listed below
1	a wrong length record was detected
2	end of file was detected during sequential retrieval
3	record not found in file
4	record i.d. (CCHHR) specified in SETL is not in prime area
5	duplicate record detected: the new record to be added has the same record key as an existing record in the file
6	the cylinder or independent overflow area that was to be used for adding a record is full, and the record can't be added
7	the retrieved record is stored in an overflow area

Figure 21.11c   Error code bits if IOROUT=LOAD in DOS. (See also IBM Publication GC33-5373.)

error code bit position	meaning when bit is set to '1'
0	an uncorrectable I/O error other than those listed below
1	a wrong length record was detected
2	prime data area full: new extents must be allocated
3	cylinder index area not large enough: must allocate more
4	master index area not large enough: must allocate more
5	duplicate record detected: the record being added has the same key as the previous one that was added
6	sequence check: the record being added is not in proper sequence
7	prime data area does not have enough space left to write an end-of-file (EOF) record

Ordinarily, there is not much that can be done except to terminate the program by means of the abnormal termination macro (CANCEL), perhaps preceding that by writing an error message. However, two of the eight error bits correspond to invalid key conditions; the user's program need not be terminated when these occur.

If bit 3 (**record not found**) is on, this may simply have been caused by a transaction request to update a record that does not exist on the master file. The invalid transaction can be written to an error message file and the program can process the next transaction. Similarly, if bit 5 (**duplicate record**) is on, it may be due to a request to add a new record to the file when a record with that key already exists in the file. After writing an appropriate error message, the program can process the next transaction. The processing steps that will accomplish these invalid key procedures are presented in the next section.

Invalid Key Conditions

21.7   UPDATING IN RANDOM MODE

In random-mode update procedures, the transaction records need not be in the same key sequence as the master file records. Nevertheless, it is customary (and it can conserve overall processing time) to place all transaction records for a given key together, in sequence by transaction code. When this is done, there need only be one READ and one WRITE per updated record and only one WRITE per new record.

Note that all four updating actions are possible in random mode: new records can be inserted in their proper sequence or added to the end of the data set, and existing records can be changed or deleted. Remember that in the general updating procedures used for sequential data sets, we have to create a new data set consisting of all the new, changed, and unchanged records of the existing data set, but excluding the deleted records. In that procedure, the existing data set is not altered in any way. In random-mode updating, *the existing data set is altered:* it is not copied to a new data set. Records for which there are no update transactions are not read at all.

Figure 21.12

The updating procedures may be divided into three main phases: initialization, main processing, and end-of-data. This is shown in Figures 21.12a–21.12c, to which the following discussion is oriented.

Initialization

In the initialization phase, the master and transaction files are opened and the first transaction record is read. An error report file (SYSOUT or SYSLST, for example) may also be opened if we intend to list transactions that cause invalid key conditions or uncorrectable errors. The first master record is not read in the initialization phase. A master record is read only when it is determined that a record is to be changed or deleted in the main processing phase. That record may then be read without having to read any records that precede it in sequence.

Main Processing

The first step in each iteration of the main processing phase is to move the key of the current transaction record to the area that is designated by the key-address parameter in an OS READ or WRITE macro and by the KEYARG= parameter in a DOS DTFIS macro. The key in the key-address area is used by the operating system to determine the location in secondary memory of the record that is to be read or written. *When adding a new record,* the data in the transaction record is used to begin construction of the new record in the area reserved for that purpose. Since successive transaction records may contain additional information for the same new record, the new record is not written until all consecutive transaction records with that new record's key have been processed. New records are written in OS by the WRITE KN macro and in DOS by the WRITE NEWKEY macro.

When updating an existing record, that record must first be read from the master file by means of the OS READ KU or DOS READ KEY macro. If the update request is to delete the record, the delete flag (X'FF') is moved into the first position of the record, the record is rewritten in OS via WRITE K and in DOS via WRITE KEY, and the next transaction is read to repeat the main processing phase. If the update request is to change an existing record, the record is rewritten only after all transaction records with that master record's key have been processed.

End-of-Data

When the transaction file end-of-data condition occurs, one of three possible situations can exist:

1. If a new record was being constructed at the time end-of-data occurred, that record must be written before processing can be terminated.
2. If an existing record was being changed, it must be rewritten.
3. If an existing record had just been deleted, there is no record to write or rewrite.

Note that the master file will never reach an end-of-data condition because records are read from it in random order, not sequentially.

Invalid Key

Also note that an invalid key condition can occur when reading or writing a master record, unless it is assumed that the transaction data are "perfect," as was the case for previous discussions in the text. To illustrate how to process these conditions, assume that they may occur as follows: When attempting to read a record that is to be updated, an invalid key condition would occur if that record were not on the master file. If this happens, the transaction causing the error is printed and the next transaction is read. When attempting to write a new record, an invalid key condition would occur if a record with that key were already on the master file. If this happens, the transaction causing the error is printed, and—except during end-of-data processing—the next transaction record is read. When attempting to rewrite an updated record, an invalid key condition cannot occur due to a transaction record error. Since an error detected during a rewrite operation will either be due to a hardware malfunction or to a programming error—for example, an unintended alteration of the key or of the data event control block—it will be treated as an uncorrectable error.

Figure 21.12a   Overview of random-mode updating procedure.

```
RANDOM_UPDATE:

   INITIALIZATION;
   MAIN_PROCESSING;
   END_OF_TRANSACTION_DATA;

EXIT RANDOM_UPDATE.



INITIALIZATION:

   open master file for updates and additions;
   open error report file;
   open transaction file for input;
   get first transaction record;

EXIT INITIALIZATION.



MAIN_PROCESSING:

   REPEAT UNTIL there is no more transaction data to process

      move transaction key to key-address area;

      IF transaction is update
      THEN
        process consecutive transactions to update existing record
           and get next transaction;  { see figure 21.12b }
      ELSE  { transaction is add }
        process consecutive transactions to add new record
           and get next transaction;  { see figure 21.12c }
      END IF;

   END UNTIL;

EXIT MAIN_PROCESSING.



END_OF_TRANSACTION_DATA:

   IF end-of-data flag indicates rewrite
   THEN
     rewrite last record;
   ELSE
     IF end-of-data flag indicates write
     THEN
       write last record;
     ELSE
       { end-of-data flag indicates bypass -- no action }
     END IF;
   END IF;

EXIT END_OF_TRANSACTION_DATA.
```

Figure 21.12b   Random-mode processing to update existing records.

```
set end-of-data flag to rewrite;
read master record and wait for completion;

IF uncorrectable error
THEN
  terminate program;
END IF;

IF invalid key error
THEN

  print error message;
  set end-of-data flag to bypass;
  get next transaction record;

ELSE { no errors }
  REPEAT UNTIL (delete has been processed)
               OR
               (transaction record key different from record being changed)

    IF transaction is delete
    THEN
      flag record for deletion;
      rewrite master record and wait for completion;
      IF any rewrite errors
      THEN
        terminate program;
      END IF;
      set end-of-data flag to bypass;
      get next transaction record;

    ELSE  { transaction is change }
      change record in buffer;
      get next transaction record;
      IF transaction record key different from record being changed
      THEN
        rewrite master and wait for completion;
        IF any rewrite errors
        THEN
          terminate program;
        END IF;
      END IF;
    END IF;

  END UNTIL;

END IF;
```

Figure 21.12c Random-mode processing to add new records.

```
set end-of-data flag to write;
begin constructing new master record;

REPEAT UNTIL transaction key is different from record being constructed

   get next transaction record;
   IF transaction key is same as record being constructed
   THEN
      continue constructing new record;
   END IF;

END UNTIL;

write new record and wait for completion;

IF uncorrectable error
THEN
   terminate program;
END IF;

IF invalid key error
THEN
   print error message;
END IF;
```

The program in Figure 21.13 illustrates the BISAM updating procedures for the dorm room master file, using the transaction record format that was described in Figure 20.5. When studying this program, note that a DSECT directive has been used to define the record fields for the master file records. For records that are to be updated, the dummy base register is loaded with the logical record address made available in the data event control block following the READ KU macro. For new records that are to be added, the dummy base register is loaded with the address of the logical record area reserved for new records. Interspersed comment statements show how similar actions would be accomplished in DOS systems.

Figure 21.13

21.8 RETRIEVAL

To retrieve information from an indexed sequential data set without updating, one of three procedures can be followed:

1. The procedure outlined for sequential data sets in Section 20.11 can be used with sequential-mode processing methods.
2. The procedure outlined for sequential data sets can be used in conjunction with the SETL macro with sequential-mode processing.
3. A random retrieval procedure can be used.

In all three retrieval procedures, the DCB macro parameters—BLKSIZE, CYLOFL, KEYLEN, LRECL, NTM, OPTCD, RECFM, and RKP—are not specified in the DCB macro or DD statement; instead, their values are obtained at open time from the data set control block. There is no similar constraint for DTFIS parameters.

Figure 21.13 *Updating the dorm room master file in BISAM.*

```
FLAG LOCTN OBJECT CODE      ADDR1   ADDR2  STMNT M SOURCE STATEMENT

       000000                               3   BISAM     CSECT
                                            4   *
                                            5   *
                                            6   * THIS PROGRAM UPDATES THE DORM ROOM MASTER FILE,
                                            7   *   IN RANDOM MODE USING  BISAM .
                                            8   *
                                            9   * TRANSACTIONS ARE NOT NECESSARILY IN KEY SEQ, BUT ALL CONSECUTIVE
                                           10   *   TRANS RECORDS FOR A GIVEN KEY ARE PROCESSED BEFORE WRITING THE
                                           11   *   CORRESPONDING MASTER RECORD.
                                           12   *
                                           13   * INVALID KEY ERRORS ARE REPORTED ON 'SYSOUT' WITHOUT TERMINATING
                                           14   *   THE PROGRAM.  THE FIRST UNCORRECTABLE ERROR TO OCCUR CAUSES
                                           15   *   PROGRAM TERMINATION.
                                           16   *
       000000 90 EC D0CC                   17             STM    14,12,12(13)      STANDARD ENTRY
       000004 05 C0                        18             BALR   12,0
       000006                              19             USING  *,12
       000006 50 D0 C672       000678      20             ST     13,SAVE+4
       00000A 41 D0 C66E       000674      21             LA     13,SAVE
       000000                              22             USING  MAREA,11           DUMMY BASE REG FOR MASTER RECD AREA
                                           23   * OS ONLY ------------------------------------------------
       000000                              24             USING  DECBD,9            DUMMY BASE REG FOR DATA EVENT CTL BLOCK
       00000E 41 90 C2B6       0002BC      25             LA     9,MSTRDECB
                                           26   *------------------------------------------------
                                           27   * INITIALIZATIONS
                                           28   *
       000012                              29             OPEN   (MASTER)           OPEN MASTER FOR UPDATES & ADDITIONS
       00001E                              35             OPEN   (REPORT,(OUTPUT))  OPEN ERROR REPORT FILE
       00002A                              41             OPEN   (TRANS,(INPUT))    OPEN TRANSACTION FILE
                                           47   * DOS ******
                                           48   *         OPEN   MASTER
                                           49   *         OPEN   REPORT
                                           50   *         OPEN   TRANS
                                           51   ***************
       000036                              52             GET    TRANS,TAREA        GET 1ST TRANS RECD
                                           57   *
                                           58   * MAIN PROCESSING
                                           59   *
       000044 D2 03 C37DC38C 000383 000392 60   MAINLOOP  MVC    KDORM,TDORM        MOVE TRANSACTION KEY TO KEY-ADDRESS AREA
       00004A D2 03 C381C394 000387 00039A 61             MVC    KROOM,TROOM
       000050 95 F1 C388       00038E      62             CLI    TTYPE,C'1'         TRANS CODE = '1' MEANS ADD NEW RECORD
       000054 47 80 C09E       0000A4      63             BE     NEWADD
       000058 47 F0 C0E2       0000E8      64             B      UPDATE             OTHERWISE, GO PROCESS UPDATES
                                           65   * END-OF-TRANSACTION-DATA
                                           66   *
                                           67   *     END-OF-DATA FLAG  'EODFLG' CONTROLS PROCESSING DECISIONS
                                           68   *             IF 'EODFLG' = WR   = X'0F', THEN WRITE LAST MASTER RECORD.
                                           69   *             IF 'EODFLG' = REWR = X'F0', THEN REWRITE LAST MASTER RECORD.
                                           70   *             IF 'EODFLG' = BYP  = X'FF', THEN DON'T WRITE OR REWRITE.
                                           71   *
       00005C 95 FF C4C1       0004C7      72   EOJ       CLI    EODFLG,BYP         EODFLG=BYP  IF END-OF-DATA OCCURRED AFTER
       000060 47 80 C072       000078      73             BE     XBYPASS            A MASTER RECD HAD BEEN DELETED.
       000064 95 0F C4C1       0004C7      74             CLI    EODFLG,WR          EODFLG=WR   IF END-OF-DATA OCCURRED WHILE
       000068 47 80 C06E       000074      75             BE     XWRITE             A NEW MASTER RECD WAS BEING CONSTRUCTED.
       00006C 45 E0 C1EC       0001C2      76   XREWRITE  BAL    14,REWRITE         EODFLG=REWR IF END-OF-DATA OCCURRED WHILE
       000070 47 F0 C072       000078      77             B      XBYPASS            AN EXISTING MSTR RECD WAS BEING UPDATED.
       000074 45 E0 C1EA       0001F0      78   XWRITE    BAL    14,WRITE
       000078                              79   XBYPASS   CLOSE  (TRANS)            AFTER HANDLING LAST MASTER RECD, CLOSE
       000082                              85             CLOSE  (MASTER)           ALL FILES, AND EXIT FROM PROGRAM
       00008E                              91             CLOSE  (REPORT)
       00009A 58 D0 C672       000678      97             L      13,SAVE+4
       00009E 98 EC D00C                   98             LM     14,12,12(13)
       0000A2 07 FE                        99             BR     14
                                          100   * DOS ******
                                          101   *XBYPASS  CLOSE  TRANS
                                          102   *         CLOSE  MASTER
                                          103   *         CLOSE  REPORT
                                          104   *         EOJ
                                          105   ***************
                                          106   *
                                          107   * ADD NEW RECORD TO MASTER FILE
                                          108   *
       0000A4 92 0F C4C1       0004C7     109   NEWADD    MVI    EODFLG,WR          SET END-OF-DATA FLAG TO WRITE LAST RECD.
       0000A8 41 B0 C312       000318     110             LA     11,NEWRECD         SET DUMMY BASE REG TO NEW-RECD AREA.
                                          111   * DOS ******
                                          112   *         LA     11,RECDL
                                          113   ***************
       0000AC 45 E0 C24C       000252     114             BAL    14,CONSTRCT        GO BEGIN CONSTRUCTION OF NEW RECD.
       0000B0 D2 4F C305C385 0003DB 00038B 115            MVC    ERRTRANS,TAREA     SET ERR MSG FOR POSSIBLE INVALID KEY.
       0000B6                             116   ADDLOOP   GET    TRANS,TAREA        GET NEXT TRANS RECD (IF ANY), AND
       0000C0 D5 03 C37DC38C 000383 000392 121            CLC    KDORM,TDORM        SEE IF ITS KEY MATCHES THAT OF RECD BE-
       0000CA 47 70 C0DA       0000E0     122             BNE    ADDEND             ING CONSTRUCTED.  IF NOT, GO WRITE NEW
       0000CE D5 03 C381C394 000387 00039A 123            CLC    KROOM,TROOM        RECD TO MASTER FILE.
```

Figure 21.13 continued

```
FLAG LOCTN OBJECT CODE      ADDR1  ADDR2   STMNT M SOURCE STATEMENT

     0000D4 47 70 C0DA      0000E0          124          BNE     ADDEND
     0000D8 45 E0 C26E      000274          125          BAL     14,UPDATING     OTHERWISE, CONTINUE CONSTRCTING NEW RECD
     0000DC 47 F0 C0B0      0000B6          126          B       ADDLOOP         USING INFO IN TRANS RECD.
     0000E0 45 E0 C1EA      0001F0          127 ADDEND   BAL     14,WRITE        AFTER WRITING NEW RECD TO MASTER, THEN
     0000E4 47 F0 C03E      000044          128          B       MAINLOOP        DETERMINE WHAT TO DO WITH NEXT TRANS.
                                            129 *
                                            130 *
                                            131 * UPDATE EXISTING RECORD IN MASTER FILE
                                            132 *
     0000E8 92 F0 C4C1      0004C7          133 UPDATE   MVI     EODFLG,REWR     SET END-OF-DATA FLG TO REWRITE LAST RECD
     0000EC 45 E0 C15E      000164          134          BAL     14,READ         THEN READ MASTER RECD THAT MATCHES KEY IN
     0000F0 12 BB                           135          LTR     11,11           KEY-ADDRESS AREA.  RETURN WITH ADDR OF
     0000F2 47 70 C106      00010C          136          BNZ     VALIDKEY        LOGICAL RECD IN REG 11, UNLESS INVALID
     0000F6 92 FF C4C1      0004C7          137          MVI     EODFLG,BYP      KEY ERROR.  IF INVALID KEY, THEN RESET
     0000FA                                 138          GET     TRANS,TAREA     END-OF-DATA FLAG TO BYPASS REWRITE, AND
     000108 47 F0 C03E      000044          143          B       MAINLOOP        GET NEXT TRANS AND GO PROCESS IT.
                                            144 *
     00010C 95 F4 C388      00038E          145 VALIDKEY CLI     TTYPE,C'4'      IF VALID KEY, SEE IF TRANS IS CHANGE OR
     000110 47 80 C140      000146          146          BE      DELETE          DELETE REQUEST.
     000114 45 E0 C26E      000274          147 CHANGE   BAL     14,UPDATING     IF CHANGE, THEN GO MAKE CHANGES.
     000118                                 148          GET     TRANS,TAREA     THEN GET NEXT TRANS RECD (IF ANY).
     000126 D5 03 C37DC38C  000383 000392   153          CLC     KDORM,TDORM     SEE IF ITS KEY MATCHES THAT OF RECD BE-
     00012C 47 70 C138      00013E          154          BNE     DIFFKEY         ING UPDATED.  IF NOT, GO REWRITE THAT
     000130 D5 03 C381C394  000387 00039A   155          CLC     KROOM,TROOM     RECD BACK TO MASTER FILE.
     000136 47 70 C138      00013E          156          BNE     DIFFKEY
     00013A 47 F0 C106      00010C          157          B       VALIDKEY        OTHERWISE, CONTINUE MAKING CHANGES.
     00013E 45 E0 C1BC      0001C2          158 DIFFKEY  BAL     14,REWRITE      AFTER REWRITING CHANGED RECD, DETERMINE
     000142 47 F0 C03E      000044          159          B       MAINLOOP        WHAT TO DO WITH NEXT TRANSACTION RECD.
                                            160 *
     000146 92 FF B000      000000          161 DELETE   MVI     MDELETE,X'FF'   WHEN THE REQUEST IS TO DELETE THE MASTER
     00014A 45 E0 C1BC      0001C2          162          BAL     14,REWRITE      RECD, THEN SET DELETE FLAG AND REWRITE
     00014E 92 FF C4C1      0004C7          163          MVI     EODFLG,BYP      THE RECD.  SET END-OF-DATA FLAG TO BYPASS
     000152                                 164          GET     TRANS,TAREA     WRITING OR REWRITING LAST MASTER RECD.
     000160 47 F0 C03E      000044          169          B       MAINLOOP        GET NEXT TRANS RECD AND PROCESS IT.


                                            170 * INTERNAL SUBROUTINES  'READ'     READS FOR UPDATING
                                            171 *                       'REWRITE' WRITES AN UPDATED RECORD
                                            172 *                       'WRITE'   WRITES A NEW RECORD
                                            173 * ALL THREE CALLED VIA  BAL 14,XXX.
                                            174 *  OS USES ERROR BYTE NAMED 'EXCODE' IN DECB NAMED 'MSTRDECB'.
                                            175 * DOS USES ERROR BYTE NAMED 'MASTERC' IN DTFIS NAMED 'MASTER'.
                                            176 *
     000164 18 2E                           177 READ     LR      2,14            SAVE RETURN ADDRESS
     000166                                 178          READ    MSTRDECB,KU,,'S',MF=E  USE DYNAMIC INPUT BUFFER
     00017C                                 185          WAIT    ECB=MSTRDECB    WAIT FOR I/O COMPLETION
     000186 58 B0 9010      000010          189          L       11,RECDADDR     GET ADDR OF LOGICAL RECORD.
     00018A 91 7D 9018      000018          190          TM      EXCODE,X'FF'-OVF-RNF  GIVE ERR MSG IF OTHER THAN
     00018E 47 70 C23C      000242          191          BNZ     ABEND           OVERFLOW OR RECD-NOT-FOUND.
     000192 91 80 9018      000018          192          TM      EXCODE,RNF      IF RECD NOT FOUND, GIVE NON-
     000196 47 70 C19C      0001A2          193          BNZ     RDERR           FATAL MSG.  OTHERWISE,
                                            194 * DOS *******
                                            195 *        READ    MASTER,KEY
                                            196 *        WAITF   MASTER
                                            197 *        LA      11,RECDR
                                            198 *        TM      MASTERC,X'FF'-OVF-RNF
                                            199 *        BNZ     ABEND
                                            200 *        TM      MASTERC,RNF
                                            201 *        BNZ     RDERR
                                            202 ***************
     00019A 95 FF B000      000000          203          CLI     MDELETE,X'FF'   SEE IF RECORD IS 'DELETED'
     00019E 47 70 C1B8      0001BE          204          BNE     RDEXIT          IF NOT, THEN READ WAS O.K.
     0001A2 D2 33 C425C48D  00042B 000493   205 RDERR    MVC     ERRMSG,NOTFMSG  ELSE, PRINT 'RECD-NOT-FOUND'
     0001A8 D2 4F C3C5C385  0003DB 00038B   206          MVC     ERRTRANS,TAREA  MSG WITH CURRENT TRANSACTION.
     0001AE                                 207          PUT     REPORT,ERRLINE
     0001BC 1B BB                           212          SR      11,11           RESET RECD ADDR SINCE IT'S BAD.
     0001BE 18 E2                           213 RDEXIT   LR      14,2            RECOVER RETURN ADDRESS, AND
     0001C0 07 FE                           214          BR      14              RETURN TO CALLER.
                                            215 *
     0001C2 18 2E                           216 REWRITE  LR      2,14            SAVE RETURN ADDRESS
     0001C4                                 217          WRITE   MSTRDECB,K,,'S',MF=E  USE INPUT BUFFER FOR OUTPUT.
     0001DA                                 224          WAIT    ECB=MSTRDECB    WAIT FOR I/O COMPLETION.
     0001E4 91 FF 9018      000018          228          TM      EXCODE,X'FF'    SEE IF ANY EXCEPTION CODES ON.
     0001E8 47 70 C23C      000242          229          BNZ     ABEND           IF ANY ERRORS, THEN TERMINATE.
                                            230 * DOS *******
                                            231 *        WRITE   MASTER,KEY
                                            232 *        WAITF   MASTER
                                            233 *        TM      MASTERC,X'FF'
                                            234 *        BNZ     ABEND
                                            235 ***************
     0001EC 18 E2                           236          LR      14,2
     0001EE C7 FE                           237          BR      14              OTHERWISE, RETURN TO CALLER.
                                            238 *
     0001F0 18 2E                           239 WRITE    LR      2,14            SAVE RETURN ADDRESS
     0001F2                                 240          WRITE   MSTRDECB,KN,,NEWBUF,MF=E  USE NEW RECD BUFFER AREA.
     000210                                 249          WAIT    ECB=MSTRDECB    WAIT FOR I/O COMPLETION.
     00021A 91 FF 9018      000018          253          TM      EXCODE,X'FF'    SEE IF ANY EXCEPTION CODES ON.
    C00021E 47 80 C238      00023E          254          BZ      WREXIT          IF NONE, THEN NO ERRORS.
     000222 91 FE 9018      000018          255          TM      EXCODE,X'FF'-DUP  IF ANY BUT DUPL-RECD, THEN
```

Figure 21.13   continued

```
FLAG LOCTN OBJECT CODE     ADDR1  ADDR2  STMNT M SOURCE STATEMENT

     000226 47 70 C23C     000242        256            BNZ    ABEND                TERMINATE PROGRAM.
                                         257  *   DOS  ******
                                         258  *          WRITE  MASTER,NEWKEY
                                         259  *          WAITF  MASTER
                                         260  *          TM     MASTERC,X'FF'
                                         261  *          BZ     WREXIT
                                         262  *          TM     MASTERC,X'FF'-DUP
                                         263  *          BNZ    ABEND
                                         264  ***************
     00022A D2 33 C425C459 00042B 00045F 265            MVC    ERRMSG,DUPLMSG       IF DUPL-RECD ONLY, THEN PRINT
     000230                              266            PUT    REPORT,ERRLINE       MSG WITH CURRENT TRANSACTION.
     00023E 18 E2                        271  WREXIT    LR     14,2                 RETURN TO CALLER.
     000240 07 FE                        272            BR     14


                                         273  * 'ABEND' ROUTINE IS CALLED WHEN I/O ERROR OTHER THAN INVALID KEY IS
                                         274  * DETECTED DURING A READ, REWRITE, OR WRITE OPERATION.
                                         275  * 'ABEND' TERMINATES THE PROGRAM AND ITS JOB STEP, VIA 'ABEND' MACRO.
                                         276  * COMPLETION CODE FOR TERMINAION IS ARBITRARILY CHOSEN AS 4095.

     000242                              277  ABEND     ABEND 4095,DUMP,STEP
                                         284  *
                                         285  * DOS  ******
                                         286  *ABEND    DUMP
                                         287  ***************
                                         288  *


                                         289  * INTERNAL SUBROUTINE WITH TWO ENTRY POINTS, 'CONSTRCT' & 'UPDATING'
                                         290  * BOTH ENTERED WITH BAL 14,...  WITH NO PARAMETERS.
                                         291  *
                                         292  * TRANSACTION CODE 'TTYPE' DETERMINES UPDATING ACTION
                                         293  *    TTYPE = C'1'  ...  ADD A NEW ROOM WITH NO STUDENTS
                                         294  *          = C'2'  ...  ADD A STUDENT NAME & I.D.
                                         295  *          = C'3'  ...  DELETE A STUDENT NAME & I.D.
                                         296  *          = C'4'  ...  DELETE ENTIRE MASTER RECD.
                                         297  *
                                         298  *'CONSTRCT' BEGINS CONSTRUCTION OF NEW OUTPUT MASTER RECD USING TRANS
                                         299  * RECD.  'UPDATING' CONTINUES CONSTRUCTION OF NEW OUTPUT MASTER RECD.
                                         300  *
     000252 D2 03 B001C38C 000001 000392 301  CONSTRCT  MVC    MDORM,TDORM          WHEN CONSTRUCTING A NEW RECD, MOVE
     000258 D2 03 B005C394 000005 00039A 302            MVC    MROOM,TROOM          DORM AND ROOM NUMBER FROM TRANS
     00025E D2 30 B009C2D0 000009 0002D6 303            MVC    MDATA1,BLANKS        TO OUTPUT AREA, AND BLANK OUT STU-
     000264 D2 30 B03AC2D0 00003A 0002D6 304            MVC    MDATA2,BLANKS        DENT DATA AREAS.
     00026A 95 F2 C388     00038E         305            CLI    TTYPE,C'2'           IF TRANS CODE IS '2', INSTEAD OF '1',
     00026E 47 80 C26E     000274         306            BE     UPDATING             CONTINUE CONSTRUCTION.
     000272 07 FE                         307            BR     14                   OTHERWISE, EXIT.
                                         308  *
     000274 18 AB                         309  UPDATING  LR     10,11                SAVE LOGICAL RECD AREA ADDR IN REG 10.
     000276 95 F2 C388     00038E         310            CLI    TTYPE,C'2'           IF TRANS CODE = '2', THEN ADD STUDENT
     00027A 47 80 C296     00029C         311            BE     ADD                  NAME AND I.D.
     00027E D5 08 B031C3C2 000031 0003C8  312  DEL       CLC    MID,TID              OTHERWISE, ASSUME CODE = '3', AND
     000284 47 80 C286     00028C         313            BE     DEL1                 DELETE EITHER 1ST OR 2ND NAME & I.D.
     000288 41 BB 0031     000031         314            LA     11,DATALNG(11)       IF NOT 1ST, MUST BE 2ND  INCR ADDR.
     00028C D2 27 B009C2D0 000009 0002D6  315  DEL1      MVC    MNAME,BLANKS         DELETE BY REPLACING NAME & I.D. WITH
     000292 D2 08 B031C2D0 000031 0002D6  316            MVC    MID,BLANKS           BLANKS.
     000298 47 F0 C2B0     0002B6         317            B      EXIT
     00029C D5 08 B031C2D0 000031 0002D6  318  ADD       CLC    MID,BLANKS           WHEN ADDING, SEE WHICH STUDENT DATA
     0002A2 47 80 C2A4     0002AA         319            BE     ADD1                 AREA IS BLANK, AND MOVE NAME & I.D.
     0002A6 41 BB 0031     000031         320            LA     11,DATALNG(11)       INTO THAT AREA.  IF NOT 1ST AREA,
     0002AA D2 27 B0C9C399 000009 00039F  321  ADD1      MVC    MNAME,TNAME          THEN ASSUME IT'S 2ND AREA.
     0002B0 D2 08 B031C3C2 000031 0003C8  322            MVC    MID,TID
     0002B6 18 BA                         323  EXIT      LR     11,10                BEFORE EXITING,  RESTORE  DUMMY  BASE
     0002B8 07 FE                         324            BR     14                   REG CONTENTS.


                                         325  *   THE FOLLOWING  READ MACRO  AND  DECBD DSECT  ARE FOR  OS  ONLY .
                                         326  * -------------------------------------------------------------------
                                         327  *
                                         328  * LIST FORM OF READ MACRO TO DEFINE DATA EVENT CONTROL BLOCK AREA

     0002BA                              329            READ   MSTRDECB,KU,MASTER,'S','S',KAREA,MF=L

                                         339  * DUMMY SECTION FOR DATA EVENT CONTROL BLOCK TO DEFINE FIELDS.
                                         340  *
     000000                              341  DECBD     DSECT
     000000                              342            DS     4F                    1ST FOUR WORDS NOT REFERRED TO.
     000010                              343  RECDADDR  DS     F                     5TH WORD IS LOGICAL RECORD ADDRESS.
     000014                              344  KEYADDR   DS     F                     6TH IS ADDRESS OF KEY AREA.
     000018                              345  EXCODE    DS     H                     7TH IS EXCEPTION CODES
     000080                              346  RNF       EQU    B'10000000'           BIT 0 = RECD-NOT-FOUND
     000002                              347  OVF       EQU    B'00000010'           BIT 6 = OVERFLOW-RECORD
     000001                              348  DUP       EQU    B'00000001'           BIT 7 = DUPLICATE-RECORD
     0002D6                              349  BISAM     CSECT
                                         350  * -------------------------------------------------------------------
                                         351  *
                                         352  * DUMMY SECTION TO DEFINE 107-BYTE MASTER FILE LOGICAL RECORD AREA.
```

Figure 21.13 **continued**

```
FLAG LOCTN OBJECT CODE     ADDR1  ADDR2  STMNT M SOURCE STATEMENT

    000000                                 353  *
    000000                                 354  MAREA    DSECT
    000000                                 355  MDELETE  DS     CL1           BYTES 0      DELETE FLAG BYTE
    000001                                 356  MDORM    DS     CL4                1-4     DORM ABBREVIATION
    000005                                 357  MROOM    DS     CL4                5-8     DORM ROOM
    000009                                 358  MDATA1   DS     CL49               9-57    1ST STUDENT DATA AREA
    00003A                                 359  MDATA2   DS     CL49               58-106  2ND STUDENT DATA AREA
    000009             000006B             360           ORG    MDATA1       REDEFINE STUDENT DATA AREA
    000009                                 361  MNAME    DS     CL40               9-48    STUDENT NAME FIELD
    000031                                 362  MID      DS     CL9                49-57   STUDENT I.D. FIELD
    000031                                 363  DATALNG  EQU    *-MNAME            LENGTH OF STUDENT AREA
    0002D6                                 364  BISAM    CSECT
                                           365  *
                                           366  * BLANKS USED TO INITIALIZE STUDENT DATA AREAS
    0002D6 40                              367  BLANKS   DC     (DATALNG)C' '  'DATALNG' IS SIZE OF STUDENT DATA AREA
                                           368  *
                                           369  * LOGICAL RECORD AREA FOR NEW ADDITIONS TO MASTER FILE
                                           370  *
    000308                                 371           DS     0D            RESERVE 123  BYTES ON DBL-WD BDY
    000308                                 372  NEWBUF   DS     CL123
    000308             000383              373           ORG    NEWBUF
    000308                                 374           DS     CL16          16-BYTE SYSTEM  AREA
    000318                                 375  NEWRECD  DS     CL107         107-BYTE LOGICAL RECD, AS IN 'MAREA'
    000383             000383              376           ORG
                                           377  *
                                           378  * KEY AREA FOR USE WITH READ AND WRITE MACROS
                                           379  *
    000383                                 380  KAREA    DS     CL8           8-BYTE KEY
    000383             00038B              381           ORG    KAREA
    000383                                 382  KDORM    DS     CL4           1ST 4 BYTES = DORM ABBREVIATION
    000387                                 383  KROOM    DS     CL4           2ND 4 BYTES = DORM ROOM NUMBER
    00038B             00038B              384           ORG
                                           385  *

                                           386  * TRANSACTION INPUT AREA
                                           387  *
    00038B                                 388  TAREA    DS     CL80          RESERVE 80 BYTES FOR CARD IMAGE.
    00038B             0003DB              389           ORG    TAREA         BEGIN REDEFINITION OF INPUT AREA.
    00038B                                 390           DS     CL3           COL 1-3     UNUSED
    00038E                                 391  TTYPE    DS     CL1                4      TRANS TYPE CODE
    00038F                                 392           DS     CL3                5-7    UNUSED
    000392                                 393  TDORM    DS     CL4                8-11   DORM ABBREVIATION
    000396                                 394           DS     CL4                12-15  UNUSED
    00039A                                 395  TROOM    DS     CL4                16-19  DORM ROOM NUMBER
    00039E                                 396           DS     CL1                20     UNUSED
    00039F                                 397  TNAME    DS     CL40               21-60  STUDENT NAME
    0003C7                                 398           DS     CL1                61     UNUSED
    0003C8                                 399  TID      DS     CL9                62-70  STUDENT I.D.
    0003DB             0003D1              400           ORG
                                           401  *

                                           402  * LOGICAL RECORD AREA FOR 'SYSOUT' PRINT LINE
                                           403  *
    0003DB                                 404  ERRLINE  DS     0CL132        RESERVE 132  BYTES
    0003DB                                 405  ERRTRANS DS     CL80          80-BYTE TRANS RECD AREA
    00042B                                 406  ERRMSG   DS     CL52          52-BYTE ERR MESSAGE AREA
                                           407  *
    00045F 40C3C1D5E340C1C4                408  DUPLMSG  DC     CL52' CANT ADD  RECD KEY ALREADY EXISTS ON MASTER FILE'
    000493 40C3C1D5E340D4E4D7              409  NOTFMSG  DC     CL52' CANT UPDATE  RECD KEY DOESNT EXIST ON MASTER FILE'

                                           410  *
                                           411  * EODFLG USED TO CONTROL PROCESSING WHEN AT END OF TRANSACTION FILE.
                                           412  *
    0004C7 FF                              413  EODFLG   DC     X'FF'         END-OF-DATA FLAG  FOR LAST MASTER RECD
    0000FF                                 414  BYP      EQU    X'FF'         BYP  = DONT WRITE OR REWRITE WHEN AT END
    00000F                                 415  WR       EQU    X'0F'         WR   = WRITE MSTR RECD WHEN AT END
    0000F0                                 416  REWR     EQU    X'F0'         REWR = REWRITE MSTR RECD WHEN AT END

                                           417  *
                                           418  * DCB'S FOR TRANS FILE, INPUT MASTER FILE, AND REPORT FILE
                                           419  *
    0004C8                                 420  TRANS    DCB    DSORG=PS,MACRF=(GM),DDNAME=SYSIN,EODAD=EOJ,         X
                                           421                  RECFM=FB,LRECL=80,BLKSIZE=4080
                                           473  *
    000528                                 474  MASTER   DCB    DSORG=IS,MACRF=(RUS,WUA),DDNAME=DORMS
                                           541  *
    000614                                 542  REPORT   DCB    DSORG=PS,MACRF=(PM),DDNAME=SYSPRINT,               X
                                           543                  RECFM=FB,LRECL=132,BLKSIZE=4092

                                           595  *  DOS  ******
                                           596  *TRANS    DTFCD DEVADDR=SYSIPT,WORKA=YES,IOAREA1=INBUF,EOFADDR=EOJ,   X
                                           597  *                DEVICE=2540
                                           598  *INBUF    DS     CL80
                                           599  *
                                           600  *REPORT   DTFPR DEVADDR=SYSLST,WORKA=YES,IOAREA1=OUTBUF,BLKSIZE=132,   X
                                           601  *                DEVICE=1403
                                           602  *OUTBUF   DC     CL132' '
```

Figure 21.13 continued

```
FLAG LOCTN OBJECT CODE     ADDR1  ADDR2  STMNT M SOURCE STATEMENT

                                          603   *
                                          604   *MASTER   DTFIS DEVADDR=SYS001,DEVICE=3330,DSKXTNT=3,HINDEX=3330,      X
                                          605   *               RECFORM=FIXBLK,RECSIZE=107,NRECDS=38,                 X
                                          606   *               IOAREAR=MSTBUF,WORKR=RECDR,KEYLEN=8,KEYLOC=2,CYLOFL=2, X
                                          607   *               IOAREAL=MSTNBUF,WORKL=RECDL,                          X
                                          608   *               IOROUT=ADDRTR,TYPEFLE=RANDOM,KEYARG=KAREA
                                          609   *
                                          610   * ERROR BYTE IN 'MASTER' DTFIS HAS FOLLOWING RELEVANT BITS
                                          611   * RNF      EQU   B'00010000'       BIT 3 = RECD-NOT-FOUND
                                          612   * DUP      EQU   B'00000100'       BIT 5 = DUPLICATE-RECORD
                                          613   * OVF      EQU   B'00000001'       BIT 7 = OVERFLOW-RECORD
                                          614   *
                                          615   *RECDR    DS    CL107
                                          616   *RECDL    DS    CL107
                                          617   ****************

      000674                              618   SAVE     DS    18F         REGISTER SAVE AREA.

                                          619   * DOS  ******
                                          620   *SAVE     DS    9D
                                          621   *        LTORG
                                          622   *        DS    0D
                                          623   *MSTBUF   DS    CL4066      DOS ISAM BUFFER FOR RETRIEVAL & UPDATE
                                          624   *KL       EQU   8           KEY LENGTH
                                          625   *MSTNBUF  DS    CL(8+KL+4066)  DOS ISAM BUFFER FOR NEW RECDS
                                          626   ****************
                                          627            END
```

CROSS-REFERENCE

```
SYMBOL     LEN   VALUE  DEFN    REFERENCES

ABEND      00002 000242 00278   00191 00229 00256
ADD        00006 00029C 00318   00311
ADDEND     00004 0000E0 00127   00122 00124
ADDLOOP    00004 0000B6 00117   00126
ADD1       00006 0002AA 00321   00319
BISAM      00001 0000C0 00364
BLANKS     00001 0002C6 00367   00303 00304 00315 00316 00318
BYP        00001 0000FF 00414   00072 00137 00163
CHANGE     00004 000114 00147
CONSTRCT   00006 000252 00301   00114
DATALNG    00001 000031 00363   00314 00320 00367
DECBD      00001 000000 00341   00024
DEL        00006 00027E 00312
DELETE     00004 000146 00161   00146
DEL1       00006 00028C 00315   00313
DIFFKEY    00004 00013E 00158   00154 00156
DUP        00001 0000C1 00348   00255
DUPLMSG    00034 00045F 00408   00265
EODFLG     00001 0004C7 00413   00072 00074 00109 00133 00137 00163
EOJ        00004 00005C 00072   00442
ERRLINE    00084 0003CB 00404   00209 00268
ERRMSG     00034 00042B 00406   00205 00265
ERRTRANS   00050 0003CB 00405   00115 00206
EXCODE     00002 000018 00345   00190 00192 00228 00253 00255
EXIT       00002 0002B6 00323   00317
KAREA      00008 000383 00380   00337 00381
KDORM      00004 000383 00382   00060 00121 00153
KEYADDR    00004 000014 00344
KROOM      00004 000387 00383   00061 00123 00155
MAINLOOP   00006 000044 00060   00128 00143 00159 00169
MAREA      00001 0000C0 00354   00022
MASTER     00004 000518 00476   00033 00089 00334
MDATA1     00031 000009 00358   00303 00360
MDATA2     00031 00003A 00359   00304
MDELETE    00001 0000C0 00355   00161 00203
MDORM      00004 000001 00356   00301
MID        00009 000031 00362   00316 00318 00322
MNAME      00028 0000C9 00361   00315 00321 00363
MROOM      00004 000005 00357   00302
MSTRDECB   00004 0002BC 00330   00025 00179 00186 00218 00225 00241 00250
NEWADD     00004 0000A4 00109   00063
NEWBUF     0007B 0003C8 00372   00244 00373
NEWRECD    0006B 000318 00375   00110
NOTFMSG    00034 000493 00409   00205
OVF        00001 000002 00347   00190
RDERR      00006 0001A2 00205   00193
RDEXIT     00002 0001BE 00213   00204
READ       00002 000164 00177   00134
RECDADDR   00004 000010 00343   00189
REPORT     00004 000614 00543   00039 00095 00208 00267
```

Figure 21.13   continued

CROSS-REFERENCE

SYMBOL	LEN	VALUE	DEFN	REFERENCES					
REWR	00001	0000F0	00416	00133					
REWRITE	00002	0001C2	00216	00076	00158	00162			
RNF	00001	000080	00346	00190	00192				
SAVE	00004	000674	00618	00020	00021	00097			
TAREA	00050	0003BB	00388	00054	00115	00118	00140	00150	00166	00206	00389
TDORM	00004	000392	00393	00060	00121	00153	00301		
TID	00009	0003C8	00399	00312	00322				
TNAME	00028	00039F	00397	00321					
TRANS	00004	0004C8	00421	00045	00053	00083	00117	00139	00149	00165
TROOM	00004	00039A	00395	00061	00123	00155	00302		
TTYPE	00001	00038E	00391	00062	00145	00305	00310		
UPDATE	00004	0000E8	00133	00064					
UPDATING	00002	000274	00309	00125	00147	00306			
VALIKEY	00004	0001CC	00145	00136	00157				
WR	00001	00000F	00415	00074	00109				
WREXIT	00002	00023E	00271	00254					
WRITE	00002	0001F0	00239	00078	00127				
XBYPASS	00004	000078	00081	00073	00077				
XREWRITE	00004	00006C	00076						
XWRITE	00004	000074	00078	00075					

Sequential Retrieval

In strict sequential retrieval, the data set must be opened for input, and either move mode or locate mode buffering can be used. In OS, this is done as follows:

```
        OPEN    (MASTER,(INPUT))
        .
        .
MASTER  DCB     DSORG=IS,MACRF=(GM),DDNAME=DORMS,EODAD=EOJ
```

In DOS, the corresponding DTFIS macro for strict sequential retrieval must designate IOAREAS and WORKS areas and specify sequential retrieval as follows:

```
MASTER  DTFIS   ...,TYPEFLE=SEQNTL,IOROUT=RETRVE,EOFADDR=EOJ,      X
                IOAREAS=buffername,WORKS=workareaname,...
```

Sequential Retrieval Using SETL

When the SETL macro is to be used, the data set is opened for input using either move mode or locate mode. In OS, the intention to use SETL must be indicated in the MACRF parameter, as when updating:

```
        OPEN    (MASTER,(INPUT))
        .
        .
MASTER  DCB     DSORG=IS,MACRF=(GM,SK),DDNAME=DORMS,EODAD=EOJ
```

In DOS a DTFIS macro must specify sequential retrieval with IOAREAS and WORKS areas and also must specify the KEYARG field name:

```
MASTER  DTFIS   ...,TYPEFLE=SEQNTL,IOROUT=RETRVE,EOFADDR=EOJ,      X
                IOAREAS=buffername,WORKS=workareaname,            X
                KEYARG=keyfieldname,...
```

Figure 21.14   Sequential retrieval using SETL.

```
SEQUENTIAL_RETRIEVAL:

   INITIALIZATIONS;
   MAIN_PROCESSING;
   END_OF_TRANSACTION_DATA;

EXIT SEQUENTIAL_RETRIEVAL.



   INITIALIZATIONS:

      open master file for input only;
      open report file for output;
      open transaction file for input;

   EXIT INITIALIZATIONS.



   MAIN_PROCESSING:

      REPEAT WHILE there is more transaction data to process

         get transaction record;
         move key class to work area;
         SETL for key class;
         get master record;
         REPEAT WHILE (master record found) AND (record key equal to key class)
            print transaction record;
            get next master record;
         END WHILE;
         ESETL;

      END WHILE;

   EXIT MAIN_PROCESSING.



   END_OF_TRANSACTION_DATA:

      close all files;

   EXIT END_OF_TRANSACTION_DATA.
```

Figure 21.14

The processing logic required for this procedure is depicted in Figure 21.14. As in the updating procedures, the transaction records may designate either a specific record key or a record key class. Figure 21.14 assumes a record key class is being designated. For example, a request for retrieval of information for an entire dorm would use the key class method.

Whether the key or key class method is used, there is a possibility that a transaction record will contain a record key or key class not represented in the master file. In such a case, a "record-not-found" error condition will occur when the SETL macro is executed.

Random Retrieval

The processing logic required for random retrieval is probably the simplest of the three methods. The transaction records need not be in key sequence. However, the key class method cannot be used; each transaction must designate a specific record key to identify the record that is to be retrieved. For this reason, the random retrieval method is usually reserved for interactive systems, where the sequence of requests cannot be predicted in advance.

In **OS,** when using BISAM for retrieval, the READ K instead of the READ KU macro is used. The list and execute forms are usually not required. A dummy section is used to define the record fields, and a dummy base register is established to access those fields beginning at the record address provided in the data event control block. The data set can be opened for input only, using dynamic buffering to retrieve records without updating them. For example, in the dorm room master file, this could be done as shown here:

```
            OPEN   (MASTER)
            .
            .
            .
            READ   MSTRDECB,K,MASTER,'S','S',KAREA
            WAIT   ECB=MSTRDECB
            .
            .
MASTER  DCB    DSORG=IS,MACRF=(RS),DDNAME=DORMS
```

The key of the desired record must be moved to the area designated by the key-address parameter in the READ macro. In this example, the key-address parameter is KAREA. After the READ operation has been completed, i.e., following the WAIT macro, the exception codes can be tested for "record-not-found" or uncorrectable error situations, and appropriate action can be taken. If there are no errors, the logical record address can be obtained from the data event control block.

In **DOS,** the DTFIS macro must specify random retrieval, together with the IOAREAR and WORKR areas and the KEYARG field name:

```
MASTER  DTFIS  ...,IOROUT=RETRVE,TYPEFLE=RANDOM,           X
               IOAREAR=buffername,WORKR=workareaname,      X
               KEYARG=keyfieldname,...
```

The WAITF macro must immediately follow the READ KEY macro in order to synchronize I/O operations with run-time CPU operations:

```
            READ   MASTER,KEY
            WAITF  MASTER
```

The error code bits can then be tested for "record-not-found" or other I/O error conditions. Of course, any condition except record-not-found would be a fatal error, and the program would normally have to be terminated.

The pseudocode in Figure 21.15 illustrates the principal processing steps required to retrieve records in random order from an indexed sequential data set. The programming required to carry out these processes is left as an exercise for you.

Figure 21.15

21.9   CONCLUDING REMARKS

Perhaps the most important aspect of using indexed sequential data sets is the choice of an appropriate key by which the records can be sequenced. Once that key is chosen, all further processing logic is essentially dependent on it. For example, in our dorm room file, having chosen the dorm and room number as the key, a request such as "In what room is John Doe?" would normally have to be answered by processing every record until John Doe's name is found. On the other hand, the dorm and room number key is more natural if the purpose of the data set is to maintain records about room assignments.

Compared to sequential data set processing, the capabilities for updating in random mode, without having to re-create the data set, can provide a significant time and space saving if the number of records in the overflow areas is relatively small compared to the number in the data set. The need to reorganize the data set periodically stems from the decrease in performance that results when more and more records are placed into the poorly utilized overflow areas.

Reorganization

Methods for handling error conditions that can occur during processing deserve more discussion than has been given in this introductory chapter. For such a discussion, the OS Assembly Language programmer should consult the descriptions of the SYNAD error-processing conventions in the *OS/*

Error-Handling

Figure 21.15   Random retrieval.

```
RANDOM_RETRIEVAL:

   INITIALIZATIONS;
   MAIN_PROCESSING;
   END_OF_DATA;

EXIT RANDOM_RETRIEVAL.



INITIALIZATIONS:

   open master file for input only;
   open report file for output;
   open transaction file for input;

EXIT INITIALIZATIONS.



MAIN_PROCESSING:

   REPEAT WHILE there is more transaction data to process

      get transaction record;
      move transaction key to work area;
      read master record and wait for completion;

      IF uncorrectable read error
      THEN
         terminate program;
      END IF;

      IF no read error
      THEN
         print transaction record;
      ELSE  { invalid key error }
         print appropriate error message;
      END IF;

   END WHILE;

EXIT MAIN_PROCESSING.



END_OF_DATA:

   close all files;

EXIT END_OF_DATA.
```

VS1 Data Management Services Guide and the descriptions of the exception code bits for BISAM and QISAM in *Appendix A* of the *OS/VS1 Data Management Macro Instructions* reference manual. The DOS programmer should investigate the use of ERREXT=YES by consulting the *DOS/VS Supervisor and I/O Macros* reference manual.

Performance Improvement

Descriptions of methods for improving the performance of indexed sequential processing procedures not mentioned in this chapter can also be found in the aforementioned manuals. In OS, these methods include improvements to the index handling procedures of the operating system (via OPTCD=U and the MSHI and SMSI parameters in the BISAM DCB macro) and improvements to the buffering procedures used when adding new records via BISAM (via the MSWA and SMSW parameters in the DCB macro). In DOS, similar improvements can be made by using the INDAREA= and INDSKIP= parameters of the DTFIS macro and by utilizing statistics that the operating system makes available in the DTFIS macro expansion. These statistics are described in the previously referenced manual, Part 4, in the section titled *Organization of Records on DASD: Programming Considerations*.

21.10 SUMMARY

Indexed sequential data sets provide a means of processing records either sequentially or randomly. In sequential-mode processing, most of the concepts that apply to sequential data sets are equally applicable to indexed sequential data sets. This includes blocking and deblocking and double buffering. In random-mode processing, the task of determining the relative and physical positions of a record in secondary memory is performed by the operating system, which uses the index it maintains for this purpose. The user's program need take little special action other than to provide the key of the record that is to be read or written.

Each record in an indexed sequential data set must be uniquely identified by the contents of its key field. Moreover, the key field of each record must begin in the same relative position and have the same length (from 1 to 255 bytes) as the key fields of all other records in the data set. When creating the data set, the records must be written in increasing key sequence. QISAM must be used in OS systems; the WRITE macro together with the SETFL/ENDFL macros are required in DOS. At the time the data set is created, the operating system allocates space for the prime, independent overflow, and cylinder index areas (all in count-key-data format) according to the specifications of the job control statements. The new records are written into the prime area and appropriate entries are made in the track and cylinder indexes by the operating system. A portion of the prime area (one or more tracks per cylinder) is always used for track indexes; it may also be used for cylinder overflow. For very large data sets—for example, those requiring more than t tracks for the cylinder index where t exceeds a cylinder's capacity—we can also request that a master index be created.

Sequential-mode processing can begin at any arbitrary record in an existing indexed sequential data set by using the SETL macro to identify the first record that is to be processed. If SETL is not executed, sequential processing begins at the first record in the data set. It is not necessary to create a new data set when updating in sequential mode, provided that new records are not being inserted and that existing variable-length records are not having their lengths changed. Records can, however, be added to the end of the data set (in the prime area), records can be deleted logically (though not physically), and record contents can be replaced without having to create a new data set. In OS, a record whose delete-flag byte is X'FF' is considered to be deleted and is ignored by all subsequent QISAM I/O requests even though physically it might still be in the prime data area. In DOS, the user's program must check the delete-flag byte to determine whether a record has been flagged for deletion.

In random-mode processing, all four updating actions (described in Section 21.6) are permitted without having to create a new data set. The operating system uses the prime and/or overflow areas when new records are inserted and when the lengths of variable-length records are changed. However, as more and more records are added to the overflow areas, processing efficiency may decrease significantly due to the poor organization of overflow records. For this reason, you should periodically reorganize an indexed sequential data set, for example, by using sequential-mode processing to copy the records in sequence from the existing data set to a new one.

Contrary to what happens in sequential processing, the operating system detects and rejects attempts to read or write records under certain data error conditions. The most common conditions for sequential mode are these:

1. When creating a data set, the key of each record written must be greater than the key of the immediately preceding record. If it is less, an out-of-sequence error condition will occur; if it is equal, a duplicate-key error condition will occur. The same conditions can arise when adding records to the end of a data set in EXTEND mode.
2. If not enough prime space was allocated to anticipate the number of records being added (either when creating or extending a data set), a space-not-found error condition will occur.
3. If there is not a key or key class in the data set that matches the one specified when a SETL macro is executed, a record-not-found error condition will occur (see Section 21.4).

In random mode, the most common conditions are:

1. When attempting to read a record that is to be updated, an invalid key condition occurs if the key specified by the READ macro does not match the key of any record in the data set.
2. When attempting to insert a new record into the data set, an invalid key condition occurs if the key specified by the WRITE macro is equal to the key of a record that is already in the data set. (If the matching data set record is flagged for deletion, however, then in OS but not DOS it is simply replaced and no error condition is posted.)

Methods for handling these errors were discussed in Sections 21.5 through 21.7.

21.11 REVIEW

Topics Common to OS and DOS

Indexed Sequential File   This is a file whose logical records are maintained in sequence by a fixed-length key field that must be in the same position of each record. The operating system maintains an index of keys that enables it to locate the position of any record on the basis of its key value, so that access to a record can be either by random-mode or sequential-mode processing.

Sequential Mode   Processing in this mode is the same as when processing sequential files, except that the records must be in ascending sequence by their keys when doing I/O. If not, a "sequence error" occurs.

Random Mode   In this mode, a program can access an existing record or write a new record in its proper sequence without having to process any other records in the file. To do so, several things are required:

1. The DCB or DTFIS parameters must have specified random-mode processing at the time the file was opened.
2. Certain buffering rules must be adhered to.
3. The key of the desired record must be in a separate area (akin to the "symbolic key" area in Cobol) when an appropriate READ or WRITE macro is invoked.
4. The program must provide for its own I/O synchronization and invalid key processing.

Invalid Key Conditions   (1) "Record not found" means that an attempt was made to retrieve a record whose key is not in the file; (2) "duplicate key" means that an attempt was made to write a new record whose key matches that of an existing record.

Space Allocation   Auxiliary memory space must be allocated for the prime data and cylinder index areas, and it may optionally be allocated for master index and independent overflow areas. Space for the track index and cylinder overflow areas is acquired from within the prime data area. See Figures 21.1a and 21.1b.

Prime Data Area   This auxiliary memory area contains data blocks that were written at the time the file was created. Logical records are in ascending key sequence within each block, and the blocks are in ascending sequence by the highest key of their records.

Cylinder Overflow Area (optional)   This auxiliary memory area contains logical records bumped off a prime area's tracks when new records are inserted in sequence. There is one cylinder overflow area for each cylinder in the prime area. A DCB or DTFIS parameter must request this option (see CYLOFL in Figs. 21.5a or 21.5b).

Independent Overflow Area (optional)   This auxiliary memory area contains logical records bumped off a prime area's tracks when new records are inserted and when there is no room for the bumped records in the cylinder overflow area. A JCL statement must request this option (see the "dsname(OVFLOW)" variable in Figure 21.1a, or the last EXTENT statement in Fig. 21.1b).

Track Index   The location and highest key of each data block in a prime area cylinder is recorded in the track index of that cylinder. Each track index is stored in the cylinder to which it pertains.

Cylinder Index   This auxiliary memory area contains the address and highest key of each prime area cylinder's track index.

Master Index (optional)   This auxiliary memory area contains the address of tracks in the cylinder index, together with the highest key in those tracks. A master index is needed only for exceptionally large files. A DCB or DTFIS parameter must request this option (see NTM in Fig. 21.5a or MSTIND in Fig. 21.5b).

Delete Flag (optional)   This is a one-byte code placed by the program in the first position of each record. If its value is X'FF', then the record has been flagged for deletion; otherwise, its value should be X'40' (blank). In OS, a DCB parameter (OPTCD=L) must request this option. In DOS, the option is not supported; it must be provided by the user's program.

Topics for OS Only

QISAM (Queued Indexed Sequential Access Method)   This access method must be used when creating an indexed sequential file. It can also be used for sequential retrieval and for updating in place sequentially, but cannot be used to insert new records into an existing file.

BISAM (Basic Indexed Sequential Access Method)   This access method is used for random-mode retrieval and for random-mode updating. It cannot be used to create an indexed sequential data set.

MACRF Parameter   This DCB parameter specifies the processing mode or modes when the file is opened.

I/O Buffers   Buffering with QISAM is no different than buffering with sequential SAM files. For BISAM, "dynamic buffering" is used.

READ K, READ KU, WRITE K, WRITE KN   These macros are used in random-mode processing. The "READ K" macro reads a record for retrieval only; "READ KU" reads it with the intent to update it. The "WRITE K" macro writes an updated record that had been read via "READ KU"; the "WRITE KN" macro is used to add a new record to the data set.

MF=E and MF=L   The MF (Macro Format) parameter must be used in a READ and WRITE macro in random-mode processing. MF=E states that when the macro is executed at run time, it will use additional parameters as well as the data event control block from an MF=L macro. An MF=L macro can't be executed at run time; its purpose is to allocate a common data area for the data event control block, and for parameters that are passed between the program and the operating system. See the discussion on READ and WRITE macros in Section 21.5.

DCB Parameters The DCB parameters of particular importance when creating a file are described in Figure 21.5a. Most of these are not specified when updating or retrieving from the file.

"Deleted" Records For input, QISAM does not retrieve records flagged for deletion but BISAM does. For output, when a new record that has the same key as the deleted one is written to a file, both QISAM and BISAM will replace the flagged record with the new one. Otherwise, a deleted record that is in the prime area remains there as a logically deleted but not physically deleted record until it is bumped off its track by other insertions, at which time it is discarded.

Topics for DOS Only

ISAM (Indexed Sequential Access Method) This is the only access method in DOS for indexed sequential files. It must be used for file creation, file updating, and file retrieval. File creation must be done in sequential mode. Updating and retrieval can be sequential or random.

ISC and ISE Parameters The //DLBL job control statement must specify ISC when creating a file, and ISE when adding records to the end of a file in sequential mode.

SETFL and ENDFL Macros When creating an indexed sequential file in DOS, the SETFL (set file load mode) macro must be invoked after opening the file and before writing the first record. ENDFL is invoked before closing the newly created file.

DTFIS Parameters The parameters of particular importance when creating a file are described in Figure 21.5b.

IOROUT, TYPEFLE, KEYARG These DTFIS parameters are used when retrieving from or updating a file in sequential or random mode.

"Deleted" Records ISAM ignores the delete flag in all operations. Each program should provide its own method of flagging records for deletion, and of subsequently recognizing and taking appropriate action on records that are flagged for deletion.

I/O Buffers Buffers and work areas are reserved with DS directives and designated with DTFIS parameters. IOAREAL always designates the buffer for new records: WORKL designates the work area where a new record is processed by the program. For retrieving and updating existing records, the DTFIS parameters are as follows: In sequential mode, IOAREAS designates the buffer, and WORKS the work area. In random mode, IOAREAR designates the buffer, and WORKR the work area. (**Note:** In this text we've assumed that RECFORM=FIXBLK [fixed-length, blocked records].)

READ KEY, WRITE KEY, WRITE NEWKEY These macros must be used in random-mode processing. The "READ KEY" macro reads a record for retrieval or updating; "WRITE KEY" writes an updated record; the corresponding areas for both are designated by IOAREAR and WORKR. The "WRITE NEWKEY" macro is used to add a new record; the areas used are designated by IOAREAL and WORKL.

21.12 REVIEW QUESTIONS

1. What parameters and/or other provisions in an assembly language program indicate that an indexed sequential file is going to be created by the program? What if the file was going to be extended rather than created?
2. What parameters and/or other provisions indicate that an indexed sequential file is going to be updated by the program in sequential mode? In random mode?
3. What parameters must be used to specify each record key's length and relative position?

4. a. What are the advantages and disadvantages of using SETL?
   b. What are the advantages of specifying a "key class" rather than an exact key when using SETL?
   c. What types of error conditions could occur when SETL is invoked?
5. What is meant by the concept of "reorganizing" an indexed sequential file, and why is it important?
6. What is meant by the concept of "I/O synchronization," and why is it important?
7. How is I/O synchronization accomplished in sequential-mode processing? In random-mode processing?
8. a. What is the definition of an "invalid key" condition?
   b. Do you think the occurrence of an invalid key condition is likely to be a rare event in the life of a program? Why or why not?
9. In random-mode processing, how do you specify the symbolic address of the byte containing the error exception bits?
10. In the random-mode updating program of Figure 21.13, why is each record that is read from the master file tested to see if it had been flagged for deletion (see statement #203)? If a record had indeed been flagged for deletion, does the program handle it properly? Why or why not?

21.13 EXERCISES

1. If we wish to process an indexed sequential data set with an assembly language program, what factors determine whether we should use QISAM or BISAM?

2. What capabilities exist in QISAM processing mode that do not exist in BISAM processing mode, and vice versa?

3. What capabilities exist both in QISAM processing and in BISAM processing?

4. What is the difference in purpose between the prime data area, the overflow areas, and the index area as specified in a DD statement or EXTENT statements for an indexed sequential data set?

5. What is the difference in purpose between the independent overflow area and the cylinder overflow areas for an indexed sequential data set?

6. Explain why the statement "overflow track space is used inefficiently, both for storage and for searching" is true.

7. What is the reason for designating the delete-flag option (OPTCD=L)? What are the requirements for use of the delete-flag option in QISAM processing? In BISAM processing? In DOS ISAM?

8. Write the SPACE= parameter of the DD statement or the EXTENT statements required to reserve space for an indexed sequential data set under each of the following sets of conditions (for an IBM 3330 disk system):

   a. Separate prime, index, and independent overflow areas for 100,000 80-byte records with 10-byte keys
   b. Separate prime and independent overflow areas (with the index at the end of the overflow area), for 10,000 200-byte records with 16-byte keys
   c. A prime area subdivided by the operating system for the index and independent overflow areas, for 10,000 100-byte records with 8-byte keys

9. Analogous to the formula for the IBM 3330 disk system, the track capacity formula for the IBM 3350 disk system is

$$\text{number of blocks per track} = \frac{19254}{267 + KL + DL}, \text{ in count-key-data format}$$

There are 30 tracks per cylinder and 555 cylinders in a disk pack of the IBM 3350 disk system.

a. Assuming that $KL + DL = 18987$ (i.e., one data block per track), what is the capacity of a disk pack in the IBM 3350 disk system if all the tracks are recorded in count-key-data format?

b. Denoting the number of blocks per track as given by the above formula by N, what is the maximum value of $KL + DL$ for each of the values $N = 1,2,3,..., 10$?

c. Assuming 8-byte keys and 10-byte data blocks in all the index areas, what would be the maximum number of track-index tracks required per cylinder of a disk pack in the IBM 3350 disk system?

d. Assuming 8-byte keys and 107-byte logical records (e.g., the dorm room master file), how many logical records could be stored per *track* in the IBM 3350 disk system if the blocksize were 4066 bytes? How many if the blocksize were 2889 bytes? Using the track capacity formula given above, show that a blocksize of 2889 bytes is the best choice that is less than or equal to 4096 bytes, from the standpoint of track-space utilization in the IBM 3350 for the dorm room master file.

e. Calculate the number of prime data area cylinders that would be required for a 5000-record dorm room master file stored in the IBM 3350 disk system; one track per cylinder is used for the track index and two tracks are reserved for cylinder overflow. Assume that $KL=8$, $DL=BLKSIZE=2889$, and $LRECL=107$. What would be the significance of the answer to this problem if prime data space were allocated only in units of whole cylinders?

10. What assembly language statements would be required to accomplish the same purpose as each of the following IBM Cobol clauses:

a. `APPLY CYL-OVERFLOW OF 2 TRACKS ON filename`
b. `ACCESS IS RANDOM...OPEN INPUT`
c. `ACCESS IS RANDOM...OPEN I/O`
d. `ACCESS IS SEQUENTIAL...OPEN OUTPUT`

11. What DCB macro parameters are required to describe each of the following situations for an indexed sequential data set for which the record format is fixed block:

a. A record key that occupies the last 8 bytes of an 80-byte record, the first byte of the record being reserved for the delete flag

b. Up to three levels of master index, each level consisting of two tracks

c. Use of both independent and cylinder overflow, the latter consisting of three tracks per cylinder

d. The data set is opened in QISAM EXTEND mode

e. The data set is opened for updating in place, using the SETL macro for positioning to the appropriate record

12. Prepare suitable test data to create an indexed sequential dorm room master file in accordance with the specifications given in this and the preceding chapter. Ensure that your test data covers at least the following situations: no students assigned to a room, one student assigned to a room, two students assigned to the same room. Ensure that the transaction records are in proper sequence by sorting them via the IBM Sort/Merge program (see IBM Publication SC33–4035, *Sort/Merge Programmer's Guide*).

13. Using the test data from Exercise 12 and the program in Figure 20.8 (suitably modified for indexed sequential processing), create a sample dorm room master file. To verify that its contents are correct, print the master file via the OS utility program IEBISAM (see IBM Publication GC26–3901, *Utilities*) or the corresponding DOS utility program (see Publication GC33–5381).

14. Write an assembly language program that could be used to reorganize the dorm room master file. (Assume that it already existed as an indexed sequential data set, as discussed at the end of Section 21.3.)

15. Write a program that will print the entire contents of the dorm room master file in some suitably readable format, with the following specifications: your program should be written to allow for an arbitrary number of records on the master file, there should be no more than 50 lines printed per page, each page should begin with an appropriate title line with date and page number on each page, and a new page should be started each time there is a change in dorm building.

16. Write a program in accordance with the same printing specifications as those given in Exercise 15, except that instead of printing the entire contents of the master file only those records containing two students per dorm room should be printed.

17. Write a program that will delete all those records in the dorm room master file that contain no student names and i.d.'s.

18. Assume that there is a transaction file in which each record contains a dorm building abbreviation in columns 8–11, and a dorm room number in that building in columns 16–19. There is no other information in the transaction file records. Write a program using BISAM to print the dorm room master file records that correspond to the transaction file records. (**Hint:** See Figure 21.15.)

19. Assume that there is a transaction file in which each record contains a dorm building abbreviation in columns 8–11. There is no other information in the transaction file records. Write a program using the SETL macro to print all the dorm room master file records for the dorm building given in each transaction record. Each set of records for a given dorm building should be printed starting on a new page. (**Hint:** See Figure 21.14.)

20. A government agency has decided to create a computer file that records the name, model year, and average city and highway gas mileage ratings (miles per gallon) of each model of automobile manufactured in the United States since 1975.

    a. Design a transaction record format that can be used to create an indexed sequential master file consisting of all the information mentioned. Design a master file format for these records.

    b. Design a transaction record format that can be used to update the gas mileage master file, with capability to add or delete records and to correct errors in existing records.

    c. Write a program to create the gas mileage master file as an indexed sequential data set. Prepare appropriate test data to verify that your program is correct.

    d. Write programs that will update the master file in EXTEND mode, UPDAT mode, and random mode. Prepare appropriate test data to verify that your programs are correct.

    e. Write a program that will produce a report giving all the information in the master file for a given year, listed in ascending sequence by city gas mileage rating (major field) and automobile model name (minor field).

22

VSAM (Virtual Storage Access Method)

The Virtual Storage Access Method has been designed for several purposes; it is intended as a replacement for the OS and DOS indexed sequential access methods (QISAM,BISAM; ISAM). It may also be used instead of the OS and DOS sequential access methods (QSAM,BSAM; SAM). And it can be used in data base management applications such as IBM's Information Management System (IMS). As will be seen, the Access Method Services utility program (AMS) provides a relatively simple means of creating VSAM data sets, and the VSAM I/O macros provide a variety of processing options.

VSAM must be used with one of the IBM virtual storage operating systems, e.g., OS/VS, DOS/VS, and their variations and extensions. In this chapter we will refer to these systems as simply OS and DOS, respectively.

Readers who have studied the preceding three chapters in this text will soon notice conceptual similarities among the sequential, indexed sequential, and virtual storage access methods. However, though very useful as background information, such prior study is not absolutely essential. The I/O macros and associated parameters available in VSAM differ in considerable detail from those of the other access methods; there are a large number of parameters and processing options that have no counterparts in the other access methods. This extensive variety exists in part to provide alternative means of accomplishing a task and in part to provide mechanisms for optimizing VSAM performance and memory space utilization.

Unlike the sequential and indexed sequential access methods, VSAM macros and associated parameters are essentially the same in both OS and DOS systems. Similarly, the use of the Access Method Services program is essentially the same in OS and DOS. Therefore, except for examples involving job control language, there are no separate OS and DOS descriptions of these facilities in this chapter. The differences that do exist between OS and DOS are noted in context.

This chapter is intended as an introduction to VSAM. It is concerned only with its use as a replacement for sequential and indexed sequential access methods. Even in this context, many processing options are either treated very briefly or are omitted. Our purpose is to provide enough information for the beginning VSAM programmer to understand basic concepts, to be able to write programs for elementary applications, and to then be able to progress to more advanced applications with the aid of the IBM reference manuals listed at the end of the chapter.

The author is indebted to his former student, Mr. Bruce Barton, for providing invaluable assistance in the formulation of this chapter.

22.1 INTRODUCTORY CONCEPTS

VSAM provides support for three types of data sets, known as Entry-Sequenced Data Sets (ESDS), Key-Sequenced Data Sets (KSDS), and Relative Record Data Sets (RRDS). All three types must be stored on and processed from direct-access storage devices, e.g., disks. ESDS is conceptually similar to sequential organization; KSDS, to indexed sequential organization; and RRDS, to relative organization. We will discuss only ESDS and KSDS in this text.

Physical Organization

The memory space in which a VSAM data set is stored on a direct-access storage device is organized into discrete units known as control intervals. A **control interval** is the unit of information that is read from and written to a storage device by the operating system. Depending on its size, a control interval can contain one or more fixed-length or variable-length logical records, one or more physical data blocks, and some unused space. It also contains information that defines the length of the records contained in it, as shown in Figure 22.1.

Control Interval Size

The size of a control interval can be independent of a track's capacity, of the physical blocksize, and of the logical record lengths. If data records are larger than the control interval size, it is permissible to specify that they be allowed to extend across (i.e., *span*) control interval boundaries. In many applications, however, use of spanned records is not necessary. Moreover, a suitable choice of control interval size will result in each control interval containing exactly one data block.

Control Area Size

Control intervals are grouped by VSAM into regions of storage known as **control areas.** Each area occupies contiguous space (e.g., consecutive tracks) on the storage device. The maximum size of a control area is one cylinder; its minimum size is one track. Every physical space extent of a data set consists of one or more control areas. VSAM data sets therefore always consist of one or more control areas, depending on how much space is allocated.

Logical Organization

ESDS

ESDS records are stored in a data set in the sequence in which they are presented to the operating system. They can, but need not, be sorted prior to being presented for storage. In this sense the sequencing of ESDS records is analogous to that of sequential data-set records.

KSDS

KSDS records are stored in a data set in ascending key sequence. The key field that controls sequencing is known as the **primary key** field. The primary key must be the same length (from 1 to 255 bytes) in each record, must be in the same relative position within each record, and must uniquely identify the record in which it exists. In this sense the primary keys and sequencing of KSDS data records are analogous to those of indexed sequential data-set records.

RBA

The relative location of a logical record in a VSAM data set is defined by its **relative byte address** (RBA), a full-word binary integer that specifies the position of the record relative to the beginning of the data set. The RBA of the Nth record is equal to the total number of bytes contained in the preceding N-1 records. For example, the RBA of the first record is zero, and the RBA of the second record is equal to the length (in bytes) of the first record. The record lengths used in calculating RBA's include all control information and unused space stored with each record (see Fig. 22.2).

Figure 22.1 *Physical space organization.*

A control interval always consists of a whole number of physical blocks.

The size of control intervals depends on the device. It can be chosen when a data set is defined and must be either 512m with m = 1,2,..., 16 (i.e., 512, 1024, 1536, ..., 8192)
or 8192 + 2048n , n = 1,2,..., 12 (i.e., 10240, 12288, ..., 32768)

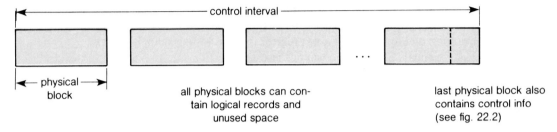

Physical blocksize is chosen by VSAM and is always either 512, 1024, 2048, or 4096.

Example 1: CISZ = 12288, BLKSZ = 4096. Device is IBM 3330.

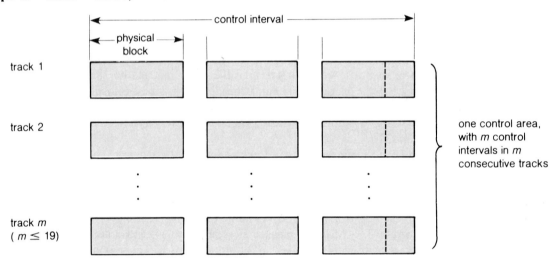

Example 2: CISZ = 4096, BLKSZ = 4096. Device is IBM 3330.

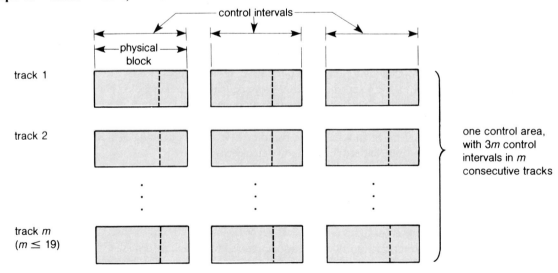

Figure 22.2 RBA's and control interval formats.

Note: The formats shown below apply only to *un*spanned records.

If in both Case 1 and Case 2 we assume that the records are in the Nth control interval (N = 1,2,...), then the RBA of record 1 is $RBA_1 = (N-1) \times CISZ$, and the RBA of record k is $RBA_k = RBA_1 + L_1 + L_2 + ... + L_{k-1}$ for k > 1. For example, if N = 2 and CISZ = 4096, then $RBA_1 = 4096$ and $RBA_3 = 4096 + L_1 + L_2$.

Case 1: No two consecutive records have the same length.

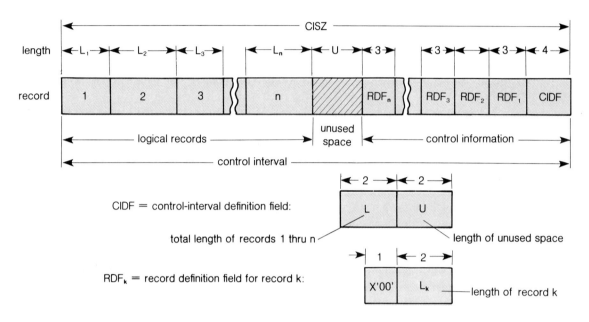

Case 2: *m* consecutive records (*m* > 1) have the same length.

In this case what would have been the *m* RDF's by the above scheme are collapsed into 2 RDF's, thereby saving space in the control interval. The 2 RDF's have the following format:

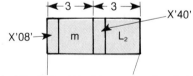

For example, suppose there are n=m+2 records in the control interval, and all but the first and last have same length L_2. Then only 4 RDF's are needed, as shown here:

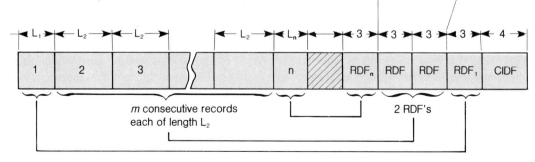

VSAM always uses the RBA to determine a record's location in a data set. But except in certain advanced applications of VSAM, RBA's are not normally needed by user programs to access records. There are other, simpler means available to user programs. If needed, however, RBA's can be obtained at run time via the SHOWCB macro, which will be discussed in Section 22.6.

Data Components, Index Components, and Clusters

VSAM maintains an *index component* (i.e., a set of index records) with each key-sequenced data set. Its function is analogous to that of the index maintained for indexed sequential data sets. Namely, it enables the VSAM modules to translate a primary key of a KSDS record into the RBA of that record. Thus, if a user program presents a primary key to VSAM, that key can be used by VSAM to locate the KSDS record that the key identifies, and thereby make it possible to read or write that record without having to read or write all the preceding records.

The term **base cluster** (and sometimes just *cluster*) describes the totality of basic information that VSAM always maintains about a data set. An ESDS cluster consists of one component, namely, the *data component*—i.e., the set of all control areas that contain control intervals in which data records are stored. A KSDS cluster consists of two components: the data component and the index component.

Indexes

The index component is organized by VSAM into a tree-structured hierarchy (see Fig. 22.3). The lowest-level nodes of this tree are known as the **sequence set** of the index. Each node in the sequence set is analogous to a track index of an indexed sequential data set. In all the applications that we will discuss, one sequence set node resides on the first track of each control area. In VSAM this positioning of the sequence set nodes is known as *imbedding* the index.

Each entry in a sequence set node points to one of the control intervals in the corresponding control area. Each entry in a higher-level node points to one of the nodes in the next-lower level. VSAM always generates as many higher-level nodes as are needed for the highest level to fit on one track—the root node of the index tree.

The manner in which index entries are formatted is a topic beyond the scope of this text. But two aspects are worth noting: (1) the entries in any index node are stored in a fixed-length data block known as an *index control interval;* and (2) the size of index control intervals is always either 512 bytes, 1024 bytes, 2048 bytes, or 4096 bytes. The size of an index control interval can be specified when defining a KSDS. The choice of size obviously determines the number of entries that can be stored in a node; for many applications, an appropriate size is 512 bytes.

Alternate Indexes

In addition to the base cluster, an ESDS or KSDS can also optionally consist of one or more alternate indexes. Each alternate index is itself a key-sequenced data set. Its purpose is to permit one or more records in the data component of the base cluster to be identified and accessed by a key other than the primary key. That key is known as an **alternate key.** More than one record of a KSDS or ESDS data component can be identified by a single alternate key value. In other words, unlike the value of a primary key, the value of an alternate key need not uniquely identify a record. The use of alternate keys and alternate key indexes will be discussed in Section 22.7.

Accessing Records

ESDS and KSDS organizations permit both sequential accessing and direct accessing, with or without alternate indexes. **Sequential accessing** means that the Nth record must be accessed before the $(N+1)$st record can be accessed and only after the $(N-1)$st record is accessed. **Direct accessing** means that any logical record can be accessed at any time, provided that the record is appropriately identified when the access request is made.

Sequential Access

ESDS records are sequentially accessed in ascending RBA sequence. This mode is known as **addressed sequential access.** VSAM maintains the value of the current record's length and RBA so that it can calculate the RBA of the next record. The user program need not present an RBA in order to access a record in this mode.

Figure 22.3 Schematic of KSDS index structure.

In these diagrams, only the prime keys are shown. They are assumed to be 3 bytes long. It is also assumed that two sets of higher-level indexes are needed.

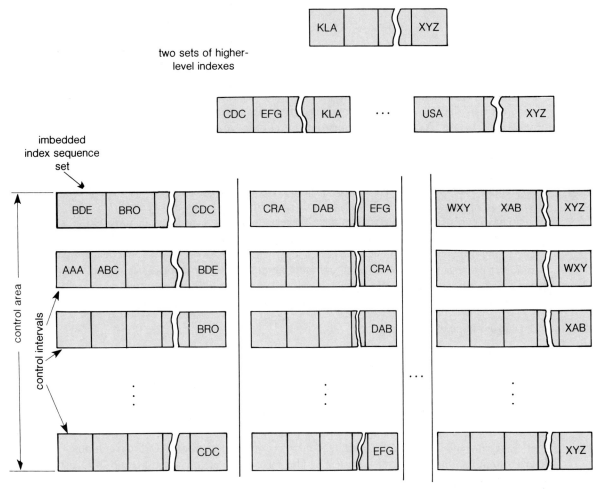

Note: Like the logical records in a control interval, the entries in an index record are stored in ascending prime key sequence.

The imbedded index sequence set (the lowest-level index) contains the highest key and a pointer for each control interval that contains data in the control area that the sequence set pertains to.

Each higher-level index contains the highest key and a pointer for each of the immediately lower-level indexes that it pertains to.

No attempt is made in the above diagrams to account for spanned records or for unused (i.e., free) control intervals.

Addressed sequential access is always used to create a new ESDS. It can also be used to add new records to the end of an existing data set, and to retrieve, update (without changing record length), and mark existing records for deletion. An ESDS record that is marked for deletion remains in the data set; it is up to the user's program to ignore or to reuse the space of such records during subsequent operations.   *ESDS*

KSDS records that are sequentially accessed must be read or written in primary key sequence. In this case the accessing mode is known as **keyed sequential access.** This mode is always used to create a new KSDS, and may also be used to sequentially retrieve, update, and delete records, and to add new records to an existing KSDS. VSAM erases deleted records from a KSDS.   *KSDS*

It is possible to begin sequential accessing at any arbitrary record position in an ESDS or KSDS. To do this, the user's program must inform VSAM of the desired beginning record position. For ESDS, this must be done by specifying the RBA of the desired record position as the search argument in a POINT macro. For KSDS, the POINT macro is also used to specify the beginning record position, but instead of the RBA you must specify the primary key of the desired record as the search argument. Use of the POINT macro will be outlined in Section 22.8.

Direct Access

If alternate keys are not used, there are two modes of direct accessing for KSDS and one for ESDS. We will refer to these modes as *ordinary* direct accessing to distinguish them from direct accessing via alternate keys. (Note: The term "ordinary" is the author's, not IBM's.)

The ESDS mode of ordinary direct accessing is known as **addressed direct access.** This mode requires that the RBA of each desired record be presented to the operating system in order to read or write a record. As in ESDS sequential processing, this mode permits existing records to be retrieved, updated without changing length, and marked for deletion. However, this mode may not be used to add new records to the data set.

The two KSDS modes of ordinary direct accessing are known as **keyed direct** and **keyed skip-sequential access.** In both modes, the primary key of a record must be presented to the operating system in order to read or write that record. Existing records can be retrieved, updated, and deleted, and new records can be inserted or added. However, whereas records can be processed in any sequence with keyed direct accessing, the keyed skip-sequential mode requires that records be processed in ascending primary key sequence. The method by which VSAM searches the index component results in faster processing for the keyed direct method under some circumstances and in faster processing for keyed skip-sequential under others. Keyed skip-sequential is faster only if there are relatively few records to be processed *and* only if those records have reasonably closely grouped primary key values.

I/O Programming Considerations

VSAM data sets must be defined, and space must be allocated for them, before any records can be stored in them. The process of defining a data set and allocating space for it is accomplished via the Access Method Services program (AMS) and will be described in the next section. The process of storing records into an empty data set, known as **loading the data set,** can be accomplished either via AMS or via a user program. Once an ESDS or KSDS is loaded, it must be closed and reopened before any other processing of that data set can occur.

As in sequential and indexed sequential assembly language I/O programming, VSAM I/O programming is accomplished via macros. There are two types of macros: request macros and control block macros (see Fig. 22.4).

Request macros are designed to be executed at run time. They initiate actions such as opening a data set, and retrieving and updating records.

Some of the **control block macros** are also designed to be executed. They can, for example, be used to create, modify, obtain, or test selected fields of the control blocks. The control blocks themselves are similar in purpose to the DTFxx areas in DOS and the DCB areas in OS systems. They provide information that is used at run time by the operating system when it responds to a request macro or to an executable control block macro. That information is generated by the ACB, RPL, and EXLST macros in both DOS and OS systems.

The ACB macro must be referred to when opening and closing a VSAM data set. The basic options specified in an ACB are these: the identity of an OS DD statement or DOS DLBL statement that in turn identifies the VSAM data set to be processed and the anticipated logical record accessing modes. Among the other options that may be specified in an ACB are the buffer space requirements for reading and writing control intervals and the address of the EXLST macro that pertains to this ACB. A password can also be specified, if needed to access the data set. (DOS users should note that unlike the other access methods, DOS VSAM allocates buffer space for use at run time. You can designate how many buffers are to be allocated by VSAM, but you do not reserve space for those buffers at assembly time. The same is true in OS VSAM.)

The RPL macro must be referred to each time any macro other than OPEN or CLOSE (or GENCB) is executed at run time. The basic options specified in an RPL are these: the name of the ACB that the RPL is associated with (see Fig. 22.5); the address and length of the I/O record work

Figure 22.4   VSAM macro summary.

Nonexecutable Control Block Macros

ACB	generates an access-method control block at assembly time
EXLST	generates a list of exit-routine addresses at assembly time
RPL	generates a request parameter list at assembly time

Executable Control Block Macros

GENCB	generates the same information that an ACB, EXLST, or RPL macro does but does so at run time rather than assembly time
MODCB	modifies the contents of any of the control blocks that were generated by ACB, EXLST, RPL, or GENCB
SHOWCB	obtains the contents of one or more fields of any control block
TESTCB	tests the contents of any one of the fields in a control block

Request Macros for General Use

CHECK	waits for completion of an asynchronous I/O request
CLOSE	disconnects a program from a data set
ENDREQ	terminates an asynchronous I/O request
ERASE	deletes a record from a key-sequenced or relative-record data set
GET	retrieves a record from a data set
OPEN	connects a program to a data set
POINT	positions a data set at a designated record or class of records
PUT	stores a record into a data set

Request Macros for Advanced Applications

BLDVRP	builds a VSAM resource pool
DLVRP	deletes a VSAM resource pool
GETIX	retrieves a specified index control interval (OS only)
MRKBFR	marks a buffer for output, or to release it from exclusive control or shared status (OS only)
PUTIX	stores a specified index control interval (OS only)
SCHBFR	searches a buffer for an RBA within specified ranges (OS only)
SHOWCAT	retrieves information from a VSAM catalog
VERIFY	ensures that the end-of-data information contained in the catalog for a specific data set is accurate (OS only)
WRTBFR	writes a deferred buffer or (in OS only) writes a buffer that was marked for output via MRKBFR

Note: All the request macros are executable macros.

---

area; the record accessing mode to be used for a particular request; the address of the search argument for direct accessing and for record positioning; and whether or not the request is for updating a record.

EXLST Macro

The EXLST macro specifies the symbolic names of user-program routines that are to be executed when certain run-time exceptions (such as end-of-data or I/O error conditions) occur.

The ACB and RPL macros are required; the EXLST macro is optional. EXLST is used primarily in applications where program execution and I/O operations proceed concurrently. It will not be discussed further until Section 22.8. ACB and RPL are used in all applications. Examples of their use will be given beginning in Section 22.3.

Error Codes

As will be seen from the examples later in this chapter, omitting the EXLST macro requires that compensating action be taken by the program. For when EXLST is omitted, VSAM always puts a code in Register 15 and returns to the instruction following execution of an I/O macro *whether or not an error has occurred!* The Register 15 code is =F'0' if no errors occurred, =F'8' if a logical (software) error occurred, and =F'12' if a physical (hardware) error occurred. It is of critical importance that the program test that code before proceeding; if there is an error and it is not handled by the program in some way, the program will in all likelihood blow up at some later instruction, and tracing the cause of the problem may prove exceedingly difficult at that point.

Figure 22.5 Relationship of JCL and VSAM macros.

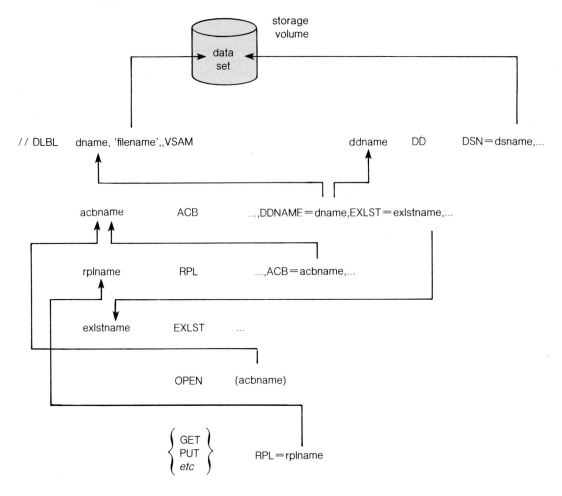

22.2   ACCESS METHOD SERVICES (AMS)

AMS is the VSAM utility program, executable under the name IDCAMS in both OS and DOS systems. The most important of its functions are:

1. It defines VSAM catalogs and data sets and allocates space for them.
2. It loads VSAM data sets from the input data stream and from other nonVSAM data sets and VSAM data sets.
3. It prints the contents of VSAM catalogs and data sets.

AMS *must* be used to define VSAM catalogs and data sets and to allocate space for them. Its other functions are optional; their use depends on your needs.

Brief definitions of all the AMS commands are given in Figure 22.6. A definitive description of the commands is in the AMS manuals noted at the end of this chapter. Here, we will discuss only the elementary aspects of the DEFINE and REPRO commands. This will provide the essential tools needed by beginning VSAM programmers.

In general a fairly substantial number of parameters can be specified with each command to indicate the precise nature of the function that is desired. The parameters and their formats are virtually the same in both OS and DOS. In addition, a certain minimal amount of job control language (JCL) must accompany execution of the AMS program. The OS JCL is of course different from the DOS JCL.

Figure 22.6   AMS command summary.

General Usage

DEFINE	creates a catalog entry for a VSAM object
DELETE	deletes one or more VSAM objects and their catalog entries
LISTCAT	lists information contained in a VSAM catalog
PRINT	prints the contents of a VSAM data set or of a sequential or indexed-sequential data set
REPRO	copies a VSAM or sequential or indexed sequential data set into another VSAM or sequential data set, or copies a catalog to another catalog
VERIFY	verifies and corrects certain information about a data set in a catalog

Special Usage

ALTER	changes catalog information about a VSAM object that was previously defined
BLDINDEX	initially loads a newly defined alternate index
CHKLIST	lists tape data sets that were open at the time a checkpoint was taken (OS only)
CNVTCAT	converts OS catalog entries into VSAM catalog entries (OS only)
EXPORT	unloads a VSAM base cluster or alternate index, together with its catalog entry, onto a movable storage volume; alternatively, copies a user catalog onto a movable volume and then disconnects that catalog from the system's master catalog
EXPORTRA	unloads data sets whose catalog entries are damaged, using the information about the data set that is in the catalog recovery area instead of the information in the catalog itself
IMPORT	defines and loads a data set or catalog that had been unloaded via EXPORT
IMPORTRA	reconstructs a data set that had been unloaded via EXPORTRA, by redefining it and reloading it
LISTCRA	lists the contents of a catalog recovery area and (optionally) compares it with the contents of the associated catalog
RESETCAT	adjusts information in a catalog to be consistent with that which is in its associated catalog recovery area and in the VTOC

There are several considerations of overriding importance when using AMS:

1. Every computer system that supports VSAM must have exactly one master catalog that is created by AMS for the entire system. The master catalog is usually defined by the system administrator and will not be considered here. *Master Catalog*

2. Every VSAM user data set must be described either in the master catalog or in a user catalog that is created by AMS. For various reasons (e.g., increased processing efficiency and easier transportability to other computer systems), a user catalog should be used for this purpose rather than the master catalog. *User Catalog*

3. There can be no more than one user catalog per storage volume (e.g., one per disk pack). Like the master catalog, user catalogs are ordinarily defined by a system administrator rather than by a programmer.

4. No two VSAM data sets that are listed in the same catalog can have the same data-set name. Indeed, no two VSAM *objects* that are listed in the same catalog can have the same name.

In (4) above, the term *object* means any of the following: master catalog, user catalog, data space, cluster (i.e., VSAM data set), non-VSAM data set, alternate index, and path (a path connects an alternate index to a VSAM data set and will be discussed in Section 22.7).

The names of VSAM objects must contain from 1 to 44 characters, of which the first must be a letter (A through Z, and @ $ #) and the others can be letters or digits. Names longer than eight characters must be segmented by periods into groups of 8 or fewer letters and digits (e.g., **VSAM.DATA.SET**). Consecutive periods are not permitted, and the last character of a name cannot be a period. That portion of a name consisting of a period and all characters to the left of that period is known as a *qualifier;* names containing qualifiers are known as *qualified names*. For example, **VSAM.** is a qualifier, as is **VSAM.DATA.**, but **VSAM.DATA.SET** is not a qualifier; it is a qualified name. *Un*qualified names are permitted but not recommended, because just as no two objects in a catalog can have the same name, so also no unqualified name can be the same as the first qualifier in a qualified name. For example, the two names **DATA** and **DATA.SET** cannot both exist in the same catalog. *VSAM Object Names*

The DEFINE Command

The AMS *DEFINE* command must be used to create a new catalog and must be used to create an entry in an existing catalog for any VSAM object. There are seven variations of this command, corresponding to the seven VSAM objects:

in full	abbreviated
DEFINE MASTERCATALOG	DEF MCAT
DEFINE USERCATALOG	DEF UCAT
DEFINE SPACE	DEF SPC
DEFINE CLUSTER	DEF CL
DEFINE NONVSAM	DEF NVSAM
DEFINE ALTERNATEINDEX	DEF AIX
DEFINE PATH	DEF PATH

A few of the parameters that can be specified with each DEFINE command are required; the others are optional.

Space Allocation   Probably the most important consideration in using the DEFINE command is the allocation of storage space for objects. AMS provides several methods by which this can be done. These depend of course on your ability to estimate how much space is required (see below). The methods of space allocation that seem to the author to be appropriate for most applications consist of three steps:

1. Use the DEF UCAT command to allocate space for a user catalog.
2. Use the DEF SPC command to allocate space to be shared by all VSAM clusters and alternate indexes that are defined in that user catalog.
3. Use the DEF CL command to request space for a cluster and the DEF AIX command to request space for an alternate index.

If these three steps are followed, then the storage space required for all objects (except the catalog itself) is allocated by VSAM from the single DEF SPC data space on an as needed basis. That single space is then known as a *suballocatable* data space.

Whoever supervises the use of VSAM at your computer installation will most likely be responsible for doing steps (1) and (2), i.e., DEF UCAT and DEF SPC. Consequently, here we will discuss only the required parameters and a few of the optional parameters for DEF CLUSTER.

To estimate the space requirements for a cluster, we note that its size is roughly $n \cdot k$ bytes, where n is the approximate number of logical records in the cluster and k is the average record length. Thus, *for a given n and k, the number of tracks required for the data component depends on the size of a control interval and on the number of control intervals per track.*

Given this, the estimated space requirements can be summarized as in the following table. It should be noted that for KSDS, we have introduced the factor A to account for various control area sizes. You will recall from Section 22.1 that one track of each control area is used by the imbedded index sequence set; thus that track must be subtracted from each KSDS control area in a cylinder to determine the number of tracks available to the data component in that control area (see Fig. 22.3).

Approximate Space Requirements   Estimates of a cluster's space requirements can be determined from the following formulas:

	K = #tracks per data component	Y = #cylinders per data component	J = #tracks per index component
ESDS	$K = (n \cdot k)/(C \cdot S)$	$Y = K / X$	---
KSDS	$K = (n \cdot k)/(C \cdot S)$	$Y = K / (X-A)$	$J = 1 + (A \cdot Y)/B$

where
- n = approximate number of logical records in the cluster
- k = average length of a record in the cluster
- S = number of bytes per data control interval
- C = number of data control intervals per track
- X = number of tracks per cylinder
- A = number of control areas per cylinder
- B = number of entries in an index record

It must be stressed that the above formulas are only approximations. More accurate estimates can be obtained by following the procedures described in the AMS manuals. Whichever method is used, the quantities n and k must be estimated; the quantities S, C, and X are device dependent (see below); $A = 1$ if space is requested in units of cylinders; and B depends on the size of the index control interval.

Size of Control Interval

The data component control interval size S is an important quantity that should be designated in the DEF CLUSTER command. Once its value is chosen, then the value of C is determined by the device characteristics. Recommended values of S, with corresponding values of C and X, are:

	IBM 2314	IBM 3330	IBM 3340	IBM 3350	
S	2048	4096	4096	4096	bytes per CI
C	3	3	2	4	CI's per track
X	20	19	12	30	tracks per cyl.

Size of Index Control Interval with Key ≤ 10 Bytes

As mentioned, the quantity B in the formula for J is the number of entries in an index record. B depends on the size of the index control interval. This size should also be designated in the DEF CLUSTER command for KSDS clusters. Recommended values of the index control interval size, with the corresponding approximate values of B, are:

	IBM 2314	IBM 3330	IBM 3340	IBM 3350	
index CI	512	512	512	1024	bytes per index CI
B	60	60	60	120	#entries per record

There are a number of reasons for the above recommendations. They result in good track-space utilization. They result in each data control interval being equal in size to one physical data block. And they make reasonably efficient use of the index control intervals. However, there is one important underlying assumption. That is that the length of the primary key in a KSDS is not more than about 10 bytes. If it is longer than this, then the index CI size may have to be doubled or quadrupled (see the AMS manuals and the VSAM Primer noted at the end of the chapter).

Dorm Room File Space

To illustrate the above formulas, we will use the dorm room master file described in Chapters 20 and 21. As you will recall, that file contained approximately 5000 fixed-length records, with a record length of 106 bytes for the sequential version and 107 bytes for the indexed sequential version. For an IBM 3330 disk system, the number of data component tracks for an ESDS version of that file is $K = (5000 \cdot 106)/(4096 \cdot 3) \approx 44$, and for a KSDS version it is also 44 tracks. The number of index component tracks for the KSDS version is (assuming one control area per cylinder) $J = 1 + (1 \cdot Y)/60$, where $Y = 44/18$. Thus $J = 2$. Therefore the total number of tracks required for the KSDS version of the dorm room file is 46, and the total for the ESDS version is 44. In either case we therefore request an allocation of 3 cylinders for an IBM 3330. (When allocation is in units of cylinders, the control area size is always one cylinder, i.e., $A = 1$ in the formula for J. When allocation is in units of tracks, the control area size will be an integral number of tracks equal to the lesser value of the primary and secondary allocation, but not exceeding one cylinder. In this case A can be greater than or equal to 1.)

Referring to the DEF CLUSTER parameters given in Figure 22.7, it is now a relatively simple matter to define the dorm room cluster. The definition will specify the cluster's name, space requirements, type (ESDS or KSDS), and the device on which it is stored. It will also specify names and control interval sizes for the data component and (KSDS only) index component. Logical record length and KSDS key length and key position complete the specifications. The requested space will be suballocated from the data space defined by DEF SPC. That is the default, and no special parameter is needed to request this. However, if suballocation were not desired, then the UNIQUE parameter would have to be specified for the cluster and for the data and index components.

The job control language required in OS systems to define an ESDS cluster is the same as that required for a KSDS cluster. Similarly, the DOS job control is the same for ESDS and KSDS clusters. If the name of the cluster is DORM.FILE and the name of the user catalog is SAMPLE.UCAT, then the job control statements can be written as follows:

JCL for Dorm Room File

For OS systems:

```
//STEP003  EXEC  PGM=IDCAMS
//STEPCAT  DD    DSN=SAMPLE.UCAT,DISP=SHR
//CLDD     DD    VOL=SER=VOLA,DISP=OLD,UNIT=3330
//SYSPRINT DD    SYSOUT=A
//SYSIN    DD    *
```

Figure 22.7 DEFINE CLUSTER parameters.

Note: Only a small subset of the many possible options is shown here. Consult the AMS manual for restrictions and other options. In the notation below, a long vertical bar separates two choices of which either but not both can be specified. Uppercase represents keywords; lowercase represents values.

General Format

```
DEFINE CLUSTER (cluster options)—
        DATA (data options)—
        INDEX (index options)—
        CATALOG (catalog options)
```

cluster options

NAME (entryname)	specifies the name of the cluster
VOLUME (volser)	identifies the volume where the cluster will reside
CYL (p s) I TRK(p s) I REC(p s)	specifies the amount of space to be allocated; p is the primary allocation, s the secondary
FILE (dname)	identifies the DD or DLBL statement linked to the cluster
NONINDEXED I INDEXED	NONINDEXED means it's an ESDS; INDEXED means it's a KSDS
NOREUSE I REUSE	specifies whether or not it is a "reusable" data set
SUBALLOCATION I UNIQUE	specifies whether the data set shares a suballocatable data space or is allotted its own space
NOIMBED I IMBED	(KSDS only) specifies whether or not to imbed the index sequence set

Note: NONINDEXED, NOREUSE, SUBALLOCATION, and NOIMBED are the defaults.

data options

NAME (entryname)	specifies the name of the data component
RECSZ (avg max)	specifies the average and maximum length of data records
CISZ (size)	specifies the data component control interval size
KEYS (length offset)	for KSDS only, specifies the length of the prime key and its displacement from the beginning of a record
FSPC (ci ca)	for KSDS only, ci specifies the percent of space in each control interval and ca the percent in each control area that is to be left free when the cluster is loaded

index options (for KSDS only)

NAME (entryname)	specifies the name of the index component
CISZ (size)	specifies the index component control interval size

catalog options

catalogname/password	identifies the name of the catalog in which the cluster is to be defined and specifies the password (if any) required to update the catalog; the slash / between catalogname and password must be included if a password is specified

For DOS systems:

```
//  DLBL     CLDD,'DORM.FILE',,VSAM
//  EXTENT   SYS010,VOLA
//  ASSGN    SYS010,DISK,VOL=VOLA,SHR
//  EXEC     IDCAMS,SIZE=AUTO
```

If DORM.FILE is a KSDS cluster, then the AMS commands that should follow the previous job control statements for both OS and DOS are these (recall that the dorm room file primary key was 8 bytes long and occupied positions 2 through 9 of each record):

```
DEF    CL   (                                   -        AMS for Dorm
             NAME (DORM.FILE)                    -        Room File
             FILE (CLDD)                         -        (KSDS)
             VOL (VOLA)                          -
             CYL (3 1)                           -
             INDEXED IMBED                       -
             )                                   -
       DATA (                                    -
             NAME (DORM.FILE.DATA)               -
             RECORDSIZE (107 107)               -
             KEYS (8 1)                          -
             CISZ (4096)                         -
             )                                   -
       INDEX (                                   -
             NAME (DORM.FILE.INDEX)              -
             CISZ (512)                          -
             )
                                                 -
       CAT (SAMPLE.UCAT/updatepassword)
```

If DORM.FILE is an ESDS cluster instead of a KSDS cluster, then the AMS commands that would follow the previous job control statements are:

```
DEF    CL   (                                   -        AMS for Dorm
             NAME (DORM.FILE)                    -        Room File
             FILE (CLDD)                         -        (ESDS)
             VOL (VOLA)                          -
             CYL (3 1)                           -
             NONINDEXED                          -
             )                                   -
       DATA (                                    -
             NAME (DORM.FILE.DATA)               -
             RECORDSIZE (106 106)               -
             CISZ (4096)                         -
             )                                   -
       CAT (SAMPLE.UCAT/updatepassword)
```

The format for the AMS commands and parameters shown above is recommended for most needs. All information is in columns 2 through 72. One or more blanks can be used to separate command and parameter words and values. The continuation indicator (a hyphen) is, for ease of visual checking, placed in the same column of all lines that are being continued. You should ordinarily avoid continuing a parameter or its value from one line to the next, but if it must be done the continuation character in that case is a plus ($+$) rather than a hyphen ($-$), and the continuation of the parameter or value must begin in column 2. Other aspects of the AMS statement formats are described in the manuals.

The REPRO Command

The AMS *REPRO* command can be used to load a new VSAM data set with records obtained from a non-VSAM data set, or from another VSAM data set. Other important uses of REPRO, such as copying catalogs and clusters, are described in the AMS manuals.

The VSAM data set that is loaded by REPRO must have been previously defined by the DEFINE command. The type of data set that is being loaded does not have to match the type of data set from which the records are obtained. To illustrate this flexibility, the example below assumes that a sequential data set is the input to the REPRO command and that the output is a KSDS cluster. The input data set is the one created in Chapter 20—i.e., the sequential dorm room file. The output data set is the one defined earlier in this section. As can be seen, DOS AMS requires that non-VSAM input data-set characteristics be described; OS AMS doesn't.

Two points are worth noting: (1) the only change required to load an ESDS cluster rather than a KSDS cluster is to change the job control statements that identify the cluster that is being loaded; and (2) the cluster being loaded must be identified in the JCL by its base cluster name, not by its data or index component names.

Copying a SAM File to a KSDS File

For OS systems:

```
//STEP004   EXEC   PGM=IDCAMS
//STEPCAT   DD     DSN=SAMPLE.UCAT,DISP=SHR
//NEWDD     DD     DSN=DORM.FILE,DISP=OLD
//OLDDD     DD     VOL=SER=VOLB,UNIT=3330,DISP=(OLD,KEEP),
//                 DSN=SEQTL.DORM.FILE,DSORG=PS,
//                 DCB=(RECFM=FB,LRECL=106,BLKSIZE=4028)
//SYSPRINT  DD     SYSOUT=A
//SYSIN     DD     *
          REPRO                      -
               INFILE (OLDDD)        -
               OUTFILE (NEWDD)
      /*
```

For DOS systems:

```
// DLBL     OLDDD,'SEQTL.DORM.FILE'
// EXTENT   SYS020,,,,50,130
// ASSGN    SYS020,DISK,VOL=VOLB,SHR
// DLBL     NEWDD,'DORM.FILE',,VSAM
// EXTENT   SYS010,VOLA
// ASSGN    SYS010,DISK,VOL=VOLA,SHR
// EXEC     IDCAMS,SIZE=AUTO
          REPRO                              -
               INFILE (OLDDD                 -
                   ENV (RECFM (FB)           -
                       BLKSZ (4028)          -
                       RECSZ (106)           -
                       PDEV (3330))          -
                   )                         -
               OUTFILE (NEWDD)
       /&
```

A VSAM data set that has been defined in a catalog via the AMS program is ready to be processed. The first act of processing the data set must be to load it. This can be done via the AMS *REPRO* command or via a user program. Thereafter, the data set can be updated, copied, printed, or just accessed for retrieval only.

In this section we discuss the basic input/output macros that are used to process VSAM data sets in Assembly Language. These include the two principal control block macros (ACB and RPL) and the five principal request macros (OPEN,CLOSE,GET,PUT,ERASE) that were summarized in Figure 22.4. Examples of their use will be given in subsequent sections.

ACB Macro

Permission to process a VSAM data set must be requested at run time by an OPEN macro. That macro must in turn specify the address of an ACB macro that describes the anticipated processing requirements. Figure 22.8 summarizes the parameters that can be specified in an ACB macro. A subset of these should always be specified, while the others are applicable only in special processing situations. All the accessing modes that are going to be used while the data set is being processed must be specified in the ACB macro.

Errors at Open Time

When the OPEN macro is executed, VSAM determines whether the data set identified by the ACB macro had been defined via AMS and is currently specified by appropriate job control statements. It also determines whether the access parameters—e.g., password, updating, access modes, etc.—are consistent with what is specified for the data set in the catalog. If all these conditions are met, then the OPEN request is granted, i.e., the data set is then said to be "open" and is available for processing. If any of the conditions are not met, VSAM puts an explanatory error code in the ERROR field of the ACB and puts a nonzero indicator in Register 15 before returning to the user program. If the program finds that Register 15 is not zero, it can take appropriate action after examining the ACB error code via the SHOWCB macro (see Section 22.6).

Errors with GET, PUT, ERASE

Once a data set is open, the GET, PUT, and ERASE macros can be used to access logical records. GET is used to retrieve an existing record, and PUT is used to update an existing record and to add or insert a new record. PUT is therefore also used to load a data set. ERASE is used to delete existing KSDS (but not ESDS) records. All three macros have identical operand formats, as shown in Figure 22.9a. If any error is detected while VSAM is responding to a GET, PUT, or ERASE request, an error code is placed in the FDBK field of the corresponding RPL macro, and VSAM puts a nonzero indicator in Register 15 before returning to the user program. As with OPEN errors, the user program can use the SHOWCB macro to determine the precise cause of the error.

It is important to note that execution of a PUT macro to update an existing record must be preceded by execution of a GET macro for that same record. The same is true for the ERASE macro: it must be preceded by a GET for the record that is to be erased. In both cases the GET is known as "GET-for-update." The PUT is similarly known as "PUT-for-update." The parameter that specifies the update mode for GET and PUT is one of the RPL's OPTCD parameters, 'UPD'.

Figure 22.9b summarizes the parameters that can be specified in an RPL macro. As with ACB, certain RPL parameters always should be specified, while the others apply only in special cases. Unlike the ACB, in which all anticipated accessing modes must be specified, only one accessing mode can be specified in an RPL macro. It must be the mode for which the GET, PUT, or ERASE is being used.

Processing Modes

Regardless of the access mode, and regardless of whether the data set is a KSDS or an ESDS, the input/output processing mode should be specified in the RPL macro as follows:

	with GET	with PUT
for retrieval only	OPTCD=(...,NUP,LOC,...) OPTCD=(...,NUP,MVE,...)	-----
for updating	OPTCD=(...,UPD,MVE,...)	OPTCD=(...,UPD,MVE,...)
for adding new records	----	OPTCD=(...,NUP,MVE,...)

Figure 22.8   ACB macro parameters.

General format: acbname   ACB   keyword$_1$=value$_1$,...,keyword$_n$=value$_n$

Only those keywords that pertain to your processing needs have to be specified. They can be specified in any order.

An asterisk (*) in the left-hand margin denotes keywords and options available in OS/VS but not in DOS/VS. See the OS/VS VSAM Programmer's Guide or the DOS/VS Supervisor and I/O Macros manual for further restrictions and explanations.

keywords commonly used
    AM=VSAM   states that the access method is VSAM
    DDNAME=dname   dname identifies the associated JCL statement
    MACRF=(macrf-options)   specifies options for run-time processing (see below)

keywords for error handling
    EXLST=exlstname   identifies this ACB's EXLST macro
    MAREA=address   names an area to receive OPEN/CLOSE error messages
    MLEN=length   specifies the length of the MAREA area

keywords for buffers
    BUFND=n$_1$ n$_1$ = # I/O buffers used for data component CIs
    BUFNI=n$_2$ n$_2$ = # I/O buffers used for index component CIs
    BUFSP=s   s = maximum number of bytes for all data and index buffers
    STRNO=n$_3$ n$_3$ = max number of requests requiring concurrent data-set positioning (such requests are known as *strings*)
*   BSTRNO=n$_4$ n$_4$ = # strings accessing the base cluster of a path

                            Note: Defaults are n$_3$=1, n$_1$=n$_3$+1, n$_2$=n$_3$, n$_4$=n$_3$.
                                 Default for s is consistent with n$_1$ and n$_2$ and with catalog info.

keywords for catalogs
    PASSWD=address   names a field that contains the highest-level password required for the type of access specified in MACRF=
*   CATALOG=NO|YES   specifies whether a catalog is being opened as a catalog (YES) or as a data set (NO); default is NO
*   CRA=SCRA|UCRA   requests system or user storage be used when processing a catalog recovery area

macrf-options for data set access
    KEY|ADR|CNV   keyed, addressed, or control-interval access
    SEQ|DIR|SKP   sequential, direct, or skip-sequential access
    IN|OUT   IN means retrieval only; OUT means loading or updating
    NRM|AIX   NRM means process the object named by DDNAME=; AIX means process the alt index whose path is named by DDNAME=
    NRS|RST   NRS: not a reusable data set, or else do not set high-RBA to zero; RST: reset high-RBA of reusable data set to zero

                            Note: Defaults are KEY, SEQ, IN, NRM, and NRS.

macrf-options for performance improvement
    NUB|UBF   whether or not user program manages use of I/O buffers
*   NFX|CFX   whether or not buffers and control blocks are swappable
*   NCI|ICI   whether or not to use improved control-interval processing
*   NIS|SIS   whether or not to split control intervals/areas at the position where a record is inserted

                            Note: Defaults are NUB, NFX, NCI, and NIS. *N* means *not.*

macrf-options for shared resources
    NSR|LSR|GSR   nonshared, locally shared, or globally shared resources
    NDF|DFR   nondeferred or deferred writing of shared buffers
*   DDN|DSN   shared control blocks are based on ddnames/dsnames

                            Note: Defaults are DDN, NDF, and NSR. GSR is for OS/VS only.

Figure 22.9a   OPEN, CLOSE, GET, PUT, and ERASE macro parameters.

```
OPEN    (acbname) I (r)

CLOSE   (acbname) I (r)                OS and DOS close and disconnect

CLOSE   (acbname) I (r), TYPE=T        OS/VS closing without disconnecting
TCLOSE  (acbname) I (r)                DOS/VS closing without disconnecting

GET     RPL=rplname I (r)
PUT     RPL=rplname I (r)
ERASE   RPL=rplname I (r)
```

Note: acbname and rplname are the name-field symbols that identify the ACB and RPL macros, respectively.
r is the address of a register (2 thru 12, enclosed in parentheses) that contains the address of an ACB or RPL macro.

Figure 22.9b   RPL macro parameters.

General format: rplname   RPL   keyword$_1$=value$_1$,...,keyword$_n$=value$_n$

Only those keywords that pertain to your processing needs have to be specified. They can be specified in any order.

An asterisk (*) in the left-hand margin denotes keywords and options available in OS/VS but not in DOS/VS. See the *OS/VS VSAM Programmer's Guide* or the *DOS/VS Supervisor and I/O Macros* manual for further restrictions and explanations.

keywords commonly used

AM=VSAM	states that the access method is VSAM
ACB=acbname	identifies the associated ACB control block
AREA=areaname	identifies the work area for logical records in move mode
AREALEN=m	m is the length of the work area, and should be no less than the length of the longest record to be processed
ARG=fieldname	identifies the field that contains the search key or RBA used in direct and skip-sequential access, and in positioning
KEYLEN=k	k is the length of the generic key used when OPTCD=GEN
RECLEN=r	r is the length of the record that PUT adds or inserts
OPTCD=(optcd-options)	specifies options for run-time processing (see below)

keywords for advanced applications

TRANSID=i	i is a number that identifies all the modified buffers associated with a given transaction ($0 \leq i \leq 31$)
* ECB=address	identifies an event control block used with asynchronous I/O
* MSGAREA=address	names an area to receive physical I/O error messages from VSAM
* MSGLEN=length	specifies the length of the MSGAREA area; must be $\geq$ 128
NXTRPL=address	specifies the address of the next RPL in a chain of RPL's

optcd-options

KEY I ADR I CNV	keyed, addressed, or control-interval access
SEQ I DIR I SKP	sequential, direct, or skip-sequential access
MVE I LOC	move mode or locate mode
NUP I UPD I NSP	is not for update, is for update, or note sequential position
KEQ I KGE	with keyed access, find the first record with a key that is either equal to, or greater than or equal to, the search key
FKS I GEN	specifies whether the search key is a full key or a generic key
FWD I BWD	record accessing is either in the forward or the backward direction; if BWD, then KEQ and FKS are assumed
ARD I LRD	ARD: record accessing is as specified in other parameters; LRD: locate or retrieve the last record in the data set (BWD)
* SYN I ASY	synchronous or asynchronous accessing
* NWAITX I WAITX	specifies whether or not to give control to the user's UPAD error-exit routine to synchronize processing of shared resources

Note: Defaults for all optcd-options are specified above as the first choice in each group of two or three options.

GET can be used in either move mode or locate mode, but both PUT and ERASE must always be used in move mode. **Move mode** (OPTCD=MVE) means that VSAM moves a logical record to and from the area specified by the AREA= parameter in the RPL macro. **Locate mode** (OPTCD=LOC) means that for the GET macro VSAM doesn't move the record to the AREA area. Instead it puts its *address* in that area. That address is the location of the record in the VSAM I/O buffer. As is indicated above, the author recommends that except when retrieving without updating, move mode should be used for all but the most performance sensitive situations. The extra processing incurred by move mode will usually be offset by the processing incurred when switching from locate mode to move mode during update operations. It should be noted, however, that move mode requires that the AREA and AREALEN parameters be specified in the RPL macro.

A final point to observe is that when PUT is used to store new records (as when loading a data set), the RPL's RECLEN= parameter must specify the length of each record that is being stored. If the records are all the same length, this is a simple matter; the length can just be coded in the RPL at assembly time. If the records are of varying length, then RECLEN= must be specified via a MODCB macro prior to each execution of a PUT macro (see Section 22.6). RECLEN= is not required for GET or ERASE; the length of existing records is known by VSAM.

22.4   LOADING A VSAM DATA SET

In Section 22.2, we showed how the AMS *REPRO* command could be used to load a key-sequenced data set. The input was a sequential data set, and the example was based on the dorm room file described in Chapter 20.

In this section, we illustrate how to load a VSAM data set via an assembly language program. By writing your own program instead of using REPRO, you are of course better able to interpret and utilize the input records.

We will again base our illustration on the dorm room master file. For this you should be familiar with Section 20.9 and the program given in Figure 20.8 that creates the master file as a sequential data set. There, it will be recalled, we showed how more than one input record could result in a single master file record. That same processing logic will be used here. The only differences between what follows now and what was done in Chapter 20 are in the use of the request macros OPEN, GET, PUT, and CLOSE, and in the use of the ACB and RPL control block macros instead of the OS DCB or DOS DTFSD macros.

Figure 22.10 shows the changed portions of the program that was given in Figure 20.8. Not changed (and therefore not shown) are the standard program entry and exit sequences, the internal subroutine to construct a master record, the input and output record areas, and the OS DCB (or DOS DTFCD) macros describing the input transaction file.

The output data set in Figure 22.10 is being loaded as an entry-sequenced data set (ESDS). From our prior discussions it should be clear that this data set must have already been defined in a VSAM catalog via AMS. In Figure 22.10 the ACB MACRF and RPL OPTCD parameters both specify ADR, SEQ (addressed sequential access), because no other accessing mode is permitted when loading an ESDS.

If the data set had been defined as a KSDS rather than an ESDS, the only changes required in the statements of Figure 22.10 would be to code MACRF=(KEY,SEQ,...) and OPTCD=(KEY,SEQ,...) instead of =(ADR,SEQ,...), and to change the record length to 107 instead of 106 by defining one blank to be the first character of the record. The record length change must also be reflected in the RECLEN= parameter of the RPL macro. The extra blank character that is introduced in this way is included only for compatibility with the indexed sequential delete flag (see Chap. 21) and is not absolutely necessary. However what *is* necessary is that the KSDS be loaded using keyed sequential access and that the records that are loaded be in ascending prime key sequence.

It is of crucial importance to note that we have not used an EXLST macro in the statements of Figure 22.10. As mentioned at the end of Section 22.1, this means that we *must* test the Register 15 code returned by VSAM after each I/O macro is executed. That code will be zero if no error occurred, and nonzero if some error did occur. Failure to test that code and take some appropriate action would most likely result in a subsequent fatal error causing the program to blow up. As can be seen, we have simply terminated the program if a nonzero code is returned in Register 15 by VSAM. (It might have been more appropriate to print a message telling the user why the program

Figure 22.10   Loading a VSAM data set.

```
1    CREATE    CSECT
2    *
3    *  THESE PROGRAM SEGMENTS ARE CHANGES TO THE PROGRAM GIVEN
4    *    IN CHAPTER 20, FIG. 20.8. THEY ARE INTENDED TO INDICATE
5    *  HOW TO CODE THE  OPEN,  PUT,  AND  CLOSE  MACROS  AND THE
6    *  ASSOCIATED  ACB  AND  RPL  MACROS WHEN LOADING A VSAM
7    *  ENTRY SEQUENCED DATA SET.
8    *
9              ...                    STANDARD ENTRY NOT SHOWN
10   *
11   * INITIALIZATIONS
12   *
13            OPEN    (MASTER)        OPEN VSAM MASTER FILE
14            LTR     15,15           SEE IF OPEN WAS SUCCESSFUL
15            BNZ     STDXIT          IF NOT, TERMINATE.
16            OPEN    (TRANS,(INPUT))  OPEN 'SYSIN' TRANSACTION FILE
17   *  DOS ********
18   *        OPEN    TRANS
19   ***************
20   *
21            GET     TRANS,INAREA    GET FIRST TRANSACTION RECORD
22            BAL     14,CONSTRCT     BEGIN CONSTRUCTING FIRST OUTPUT RECD
23   *
24   * MAIN PROCESSING
25   *
26   READ     GET     TRANS,INAREA    GET NEXT TRANS RECD (IF ANY)
27            ...                    PROCESS IT AS IN FIG. 20.8
28   *
29   WRITE    PUT     RPL=LOADIT      MOVE OUTPUT RECD TO OUTPUT BUFFER.
30            LTR     15,15           SEE IF ANY I/O ERRS
31            BNZ     EOJX            IF SO, TERMINATE.
32            BAL     14,CONSTRCT     BEGIN CONSTRUCTING NEXT OUTPUT RECD.
33            B       READ            THEN GET NEXT TRANS RECD.
34   *
35   * END-OF-DATA PROCESSING
36   *
37   EOJ      PUT     RPL=LOADIT      MOVE LAST OUTPUT RECD TO OUTPUT BUF.
38   EOJX     CLOSE   (MASTER)        CLOSE ALL FILES.
39            CLOSE   (TRANS)
40   *  DOS ********
41   *        CLOSE   TRANS
42   ***************
43   STDXIT   ...                    STANDARD EXIT NOT SHOWN.
44   *
45   *
46   * INTERNAL SUBRS  'CONSTRCT'  AND  'UPDATING'  ARE THE SAME AS
47   *    IN FIG.20.8,  AND ARE NOT SHOWN HERE.
48   * OS DCB  AND  DOS DTFCD  FOR TRANS FILE ARE ALSO THE SAME,
49   *    AS ARE THE I/O RECORD AREAS FOR THE TRANS AND MASTER FILES.
50   * BUT  OS DCB  AND  DOS DTFSD  FOR MASTER FILE ARE REPLACED BY
51   *    THIS VSAM  ACB / RPL PAIR.
52   *
53   MASTER   ACB     AM=VSAM,DDNAME=DORMS,MACRF=(ADR,SEQ,OUT)
54   LOADIT   RPL     AM=VSAM,ACB=MASTER,RECLEN=106,               X
55            AREA=OUTAREA,AREALEN=106,OPTCD=(ADR,SEQ,NUP,MVE)
56   *
57   * REGISTER SAVE AREA IS SAME AS IN FIG. 20.8
58            END
```

terminated, but we leave that for you. The precise nature of the error can be determined by examining the ERROR or FDBK codes supplied by VSAM, as will be described in Section 22.6.)

Finally, it may be noted that the information about record format and blocksize is not coded in an ACB or RPL because VSAM gets that information from the catalog. The same is true of key length and key position for key-sequenced data sets.

22.5   UPDATING AN ENTRY-SEQUENCED DATA SET

There are two principal techniques for updating an entry-sequenced data set. One technique requires the creation of a new data set. The other updates the existing data set in place.

If a new data set is to be created, it must have been previously defined via AMS. The existing data set is opened in input mode (ACB *IN* parameter), and the new data set is opened in output mode (ACB *OUT*). Both are processed with RPL OPTCD=NUP i.e., not an update. The new data set is in effect loaded with all the unchanged and changed records of the old data set, excluding the records that are being deleted. New records (i.e., records not in the existing data set) can also be added to the new data set during processing.

Updating to a New Data Set

This method is the same as that used with sequential data sets (see Section 20.10 and the pseudocode of Figures 20.12a–c), except of course for the differences in I/O macros that are required for VSAM. Changes to the sequential update program in Chapter 20, Figure 20.13, that are similar to those shown in Figure 21.10 would serve to update an ESDS dorm room master file.

Updating in Place

The other method of updating an ESDS is akin to the sequential UPDAT mode of OS systems, except that in VSAM the update-in-place can be done either by addressed sequential access or by addressed direct access. Whichever access mode is used, changes to the data set are made by replacing existing records rather than by copying them to a new data set. The lengths of updated records cannot be changed; neither can records be erased. However, a record can be "marked for deletion" to indicate that they are subsequently to be ignored or replaced (see the following).

In this section we will discuss only the addressed sequential access mode. Addressed direct is a more complex process because it requires that the program specify the RBA (relative byte address) of each record that is to be updated. That in turn requires that the program somehow know the RBA *before* it can read a record. In addressed sequential you do not have to specify the RBA because the records are read in the sequence in which they exist in the data set and VSAM therefore can calculate the RBA of each record.

OPTCD Parameter

Each data-set record is read one at a time by the GET macro into the work area designated by the RPL AREA= parameter. The GET macro must be a GET-for-update, i.e., with OPTCD=UPD coded in the associated RPL.

When the program's logic determines that a particular record is to be updated, the desired changes are made to the record in the AREA= work area. The record must then be rewritten by the PUT-for-update macro (PUT with OPTCD=UPD) before the next GET-for-update is executed.

If on the other hand the program determines that a record is not to be updated, then it bypasses execution of the PUT-for-update, i.e., the record is not rewritten. Instead, the program just executes the next GET-for-update.

The process continues until all records that were intended to be updated were in fact updated. As we can see, the advantage of updating in place instead of updating by creating a new data set is that computer processing time is not wasted on writing unchanged records. The disadvantage is that there is not as much flexibility: Records cannot be inserted, the lengths of existing records cannot be changed, and deleted records cannot be erased but can only be marked for deletion. Despite these disadvantages, updating in place is often used.

Delete Flag

A program that carries out this procedure for the dorm room master file is outlined in Figure 22.11. It is based on the pseudocode of Figure 20.10 and is similar to the program of Figure 20.11 that updates sequential data sets in the OS UPDAT mode. The only difference in the procedures is that VSAM update-in-place includes marking records for deletion. This is done by putting a distinguishing code (X'FF' in our program) in the record before rewriting it. By studying Figure 22.11, you will see that records previously marked for deletion are either ignored or replaced by new records of the same length after they are read by the program.

22.6 UPDATING A KEY-SEQUENCED DATA SET

As with ESDS updating, there are two principal methods for KSDS updating: either by creating a new data set, which is the updated version of an existing data set, or by updating existing records in place. However, we rarely update a KSDS cluster by creating a new data set; the main purpose of using KSDS is to be able to use its capabilities for direct updating and retrieval.

Access Modes Via MACRF

KSDS updating in place can be accomplished by keyed sequential access, keyed direct access, and keyed skip-sequential access. Only one of these can be used with a given request macro, but a program can switch from one mode to another after opening the data set. The MACRF= parameter of an ACB must specify all the access modes that are to be used during updating. Then when a GET, PUT, or ERASE macro is executed, the OPTCD= parameter of the corresponding RPL macro must designate the particular access mode being used: (KEY,SEQ,...), (KEY,DIR,...), or (KEY,SKP,...).

Keyed Seq'tl

Use of keyed sequential access to update KSDS records in place is similar to updating ESDS records in place, except that the data set can be positioned to any arbitrary point before beginning sequential updating from that point on. The positioning is done with a POINT macro. Either a primary key or a high-order portion of a primary key (the latter being known as a *generic* key) can be used to designate the starting position. This is analogous to the use of the SETL macro when updating indexed sequential data sets.

Figure 22.11   ESDS updating in place.

```
  1   UPDAT    CSECT
  2   *
  3   *THIS PROGRAM UPDATES THE ESDS DORM ROOM MASTER FILE USING ADDRESSED-
  4   * SEQUENTIAL ACCESSING, WITH FIXED-LENGTH RECORDS AND MOVE MODE.
  5   *
  6   * THE PROGRAM IS SIMILAR TO THE ONE IN FIG. 20.11 FOR UPDATING A SE-
  7   * QUENTIAL DATA SET, EXCEPT FOR THE USE OF MOVE MODE, MARKING RECORDS
  8   * FOR DELETION, AND BYPASSING/REPLACING DELETED RECDS.
  9   *
 10   *NO RECORDS ARE ADDED OR INSERTED. RECORDS MAY BE MARKED FOR DELE-
 11   * TION OR MODIFIED BY THE ADDITION OR DELETION OF STUDENT NAMES AND
 12   * I.D.'S. WHEN A NAME AND I.D. IS DELETED, IT IS SIMPLY REPLACED
 13   * BY BLANKS. WHEN A NAME AND I.D. IS ADDED TO A RECORD, IT IS PUT
 14   * INTO THE STUDENT DATA AREA THAT IS BLANK. IT IS ASSUMED THAT THE
 15   * INPUT TRANSACTION DATA ARE 'PERFECT'  NO ERRORS, NO DUPLICATES,
 16   * NO INVALID TRANSACTIONS.
 17   *
 18            ...                   STD ENTRY NOT SHOWN HERE.
 19   *
 20            OPEN   (MASTER)       OPEN MASTER FILE
 21            LTR    15,15          SEE IF OPEN WAS SUCCESSFUL
 22            BNZ    STDXIT         IF NOT, TERMINATE.
 23            OPEN   (TRANS,(INPUT)) OPEN 'SYSIN' DATA SET.
 24   * DOS *******
 25   *        OPEN   TRANS
 26   ***************
 27   *
 28            GET    TRANS,INAREA   GET FIRST TRANSACTION RECORD.
 29            BAL    14,GETMSTR     GET FIRST MASTER RECORD
 30   *
 31   * MAIN PROCESSING PROCEDURES
 32   *
 33   MAINLOOP CLC    TDORM,MDORM    IF DORM AND ROOM OF TRANS RECD ARE
 34            BNE    REWRITE           NOT EQUAL TO THOSE OF MASTER RECD,
 35            CLC    TROOM,MROOM    THEN RE-WRITE MASTER (IF NECESSARY)
 36            BNE    REWRITE           AND THEN GET NEXT MASTER RECD.
 37            BAL    14,UPDATING    OTHERWISE, GO DO UPDATING, AND THEN
 38            GET    TRANS,INAREA      GET NEXT TRANS RECD AND REPEAT THE
 39            B      MAINLOOP          PROCESS TILL END-OF-DATA.
 40   *
 41   REWRITE  CLI    MFLAG,BYP      MFLAG NOT 'BYP' IF CHANGES HAD BEEN
 42            BE     BYPASS            MADE TO MASTER RECORD.
 43            PUT    RPL=UPDIT      WHEN THAT IS THE CASE, RE-WRITE IT.
 44            LTR    15,15          IF ANY I/O ERR, TERMINATE.
 45            BNZ    EOJX
 46   BYPASS   BAL    14,GETMSTR     OTHERWISE, GET NEXT MASTER RECD,
 47            B      MAINLOOP          AND CONTINUE PROCESSING.
 48   *
 49   * END-OF-DATA PROCESSING
 50   *
 51   EOJ      CLI    MFLAG,BYP      BEFORE CLOSING, SEE IF MASTER RECD
 52            BE     EOJX              MUST BE RE-WRITTEN.
 53            PUT    RPL=UPDIT      IF SO, REWRITE IT.
 54   EOJX     CLOSE  (MASTER)       THEN CLOSE ALL DATA SETS, AND EXIT.
 55            CLOSE  (TRANS)
 56   * DOS *******
 57   *        CLOSE  TRANS
 58   ***************
 59   *
 60   STDXIT   ...                   STD EXIT NOT SHOWN
 61   *
 62   * INTERNAL SUBROUTINE 'GETMSTR' ENTERED VIA BAL 14,GETMSTR
 63   * GETS NEXT MASTER RECD IN MOVE MODE, AFTER RESETTING RECD-CHGD FLAG.
 64   * BYPASSES RECDS MARKED FOR DELETION UNLESS TRANS RECD IS FOR SAME
 65   * DORM & ROOM AS MASTER. IF SO, TRANS DATA REPLACES MASTER DATA.
 66   *
 67   GETMSTR  LR     2,14           SAVE RETURN ADDRESS
 68            MVI    MFLAG,BYP      RESET RECORD-CHANGED FLAG, TO INDI-
 69   GETMSTRA GET    RPL=UPDIT         CATE NO CHANGES HAVE YET BEEN MADE.
 70            LTR    15,15          IF END-OF-DATA OR I/O ERR,
 71            BNZ    EOJX              IGNORE REST OF TRANS FILE.
 72            CLI    DELMARK,X'FF'  SEE IF RECD MARKED FOR DELETION.
 73            BNE    GETMSTRX       IF NOT, O.K.
 74            CLC    TDORM,MDORM    ELSE, SEE IF TRANS RECD IS FOR
 75            BNE    GETMSTRA          SAME DORM & ROOM AS MSTR RECD.
 76            CLC    TROOM,MROOM    IF NOT, BYPASS MSTR RECD BY
 77            BNE    GETMSTRA          READING NEXT MSTR RECD.
 78            BAL    14,CONSTRCT    ELSE, REPLACE MSTR WITH TRANS DATA.
 79   GETMSTRX LR     14,2              THEN RETURN TO CALLER.
 80            BR     14
 81   *
 82   * INTERNAL SUBROUTINE 'UPDATING' ENTERED VIA  BAL 14,UPDATING
 83   * MARKS RECORDS FOR DELETION IF TRANSACTION CODE IS '4'; ELSE,
 84   * ADDS OR DELETES STUDENT NAME & I.D. FROM STUDENT DATA AREA
 85   * IN MASTER RECD. SETS FLAG INDICATING MSTR RECD HAS BEEN CHANGED.
 86   *
 87   * TRANSACTION CODE 'TTYPE' DETERMINES UPDATING ACTION
 88   *        TTYPE = C'1'  ...  ADD A NEW ROOM WITH NO STUDENTS
 89   *              = C'2'  ...  ADD A STUDENT NAME & I.D.
 90   *              = C'3'  ...  DELETE A STUDENT NAME & I.D.
 91   *              = C'4'  ...  DELETE ENTIRE MASTER RECD.
```

Figure 22.11   continued

```
 92  *
 93  UPDATING EQU    *
 94          USING SDAREA,11              SET DUMMY BASE REG TO ACCESS
 95          LA    11,MDATA1              STUDENT DATA AREA.
 96          CLI   TTYPE,C'4'       TRANS CODE '4' MEANS DELETE RECD
 97          BE    ERASE
 98          CLI   TTYPE,C'3'       TRANS CODE '3' MEANS DELETE STUDENT
 99          BNE   ADD              OTHERWISE ASSUME IT'S CODE '2' (ADD)
100  DEL     CLC   MID,TID          IF IT'S A DELETE, THEN MUST LOOK
101          BE    DEL1             FOR STUDENT I.D. IN 1ST & 2ND DATA AREAS
102          LA    11,DATALNG(11)   IF NOT IN 1ST, MUST BE IN 2ND  INCR ADDR
103  DEL1    MVC   MDATA1,BLANKS    REPLACE NAME & I.D. WITH BLANKS WHEN DE-
104          B     EXIT             LETING.
105  ADD     CLC   MID,BLANKS       WHEN ADDING, LOOK FOR VACANT STUDENT DATA
106          BE    ADD1             AREA.  IF NOT 1ST ONE, THEN ASSUME THAT
107          LA    11,DATALNG(11)   2ND AREA IS VACANT, AND INCR ADDR TO IT.
108  ADD1    MVC   MNAME,TNAME      MOVE NAME & I.D. FROM TRANS RECD TO STU-
109          MVC   MID,TID          DENT DATA AREA.
110          B     EXIT
111  ERASE   MVC   MDATA1,BLANKS    WHEN "ERASING", BLANK OUT STUDENT
112          MVC   MDATA2,BLANKS    INFO IN MSTR WORK AREA.
113          MVI   DELMARK,X'FF'    THEN MARK RECD FOR DELETION
114  EXIT    MVI   MFLAG,REWR       BEFORE RETURNING, SET FLAG TO INDICATE
115          BR    14               THAT RECD MUST BE REWRITTEN.
116  *
117  * INTERNAL SUBR 'CONSTRCT' ENTERED VIA  BAL  14,CONSTRCT
118  * REPLACES MSTR RECD DATA WITH TRANS DATA.
119  *
120  CONSTRCT EQU   *
121          USING SDAREA,11              SET DUMMY BASE REG FOR ACCESS
122          LA    11,MDATA1              TO STUDENT DATA AREA.
123          MVC   MNAME,TNAME      PUT STUDENT NAME & I.D. INTO
124          MVC   MID,TID          1ST STUDENT AREA, AND BLANK OUT
125          MVC   MDATA2,BLANKS    2ND AREA.
126          MVI   MFLAG,REWR       SET FLAG TO REWRITE MSTR RECD.
127          BR    14
128  *
129  * TRANSACTION INPUT RECORD AREA
130  *
131  INAREA  DS    CL80             RESERVE 80 BYTES FOR CARD IMAGE.
132          ORG   INAREA           BEGIN REDEFINITION OF INPUT AREA.
133          DS    CL3              COL 1-3  UNUSED
134  TTYPE   DS    CL1                4      TRANS TYPE CODE
135          DS    CL3                5-7    UNUSED
136  TDORM   DS    CL4                8-11   DORM ABBREVIATION
137          DS    CL4               12-15   UNUSED
138  TROOM   DS    CL4               16-19   DORM ROOM NUMBER
139          DS    CL1               20      UNUSED
140  TNAME   DS    CL40              21-60   STUDENT NAME
141          DS    CL1               61      UNUSED
142  TID     DS    CL9               62-70   STUDENT I.D.
143          ORG
144  *
145  * MASTER FILE LOGICAL RECORD AREA (FIXED LENGTH RECDS)
146  *
147  OUTAREA DS    OCL106
148  MDORM   DS    CL4              BYTES 0-3     DORM ABBREVIATION
149  MROOM   DS    CL4                    4-7     DORM ROOM NUMBER
150  MDATA1  DS    CL49                   8-56     1ST STUDENT DATA AREA
151  DELMARK EQU   MDATA1                 8      X'FF' MARKS DELETED RECDS
152  MDATA2  DS    CL49                   57-105   2ND STUDENT DATA AREA
153  *
154  * DUMMY SECTION TO ACCESS STUDENT WORK AREA
155  *
156  SDAREA  DSECT
157  MNAME   DS    CL40                   8-47    STUDENT NAME FIELD
158  MID     DS    CL9                    48-56   STUDENT I.D. FIELD
159  DATALNG EQU   *-MNAME                        LENGTH OF STUDENT AREA
160  UPDAT   CSECT
161  *
162  * BLANKS USED TO INITIALIZE STUDENT DATA AREAS
163  * MFLAG INDICATES WHEN A MASTER RECD MUST BE REWRITTEN.
164  *
165  BLANKS  DC    (DATALNG)C' '    'DATALNG' IS SIZE OF STUDENT DATA AREA
166  MFLAG   DC    X'FF'            X'FF' = DON'T REWRITE; X'00' = REWRITE
167  REWR    EQU   X'00'            REWR = RECORD HAS BEEN CHGD, REWRITE OK
168  BYP     EQU   X'FF'            BYP = RECD NOT CHGD, DONT REWRITE
169  *
170  *
171  * OS DCB  AND  DOS DTFCD  FOR TRANS FILE IS SAME AS IN  FIG.20.11
172  *    AND IS NOT SHOWN HERE.
173  *  BUT DCB / DTFSD  FOR MASTER IS REPLACED BY  VSAM ACB / RPL PAIR
174  *
175  MASTER  ACB   AM=VSAM,DDNAME=DORMS,MACRF=(ADR,SEQ,OUT)
176  UPDIT   RPL   AM=VSAM,ACB=MASTER,                                       X
177                AREA=OUTAREA,AREALEN=106,OPTCD=(ADR,SEQ,UPD,MVE)
178  *
179  * REGISTER SAVE AREA NEEDED BUT NOT SHOWN HERE
180          END
```

Use of keyed direct access to update KSDS records in place is similar to random-mode updating of indexed sequential data sets. The only records that have to be read from the master file are those that are to be updated. The program identifies each such record by specifying its prime key when a GET macro is executed. That key must be stored in the work area designated by the ARG= parameter of the RPL macro prior to executing the GET. Alternatively, a generic key can be used instead of the full prime key. The RPL parameter requirements are the same in this case as those for the POINT macro (see Section 22.8) and won't be discussed here. *Keyed Direct*

In on-line applications, keyed direct access is indispensable because records can be read in any sequence from the master file. In batch applications, this mode is also very useful and efficient provided the number of records that need to be updated is not a large proportion of the total number of KSDS records.

Use of keyed skip-sequential access to update KSDS records in place uses essentially the same program processing logic as keyed direct access. The main difference other than the OPTCD parameter is that the keys have to be presented in ascending key sequence. This is because in this mode VSAM does a sequential search of the index sequence sets to determine the location of records, and the search for each prime key that is presented begins where the search for the preceding prime key left off. Since the keys in the sequence sets are in ascending sequence, the keys that are presented by the user program must also be in ascending sequence. In keyed direct access this isn't necessary because in that mode VSAM does a top-down tree search on the entire index for each key that is presented. *Keyed Skip Seq'tl*

A program that uses keyed direct access to update the KSDS dorm room master file is outlined in Figure 22.12. The program uses a sequential data set of transactions to identify the records that are to be updated. It is based on the pseudocode of Figures 21.12a–c, and is similar to the program of Figure 21.13 that updates indexed sequential data sets in random mode. *Figure 22.12*

There are several differences between the indexed sequential and VSAM update procedures. These have to do with the manner in which existing records are erased or updated, the manner in which new records are inserted, and the manner in which invalid key conditions are detected.

In VSAM, records that are to be deleted are erased by the ERASE macro. There is no delete-flag mechanism comparable to that of indexed sequential processing. Instead of marking a record for eventual deletion, VSAM removes the record from its control interval when an ERASE macro is executed. *ERASE Macro*

To update a record, the record must be retrieved by a GET-for-update macro and rewritten (after suitable changes have been made to it in the user's work area) by a PUT-for-update macro. The RPL's OPTCD parameter must specify OPTCD=UPD for the GET and for the PUT. Any field in a record can be changed except the prime key field. To change a prime key, you must first erase the record that has the old prime key, and then insert a new record with the new prime key. *GET-for-Update* *PUT-for-Update*

To insert a new record, the record must be written by a PUT macro with OPTCD=NUP (not an update). The same output record area can be used for an insertion as is used for an update. As will be seen, rather than having two different RPL's for the two different OPTCD parameters, the program uses the MODCB macro to change the parameter from UPD to NUP (and vice versa) in a single RPL. *New Records*

The manner in which an invalid key condition is detected also deserves some comment. You will recall from Chapter 21 that an invalid key condition is said to exist in either of two situations: (1) when there is no master file record corresponding to the primary key presented by a GET-for-update; and (2) when there already exists a master file record with the same primary key as that of a new record that PUT attempts to add to the file. The first situation is known as "record not found"; the second, as "duplicate record". *Invalid Key*

When an invalid key or other exception condition occurs, VSAM puts an appropriate error code in the FDBK field of the RPL and also puts a code in Register 15. Then it returns to the user program. The code in Register 15 is =F'0' if no exception occurred, =F'8' if a logical error (including invalid key) occurred, and =F'12' if a physical I/O error occurred. The 1-byte FDBK code is stored in the low-order byte of a full-word work area whose address is designated in a SHOWCB macro (see p. 619).

Figure 22.12   *KSDS updating in place.*

```
 1   KSDSUPD   CSECT
 2   *
 3   * THIS PROGRAM UPDATES THE KSDS DORM ROOM MASTER FILE,
 4   *   USING  KEYED DIRECT  ACCESS.
 5   * IT IS SIMILAR TO THE PROGRAM OF FIG. 21.13 THAT UPDATES AN IN-
 6   *   DEXED SEQUENTIAL FILE IN RANDOM MODE, EXCEPT IN CHECKING FOR
 7   *   INVALID KEY VIA 'SHOWCB', AND USING 'ERASE' TO DELETE RECORDS.
 8   *
 9   * TRANSACTIONS ARE NOT NECESSARILY IN KEY SEQ, BUT ALL CONSECUTIVE
10   *   TRANS RECORDS FOR A GIVEN KEY ARE PROCESSED BEFORE WRITING THE
11   *   CORRESPONDING MASTER RECORD.
12   * INVALID KEY ERRORS ARE REPORTED ON 'SYSOUT' WITHOUT TERMINATING
13   *   THE PROGRAM.  THE FIRST UNCORRECTABLE ERROR TO OCCUR CAUSES
14   *   PROGRAM TERMINATION.
15   *
16             ...                 STANDARD ENTRY NOT SHOWN
17   *
18   * INITIALIZATIONS
19   *
20             OPEN   (MASTER)       OPEN MASTER FOR UPDATES & ADDITIONS
21             LTR    15,15          SEE IF OPEN WAS SUCCESSFUL
22             BNZ    STDXIT         IF NOT, TERMINATE.
23             OPEN   (REPORT,(OUTPUT))  OPEN ERROR REPORT FILE
24             OPEN   (TRANS,(INPUT))    OPEN TRANSACTION FILE
25   * DOS *******
26   *         OPEN   REPORT
27   *         OPEN   TRANS
28   ***************
29             GET    TRANS,TAREA      GET 1ST TRANS RECD
30   *
31   * MAIN PROCESSING
32   *
33   MAINLOOP MVC    KDORM,TDORM    MOVE TRANSACTION KEY TO KEY ARGUMENT
34            MVC    KROOM,TROOM         FOR KEYED DIRECT 'GET-FOR-UPDATE'.
35            CLI    TTYPE,C'1'     TRANS CODE = '1' MEANS ADD NEW RECORD
36            BE     NEWADD
37            B      UPDATE         OTHERWISE, GO PROCESS UPDATES
38   *
39   * END-OF-TRANSACTION-DATA
40   *
41   *     END-OF-DATA FLAG 'EODFLG'  CONTROLS PROCESSING DECISIONS
42   *          IF 'EODFLG' = WR   = X'0F', THEN WRITE LAST MASTER RECORD.
43   *          IF 'EODFLG' = REWR = X'F0', THEN REWRITE LAST MASTER RECORD.
44   *          IF 'EODFLG' = BYP  = X'FF', THEN DON'T WRITE OR REWRITE.
45   *
46   EOJ      CLI    EODFLG,BYP     EODFLG=BYP  IF END-OF-DATA OCCURRED AFTER
47            BE     XBYPASS        A MASTER RECD HAD BEEN DELETED.
48            CLI    EODFLG,WR      EODFLG=WR   IF END-OF-DATA OCCURRED WHILE
49            BE     XWRITE         A NEW MASTER RECD WAS BEING CONSTRUCTED.
50   XREWRITE BAL    14,REWRITE     EODFLG=REWR IF END-OF-DATA OCCURRED WHILE
51            B      XBYPASS        AN EXISTING MSTR RECD WAS BEING UPDATED.
52   XWRITE   BAL    14,WRITE
53   XBYPASS  CLOSE  (MASTER)       AFTER HANDLING LAST MASTER RECD, CLOSE
54            CLOSE  (TRANS)        ALL FILES, AND EXIT FROM PROGRAM
55            CLOSE  (REPORT)
56   * DOS *******
57   *         CLOSE  TRANS
58   *         CLOSE  REPORT
59   ***************
60   STDXIT   ...                   STD EXIT NOT SHOWN
61   *
62   * ADD NEW RECORD TO MASTER FILE
63   *
64   NEWADD   MVI    EODFLG,WR      SET END-OF-DATA FLAG TO WRITE LAST RECD.
65            BAL    14,CONSTRCT    GO BEGIN CONSTRUCTION OF NEW RECD.
66            MVC    ERRTRANS,TAREA  SET ERR MSG FOR POSSIBLE INVALID KEY.
67   ADDLOOP  GET    TRANS,TAREA    GET NEXT TRANS RECD (IF ANY), AND
68            CLC    KDORM,TDORM    SEE IF ITS KEY MATCHES THAT OF RECD BE-
69            BNE    ADDEND          ING CONSTRUCTED.  IF NOT, GO WRITE NEW
70            CLC    KROOM,TROOM    RECD TO MASTER FILE.
71            BNE    ADDEND
72            BAL    14,UPDATING    OTHERWISE, CONTINUE CONSTRCTING NEW RECD
73            B      ADDLOOP        USING INFO IN TRANS RECD.
74   ADDEND   BAL    14,WRITE       AFTER WRITING NEW RECD TO MASTER, THEN
75            B      MAINLOOP       DETERMINE WHAT TO DO WITH NEXT TRANS.
76   *
77   * UPDATE EXISTING RECORD IN MASTER FILE
78   *
79   UPDATE   MVI    EODFLG,REWR    SET END-OF-DATA FLG TO REWRITE LAST RECD
80            BAL    14,READ        THEN READ MASTER RECD THAT MATCHES KEY IN
81            LTR    15,15          KEY-ADDRESS AREA.  RETURN WITH CODE IND-
82            BNZ    VALIDKEY       ICATING WHETHER OR NOT IT WAS INVALID
83            MVI    EODFLG,BYP     KEY ERROR.  IF INVALID KEY, THEN RESET
84            GET    TRANS,TAREA    END-OF-DATA FLAG TO BYPASS REWRITE, AND
85            B      MAINLOOP       GET NEXT TRANS AND GO PROCESS IT.
86   *
87   VALIDKEY CLI    TTYPE,C'4'     IF VALID KEY, SEE IF TRANS IS CHANGE OR
88            BE     DELETE         DELETE REQUEST.
89   CHANGE   BAL    14,UPDATING    IF CHANGE, THEN GO MAKE CHANGES.
90            GET    TRANS,TAREA    THEN GET NEXT TRANS RECD (IF ANY).
91            CLC    KDORM,TDORM    SEE IF ITS KEY MATCHES THAT OF RECD BE-
```

Figure 22.12 continued

```
92                BNE    DIFFKEY      ING UPDATED.  IF NOT, GO REWRITE THAT
93                CLC    KROOM,TROOM  RECD BACK TO MASTER FILE.
94                BNE    DIFFKEY
95                B      VALIDKEY     OTHERWISE, CONTINUE MAKING CHANGES.
96       DIFFKEY  BAL    14,REWRITE   AFTER REWRITING CHANGED RECD, DETERMINE
97                B      MAINLOOP     WHAT TO DO WITH NEXT TRANSACTION RECD.
98       *
99       DELETE   DS     OH           WHEN THE REQUEST IS TO DELETE THE MASTER
100               BAL    14,ERASE     RECD, THEN SET DELETE FLAG AND REWRITE
101               MVI    EODFLG,BYP   THE RECD. SET END-OF-DATA FLAG TO BYPASS
102               GET    TRANS,TAREA  WRITING OR REWRITING LAST MASTER RECD.
103               B      MAINLOOP     GET NEXT TRANS RECD AND PROCESS IT.
104      *
105      * INTERNAL SUBROUTINES   'READ'    READS FOR UPDATING
106      *                        'REWRITE' WRITES AN UPDATED RECORD
107      *                        'ERASE'   ERASES AN EXISTING RECORD
108      *                        'WRITE'   WRITES A NEW RECORD
109      * ALL FOUR CALLED VIA  BAL 14,....
110      *
111      READ     LR     2,14                   SAVE RETURN ADDRESS
112               MODCB  RPL=UPDIT,OPTCD=(UPD)   SET GET-FOR-UPDATE MODE
113               LTR    15,15        SEE IF 'MODCB' WAS O.K.
114               BNZ    ABEND        IF NOT, TERMINATE.
115               GET    RPL=UPDIT    GET RECD VIA SEARCH ARGUMENT
116               LTR    15,15
117               BZ     RDEXIT       BRANCH IF NO I/O ERR.
118               SHOWCB RPL=UPDIT,                                        X
119                      AREA=FDBKAREA,LENGTH=4,FIELDS=(FDBK)
120               LTR    15,15        SEE IF 'SHOWCB' WAS O.K.
121               BNZ    ABEND        IF NOT, TERMINATE.
122               CLI    FDBKCODE,RNF ELSE, SEE IF RECD-NOT-FOUND
123               BNE    ABEND        IF NOT, THEN I/O ERR IS FATAL.
124      RDERR    MVC    ERRMSG,NOTFMSG ELSE, PRINT 'RECD-NOT-FOUND'
125               MVC    ERRTRANS,TAREA  MSG WITH CURRENT TRANSACTION.
126               PUT    REPORT,ERRLINE
127               LH     15,=H'-1'    SET ERROR RETURN CODE
128      RDEXIT   LR     14,2         RECOVER RETURN ADDRESS, AND
129               BR     14                RETURN TO CALLER.
130      *
131      REWRITE  LR     2,14         SAVE RETURN ADDRESS
132               PUT    RPL=UPDIT    PUT-FOR-UPDATE  REWRITES THE RECD
133               LTR    15,15        SEE IF ANY I/O ERR
134               BNZ    ABEND        IF SO, TERMINATE
135               LR     14,2
136               BR     14           OTHERWISE, RETURN TO CALLER.
137      *
138      ERASE    LR     2,14         SAVE RETURN ADDRESS
139               ERASE  RPL=UPDIT    DELETE THE MOST-RECENTLY-READ RECD
140               LTR    15,15        SEE IF ANY ERR
141               BNZ    ABEND        IF SO, IT'S FATAL.
142               LR     14,2         ELSE, RETURN TO CALLER.
143               BR     14
144      *
145      WRITE    LR     2,14                   SAVE RETURN ADDRESS
146               MODCB  RPL=UPDIT,OPTCD=(NUP)  SET 'PUT NOT-AN-UPDATE'
147               LTR    15,15        SEE IF 'MODCB' ERR
148               BNZ    ABEND        IF SO, TERMINATE.
149               PUT    RPL=UPDIT    WRITE NEW RECORD.
150               LTR    15,15        SEE IF I/O ERR
151               BZ     WREXIT       IF NOT, O.K.
152               SHOWCB RPL=UPDIT,                                        X
153                      AREA=FDBKAREA,LENGTH=4,FIELDS=(FDBK)
154               LTR    15,15        SEE IF 'SHOWCB' ERR
155               BNZ    ABEND        IF SO, IT'S FATAL.
156               CLI    FDBKCODE,DUP ELSE SEE IF 'DUPLICATE-RECD'
157               BNE    ABEND        ANY OTHER ERR IS FATAL.
158               MVC    ERRMSG,DUPLMSG IF DUPL-RECD ONLY, THEN PRINT
159               PUT    REPORT,ERRLINE  MSG WITH CURRENT TRANSACTION.
160      WREXIT   LR     14,2         RETURN TO CALLER.
161               BR     14
162      *
163      *
164      * 'ABEND' ROUTINE IS CALLED WHEN I/O ERROR OTHER THAN INVALID KEY IS
165      *   DETECTED DURING A READ, REWRITE, OR WRITE OPERATION.
166      * 'ABEND' TERMINATES THE PROGRAM AND ITS JOB STEP, VIA 'ABEND' MACRO.
167      *   COMPLETION CODE FOR TERMINAION IS ARBITRARILY CHOSEN AS 4095.
168      *
169      ABEND    ABEND  4095,DUMP,STEP
170      *
171      * DOS *******
172      *ABEND   DUMP
173      ************** **
174      *
175      * INTERNAL SUBROUTINE WITH TWO ENTRY POINTS, 'CONSTRCT' & 'UPDATING'
176      * BOTH ENTERED WITH BAL 14,... WITH NO PARAMETERS.
177      *
178      * TRANSACTION CODE 'TTYPE' DETERMINES UPDATING ACTION
179      *   TTYPE = C'1' ... ADD A NEW ROOM WITH NO STUDENTS
180      *         = C'2' ... ADD A STUDENT NAME & I.D.
181      *         = C'3' ... DELETE A STUDENT NAME & I.D.
182      *         = C'4' ... DELETE ENTIRE MASTER RECD.
```

Figure 22.12   continued

```
183  *
184  *'CONSTRCT' BEGINS CONSTRUCTION OF NEW OUTPUT MASTER RECD USING TRANS
185  * RECD.  'UPDATING' CONTINUES CONSTRUCTION OF NEW OUTPUT MASTER RECD.
186  *
187  CONSTRCT MVC   MDORM,TDORM          WHEN CONSTRUCTING A NEW RECD, MOVE
188           MVC   MROOM,TROOM          DORM AND ROOM NUMBER FROM TRANS
189           MVC   MDATA1,BLANKS        TO OUTPUT AREA, AND BLANK OUT STU-
190           MVC   MDATA2,BLANKS        DENT DATA AREAS.
191           CLI   TTYPE,C'2'           IF TRANS CODE IS '2', INSTEAD OF '1',
192           BE    UPDATING             CONTINUE CONSTRUCTION.
193           BR    14                   OTHERWISE, EXIT.
194  *
195  UPDATING LA    11,MDATA1            SET UP DUMMY BASE REG TO ACCESS STUDENT
196           USING SDAREA,11            DATA FIELDS IN MSTR RECD AREA.
197           CLI   TTYPE,C'2'           IF TRANS CODE = '2', THEN ADD STUDENT
198           BE    ADD                  NAME AND I.D.
199  DEL      CLC   MID,TID              OTHERWISE, ASSUME CODE = '3', AND
200           BE    DEL1                 DELETE EITHER 1ST OR 2ND NAME & I.D.
201           LA    11,DATALNG(11)       IF NOT 1ST, MUST BE 2ND  INCR ADDR.
202  DEL1     MVC   MNAME,BLANKS         DELETE BY REPLACING NAME & I.D. WITH
203           MVC   MID,BLANKS           BLANKS.
204           B     EXIT
205  ADD      CLC   MID,BLANKS           WHEN ADDING, SEE WHICH STUDENT DATA
206           BE    ADD1                 AREA IS BLANK, AND MOVE NAME & I.D.
207           LA    11,DATALNG(11)       INTO THAT AREA.  IF NOT 1ST AREA,
208  ADD1     MVC   MNAME,TNAME          THEN ASSUME IT'S 2ND AREA.
209           MVC   MID,TID
210  EXIT     BR    14
211  *
212  *
213  *   MASTER FILE I/O RECORD AREA
214  *
215  MAREA    DS    OCL107
216  MDELETE  DS    CL1         BYTES 0     FOR ISAM COMPATIBILITY ONLY
217  MDORM    DS    CL4               1-4   DORM ABBREVIATION
218  MROOM    DS    CL4               5-8   DORM ROOM
219  MDATA1   DS    CL49              9-57  1ST STUDENT DATA AREA
220  MDATA2   DS    CL49             58-106 2ND STUDENT DATA AREA
221  *
222  * DUMMY SECTION TO PERMIT ACCESS TO STUDENT DATA FIELDS
223  SDAREA   DSECT
224  MNAME    DS    CL40              9-48  STUDENT NAME FIELD
225  MID      DS    CL9              49-57  STUDENT I.D. FIELD
226  DATALNG  EQU   *-MNAME                 LENGTH OF STUDENT AREA
227  KSDSUPD  CSECT
228  *
229  * BLANKS USED TO INITIALIZE STUDENT DATA AREAS
230  BLANKS   DC    (DATALNG)C' '   'DATALNG' IS SIZE OF STUDENT DATA AREA
231  *
232  * KEY AREA FOR USE AS SEARCH ARGUMENT FOR 'GET' AND 'PUT'
233  *
234  KAREA    DS    CL8               8-BYTE KEY
235           ORG   KAREA
236  KDORM    DS    CL4               1ST 4 BYTES = DORM ABBREVIATION
237  KROOM    DS    CL4               2ND 4 BYTES = DORM ROOM NUMBER
238           ORG
239  *
240  *   AREA RESERVED FOR  'SHOWCB' FDBK CODES
241  FDBKAREA DS    OF                 MUST BE ON FULLWORD BOUNDARY
242           DS    XL1         BYTE 0      UNUSED
243  R15CODE  DS    XL1              1      R15 RETURN CODE
244  FTNCODE  DS    XL1              2      FTNCD (FOR ALT INDEXES)
245  FDBKCODE DS    XL1              3      FDBK FROM I/O MACROS
246  DUP      EQU   X'08'              DUPLICATE-RECD FDBK CODE
247  RNF      EQU   X'10'              RECD-NOT-FOUND FDBK CODE
248  *
249  * TRANSACTION INPUT AREA
250  *
251  TAREA    DS    CL80              RESERVE 80 BYTES FOR CARD IMAGE.
252           ORG   TAREA             BEGIN REDEFINITION OF INPUT AREA.
253           DS    CL3         COL 1-3    UNUSED
254  TTYPE    DS    CL1              4      TRANS TYPE CODE
255           DS    CL3              5-7    UNUSED
256  TDORM    DS    CL4              8-11   DORM ABBREVIATION
257           DS    CL4             12-15   UNUSED
258  TROOM    DS    CL4             16-19   DORM ROOM NUMBER
259           DS    CL1             20      UNUSED
260  TNAME    DS    CL40            21-60   STUDENT NAME
261           DS    CL1             61      UNUSED
262  TID      DS    CL9             62-70   STUDENT I.D.
263           ORG
264  *
265  * LOGICAL RECORD AREA FOR 'SYSOUT' PRINT LINE
266  *
267  ERRLINE  DS    OCL132            RESERVE 132 BYTES
268  ERRTRANS DS    CL80              80-BYTE TRANS RECD AREA
269  ERRMSG   DS    CL52              52-BYTE ERR MESSAGE AREA
270  *
271  DUPLMSG  DC    CL52' CANT ADD    RECD KEY ALREADY EXISTS ON MASTER FILE'
272  NOTFMSG  DC    CL52' CANT UPDATE RECD KEY DOESNT EXIST ON MASTER FILE'
```

Figure 22.12   continued

```
273  *
274  * EODFLG USED TO CONTROL PROCESSING WHEN AT END OF TRANSACTION FILE.
275  *
276  EODFLG    DC    X'FF'       END-OF-DATA FLAG  FOR LAST MASTER RECD
277  BYP       EQU   X'FF'         BYP  = DONT WRITE OR REWRITE WHEN AT END
278  WR        EQU   X'0F'         WR   = WRITE MSTR RECD WHEN AT END
279  REWR      EQU   X'F0'         REWR = REWRITE MSTR RECD WHEN AT END
280  *
281  *
282  * OS DCB'S  AND  DOS DTF'S  FOR TRANS FILE AND REPORT FILE
283  *   ARE NOT SHOWN HERE.  THEY ARE THE SAME AS IN  FIG.21.13 .
284  *
285  * OS DCB  AND  DOS DTFIS  FOR MASTER FILE  ARE REPLACED BY
286  *  THIS  VSAM  ACB / RPL  PAIR.
287  *
288  *
289  MASTER    ACB   AM=VSAM,DDNAME=DORMS,MACRF=(KEY,DIR,OUT)
290  UPDIT     RPL   AM=VSAM,ACB=MASTER,RECLEN=107,                      X
291                  AREA=MAREA,AREALEN=107,ARG=KAREA,                   X
292                  OPTCD=(KEY,DIR,SYN,MVE,UPD)
293  *
294  * REGISTER SAVE AREA NEEDED BUT NOT SHOWN.
295            END
```

The most important FDBK codes for beginning VSAM programmers are these[1]:

FDBK Error Codes

$$X'04' = \text{end-of-data (for ESDS as well as for KSDS)}$$
$$X'08' = \text{duplicate record}$$
$$X'10' = \text{record not found}$$

As can be seen from the program in Figure 22.12, a branch is made to an error-handling routine whenever a nonzero code is detected in Register 15 following execution of a GET or PUT macro. That error routine obtains the FDBK code via a SHOWCB macro and then determines whether the error was caused by an invalid key condition. An invalid key is a nonfatal error; the program can just inform the user and then proceed to the next transaction.

It is important to note that underlying the above method of detecting invalid key conditions is the fact that our program is running in synchronous I/O mode. This means that VSAM does not return to the program until it has finished processing a request macro. You will recognize that this is different from indexed sequential random-mode processing. There, a program must issue a WAIT or CHECK macro to synchronize I/O operations with program execution. In VSAM, the program must explicitly request asynchronous operations via OPTCD=ASY; only then is a CHECK macro used to synchronize operations. In our case we haven't designated OPTCD=ASY; instead, we are using the default OPTCD=SYN—i.e., synchronous mode.

I/O Synchronization

The SHOWCB macro used in Figure 22.12 copies information from the designated control block into a user work area. The work area address and length are specified by the AREA= and AREALEN= parameters, respectively (see Fig. 22.13). In general, the control block from which information is to be copied must be indicated by one of three parameters: ACB=*address,* RPL=*address,* and EXLST=*address.* In each case *address* identifies the location of the control block and can be specified symbolically, or as a relocatable expression, or in register notation. For the FDBK code, the appropriate control block is the request parameter list (RPL).

SHOWCB Macro

The information that is copied into the work area is requested by one or more options specified in the SHOWCB FIELDS= parameter. Values corresponding to those options are placed in the work area in the order in which the options are specified. Each value requires one full word (except those for the DDNAME and STMST options of the SHOWCB for ACB, which require two consecutive full words each). As can be expected, the user work area must begin on a full-word boundary and be long enough to contain all the values requested.

---

1. Other FDBK codes are listed in the section on "Return Codes" in the *VSAM Programmer's Guide.* Also to be found there is a description of ACB ERROR codes for OPEN and CLOSE macros.

Figure 22.13   SHOWCB and MODCB macro formats.

There are three separate SHOWCB and three separate MODCB macro operand formats, corresponding to the three separate control blocks ACB, EXLST, and RPL:

$$\text{showname SHOWCB} \left\{ \begin{array}{c} \text{ACB}= \\ \text{RPL}= \\ \text{EXLST}= \end{array} \right\} \text{address,keyword}_1=\text{value}_1,..., \text{keyword}_n=\text{value}_n$$

$$\text{modname MODCB} \left\{ \begin{array}{c} \text{ACB}= \\ \text{RPL}= \\ \text{EXLST}= \end{array} \right\} \text{address,keyword}_1=\text{value}_1,...,\text{keyword}_m=\text{value}_m$$

As can be seen, you must designate the address of the particular control block being referenced in each of the operand formats.

The keyword parameters and values in the SHOWCB operand are different from those in the MODCB operand.

SHOWCB keywords

AREA=address	designates the address of the area that will receive the values corresponding to the options specified in the FIELDS= parameter
LENGTH=m	m is the length of the AREA area
OBJECT=DATA I INDEX	specifies whether the fields that are specified are for the data component or for the index component (used with SHOWCB for ACB only)
FIELDS=(*field options*)	*field options* is a list of one or more mnemonic code words that identify the control block fields whose values are to be received in the AREA area

Note: For definition of the field-option mnemonics, see either the *OS/VS VSAM Programmer's Guide* or the *DOS/VS Supervisor and I/O Macros* manual.

MODCB keywords

The keywords and options in MODCB are (with but a few minor exceptions) the same as those in the respective ACB, RPL, and EXLST macros. For details, see either of the two manuals mentioned above.

The exact meanings of all the FIELDS= options are explained in the *VSAM Programmer's Guide*. Those that are probably of most use to beginning VSAM programmers are:

for SHOWCB ACB: FIELDS=ERROR obtains the error code that is placed in the ACB by VSAM after execution of an OPEN or CLOSE macro

for SHOWCB RPL: FIELDS=FDBK obtains the error code that is placed in the RPL by VSAM after execution of a request macro other than OPEN or CLOSE

FIELDS=RBA obtains the relative byte address of the most recently processed logical record

FIELDS=RECLEN obtains the length of the most recently processed logical record

In the program of Figure 22.12, we have used only the FIELDS=FDBK option.

MODCB Macro

The MODCB macro used in Figure 22.12 changes the value of one of the OPCTD parameters in the designated RPL control block. In general, MODCB can be used to change values of one or more parameters in an ACB, RPL, or EXLST control block. As can be seen from Figure 22.13, its operand format is similar to that of SHOWCB in that the control block must be identified by *address*. Beyond that the similarity breaks down, for MODCB's other operands are identical in format to those of the control block macro whose fields are to be modified.

Any number of valid parameters can be specified in a single MODCB macro. However, there is one precaution: you cannot modify the contents of an ACB that has not been opened by an OPEN macro; you cannot modify the contents of an RPL that is active, i.e., currently being used by VSAM at the same time that MODCB is executed; and you cannot modify an EXLST parameter unless that parameter was specified when the EXLST was generated.

Figure 22.14   Schematic structure of an alternate index.

An alternate index is a key sequenced data set. The base cluster to which it is related can be an entry sequenced or key sequenced data set.

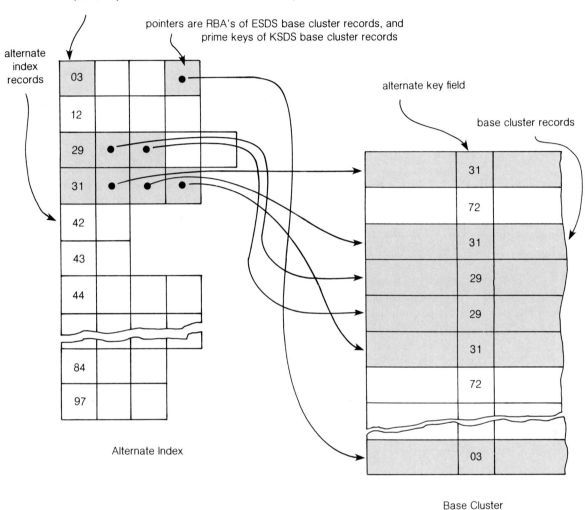

In our case we are safe. We are modifying an RPL that is inactive, i.e., although it is being used in the program it is not being used at the moment that the MODCB is executed. The OPTCD=SYN (synchronous) parameter ensures that the preceding GET, PUT, or ERASE macro has completed its use of the RPL before the MODCB is executed.

22.7   ALTERNATE INDEXES

An alternate index enables records in an ESDS or KSDS base cluster to be identified and accessed by key. That key is known as an alternate key, to distinguish it from the prime key of KSDS clusters. Its value is stored in what is known as an alternate key field of the base cluster records (see Figure 22.14).

As an example, we once again consider the dorm room file as a KSDS cluster. The second through ninth bytes of each record contain a 4-byte dorm identity and a 4-byte room number. Each record identifies the occupants of one room in a dormitory building (see Chap. 21). If we select the first two digits of the *room* number as an alternate key field, we can then use the values of that field as an alternate key to access records for a given *floor* of the dorms without having to access all records. In other words, the alternate key gives us access to just those records that contain that alternate key value.

Any field in the base cluster's records can be defined to be an alternate key field, provided it has a fixed length (1 to 255 bytes) and the same fixed position in all records of the cluster. There can be several different alternate key fields in a base cluster record. They can overlap one another, and they can overlap the prime key field if it's a KSDS cluster. For each alternate key field there must be one alternate index.

AMS Considerations

Each alternate index is itself a key-sequenced data set and must be defined by an Access Method Services DEF AIX (Define Alternate Index) command. That definition must allocate space for the alternate index and identify the base cluster to which the index is related. It must also identify the alternate key field's length and position in the base cluster records, and state whether or not the alternate key values should uniquely identify those records. We will illustrate how to do this for the dorm room master file, using as the alternate key field the first two digits of the room number.

Corresponding to each DEF AIX command there must be a DEF PATH command and a BLDINDEX command. The BLDINDEX command causes AMS to construct the alternate index records. Obviously, it cannot be used until after the base cluster has been loaded, and until after the two DEFINE commands have entered the appropriate alternate index information into a VSAM catalog. The DEF PATH command defines the means by which alternate key access to records in the base cluster is achieved at run time.

All three commands have the same formats in OS and DOS systems. The job control statements in each system must of course identify the alternate index and base cluster data sets, and in DOS the path itself must also be identified by JCL. No distinction is made in either system's job control statements as to whether the base cluster is a key-sequenced or entry-sequenced data set. AMS obtains that information from the catalog.

If the names we choose for the alternate index and path are DORM.FILE.AIX1 and DORM.FILE.PATH1, respectively, and if the names of the base cluster and user catalog are DORM.FILE and SAMPLE.UCAT, respectively, then the job control statements that precede the DEF AIX and DEF PATH commands can be written as follows (see also Section 22.2):

Job Control for Alternate Index

for OS systems:

```
//STEP006  EXEC  PGM=IDCAMS
//STEPCAT  DD    DSN=SAMPLE.UCAT,DISP=SHR
//AIXDD    DD    VOL=SER=VOLA,DISP=OLD,UNIT=3330
//SYSPRINT DD    SYSOUT=A
//SYSIN    DD    *
```

for DOS systems:

```
// DLBL    CLDD,'DORM.FILE',,VSAM
// EXTENT  SYS010,VOLA
// DLBL    AIXDD,'DORM.FILE.AIX1',,VSAM
// EXTENT  SYS010,VOLA
// DLBL    PATHDD,'DORM.FILE.PATH1',,VSAM
// EXTENT  SYS010,VOLA
// ASSGN   SYS010,DISK,VOL=VOLA,SHR
// EXEC    IDCAMS,SIZE=AUTO
```

The AMS commands that can then be used to define the alternate index and path are:

```
DEF AIX     ( NAME (DORM.FILE.AIX1), FILE (AIXDD) -
              RELATE (DORM.FILE), KEYS (2 5)       -
              VOL (VOLA), TRK (4 4)                -
              NONUNIQUEKEY, UPGRADE )              -
    DATA    ( NAME (DORM.FILE.AIX1.DATA)           -
              CISZ (4096) )                        -
    INDEX   ( NAME (DORM.FILE.AIX1.INDEX)          -
              CISZ (512) )                         -
            CAT (SAMPLE.UCAT/updatepassword)
DEF PATH    ( NAME (DORM.FILE.PATH1), FILE (xxx)   -
              PATHENTRY (DORM.FILE.AIX1) )         -
            CAT (SAMPLE.UCAT/updatepassword)
```

In the DEF PATH FILE parameter, *xxx* is AIXDD if the previous OS job control statements are used and is PATHDD if the DOS ones are used.

As was mentioned earlier, we have used the first two digits of the dormitory room number as the alternate key field. For the KSDS version of that file, those two digits occupy the sixth and seventh bytes of each record; hence the *offset* of the field from the beginning of each record is 5 bytes, while the length is 2 bytes: KEYS (2 5).

We specified NONUNIQUEKEY, meaning that an alternate key value need not uniquely identify a base cluster record. That is certainly the case in our example; since there are several rooms on each dormitory floor, there will be several records with the same first two digits of the room number.

We specified UPGRADE, meaning that VSAM is to keep the contents of the alternate index accurate and up-to-date. (In VSAM parlance, the alternate index is then part of the *upgrade set* of alternate indexes.) If we had not specified UPGRADE, then the information in the alternate index would have had to be kept accurate by a user program.

The space allocation TRK (4 4) was determined as discussed in Section 22.2: with a control interval size of 4096 bytes on an IBM 3330, then the number of tracks required for the data component of the alternate index is $(n \cdot k)/(4096 \cdot 3)$, where n = number of records in the alternate index, and k = average length of each record. The number n is easy to estimate, because *there is only one record in the alternate index for each different alternate key value.* Thus if there are no more than 10 floors per dormitory building, then $n = 10$, since there can be no more than ten different values of the first two digits of the room number. Somewhat more difficult to estimate is k, because the length of each alternate index record depends on how many base cluster records contain a given key value (see Fig. 22.14).

One simple estimate is to assume that $k = (1/n) \cdot N \cdot L$, where N is the total number of base cluster records and L is the length of each pointer in the alternate index. This estimate assumes that the different key values are fairly evenly distributed over the base cluster records. In our case, $N = 5000$, so with $n = 10$ we then have $k = 500 \cdot L$ bytes per alternate index record. For an ESDS cluster, the pointers are just the RBA's, so $L = 4$; for a KSDS cluster, the pointers are the prime keys, so L is the length of a prime key.

For our KSDS dorm room master file, we therefore have $k = 4000$. The number of tracks required is thus $(10 \cdot 4000)/(4096 \cdot 3) \approx 3$. To this we added one track for the index component of the alternate index. More accurate methods of estimating an alternate index's space requirements can be found in the AMS manuals.

To complete this brief discussion of the AMS commands for alternate indexes, we recall that the BLDINDEX command is required to construct the alternate index records once the definitions have been made. This command is much simpler than the DEF AIX or DEF PATH command. It consists of just one line:

```
BLDINDEX  INFILE (CLDD), OUTFILE (AIXDD)
```

The associated job control statements are almost identical to those given previously for DEF AIX and DEF PATH. The differences are that in OS systems you must *insert* this statement prior to the //SYSPRINT :

```
//CLDD      DD    DSN=DORM.FILE,VOL=SER=VOLA,DISP=OLD,UNIT=3330
```

and in DOS systems the //DLBL and //EXTENT statements for PATHDD are not included in the BLDINDEX JCL.

Programming Considerations

Having defined and constructed the alternate index via AMS, we are now able to use it to access the dorm room master file. The program statements in Figure 22.15 show the essential aspects of retrieving base cluster records through an alternate index.

Opening the Path

There are several things to notice. First, in order to access records at run time via an alternate key, a program must open the path, *not* the alternate index itself. *Opening the path simultaneously opens the alternate index* and *the base cluster.* (If you open the alternate index itself you just gain access to the records in that index; if you open the cluster, you just gain access to the records in the cluster without benefit of the alternate index. Opening the path is what is required to gain access to the cluster's records through the alternate index.) Therefore the JCL statement identified by the DDNAME= parameter of the ACB macro must refer to the *path* name, not to the base cluster or alternate index name.

Keyed Direct vs. Keyed Seq'tl

Second, once a path is opened at run time, an alternate key is used as the search argument for a GET macro executed with keyed direct access. That GET retrieves the first record in the base cluster that contains the key value. Any other records containing that same key value must then be retrieved by a GET executed with keyed sequential access. Each GET retrieves one record. The program determines whether there is another record with the same alternate key value by examining the FDBK code, which is returned by VSAM. Note that this is done when the Register 15 return code is *zero;* i.e., the existence of another record with the same alternate key is not an error condition.

Use of MODCB Macro

The third thing to notice is that the program must switch access modes from keyed direct to keyed sequential when more than one record with the same alternate key exists. This is done via the MODCB macro, by modifying the RPL's OPTCD=DIR parameter to OPTCD=SEQ. Then when there are no more records for a given alternate key, the program switches back to keyed direct and moves the next alternate key into the search argument field in preparation for the GET that retrieves the first record corresponding to that key.

In the statements of Figure 22.15, the ACB macro designates both keyed sequential *and* keyed direct access. This illustrates the rule that when opening a VSAM data set, the ACB must specify all the accessing techniques that might be used during processing. The RPL, on the other hand, designates only one access technique, namely, the one that is being used at that moment.

The ACB of Figure 22.15 also specifies the *IN* parameter, meaning that the base cluster's records will be retrieved but not updated. If updating were to be done, *OUT* would have been specified instead of *IN*. But when updating via an alternate index, you are not permitted to change the alternate key value. Changing the alternate key value must be done when updating with ordinary direct or sequential access, i.e., opening the base cluster itself rather than going through the alternate index.

OPTCD=NSP

Finally, it should be noted that OPTCD=NSP has been specified in the RPL. NSP (Note Sequential Position) means that VSAM will remember the position of the record that is retrieved in keyed direct mode so that the subsequent keyed sequential retrievals can be made without having to specify an RBA or key in the user program. NSP must be used instead of NUP (No Update), because when NUP is specified with keyed direct access, VSAM does not remember the position of the record that is retrieved.

22.8 TOPICS FOR FURTHER STUDY

The following brief list of topics is intended to introduce beginning VSAM programmers to some of the other VSAM processing capabilities not covered in this chapter. Details of these and other capabilities are in the manuals listed in the next section.

Figure 22.15   Retrieval via alternate index.

```
1   *
2   * THE FOLLOWING PROGRAM SEGMENTS SHOW THE ESSENTIAL ASPECTS
3   * OF RETRIEVING LOGICAL RECORDS FROM THE  KSDS  DORM-ROOM
4   * MASTER FILE THROUGH AN ALTERNATE INDEX.  SEE TEXT FOR ADDI-
5   * TIONAL COMMENTS.
6   *
7            OPEN   (MASTER)           OPEN FOR RETRIEVAL VIA ALT INDEX
8            LTR    15,15              SEE IF 'OPEN' FAILED
9            BNZ    ABERR              IF SO, TELL USER.
10           ...                       OPEN TRANSACTION FILE
11  *
12  GETNEW   GET    TRANS,TAREA        GET TRANS RECD WITH DESIRED ALT KEY
13           MVC    ALTKEY,TFLOOR      MOVE KEY TO RPL'S  ARG=  FIELD
14           MODCB  RPL=ALTRPL,OPTCD=(DIR)    SET KEYED-DIRECT ACCESS
15           LTR    15,15              SEE IF 'MODCB' O.K.
16           BNZ    ABERR              IF NOT, TELL USER
17           GET    RPL=ALTRPL         GET 1ST RECD WITH ALTKEY VALUE
18           LTR    15,15              SEE IF I/O ERRS
19           BNZ    NOGO               IF SO, MAY BE RECD-NOT-FOUND
20  PROCESS  ...                       ELSE, CAN NOW PROCESS THE RECD
21  *
22  * WHEN PROCESSING IS FINISHED, SEE IF THERE ARE ANY MORE
23  *  RECORDS WITH THE SAME ALT KEY VALUE.
24  *
25  PROCESSX SHOWCB RPL=ALTRPL,                                           X
26                  AREA=FDBKAREA,LENGTH=4,FIELDS=(FDBK)
27           LTR    15,15              SEE IF 'SHOWCB' O.K.
28           BNZ    ABERR              IF NOT, TELL USER.
29           CLI    FDBKCODE,DUP       ELSE FDBK CODE TELLS IF MORE RECDS
30           BNE    GETNEW             EXIST WITH SAME ALT KEY.
31           MODCB  RPL=ALTRPL,OPTCD=(SEQ) IF SO, NEED KEYED-SEQTL ACCESS
32           LTR    15,15              SEE IF 'MODCB' O.K.
33           BNZ    ABERR              IF NOT, TELL USER
34           GET    RPL=ALTRPL         ELSE, GET NEXT RECD WITH SAME KEY
35           LTR    15,15              SEE IF 'GET' FAILED
36           BNZ    ABERR              IF SO, TELL USER
37           B      PROCESS            ELSE, GO PROCESS THE RECD.
38  *
39  * IF 'GET' GAVE NONZERO ERR CODE IN REG 15, MAY BE RECD-NOT-FOUND.
40  * DETERMINE THAT WITH 'SHOWCB' FOR FDBK CODE.
41  *
42  NOGO     SHOWCB RPL=ALTRPL,                                           X
43                  AREA=FDBKAREA,LENGTH=4,FIELDS=(FDBK)
44           LTR    15,15              SEE IF 'SHOWCB' O.K.
45           BNZ    ABERR              IF NOT, TELL USER.
46           CLI    FDBKCODE,RNF       ELSE SEE IF RECD-NOT-FOUND ERR
47           BNE    ABERR              IF NOT, THEN ERR WAS SERIOUS.
48           ...                       ELSE, CAN WRITE NON-FATAL ERR MSG
49           B      GETNEW             AND THEN GET NEXT TRANSACTION.
50  *
51  * TAKE REMEDIAL ACTION (E.G., WRITE MSG TO USER) AND/OR TERMINATE.
52  *
53  ABERR    ...
54  *
55  * TERMINATE WHEN TRANS FILE REACHES END-OF-DATA
56  *
57  EOD      ...                       CLOSE ALL FILES
58           B      STDXIT
59  *
60  STDXIT   ...                       STANDARD EXIT FROM PROGRAM.
61  *
62  *
63  * TRANSACTION INPUT RECORD AREA
64  TAREA    DS     0CL80              DEFINE 80-BYTE AREA
65           DS     CL15               COL 1-15  UNUSED
66  TFLOOR   DS     CL02                  16-17  1ST TWO DIGITS OF ROOM#
67           DS     CL63                  18-80  UNUSED
68  *
69  * MASTER FILE LOGICAL RECORD AREA
70  MAREA    DS     0CL107             DEFINE 107-BYTE AREA FOR KSDS RECORD
71           ...                       SPECIFY OTHER FIELDS FOR PROCESSING
72  *
73  * SEARCH ARGUMENT AREA FOR 2-BYTE ALTERNATE KEY.
74  ALTKEY   DS     CL2                CONTAINS 1ST TWO DIGITS OF ROOM#
75  *
76  * FDBK AREA FOR USE WITH 'SHOWCB' MACRO
77  FDBKAREA DS     0F                 MUST BE ON FULLWORD BOUNDARY
78           DS     XL3                BYTES 0-2  UNUSED
79  FDBKCODE DS     XL1                     3   FDBK CODE
80  DUP      EQU    X'08'              DUPLICATE-RECD CODE
81  RNF      EQU    X'10'              RECD-NOT-FOUND CODE
82  *
83  * ACB/RPL PAIR FOR ACCESS TO KSDS CLUSTER THROUGH ALT INDEX
84  *
85  MASTER   ACB    AM=VSAM,DDNAME=FLPATH,MACRF=(KEY,DIR,SEQ,IN)
86  ALTRPL   RPL    AM=VSAM,ACB=MASTER,                                   X
87                  AREA=MAREA,AREALEN=107,                               X
88                  OPTCD=(KEY,DIR,SYN,MVE,NSP),ARG=ALTKEY,KEYLEN=2
89  *
```

EXLST Macro. This macro establishes the addresses of user-program routines that VSAM branches to when logical or physical errors prevent VSAM from successfully processing a request macro. It can also be used to obtain notification of so-called journalizing events, i.e., events that are not necessarily errors but that a user program may wish to know about in order to keep a record, or journal, of their occurrence. An example of such an event is a change in the RBA of a record.

TESTCB Macro. This is similar to the SHOWCB macro, but instead of putting control block information into a user work area as SHOWCB does, TESTCB simply compares the value of a control block field to a value that you supply and sets the condition code to indicate the result of the comparison.

POINT Macro. This positions a VSAM data set for subsequent sequential processing. Positioning can be done by an RBA, a prime key, or a generic key. If done with a generic key (i.e., a high-order portion of a prime key), then the associated RPL macro's OPTCD parameter must specify whether POINT should find a record with the exact generic key (GEN,KEQ) or with a key that is greater than or equal to the generic key (GEN,KGE). Whether an RBA or a full or generic key is used, it must be moved to the field designated by the ARG= parameter before POINT is executed. If a generic key is used, the RPL KEYLEN= parameter must specify the generic key's length.

GENCB Macro. This is an executable macro that creates an access-method control block (ACB), request parameter list (RPL), or list of exception-routine addresses (EXLST) at run time rather than at assembly time. One advantage of using GENCB instead of ACB, RPL, or EXLST is that if VSAM control block formats change in the future, programs assembled with older versions of VSAM may not have to be reassembled to run under the newer versions.

VSAM Processing Statistics. The SHOWCB-ACB macro can obtain a number of statistics that characterize the processing that has occurred on a given data set. The statistics are full-word integers whose names are specified via the FIELDS= parameter in SHOWCB. Most of the names begin with the letter *N;* for example, NLOGR obtains the number of logical records that exist in the data component of the designated base cluster.

PRINT, LISTCAT, and DELETE Commands in AMS. These Access Method Services commands print the contents of a VSAM data set, list the contents of a VSAM catalog, and delete a data set or other VSAM object. LISTCAT is particularly useful for determining the names of your data sets (in case you've forgotten them) and for determining how much space was actually allocated to each data set.

Reusable Data Sets. Any VSAM data set can be defined as a temporary, i.e., reusable, data set via the DEF CLUSTER *REUSE* parameter. When opening such a data set, you can specify MACRF=(OUT,RST) in the ACB. The RST resets the highest RBA of records in that data set to zero, so that in effect the data set is considered to be empty when it is opened. Alternate indexes cannot be defined for reusable data sets.

FREESPACE Option for KSDS. A portion of the data space that is allocated to a key-sequenced data set can be reserved for use in subsequent record insertions. The reserved space is known as *free* space. The amount that is to be reserved is specified as a percentage of the total allocation of each control interval and/or control area, via the FREESPACE parameter in the DEF CL, ALTER, or DEF AIX commands. If not specified, then no free space is reserved.

Performance Improvements. The *VSAM Programmer's Guide* contains a number of guidelines on how VSAM processing performance may be improved. These include the use of free space, the choice of control interval size, the allocation of additional buffers, and the use of separate volumes for the data and index components of a key-sequenced data set.

The IBM reference manuals listed below provide conceptual and detailed information about the use of VSAM facilities. The "Primer" is especially useful for its many detailed examples of the use of Access Method Services (both OS and DOS) and of space allocation calculations.

IBM Publication #	Title of Reference Manual
G320-5774	VSAM Primer and Reference
GC26-3838	OS/VS VSAM Programmer's Guide
GC26-3840	OS/VS1 Access Method Services
GC26-3841	OS/VS2 Access Method Services
GC33-5382	DOS/VS Access Method Services User's Guide
GC33-5371	DOS/VS System Management Guide
GC33-5372	DOS/VS Data Management Guide
GC33-5373	DOS/VS Supervisor & I/O Macros

22.10   SUMMARY

You may find it useful to review VSAM concepts by rereading Section 22.1. Here we simply summarize the principal terms that have been introduced by IBM for VSAM entities discussed in this chapter.

Access Method Services (AMS).   The utility program that must be used to define VSAM objects and can also be used to load, delete, and print the contents of VSAM catalogs and data sets.

Addressed Direct Access.   Retrieval or storage of a data record that is identified by its relative byte address.

Addressed Sequential Access.   Retrieval or storage of the data record that sequentially follows the previously retrieved or stored record.

Alternate Index.   A key-sequenced data set whose records identify and permit access to base cluster records via an alternate key value.

Alternate Key.   From 1 to 255 consecutive characters of a base cluster record that can be used to access that record via an alternate index. An alternate key's length and position must be the same in each record and must be specified in the AMS DEF AIX command that defines the alternate index.

Base Cluster.   A relative-record, key-sequenced, or entry-sequenced data set other than an alternate index.

Control Area.   A set of one or more control intervals, the total size of which does not exceed one cylinder of a direct access storage device.

Control Block.   The memory area in a program that contains information generated by an ACB, EXLST, GENCB, or RPL macro for use by VSAM when it processes a request macro.

Control Interval.   The fixed-length unit of information that is read from or written to a direct access storage device by VSAM when it retrieves or stores records of a data set.

Data Component.   That portion of a data set that contains the logical records.

Entry-Sequenced Data Set (ESDS).   A VSAM data set whose logical records are stored in the sequence in which they are first presented to the operating system.

Generic Key.   One or more consecutive high-order characters of a key.

Imbedded Index. The situation that prevails when each sequence set node of a key-sequenced data set's index is stored in the first track of the control area that the node pertains to.

Index Component. That portion of a key-sequenced data set that contains the index records.

Keyed Direct Access. Retrieval or storage of a data record that is identified by its key.

Keyed Sequential Access. Retrieval or storage of the data record whose key sequentially follows that of the previously retrieved or stored data record.

Keyed Skip-Sequential Access. Retrieval or storage of a data record that is identified by a key whose value is greater than that of the previously retrieved or stored record. Used only with KSDS.

Key-Sequenced Data Set (KSDS). A VSAM data set whose logical records are stored in ascending prime key sequence, and whose index component records contain the highest prime key and relative byte address of each control interval in the data component.

Loading a Data Set. The act of storing records in a previously empty data set.

Path. The VSAM object that connects an alternate index to its associated base cluster.

Prime Key (or Primary Key). From 1 to 255 consecutive characters of a KSDS logical record, whose value uniquely identifies that record when the data set is stored or retrieved via keyed direct or keyed skip-sequential access. The prime key's length and position must be the same in each record and must be specified in the AMS DEF CLUSTER command that defines the data set.

Relative Byte Address (RBA). A full-word binary integer that specifies the position of a logical record relative to the beginning of a data set.

Reusable Data Set. A data set defined in such a way that its highest RBA can be reset to zero when it is opened, so that the data set is in effect empty immediately after it is opened.

Sequence Set. The lowest-level nodes in a KSDS index. Each sequence set node is associated with a control area, and each entry in a sequence set node points to one of the control intervals in the control area.

Suballocatable Data Space. A portion of the memory of a direct access storage device that is reserved by the AMS DEF SPACE command so that it can be allocated among one or more VSAM data sets.

Upgrade Set. Alternate indexes whose contents are kept accurate and up-to-date by VSAM.

VSAM Catalog. A set of records that VSAM uses to keep track of the characteristics of data sets. There is exactly one VSAM master catalog per computer installation, and there can be one or more user catalogs per installation. There can be no more than one user catalog per storage volume.

VSAM Object. The term used to denote any of the following: master catalog, user catalog, VSAM data set, non-VSAM data set, alternate index, path, and data space.

22.11 REVIEW QUESTIONS

1. a. What determines the sequence of records in an ESDS data set?
   b. Can an ESDS data set include an alternate index even when the data set's records do not include a primary key?
2. What parameters (if any) in the ACB and/or RPL macro are required to indicate what type of data set (ESDS or KSDS) is being processed? If no parameters are required, then how does the operating system know whether it's an ESDS or KSDS data set?
3. What parameters (if any) in the ACB and/or RPL macro are required to indicate what the processing mode for a VSAM data set—e.g., loading, updating in place, retrieval only—will be at run time?

4. a. What is the purpose of the primary key in a KSDS data set? What is the minimum permissible length of a primary key? The maximum permissible length?
   b. What is the purpose of the "sequence set" in a KSDS data set?
5. What are the rules for assigning names to a VSAM data set?
6. What job control or AMS commands (if any) are required to allocate space for a VSAM data set *within* a "suballocatable data space"? If no such commands are required, then what causes the data set's space to be allocated, and how much is allocated?
7. As was discussed, the AMS DEFINE command must be used to create an entry in an existing catalog for a VSAM data set, but it does not create the VSAM data set itself. By what method or methods is it possible to create the data set?
8. When using "move mode," what parameters (if any) are required to specify the location and length of a logical record's I/O work area? Of a control interval's I/O buffer area?
9. Although the EXLST macro lets a programmer specify the addresses of I/O error-handling routines within a program, we did not use EXLST in any of the sample programs in this chapter. Instead, we used another method for detecting when errors occurred. What was that method?
10. One of the OPTCD parameters that we specified in each of our sample programs was the SYN parameter. What does this mean, and what effect would it have on our programs at run time?
11. How can an assembly language program determine whether (and if so, which) invalid key conditions have occurred when updating a KSDS data set in random mode?
12. Since VSAM does not provide for a "delete flag" option for either an ESDS or a KSDS data set, what is the mechanism for deleting VSAM records when "updating in place"?
13. Before using an alternate index, three AMS tasks must be completed, as described in Section 22.7: (1) the alternate index must be defined; (2) a "path" between the alternate index and the base cluster file must be defined; and (3) the alternate index records must be constructed.
   a. With the above ideas in mind, explain each parameter that was used in the text's definition for the dorm room master file's alternate index and path.
   b. What job control statements and AMS commands are sufficient to construct the alternate index records for the dorm room master file?
14. What is the purpose of each of the two uses of the MODCB macro in the retrieval example of Figure 22.15, and under what conditions would the second of these (namely the one in Statement #31) be executed at run time?

22.12 EXERCISES

1. What are the similarities and differences between a control interval and a physical data block? Between a control interval and a control area?

2. What are the similarities and differences between addressed sequential and keyed sequential access? Between keyed direct and keyed skip-sequential access?

3. What parameters of the ACB macro have counterparts in an OS DCB (or DOS DTF) macro? What parameters of the RPL macro have counterparts in an OS DCB (or DOS DTF) macro?

4. What is the difference in purpose between the AREA= and ARG= parameters of an RPL macro? Between the AREALEN= and KEYLEN= parameters? Between the AREALEN= and RECLEN= parameters?

5. What is the difference between a GET and a GET-for-update when used with entry-sequenced data sets? When used with key-sequenced data sets?

6. What is the name and update password of the VSAM user catalog that you will be using when defining data sets at your computer installation? Under what conditions does your installation use suballocatable data spaces? Under what conditions are you permitted to use the UNIQUE parameter when allocating space for a data set at your installation?

7. Suppose that all but two cylinders of a disk pack at your computer installation are available for allocation to a VSAM data set. What is then the largest number of records that can be stored in an entry-sequenced data set on a single disk pack if the record length is 100 bytes? 200 bytes? 500 bytes? 1000 bytes? You can assume that each control area consists of one cylinder.

8. Under the same conditions as in Exercise 7, what is the largest number of records that can be stored in a key-sequenced data set on a single disk pack, assuming that the prime key length is 10 bytes?

9. Which of the statements in Figure 22.10 have to be modified, and what must those modifications be in order to load a key-sequenced data set instead of an entry-sequenced data set?

10. Write a program that will print the contents of the ESDS dorm room master file. Write the AMS commands that will print the contents of that file (for this you will need to learn about the PRINT command from the AMS manuals).

11. What modifications have to be made to the statements of Figure 22.11, and what new statements must be added to those in the figure in order to process transactions that would add new records to the end of the existing data set?

12. What modifications have to be made to the statements of Figure 22.12, and what new statements must be added to those in the figure in order to process transactions that would change the prime key of an existing record? You can assume that a transaction record with type code '5' (not shown in the figure) contains both the prime key of an existing record and the key that is to replace it.

13. If the student i.d. fields of the KSDS dorm room master file were to be used as alternate keys, one alternate index would have to be defined for each student i.d. field. Write the AMS commands that would accomplish this. (Note: Neither field can be defined as a UNIQUEKEY because some master file records may contain information about just one student, and some may not contain information about any students. In those cases the i.d. field is blank.)

14. What changes and additions would have to be made to the program statements of Figure 22.15 in order to access the KSDS dorm room master file through the alternate indexes defined in Exercise 13? (**Hint:** You have to open two paths, not just one.)

VI

The Assembler

23

Assembler Concepts

The purpose of this chapter is to provide some understanding of the processes that take place when a source module is assembled. We begin by explaining the need for a two-pass assembler and then describe several of the concepts and techniques used in an assembler. The discussion is totally oriented to the IBM 360 and 370 assemblers, though a number of simplifying assumptions have been made. Thus, the chapter essentially constitutes a conceptual, not a detailed, description of those assemblers.

Some of the data structures for representing information about source module statements and machine language are discussed in detail: the symbol table, the object module tables, and cross-reference lists. In addition, an overview of the assembler's Pass 1 and Pass 2 processing logic and a brief description of table-searching and table-sorting techniques used in an assembler have been included.

23.1   INTRODUCTORY CONCEPTS

In simple terms, the assembly process can be depicted by the diagram of Figure 23.1. The machine language representation of the source module is produced by the assembler and stored in an object module, where it is available to the loader program and/or the linkage editor. In addition to the object module, the assembler produces a listing that correlates the source and object module contents and provides certain diagnostic information.

Let us consider the source statements in Figure 23.2. We can begin to appreciate the processes by which the transformation from source to object module takes place by pretending to *be* the assembler. As the assembler, we must process the source statements one by one, in the order of their

Figure 23.1 Assembler input and output.

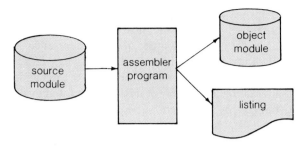

Figure 23.2 Creating object code.

			addr	object code	addr	object code
1	MAIN	CSECT	0000		0000	
2		STM	14,12,12(13)	0000	90EC D00C	0000	90EC D00C
3		BALR	12,0	0004	05C0	0004	05C0
4		USING	*,12	0006		0006	
5		ST	13,SAVE+4	0006	50D0 ----	0006	50D0 C02A
6		LA	13,SAVE	000A	41D0 ----	000A	41D0 C026
7	*					
8		L	3,X	000E	5830 ----	000E	5830 C01E
9		A	3,=F'8'	0012	5A30 ----	0012	5A30 C072
10		ST	3,Y	0016	5030 ----	0016	5030 C022
11	*					
12		L	13,SAVE+4	001A	58D0 ----	001A	58D0 C02A
13		LM	14,12,12(13)	001E	98EC D00C	001E	98EC D00C
14		BR	14	0022	07FE	0022	07FE
15	*					
16	X	DC	A(N)	0024	---- ----	0024	0000 0074
17	Y	DS	F	0028		0028	
18	*					
19	SAVE	DS	18F	002C		002C	
20	*					
21	LAST	EQU	*	0074		0074	
22	N	EQU	LAST-MAIN	0074		0074	
23		END		0078	0000 0008	0078	0000 0008

source code	object code end of Pass 1	object code end of Pass 2

occurrence. Therefore, to save time, we should attempt to get all the information we possibly can from one reading of each statement (i.e., from one pass through the entire set of statements). At this point, it might help you to review the address concepts and instruction formats presented in Chapter 3. We can then proceed in the following manner.

Before processing the first statement, we set our memory location counter (MLC) to zero. The *The MLC* first statement, a CSECT directive, gives the name of the control section. Since it is the first CSECT with that name, we assign the value of MLC to MAIN. The second and third statements can be translated into object code immediately, since both contain valid mnemonic instructions and since neither contains symbols in the operand field. The address assigned to each statement is obtained by increasing MLC by an amount that depends on the preceding statement. Since the CSECT results in no object code or memory space being reserved, the STM instruction will be assigned to address 0000, and since the STM requires 4 bytes, the BALR is assigned to address 0004.

The USING directive is a note to the assembler that Register 12 should be used as the implied base register and that the base address in Register 12 is the current value of MLC; this value was obtained from the address of the previous instruction plus its length; 0004 +2 = 0006.

The next six instructions pose a problem: although we can assign addresses to those instructions (since we know the length of each one), and although we can translate the mnemonic instruction code into machine language, *we cannot create the machine language corresponding to the second operand field* because we do not yet know the value of the symbols SAVE, X, and Y. Nor have we assigned an address to the literal =F'8' appearing in Statement 9. This is a consequence of having to process the statements one at a time, in the order of their occurrence. We can see immediately that we will have to return to these six statements and others, e.g., Statement 16, after we have obtained the necessary information. Therefore, we proceed with the remaining statements, assigning addresses to symbols and to literals and taking any other action dictated by directives that we process.

For example, the DC directive in Statement 16 requires the allocation of four bytes beginning on a full-word boundary, but we can't assemble the constant until the value of N is known. The DS directives of Statements 17 and 19 require the allocation of one and eighteen full words, respectively. The two EQU directives define values for the symbols LAST and N. Finally, when we reach the END directive, we assign addresses to any literals in the literal pool.

At the completion of our first pass through the source statements, we have compiled the following information (see the middle column of Fig. 23.2):

literals	address
=F'8'	00078

symbol	value
LAST	00074
MAIN	00000
N	00074
SAVE	0002C
X	00024
Y	00028

base register	base address
12	00006

To complete the transformation to object code, we must make a second pass over the source statements using this information. In doing so, we shall have to calculate the implied displacements to use in the base-displacement form of addresses in the operands of instructions. As discussed previously, this is done according to the formula

$$\left\{ \begin{array}{c} \text{implied} \\ \text{displacement} \end{array} \right\} = \left\{ \begin{array}{c} \text{desired} \\ \text{address} \end{array} \right\} - \left\{ \begin{array}{c} \text{base} \\ \text{address} \end{array} \right\}$$

You should verify that the object code given in the right-hand column of Figure 23.2 is consistent with the information given here.

To recapitulate, the constraint that each statement must be processed in the order of its occurrence, plus the fact that some symbols will be used in operand fields before they are defined, has led us to make two passes over the source statements. In the first pass, our main function was to determine and remember the values of all symbols and to assign addresses to literals. In the second pass, our main function was to complete the transformation from source code to object code, using the information that was gathered in the first pass. To perform these two passes, we also needed certain reference information: the hexadecimal opcode and instruction format and length corresponding to each mnemonic instruction code, and the definition of each directive. As we will learn in the next section, this information must also be available to the assembler during the assembly process.

There is one other observation to be made. Suppose that in the source statements of Figure 23.2, we reverse Statements 21 and 22, so that instead of the sequence

```
21      LAST    EQU     *
22      N       EQU     LAST-MAIN
```

we have the following Statements 21' and 22'

```
21'    N      EQU    LAST-MAIN
22'    LAST   EQU    *
```

If this were done, we would be unable to compute the value of LAST-MAIN when Statement 21' is processed in Pass 1, since the value of LAST will not be defined until Statement 22' is processed. Thus, the value of N would not be known at the end of Pass 1. As a consequence, when Statement 16—X DC A(N)—is processed in Pass 2, we will be unable to translate its operand into object code. To determine the value of N and to complete the translation of Statement 16, we would have to wait until Statement 21' was processed in Pass 2.

There are several ways to avoid this apparent dilemma. The simplest, and the one used in most assemblers, including that of the IBM 360 and 370, is simply to forbid a sequence such as the one represented by Statements 21' and 22': all symbols in the operand of an EQU directive are required to be defined in statements preceding that EQU, as was done in Figure 23.2. Thus, if the source module contains no errors, the value of all symbols will be known at the end of Pass 1 and all instructions and constants will be translatable in Pass 2.

23.2   FUNDAMENTALS OF THE ASSEMBLY PROCESS

The outline presented in Section 23.1 illustrates the need for a two-pass assembler. But the outline differs in two essential ways from the sequence of steps taken in an assembler. First, the assembler does not attempt to generate any object code in Pass 1, not even for instructions or constants where this could be done. This is because it is simpler, from a design and implementation standpoint, to generate all the object code in Pass 2. Second, the assembler does not process the original source module in Pass 2. Instead, it processes an augmented version of that source module, produced by Pass 1. This **intermediate file,** as it is often called, contains not only the source statements but also some of the information determined by Pass 1: information about the opcode and the MLC associated with each statement.

Information Requirements

Nevertheless, for the assembler to carry out the types of processes outlined in Section 23.1, it needs descriptions of the instructions and directives and it must be able to determine and remember the values of symbols, the identities and addresses of literals, and the base register and base address. It also must be prepared to handle multiple base registers, external symbols, arithmetic expressions in operands, and other aspects of assembly language. To do these things it must be able to store and process a variety of types of information.

One of the principal information-handling techniques used by an assembler is based on the concept of a table. A **table** is simply a collection of data arranged in some orderly fashion so that the data items are relatively easy to locate and process. The data items are organized into a number of subcollections called **entries,** all of which usually contain the same types of items. One of the items, called a **key,** is used to identify each entry. The value of each key is often distinct from that of all other keys in the table, so that the identity is unique.

Figure 23.3 shows how the table that describes instructions will be defined for our descriptions of the assembly process. Each entry, shown as a single line of the table, consists of 8 bytes that are unevenly divided into five items, or **fields.** The key field is the mnemonic instruction code; entries are in ascending sequence by the values of this field. The other fields provide information that the assembler will need to process an instruction: the machine language opcode, the instruction's type and length, the 4-bit mask defining conditional branch instructions such as BE, and a few other pieces of information described by 1-bit flags. The information in a table is represented as concisely as possible in order to conserve memory space. However, since it would be impracticable to have an entry's length be other than an integral multiple of bytes and inefficient from a processing standpoint if we did not align counters, addresses, etc., on appropriate boundaries, the table formats presented here represent an attempt at a reasonable compromise between memory and processing efficiency.

Figure 23.4 shows the table that will be used to process directives. Because of the diversity of operand formats in directives, the table simply contains the address of a routine within the assembler that processes each directive. Like the opcode table of Figure 23.3, the directive table can be used to determine whether a given character string represents a valid directive, and, if it does, what should be done with it. But, unlike the opcode table, the action to be taken is decentralized; each directive has its own processing routine.

Figure 23.3 *Opcode table format.*

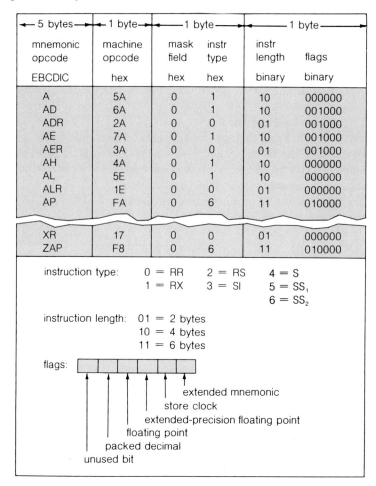

mnemonic opcode	machine opcode	mask field	instr type	instr length	flags
EBCDIC	hex	hex	hex	binary	binary
A	5A	0	1	10	000000
AD	6A	0	1	10	001000
ADR	2A	0	0	01	001000
AE	7A	0	1	10	001000
AER	3A	0	0	01	001000
AH	4A	0	1	10	000000
AL	5E	0	1	10	000000
ALR	1E	0	0	01	000000
AP	FA	0	6	11	010000
XR	17	0	0	01	000000
ZAP	F8	0	6	11	010000

instruction type: 0 = RR 2 = RS 4 = S
1 = RX 3 = SI 5 = SS₁
6 = SS₂

instruction length: 01 = 2 bytes
10 = 4 bytes
11 = 6 bytes

flags:

- extended mnemonic
- store clock
- extended-precision floating point
- floating point
- packed decimal
- unused bit

Figure 23.4 *Directive table format.*

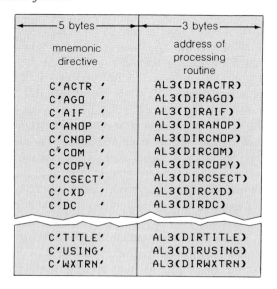

mnemonic directive	address of processing routine
C'ACTR '	AL3(DIRACTR)
C'AGO '	AL3(DIRAGO)
C'AIF '	AL3(DIRAIF)
C'ANOP '	AL3(DIRANOP)
C'CNOP '	AL3(DIRCNOP)
C'COM '	AL3(DIRCOM)
C'COPY '	AL3(DIRCOPY)
C'CSECT'	AL3(DIRCSECT)
C'CXD '	AL3(DIRCXD)
C'DC '	AL3(DIRDC)
C'TITLE'	AL3(DIRTITLE)
C'USING'	AL3(DIRUSING)
C'WXTRN'	AL3(DIRWXTRN)

The opcode and directive tables are examples of tables in which all the entries are known in advance, so to speak, so that the information in each entry can be coded in the source module of the assembler itself. By placing the entries in key sequence, the process of finding an entry, which is required each time a statement is processed by the assembler, can be made more efficient.

The assembler also needs tables in which the entries are not known until assembly time. Among these are the symbol table, the literal table, and the base register table. Since the entries in these tables depend on the statements processed by the assembler, they must be created and inserted at assembly time. Before discussing these tables, it might prove useful to summarize where we are heading.

As demonstrated, the assembly process depends on information represented in tables. Some of these tables are generated as part of the assembler source module, some at assembly time. The assembler itself operates in two phases, or passes: the primary function of the first pass is to determine the values of symbols; the primary function of the second pass is to produce the object code. The second pass relies on information generated in the first pass, and both passes rely on the opcode and directive tables, as well as on the source module statements.

This interdependence is depicted in Figure 23.5. The arrowheads indicate the direction in which information is transferred. For example, Pass 1 creates the symbol table by transferring information into it, and Pass 2 uses that information. In the next section we will describe the contents of the assembler's tables in more detail. Following that, the activities in Pass 1 and Pass 2 will be examined; first in overview fashion, then to see how information might be inserted into and retrieved from the tables, how the symbol table can be sorted into sequence at the end of Pass 1, and how the object module and cross-reference information is compiled.

Even at this stage of the discussion, it should be clear that the assembler is a complex program. If it is written in assembly language, it will require tens of thousands of statements to adequately handle all the potential situations that could occur in a user's source module. In addition to the nearly 150 instruction codes and 7 instruction formats with implied or explicit lengths and base registers, there are 15 data-type codes and nearly 50 directives in the IBM 360 and 370 Assembly language. Arithmetic expressions must be analyzed, macros expanded, control sections segregated, errors detected, and a listing and object module created. Further, since the assembler is a frequently used program, its design and implementation must use memory space and processing time efficiently.

It is therefore simply not practicable to describe in one chapter all the processes that take place in an assembler. Consequently, we will impose four major simplifications in order to concentrate on a few underlying principles:

1. We will consider only ten of the most frequently used directives, and will not consider macro processing at all. The ten directives are CSECT, DSECT, ENTRY, EXTRN, USING, DROP, DC, DS, EQU, END.
2. We will consider only five of the data-type codes: C-, X-, F-, A-, and V- and will exclude any discussion of exponent and scale factors in F-type constants.
3. We will not discuss the procedures involved in translating operand expressions such as SAVE+4.
4. We will not be concerned with the process of creating a listing but will focus attention on the creation of the object module instead.

23.3 ASSEMBLER TABLES

In this section, we will describe a few of the principal tables used by an assembler: the symbol table, the literal table, the base-register table, and the intermediate file. The ESD, TXT, and RLD tables used for the creation of the object module (see Fig. 23.5) will be discussed in Section 23.6.

Note that although the descriptions given here are meant to be accurate in their portrayal of the kinds of information contained in the tables, they are not necessarily accurate in terms of field size or position within an entry, or even in terms of all the fields that might be in an entry. These details depend on design considerations that will not be discussed in this chapter.

Figure 23.5   Assembler table and file usage.

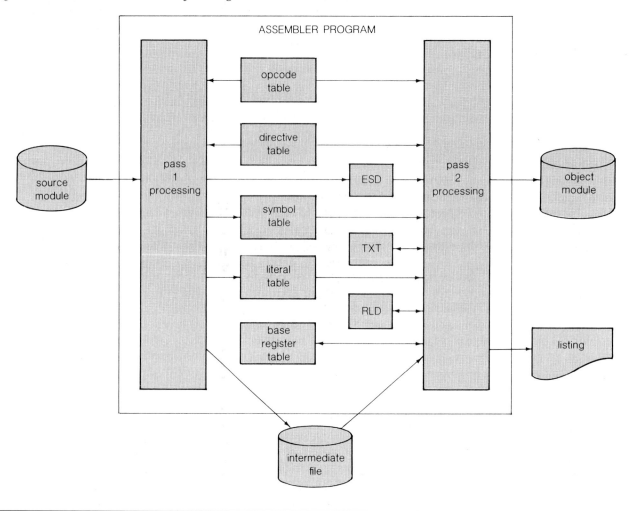

Figure 23.6   Symbol table format.

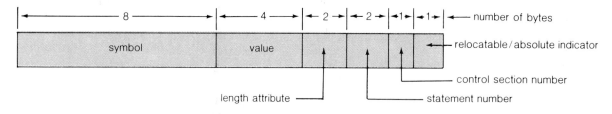

The Symbol Table

An entry is made in the symbol table (see Fig. 23.6) in Pass 1 for each symbol that occurs in the name field of an instruction or directive. An entry is also made in Pass 1 for each symbol that occurs in the operand of an EXTRN directive. At the end of Pass 1, the entries are sorted into ascending order by the key field values. Duplicates (multiply-defined symbols) are kept in the table so that they can be reported in the cross-reference portion of the listing and flagged as errors.

As indicated in Figure 23.6, each entry contains several fields: the symbol itself, its value, its length attribute, the number assigned by the assembler to the statement in which the symbol was defined, and a number identifying the control section in which the statement appeared. In addition, each entry contains information characterizing the symbol as being relocatable or absolute.

Figure 23.7   Literal table format.

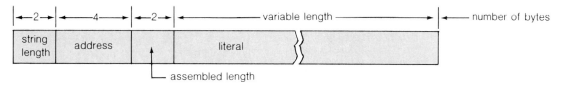

Except for external symbols and symbols defined by an EQU directive, the **value of a symbol** is the address of the instruction, constant, or data area for which it has been defined. The value of a symbol defined by an EQU directive is the value of the operand in that directive. The value of an external symbol is arbitrarily set to zero, since it is the loader or linkage editor, not the assembler, that must determine that value.

The **length attribute of a symbol** is the number of bytes in the object code that are identified by that symbol. This clearly depends on the statement in which the symbol is defined. If a symbol is defined in the name field of an instruction, its length attribute is the instruction's length. If a symbol is defined in the name field of a DC or DS directive, its length attribute is either the number of bytes explicitly represented in the length modifier Ln, or, in the absence of a length modifier, it is the number of bytes implied by the constant or data-type code. (For most other directives, the length attribute is arbitrarily set to 0 or 1; in these cases, its value is unimportant.) The assembler inserts a symbol's length attribute into the length field of an SS_1 or SS_2 machine language instruction whenever the corresponding source language operand references that symbol but does not include an explicit length-field specification.

Each symbol's value (and, by definition, the symbol itself) is always considered to be either relocatable or absolute. The word **relocatable** means that the value of the symbol is a function of the starting memory address of the object code being assembled. When the loader or linkage editor assigns a starting memory address to the object code, that starting address is added to all relocatable addresses in order to make it possible for the object code to be executed in that area of memory. Correspondingly, the word *absolute* in this context means that the value of the symbol is not dependent on the starting address assigned by the loader or linkage editor. *The only absolute symbols are those defined by an EQU directive whose operand value is absolute. All other symbols are relocatable.*

The assembler assigns a number, the *statement number,* to each statement that it processes. This number makes it easy to identify statements in the cross-reference portion of a listing. The assembler also assigns a **control section number,** or i.d., to each separate control section in a source module. This number is used by the assembler to determine which base register is eligible for use in the base-displacement address calculation for a symbol. Both these numbers are inserted into the symbol table at the time a symbol is defined.

The Literal Table

A literal is entered into this table (see Fig. 23.7) when it is obtained from an instruction's operand field in Pass 1. Since the number of bytes in each entry depends on the number of characters in the literal string, each entry includes its length. There are no duplicates. If two instructions specify the same literal in exactly the same way, there will be only one entry for that literal in the table. (In the terminology of earlier chapters, the literal table is identical to the literal *pool.*)

Addresses are assigned to any literals in the table when an END directive is processed and also when the LTORG directive is processed (see Chap. 15). In the IBM 360 and 370 systems, the first address assigned to a literal is always on a double-word boundary. The addresses are assigned in the following order: first, to all literals whose assembled lengths are a multiple of eight; next, to all whose assembled lengths are a multiple of four but not of eight; third, to those whose assembled lengths are a multiple of two but not four; and, last, to all remaining literals. This hierarchy removes the need to adjust address values (and possibly leave unused bytes) for the proper boundary alignment each time an address is assigned to a literal.

Figure 23.8   Base-register table format.

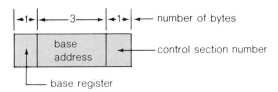

Figure 23.9   Intermediate file format.

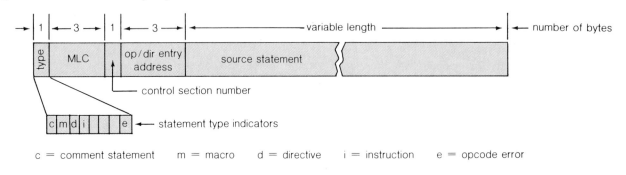

c = comment statement   m = macro   d = directive   i = instruction   e = opcode error

The Base-Register Table

The entries in this table (see Fig. 23.8) reflect the information obtained from the USING and DROP directives. As discussed in Chapter 9, the general format of these directives is

        USING   base-address, base-register-1, base-register-2,...
        DROP   base-register-1, base-register-2,...

To allow for the designation of symbolic base registers and symbolic base addresses, entries are not made in this table until Pass 2. (This differs from the scheme used in Section 23.1.) There is one entry per base register. A USING directive causes an entry to be made in the table for each base register designated in its operand; a DROP directive causes entries to be deleted.

Base-Displacement Addresses
To compute a base-displacement address corresponding to a relocatable symbolic address, the assembler chooses the base register whose base address is in the same control section as the symbolic address, and whose value is closest to but not greater than the value of the symbolic address. If there are no addressing errors in the source module, this procedure guarantees that the displacement will be as small as possible but nonnegative.

The Intermediate File

A file is essentially a table in which all the entries either cannot fit or need not be in main memory at the same time. Since file processing was discussed in Part Five, we need only note here that each entry in the intermediate file (Fig. 23.9) is created in Pass 1 and used in Pass 2. The sequence of the entries is the same as that of the statements in the source module.

As illustrated in Figure 23.9, each entry contains a copy of a source module statement plus some additional information determined in Pass 1. This includes the value of the MLC at the time the statement was processed, the address of the opcode or directive table entry corresponding to the mnemonic instruction code in the source statement, and a summarization of the statement's type. This information is included in order to eliminate the need to repeat the process of determining it in Pass 2; this saves some processing time in Pass 2.

The statement-type byte in an intermediate file entry illustrates a technique often used to represent information: 1-bit indicators whose status (1 or 0) indicates a true or false condition. For example, if the statement is a comment, the first bit (labeled as lowercase *c*) will be set to 1; the

Figure 23.10   Sample source module.

```
1       MAIN       CSECT
2       MAINLINE   STM     14,12,12(13)
3                  BALR    12,0
4                  USING   *,12
5                  ST      13,SAVE+4
6                  LA      13,SAVE
7       *
8                  ENTRY   MAINLINE
9                  EXTRN   ARRAY1
10      *
11                 LA      1,=A(ARRAY1,ARRAY2)
12                 L       15,=V(SUBR)
13                 BALR    14,15
14      *
15                 USING   ARRAYFLD,DUMMYREG
16                 LA      DUMMYREG,ARRAY2
17                 MVC     A1,=C'ABC'
18                 MVC     A3,ZEROES
19                 DROP    DUMMYREG
20      *
21                 L       13,SAVE+4
22                 LM      14,12,12(13)
23                 BR      14
24      *
25      ARRAYFLD   DSECT
26      A1         DS      CL3
27      A2         DS      CL4
28      A3         DS      CL5
29      A4         DS      CL2
30      A5         DS      C
31      MAIN       CSECT
32      *
33      N          EQU     15
34      ARRAY2     DS      (N)F
35      SAVE       DS      18F
36      DUMMYREG   EQU     11
37      ZEROES     DC      15X'00'
38                 END
```

other bits are irrelevant. If the statement is not a comment, then the first bit will be set to 0, and one of the other bits will be set to 1 (the remaining bits being set to 0). The second bit will be 1 if the statement is a macro, the third if it is a directive, the fourth if an instruction, and the right-most bit if the opcode is undecipherable. The setting of these bits can easily be tested in Pass 2 by means of the TM instruction.

23.4   ASSEMBLER TABLE EXAMPLE

To illustrate the ideas presented in the previous section, we will describe the contents of the assembler tables that would result from the assembly of the source module shown in Figure 23.10. (The statements in the source module do not constitute a meaningful program; they are for illustrative purposes only.)

Pass 1 Processing

All the tables except the base-register table are created in Pass 1. For each statement that is processed in Pass 1, the following procedures take place:

1. The current value of the MLC, adjusted if necessary for boundary alignment requirements, is assigned to the name-field symbol (if any), and that symbol is entered into the symbol table along with the other information that characterizes that symbol.

Symbol Table

symbol	value (hex)	length attribute	statement number (decimal)	control section	rel/abs flag
ARRAYFLD	000000	1	25	2	R
ARRAY1	000000	1	9	1	R
ARRAY2	000034	4	34	1	R
A1	000000	3	26	2	R
A2	000003	4	27	2	R
A3	000007	5	28	2	R
A4	00000C	2	29	2	R
A5	00000E	2	30	2	R
DUMMYREG	00000B	1	36	1	A
MAIN	000000	1	1	1	R
MAINLINE	000000	4	2	1	R
N	00000F	1	33	1	A
SAVE	000070	4	35	1	R
ZEROES	0000B8	1	37	1	R

Literal Table

string length (hex)	address (hex)	assembled length (hex)	literal string
0011	0000C8	0008	=A(ARRAY1,ARRAY2)
0008	0000D0	0004	=V(SUBR)
0007	0000D4	0003	=C'ABC'

2. Directives that affect the value of the MLC are processed just enough so that the new MLC can be computed. This includes not only DC and DS directives, but also CSECT and DSECT directives. (There is a separate MLC maintained for each reference control section, as discussed in Chap. 15.) It should be noted that in Statement 34 of Figure 23.10—ARRAY2 DS (N)F—the value of N is required in Pass 1 in order that the number of full words, and thus the number of assembled bytes, can be determined. For this reason, a symbol must be defined before it is used in the duplicator field of a DC or DS directive's operand.

3. For instructions, the operand is scanned for the presence of a literal, and whenever one is found it is entered into the literal table along with its string length (provided it is not already there).

4. When the END directive is processed, the symbol table is sorted into sequence and addresses are assigned to literals.

Note that the symbol and literal tables for the source module of Figure 23.10 are as shown in Figure 23.11. Note also that all the symbol values and length attributes are known; if this were not the case, undefined symbols would be detected in Pass 2.

Pass 2 Processing   In Pass 2, each statement is processed again, this time using the copy in the intermediate file. Each instruction is assembled into machine language by substituting the values for symbols in the operand fields and by using the instruction format given in the opcode table. Constants defined by DC directives are assembled in accordance with the rules governing the various type codes, including padding, truncation, duplication, conversion to machine language, and so forth. The DS, EQU, and EXTRN directives are effectively skipped over (they are of course printed on the listing), since all the information provided by them was obtained and utilized in Pass 1. The CSECT and DSECT directives determine the control section that is being assembled. When a USING directive is processed, an appropriate entry is made in the base-register table, and when a DROP directive is processed an appropriate entry is deleted.

For example, when Statement 4—USING *,12—is processed, the following entry is made in the base-register table:

base register	base address	control section
12	000006	1

This entry remains in the table and is used by the assembler to determine the base-displacement addresses in subsequent operands, until one of three events is detected: (1) the END directive is processed, thereby terminating Pass 2 except for the assembling of literals; (2) another USING directive for the same base register is processed, thereby causing the previous entry to be replaced by a new entry; or (3) a DROP directive for that base register is processed, thereby causing the previous entry to be deleted from the table.

When Statement 15—USING ARRAYFLD,DUMMYREG—is processed, the values of the base-address and base-register symbols in the USING operand are determined from the symbol table, and an entry is added to the base-register table so that it now contains

base register	base address	control section
12	000006	1
11	000000	2

Choosing an Implied Base Register

Now when an instruction is processed, the assembler must decide which base register to use. For example, when Statement 18—MVC   A3,ZEROES—is processed, the assembler determines from the symbol table that A3 is in control section 2, and ZEROES is in control section 1. From the base-register table, it finds that Register 11 governs control section 2, and Register 12, control section 1. It then computes the implied displacements as follows:

$$\left\{\begin{array}{c} \text{implied} \\ \text{displacement} \\ \text{for A3} \end{array}\right\} = \left\{\begin{array}{c} \text{value} \\ \text{of A3} \end{array}\right\} - \left\{\begin{array}{c} \text{base address} \\ \text{in Register 11} \end{array}\right\}$$

$$= \quad 000007 \quad - \quad 000000$$

$$\left\{\begin{array}{c} \text{implied} \\ \text{displacement} \\ \text{for ZEROES} \end{array}\right\} = \left\{\begin{array}{c} \text{value} \\ \text{of ZEROES} \end{array}\right\} - \left\{\begin{array}{c} \text{base address} \\ \text{in Register 12} \end{array}\right\}$$

$$= \quad 0000B8 \quad - \quad 000006$$

In addition, since MVC is an SS_1 instruction and since no length field is specified in the source statement, the assembler substitutes the length attribute of A3, which it obtains from the symbol table, reduced by +1 for machine language. Thus the assembled instruction is created as follows:

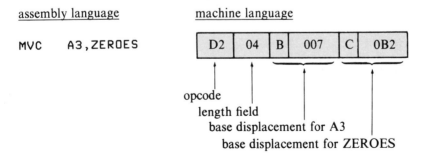

The DROP directive in Statement 19 causes the entry for Register 11 to be removed from the base-register table. If any subsequent instruction referred to a symbol in control section 2, the assembler would report an **"addressability error,"** i.e., an error in which the base-displacement address cannot be calculated due to lack of a base register for control section 2.

Figure 23.12   Assembly listing for Figure 23.10.

```
FLAG LOCTN OBJECT CODE      ADDR1   ADDR2  STMNT M SOURCE STATEMENT

     000000                                  3      MAIN      CSECT
     000000 90 EC D00C                        4      MAINLINE  STM     14,12,12(13)
     000004 05 C0                             5                BALR    12,0
     000006                                   6                USING   *,12
     000006 50 D0 C06E       000074           7                ST      13,SAVE+4
     00000A 41 D0 C06A       000070           8                LA      13,SAVE
                                              9      *
     000000                                  10                ENTRY   MAINLINE
                                             11                EXTRN   ARRAY1
                                             12      *
     00000E 41 10 C0C2       0000C8          13                LA      1,=A(ARRAY1,ARRAY2)
     000012 58 F0 C0CA       0000D0          14                L       15,=V(SUBR)
     000016 05 EF                            15                BALR    14,15
                                             16      *
     000000                                  17                USING   ARRAYFLD,DUMMYREG
     000018 41 B0 C02E       000034          18                LA      DUMMYREG,ARRAY2
     00001C D2 02 B000C0CE 000000 000004     19                MVC     A1,=C'ABC'
     000022 D2 04 B007C0B2 000007 0000B8     20                MVC     A3,ZEROES
                                             21                DROP    DUMMYREG
                                             22      *
     000028 58 D0 C06E       000074          23                L       13,SAVE+4
     00002C 98 EC D00C                       24                LM      14,12,12(13)
     000030 07 FE                            25                BR      14
                                             26      *
     000000                                  27      ARRAYFLD  DSECT
     000000                                  28      A1        DS      CL3
     000003                                  29      A2        DS      CL4
     000007                                  30      A3        DS      CL5
     00000C                                  31      A4        DS      CL2
     00000E                                  32      A5        DS      C
     000032                                  33      MAIN      CSECT
                                             34      *
     00000F                                  35      N         EQU     15
     000034                                  36      ARRAY2    DS      (N)F
     000070                                  37      SAVE      DS      18F
     00000B                                  38      DUMMYREG  EQU     11
     0000B8 00                               39      ZEROES    DC      15X'00'
     0000C8 0000000000000034                 40
     0000D0 00000000
     0000D4 C1C2C3
                                             41                END
```

Figure 23.12 is the listing that would be produced for the Figure 23.10 source module. Pretend once more to be the assembler, this time using the symbol table, literal table, and base-register table as described, and verify that the object code shown on the listing is consistent with the descriptions provided in this section. Note that, although there are two occurrences of the CSECT directive, both with the name-field symbol MAIN, this does not result in MAIN being multiply-defined. The first CSECT defines the beginning of control section MAIN, while the second defines the resumption of that section and, consequently, a resumption of the addresses assigned in that section. The second CSECT thus permits the assembler to switch from assembling the dummy section ARRAYFLD back to assembling the control section MAIN. Further discussion of this concept can be found in Section 15.1.

23.5   ASSEMBLER PROCESSING LOGIC

Based on the discussion and simplifications presented in the preceding sections, the overall processing logic of Pass 1 and Pass 2 is summarized in Figures 23.13 and 23.14. The pseudocode is virtually identical to the descriptions already given, except for the processes associated with creating the object module and cross-reference information. The latter will be discussed in Section 23.9, after some characteristics of table processing have been presented. The object module is described in Section 23.6.

Pass 1

The principal ideas in **Pass 1** processing shown in Figure 23.13 are

1. Comment statements are processed by simply putting an appropriate entry on the intermediate file.
2. Instructions must be aligned on a half-word boundary; literals and name-field symbols must be placed in the appropriate tables; and the MLC must be increased by the instruction length.

Figure 23.13   Pass 1 processing logic summary.

```
PASS_1:

  MLC := 0;
  statement_number := 0;

  REPEAT UNTIL instruction = "END"

    get source module statement;

    IF statement is a comment
    THEN
      { no action }
    ELSE

      IF mnemonic instruction is in opcode table
      THEN   { opcode found }
        adjust MLC to next half-word boundary;
        save length of instruction;
        put literal (if any) in literal table;
        put name-field symbol (if any) in symbol table;
        increase MLC by instruction length;
      ELSE

        IF mnemonic instruction is in directive table
        THEN
          CASE mnemonic instruction OF
            "END"   : assign addresses to literals;
            "CSECT",
            "DSECT" : assign section number;
                      put name-field symbol in symbol and ESD tables;
            "EQU"   : evaluate operand;
                      put name-field symbol in symbol table;
            "EXTRN" : put operand symbols in ESD table;
                      put operand symbols in symbol table;
            "ENTRY" : put operand symbol in ESD table;
            "DC",
            "DS"    : adjust MLC to appropriate boundary;
                      put name-field symbol in symbol table;
                      increase MLC by size of constant or data area;
          END CASE;
        ELSE
          { instruction error }
        END IF;

      END IF;

    END IF;

    put appropriate entry on intermediate file;

  END UNTIL;

EXIT PASS_1.
```

Figure 23.14   Pass 2 processing logic summary.

```
PASS_2:

   put ESD entries on object module file;

   REPEAT WHILE there are more entries in intermediate file

     get entry from intermediate file;

     IF entry is comment or error
     THEN
       put source code on listing
     ELSE

       IF entry is instruction
       THEN
         evaluate operand fields and assemble object code
           according to instruction type, based on information
           in symbol, literal, and base register tables;
         TXT_ENTRY;
       ELSE { entry is directive }
         CASE directive OF
             "END"   : assemble literals;
                       put address constants in RLD table;
                       TXT_ENTRY;
             "DC"    : assemble constants;
                       put address constants in RLD table;
                       TXT_ENTRY;
             "USING" : enter data in base register table;
             "DROP"  : delete entry from base register table;
         END CASE;
       END IF;

       put operand symbols (if any) in cross reference table;
       put object code (if any) and source code on listing;

     END IF;

   END WHILE;

   put last TXT entry (if any) on object module file;
   put RLD entries (if any) on object module file;
   put END entry on object module file;
   put cross reference information on listing;

EXIT PASS_2.


TXT_ENTRY;

   IF object code does not fit in current TXT entry
   THEN
     put current TXT entry on object module file;
     begin new entry;
   END IF;
   put object code in TXT entry;

EXIT TXT_ENTRY.
```

3. Each directive has separate processing requirements. Some, like USING and DROP, are not processed at all except to put the statements in which they occur on the intermediate file. The CSECT, DSECT, EXTRN, and ENTRY directives contain information that must be placed in the ESD table for use in the creation of the object module. The DC and DS directives affect the MLC in two ways: (1) through the boundary alignment that may be required for the constant or data area and (2) through the increase due to the size of the constant or data area. Most directives will include a name-field symbol that must be entered into the symbol table, but in the EXTRN directive it is the operand symbols that are entered into the symbol table so that they may be referred to by A-type address constants.

The principal ideas in **Pass 2** processing depicted in Figure 23.14 are

1. Since there is sufficient information in the intermediate file to describe the statement type, the opcode and directive tables need not be searched.
2. Each instruction requires extensive processing that depends on its type, e.g., RR, RX. This processing is summarized in Figure 23.14. After the object code has been created, it is not immediately written onto the object module but instead is placed in the TXT table. This is because each TXT entry may contain more than one assembled instruction or constant.
3. Of the ten directives under consideration, only four require special processing: END, DC, USING, and DROP. In particular, it should be noted that even though the DS directive causes the MLC to be changed during Pass 1 processing, it does not cause any object code to be generated during Pass 2. For this reason, you should not assume that an area reserved by a DS will contain blanks, or zeroes, or whatever, at the start of program execution.
4. The listing is created in Pass 2, one line at a time, as each statement is processed. The cross-reference information is accumulated by putting the operand symbols in a cross-reference table to be printed at the end of Pass 2. Address constants created by DC directives and literals are accumulated in the RLD table to be written on the object module at the end of Pass 2.

23.6 THE OBJECT MODULE

An object module is a file containing four types of entries: External Symbol Dictionary (ESD) entries, which identify each control section, entry point, and external reference; Text (TXT), or object code entries, which consist of the machine language instructions and data; Relocation Dictionary (RLD) entries, which describe each A- and V-type address constant; and an END entry, which specifies the address of the first instruction to be executed at run time.

The reason that there is more than just object code (TXT) data in an object module is to provide the loader and linkage editor programs with the information they need to link together external subroutines and to relocate the object code into whatever main memory area is allocated by the operating system.

The process of relocation does not alter the manner in which the object code is executed, but it does involve increasing each A- and V-type constant by a nonnegative integer, known as the **relocation factor.** For example, if the object code corresponding to the source module of Figure 23.10 were loaded into memory location 4000_x, then, at run time, the address of ARRAY2 would be 004034_x, not 000034_x as it was at assembly time. Therefore, the address constant defined by the literal $=A(ARRAY1,ARRAY2)$ would have to be increased by 4000_x in order to be consistent with the run-time address. 4000_x is the relocation factor. The loader obtains the relocation factor from the operating system; it obtains the information about the literal address constant from the RLD entries.

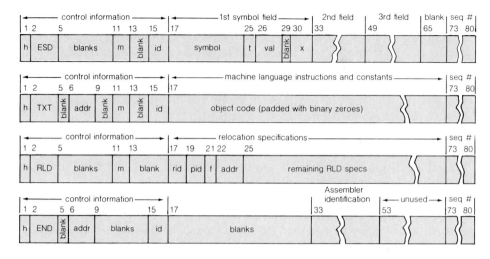

Figure 23.15 Overview of ESD, TXT, RLD, and END entry formats.

The process of linking subroutines together requires that each address constant referring to an external symbol be replaced with the memory address with which that symbol is associated. For example if the subroutine named SUBR in Figure 23.10 were loaded into memory location 6000_x, the address constant $=V(SUBR)$ would be replaced with the binary representation of 006000_x. Similarly, if there were another program that referred to ours by a V-type constant, say $=V(MAIN)$, then, in that program, the constant would be replaced by 004000_x, since that is the address associated with the symbol MAIN. The loader obtains the information it needs about external references, control section names, and entry points from the ESD entries.

Although there are a number of other considerations in the processes of loading, linking, and relocation that will not be discussed in this text, the brief descriptions given should serve as a rationale for the formats of the ESD, TXT, and RLD entries. These formats are presented in summary form in Figure 23.15 and in detail in Figures 23.16a–23.16d. The examples presented in the detailed figures represent the object module formats for the same source module we discussed previously (see Fig. 23.12). You should verify that the TXT data of Figure 23.16b corresponds to the object code in the listing in Figure 23.12.

Perhaps the main concept to be noted is that of the External Symbol Dictionary Identification Number (ESDID). As pointed out in the discussion of the symbol table entries, the assembler assigns a control section number to each control section in the source module. This makes it simple to correlate a symbol with the control section in which it is defined, for purposes of choosing a base register and base address from the base-register table. A similar numbering technique is used in the object module. In fact, it is the same numbering technique just mentioned but extended to include not only control sections but also external references. ESDID's are assigned sequentially, in the order in which the control section names and external references occur in the source module. The ESDID of each such symbol is represented in the ESD entries.

In TXT entries, the ESDID of the control section to which the object code belongs is given in positions 15 and 16. In Figure 23.16c, there are three TXT entries, each containing a portion of the object code in the control section whose ESDID is 0001_x, which, as may be seen from the first ESD entry in Figure 23.16a, is the ESDID of MAIN. Thus, the two-byte ESDID serves as a kind of shorthand for the 8-byte symbol C'MAIN   '.

Figure 23.16a ESD explanation and example.

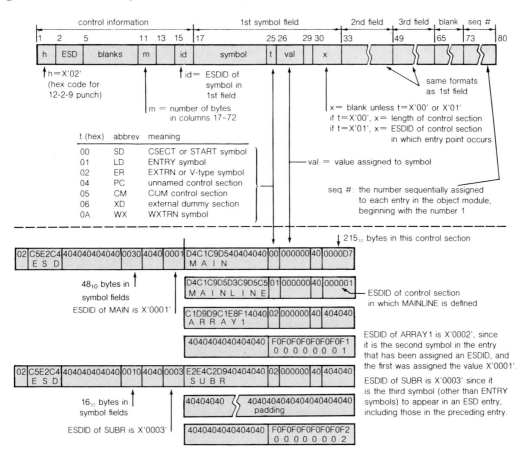

Figure 23.16b TXT explanation and example.

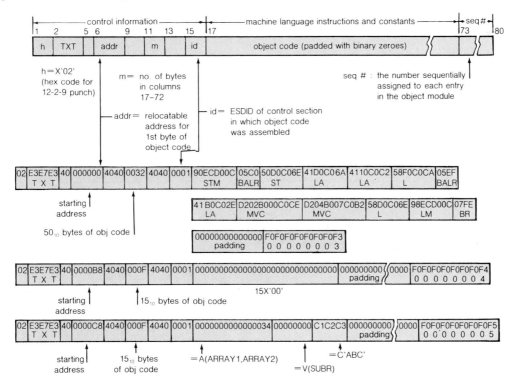

Figure 23.16c *RLD explanation and example.*

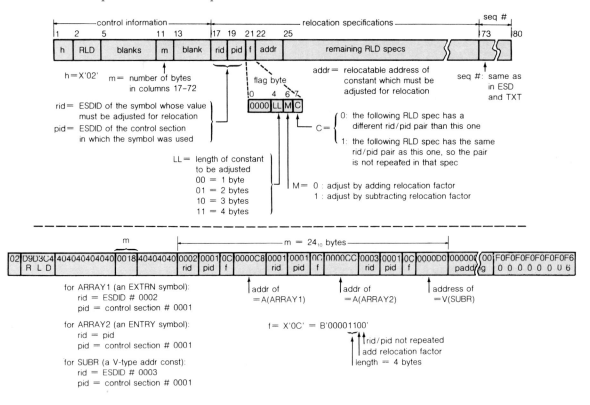

Figure 23.16d *END explanation and example.*

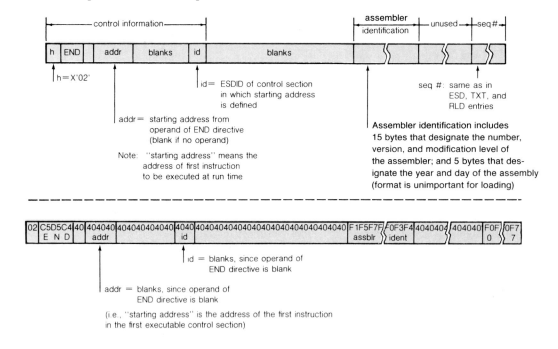

The Assembler

In RLD entries, it is not only necessary to identify the control section in which an A- or V type constant occurs but also to identify the address of that constant, the symbol used to create it, and whether that symbol is an external or internal symbol. Referring to Figure 23.16c, we see that this information is coded as follows:

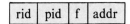

| rid | pid | f | addr |

where
rid = ESDID of the symbol
pid = ESDID of the control section in which the symbol occurs
f = indicators describing the length of the constant, whether it is negative or positive, and whether the following constant has the same or different "rid" and "pid" numbers
addr = address of the constant

The "rid" number leads back to an ESD entry, where further information about that symbol may be found. For example, for the address constant =A(ARRAY1), we have, in the above format,

| 0002 | 0001 | 0C | 0000C8 |

meaning that this constant is at address $0000C8_x$ in the control section whose ESDID is 0001_x, that it is defined further in the ESD field for ESDID 0002_x, and that the constant is 4 bytes long, positive, and not followed by another RLD field for the same symbol. Referring back to Figure 23.16a, we find that ESDID 0002_x identifies the symbol ARRAY1, an external symbol whose value therefore must be determined by the loader or linkage editor.

Further discussion of the object module and the manner in which it is processed by the loader and linkage editor will not be pursued.

23.7 TABLE SEARCHING

Linear Search

In the preceding discussions of the assembler, the role of tables was seen to be fundamental. The problem we now wish to touch upon is that of determining by what processing technique a sought-for table entry can be found. The most obvious solution is to examine each entry in turn, starting at the first one, until the desired entry is found. This is known as a **linear search** procedure (Fig. 23.17). Linear searching has the advantage of being simple to implement; it has the disadvantage of being time-consuming if there are a large number of entries in the table.

If many searches have to be made through a table, a linear search will require that half the entries, on the average, be examined. If there are N entries, the average search time will be $A(N/2)$, where the constant A is a function of the speed of the computer and of the number and type of instructions used in each iteration of the search procedure. If the entries are not in sequence, every entry would have to be examined to determine that the sought-for entry is not in the table. If the entries are in sequence, the search could be terminated at the point beyond which the sought-for entry could not occur.

It may be helpful to visualize the linear search technique by imagining oneself searching through a small dictionary or glossary for a particular word and its definition. Starting at the first word, you would eventually come to a word beyond which the word being sought could not occur. This, of course, is a consequence of the fact that the words are in alphabetical sequence. Obviously, you would not use a linear search to look for a word in a dictionary, because a faster method is available. You would start looking somewhere near where the word is expected to occur, and work forward or backward, perhaps reversing direction several times in the process, until you found the word or were certain it wasn't there. A similar technique, known as the **binary search technique,** has long been used in searching tables in computer memory.

Binary Search

Simply stated, the binary search technique involves starting at the middle of the table, not the beginning, and proceeding in the following manner. First, we determine, by comparing the search key to the key of the middle entry, whether the sought-for entry is in the first half or the last half of

Figure 23.17 Linear search procedure for table with M entries.

```
LINEAR_SEARCH:

  j := 1;

  REPEAT WHILE j <= number of entries in table

    IF search_key = key of jth entry of table
    THEN
      { key found in jth entry }
      EXIT LINEAR_SEARCH;
    END IF;
    increase j by 1;

  END WHILE;

  { key not found }

  EXIT LINEAR_SEARCH.
```

the table. Then, when the appropriate area is determined, we examine the middle entry of *that* half, to determine which of the two halves of that half is the appropriate area in which to look further. The process continues in this way, with further subdivisions into smaller and smaller halves, until the entry is either found or not found.

It can be shown that on the average the search time using the binary search technique will be $B(\log_2 N)$, where B is some constant. The technique is depicted in Figure 23.18. It is somewhat more complex than a linear search; consequently, the constant B will be somewhat larger than A for a given computer system. A comparison of $B(\log_2 N)$ and $A(N/2)$ is described by the curves in Figure 23.19, so that for reasonably large N, a binary search is to be preferred. For example, if $B = 10 \times A$, then the cutover point will be approximately $N = 150$. If $B = 5 \times A$, the cutover is approximately $N = 50$.

Linear vs. Binary Search Time

Suppose that $B = 5A$, i.e., that each iteration in the binary search takes five times as much processing time as an iteration in the linear search. Then, by calculating the ratio $\dfrac{B(\log_2 N)}{A(N/2)}$, we see that, if $N = 100$, the average table search time using the binary technique will be half as long as that using the linear technique; if $N = 500$, it will take one fifth the time; if $N = 1000$, one tenth the time. If, as in the assembler, hundreds if not thousands of table searches must be made each day, the appropriate choice of search technique can yield large dividends in terms of reduced processing time.

To search a table by any method, the values of several variables must be known: the number of entries in the table, the size (number of bytes) of each entry, the position and length of the key field in each entry, and the key of the sought-for entry. From a programming standpoint, it is clearly desirable that the size of all entries be the same and the length of the key field be the same in each entry. However, this is not always possible. It depends on the table. For example, in the opcode table each entry is 8 bytes long, and the key occupies the first 5 bytes of each entry; but in the literal table, the length of each entry depends on the length of the literal string, and that string is itself the key of each entry. The opcode table entries are said to be **fixed-length,** the literal entries **variable-length.** Similar terminology is used to describe the keys.

Since in a program such as the assembler there are several tables to be searched, it is convenient to have a single subroutine that will search any table. The subroutine should be general enough to handle any values of the variables mentioned above, and it must be programmed to return one of two results: (1) the address of the sought-for entry if it is found, or (2) an indication that it wasn't found. The subroutine in Figure 23.20 is a binary search routine that satisfies most of the requirements discussed. The constraints are that the entries and keys be fixed-length and that the key length be less than or equal to 256 bytes. The first constraint makes the programming simpler; the key-length constraint allows us to use the CLC instruction (via the EX instruction) for the key comparisons. The routine closely follows the processing logic depicted in Figure 23.18.

Figure 23.18   Binary search procedure for table with M entries.

```
BINARY_SEARCH:

  { set initial group to entire table }
  LOWPT := 1;  { first entry }
  HIPT := M;  { number of entries in table }

  REPEAT WHILE LOWPT < HIPT

    MIDPT := integer portion of (LOWPT + HIPT)/2; {index of current middle}
    IF search_key = key of entry of table at position MIDPT
    THEN
      { key found in MIDPT entry }
      EXIT BINARY_SEARCH;
    ELSE
      IF search_key < key of entry of table at position MIDPT
      THEN
        HIPT := MIDPT - 1;  { use lower half of current group }
      ELSE
        LOWPT := MIDPT + 1;  { use upper half of current group }
      END IF;
    END IF;

  END WHILE;

  IF LOWPT = HIPT
  THEN { one entry remains to be checked }
    IF search_key = key of remaining entry of table
    THEN
      { key found in MIDPT +/- 1 entry }
      EXIT BINARY_SEARCH;
    END IF;
  END IF;
  { key not found }

EXIT BINARY_SEARCH.
```

Figure 23.19   Comparison of N/2 with Log₂N.

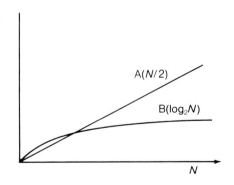

Figure 23.20 *Binary search subroutine for fixed-length entries.*

```
BISRCH    CSECT
*
* BINARY SEARCH SUBROUTINE, ENTERED WITH CALL BISRCH(TBL,M,L,KP,KL,SK)
*       WHERE   TBL = ADDRESS OF FIRST ENTRY IN TABLE TO BE SEARCHED
*               M   = NUMBER OF ENTRIES IN TABLE
*               L   = LENGTH OF EACH ENTRY (NUMBER OF BYTES)
*               KP  = RELATIVE POSITION OF ENTRY KEY (0=1ST BYTE OF ENTRY)
*               KL  = LENGTH OF KEY (NUMBER OF BYTES)
*               SK  = ADDR OF KEY OF SOUGHT-FOR ENTRY
* IF SOUGHT-FOR ENTRY IS FOUND, ITS ADDRESS IS RETURNED IN REG 15
* IF SOUGHT-FOR ENTRY IS NOT FOUND, A ZERO IS RETURNED IN REG 15
*
* USES FOLLOWING INDEXES:
*       LOWPT   = RELATIVE POSITION OF THE LOWEST ENTRY IN THAT
*                    'HALF' OF THE TABLE CURRENTLY BEING EXAMINED
*       HIPT    = REL POSITION OF HIGHEST ENTRY IN CURRENT HALF
*                    OF TABLE
*       MIDPT   = REL POSITION OF MID-ENTRY IN CURRENT HALF OF
*                    TABLE (INTEGER PORTION OF (LOWPT+HIPT)/2  )
*
* USES FOLLOWING SYMBOLIC REGISTER ADDRESSES:
TBL       EQU   1             REG 1 (TEMPORARY) ADDR OF 1ST TABLE ENTRY
KPA       EQU   1             REG 1 = KPA, ADDR OF KEY IN 1ST ENTRY
M         EQU   2             REG 2 = M, # ENTRIES IN TBL
L         EQU   3             REG 3 = L, LENGTH OF EACH ENTRY
KP        EQU   4             REG 4 = KP, REL BYTE POSITION OF KEY
KL        EQU   5             REG 5 = KL, LENGTH OF KEY
SK        EQU   6             REG 6 = SK, ADDR OF SOUGHT-FOR KEY
LOWPT     EQU   7             REG 7 = POSITION OF LOWEST ENTRY IN THIS HALF
HIPT      EQU   8             REG 8 = POSITION OF HIGHEST ENTRY, THIS HALF
MIDPT     EQU   9             REG 9 = POSITION OF MID-ENTRY IN THIS HALF
X         EQU   10            REG 10= SCRATCH REGISTER
CUR       EQU   11            REG 11= ADDR OF KEY OF CURRENT MID-ENTRY
BASE      EQU   12            REG 12= BASE REGISTER FOR SUBROUTINE
*
          STM   14,12,12(13)      STANDARD ENTRY
          BALR  BASE,0
          USING *,BASE
          ST    13,SAVE+4
          LA    13,SAVE
*
          LM    TBL,SK,0(1)       GET PARAMETERS FROM CALLER
          L     M,0(M)            # ENTRIES IN TABLE
          LTR   M,M               SEE IF TABLE IS EMPTY
          BNP   NOTFOUND          IF SO, CAN'T FIND SOUGHT-FOR ENTRY
          L     L,0(L)            LENGTH OF EACH ENTRY
          L     KP,0(KP)          REL BYTE POSITION OF KEY
          AR    TBL,KP            COMPUTE ADDR OF KEY IN 1ST ENTRY
          L     KL,0(KL)          LENGTH OF KEY
          SH    KL,=H'1'          SUBTRACT 1 FOR EXECUTE INSTRUCTION
*
          LH    LOWPT,=H'1'       INITIALIZE LOWPT TO FIRST ENTRY
          LR    HIPT,M            INITIALIZE HIPT TO LAST ENTRY
*
*
* COMPUTE INDEX OF MID-ENTRY, AND ADDRESS OF MID-ENTRY'S KEY
LOOP      LA    MIDPT,0(LOWPT,HIPT)    MIDPT=(LOWPT+HIPT)/2
          SRA   MIDPT,1           (RIGHT-SHIFT 1 BIT TO DIVIDE BY 2)
          LR    CUR,MIDPT         ADDR OF MID-ENTRY'S KEY EQUALS
          SH    CUR,=H'1'         ADDR OF 1ST ENTRY'S KEY, PLUS
          MR    X,L               L*(MIDPT-1)
          AR    CUR,KPA
*
```

Figure 23.20   continued

```
* COMPARE KEY OF SOUGHT-FOR ENTRY TO KEY OF MID-ENTRY
         EX      KL,COMPARE      COMPARE KEYS
         BH      UPPER           HI MEANS LOOK IN UPPER HALF
         BL      LOWER           LO MEANS LOOK IN LOWER HALF
         B       FOUND           EQ MEANS IT'S FOUND
*
* SET HIPT = MIDPT-1     IF SOUGHT-FOR KEY MUST BE IN LOWER HALF
LOWER    SH      MIDPT,=H'1'
         LR      HIPT,MIDPT
         B       MORE
*
* SET LOWPT = MIDPT+1    IF SOUGHT-FOR KEY MUST BE IN UPPER HALF
UPPER    AH      MIDPT,=H'1'
         LR      LOWPT,MIDPT
*
* SEE IF THERE ARE AT LEAST TWO ENTRIES THAT HAVEN'T BEEN EXAMINED
MORE     CR      HIPT,LOWPT      IS  HIPT>LOWPT ?
         BH      LOOP            IF SO, CONTINUE SEARCHING
         BE      ONEMORE         IF EQUAL, THERE'S ONE MORE ENTRY TO BE
         B       NOTFOUND            EXAMINED; OTHERWISE, IT'S NOT FOUND.
*
* EXAMINE SOLE REMAINING ENTRY
ONEMORE  LR      CUR,MIDPT       COMPUTE ADDR OF REMAINING ENTRY'S KEY
         SH      CUR,=H'1'
         MR      X,L
         AR      CUR,KPA
         EX      KL,COMPARE      COMPARE KEYS
         BE      FOUND
*
* SOUGHT-FOR KEY NOT IN TABLE, SO RETURN  0  IN REG 15.
NOTFOUND SR      15,15
         B       EXIT
*
* SOUGHT-FOR ENTRY FOUND IN TABLE, SO RETURN ADDR OF ENTRY IN REG 15.
FOUND    LR      15,CUR          ADDR OF ENTRY IS ADDR OF KEY IN THAT
         SR      15,KP           ENTRY, MINUS POSITION OF KEY
*
* EXIT FROM SUBROUTINE
EXIT     L       13,SAVE+4
         L       14,12(13)       PRESERVE CONTENTS OF REG 15
         LM      0,12,20(13)
         BR      14
*
* COMPARE INSTRUCTION FOR EXECUTE INSTR.
COMPARE  CLC     0(0,SK),0(CUR)
*
SAVE     DS      18F
         END
```

If the keys are of variable length, as in the literal table, or if their length exceeds 256 bytes, it might be more convenient to use the CLCL instruction discussed in Section 7.8. This instruction allows strings of virtually arbitrary length to be compared; the two strings being compared need not have the same length. As an exercise, you should alter the binary search routine of Figure 23.20 so that it utilizes the CLCL instruction and could thereby be used to search a table such as the literal table.

The comprehensive analysis and comparison of linear, binary, and other search techniques given in Donald E. Knuth's *The Art of Computer Programming, vol. 3: Sorting and Searching* (Addison-Wesley, 1973) is recommended for those who wish further details of these techniques.

Sorting involves rearrangement of entries into some prescribed order. The rearrangement is usually physical, much like the physical rearrangement of personal canceled checks into check number sequence, or the rearrangement of a deck of cards into sequence within each suit. Clearly, any rearrangement that places entries into some prescribed order must be based on some property of each entry. In sorting, this property is invariably the value of one or more fields in the entry. For example, the entries in the assembler's opcode table are in sequence by the mnemonic instruction code. But if the entries in the symbol table were not sorted into sequence based on the alphanumeric symbols that constitute the key field of each entry, then symbol table searching would not be as efficient as it could be.

We mention table sorting in the title of this section to emphasize that all the entries that are to be sorted can fit in main memory throughout the sorting process. This is commonly known as **internal sorting**—internal to main memory. When the number of entries is so large that only a portion can be in main memory at one time, the rest being in secondary memory, the process is known as *external* sorting. Since external sorting must involve input and output, it entails considerations that are qualitatively different from those in internal sorting. We will restrict our discussions to internal sorting.

Criteria for Best Sort

Many studies have been made to devise fast sorting algorithms. Knuth discusses five major internal sorting techniques and describes some two dozen algorithms. But as Knuth points out, this "is only a fraction of the algorithms that have been devised so far." The main reason for the existence of so many algorithms is the importance of using one that is in some sense best suited to the data and the computer system. *There is no known best way to sort an arbitrary set of data in an arbitrarily chosen computer system.* The best way for a given situation would be one that used the least amount of time and the least amount of memory space. This will certainly depend on the computer and on the instructions used in the algorithm on that computer, and it will also depend on the data—how many entries are to be sorted and how badly out of sequence (or how nearly in sequence) they are when the sort is begun.

Straight Insertion Sort Technique

Let us illustrate a simple sorting procedure, known as **straight insertion,** by considering the symbol table that would exist at the end of Pass 1 for the sample source module of Figure 23.10. To simplify the discussions, we will adopt the notation and terminology used in Knuth's book:

Let R_j denote the jth entry, or *record,* in the table

Let K_j denote the key field in record R_j

Assume that there are N entries or records in the table

Then the straight insertion technique can be summarized as follows: Assume that $1 < j \leq N$, and that records $R_1,...,R_{j-1}$ have been sorted. We now compare the jth key K_j to the keys preceding it in the table, in the following order: K_{j-1}, $K_{j-2},...,K_1$. When we discover a key, K_i, such that $K_j \geq K_i$, the record R_j is inserted between records R_i and R_{i+1}. To make this insertion, the records R_{i+1}, $R_{i+2},...,R_{j-1}$ are moved back one position in the table.

Figure 23.21 illustrates the procedure for our symbol table; Figure 23.22a depicts the steps in the procedure. Note that the comparison and moving operations are interleaved to avoid another loop. Note also that very little temporary memory space is required: the records are sorted "in place," so to speak. Finally, note from Figure 23.21 that when a record is already in its correct position for a given j, all the comparisons must be made (the computer having no other way to determine that the record is in its proper position) although no records are moved. For simplicity, only the keys K_i are shown in Figure 23.21. In actuality, the entire record containing each key would be moved as appropriate. The subroutine in Figure 23.22b illustrates this; it uses the algorithm of Figure 23.22a to sort any table that contains fixed-length entries.

The straight insertion technique moves records one position at a time. This is satisfactory from the standpoint of overall processing time only if the records are nearly in their final position or if, as in Figure 23.21, there are relatively few records to be sorted. The technique would be rather slow under other conditions. Consequently, a number of variations of the straight insertion technique have been developed to reduce the number of comparisons and/or to reduce the amount of data movement.

Figure 23.21 *Symbol table sorted by straight insertion. (The original table is given in the order of occurrence in Figure 23.10.)*

i	j=2 original table	j=3	j=4	j=5	j=6	j=7	j=8	j=9	j=10	j=11	j=12	j=13	j=14	j=15	sorted table
1	MAIN	MAIN	ARRAY1	ARRAYFLD	ARRAYFLD	ARRAYFLD	ARRAYFLD	ARRAYFLD	ARRAYFLD	ARRAYFLD	ARRAYFLD	ARRAYFLD	ARRAYFLD	ARRAYFLD	ARRAYFLD
2	MAINLINE	MAINLINE	MAIN	ARRAY1	ARRAY1	ARRAY1	ARRAY1	ARRAY1	ARRAY1	ARRAY1	ARRAY1	ARRAY1	ARRAY1	ARRAY1	ARRAY1
3	ARRAY1	ARRAY1	MAINLINE	MAIN	A1	A1	A1	A1	A1	A1	A1	ARRAY2	ARRAY2	ARRAY2	ARRAY2
4	ARRAYFLD	ARRAYFLD	ARRAYFLD	MAINLINE	MAIN	A2	A2	A2	A2	A2	A2	A1	A1	A1	A1
5	A1	A1	A1	A1	MAINLINE	MAIN	A3	A3	A3	A3	A3	A2	A2	A2	A2
6	A2	A2	A2	A2	A2	MAINLINE	MAIN	A4	A4	A4	A4	A3	A3	A3	A3
7	A3	A3	A3	A3	A3	A3	MAINLINE	MAIN	A5	A5	A5	A4	A4	A4	A4
8	A4	A4	A4	A4	A4	A4	A4	MAINLINE	MAIN	MAIN	MAIN	A5	A5	A5	A5
9	A5	A5	A5	A5	A5	A5	A5	A5	MAINLINE	MAIN	MAIN	MAIN	MAIN	DUMMYREG	DUMMYREG
10	MAIN	MAIN	MAIN	MAIN	MAIN	MAIN	MAIN	MAIN	MAIN	MAINLINE	MAINLINE	MAIN	MAIN	MAIN	MAIN
11	N	N	N	N	N	N	N	N	N	N	N	MAINLINE	MAINLINE	MAIN	MAIN
12	ARRAY2	ARRAY2	ARRAY2	ARRAY2	ARRAY2	ARRAY2	ARRAY2	ARRAY2	ARRAY2	ARRAY2	ARRAY2	N	N	MAINLINE	MAINLINE
13	SAVE	SAVE	SAVE	SAVE	SAVE	SAVE	SAVE	SAVE	SAVE	SAVE	SAVE	SAVE	SAVE	N	N
14	DUMMYREG	DUMMYREG	DUMMYREG	DUMMYREG	DUMMYREG	DUMMYREG	DUMMYREG	DUMMYREG	DUMMYREG	DUMMYREG	DUMMYREG	DUMMYREG	DUMMYREG	SAVE	SAVE
15	ZEROES	ZEROES	ZEROES	ZEROES	ZEROES	ZEROES	ZEROES	ZEROES	ZEROES	ZEROES	ZEROES	ZEROES	ZEROES	ZEROES	ZEROES

Several of these techniques are described in Knuth's book. In addition to the straight insertion technique, Knuth investigated four other categories of techniques, each with their own set of algorithms. These may be summarized in a simplified fashion as follows:

Other Sort Techniques

1. **Exchange** techniques, which interchange pairs of entries that are out of order until no more such pairs exist in the table.
2. **Selection** techniques, which search first for the smallest (or largest) entry, then for the next smallest (or largest), and so on.
3. **Merge** techniques, which combine two or more already sequenced subsets of entries to produce a new sequenced subset and continue in this way until all the sequenced subsets have been merged into one, which is the final sorted table.
4. **Distribution** techniques, in which a portion of each key is examined and the entries separated (or distributed) into subsets, one for each different value of the key portion being examined. A different portion of the key is then used and the process repeated, maintaining the order of the entries that was established by the previous distribution. The process continues in this way until the final portion of the key has been examined. The final subset produced consists of all the entries in sequence.

Of course, these summaries convey only the broadest differences among the techniques. Further discussion of these techniques is beyond the scope of this text.

23.9 CROSS-REFERENCES

The task of producing cross-reference information for a source module requires some mechanism for remembering the statement numbers of all statements in which the symbol appears in an operand field, in order that they can be printed at the end of Pass 2.

One way to meet this requirement would be to have one cross-reference table for each symbol. But this poses two immediate problems: (1) how many tables should there be and (2) how much space should be reserved for each table? We don't know how many tables there should be, because we don't know how many symbols there will be in a given source module until that module is processed. Nor do we know how much space to reserve for each table since we don't know ahead of time how many

Space Considerations

```
INSERTION_SORT:

  REPEAT FOR j := 2, 3, ..., N

    K := key from record j;
    R := copy of record j;
    i := j - 1;

    { i will be the position to the left of the inserted jth record }

    REPEAT WHILE ( i > 0 ) AND ( K < key from record i )
      move record i to record i+1;
      subtract 1 from i;
    END WHILE;

    move R to record i+1;

  END FOR;

EXIT INSERTION_SORT.
```

references there will be to each symbol in a source module. It would be a waste of memory space to make each table big enough to hold all the expected cross-references to a symbol; some symbols will clearly never be referenced, others may be referenced only a few times, and some may be referenced many times. We need a scheme that will accommodate these differences and uncertainties without undue waste of memory space.

One such scheme would be to reserve space for just one table, instead of having one table for each symbol. This space must be large enough to hold the totality of all cross-references in the source module. We could then allocate the space at assembly time by adding each new cross-reference entry to the then current end of the table, much as we would add a symbol table entry to the end of the symbol table. To identify the symbol to which each cross-reference entry pertains, it would seem logical to reserve 8 bytes in each entry for that symbol, similar to the definition of a symbol table entry. However, we can avoid doing this, and thereby save even more space, by using the concept of a list.

A **list** is a set of entries that may be scattered in memory, instead of being consecutive as in a table. Each list entry contains at least one field that is used in locating another entry of the list. The content of this field is known as a **pointer,** since it points to the location of an entry. The pointer can be an address or any other number that can be used in calculating an address.

*Cross-Reference
List Structure*

The list structure we have in mind for the cross-reference table is illustrated in Figure 23.23. The entries are shown in the order in which they would be placed there in Pass 2 of the assembler when the intermediate file corresponding to Figure 23.10 is processed. The structure has these properties. Each entry consists of two fields of 2 bytes each: a statement number field that identifies the statement in which the cross-reference occurs and a pointer field that identifies the next entry in the structure that contains a cross-reference for the same symbol. (If the pointer is zero, there are no more entries in the structure for that symbol.) If we know where the first entry for a given symbol is located in the structure, we can find the other entries for that symbol by using the pointer in each entry to locate the next entry. Moreover, since the entries on a given list were added in the order in which they were discovered in Pass 2, they are in statement number sequence and need not be sorted before printing.

For example, the entries for the symbol SAVE are in positions 1, 2, and 15 of the structure. The entry in position 1 corresponds to the reference made in Statement 5—ST 13,SAVE+4; the entry in position 2 corresponds to the reference in Statement 6—LA 13,SAVE; and the entry in position 15 corresponds to the reference in Statement 21—L 13,SAVE+4. Between position 2 and position 15, a number of references to other symbols occurred; these were assigned to consecutively available positions in the structure.

```
STSORT     CSECT
*
*    STRAIGHT INSERTION SORT SUBROUTINE STSORT(TBL,N,L,KP,KL)
*       WHERE TBL = ADDRESS OF FIRST ENTRY IN TABLE TO BE SORTED
*             N   = NUMBER OF ENTRIES IN THE TABLE
*             L   = LENGTH OF EACH ENTRY (NUMBER OF BYTES)
*             KP  = RELATIVE POSITION OF ENTRY KEY (0=1ST POSITION)
*             KL  = LENGTH OF KEY (NUMBER OF BYTES)
*
*    THIS ROUTINE ASSUMES THE PARAMETERS SATISFY THESE CONSTRAINTS:
*       N>0,  0<L≤256,  0≤KP≤256,  0≤KP+KL≤256.
*    THE ENTRIES ARE SORTED 'IN PLACE', I.E., THE SORTED ENTRIES
*       REPLACE THE ORIGINAL UNSORTED ENTRIES.
*    'STSORT' USES THE FOLLOWING SYMBOLIC REGISTER ADDRESSES:
*    (NOTE THAT THE USE OF REGS 1-5 MATCHES THE SEQUENCE OF PARAMS)
*
TBL        EQU   1          REG 1 = ADDR OF 1ST TABLE ENTRY
N          EQU   2          REG 2 (TEMPORARY) = # ENTRIES IN TBL
NADDR      EQU   2          REG 2 = ADDR OF LAST TABLE ENTRY
L          EQU   3          REG 3 = L, LENGTH OF EACH ENTRY
KP         EQU   4          REG 4 = KP, RELATIVE BYTE POSITION OF KEY
KLX        EQU   5          REG 5 = KL-1, ONE LESS THAN KEY LENGTH
KL         EQU   KLX
LX         EQU   6          REG 6 = L-1, ONE LESS THAN ENTRY LENGTH
RI         EQU   7          REG 7 = ADDR OF RECORD 'I'
KI         EQU   8          REG 8 = ADDR OF KEY IN RECORD 'I'
RI1        EQU   9          REG 9 = ADDR OF RECORD 'I+1'
RJ         EQU   10         REG 10= ADDR OF RECORD 'J'
KJ         EQU   11         REG 11= ADDR OF KEY IN 'RECDJ' TEMP AREA
XEVEN      EQU   10         REG 10= (TEMP) EVEN# REG FOR COMPUTING (N-1)*L
XODD       EQU   11         REG 11= (TEMP) ODD #       ''              ''
*
           STM   14,12,12(13)    ENTRY TO SUBR
           BALR  12,0
           USING *,12
           ST    13,SAVE+4
           LA    13,SAVE
           LM    TBL,KL,0(1)     GET PARAMS IN REG 1 THRU 5
*
*    INITIALIZATIONS
           L     N,0(N)          N = NUMBER OF ENTRIES
           C     N,=F'1'
           BNH   FINIS           IF 'N' NOT GREATER THAN 1, DON'T SORT
           L     L,0(L)          L = ENTRY LENGTH
           LR    LX,L            LX= L-1  FOR 'EX' INSTRUCTION
           SH    LX,=H'1'
           LR    XODD,N
           SH    XODD,=H'1'          COMPUTE  (N-1)*L  IN REG 'XODD'
           MR    XEVEN,L             NADDR = (N-1)*L + ADDR OF TABLE
           LA    NADDR,0(XODD,TBL)        = ADDR OF LAST TBL ENTRY
           L     KP,0(KP)        KP= RELATIVE KEY POSITION IN ENTRY
           L     KLX,0(KL)       KL= KEY LENGTH
           SH    KLX,=H'1'       KLX = KL-1  FOR 'EX' INSTRUCTION
           LA    RJ,0(L,TBL)     RJ= ADDR OF JTH ENTRY
*                                INITIALLY, J = 2
*
*    MAIN LOOP FOR COMPARING RECDS, AND MOVING THEM WHEN NECESSARY
*
MAINLOOP   EX    LX,MOVEJ        MOVE JTH RECD TO TEMP AREA
           LA    KJ,RECDJ(KP)    KJ = ADDR OF KEY IN TEMP AREA
           LR    RI,RJ           RI = ADDR OF ITH RECD
           SR    RI,L            INITIALLY, I = J-1
*
COMPLOOP   LA    RI1,0(L,RI)     RI1 = ADDR OF (I+1)ST RECD
```

Figure 23.22b   continued

```
            LA      KI,0(KP,RI)         KI = ADDR OF KEY IN ITH RECD
            EX      KLX,COMPARE         IS JTH RECD > OR = ITH RECD ?
            BNL     COMPYES             IF SO, BRANCH TO 'COMPYES'
            EX      LX,MOVEI            ELSE, MOVE ITH RECD TO (I+1)ST
            SR      RI,L                BACK UP TO (I-1)ST RECD
            CR      RI,TBL              IS THIS THE ZEROTH RECD ?
            BNL     COMPLOOP            IF NOT, REPEAT THE COMPARE/MOVE LOOP
            LR      RI1,TBL             IF I=0, SET RI1 = ADDR OF 1ST ENTRY
*
* IF JTH RECD GREATER THAN ITH, OR IF 'I' HAS BEEN REDUCED TO ZERO,
COMPYES     EX      LX,MOVE             MOVE JTH RECD FROM TEMP TO (I+1)ST
            AR      RJ,L                INCR TO (J+1)ST RECD
            CR      RJ,NADDR            WAS JTH RECD THE NTH (LAST) RECD ?
            BNH     MAINLOOP            IF NOT, GO DO NEXT PASS WITH J = J+1
*
FINIS       L       13,SAVE+4
            LM      14,12,12(13)        EXIT FROM SUBR
            BR      14
*
MOVEI       MVC     0(0,RI1),0(RI)      MOVE ITH RECD TO (I+1)ST
MOVEJ       MVC     RECDJ(0),0(RJ)      MOVE JTH RECD TO TEMP AREA
MOVE        MVC     0(0,RI1),RECDJ      MOVE JTH RECD FROM TEMP TO (I+1)ST
COMPARE     CLC     0(0,KJ),0(KI)       COMPARE JTH RECD (IN TEMP AREA) TO ITH
*
RECDJ       DS      CL256       TEMP SPACE FOR MAX LENGTH JTH RECORD
SAVE        DS      18F         REGISTER SAVE AREA
            END
```

Figure 23.23   *Cross-reference list structure and example.*

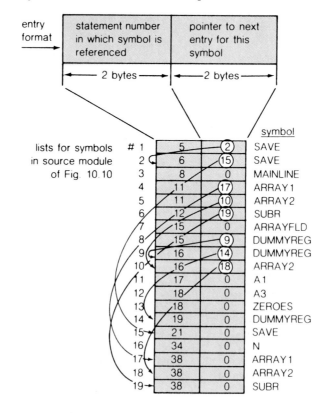

Clearly, the problems that now need to be resolved to use this scheme in the assembler are

1. Where is the first entry for a given symbol located?
2. When adding a new entry to a given list (for example, when adding the entry in position 15 for the symbol SAVE), how would we find the previous last entry on that list in order to replace its "zero" pointer with a pointer to the new entry (e.g., how would we find that 15 should be placed in the pointer field of position 2 when we add the reference to SAVE that occurs in Statement 21)?
3. When adding a new entry to a given list, how do we determine which position in the structure to use for that new entry?

For the first two problems, it is convenient to provide the information in the symbol table itself. This requires a change to the symbol table entry format, as follows. Instead of the format that was defined in Figure 23.5,

symbol	value	length attr	stmnt #	ctl sect	rel/ abs

we define the following format:

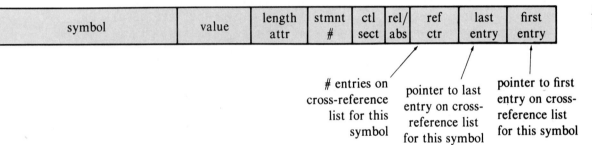

Revised Symbol Table Format

Each of the last three fields is 2 bytes long. The content of the last field does not change after the first cross-reference for that symbol is added to the list structure. The content of the other two fields changes each time a cross-reference for the symbol is added in Pass 2.

For example, after Statement 6 of the source module has been processed in Pass 2, the symbol table entry for SAVE would be this:

symbol	value	length attr	stmnt #	ctl sect	rel/ abs	ref ctr	last entry	first entry
SAVE	000070	4	35	1	R	2	2	1

After Statement 21 has been processed in Pass 2, the symbol table entry for SAVE would be this:

symbol	value	length attr	stmnt #	ctl sect	rel/ abs	ref ctr	last entry	first entry
SAVE	000070	4	35	1	R	3	15	1

We still need a mechanism for determining where to place each new entry in the cross-reference list structure. The mechanism for this is quite simple. In conjunction with the cross-reference table area, two fields are defined to control the information that is placed in that area: (1) a quantity that specifies the maximum number of entries that may be placed in the table, and (2) a pointer to the last-used entry position in the table. The maximum prevents the assembler from exceeding the capacity of the cross-reference area; if a source module has more references than this maximum allows, the assembly must be aborted and the user must segment the module into two or more modules before reassembly. The pointer is initially set to 0 and is increased each time a cross-reference entry is added to the structure.

List Pointers

Figure 23.24 Cross-reference list maintenance subroutine.

```
CROSSREF  CSECT
*
*    SUBROUTINE  CROSSREF(XREFTBL,SYMBOL,STMT#)
*    APPENDS A CROSS REF ENTRY TO THE CROSS REF TABLE.
*    PARAMS = ADDR OF BEGINNING OF CROSS REF TABLE
*           = ADDR OF SYMBOL TABLE ENTRY TO WHICH CROSS REF APPLIES
*           = ADDR OF NEW CROSS REF STMT #
*    RETURNS  0  IN  R15  IF CROSS REF (XREF) ADDED SUCCESSFULLY
*             4  IN  R15  IF XREF TBL WAS FULL AND NO CROSS REF ADDED.
*
          STM    14,12,12(13)       ENTRY TO SUBR
          BALR   12,0
          USING  *,12
          ST     13,SAVE+4
          LA     13,SAVE
*                             PARAMS...
          LM     2,4,0(1)             R2 = ADDR OF CROSS REF TABLE
*                                     R3 = ADDR OF SYMBOL TBL ENTRY
*                                     R4 = ADDR OF CROSS REF STMT #
*
          USING SYMENTRY,3     R3 =BASE REG FOR SYMBOL TABLE DSECT
          USING STKENTRY,11    R11=BASE REG FOR CROSS REF DSECT
          LR     11,2
*
          LH     8,STKPTR       SEE IF CROSS REF TBL IS FULL
          CH     8,STKMAX
          BNL    STKFULL         BRANCH IF IT'S FULL.
          AH     8,=H'1'         OTHERWISE,
          STH    8,STKPTR          UPDATE PTR TO NEXT AVAILABLE ENTRY
*
```

Let us assume that the assembler has determined the address of the symbol table entry for a symbol that has been referenced in the operand of a source module statement. Then, to make an entry in the cross-reference table, the following procedure may be used:

1. The pointer to the next available position in the cross-reference area is determined.
2. If the reference counter field in the symbol table entry is zero, this is the first cross-reference for that symbol. Therefore, the pointer to the next available position is placed in both the first and last entry pointer fields, the reference counter is set to 1, and an entry is made in the cross-reference area with a pointer of 0.
3. If the reference counter in the symbol table entry is not zero, the pointer to the last cross-reference entry for that symbol tells the assembler where to insert the new pointer in the list. The new entry is added in the first available position, and *its* pointer field is set to 0. Both the reference counter and the last entry pointer fields in the symbol table entry are updated accordingly.

The subroutine in Figure 23.24 illustrates one method of implementing this procedure. Note that the cross-reference control data (maximum number of entries, pointer to last-used entry position) is maintained in the first position of the cross-reference table.

The structure described for the cross-reference data is known as a *one-way list,* since the pointers always point to the *next* entry on the list, not to the previous or any other entry. In addition, the structure is known as a first-in, first-out (FIFO) list, because we start at the first entry that was made when retrieving entries from the list. A FIFO list is a queue of entries, the last entry on the queue being the last one to be retrieved for further processing, such as printing the cross-reference information.

Figure 23.24   continued

```
              LH       9,REFCTR            SEE IF THIS IS FIRST REF FOR SYMBOL
              LTR      9,9
              BNZ      NOTFIRST            BRANCH IF OTHER REFS ALREADY EXIST
              STH      8,REF1ST     ELSE, SET PTR TO 1ST CROSS REF TBL ENTRY,
              STH      8,REFLAST           AND TO LAST ENTRY (THE SAME ENTRY).
              MVC      REFCTR,=H'1'        ALSO, SET COUNT OF CROSS REFS TO 1.
              B        NEWENTRY            THEN GO MAKE NEW ENTRY IN XREF TBL.
*
NOTFIRST      AH       9,=H'1'             UPDATE # CROSS REFS FOR THIS SYMBOL.
              STH      9,REFCTR
              LH       10,REFLAST   R10= PTR TO PREV LAST CROSS REF.
              STH      8,REFLAST           STORE PTR TO NEW REF IN SYMB TBL.
*
* COMPUTE  (ADDR OF XREF ENTRY) = (ADDR OF XREF TBL) + ( 4*PTR ),
*     THE FACTOR '4' BECAUSE EACH XREF ENTRY IS 4 BYTES.
*
              SLL      10,2       R10 = 4*PTR  = INDEX TO PREV LAST CROSS REF.
              LA       11,0(10,2)          R11 = ADDR OF PREV LAST CROSS REF.
              STH      8,NEXTREF           STORE PTR TO NEW REF IN PREV REF.
*
NEWENTRY      SLL      8,2                 R8  = INDEX TO NEW CROSS REF.
              LA       11,0(8,2)           R11 = ADDR OF NEW CROSS REF.
              MVC      NEXTREF,=H'0'       SET NEW REF'S FWD PTR TO ZERO.
              MVC      STMTREF,0(4)        SET NEW REF'S STMT# FIELD VIA REG 4.
              LH       15,=H'0'            SET RETURN CODE 'O.K.'
*
REFXIT        L        13,SAVE+4           EXIT FROM SUBR
              L        14,12(13)
              LM       0,12,20(13)         DON'T RESTORE R15
              BR       14
*
STKFULL       LH       15,=H'4'            SET ERR CODE WHEN XREF TBL IS FULL
              B        REFXIT
*
*   DATA AREAS AND DSECTS
*
SAVE          DS       18F                 REGISTER SAVE AREA
*
SYMENTRY      DSECT                        , DSECT FOR SYMBOL TABLE ENTRY ...
SYMNAME       DS       CL8          BYTES  0-7     SYMBOL
SYMVALUE      DS       CL4                 8-11    SYMBOL VALUE
SYMLNG        DS       CL2                 12-13   LENGTH ATTRIBUTE
SYMDEFN       DS       CL2                 14-15   STMT# WHERE DEFINED
SYMSECT       DS       CL1                 16      SYMBOL'S SECTION#
SYMTYPE       DS       CL1                 17      REL/ABS INDICATOR
REFCTR        DS       H                   18-19   CROSS REF COUNT
REFLAST       DS       H                   20-21   PTR TO LAST XREF ENTRY
REF1ST        DS       H                   22-23   PTR TO 1ST XREF ENTRY
*
STKENTRY      DSECT                        , DSECT FOR CROSS REF TBL STRUCTURE
*                              TYPICAL XREF ENTRY . . .
STMTREF       DS       H           BYTES  0-1    STMT# THAT REF'D SYMBOL
NEXTREF       DS       H                   2-3    PTR TO NEXT XREF IN TBL
*                              FIRST ENTRY ONLY . . .
STKMAX        EQU      STMTREF             1ST HALF-WORD HAS MAX # XREF ENTRIES
STKPTR        EQU      NEXTREF             2ND HALF-WD POINTS TO LAST USED ENTRY
*                                          (ASSUMING STKPTR = 0 INITIALLY)
              END
```

The concept and use of lists is one of the fundamental mechanisms for structuring data in computer memories. The use of pointers allows us to break free of the essentially linear constraint imposed by the physical organization of memory and to interrelate data that need not be stored in consecutive locations of memory. List entries may contain more than one pointer: a pointer back to the previous entry, a pointer to the first and/or last entry, pointers to entries on other lists. Each such pointer allows a relationship to be represented without requiring that the two entries be adjacent in memory or that they belong to the same table or file. The study of these techniques is not within the scope of this text; the reader may find that Donald Knuth's *The Art of Programming, vol I: Fundamental Algorithms* provides a good starting point for further study.

23.10 SUMMARY

The assembly process we have described is typical of that used in many computer systems, particularly the IBM 360 and 370 systems. It requires two passes over the source module statements and depends on mechanisms that permit reasonably efficient processing of information.

The first pass assigns addresses to all instructions, constants, and data areas and thereby also assigns values to name-field symbols. The second pass generates the object module and the listing. If there were only one pass, it would be impracticable to assemble source statements in which the operand referred to symbols that had not yet been defined. Even with two passes, the operands of a few directives, most notably EQU, are restricted to already defined symbols and to self-defining terms.

The mechanisms for processing information are based on the concepts of tables and lists. These data structures consist of entries (also known as records) that are usually subdivided into a number of fields. The contents of one or more fields in an entry serve to identify that entry; the contents of other fields describe certain characteristics of whatever the entry represents. In a table, the addresses of the entries can be inferred once the address of the first entry is known (or at worst they can be calculated from it). This is so because table entries are stored in consecutive locations in memory. In a list, the entries are not necessarily stored in consecutive memory locations. Consequently, an explicit representation of each entry's address is required. This representation, often called a pointer, must be available in order to process an entry. In the cross-reference list described in this chapter, the pointer to each entry other than the first was stored in the entry logically preceding that entry. Other schemes, not discussed in this chapter, are also possible.

The principal assembler tables and lists covered in this chapter are the opcode and directive tables; the symbol, literal, and base-register tables; the object module tables (ESD, TXT, RLD, END); and the cross-reference list. In addition, the intermediate file, consisting of the source module statements and certain information about these statements determined in Pass 1, was described. The content of two of these tables—the opcode and directive tables—is known at the time the assembler program is written. The entries in these two tables are thus "built into" the assembler. The entries in the other data structures mentioned must be determined at assembly time. The intermediate file and the symbol, literal, and ESD tables are created in Pass 1; the base-register, cross-reference, and remaining object module tables are created in Pass 2.

The assembler may have to search one or more tables in order to complete the processing of a given source module statement. One of the most efficient and frequently used methods of table searching is known as the binary search technique. In this technique, the middle table entry is the first one examined, to determine which half of the table to search further. Then the middle entry of that half is examined to further restrict the search domain, and so forth until the sought-for entry is either found or not found. Use of this technique requires that the entries be in sequence, and that the field controlling the sequence be the same as the field used in the search. Built-in tables, such as the opcode and directive tables, can be created in sequence and are thus directly amenable to the binary search technique. Tables that are created, such as the symbol table, might not be created in the sequence needed for searching. In such a case, the entries must be sorted before a binary search can be used. One method of sorting—straight insertion—was summarized in this chapter. It is one of the simpler methods of sorting. Many other sorting methods have been devised; their relative merits depend in large part on the characteristics of the data and of the computer system. There is no known best method to be used under all conditions.

Two-Pass Assembler The entire source module is processed twice in succession, statement by statement. The first pass assigns values to symbols and addresses to literals; the second creates the object module, the listing, and related information.

The EQU Directive For a two-pass assembler, a symbol must be defined prior to its occurrence in an EQU's operand.

Tables A table is a collection of data entries usually arranged so that they are easy to locate and to process. The simplest form of table is a one-dimensional integer array, in which each of the array's integers is an entry in the table. Typically, table entries contain more than one data item; among the items is a key that identifies the entry.

Built-In Assembler Tables These tables contain entries whose values are all known at the time the assembler itself is created. Examples are the opcode and directive tables.

Assembly-Time Assembler Tables These tables contain entries whose values depend on the source module statements being assembled. Examples are the symbol, literal, and base-register tables.

Intermediate File The use of this file enables Pass 2 to avoid having to retranslate mnemonic opcodes, to recalculate the memory location counter, and to do other tasks already accomplished in Pass 1.

ESD, TXT, RLD, END These are the four types of records contained in an object module.

ESD The External Symbol Dictionary identifies the name and length of the module and each of its control sections, as well as all of its other entry points. It also identifies the symbols that are referenced within the module but defined in other modules.

TXT The "text" portion of an object module contains the object code itself: machine language instructions and machine language data.

RLD The Relocation Dictionary identifies the address and characteristics of each relocatable constant in the module, including those of external address constants.

END The final record in an object module identifies the address of the module's first executable instruction.

Linear Search A linear search examines table entries in the order in which they occur in the table. The entries need not be in sequence.

Binary Search For this technique, table entries must be in sequence. A binary search examines the middle entry to determine whether to continue searching in the top half or the bottom half of the table, and it then repeats this tactic on the half that it selects and continues in this way until the sought item is either found or not.

Sorting Tables Tables that are sorted can be searched more rapidly than those that aren't. Choice of an appropriate sort algorithm depends on the characteristics of the data as well as on those of the computer in which the sorting is done.

Cross-References Linked lists provide an elegant way to collect and organize the data that identifies the statements in which each symbol is referenced.

Linked Lists Unlike a table, the entries of a linked list need not be in consecutive memory locations, and the memory requirements need not be precisely known in advance of its use. The location of each entry is determined by a pointer in another entry. A pointer is either an address or a number (such as a subscript) from which an address can be calculated.

1. What single fact about assembly language programs makes it highly desirable if not imperative to have a two-pass assembler?
2. What does it mean for a symbol to be "defined"? Why must a symbol be defined prior to its occurrence in an EQU's operand?
3. What is the primary purpose of the assembler's opcode table? Of its directive table?
4. What is the primary purpose of the assembler's symbol table? Of its literal table? Its base-register table?
5. Why is the MLC (memory location counter) calculated in Pass 1?
6. By what rule does the assembler choose a base register when assembling an implicit operand?
7. What is the "relocation factor," when is its value determined, and how is its use related to the RLD entries of an object module?
8. When the assembler assembles a DC directive, what information about it is placed in a TXT record?
9. When the assembler assembles a DS or EQU directive, why doesn't it put any information about it in a TXT record?
10. What information in the object module indicates that a source module is calling an external subroutine?
11. What are the main purpose and advantages of using ESDID's?
12. What is the principal advantage of using a binary search instead of a linear search?
13. Explain how it is possible that a linear search can be faster if a table is in sequence than if it isn't in sequence.
14. Why was a linked-list structure instead of a table used for the cross-reference information?

23.13   EXERCISES _____

1. Compared to the two-pass assembly process described in this chapter, what would be the disadvantage of having a one-pass assembly instead? What would be the advantage of having a three-pass assembly?

2. Explain why entries are not made in the base-register table until Pass 2 (as shown in Fig. 23.8 and the accompanying text).

3. Why is it that no object code is generated by the assembler when it processes an EQU directive (see, for example, Fig. 23.2)?

4. Which of the symbols in the source module of Figure 23.2 are relocatable and which are absolute constants? Except for the entry that would be made in the symbol table for the relocatable constants of Figure 23.2, is there any other way in which they would be processed differently from the absolute constants? Would the address constant of Statement 16 in Figure 23.2 be considered a relocatable constant or an absolute constant? Why?

5. If an assembly language program is large enough to warrant use of two or more implied base registers in a single control section, by what rule would the assembler most likely choose one of those registers when creating the base-displacement form of address corresponding to an implicit operand?

6. In Chapter 14, we discussed how the OPSYN directive may be used to define a new opcode that is synonymous with (has the same properties as) an existing opcode and how it may be used to remove an opcode from the set of allowable opcodes. In the context of the discussions in the present chapter, explain how these two functions of the OPSYN directive might be implemented in the assembler. Would the implementation of the OPSYN directive be part of Pass 1 processing, Pass 2 processing, or both?

7. Suppose that you wanted to provide a new directive in assembly language, call it OPDEF, whose purpose would be to allow a programmer to define an entirely new instruction opcode. For example, if you had an assembler for the IBM 360, you might use the OPDEF directive to define the instruction opcodes such as CLCL, MVCL, and the other IBM 370 instructions so that the 360 assembler could be used to assemble 370 programs. In the context of the discussions in this chapter, explain how the OPDEF directive might be implemented in the assembler. Would the implementation be part of Pass 1 processing, Pass 2 processing, or both?

8. What would be the contents of the object module for the source code shown in Figure 23.2? Write your answer in the same form as that shown in Figures 23.16a–23.16d.

9. From Figure 23.14, it can be seen that entries are placed in an object module in the following order: (1) all the ESD entries, (2) all the TXT entries, (3) the RLD entries, and (4) the END entry. What is the minimum number of each type of entry that can occur in an object module? From the standpoint of the linkage editor program, what advantage is gained by having the entries in the order just described and not in some other order?

10. Based on Figure 23.17, write an assembly language subroutine that will perform a linear search of a table of M entries subject to the following criteria:

   a. Each entry in the table has the fixed-length symbol table entry format shown in Figure 23.5.

   b. The search key is an 8-byte symbol to be matched against the symbol field in each entry.

   c. The subroutine should return the address of the entry in Register 15 if the entry is found, and a full-word zero in Register 15 if the entry is not found. The table entries should not be assumed to be in any particular sequence. The number of entries in the table should be permitted to be any integer M such that $M \geq 0$.

11. Modify your subroutine solution to Exercise 10 so that if the sought-for entry is not found, it adds an entry to the end of the table. The entry to be added must be provided by the calling program and the subroutine must increase the caller's entry-count M by $+1$ and return the address of the newly inserted entry in Register 15.

12. What modifications should be made to your subroutine solution to Exercise 10 if

   a. The symbol table entries are in ascending sequence by key field?

   b. No symbol occurs more than once in the table?

13. Modify your solution to Exercise 10 so that your subroutine can search a table all of whose entries have the same fixed length, L, and a key field of length KL, and in which the key field in each entry begins in byte position KP relative to the beginning of the entry. The integers L, KL, and KP are to be passed as parameters to your subroutine, and each can be assumed to be in the range from 1 to 256. As in Exercise 10, the number of entries in the table should be permitted to be any nonnegative integer M, and the key field should be assumed to be an EBCDIC string.

14. Write an assembly language program that will read input data consisting of assembly language source module statements, and create a symbol table according to these criteria: Your program should assign a statement number to each statement it processes and create an entry to be added to the symbol table for each statement that contains a valid name-field entry. The entry should be in the format of Figure 23.5, although all but the symbol and statement number fields will be blank. The symbol table should be created using your subroutine solution to Exercise 11. After all input statements have been processed, print the contents of the symbol table.

15. Modify the assembly language subroutine of Figure 23.22b so that it is tailored to the format of the symbol table given in Figure 23.5. In other words, your subroutine should assume that the table being sorted consists of fixed-length entries of length L = 18, key length KL = 8, and key position KP = 0. The number of entries in the table is a parameter that must be passed to your subroutine. The symbol table entries should be sorted "in place" as in Figure 23.22b, i.e., at each stage of the sorting process the partially sorted entries should occupy the same area of memory that was occupied by the original, unsorted entries.

16. Modify your solution to Exercise 14 so that after printing the symbol table it calls your sort subroutine of Exercise 15 and then prints the sorted symbol table.

17. Describe the processing that must take place in order that an entry may be made for a given symbol reference in the cross-reference list structure of Figure 23.23. Your description should be consistent with the discussions of Section 10.9 regarding the revisions to the symbol table entry format and be general enough to be applicable to any symbol and any cross-reference entry. (**Hint:** See Fig. 23.24.)

18. Describe the processes that must take place in order that all the cross-reference entries for a given symbol may be removed from the list structure of Figure 23.23 and printed as on a cross-reference listing.

19. Write a subroutine that will accomplish the task described in Exercise 18.

Appendixes

	mnemonic code	machine code	type	instruction name	text section
c	A	5A	RX	add	5.3
c	AD	6A	RX	add normalized (long)	13.7
c	ADR	2A	RR	add normalized (long)	13.7
c	AE	7A	RX	add normalized (short)	13.7
c	AER	3A	RR	add normalized (short)	13.7
c	AH	4A	RX	add halfword	5.3
c	AL	5E	RX	add logical	5.3
c	ALR	1E	RR	add logical	5.3
c	AP	FA	SS$_2$	add decimal	12.3
c	AR	1A	RR	add	5.3
c	AU	7E	RX	add unnormalized (short)	13.7
c	AUR	3E	RR	add unnormalized (short)	13.7
c	AW	6E	RX	add unnormalized (long)	13.7
c	AWR	2E	RR	add unnormalized (long)	13.7
c	AXR	36	RR	add normalized (extended)	13.7
	BAL	45	RX	branch and link	9.2
	BALR	05	RR	branch and link	10.3
*	BAS	4D	RX	branch and save	9.2
*	BASR	0D	RR	branch and save	10.3
	BC	47	RX	branch on condition	8.4
	BCR	07	RR	branch on condition	8.4
	BCT	46	RX	branch on count	4.5
	BCTR	06	RR	branch on count	---
	BXH	86	RS	branch on index high	4.6
	BXLE	87	RS	branch on index low or equal	4.6
c	C	59	RX	compare	5.5
c	CD	69	RX	compare (long)	13.5
c	CDR	29	RR	compare (long)	13.5
*c	CDS	BB	RS	compare double and swap	---
c	CE	79	RX	compare (short)	13.5
c	CER	39	RR	compare (short)	13.5
c	CH	49	RX	compare halfword	5.5
c	CL	55	RX	compare logical	7.3
c	CLC	D5	SS$_1$	compare logical characters	7.3
*c	CLCL	0F	RR	compare logical characters long	7.8
c	CLI	95	SI	compare logical immediate	7.3
*c	CLM	BD	RS	compare logical under mask	7.3
c	CLR	15	RR	compare logical	7.3
c	CP	F9	SS$_2$	compare decimal	12.4
c	CR	19	RR	compare	5.5
*c	CS	BA	RS	compare and swap	---
	CVB	4F	RX	convert to binary	12.8
	CVD	4E	RX	convert to decimal	12.8
	D	5D	RX	divide	5.3
	DD	6D	RX	divide (long)	13.7
	DDR	2D	RR	divide (long)	13.7
	DE	7D	RX	divide (short)	13.7
	DER	3D	RR	divide (short)	13.7
	DP	FD	SS$_2$	divide decimal	12.3
	DR	1D	RR	divide	5.3
c	ED	DE	SS$_1$	edit	12.9
c	EDMK	DF	SS$_1$	edit and mark	12.9
	EX	44	RX	execute	7.7
	HDR	24	RR	halve (long)	13.7
	HER	34	RR	halve (short)	13.7
	IC	43	RX	insert character	7.2
*c	ICM	BF	RS	insert characters under mask	7.2
	L	58	RX	load	5.2
	LA	41	RX	load address	4.5
c	LCDR	23	RR	load complement (long)	13.6
c	LCER	33	RR	load complement (short)	13.6
c	LCR	13	RR	load complement	5.6
	LD	68	RX	load (long)	13.4
	LDR	28	RR	load (long)	13.4
	LE	78	RX	load (short)	13.4
	LER	38	RR	load (short)	13.4
	LH	48	RX	load halfword	5.2
	LM	98	RS	load multiple	5.2
c	LNDR	21	RR	load negative (long)	13.6
c	LNER	31	RR	load negative (short)	13.6
c	LNR	11	RR	load negative	5.6
c	LPDR	20	RR	load positive (long)	13.6
c	LPER	30	RR	load positive (short)	13.6
c	LPR	10	RR	load positive	5.6
	LR	18	RR	load	5.2
	LRDR	25	RR	load rounded (extended to long)	13.7
	LRER	35	RR	load rounded (long to short)	13.7
c	LTDR	22	RR	load and test (long)	13.5
c	LTER	32	RR	load and test (short)	13.5
c	LTR	12	RR	load and test	5.4
	M	5C	RX	multiply	5.3
*	MC	AF	SI	monitor call	---
	MD	6C	RX	multiply (long)	13.7
	MDR	2C	RR	multiply (long)	13.7
	ME	7C	RX	multiply (short)	13.7
	MER	3C	RR	multiply (short)	13.7
	MH	4C	RX	multiply halfword	5.3
	MP	FC	SS$_2$	multiply decimal	12.3
	MR	1C	RR	multiply	5.3
	MVC	D2	SS$_1$	move characters	7.2
*	MVCIN	E8	SS$_1$	move inverse	7.2
*c	MVCL	0E	RR	move characters long	7.8
	MVI	92	SI	move immediate	7.2
	MVN	D1	SS$_1$	move numerics	12.6
	MVO	F1	SS$_2$	move with offset	12.6
	MVZ	D3	SS$_1$	move zones	12.6
	MXD	67	RX	multiply (long to extended)	13.7
	MXDR	27	RR	multiply (long to extended)	13.7
	MXR	26	RR	multiply (extended)	13.7
c	N	54	RX	and	8.2
c	NC	D4	SS$_1$	and characters	8.2
c	NI	94	SI	and immediate	8.2
c	NR	14	RR	and	8.2
c	O	56	RX	or	8.2
c	OC	D6	SS$_1$	or characters	8.2
c	OI	96	SI	or immediate	8.2
c	OR	16	RR	or	8.2
	PACK	F2	SS$_2$	pack	12.8
c	S	5B	RX	subtract	5.3
c	SD	6B	RX	subtract normalized (long)	13.7
c	SDR	2B	RR	subtract normalized (long)	13.7
c	SE	7B	RX	subtract normalized (short)	13.7
c	SER	3B	RR	subtract normalized (short)	13.7
c	SH	4B	RX	subtract halfword	5.3
c	SL	5F	RX	subtract logical	5.3
c	SLA	8B	RS	shift left single	8.1
c	SLDA	8F	RS	shift left double	8.1
	SLDL	8D	RS	shift left double logical	8.1
	SLL	89	RS	shift left single logical	8.1
c	SLR	1F	RR	subtract logical	5.3
c	SP	FB	SS$_2$	subtract decimal	12.3
c	SPM	04	RR	set program mask	11.4
c	SR	1B	RR	subtract	5.3
c	SRA	8A	RS	shift right single	8.1
c	SRDA	8E	RS	shift right double	8.1
	SRDL	8C	RS	shift right double logical	8.1
	SRL	88	RS	shift right single logical	8.1
*c	SRP	F0	SS$_1$	shift and round decimal	12.5
	ST	50	RX	store	5.2
	STC	42	RX	store character	7.2

c = condition code is set   * = IBM System 370

mnemonic code	machine code	type	instruction name	text section		mnemonic code	machine code	type	instruction name	text section
* STCK	B205	S	store clock	---		c SWR	2F	RR	subtract unnormalized (long)	13.7
* STCM	BE	RS	store characters under mask	7.2		c SXR	37	RR	subtract normalized (extended)	13.7
STD	60	RX	store (long)	13.4		c TM	91	SI	test under mask	8.3
STE	70	RX	store (short)	13.4		TR	DC	SS₁	translate	7.9
STH	40	RX	store halfword	5.2		c TRT	DD	SS₁	translate and test	7.9
STM	90	RS	store multiple	5.2		c TS	93	S	test and set	8.3
c SU	7F	RX	subtract unnormalized (short)	13.7		UNPK	F3	SS₂	unpack	12.8
c SUR	3F	RR	subtract unnormalized (short)	13.7		c X	57	RX	exclusive or	8.2
SVC	0A	RR	supervisor call	19.4		c XC	D7	SS₁	exclusive or characters	8.2
c SW	6F	RX	subtract unnormalized (long)	13.7		c XI	97	SI	exclusive or immediate	8.2
						c XR	17	RR	exclusive or	8.2
						c ZAP	F8	SS₂	zero and add decimal	12.3

c = condition code is set   * = IBM System 370

Instruction Format Summary

type	machine language instruction formats	assembly language operand formats	notes
RR	op R1 R2 (0, 8, 12)	explicit R1,R2	
RX	op R1 X2 B2 D2 (0, 8, 12, 16, 20, 31)	explicit R1(X2,B2) / R1,D2(,B2) / R1,D2(X2) / R1,D2 ; implicit R1,S2(X2) / R1,S2	1
RS	op R1 R2 B3 D3 (0, 8, 12, 16, 20, 31)	explicit R1,R2,D3(B3) ; implicit R1,R2,S3	2
SI	op I2 B1 D1 (0, 8, 16, 20, 31)	explicit D1(B1),I2 ; implicit S1,I2	3
S	op B1 D1 (0, 16, 20, 31)	explicit D1(B1) ; implicit S1	
SS₁	op L B1 D1 B2 D2 (0, 8, 16, 20, 32, 36, 47)	explicit D1(L,B1),D2(B2) ; implicit S1,S2 ; mixed D1(L,B1),S2 / S1(L),D2(B2) / S1(L),S2 / S1,D2(B2)	4,5
SS₂	op L1 L2 B1 D1 B2 D2 (0, 8, 12, 16, 20, 32, 36, 47)	explicit D1(L1,B1),D2(L2,B2) ; implicit S1,S2 ; mixed D1(L1,B1),S2(L2) / D1(L1,B1),S2 / S1(L1),S2(L2) / S1(L1),S2 / S1,S2(L2) / S1(L1),D2(L2,B2) / S1,D2(L2,B2)	5,6

Notes:
1. RX: When the index field X2 is omitted, it is assumed to be 0. An X2 field of 0 means no indexing.

2. RS: IBM manuals give R1,R3,D2(B2) where we have given R1,R2,D3(B3).

3. SI: The I2 field is 1 byte, used as immediate data.

4. SS₁: In machine language, the length field L is represented by a number that is one less than that used in assembly language.

5. SS₁, SS₂: Any of the length fields can be omitted in assembly language when a symbolic address is used. If so omitted, the assembler uses the length attribute of the corresponding symbol.

6. SS₂: In machine language the length fields L1 and L2 are represented by numbers that are one less than those used in the corresponding assembly language fields.

Appendix B   Extended Mnemonic Codes for BC and BCR Instructions

RX-type instructions				**RR-type instructions**		
extended mnemonic code	mnemonic code	machine code	instruction name	extended mnemonic code	mnemonic code	machine code
B	BC 15,	47F	unconditional branch	BR	BCR 15,	07F
NOP	BC 0,	470	unconditional no operation	NOPR	BCR 0,	070
			used after compare instructions			
BE	BC 8,	478	branch if equal	BER	BCR 8,	078
BL	BC 4,	474	branch if low	BLR	BCR 4,	074
BH	BC 2,	472	branch if high	BHR	BCR 2,	072
BNE	BC 7,	477	branch if not equal	BNER	BCR 7,	077
BNL	BC 11,	47B	branch if not low	BNLR	BCR 11,	07B
BNH	BC 13,	47D	branch if not high	BNHR	BCR 13,	07D
			used after arithmetic instructions			
BZ	BC 8,	478	branch if zero	BZR	BCR 8,	078
BM	BC 4,	474	branch if minus	BMR	BCR 4,	074
BP	BC 2,	472	branch if plus	BPR	BCR 2,	072
BO	BC 1,	471	branch if overflow	BOR	BCR 1,	071
BNZ	BC 7,	477	branch if not zero	BNZR	BCR 7,	077
BNM	BC 11,	47B	branch if not minus	BNMR	BCR 11,	07B
BNP	BC 13,	47D	branch if not plus	BNPR	BCR 13,	07D
BNO	BC 14,	47E	branch if not overflow	BNOR	BCR 14,	07E
			used after test under mask instructions			
BZ	BC 8,	478	branch if zeroes	BZR	BCR 8,	078
BO	BC 1,	471	branch if ones	BOR	BCR 1,	071
BM	BC 4,	474	branch if mixed	BMR	BCR 4,	074

Appendix C   Condition Code Settings for Nonprivileged Instructions

	instruction		--------- condition code setting depends on the instruction and its result, as shown ---------			
			condition code 0	condition code 1	condition code 2	condition code 3
INTEGER OPERATIONS	add subtract	A, AR, AH S, SR, SH	result is zero	result is negative	result is positive	operation generated an overflow
	add subtract	AL, ALR SL, SLR	result is zero, with no carry (AL, ALR only)	result is not zero, with no carry	result is zero, with carry	result is not zero, with carry
	compare	C, CR, CH	both operands are equal	first operand less than second	first operand greater than second	---
	load	LCR	result is zero	result is negative	result is positive	overflow generated
		LNR	result is zero	result is negative	---	---
		LPR	result is zero	---	result is positive	overflow generated
		LTR	result is zero	result is negative	result is positive	---
	shift	SLA, SLDA	result is zero	result is negative	result is positive	overflow generated
		SRA, SRDA	result is zero	result is negative	result is positive	---
BYTE OPERATIONS	insert	ICM	all inserted bits 0, or all mask bits 0	1st inserted bit is 1	1st inserted bit is 0, but not all are 0	---
	compare	CL, CLR CLC, CLI	both operands are equal	first operand less than second	first operand greater than second	---
		CLCL	operands are equal, or have zero lengths	first operand less than second	first operand greater than second	---
		CLM	bytes selected are equal or mask bits are all 0	first operand field less than second	first operand field greater than second	---
	copy	MVCL	first operand's length equals second operand's	first operand's length less than second's	first operand's length greater than second's	destructive overlap (no bytes copied)
	translate	TRT	all argument bytes tested; all function bytes zero	one or more argument bytes not tested	search stopped on last argument byte	---

	instruction		condition code 0	condition code 1	condition code 2	condition code 3
BIT OPERATIONS	AND	N, NC, NI, NR	result is zero	result is not zero	---	---
	OR	O, OC, OI, OR	result is zero	result is not zero	---	---
	EXCL-OR	X, XC, XI, XR	result is zero	result is not zero	---	---
	test	TM	all selected bits 0, or all mask bits 0	some selected bits are 0, and some are 1	---	all selected bits are 1's
		TS	left-most bit of tested byte is 0	left-most bit of tested byte is 1	---	---
DECIMAL	add subtract	AP, ZAP SP	result is zero	result is negative	result is positive	operation generated an overflow
	compare	CP	both operands are equal	first operand less than second	first operand greater than second	---
	shift	SRP	result is zero	result is negative	result is positive	overflow generated
FLOATING POINT	add	AE, AER, AD, ADR, AU, AUR, AW, AWR, AXR	mantissa of result is zero	result is negative	result is positive	---
	subtract	SE, SER, SD, SDR, SU, SUR, SW, SWR, SXR	mantissa of result is zero	result is negative (mantissa not zero)	result is positive (mantissa not zero)	---
	load	LCER, LCDR	result mantissa is zero	result is negative	result is positive	---
		LNER, LNDR	result mantissa is zero	result is negative	---	---
		LPER, LPDR	result mantissa is zero	---	result is positive	---
		LTER, LTDR	result mantissa is zero	result is negative	result is positive	---
	compare	CE, CER CD, CDR	both operands are equal	first operand less than second	first operand greater than second	---
MISCELLANEOUS	compare and swap	CS, CDS	compared operands equal, second one is replaced	compared operands not equal, first is replaced	---	---
	set program mask	SPM	(the condition code is set to the value of bits 2 and 3 of the designated register)			
	store clock	STCK	clock in set state	clock in not-set state	clock in error state	clock in stopped state or not-operational
	editing	ED, EDMK	last edited field is zero	last edited field is negative	last edited field is positive	---

--------- condition code setting depends on the instruction and its result, as shown ---------

	name of exception	cause of exception	instructions in which exceptions can occur
binary integer arithmetic instructions	Fixed-Point Overflow*	occurs when there is a carry out of the high-order numeric bit position different from the carry out of the sign-bit position	A, AR, AH, S, SR, SH, LCR, LPR, SLA, SLDA
	Fixed-Point Divide	occurs when the divisor is zero or when the quotient or the result of a CVB instruction is greater than $2^{31} - 1$ or less than -2^{31}	D, DR, CVB
	Specification	occurs when the first operand does not specify an even-numbered register address	D, DR, M, MR, SLDA, SRDA, SLDL, SRDL
decimal arithmetic instructions	Decimal Overflow*	occurs when one or more significant high-order digits are lost because the destination field is too small to contain the result	AP, SP, ZAP, SRP
	Decimal Divide	occurs when the divisor is zero or when the quotient exceeds the specified data-field size	DP
	Specification	occurs when the multiplier or divisor exceeds fifteen digits and sign, or when the first operand field is not longer than the second operand field in a multiplication or division	DP, MP
	Data	occurs when any of the following conditions occur	
		1. the sign or digit codes of operand fields in any packed-decimal or CVB instruction are invalid	AP, CP, DP, MP, SP, SRP, ZAP, ED, EDMK, CVB
		2. the first operand field in an MP instruction has an insufficient number of high-order zeroes	MP
		3. the operand fields in AP, CP, DP, MP, and SP overlap in a way other than with coincident right-most bytes	AP, CP, DP, MP, SP
		4. the operand fields in ZAP overlap, and the right-most byte of the second operand is to the right of the right-most byte of the first operand	ZAP
floating-point arithmetic instructions	Exponent Overflow	occurs when the result characteristic exceeds 127 and the result mantissa is not zero	all floating-point Add, Subtract, Multiply, Divide, and Round instructions
	Exponent Underflow*	occurs when the result characteristic is less than zero and the result mantissa is not zero	all floating-point Add Normalized, Subtract Normalized, Multiply, Divide, and Halve instructions
	Significance*	occurs when the result mantissa in floating-point addition or subtraction is zero	all floating-point Add and Subtract instructions
	Floating-Point Divide	occurs when the mantissa of the divisor is zero.	DD, DDR, DE, DER
	Specification	occurs when an invalid floating-point register address is specified in a floating-point instruction	all floating-point instructions
nonprivileged instructions in general	Specification	occurs under any of the following conditions	
		1. an instruction address does not designate a location on an even-byte boundary	all branch instructions, and the EX instruction
		2. an operand address does not designate a half-, full-, or double-word boundary in an instruction requiring such a boundary designation	various instructions**
		3. even-numbered register addresses are not specified in the CLCL or MVCL instructions	CLCL, MVCL
		4. bit positions 8–11 of an MC instruction do not contain all zeroes	MC
	Execute	occurs when the target instruction of an EX instruction is another EX instruction	EX
	Privileged	occurs when a privileged instruction is executed in problem mode	all privileged instructions
	Operation	occurs when an attempt is made to execute an instruction that has an invalid opcode.	all invalid opcodes
	Access	occurs under a variety of conditions, perhaps best summarized as follows: whenever an attempt is made to obtain or store information in an area of memory to which the program is not allowed to have access, this exception occurs. These errors are separately categorized as protection, addressing, segment-translation, page-translation, and translation-specification exceptions. The reader is referred to the *Principles of Operation* manual for the IBM System 360 or 370, for explanatory details.	all instructions that require access to a main memory location in order to complete their execution cycle

Footnotes to Run-Time Errors

*NOTE: Through appropriate execution of the SPM instruction (see Section 11.4), program interruption may be prohibited for fixed-point overflow, floating-point overflow, exponent underflow, and significance error exceptions. All other exceptions always cause program interruption.

**Specification errors occur when operand addresses are not aligned as follows:

	IBM 360	IBM 370
on half word	EX and all branch instructions AH, CH, LH, MH, SH, STH	EX and all branch instructions
on full word	A, AL, C, CL, D, L, LM, M, S, SL, ST, STM AE, AU, CE, DE, LE, ME, SE, STE, SU N, O, X	CS
on double word	AD, AW, CD, DD, LD, MD, MXD, SD, STD, SW, CVB, CVD	CDS

Debugging Tips

Listed below are some things to keep in mind while you are looking for the cause of a crash or other run-time error.

The first rule of debugging is to suspect every statement in your program of a possible error until proven otherwise. Do NOT assume that a statement is correct until you can convince yourself *beyond any doubt* that it is correct in the context in which it is used. Your eyes and mind will then be receptive to finding subtle as well as elementary errors.

Debugging Tools

Obviously one major debugging tool is the snapshot dump; another is the full-memory dump; and a third is interactive debugging, in which selected portions of memory and registers can be displayed at breakpoints. To use any of these tools, you may need one of the relevant IBM reference manuals, such as the *OS/VS1 Debugging Guide* (#GC24-5093) or the *OS/VS2 System Programming Library: Debugging Handbook* (#GC28-1047,-1048,-1049).

There are also several good books on debugging. Robert Binder's *Application Debugging* is one of the most comprehensive; Barbara Burian's *Simplified Approach to S/370 Assembly Language Programming* has excellent discussions and examples on how to read a memory dump, as does *Debugging System 360/370 Programs using OS and VS Storage Dumps*, by Daniel Rindfleisch. Other useful books and manuals can be discovered through the references provided by the three books just mentioned.

Another debugging tool is the assembler's cross-reference listing, which can show you whether or not (and if so, where) you have initialized, referenced, and changed any variable or constant. Among other items, it will also show you what statements called subroutines, and which macros were invoked and where they were invoked. Many interactive debuggers also provide cross-reference information on-line.

One final comment: In addition to the use of debugging tools, be sure that you know exactly what data your program was processing. If the data was in a file, then get a printout of that file. If the data and/or commands were provided interactively, then try to reconstruct—or make your program save on a file—exactly what was typed into the program up to the moment it crashed. Often the input will help you locate the source of your program error, especially if the data wasn't typed in the format you expected.

Check the Register Contents for Clues

When your program crashes with one of the exception conditions listed above, then one of the first things to do after you've determined the system completion code and the address of the offending instruction is to look at the contents of the registers at the point where the crash occurred. The register contents frequently provide a clue about what might have gone wrong. Here are some of the things you should look for:

1. What is the value of the most recently used loop-control counter?
2. Is the address and/or index used for loop iterations correct?
3. Is the implied base address correct in R12?
4. Is the save-area address correct in R13?
5. Does R14 give the reentry point for the most recent subroutine or macro call?
6. Does R15 contain an error code from the most recent subroutine or macro call, and if so, did your program detect it and take a valid action?
7. Is any other register's contents different from what you think it should be, and if so, can you locate the instructions in your program that might have affected that register?

Check Your Listing for Common Programming Errors

You should try to eliminate obvious errors as soon as you can. Do not make the mistake of just looking near the point where the program crashed. Instead, *look through your entire program for possible errors.* Start by looking for these (and similar) common programming errors:

errors in standard entry/exit

Do not use L instead of LA (or vice versa).

Do not use LM instead of STM (or vice versa).

Do not code LM/STM operand as 12,14,12(13); it should be 14,12,12(13).

Do not code B 14 instead of BR 14.

errors in conditional branch instructions

BM does not mean "branch if less than or equal to zero."

BP does not mean "branch if greater than or equal to zero."

BNH does not mean "branch if less than."

BNL does not mean "branch if greater than."

errors in use of registers

Do not use the linkage registers (R0,R1,R13,R14,R15) for other than linkage purposes; the contents of R0, R1, R14, R15 are very likely to be different when the program returns from an I/O or other system macro than they were when it invoked the macro.

Do not use Register 13 (R13) for anything except the register save-area address.

Do not use the implied base register (R12) for anything except the implied base address.

Do not use registers inconsistently when calling/returning from an internal subroutine—e.g., don't pass a parameter in a different register than the one in which it is expected by the subroutine.

Do not forget to save/restore registers that are used in an internal subroutine.

errors in initializations

Do not forget to initialize and/or reset a memory location or register at the right time and place in the program.

Note: Here is where the assembler's cross-reference listing or a similar interactive capability can be of great help in locating errors.

Check for Misused Instructions

It is imperative that you know the exact manner in which each of the instructions operate. Here are some of the types of things that you should be aware of:

M/MR: Both generate a double-word product in an even-odd register pair, so be sure you know the maximum size a product can attain.

MH: Generates a full-word product but does *not* cause an overflow if the product is outside the range of 32-bit integers.

D/DR: Both require a double-word dividend, with its sign correctly propagated.

LTR: No multiply or divide instruction sets the condition code—so, use LTR to set the code for product, quotient, remainder. Note that, in this and other RR-type instructions, the destination register is specified in the first operand field.

LH: Replaces a register's entire contents with a half word from memory.

STH: Stores the low-order half of a register into a memory half word.

CH: Algebraically compares a register's entire contents to a half word in memory.

EX: Executes no matter what is in the designated register, and treats bits 24–31 of the designated register as an unsigned positive number—e.g., X'FF' is 255, *not* –1.

TRT: Sets the condition code and alters Registers 1 and 2 as follows: inserts a copy of the selected nonzero function byte into bits 24–31 of Register 2, and inserts the address of the corresponding argument byte into bits 8–31 of Register 1.

TM: Sets the condition code, which should be interrogated via BZ (branches if the tested bits were all **Z**eroes), BM (branches if the tested bits were **M**ixed—some 0's and some 1's), or BO (branches if the tested bits were all **O**nes).

EDMK: Sets the condition code and may replace Register 1's contents with the address of the first significant digit in the pattern.

Comparisons: The result of all compare instructions is relative to the quantity designated by the first operand field.

Check your Program for Less Obvious Pitfalls

The types of errors listed below represent but a tiny fraction of the possible causes of a crash. If you become familiar with this list it should help you to think of other possible causes.

Using a register for two or more different purposes during a loop or other sequence of related statements

Using an instruction that does not match the type of data being operated on—e.g., LE instead of LD for long-format floating-point data, or CLI instead of CLC for strings whose length exceeds one character

Incrementing an address by the wrong amount—increment should be $+1$ for character strings, $+2$ for half-word array components, $+4$ for full-word array components, etc.

Referencing a different symbol or register than the one that should be referenced in a given situation

Using DS instead of DC to define a constant

Losing significant data from a DC directive due to truncation by the assembler when the length modifier Ln is too small

Using an incorrect DC or DS length attribute (e.g., DS 10C instead of DS CL10) causing a wrong implied length in an SS_1 or SS_2 instruction, with likely error due to data being overwritten

Failing to include a branch instruction that would prevent "falling through" from one instruction to the following memory location

Moving too many bytes via MVC or MVCL due to a wrong length, or due to a loop with too many repetitions

Failing to follow a comparison or other test instruction with a conditional branch instruction

Putting a conditional branch instruction too far from the instruction whose result it was intended to interrogate, so that what's actually being interrogated is the result of an intervening code-setting instruction

Appendix E   Assembler Directives

| name field[1] | | | | | | | text |
b	o	v	s	opcode[7]	operand[2]	meaning	summary of action taken by assembler	section
X			X	REPRO		produce punched card output	punches one card, whose contents are given in the statement line following the REPRO directive	none
		X		SETx	3, 6	assign value to assembly variable	assigns value specified by operand to assembly variable identified in name field	16.2
X			X	SPACE	n, or blank	line spacing	inserts n lines in listing (if operand blank, $n = 1$)	14.3
X	X	X	X	START	self-defining term, or blank	control section	defines the beginning of the first executable control section in a source module	15.3
X			X	TITLE	'text-string'	page title	prints text string at top of each page until subsequent TITLE processed	14.2
X			X	USING	base-addr,base-reg-list	specifies implied base registers & base addresses	determines base-displacement form of address corresponding to implicit operand, using base register whose base address gives smallest displacement	3.5 9.7
X			X	WXTRN	list of symbols	weak external symbol	same as EXTRN, except that automatic search of libraries is suppressed	none

Footnotes to Assembler Directives

1. The name field for each directive will either be a blank (b), an ordinary symbol (o), a variable symbol (v), or a sequence symbol (s). Whichever of these is permitted for a given directive is indicated by an X in the appropriate column of the name-field heading. Absence of an X means that that type of name field is not permitted in that directive. For example, in the END directive, the name field can only be blank *or* a sequence symbol.

2. The following abbreviations are used:

abs-expr	absolute expression	dupl	duplicator
arithm-expr	arithmetic expression	logic-expr	logical expression
base-addr	base address	MLC	memory location counter
base-reg-list	base register list	modf	modifier
const	constant	relo-expr	relocatable expression
		vars	variables

3. In the GBLx, LCLx, and SETx directives, the letter "x" stands for either A, B, or C, indicating, respectively, an arithmetic assembly variable, a Boolean assembly variable, or a character assembly variable.

4. The operands of the PUSH and POP directives must be one of the following four strings:

        PRINT
        PRINT,USING
        USING,PRINT
        USING

5. The operand of the PRINT directive must contain one or more of the following keywords, separated by commas: ON, OFF, GEN, NOGEN, DATA, NODATA.

6. The operand of a SETx directive must be an arithmetic expression, a Boolean expression, or a character expression, whichever is appropriate for the assembly variable identified in the SETx name field.

7. The following directives are not available in DOS/VS: CXD, DXD, OPSYN, POP, PUSH.

Appendix F   EBCDIC and ASCII Schemes

bits 0,1,2,3   EBCDIC   bits 4,5,6,7

0000	0001	0010	0011	0100	0101	0110	0111	1000	1001	1010	1011	1100	1101	1110	1111	bits 4,5,6,7
NUL	DLE	DS	SP	&	-							{	}	\	0	0000
SOH	DC1	SOS	RSP		/			a	j	~		A	J	NSP	1	0001
STX	DC2	FS	SYN					b	k	s		B	K	S	2	0010
ETX	DC3	WUS	IR					c	l	t		C	L	T	3	0011
SEL	RES	BYP	PP					d	m	u		D	M	U	4	0100
HT	NL	LF	TRN					e	n	v		E	N	V	5	0101
RNL	BS	ETB	NBS					f	o	w		F	O	W	6	0110
DEL	POC	ESC	EOT					g	p	x		G	P	X	7	0111
GE	CAN	SA	SBS					h	q	y		H	Q	Y	8	1000
SPS	EM	SFE	IT				`	i	r	z		I	R	Z	9	1001
RPT	UBS	SM	REF	¢	!	¦	:					SHY			|	1010
VT	CU1	CSP	CU3	.	$	,	#									1011
FF	IFS	MFA	DC4	<	*	%	@					⌐		rt		1100
CR	IGS	ENQ	NAK	(	)	_	'									1101
SO	IRS	ACK		+	;	>	=					Y				1110
SI	IUS	BEL	SUB	|	¬	?	"							EO		1111

bits 1,2,3   ASCII   bits 4,5,6,7

000	001	010	011	100	101	110	111	bits 4,5,6,7
NUL	DLE	SP	0	@	P	`	p	0000
SOH	DC1	!	1	A	Q	a	q	0001
STX	DC2	"	2	B	R	b	r	0010
ETX	DC3	#	3	C	S	c	s	0011
EOT	DC4	$	4	D	T	d	t	0100
ENQ	NAK	%	5	E	U	e	u	0101
ACK	SYN	&	6	F	V	f	v	0110
BEL	ETB	'	7	G	W	g	w	0111
BS	CAN	(	8	H	X	h	x	1000
HT	EM	)	9	I	Y	i	y	1001
LF	SUB	*	:	J	Z	j	z	1010
VT	ESC	+	;	K	[	k	{	1011
FF	FS	,	<	L	\	l	|	1100
CR	GS	-	=	M	]	m	}	1101
SO	RS	.	>	N	^	n	~	1110
SI	US	/	?	O	_	o	DEL	1111

NOTE: The seven ASCII bits are numbered so as to enable direct comparison with EBCDIC. For example, the letter J is

1001010   in ASCII
11010001   in EBCDIC

The control character mnemonics are defined below. Note that SP is the space, or blank, character.

Sources: IBM Publications GA22–7000, *System/370 Principles of Operation* and GX20–1850, *System/370 Reference Booklet.*

* ACK	Acknowledge	* EM	End of Medium	ITB	Intermed. Transmission Block	SBS	Subscript
* BEL	Bell	* ENQ	Enquiry	* LF	Line Feed	SEL	Select
* BS	Backspace	EO	Eight Ones	MFA	Modify Field Attribute	SHY	Syllable Hyphen
BYP/	Bypass/	* EOT	End of Transmission	* NAK	Negative Acknowledge	* SI	Shift In
INP	Inhibit Presentation	* ESC	Escape	NBS	Numeric Backspace	SM/	Set Mode/
* CAN	Cancel	* ETB	End of Transmission Block	* NL	New Line	SW	Switch
* CR	Carriage Return	* ETX	End of Text	NSP	Numeric Space	* SO	Shift Out
CSP	Control Sequence Prefix	* FF	Form Feed	* NUL	Null	* SOH	Start of Heading
CU1	Customer Use 1	* FS	Field Separator	POC	Program-Operator Communication	SOS	Start of Significance
CU2	Customer Use 2	GE	Graphic Escape	PP	Presentation Position	* SP	Space
CU3	Customer Use 3	* GS	Group Separator	RES/	Restore/	SPS	Superscript
* DC1	Device Control 1	* HT	Horizontal Tab	ENP	Enable Presentation	* STX	Start of Text
* DC2	Device Control 2	IFS	Interchange File Separator	RFF	Required Form Feed	* SUB	Substitute
* DC3	Device Control 3	IGS	Interchange Group Separator	RNL	Required New Line	* SYN	Synchronous Idle
* DC4	Device Control 4	IR	Index Return	RPT	Repeat	UBS	Unit Backspace
* DEL	Delete	IRS	Interchange Record Separator	* RS	Record Separator	* US	Unit Separator
* DLE	Data Link Escape	IT	Indent Tab	RSP	Required Space	* VT	Vertical Tab
DS	Digit Select	IUS/	Interchange Unit Separator/	SA	Set Attribute	WUS	Word Underscore

* Indicates that definitions of purpose may be found in the *American National Dictionary for Information Processing*, Technical Report X3/TR–1–77, September 1977, published by the Computers and Business Equipment Manufacturers Association, 1828 L Street NW, Washington, DC 20036. Definitions for the remaining control characters may be found in the various IBM reference manuals describing individual device characteristics.

Appendix G Sample Assembler Listing

The sample assembler listing shown below exhibits most of the items that may be found on the printout produced by an assembler. The accompanying explanations should suffice for almost all uses of a listing. The definitive explanations, however, are to be found in the assembler guides published by IBM for its various systems. You should consult the guide for your system if there are differences between this sample and the listing prepared by your assembler.

In general, the listing produced when a source module is assembled on an IBM 360 or 370 system will have most if not all of the following components or ones similiar to them, though not necessarily in the order shown here:

1. The **source and object program listing,** which displays the object code produced by the assembler and all source module statements except those whose printing was suppressed by a PRINT directive
2. The **External Symbol Dictionary,** which summarizes what is in the object module's ESD records
3. The **Relocation Dictionary,** which summarizes the contents of the object module's RLD records
4. The **cross-reference list for symbols,** which identifies the statement where each ordinary symbol is defined and the statements where each one is used
5. The **cross-reference list for literals,** which identifies the statement at which each literal has been assembled and the statements in which each literal has been used
6. A **diagnostics and statistics** section, which briefly explains the causes of assembly-time errors that were noted on the source and object program portion of the listing, shows what assembler options were selected explicitly or by default when the module was assembled, and lists some elementary statistics about the program

Of these six components, all but (3) and (6) are illustrated and explained below. As will be seen, the listings all refer to the same source module.

The Source and Object Listing

The first line of each page of the source and object code listing, which is the main body of the listing, contains the phrase (if any) that was specified in the operand of a TITLE directive. Reading from left to right, the columns are interpreted as follows:

LOC: This column contains the hex address (the memory location counter) assigned to the instruction, constant, or data area defined by the corresponding source statement. It may also contain the following data:

For COM, CSECT, DSECT: the double-word address of the control section
For ORG: the current value of LOC
For LTORG: the double-word address assigned to the literal pool
For ENTRY, EXTRN, WXTRN, DXD: nothing is printed
For END with an operand: the operand's value

OBJECT CODE: This is the run-time machine language code (in hex) corresponding to the instruction or constant given in the corresponding source statement, except that PRINT NODATA restricts the amount of code printed for constants. Note that EQU and DS do not produce any run-time code. For EQU, DS, and all other directives except DC, the object code columns are blank.

ADDR1: This column gives the effective memory address (base address plus displacement) for the second operand in RS-, RX-, SS-type instructions, and for the first operand in SI- and SS-type instructions.

ADDR2: This column gives the effective memory address (base address plus displacement) for the second operand of an SS-type instruction. It also gives data for these directives:

For ORG: the memory location counter's value after the ORG has been processed
For EQU: the value of the EQU operand
For USING: the value of USING's first operand

STMT: This column lists the statement number assigned by the assembler to each source statement. Statement numbers identify the statements in the cross-reference listings.

STMT+: Adjacent to the STMT column, a plus (+) or other character indicates that the source statement shown is part of a macro's expansion. Macro expansions are displayed unless the PRINT NOGEN directive is in effect. Compare statements #25 and #26, generated by the RETURN macro, to the numbering gap between #42 and #59: The PRINT NOGEN directive in #41 prevents the expansion of the REGS macro from being on the listing. But note that the cross-reference listing is independent of PRINT NOGEN: The symbols in the REGS expansion (R0, R1, etc.) are shown in the cross-reference listing despite the PRINT NOGEN directive.

SOURCE STATEMENT: Columns 1–80 of the source statements (except for SPACE, EJECT, and TITLE directives) are listed here, unless otherwise requested by PRINT directive operands or listing control options specified in job control language.

External Symbol Dictionary

The External Symbol Dictionary listing contains the following data:

SYMBOL: This column lists each symbol that is defined as the name of a control section, as an entry point other than a control section name, or as an external reference.

TYPE: This column identifies the type of statement the symbol was specified in, as follows:

SD: CSECT or START section name*
CM: COM (common) section name
LD: ENTRY symbol
ER: EXTRN or V-type symbol
XD: External dummy section symbol
WX: WXTRN symbol

*Note: If a CSECT or START directive does not contain a name-field symbol, then the SYMBOL column for that CSECT or START directive is blank, and the corresponding TYPE is PC, meaning private (unnamed) control section.

ID: This column gives the ESDID (external symbol identification number) that identifies the symbol in the object module's ESD, TXT, and RLD records.

ADDR: This column gives the address assigned to the symbol by the assembler. For external references (ER and WX) this column is blank.

LENGTH: This column gives the length in bytes of the SD, CM, XD, or PC control section identified in the SYMBOL column.

LDID: This column is only for "entry" symbols (type LD). It gives the ID of the control section in which the entry symbol is defined.

Cross-References

The Cross-Reference listing contains the following data:

SYMBOL: This column alphabetically lists every symbol that appears in the source module except those that appear in the operand of a V-type address constant. Even if a symbol is referenced but not defined, or is defined more than once, or is properly defined but was suppressed from the source statement listing by a PRINT directive, it will still appear in this listing.

LEN: This column gives the length attribute of the symbol, as defined by the assembler. Normally, this is the number of bytes allocated to the memory area associated with the symbol. But for directives such as EQU that are not associated with a memory area, the length attribute is usually 0 or 1.

VALUE: This column gives the address associated with the symbol, or the value assigned to it.

DEFN: This column lists the statement number of the statement in which the symbol is defined.

REFERENCES: The numbers appearing in this portion of the cross-reference listing are the statement numbers of statements in which the symbol is used, i.e., appears in an operand.

Literal Cross-References

The Literal Cross-Reference listing lists all the literals that are used in a source module, and it identifies the statements where each literal is used.

SYMBOL: This column lists the literal to which the remaining columns refer.

LEN: This column gives the number of memory bytes allocated to the first or only constant specified in the literal.

VALUE: This column gives the memory address assigned by the assembler to the first or only constant specified in the literal.

DEFN: This column gives the statement number assigned to the literal at the point where its object code appears on the listing.

REFERENCES: This column lists the statement numbers of all statements in which the literal appears in an operand.

```
  LOC     OBJECT CODE        ADDR1   ADDR2   STMT       SOURCE STATEMENT

                                                2              PRINT GEN,NODATA
000000                                          3    MAIN      CSECT
000000   90EC D00C                              4    MAINLINE  STM   R14,R12,12(R13)
000004   05C0                                   5              BALR  R12,0
                                     000006     6              USING *,R12
000006   50D0 C06E         000074               7              ST    R13,SAVE+4
00000A   41D0 C06A         000070               8              LA    R13,SAVE
                                                9    *
                                               10              ENTRY MAINLINE
                                               11              EXTRN ARRAY1
                                               12    *
00000E   4110 C0C2         0000C8              13              LA    R1,=A(ARRAY1,ARRAY2)
000012   58F0 C0CA         0000D0              14              L     R15,=V(SUBR)
000016   05EF                                  15              BALR  R14,R15
                                               16    *
                                     000000    17              USING ARRAYFLD,DUMMYREG
000018   41B0 C02E         000034              18              LA    DUMMYREG,ARRAY2
00001C   D202 B000 C0CE   000000 0000D4        19              MVC   A1,=C'ABC'
000022   D204 B007 C0B2   000007 0000B8        20              MVC   A3,ZEROES
                                               21              DROP  DUMMYREG
                                               22    *
000028   58D0 C06E         000074              23              L     R13,SAVE+4
                                               24              RETURN (14,12)
00002C   98EC D00C                             25+             LM    14,12,12(13)
000030   07FE                                  26+             BR    14
                                               27    *
000000                                         28    ARRAYFLD  DSECT
000000                                         29    A1        DS    CL3
000003                                         30    A2        DS    CL4
000007                                         31    A3        DS    CL5
00000C                                         32    A4        DS    CL2
00000E                                         33    A5        DS    CL1
000032                                         34    MAIN      CSECT
                                               35    *
                                     00000F    36    N         EQU   15
000034                                         37    ARRAY2    DS    (N)F
000070                                         38    SAVE      DS    18F
                                     00000B    39    DUMMYREG  EQU   R11
0000B8   00                                    40    ZEROES    DC    15X'00'
                                               41              PRINT NOGEN
                                               42              REGS
0000C8   0000000000000034                      59                    =A(ARRAY1,ARRAY2)
0000D0   00000000                              60                    =V(SUBR)
0000D4   C1C2C3                                61                    =C'ABC'
000000                                         62              END   MAIN
```

EXTERNAL SYMBOL DICTIONARY

SYMBOL	TYPE	ID	ADDR	LENGTH	LDID
MAIN	SD	0001	000000	0000D7	
MAINLINE	LD		000000		0001
ARRAY1	ER	0002			
SUBR	ER	0003			

CROSS-REFERENCE

SYMBOL	LEN	VALUE	DEFN	REFERENCES		
ARRAYFLD	00015	00000000	00028	00017		
ARRAY1	00001	00000000	00011	00013	00059	
ARRAY2	00004	00000034	00037	00013	00018	00059
A1	00003	00000000	00029	00019		
A2	00004	00000003	00030			
A3	00005	00000007	00031	00020		
A4	00002	0000000C	00032			
A5	00001	0000000E	00033			
DUMMYREG	00001	00000011	00039	00017	00018	00021
MAIN	00001	00000000	00003	00034	00062	
MAINLINE	00004	00000000	00004	00010		
N	00001	0000000F	00036	00037		
R0	00001	00000000	00043			
R1	00001	00000001	00044	00013		
R10	00001	0000000A	00053			
R11	00001	0000000B	00054	00039		
R12	00001	0000000C	00055	00004	00005	00006
R13	00001	0000000D	00056	00004	00007	00008
R14	00001	0000000E	00057	00004	00015	
R15	00001	0000000F	00058	00014	00015	
R2	00001	00000002	00045			
R3	00001	00000003	00046			
R4	00001	00000004	00047			
R5	00001	00000005	00048			
R6	00001	00000006	00049			
R7	00001	00000007	00050			
R8	00001	00000008	00051			
R9	00001	00000009	00052			
SAVE	00004	00000070	00038	00007	00008	00024
ZEROES	00001	000000B8	00040	00020		

LITERAL CROSS-REFERENCE

SYMBOL	LEN	VALUE	DEFN	REFERENCES
=A(ARRAY1,ARRAY2)				
	00004	000000C8	00058	00013
=V(SUBR)				
	00004	000000D0	00059	00014
=C'ABC'				
	00003	000000D4	00060	00019

Listed below are the definitions of two macros. One, named EBCBIN, makes it rather simple to convert an integer to its full-word binary representation after it has been read in EBCDIC format. The other one, named BINEBC, makes it rather simple to convert a full-word binary integer to its EBCDIC representation prior to printing or writing it.

To use these macros, either their definitions must be in your source module or they must be in a macro library file accessible to the assembler. Once they are located in one or the other of these two places, they can be used any number of times in your source module merely by putting their name in the opcode field and two appropriate symbolic addresses in the operand field. The example in each definition's comments illustrates how to do this. The comments themselves describe the capabilities and restrictions you need to be aware of when using these macros.

```
            MACRO
&L          EBCBIN  &A,&X
.*
.*  EBCBIN macro converts an integer from its EBCDIC representation at
.*     the address given symbolically by  &A  to its full-word binary
.*     representation at the address given symbolically by  &X.
.*
.*  This macro is based on the procedure given at the end of Sect. 12.8.
.*
.*  The restrictions are as follows:
.*     (1) Both  &A  and  &X  must be symbolic memory addresses, not
.*         register addresses.
.*     (2) The length attribute of  &A  must be the length of the EBCDIC
.*         field, and must not exceed 16.
.*     (3) The EBCDIC representation must be right-justified with
.*         either leading zeroes or leading blanks, but with no other
.*         punctuation (e.g., no commas) except an optional minus sign.
.*     (4) The value of the integer must not exceed (2**31)-1, nor be
.*         less than  -(2**31).
.*     (5) The symbolic address represented by &X should be a full word.
.*
.*  Example:
.*              EBCBIN  DATA,NUMBER
.*  converts the EBCDIC integer given at symbolic address DATA to a
.*   full-word binary integer and stores it in symbolic address NUMBER.
.*  DATA and NUMBER --- or whatever symbols you use in their place ---
.*   must be defined by statements like these:
.*      NUMBER  DS   F
.*      DATA    DS   CLn   ( n  is an integer from  1  to  16 )
.*
.*
&L          STM   5,6,R&SYSNDX
            PACK  N&SYSNDX,&A
            MVN   N&SYSNDX+7(1),=P'-1'
            LH    5,=Y(L'&A)
            LA    6,&A
L&SYSNDX    CLI   0(6),C'-'
            BE    M&SYSNDX
            LA    6,1(6)
            BCT   5,L&SYSNDX
            MVN   N&SYSNDX+7(1),=P'+1'
M&SYSNDX    CVB   5,N&SYSNDX
            ST    5,&X
            LM    5,6,R&SYSNDX
            B     Q&SYSNDX
N&SYSNDX    DS    D
R&SYSNDX    DS    2F
Q&SYSNDX    DS    0H
            MEND
```

```
              MACRO
&L            BINEBC  &X,&A
.*
.*   BINEBC macro converts an integer from its full-word binary represen-
.*      tation at the address given symbolically by  &X  to its EBCDIC
.*      representation at the address given symbolically by &A.
.*
.*   This macro is based on Example 6 given at the end of Sect. 12.9.
.*
.*   The restrictions are as follows:
.*      (1) Both  &X  and  &A  must be symbolic memory addresses, not
.*          register addresses.
.*      (2) The symbolic address represented by  &X  should be a full word.
.*      (3) The length attribute of &A  must be the length of the EBCDIC
.*          field, and must not exceed 16.
.*      (4) The resulting EBCDIC representation will be right-justified
.*          with leading blanks instead of leading zeroes, but with no
.*          other punctuation (e.g., no commas) except a minus sign if
.*          the number is negative.
.*
.*   Example:
.*              BINEBC  NUMBER,DATA
.*   converts the binary integer given at symbolic address NUMBER to its
.*    EBCDIC representation and stores it at symbolic address DATA.
.*   DATA and NUMBER --- or whatever symbols you use in their place ---
.*    must be defined by statements like these:
.*          NUMBER  DS    F
.*          DATA    DS    CLn    ( n  is an integer from  1  to  16 )
.*
.*
&L            ST      1,R&SYSNDX
              L       1,&X
              CVD     1,N&SYSNDX
              MVC     T&SYSNDX,=X'40202020202020202020202020202120'
              LA      1,T&SYSNDX+15
              EDMK    T&SYSNDX,N&SYSNDX
              BNM     C&SYSNDX
              SH      1,=H'1'
              MVI     0(1),C'-'
C&SYSNDX      MVC     &A,T&SYSNDX+16-L'&A
              B       Q&SYSNDX
N&SYSNDX      DS      D
R&SYSNDX      DS      F
T&SYSNDX      DS      CL16
Q&SYSNDX      DS      0H
              MEND
```

Appendix I References

Abel, Peter. *Programming Assembler Language.* 2d ed. Reston, VA: Reston Publishing Co., 1984.

ANDIP: American National Dictionary for Information Processing. American National Standards Committee X3 Technical Report X3/TR-1-77. Washington D.C.: Computers and Business Equipment Manufacturers Association, 1977.

Bailes, Gordon L., and Riser, Robert R. *IBM 370 Computer Organization and Assembly Language.* St. Paul, MN: West Publishing Co., 1986.

Beizer, Boris. *Software Testing Techniques.* New York: Van Nostrand, 1983.

Binder, Robert. *Application Debugging: An MVS Handbook for COBOL, Assembly, PL/I, and Fortran Programmers.* Englewood Cliffs, NJ: Prentice-Hall, 1985.

Brearley, Harrington C., Jr. *Introduction to Assembler Language Programming for the IBM System 360–370.* New York: Macmillan, 1974.

Brown, Gary DeWard. *System/370 Job Control Language.* New York: Wiley, 1977.

Burian, Barbara J. *A Simplified Approach to S/370 Assembly Language Programming.* Englewood Cliffs, NJ: Prentice-Hall, 1977.

Calingaert, Peter. *Assemblers, Compilers, and Program Translation.* Potomac, MD: Computer Science Press, 1979.

Campbell-Kelly, M. *An Introduction to Macros.* New York: American Elsevier, 1973.

Cashman, Thomas, and Shelly, Gary B. *Introduction to Computer Programming: IBM System/360 Assembler Language.* Anaheim, CA: Anaheim Publishing Co., 1984.

Chapin, Ned. *Three-Sixty—Three-Seventy Programming in Assembly Language.* New York: McGraw-Hill, 1973.

Computing Surveys (Special Issue). *Programming.* December 1974.
   Brown, P. J., "Programming and Documenting Software Projects," 213–20.
   Kernighan, B. W. and Plauger, P. J., "Programming Style: Examples and Counterexamples," 303–19.
   Knuth, D. E., "Structured Programming with Go-To Statements," 261–301.
   Wirth, N., "On the Composition of Well-Structured Programs," 247–59.
   Yohe, J. M., "An Overview of Programming Practices," 221–45.

Dahl, O.-J., Dijkstra, E. W., and Hoare, C. A. R. *Structured Programming.* New York: Academic Press, 1972.

Denning, P. J. *"A Hard Look at Structured Programming."* In *Structured Programming,* D. Bates, editor. pp. 183–202. Maidenhead, England: Infotech International Ltd., 1976.

Eckols, Steve. *DOS/VSE JCL.* Fresno, CA: M. Murach & Associates, 1985.

Feingold, Carl. *Introduction to Assembler Language Programming.* Dubuque, IA: Wm. C. Brown, 1978.

Flores, Ivan. *Job Control Language and File Definition.* Englewood Cliffs, NJ: Prentice-Hall, 1971.

Freeman, Peter, and Wasserman, Anthony. *Tutorial on Software Design Techniques.* Washington, D.C.: IEEE Computer Society, 1976.

Gust, Philip. *Introduction to Machine and Assembly Language Programming.* Englewood Cliffs, NJ: Prentice-Hall, 1985.

Hannula, Reino. *Computers and Programming: A System Three Sixty-Three Seventy Assembler Language Approach.* San Luis Obispo, CA: Quality Hill Books, 1983.

Johnson, David L. *Structured Assembly Language for IBM Computers.* Palo Alto, CA: Mayfield, 1982.

Katzan, Harry, Jr. *Computer Systems Organization and Programming.* Chicago, Il: Science Research Associates, 1976.

Kent, W. "Assembler-Language Macroprogramming: A Tutorial Oriented Toward the IBM 360." In *Computing Surveys,* pp. 183–96. December 1969.

Kindred, Alton R. *Structured Assembly Language for IBM Computers.* Chicago, IL: Harcourt Brace Jovanovich, 1987.

Knuth, Donald E. *The Art of Computer Programming.* Reading, MA: Addison-Wesley.
    Vol. 1: *Fundamental Algorithms,* 2d ed. 1973.
    Vol. 2: *Semi-Numerical Algorithms,* 2d ed. 1981.
    Vol. 3: *Sorting and Searching,* 1973.

Kuo, Shan Sun. *Assembler Language for FORTRAN, COBOL, and PL/1 Programmers IBM 360/370.* Reading, MA: Addison-Wesley, 1974.

Lavery, Robert G. *Programming with System 370 Assembler Language.* Dubuque, IA: Kendall-Hunt, 1981.

Lowe, Doug. *MVS JCL.* Fresno, CA: M. Murach & Associates, 1987.

Martin, James, et al. *VSAM: Access Methods Services and Programming Techniques 1987.* Englewood Cliffs, NJ: Prentice-Hall, 1987.

Massie, Paul. *IBM Assembler Language Programming.* New York: MacMillan, 1985.

McBeth, Robert W., and Ferguson, J. Robert. *IBM Assembler: An Intuitive Approach.* New York: Wiley, 1987.

McQuillen, Kevin, and Prince, Anne. *DOS/VSE Assembler Language.* Fresno, CA: M. Murach & Associates, 1986.

McQuillen, Kevin, and Prince, Anne. *OS/MVS Assembler Language.* Fresno, CA: M. Murach & Associates, 1986.

Overbeek, Ross A., and Singletary, Wilson E. *Assembler Language with ASSIST and ASSIST-I.* 3d ed. Chicago, IL: Science Research Associates, 1986.

Peterson, James L. *Computer Organization and Assembly Language Programming.* New York: Academic Press, 1978.

Presser, L., and White, J. R. "Linkers and Loaders." In *Computing Surveys,* pp. 149–67. September 1972.

Rindfleisch, Daniel H. *Debugging System 360/370 Programs Using OS and VS Storage Dumps.* Englewood Cliffs, NJ: Prentice-Hall, 1976.

Rindfleisch, Daniel H. *OS & VS Job Control Language and Utility Programs.* 2d ed. Englewood Cliffs, NJ: Prentice-Hall, 1987.

Rosenberg, Jerry M. *Dictionary of Computers, Data Processing, and Telecommunications.* New York: Wiley, 1984

Rudd, Walter G. *Assembly Language Programming and the IBM 360 & 370 Computers.* Englewood Cliffs, NJ: Prentice-Hall, 1976.

Schneider, Michael. *The Principles of Computer Organization.* New York: Wiley, 1985.

Shelly, Gary B., and Cashman, Thomas J. *DOS Job Control for Assembler Programmers.* Anaheim, CA: Anaheim Publishing Co., 1972.

Shelly, Gary B., and Cashman, Thomas J. *IBM 360 Assembler Language Disk-Tape Advanced Concepts.* Anaheim, CA: Anaheim Publishing Co., 1978.

Shelly, Gary B., and Cashman, Thomas J. *OS Job Control Language*. Anaheim, CA: Anaheim Publishing Co., 1984.

Silver, Gerald A. *Computer Algorithms and Flowcharting*. New York: McGraw-Hill, 1975.

Silver, James. *Structured Assembly Language Programming for the IBM 370*. New York: MacMillan, 1986.

Stabley, Don H. *Assembler Language for Application Programming*. Princeton, NJ: Petrocelli Books, 1982.

Stark, Richard, and Dearholt, Donald M. *Computer Concepts and Assembler Programming: 360/370 Systems*. New York: Academic Press, 1975.

Stern, Nancy, et al. *Assembler Language Programming for IBM Registered and IBM Registered Compatible Computers*. (Formerly *370/360 Assembler Language Programming*.) New York: Wiley, 1986.

Stoddard, Spotswood D. *Principles of Assembler Language Programming for the IBM 370*. New York: McGraw-Hill, 1985.

Struble, George. *Assembler Language Programming: The IBM System/370 Family*. 3d ed. Reading, MA: Addison-Wesley, 1984.

Tabler, Donna, and Ashley, Ruth. *IBM OS Assembler Language: Language Basics*. New York: Wiley, 1985.

Tabler, Donna, et al. *IBM OS Assembler Language: Subroutines, Macros, and Tables*. New York: Wiley, 1986.

Trombetta, Michael, and Finkelstein, Sue. *OS JCL and Utilities*. Reading, MA: Addison-Wesley, 1984.

Tuggle, Sharon K. *Assembler Language Programming: Systems/360 and 370*. 2d ed. Chicago, IL: Science Research Associates, 1986.

Turski, W. M. *Computer Programming Methodology*. Philadelphia, PA: Heyden and Sons, 1978.

Weik, Martin H. *Standard Dictionary of Computers and Information Processing*. Revised 2d ed. Rochelle Park, NJ: Hayden, 1977.

Yarmish, Rina, and Yarmish, Joshua. *Assembly Language Fundamentals 360/370 OS/VS DOS/VS*. Reading, MA: Addison-Wesley, 1979.

Selected IBM Reference Manuals for Assembly Language Programmers

GC20–0001 *IBM System/370, 30xx, and 4300 Processors Bibliography*   (Lists all the publications for the indicated processors, including those given below.)
A22–6821 *System/360 Principles of Operation*
GA22–7000 *System/370 Principles of Operation*
GC22–7070 *IBM 4300 Processors: Principles of Operation*
GA26–1615 *Reference Manual for IBM 3330 Series Disk Storage*
GA26–1638 *Reference Manual for IBM 3350 Direct Access Storage*
GC26–4193 *IBM 3380 Direct Access Storage: General Information*
GC20–1699 *IBM Vocabulary for Data Processing, Telecommunications, and Office Systems*
GX20–1850 *System/370 Reference Summary* (the "yellow booklet")
GC26–3813 *OS/VS Linkage Editor and Loader*
GC33–4010 *OS/VS-DOS/VSE-VM/370 Assembler Language*
GC33–4021 *OS/VS-VM/370 Assembler Programmer's Guide*
GC33–4024 *Guide to the DOS/VSE Assembler*

GC24–5093 *OS/VS1 Debugging Guide*
GC24–5099 *OS/VS1 JCL Reference*
GC24–5100 *OS/VS1 JCL Services*
GC24–5103 *OS/VS1 Supervisor Services and Macros*

GC26–3872 *OS/VS1 Data Management Macro Instructions*
GC26–3874 *OS/VS1 Data Management Services Guide*
GC26–3901 *OS/VS1 Utilities*
GC38–1001 *OS/VS1 Message Library: System Messages*

GC26–3873 *OS/VS2 MVS Data Management Macro Instructions*
GC26–3875 *OS/VS2 MVS Data Management Services Guide*
GC26–3902 *OS/VS2 MVS Utilities*
GC28–0683 *OS/VS2 Supervisor Services and Macro Instructions*
GC28–1047 *OS/VS2 System Programming Library: Debugging Handbook, Vol. 1*
GC28–1048 *OS/VS2 System Programming Library: Debugging Handbook, Vol. 2*
GC28–1049 *OS/VS2 System Programming Library: Debugging Handbook, Vol. 3*
GC28–1300 *OS/VS2 MVS JCL*
GC38–1002 *OS/VS Message Library: VS2 System Messages*

GC33–5371 *DOS/VS System Management Guide*
GC33–5372 *DOS/VS Data Management Guide*
GC33–5373 *DOS/VS Supervisor and I/O Macros*
GC33–5376 *DOS/VS System Control Statements*
GC33–5380 *DOS/VS Serviceability Aids and Debugging Procedures*
GC33–5381 *DOS/VS System Utilities*

G320–5774 *VSAM Primer and Reference*
GC26–3838 *OS/VS VSAM Programmer's Guide*
GC26–3841 *OS/VS Access Method Services*

Index